Cambridge Grammar of Classical C

D1388496

This is the first full-scale reference grammar c
century. The first work of its kind to reflect the ᵕ _
made in recent decades, it offers students, teachers and academics a comprehensive
yet user-friendly treatment. The chapters on phonology and morphology make full
use of insights from comparative and historical linguistics to elucidate the complex
systems of roots, stems and endings. The syntax offers linguistically up-to-date
descriptions of such topics as case usage, tense and aspect, voice, subordinate
clauses, infinitives and participles. An innovative section on textual coherence
treats particles and word order and discusses several sample passages in detail,
demonstrating new ways of approaching Greek texts. Throughout the book
numerous original examples are offered, all with translations and often with
clarifying notes. Clearly laid-out tables, helpful cross-references and full indexes
make this essential resource accessible to users of all levels.

EVERT VAN EMDE BOAS specializes in the application of modern linguistic and
cognitive approaches to ancient Greek literature. He currently serves as Leventis
Research Fellow in Ancient Greek at Merton College, Oxford. His publications include
a monograph and articles on Greek tragedy, as well as several interdisciplinary studies
on the psychology of theatre audiences. He has previously held various teaching and
research positions at the University of Oxford, the University of Amsterdam, VU
University Amsterdam, the University of Groningen and Leiden University.

ALBERT RIJKSBARON is emeritus professor of Ancient Greek Linguistics at the
University of Amsterdam. His publications include highly acclaimed and widely
used Greek linguistics titles as well as numerous articles. He has edited and co-
edited collaborative works in this field.

LUUK HUITINK is currently employed as a postdoctoral research fellow on the ERC
Project 'Ancient Narrative' at Heidelberg University, where he examines the rela-
tionship between ancient rhetoric and cognitive linguistics in order to shed light on
the ancient readerly imagination. He previously was the Leventis Research Fellow in
Ancient Greek at Merton College, Oxford, and held a Spinoza Visiting Fellowship at
Leiden University. He has published on linguistic and narratological topics in
classical and post-classical Greek and is the author of a CUP commentary on
Xenophon's *Anabasis* III (together with Tim Rood), which is keyed to this grammar.

MATHIEU DE BAKKER is university lecturer at the classics department of the
University of Amsterdam, where he teaches courses on all aspects of ancient
Greek. He has published on the Greek historians and orators and previously
lectured at the University of Oxford.

Cambridge Grammar of Classical Greek

EVERT VAN EMDE BOAS *University of Oxford*

ALBERT RIJKSBARON *Universiteit van Amsterdam*

LUUK HUITINK *Universität Heidelberg*

MATHIEU DE BAKKER *Universiteit van Amsterdam*

CAMBRIDGE
UNIVERSITY PRESS

Shaftesbury Road, Cambridge CB2 8EA, United Kingdom

One Liberty Plaza, 20th Floor, New York, NY 10006, USA

477 Williamstown Road, Port Melbourne, VIC 3207, Australia

314–321, 3rd Floor, Plot 3, Splendor Forum, Jasola District Centre, New Delhi – 110025, India

103 Penang Road, #05–06/07, Visioncrest Commercial, Singapore 238467

Cambridge University Press is part of Cambridge University Press & Assessment,
a department of the University of Cambridge.

We share the University's mission to contribute to society through the pursuit of
education, learning and research at the highest international levels of excellence.

www.cambridge.org
Information on this title: www.cambridge.org/9780521198608
DOI: 10.1017/9781139027052

First published 2019 (version 4, August 2022)

Printed in the United Kingdom by TJ Books Limited, Padstow Cornwall

A catalogue record for this publication is available from the British Library.

Library of Congress Cataloging-in-Publication Data
Names: Emde Boas, Evert van, 1982– author. | Rijksbaron, Albert, author. |
Huitink, Luuk, 1981– author. | Bakker, Mathieu de, author.
Title: Cambridge grammar of classical Greek / Evert van Emde Boas,
Albert Rijksbaron, Luuk Huitink, Mathieu de Bakker.
Description: Cambridge ; New York : Cambridge University Press, 2017.
Identifiers: LCCN 2017024372 | ISBN 9780521198608
Subjects: LCSH: Greek language – Grammar.
Classification: LCC PA258 .E45 2017 | DDC 488.2421–dc23
LC record available at https://lccn.loc.gov/2017024372

ISBN 978-0-521-19860-8 Hardback
ISBN 978-0-521-12729-5 Paperback

Contents

Preface

On Cs and Gs: History and Aims of the Book

Conception and Development

Readers picking up this hefty tome may be surprised to learn that the first C of *CGCG* (as we like to call it) once stood for *Concise*. The syntax part of that *Concise Grammar of Classical Greek* began, as so many grammar books no doubt have, as lecture handouts – to be precise, as EvEB's handouts used in first-year Greek syntax classes at the University of Oxford. The work grew from a dissatisfaction with existing teaching materials in English: the main concern was that those materials did not reflect decades' worth of advances in the linguistic description of Ancient Greek, inspired by the incorporation of insights from various areas of general linguistics. The last good full-scale reference grammar in English, Smyth's *Greek Grammar*, for all its excellence, stemmed from a time long before such advances had even been possible, and more recent grammar books had done nothing to bridge the gap. The truth was that no book existed that represented the current state of knowledge on the Greek language. There were other problems, too: Smyth was often perceived by undergraduates as daunting and dense, but alternatives were typically too limited in their coverage; examples used in existing grammars were not always representative, and based on antiquated text editions; terminology was confusing and outmoded; and so forth.

The lecture handouts began to look more like a book when EvEB was joined by AR in revising the material and producing additional chapters. LH, who had also been teaching at Oxford and who had run into similar difficulties with existing materials, then joined, and he and EvEB wrote the first version of the section on textual coherence – a particular *desideratum* in view of the advances in linguistics mentioned above.

Late in 2009, at the instigation of Juliane Kerkhecker, Grocyn Lecturer at Oxford, the material was sent, in the state that it had now attained (still without a morphology), to Cambridge University Press – not so much as a full-fledged book proposal (in the minds of the authors, at least: without the morphology the work could not yet lay full claim to its first G), but as an opening gambit. To our delight, the Press took the submission very seriously, and engaged a large number of readers to judge the work. This led to a contract, and a change of title to *Cambridge Grammar of Classical Greek*.

A very great deal of labour, however, was still to be done at this point. Over the next few years – with many delays as the result of other obligations – we drafted the phonology and morphology chapters, and overhauled the existing parts to take into account the readers' reports (which had been gratifyingly favourable and detailed). It is in this period that MdB, former Grocyn Lecturer at Oxford, who had himself been planning a similar effort, joined the writing team.

The revised work, which had grown considerably due to addition of the phonology/morphology and further additions requested by our readers, was resubmitted to the Press in the final months of 2013, and another full set of readers' reports on the complete text followed in the subsequent year. These reports were once again very helpful and detailed, eliciting not only a final round of revision, but also a complete overhaul of the numbering system used for our sections. These changes were completed early in 2015; this was followed by a lengthy and complex production process (in our Bibliography, we have not systematically added references to works from 2016 or later).

The end product is in every way the result of a joint effort: although individual authors wrote first drafts of particular chapters, or took the initiative in revising chapters or sections, we discussed every page of the book as a group, and all four of us have reflected extensively on the entire work. Each of us is happy to share responsibility for the whole.

Target Audience and Scope

Our particular hope is that university students (at all levels) and teachers will profit from *CGCG*. Professional scholars whose main area of expertise is not Greek linguistics may also benefit from our presentation, particularly where it concerns areas which are less often covered in traditional grammars (word order is a prime example), but also more generally because of the manner in which we have tried to reflect current thinking in the field (on such issues as verbal aspect, the use of tenses, voice, the representation of reported discourse, complement constructions, particles, etc.).

CGCG's coverage is such, we suggest, that it could be used in the context of undergraduate and graduate language courses, and that a commentary on a classical text geared primarily to a student audience could refer to it for most grammatical features, except those so rare that they deserve fuller discussion anyway. Still, there are many subjects about which we might have said much more, and some about which we have said almost nothing at all (syllable structure, the interjections, and forms of address spring to mind here). Other expansions, such as a section on metre and/or prose rhythm, or the kind of stylistic glossary often found in grammars, were never seriously considered: to our mind, readers are much better served on these issues by specialized resources.

On the point of coverage, a few words must also be said about the second C and G of our title. There was a temptation (and a desire among a minority of our readers) to increase the diachronic and dialectological scope of the work to cover Homer, archaic lyric, the Koine, etc.; we also would have loved to say more about the Greek of inscriptions. However, as any such move would have drastically increased the size and complexity of the book (and accordingly decreased its accessibility), we decided to limit our purview to classical Greek. Again, such omissions seemed all the more feasible given the availability of specialized resources on the dialects, Homeric grammar, etc. Since Herodotus and the dramatists fall clearly under the heading of classical Greek, we did include a chapter on Ionic prose and some dialectal features of drama (particularly the 'Doric' alpha).

Some Principles of Presentation

Although we abandoned *Concise* for our first C early on, we have still strived for concision and accessibility in our presentation. Implicated in this is our decision not to clutter the book's pages with bibliographical references or extensive discussion of diverging views. We do provide a brief, thematically organized bibliography at the end of the book, and trust that the resources listed there will allow interested readers to follow up particular subjects. We are well aware, of course, that at some points our presentation is open to genuine debate or uncertainty. Where we have elided such discussions, it is not from dogmatism but from a desire for consistency and clarity.

Another way in which we have attempted to keep the book accessible is by making it 'theory-light' and by taking a considered approach towards our terminological apparatus. Whether or not we have succeeded in this must be judged by our users: we provide some further discussion of our choices in terminology at pp. xl–xlii.

Keeping the book approachable also meant forgoing radical departures from 'normal' ways of organizing a grammar. Our syntax chapters, for instance, follow a traditional pattern, moving from the constructions of simple sentences (including basic nominal syntax and verbal categories such as tense, aspect and mood), to various kinds of subordinate constructions, gathered under such headings as 'causal clauses', 'purpose clauses', 'the participle', etc., which are strongly correlated to form. Another approach – one more attuned to the fact that language is not merely a system of forms, but a medium used by speakers and writers to accomplish certain goals and effects – might have been to give much more prominence to function, for instance by discussing all ways of expressing 'cause' or 'purpose' under one heading. This is not, in the end, the course we took, but gestures towards such an approach may be found throughout the book, and some chapters (e.g. the chapter on wishes, directives, etc.) more expressly align with such organizing principles.

We have put considerable effort into the selection of our Greek examples: some, of course, were found in our predecessors and recommissioned, but most were newly culled from a wide range of texts. Our aim has been to find, in varied sources, examples that are clear and actually representative of the phenomenon they are meant to exemplify. Digital search corpora such as the *Thesaurus Linguae Graecae* and *Perseus under PhiloLogic* were of great help in finding suitable material. We also decided to dispense almost entirely with fabricated sentences, from a conviction that working with real Greek examples is the best way of learning how to deal with real Greek texts (and from what we consider a healthy mistrust of our own ability to produce Greek that would have sounded true to an ancient hearer).

In the phonology/morphology part, too, our presentation of forms is often based on a fresh examination of the corpus. Some exceptional forms that are often listed in grammars but do not actually occur in classical Greek have been left out. This is particularly relevant in the case of our list of principal parts, where we have generally avoided giving forms which are non-existent (or nearly so) in classical Greek.

While on the topic of the phonology/morphology: we have in those chapters provided rather more historical information than is now usual in university-level grammars. Much of what is 'irregular' in Greek forms and paradigms can be explained with a little historical background, and it is our experience that students benefit greatly from being provided with such information. It should be stressed that our aim in this was expressly didactic, not to provide a proper historical grammar. This is the only excuse we can offer to experts wondering about our principles of selection (no labiovelars?), or our manner of presentation (e.g. the use of the Greek alphabet for reconstructed forms, yielding, for instance, such infelicitous reconstructions as *σεχ- instead of *seg^h-). Students interested in finding out more about the historical background of the language are strongly encouraged to refer to the works on this topic listed in the bibliography.

In the phonology/morphology part we have given indications of vowel quantity (ă/ā, ĭ/ī, ŭ/ū) where we deemed such indications helpful for the analysis of forms, or for students' memorization of prevalent patterns (e.g. vowel quantities in endings). We often give full indications only once within a section, or only when a form or ending first appears. We have not strived for complete consistency, nor attempted to replicate the information about individual lexical items available in dictionaries.

Finally, one other point of principle in the morphology has been to analyse forms explicitly: we find in our teaching that there is a crucial difference between telling a student that the acc. pl. masc. aor. ppl. act. of παιδεύω is παιδεύσαντας, and explaining that the form is built up from a sigmatic aorist stem παιδευσ(α)- (itself the product of regular processes of formation), the participle-suffix -ντ-, and a third-declension accusative ending -ας. Our aim throughout has been to stimulate the second, analytical approach to Greek morphology.

Using *CGCG*: A Few Points of Guidance

The chapters of the book were written so as to be suitable for continuous reading, yet we recognize that most users of a reference grammar will come to it looking for discussion of a particular topic. A detailed table of contents and extensive indexes should allow for easy navigation to the right place.

We have also included many cross-references throughout the book, so that related topics or terms may be followed up quickly. In some cases the 'target' of these references is a (more) complete treatment of a topic which is not (fully) discussed at the 'source'; in others, a cross-reference is inserted when a grammatical term or concept is used which users may not know, or which they may wish to see treated in more detail; we also use cross-references in the discussion of examples, helping readers with difficult points of grammar. Some readers will want to follow up more of these cross-references than others: we trust that individual users will soon develop their own preferences and practices in this respect.

A difference in type-size represents the difference between sections discussing features of the language that are more frequent, central, or significant (to our mind), and those that are less so. Notes are added to sections for further discussion, exceptions, etc. The general idea is that text in larger type presents the main features of a particular grammatical topic – those which an undergraduate student might be expected to know – whereas the notes and smaller-type sections offer additional information, or features with which students will be confronted when reading texts, but which they may not be expected to know by heart. Naturally, when *CGCG* is used as a teaching resource, instructors will determine for themselves which material they wish to emphasize.

In the morphology, tables of forms are presented before a paradigm is discussed in detail. Those looking for nothing but the tables, gathered together in one place, may find them online, at the book's page on the Cambridge University Press website.

Acknowledgements

CGCG has been a long time in the making, and over the years many have contributed to its improvement. Where it falls short the responsibility is of course ours. It is a genuine pleasure to record here some of the debts we have incurred.

A first word of thanks must go out to the community of scholars working on Greek linguistics at large. Many of them will see their ideas reflected in these pages, and although, outside of our bibliography, we do not cite individuals by name (for reasons outlined above), their contribution in shaping our thinking is no less significant.

The Cambridge University Press-assigned readers offered generously of their time (twice!) to comment on a large manuscript in detail. Their general endorsement has been gratifying, their criticism has sharpened our presentation in many places, and their corrections have saved us from a large number of mistakes. We are pleased to be able to mention some of the readers by name: Patrick Finglass wrote acute comments and was the ideal person to comment on our *Ajax*-passage; Helma Dik provided superior input and has continued doing so even after her task was done; Coulter George deserves a special deal of gratitude for the breadth and detail of his report.

Benjamin Allgaier, Maurits de Leeuw, Karel Stegeman and David Cohen checked the text and citation of all of our examples, working with precision and speed. Mirte Liebregts took on the mammoth task of drafting our Index Locorum and parts of the other indexes: we are grateful for her diligent efforts.

Juliane Kerkhecker provided early encouragement and was instrumental in making contact with the Press. Gerry Wakker was intimately involved in early discussions, and commented on the first draft of the section on textual coherence. Rutger Allan offered insightful comments on several chapters, and more generally we have profited from his published work in many places.

At the Press, we would like to thank Michael Sharp as well as our successive Content Managers, Liz Hanlon, Christina Sarigiannidou, Ross Stewart, and especially Sarah Lambert. Malcolm Todd, our swift and precise copyeditor, was a trusted ally during the production phase.

The book uses a specially modified version of the Press's house font for Greek, Neohellenic. Additional characters were designed by EvEB and by George Matthiopoulos of the Greek Font Society. For his elegant designs, produced at very short notice, George has our sincere thanks.

Friends and colleagues at our various institutions offered moral support, and patience when we were once again preoccupied with work on the grammar. EvEB wishes to thank, in Oxford, the Faculty of Classics, Corpus Christi College, and Magdalen College (particularly his colleagues at the Calleva Centre); and in the Netherlands, the members of the departments of Classics at the University of Amsterdam, VU University Amsterdam, the University of Groningen, and the University of Leiden. Each of these institutions provided a welcoming home and a base of operations on one or more occasions during the years that *CGCG* was written. AR is indebted to the Amsterdam Center for Language and Communication of the Faculty of Humanities of the University of Amsterdam, which continued to provide material support of various kinds after his retirement. LH wishes to record a debt of gratitude to the Provost and Fellows of Worcester College, Oxford, where the work was begun, to the Warden and Fellows of Merton College, Oxford, where most of it was done, and to the Seminar für klassische Philologie of the Ruprecht-Karls-Universität Heidelberg, where it was finally seen through; at the last institution Jonas Grethlein in particular has shown great patience and support. MdB wishes to thank his colleagues from the Classics team at the University of Amsterdam, and Irene de Jong in particular for her support and encouragement.

Even more patience was shown by our families, who relentlessly supported the enterprise and cheerfully indulged our nocturnal email exchanges. The four of us spent many hours in each other's (often digital) company, including evenings and weekends. We are all too aware that those hours might also have been spent elsewhere.

Students in Oxford (especially at Merton College), Amsterdam, Groningen and Leiden have been using pages from the book or earlier versions of the whole for some time, and have offered their views. To all our students, we owe a great debt. It is with them in mind that we wrote this book.

Abbreviations, Symbols, Editions

Abbreviations Used in This Book

1	first person	ind.	indicative
2	second person	inf.	infinitive
2x acc.	double accusative	intr.	intransitive
3	third person	Ion.	Ionic
acc.	accusative	Ital.	Italian
act.	active	Lat.	Latin
adj.	adjective	lit.	(more) literally
adv.	adverb	masc./m.	masculine
Afrik.	Afrikaans	mid.	middle
aor.	aorist	mp.	middle-passive
athem.	athematic	n.	note
Att.	Attic	neut./n.	neuter
augm.	augment(ed)	nom.	nominative
cf.	compare (*confer*)	opt.	optative
class.	classical	pass.	passive
dat.	dative	pf.	perfect
decl. inf.	declarative infinitive	pl.	plural
du.	dual	plpf.	pluperfect (=secondary perfect indicative)
dyn. inf.	dynamic infinitive	ppl.	participle
Engl.	English	pres.	present
fem./f.	feminine	redupl.	reduplication/ reduplicated
Fr.	French	refl.	reflexive
fut.	future	sec.	secondary
fut. pf.	future perfect	sg.	singular
gen.	genitive	sigm.	sigmatic
Germ.	German	subj.	subjunctive
Gk.	Greek	them.	thematic
imp.	imperative	voc.	vocative
impf.	imperfect (=secondary present indicative)		

Abbreviations of authors and works used in the examples follow those of the *Oxford Classical Dictionary*, except that the orators are cited, where possible, by speech number, and that Euripides' *Heracles* is abbreviated (*Her.*). Fragments are cited (fr.) with the edition from which they (and their numbering) are taken. When scholarly consensus holds a work to be spurious, this is indicated by square brackets (e.g. '[Andoc.] 4'). For a complete list see the Index of Examples at the end of the book.

Other Symbols

The symbol → ('see') indicates a cross-reference to another chapter (e.g. →1), section (e.g. →1.2) or range of sections (e.g. →1.2–4). In some cases a cross-reference points to a specific note (e.g. →1.2 n.1).

Greek examples are numbered (1), (2), (3), etc. (the numbering restarts each chapter), and referred to using that format. Three dots (...) in Greek examples indicate that a part of the text has been left out for the sake of brevity or clarity. A vertical bar (|) indicates a line division in the Greek text. A double semicolon (::) is used to indicate a change of speaker. Explanatory notes in and following the translations of Greek examples are given in *italics*.

For the signs > and <, the asterisk * and the symbol †, →1.48.

For the representation of (reconstructed) sounds using the International Phonetic Alphabet (IPA), →1.14.

Texts and Translations of Examples

Our examples were typically taken from electronic sources – we have made extensive usage of the online edition of *Thesaurus Linguae Graecae*, as well as the excellent search functionality of *Perseus under PhiloLogic*. All examples were subsequently checked against printed editions, normally the most recent Oxford Classical Text, in a few cases a Budé or Teubner edition. We have indicated any material left out, but have freely added full stops (or question marks) to sentences which are syntactically complete in our example but run on in the original. We have also indicated line divisions and speaker changes (see above, 'Other Symbols').

All translations are our own, although we have often borrowed phrasing from published translations (particularly those in the Loeb Classical Library series).

On Terminology

Problems and Principles

Greek grammar is something of a terminological morass. All kinds of phenomena are known by different overlapping – or not quite overlapping – labels, variously popular in different periods or different regions. Conversely, for some features of the language no good term has ever been firmly established. Matters are not helped by the fact that, outside of Greece, the traditional terminology for Greek grammar is largely based on Latin grammar, even though there are some fundamental differences between the two languages (particularly in the verbal system).

The challenges for the grammar writer are many, ranging from the trivial to the serious: should we call εἰ + optative a 'hypothetical' condition, a 'remote' condition, a 'should-would' condition, a 'potential' condition, or perhaps a 'future less vivid'? Should we refer to μήν as a 'modal', 'attitudinal' or 'interactional' particle, or perhaps as a particle which 'expresses a mode of thought in isolation' (all the while well aware that the term 'particle' itself has fallen out of favour with linguists today)? Being no real fans of the 'declarative' and 'dynamic' infinitive, should we yet abandon those terms – now fairly well established in Greek linguistics, if not in Classics at large – for an older apparatus which blurs the crucial distinctions? Are 'imperfective' and 'perfective', the fully standardized terms in the linguistic literature on verbal aspect, too confusing to use when there are also imperfects and (not at all perfective) perfects to contend with?

Any answer to such problems is inevitably a compromise, and one which will leave a number of people unhappy to see no preference accorded to their preferred terms. What remains is to briefly state our general principles in selecting and using terminology in this book:

- We aim to use, whenever possible, terms which have some currency in general linguistics, not merely in Greek grammar.
- We wish to reflect, through our selection of terms, some of the significant advances made in Greek linguistics in recent decades.
- We aim to use terminology which is accurate and discrete (i.e. terms cover the phenomena they are meant to cover, and no more or less).
- Taking the above principles into account, we aim to use terminology which is intuitive (ideally, self-explanatory) and, where possible, familiar.
- Finally, and most importantly, we have strived for 'terminological inclusiveness' throughout: our notes and our Index of Subjects provide many alternative terms for the phenomena we treat (sometimes we also indicate why those alternative terms were not chosen).

Verbal Terminology

Separate attention in this context is demanded by the verb. A satisfying description of the Greek verbal system is made especially difficult by the confusion plaguing traditional grammatical terminology. This confusion is not easily resolved, other than by completely abandoning that traditional terminology (a course we decided not to take). Although we aim to be precise in our use of verbal terminology, some overlaps and forms of shorthand will remain, and it is good to be clear about these at the outset (reference to the table that opens chapter 11 may be helpful here; fuller discussion of the relevant terms may be found in that chapter).

Tenses, Aspects and Moods

- The term **tense** is found used as (i) a morphological concept identifying certain indicatives ('the imperfect tense', 'the aorist tense', 'narrative tenses', etc.), (ii) as the equivalent of what we will call tense-aspect stems ('a participle of the aorist tense', 'a present-tense optative', 'the tenses outside the indicative', etc.) and (iii) as a grammatical concept referring to the expression of temporal relationships ('past tenses', 'present tenses', etc.; 'anteriority', 'simultaneity', etc.). In this grammar 'tense' is primarily used in the third sense, occasionally in the first. The second use will (and should) be avoided, since the term 'tense' is much less relevant to the description of (e.g.) participles and optatives.
- Similarly, the terms **present, aorist, future** and **perfect** are used both (i) to refer to tense-aspect stems ('a perfect infinitive', 'the aorist optative does not have an augment') and (ii) to refer to the indicatives of these tense-aspect stems ('aorists and imperfects', 'the aorist has an augment') . It may be noted that in the latter use, 'aorist' is a direct equivalent of 'imperfect', but not in the former (there is, in Greek, no 'imperfect subjunctive' parallel to the 'aorist subjunctive'). In this book we write 'aorist' for 'aorist indicative' (etc.) only when there can be no doubt about the intended meaning.

Note 1: Thus, most often, 'aorist' in this book stands for a stem which expresses a kind of aspect (perfective aspect), 'present' for a stem which expresses another kind (imperfective aspect), etc.: for these distinctions, →33.4–7. We observe that in some recent treatments in general linguistics, the stems are in fact referred to by these names (yielding such terminology as 'primary imperfective indicative' for Greek forms which we will call 'present indicative', and 'perfective infinitive' for what we call 'aorist infinitive'). Such a system has considerable advantages, but strays, perhaps, too far from territory familiar to most students and scholars of Greek.

- We prefer simple **imperfect** and **pluperfect** over 'imperfect indicative' and 'pluperfect indicative', since the latter formulations are tautologous (Greek imperfects and pluperfects are by definition indicatives), and may suggest that

other variables could go into the indicative 'slot' (which they cannot: there is no 'imperfect subjunctive'). For the definition of the imperfect as 'secondary present indicative' and the pluperfect as 'secondary perfect indicative', →11.7.
- We identify only indicatives, subjunctives, optatives and imperatives as **moods**: the infinitive and participle should not be classed as such.

On 'First' and 'Second' Aorists and Perfects

Finally, there is a persistent tradition in handbooks to distinguish between 'first' (or 'weak') and 'second' (or 'strong') forms in the aorist, aorist passive and perfect stems:

- An aorist stem is called first (or 'weak') when σ is added to the verb stem (e.g. παιδευσ(α)-), an aorist passive stem when θ is added (e.g. παιδευθη-), a perfect stem when κ is added (e.g. πεπαιδευκ-).
- Otherwise, forms are second (or 'strong').

We have not followed this use: 'first' and 'second' are, in our view, unhelpful terms which provide insufficient morphological information (note, for instance, that the 'second' thematic aorist ἐ-λίπ-ο-μεν has a thematic vowel, whereas 'second' root aorist ἔ-γνω-μεν does not; these should not be classed together), and which misleadingly suggest that phenomena which are in fact highly regular (e.g. perfect active stems ending in χ or φ) are irregular. Instead, we distinguish between three types of aorist stem (sigmatic, thematic, root; →13), between two types of aorist passive stem (θη- and η-; →14), and between three types of perfect active stem (κ-, aspirated, stem; →18).

Part I

Phonology and Morphology

1

The Signs and Sounds of Classical Greek

Writing: the Alphabet, Accent and Breathing Marks, Punctuation

The Alphabet

1.1 The standard Greek alphabet consists of twenty-four letters:

	capital	lower case	name		capital	lower case	name
1	**A**	α	ἄλφα *alpha*	13	**N**	ν	νῦ *nu*
2	**B**	β	βῆτα *beta*	14	**Ξ**	ξ	ξεῖ (ξῖ) *xi*
3	**Γ**	γ	γάμμα *gamma*	15	**O**	ο	ὂ μικρόν omicron
4	**Δ**	δ	δέλτα *delta*	16	**Π**	π	πεῖ (πῖ) *pi*
5	**E**	ε	ἒ ψιλόν *epsilon*	17	**P**	ρ	ῥῶ *rho*
6	**Z**	ζ	ζῆτα *zeta*	18	**Σ, C**	σ, ς, c	σῖγμα/σίγμα sigma
7	**H**	η	ἦτα *eta*	19	**T**	τ	ταῦ *tau*
8	**Θ**	θ	θῆτα *theta*	20	**Y**	υ	ὖ ψιλόν upsilon
9	**I**	ι	ἰῶτα *iota*	21	**Φ**	φ	φεῖ (φῖ) *phi*
10	**K**	κ	κάππα *kappa*	22	**X**	χ	χεῖ (χῖ) *chi*
11	**Λ**	λ	λά(μ)βδα la(m)bda	23	**Ψ**	ψ	ψεῖ (ψῖ) *psi*
12	**M**	μ	μῦ *mu*	24	**Ω**	ω	ὦ μέγα omega

1.2 Several other letters were used in Greek alphabets during and before the classical period. Of these, the following will be used in this book:

letter   *name*

ϝ   *digamma* or *wau* (→1.31, 1.74, 9.13); the symbols ṷ or *w* are also used as an equivalent of this.

ϙ   *koppa* (→9.13)

ϛ   *stigma* (→9.13)

ϡ   *san* or *sampi* (→9.13)

Not part of any Greek alphabet, but frequently used in the transcription of reconstructed Greek, is the sign y, *yod* (→1.31, 1.74); this is also often written as i̯ or as j.

Particulars

1.3   For the pronunciation (and phonetic categorization) of the letters, →1.14–33. α, ε, η, ι, ο, υ and ω represent vowels; the other letters represent consonants, apart from ζ, ξ and ψ, which each represent two consonants.

1.4   **Lower case sigma** is conventionally written σ in all positions except at the end of a word, where it is written ς: e.g. Σώστρατος, στάσις. Some text editions use so-called 'lunate' sigma C/c in all positions: e.g. Cώcτρατοc, cτάcιc.

1.5   Some specific spelling conventions pertain to **diphthongs** (combinations of two vowels that are pronounced in a single syllable):

   – Only the first part of diphthongs is **capitalized**: e.g. Αἴγυπτος, Εὐριπίδης.
   – In three diphthongs ending in iota, the iota is conventionally printed underneath the first vowel: ᾳ, ῃ and ῳ. This is called **iota subscript**. Alternatively, these diphthongs are sometimes printed with **iota adscript**: αι, ηι, ωι. Iota subscript is not used with capitals: e.g. Ἅιδης, Ὠιδή (lower case ᾠδή).

   For a complete list of diphthongs, their pronunciation, and details concerning iota subscript, →1.20–3. For accents and breathings on diphthongs, →1.8.

Accents and Breathings

1.6   Three accent signs are conventionally used in Greek texts:

   – the **acute** accent ´ : e.g. ά, έ, ό, αί, οί;
   – the **grave** accent ` : e.g. ὰ, ὲ, ὸ, ὺ, αὶ, οὶ (written only on the final syllable of a word);
   – the **circumflex** accent ˜ (also frequently written ^): e.g. ᾶ, ῆ, αῦ, οῖ (written only on long vowels or diphthongs).

   For the value of these accents and the basic principles of Greek accentuation, →24.

1.7   Two breathing signs are conventionally used in Greek texts, written on words that begin with a vowel or diphthong, or with ρ:

   – the **smooth breathing** (*spiritus lenis*) ᾿ : e.g. ὄρος, αὐτή, ᾖ;
   – the **rough breathing** (*spiritus asper*) ῾ : e.g. ὅρος, αὕτη, ᾗ.

   A rough breathing indicates **aspiration**, i.e. a [h]-sound preceding the opening vowel/diphthong of a word (→1.27). In addition, words beginning with ρ are written with a rough breathing (e.g. ῥίπτω). A smooth breathing indicates the lack of aspiration.

1.8   The following conventions pertain to the placement of accents and breathing marks:

– Accents and breathing marks are written only on vowels (and the rough breathing on ρ). When written on a **capitalized** vowel or ρ, accents and breathings are placed **before** the letter:

ὁ Ἐρατοσθένης   ὁ Ἄδμητος   ἡ Ῥόδος

– When written on a **diphthong**, accents and breathings are written on the second vowel:

αἰτεῖν   οἷος   ποίησον

οὔκουν   Εὐριπίδης   παιδεῦον

However, when an accent and/or breathing is written on a **diphthong with an iota subscript**, it is written on the first vowel. This convention is followed even in cases where adscript iota is used (in certain text editions, or if the diphthong is capitalized):

ᾤκουν (adscript: ὤικουν)   ᾖ (adscript: ἦι)   Ἅιδης

– In combinations of breathing marks and accents, acute or grave accents are written after (i.e. to the right of) breathing marks (e.g. οὔκουν, ἃ, Ἄδμητος); the circumflex is placed above breathing marks (e.g. εἶδος, ᾧ, Ἧρα).

Punctuation

1.9   Modern editions of Greek texts use the following signs of punctuation:

– the **period** (.): serves the same function as in English usage;
– the **comma** (,): serves the same function as in English usage;
– the **high dot** (·): roughly the equivalent of the English semi-colon (;) and colon (:);
– the **question mark** (;): the equivalent of the English question mark (?);
– the **apostrophe** (’): used to indicate elision of a vowel (→1.34–8);
– dashes (—) or parenthesis signs (( )) are used to mark parentheses; the dash is also used by some editors to mark interrupted/incomplete utterances in dramatic texts; other editors use three dots (. . .).

Modern editions are inconsistent in their use of **quotation marks**: some editions are printed entirely without quotation marks (often with a capital letter at the start of the quoted speech – this convention is followed in this book), some use “ . . . ” or ‘ . . . ’; finally, some text editions (particularly those printed in France and Italy) use « . . . ».

Note 1: Modern punctuation of Ancient Greek texts traditionally follows the conventions used in modern languages (and therefore varies according to where an edition is printed): it often does not reflect the probable ancient intonation and/or writing conventions.

Further Diacritical Signs

1.10   Apart from the breathings, accents and punctuation signs listed above, the following signs are used:

- the **diaeresis** ¨ : written on the second of two vowels to indicate that they do not form a diphthong (e.g. δαΐζω, ἄϋπνος);
- the **coronis** ʼ (sign identical to a smooth breathing): used to indicate **crasis**, the merging of a word ending with a vowel/diphthong and a word beginning with a vowel/diphthong: e.g. ταὐτό (= τὸ αὐτό), κᾆτα (= καὶ εἶτα); for details, →1.43–5.

The Alphabet, Breathings, Accents, Punctuation: a Very Brief Historical Overview

1.11   The Greeks adopted the **alphabet** from the Phoenicians, presumably in the ninth century BCE, with the first securely dated inscriptions attested in the eighth century BCE. The letters of the Phoenician alphabet all represented consonants, but the Greeks re-assigned the value of some of the letters to represent vowels, and added some letters. Most of the names of the Greek letters are derived from the Phoenician names.

Early Greek alphabets differed strongly from each other, with respect to both the inventory and the shape of the symbols. The East-Ionic alphabet (which had some particular innovations, such as assigning a vowel-sound to the letter H) was eventually adopted throughout the Greek world; in Athens, it was adopted for official state documents in 403/402 BCE, although it may have been introduced earlier for literary works. This is the standardized alphabet given above.

The division between upper and lower case letters is not ancient: small letters (minuscules) were introduced in the ninth/tenth centuries CE by Byzantine scholars; the ancient Greeks themselves only wrote in capital letters (majuscules/uncials). In modern editions, capital letters are conventionally used only at the beginning of names and sometimes at the beginning of a new sentence, a new paragraph, a new speech turn (in dialogues), or to mark the beginning of cited direct speech (the latter convention is followed in this book). Inscriptions are sometimes printed entirely in capital letters in modern editions.

Note 1: For the use of the letters of the alphabet as numerals, →9.13.

1.12   **Breathing marks** and **accents** were introduced by scholars working in the Library of Alexandria in the Hellenistic period. The system of accentuation adopted in modern text editions, although deriving indirectly from these Hellenistic scholars, is based on treatises by Byzantine scholars.

1.13   The Greeks also did not avail themselves systematically of **punctuation** or **word divisions** (although early inscriptions sometimes used the signs : or ⁝ for divisions between words or word groups). Both were introduced in Byzantine times and adopted in modern editions.

Pronunciation: Vowels and Diphthongs

1.14   The (reconstructed) pronunciation of sounds in classical Greek in the following sections is given in the International Phonetic Alphabet (IPA), and with as close an approximation in English or another modern language as possible. IPA symbols are given between square brackets (e.g. [a]). Many IPA symbols are predictable and correspond to standard English usage; some, however, diverge (for these, a guide or the website of the *International Phonetic Association* may be consulted). The symbol : in IPA indicates a long vowel (e.g. [aː]).

Vowels

1.15   The following are the Greek **vowels**, and their pronunciation. In addition, an approximation of the classical pronunciation is given in English and/or another modern language.

vowel	sound	example	approximation
α	[a]	γάρ [gár] *for*	*aha*, Germ. *Mann*, Ital. *amare*
	[aː]	χώρα [kʰɔ́ːraː] *land*	*aha*, Ital. *amare*
ε	[e]	ψέγω [ségɔ:] *rebuke*	*fatal*, Fr. *clé*
η	[ɛː]	ἦθος [ɛ̂ːtʰos] *character*	*air*, Fr. *tête*
ι	[i]	πόλις [pólis] *city*	*fancy*, Fr. *écrit*
	[iː]	δελφῖνος [delpʰîːnos] *dolphin* (gen.)	*weed*
ο	[o]	ποτε [pote] *once*	*go*, *notorious*, Germ. *Motiv*
υ	[y]	φύσις [pʰýsis] *nature*	Fr. *lune*
	[yː]	μῦθος [mŷːtʰos] *word, story*	Fr. *muse, écluse*
ω	[ɔː]	Πλάτων [plátɔːn] *Plato*	*more*, *notorious*

Below, to distinguish short and long α, ι and υ, the marks ˘ (*breve*, short) and ˉ (*macron*, long) will frequently be used: ᾰ, ῐ, and ῠ are short, ᾱ, ῑ and ῡ are long. ε and ο are always short. η and ω are always long.

Note 1: In conventional Anglophone pronunciation of Ancient Greek, ε is usually pronounced [ɛ] as in *get*, η is often (especially in America) pronounced [eː] as in *made*, ι is usually pronounced [ɪ] as in *win*, and ο is often pronounced [ɒ] as in *got*.

Phonetic Details

1.16   Vowels are produced by the uninterrupted flow of air from the vocal cords through
the mouth (as opposed to consonants, which involve a complete or partial interruption of the air flow, →1.25).

1.17   The **quality** of a vowel (its sound) is determined by three factors:
–   **height** (or 'openness'): the vertical position of the tongue relative to the roof of
the mouth: for example, ι and υ are 'high' ('close') vowels, because the tongue is
high in the mouth when they are pronounced; α is a 'low' ('open') vowel;
–   **backness**: the position of the tongue relative to the back of the mouth: for
example, ι is a 'front' vowel, because the tongue is positioned towards the front
of the mouth when it is pronounced; ο is a 'back' vowel; α is a 'central' vowel;
–   **roundedness**: whether the lips are rounded or not: for example, υ and ο are
'rounded' because the lips are rounded when they are pronounced; ι, ε and α are
'unrounded'.

1.18   The **quantity** (length) of a vowel is determined primarily by the duration of its
pronunciation, although there are often changes in quality between long and short
vowels as well. Note that the letters α, ι and υ are used to represent both short and
long vowels. The long equivalent of ε is either η or 'spurious' ει; the long equivalent
of ο is either ω or 'spurious' ου (→1.23).

1.19   Using these variables, the vowel system of classical Attic may be represented as
follows (the outer triangle represents long vowels, the inner triangle short vowels;
rounded vowels are underlined):

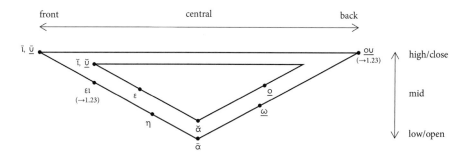

Figure 1.1: Vowel triangle: the vowel system of classical Attic

Diphthongs

1.20   Greek has thirteen **diphthongs**, combinations of two vowels that are pronounced in a
single syllable. The second part of a diphthong is always either ι or υ. On the basis of
the quantity of the first vowel, a distinction is made between 'short' and 'long'
diphthongs (although the resulting syllable is always long for the purposes of metre
and accentuation, except for final -οι/-αι in certain words; for details →24.7, 24.10).

Short Diphthongs

1.21   The following are the **short diphthongs**:

diphthong	sound	example	approximation
αι	[ai]	καινός [kainós] *new*	*high, eye* (with short first vowel)
ει	[eː] (earlier [ei])	πείθω [péːtʰɔː] *persuade*	*made*, Germ. *Beet* (earlier *eight, hey*)
οι	[oi]	λοιπός [loipós] *remaining*	Afrik. *rooibos* (with short first vowel)
υι	[yj]	μυῖα [myĵa] *fly*	Fr. *huit, halleluja*
αυ	[au]	ταῦρος [taûros] *bull*	*how* (with short first vowel)
ευ	[eu]	εὖρος [eûros] *width*	(no close equivalent available) a glide from *get* to *wide*; cf. Cockney *bell*
ου	[oː] (earlier [ou], later [uː])	πούς [póːs] *foot*	*mode* (earlier *low*, later *pool*)

Note 1: υ as second part of a diphthong was presumably closer to [u] (as in Engl. *do*) than to [y]. Moreover, ι and υ in diphthongs were not pronounced exactly like the equivalent single vowels, but as sounds approximating 'semivowels' [j] and [w] (as in Engl. *you* and *wave*); this was particularly the case when the diphthong preceded a vowel, in which case ι/υ was pronounced as a glide between the vowel sounds (as in Engl. *hey you* and *new wave*). For the semivowels, also →1.31.
Note 2: υι occurs only before vowels.

Long Diphthongs

1.22   In **long** diphthongs, if the second part is ι, it is written in most texts *under* the first letter (**iota subscript**):

diphthong	sound	example	approximation
ᾳ	[aːi]	ᾄδω [aːídɔː] *sing*	*rye*
ῃ	[εːi]	κομιδῇ [komidɛ̂ːi] *entirely*	Fr. *appareil*
ῳ	[ɔːi]	τραγῳδία [tragɔːidíaː] *tragedy*	*noise* (with long first vowel)
αυ	[aːu]	ταὐτό [taːutó] *the same*	*how* (with long first vowel)
ηυ	[εːu]	ηὗρον [hɛ̂ːuron] *found*	(similar to ευ, but with long first vowel)
ωυ	[ɔːu]	ἑωυτόν [heɔːutón] *himself* (Ion., →25.14)	a glide from *more* to *wide*; cf. *saw*

Note 1: The ι as second part of long diphthongs was gradually lost in the pronunciation of post-classical Greek, and subsequently also in writing. Iota subscript was then introduced to indicate the original presence of the sound. In an increasing number of modern text editions, the iota is written as a full letter: **iota adscript** (ηι instead of ῃ, αι instead of ᾳ, ωι instead of ῳ). Observe that αι in this system is ambiguous (it can be both a 'short' and a 'long' diphthong; but →1.8 above for the position of accents and breathing marks).

Note 2: The ι as second part of ῃ was probably lost already in the classical period. This sound then appears to have merged with ει.

Note 3: In conventional Anglophone pronunciation of Ancient Greek, iota subscript is usually not pronounced (i.e. ῃ is pronounced as η, etc.).

'Spurious' Diphthongs ει and ου

1.23   Two developments contributed to a peculiar feature of Greek (particularly Attic-Ionic) spelling:

- a long e-sound and a long o-sound, [eː] and [oː], came into use as the result of contraction (→1.58–65) or compensatory lengthening (→1.67–9); these were distinct from – namely 'higher' (→1.17–19) than – the older long vowels [ɛː] (eventually written η) and [ɔː] (eventually written ω);
- the pronunciation of the diphthongs [ei] and [ou] gradually shifted towards [eː] and [oː] as well (they were monophthongized).

As a result, in the late fifth century, the digraphs **ει** and **ου** began to be used to represent [eː] and [oː], not just when these sounds developed from the older 'genuine' diphthongs (at that time no longer pronounced as such), but *also* when they resulted from contraction or compensatory lengthening. This spelling was later standardized.

Because ει and ου in such cases represent sounds which were never genuine diphthongs, they are normally called '**spurious' diphthongs**.

Note 1: Below, ε̄ and ō will occasionally be used to represent [eː] and [oː] when resulting from contraction or compensatory lengthening, in order to distinguish them from 'genuine' diphthongs. It may be noted that E and O was the spelling for both long [eː]/[oː] and short [e]/[o] in Attic inscriptions up to the late fifth century BCE: the use of EI and OY made it possible to distinguish the long vowels from short [e] and [o].

Note 2: The pronunciation of ου (whether originally genuine or 'spurious') soon shifted to [uː] (the pronunciation was fronted and raised, →1.17–19).

Pronunciation: Consonants

List of Consonants

1.24   The following are the Greek **consonants**, and their pronunciation:

consonant	sound	example	approximation
β	[b]	βαίνω [baínɔ:] *go, walk*	*bed*
γ	[g]	γυνή [gynέ:] *woman*	*guy*
	before γ, κ, χ: [ŋ]	συγγενής [syŋgenέ:s] *akin*	li*v*i*ng*,
			ha*ng*man
δ	[d]	διά [diá] *through*	*dear*
ζ	[zd]	ζοή [zdoέ:] *life*	wi*sd*om
θ	[tʰ]	θάνατος [tʰánatos] *death*	(word-initial t)
			*T*om
κ	[k]	ἐκ [ek] *out of, from*	s*c*an
λ	[l]	καλός [kalós] *beautiful*	*l*esson
μ	[m]	ῥῆμα [rʰɛ̂:ma] *word*	*m*other
ν	[n]	νύξ [núks] *night*	*n*othing
ξ	[ks]	ξίφος [ksípʰos] *sword*	e*x*
π	[p]	λείπω [lé:pɔ:] *leave*	s*p*ot
ρ	[r]	ῥέω [rʰéɔ:] *flow*	*rh*yme (rolling r)
σ/ς	[s]	βάσις [básis] *step*	*s*ound
τ	[t]	κράτος [krátos] *power*	s*t*ill
φ	[pʰ]	γράφω [grápʰɔ:] *write*	(word-initial p)
			*p*ot
χ	[kʰ]	ταχύς [takʰýs] *quick*	*ch*orus
ψ	[ps]	ῥαψῳδός [rʰapsɔ:idós] *rhapsode*	la*ps*e

Phonetic Details

1.25   Consonants are sounds produced by the complete or partial interruption of the flow of air by a constriction at some point in the vocal tract: the Greek consonants may be divided into the following categories: stops (labial, velar and dental stops), fricatives, liquids, and nasals (for semivowels, →1.31).

Stops

1.26   **Stops** (or **plosives**): sounds produced by the complete interruption of the flow of air. Within this category, three groups may be distinguished, depending on the place of articulation:

–   **(bi)labial stops**: the flow of air is interrupted by pressing the lips (Lat. *labia*) together;

–   **dental stops**: the flow of air is interrupted by pressing the tongue against the teeth (Lat. *dentes*);

- **velar stops**: the flow of air is interrupted by pressing the tongue against the roof of the mouth (Lat. *velum*).

The stops may be further divided between:

- **voiced stops**: the vocal cords vibrate;
- **voiceless stops**: the vocal cords do not vibrate;
- **aspirated (voiceless) stops**: the sound is produced together with aspiration (an h-sound: →1.27).

The following are the nine stops of Greek:

	voiced	*voiceless*	*aspirated (voiceless)*
labial stops	β [b]	π [p]	φ [pʰ]
dental stops	δ [d]	τ [t]	θ [tʰ]
velar stops	γ [g]	κ [k]	χ [kʰ]

Note 1: In conventional Anglophone pronunciation, φ and θ are often pronounced as fricatives ([f] as in Engl. *fast* and [θ] as in *theatre*, respectively). This corresponds to the pronunciation of medieval and modern Greek.

Note 2: γ may also be a nasal, →1.29, with n.1.

Fricatives

1.27 **Fricatives**: sounds produced by 'squeezing' air through a constriction at some point in the mouth. The standard Greek alphabet has only one fricative, **σ**, a voiceless **sibilant** (a sharp 'hissing' sound; the obstruction is formed by pressing the tongue against the gums).

In addition, the rough breathing (ʽ) represents a fricative, [h].

Resonants

1.28 The category of **resonants** consists of the nasal consonants μ and ν (and in certain cases γ) and the so-called 'liquids' λ and ρ.

1.29 **Nasals**: the air flow is completely obstructed in the mouth, but flows through the nose. The Greek alphabet has three nasals (all voiced):

- a **labial nasal, μ** [m]: the flow of air is interrupted by pressing the lips together; air escapes through the nose;
- a **dental nasal, ν** [n]: the flow of air is interrupted by pressing the tongue against the teeth or gums; air escapes through the nose;
- a **velar nasal, γ** [ŋ] (only when written before a velar stop – γ, κ, χ): the flow of air is interrupted by pressing the tongue against the roof of the mouth; air escapes through the nose.

Note 1: The letter γ was, according to scholars in antiquity, pronounced as [ŋ] also before the nasal μ, e.g. in πρᾶγμα [praːŋma]. This sound was then called 'angma'. In modern convention, however, this pronunciation is usually not followed, and γ before μ is given its 'regular' pronunciation as a voiced velar stop [g].

1.30   **Liquids:** two Greek letters belong to the class of liquids – λ and ρ:

– a **lateral consonant, λ** [l]: air escapes along the sides of the tongue, but not through the middle of the mouth;
– a **rhotic consonant** (or 'tremulant'), **ρ** [r]: this was pronounced as a rolling, 'alveolar trill' sound, with the tongue vibrating against the gums. At the beginning of a word (and in some cases in the middle of a word), this sound was pronounced with aspiration (hence word-initial *rho* is always written ῥ-).

1.31   To the category of resonants also belong the so-called **semivowels**:

– [j], as in Engl. *you*: in the notation of Greek, the letter *yod* (y, also j) is used to represent this sound; some modern treatments use the symbol *i̯*;
– [w], as in Engl. *wave*: various Greek alphabets used the letter *digamma* (ϝ, also known as *wau*) for this sound; some modern treatments use the symbol *w* or *u̯*.

The semivowels are the equivalents of the vowels ι and υ, but they occur in different environments; for this, and for their disappearance from Greek, →1.74–82.

Geminates

1.32   Most of the consonants discussed above can be doubled (so-called 'geminates'), e.g. κκ, μμ, σσ: these stand for 'lengthened' versions of the same sounds (cf. the pronunciation of English compounds such as *unnamed*, *part-time*). In geminates with an aspirated stop (πφ, τθ, κχ), only the second letter is written in its aspirated form (thus e.g. Σαπφώ *Sappho*). Geminates affect the metrical quantity of a syllable: thus e.g. the first syllable of ὄμμα *eye* is long for the purpose of metre, even though the o is a short vowel.

Letters Representing Two Consonants

1.33   **Single letters, two consonants:** three letters in the Greek alphabet represent a combination of two consonants:

– ζ [zd]: voiced sibilant, followed by voiced dental stop;
– ξ [ks]: voiceless velar stop, followed by voiceless sibilant;
– ψ [ps]: voiceless labial stop, followed by voiceless sibilant.

Note 1: In conventional Anglophone pronunciation, ζ is sometimes pronounced as a single voiced sibilant [z] (as in Engl. *zoo*). This corresponds to that of post-classical and later Greek.

Elision, 'Movable' Consonants, Crasis, Hiatus

Elision

1.34   Most short vowels at the end of a word may be dropped before a word beginning with a vowel or diphthong; this is called **elision**. That a vowel has been elided is indicated by an **apostrophe** ('):

ἀπ' αὐτοῦ (= ἀπ(ὸ) αὐτοῦ) *from him*

(1) ἔτ' ἄρ' Ἀθηνῶν ἔστ' ἀπόρθητος πόλις; (= ἔτ(ι) ἄρ(α) Ἀθηνῶν ἔστ(ι) ἀπόρθητος πόλις;) (Aesch. *Pers.* 348)
Is, then, the city of the Athenians still not sacked?

When π, κ or τ precedes the elided vowel, and the following word begins with a vowel/diphthong with rough breathing, the stop is aspirated (φ, χ, θ; 'assimilation', →1.88–9):

ἀφ' οὖ (= ἀπ(ὸ) οὖ) *since*

(2) ἀλλ' ἔσθ' ὅθ' ἡμᾶς αἰνέσεις. (= ἀλλ(ὰ) ἔστ(ι) ὅτ(ε) ἡμᾶς αἰνέσεις.) (Eur. *Alc.* 1109)
But there will be a day when you will praise me.

1.35   Elision also takes place in **compound words**, although this is not marked in writing:

ἐπέρχομαι *come upon* (ἐπί + ἔρχομαι), ἄφεσις *discharge* (ἀπό + ἔσις)

1.36   In monosyllabic words, the final vowel can only be elided if it is ε: e.g. γ' (γε), δ' (δέ), μ' (με), but not, for instance, the vowel of τό, τά, τί, πρό, etc.

The -ῐ of περί and ὅτι is never elided; the final ι of third-declension dative singular forms ending in ι (e.g. φύλακι) is elided only very rarely. Final -ῠ is never elided.

1.37   In poetry, the first vowel of a word (usually ἐ-) may be elided when it *follows* a word ending in a long vowel or diphthong. This is called '**prodelision**' or 'aphaeresis'. E.g. ποῦ 'στι (= ποῦ (ἐ)στι), ἐγὼ 'κ (= ἐγὼ (ἐ)κ).

1.38   Rarely, and only in poetry, final -αι or -οι is elided: e.g. εἶν' ἐν τῇ πόλει (= εἶν(αι) ἐν τῇ πόλει) *to be in the city*, οἴμ' ὡς ἀθυμῶ (= οἴμ(οι) ὡς ἀθυμῶ) *woe, how I suffer*.

'Movable' Consonants

1.39   Some verb forms and nominal forms normally get an additional -ν when a word beginning with a vowel or diphthong follows, and often at the end of a clause or sentence. This is called '**movable** *nu*' (Gr. νῦ ἐφελκυστικόν). It occurs with the following forms:

  – nominal forms with a dative plural ending in -σι: e.g. πατράσι(ν), Ἕλλησι(ν), τοῖσι(ν);

– third-person verb forms ending in -ε or -ι: e.g. ἔλεγε(ν), φέρουσι(ν), τίθησι(ν), ἐστί(ν);

– the 3 sg. impf. ᾔει(ν) *he went*, and 3 sg. pluperfects ending in -ει(ν): e.g. ᾔδει(ν) *he knew*; and in the 1 sg. impf. ἦ(ν) *I was*.

ἔλεγεν αὐτοῖς *she said to them*	ἔλεγε τοιάδε *she said the following*
φέρουσιν αἵδε πρόσπολοι *these servants carry*	διαφέρουσι δ' αἱ φύσεις *natures differ*
πᾶσιν ἀνθρώποις *all men*	πᾶσι θεοῖς *all the gods*

The optional presence of movable *nu* is indicated in this book by '-(ν)'.

Note 1: Especially in poetry, movable *nu* is written even before consonants: e.g. πᾶσιν βροτοῖς *all mortals* (often for metrical purposes, as it makes the final syllable of its word metrically 'long'). This occurs sometimes in prose texts as well, however.

1.40   The word **οὕτως** *so, thus* is usually spelled **οὕτω** (without final -ς) when a word beginning with a consonant follows. This -ς is therefore sometimes also called 'movable':

οὕτως ἐτελεύτησεν *so he died*   οὕτω δέχονται τὸν στρατόν *so
                                                                        they receive the army*

1.41   The preposition **ἐκ** takes the form **ἐξ** when followed by a word beginning with a vowel:

ἐξ ἀνδρῶν *from men*   ἐκ βροτῶν *from mortals*

1.42   The negative **οὐ** *not* has three forms: οὐ before consonants, οὐκ before vowels/diphthongs, but οὐχ before vowels/diphthongs with rough breathing:

οὐ θέμις *it is not allowed*   οὐκ οἶδα *I do not know*   οὐχ ὁρᾷς; *don't you see?*

Note 1: For the forms οὔ/οὔκ/οὔχ (with accent) and οὐχί, →24.36, 56.1.
Note 2: μηκέτι *no longer* (negative μή + ἔτι) has its κ by analogy with οὐκέτι *no longer* (οὐκ + ἔτι).

Crasis

1.43   Two words of which the first (a word of at most two syllables) ends in a vowel/diphthong, and the second begins with a vowel/diphthong, may 'blend' together, the two blended syllables forming a single new syllable. This is known as **crasis** (κρᾶσις *mixing*), and is indicated in texts by the addition of a **coronis** (→1.10) on the new vowel/diphthong:

ταὐτά (= τὰ αὐτά)   τοὐναντίον (= τὸ ἐναντίον)   ἐγᾦδα (= ἐγὼ οἶδα)
    the same things   *the opposite*   *I know*

If π, κ or τ precedes the new vowel/diphthong, and the second word started with a rough breathing, the aspiration is transferred to this stop (the coronis has its usual shape):

θοἰμάτιον (= τὸ ἱμάτιον)	τῇδε θἠμέρᾳ (= τῇδε τῇ ἡμέρᾳ)	χὠ (= καὶ ὁ)
the cloak	*this day*	*and the*

Note 1: Some editors incorrectly print θοἰμάτιον, θἠμέρᾳ, etc.

1.44   No coronis is present if the first word consists of only a single vowel or diphthong (this occurs especially with forms of the article). In such cases, only the breathing mark of the first word is written:

ὦνερ (= ὦ ἄνερ)	αὑτή (= ἡ αὐτή)	αὑτός (= ὁ αὐτός)	οὑμοί (= οἱ ἐμοί)
sir!	*the same woman*	*the same man*	*my men*

1.45   The vowel/diphthong resulting from crasis depends on the **rules of contraction** (→1.58–66). Thus e.g. τὸ ἐναντίον gives τοὐναντίον because ο + ε contracts to ('spurious') ου, τὰ ἐναντία gives τἀναντία because α + ε contracts to ᾱ.

Note 1: In some cases the rules of contraction are not observed, in order to preserve the vowel quality of the second word's initial vowel: e.g. ἁνήρ *the man* (= ὁ ἀνήρ, although ο + α normally gives ω), αὑτή, αὑτός (→1.44 above).

Note 2: When a diphthong with ι merges with a following word, the ι is lost: κἀγώ (= καὶ ἐγώ) *and I*, τἄρα (= τοι ἄρα), μεντἄν (= μέντοι ἄν); also θἠμέρᾳ, χὠ, αὑταί, and οὑμοί (→1.43–4 above).

Note 3: Most crasis-forms of ὁ ἕτερος *the other (of two)* are based on an older form ἅτερος: e.g. ἅτερος (= ὁ ἅτερος), ἅτεροι (= οἱ ἅτεροι), θάτερον (= τὸ ἅτερον), θἠτέρᾳ (= τῇ ἁτέρᾳ). θάτερ-forms are often written without coronis; from this developed a fully-fledged alternative pronoun θάτερος.

Hiatus

1.46   **'Hiatus'** is the term for any instance of a word ending with a vowel followed by a word beginning with a vowel, e.g. τὰ δὲ ἐναντία, τοῦτο ἄρα. Hiatus is generally avoided in poetry and sometimes by prose writers: this is done by elision, the addition of movable consonants, or crasis.

Historical Developments: Introduction

1.47   The remaining sections of this chapter treat certain historical developments in the Greek language before the classical period. These sections are designed to elucidate many of the 'irregularities' of (Attic) Greek morphology. Contrast, for instance, the following pairs of nominatives and genitives of some third-declension nouns:

nom. sg. ἀγών *contest*	gen. sg. ἀγῶνος
nom. sg. γένος *race, offspring*	gen. sg. γένους
nom. sg. βασιλεύς *king*	gen. sg. βασιλέως

The endings of these genitives seem at first sight unrelated, but may in fact be explained as three instances of the same genitive singular ending -ος seen in ἀγῶν-ος:

- γένους derives from a form which is reconstructed as *γένεσ-ος, from which the first σ disappeared, giving γένεος; εο subsequently contracted to ō ('spurious' ου) (for these steps, →1.83, 1.58–60);
- βασιλέως derives from *βασιλῆϝ-ος, from which ϝ disappeared, and ηο changed by a process known as *quantitative metathesis* to εω (for these steps, →1.80, 1.71).

Such changes are found to have occurred consistently in certain environments at certain periods, and are therefore sometimes referred to as **sound change 'laws'**: for instance, the disappearance of ϝ between vowels is such a law of Greek historical grammar. Most of the apparent irregularities of Greek morphology can be explained with reference to such laws, and it is therefore useful to have some familiarity with them.

Reference to the sections below will be made throughout the morphology.

1.48 The following conventions of **notation** will be used in the description of historical developments:

- Earlier forms which are not actually attested in our extant texts, but which are reconstructed on the basis of our knowledge of historical developments, are marked with the symbol * (**asterisk**).
- Non-existent hypothetical forms and impossible forms are marked with the symbol †.
- The symbol > stands for '**develops into**'; the symbol < stands for '**is derived from**'; these symbols are used both for changes in individual forms (e.g. *γένεσος > γένεος), and for more general laws (e.g. ā > η in Attic, →1.57).

1.49 In principle, the sound laws detailed below took place without exception (though they are often restricted to certain phonological 'environments' (e.g. between vowels), to certain dialect-regions, and always to certain periods in the development of the language). Still, numerous forms then remain which appear to violate the laws. Such unexpected forms are often the result of '**analogy**', the process by which certain forms are remodelled after certain familiar other forms.

For instance, the nom./acc. pl. neut. form of the noun ὀστοῦν *bone* is ὀστᾶ, and derives from ὀστέα; yet the combination εα normally contracted to η (→1.59). The 'unexpected' form ὀστᾶ was presumably modelled on other nom./acc. pl. neut. forms, which nearly always end in -α (e.g. δῶρα *gifts*).

Analogical remodelling often functioned to 'level' (i.e. regularize) nominal or verbal paradigms: for instance, the aor. pass. (θη-aor.) of the verb χέω *pour* is ἐχύθην, etc., even though the expected form, given sound change laws, would have been †ἐκύθην (-κυθ-<*-χυθ-, →1.97). Forms with χυθ- may be explained as levelling of the verb paradigm, given that all other forms of the verb have χ-.

1.50 Several of the developments detailed below apply only to **Attic Greek** (for other dialects, →25).

Historical Developments: Ablaut (Vowel Gradation)

Introduction; Qualitative and Quantitative Ablaut

1.51   In Greek, as in all Indo-European languages, there are often different **grades** (variants) of an individual root (for roots, →23.2): the different grades have **different vowels**. The German term *Ablaut* is normally used for this alternation.

For instance, the following grades of the root meaning 'father' are found, depending on the word in which that root is used, and the grammatical case:

πατερ-	e.g. in the voc. sg. πάτε̱ρ, nom. pl. πατέρες	(normal) e-grade
πατηρ-	in the nom. sg. πατή̱ρ *father*	lengthened e-grade
πατορ-	e.g. in the gen. sg. ἀπάτο̱ρος, acc. sg. ἀπάτο̱ρα	(normal) o-grade
πατωρ-	e.g. in the nom. sg. of the adj. ἀπάτω̱ρ *fatherless*	lengthened o-grade
πατρ-	e.g. in the gen. sg. πατ̱ρός, dat. sg. πατ̱ρί	zero-grade

Different grades also frequently appear in **different tense-aspect stems of a verb** (→11.11–12), for instance with the verb λείπω *leave*:

λειπ-	e.g. in the pres. ind. λε̱ίπω, fut. ind. λε̱ίψω	diphthong with e-grade
λοιπ-	e.g. in the pf. ind. λέλο̱ιπα	diphthong with o-grade
λῐπ-	e.g. in the aor. ind. ἔλῐ̱πον	no diphthong, zero-grade

Note 1: Indo-European ablaut is the cause of similar variation in English roots, such as *drink, drank, drunk*; and *blood, bleed*.
Note 2: Ablaut is in some older works called 'apophony'.

1.52   Two dimensions of ablaut may be distinguished:

– **qualitative ablaut**: variation between **e-grades** and **o-grades**;
– **quantitative ablaut**: variation between the **zero-grade** (or 'weak' grade), **normal grade** (or 'strong', 'full' grade), and **lengthened grades**.

This gives the following possibilities:

	e-grade	*o-grade*
normal grade	πάτε̱ρ	ἀπάτο̱ρος
lengthened grade	πατή̱ρ	ἀπάτω̱ρ
zero-grade		πατ̱ρός

1.53   Often, the ablaut patterns outlined above are not immediately transparent in Greek variants of a root because historical sound changes and/or subsequent analogical remodelling have obscured them. For instance:

– Roots with a nasal or liquid consonant often have a zero-grade with ᾰ (→1.85–7):

	e-grade	*o-grade*	*zero-grade*
τρέπω *turn*	τρεπ-	τροπ-	τρᾰπ- (<*τρ̥π-)
στέλλω *dispatch*	στελ-	στολ-	στᾰλ- (<*στλ̥-)
σπείρω *sow*	σπερ-	σπορ-	σπᾰρ- (<*σπρ̥-)
πάσχω *suffer*, πένθος *pain*	πενθ-	πονθ-	πᾰθ- (<*πn̥θ-)

- The stems of some frequently occurring verbs, which alternate between a long and a short vowel, are reconstructed as e-grades and zero-grades. For instance:

	e-grade	*zero-grade*
δίδωμι *give*	δω̄-	δο-
ἵστημι *make stand, set up*	στη- (<στᾱ-, →1.57)	στᾰ-
τίθημι *put, place*	θη-	θε-
ἵημι *send, let go*	ἡ̄-	ἑ-

Note 1: The reconstruction of stems such as δω-/δο-, στη-/στᾰ-, etc. involves a series of consonants called 'laryngeals': for instance, δω-/δο- is reconstructed as *deh_3-/*dh_3-, στη-/στᾰ- as *$steh_2$-/*sth_2- (where h_2 and h_3 are symbols for laryngeals). These laryngeals disappeared from the language very early in its history, but left several traces. For treatments of laryngeal theory, consult the works on historical grammar listed in the Bibliography at the end of this book.

Some Typical Greek Ablaut Patterns

1.54 **Lengthened grade** forms are found primarily in the nominative singular masculine/feminine of nominal forms of the third declension (→4.31–92). Contrast e.g. the following pairs:

lengthened grade	*normal grade*
nom. sg. masc. δαίμων *daemon*	acc. sg. δαίμονα
nom. sg. fem. μήτηρ *mother*	acc. sg. μητέρα

1.55 Many first-declension **nouns** ending in η/ᾱ (→4.3–7) and most second-declension nouns in -ος (→4.19–23) have a stem in the (normal) o-grade:

o-grade	*contrast:*
λόγος *word, speech*	λέγω *say, speak*, e-grade
στόλος *expedition*, στολή *garment*	στέλλω *dispatch, dress*, e-grade

---

Note 1: Again, this pattern is sometimes obscured by sound changes (frequently involving laryngeals, →1.53 n.1 above):

φωνή *voice* (o-grade, <*b^hoh_2-)

φημί *say, claim* (<*φᾱμί, e-grade, <*b^heh_2-; cf. 1 pl. φᾰμεν, zero-grade, <*b^hh_2-; cf. στη-/στᾰ-)

Neuter third-declension nouns in -ος (→4.65–7) and -μα (→4.40–2) often have a stem in the e-grade (for ablaut in the *endings* of neuter nouns in -ος, →4.66).

e-grade   *contrast:*

γένος *race, offspring*   γί-γν-ομαι *become, be born* (zero-grade), γόνος *child*
                             (o-grade)

σπέρμα *seed*   ἐσπάρην *I was sown* (zero-grade, <*σπr̥-), σπόρος
                             sowing (o-grade)

1.56   Many **verbs** originally had:

– e-grade in thematic present, future, and sigmatic aorist stems;
– o-grade in perfect active stems;
– zero-grade in thematic aorist, aorist passive, and perfect middle-passive stems.

In the following example, this pattern is retained:

	e-grade	*o-grade*	*zero-grade*
τρέπω *turn*	pres. τρέπω	pf. τέτροφα	them. aor. ἐτραπόμην (<*τr̥π-)
	fut. τρέψω		aor. pass. ἐτράπην
	sigm. aor. ἔτρεψα		pf. mp. τέτραμμαι

However, this pattern has often been obscured by subsequent changes or analogical remodelling (→1.49).

Historical Developments: Vowels

Attic-Ionic ᾱ > η

1.57   In Attic, **long ᾱ** was gradually 'raised' to η (for vowel height, →1.17):

μήτηρ *mother* (<μάτηρ), φυγή *flight* (<φυγά), νίκη *victory* (<νίκᾱ), δεσπότης *master*
(<δεσπότᾱς), fem. δεινή *impressive* (<δεινά), ἵστημι *make stand, set up* (<ἵστᾱμι),
aor. ἐτίμησα *honoured* (<ἐτίμᾱσα), fut. νικήσω *will conquer* (<νικάσω).

But this sound change was reversed if ᾱ stood immediately **after ε, ι or ρ**:

θέᾱ *sight*, αἰτίᾱ *cause*, σοφίᾱ *wisdom*, χώρᾱ *land*, νεανίᾱς *young man*, fem. δικαίᾱ
just, aor. ἔδρᾱσα *did*, fut. ἀνιάσω will grieve.

Note 1: The change ᾱ > η is peculiar to the Attic-Ionic dialect group. In Ionic, the change to η took place also after ε, ι or ρ: thus e.g. χώρη, →25.5.

Note 2: If ᾱ stands in other places than after ε/ι/ρ in Attic, it is itself the result of another development, usually contraction (e.g. imp. τίμᾱ <*-άε, →1.58–66) or compensatory lengthening (e.g. πᾶς *every, all* <*πάντς, →1.68).

Note 3: Quantitative metathesis (→1.71) took place after this change: thus e.g. gen. sg. νεώς *ship* (<*νη(ϝ)ός <*νᾱϝός). So too the disappearance of ϝ (→1.80): thus e.g. κόρη *girl* (with η after ρ, <*κόρϝη <*κόρϝᾱ).

Contraction of Vowels

1.58   **Contraction** is the merging of two vowels, or a vowel and a diphthong, into a single **long vowel** or a **diphthong**. This occurred especially when ϝ, y or σ disappeared between vowels (→1.74–84): e.g. 1 sg. τιμῶ *I honour* (<*-ἀ(y)ω); dat. sg. γένει *race* (<*-ε(σ)ι). For a complete overview of possible contractions, see the table below (1.63).

Contraction of α, ε, η, o and ω

1.59   Contraction of the vowels α, ε, η, o and ω involves two of the main factors determining vowel quality: **height** and **roundedness** (→1.17–19):

	unrounded	*rounded*
high	ε̄ (spelling: 'spurious' diphthong ει)	ō (spelling: 'spurious' diphthong ου)
	ε	o
	η	ω
low	ᾰ, ᾱ	

If at least one of the component vowels is (relatively) low, the product will be low; if at least one of the component vowels is rounded, the product will be rounded (roughly speaking: α-sounds 'beat' ε-sounds, o-sounds 'beat' everything else). The product is always a long vowel or a diphthong. Thus e.g.:

- ε + ε (none of the component vowels is rounded or low) > ε̄ (high/unrounded, long); e.g. 2 pl. ποιεῖτε (= -ε̄̃τε <-έετε);
- ε + o (none of the component vowels is low, one is rounded) > ō (high/rounded, long); e.g. 1 pl. ποιοῦμεν (= -ō̃μεν <-έομεν);
- o + o (none of the component vowels is low, both are rounded) > ō (high/ rounded, long); e.g. 1 pl. δηλοῦμεν (= -ō̃μεν <-όομεν);
- α + o (one of the component vowels is low, one of the component vowels is rounded) > ω (low, rounded); e.g. 1 pl. τιμῶμεν (<-άομεν).

If contraction leads to a low, unrounded product (i.e. contraction of α with ε/η), the rule is: α first > ᾱ; ε/η first > η. Thus e.g.:

- ε + α (one of the component vowels is low, ε first) > η (low, unrounded); e.g. nom./acc. pl. neut. γένη (<-εα);
- α + ε (same, but with α first) > ᾱ; e.g. 2 pl. τιμᾶτε (<-άετε).

Note 1: For the sequences ηᾰ, ηᾱ, ηo, ηō, and ηω, →1.71.

1.60   Long vowels ε̄ and ō were spelled in classical Greek as '**spurious' diphthongs ει and ου** (→1.23). Their behaviour in contraction, however, is entirely according to the rules given above. This means that when these sounds contract with another vowel, **no ι or υ is involved**. Thus e.g.:

– α + spurious ει > ᾱ (<u>not</u> ᾳ): e.g. inf. τιμᾶν (<*-ά-ε̄ν);
– ο + spurious ει > spurious ου (= ō): e.g. inf. δηλοῦν (= -όν <*-ό-ε̄ν);
– α + spurious ου > ω (<u>not</u> ωυ): e.g. 2 sg. imp. mp. τιμῶ (<*-α-ō).

Diphthongs

1.61   Contraction of a vowel with ι/υ generally leads to a **diphthong**: e.g. dat. sg. πόλει (<*πόλε(y)ι), 3 sg. opt. παιδεύοι (-ο-ι).

1.62   When a vowel contracts with a diphthong, the product is a diphthong with the same ι or υ as its second part; for the first part of the diphthong, the rules given above apply (so e.g. ε + αι > ῃ, because ε + α > η).
   Exception: ο + η > οι (e.g. 3 sg. subj. δηλοῖ <*-ο-η).

Note 1: Diphthongs ε̄ι, ōι and ōυ are 'shortened' to regular ει, οι, ου (so e.g. 3 sg. ind. δηλοῖ <*-ό-ει (ο + ε > ō)).
Note 2: The endings -εις and -ει of 2/3 sg. pres. act. ind. have a 'real' diphthong, but in the infinitive ending -ειν the diphthong is 'spurious' (contracted from -ε-εν): thus 3 sg. ind. τιμᾷ (<*-α-ει), but inf. τιμᾶν (<*-α-ε̄ν); 3 sg. ind. δηλοῖ (<*-ο-ει), but inf. δηλοῦν (= -όν <*-ο-ε̄ν).

Summary Table of Contractions

1.63   The principles outlined above lead to the following possibilities for contraction:

first vowel	second vowel								
	ᾰ/ᾱ	ε	ει (ε̄)	η	ι	ο	ου (ō)	ω	υ
ᾰ/ᾱ	ᾱ	ᾱ	ᾱ	ᾱ	αι/ᾳ	ω	ω	ω	αυ
ε	η	ει (ε̄)	ει (ε̄)	η	ει	ου (ō)	ου (ō)	ω	ευ
η	η →1.71	η	η	η	η	ω →1.71	ω →1.71	ω →1.71	ηυ
ο	ω	ου (ō)	ου (ō)	ω	οι	ου (ō)	ου (ō)	ω	ου
ω	ω	ω	ω	ω	ῳ	ω	ω	ω	ωυ

first vowel	second vowel (diphthongs)						
	ει	ῃ	αι	ᾳ	οι	ου	ῳ
ᾰ/ᾱ	ᾳ	ᾳ	(ᾳ)	ᾳ	ῳ	n/a	n/a
ε	ει	ῃ	ῃ	ῃ	οι	n/a	ῳ
η	ῃ	ῃ	ῃ →1.71	n/a	ῳ →1.71	n/a	n/a
ο	οι	οι	n/a	n/a	οι	n/a	ῳ
ω	ῳ	ῳ	n/a	n/a	ῳ	n/a	ῳ

Occasionally, ι or υ contracts with a following vowel, generally 'swallowing' it: e.g. nom. pl. ἰχθύες > ἰχθῦς *fishes*, Χίιος > Χῖος *Chios*.

1.64   Some further examples:

– contraction beginning with α-:

α + ε/spurious ει/η > ᾱ   e.g. τίμαε > τίμα; τιμάειν (= -αεν) >
                                                τιμᾶν; τιμάητε > τιμᾶτε

α + ο/spurious ου/ω > ω   e.g. τιμάομεν > τιμῶμεν; τιμάου > τιμῶ;
                                                τιμάω > τιμῶ

α + real ει > ᾳ; α + οι > ῳ   e.g. τιμάει > τιμᾷ; τιμάοιμεν > τιμῷμεν

– contraction beginning with ε-:

ε + ε/spurious ει > spurious ει   e.g. ποίεε > ποίει; ποιέειν (= -εεν) > ποιεῖν

ε + ο/spurious ου > spurious ου   e.g. ποιέομαι > ποιοῦμαι; χρυσέου (= -εο) >
                                                χρυσοῦ

ε + α > η; ε + αι > ῃ   e.g. γένεα > γένη; παιδεύεαι > παιδεύῃ.

ε 'dissolves' into ει, οι, η, ω   e.g. ποιέει > ποιεῖ; ποιέοιμεν > ποιοῖμεν;
                                                ποιέητε > ποιῆτε; ποιέω > ποιῶ

– contraction beginning with ο-:

ο + ε/spurious ει > spurious ου   e.g. δήλοε > δήλου; δηλόειν (= -οεν) > δηλοῦν

ο + α/η/ω > ω   e.g. αἰδόα > αἰδῶ; δηλόητε > δηλῶτε;
                                                δηλόω > δηλῶ

ο + ει/οι > οι; ο + η > οι (!)   e.g. δηλόει > δηλοῖ; δηλόοιμεν > δηλοῖμεν;
                                                δηλόη > δηλοῖ

– contraction beginning with η- or ω-:

η + ε > η; ω + ε/α > ω   e.g. χρήεται > χρῆται; ἥρωες > ἥρως ; ἥρωα
                                                > ἥρω

η + η > η; ω + οι > ῳ   e.g. ζήῃ > ζῇ; λαγώοι > λαγῴ

Further Particulars and Exceptions

1.65   If ϝ **disappeared** (→1.80) between ε/η and another vowel, contraction only
occurred if the second vowel was ε/η (or a diphthong with those sounds) as well.
Thus e.g. 3 sg. πλεῖ *sails* (<*πλέϝ-ει), Περικλῆς *Pericles* (<*-κλέϝ-ης); but 1 pl. πλέομεν
(<*πλέϝομεν), gen. Περικλέους (<*-κλέϝ-ος <*-κλέϝε(σ)ος).

If ϝ disappeared between other vowels, these did not contract: e.g. pf. ἀκήκοα
have heard (<*ἀκήκοϝα).

Note 1: Even if ϝ disappeared between two instances of ε/η, contraction did not occur
consistently: contrast 3 sg. impf. κατέχεε with ἐνέχει (both <*-έχεϝε, of the verbs καταχέω
pour down and ἐγχέω *pour in*, respectively), and nom. pl. νῆες *ships* with βασιλῆς *kings* (both
<*-ῆϝες).

1.66 Frequently, **analogy** (→1.49) cancels the effects of contraction: e.g. nom./acc. neut. pl. ὀστέ-α > ὀστᾶ *bones* (not †ὀστῆ; by analogy with other neut. pl. forms in -α); nom. fem. pl. μνάαι > μναῖ *minae* (not †μνᾷ; by analogy with other fem. pl. forms in -αι), nom. fem. pl. χρυσέαι > χρυσαῖ *golden* (not †χρυσῆ).

Long and Short: the Augment, Stem Formation, Compensatory Lengthening

1.67 A number of grammatical rules and sound changes cause variants of certain forms to occur with either a long or a short vowel/diphthong:

- the formation of many verbal and nominal **stems**: e.g. nom. sg. δαίμων *spirit*, contrast gen. sg. δαίμονος; ποιη- (e.g. in fut. ποιήσω), contrast ποιε- (pres. stem of ποιέω *make, do*);
- the formation of the **augment** with verbs starting with a vowel or diphthong: e.g. impf. ἤκουον (ἀκούω *hear*); for details, →11.37–8;
- so-called **compensatory lengthening**, usually caused by the disappearance of a consonant in a cluster consisting of **resonant + σ/y**: e.g. aor. ἔφηνα *showed* (<*ἔ-φᾰν-σα).

All of these phenomena are often referred to as 'lengthening', but the sound changes underlying them are not the same, and occurred at different moments in the development of the language (in fact the heading 'lengthening' is often not accurate, particularly in the case of stem formation, where the alternation is typically the result of ablaut, →1.51–6). They therefore lead to different results, especially where it concerns the long counterparts of ᾰ, ε and ο. For an overview of the different results, see the table below (→1.69).

Compensatory Lengthening

1.68 **Compensatory lengthening**, most often caused by the disappearance of a consonant from the cluster **nasal/liquid + σ or y**, occurs regularly in the following cases:

- in the **pseudo-sigmatic aorist** (with verb stems ending in a resonant, →13.24–6); e.g. κρίνω *judge*, verb stem κρῑ(ν)-, aor. ἔκρῑνα (<*ἔ-κρῐν-σα); with φαίνω *show*, verb stem φην-/φᾰν-, aor. ἔφηνα (<*ἔ-φᾰν-σα);
- in the **present stem** of verbs in -είνω/-είρω, -ῑνω/-ῑρω, and -ῠνω/-ῠρω, e.g. σπείρω *sow* (= σπέρω <*σπέρ-yω), κρίνω *judge* (<*κρῐν-yω), φύρω *mix* (<*φῠρ-yω);
- in the dat. pl. masc./neut., the fem., and sometimes the nom. sg. masc. of nominal **ντ-stems** (→4.45–8, 5.15–18), e.g. nom. sg. masc. ppl. δεικνύς *showing* (<*δεικνῠνς <*δεικνῠντς), dat. pl. δεικνῦσι (<*-ῠνσι <*-ῠντσι), fem. δεικνῦσα (<*-ῠνσα <*-ῠντyα), but gen. sg. masc. δεικνῠντος, dat. δεικνῠντι;

- in the **3 pl. pres. act. ind.** of -ω verbs (thematic, →11.27, 12.3–7): e.g. 3 pl. παιδεύουσι *educate* (= παιδεύο͞σι <*παιδεύο̱νσι), contrast 1 pl. παιδεύο̱μεν;
- in the **accusative plural endings** of the first and second declensions: τᾱ́ς (<*τᾰ́νς), τούς (= τό̄ς <*τόνς);
- other, incidental, cases, e.g. εἷς *one* (= ἕ̄ς <*ἕνς), contrast gen. ἑνός; εἰς *(in)to* (= ἐ̄ς <*ἐ̱νς); εἰμί *be* (= ἐ̄μί <*ἐ̱σμί), contrast 2 pl. ἐστέ.

Two stages of compensatory lengthening are distinguished: in the first, σ or y disappeared and a resonant remained (e.g. ἔκρῑνα <*ἔκρῐνσα); in the second, (word-final or 'secondary', →1.84) σ remained and a resonant disappeared (e.g. τούς <*τόνς).

In Attic, the two stages led to different results in the case of lengthened α, as one stage occurred before the change ᾱ > η (→1.57), the other after it; thus first-stage lengthened ᾱ could subsequently change to η (e.g. ἔφηνα <*ἔφᾱνα <*ἔφᾰνσα), whereas second-stage ᾱ did not (e.g. τᾱ́ς <*τᾰ́νς).

Note 1: Results such as τᾱ́ς, τούς, and εἰς originally would have occurred only when these words were followed by a vowel, but were generalized. Sometimes different dialects/authors generalized different forms (e.g. Ion. ἐς).

Note 2: In the dat. pl. of nominal ν-stems, the ν seems to disappear without compensatory lengthening: e.g. with δαίμων *spirit* (stem δαιμον-), dat. pl. δαίμοσι; with σώφρων *prudent* (stem σωφρον-), dat. pl. σώφροσι. This is presumably the result of analogical levelling of paradigms rather than a regular change: →4.51 n.1.

Summary Table

1.69   The following table summarizes the different vowel alternations:
(the table on the next page)

Shortening: Osthoff's Law

1.70   **Long vowels** (ᾱ, η, ῑ, ῡ, ω) were **shortened** (to ᾰ, ε, ῐ, ῠ, o, respectively) when they were followed by a **resonant** (μ, ν, λ, ρ) and **another consonant**. This sound change is known as **Osthoff's Law**. Some examples:

gen. sg., ppl. aor. pass. παιδευθέντος (<*-θη̱ντος), gen. pl. παιδευθέντων (<*-θη̱ντων); cf. ἐπαιδεύθην;

ppl. aor. γνόντες (<*γνω̱ντες), dat. pl. γνοῦσι (= γνõσι <*γνό̱ντσι <*γνω̱ντσι); cf. ἔγνων.

To this sound change also belongs the **shortening of long diphthongs** before a consonant (or at word end), since the second part of diphthongs (ι, υ) counts as a resonant (cf. y, ϝ, →1.31). This explains such cases as:

βασιλεύς *king* (<*-η̱υς), voc. sg. βασιλεῦ (<*-η̱υ), cf. nom. pl. βασιλῆς (<*-ῆϝες, →1.79–80);

short vowel / long vowel		augmentation/stem formation	
		augmentation	stem formation
ᾰ	η	ἀ̱κούω impf. ἤκουον	τιμᾰ̱́ω fut. τιμή̱σω
	ᾱ (after ε, ι or ρ)		δρᾰ̱́ω fut. δρᾱ́σω
ε	η	ἐρωτάω impf. ἠ̱ρώτων	ποιέω fut. ποιή̱σω
ῐ	ῑ	ἵ̱ημι impf. ἵ̱ην	—
ο	ω	ὀ̱νομάζω impf. ὠ̱νόμαζον	δηλό̱ω fut. δηλώ̱σω
ῠ	ῡ	ὑ̱βρίζω impf. ὕ̱βριζον	—
long vowel	unchanged	ἥ̱κω impf. ἥ̱κον	n/a
diphthong	first part as above, second part (ι/υ) unchanged	αἰ̱σχύνομαι impf. ᾐ̱σχυνόμην εὑ̱ρίσκω aor. ηὗ̱ρον οἰ̱κέω impf. ᾤ̱κουν	n/a

short vowel / long vowel		compensatory lengthening	
		first stage (result: σ/y disappears, resonant remains)	second stage (result: σ remains, resonant disappears)
ᾰ	η	stem φᾱ̆ν- aor. ἔφη̱να (<*ἔφᾰνσα)	ᾱ dat. pl. ἱστᾱσι (<*ἱστᾰντσι)
	ᾱ (after ε, ι or ρ)	stem μιᾱ̆ν- aor. ἐμίᾱνα (<*ἐμίᾰνσα)	
ε	'spurious' ει (= ē̄)	stem μεν- aor. ἔμει̱να (<*ἔμενσα)	dat. pl. τιθεῖσι (<*τιθέντσι)
ῐ	ῑ	stem κρῑ̆ν- aor. ἔκρῑ̱να (<*ἔκρῐνσα)	Ion. acc. pl. πόλῑ̄ς (<*πόλῐνς, →25.22)
ο	'spurious' ου (=ō̄)	—	dat. pl. διδοῦσι (<*διδόντσι) 3 pl. ind. λύουσι (<*λύονσι)
ῠ	ῡ	stem ἀμῡ̆ν- aor. ἤμῡ̱να (<*ἤμῠνσα)	dat. pl. δεικνῦσι (<*δεικνῠντσι)
long vowel	n/a		
diphthong	n/a		

Note 1: There are several exceptions to these 'rules' for the formation of the augment. For details, →11.40–1.

ναῦς *ship* (<*ναῦς, rather than > νηῦς), dat. pl. ναυσί (<*ναυσί, rather than > νηυσί), cf. nom. pl. νῆες (<*νῆϝες).

Note 1: The diphthong formed by the optative marker ι/ιη (→11.16) is always short, even when it is added to stems which are otherwise long: e.g. γνοίην, σταῖεν, παιδευθεῖμεν (contrast ἔγνων, ἔστην, ἐπαιδεύθην). Osthoff's Law was presumably involved at least in forms whose endings begin with a consonant (e.g. παιδευθεῖμεν <*παιδευθή-ι-μεν); the reasons for the short diphthong in some other cases are controversial.

Quantitative Metathesis

1.71 The following changes are referred to as **quantitative metathesis** (= exchange of (vowel) quantity):

– When η was followed by long ᾱ or ω, it was shortened in Attic-Ionic (i.e. **ηᾱ > εᾱ, ηω > εω**); if it was followed by ō ('spurious' ου), it was shortened and ō changed to ω (i.e. **ηō > εω**).

– When η was followed by short ᾰ or ο, it was shortened and the second vowel lengthened to ᾱ or ω (i.e. **ηᾰ > εᾱ, ηο > εω**):

Contraction of the two resulting vowels then took place, unless ϝ stood between them (→1.65).

θέᾱ *sight* (<*θή(ϝ)ᾱ); gen. sg. νεώ *temple* (<*νη(ϝ)ō); gen. pl. βασιλέων *kings* (<*βασιλή(ϝ)ων), 1 sg. aor. subj. θῶ (<θέω <*θήω), 3 pl. aor. subj. στῶσιν (<στέωσιν <*στήωσιν).

acc. sg. βασιλέᾱ (<*βασιλή(ϝ)ᾰ); gen. sg. βασιλέως (<*βασιλή(ϝ)ος), nom. sg. νεώς (<*νη(ϝ)ός <*νᾱϝός), nom. pl. ἵλεω *favourable* (<*ἵλη(ϝ)οι).

Note 1: The term 'quantitative metathesis' is inaccurate in cases such as θέᾱ, νεώ, etc., as there is no 'exchange' of vowel length, merely a shortening of the first. Nevertheless, the term tends to be used for such instances as well.

Historical Developments: Consonants

Consonants at Word End

1.72 Apart from vowels, only **ν, ρ** and **ς** (including **ξ** and **ψ**) can occur at word end.

Note 1: There are two exceptions (both proclitics, →24.33–5): the preposition ἐκ and the negative οὐκ/οὐχ.

1.73 Other original consonants at word end **were lost** or changed:

– **stops** at word end disappeared:

voc. sg. γύναι *woman* (<*γύναικ, cf. γυναικός), nom. sg. γάλα *milk* (<*γάλακτ, cf. γάλακτος);

voc. sg. παῖ *child* (<*παῖδ, cf. παιδός), neut. ppl. παιδεῦον (<*-οντ, cf. gen. παιδεύοντος), 3 pl. impf. ἔφερον *carried* (<*ἔφεροντ, cf. Lat. *ferebant*).

- -**μ** at word end after a vowel became -**ν** (for -μ at word end after consonants, →1.85–6):

neut. ἕν *one* (<*σέμ, cf. fem. σμία), acc. sg. λύκον *wolf* (<*λύκομ, cf. Lat. *lupum*), 1 sg. impf. ἔφερον (<*ἔφερομ, cf. Lat. *ferebam*).

The Disappearance of ϝ, y and σ

1.74   Many peculiarities of Greek morphology are due to the disappearance or change of the semivowels y and ϝ (→1.31) and the fricative σ at different points in the history of the language. The most important sound changes involving these consonants are detailed below.

Semivowel ϝ and vowel ῠ are in fact the same sound in different environments (so e.g. ταχῠ́ς *quick* (nom. sg., zero-grade) between consonants, but *ταχέϝος (gen. sg., e-grade, > ταχέος between vowels). The same holds for semivowel y and vowel ῐ (so e.g. πόλῐς *city* (nom. sg., zero-grade) between consonants, but *πόλεyες (nom. pl., e-grade, > πόλεις) between vowels).

Sound Changes Involving ῐ/y

1.75   The **vowel ῐ** is found:

- **Between consonants** or **at word end after a consonant**. So e.g. πόλῐς, voc. πόλῐ.
- **Between a vowel and a consonant** or **at word end after a vowel**, forming a **diphthong** with the preceding vowel. So e.g. εἶμι *go*, ᾄδω *sing* (<ἀείδ-), ᾠδή *song* (<ἀοιδ-), opt. παιδεύοιμι, 3 sg. παιδεύοι.

1.76   When semivowel **y** stood **between vowels**, it **disappeared without trace**; the vowels then contracted (→1.58–66): e.g. dat. sg. πόλει (<*πόλεyι), nom. pl. πόλεις (= πόλēς <*πόλεy-ες), 1 sg. ind. τιμῶ (<*τιμάyω), nom. τρεῖς *three* (= τρ͂ες <*τρέyες).

Note 1: When ι occurs between vowels, i.e. in a diphthong followed by a vowel, this is usually due to the loss of ϝ or σ (e.g. ποιέω *do, make* <*ποιϝε-; τοῖος *such* <*τόσyος), or analogy (→1.49, e.g. 2 sg. opt. δοίης (<*δοΐης), presumably modelled on e.g. 1 pl. δοῖμεν; 1 sg. impf. ἦα *went*, modelled on forms such as 1 pl. ἦμεν).

1.77   **Stop + y before a vowel** had various results:

- Labial stop + y (i.e. **πy/φy**) > **ττ**: e.g. βλάπτω *harm* (<*βλάπyω), θάπτω *bury* (<*θάφyω).
- Voiceless dental or velar stop + y (i.e. **τy/θy, κy/χy**) > **ττ**: e.g. μέλιττα *bee* (<*μέλιτyα), κορύττω *equip* (<*κορύθyω), φυλάττω *guard* (<*φυλάκyω), ὀρύττω *dig* (<*ὀρύχyω).

But in some cases **τy > σ**: e.g. fem. πᾶσα *every, all* (<*πᾰ́νσα <*πᾰ́ντyα), τόσος *so large* (<*τότyος).

- Voiced dental or velar stop + y (i.e. **δy** or **γy**) > ζ: e.g. Ζεύς (<*Δyεύς), νομίζω *believe* (<*νομίδyω); κράζω *shout* (<*κράγyω), ἅζομαι *revere* (<*ἅγyομαι).

  But also sometimes **γy > ττ**, e.g. τάττω *array* (<*τάγyω), probably by analogy with voiceless velars.

ττ as the result of these changes is specifically Attic; other dialects, including Ionic, have σσ, which is also preferred in tragedy, by Thucydides, and in Koine Greek (→25.10).

1.78 **Resonant + y before a vowel** also had various results:

- **λy > λλ**: e.g. ἀγγέλλω *report* (<*ἀγγέλyω), βάλλω *throw* (<*βάλyω), ἄλλος *other* (<*ἄλyος).
- **νy/ρy after α/ο> αιν/αιρ, οιν/οιρ** (inversion of the ν/ρ and y): e.g. φαίνω *show* (<*φᾰ́νyω), μέλαινα *black* (<*μέλᾰνyα), καθαίρω *cleanse* (<*καθᾰ́ρyω), μοῖρα *fate* (<*μόρyα).
- **νy/ρy after ε/ι/υ > ειν/ειρ (= ε̄ν/ε̄ρ), ῑν/ῑρ, ῡν/ῡρ** (y disappears with compensatory lengthening (→1.68–9) of the vowel before ν/ρ): e.g. κτείνω *kill* (<*κτένyω), σπεῖρα *coil* (<*σπέρyα), κρῑ́νω *judge* (<*κρῐ́νyω), ἀμῡ́νω *defend* (<*ἀμῠ́νyω), φῡ́ρω *mix* (<*φῠ́ρyω).

Note 1: σy and ϝy between vowels > y, resulting in a diphthong: e.g. τοῖος *such* (<*τόσyος), καίω *burn* (<*κάϝyω); sometimes the y disappeared, e.g. κάω next to καίω.

Sound Changes Involving ῠ/ϝ

1.79 The **vowel ῠ** is found:

- **Between consonants** or **at word end after a consonant**. So e.g. ταχῠ́ς *quick*, neut. ταχῠ́, acc. sg. ἰσχῠ́ν *strength*, ἄστῠ *town*.
- **Between a vowel and a consonant** or **at word end after a vowel**, forming a **diphthong** with the preceding vowel. So e.g. Ζεῦς, voc. sg. Ζεῦ, βοῦς *ox*. If the preceding vowel was long, it was shortened (Osthoff's Law, →1.70): βασιλεύς *king* (<*βασιληῠ́-ς), ναῦς *ship* (<*νᾱῦ-ς).

1.80 In other environments, the **semivowel ϝ disappeared**:

- **At word beginning before a vowel**: so e.g. οἶκος *house* (<*ϝοῖκος), ἄναξ *lord* (<*ϝάναξ), ἔργον *work* (<*ϝέργον).
- **Between vowels**: 1 pl. pres. ind. πλέομεν *sail* (<*πλέϝομεν), gen. sg. Διός *Zeus* (<*Διϝός). When ϝ disappeared between two instances of ε or η, these vowels usually contracted (→1.65): Περικλῆς (<*Περικλέϝης), 3 sg. pres. ind. πλεῖ (<*πλέϝει), nom. pl. βασιλῆς (<*βασιλῆϝες).

1.81 σϝ- at word beginning before a vowel disappeared leaving a rough breathing: e.g. ἡδύς (<*σϝᾱδύς, cf. Lat. *suavis*, Engl. *sweet*), ἀνδάνω *please* (<*σϝα-).

1.82   In the combination resonant + ϝ between vowels, ϝ disappeared without trace: e.g. ξένος *stranger* (<*ξένϝος) – but for Ion. ξεῖνος, →25.11.

Sound Changes Involving σ

1.83   **σ disappeared** between vowels or at word beginning before a vowel, leaving the sound [h]:

– **at word beginning before a vowel**: the [h] appears as a **rough breathing**: so e.g. ἕπομαι *follow* (<*σε-; cf. Lat. *sequor*), ἵστημι *make stand* (<*σίστ-, →11.49), εἷς *one* (= ἕς <*ἕνς (→1.68) <*σένς), ἑπτά *seven* (<*σεπτή̣, →1.86; cf. Lat. *septem*).
– **between vowels**: the [h] subsequently disappeared, and contraction normally followed (→1.58–66): gen. sg. γένους *race* (<γένε(h)ος <*γένεσος), acc. Σωκράτη (<*-κράτεσα), 2 sg. mp. ind. ἐπαιδεύου (<*ἐπαιδεύεσο), fut. βαλῶ *will throw* (<*βαλέσω).

Note 1: If σ is found in classical Greek in these environments (i.e. between vowels or word-initially before a vowel), it is normally itself the product of sound changes (e.g. dat. pl. γένεσι *races* (<γένεσσι, →1.92), fut. ὀνομάσω *will name* (<*ὀνομάδσω, →1.91), τόσος *so large* (<*τότγος, →1.77)), or due to analogy (→1.49; e.g. dat. pl. ἰσχύσι *strengths* (modelled on e.g. φύλαξι), fut. παιδεύσω *strengths* (modelled on e.g. δείξω), aor. ἐπαίδευσα (modelled on e.g. ἔδειξα)).

Such instances of σ are often called **secondary**, or, together with instances where an original σ did not disappear (e.g. at word end), 'strong'.

1.84   In a cluster of **resonant + σ**, the σ usually disappeared, with compensatory lengthening of any preceding vowel (→1.68): so e.g. fem. μία *one* (<*σμία), and pseudo-sigmatic aor. ἔνειμα *dealt out* (= ἔνημα <*ἔνεμσα), ἔφηνα *showed* (<ἔφᾱνσα <*ἔφᾰνσα).

Word-final or 'secondary' σ (→1.83 n.1) in such clusters was not lost; instead the resonant disappeared, again with compensatory lengthening: so e.g. fem. πᾶσα *every, all* (<*πᾶνσα <*πάντγα), 3. pl. ind. παιδεύουσι (= -ōσι <*-ονσι <*-οντι), εἷς *one* (= ἕς <*ἕν̣ς).

Note 1: The cluster ρσ changed to ρρ in Attic: θάρρος *courage* < θάρσος, ἄρρην *masculine* < ἄρσην.

Note 2: The cluster λσ sometimes remained unchanged: e.g. ἄλσος *grove*, aor. ἔκελσα *put to shore*.

Other Consonant Clusters: Vocalization of Resonants, Assimilation, Loss of Consonants

Vocalization of Syllabic Resonants

1.85   Resonants (nasals and liquids) could originally occur **between consonants** or at **word end** after a consonant: such nasals/liquids were pronounced in a separate syllable, and are therefore called '**syllabic resonants**'; they are commonly written ṃ, ṇ, ḷ, ṛ.

Note 1: The pronunciation of such nasals and liquids may be compared to English examples such as *seventh* [sɛvᵊnθ] and *bottle* [bɒtᵊl].
Note 2: The relation between (e.g.) μ and ṃ is identical to that between y and ι, and between ϝ and υ: →1.74.

1.86 In Greek syllabic nasals ṃ and ṇ were 'vocalized' to ᾰ:

ἑκᾰτόν *hundred* (<*ἑ-ḳṇτόν, cf. Lat. *centum*), δέκᾰ *ten* (<*δέκ-ṃ, cf. Lat. *decem*), ὄνομᾰ *name* (<*ὄ-νομ-ṇ, cf. Lat. *nomen*).

Note especially the endings -ᾰ/-ᾰς of the acc. sg./pl. of many third-declension nominal forms (→2.4 n.1, 2.6), and the zero-grade stem of some verbs (→1.53, 1.56):

acc. sg. πόδᾰ *foot* (<*πόδ-ṃ, cf. e.g. Lat. *pedem*), γῦπᾰ *vulture* (<*γῦπ-ṃ), cf. e.g. τόν (<*τόμ, →1.73);

acc. pl. πόδᾰς (<*πόδ-ṇs), γῦπᾰς (<*γῦπ-ṇs), cf. e.g. τούς (<*τόνς, →1.68);

zero-grade stems: aor. pass. ἐτάθην (<*ἐ-ṭṇ-θην), pf. τέτᾰκα (<*τέ-ṭṇ-κα), cf. τείνω *stretch* (<*τέν-yω, →1.78); aor. ἔπᾰθον *suffered* (<ἔ-ṗṇθ-ον); cf. πένθος *grief*.

This change also explains the -ᾰ of the (pseudo-)sigmatic aorist (→13.7):

1 sg. aor. act. ind. ἔδειξᾰ *showed* (<*ἔ-δειξ-ṃ; cf. 1 sg. impf. act. ἔδεικνυν <*-νυ-μ, →1.73)

1.87 Syllabic **liquids** ḷ, ṛ were also vocalized, becoming **λᾰ/ρᾰ** (or ᾰλ/ᾰρ), respectively:

dat. pl. πατράσι *fathers* (<*πατṛ́-σι, cf. gen. sg. πατρ-ός), πλᾰτύς *wide* (<*pḷτύς).

Note especially the zero-grade stem of some verbs (→1.53, 1.56):

aor. pass. ἐστράφην (<*ἐ-στṛ́φ-ην, cf. στρέφω *turn*), pf. mp. διέφθαρμαι (<*δι-ε-φθṛ-μαι, cf. διαφθείρω *destroy*);

aor. pass. ἐκλᾰ́πην (<*ἐ-ḳḷπ-ην, cf. κλέπτω *steal*), pf. mp. ἔστᾰλμαι (<*ἔ-στḷμαι, cf. στέλλω *dispatch*).

Assimilation in Consonant Clusters

1.88 **Assimilation** is a common morphological process by which one sound becomes more like another, nearby sound. In Greek sequences of two consonants, the first often changed under influence of the second ('regressive assimilation', as in e.g. συλλέγω *collect* <συν-λέγω); very rarely the reverse process occurred ('progressive assimilation', as in e.g. ὄλλυμι *lose* <*ὄλ-νυμι). The most common forms of assimilation are detailed below.

1.89 Assimilation in clusters of stops:

 – A **labial or velar stop** before a **dental stop** became voiceless, voiced, or aspirated (→1.26) in the same manner as that dental stop: thus the only possible combinations are πτ/κτ (voiceless), βδ/γδ (voiced), and φθ/χθ (aspirated):

3 sg. pf. mp. τέτριπται (<*τέτριβ-ται, cf. τρίβω *rub*), aor. pass. ἐλέχθην (<*ἐλέγ-θην, cf. λέγω *say*), πλέγδην *entwined* (<*πλέκ-δην, cf. πλέκω *plait*).

- A **dental stop** before another **dental stop** changed to σ:

aor. pass. ἐπείσθην (<*ἐπείθ-θην, cf. πείθω *persuade*), 3 sg. pf. mp. κεκόμισται (<*κεκόμιδ-ται, cf. κομιδή *attendance*), ψεύστης *liar* (<*ψεύδ-της, cf. ψεύδομαι *lie*).

Note 1: The preposition ἐκ- does not change in compounds, e.g. ἔκγονος *descendant*, ἐκδίδωμι *give up*, ἔκθετος *put out*.
Note 2: For 'geminates' such as ττ, →1.32.

1.90   Assimilation in clusters of **stop + nasal**:

- Clusters of **velar or dental stop** with a **nasal** normally remained unchanged: e.g. ἀκμή *point*, ὀκνῶ *shrink from*, κεδνός *diligent*.

    However, before μ in the conjugation of the middle-passive perfect, velars changed to γ, dentals to σ (i.e. κμ/χμ > γμ; τμ/δμ/θμ > σμ); this also occurs before some suffixes such as -μα and -μος (→23.21–2):

    pf. mp. πεφύλαγμαι (<*πεφύλακ-μαι, cf. gen. sg. φύλακος *guard*); δεῖγμα *evidence* (<*δεῖκ-μα, cf. δείκνυμι *show*);

    pf. mp. πέπεισμαι (<*πέπειθ-μαι, cf. πείθω *persuade*), ψεῦσμα *lie* (<*ψεῦδ-μα, cf. ψεύδομαι *lie*).

- **Labial stops** assimilate fully to a following **μ** (i.e. πμ/βμ/φμ > μμ;); also βν > μν:

    pf. mp. τέτριμμαι (<*τέτριβ-μαι, cf. τρίβω *rub*); γράμμα *writing* (<*γράφ-μα, cf. γράφω *write*); σεμνός *revered* (<*σεβ-νός, cf. σέβομαι *revere*).

- **Nasals before stops** got the same place of articulation as the stop (→1.26, 1.29): the labial nasal μ before a labial stop, dental nasal ν before a dental stop, velar nasal γ before a velar stop:

    συμβάλλω *throw together*, συντάττω *array*, συγκαλῶ *convene* (all <συν-). Cf. also the 'nasal infix' (→12.30) in verbs like λαμβάνω *get*, λανθάνω *go unnoticed*, λαγχάνω *obtain by lot* (cf. aor. ἔλαβον, ἔλαθον, ἔλαχον).

1.91   Assimilation in clusters of **stop + σ**:

- A dental stop before σ disappeared without trace:
    aor. ἔψευσα (<*ἔψευδ-σα, cf. ψεύδω *cheat*); fut. πείσω (<*πείθ-σω, cf. πείθω *persuade*); dat. pl. πράγμασι *things* (<*πράγματ-σι, cf. πράγματος), νύξ *night* (<*νύκ-ς <*νύκτ-ς, cf. νυκτός); dat. pl. πᾶσι *all* (<*πάνσι (→1.68) <*πάντ-σι, cf. παντός).

Note 1: With some adverbs of direction in -δε (→6.11), sibilant σ became voiced before the voiced dental δ, and the resulting cluster was spelled ζ ([zd], →1.33): e.g. Ἀθήναζε *to Athens* (<-ασ-δε).

- **Labial stop + σ > ψ; velar stop + σ > ξ** (this is to some extent a matter of spelling rather than assimilation):

  aor. ἔτριψα (<*ἔτριβ-σα, cf. τρίβω *rub*); fut. γράψω (<*γράφ-σω, cf. γράφω *write*); γύψ *vulture* (<*γύπ-ς, cf. gen. sg. γυπός);

  aor. ἔπλεξα (<*ἔπλεκ-σα, cf. πλέκω *plait*); fut. τάξω *will array* (<*τάγ-σω, cf. ταγή *battle line*); φύλαξ *guard* (<*φύλακ-ς, cf. gen. sg. φύλακος).

1.92   A sequence of two sibilants (σ + σ) was simplified to σ: e.g. dat. pl. γένεσι *races* (<γένεσ-σι), aor. ἐγέλασα *laughed* (<ἐγέλασ-σα).

1.93   Assimilation in clusters of **liquids and nasals**:

- In a sequence of **ν before μ**, the first nasal assimilated to the second: e.g. ἐμμένω *abide* (<ἐν-μένω), σύμμαχος *ally* (<σύν-μαχος). However, in the conjugation of the middle-passive perfect, νμ was sometimes replaced analogically by σμ; this also occurs before some suffixes such as -μα:

  pf. mp. πέφασμαι (*πέφαν-μαι, cf. φαίνω *show*); μίασμα *pollution* (*μίαν-μα, cf. μιαίνω *defile*); but contrast regularly formed pf. mp. ᾔσχυμμαι (<*ᾔσχυν-μαι, cf. αἰσχύνομαι *be ashamed*)

- The sequences **νρ, μρ** and **μλ** were expanded with a transitional sound, a voiced stop with the same point of articulation (i.e. labial or dental) as the nasal (→1.26, 1.28), i.e. **νδρ, μβρ, μβλ**. At the beginning of a word, the nasal was lost:

  acc. sg. ἄνδρα *man* (<*ἄνρα (zero-grade), cf. voc. ἄνερ (e-grade)); βλώσκω *come* (<*μλω- (zero-grade), cf. aor. ἔ-μολ-ον (o-grade)).

Note 1: Exceptions: especially in compounds with συν- and παν-, the nasal often assimilates fully to the following liquid: e.g. συρρέω *flow together* (<συν-ρ-), συλλέγω *collect* (<συν-λ-), παρρησία *freedom of speech* (<παν-ρ-).

Loss of Consonants

1.94   In clusters of three or more consonants, one was sometimes lost. This occurs especially in sequences consonant–σ–consonant in the conjugation of the perfect middle-passive, where the σ normally disappears:

  pf. mp. inf. ἠγγέλθαι (<*ἠγγέλσθαι; ἀγγέλλω *report*), τετράφθαι (<*τετράπθαι <*τετράπσθαι; τρέπω *turn*); 2 pl. pf. mp. ind. τέταχθε (<*τέταχθε <*τέταγσθε; τάττω *array*).

1.95   When σ stood between two stops with the same place of articulation, the first stop disappeared: e.g. λάσκω *rattle* (<*λάκσκω, cf. aor. ἔλακον).

1.96   For clusters with a dental stop before σ, →1.91 (dental disappears; e.g. νύξ *night* <*νύκτς; πάσχω *suffer* <*πάθσκω (<πήθ-σκ-ω, →1.86), with transference of aspiration).

Loss of Aspiration: Grassmann's Law

1.97   In a sequence **aspirated stop–vowel–aspirated stop**, the **first** aspirated stop **lost its aspiration** (this sound change is known as **Grassmann's law**). The change also occurred in such sequences with an intervening resonant:

τίθημι *put, place* (<*θίθ-), pf. τέθηκα (<*θέθ-), aor. pass. ἐτέθην (<*ἐθέθ-); pf. πέφηνα (<*φέφ-; φαίνομαι *appear*), pf. κέχυμαι (<*χέχ-; χέω *pour*), τρέφω *nourish* (<*θρέφ-), τρέχω *run* (<*θρέχ-).

By the same process, a vowel with a rough breathing before an aspirated stop lost its aspiration:

ἔχω *have* (<*ἕχω <*σέχω; for the disappearance of σ, →1.83).

Note 1: ξ and ψ were not aspirated when this sound change occurred, so they had no effect on a preceding aspirated stop or rough breathing. This explains variations such as ἔχω (<*ἕχω <*σέχω) but fut. ἕξω (<*σέχσω); fut. θάψω but aor. pass. ἐτάφην (<*ἐθάφην; θάπτω *bury*); τρέφω (<*θρέφ-) but fut. θρέψω; nom. sg. θρίξ *hair* but gen. sg. τριχός (<*θριχός).

The change occurred after the disappearance of y, hence e.g. θάπτω *bury* (<*θάφyω, →1.77, not †τάπτω).

Note 2: Exceptions to this rule occur frequently, especially in later forms; these can normally be explained as the result of analogy (→1.49): e.g. aor. pass. ὠρθώθην (ὀρθόω *set straight*), ἐχύθην (χέω *pour*), ἐφάνθην (φαίνω *show*; cf. also πεφάνθαι), ἐκαθάρθην (καθαίρω *cleanse*), etc.

Note also the 'inverse' application of the rule (with the second aspirated stop losing its aspiration) in the case of the 2 sg. imp. of θη-aorists, e.g. παιδεύθητι (<*παιδεύθη-θι), →14.6.

2

Introduction to Nominal Forms

Basic Categories

2.1 All nominal forms (the article, nouns, adjectives, participles, pronouns) express each of the following three categories:

- **case**: nominative, genitive, dative, accusative or vocative;
- **number**: singular, plural or dual (referring to a group of exactly two);
- **gender**: masculine, feminine or neuter.

Some examples of nominal forms and the categories they express:

δώρῳ *gift*: a noun marked for case (dative), number (singular) and gender (neuter).

παιδεύοντες *educating*: a participle marked for case (nominative), number (plural) and gender (masculine); the participle also expresses tense-aspect and voice (→11.2–4).

τοῖν *the*: an article marked for case (genitive *or* dative), number (dual) and gender (masculine, feminine *or* neuter).

> **Note 1:** Nouns can have any case and number, but (usually) have only one gender: for instance, in the case of the noun οἶκος *house*, the form οἴκου is genitive singular, οἴκοις dative plural, and οἴκους accusative plural, but they are all masculine, as the noun is masculine.
>
> The article, adjectives, participles and pronouns can have any combination of case, number and gender: for instance, in the case of the adjective δεινός *impressive, awful* the form δεινοί is nominative plural masculine, δειναῖς dative plural feminine.
> **Note 2:** The genitive, dative and accusative are often referred to as **oblique cases**.

Building Blocks: Stems and Endings

2.2 All forms of a certain nominal word share a **stem**, which identifies the forms as deriving from that particular noun/adjective/etc.: for example, in any form of the adjective δεινός (e.g. δεινοῦ, δειναῖς, δεινά), the nominal stem δειν- identifies the form as belonging to that particular adjective and thus expressing the meaning *impressive*.

Some Greek nominal stems occur in different variants due to 'ablaut' vowel change (→1.51–6). For example, the stem of the noun γένος *race* occurs as either γενοσ- (o-grade) or γενε(σ)- (e-grade), and the stem of the noun δαίμων *spirit* occurs as either δαιμων- (lengthened grade) or δαιμον- (full-grade). Which grade is used depends on the type of stem, case and number.

Some other nouns and adjectives use more strongly different variants of nominal stems. For instance, the adjective πολύς *much, many* has some forms built on the stem πολυ- (e.g. πολύς, πολύν), and some on the stem πολλ- (e.g. πολλοῦ, πολλαῖς).

With any such forms, all different variants of the stem are normally given in the following chapters.

2.3   Every nominal form also has an **ending**, which provides the information required to identify the case, number and (in the case of articles, adjectives and pronouns) gender of the form:

πατρός: the ending -ος identifies the form as a genitive singular; the noun πατήρ *father* is masculine.

ὁδοῖς: the ending -οις identifies the form as a dative plural; the noun ὁδός *road* is feminine.

αὐτοί: the ending -οι identifies the form as a nominative plural masculine.

In a significant number of cases, a single ending may represent two or three different combinations of case, number and gender:

αὐτοῖς: the ending -οις identifies the form as a dative plural masculine *or* neuter.

ἐκεῖνο: the ending -ο identifies the form as a nominative *or* accusative singular neuter.

δεινῶν: the ending -ων identifies the form as a genitive plural, masculine *or* feminine *or* neuter.

Declensions and Endings

Declensions

2.4   Greek nominal forms are constructed according to regular patterns, called **declensions**:

- **first** or **a-declension**: nearly all forms show the presence of an α-sound in the ending (either ᾰ or ᾱ – in Attic, ᾱ has changed to η, except after ε, ι, ρ, →1.57);
- **second** or **o-declension**: nearly all forms show the presence of an o-sound in the ending (either ο, ου, or ω);
- **third** or **consonant-declension** (sometimes also called 'mixed' declension): a distinct set of endings is added to a stem, which ends in a consonant or ι or υ (or semivowels y/ϝ, →1.74).

Some examples:

δειν-<u>ᾱς</u> *impressive*: a first-declension form, with ending -ᾱς for accusative plural.

δούλ-<u>ους</u> *slaves*: a second-declension form, with ending -ους for accusative plural.

γῦπ-<u>ες</u> *vultures*: a third-declension form, with ending -ες for nominative plural.

Note 1: Historically, the endings used in each of the declensions were largely the same. The differences between the declensions may be explained as follows:

- The second declension is 'thematic', i.e. includes a thematic vowel ο (ε in the vocative singular; for thematic vowels, →11.18–19). Thus the second-declension nom. sg. δοῦλος *slave* can be analysed as consisting of a stem δουλ-, thematic vowel -ο- and an original ending -ς. The thematic vowel is often considered to be part of the stem, so that the second declension consists of stems (usually) ending in ο, such as δουλο-.
- The first declension (with stems ending in α) and third declension (with stems ending in a consonant or ι/υ) are 'athematic', i.e. endings are added directly to the stem. Thus the first-declension nom. sg. νεανίας *young man* and the third-declension nom. sg. γύψ *vulture* may be analysed as νεανία-ς and γύπ-ς, respectively, with the same ending -ς.

In many cases, however, such similarities between the declensions have been obscured by sound changes or variations in the use of endings. Thus, for instance, an original accusative singular ending *-μ has led to a -ν in the first/second declension (e.g. δοῦλον <*δοῦλ-ο-μ, →1.73) but in most subtypes of the third declension to an -ἄ (e.g. γῦπἄ <*γῦπ-μ̥, →1.86); similarly, compare the accusative plural forms (original ending *-νς) of the first declension (e.g. νεανίᾱς <*νεανία-νς, →1.68), second declension (e.g. δούλους = δούλōς <*δούλ-ο-νς, →1.68), and third declension (e.g. γῦπᾶς <*γῦπ-ν̥ς, →1.86).

For clarity's sake, the α-sound of the first declension and the ο/ε of the second declension will be treated as **part of the endings** below.

2.5   It is often impossible to derive the stem and pattern of declension of a noun from the nom. sg. form alone: dictionaries therefore provide the article and/or gen. sg. form in addition. These forms together generally provide sufficient information to determine which subtype the noun belongs to. Compare, for example:

ὁ δοῦλ<u>ος</u> *slave*, gen. δούλ<u>ου</u> (second decl.)	*but*	τὸ γέν<u>ος</u> *race*, gen. γέν<u>ους</u> (third decl.)
ὁ Ξέρξ<u>ης</u> *Xerxes*, gen. Ξέρξ<u>ου</u> (first decl.)	*but*	ὁ Σωκράτ<u>ης</u> *Socrates*, gen. Σωκράτ<u>ους</u> (third decl.)

In the third declension, the nom. sg. and gen. sg. are usually needed to determine which 'subtype' of the third declension a noun belongs to: →4.33.

Table of Endings

2.6   The regular case endings for each of the declensions are given in the table below. Fuller information and exceptions will be given in the following chapters:

	first declension		second declension		third declension	
sg. nom.	-ᾰ or -ᾱ/-η (fem.)	-ᾱς/-ης (masc.)	-ος (masc./fem.)	-ον or -ο (neut.)	-ς or -ø[1] (masc./fem.)	-ø[1] (neut.)
gen.	-ᾱς/-ης (fem.)	-ου (=-ō →1.23) (masc.)	-ου (=-ō →1.23)		-ος	
dat.	-ᾳ/-η		-ῳ		-ῐ	
acc.	-ᾱν or -ᾱν/-ην		-ον (masc./fem.)	= nom.[2] (neut.)	-ᾰ or -ν (masc./fem.)	= nom.[2] (neut.)
voc.	= nom.[3] (fem.)	-ᾰ or -ᾱ/-η (masc.)	-ε	= nom.[2] (neut.)	= nom./-ø[1]	
pl. nom.	-αι		-οι (masc./fem.)	-ᾰ (neut.)	-ες (masc./fem.)	-ᾰ (neut.)
gen.	-ῶν (<-άων)		-ων		-ων	
dat.	-αις[4]		-οις[4]		-σῐ(ν)	
acc.	-ᾱς		-ους (=-ōς →1.23) (masc./fem.)	= nom.[2] (neut.)	-ᾰς	= nom.[2] (neut.)
voc.	= nom.[3]		= nom.[3]		= nom.[3]	

[1] The symbol ø stands for 'no ending'. E.g. nom. sg. masc. Ἕλλην *Greek* (compare gen. sg. Ἕλλην-ος).
[2] In the neuter, the nominative, accusative and vocative are always identical to each other.
[3] The voc. sg. of feminine first-declension nouns is always identical to the nom. sg.; the voc. pl. of all nominal forms is identical to the nom. pl.
[4] In poetry, the epic/Ionic (→25) dative plural endings -οισι(ν) and -αισι(ν) are frequently found; they are found occasionally in prose. The regular first-declension dative plural ending in Ionic prose is -ῃσι(ν).

2.7   For the endings of the dual, →10.1.

3

The Article

3.1   For the meanings and uses of the article, →28. The forms are as follows:

		article		
		ὁ, ἡ, τό *the*		
		masc.	fem.	neut.
sg.	nom.	ὁ	ἡ	τό
	gen.	τοῦ	τῆς	τοῦ
	dat.	τῷ	τῇ	τῷ
	acc.	τόν	τήν	τό
pl.	nom.	οἱ	αἱ	τά
	gen.	τῶν	τῶν	τῶν
	dat.	τοῖς	ταῖς	τοῖς
	acc.	τούς	τάς	τά

Except for the nom. sg. masc. ὁ (which has no ending), the article uses second-declension endings in the masculine and neuter, and first-declension endings in the feminine. The forms start with τ-, except the nominatives of the masculine and feminine, which start with a rough breathing.

Note 1: The forms of the article are prepositive (→60.4–6, 60.13). For the purpose of accentuation they count as proclitics (24.33–9).
Note 2: In poetry, the dat. pl. forms τοῖσι and ταῖσι are frequently found. In some prose uses, the form of the nom. sg. masc. is ὅς (→28.29–30).
Note 3: For Ionic forms, →25.26.

4

Nouns

First-Declension Nouns

Stems, Types and Gender of First-Declension Nouns

4.1 The first declension is also known as the **a-declension**, since it consists of nouns with a stem ending in an a-sound (this sound is considered to be part of the endings, →2.4 n.1).

4.2 The following types of noun belong to the first declension:

– **feminine nouns**, with a nominative singular ending either in short -ᾰ or long -ᾱ (which in Attic has changed to -η, except after ε, ι or ρ, →1.57);
– **masculine nouns**, with a nominative singular ending in -ης/-ᾱς.

The first declension does not have neuter nouns.

Feminine Nouns in -η, -ᾱ or -ᾰ

4.3 Overview of forms:

		with long ᾱ/η		with short ᾰ	
		-	after ε, ι or ρ	-	after ε, ι or ρ
		ἡ φυγή *flight*	ἡ χώρᾱ *land*	ἡ μοῦσᾰ *muse*	ἡ διάνοιᾰ *thought*
sg.	nom. / voc.	φυγή	χώρᾱ	μοῦσᾰ	διάνοιᾰ
	gen.	φυγῆς	χώρᾱς	μούσης	διανοίᾱς
	dat.	φυγῇ	χώρᾳ	μούσῃ	διανοίᾳ
	acc.	φυγήν	χώρᾱν	μοῦσᾰν	διάνοιᾰν
pl.	nom. / voc.	φυγαί	χῶραι	μοῦσαι	διάνοιαι
	gen.	φυγῶν	χωρῶν	μουσῶν	διανοιῶν
	dat.	φυγαῖς	χώραις	μούσαις	διανοίαις
	acc.	φυγάς	χώρᾱς	μούσᾱς	διανοίᾱς

Note 1: For Ionic forms, →25.15.

4.4 Most nouns of the first declension are **feminine**. There are two main types:

- with a **nominative singular in a long** -η/-ᾱ: for example ἡ φυγή *flight*, ἡ τύχη *fate*, ἡ νίκη *victory*, ἡ ἀδελφή *sister*; ἡ Ἑλένη *Helen*; ἡ χώρᾱ *land*, ἡ θέᾱ *sight*, ἡ αἰτίᾱ *cause*; ἡ Ἠλέκτρᾱ *Electra*;

- with a **nominative singular in a short** ᾰ: for example ἡ μοῦσᾰ *muse*, ἡ θάλαττᾰ *sea*, ἡ δόξᾰ *opinion*; ἡ διάνοιᾰ *thought*; ἡ μοῖρᾱ *fate*; ἡ Ἰφιγένειᾰ *Iphigenia*.

4.5 Endings in the **singular** (→2.6):

- Type with long η/ᾱ: long vowel throughout the singular (η, but ᾱ when ε, ι or ρ precedes):

τύχη: nom. sg.	χώρᾱ: nom. sg.
φυγῆς: gen. sg.	αἰτίᾱς: gen. sg.
ἀδελφῇ: dat. sg.	χώρᾳ: dat. sg.
νίκην: acc. sg.	αἰτίᾱν: acc. sg.

- Type with **short** ᾰ: short vowel in the nominative, accusative and vocative singular:

θάλαττᾰ: nom. sg.	μοῦσᾰ: voc. sg.
διάνοιᾰν: acc. sg.	

- In the other cases in the singular, the endings have either η or (after ε, ι or ρ) long ᾱ:

θαλάττης: gen. sg.	διανοίᾱς: gen. sg.
μούσῃ: dat. sg.	μοίρᾳ: dat. sg.

4.6 Endings in the **plural** (→2.6) are the same in all types:

φυγαί: nom. pl.	θαλάτταις: dat. pl.
μοῦσαι: nom. pl.	αἰτίαις: dat. pl.

4.7 Observe that there is no distinction in spelling between the endings of the two main types if ε, ι or ρ precedes (indications of vowel length are not given in standard texts): it is, however, often possible to determine the length of α from accentuation (e.g. in the case of nom. sg. διάνοιᾰ, →24.8–9, 24.27), and sometimes from the use of a word in certain metrical positions (for example if the final syllable occupies a position which must scan short).

Masculine Nouns in -ης or -ᾱς

4.8   Overview of forms:

		nouns in -ης ὁ δεσπότης *master*	nouns in -ᾱς (after ε, ι or ρ) ὁ νεανίᾱς *young man*
sg.	nom.	δεσπότης	νεανίᾱς
	gen.	δεσπότου	νεανίου
	dat.	δεσπότῃ	νεανίᾳ
	acc.	δεσπότην	νεανίᾱν
	voc.	δέσποτᾰ	νεανίᾱ
pl.	nom. / voc.	δεσπόται	νεανίαι
	gen.	δεσποτῶν	νεανιῶν
	dat.	δεσπόταις	νεανίαις
	acc.	δεσπότᾱς	νεανίᾱς

Note 1: For Ionic forms, →25.16.

4.9   Nouns of the first declension with a nom. sg. in -ς are **masculine** (most are proper names or professions): for example ὁ δεσπότης *master*, ὁ πολίτης *citizen*, ὁ κριτής *judge*; ὁ Ἀτρείδης *son of Atreus*, ὁ Εὐριπίδης *Euripides*, ὁ Πέρσης *Persian*; ὁ νεανίᾱς *young man*, ὁ ταμίᾱς *treasurer*; ὁ Ξανθίᾱς *Xanthias*.

4.10   Masculine nouns of the first declension have the same endings as feminine ones, with two exceptions:

– the **nominative singular ends in -ς**: contrast e.g. ὁ κριτή̲ς̲ with ἡ τύχη̲;
– the ending **-ου** is used in the **genitive singular**: contrast e.g. τοῦ κριτο̲ῦ̲ with τῆς τύχη̲ς̲.

Note 1: This genitive ending was presumably formed with the genitive ending -(σ)ο, via a process -ᾱ(σ)ο > -ηο (→1.57, 1.83) > -εω (→1.71) > -εο (by analogy, →1.49) > -ō (→1.58–60; =-ου). The second-declension ending -ου (itself < -ο(σ)ο), used for many masculine nouns, may also have directly influenced this formation.

4.11   There are no masculine nouns of the first declension with short ᾰ; thus the **endings in the singular are always long** (e.g. nom. sg. πολίτη̲ς̲, acc. sg. νεανίᾱ̲ν), except sometimes in the vocative.

4.12   The voc. sg. is formed as follows:

– with nouns in -της and with the names of races/peoples: -ᾰ (e.g. with κριτής, voc. κριτᾰ; with Πέρσης, voc. Πέρσᾰ);

– with other first-declension nouns in -ης/-ᾱς, including all proper names in -άδης and -ίδης: voc. in -η/-ᾱ (e.g. with Ἀτρείδης, voc. sg. Ἀτρείδη; with νεανίᾱς, voc. sg. νεανίᾱ, with Ξανθίᾱς, voc. sg. Ξανθίᾱ).

4.13 Proper names in -ης may also belong to the third declension: e.g. ὁ Σωκράτης (gen. Σωκράτους, →4.65–9). All names in -άδης and -ίδης are first-declension.

Further Notes and Exceptions

4.14 A few nouns of the first declension have endings resulting from **contraction with ε or α**. In α-contracts the long ᾱ resulting from the contraction is found in all forms. In ε-contracts, the endings are like those of the type φυγή (→4.3–7), but with differences in accentuation (→24.12):

– α-contracts: ἡ μνᾶ *mina* (<*μνά-ᾱ), gen. μνᾶς, etc.; ἡ Ἀθηνᾶ *Athena* (<Ἀθηνα(ί)-ᾱ), gen. Ἀθηνᾶς, etc;
– ε-contracts: ἡ γαλῆ *weasel* (<*γαλέ-ᾱ), gen. γαλῆς, etc.; ὁ Ἑρμῆς *Hermes* (<*Ἑρμέ-ᾱς), gen. Ἑρμοῦ, etc.; ὁ Βορρᾶς *north wind* (<Βο(ρ)ρέ-ᾱς, with ᾱ because of the preceding ρ), etc.

Note that in the ε-contracts, various forms are different from what the rules of contraction ought to have produced, by analogy with uncontracted first-declension endings (→1.49): e.g. nom. pl. γαλαῖ (rather than γαλῆ <*γαλέ-αι).

4.15 Occasionally, a genitive in -ᾱ is used with proper names ending in -ᾱς (the 'Doric' genitive, →25.47): e.g. gen. Εὐρώτᾱ (with ὁ Εὐρώτᾱς *Eurotas*), gen. Καλλίᾱ (with ὁ Καλλίᾱς *Callias*).

4.16 ἡ κόρη *girl* and ἡ δέρη *neck* have -η in the sg., even though ρ precedes (originally, ϝ intervened: e.g. κόρη <*κόρϝη <*κόρϝᾱ, →1.57 n.3).

Second-Declension Nouns

Stems, Types and Gender of Second-Declension Nouns

4.17 The second declension is also known as the **o-declension**, since it consists of nouns with a stem which normally ends in o (the o is treated here as part of the endings, →2.4 n.1).

4.18 The following types of noun belong to the second declension:

– **masculine** (and several feminine) nouns, with a nominative singular ending in **-ος** (or -ους or -ως);
– **neuter** nouns, with a nominative singular ending in **-ον** (or -ουν).

Masculine (and Feminine) Nouns in -ος or -ους

4.19   Overview of forms:

		nouns in -ος	nouns in -ους	
		ὁ δοῦλος *slave*	ὁ νοῦς *mind*	
sg.	nom.	δοῦλος	νοῦς	(<-ό-ος)
	gen.	δούλου	νοῦ	(<-ό-ου)
	dat.	δούλῳ	νῷ	(<-ό-ῳ)
	acc.	δοῦλον	νοῦν	(<-ό-ον)
	voc.	δοῦλε	νοῦ	(<-ό-ε)
pl.	nom. / voc.	δοῦλοι	νοῖ	(<-ό-οι)
	gen.	δούλων	νῶν	(<-ό-ων)
	dat.	δούλοις	νοῖς	(<-ό-οις)
	acc.	δούλους	νοῦς	(<-ό-ους)

Note 1: For Ionic forms, →25.18.

4.20   Most nouns of the second declension are **masculine**: these have a nom. sg. in -ος. E.g. ὁ δοῦλος *slave*, ὁ ἰατρός *physician*, ὁ πόλεμος *war*, ὁ ποταμός *river*; ὁ Αἴσχυλος *Aeschylus*.

4.21   With a few masculine nouns of the second declension, the vowels of the endings have **contracted** (→1.58–64) with a preceding ο in the stem. For example ὁ νοῦς *mind* (<νό-ος) and ὁ ἔκπλους *sailing away* (<ἔκπλο-ος).

4.22   Several nouns of the second declension are **feminine**. These include:

- ἡ παρθένος *maiden*, ἡ ἤπειρος *mainland*, ἡ νόσος *disease*, ἡ νῆσος *island*, ἡ ὁδός *road* (and compounds, e.g. ἡ εἴσοδος *entrance*);
- many geographical entities, e.g. ἡ Αἴγυπτος *Egypt*, ἡ Κόρινθος *Corinth*, ἡ Ῥόδος *Rhodes*;
- most trees and plants, e.g. ἡ ἄμπελος *vine*, ἡ πλάτανος *plane-tree*.

They are declined exactly like second-declension masculine nouns:

τῆς ὁδοῦ: gen. sg. fem.

ταῖς νήσοις: dat. pl. fem.

A few others occur both as **masculine and feminine** nouns (these are often called 'common gender' nouns), again with no changes in the declension: ὁ/ἡ θεός *god/goddess*, ὁ/ἡ ἄνθρωπος *man/woman*, ὁ/ἡ τροφός *nurse*, etc.:

τοῦ ἀνθρώπου: gen. sg. masc.

τῆς ἀνθρώπου: gen. sg. fem.

4.23 There are also nouns with a nominative in -ος which belong to the third declension, always neuter: e.g. τὸ γένος (gen. γένους, →4.65–7); these should not be confused with second-declension nouns.

Neuter Nouns in -ov or -ouv

4.24 Overview of forms:

		nouns in -ov	nouns in -ouv	
		τὸ δῶρον *gift*	τὸ ὀστοῦν *bone*	
sg.	nom. / voc.	δῶρον	ὀστοῦν	(<-έ-ον)
	gen.	δώρου	ὀστοῦ	(<-έ-ου)
	dat.	δώρῳ	ὀστῷ	(<-έ-ῳ)
	acc.	δῶρον	ὀστοῦν	(<-έ-ον)
pl.	nom. / voc.	δῶρᾰ	ὀστᾶ	
	gen.	δώρων	ὀστῶν	(<-έ-ων)
	dat.	δώροις	ὀστοῖς	(<-έ-οις)
	acc.	δῶρᾰ	ὀστᾶ	

Note 1: For Ionic forms, →25.18.

4.25 There are many **neuter** second-declension nouns: for example τὸ ἄστρον *star*, τὸ δεῖπνον *meal*, τὸ δῶρον *gift*, τὸ ἱμάτιον *cloak*. Note that nominative and accusative are identical, and that in the plural these end in -ᾰ.

4.26 With a few neuter nouns of the second declension, the vowels of the endings have **contracted** (→1.58–66) with a preceding ε in the stem. For example τὸ κανοῦν *basket* (<κανέ-ον) and τὸ ὀστοῦν *bone* (<ὀστέ-ον).

Note 1: The ending of the nom./acc. pl. in -ᾱ (ὀστᾶ) is due to analogy with the a-sound in e.g. δῶρᾰ (→1.49; regular contraction of -εᾰ would have resulted in -η, cf. e.g. γένη < γένεᾰ, →1.59).

Further Notes and Exceptions

4.27 The so-called **Attic second declension** consists of a few masculine and feminine nouns whose nominative singular ends in -ως, for example ὁ νεώς *temple*, ὁ λεώς *people*, ἡ ἕως *dawn*; ὁ Μενέλεως *Menelaus*. Their endings throughout the declension include ω. These endings are usually the result of quantitative metathesis (→1.71):

			nouns in -ως (Attic second declension)	
			ὁ νεώς *temple*	
sg.	nom. / voc.	νεώς	(<*νηϝός)
	gen.	νεώ	(<*νηϝō)
	dat.	νεῴ	(<*νηϝῷ)
	acc.	νεών	(<*νηϝόν)
pl.	nom. / voc.	νεῴ	(<*νηϝοί)
	gen.	νεών	(<*νηϝῶν)
	dat.	νεῴς	(<*νηϝοῖς)
	acc.	νεώς	(<*νηϝός)

Also in the Attic declension, but not the result of quantitative metathesis, are a few nouns like ὁ λαγώς *hare* (<*λαγωός), ὁ κάλως *cable* (<*κάλωος). The resulting endings are identical to those of νεώς.

The acc. sg., particularly with nouns of the λαγώς type, sometimes ends in -ω. This is always the case with ἕως *dawn* (originally declined like αἰδώς, →4.71): τὴν ἕω.

Note 1: The Attic declension is not used consistently in Attic poetry, or in Ionic (→25.19), and was not adopted in the Koine; these use e.g. Μενέλαος, λαός, etc. The term 'Attic' derives, in fact, from the contrast with Koine Greek.

Note 2: For the accentuation of forms such as Μενέλεως, →24.10 n.2.

4.28   Some second-declension nouns have both masculine and neuter forms (such words, following different patterns of declension, are often called **heteroclitic**):

- ὁ δεσμός *band, bond, chain* has both masculine and plural neuter forms: nom. pl. δεσμά as well as δεσμοί/δεσμούς (only the masculine forms are used when δεσμοί refers to chains or bonds used for imprisonment).
- ὁ σῖτος *grain* has neuter plural forms: nom./acc. pl. τὰ σῖτα.
- τὸ στάδιον *stade* has both neuter and masculine plural forms: nom./acc. pl. οἱ στάδιοι/τοὺς σταδίους as well as τὰ στάδια.

4.29   With θεός *god*, the nom. sg. is used as voc. sg., rather than a form in -ε: ὦ θεός.

4.30   For the declension of τὸ δάκρυον *tear*, ὁ ὄνειρος *dream*, ὁ σκότος *shade* and ὁ υἱός *son*, →4.91.

Third-Declension Nouns

Stems, Types and Gender of Third-Declension Nouns

4.31   All third-declension nouns have a **stem ending in a consonant or ι or υ** (or semivowels y or ϝ).

4.32 Although the endings used are generally the same throughout the entire declension (→2.6, for exceptions see the individual sections below), a number of different **subtypes** of the third declension are distinguished: the differences between these types largely depend on two factors:

– the (type of) consonant, or ι/υ, in which the stem ends;
– whether or not there is ablaut (→1.51–6) in the stem.

4.33 It is often impossible to derive the stem of a third-declension noun (and thus the exact pattern of that noun's declension) from the nominative singular alone: the genitive is required to determine which subtype the noun belongs to. Compare, for example:

ὁ ἀγών *contest*, gen. ἀγῶνος,   *but*   ὁ γέρων *old man*, gen. γέροντος,
     stem in ν   stem in ντ

ἡ ἐλπίς *hope*, gen. ἐλπίδος,   *but*   ἡ πόλις *city*, gen. πόλεως,
     stem in δ   stem in ι

ἡ κόρυς *helmet*, gen. κόρυθος,   *but*   ὁ ἰχθῦς *fish*, gen. ἰχθύος,
     stem in θ   stem in υ

                                               but   ὁ πῆχυς *forearm*, gen. πήχεως,
                                                     stem in υ, with ablaut

ὁ σωτήρ *saviour*, gen. σωτῆρος,   *but*   ὁ πατήρ *father*, gen. πατρός,
     stem in ρ   stem in ρ, with ablaut

For a complete overview of noun types, →4.93 below.

4.34 Third-declension nouns are masculine, feminine or neuter. Some subtypes occur only in certain genders, however: see the individual sections below.

Stems in a Labial Stop (π, β, φ) or Velar Stop (κ, γ, χ)

4.35   Overview of forms:

		nouns in -ψ ὁ γύψ *vulture* stem γυπ-	**nouns in -ξ** ὁ φύλαξ *guard* stem φυλακ-
sg.	nom. / voc.	γύψ	φύλαξ
	gen.	γυπός	φύλακος
	dat.	γυπΐ	φύλακῐ
	acc.	γῦπᾰ	φύλακᾰ
pl.	nom. / voc.	γῦπες	φύλακες
	gen.	γυπῶν	φυλάκων
	dat.	γυψΐ(ν)	φύλαξῐ(ν)
	acc.	γῦπᾶς	φύλακᾰς

4.36   Third-declension nouns with a **stem ending in a labial or velar stop** are either **masculine** or **feminine**: e.g. ὁ γύψ *vulture* (γυπ-), ἡ φλέψ *vein* (φλεβ-), ὁ Πέλοψ *Pelops* (Πελοπ-); ὁ φύλαξ *guard* (φυλακ-), ὁ/ἡ αἴξ *goat* (αἰγ-), ἡ σάλπιγξ *trumpet* (σαλπιγγ-), ἡ θρίξ *hair* (θριχ-), ὁ ὄνυξ *claw* (ὀνυχ-).

4.37   Labial + σ = ψ; velar + σ = ξ:

– in the nom. sg.: γύπ-ς> γύψ; φλέβ-ς > φλέψ; ὄνυχ-ς > ὄνυξ;

– in the dat. pl.: γυπ-σί> γυψί; φλεβ-σί > φλεψί; ὄνυχ-σι > ὄνυξι.

4.38   The noun ἡ γυνή *woman* is, apart from its irregularly formed nom. sg., declined according to this type (stem γυναικ-): gen. sg. γυναικός, dat. pl. γυναιξί, etc.

The voc. sg. is γύναι (<*γύναικ, →1.73).

4.39   The stem of θρίξ *hair* has lost its initial aspiration in all cases where aspirated χ is retained (→1.97 n.1): gen. sg. τ̱ριχός, dat. τ̱ριχί, acc. τ̱ρίχα; nom. pl. τ̱ρίχες, gen. τ̱ριχῶν, acc. τ̱ρίχας; but nom. sg. θ̱ρίξ, dat. pl. θ̱ριξί.

Stems in a Dental Stop (τ, δ, θ, except ντ)

4.40 Overview of forms:

		stems in a dental stop			
		nouns in -μα (always neuter)	nouns in -ίς (with accented final syllable)	nouns in -ις (or -υς) (with unaccented final syllable)	other nouns
		τὸ πρᾶγμα *thing* stem πραγματ-	ἡ ἐλπίς *expectation* stem ἐλπιδ-	ἡ ἔρις *strife* stem ἐριδ-	ἡ ἐσθής *clothing* stem ἐσθητ-
sg.	nom.	πρᾶγμα	ἐλπίς	ἔρις	ἐσθής
	gen.	πράγματος	ἐλπίδος	ἔριδος	ἐσθῆτος
	dat.	πράγματι	ἐλπίδι	ἔριδι	ἐσθῆτι
	acc.	πρᾶγμα	ἐλπίδα	ἔριν	ἐσθῆτα
	voc.	= nom.	ἐλπί	ἔρι	= nom.
pl.	nom. / voc.	πράγματα	ἐλπίδες	ἔριδες	ἐσθῆτες
	gen.	πραγμάτων	ἐλπίδων	ἐρίδων	ἐσθήτων
	dat.	πράγμασι(ν)	ἐλπίσι(ν)	ἔρισι(ν)	ἐσθῆσι(ν)
	acc.	πράγματα	ἐλπίδας	ἔριδας	ἐσθῆτας

Note 1: For Ionic forms, →25.20.

4.41 Third-declension nouns with a **stem ending in a dental stop** may be:

– **neuter**, usually with a stem in μᾰτ: e.g. τὸ πρᾶγμα *thing* (πραγματ-), τὸ σῶμα *body* (σωματ-), τὸ ὄνομα *name* (ὀνοματ-);

Note 1: There are a few other neuter nouns with a stem in τ: e.g. τὸ γόνυ *knee* (γονατ-), τὸ δόρυ *spear* (δορατ-), τὸ μέλι *honey* (μελιτ-), τὸ οὖς *ear* (ὠτ-), τὸ τέρας *omen* (τερατ-), τὸ ὕδωρ *water* (ὑδατ-), τὸ φῶς *light* (φωτ-). Also →4.90–1.

– **feminine**: e.g. ἡ ἐλπίς *expectation* (ἐλπιδ-), ἡ ἔρις *strife* (ἐριδ-), ἡ ἐσθής *clothing* (ἐσθητ-), ἡ κακότης *baseness* (κακοτητ-), ἡ κόρυς *helmet* (κορυθ-), ἡ χάρις *favour, gratitude* (χαριτ-); ἡ Ἄρτεμις *Artemis* (Ἀρτεμιδ-);

– occasionally **masculine**: e.g. ὁ πούς *foot* (ποδ-); **common gender**: ὁ/ἡ ὄρνις *bird* (ὀρνιθ-), ὁ/ἡ παῖς *child* (παιδ-).

4.42 Dental stops **disappear without trace before σ** (→1.91):

– in the nom. sg.: e.g. *ἐλπίδ-ς > ἐλπίς;

– in the dat. pl.: e.g. *ἐλπίδ-σι > ἐλπίσι; *τέρατ-σι > τέρασι.

Neuter nouns with a stem in ματ have no ending in the nom./acc. sg., and the final τ is lost (→1.73): *πρᾶγματ > πρᾶγμα.

Note 1: ἡ νύξ *night* derives from νύκ(τ)-ς (stem νυκτ-, cf. gen. sg. νυκτός); dat. pl. νυξί < νυκ(τ)-σί. Similarly ὁ ἄναξ *lord* (gen. ἄνακτος). Also cf. neut. τὸ γάλα *milk* (stem γαλακτ-, nom./acc. <*γάλα(κτ), gen. γάλακτος; sg. only).

4.43   Nouns in -ις (or -υς) which do not have the accent on the final syllable of the stem (i.e. on the ι or υ) have an **accusative singular in -ιν** (or -υν):

ὄρνις, gen. ὄρνιθος	acc. ὄρνιν
χάρις, gen. χάριτος	acc. χάριν
Ἄρτεμις, gen. Ἀρτέμιδος	acc. Ἄρτεμιν
κόρυς, gen. κόρυθος	acc. κόρυν

but:

ἐλπίς, gen. ἐλπίδος	acc. ἐλπίδα

4.44   The **voc. sg.** is usually formed without ending and with loss of the final dental: e.g. ὦ παῖ (<*παῖδ, →1.73). In other cases it is identical to the nominative.

Stems in ντ

4.45   Overview of forms:

		stems in ντ	
		ὁ γίγᾱς *giant* stem γιγᾰντ-	ὁ γέρων *old man* stem γεροντ-
sg.	nom.	γίγᾱς	γέρων
	gen.	γίγᾰντος	γέροντος
	dat.	γίγᾰντι	γέροντι
	acc.	γίγᾰντα	γέροντα
	voc.	γίγᾰν	γέρον
pl.	nom. / voc.	γίγᾰντες	γέροντες
	gen.	γιγᾰντων	γερόντων
	dat.	γίγᾱσι(ν)	γέρουσι(ν)
	acc.	γίγᾰντας	γέροντας

4.46   Third-declension nouns with a **stem in ντ** are **masculine**: e.g. ὁ γέρων *old man* (γεροντ-), ὁ γίγᾱς *giant* (γιγᾰντ-), ὁ δράκων *serpent* (δρακοντ-), ὁ λέων *lion* (λεοντ-), ὁ ὀδούς *tooth* (ὀδοντ-); ὁ Ξενοφῶν *Xenophon* (Ξενοφωντ-).

4.47 The combination **ντ disappeared before** σ, with **compensatory lengthening** (→1.68–9):

- in the nom. sg., when it is formed with -ς: *γίγᾰντ-ς > γίγᾱς; *ὀδοντ-ς > ὀδούς (= ὀδός); note, however, that some nouns have a nom. sg. ending not in -ς, but with a long vowel and no τ: e.g. γέρων; δράκ<u>ω</u>ν;
- in the dat. pl.: *γέροντ-σι > γέρ<u>ου</u>σι (= γέρ<u>ο</u>σι); *γίγᾰντ-σι > γίγᾱσι.

4.48 The **voc. sg.** is formed without ending (→2.6) and without -τ: e.g. ὦ γέρ<u>ο</u>ν.

Stems in ν

4.49 Overview of forms:

		stems in ν		
			(with ablaut)	
		ὁ ἀγών *contest* stem ἀγων-	ὁ ποιμήν *shepherd* stem ποιμεν-/ποιμην-	ὁ δαίμων *spirit* stem δαιμον-/δαιμων-
sg.	nom.	ἀγών	ποιμήν	δαίμων
	gen.	ἀγῶνος	ποιμένος	δαίμονος
	dat.	ἀγῶνι	ποιμένι	δαίμονι
	acc.	ἀγῶνα	ποιμένα	δαίμονα
	voc.	= nom.	ποιμήν	δαῖμον
pl.	nom. / voc.	ἀγῶνες	ποιμένες	δαίμονες
	gen.	ἀγώνων	ποιμένων	δαιμόνων
	dat.	ἀγῶσι(ν)	ποιμέσι(ν)	δαίμοσι(ν)
	acc.	ἀγῶνας	ποιμένας	δαίμονας

4.50 Third-declension nouns with a **stem in ν** may be:

- **masculine**: e.g. ὁ ἀγών *contest* (ἀγων-), ὁ δαίμων *spirit* (δαιμον-), ὁ δελφίς *dolphin* (δελφιν-), ὁ ἡγεμών *guide* (ἡγεμον-), ὁ ποιμήν *shepherd* (ποιμεν-); ὁ Ἀγαμέμνων *Agamemnon* (Ἀγαμεμνον-), ὁ Ἕλλην *Greek* (Ἑλλην-), ὁ Πλάτων *Plato* (Πλατων-);
- in fewer cases, **feminine**: e.g. ἡ εἰκών *image* (εἰκον-), ἡ σταγών *drop* (σταγον-), ἡ ὠδίς *childbirth pain* (ὠδιν-); ἡ Σαλαμίς *Salamis* (Σαλαμιν-).

4.51 The final ν of the stem has **disappeared before** σ:

- in the nom. sg. of a few nouns: *δελφίν-ς > δελφίς (gen. δελφῖνος), *Σαλαμίν-ς > Σαλαμίς (gen. Σαλαμῖνος); observe, however, that most nouns of this type form a nom. sg. without an ending (→2.6), and with a long vowel (→1.54): e.g. ἀγ<u>ών</u> (stem ἀγων-); δαίμ<u>ων</u> (stem δαιμον-);
- in the dat. pl.; there is *no* compensatory lengthening: e.g. ἀγῶσι, δαίμ<u>ο</u>σι, σταγ<u>ό</u>σι.

Note 1: The dat. pl. was presumably formed through the process *δαίμη̯-σι (zero-grade, →1.51–3) > *δαίμᾱσι (η̯ > ᾰ, →1.86) > δαίμοσι (analogical levelling of the paradigm, →1.49, with o for α). It is thus more accurate to say that there was, in the dat. pl., never a cluster -νσ- between vowels which could have resulted in compensatory lengthening. This pattern is found in all nominal ν-stems (adjectives, →5.24, 5.27; pronouns, →7.24).

4.52   The **voc. sg.**, without ending (→2.6), is often identical to the nominative (e.g. ὦ Πλάτων, ὦ ποιμήν), although with some nouns a short vowel grade is used: e.g. ὦ Ἀγάμεμνο̱ν, ὦ δαῖμο̱ν, ὦ Ἄπολλο̱ν (also →4.53).

4.53   **ὁ Ἀπόλλων** *Apollo* has acc. Ἀπόλλω̱ next to Ἀπόλλωνα. So too **ὁ Ποσειδῶν** *Poseidon*, acc. sg. Ποσειδῶ̱ next to Ποσειδῶνα. Their voc. is Ἄπολλο̱ν, Πόσειδο̱ν.

4.54   **ὁ κύων** *dog* uses the stem κυν- throughout the rest of its declension (gen. sg. κυνός, dat. sg. κυνί, etc.), except for the voc. sg. κύον.

Stems in a Liquid (λ or ρ)

4.55   Overview of forms:

		stems in a liquid	
		ὁ ἅλς *salt* stem ἁλ-	ὁ ῥήτωρ *orator* stem ῥητορ-
sg.	nom.	ἅλς	ῥήτωρ
	gen.	ἁλός	ῥήτορος
	dat.	ἁλί	ῥήτορι
	acc.	ἅλα	ῥήτορα
	voc.	—	ῥῆτορ
pl.	nom. / voc.	ἅλες	ῥήτορες
	gen.	ἁλῶν	ῥητόρων
	dat.	ἁλσί(ν)	ῥήτορσι(ν)
	acc.	ἅλας	ῥήτορας

4.56   Third-declension nouns with a **stem ending in a liquid** are:
- normally **masculine**: e.g. ὁ ῥήτωρ *orator* (ῥητορ-), ὁ κρατήρ *mixing bowl* (κρατηρ-), ὁ σωτήρ *saviour* (σωτηρ-), ὁ φώρ *thief* (φωρ-); ὁ Ἕκτωρ *Hector* (Ἑκτορ-). A few feminine nouns occur: e.g. ἡ κήρ *fate* (κηρ-), ἡ χείρ *hand* (χειρ-);
- masculine *or* feminine are ὁ ἅλς *(grain of) salt*, ἡ ἅλς *sea* (ἁλ-); ὁ/ἡ ἀήρ *air* (ἀερ-); ὁ/ἡ αἰθήρ *heaven* (αἰθερ-);
- two nouns are neuter: τὸ ἔαρ *spring* and τὸ πῦρ *fire* (→4.61).

4.57 The **nom. sg.** is normally without ending. Several nouns of this type have ablaut in the stem, and then use the lengthened vowel in the nom. sg. (→1.54): e.g. αἰθήρ (gen. αἰθέρος), ῥήτωρ (gen. ῥήτορος); other nouns have a long vowel throughout the declension: e.g. κρατήρ (gen. κρατῆρος), φώρ (gen. φωρός).

In ἅλς, -ς is added to the stem (without change) to form the nom. sg.

4.58 The **voc. sg.** is formed without ending (→2.6), normally with a short vowel: ὦ ῥῆτορ, ὦ σῶτερ, ὦ Ἕκτορ.

4.59 ἡ **χείρ** hand (stem χειρ-, gen. χειρός) has dat. pl. χερσί: this shorter variant of the stem (χερ-) is found in the other cases as well, especially in poetry.

4.60 ὁ **μάρτυς** witness (stem μαρτυρ-, gen. μάρτυρος, dat. μάρτυρι, etc.) has dat. pl. μάρτυσι.

4.61 The neuter nouns τὸ **πῦρ** fire and τὸ **ἔαρ** spring occur only in the singular. They are declined πῦρ, πυρός, πυρί, πῦρ and ἔαρ, ἔαρος (often > ἦρος), ἔαρι (often > ἦρι), ἔαρ.

Stems in (ε)ρ, with Three Ablaut Grades (Type πατήρ, ἀνήρ)

4.62 Overview of forms:

		type πατήρ ὁ πατήρ father stem πατ(ε)ρ-	**ἀνήρ** ὁ ἀνήρ man stem ἀν(ε)ρ-
sg.	nom.	πατήρ	ἀνήρ
	gen.	πατρός	ἀνδρός
	dat.	πατρί	ἀνδρί
	acc.	πατέρα	ἄνδρα
	voc.	πάτερ	ἄνερ
pl.	nom. / voc.	πατέρες	ἄνδρες
	gen.	πατέρων	ἀνδρῶν
	dat.	πατράσι(ν)	ἀνδράσι(ν)
	acc.	πατέρας	ἄνδρας

4.63 Four nouns ending in -τηρ – ὁ **πατήρ** father, ἡ **μήτηρ** mother, ἡ **θυγάτηρ** daughter, ἡ **γαστήρ** belly – show three different ablaut variations (→1.51–2) through their declension:

- lengthened e-grade in the nom. sg.: e.g. πατήρ, μήτηρ;
- e-grade in the acc. and voc. sg.; nom., gen. and acc. pl.: e.g. πατέρα, θυγατέρων, γαστέρας;

– zero-grade in the gen. and dat. sg., and in the dat. pl., e.g. μητρός, θυγατρός; in the resulting combination of the dat. pl., *-τρ-σι, the ρ has expanded to ρᾰ (→1.87): e.g. πατρᾰ́σι, γαστρᾰ́σι.

4.64   ὁ **ἀνήρ** *man* is similarly declined using three ablaut variations: lengthened grade in the nom. sg. (ἀνή̱ρ), e-grade in the voc. sg. (ἄνερ); however, the zero-grade appears in all the other cases, where the resulting combination νρ has changed to νδρ (→1.93): e.g. ἀνδρί, ἀνδρῶν. Note the dat. pl. ἀνδρᾰ́σι.

Stems in σ (Neuter Nouns in -ος, Names in -ης)

4.65   Overview of forms:

		neuter nouns in -ος		proper names in -ης			
		τὸ γένος *race* stem γενοσ-/γενεσ-		Σωκράτης *Socrates* stem Σωκρατεσ-		Περικλῆς *Pericles* stem Περικλε(ϝ)εσ-	
sg.	nom.	γένος		Σωκράτης		Περικλῆς	(<*-έ(ϝ)ης)
	gen.	γένους	(<*-ε(σ)ος)	Σωκράτους	(<*-ε(σ)ος)	Περικλέους	(<*-έ(ϝ)ε(σ)ος)
	dat.	γένει	(<*-ε(σ)ι)	Σωκράτει	(<*-ε(σ)ι)	Περικλεῖ	(<*-έ(ϝ)ε(σ)ι)
	acc.	γένος		Σωκράτη	(<*-ε(σ)α)	Περικλέᾱ	(<*-έ(ϝ)ε(σ)α)
				or Σωκράτην			
	voc.	= nom.		Σώκρατες		Περίκλεις	(<*-ε(ϝ)ες)
pl.	nom. / voc.	γένη	(<*-ε(σ)α)	—		—	
	gen.	γενῶν	(<*-ε(σ)ων)				
	dat.	γένεσι(ν)	(<*-εσσι(ν))				
	acc.	γένη	(<*-ε(σ)α)				

Note 1: For Ionic forms, →25.21.

4.66   Third-declension nouns with a **stem ending in σ** may be:

– **neuter**: nouns ending in -ος, with two ablaut variations in the stem, οσ- (used in nom./acc. sg.) and εσ- (used in all other cases): e.g. τὸ γένος *race* (γενεσ-), τὸ ἔπος *word* (ἐπεσ-), τὸ ἔτος *year* (ἐτεσ-), τὸ κράτος *might* (κρατεσ-), τὸ τεῖχος *wall* (τειχεσ-);

– **masculine**: a number of masculine proper names in -ης, with a stem in εσ-: e.g. ὁ Διογένης *Diogenes* (Διογενεσ-), ὁ Σωκράτης *Socrates* (Σωκρατεσ-); also names in -κλῆς, with a stem originally ending in ε(ϝ)εσ-: e.g. ὁ Περικλῆς *Pericles* (Περικλε(ϝ)εσ-), ὁ Σοφοκλῆς *Sophocles* (Σοφοκλε(ϝ)εσ-).

The masculine proper names are built on the same stems as some of the neuter nouns: Διογένης (γένος), Σωκράτης (κράτος), Περικλῆς (κλέος *fame*, <*κλέϝος).

4.67   Between vowels, the **σ of the stem has disappeared** (→1.83), and the remaining vowels have contracted (→1.58–66): e.g. gen. sg. Σωκράτ<u>ους</u> (= -τ<u>ο͂</u>ς) < -εος < *-εσος; nom./acc. pl. γένη < -εα < *-εσα.

In the dat. pl., the combination -εσ-σι has been simplified to -εσι: e.g. γένε<u>σι</u>, ἔτε<u>σι</u> < -εσσι.

4.68   Proper names in -ης often get an **acc. in -ην** (modelled on the first declension): e.g. τὸν Σωκράτην, τὸν Διογένην.

4.69   In the declension of names ending in -κλῆς, both the σ and the ϝ have disappeared between vowels. After the disappearance of ϝ further contraction has occurred in the nom., dat. and voc. (Περικλῆς <*-κλέϝης; Περικλ<u>ε͂ι</u> <*-κλέϝεσι; Περίκλ<u>εις</u> <*-κλεϝες), but not in the gen. and acc. (Περικλέους <*-κλέϝεσος; Περικλέ<u>ᾶ</u> <*-κλέϝεσα; with ᾱ after ε, →1.57).

4.70   There are a few **neuter nouns with a stem in ασ-**: e.g. τὸ γέρας *gift of honour*, τὸ γῆρας *old age*, τὸ κρέας *flesh*. These are declined as follows: nom./acc. sg. γέρας, gen. γέρως (<*-α(σ)ος), dat. γέρᾳ (<*-α(σ)ι); nom./acc. pl. γέρᾱ (<*-α(σ)α), gen. γερῶν (<*-ά(σ)ων), dat. γέρασι (<*-α(σ)σι).

4.71   To the σ-stems also belong two feminine nouns – **ἡ τριήρης** *trireme* and **ἡ αἰδώς** *shame*. They are declined as follows:

– τριήρης (properly an adjective with an unexpressed form of ἡ ναῦς *ship*): gen. τριήρους, dat. τριήρει, acc. τριήρη; nom. pl. τριήρεις, gen. τριήρων, dat. τριήρεσι, acc. τριήρεις (for the declension, cf. ἀληθής, →5.28–9);

– αἰδώς (sg. only): gen. αἰδοῦς (<*-ό(σ)ος), dat. αἰδοῖ (<*-ό(σ)ι), acc. αἰδῶ (<*-ό(σ)α).

4.72   **ὁ Ἄρης** *Ares* has gen. Ἄρεως or (poetic) Ἄρεος, dat. Ἄρει, acc. Ἄρη or (poetic) Ἄρεα, voc. Ἄρες.

4.73   Proper names ending in -ης may also be of the first declension (→4.8–13): e.g. ὁ Εὐριπίδης, gen. Εὐριπίδου. But all names in -γένης, -κράτης, -μένης and -σθένης are third-declension.

Stems in ι/ε(y) (Type πόλις)

4.74   Overview of forms:

		stems in ι/ε(y) ἡ πόλις *city* stem πολι-/πολε(y)-	
sg.	nom.	πόλῐς	
	gen.	πόλεως	
	dat.	πόλει	(<*-ε(y)ι)
	acc.	πόλῐν	
	voc.	πόλῐ	
pl.	nom. / voc.	πόλεις	(<*-ε(y)ες)
	gen.	πόλεων	(<*-ε(y)ων)
	dat.	πόλεσῐ(ν)	
	acc.	πόλεις	

Note 1: For Ionic forms, →25.22 (the Ionic paradigm differs strongly from the Attic one).

4.75   Third-declension nouns with a **stem ending in ῐ** are nearly all **feminine**: e.g. ἡ πόλις *city*, ἡ δύναμις *power*, ἡ ὕβρις *brutality*. Many such nouns end in -σις (→23.27): e.g. ἡ ποίησις *poetry*, ἡ λύσις *release*, ἡ πρᾶξις *act*. A few nouns are masculine: e.g. ὁ μάντις *seer*, ὁ ὄφις *serpent*.

These nouns show two ablaut variations in the stem:

– (zero-grade) in ι: in nom., acc. and voc. sg.: e.g. πόλι-ς, πόλι-ν, πόλι;
– (e-grade) in εy, the y of which disappeared (→1.76): in dat. sg. πόλει (<*πόλε(y)-ι), nom. pl. πόλεις (= πόλες <*πόλε(y)-ες, with contraction).

4.76   The dat. pl. was probably modelled on the nom. pl., using a stem πολε-: dat. πόλε-σι. The acc. pl. also derives from the nom. pl., either directly or building on the stem πολε-: acc. πόλεις = πόλες <*πόλε-νς (→1.68).

The gen. sg. and pl. in -εως/-εων is built on a stem πολη- (attested in Homer): πόλεως < πόληος; πόλεων <*πολήων (quantitative metathesis, →1.71; for the accentuation of πόλεως/πόλεων, →24.10 n.2).

4.77   The ι-stem noun οἶς *sheep* has a declension without ablaut: nom. sg. οἶς (<*ὄ(ϝ)ι-ς) gen. οἰός, dat. οἰΐ, acc. οἶν; nom. pl. οἶες, gen. οἰῶν, dat. οἶσι, acc. οἶς (<*ὄ(ϝ)ι-νς).

4.78   A few compound proper names in -πόλις are declined as dental-stem nouns (→4.40–4; i.e., not according to the declension of πόλις): so e.g. ὁ Δικαιόπολις *Dicaeopolis*, gen. Δικαιοπόλιδος, dat. Δικαιοπόλιδι, acc. Δικαιόπολιν, voc. Δικαιόπολι.

Stems in υ (Type ἰσχύς) or in υ/ε(ϝ) (Type πῆχυς)

4.79 Overview of forms:

		stems in υ		
		(without ablaut)	(with ablaut)	
		ἡ ἰσχύς *strength* stem ἰσχυ-	ὁ πῆχυς *forearm* stem πηχυ-/πηχε(ϝ)-	
sg.	nom.	ἰσχύς	πῆχῠς	
	gen.	ἰσχύος	πήχεως	
	dat.	ἰσχύϊ	πήχει	(<-ε(ϝ)ι)
	acc.	ἰσχύν	πῆχῠν	
	voc.	ἰσχύ	πῆχυ	
pl.	nom. / voc.	ἰσχύες *or* ἰσχῦς	πήχεις	(<-ε(ϝ)ες)
	gen.	ἰσχύων	πήχεων	(<-έ(ϝ)ων)
	dat.	ἰσχύσι(ν)	πήχεσι(ν)	
	acc.	ἰσχῦς *or* ἰσχύας	πήχεις	

Note 1: For Ionic forms, →25.23.

4.80 Third-declension nouns with a **stem ending in υ** are of two types:

- **without ablaut**: feminine and a few masculine nouns in -υς, with a gen. in -υος:
  e.g. ἡ ἰσχύς *strength*, ἡ χέλυς *tortoise*, ἡ Ἐρινύς *Fury*; ὁ ἰχθῦς *fish*, ὁ νέκυς *corpse*.
- (infrequently) **with ablaut** in the stem (ῠ/εϝ, →1.74): these nouns have a gen. sg.
  in -εως and are masculine: e.g. ὁ πῆχυς *forearm*, ὁ πέλεκυς *axe*, ὁ πρέσβυς *elder*.

4.81 In the type without ablaut, the regular third-declension endings are added to the
stem in υ; note acc. sg. ἰσχύ-ν and acc. pl. ἰσχῦς (<*ἰσχύ-νς, →1.68; ἰσχύας occurs
sometimes). The nom. pl. is usually ἰσχύες, but the (contracted) form ἰσχῦς occurs
as well.

Note 1: The quantity of υ in this type varies. For instance, of ἰσχύς, metrical texts attest both
nom. sg. ἰσχύς/acc. sg. ἰσχύν and ἰσχῦς/ἰσχῦν. However, the gen. and dat. regularly have -ῠος,
-ῠι, -ῠων, -ῠσι(ν).

4.82 The type with ablaut corresponds in most of its declension with type πόλις
(→4.74–6), since ϝ has disappeared in the same place as y there. The irregular
forms in the gen. sg., dat. pl. and acc. pl. were, in fact, probably modelled on the
πόλις-type (the acc. pl. πήχεις may also have been modelled on the nom. pl.).

Note 1: The accentuation of these nouns is also analogous to that of the πόλις-type
(→24.10 n.2).

4.83   There is one neuter noun of the type with ablaut, **τὸ ἄστυ** *town*: the rest of the declension is gen. sg. ἄστεως, dat. ἄστει, nom./acc. pl. ἄστη (<*-εϝα), gen. ἄστεων, dat. ἄστεσι(ν). For the accentuation, →24.10 n.2.

Stems in ηυ/η(ϝ) (Type βασιλεύς)

4.84   Overview of forms:

		nouns ending in -εύς	
		ὁ βασιλεύς *king* stem βασιλη(ϝ)-	
sg.	nom.	βασιλεύς	(<-ηυς)
	gen.	βασιλέως	(<-η(ϝ)ος)
	dat.	βασιλεῖ	(<-η(ϝ)ι)
	acc.	βασιλέᾱ	(<-η(ϝ)ᾰ)
	voc.	βασιλεῦ	(<-ηυ)
pl.	nom. / voc.	βασιλῆς *or* βασιλεῖς	(<-η(ϝ)ες)
	gen.	βασιλέων	(<-η(ϝ)ων)
	dat.	βασιλεῦσι(ν)	(<-ηυσι)
	acc.	βασιλέᾱς *later* βασιλεῖς	(<-η(ϝ)ᾰς)

Note 1: For Ionic forms, →25.24.

4.85   Third-declension nouns ending in **-εύς** are all **masculine**; they are proper names or indications of profession or geographical origin: e.g. ὁ βασιλεύς *king*, ὁ ἱππεύς *horseman*, ὁ χαλκεύς *metal-worker*, ὁ Πρωτεύς *Proteus*, ὁ Ἀχαρνεύς *Acharnian* (from the deme Acharnae). The forms of these nouns derive from a stem in ηυ/ηϝ (→1.74, 1.79–80):

– before a consonant (and in the voc. sg.): diphthong ηυ, which was shortened to ευ (→1.70): so nom. sg. βασιλεύ-ς, dat. pl. βασιλεῦ-σι.
– before a vowel: ηϝ, from which ϝ disappeared, followed in many cases by quantitative metathesis (→1.71): gen. sg. βασιλέως <*-ηϝος; acc. sg. βασιλέᾱ <*-ηϝᾰ; gen. pl. βασιλέων < *-ηϝων; acc. pl. βασιλέᾱς <*-ηϝᾰς. In two cases contraction has taken place: dat. sg. βασιλεῖ <*-ῆϝι (with ει shortened from η); nom. pl. βασιλῆς <*-ῆϝες.

Note 1: A later nom. pl. form βασιλεῖς, modelled on the ε-forms of the sg. (-εῖς <*-ε-ες) gradually replaced the form in -ῆς from the fourth century onwards. Later an acc. pl. in -εῖς was modelled on the new nominative (cf. πόλις, →4.76).

Ζεύς, ναῦς, βοῦς

4.86   Overview of forms:

		Ζεύς		ναῦς		βοῦς	
		ὁ Ζεύς *Zeus*		ἡ ναῦς *ship*		ὁ/ἡ βοῦς *ox/cow*	
		stem Δγευ-/Διϝ-		stem ναυ-/ναϝ-		stem βου-/βοϝ-	
sg.	nom.	Ζεύς	(<*Δγευς <*Δγηύς)	ναῦς	(<*ναῦς)	βοῦς	
	gen.	Διός	(<*Διϝός)	νεώς	(<*νηϝός <*νᾱϝός)	βοός	(<*βοϝός)
	dat.	Διΐ	(<*Διϝί)	νηΐ	(<*νηϝί <*νᾱϝί)	βοΐ	(<*βοϝί)
	acc.	Δία *also* Ζῆνα	(<*Δίϝα)	ναῦν	(<*ναῦν)	βοῦν	
	voc.	Ζεῦ	(<*Δγευ)	ναῦ		βοῦ	
pl.	nom.	—		νῆες	(<*νῆϝες <*νᾶϝες)	βόες	(<*βόϝες)
	gen.			νεῶν	(<*νηϝῶν <*νᾱϝῶν)	βοῶν	(<*βοϝῶν)
	dat.			ναυσί(ν)	(<*νᾱυσί(ν))	βουσί(ν)	
	acc.			ναῦς		βοῦς	

Note 1: For the Ionic declension of ναῦς, →25.25.

4.87   The nouns ὁ **Ζεύς** *Zeus*, ἡ **ναῦς** *ship* and ὁ/ἡ **βοῦς** *ox/cow*, like nouns in -εύς (→4.84–5), had a stem ending in υ/ϝ that formed a diphthong with the preceding vowel before a consonant (and in the voc.), but disappeared between vowels (→1.74, 1.79–80).

– ὁ Ζεύς in addition shows three ablaut variations in the stem: lengthened grade *Δγηυ- (in the nom.; ηυ shortened to ευ, →1.70), normal e-grade *Δγευ-, and zero-grade *Δι(ϝ)-. Apart from the different results of υ/ϝ, the declension was complicated by the change δy > ζ (→1.77).

– In the declension of ἡ ναῦς, the long ᾱ of the stem (ναυ-/ναϝ-) became short in those cases where it formed diphthong αυ (before a consonant), but remained long in those where ϝ disappeared (between vowels). Long ᾱ changed to η (→1.57), resulting in quantitative metathesis (→1.71) in the gen. sg. and gen. pl. (e.g. νεώς < νηός <*νᾱϝός).

4.88   The declension of ἡ **γραῦς** *old lady* is in origin identical to that of ναῦς, but Attic forms differ in various cases because of ρ preceding ᾱ (→1.57): nom sg. γραῦς, gen. γρᾱός, dat. γρᾱΐ, acc. γραῦν, voc. γραῦ; nom. pl. γρᾶες, gen. γρᾱῶν, dat. γραυσί, acc. γραῦς.

Further Notes and Exceptions

4.89   There are a few feminine nouns, usually of women's names, with a stem in ωy/oy: e.g. ἡ Σαπφώ *Sappho*, ἡ πειθώ *persuasion*. For their declension, see below, and compare the declension of αἰδώς (→4.71).

Very few nouns, all masculine, have a stem in ωϝ, e.g. ὁ ἥρως *hero*, ὁ μητρώς *maternal uncle*, ὁ δμώς *slave*. The complete declension is given below. An occasionally occurring gen. sg. in -ω (e.g. ἥρω) is modelled on the Attic second declension (→4.27):

		stems in ω(y)/o(y)		stems in ω(ϝ)	
		ἡ Σαπφώ *Sappho*		ὁ ἥρως *hero*	
		stem Σαπφο(y)-		stem ἡρω(ϝ)-	
sg.	nom.	Σαπφώ	(<*Σαπφώ(y))	ἥρως	(<*ἥρω(ϝ)ς)
	gen.	Σαπφοῦς	(<*-ό(y)ος)	ἥρωος *or* ἥρω	(<*ἥρω(ϝ)ος)
	dat.	Σαπφοῖ	(<*-ό(y)ι)	ἥρωϊ *or* ἥρῳ	(<*ἥρω(ϝ)ι)
	acc.	Σαπφώ	(<*-ό(y)α)	ἥρωα *or* ἥρω	(<*ἥρω(ϝ)α)
	voc.	Σαπφοῖ		= nom.	
pl.	nom. / voc.	—		ἥρωες *or* ἥρως	(<*ἥρω(ϝ)ες)
	gen.	—		ἡρώων	(<*ἡρώ(ϝ)ων)
	dat.	—		ἥρωσι(ν)	(<*ἥρω(ϝ)σι)
	acc.	—		ἥρωας *or* ἥρως	(<*ἥρω(ϝ)ας)

4.90   Several third-declension nouns have forms built on different stems (**heteroclitic** nouns):

– **τὸ κέρας** *horn* has dental-stem *and* σ-stem forms (→4.40–4 and cf. σ-stem γέρας, →4.70): thus gen. sg. κέρατος or κέρως, dat. sg. κέρατι or κέρᾳ, etc.

– So too **ὁ χρώς** *skin* (sg. only, cf. σ-stem αἰδώς, →4.71) gen. χρωτός or χροός (uncontracted), χρωτί or χροΐ, acc. χρῶτα or χρόα. The dat. sg. χρῷ also occurs. The σ-stem forms are poetic.

– **τὸ γόνυ** *knee* and **τὸ δόρυ** *spear* have nom./acc. sg. of the υ-type (cf. ἄστυ, →4.83), but other forms built on a stem in ατ- (→4.40–4; e.g. gen. sg. δόρατος, dat. pl. γόνασι).

– **τὸ ὕδωρ** *water* similarly has a stem in ατ (ὑδατ-): e.g. gen. sg. ὕδατος, dat. ὕδατι.

– So too **τὸ ἧπαρ** *liver*, gen. ἥπατος, dat. ἥπατι; and ἧμαρ *day*, gen. ἥματος (poetic).

– **τὸ κάρα** *head* (poetic) has gen. sg. κρατός, dat. κρατί (but also κάρᾳ), gen. pl. κράτων. The nom./acc. sg. τὸ κρᾶτα also occurs.

– For ἡ γυνή, →4.38.

4.91   Other heteroclitic nouns have both second-declension *and* third-declension forms:

– **ὁ ὄνειρος** *dream* (in poetry also τὸ ὄνειρον) has alternative dental-stem type forms: so e.g. gen. sg. ὀνείρου or ὀνείρατος, etc. The nom./acc. sg. τὸ ὄναρ also occurs.

– **ὁ γέλως** *laughter*, gen. γέλωτος is normally declined as a dental stem; in poetry, 'Attic' second-declension acc. sg. γέλων also occurs.

- ὁ ἔρως *love*, gen. ἔρωτος is normally declined as a dental stem; in poetry, second-declension ἔρος, dat. ἔρῳ, acc. ἔρον also occur.
- ὁ σκότος *shade*, second-declension, also occurs as a neuter third-declension σ-stem noun: nom./acc. sg. τὸ σκότος, gen. σκότους, dat. σκότει, etc.
- τὸ δένδρον *tree* similarly has dat. sg. δένδρει, nom./acc. pl. δένδρη, dat. pl. δένδρεσι next to δένδρῳ, δένδρα, δένδροις.
- ὁ υἱός *son* has, next to its regular second-declension forms, alternative υ-stem type forms: gen. sg. υἱέος, dat. υἱεῖ; nom. pl. υἱεῖς, gen. υἱέων, dat. υἱέσι, acc. υἱεῖς (for these forms, cf. the declension of ἡδύς, →5.21)
- Similarly, τὸ δάκρυον *tear* has dat. pl. δάκρυσι next to δακρύοις. Nom./acc. sg. δάκρυ is found in poetry, next to δάκρυον.

4.92   The form τᾶν (indeclinable) occurs only as a form of address: ὦ τᾶν *dear man, good sir.*

Conspectus of Noun Types

4.93   Listed below, alphabetically, are the endings of nom. sg. and gen. sg. of most types of noun (excluding individual exceptions), followed by an indication of the declension (with subtype), gender, and a reference to the sections above where that type is treated:

nom. sg.	gen. sg.	declension		gender	section(s)
-ᾰ	-ᾱς	1	(after ε, ι, ρ)	fem.	→4.3–7
-ᾰ	-ης	1		fem.	→4.3–7
-ᾱ	-ᾱς	1	(after ε, ι, ρ)	fem.	→4.3–7
-ᾱς	-ου	1	(after ε, ι, ρ)	masc.	→4.8–13
-ᾱς	-ᾰντος	3	ντ-stem	masc.	→4.45–8
-ᾰς	-ᾰτος	3	dental-stem	neut.	→4.40–2
-ᾰς	-ως	3	σ-stem	neut.	→4.70
-εύς	-έως	3	ευ-stem	masc.	→4.84–5
-η	-ης	1		fem.	→4.3–7
-ην	-ηνος	3	ν-stem	masc.	→4.49–52
-ην	-ενος	3	ν-stem	masc. or fem.	→4.49–52
-ηρ	-ηρος	3	liquid-stem	masc.	→4.55–8
-ηρ	-ερος	3	liquid-stem	mostly masc.	→4.55–8
-(τ)ηρ	-(τ)ρος	3	ρ-stem with ablaut	masc. or fem.	→4.62–4

nom. sg.	gen. sg.	declension		gender	section(s)
-ῆς	-έους	3	σ-stem	masc. proper names	→4.65–9
-ης	-ητος	3	dental-stem	fem. or masc.	→4.40–2
-ης	-ου	1		masc.	→4.8–13
-ης	-ους	3	σ-stem	masc. proper names	→4.65–8
-ῐς	-εως	3	ι/ε(y)-stem	mostly fem.	→4.74–7
-ῐς	-ῐδος/-ῐθος/-ῐτος	3	dental-stem	mostly fem.	→4.40–4
-ῑς	-ῑνος	3	ν-stem	mostly fem.	→4.49–52
-μα	-ματος	3	dental-stem	neut.	→4.40–2
-ξ	-γος/-κος/-χος	3	velar-stem	masc. or fem.	→4.35–7
-ος	-ου	2		mostly masc.	→4.19–22
-ος	-ους	3	σ-stem	neut.	→4.65–7
-ον	-ου	2		neut.	→4.24–6
-ουν	-ου	2	(with contraction)	neut.	→4.24–6
-ους	-οντος	3	ντ-stem	masc.	→4.45–8
-ους	-ου	2	(with contraction)	masc.	→4.19–22
-υ	-εως	3	υ/ε(ϝ)-stem	neut.	→4.83
-υς	-υος	3	υ-stem	mostly masc.	→4.79–81
-υς	-εως	3	υ/ε(ϝ)-stem	masc.	→4.79–82
-ψ	-βος/-πος/-φος	3	labial-stem	masc. or fem.	→4.35–7
-ω	-ους	3	oy-stem	fem.	→4.89
-ων	-ονος	3	ν-stem	masc. or fem.	→4.49–52
-ων	-οντος	3	ντ-stem	masc.	→4.45–8
-ων	-ωνος	3	ν-stem	mostly masc.	→4.49–53
-(τ)ωρ	-(τ)ορος	3	liquid-stem	masc.	→4.55–8
-ως	-ω	2	'Attic'	mostly masc.	→4.27
-ως	-ωος (or -ω)	3	ϝ-stem	masc.	→4.89

5

Adjectives and Participles

First-and-Second-Declension Adjectives and Participles

Of Three Endings (-ος, -η/-ᾱ, -ον)

Adjectives

5.1   Overview of forms:

		-ος, -η, -ον			-ος, -ᾱ, -ον (after ε, ι, ρ)		
		δεινός *impressive*			δίκαιος *just*		
		masc.	fem.	neut.	masc.	fem.	neut.
sg.	nom.	δεινός	δεινή	δεινόν	δίκαιος	δικαίᾱ	δίκαιον
	gen.	δεινοῦ	δεινῆς	δεινοῦ	δικαίου	δικαίᾱς	δικαίου
	dat.	δεινῷ	δεινῇ	δεινῷ	δικαίῳ	δικαίᾳ	δικαίῳ
	acc.	δεινόν	δεινήν	δεινόν	δίκαιον	δικαίᾱν	δίκαιον
	voc.	δεινέ	= nom.	= nom.	δίκαιε	= nom.	= nom.
pl.	nom./voc.	δεινοί	δειναί	δεινά	δίκαιοι	δίκαιαι	δίκαιᾰ
	gen.	δεινῶν	δεινῶν	δεινῶν	δικαίων	δικαίων	δικαίων
	dat.	δεινοῖς	δειναῖς	δεινοῖς	δικαίοις	δικαίαις	δικαίοις
	acc.	δεινούς	δεινάς	δεινά	δικαίους	δικαίᾱς	δίκαιᾰ

5.2   The most common type of adjective has second-declension forms in the masculine and neuter, and first-declension forms in the feminine. E.g. δεινός, -ή, -όν *impressive*, καλός, -ή, -όν *beautiful*, ὀλίγος, -η, -ον *little, few*, λεπτός, -ή, -όν *fine*, φίλος, -η, -ον *dear*, δίκαιος, -ᾱ, -ον *just*, αἰσχρός, -ά, -όν *shameful*, νέος, -ᾱ, -ον *young, new*.

These adjectives are declined:

– like δοῦλος (→4.19, second declension) in the **masculine**;
– like φυγή in the **feminine**, or if ε, ι, or ρ precedes the endings like χώρᾱ (→4.3, first declension); the endings of the fem. sg. have a long vowel throughout;
– like δῶρον (→4.24, second declension) in the **neuter**.

Note 1: But the accentuation does not necessarily correspond to such nouns, depending, rather, on the 'base accent' of the adjective's nom. sg. masc. (→24.14); for the accentuation of the gen. pl. fem., →24.22 n.1.

Participles

5.3   Overview of forms:

		-μενος, -μένη, -μενον		
		pres. mp. ppl. παιδεύω *educate*		
		masc.	fem.	neut.
sg.	nom.	παιδευόμενος	παιδευομένη	παιδευόμενον
	gen.	παιδευομένου	παιδευομένης	παιδευομένου
	dat.	παιδευομένῳ	παιδευομένῃ	παιδευομένῳ
	acc.	παιδευόμενον	παιδευομένην	παιδευόμενον
	voc.	παιδευόμενε	= nom.	= nom.
pl.	nom./voc.	παιδευόμενοι	παιδευόμεναι	παιδευόμενα
	gen.	παιδευομένων	παιδευομένων	παιδευομένων
	dat.	παιδευομένοις	παιδευομέναις	παιδευομένοις
	acc.	παιδευομένους	παιδευομένας	παιδευόμενα

5.4   Like δεινός, -ή, -όν are declined all **middle-passive participles** ending in -μενος, -μένη, -μενον:

pres. mp. ppl.	e.g. παιδευόμενος, ποιούμενος, τιμώμενος, δηλούμενος, δεικνύμενος
aor. mid. ppl.	e.g. παιδευσάμενος, λαβόμενος, δόμενος
fut. mid. ppl.	e.g. παιδευσόμενος, νεμούμενος
fut. pass. (θη-/η-) ppl.	e.g. παιδευθησόμενος, βουλησόμενος
pf. mp. ppl.	e.g. πεπαιδευμένος, τετριμμένος (note the different accentuation, →24.20)

Of Three Endings, with Contraction (-οῦς, -ῆ/-ᾶ, -οῦν)

5.5   Overview of forms:

		-οῦς, -ῆ, -οῦν			-οῦς, -ᾶ, -οῦν (after ε, ι, ρ)		
		χρυσοῦς *gold(en)*			ἀργυροῦς *silver*		
		masc.	fem.	neut.	masc.	fem.	neut.
sg.	nom./voc.	χρυσοῦς	χρυσῆ	χρυσοῦν	ἀργυροῦς	ἀργυρᾶ	ἀργυροῦν
	gen.	χρυσοῦ	χρυσῆς	χρυσοῦ	ἀργυροῦ	ἀργυρᾶς	ἀργυροῦ
	dat.	χρυσῷ	χρυσῇ	χρυσῷ	ἀργυρῷ	ἀργυρᾷ	ἀργυρῷ
	acc.	χρυσοῦν	χρυσῆν	χρυσοῦν	ἀργυροῦν	ἀργυρᾶν	ἀργυροῦν
pl.	nom./voc.	χρυσοῖ	χρυσαῖ	χρυσᾶ	ἀργυροῖ	ἀργυραῖ	ἀργυρᾶ
	gen.	χρυσῶν	χρυσῶν	χρυσῶν	ἀργυρῶν	ἀργυρῶν	ἀργυρῶν
	dat.	χρυσοῖς	χρυσαῖς	χρυσοῖς	ἀργυροῖς	ἀργυραῖς	ἀργυροῖς
	acc.	χρυσοῦς	χρυσᾶς	χρυσᾶ	ἀργυροῦς	ἀργυρᾶς	ἀργυρᾶ

Note 1: For Ionic forms, →25.27.

5.6   In some first-and-second-declension adjectives, the endings are contracted with a preceding ε or ο in the stem. These are adjectives expressing material, e.g. χρυσοῦς, -ῆ, -οῦν *gold(en)* (-έος, -έᾱ, -έον), ἀργυροῦς, -ᾶ, -οῦν *silver*, πορφυροῦς, -ᾶ, -οῦν *purple*; and those expressing multiplication ending in -πλοῦς, e.g. ἁπλοῦς, -ῆ, -οῦν *single* (-όος, -έᾱ, -όον); διπλοῦς, -ῆ, -οῦν *double*.

These adjectives are declined:

– like νοῦς (→4.21) in the **masculine**;
– like φυγή in the **feminine**, or if ε, ι, or ρ precedes the endings like χώρᾱ (→4.3, first declension). The endings of the fem. sg. have a long vowel throughout;
– like ὀστοῦν (→4.24) in the **neuter**.

> **Note 1:** Even if the stem has ο, the feminine endings are as if contracted with ε: thus ἁπλοῦς (-όος), but ἁπλῆ (-έᾱ).
>
> **Note 2:** The ending of the nom./acc. pl. neut. in -ᾱ (χρυσᾶ, ἀργυρᾶ) is due to analogy with e.g. δεινά (→1.49; regular contraction of -εᾰ would have resulted in -η, cf. γένη < γένεᾰ, →1.59). The same holds for the endings of the feminine (e.g. nom. pl. χρυσαῖ rather than expected †χρυσῇ < -έαι).

Of Two Endings (-ος, -ον or -ους, -ουν)

5.7   Overview of forms:

		-ος, -ον		-ους, -ουν	
		ἄδικος *unjust*		εὔνους *well-disposed*	
		masc. and fem.	neut.	masc. and fem.	neut.
sg.	nom.	ἄδικος	ἄδικον	εὔνους	εὔνουν
	gen.	ἀδίκου	ἀδίκου	εὔνου	εὔνου
	dat.	ἀδίκῳ	ἀδίκῳ	εὔνῳ	εὔνῳ
	acc.	ἀδίκῳ	ἄδικον	εὔνουν	εὔνουν
	voc.	ἄδικε	= nom.	= nom.	= nom.
pl.	nom/voc.	ἄδικοι	ἄδικα	εὖνοι	εὔνοα
	gen.	ἀδίκων	ἀδίκων	εὔνων	εὔνων
	dat.	ἀδίκοις	ἀδίκοις	εὔνοις	εὔνοις
	acc.	ἀδίκους	ἄδικα	εὔνους	εὔνοα

5.8   Some adjectives have **no distinct forms for the feminine**. With such adjectives, second-declension forms are used for all three genders, and the feminine forms are identical to the masculine ones ('of two endings' thus means one set of forms for the masculine *and* feminine, and one set for the neuter). Compare e.g.:

ὁ ἄδικο<u>ς</u> ἀνήρ	*the unjust man*
ἡ ἄδικο<u>ς</u> δίκη	*the unjust trial*
τὸ ἄδικ<u>ον</u> ἔργον	*the unjust deed*

5.9   Adjectives of two endings are declined:

- like δοῦλος (→4.19, second declension) in the **masculine *and* feminine**;
- like δῶρον (→4.24, second declension) in the **neuter**.

A few adjectives of two endings show contraction (e.g. εὔνους, -ουν, *well-disposed*; ἄπλους, -ουν *unseaworthy*); such adjectives are declined:

- like νοῦς (→4.19) in the **masculine *and* feminine**;
- like ὀστοῦν (→4.24) in the **neuter**; but note that the endings of the nom. and acc. pl. are not contracted (-οᾰ).

5.10   Adjectives of two endings fall into two groups.

- **compound adjectives**, formed from two or more distinct components (→23.37–40), regularly have two endings:

ἔν-δοξος, -ον	*famous*
περί-οικος, -ον	*dwelling round*
εὔ-φημος, -ον	*reverentially silent, well-spoken*
θεήλατος, -ον	*god-driven* (θεός, ἐλαύνω)

Note adjectives with so called 'privative' ἄ-:

ἄ-δικος, -ον	*unjust*
ἄ-λογος, -ον	*without reason*
ἄ-φιλος, -ον	*friendless*
ἀ-κίνητος, -ον	*motionless*

- a few non-compound adjectives, e.g.:

βάρβαρος, -ον	*non-Greek*
βέβαιος, -ον	*safe, secure, clear*
ἔρημος, -ον	*abandoned, uninhabited*
ἥσυχος, -ον	*calm*
φρόνιμος, -ον	*thoughtful, careful*
χρήσιμος, -ον	*useful*

Note 1: Comparatives and superlatives (→5.36–8) of these adjectives are of three endings: e.g. with ἄδικος, comparative ἀδικώτερος, -ᾱ, -ον, with βέβαιος, superlative βεβαιότατος, -η, -ον.

5.11 Adjectives which regularly have three endings sometimes appear as adjectives of two endings, and vice versa, in specific authors, texts or in individual places. This occurs frequently in poetry. Thus e.g. with the adjective βέβαιος (usually -ος, -ον):

(1) σοὶ δ᾽ ὁμιλία πρὸς τόνδε . . . βέβαιος. (Soph. *Phil.* 70–1)
Your relationship with him is safe. *Of two endings, as usual.*

(2) ἀρετῆς βέβαιαι . . . αἱ κτήσεις μόνης. (Soph. fr. 194 Radt)
Only of valour are the gains safe. *Of three endings.*

Further Particulars

5.12 A few (first-and-)second-declension adjectives are declined in the masculine and neuter following the 'Attic' second declension (→4.27). Of these, only πλέως, -έᾱ, -έων *full* has three endings; others, such as ἵλεως, -εων *favourable*, and compound adjectives such as ἔκπλεως, -εων *completely full*, all have two endings. The full declension of these adjectives is as follows:

		-εως, -έᾱ, -έων			-εως, -εων	
		πλέως *full*			ἵλεως *favourable*	
		masc.	fem.	neut.	masc. and fem.	neut.
sg.	nom./voc.	πλέως	πλέᾱ	πλέων	ἵλεως	ἵλεων
	gen.	πλέω	πλέᾱς	πλέω	ἵλεω	ἵλεω
	dat.	πλέῳ	πλέᾳ	πλέῳ	ἵλεῳ	ἵλεῳ
	acc.	πλέων	πλέᾱν	πλέων	ἵλεων	ἵλεων
pl.	nom./voc.	πλέῳ	πλέαι	πλέᾱ	ἵλεῳ	ἵλεᾱ
	gen.	πλέων	πλέων	πλέων	ἵλεων	ἵλεων
	dat.	πλέῳς	πλέαις	πλέῳς	ἵλεῳς	ἵλεῳς
	acc.	πλέως	πλέᾱς	πλέᾱ	ἵλεως	ἵλεᾱ

Note 1: For Ionic forms of πλέως, →25.27.

Mixed-Declension Adjectives

5.13   Overview of forms:

| | | πολύς, πολλή, πολύ | | | μέγας, μεγάλη, μέγα | | |
| | | πολύς *great, many* | | | μέγας *large, great* | | |
		masc.	fem.	neut.	masc.	fem.	neut.
sg.	nom.	πολύς	πολλή	πολύ	μέγας	μεγάλη	μέγα
	gen.	πολλοῦ	πολλῆς	πολλοῦ	μεγάλου	μεγάλης	μεγάλου
	dat.	πολλῷ	πολλῇ	πολλῷ	μεγάλῳ	μεγάλῃ	μεγάλῳ
	acc.	πολύν	πολλήν	πολύ	μέγαν	μεγάλην	μέγα
	voc.	= nom.	= nom.	= nom.	μεγάλε	= nom.	= nom.
pl.	nom./voc.	πολλοί	πολλαί	πολλά	μεγάλοι	μεγάλαι	μεγάλα
	gen.	πολλῶν	πολλῶν	πολλῶν	μεγάλων	μεγάλων	μεγάλων
	dat.	πολλοῖς	πολλαῖς	πολλοῖς	μεγάλοις	μεγάλαις	μεγάλοις
	acc.	πολλούς	πολλάς	πολλά	μεγάλους	μεγάλας	μεγάλα

Note 1: For Ionic forms (regular πολλός, πολλή, πολλόν), →25.27.

5.14   The adjectives **πολύς** *great, many* and **μέγας** *great, large* have a mixed declension, and are built on two different stems:

– The **nom. and acc. sg. in the masc. and neut**. are third-declension forms built on the stems πολῠ- and μεγᾰ-; the nom. sg. masc. ends in -ς, the acc. sg. masc. in -ν; the nom./acc. sg. neut. has no ending. So:

nom. sg. masc.	πολύ-ς, μέγα-ς
acc. sg. masc.	πολύ-ν, μέγα-ν
nom./acc. sg. neut.	πολύ, μέγα

– **All other forms** are built on the stems πολλ- and μεγᾰλ-, and are of the first-and -second declension type, declined like δεινός (→5.1). So e.g.:

| nom. pl. masc. | πολλ-οί, μεγάλ-οι |
| gen. sg. fem. | πολλ-ῆς, μεγάλ-ης |

First-and-Third-Declension Adjectives and Participles

Of Three Endings, Stems in ντ (-ων, -ουσα, -ον and πᾶς, πᾶσα, πᾶν)

Adjectives

5.15 Overview of forms:

		-ων, -ουσα, -ον			πᾶς, πᾶσα, πᾶν		
		ἑκών *willing*			πᾶς *every, whole, all*		
		masc.	fem.	neut.	masc.	fem.	neut.
sg.	nom./voc.	ἑκών	ἑκοῦσᾰ	ἑκόν	πᾶς	πᾶσᾰ	πᾶν
	gen.	ἑκόντος	ἑκούσης	ἑκόντος	πάντός	πάσης	πάντός
	dat.	ἑκόντῐ	ἑκούσῃ	ἑκόντῐ	πάντί	πάσῃ	πάντί
	acc.	ἑκόντᾰ	ἑκοῦσᾰν	ἑκόν	πάντᾰ	πᾶσᾰν	πᾶν
pl.	nom./voc.	ἑκόντες	ἑκοῦσαι	ἑκόντᾰ	πάντες	πᾶσαι	πάντᾰ
	gen.	ἑκόντων	ἑκουσῶν	ἑκόντων	πάντων	πασῶν	πάντων
	dat.	ἑκοῦσῐ(ν)	ἑκούσαις	ἑκοῦσῐ(ν)	πᾶσι(ν)	πάσαις	πᾶσι(ν)
	acc.	ἑκόντᾱς	ἑκούσᾱς	ἑκόντᾰ	πάντᾱς	πάσᾱς	πάντᾰ

5.16 The adjectives **ἑκών** *willing* (ἑκοντ-), **ἄκων** *unwilling* (ἀκοντ-) and **πᾶς** *whole, every, all* (πάντ-) have a **stem ending in ντ**. They are declined:

- in the **masculine**: following the third declension, like γέρων or γίγας (→4.46). With ἑκών and ἄκων the nom. sg. masc. has a long stem-vowel and no final τ (so ἑκών with stem ἑκόντ-). With πᾶς the ending -ς was added and ντ disappeared with compensatory lengthening (πᾶς <*πάντς, →1.68). In the dat. pl. of each of these adjectives, again, ντ disappeared with compensatory lengthening (ἑκοῦσι = ἑκόσι <*ἑκόντ-σι; πᾶσι <*πάντ-σι);
- in the **feminine**: the suffix *-yᾰ (→23.9) was added to the stem, resulting in -σᾰ (<*-ντyᾰ, →1.77) with compensatory lengthening of the preceding vowel (→1.68). So e.g. ἑκοῦσᾰ (<*ἑκόντ-yᾰ), πᾶσᾰ (<*πάντ-yᾰ). The resulting forms are declined following first declension nouns with short ᾰ, like μοῦσᾰ (→4.3);
- in the **neuter**: the nom./acc. sg. is identical to the stem but has lost the final τ: e.g. ἑκόν (<*ἑκόντ), πᾶν (<*πάντ, but →n.1). The nom./acc. pl. ends in -ᾰ. Other forms are identical to the masc.

Note 1: The long ᾱ in the nom./acc. sg. neut. πᾶν is irregular; it is modelled on other cases throughout the paradigm, such as (regular) πᾶς, πᾶσα (analogy, →1.49).

Participles

5.17   Overview of forms:

		-ων, -ουσα, -ον pres. act. ppl. of παιδεύω *educate*			**-ῶν, -οῦσα, -οῦν** pres. act. ppl. of ποιέω *make, do*		
		masc.	fem.	neut.	masc.	fem.	neut.
sg.	nom.	παιδεύων	παιδεύουσα	παιδεῦον	ποιῶν	ποιοῦσα	ποιοῦν
	gen.	παιδεύοντος	παιδευούσης	παιδεύοντος	ποιοῦντος	ποιούσης	ποιοῦντος
	dat.	παιδεύοντι	παιδευούσῃ	παιδεύοντι	ποιοῦντι	ποιούσῃ	ποιοῦντι
	acc.	παιδεύοντα	παιδεύουσαν	παιδεῦον	ποιοῦντα	ποιοῦσαν	ποιοῦν
pl.	nom.	παιδεύοντες	παιδεύουσαι	παιδεύοντα	ποιοῦντες	ποιοῦσαι	ποιοῦντα
	gen.	παιδευόντων	παιδευουσῶν	παιδευόντων	ποιούντων	ποιουσῶν	ποιούντων
	dat.	παιδεύουσι(ν)	παιδευούσαις	παιδεύουσι(ν)	ποιοῦσι(ν)	ποιούσαις	ποιοῦσι(ν)
	acc.	παιδεύοντας	παιδευούσας	παιδεύοντα	ποιοῦντας	ποιούσας	ποιοῦντα

		-ῶν, -ῶσα, -ῶν pres. act. ppl. of τιμάω *honour*			**-ῶν, -οῦσα, -οῦν** pres. act. ppl. of δηλόω *make clear*		
		masc.	fem.	neut.	masc.	fem.	neut.
sg.	nom.	τιμῶν	τιμῶσα	τιμῶν	δηλῶν	δηλοῦσα	δηλοῦν
	gen.	τιμῶντος	τιμώσης	τιμῶντος	δηλοῦντος	δηλούσης	δηλοῦντος
	dat.	τιμῶντι	τιμώσῃ	τιμῶντι	δηλοῦντι	δηλούσῃ	δηλοῦντι
	acc.	τιμῶντα	τιμῶσαν	τιμῶν	δηλοῦντα	δηλοῦσαν	δηλοῦν
pl.	nom.	τιμῶντες	τιμῶσαι	τιμῶντα	δηλοῦντες	δηλοῦσαι	δηλοῦντα
	gen.	τιμώντων	τιμωσῶν	τιμώντων	δηλούντων	δηλουσῶν	δηλούντων
	dat.	τιμῶσι(ν)	τιμώσαις	τιμῶσι(ν)	δηλοῦσι(ν)	δηλούσαις	δηλοῦσι(ν)
	acc.	τιμῶντας	τιμώσας	τιμῶντα	δηλοῦντας	δηλούσας	δηλοῦντα

		-ύς, -ῦσα, -ύν pres. act. ppl. of δείκνῡμι *show*			**-άς, -ᾶσα, -άν** pres. act. ppl. of ἵστημι *make stand*		
		masc.	fem.	neut.	masc.	fem.	neut.
sg.	nom.	δεικνύς	δεικνῦσα	δεικνύν	ἱστάς	ἱστᾶσα	ἱστάν
	gen.	δεικνύντος	δεικνύσης	δεικνύντος	ἱστάντος	ἱστάσης	ἱστάντος
	dat.	δεικνύντι	δεικνύσῃ	δεικνύντι	ἱστάντι	ἱστάσῃ	ἱστάντι
	acc.	δεικνύντα	δεικνῦσαν	δεικνύν	ἱστάντα	ἱστᾶσαν	ἱστάν
pl.	nom.	δεικνύντες	δεικνῦσαι	δεικνύντα	ἱστάντες	ἱστᾶσαι	ἱστάντα
	gen.	δεικνύντων	δεικνῡσῶν	δεικνύντων	ἱστάντων	ἱστασῶν	ἱστάντων
	dat.	δεικνῦσι(ν)	δεικνύσαις	δεικνῦσι(ν)	ἱστᾶσι(ν)	ἱστάσαις	ἱστᾶσι(ν)
	acc.	δεικνύντας	δεικνύσας	δεικνύντα	ἱστάντας	ἱστάσας	ἱστάντα

| | | -εἰς, -εῖσα, -έν | | | -ούς, -οῦσα, -όν | | |
| | | pres. act. ppl. of τίθημι *put, place* | | | pres. act. ppl. of δίδωμι *give* | | |
		masc.	fem.	neut.	masc.	fem.	neut.
sg.	nom.	τιθείς	τιθεῖσα	τιθέν	διδούς	διδοῦσα	διδόν
	gen.	τιθέντος	τιθείσης	τιθέντος	διδόντος	διδούσης	διδόντος
	dat.	τιθέντι	τιθείσῃ	τιθέντι	διδόντι	διδούσῃ	διδόντι
	acc.	τιθέντα	τιθεῖσαν	τιθέν	διδόντα	διδοῦσαν	διδόν
pl.	nom.	τιθέντες	τιθεῖσαι	τιθέντα	διδόντες	διδοῦσαι	διδόντα
	gen.	τιθέντων	τιθεισῶν	τιθέντων	διδόντων	διδουσῶν	διδόντων
	dat.	τιθεῖσι(ν)	τιθείσαις	τιθεῖσι(ν)	διδοῦσι(ν)	διδούσαις	διδοῦσι(ν)
	acc.	τιθέντας	τιθείσας	τιθέντα	διδόντας	διδούσᾱς	διδόντα

5.18   All active participles (except perfect active participles in -ώς, -υῖα, -ός, →5.19–20), and aorist passive (θη-/η-aorist) participles, are built on a stem ending in ντ, and thus follow the pattern of declension of ἑκών or πᾶς:

– like ἑκών (with a nom. sg with a long stem-vowel, without τ):

pres. act. of -ω verbs	e.g. παιδεύων (gen. -οντος), παιδεύουσα, παιδεῦον
pres. act. of εἰμί *be*	ὤν (gen. ὄντος), οὖσα, ὄν
pres. act. of εἶμι *go*	ἰών (gen. ἰόντος), ἰοῦσα, ἰόν
fut. act.	e.g. παιδεύσων (gen. -οντος), παιδεύσουσα, παιδεῦσον
aor. act., thematic	e.g. λαβών (gen. -όντος), λαβοῦσα, λαβόν

Note the forms of participles with contraction:

pres. act. of -έω verbs	e.g. ποιῶν (gen. -οῦντος), ποιοῦσα, ποιοῦν
pres. act. of -άω verbs	e.g. τιμῶν (gen. -ῶντος), τιμῶσα, τιμῶν
pres. act. of -όω verbs	e.g. δηλῶν (gen. -οῦντος), δηλοῦσα, δηλοῦν
fut. act., Attic	e.g. νεμῶν (gen. -οῦντος), νεμοῦσα, νεμοῦν

– like πᾶς (with a nom. sg. ending in -ς and compensatory lengthening):

pres. act. of -μι verbs	e.g. δεικνύς (gen. -ύντος), δεικνῦσα, δεικνύν
	e.g. ἱστάς (gen. -άντος), ἱστᾶσα, ἱστάν
	διδούς (gen. -όντος), διδοῦσα, διδόν
	τιθείς (gen. -έντος), τιθεῖσα, τιθέν
	ἱείς (gen. -έντος), ἱεῖσα, ἱέν
aor. act., sigmatic	e.g. παιδεύσᾱς (gen. -αντος), παιδεύσᾱσα, παιδεῦσᾱν
aor. act., root	e.g. δύς (gen. δύντος), δῦσα, δύν
	e.g. στάς (gen. -άντος), στᾶσα, στάν
	e.g. θείς (gen. -έντος), θεῖσα, θέν
	e.g. δούς (gen. -όντος), δοῦσα, δόν
aor. θη-/η-	e.g. παιδευθείς (gen. -έντος), παιδευθεῖσα, παιδευθέν
	e.g. φανείς (gen. -έντος), φανεῖσα, φανέν

Of Three Endings, Perfect Active Participles in -ώς, -υῖα, -ός

5.19   Overview of forms:

		-ώς, -υῖα, -ός		
		ppl. pf. act. of παιδεύω *educate*		
		masc.	fem.	neut.
sg.	nom.	πεπαιδευκώς	πεπαιδευκυῖᾰ	πεπαιδευκός
	gen.	πεπαιδευκότος	πεπαιδευκίας	πεπαιδευκότος
	dat.	πεπαιδευκότι	πεπαιδευκυίᾳ	πεπαιδευκότι
	acc.	πεπαιδευκότα	πεπαιδευκυῖᾰν	πεπαιδευκός
pl.	nom.	πεπαιδευκότες	πεπαιδευκυῖαι	πεπαιδευκότα
	gen.	πεπαιδευκότων	πεπαιδευκυιῶν	πεπαιδευκότων
	dat.	πεπαιδευκόσι(ν)	πεπαιδευκυίαις	πεπαιδευκόσι(ν)
	acc.	πεπαιδευκότας	πεπαιδευκυίας	πεπαιδευκότα

5.20   The participle of the perfect active has, in the masculine and neuter, some forms with a stem in οσ and other forms with a stem in οτ. Feminine forms are built on a stem in υι. The forms are declined as follows:

- in the **masculine**: following the third declension; in the nom. sg., the stem in οσ- is used, without ending, but with lengthened stem-vowel (i.e. -ως), e.g. πεπαιδευκ<u>ώς</u>; in all other cases the stem in οτ- is used, e.g. gen. sg. πεπαιδευκ<u>ότος</u>, dat. pl. πεπαιδευκ<u>όσι</u> (dental τ disappears before -σι);
- in the **feminine**: following the first declension, type διάνοιᾰ (→4.3, note the ι preceding the α), hence gen. sg. πεπαιδευκυ<u>ίας</u>, dat. sg. -υί<u>ᾳ</u>;
- in the **neuter**: in the nom./acc. sg. the stem in οσ- is used, without ending (e.g. πεπαιδευκός); other cases use the stem in οτ-, e.g. nom./acc. pl. πεπαιδευκότα; gen. and dat. forms are thus identical to the masc.

Note 1: The suffix originally used in these participles was (o-grade) *-ϝοσ-, with the feminine based on zero-grade *-ϝσ- followed by the suffix *-yᾰ (→23.9) (*-ϝσ-yᾰ > -υιᾰ). The suffix *-ϝοτ- then replaced *-ϝοσ- in most cases of the masculine and neuter. The resulting heteroclitic pattern of declension was originally found in stem perfects such as εἰδώς, εἰδυῖα, etc. (οἶδα, →18.23) and extended from there (with ϝ no longer felt) to later, regularly formed κ-perfects and aspirated perfects (for these types of perfect stem, →18.2).

Of Three Endings, Stems in υ/εϝ (-υς, -εια, -υ)

5.21   Overview of forms:

| | | -υς, -εια, -υ | | |
| | | ἡδύς *sweet* | | |
		masc.	fem.	neut.
sg.	nom.	ἡδύς	ἡδεῖα	ἡδύ
	gen.	ἡδέος	ἡδείᾱς	ἡδέος
	dat.	ἡδεῖ	ἡδείᾳ	ἡδεῖ
	acc.	ἡδύν	ἡδεῖαν	ἡδύ
	voc.	ἡδύ	= nom.	= nom.
pl.	nom./voc.	ἡδεῖς	ἡδεῖαι	ἡδέᾰ
	gen.	ἡδέων	ἡδειῶν	ἡδέων
	dat.	ἡδέσῐ(ν)	ἡδείαις	ἡδέσῐ(ν)
	acc.	ἡδεῖς	ἡδείᾱς	ἡδέᾰ

Note 1: For Ionic forms, →25.27.

5.22   A group of adjectives ending in -υς, -εια, -υ is built on stems with two ablaut variants ending in zero-grade ŭ or e-grade εϝ (for ŭ/ϝ, →1.79): e.g. ἡδύς *sweet*, βαρύς *heavy*, εὐρύς *wide*, ὀξύς *sharp*, ταχύς *quick*.

– in the **masculine**: following the third declension, similar to πῆχυς (→4.79, but note the different gen. sg.). The zero-grade stem in υ is used in the nom. and acc. sg. ἡδύ-ς, ἡδύ-ν. The other cases use the full e-grade *ἡδεϝ-, the ϝ of which disappeared: gen. sg. ἡδέ(ϝ)ος, gen. pl. ἡδέ(ϝ)ων; there is contraction in the dat. sg. ἡδεῖ (<*ἡδέ(ϝ)ι) and nom. pl. ἡδεῖς (= ἡδές <*ἡδέ(ϝ)ες);

Note 1: The forms of the dat. pl. and acc. pl. were presumably built on a stem ἡδε-, analogous to (e.g.) the nom. pl.; for this kind of formation, cf. πόλις (→4.76) and πῆχυς (→4.82).

– in the **feminine**: the suffix *-yᾰ (→23.9) was added to the e-grade stem ἡδεϝ-, producing ἡδεῖα (<*ἡδέ(ϝ)yα). The forms are declined according to the first declension, like διάνοια (→4.3, note 1 preceding ᾰ);
– in the **neuter**: following the third declension, similar to ἄστυ (→4.83, but note the uncontracted gen. sg. and nom./acc. pl.). The nom./acc. sg. is built on the zero-grade and has no ending: ἡδύ; other cases use the full e-grade. The nom./acc. pl. ends in -ᾰ (ἡδέᾰ <*ἡδέ(ϝ)ᾰ, without contraction). Other forms are identical to the masc.

Of Three Endings, Stems in ν (-ας, -αινα, -αν)

5.23   Overview of forms:

		-ας, -αινα, -αν		
		μέλας *dark*		
		masc.	fem.	neut.
sg.	nom.	μέλᾱς	μέλαινα	μέλᾰν
	gen.	μέλᾰνος	μελαίνης	μέλᾰνος
	dat.	μέλᾰνι	μελαίνῃ	μέλᾰνι
	acc.	μέλᾰνα	μέλαιναν	μέλᾰν
	voc.	μέλᾰν	= nom.	= nom.
pl.	nom./voc.	μέλᾰνες	μέλαιναι	μέλᾰνα
	gen.	μελᾰνων	μελαινῶν	μελᾰνων
	dat.	μέλᾰσι(ν)	μελαίναις	μέλᾰσι(ν)
	acc.	μέλᾰνας	μελαίνας	μέλᾰνα

5.24   The adjectives **μέλας** *dark* (stem μελᾰν-) and **τάλας** *miserable* (stem ταλᾰν-) have stems ending in ν. Their declension is as follows:

– in the **masculine**: following third-declension ν-stems (→4.49). In the nom. sg. μέλας and τάλας have the ending -ς, with loss of ν and compensatory lengthening (μέλᾱς <*μέλᾰνς, →1.68).

Note 1: The short vowel in the dat. pl. (μέλᾰσι) is presumably the result of analogy, cf. ν-stem forms such as δαίμοσι, →4.51 n.1.

– in the **feminine**: the suffix *-yᾰ (→23.9) was added to the stem, producing μέλαινα, τάλαινα through inversion (<*τάλανyα, →1.78);
– in the **neuter**: the nom./acc. sg. has no ending: μέλαν, τάλαν. The nom./acc. pl. ends in -ᾰ: μέλανα. Other forms are identical to the masc.

Note 2: Also with a stem in ν is the adjective **τέρην** *tender* (stem τερεν-). The nom. sg. masc. τέρην has no ending and a long stem-vowel; the fem. is τέρεινα (= τέρεˉνα <*τέρενyα, →1.78), gen. τερείνης; neut. τέρεν, gen. τέρενος. Declined like the masc./neut. of τέρην is ἄρρην *male* (of two endings).
Note 3: There are also adjectives with a stem in ν of two endings (in -ον): →5.26 below.

Of Three Endings, Stems in εντ (-εις, -εσσα, -εν)

5.25   A few first-and-third-declension adjectives chiefly found in poetry and meaning *rich in . . .* or *. . .-ful* have the endings -εις, -εσσα, -εν: e.g. χαρίεις *graceful*, φωνήεις *voiced*, δακρυόεις *tearful*. The stem of these adjectives ends in ντ, and they are declined in most of the masculine and neuter as in 5.17 above (cf. e.g. τιθείς, τιθέν). In the feminine, however, forms with -εσσ- (known from epic poetry) are used. The full declension is as follows:

| | | -εις, -εσσα, -εν | | |
| | | χαρίεις *graceful* | | |
		masc.	fem.	neut.
sg.	nom./voc.	χαρίεις	χαρίεσσα	χαρίεν
	gen.	χαρίεντος	χαριέσσης	χαρίεντος
	dat.	χαρίεντι	χαριέσσῃ	χαρίεντι
	acc.	χαρίεντα	χαρίεσσαν	χαρίεν
pl.	nom./voc.	χαρίεντες	χαρίεσσαι	χαρίεντα
	gen.	χαριέντων	χαριεσσῶν	χαριέντων
	dat.	χαρίεσι(ν)	χαριέσσαις	χαρίεσι(ν)
	acc.	χαρίεντας	χαριέσσας	χαρίεντα

Third-Declension Adjectives

Of Two Endings, Stems in ον (-ων, -ον)

5.26   Overview of forms:

| | | -ων, -ον | |
| | | σώφρων *prudent* | |
		masc. and fem.	neut.
sg.	nom.	σώφρων	σῶφρον
	gen.	σώφρονος	σώφρονος
	dat.	σώφρονι	σώφρονι
	acc.	σώφρονα	σῶφρον
	voc.	σῶφρον	= nom.
pl.	nom./voc.	σώφρονες	σώφρονα
	gen.	σωφρόνων	σωφρόνων
	dat.	σώφροσι(ν)	σώφροσι(ν)
	acc.	σώφρονας	σώφρονα

5.27   A group of adjectives of two endings (i.e., with no separate forms for the feminine) have stems ending in ον. E.g. σώφρων *prudent* (σωφρον-), εὐδαίμων *fortunate* (εὐδαιμον-), μνήμων *mindful* (μνημον-). Their declension is as follows:

– in the **masculine *and* feminine**: like δαίμων (→4.49). The nom. sg. uses a long stem-vowel and no ending (e.g. σώφρων with stem σωφρον-).

– in the **neuter**: the nom./acc. sg. has no ending, e.g. σῶφρον. The nom./acc. pl. ends in -ᾰ. Other forms are identical to the masc./fem.

Note 1: In the dat. pl. ν disappears without compensatory lengthening (e.g. σώφρο̱σι). For this type of formation, →4.51 n.1.

Of Two Endings, Stems in σ (-ης, -ες)

5.28   Overview of forms:

		-ης, -ες			
		ἀληθής *true*		ὑγιής *healthy*	
		masc. and fem.	neut.	masc. and fem.	neut.
sg.	nom.	ἀληθής	ἀληθές	ὑγιής	ὑγιές
	gen.	ἀληθοῦς (<-έ(σ)ος)	ἀληθοῦς	ὑγιοῦς	ὑγιοῦς
	dat.	ἀληθεῖ (<-έ(σ)ι)	ἀληθεῖ	ὑγιεῖ	ὑγιεῖ
	acc.	ἀληθῆ (<-έ(σ)α)	ἀληθές	ὑγιᾶ	ὑγιές
	voc.	ἀληθές	= nom.	ὑγιές	= nom.
pl.	nom./voc.	ἀληθεῖς (<-έ(σ)ες)	ἀληθῆ (<-έ(σ)α)	ὑγιεῖς	ὑγιᾶ
	gen.	ἀληθῶν (<-έ(σ)ων)	ἀληθῶν	ὑγιῶν	ὑγιῶν
	dat.	ἀληθέσι(ν) (<-έσσι(ν))	ἀληθέσι(ν)	ὑγιέσι(ν)	ὑγιέσι(ν)
	acc.	ἀληθεῖς	ἀληθῆ (<-έ(σ)α)	ὑγιεῖς	ὑγιᾶ

Note 1: For Ionic forms, →25.27.

5.29   A group of adjectives of two endings in -ης, -ες have stems ending in εσ. E.g. ἀληθής *true* (ἀληθεσ-), εὐγενής *well-born* (εὐγενεσ-), εὐκλεής *famous* (εὐκλεεσ-), ὑγιής *healthy* (ὑγιεσ-). Their declension is as follows:

– in the **masculine *and* feminine**: the nom. sg. uses a long stem-vowel and no ending (e.g. ἀληθής, stem in other cases ἀληθε̱σ-). The other case forms are the result of contraction (→1.58–64) after the σ of the stem disappeared (→1.83). Note the acc. pl. in -εῖς (for which cf. πόλεις, →4.76);

– in the **neuter**: the nom./acc. sg. has no ending, e.g. ἀληθές, εὐκλεές. The nom./acc. pl. ends in -η (contracted from -ε(σ)α). The gen. and dat. sg./pl. are identical to the masc./fem.

5.30   With adjectives that have **ε or ι** preceding the εσ of the stem, e.g. εὐκλε̱ής, ὑγι̱ής, the forms of the acc. sg. masc./fem. and nom./acc. pl. neut. normally do not contract to -η, but to -ᾱ (→1.57): e.g. εὐκλεᾱ̱, ὑγιᾱ̱ (however, ὑγιῆ also occurs).

Further Particulars

Adjectives Formed with Dental-Stem Nouns

5.31 A few third-declension adjectives are compounds (thus of **two endings**, →5.10) formed with a **dental-stem noun** as their second part: e.g. εὔελπις *hopeful* (compounded with ἐλπίς, stem ἐλπῐδ-; gen. εὐέλπιδος), ἄχαρις *graceless* (compounded with χάρις, stem χαρῐτ-; gen. ἀχάριτος), ἄπολις *city-less* (compounded with πόλις, treated as if from stem πολῐδ-; gen. ἀπόλιδος; cf. proper names in -πολις, →4.78).

The forms of such adjectives are largely declined as the relevant nouns (→4.40; the nom./acc. pl. neut. ends in -α, e.g. ἀχάριτα). But the acc. sg. masc. always ends in -ιν (→4.43), the nom./acc. sg. neut. in -ι (e.g. εὔελπι).

Adjectives of One Ending

5.32 There are also a few other adjectives of two endings with stems ending in a dental stop (or in some cases another type of consonant). Since no separate neuter forms of these adjectives are found, they are sometimes called 'of one ending':

πένης *poor*	gen. πένητος	ἀγνώς *unknown, ignorant*	gen. ἀγνῶτος
φυγάς *fugitive*	gen. φυγάδος	ἅρπαξ *thieving, raping*	gen. ἅρπαγος

Used only in the masculine is ἐθελοντής, -οῦ *volunteer-* (first declension, →4.8). Only used in the feminine are adjectives in -ίς, gen. -ίδος (third declension, →4.40), such as Ἑλληνίς *Greek*, συμμαχίς *allied*.

μάκαρ *blessed*, gen. μάκαρος, may also be listed here (μάκαρ may be masc./fem./neut.), although a separate fem. μάκαιρᾰ (<*-αρ-yᾰ, →23.9, 1.78) also occurs in poetry.

5.33 Many of these adjectives are **used regularly as nouns** (e.g. ὁ/ἡ φυγάς *fugitive*, ὁ πένης *poor man*, ἡ Ἑλληνίς *Greek woman*).

Comparison of Adjectives

Introduction

5.34 The **comparative** (expressing greater degree) and **superlative** (expressing greatest degree) of adjectives are formed in two different ways:

- most adjectives form comparatives using the suffix -τερος, -τέρᾱ, -τερον; corresponding superlatives are formed using the suffix -τατος, -τάτη, -τατον. E.g. δικαιότερος *more just, fairly just, too just, most just* (*of two*); δικαιότατος *most just, very just*;
- a smaller group of adjectives forms comparatives using the suffix -(ί)ον- (nom. -(ί)ων); corresponding superlatives are formed using the suffix -ιστος, -ίστη, -ιστον. E.g. κακίων *worse, fairly bad, too bad, worst* (*of two*), κάκιστος *worst, very bad*.

5.35   For the meanings and uses of comparatives and superlatives, →32.

Note 1: Apart from by single forms, comparison may also be expressed by the adverb μᾶλλον *more* (itself the comparative form of μάλα *very*): e.g. μᾶλλον φίλος *dearer*.

Similarly, an alternative for the superlative is the use of the adverb μάλιστα *most* (itself superlative of μάλα): e.g. μάλιστα φίλος *dearest*.

Comparatives in -τερος and Superlatives in -τατος

5.36   The **comparative degree** of most adjectives is formed with the suffix -τερος, -τέρᾱ, -τερον, added to the (masculine) stem of the adjective's positive degree (for details see below). Such comparatives are declined as first-and-second-declension adjectives, like δίκαιος (→5.1–2, note -τέρᾱ).

5.37   The **superlative degree** of these adjectives is formed by adding the suffix -τατος, -τάτη, -τατον to the same stem. Such superlatives are declined as first-and-second-declension adjectives, like δεινός (→5.2).

5.38   The following individual types may be distinguished:

- For adjectives with a masc. in -ος (→5.1–2, 5.7–10), if the preceding **syllable is long** (i.e. its vowel is long or followed by two or more consonants), the comparative has the form -ότερος, superlative -ότατος:

positive	comparative	superlative
δεινός *impressive*	δεινότερος	δεινότατος
δίκαιος *just*	δικαιότερος	δικαιότατος
ἰσχῡρός *strong*	ἰσχῡρότερος	ἰσχῡρότατος
λεπτός *fine*	λεπτότερος	λεπτότατος
πικρός *painful*	πικρότερος	πικρότατος

- If the preceding **syllable is short** (i.e. its vowel is short) the comparative has the form -ώτερος, superlative -ώτατος:

ἄξιος *worthy*	ἀξιώτερος	ἀξιώτατος
ἱκανός *suitable, sufficient*	ἱκανώτερος	ἱκανώτατος
νέος *young*	νεώτερος	νεώτατος
χαλεπός *difficult*	χαλεπώτερος	χαλεπώτατος

- Adjectives with a masc. in -ας (stem in ν, →5.23–4) have -άντερος, -άντατος:

μέλας *dark*	μελάντερος	μελάντατος

- Adjectives with a masc. in -υς (→5.21–2) have -ύτερος/-ύτατος (but for exceptions, →5.43 below):

βαρύς *heavy*	βαρύτερος	βαρύτατος
βραχύς *short*	βραχύτερος	βραχύτατος

- Adjectives with a masc. in -ης (→5.28–30) have -έστερος/-έστατος:

ἀληθής *true*   ἀληθέστερος   ἀληθέστατος

εὐκλεής *famous*   εὐκλεέστερος   εὐκλεέστατος

- Adjectives with a masc. in -ων (→5.26–7) add -εσ- to the stem, giving **-ονέστερος/-ονέστατος**:

εὐδαίμων *fortunate*   εὐδαιμονέστερος   εὐδαιμονέστατος

σώφρων *prudent*   σωφρονέστερος   σωφρονέστατος

- So too, in most cases, adjectives with a contracted masc. in **-ους** (→5.5–6, 5.7–10), giving **-ούστερος** (<-οέστερος), **-ούστατος**:

ἁπλοῦς *single*   ἁπλούστερος   ἁπλούστατος
                       but also: ἁπλοώτερος

εὔνους *well-disposed* εὐνούστερος   εὐνούστατος

- And adjectives with a masc. in **-εις** (→5.25) also have **-έστερος, -έστατος**:

χαρίεις *graceful*   χαριέστερος   χαριέστατος

5.39   The following exceptions may be noted:

- The adjective φίλος *dear* has comparative and superlative forms without o: φίλτερος *dearer*, φίλτατος *dearest* (occasionally φιλαίτερος, φιλαίτατος, see below). So too ἐνέρτερος *lower*, ἐνέρτατος *lowest* with οἱ ἔνεροι *those below* (only masc. pl.).

- Also without o are the comparative and superlative of several adjectives ending in -αιος, e.g.:

γεραιός *old, grey*   γεραίτερος   γεραίτατος

παλαιός *ancient*   παλαίτερος   παλαίτατος

σχολαῖος *leisurely*   σχολαίτερος   σχολαίτατος
                       but also: σχολαιότερος   but also: σχολαιότατος

- Some other adjectives also get a comparative and superlative in -αίτερος, -αίτατος, e.g.:

ὄψιος *late*   ὀψιαίτερος   ὀψιαίτατος

ἥσυχος *calm*   ἡσυχαίτερος   ἡσυχαίτατος
                       but also: ἡσυχώτερος   but also: ἡσυχώτατος

- κενός *empty* and στενός *narrow* (<*κενϝός, *στενϝός, →1.82) normally have -ότερος/-ότατος, even though the preceding syllable is short/open in Attic.

- πένης *poor* (gen. πένητος) shortens its vowel, giving πενέ̆στερος (<*πενέτ-τερος, →1.89), πενέ̆στατος.

- Some adjectives form a comparative in -ίστερος, superlative in -ίστατος: e.g. λάλος *babbling*, comparative λαλίστερος, superlative λαλίστατος.

5.40   Some comparatives and superlatives of this type are **not based on an adjective**, but on a preposition/adverb or no positive degree whatsoever:

positive	comparative	superlative
(ἐκ out)	—	ἔσχατος extreme, utmost
(πρό before)	πρότερος earlier, before	πρῶτος first
(ὑπέρ above)	ὑπέρτερος higher	ὑπέρτατος highest
—	ὕστερος later	ὕστατος latest

Comparatives in -(ῐ)ων and superlatives in -ιστος

5.41   Several frequently occurring adjectives form their **comparative degree** by adding the suffix -ῑον-/-(y)ον- to the adjective's stem (this occurs especially with adjectives in -υς), or to an entirely different stem. For the declension of such comparatives, →5.44 below.

5.42   The **superlative degree** of these adjectives is formed by adding the suffix -ιστος, -ιστη, -ιστον to the same stem. Such superlatives are declined as first-and-second-declension adjectives of three endings, like δεινός, -ή, -όν (→5.1–2).

5.43   The following comparatives and superlatives belong to this type:

positive	comparative	superlative
ἀγαθός good, strong	ἀμείνων	ἄριστος (see below)
"	ἀρείων (poetry only)	ἄριστος
"	βελτίων	βέλτιστος
"	λῴων	λῷστος
(κρατύς strong (Homer only))	κρείττων better	κράτιστος best
αἰσχρός ugly	αἰσχίων	αἴσχιστος
ἐχθρός hostile	ἐχθίων	ἔχθιστος
ἡδύς sweet	ἡδίων	ἥδιστος
κακός bad, evil	κακίων	κάκιστος
"	but also: κακώτερος (poetry only)	
"	χείρων	χείριστος
"	ἥττων worse	ἥκιστος worst (usually adv. ἥκιστα)
καλός beautiful	καλλίων	κάλλιστος
μακρός long	(μάσσων (<*μάκ-yων, →1.77), poet.)	μήκιστος
	but normally: μακρότερος	but also: μακρότατος
μέγας large, great	μείζων (Ion. μέζων <*μέγ-yων, →1.77)	μέγιστος

μικρός *small*	ἐλάττων (<*ἐλάχ-γων, →1.77)	ἐλάχιστος
"	μείων	—
	but also: μικρότερος	μικρότατος
ὀλίγος *little, few*	ἐλάττων (<*ἐλάχ-γων, →1.77)	ἐλάχιστος
"	μείων	ὀλίγιστος
"	ἥττων *less*	ἥκιστος *least* (usually adv. ἥκιστα)
πολύς *great, many*	πλέων or πλείων	πλεῖστος
ῥᾴδιος *easy*	ῥᾴων	ῥᾷστος
ταχύς *quick* (<*θαχ-, →1.97)	θάττων (<*θάχ-γων, →1.77)	τάχιστος

Note 1: The various comparatives and superlatives of ἀγαθός (each translatable by *better* and *best*) and κακός (each translatable by *worse* and *worst*) have different nuances of meaning: broadly speaking, ἀρείων/ἄριστος refer to capability/prowess, βελτίων/βέλτιστος to (moral) suitability, λῴων/λῷστος to usefulness, benefit. χείρων/χείριστος refer to lack of worth, ἥττων/ἥκιστος to weakness. ἀμείνων and κακίων share the range of meanings of ἀγαθός and κακός. These shades of meaning are not always fully clear in individual examples.

5.44   Comparatives in -(ί)ων are **declined** as third-declension adjectives of two endings with a stem in ον-, like σώφρων (→5.26–7; the nom. sg. masc./fem. uses a long stem-vowel).

In some cases (acc. sg. masc./fem.; nom./acc. pl. masc./fem. and neut.), alternative forms based on an older suffix *-yοσ- are used more frequently than the ον-forms (for these forms, cf. αἰδώς, →4.71).

The full declension is as follows:

| | | -(ῐ)ων, -(ῐ)ον ||
| | | μείζων *larger, more* ||
		masc. and fem.	neut.
sg.	nom.	μείζων	μεῖζον
	gen.	μείζονος	μείζονος
	dat.	μείζονι	μείζονι
	acc.	μείζονα	μεῖζον
		more often μείζω (<*-ο(σ)α)	
	voc.	μεῖζον	= nom.
pl.	nom./voc.	μείζονες	μείζονα
		more often μείζους (<*-ο(σ)ες)	*more often* μείζω (<*-ο(σ)α)
	gen.	μειζόνων	μειζόνων
	dat.	μείζοσι(ν)	μείζοσι(ν)
	acc.	μείζονας	μείζονα
		more often μείζους (= nom.)	*more often* μείζω (<*-ο(σ)α)

Note 1: For the accentuation of this type of comparative, →24.32.

6

Adverbs

Formation of Adverbs

Introduction

6.1 Nearly all adverbs derive from original case-forms of an adjective or noun.

- A few of these case endings developed into suffixes specifically used for the formation of adverbs; chief among these is -ως (an old case-ending -ω, with a suffix -ς); this suffix -ως was freely added (i.e. it was productive) to the stems of adjectives to create manner adverbs, e.g. adv. ἡδέως *sweetly*, with the adj. ἡδύς *sweet*. →6.3.

  Less productive, but still widely used, were various endings indicating various local relationships, e.g. -δε/-σε (indicating place to which), -θεν (indicating place from which), etc. →6.7–11.

- In numerous other cases, another case-form came to be used as adverb: in some instances the derivation was still transparent in classical Greek (as the case-form in question was still used, e.g. adv. πολύ *very, greatly*, originally acc. sg. neut. πολύ of the adj. πολύς *great, many*); however, in other cases, the original noun/adjective had gone out of use, and the adverb remained as a fossilized, isolated form. →6.4–6.

Note 1: Even in the case of adverbs whose derivation was transparent, however, they were presumably no longer 'felt' to be adjectives; this may be seen most clearly in cases where the adverb is accented differently from the original adjective form: e.g. σφόδρα *very, strongly* (originally acc. pl. neut. σφοδρά of σφοδρός *vehement*).

6.2 A few adverbs did not originate as case forms of a noun or adjective. Some of these are treated below. For adverbs formed from (the stems of) pronouns (e.g. πότε, ὁπότε, τότε, τῇδε, ταύτῃ), →8.2. For adverbs formed from numerals (usually in -άκις), →9.12.

Manner Adverbs in -ως

6.3 The productive adverbial suffix -ως formed primarily adverbs of manner. The suffix is added directly to the stem.

Note 1: This means that the form of these adverbs is nearly identical to the gen. pl. masc. of the corresponding adjectives, except for the final -ς (in short, replacing -ων in the gen. pl. masc. with -ως forms the adverb); the parallelism in the formation extends to accentuation. E.g. with ἄξιος *worthy*, adv. ἀξίως *in a worthy manner* (cf. gen. pl. ἀξίων); with καλός *beautiful, fine, noble*, adv. καλῶς *well, nobly* (cf. gen. pl. καλῶν).

Such adverbs are formed from all types of adjectives, and occasionally from participles.

Formed from adjectives:

ἀξίως	in a worthy manner	(ἄξιος *worthy*)
ἄλλως	otherwise; in vain	(ἄλλος *other*)
καλῶς	well, nobly	(καλός *beautiful, fine, noble*)
ἁπλῶς	simply	(ἁπλοῦς *simple*)
πάντως	wholly, in every way	(πᾶς *all, whole*)
ἀληθῶς	truly, really	(ἀληθής *true*)
ἡδέως	sweetly, pleasantly	(ἡδύς *sweet*)
ἀφρόνως	senselessly	(ἄφρων *senseless*)
χαριέντως	gracefully	(χαρίεις *graceful*)

Formed from participles:

ὄντως	truly, really, actually	(ppl. ὤν, with εἰμί *be*)
διαφερόντως	differently	(ppl. διαφέρων, with διαφέρω *differ*)

Note 2: ὁμῶς *likewise, similarly* and ὅμως *nevertheless, still* (cf. Engl. *all the same*) are related to an adjective ὁμός *one and the same* (in classical Greek the adj. ὅμοιος *similar* is used instead of ὁμός; this has its own, regularly formed adverb, ὁμοίως *in a similar manner*).

Note 3: The suffix -ως also functions as an adverbial suffix in its own right, e.g. in:

- the demonstrative manner adverb οὕτως *thus, in that way* (also οὕτω →1.40; this adverb corresponds to οὗτος; note that its formation is not parallel to that of the gen. pl. masc. τούτων);
- the interrogative adverb πῶς; *how?, in what way?*;
- the relative manner adverb ὡς *(such) as, like*.

For these forms, also →8.2.

Adverbs Based on Other Case-Forms

6.4   Various adverbs derive from other **case-forms of adjectives**.

- **accusative neuter** (singular or plural); →30.18 for the adverbial accusative:

μέγα (also μεγάλως)	greatly, very, loudly	(μέγας *great*)
μικρόν	a little	(μικρός *small*)
ὀλίγον	a little	(ὀλίγος *few, small*)
πολλά	often	(πολύς *large, many*)

| πολύ | much, very | (πολύς *large, many*) |
| ταχύ (also ταχέως) | fast, quickly | (ταχύς *quick*) |

Note 1: Also based on an accusative is the adverb μακράν *far, long* (μακρός *long*; fem., supply ὁδόν: *a long way*; cf. superlative (τὴν) ταχίστην *in the quickest possible way*, →6.13 below).
Note 2: For forms in -η, also →8.2.

– **genitive** (neuter):

| μικροῦ | almost | (μικρός *small*) |
| ὀλίγου | almost | (ὀλίγος *few, small*) |

– **dative** (usually feminine: ὁδῷ may be supplied; cf. above n.1):

ἰδίᾳ	privately	(ἴδιος *private*)
κοινῇ	in common, commonly	(κοινός *communal, shared*)
πεζῇ	on foot, by land	(πεζός *on land*)

6.5 Some adverbs are based on **case-forms of nouns**: these are often difficult to distinguish from particular usages of cases, such as the accusative of the internal object (→30.12), accusative of respect (→30.14) or dative of manner (→30.44).

τέλος	in the end	(τὸ τέλος *end*)
δωρεάν	for free, freely	(ἡ δωρεά *gift*)
κύκλῳ	in a circle, round about	(ὁ κύκλος *circle*)
σιγῇ	in silence	(ἡ σιγή *silence*)

6.6 For many adverbs which derive from an original case-form, there is no longer a corresponding adjective or noun in classical Greek: only the adverb remains as an isolated, **fossilized** form. Some examples are (there are many more):

– Originally accusative:

ἄγαν, λίαν	too, excessively
μάτην	in vain
εὖ	well (*adverb with* ἀγαθός '*good*'; ἐΰς '*good, brave*' *occurs in epic*)
πάλιν	back, again

– Originally genitive:

| ἑξῆς | in a row, one after the other |

– Originally dative:

| εἰκῇ | randomly |
| λάθρα | in secret, secretly |

– Formed with adverbial -ς (cf. -(ω)ς):

| ἅπαξ | once |
| ἅλις | sufficiently |

| μόγις, μόλις | with difficulty, hardly, scarcely |
| εὐθύς (also εὐθύ, εὐθέως) | directly, immediately, straight |

– Other, in some cases obscure derivations (only a few examples are given):

πέλας	nearby
μάλα	very
πάνυ	altogether, completely, very (*related to* πᾶς)
νῦν	now
χθές	yesterday

Specific Formations of Adverbs Indicating Space

6.7   With place names and a few other nouns of the first declension (in -η/-α), which have a dative plural in -αις, an older form of the dative plural, in -ᾱσι or -ησι, is still used as a **locative** (denoting **place where**):

| Ἀθήνησι | in Athens |
| Πλαταιᾶσι | in Plataea |

6.8   There also remain in classical Greek a few fossilized examples of an original **locative in -ι.**

οἴκοι	(at) home
χαμαί	on the ground
Πυθοῖ	at Delphi

Note 1: This ending is also found in ἀ(ὶ)εί *always*.

6.9   Some **genitives** are also used to indicate place where:

αὐτοῦ   here, there, in this very place   (αὐτός)
ὁμοῦ   in the same place, together, at once, close at hand   (ὁμός, →6.3 n.2 above)

6.10   An old instrumental ending -**ω** is used in various adverbs indicating direction, often related to prepositions:

ἄνω	above, upwards	(ἀνά *above*)
κάτω	below, downwards	(κατά *below*)
ἔξω	(to) outside, away	(ἐξ *(away) from*)
πόρρω	forward	
ὀπίσω	backward	

Note 1: This ending is also found in οὔπω/μήπω *not yet*, οὐ πώποτε/μὴ πώποτε *never yet*.

6.11   Several other suffixes (originally case endings) are used to form spatial modifiers:

– The suffixes -**σε** and -**δε** (attached to the accusative) indicate place to which:

πανταχόσε	in all directions
ὁμόσε	to the same place
Ἀθήναζε (<Ἀθήνασ-δε)	to Athens (*for ζ, →1.91 n.1*)
οἴκαδε	(to) home

– The suffix -**θεν** indicates place from where:

πανταχόθεν	from every direction
Ἀθήνηθεν	from Athens
οἴκοθεν	from home

– The suffix -**θι** indicates (with certain stems only) place where:

ἄλλοθι	elsewhere
ἀμφοτέρωθι	on both sides (= in both ways)
αὐτόθι (≈ αὐτοῦ)	in that very place

For the use of these suffixes in the system of correlative adverbs, →8.2.

Adverbs Deriving from Prepositions/Prepositional Phrases

6.12   Finally some adverbs derive from a preposition or prepositional phrase:

– Adverbs deriving from a combination of **preposition and noun** (for this type of formation, →23.38):

ἐκποδών	out of the way	(ἐκ ποδῶν)
παραχρῆμα	immediately	(παρὰ χρῆμα)
παράπαν	altogether, absolutely	(παρὰ πᾶν)

– Many **prepositions** are used also as adverbs (→31.6):

μετά	thereafter
πρός	furthermore, besides

– For adverbs such as ἄνω (ἀνά), κάτω (κατά), etc., →6.10 above.

Comparison of Adverbs

6.13   The comparative and superlative degrees of adverbs are identical to the **neuter accusative** of the corresponding comparative and superlative adjectives. The acc. neut. **singular** of the comparative adjective is used for the **comparative** adverb; the acc. neut. **plural** of the superlative adjective is used for the **superlative** adverb. Thus:

positive	comparative	superlative
ἀληθῶς	ἀληθέστερον *more truly*	ἀληθέστατα *most truly*
ἀξίως	ἀξιώτερον *in a more worthy manner*	ἀξιώτατα *in the most worthy manner*
ἁπλῶς	ἁπλούστερον *more simply*	ἁπλούστατα *most simply*
ἀφρόνως	ἀφρονέστερον *more senselessly*	ἀφρονέστατα *most senselessly*
χαριέντως	χαριέστερον *more gracefully*	χαριέστατα *most gracefully*

The same rules apply to superlative adverbs based on 'irregular' comparatives and superlatives (→5.41–4):

εὖ (ἀγαθῶς)	ἄμεινον *in a better manner*	ἄριστα *in the best manner*
ἡδέως	ἥδιον *more pleasantly*	ἥδιστα *most pleasantly*
μεγάλως, μέγα	μεῖζον *more greatly*	μέγιστα *most greatly*
καλῶς	κάλλιον *more beautifully*	κάλλιστα *most beautifully*
ὀλίγον	ἧττον *less*	ἥκιστα *least*
πολύ	πλεῖον *more*	πλεῖστα *most*
ταχέως, ταχύ	θᾶττον *more quickly*	τάχιστα *most quickly*; also: (τὴν) ταχίστην *(in) the fastest way*

Observe that some comparative/superlative adverbs have no directly corresponding adverb in the positive degree (→5.40):

(πρό)	πρότερον *earlier, before* also: τὸ πρότερον *the previous time*	πρῶτον/πρῶτα *firstly* also: τὸ πρῶτον/τὰ πρῶτα *the first time*
—	ὕστερον *later* also: τὸ ὕστερον *the next time*	ὕστατον *lastly* also: τὸ ὕστατον/τὰ ὕστατα *the last time*

In some cases, comparative and superlative adverbs are formed from a positive adverb. Note especially:

μάλα *very*	μᾶλλον *more*	μάλιστα *most*

Note 1: A few adverbs, e.g. ἄλλως and πάντως, due to their meaning, have no comparative and superlative.

6.14   In addition to the above forms, comparative adverbs in **-τέρως** are fairly frequent. E.g.:

δικαιοτέρως *more justly*   (δίκαιος, next to δικαιότερον)
χαλεπωτέρως *in a more difficult way*   (χαλεπός, next to χαλεπώτερον)
σωφρονεστέρως *more prudently*   (σώφρων, next to σωφρονέστερον)

Superlative adverbs in **-τάτως** occur infrequently, e.g.:

συντομωτάτως *in the most summary fashion*   (σύντομος, next to συντομώτατα)

7

Pronouns

Personal Pronouns

7.1   For the meanings and uses of the personal pronouns, →29.1–6. The forms are as follows:

		first person		second person	
		ἐγώ *I, me*; ἡμεῖς *we, us*		σύ *you* (sg.); ὑμεῖς *you* (pl.)	
		accented	unaccented	accented	unaccented
sg.	nom.	ἐγώ	—	σύ (also voc.)	—
	gen.	ἐμοῦ	μου	σοῦ	σου
	dat.	ἐμοί	μοι	σοί	σοι
	acc.	ἐμέ	με	σέ	σε
pl.	nom.	ἡμεῖς		ὑμεῖς (also voc.)	
	gen.	ἡμῶν		ὑμῶν	
	dat.	ἡμῖν		ὑμῖν	
	acc.	ἡμᾶς		ὑμᾶς	

Note 1: For Ionic forms, →25.28.

Note 2: The unaccented forms are enclitic (→24.33–4).

In poetry some editors follow the ancient grammatical tradition of distinguishing unaccented forms of the oblique cases of the plural (these have their accent on the first syllable): ἥμων; ἥμῑν (or ἣμῑν), ἥμεας/ἥμᾱς (or ἣμᾱς), ὕμεων/ὕμων, ὕμῑν (or ὓμῑν), ὕμεας/ὕμᾱς (or ὓμᾱς). In poetry, the last syllable -ιν in the dat. pl. often scans short, so that there is indeed good reason to print ἥμιν/ὕμιν in those cases.

7.2   For the **third-person** personal pronoun, classical Greek uses primarily oblique forms of αὐτός (→29.5, 29.7). A separate third-person pronoun is almost entirely absent from classical Greek. However:

- In poetry and Ionic, the form μιν is frequently found as accusative third-person pronoun. In poetry, νιν is also found as accusative singular and plural.
- Forms of an older separate third-person pronoun, still used in Homeric epic, are used in Attic as indirect reflexives (→29.18); in Herodotus they are also used as personal pronoun, →25.28. The complete paradigm is (in Attic):

		third person	
		him, her, it; they, them	
		accented	unaccented
sg.	nom.	—	—
	gen.	οὗ	οὑ
	dat.	οἷ	οἱ
	acc.	ἕ	ἑ
pl.	nom.	σφεῖς	—
	gen.	σφῶν	σφων
	dat.	σφίσι(ν)	σφισι(ν)
	acc.	σφᾶς	σφᾶς

Note 1: For Ionic forms, →25.28
Note 2: The unaccented forms are enclitic (→24.33–4).

Reflexive Pronouns

7.3   For the meanings and uses of the reflexive pronouns, →29.14–20. The forms of
the 'direct' reflexive pronoun are as follows:

		first person		**second person**	
		ἐμαυτοῦ, -ῆς *myself, ourselves*		σ(ε)αυτοῦ, -ῆς *yourself, yourselves*	
		masc.	fem.	masc.	fem.
sg.	nom.	—	—	—	—
	gen.	ἐμαυτοῦ	ἐμαυτῆς	σ(ε)αυτοῦ	σ(ε)αυτῆς
	dat.	ἐμαυτῷ	ἐμαυτῇ	σ(ε)αυτῷ	σ(ε)αυτῇ
	acc.	ἐμαυτόν	ἐμαυτήν	σ(ε)αυτόν	σ(ε)αυτήν
pl.	nom.	—	—	—	—
	gen.	ἡμῶν αὐτῶν	ἡμῶν αὐτῶν	ὑμῶν αὐτῶν	ὑμῶν αὐτῶν
	dat.	ἡμῖν αὐτοῖς	ἡμῖν αὐταῖς	ὑμῖν αὐτοῖς	ὑμῖν αὐταῖς
	acc.	ἡμᾶς αὐτούς	ἡμᾶς αὐτάς	ὑμᾶς αὐτούς	ὑμᾶς αὐτάς

		third person		
		ἑαυτοῦ, -ῆς, -οῦ *himself, herself, itself; themselves*		
		masc.	fem.	neut.
sg.	nom.	—	—	—
	gen.	ἑαυτοῦ, αὑτοῦ	ἑαυτῆς, αὑτῆς	ἑαυτοῦ, αὑτοῦ
	dat.	ἑαυτῷ, αὑτῷ	ἑαυτῇ, αὑτῇ	ἑαυτῷ, αὑτῷ
	acc.	ἑαυτόν, αὑτόν	ἑαυτήν, αὑτήν	ἑαυτό, αὑτόν
pl.	nom.	—	—	—
	gen.	ἑαυτῶν, αὑτῶν σφῶν αὐτῶν	ἑαυτῶν, αὑτῶν σφῶν αὐτῶν	ἑαυτῶν, αὑτῶν
	dat.	ἑαυτοῖς, αὑτοῖς σφίσιν αὐτοῖς	ἑαυταῖς, αὑταῖς σφίσιν αὐταῖς	ἑαυτοῖς, αὑτοῖς
	acc.	ἑαυτούς, αὑτούς σφᾶς αὐτούς	ἑαυτάς, αὑτάς σφᾶς αὐτάς	ἑαυτά, αὑτά

Note 1: There is no nominative of the reflexive pronoun.

Note 2: The genitives ἐμαυτοῦ, σεαυτοῦ, and ἑαυτοῦ originally result from crasis of ἐμέο αὐτοῦ, σέο αὐτοῦ and ἕο αὐτοῦ (ἕο (so found in Homeric epic) = classical Attic οὗ). The other cases were generalized from these forms (analogy, →1.49), and built on ἐμ-, σε-, ἑ-.

7.4   Third-person ἑαυτοῦ was gradually generalized to the first and second person as well; for details, →29.19.

7.5   For the use of the obsolete third-person pronoun οὗ/οὑ, οἷ/οἱ, ἕ/ἑ; σφῶν/σφων, etc. (→7.2 above) as 'indirect' reflexive pronoun, →29.18.

The Reciprocal Pronoun

7.6   For the uses of the reciprocal pronoun ἀλλήλων *each other*, →29.26. It has the following forms:

		reciprocal pronoun		
		ἀλλήλων *each other*		
		masc.	fem.	neut.
pl.	nom.	—	—	—
	gen.	ἀλλήλων	ἀλλήλων	ἀλλήλων
	dat.	ἀλλήλοις	ἀλλήλαις	ἀλλήλοις
	acc.	ἀλλήλους	ἀλλήλας	ἄλληλα

The Possessive 'Pronoun'

7.7   For the uses of possessive adjectives, →29.21–5. They are:

	singular	plural
first	ἐμός, ἐμή, ἐμόν *my, mine*	ἡμέτερος, -τέρᾱ, -τερον *our, ours*
second	σός, σή, σόν *your, yours*	ὑμέτερος, -τέρᾱ, -τερον *your, yours*
third	—	σφέτερος, -τέρᾱ, -τερον *their*

They are declined like the adjectives in -ος, -η/-ᾱ, -ον (→5.1).

Note 1: The term 'pronoun' for these adjectives is somewhat misleading: they are properly adjectives, and not used pronominally (→26.22, although they may, like all adjectives, be used as head of a noun phrase (→26.20), e.g. τὰ ἐμά *my things*).

7.8   In Attic, there is no third person singular possessive adjective, and for 'plural possession' σφέτερος is relatively infrequent. Instead, the genitive of αὐτός, of the reflexive pronoun, or more rarely, of a demonstrative pronoun is used.

Note 1: σφέτερος is properly a form of an older third-person possessive pronoun, which is still used regularly in Homeric epic. In the singular, its forms are ὅς/ἑός, ἥ/ἑή, ὅν/ἑόν.

7.9   Especially in the plural, the possessive pronouns are occasionally strengthened by a gen. of αὐτός when they are used for 'reflexive' possession: e.g. ἐμὸν αὐτῆς *my own*, ἡμέτερος αὐτῶν *our own*, σφετέροις αὐτῶν *their own*, etc.

αὐτός

7.10   For the meanings and uses of **αὐτός**, →29.7–13. The forms are as follows:

		αὐτός, -ή, -ό		
		masc.	fem.	neut.
sg.	nom.	αὐτός	αὐτή	αὐτό
	gen.	αὐτοῦ	αὐτῆς	αὐτοῦ
	dat.	αὐτῷ	αὐτῇ	αὐτῷ
	acc.	αὐτόν	αὐτήν	αὐτό
pl.	nom.	αὐτοί	αὐταί	αὐτά
	gen.	αὐτῶν	αὐτῶν	αὐτῶν
	dat.	αὐτοῖς	αὐταῖς	αὐτοῖς
	acc.	αὐτούς	αὐτάς	αὐτά

αὐτός is declined like the adjectives in -ος, -η, -ον, with the exception of nom. and acc. sg. neut., which is αὐτό, using the pronominal ending -ο found also with the article (τό), οὗτος (τοῦτο), ἐκεῖνος (ἐκεῖνο, →7.14–15).

7.11   Forms of the article ending in a vowel or diphthong frequently coalesce with αὐτ- (**crasis**, →1.43–5), as follows:

αὑτός = ὁ αὐτός, αὑτή = ἡ αὐτή, ταὐτό = τὸ αὐτό (but ταὐτόν is also found)
ταὐτοῦ = τοῦ αὐτοῦ, ταὐτῷ = τῷ αὐτῷ
ταὐτῇ = τῇ αὐτῇ
αὑτοί = οἱ αὐτοί, αὑταί = αἱ αὐταί, ταὐτά = τὰ αὐτά

Note 1: For Ionic forms in crasis, →25.14.
Note 2: Forms of αὐτός and ὁ αὐτός (with crasis) are often confused with each other or with forms of οὗτος or ἑαυτοῦ: for the differences between the forms, →7.26.

Demonstrative Pronouns

7.12   For the uses of the demonstrative pronouns, →29.27–37.

ὅδε

7.13   ὅδε is declined as follows:

		ὅδε		
		ὅδε, ἥδε, τόδε *this (here)*		
		masc.	fem.	neut.
sg.	nom.	ὅδε	ἥδε	τόδε
	gen.	τοῦδε	τῆσδε	τοῦδε
	dat.	τῷδε	τῇδε	τῷδε
	acc.	τόνδε	τήνδε	τόδε
pl.	nom.	οἵδε	αἵδε	τάδε
	gen.	τῶνδε	τῶνδε	τῶνδε
	dat.	τοῖσδε	ταῖσδε	τοῖσδε
	acc.	τούσδε	τάσδε	τάδε

ὅδε is declined by adding the 'deictic' suffix -**δε** to the forms of the **article** (→3.1):

οὗτος

7.14   οὗτος is declined as follows:

		οὗτος		
		οὗτος, αὕτη, τοῦτο *this, that*		
		masc.	fem.	neut.
sg.	nom.	οὗτος	αὕτη	τοῦτο
	gen.	τούτου	ταύτης	τούτου
	dat.	τούτῳ	ταύτῃ	τούτῳ
	acc.	τοῦτον	ταύτην	τοῦτο
pl.	nom.	οὗτοι	αὗται	ταῦτα
	gen.	τούτων	τούτων	τούτων
	dat.	τούτοις	ταύταις	τούτοις
	acc.	τούτους	ταύτας	ταῦτα

The endings of οὗτος are those of e.g. αὐτός (i.e. those of adjectives ending in -ος, -η, -ον, but with pronominal ending -ο in nom./acc. sg. neut.). With regard to the stem(s) of the forms, note that:

– they start with τ-, except in the nominatives of the masc. and fem., which start with a rough breathing (compare the article, →3.1);
– the stem is (τ)ουτ- or (τ)αυτ- depending on the ending (not the gender): if an α/η-sound follows, (τ)αυτ- is used; if an o-sound follows, (τ)ουτ- is used. Note particularly gen. pl. fem. το<u>ύ</u>των and nom./acc. pl. neut. τα<u>ῦ</u>τα.

ἐκεῖνος

7.15   ἐκεῖνος is declined as follows:

		ἐκεῖνος		
		ἐκεῖνος *that (there)*		
		masc.	fem.	neut.
sg.	nom.	ἐκεῖνος	ἐκείνη	ἐκεῖνο
	gen.	ἐκείνου	ἐκείνης	ἐκείνου
	dat.	ἐκείνῳ	ἐκείνῃ	ἐκείνῳ
	acc.	ἐκεῖνον	ἐκείνην	ἐκεῖνο
pl.	nom.	ἐκεῖνοι	ἐκεῖναι	ἐκεῖνα
	gen.	ἐκείνων	ἐκείνων	ἐκείνων
	dat.	ἐκείνοις	ἐκείναις	ἐκείνοις
	acc.	ἐκείνους	ἐκείνας	ἐκεῖνα

ἐκεῖνος is declined like αὐτός (→7.10).

Note 1: ἐκεῖνος has an alternative form κεῖνος, which is used in poetry for metrical reasons, and occasionally in Herodotus.

Further Particulars

Other Demonstratives

7.16   The following pronominal adjectives are also demonstrative (for details on these, →8.1):

τοσόσδε, τοσήδε, τοσόνδε	of such a size, so great, so much; *plural*: so many
τοιόσδε, τοιάδε, τοιόνδε	of such a kind/nature/quality, such
τοσοῦτος, τοσαύτη, τοσοῦτο *or* -ον	of such a size; so great, so much, *plural*: so many
τοιοῦτος, τοιαύτη, τοιοῦτο *or* -ον	such (as) . . . , of such a kind/quality/nature

Note 1: τοσόσδε and τοιόσδε combine the adjectives τόσος and τοῖος (which are found in poetry with the same meaning), and the suffix -δε (compare ὅδε, →7.13). τοσοῦτος and τοιοῦτος are built from τοσ- and τοι- + οὗτος, respectively.

7.17   Less frequent are τηλικόσδε, τηλικήδε, τηλικόνδε *so old, so big*, and τηλικοῦτος, τηλικαύτη, τηλικοῦτο(ν) *so old, so big*.

Deictic Iota

7.18   Forms of demonstrative pronouns, adjectives or adverbs are sometimes expanded with the suffix -ί, usually called the **deictic iota**. When this suffix is present, the pronoun is always accented on it. Before the suffix the short vowels α, ε and ο disappear.

e.g. ὁδί, τουδί, τῳδί, τονδί; ἡδί, τοδί; οὑτοσί, τουτουί, τουτῳί, τουτονί; αὑτηί, τουτί; ἐκεινοσί, ἐκεινηί

For the use of deictic iota and further examples, →29.36.

Note 1: In comedy, long vowels and diphthongs preceding deictic iota count as short: αὐτηί, τουτουί, etc.

Relative Pronouns

7.19   For the uses of relative pronouns, →50.

ὅς and ὅστις

7.20   Overview of forms:

		ὅς			ὅστις		
		ὅς, ἥ, ὅ *who, which, that*			ὅστις, ἥτις, ὅτι *whoever, anyone who*		
		masc.	fem.	neut.	masc.	fem.	neut.
sg.	nom.	ὅς	ἥ	ὅ	ὅστις	ἥτις	ὅτι
	gen.	οὗ	ἧς	οὗ	οὗτινος / ὅτου	ἧστινος / ὅτου	οὗτινος / ὅτου
	dat.	ᾧ	ᾗ	ᾧ	ᾧτινι / ὅτῳ	ᾗτινι / ὅτῳ	ᾧτινι / ὅτῳ
	acc.	ὅν	ἥν	ὅ	ὅντινα	ἥντινα	ὅτι
pl.	nom.	οἵ	αἵ	ἅ	οἵτινες	αἵτινες	ἅτινα / ἅττα
	gen.	ὧν	ὧν	ὧν	ὧντινων / ὅτων	ὧντινων / ὅτων	ὧντινων / ὅτων
	dat.	οἷς	αἷς	οἷς	οἷστισι(ν) / ὅτοις	αἷστισι(ν) / ὅτοις	οἷστισι(ν) / ὅτοις
	acc.	οὕς	ἅς	ἅ	οὕστινας	ἅστινας	ἅτινα / ἅττα

The 'definite' relative pronoun **ὅς** is declined like (the endings of) αὐτός (→7.10), beginning with a rough breathing. The 'indefinite' relative pronoun **ὅστις** is formed by adding the appropriate form of the indefinite pronoun τις (→7.24) to that of ὅς.

Note 1: In many text editions the neuter sg. nom and acc. of ὅστις is printed as ὅ τι, to differentiate it from the conjunction ὅτι *that, because*.
Note 2: The alternative forms ὅτου, ὅτῳ (indeclinable ὅ + the alternative genitive and dative of τις, →7.24) and ἅττα (<*ἅ-τϳα, →1.77), are all far more common than regularly formed οὗτινος and ᾧτινι and ἅτινα. The plural forms ὧντινων, ὅτων and οἷστισι(ν), ὅτοις are rare.
Note 3: For Ionic forms, →25.31.

7.21   Forms of ὅς are frequently followed by the enclitic particle -περ (→59.55), and then written as one word, **ὅσπερ**, etc.

7.22   For the use of the article as relative pronoun in poetry, →28.31.

Other Relative Pronouns

7.23   Some other pronouns used in relative clauses are (for details on these pronouns, →8.1):

ὁπότερος, -ᾱ, -ον	(the person of the two . . .) that, which
definite ὅσος, -η, -ον	(so much/great . . .) as, *pl.*: (so many . . .) as

indefinite ὁπόσος, -η, -ον
definite οἷος, οἵα, οἷον   (such . . .) as, (of such a kind/nature . . .) as
indefinite ὁποῖος, -ᾱ, -ον

Interrogative and Indefinite Pronouns

τίς, τί; τις, τι

7.24   For the meanings and uses of interrogative pronouns, →38.11–14 (direct questions), 42.5–6 (indirect questions). For the meanings and uses of indefinite pronouns, →29.38–42. The forms of the central interrogative pronouns τίς and τί, and the corresponding indefinite pronouns τις and τι, are as follows:

		interrogative pronoun		indefinite pronoun	
		τίς, τί		τις, τι	
		independent *who? what?*		independent *someone, something*	
		as adjective *which? what?*		as adjective *some*	
		masc./fem.	neut.	masc./fem.	neut.
sg.	nom.	τίς	τί	τις	τι
	gen.	τίνος / τοῦ	τίνος / τοῦ	τινος / του	τινος / του
	dat.	τίνι / τῷ	τίνι / τῷ	τινι / τῳ	τινι / τῳ
	acc.	τίνα	τί	τινα	τι
pl.	nom.	τίνες	τίνα	τινες	τινα / ἄττα
	gen.	τίνων	τίνων	τινων	τινων
	dat.	τίσι(ν)	τίσι(ν)	τισι(ν)	τισι(ν)
	acc.	τίνας	τίνα	τινας	τινα / ἄττα

They are declined following the third declension, with two endings and a stem ending in ν (→5.26)

Note 1: The forms τοῦ/του, τῷ/τῳ, etc. occur frequently in both prose and poetry, but are somewhat less common than τίνος/τινος, τίνι/τινι, etc. The form ἄττα (nom./acc. neut. pl. of the indefinite pronoun) is much less common than τινα, and particularly rare in poetry.
Note 2: For the accentuation of these pronouns, →24.38 n.1.
Note 3: For Ionic forms, →25.30.

Other Interrogative Pronouns

7.25   Some other interrogative pronouns are (for details on these pronouns, →8.1):
πότερος, ποτέρᾱ, πότερον   which of the two?
πόσος, πόση, πόσον   how great, how much? *pl.:* how many?
ποῖος, ποίᾱ, ποῖον   what sort/kind of?

Note 1: Also, but rarely, πηλίκος, -η, -ον *how old, how big?*

Seemingly Similar Forms of αὐτός, ὁ αὐτός, ἑαυτοῦ and οὗτος

7.26   Forms of αὐτός, ὁ αὐτός (with crasis), ἑαυτοῦ (when contracted) and οὗτος can easily be confused. They may be distinguished by looking at the position of the accent, and at breathings. Note that *no* form or combination is ambiguous:

	αὐτός	ἑαυτοῦ (contracted)	ὁ αὐτός (in crasis)	οὗτος
	–smooth breathing –accent on the last syllable	–rough breathing –accent on the last syllable –oblique cases only	–rough breathing in nom. masc./fem. –τ/coronis in other forms –accent on the last syllable	–rough breathing in nom. masc./fem. –τ in other forms –accent on the first syllable (with ου/αυ)
nom. sg./pl. masc.	αὐτός, αὐτοί	–	αὑτός, αὑτοί	οὗτος, οὗτοι
nom. sg./pl. fem.	αὐτή, αὐταί	–	αὑτή, αὑταί	αὕτη, αὗται
nom./acc. sg. neut.	αὐτό	αὑτό (acc.)	ταὐτό(ν)	τοῦτο
nom./acc. pl. neut.	αὐτά	αὑτά (acc.)	ταὐτά	ταῦτα
gen./dat. sg. m./n.	αὐτοῦ, αὐτῷ	αὑτοῦ, αὑτῷ	ταὐτοῦ, ταὐτῷ	τούτου, τούτῳ
dat. sg. fem.	αὐτῇ	αὑτῇ	ταὐτῇ	ταύτῃ
other forms	αὐτῆς, αὐτόν, αὐτήν, αὐτῶν, αὐτοῖς, etc.	αὑτῆς, αὑτόν, αὑτήν, αὑτῶν, αὑτοῖς, etc.	–	ταύτης, τοῦτον, ταύτην, τούτων, τούτοις, etc.

8

Correlative Pronouns and Adverbs

The System of Correlative Pronouns and Adjectives

8.1 The (cor)relative pronouns/adjectives are as follows:

	interrogative		indefinite	personal and demonstrative	relative	
	direct	indirect			'definite'	'indefinite'
basic forms	τίς; who? which? what?	ὅστις, τίς who, which	τις someone	ὅδε this (here) οὗτος that (there) ἐκεῖνος that (far away)	ὅς who, which, that	ὅστις who(ever)
-τερος of two	πότερος; which of the two?	ὁπότερος, πότερος which of the two	πότερος[1] one/other (of two) (*very rare*)	(ὁ) ἕτερος the one/the other (of two)	-	ὁπότερος which(ever) of the two
-οσο- size, number	πόσος; how great, how much? *pl.* how many?	ὁπόσος, πόσος how great, how much, *pl.* how many	ποσος of some size/ quantity	τοσόσδε[2] τοσοῦτος so great, so much; *pl.* so many	ὅσος (as great, much) as; *pl.* (as many) as	ὁπόσος (however great, much) as; *pl.* (however many) as
-οιο- kind, sort	ποῖος; what kind?	ὁποῖος, ποῖος what kind	ποιος of some kind	τοιόσδε[2] τοιοῦτος such, of this kind	οἷος (such) as	ὁποῖος (such ever) as

The indefinite pronouns are enclitic (→24.33–4).

[1] πότερος is accented like interrogative πότερος but nonetheless enclitic, unlike the interrogative.

[2] In poetry also τόσος, τοῖος.

The System of Correlative Adverbs

8.2   The (cor)relative adverbs are as follows:

	interrogative		indefinite	demonstrative	relative	
	direct	indirect			'definite'	'indefinite'
-ου position	ποῦ; where?	ὅπου, ποῦ where	που somewhere, anywhere	αὐτοῦ on the spot, in this very place ἐνθάδε here ἐνταῦθα[1] ἐκεῖ there	(ἐνταῦθα . . .) οὗ, ἵνα, ἔνθα (there . . .) where	ὅπου (somewhere . . .) where
-η way by which, manner	πῇ; (in) which way? how?	ὅπῃ, πῇ (in) which way; how	πῃ (in) some way, somehow	τῇδε ταύτῃ ἐκείνῃ (in) that way, on that side	ᾗ (in the way . . .) in which	ὅπῃ (in some way . . .) in which
-θεν separation	πόθεν; from where?	πόθεν, ὁπόθεν from where	ποθεν from some place or other	ἔνθεν, ἐνθένδε from here ἐντεῦθεν, ἐκεῖθεν from there	ἔνθεν, ὅθεν (the place . . .) from where	ὁπόθεν (somewhere . . .) from where
-οι destination	ποῖ; (to) where? to what end?	ὅποι, ποῖ (to) where, to what end	ποι (to) somewhere	ἐνθάδε (to) here ἐνταυθοῖ, ἐνταῦθα ἐκεῖσε, κεῖσε, ἐκεῖ (to) there	οἷ (the place . . .) to which	ὅποι (some place . . .) to which
-τε time when	πότε; when?	ὁπότε, πότε when	ποτε sometime, once	νῦν now τότε, ἐνταῦθα then, on that occasion	ὅτε (the time . . .) when	ὁπότε (sometime . . .) when
-ως manner	πῶς; how?	ὅπως, πῶς how	πως somehow	ὧδε in this way, in the following way οὕτως ἐκείνως in that way	(οὕτως . . .) ὡς (in such a way . . .) as	ὅπως how

The indefinite adverbs are enclitic (→24.33–4).

The relationship between ἐνθένδε/ἐντεῦθεν/ἐκεῖθεν, ὧδε/οὕτως/ἐκείνως, etc., is similar to that between ὅδε/οὗτος/ἐκεῖνος.

[1] In poetry also ἔνθα.

9

Numerals

List of Numerals

9.1   The numerals are as follows:

	cardinal numbers (one, two, three, . . .)	ordinal adjectives (first, second, third, . . .)
1	εἷς, μία, ἕν	πρῶτος, πρώτη, πρῶτον
2	δύο	δεύτερος, -ᾱ, -ον
3	τρεῖς, τρία	τρίτος, -η, -ον
4	τέτταρες, τέτταρα	τέταρτος
5	πέντε	πέμπτος
6	ἕξ	ἕκτος
7	ἑπτά	ἕβδομος
8	ὀκτώ	ὄγδοος (not contracted)
9	ἐννέα	ἔνατος
10	δέκα	δέκατος
11	ἕνδεκα	ἑνδέκατος
12	δώδεκα	δωδέκατος
13	τρεῖς/τρία καὶ δέκα	τρίτος καὶ δέκατος
14	τέτταρες/-ρα καὶ δέκα	τέταρτος καὶ δέκατος
15	πεντεκαίδεκα	πέμπτος καὶ δέκατος[1]
16	ἑκκαίδεκα	ἕκτος καὶ δέκατος[1]
17	ἑπτακαίδεκα	ἕβδομος καὶ δέκατος[1]
18	ὀκτωκαίδεκα	ὄγδοος καὶ δέκατος[1]
19	ἐννεακαίδεκα	ἔνατος καὶ δέκατος[1]
20	εἴκοσι(ν)	εἰκοστός
21, etc.	εἷς/μία/ἕν καὶ εἴκοσι, etc.	πρῶτος καὶ εἰκοστός, etc.
30	τριάκοντα	τριακοστός
40	τετταράκοντα	τετταρακοστός
50	πεντήκοντα	πεντηκοστός
60	ἑξήκοντα	ἑξηκοστός
70	ἑβδομήκοντα	ἑβδομηκοστός
80	ὀγδοήκοντα	ὀγδοηκοστός
90	ἐνενήκοντα	ἐνενηκοστός
100	ἑκατόν	ἑκατοστός
101, etc.	εἷς καὶ ἑκατόν, etc.	πρῶτος καὶ ἑκατοστός, etc.
200	διακόσιοι, -αι, -ᾰ	διακοσιοστός

	cardinal numbers (one, two, three, …)	ordinal adjectives (first, second, third, …)
300	τριακόσιοι	etc.
400	τετρακόσιοι	
500	πεντακόσιοι	
600	ἑξακόσιοι	
700	ἑπτακόσιοι	
800	ὀκτακόσιοι	
900	ἐνακόσιοι	
1000	χίλιοι, -αι, -ᾰ	χιλιοστός
1001, etc.	εἷς καὶ χίλιοι, etc.	
2000	δισχίλιοι (lit. 'twice thousand')	
10,000	μύριοι, -αι, -ᾰ	μυριοστός
20,000, etc.	δισμύριοι, etc.	

[1] Outside classical Attic, the forms πεντεκαιδέκατος, ἑκκαιδέκατος, ἑπτακαιδέκατος, ὀκτωκαιδέκατος, ἐννεακαιδέκατος are also used.

Declension of Numerals

9.2   The declension of the **first four cardinal numbers** is as follows:

	εἷς *one*			δύο *two*	τρεῖς *three*		τέτταρες *four*	
	masc.	fem.	neut.	m./f./n.	m./f.	n.	m./f.	n.
nom.	εἷς	μία	ἕν	δύο	τρεῖς	τρία	τέτταρες	τέτταρα
gen.	ἑνός	μιᾶς	ἑνός	δυοῖν	τριῶν	τριῶν	τεττάρων	τεττάρων
dat.	ἑνί	μιᾷ	ἑνί	δυοῖν	τρισί(ν)	τρισί(ν)	τέτταρσι(ν)	τέτταρσι(ν)
acc.	ἕνα	μίαν	ἕν	δύο	τρεῖς	τρία	τέτταρας	τέτταρα

9.3   Like εἷς is declined:

– **οὐδείς**, gen. οὐδενός; fem. οὐδεμία, -ᾶς; neut. οὐδέν, οὐδενός *no one, nothing, no*
– so too **μηδείς**, μηδεμία, μηδέν, in constructions where μή can occur (→56).

Unlike εἷς, μία, ἕν, the forms οὐδείς and μηδείς also have plural forms: οὐδένες, οὐδένων, οὐδέσι(ν), οὐδένας (these are infrequent, however). The non-contracted forms οὐδὲ εἷς, οὐδὲ μία, οὐδὲ ἕν are also used, as emphatic variants: *not even one*.

9.4   The numerals ending in **-κόσιοι, χίλιοι**, etc. and **μύριοι**, etc. are declined like the plurals of adjectives in -ος, -ᾱ, -ον (→5.1–2).

9.5   Other numerals are not declined: e.g. ἑξήκοντα καὶ πέντε νεῶν *sixty-five ships* (gen. pl. fem.), ὀγδοήκοντα καὶ πέντε ἔτεσι *eighty-five years* (dat. pl. neut.).

Further Particulars

9.6 Complex numbers above 20 may be **ordered** in two ways:

 – in the order units-tens-hundreds-thousands, in which case they *must* be connected by καί (in Herodotus also τε καί);

 – or, more rarely, in the reverse order, in which case they *may* but need not be connected by καί:

πέντε καὶ εἴκοσι *or* εἴκοσι (καὶ) πέντε	twenty-five
πέντε (τε) καὶ πεντακόσια (neut.)	five hundred and five

Also with ordinals: e.g. ἔτει πέμπτῳ καὶ τετταρακοστῷ *in the forty-fifth year*.

9.7 Our two-digit numerals ending in 8 or 9 (18, 19, etc.) can also be expressed by means of the participle of δέω *lack* + δυοῖν and ἑνός/μιᾶς, respectively:

δυοῖν δέοντα εἴκοσιν ἔτη	eighteen years (*lit. 'twenty years lacking two'*)
μιᾶς δέουσαι τετταράκοντα νῆες	thirty-nine ships (*lit. 'forty ships lacking one'*)

Also with ordinals: e.g. ἔτος ἑνὸς δέον εἰκοστόν *the nineteenth year* (lit. 'the twentieth year lacking one')

9.8 There are also abstract and collective numeral nouns, ending in -άς, -άδος: e.g. ἡ δεκάς *decade*, ἡ μυριάς (*a number of*) *ten thousand*. μυριάς is frequently used to express large numbers: e.g. πέντε καὶ εἴκοσι μυριάδες ἀνδρῶν *twenty-five ten thousands of men* (= 250,000).

9.9 Ancient grammarians made a distinction (in accent) between:

 – μύριοι, -αι, -α *ten thousand*
 – μυρίοι, -αι, -α *innumerable, countless* (also singular, e.g. μυρίον ἄχθος an endless burden, etc.)

For the oblique cases, however, rules of accentuation usually render this distinction void (e.g. both have acc. μυρίους, →24.8–10). In such cases, the context (e.g. the presence of another numeral) usually clarifies which meaning is meant: τρισχιλίους καὶ μυρίους *thirteen thousand*, ὑπὲρ μυρίους *more than ten thousand*, ἢ Ὀδυσσέα ἢ Σίσυφον ἢ ἄλλους μυρίους *Odysseus or Sisyphus or countless others*.

9.10 Note that Greek counts '**inclusively**' from a certain point of orientation, i.e. that point of orientation is included in the number counted: e.g. τρίτον ἔτος τουτί *two years ago* (lit. 'this is the third year'; for τουτί, →7.18, 29.36).

9.11 **Fractions** are expressed e.g. by ἥμισυς *half* (declined like ἡδύς, →5.21–2). Some examples:

τάλαντον καὶ ἥμισυ	one and a half talents
τὸ ἥμισυ τῆς ὅλης μισθώσεως	half of the whole rent
τὸν ἥμισυν τοῦ χρόνου	half of the time (acc.)
τὰς ἡμισείας τῶν νεῶν	half of the ships (acc.)

Some other expressions: ἡμιτάλαντον *half a talent*; τριτημόριον *one third*; τρίτον μέρος ἀνθ' ἡμίσεος *one third instead of half*; τρίτον ἡμιτάλαντον *two and a half talents* (lit. 'the third half', i.e. the one between two and three = 2½); Πελοποννήσου τῶν πέντε τὰς δύο μοίρας *two fifths of the Peloponnese* (lit. 'the two parts of the five of . . .')

9.12   **Multiplication** is expressed by adverbs and adjectives:

- adverbs: ἅπαξ *once*, δίς *twice*, τρίς *three times*; all other adverbs are formed with the suffix -άκις: τετράκις *four times*, πεντάκις *five times*, etc. (cf. the adverb πολλάκις *often*):

  τὰ δὶς πέντε δέκα ἐστίν   two times five equals ten

- adjectives: either formed with -πλοῦς, -πλῆ, -πλοῦν *-fold*: ἁπλοῦς *single, simple*, διπλοῦς *twofold, double*, etc. (for the declension, →5.5–6); or with -πλάσιος, -ᾱ, -ον: διπλάσιος *double, twice as great/much/many*, τριπλάσιος *triple, three times as great/much/many*, etc.

9.13   The Greeks usually wrote out numbers in full. In manuscripts and inscriptions, two **sign-systems** were in use:

- (In inscriptions of the classical period:) a vertical stroke Ι for one unit, and the initial letter of words designating certain numbers, e.g. Γ = πέντε = 5, Δ = δέκα = 10, ΔΙ = 11, ⊩ = πεντάκις δέκα = 50, Η = ἑκατόν (hεκατόν) = 100, Χ = χίλιοι = 1000, etc. This system was used especially to indicate value, weight and measure.

- (In later inscriptions, papyri and manuscripts:) the letters of the alphabet as 'numbers' in a decimal system; these were often modified by an oblique stroke above and to the right of the letter for numbers up to and including 999:

α′	β′	γ′	δ′	ε′	ϛ′ or ϝ′	ζ′	η′	θ′
1	2	3	4	5	6	7	8	9
ι′	κ′	λ′	μ′	ν′	ξ′	ο′	π′	ϟ′
10	20	30	40	50	60	70	80	90
ρ′	σ′	τ′	υ′	φ′	χ′	ψ′	ω′	ϡ′
100	200	300	400	500	600	700	800	900

(The letters ϛ (stigma), ϝ (digamma/wau), ϟ (koppa), and ϡ (sampi), which were no longer in common use, were introduced into this numeral system to supplement the standardized 24, insufficient by themselves to write all numbers up to 999.)

The same letters were used with a stroke below and to the left of the letter for numbers starting with 1000: ͵α = 1000, ͵β = 2000, etc.

Complex numbers are formed by combining the letter symbols. Only the rightmost letter (and the leftmost with numbers over 1000) have the stroke:

τιθ′ = 319 (any ordering was possible: τθι′, θτι′, etc.)
͵ατιθ′ = 1319

- Until Hellenistic times, Greek had no letter-symbol for 0 ('zero'; the Hellenistic symbol was ō). The corresponding item in written form was οὐδέν.

10

The Dual: Nominal Forms

Endings

10.1 Nominal forms of the dual number (referring to groups of exactly two) are formed in exactly the same manner as the forms treated in the preceding chapters. The only respect in which they differ is their **endings**.

The dual endings for the different declensions are as follows:

	first declension	second declension	third declension
nom.	-ᾱ	-ω	-ε
gen.	-αιν	-οιν	-οιν
dat.	-αιν	-οιν	-οιν
acc.	-ᾱ	-ω	-ε
voc.	= nom.	= nom.	= nom.

Forms

The Article

10.2 The forms of the dual article are as follows:

	ὁ, ἡ, τό masc./fem./neut.
nom.	τώ
gen.	τοῖν
dat.	τοῖν
acc.	τώ

Note 1: Occasionally the feminine dual article ταῖν is found, e.g. ταῖν χειροῖν *the two hands* (gen./dat.). The nom./acc. form τά is not frequently found in Attic; modern editions often correct it to τώ, although this may not be justified.

Nouns and Adjectives/Participles

10.3   Examples of **first-declension** forms:

δυοῖν χώραιν   two lands
μόνᾱ νὼ λελειμμένᾱ   the two of us left all alone (*for νώ, see below*)

10.4   Examples of **second-declension** forms:

τὼ ἀνθρώπω, τοῖν ἀνθρώποιν	the two men
δυοῖν καλοῖν	two good things (*neut.*)
τὼ παρθένω, τοῖν παρθένοιν	the two maidens
τὼ θεώ, τοῖν θεοῖν	the two goddesses (*Demeter and Korê*)

10.5   Examples of **third-declension** forms:

τὼ χεῖρε, τοῖν χειροῖν	the two hands
ἄμφω τὼ πόλεε/τὼ πόλει, ἀμφοῖν τοῖν πολέοιν	both states
τὼ φύλακε κωλύοντε	the two guards, preventing
τοῖν παρόντοιν πραγμάτοιν	the two present problems
δυοῖν νεοῖν ἐναντίαιν περιπλέοντες	sailing around with two ships in different directions

Pronouns

10.6   The **personal pronouns** of the first and second person have separate dual forms:

	personal pronouns	
	first person	second person
	the two of us	*the two of you*
nom.	νώ	σφώ
gen.	νῷν	σφῷν
dat.	νῷν	σφῷν
acc.	νώ	σφώ

10.7   Examples of **other pronouns**:

– demonstrative pronouns:

τούτοιν τοῖν διαθήκαιν	these two wills
ἐκείνω τὼ λόγω	those two arguments
τωδὶ τὼ τρίποδε	these two tripods here (*for -ί, →7.18*)

(1) θερμὸν καὶ ψυχρὸν ἤ τινε δύο <u>τοιούτω</u> (Pl. *Soph.* 243d)
 warm and cold, or any such pair of things

- possessive adjectives:

 τοῖν <u>ὑμετέροιν</u> πολίταιν   your two fellow citizens
 ἀμφὶ τοῖν <u>σοῖν</u> δυσμόροιν παίδοιν   about your two unhappy sons

- relative pronouns:

(2) τὼ μὲν οὖν ἀδελφὼ αὐτῷ <u>ὥ</u> περ ἐγενέσθην ἄμφω ἄπαιδε ἐτελευτησάτην.
 (Isae. 6.6)
 The two brothers that were born to him both died childless. *For the dual verb*
 forms ἐγενέσθην and ἐτελευτησάτην, →21.

(3) δύ᾽ ... τώδ᾽ ἄνδρ᾽ ἔλεξας, <u>οἷν</u> ἐγὼ | ἥκιστ᾽ ἂν ἠθέλησ᾽ ὀλωλότοιν κλύειν. (Soph.
 Phil. 426–7)
 You have named two men there of whose death I would have least wanted to
 hear.

- indefinite/interrogative pronouns:

(4) ΣΩ. ἐστὸν δή <u>τινε</u> δύο ... :: ΠΡ. πῶς τούτω καὶ <u>τίνε</u> λέγεις; (Pl. *Phlb.* 53d)
 (Socrates:) There are two things. :: (Protarchus:) What do you mean? What are
 these two? *For the dual verb form ἐστόν,* →21.

- αὐτός, ἄλλος, ἕτερος, ἀλλήλων, etc.

 <u>ἀλλήλοιν</u>   each other
 <u>ἑκατέρω</u> τὼ γένει   each of the two races

(5) δύο γένη τινὲ <u>αὐτώ</u>, τῶν μὲν τριῶν <u>ἄλλω</u> (Pl. *Soph.* 254e)
 two certain classes by themselves, separate from the other three

---

Note 1: Feminine nom./acc. forms of these pronouns in -ᾱ (e.g. τάδε, ταὐτᾱ, etc.) are not
normally found in classical Greek. The gen./dat. forms in -αιν do occur (particularly in
Sophocles), but are rare.

11

Introduction to Verb Forms

Summary of the Greek Verbal System

		present stem		aorist stems		
		act.	mp.	act.	mid.	pass.
ind.		**present indicative**				
	1 sg.	παιδεύω	παιδεύομαι			
	2	παιδεύεις	παιδεύει/-ῃ			
	3	παιδεύει	παιδεύεται			
	1 pl.	παιδεύομεν	παιδευόμεθα			
	2	παιδεύετε	παιδεύεσθε			
	3	παιδεύουσι(ν)	παιδεύονται			
sec. ind.		**imperfect**		**aorist indicative**		
	1 sg.	ἐπαίδευον	ἐπαιδευόμην	ἐπαίδευσα	ἐπαιδευσάμην	ἐπαιδεύθην
	2	ἐπαίδευες	ἐπαιδεύου	ἐπαίδευσας	ἐπαιδεύσω	ἐπαιδεύθης
	3	ἐπαίδευε(ν)	ἐπαιδεύετο	ἐπαίδευσε(ν)	ἐπαιδεύσατο	ἐπαιδεύθη
	1 pl.	ἐπαιδεύομεν	ἐπαιδευόμεθα	ἐπαιδεύσαμεν	ἐπαιδευσάμεθα	ἐπαιδεύθημεν
	2	ἐπαιδεύετε	ἐπαιδεύεσθε	ἐπαιδεύσατε	ἐπαιδεύσασθε	ἐπαιδεύθητε
	3	ἐπαίδευον	ἐπαιδεύοντο	ἐπαίδευσαν	ἐπαιδεύσαντο	ἐπαιδεύθησαν
subj.		**present subjunctive**		**aorist subjunctive**		
	1 sg.	παιδεύω	παιδεύωμαι	παιδεύσω	παιδεύσωμαι	παιδευθῶ
	2	παιδεύῃς	παιδεύῃ	παιδεύσῃς	παιδεύσῃ	παιδευθῇς
	3	παιδεύῃ	παιδεύηται	παιδεύσῃ	παιδεύσηται	παιδευθῇ
	1 pl.	παιδεύωμεν	παιδευώμεθα	παιδεύσωμεν	παιδευσώμεθα	παιδευθῶμεν
	2	παιδεύητε	παιδεύησθε	παιδεύσητε	παιδεύσησθε	παιδευθῆτε
	3	παιδεύωσι(ν)	παιδεύωνται	παιδεύσωσι(ν)	παιδεύσωνται	παιδευθῶσι(ν)
opt.		**present optative**		**aorist optative**		
	1 sg.	παιδεύοιμι	παιδευοίμην	παιδεύσαιμι	παιδευσαίμην	παιδευθείην
	2	παιδεύοις	παιδεύοιο	παιδεύσειας	παιδεύσαιο	παιδευθείης
	3	παιδεύοι	παιδεύοιτο	παιδεύσειε(ν)	παιδεύσαιτο	παιδευθείη
	1 pl.	παιδεύοιμεν	παιδευοίμεθα	παιδεύσαιμεν	παιδευσαίμεθα	παιδευθεῖμεν
	2	παιδεύοιτε	παιδεύοισθε	παιδεύσαιτε	παιδεύσαισθε	παιδευθεῖτε
	3	παιδεύοιεν	παιδεύοιντο	παιδεύσειαν	παιδεύσαιντο	παιδευθεῖεν
imp.		**present imperative**		**aorist imperative**		
	2 sg.	παίδευε	παιδεύου	παίδευσον	παίδευσαι	παιδεύθητι
	3	παιδευέτω	παιδευέσθω	παιδευσάτω	παιδευσάσθω	παιδευθήτω
	2 pl.	παιδεύετε	παιδεύεσθε	παιδεύσατε	παιδεύσασθε	παιδεύθητε
	3	παιδευόντων	παιδευέσθων	παιδευσάντων	παιδευσάσθων	παιδευθέντων
inf.		**present infinitive**		**aorist infinitive**		
		παιδεύειν	παιδεύεσθαι	παιδεῦσαι	παιδεύσασθαι	παιδευθῆναι
ppl.		**present participle**		**aorist participle**		
	m.	παιδεύων, -οντος	παιδευόμενος, -ου	παιδεύσας, -αντος	παιδευσάμενος, -ου	παιδευθείς, -έντος
	f.	παιδεύουσα, -ης	παιδευομένη, -ης	παιδεύσασα, -ης	παιδευσαμένη, -ης	παιδευθεῖσα, -είσης
	n.	παιδεῦον, -οντος	παιδευόμενον, -ου	παιδεῦσαν, -αντος	παιδευσάμενον, -ου	παιδευθέν, -έντος

		future stems			perfect stems	
		act.	mid.	pass.	act.	mp.
ind.		**future indicative**			**perfect indicative**	
	1 sg.	παιδεύσω	παιδεύσομαι	παιδευθήσομαι	πεπαίδευκα	πεπαίδευμαι
	2	παιδεύσεις	παιδεύσει/-ῃ	παιδευθήσει/-ῃ	πεπαίδευκας	πεπαίδευσαι
	3	παιδεύσει	παιδεύσεται	παιδευθήσεται	πεπαίδευκε(ν)	πεπαίδευται
	1 pl.	παιδεύσομεν	παιδευσόμεθα	παιδευθησόμεθα	πεπαιδεύκαμεν	πεπαιδεύμεθα
	2	παιδεύσετε	παιδεύσεσθε	παιδευθήσεσθε	πεπαιδεύκατε	πεπαίδευσθε
	3	παιδεύσουσι(ν)	παιδεύσονται	παιδευθήσονται	πεπαιδεύκασι(ν)	πεπαίδευνται
sec. ind.					**pluperfect**	
	1 sg.				ἐπεπαιδεύκειν	ἐπεπαιδεύμην
	2				ἐπεπαιδεύκεις	ἐπεπαίδευσο
	3				ἐπεπαιδεύκει(ν)	ἐπεπαίδευτο
	1 pl.				ἐπεπαιδεύκεμεν	ἐπεπαιδεύμεθα
	2				ἐπεπαιδεύκετε	ἐπεπαίδευσθε
	3				ἐπεπαιδεύκεσαν	ἐπεπαίδευντο
subj.					**perfect subjunctive**	
	1 sg.				πεπαιδεύκω	πεπαιδευμένος ὦ
	2				πεπαιδεύκῃς	ᾖς
	3				πεπαιδεύκῃ	ᾖ
	1 pl.				πεπαιδεύκωμεν	πεπαιδευμένοι ὦμεν
	2				πεπαιδεύκητε	ἦτε
	3				πεπαιδεύκωσι(ν)	ὦσι(ν)
opt.		**future optative**			**perfect optative**	
	1 sg.	παιδεύσοιμι	παιδευσοίμην	παιδευθησοίμην	πεπαιδεύκοιμι	πεπαιδευμένος εἴην
	2	παιδεύσοις	παιδεύσοιο	παιδευθήσοιο	πεπαιδεύκοις	εἴης
	3	παιδεύσοι	παιδεύσοιτο	παιδευθήσοιτο	πεπαιδεύκοι	εἴη
	1 pl.	παιδεύσοιμεν	παιδευσοίμεθα	παιδευθησοίμεθα	πεπαιδεύκοιμεν	πεπαιδευμένοι εἶμεν
	2	παιδεύσοιτε	παιδεύσοισθε	παιδευθήσοισθε	πεπαιδεύκοιτε	εἶτε
	3	παιδεύσοιεν	παιδεύσοιντο	παιδευθήσοιντο	πεπαιδεύκοιεν	εἶεν
imp.					**perfect imperative**	
	2 sg.					πεπαίδευσο
	3					πεπαιδεύσθω
	2 pl.					πεπαίδευσθε
	3					πεπαιδεύσθων
inf.		**future infinitive**			**perfect infinitive**	
		παιδεύσειν	παιδεύσεσθαι	παιδευθήσεσθαι	πεπαιδευκέναι	πεπαιδεῦσθαι
ppl.		**future participle**			**perfect participle**	
	m.	παιδεύσων, -οντος	παιδευσόμενος, -ου	παιδευθησόμενος, -ου	πεπαιδευκώς, -ότος	πεπαιδευμένος, -ου
	f.	παιδεύσουσα, -ης	παιδευσομένη, -ης	παιδευθησομένη, -ης	πεπαιδευκυῖα, -ας	πεπαιδευμένη, -ης
	n.	παιδεῦσον, -οντος	παιδευσόμενον, -ου	παιδευθησόμενον, -ου	πεπαιδευκός, -ότος	πεπαιδευμένον, -ου

Basic Categories and Elements

Categories of the Verb

Finite versus Non-finite Verb Forms

11.1   Greek verb forms are either **finite** (indicatives, subjunctives, optatives, imperatives) or **non-finite** (infinitives, participles, and verbal adjectives in -τός or -τέος). Finite verbs have a personal ending (→11.15) and express person, number and mood; non-finite verbs do not have a personal ending and do not express person or mood.

Categories Pertaining to All Verb Forms: Tense-Aspect and Voice

11.2   All Greek verb forms, i.e. both finite and non-finite forms (except verbal adjectives in -τός or -τέος), are marked for the categories of **tense-aspect** and **voice**.

11.3   **Tense-aspect**: Greek verb forms fall into four overarching systems, depending on which stem of the verb is used (→11.12); these four systems differ primarily in their expression of aspect, although in the case of the future stems tense is the more important variable (these terms are treated in detail in 33):

- the **present-stem system**, covering the present indicative (or primary present indicative), the imperfect (or secondary present indicative), the present subjunctive, the present optative, the present imperative, the present infinitive, and the present participle;
- the **aorist-stem system**, covering the aorist indicative, the aorist subjunctive, the aorist optative, the aorist imperative, the aorist infinitive, and the aorist participle;
- the **future-stem system**, covering the future indicative, the future optative, the future infinitive, and the future participle;
- and the **perfect-stem system**, covering the perfect indicative (or primary perfect indicative), the pluperfect (or secondary perfect indicative), the perfect subjunctive, the perfect optative, the perfect imperative, the perfect infinitive, and the perfect participle.

Within these systems, **tense** is expressed by the indicatives, and by all forms of the future-stem system. **Aspect** is expressed by all forms except future-stem forms.

Note 1: For the rare future perfect (technically a fifth tense-aspect system), →17 and 33.46–7.

11.4   **Voice**: all Greek verb forms also express voice, treated in detail in 35. A basic two-way distinction between different kinds of forms may be made:

– **active** forms;

– and **middle-passive** forms.

In the aorist-stem system and in the future-stem system, further sub-divisions usually exist between different kinds of middle-passive forms, most often between **middle** forms and **passive** forms.

Note 1: In the present-stem and perfect-stem systems, a single set of forms is thus used for middle-passive voice (covering the entire range of meanings expressed by this voice). Present forms will be identified below either as 'active' (act.) or as 'middle-passive' (mp.). The three-way distinction between 'active', 'middle' (mid.) and 'passive' (pass.) forms in the aorist-stem and future-stem systems is traditional, but →35.8–29 for more accurate distinctions.

Categories Pertaining Only to Finite Verb Forms

11.5   All finite verb forms, in addition to belonging to one of the four tense-aspect systems and being marked for voice, are also marked for the categories of **person** and **number**, and the category of **mood**.

11.6   Finite verb forms express one of the following **persons**:

– **first person** ('I'/'we');

– **second person** ('you');

– or **third person**('he'/'she'/'it', 'they').

And they express one of the following **numbers**:

– **singular** ('I', 'you', 'he'/'she'/'it');

– **plural** ('we', 'you', 'they');

– in addition, Greek has a **dual number**, occurring only in the second and third person ('you two', 'the two of them', →21).

11.7   Finite verb forms also express one of the following **moods** (for the uses and meanings of these moods, →34):

– **indicative**; within this category a distinction may be made between **primary indicatives** (expressing present or future tense) and **secondary indicatives** (usually expressing past tense); both types of indicative occur in the present-stem system (present indicative and imperfect) and the perfect-stem system (perfect indicative and pluperfect); the aorist-stem system has only a secondary indicative; the future-stem system has only a primary indicative;

– **subjunctive**;

– **optative**;

– **imperative**.

11.8   Some examples of finite verb forms and the categories they express:

παιδεύεις: 2 sg. pres. act. ind.: *you are educating* – a part of the present-stem system; expresses second person, singular number, and indicative mood (primary – indicating present tense), aspect and active voice;

παιδευώμεθα: 1 pl. pres. mp. subj.: *let us be educated* – a part of the present-stem system; expresses first person, plural number, and subjunctive mood, as well as aspect and middle-passive voice;

ἐπαίδευσε(ν): 3 sg. aor. act. ind.: *he educated* – a part of the aorist-stem system; expresses third person, singular number, and indicative mood (secondary – normally indicating past tense), aspect and active voice;

παιδεύθητε: 2 pl. aor. imp. pass.: *be educated!* – a part of the aorist-stem system; expresses second person, plural number, and imperative mood, as well as aspect and passive voice;

ἐπεπαιδεύκεσαν: 3 pl. plpf. (= sec. pf. ind.) act.: *they had educated* – a part of the perfect-stem system; expresses third person, plural number, and indicative mood (secondary – normally indicating past tense), aspect and active voice.

Categories Pertaining to Non-finite Verb Forms

11.9   Non-finite verb forms are marked for the following categories:

- **Infinitives** only express tense-aspect and voice.
- **Participles** express tense-aspect and voice, and, like adjectives, are also marked for the categories of case, number and gender (→2.1).
- **Verbal adjectives** are only marked for the categories of case, number and gender.

11.10   Some examples of non-finite verb forms and the categories they express:

παιδευθῆναι: aor. pass. inf. *to be/have been educated* – an infinitive, part of the aorist-stem system; expresses aspect and passive voice;

παιδεύουσαι: nom. pl. fem., pres. act. ppl.: *educating* – a participle, part of the present-stem system; expresses nominative case, plural number, feminine gender, as well as aspect and active voice;

παιδευτέος: nom. sg. masc. *X must be educated* – a verbal adjective (a gerundive, →37.2); expresses nominative case, singular number, and masculine gender.

Morphological Building Blocks: Stems, Endings, and Other Markings

Verb Stems and Tense-Aspect Stems

11.11   All forms of a certain verb share a **verb stem**, which identifies the forms as deriving from that particular verb: for example, in any form of the verb παιδεύω (e.g.

ἐπαίδευσε(ν), ἐπεπαιδεύκεσαν, παιδεύουσαι), the verb stem παιδευ- identifies the form as belonging to that particular verb (and thus expressing in some way the meaning *educate*).

Many Greek verb stems occur in different variants due to ablaut vowel gradation (→1.51–6): for example, the verb stem of the verb λείπω *leave* occurs as either λειπ- (e-grade), λιπ- (zero-grade) or λοιπ- (o-grade). Different tense-aspect stems of such verbs differ in the vowel-grade they show.

A particular common type of variation in verb stems (originally also due to ablaut, but greatly regularized in the language) is that between long and short variants of the final vowel of a stem: η/ᾰ (or after ε, ι, ρ: ᾱ/ᾰ, →1.57), η/ε, ω/ο: for example, the verb stem of τιμάω *honour* occurs as either τιμᾱ- or τιμη-, the verb stem of ποιέω *make, do* as either ποιε- or ποιη-, and the verb stem of δηλόω *make clear* as either δηλο- or δηλω-.

For verbs which have variant verb stems, all variants are given below, where required.

11.12   Through the selection of one of the variants of a verb stem and/or the addition of various suffixes, a **tense-aspect stem** is formed. The tense-aspect stem identifies the form as having a particular combination of tense-aspect and voice – though many tense-aspect stems are used for more than one voice.

Seven different kinds of tense-aspect stems may be distinguished; these fall into the four overarching systems described above (→11.3):

– present tense-aspect: **present stems** (act./mp.);
– aorist tense-aspect: **aorist stems** (act./mid.) and **aorist passive stems** (θη-/η-aor. stems);
– future tense-aspect: **future stems** (act./mid.) and **future passive stems**;
– perfect tense-aspect: **perfect stems** (act.) and **perfect middle-passive stems**.

Note 1: Two additional (but rare) tense-aspect stems are the future perfect stem (act.) and the future perfect middle-passive stem. For these, →17.

Some examples:

πεπαιδευκέναι *to have educated*: the perfect stem πεπαιδευκ- (based on the verb stem παιδευ-) identifies the form as deriving from the verb παιδεύω, belonging to the perfect tense-aspect system, and expressing active voice.

ἐπαιδεύσαμεν *we educated*: the aorist stem παιδευσ(α)- (based on the verb stem παιδευ-) identifies the form as deriving from the verb παιδεύω, and belonging to the aorist tense-aspect system.

ἔλιπε(ν) *(s)he left*: the aorist stem λῐπ- (one of the variants of the verb stem λειπ-/λοιπ-/λῐπ-) identifies the form as deriving from the verb λείπω, and belonging to the aorist tense-aspect system.

λελοιπότες *having left*: the perfect stem λελοιπ- (based on one of the variants of the verb stem λειπ-/λοιπ-/λῐπ-) identifies the form as deriving from λείπω, belonging to the perfect tense-aspect system, and expressing active voice.

The mechanisms involved in forming tense-aspect stems from verb stems are detailed in the individual chapters on the present (→12), aorist (→13–14), future (→15–16), and perfect (→17–19) stems.

11.13   In a few cases, entirely different verb stems are used to form different tense-aspect stems of 'the same' verb: for instance, with the verb αἱρέω *take*, the verb stem αἱρη-/αἱρε- is used in the present, aorist passive (ᾑρέθην), future (αἱρήσω), perfect and perfect middle-passive (ᾕρηκα/ᾕρημαι), but not in the aorist active and middle, where the verb stem ἑλ- is used (e.g. 1 sg. act. ind. εἷλον). Such verbs are called **suppletive verbs**.

11.14   Verbs lacking certain tense-aspect stems altogether are called **defective verbs**: for instance, the verb εἴωθα *be accustomed* lacks present-stem forms in classical Greek (εἴωθα is a perfect, the present ἔθω occurs in Homer), and has no forms of other stems (aorist or future) at all.

Endings

11.15   Every verb form also has an **ending**, which provides the information required to identify the form as either finite or non-finite, and usually its voice.
- For finite verbs, the ending ('personal ending') also expresses person, number and sometimes (in the imperative) mood.
- Infinitive endings merely express voice.
- The endings of participles and verbal adjectives express case, number and gender.

Some examples:

ἐπαιδευόμην: the personal ending -μην identifies the form as first person singular, middle-passive.

γνῶθι: the personal ending -θι identifies the form as a second person singular imperative active.

πεπαιδεῦσθαι: the ending -σθαι identifies the form as a middle-passive infinitive.

πεπαιδευμένα: the ending -(μεν)α identifies the form as a nominative or accusative plural neuter participle.

The endings are treated more fully below, →11.20–34.

Thematic Vowels, Optative Suffixes, Participle Suffixes

11.16   Some elements appear **between the stem and the ending**:
- Many Greek verb forms include a **thematic vowel** (or: 'theme vowel'), either **o** or **ε**, standing between the stem and the ending, e.g. παιδεύομεν, ἐπαιδεύεσθε, λιπόντων; for details, →11.18–19 below.

- **Subjunctives** are identified by a **long thematic vowel**, either **ω or η**, e.g. παιδεύησθε, λίπωμεν.
- **Optatives** are identified by the **suffix -ι-** or in some cases -ιη-, directly preceding the ending. The ι always forms a diphthong (always 'short', →1.70 n.1) with either a preceding thematic vowel, e.g. παιδεύοιμι, παιδεύοιεν, or a preceding stem vowel, e.g. παιδευθεῖμεν, τιθείην, ἱσταίμεθα.
- **Active participles** and **aorist passive participles** are identified by the suffix **-ντ-**, e.g. παιδεύοντος, παιδευθέντων; in several cases ντ is not visible in the form, e.g. παιδεύουσα (<*παιδεύοντ-γα, →1.77, 1.68): for the full declensions, →5.17–18.

  However, **perfect active participles** are identified by **-οτ-** (masc., neut.) or **-υι-** (fem.) e.g. λελοιπότας, πεπαιδευκυῖα: for the full declension, →5.19–20.
- All **middle-passive participles** except aorist passive participles are identified by the suffix **-μεν-**, e.g. πεπαιδευμένον, λιπόμενα.

Augments and Prepositional Prefixes

11.17   Finally, some elements **precede the stem**:

- Secondary indicatives (imperfect, aorist, pluperfect) include an **augment**, which takes the form of an ε directly preceding the stem (e.g. ἔλιπον), or, if the verb stem begins with a vowel, that vowel is lengthened (e.g. ὡμολόγουν). For details, →11.35–42.
- Many compound verbs begin with a prepositional **prefix**, an original preposition integrated into the verb form, e.g. ἐκπαιδεύω, ἀπολείπω (→23.51). These prefixes are always the first element of a form, preceding even augments and reduplications (→11.51–8).

  A final consonant of such prefixes often assimilates to the following sound: e.g. ἐλ-λείπει but ἐν-έλιπε (→11.54). If the prefix ends in a vowel, this vowel usually drops out before another vowel (elision, →1.35): e.g. ἀπο-βαίνει but ἀπ-έρχεται, ἀφ-ίησι.

Note 1: For reduplications (which are themselves part of the perfect stem), →11.43–50 below.

Thematic and Athematic Conjugations

11.18   Greek verb forms are either **thematic** or **athematic**. Thematic forms include a thematic vowel (ο/ε, subj. ω/η) between the stem and the ending. Athematic forms do not include a thematic vowel: thus in athematic forms endings are attached immediately to the stem (only optative or participle suffixes can stand in between):

- **Thematic conjugations**: present-stem forms of -ω verbs, the present optative of -νυμι verbs, some imperfects of -μι verbs, aorist forms of the 'thematic' type, all future and future perfect forms, nearly all perfect active optatives. Moreover, as subjunctives are identified by a long thematic vowel (η/ω), *all* subjunctives are thematic.

– **Athematic conjugations**: present-stem forms of -μι verbs (except subjunctives, the optative of -νυμι verbs and some imperfects), all aorists of the 'sigmatic' and 'root' types (except subjunctives), all aorist passive forms (except subjunctives), all perfect forms (except subjunctives and active optatives).

Some examples with the verb δείκνυμι *show*:

δείκνυ-σι(ν): 3 sg. pres. act. ind., athematic: the ending -σι(ν) is added immediately to the present stem δείκνυ-;

δεικνύ-ο̣ι-μεν: 1 pl. pres. act. opt., thematic: a thematic vowel and optative ι (merged as diphthong οι) stand between the present stem and the ending -μεν;

δείξ-ε̣-τε: 2 pl. fut. act. ind., thematic: a thematic vowel stands between the future stem δειξ- and the ending -τε;

δέδεικ-ται: 3 sg. pf. mp. ind., athematic: the ending -ται follows directly on the perfect stem δεδεικ-.

Note 1: It is misleading to call verbs as a whole 'thematic' or 'athematic' – for example, future verb forms (no matter from what verb) are always thematic; perfect middle-passive forms are always athematic. It is only in the present and in the aorist that a significant distinction exists between verbs with thematic conjugations and those with athematic conjugations (for the present: between -ω verbs and -μι verbs).

11.19   Which thematic vowel (ε/η or ο/ω) is used depends on the sound following it:

– **o/ω** is used **before μ or ν**, and in the first person singular ending -**ω**: e.g. παιδεύω̣, παιδεύο̣μεν, παιδευ̣ό̣ντων, παιδεύω̣μαι, etc.

– **o** is used **before the optative suffix -ι-/-ιη-** (so in all thematic optatives), forming a diphthong with the following ι: e.g. παιδεύο̣ις, παιδεύο̣ισθε, πεπαιδεύκο̣ι, etc.

– in **all other cases**, **ε/η** is used: e.g. παιδεύε̣τε, παιδεύη̣σθε, παίδευε̣, etc.

Note 1: With the exception of optatives, the division of thematic vowels among persons is normally 1 sg. ο, 2 sg. ε, 3 sg. ε; 1 pl. ο, 2 pl. ε, 3 pl. ο. This 'rule' is, however, a result of the rules given above, and there are further exceptions: note e.g. the difference between 3 pl. pres. act. imp. παιδευό̣ντων (preceding ν) and its middle-passive equivalent παιδευέ̣σθων (also 3 pl., but preceding σ).

Endings

Personal Endings

11.20   The **personal endings** of finite verb forms are either active or middle-passive, and either primary or secondary (except for imperatives):

– **Active endings** are used for all active forms, and for aorist passive forms. **Middle-passive endings** are used for all middle and passive forms, apart from aorist passive forms.
– **Primary endings** are used for all indicatives referring to the present or future ('primary indicatives'), for all subjunctives, and for a few optatives. **Secondary endings** are used for all indicatives referring to the past (those indicatives that have an augment, 'secondary indicatives'), and for nearly all optatives. **Imperatives** have their own set of separate endings.

11.21   The most common forms of these endings are set out in the tables below, with examples per person/number.

Tables of Endings

11.22   **First person singular**:

	active		middle-passive	
	primary	secondary	primary	secondary
-ω[1] (them.) -μῐ (athem.)		-ν	-μαι	-μην

[1]   Includes a thematic vowel (ending and thematic vowel have inextricably fused).

Examples:

active, primary: e.g. pres. ind. παιδεύω, τιμῶ (<*-άω), δείκνυμι, εἰμί; secondary: impf. ἐπαίδευον, ἐδείκνυν, pres. opt. ποιοίην, aor. pass. ἐπαιδεύθην
middle-passive, primary: e.g. pres. ind. παιδεύομαι, δείκνυμαι, δύναμαι; pf. ind. πεπαίδευμαι; secondary: impf. ἐπαιδευόμην, plpf. ἐπεπαιδεύμην, pres. opt. παιδευοίμην

11.23   **Second person singular**:

	active		middle-passive	
	primary	secondary	primary	secondary
-εις[1] (them.) -ς[2] (athem.)		-ς[2]	-σαι[3]	-σο[3]

[1]   Includes a thematic vowel (ending and thematic vowel have inextricably fused).
[2]   Primary ending originally -σῐ (still 'visible' in pres. ind. εἶ you are (<*ἐσ-σί)); the primary/secondary ending -θα is also sometimes found (e.g. pf. ind. οἶσθα; impf. ἦσθα).
[3]   The σ in these endings has usually disappeared between vowels (→1.83); see the examples below.

Examples:

active, primary: e.g. pres. ind. παιδεύ<u>εις</u>, τιμᾷς (<*-ά<u>εις</u>), δείκνυ<u>ς</u>, τίθη<u>ς</u>; impf. ἐπαίδευε<u>ς</u>, ἐδείκνυ<u>ς</u>, aor. ind. ἐπαίδευσα<u>ς</u>, pres. opt. παιδεύοι<u>ς</u>, aor. pass. ἐπαιδεύθη<u>ς</u>

middle-passive, primary: e.g. pres. ind. δείκνυ<u>σαι</u>, παιδεύῃ (<*-ε<u>σαι</u>), pf. ind. πεπαίδευ<u>σαι</u>; secondary: impf. ἐδείκνυ<u>σο</u>, ἐπαιδεύου (<*-ε<u>σο</u>), aor. ind. ἐπαιδεύσω (<*-σα<u>σο</u>), plpf. ἐπεπαίδευ<u>σο</u>, pres. opt. παιδεύοιο (<*-οι<u>σο</u>)

11.24 **Third person singular:**

active		middle-passive	
primary	secondary	primary	secondary
-ει[1] (them.) -σῐ(ν)[2] (athem.)	**no ending**	-ται	-το

[1] Includes a thematic vowel (ending and thematic vowel have inextricably fused).
[2] Originally -τῐ(ν) (still visible in pres. ind. ἐστί(ν)).

Examples:

active, primary: e.g. pres. ind. παιδεύ<u>ει</u>, τιμᾷ (<*-ά<u>ει</u>), δείκνυ<u>σι</u>(ν), τίθη<u>σι</u>(ν); secondary: impf. ἐπαίδευε(ν) (no ending; for movable ν, →1.39), ἐδείκνυ (no ending), pres. opt. παιδεύοι (no ending), aor. pass. ἐπαιδεύθη (no ending)

middle-passive, primary: e.g. pres. ind. παιδεύε<u>ται</u>, δείκνυ<u>ται</u>, pf. ind. πεπαίδευ<u>ται</u>; secondary: impf. ἐπαιδεύε<u>το</u>, ἐδείκνυ<u>το</u>, aor. ind. ἐπαιδεύσα<u>το</u>, plpf. ἐπεπαίδευ<u>το</u>, pres. opt. παιδεύοι<u>το</u>

11.25 **First person plural:**

active		middle-passive	
primary	secondary	primary	secondary
-μεν	-μεν	-μεθᾰ[1]	-μεθᾰ[1]

[1] In poetry, especially in lyric, sometimes -μεσθᾰ.

Examples:

active, primary: e.g. pres. ind. παιδεύο<u>μεν</u>, τιμῶ<u>μεν</u>, δείκνυ<u>μεν</u>, ἐσ<u>μέν</u>; secondary: impf. ἐπαιδεύο<u>μεν</u>, ἐδείκνυ<u>μεν</u>, pres. opt. παιδεύοι<u>μεν</u>, aor. pass. ἐπαιδεύθη<u>μεν</u>

middle-passive, primary: e.g. pres. ind. παιδευό<u>μεθα</u>, δεικνύ<u>μεθα</u>, pf. ind. πεπαιδεύ<u>μεθα</u>; secondary: impf. ἐπαιδευό<u>μεθα</u>, ἐδεικνύ<u>μεθα</u>, aor. ind. ἐπαιδευσά<u>μεθα</u>, plpf. ἐπεπαιδεύ<u>μεθα</u>, pres. opt. παιδευοί<u>μεθα</u>

11.26 **Second person plural**:

active		middle-passive	
primary	secondary	primary	secondary
-τε	-τε	-σθε	-σθε

Examples:

active, primary: e.g. pres. ind. παιδεύετε, τιμᾶτε, δείκνυτε, ἐστέ; secondary: impf.
ἐπαιδεύετε, ἐδείκνυτε, pres. opt. παιδεύοιτε, aor. pass. ἐπαιδεύθητε

middle-passive, primary: e.g. pres. ind. παιδεύεσθε, δείκνυσθε, pf. ind. πεπαίδευσθε;
secondary: impf. ἐπαιδεύεσθε, ἐδείκνυσθε, aor. ind. ἐπαιδεύσασθε, plpf.
ἐπεπαίδευσθε, pres. opt. παιδεύοισθε

11.27 **Third person plural**:

active			middle-passive	
primary	secondary		primary	secondary
-[ν]σῐ(ν)[1] (them.)	-ᾱσῐ(ν) (athem.)	-ν, -σᾰν or -εν[2]	-νται	-ντο

[1] The first ν in this ending has disappeared, resulting in compensatory lengthening
 (→1.68–9) of the preceding vowel; see the examples below.
[2] -εν occurs only in the optative.

Examples:

active, primary: e.g. pres. ind. παιδεύουσι(ν) (<*-ονσι(ν)), τιμῶσι(ν) (<*-άονσι(ν)),
δεικνύᾱσι(ν); secondary: impf. ἐπαίδευον, aor. ind. ἐπαίδευσαν; impf. ἐδείκνυσαν,
aor. pass. ἐπαιδεύθησαν; pres. opt. παιδεύοιεν

middle-passive, primary: e.g. pres. ind. παιδεύονται, δείκνυνται, pf. ind.
πεπαίδευνται; secondary: impf. ἐπαιδεύοντο, ἐδείκνυντο, aor. ind.
ἐπαιδεύσαντο, plpf. ἐπεπαίδευντο, pres. opt. παιδεύοιντο

Subjunctives

11.28 As noted above, all **subjunctives** are thematic (with a long thematic vowel), and all
have primary endings: thus all subjunctives are formed by adding -ω, -ῃς, -ῃ,
-ωμεν, -ητε, -ωσῐ(ν) (act.) or -ωμαι, -ῃ, -ηται, -ώμεθᾰ, -ησθε, -ωνται (mp.) to the
stem, no matter which stem is concerned.

Note 1: 2 sg. mp. -ῃ is contracted from -ησαι (see on -σαι above, →11.23).

Examples:

active: e.g. pres. παιδεύω, τιμᾷς (<*-άῃς), δηλῶτε (<*-όητε), δεικνύῃ, aor. παιδεύσωμεν, βάλητε, aor. pass. παιδευθῶσι(ν) (<-έωσι(ν), <*-ήωσι(ν), →1.71) middle-passive: e.g. pres. παιδεύῃ, δεικνύωνται, aor. παιδεύσωμαι, θώμεθα (<θεώμεθα <*θηώμεθα, →1.71).

Imperatives

11.29   Separate endings are used in the **imperative**:

	active	middle-passive
2 sg.	**no ending** or **-θι** or **-ς** sigmatic aorist: -(σ)ον (→13.10)	**-σο**[1] sigmatic aorist: -(σ)αι (→13.10)
3 sg.	-τω	-σθω
2 pl.	-τε	-σθε
3 pl.	-ντων[2]	-σθων[2]

1 The σ in this ending has often disappeared between vowels (→1.83); see the examples below.
2 Later -τωσαν (active) and -σθωσαν (middle-passive).

Examples:

2 sg. active: pres. παίδευε (no ending), τίμα (<*-αε, no ending), δείκνυ (no ending); pres. ἴσθι, aor. στῆθι, aor. pass. (η-aor.) φάνηθι, aor. pass. (θη-aor.) παιδεύθητι (→1.97 n.2); aor. δός, σχές; sigm. aor. παίδευσον, pseudo-sigm. aor. ἄγγειλον (<*-ελ-σον);

other, active: 3 sg., pres. παιδευέτω, τιμάτω, δεικνύτω, aor. παιδευσάτω, aor. pass. παιδευθήτω; 2 pl., pres. παιδεύετε, τιμᾶτε, aor. pass. παιδεύθητε; 3 pl., pres. παιδευόντων, aor. παιδευσάντων;

2 sg. middle-passive: pres. παιδεύου (<*παιδεύεσο), τιμῶ (<*-άεσο), δείκνυσο; aor. θοῦ (<*θέσο); sigm. aor. παίδευσαι, pseudo-sigm. aor. ἄγγειλαι (<*-ελ-σαι);

other, middle-passive: 3 sg., pres. παιδευέσθω, τιμάσθω, δεικνύσθω, aor. παιδευσάσθω; 2 pl., pres. παιδεύεσθε, τιμᾶσθε, δείκνυσθε; 3 pl., pres. παιδευέσθων, aor. παιδευσάσθων.

Note 1: The 2 pl. imperative of any stem is always identical to the 2 pl. indicative, except for augments: e.g. pres. παιδεύετε (ind./imp.); aor. ἐπαιδεύσασθε (ind.)/παιδεύσασθε (imp.).

Exceptions

11.30   Although the endings discussed above are present in most forms, a few exceptions still remain. In particular, several endings in the **perfect and pluperfect active** differ from those given above: →18.5.

Endings of Non-finite Forms

Infinitives

11.31 The endings of **active infinitives** are as follows:

- **Thematic**: -εν; this contracts with the preceding thematic vowel ε to form -ειν (with 'spurious' ει, →1.23, 1.59), e.g. παιδεύειν; this may then further contract with the final vowel of a verb stem: e.g. τιμᾶν (<*τιμά-ε-εν), δηλοῦν (<*δηλό-ε-εν).
- **Athematic**: -ναι (e.g. pres. δεικνύναι, διδόναι, εἶναι, aor. pass. παιδευθῆναι) or -εναι (e.g. pres. ἰέναι, aor. δοῦναι (<*δόεναι), pf. πεπαιδευκέναι).

The ending in the sigmatic aorist is -(σ)αι: e.g. παιδεῦσαι, γράψαι, ἀγγεῖλαι (<*-ελ-σαι).

Note 1: For the differences in accentuation between e.g. aor. act. inf. παιδεῦσαι and aor. mid. imp. παίδευσαι, →24.20 n.1.

11.32 The ending of all **middle-passive infinitives** is -σθαι: e.g. pres. παιδεύεσθαι, δείκνυσθαι, aor. παιδεύσασθαι, pf. πεπαιδεῦσθαι.

Participles and Verbal Adjectives

11.33 The endings of **participles** are those of adjectives of the first and third declensions (→5.17–20).

11.34 **Verbal adjectives** (in -τέος, -τέα, -τέον, and in -τός, -τή, -τόν) have endings of the first and second declensions (→5.1–2).

Augments and Reduplications

Formation of the Augment

11.35 Secondary indicatives (imperfect, aorist indicative, pluperfect) normally include an **augment**, which immediately precedes the stem. The form of the augment is determined by the initial sound of the (tense-aspect) stem.

With Stems Beginning with a Consonant

11.36 If the stem begins with a **consonant**, the augment takes the form ἐ-:

παιδεύω *educate*	pres. stem παιδευ-	impf. ἐπαίδευον
λύω *loosen, release*	aor. stem λυσ(α)-	aor. ind. ἔλυσα
δίδωμι *give*	aor. stem δω-/δο-	aor. ἔδωκα
βλάπτω *harm, damage*	aor. pass. (η-aor.) stem βλαβη-	aor. pass. ind. ἐβλάβην

With stems beginning with ρ, that **ρ is doubled** after the augment:

ῥίπτω *throw*	pres. stem ῥιπτ-	impf. ἔρριπτον
ῥήγνυμι *(cause to) break*	aor. stem ῥηξ(α)-	aor. ind. ἔρρηξα

Note 1: This type of augment is called 'syllabic' (Lat. *augmentum syllabicum*), because a syllable is added.

With Stems Beginning with a Vowel or Diphthong

11.37   If the stem begins with a **vowel**, the augment has the form of the **lengthened** initial vowel (→1.67–9):

ᾰ > η	ἄγω *lead, bring*	aor. stem ἀγαγ-	aor. ind. ἤγαγον
ε > η	ἐλπίζω *expect*	pres. stem ἐλπιζ-	impf. ἤλπιζον
ῐ > ῑ	ἱκετεύω *beg*	pres. stem ἱκετευ-	impf. ἱκέτευον
ο > ω	ὀνομάζω *name*	aor. stem ὀνομασ(α)-	aor. ind. ὠνόμασα
ῠ > ῡ	ὑβρίζω *abuse*	aor. stem ὕβρισ(α)-	aor. ind. ὕβρισα

Long vowels stay unchanged:

ἡγέομαι *lead, guide, consider*	pres. stem ἡγε-	impf. ἡγούμην
ὠφελέω *benefit*	aor. stem ὠφελησ(α)-	aor. ind. ὠφέλησα

11.38   Stems beginning with a **diphthong** lengthen the first part of that diphthong:

αἰτιάομαι *accuse*	aor. stem αἰτιασ(α)-	aor. ind. ᾐτιασάμην
αὐξάνω *increase*	pres. stem αὐξαν-	impf. ηὔξανον
εἰκάζω *liken*	aor. stem εἰκασ(α)-	aor. ind. ᾔκασα
εὑρίσκω *find*	aor. stem εὑρ-	aor. ind. ηὗρον
οἰκέω *live*	pres. stem οἰκε-	impf. ᾤκουν

Note 1: The type of augment described in 11.37–8 is sometimes, somewhat unhelpfully, called 'temporal' (Lat. *augmentum temporale*), as it normally causes the initial vowel/diphthong to be pronounced for a greater amount of time (vowel quantity, →1.18).

Further Particulars

11.39   Augments are not part of the stem, and occur only in the secondary indicative:

1 sg. impf. act. ἦγον, but 1 sg. pres. act. opt. ἄγοιμι, pres. act. ppl. nom. sg. masc. ἄγων, etc.

1 sg. aor. act. ind. ἐπαίδευσα, but 1 sg. aor. act. subj. παιδεύσω, aor. act. inf. παιδεῦσαι, etc.

11.40   Augmentation occurred before the disappearance of consonants ϝ, y and σ (→1.74–84). The result of this is that some augments, although originally regularly formed, appear irregular in classical Greek:

ἔχω *have, hold*	verb stem ἐχ-/σχ- (<*σ(ε)χ-)	impf. εἶχον (<*ἔσεχον <*ἔ-σεχον); note aor. ἔ-σχ-ον)
ἐάω *allow*	verb stem ἐᾱ-/ἐᾰ- (<*σεϝα-)	aor. εἴᾱσα (<*ἔ-σεϝα-), impf. εἴων

ἐργάζομαι *work*	verb stem ἐργ- (<*ϝεργ-)	impf. εἰργαζόμην (<*ἐ-ϝεργ-)
ἵημι *send, let go*	verb stem ἡ-/ἑ- (<*γη-/*γε-)	aor. pass εἵθην (<*ἐ-γε-)

In some such cases, the original augment seems to have been ἠ-, resulting (through quantitative metathesis, →1.71) in augmented forms beginning with εᾱ- or εω-:

ἁλίσκομαι *be captured*	verb stem ἁλ(ω)- (<*ϝᾰλ(ω)-)	aor. ἑᾱλων (<*ἠ-ϝᾰλ-); cf. e.g. inf. ἁλῶναι; aor. ἥλων is also found)
ὁράω *see*	verb stem ὁρᾱ- (<*ϝορᾱ-), ῐδ- (<*ϝῐδ-), ὀπ-	impf. ἑώρων (<*ἠ-ϝορ-); also cf. aor. εἶδον (<*ἐ-ϝῐδ-)
(ἀν)οίγνυμι *open*	verb stem οἰγ- (<*ϝοιγ-)	impf. ἀν-έῳγον (<*-η-ϝοιγ-); rarely also ἤνοιγον (→11.57)

11.41   Observe the following further exceptions:

- Sometimes, stems beginning with a diphthong (especially εἰ-) are not augmented; stems beginning with οὐ- are never augmented:

εἰκάζω *liken*	pres. stem εἰκαζ-	impf. εἴκαζον (next to ἤκαζον)
οὐτάζω *stab*	pres. stem οὐταζ-	impf. οὔταζον

- With ᾄδω *sing*, the long diphthong ᾄ- (<ἀει-) is augmented to ᾐ- (<ἠει-): e.g. impf. ᾖδον.
- With αἴρω *lift*, the aorist stem ἀρ- (<*ἀερ-) is augmented to ἠ-: e.g. 1 sg. ind. ἦρα (cf. aor. inf. ἆραι, etc.).
- The verbs βούλομαι, δύναμαι and μέλλω are found in fourth century and later Greek with the augment ἠ- instead of ἐ-: ἠβουλόμην, ἠδυνήθην, ἤμελλον, etc.
- The form χρῆν *it was necessary* – originally combined from the noun χρή *necessity* and the augmented form ἦν *there was* (→12.44) – is often given an extra augment: ἐχρῆν.

11.42   The augment is frequently **omitted** in epic poetry and occasionally in other poetry; in tragedy the syllabic augment (→11.36 n.1) is sometimes omitted in narrative passages (messenger speeches, etc.). For the omission of the temporal augment (→11.38 n.1) in Herodotus, →25.43.

Formation of Reduplications

11.43   Perfect stems are formed by the addition of a **reduplication** to the verb stem. Reduplications either consist of a consonant + ε, or they are formed exactly like the augment, depending on the initial sound of the verb stem.

Two Types of Reduplication

11.44   With verb stems beginning

- with a single consonant (except ρ),
- or with a combination of stop + resonant (μ, ν, λ, ρ):

reduplication = initial consonant + ε:

παιδεύω *educate*	verb stem παιδευ-	pf. πεπαίδευκα
λύω *loosen, release*	verb stem λῡ-/λῠ-	pf. λέλῠκα

δίδωμι *give*	verb stem δω-/δο-	pf. δέδωκα
γίγνομαι *become, be born*	verb stem γεν(η)-/γον-/γν-	pf. γέγονα, γεγένημαι
βλάπτω *harm, damage*	verb stem βλᾰβ-	pf. βέβλαφα
κλίνω *cause to lean*	verb stem κλῐ(ν)-	pf. κέκλῐκα

With stems beginning with an aspirated stop (θ/φ/χ), the reduplication uses the **unaspirated**, voiceless stop (τ/π/κ, →1.97):

φονεύω *murder*	verb stem φονευ-	pf. πεφόνευκα
τίθημι *put, place*	verb stem θη-/θε-	pf. τέθηκα
θραύω *injure*	verb stem θραυ(σ)-	pf. τέθραυσμαι

11.45   With verbs whose stem begins

– with ῥ-,
– with two consonants other than stop + resonant (including ζ/ξ/ψ) or στρ-,
– or with a vowel:

reduplication = formed like the augment (→11.35–41):

ἄγω *lead, bring*	verb stem ᾰγ-	pf. ἦχα
ζητέω *seek*	verb stem ζητη-/ζητε-	pf. ἐζήτηκα
ξενόομαι *entertain*	verb stem ξενω-/ξενο-	pf. ἐξένωμαι
κτίζω *found*	verb stem κτῐδ-	pf. ἔκτικα
ὀρθόω *straighten*	verb stem ὀρθω-/ὀρθο-	pf. ὤρθωκα
στρατηγέω *lead*	verb stem στρατηγη-/στρατηγε-	pf. ἐστρατήγηκα
ῥίπτω *throw*	verb stem ῥῑπ-	pf. ἔρρῑφα
ῥήγνυμι *(cause to) break*	verb stem ῥηγ-/ῥωγ-/ῥᾰγ-	pf. ἔρρωγα
ὑβρίζω *abuse, maltreat*	verb stem ὑβρῐδ-	pf. ὕβρικα

Further Particulars

11.46   Reduplications, unlike augments, are **part of the stem** (even when formed like an augment), and thus occur both in non-finite and in finite forms (all moods):

1 sg. pf. act. ind. ἐστρατήγηκα, pf. act. ppl. nom. sg. masc. ἐστρατηγηκώς; contrast e.g. the aor. equivalents ἐστρατήγησα (ind., with augment), στρατηγήσας (ppl., no augment)

11.47   Reduplication occurred before the disappearance of consonants ϝ, y and σ (→1.74–84). The result of this is that some reduplications, although originally regularly formed, seem irregular in classical Greek. For example:

ἵημι *send, let go*	verb stem ἡ-/ἑ- (<*yη-/*yε-)	pf. εἷκα (<*yέyε-)
ἄγνυμι *break*	verb stem ἀγ-/ᾰγ- (<*ϝᾱγ-/*ϝᾰγ-)	pf. ἔᾱγα (<*ϝέϝᾱγ-)
with λέγω *say, speak*	verb stem ἐρ-/ρη- (<*ϝερ-/*ϝρη-)	pf. εἴρηκα (<*ϝέϝρη-)
μείρομαι *obtain by lot*	verb stem μερ-/μορ-/μᾰρ- (<*σμρ̥-, →1.87)	pf. εἵμαρται (3 sg., <*σεσμρ̥-)
λαμβάνω *get, take*	verb stem ληβ-/λᾰβ- (<*σλᾱβ-/*σλᾰβ-)	pf. εἴληφα (<*σεσλᾱβ-)

Note also:

λαγχάνω *obtain by lot*	verb stem ληχ-/λᾰχ-	pf. εἴληχα (εἰ- by analogy with εἴληφα)
συλ-λέγω *collect*	verb stem λεγ-/λογ-	pf. συν-είλεγμαι (εἰ- by analogy)

11.48   The following further exceptions may be observed:

– The verbs ἵστημι, κτάομαι, μιμνήσκω and πίπτω – though their verb stems begin with two consonants that are not stop + resonant – get reduplications including the initial consonant:

ἵσταμαι *come to stand*	verb stem στη-/στᾰ-	pf. ἕστηκα (<*σέστηκα; →1.83).
μιμνήσκω *remind*	verb stem μνη-	pf. mp. μέμνημαι
κτάομαι *acquire*	verb stem κτη-/κτᾰ-	pf. κέκτημαι (also ἔκτημαι)
πίπτω *fall*	verb stem πεσ-/πτ(ω)-	pf. πέπτωκα

– Most verb stems beginning with γν- or γλ- – though their verb stems begin with stop + resonant – get reduplications formed like the augment:

γιγνώσκω *know, recognize*	verb stem γνω-	pf. ἔγνωκα
γνωρίζω *make known*	verb stem γνωρῐδ-	pf. ἐγνώρικα

– A few verb stems beginning with α, ε or ο followed by a single consonant, get a so-called 'Attic' reduplication, by duplicating the vowel and consonant, and lengthening the initial vowel of the verb stem:

ἀκούω *hear*	verb stem ἀκο(υ)(σ)-	pf. ἀκήκοα
ἐγείρομαι *wake up, be woken*	verb stem ἐγερ-/ἐγορ-/ἐγρ-	pf. ἐγήγερμαι, also ἐγρήγορα (note ἐγρ-)
ὄμνυμι *swear*	verb stem ὀμ(ο)-	pf. ὀμώμοκα
with ἔρχομαι *go, come*	verb stem ἐλευθ-/ἐλ(υ)θ-	pf. ἐλήλυθα
with φέρω *carry, bring*	verb stem ἐνεκ-/ἐνοκ-/ἐγκ-	pf. ἐνήνοχα

Reduplications Outside the Perfect

11.49   Various **present stems** show reduplication as well, in this case **with ι**: e.g. γι-γνώσκω *know, recognize* (verb stem γνω-), τί-θημι *put, place* (verb stem θη-/θε-), ἵ-στημι *make stand, set up* (<*σιστ-, →1.83; verb stem στη-/στᾰ-).

11.50   Very few verbs have a form of reduplication in the **aorist**: e.g. with ἄγω *lead, bring*, aor. stem. ἀγαγ- (verb stem ἀγ-), aor. ind. ἤγαγον; with φέρω *carry, bring*, aor. stem. ἐνεγκ- (verb stem ἐγκ-), aor. ind. ἤνεγκον.

The Relative Position of Augments, Reduplications and Prefixes
Basic Rules

11.51   In **compound verbs** that include a prepositional prefix, any augment or reduplication comes **after the prefix**:

προσ-βαίνω *go towards*	impf. προσέβαινον	pf. προσβέβηκα
εἰσ-άγω *lead into*	impf. εἰσῆγον	pf. εἰσῆχα

11.52   Prepositional **prefixes ending in a vowel** drop that vowel before an augment (or reduplication formed like an augment), except in the case of περι- and προ-. When προ- is followed by ε, this may contract to προὐ- (by crasis, →1.43–5; also sometimes printed πρου- without coronis):

ἀνα-βαίνω *go up*	impf. ἀνέβαινον	
ἐπι-βαίνω *approach*	impf. ἐπέβαινον	
ἀπο-στερέω *rob*	aor. ind. ἀπεστέρησα	pf. ind. ἀπεστέρηκα
δια-στρέφομαι *be distorted*	aor. ind. διεστράφην	pf. ind. διέστραμμαι

but:

περι-βαίνω *go around*	impf. περιέβαινον	
προ-σκέπτομαι *consider*	aor. ind. προεσκεψάμην	pf. προέσκεμμαι or
beforehand	or προὐσκεψάμην	προὐσκεμμαι

11.53   Before vowels, and hence before an augment (or reduplication formed like an augment), **ἐκ- becomes ἐξ-** (→1.41):

ἐκ-βαίνω *go away*	impf. ἐξέβαινον	
ἐκ-ρέω *flow out*	aor. ind. ἐξερρύην	pf. ἐξερρύηκα

11.54   Prefixes whose final consonant assimilates to the first sound of the verb stem in unaugmented/unreduplicated forms (→1.90), are used in their **non-assimilated form** before an augment (a reduplication starting with a vowel):

ἐμβαίνω *go onto*	impf. ἐνέβαινον	
ἐγγράφω *write onto*	impf. ἐνέγραφον	
συρρήγνυμαι *break apart*	aor. ind. συνερράγην	pf. ind. συνέρρωγα
συλλέγω *collect*	impf. συνέλεγον	pf. ind. συνείλοχα

11.55   In the **pluperfect**, the augment precedes the stem and thus the reduplication:

παιδεύω *educate*	verb stem παιδευ-	plpf. ἐ-πεπαιδεύκειν (pf. ind. πεπαίδευκα)
θραύω *injure*	verb stem θραυ(σ)-	plpf. pass. ἐ-τεθραύσμην (pf. ind. τέθραυσμαι)

However, if the reduplication is formed like an augment or otherwise starts with a vowel, no extra augment is added in the pluperfect:

ὀρθόω *straighten*	verb stem ὀρθω-/ὀρθο-	plpf. ὠρθώκειν (pf. ind. ὤρθωκα)
στρατηγέω *lead*	verb stem στρατηγη-/ στρατηγε-	plpf. ἐστρατηγήκειν (pf. ind. ἐστρατήγηκα)
λαμβάνω *get, take*	verb stem ληβ-/λᾰβ-	plpf. εἰλήφειν (pf. ind. εἴληφα)

Further Particulars

11.56 Only compound verbs with **prepositional** prefixes get the augment between prefix and stem. Compounds formed from other elements are augmented as normal, e.g. ἀδικέω *act unjustly*, aor. ind. ἠδίκησα; δυστυχέω *be unfortunate*, aor. ind. ἐδυστύχησα. For such verbs, →23.50.

11.57 The verbs **καθεύδω, κάθημαι, καθίζω**, and **ἀμφιέννυμι** are usually treated as if they were not compounds, and thus get their augment/reduplication before the prefix:

κάθ-ημαι *sit*	impf. ἐκαθήμην
καθ-εύδω *sleep*	impf. ἐκάθευδον (but also καθηῦδον)
καθ-ίζω *make sit down, sit down*	impf. ἐκάθιζον (but also κάθιζον)
ἀμφι-έννυμι *envelop*	aor. ind. ἠμφίεσα

The verb **ἐπίσταμαι** is never treated as a compound:

ἐπίσταμαι *know, be able*	impf. ἠπιστάμην

11.58 Some compound verbs take a **double augment**, i.e. both the prefix and the stem are augmented. For instance:

ἀν-έχομαι *endure*	impf. ἠνειχόμην, aor. ἠνεσχόμην
ἀμφι-γνοέω *be doubtful*	impf. ἠμφεγνόουν, aor. ἠμφεγνόησα
ἀμφισ-βητέω *disagree, dispute*	impf. ἠμφεσβήτουν, aor. ἠμφεσβήτησα

12

The Present

Thematic (-ω) and Athematic (-μι) Presents

12.1　Forms built on the present stem follow either a **thematic** or an **athematic** conjugation.

- The **thematic** conjugation, comprising all verbs in -**ω**, is much more common. With these verbs, a thematic vowel (ε/ο) stands between the present stem and the endings: e.g. 1 pl. act. ind. παιδεύ-ο-μεν, 2 pl. παιδεύ-ε-τε.
- The **athematic** conjugation comprises all verbs ending in -**μι**. The endings follow immediately on the present stem (apart from some exceptions detailed below): e.g. 1 pl. act. ind. δείκνυ-μεν, 2 pl. δείκνυ-τε.

12.2　Apart from the thematic vowel, there are two important points of distinction between thematic and athematic presents:

- **Endings**: the endings of thematic and athematic presents differ:

  in the present indicative singular: thematic (including thematic vowels) -ω, -εις, -ει, athematic -μι, -ς, -σῐ(ν);

  in the present third person plural: thematic (including thematic vowel) -ουσι(ν) (<*-ονσῐ(ν), →11.27), athematic -ᾱσῐ(ν);

  in the imperfect third person plural: thematic -ν, athematic: -σαν;

  and in the active infinitive: thematic (including thematic vowel) -ειν (= -ēν <*-ε-εν, →11.31), athematic -ναι.

  Contrast e.g. 2 sg. pres. act. ind. παιδεύεις (thematic) with δείκνυς (athematic); pres. act. inf. παιδεύειν (thematic) with δεικνύναι (athematic).

- **Variation of vowel length in the stem**: athematic presents use a stem with a long vowel in the singular of the present active indicative, the singular of the imperfect active, and in the subjunctive, but a stem with a short vowel elsewhere. Contrast e.g. 1 sg./pl. act. ind. λύω/λύομεν (thematic) with δείκνῡμι/δείκνῠμεν (athematic). For details, →12.37–8.

The Thematic Present

Overview of Forms

12.3 **Active** forms:

			verbs in -ω	contract verbs					
				verbs in -έω		verbs in -άω		verbs in -όω	
			παιδεύω *educate*	ποιέω *make, do*		τιμάω *honour*		δηλόω *make clear*	
prim.	sg.	1	παιδεύω	ποιῶ	(<έω)	τιμῶ	(<άω)	δηλῶ	(<όω)
ind.		2	παιδεύεις	ποιεῖς	(<έεις)	τιμᾷς	(<άεις)	δηλοῖς	(<όεις)
(pres.)		3	παιδεύει	ποιεῖ	(<έει)	τιμᾷ	(<άει)	δηλοῖ	(<όει)
	pl.	1	παιδεύομεν	ποιοῦμεν	(<έομεν)	τιμῶμεν	(<άομεν)	δηλοῦμεν	(<όομεν)
		2	παιδεύετε	ποιεῖτε	(<έετε)	τιμᾶτε	(<άετε)	δηλοῦτε	(<όετε)
		3	παιδεύουσι(ν)	ποιοῦσι(ν)	(<έοσι)	τιμῶσι(ν)	(<άοσι)	δηλοῦσι(ν)	(<όοσι)
sec.	sg.	1	ἐπαίδευον	ἐποίουν	(<εον)	ἐτίμων	(<αον)	ἐδήλουν	(<οον)
ind.		2	ἐπαίδευες	ἐποίεις	(<εες)	ἐτίμας	(<αες)	ἐδήλους	(<οες)
(impf.)		3	ἐπαίδευε(ν)	ἐποίει	(<εε)	ἐτίμα	(<αε)	ἐδήλου	(<οε)
	pl.	1	ἐπαιδεύομεν	ἐποιοῦμεν	(<έομεν)	ἐτιμῶμεν	(<άομεν)	ἐδηλοῦμεν	(<όομεν)
		2	ἐπαιδεύετε	ἐποιεῖτε	(<έετε)	ἐτιμᾶτε	(<άετε)	ἐδηλοῦτε	(<όετε)
		3	ἐπαίδευον	ἐποίουν	(<εον)	ἐτίμων	(<αον)	ἐδήλουν	(<οον)
subj.	sg.	1	παιδεύω	ποιῶ	(<έω)	τιμῶ	(<άω)	δηλῶ	(<όω)
		2	παιδεύῃς	ποιῇς	(<έῃς)	τιμᾷς	(<άῃς)	δηλοῖς	(<όῃς)
		3	παιδεύῃ	ποιῇ	(<έῃ)	τιμᾷ	(<άῃ)	δηλοῖ	(<όῃ)
	pl.	1	παιδεύωμεν	ποιῶμεν	(<έωμεν)	τιμῶμεν	(<άωμεν)	δηλῶμεν	(<όωμεν)
		2	παιδεύητε	ποιῆτε	(<έητε)	τιμᾶτε	(<άητε)	δηλῶτε	(<όητε)
		3	παιδεύωσι(ν)	ποιῶσι(ν)	(<έωσι)	τιμῶσι(ν)	(<άωσι)	δηλῶσι(ν)	(<όωσι)
opt.	sg.	1	παιδεύοιμι	ποιοίην[1]	(<εοίην)	τιμῴην[1]	(<αοίην)	δηλοίην[1]	(<οοίην)
		2	παιδεύοις	ποιοίης[1]	(<εοίης)	τιμῴης[1]	(<αοίης)	δηλοίης[1]	(<οοίης)
		3	παιδεύοι	ποιοίη[1]	(<εοίη)	τιμῴη[1]	(<αοίη)	δηλοίη[1]	(<οοίη)
	pl.	1	παιδεύοιμεν	ποιοῖμεν[2]	(<έοιμεν)	τιμῷμεν[2]	(<άοιμεν)	δηλοῖμεν[2]	(<όοιμεν)
		2	παιδεύοιτε	ποιοῖτε[2]	(<έοιτε)	τιμῷτε[2]	(<άοιτε)	δηλοῖτε[2]	(<όοιτε)
		3	παιδεύοιεν	ποιοῖεν	(<έοιεν)	τιμῷεν	(<άοιεν)	δηλοῖεν	(<όοιεν)
imp.	sg.	2	παίδευε	ποίει	(<εε)	τίμα	(<αε)	δήλου	(<οε)
		3	παιδευέτω	ποιείτω	(<εέτω)	τιμάτω	(<αέτω)	δηλούτω	(<οέτω)
	pl.	2	παιδεύετε	ποιεῖτε	(<έετε)	τιμᾶτε	(<άετε)	δηλοῦτε	(<όετε)
		3	παιδευόντων	ποιούντων	(<εόντων)	τιμώντων	(<αόντων)	δηλούντων	(<οόντων)
inf.			παιδεύειν	ποιεῖν	(<έεν)	τιμᾶν	(<άεν)	δηλοῦν	(<όεν)
ppl.	masc.		παιδεύων, -οντος	ποιῶν, -οῦντος	(<έων)	τιμῶν, -ῶντος	(<άων)	δηλῶν, -οῦντος	(<όων)
	fem.		παιδεύουσα, -σης	ποιοῦσα, -σης	(<έοσα)	τιμῶσα, -σης	(<άοσα)	δηλοῦσα, -σης	(<όοσα)
	neut.		παιδεῦον, -οντος	ποιοῦν, -οῦντος	(<έον)	τιμῶν, -ῶντος	(<άον)	δηλοῦν, -οῦντος	(<όον)

[1] Also ποιοῖμι/ποιοῖς/ποιοῖ; τιμῷμι/τιμῷς/τιμῷ; δηλοῖμι/δηλοῖς/δηλοῖ.

[2] Also ποιοίημεν/ποιοίητε; τιμῴημεν/τιμῴητε; δηλοίημεν/δηλοίητε.

12.4   **Middle-passive** forms:

			verbs in -ω	contract verbs		
				verbs in -έω	verbs in -άω	verbs in -όω
			παιδεύω *educate*	ποιέω *make, do*	τιμάω *honour*	δηλόω *make clear*
prim.	sg.	1	παιδεύομαι	ποιοῦμαι (<έομαι)	τιμῶμαι (<άομαι)	δηλοῦμαι (<όομαι)
ind.		2	παιδεύῃ/ει[1] (<*-ε(σ)αι)	ποιῇ/εῖ[1] (<έῃ/έει)	τιμᾷ (<άῃ)	δηλοῖ (<όῃ)
(pres.)		3	παιδεύεται	ποιεῖται (<έεται)	τιμᾶται (<άεται)	δηλοῦται (<όεται)
	pl.	1	παιδευόμεθα	ποιούμεθα (<εόμεθα)	τιμώμεθα (<αόμεθα)	δηλούμεθα (<οόμεθα)
		2	παιδεύεσθε	ποιεῖσθε (<έεσθε)	τιμᾶσθε (<άεσθε)	δηλοῦσθε (<όεσθε)
		3	παιδεύονται	ποιοῦνται (<έονται)	τιμῶνται (<άονται)	δηλοῦνται (<όονται)
sec.	sg.	1	ἐπαιδευόμην	ἐποιούμην (<εόμην)	ἐτιμώμην (<αόμην)	ἐδηλούμην (<οόμην)
ind.		2	ἐπαιδεύου (<*-ε(σ)ο)	ἐποιοῦ (<έο)	ἐτιμῶ (<άο)	ἐδηλοῦ (<όο)
(impf.)		3	ἐπαιδεύετο	ἐποιεῖτο (<έετο)	ἐτιμᾶτο (<άετο)	ἐδηλοῦτο (<όετο)
	pl.	1	ἐπαιδευόμεθα	ἐποιούμεθα (<εόμεθα)	ἐτιμώμεθα (<αόμεθα)	ἐδηλούμεθα (<οόμεθα)
		2	ἐπαιδεύεσθε	ἐποιεῖσθε (<έεσθε)	ἐτιμᾶσθε (<άεσθε)	ἐδηλοῦσθε (<όεσθε)
		3	ἐπαιδεύοντο	ἐποιοῦντο (<έοντο)	ἐτιμῶντο (<άοντο)	ἐδηλοῦντο (<όοντο)
subj.	sg.	1	παιδεύωμαι	ποιῶμαι (<έωμαι)	τιμῶμαι (<άωμαι)	δηλῶμαι (<όωμαι)
		2	παιδεύῃ (<*-η(σ)αι)	ποιῇ (<έῃ)	τιμᾷ (<άῃ)	δηλοῖ (<όῃ)
		3	παιδεύηται	ποιῆται (<έηται)	τιμᾶται (<άηται)	δηλῶται (<όηται)
	pl.	1	παιδευώμεθα	ποιώμεθα (<εώμεθα)	τιμώμεθα (<αώμεθα)	δηλώμεθα (<οώμεθα)
		2	παιδεύησθε	ποιῆσθε (<έησθε)	τιμᾶσθε (<άησθε)	δηλῶσθε (<όησθε)
		3	παιδεύωνται	ποιῶνται (<έωνται)	τιμῶνται (<άωνται)	δηλῶνται (<όωνται)
opt.	sg.	1	παιδευοίμην	ποιοίμην (<εοίμην)	τιμῴμην (<αοίμην)	δηλοίμην (<οοίμην)
		2	παιδεύοιο (<*-οι(σ)ο)	ποιοῖο (<έοιο)	τιμῷο (<άοιο)	δηλοῖο (<όοιο)
		3	παιδεύοιτο	ποιοῖτο (<έοιτο)	τιμῷτο (<άοιτο)	δηλοῖτο (<όοιτο)
	pl.	1	παιδευοίμεθα	ποιοίμεθα (<εοίμεθα)	τιμῴμεθα (<αοίμεθα)	δηλοίμεθα (<οοίμεθα)
		2	παιδεύοισθε	ποιοῖσθε (<έοισθε)	τιμῷσθε (<άοισθε)	δηλοῖσθε (<όοισθε)
		3	παιδεύοιντο	ποιοῖντο (<έοιντο)	τιμῷντο (<άοιντο)	δηλοῖντο (<όοιντο)
imp.	sg.	2	παιδεύου (<*-ε(σ)ο)	ποιοῦ (<έο)	τιμῶ (<άο)	δηλοῦ (<όο)
		3	παιδευέσθω	ποιείσθω (<εέσθω)	τιμάσθω (<αέσθω)	δηλούσθω (<οέσθω)
	pl.	2	παιδεύεσθε	ποιεῖσθε (<έεσθε)	τιμᾶσθε (<άεσθε)	δηλοῦσθε (<όεσθε)
		3	παιδευέσθων	ποιείσθων (<εέσθων)	τιμάσθων (<αέσθων)	δηλούσθων (<οέσθων)
inf.			παιδεύεσθαι	ποιεῖσθαι (<έεσθαι)	τιμᾶσθαι (<άεσθαι)	δηλοῦσθαι (<όεσθαι)
ppl.	masc.		παιδευόμενος	ποιούμενος (<εόμενος)	τιμώμενος (<αόμενος)	δηλούμενος (<οόμενος)
	fem.		παιδευομένη	ποιουμένη (<εομένη)	τιμωμένη (<αομένη)	δηλουμένη (<οομένη)
	neut.		παιδευόμενον	ποιούμενον (<εόμενον)	τιμώμενον (<αόμενον)	δηλούμενον (<οόμενον)

[1]   For the ending of the 2 sg. pres. ind. (-η/-ει), →12.7 n.1 below.

Non-Contract and Contract Presents

12.5   Two types of thematic conjugation can be distinguished, depending on the ending of the present stem:

- Present stems **ending in ι, υ, a diphthong or a consonant**, e.g. χρίω *anoint*, λύω *loosen, release*, παιδεύω *educate*, λέγω *say, speak*. The thematic vowel and endings follow on the stem.

- Present stems **ending in other vowels** (typically ε, α, ο), e.g. ποιέ-ω *make, do*, τιμά-ω *honour*, δηλό-ω *make clear*. The thematic vowel and endings contract with the final vowel of the stem: ποιῶ, τιμῶ, δηλῶ. These are called **contract(ed) verbs**.

Endings

12.6   The endings of thematic present-stem forms are listed in 11.20–33. The forms are built as follows.

12.7   **Present indicative**: formed with primary endings: e.g. 1 sg. act. παιδεύ-ω, 2 sg. παιδεύ-εις; 1 sg. mp. παιδεύ-ο-μαι.

   Note the contraction in the 2 sg. mp., e.g. παιδεύῃ/-ει (<*-ε-(σ)αι), and compensatory lengthening in the 3 pl. act., e.g. παιδεύουσι(ν) (= -ōσιν <*-ο-(ν)σιν).

Note 1: The older (and, given the rules of contraction (→1.58–66), expected) form of the 2 sg. mp. is παιδεύῃ <*παιδεύ-ε-(σ)αι. But from the fourth century onwards, the pronunciation of η and ει approximated each other and both were in use. Modern editors differ in what they print. However, both in modern editions and in ancient sources, it is nearly always βούλει *you want*, οἴει *you think* and δέει *you need* (for the last form, also →12.17).

12.8   **Imperfect**: formed with the augment, and with secondary endings: e.g. 1 sg. act. ἐ-παίδευ-ο-ν, 2 sg. ἐ-παίδευ-ε-ς; 1 sg. mp. ἐ-παιδευ-ό-μην. Note the contraction in the 2 sg. mp., e.g. ἐπαιδεύου (= -ō<*-ε-(σ)ο).

12.9   **Imperative**: the 2 sg. act. has no ending after the thematic vowel: e.g. παίδευ-ε. Note the 2 sg. mp., e.g. παιδεύου (= -ō<*-ε-(σ)ο).

12.10   **Subjunctive**: formed with the long thematic vowel of the subjunctive and primary endings, e.g. 1 pl. act. παιδεύ-ω-μεν, 1 sg. mp. παιδεύ-ω-μαι.

12.11   **Optative**: formed with the optative suffix -ι-/-ιη- and (mostly) secondary endings, e.g. 2 sg. act. παιδεύ-οι-ς, 3 pl. mp. παιδεύ-οι-ντο. Note the 2 sg. mp., e.g. παιδεύοιο (<*-οι-(σ)ο).

12.12   **Active infinitive**: formed with -εν, which contracts with the preceding thematic vowel, e.g. act. παιδεύ-ειν (<*-ε-εν).

   Middle-passive infinitive: formed with -σθαι, e.g. παιδεύ-ε-σθαι.

12.13   **Active participle**: formed with -ντ-; for the declension, →5.17–18. E.g. gen. sg. masc. παιδεύ-ο-ντ-ος, nom. sg. fem. παιδεύ-ουσα (<*-οντγα).

   Middle-passive participle: formed with -μεν-; for the declension, →5.3–4. E.g. nom. sg. masc. παιδευ-ό-μεν-ος, nom. sg. fem. παιδευ-ο-μέν-η.

12.14   The verb οἴομαι *think* is regularly thematic, but has some forms without the thematic vowel, particularly 1 sg. pres. ind. οἶμαι and 1 sg. impf. ᾤμην.

Contract Presents

Simple Contraction Rules

12.15   The relevant contraction rules for each type of contract verb may be summarized as follows (for a more elaborate treatment of contraction, →1.58–63):

- with present stems ending in **ε**:

ε + ε/ε̄ > ει (spurious, = ε̄)
ε + ο/ō > ου (spurious, = ō)
ε + any other long vowel or diphthong: ε merges with (disappears into) the long
vowel/diphthong

- with present stems ending in **α**:

α + [e]-sound (ε/ε̄/η) > ᾱ
α + (genuine) ει or η > ᾳ
α + [o]-sound (ο/ō/ω) > ω
α + οι > ῳ

- with present stems ending in **ο**:

ο + ε/ε̄ or ο/ō > ου (spurious, = ō)
ο + η/ω > ω
ο + (genuine) ει, η or οι > οι

Note 1: Ionic forms of verbs in -έω often do not contract; verbs in -άω are conjugated in
various forms as verbs in -έω. For full details, →25.33–5.

12.16   The following points should be noted especially:

- Since no ι or υ was involved in the formation of **spurious diphthongs ει and ου**
(→1.23) in such forms as inf. act. παιδεύειν (<-ε-εν), 2 sg. imp. mp. παιδεύου
(<-ε-σο), fem. ppl. act. παιδεύουσα (<*-ο-ντγα), corresponding forms of the
contract verbs also do not have diphthongs with ι/υ (also →1.60, 1.62 n.2): thus
e.g. inf. τιμᾶν (<-α-ε-εν), δηλοῦν (spurious ου; <-ο-ε-εν); imp. τιμῶ (<-α-ε-σο);
ppl. ποιοῦσα (spurious ου; <*-έ-ο-ντγα), τιμῶσα (<*-ά-ο-ντγα). But 2/3 sg. pres.
ind. act. παιδεύεις and παιδεύει have genuine diphthongs, and corresponding
contract verb forms also have a genuine diphthong (e.g. τιμᾷς, δηλοῖ).
- The **active optative singular** of contract verbs usually has different endings
from those of the non-contract verbs, formed with optative suffix -ιη-. But next
to ποιοίην/ποιοίης/ποιοίη we occasionally find ποιοῖμι, ποιοῖς, ποιοῖ; next to
τιμῴην/τιμῴης/τιμῴη occasionally τιμῷμι/τιμῷς/τιμῷ; next to δηλοίην/δηλοίης/
δηλοίη occasionally δηλοῖμι/δηλοῖς/δηλοῖ.
- The **active optative plural** of contract verbs usually has the same endings as those of
the non-contract verbs. But occasionally we find forms with -ιη- in the first
and second person. Thus next to ποιοῖμεν/ποιοῖτε we find ποιοίημεν/ποιοίητε;
next to τιμῷμεν/τιμῷτε, we find τιμῴημεν/τιμῴητε; and next to δηλοῖμεν/δηλοῖτε
we find δηλοίημεν/δηλοίητε.

Further Particulars

12.17   Most verbs with a **monosyllabic stem in ε** (originally in εϝ, →12.25 below) only contract if the
result is ει: So, with πλέω *sail* (<*πλέϝω), pres. ind. πλέ̱ω, πλεῖς, πλεῖ, πλέ̱ομεν, πλεῖτε, πλέ̱ουσι
(ν); impf. ἔπλε̱ον, ἔπλεις, etc.; subj. πλέ̱ω, πλέῃς, etc.; opt. πλέ̱οιμι, πλέ̱οις (forms with -ιη- do not

occur); inf. πλεῖν; part. πλέων, πλέουσα, πλέον. Similarly conjugated are e.g. πνέω *blow*, ῥέω *flow*, χέω *pour* and δέω *lack*, its middle δέομαι *ask, need* (note the 2nd person singular middle δέει) and impersonal δεῖ *it is necessary* (imperfect: ἔδει; participle: δέον).

However, this conjugation is not followed by δέω *bind* (<*δέ-γω), which contracts regularly like ποιέω.

12.18   The verbs **κάω** (older καίω) *set on fire* and **κλάω** (older κλαίω) *cry, weep* do not contract (→12.29).

12.19   There is a small number of verbs whose **stem ends in η**: ζήω *live*, διψήω *be thirsty*, πεινήω *be hungry*, χρήομαι *use, need*. These verbs follow the conjugation of τιμάω, except for the following contraction rule: η + [e]-sound > η

The paradigm is as follows:

			verbs in -ήω/-ήομαι			
			active		middle-passive	
			διψήω *be thirsty*		χρήομαι *use, need*	
prim.	sg.	1	διψῶ	(<ή-ω)	χρῶμαι	(<ή-ομαι)
ind.		2	διψῆς	(<ή-εις)	χρῇ	(<ή-η)
(pres.)		3	διψῇ	(<ή-ει)	χρῆται	(<ή-εται)
	pl.	1	διψῶμεν	(<ή-ομεν)	χρώμεθα	(<ή-όμεθα)
		2	διψῆτε	(<ή-ετε)	χρῆσθε	(<ή-εσθε)
		3	διψῶσι(ν)	(<ή-όσιν)	χρῶνται	(<ή-ονται)
sec.	sg.	1	ἐδίψων	(<η-ον)	ἐχρώμην	(<ή-ομην)
ind.		2	ἐδίψης	(<η-ες)	ἐχρῶ	(<ή-ō)
(impf.)		3	ἐδίψη	(<η-ε)	ἐχρῆτο	(<ή-ετο)
	pl.	1	ἐδιψῶμεν	(<ή-ομεν)	ἐχρώμεθα	(<ή-όμεθα)
		2	ἐδιψῆτε	(<ή-ετε)	ἐχρῆσθε	(<ή-εσθε)
		3	ἐδίψων	(<η-ον)	ἐχρῶντο	(<ή-οντο)
subj.	sg.	1	διψῶ	(<ή-ω)	χρῶμαι	(<ή-ωμαι)
		2	διψῆς	(<ή-ης)	χρῇ	(<ή-η)
		3	διψῇ	(<ή-η)	χρῆται	(<ή-ηται)
	pl.	1	διψῶμεν	(<ή-ωμεν)	χρώμεθα	(<η-ώμεθα)
		2	διψῆτε	(<ή-ητε)	χρῆσθε	(<η-ησθε)
		3	διψῶσι(ν)	(<ή-ωσι)	χρῶνται	(<ή-ωνται)
opt.	sg.	1	διψῴην	(<η-οίην)	χρῴμην	(<η-οίμην)
		2	διψῴης	(<η-οίης)	χρῷο	(<ή-οιο)
		3	διψῴη	(<η-οίη)	χρῷτο	(<ή-οιτο)
	pl.	1	διψῷμεν	(<ή-οιμεν)	χρῴμεθα	(<η-οίμεθα)
		2	διψῷτε	(<ή-οιτε)	χρῷσθε	(<ή-οισθε)
		3	διψῷεν	(<ή-οιεν)	χρῷντο	(<ή-οιντο)
imp.	sg.	2	δίψη	(<η-ε)	χρῶ	(<ή-ō)
		3	διψήτω	(<η-έτω)	χρήσθω	(<η-έσθω)
	pl.	2	διψῆτε	(<ή-ετε)	χρῆσθε	(<η-εσθε)
		3	διψόντων	(<η-όντων)	χρήσθων	(<η-έσθων)
inf.			διψῆν	(<ή-ε-εν)	χρῆσθαι	(<ή-εσθαι)
ppl.	masc.		διψῶν, -ῶντος	(<ή-ων)	χρώμενος	(<η-όμενος)
	fem.		διψῶσα, -σης	(<ή-όσα)	χρωμένη	(<η-ομένη)
	neut.		διψῶν, -ῶντος	(<ή-ον)	χρώμενον	(<η-όμενον)

12.20   Two verbs have a present stem ending in ω: **ἱδρώω** *sweat* and **ῥιγώω** *shiver*. These verbs contract to ω (or ῳ) throughout their conjugation: e.g. 3 sg. act. subj. ῥιγῷ (<-ώ-η), act. inf. ῥιγῶν (<-ώ-ε-εν), dat. sg. masc. ppl. pres. act. ἱδρῶντι (<-ώ-οντι). We also find forms of these verbs, however, which are conjugated in the same way as -όω verbs, and manuscripts sometimes vary (and ῥιγέω *shiver* also occurs).

12.21   In Attic, the verb **λούω** *wash*, *bathe*, deriving from *λοϝέω, behaves sometimes like an uncontracted verb (e.g. λούει, λούειν, λουόμενοι, λούεσθαι), but in other cases, especially in earlier authors, shows contraction (e.g. ἐλοῦμεν, λοῦται, λοῦσθαι, λούμενος).

Thematic Present Stem Formation

12.22   Basic points on the formation of thematic present stems are given in the sections that follow. The formation of athematic present stems is treated separately, →12.39–44. For further details on present stem formation, →23.41–51.

12.23   In general, a distinction may be made between verbs whose present stem is unelaborated (i.e. identical to (a variant of) the verb stem), and verbs whose present stem is formed by the addition of one or more suffixes to the verb stem:

   – **unelaborated present stems**: e.g. παιδεύω *educate* (verb stem παιδευ-), γράφω *write* (verb stem γραφ-), etc.
   – **present stems with elaborations**: e.g. φυλάττω *guard* (verb stem φυλακ-), γιγνώσκω *recognize* (verb stem γνω-).

Note 1: Present stems formed with elaborations are sometimes called 'characterized presents' (the present stem is characterized by one or more additions to the verb stem). The present stem of such verbs often differs significantly from *all* other tense-aspect stems of a verb. Being aware of the most common elaborations makes it possible to derive the verb stem, and hence other tense-aspect stems, systematically from the dictionary form (i.e. from the present stem) of a verb.

Presents without Elaboration

12.24   With several verbs, the thematic present stem is simply **identical to (a variant of) the verb stem**. Some examples:

verb	verb stem
γράφω *write*	γρᾰφ-
δέρω *skin*	δερ-/δᾰρ-
διώκω *pursue*	διωκ-
λέγω *say, speak*	λεγ-/λογ-, εἰπ-, ἐρ-/ῥη-
λύω *loosen, release*	λῡ-/λῠ-
παιδεύω *educate*	παιδευ-
πέμπω *send*	πεμπ-/πομπ-
πείθω *persuade*	πειθ-/ποιθ-/πῑθ-
τρίβω *rub*	τρῑβ-/τρῐβ-
ψεύδω *cheat*	ψευδ-

Note 1: Most, but not all of these examples can be described as 'primitive verbs', meaning that the verb stem is itself an unelaborated verbal root: for details on this, →23.2 with n.3.

12.25   With a few other verbs, the present stem is identical to the (original) verb stem, but part of that verb stem is no longer visible in the present conjugation due to sound changes. This holds especially for verbs whose verb stem ended originally in σ or ϝ, both of which disappeared (→1.74–84) in the present stem, but are often visible in other tense-aspect stems of the verb. Some examples:

verb		compare
σείω *shake*	<*σείσ-ω	aor. pass. ἐσείσθην; σεισμός *earthquake*
πλέω *sail*	<*πλέϝ-ω	aor. ἔπλευσα
πνέω *blow*	<*πνέϝ-ω	aor. ἔπνευσα

Note 1: For the effect of the lost ϝ on the conjugation of πλέω, →12.17 above.

Presents with an Original Yod

12.26   To a very large number of verb stems a **yod** (→1.31) was originally added to form the thematic present stem. This yod has in many cases left traces in the present stem.

12.27   Verb stems ending in a **stop**:

– Verb stems ending in a **voiceless velar or dental stop** (κ, χ, τ, θ) have a present stem in **ττ** (σσ in Ionic, Koine, tragedy, Thucydides, etc.):

verb (present stem)	verb stem + yod	compare
φυλάττω *guard*	<*φυλάκ-yω	aor. ἐφύλαξα; φυλακή *watch*
ταράττω *confuse*	<*ταράχ-yω	aor. ἐτάραξα; ταραχή *confusion*
ἐρέττω *row*	<*ἐρέτ-yω	ἐρέτης *rower*
πλάττω *mould*	<*πλάθ-yω	κοροπλάθος *doll-maker*

– Verb stems ending in a **voiced velar or dental stop** (γ, δ) have a present stem in ζ:

οἰμώζω *lament*	<*οἰμώγ-yω	οἰμωγή *lament*
ἐλπίζω *hope, expect*	<*ἐλπίδ-yω	ἐλπίς, gen. ἐλπίδος *hope, expectation*

– Verb stems ending in a **labial** (π, φ, β), have a present stem in **ττ**. Some examples:

τύπτω *hit*	<*τύπ-yω	aor. ἔτυπον(/ἔτυψα)
κρύπτω *hide*	<*κρύφ-yω	κρυφῇ *secretly*
βλάπτω *harm, damage*	<*βλάβ-yω	βλάβη *damage*

Note 1: A few verb stems in γ do not get ζ, but ττ: for example πράττω *do, act* <*πράγ-yω (cf. pf. πέπραγα), and τάττω *array, appoint* (<*τάγ-yω, cf. ταγός *commander*). This is probably due to analogy with stems ending in voiceless velar stops (κ, χ).

Note 2: Verbs with a stem in γγ also often get a stem in ζ, e.g. κλάζω *scream* <*κλάγγ-yω (cf. fut. κλάγξω), σαλπίζω *sound the trumpet* <*σαλπίγγ-yω (cf. ἡ σάλπιγξ *trumpet*, gen. σάλπιγγος). But note φθέγγομαι *make a sound* (stem φθεγγ-), not formed with yod.

Note 3: The suffixes -ίζω/-άζω became productive in their own right (→23.48), and therefore occur often: for example, ὁπλ-ίζω *arm*, ἀναγκ-άζω *force*, ἐργ-άζομαι *work, perform*.

12.28   Verb stems ending in a **resonant**:

– Verb stems ending in **λ** have a present stem in **λλ**:

verb (present stem)	verb stem + yod	compare
ἀγγέλλω *report*	<*ἀγγέλ-yω	fut. ἀγγελῶ
βάλλω *throw, hit*	<*βάλ-yω	aor. ἔ-βαλ-ον

– Yod-presents whose verb stem ends in **ν/ρ** behave differently depending on the vowel in front of the resonant. The following rules apply (also →1.78):

-ἄνyω > **-αίνω**; -ἄρyω > **-αίρω**;

-ένyω > **-είνω**; -έρyω> **-είρω**;

-ῐνyω > **-ῑνω**; -ῐρyω > **-ῑρω**;

-ῠνyω > **-ῡνω**; -ῠρyω > **-ῡρω**

Examples:

verb (present stem)	verb stem + yod	compare
φαίνω *show*	<*φάν-yω	fut. φανῶ
καθαίρω *cleanse*	<*καθάρ-yω	fut. καθᾱρῶ
τείνω *stretch, tighten*	<*τέν-yω	fut. τενῶ; adjective ἀτενής *tight*
σπείρω *sow*	<*σπέρ-yω	σπέρμα *seed*
κρίνω *judge*	<*κρίν-yω	fut. κρῐνῶ
οἰκτίρω *pity*	<*οἰκτίρ-yω	fut. οἰκτῑρῶ
ἀμύνω *defend*	<*ἀμύν-yω	fut. ἀμῡνῶ
φύρω *mix*	<*φύρ-yω	φύρδην *mingled up*

12.29   Most verbs whose **present stem ends in a vowel** (i.e. contract verbs) also belong to the yod-presents. In this case yod simply disappeared, paving the way for contraction. For example: τιμά-ω *honour* <*τιμά-yω; ποιέ-ω *do, make* <*ποιϝέ-yω.

Note 1: With several such verbs, it is not only yod which has disappeared, but also σ or ϝ. These may again be visible in other tense-aspect stems (cf. πλέω, →12.25), and may result in other peculiarities in the conjugation. For instance:

γελάω *laugh*	<*γελάσ-yω	epic aor. ἐγέλασσα, fut. γελάσομαι
τελέω *finish*	<*τελέσ-yω	aor. pass. ἐτελέσθην, epic aor. ἐτέλεσσα
αἰδέομαι *be ashamed*	<*αἰδέσ-yομαι	pf. mp. ᾔδεσμαι, epic fut. αἰδέσσομαι
κάω *set on fire*	<*κάϝ-yω	aor. ἔκαυσα, pf. κέκαυκα

To κάω compare κλάω *cry, weep*; these verbs also have the form καίω/κλαίω. Note that they do not contract (→12.18 above).

Note 2: With some other verbs, the vowel *is* the elaboration. For example, δοκέω may be analysed as δοκ-έ-ω (cf. aor. ἔδοξα).

Note 3: Many new verbs in -έω were formed after the disappearance of yod: →23.44, 23.50; their conjugation is identical to older -έω verbs (the conjugation of the -άω, -έω and -όω types was strongly regularized).

Presents with a Nasal Infix

12.30 Numerous present stems were formed with a **nasal infix** (-ν-/-αν-/-ν-αν-):

verb (present stem)	verb stem	compare
τέμ-<u>ν</u>-ω *cut*	<u>τεμ</u>-/τμη-	aor. ἔ-τεμ-ον
αὐξ-<u>άν</u>-ω *increase*	αὐξ-	fut. αὐξ-ήσω
ὀφλ-ισκ-<u>άν</u>-ω *become a debtor*	ὀφλ-	fut. ὀφλ-ήσω
λα-<u>ν</u>-θ-<u>άν</u>-ω *go unnoticed*	ληθ-/<u>λᾰθ</u>-	aor. ἔ-λαθ-ον
λα-<u>μ</u>-β-<u>άν</u>-ω *take*	ληβ-/<u>λᾰβ</u>-	aor. ἔ-λαβ-ον
λα-<u>γ</u>-χ-<u>άν</u>-ω *acquire by lot*	ληχ-/<u>λᾰχ</u>-	aor. ἔ-λαχ-ον
τυ-<u>γ</u>-χ-<u>άν</u>-ω *hit upon, happen to*	τευχ-/<u>τῠχ</u>-	aor. ἔ-τυχ-ον
also ἐλα-<u>ύ</u>-<u>ν</u>-ω *drive*	ἐλᾰ-	aor. ἤλα-σα

Note 1: For μ/γ in λαμβάνω/λαγχάνω, →1.90.

Note 2: With a few verbs, the nasal suffix is extended to some (but not all) other stems, as if part of the verb stem: e.g. κρίνω *decide, judge* (<*κρί-ν-yω, →12.28 above), aor. ἔκρῑνα (<*ἔ-κρῑν-σα, →13.24), fut. κρῐνῶ (→15.32), but θη-aor. ἐκρίθην, pf. κέκρῐκα, pf. mp. κέκρῐμαι. Similarly κλίνω *cause to lean*, aor. ἔκλῑνα, fut. κλῐνῶ, η-aor. ἐκλίνην, but θη-aor. ἐκλίθην, pf. κέκλῐκα, pf. mp. κέκλῐμαι. Also →18.17, 19.30.

Presents with the Suffix -(ι)σκ-

12.31 A number of presents are formed with the **suffix -(ι)σκ-**:

verb (present stem)	verb stem	compare
εὑρ-<u>ίσκ</u>-ω *find*	εὑρ-	fut. εὑρ-ήσω
ὀφλ-<u>ισκ</u>-άν-ω *become a debtor*	ὀφλ-	fut. ὀφλ-ήσω
γι-γνώ-<u>σκ</u>-ω *recognize*	γνω-	aor. ἔ-γνω-ν
πάσχω *suffer* (<*παθ-<u>σκ</u>-, →1.96)	πενθ-/πονθ-/<u>πᾰθ</u>-	aor. ἔπαθον

Reduplicated Presents

12.32 A number of present stems were formed with a **reduplication**, consisting of the first consonant of the verb stem plus ι:

verb (present stem)	verb stem	compare
<u>γι</u>-γνώσκω *recognize*	γνω-	aor. ἔ-γνω-ν
<u>γί</u>-γνομαι *become*	γεν(η)-/γον-/γν-	aor. ἐ-γεν-όμην
<u>τί</u>-κτω *give birth* (<*τί-τκ-ω)	τεκ-/τοκ-/<u>τκ</u>-	aor. ἔ-τεκ-ον
<u>πί</u>-πτω *fall*	πεσ-/<u>πτ(ω)</u>-	aor. ἔ-πεσ-ον

The Athematic Present

Overview of Forms

Verbs in -νυμι

12.33   Active and middle-passive forms:

			verbs in - νυμι	
			δείκνῡμι *show* stem δεικνῡ-/δεικνῠ-	
			active	middle-passive
prim. ind. (pres.)	sg.	1	δείκνῡμι	δείκνῠμαι
		2	δείκνῡς	δείκνῠσαι
		3	δείκνῡσι(ν)	δείκνῡται
	pl.	1	δείκνῠμεν	δεικνῠμεθα
		2	δείκνῠτε	δείκνῠσθε
		3	δεικνῠᾱσι(ν)	δείκνῠνται
sec. ind. (impf.)	sg.	1	ἐδείκνῡν	ἐδεικνῠμην
		2	ἐδείκνῡς	ἐδείκνῠσο
		3	ἐδείκνῡ	ἐδείκνῠτο
	pl.	1	ἐδείκνῠμεν	ἐδεικνῠμεθα
		2	ἐδείκνῠτε	ἐδείκνῠσθε
		3	ἐδείκνῠσαν	ἐδείκνῠντο
subj.	sg.	1	δεικνῠω	δεικνῠωμαι
		2	δεικνῠῃς	δεικνῠῃ
		3	δεικνῠῃ	δεικνῠηται
	pl.	1	δεικνῠωμεν	δεικνῡωμεθα
		2	δεικνῠητε	δεικνῠησθε
		3	δεικνῠωσι(ν)	δεικνῠωνται
opt.	sg.	1	δεικνῠοιμι	δεικνῠοίμην
		2	δεικνῠοις	δεικνῠοιο
		3	δεικνῠοι	δεικνῠοιτο
	pl.	1	δεικνῠοιμεν	δεικνυοίμεθα
		2	δεικνῠοιτε	δεικνῠοισθε
		3	δεικνῠοιεν	δεικνῠοιντο
imp.	sg.	2	δείκνῡ	δείκνῠσο
		3	δεικνῠτω	δεικνῠσθω
	pl.	2	δείκνῠτε	δείκνῠσθε
		3	δεικνῠντων	δεικνῠσθων
inf.			δεικνῠναι	δείκνῠσθαι
ppl.	masc.		δεικνῠς, -νῠντος	δεικνῠμενος
	fem.		δεικνῡσα, -νῠσης	δεικνῡμένη
	neut.		δεικνῠν, -νῠντος	δεικνῠμενον

In the active, some thematic variants occasionally occur (→12.54).

Reduplicated Verbs

12.34 **Active** forms:

			verb stems in η/ᾰ	τίθημι	ἵημι	δίδωμι
			ἵστημι *make stand* stem ἱστη-/ἱστᾰ-	τίθημι *put, place* stem τιθη-/τιθε-	ἵημι *send, let go* stem ἱη-/ἱε-	δίδωμι *give* stem διδω-/διδο-
prim. ind. (pres.)	sg.	1	ἵστημι	τίθημι	ἵημι	δίδωμι
		2	ἵστης	τίθης	ἵης	δίδως
		3	ἵστησι(ν)	τίθησι(ν)	ἵησι(ν)	δίδωσι(ν)
	pl.	1	ἵστᾰμεν	τίθεμεν	ἵεμεν	δίδομεν
		2	ἵστᾰτε	τίθετε	ἵετε	δίδοτε
		3	ἱστᾶσι(ν) (<-ᾰᾰσιν)	τιθέᾶσι(ν)	ἱᾶσι(ν) (<-έᾶσιν)	διδόᾶσι(ν)
sec. ind. (impf.)	sg.	1	ἵστην	ἐτίθην	ἵειν	ἐδίδουν
		2	ἵστης	ἐτίθεις	ἵεις	ἐδίδους
		3	ἵστη	ἐτίθει	ἵει	ἐδίδου
	pl.	1	ἵστᾰμεν	ἐτίθεμεν	ἵεμεν	ἐδίδομεν
		2	ἵστᾰτε	ἐτίθετε	ἵετε	ἐδίδοτε
		3	ἵστᾰσαν	ἐτίθεσαν	ἵεσαν	ἐδίδοσαν
subj.	sg.	1	ἱστῶ	τιθῶ	ἱῶ	διδῶ
		2	ἱστῇς	τιθῇς	ἱῇς	διδῷς
		3	ἱστῇ	τιθῇ	ἱῇ	διδῷ
	pl.	1	ἱστῶμεν	τιθῶμεν	ἱῶμεν	διδῶμεν
		2	ἱστῆτε	τιθῆτε	ἱῆτε	διδῶτε
		3	ἱστῶσι(ν)	τιθῶσι(ν)	ἱῶσι(ν)	διδῶσι(ν)
opt.	sg.	1	ἱσταίην	τιθείην	ἱείην	διδοίην
		2	ἱσταίης	τιθείης	ἱείης	διδοίης
		3	ἱσταίη	τιθείη	ἱείη	διδοίη
	pl.	1	ἱσταῖμεν	τιθεῖμεν	ἱεῖμεν	διδοῖμεν
		2	ἱσταῖτε	τιθεῖτε	ἱεῖτε	διδοῖτε
		3	ἱσταῖεν	τιθεῖεν	ἱεῖεν	διδοῖεν
imp.	sg.	2	ἵστη	τίθει	ἵει	δίδου
		3	ἱστάτω	τιθέτω	ἱέτω	διδότω
	pl.	2	ἵστατε	τίθετε	ἵετε	δίδοτε
		3	ἱστάντων	τιθέντων	ἱέντων	διδόντων
inf.			ἱστάναι	τιθέναι	ἱέναι	διδόναι
ppl.	masc.		ἱστάς, -άντος	τιθείς, -έντος	ἱείς, -έντος	διδούς, -όντος
	fem.		ἱστᾶσα, -σης	τιθεῖσα, -σης	ἱεῖσα, -σης	διδοῦσα, -σης
	neut.		ἱστάν, -άντος	τιθέν, -έντος	ἱέν, -έντος	διδόν, -όντος

Some thematic variants occur in the pres. ind.: e.g. τιθεῖς (instead of τίθης), ἱεῖ (instead of ἵησι): →12.55.

12.35   **Middle-passive** forms:

			verb stems in η/ᾰ	τίθημι	ἵημι	δίδωμι
			ἵστημι *make stand*	τίθημι *put, place*	ἵημι *let go*	δίδωμι *give*
			stem ἱστη-/ἱστᾰ-	stem τιθη-/τιθε-	stem ἱη-/ἱε-	stem διδω-/διδο-
prim.	sg.	1	ἵσταμαι	τίθεμαι	ἵεμαι	δίδομαι
ind.		2	ἵστασαι	τίθεσαι	ἵεσαι	δίδοσαι
(pres.)		3	ἵσταται	τίθεται	ἵεται	δίδοται
	pl.	1	ἱστάμεθα	τιθέμεθα	ἱέμεθα	διδόμεθα
		2	ἵστασθε	τίθεσθε	ἵεσθε	δίδοσθε
		3	ἵστανται	τίθενται	ἵενται	δίδονται
sec.	sg.	1	ἱστάμην	ἐτιθέμην	ἱέμην	ἐδιδόμην
ind.		2	ἵστασο	ἐτίθεσο	ἵεσο	ἐδίδοσο
(impf.)		3	ἵστατο	ἐτίθετο	ἵετο	ἐδίδοτο
	pl.	1	ἱστάμεθα	ἐτιθέμεθα	ἱέμεθα	ἐδιδόμεθα
		2	ἵστασθε	ἐτίθεσθε	ἵεσθε	ἐδίδοσθε
		3	ἵσταντο	ἐτίθεντο	ἵεντο	ἐδίδοντο
subj.	sg.	1	ἱστῶμαι	τιθῶμαι	ἱῶμαι	διδῶμαι
		2	ἱστῇ	τιθῇ	ἱῇ	διδῷ
		3	ἱστῆται	τιθῆται	ἱῆται	διδῶται
	pl.	1	ἱστώμεθα	τιθώμεθα	ἱώμεθα	διδώμεθα
		2	ἱστῆσθε	τιθῆσθε	ἱῆσθε	διδῶσθε
		3	ἱστῶνται	τιθῶνται	ἱῶνται	διδῶνται
opt.	sg.	1	ἱσταίμην	τιθείμην	ἱείμην	διδοίμην
		2	ἱσταῖο	τιθεῖο	ἱεῖο	διδοῖο
		3	ἱσταῖτο	τιθεῖτο	ἱεῖτο	διδοῖτο
	pl.	1	ἱσταίμεθα	τιθείμεθα	ἱείμεθα	διδοίμεθα
		2	ἱσταῖσθε	τιθεῖσθε	ἱεῖσθε	διδοῖσθε
		3	ἱσταῖντο	τιθεῖντο	ἱεῖντο	διδοῖντο
imp.	sg.	2	ἵστασο	τίθεσο	ἵεσο	δίδοσο
		3	ἱστάσθω	τιθέσθω	ἱέσθω	διδόσθω
	pl.	2	ἵστασθε	τίθεσθε	ἵεσθε	δίδοσθε
		3	ἱστάσθων	τιθέσθων	ἱέσθων	διδόσθων
inf.			ἵστασθαι	τίθεσθαι	ἵεσθαι	δίδοσθαι
ppl.	masc.		ἱστάμενος	τιθέμενος	ἱέμενος	διδόμενος
	fem.		ἱσταμένη	τιθεμένη	ἱεμένη	διδομένη
	neut.		ἱστάμενον	τιθέμενον	ἱέμενον	διδόμενον

Root Presents

12.36   Forms of **εἰμί** *be*, **εἶμι** *go*, and **φημί** *say*:

			εἰμί *be* stem ἐ(σ)-	**εἶμι** *go* stem εἰ-/ἰ-	**φημί** *say, claim* stem φη-/φᾰ-
prim.	sg.	1	εἰμί	εἶμι	φημί
ind.		2	εἶ	εἶ	φής/φῄς
(pres.)		3	ἐστί(ν)	εἶσι(ν)	φησί(ν)
	pl.	1	ἐσμέν	ἴμεν	φᾰμέν
		2	ἐστέ	ἴτε	φᾰτέ
		3	εἰσί(ν)	ἴᾱσι(ν)	φᾱσί(ν)
sec.	sg.	1	ἦ(ν)	ᾔειν/ᾖα	ἔφην
ind.		2	ἦσθα	ᾔεις/ᾔεισθα	ἔφησθα/ἔφης
(impf.)		3	ἦν	ᾔει(ν)	ἔφη
	pl.	1	ἦμεν	ᾖμεν	ἔφᾰμεν
		2	ἦτε	ᾖτε	ἔφᾰτε
		3	ἦσαν	ᾖσαν/ᾔεσαν	ἔφᾰσαν
subj.	sg.	1	ὦ	ἴω	φῶ
		2	ᾖς	ἴῃς	φῇς
		3	ᾖ	ἴῃ	φῇ
	pl.	1	ὦμεν	ἴωμεν	φῶμεν
		2	ἦτε	ἴητε	φῆτε
		3	ὦσι(ν)	ἴωσι(ν)	φῶσι(ν)
opt.	sg.	1	εἴην	ἰοίην/ἴοιμι	φαίην
		2	εἴης	ἴοις	φαίης
		3	εἴη	ἴοι	φαίη
	pl.	1	εἶμεν/εἴημεν	ἴοιμεν	φαῖμεν/φαίημεν
		2	εἶτε/εἴητε	ἴοιτε	φαίητε
		3	εἶεν/εἴησαν	ἴοιεν	φαῖεν
imp.	sg.	2	ἴσθι	ἴθι	φᾰθι
		3	ἔστω	ἴτω	φᾰτω
	pl.	2	ἔστε	ἴτε	φᾰτε
		3	ἔστων	ἰόντων	φᾰντων
inf.			εἶναι	ἰέναι	φᾰναι
ppl.	masc.		ὤν, ὄντος	ἰών, ἰόντος	φᾰσκων, -οντος / φᾱς, φᾰντος
	fem.		οὖσα, οὔσης	ἰοῦσα, ἰούσης	φᾰσκουσα, -σης / φᾶσα, φάσης
	neut.		ὄν, ὄντος	ἰόν, ἰόντος	φᾰσκον, -οντος / φᾰν, φᾰντος

For the accentuation of the pres. ind. of εἰμί *be* and φημί, →24.34.

Present Stems with a Long and Short Variant

12.37   The present stem of -μι verbs nearly always has **two variants**, one with a **long** and one with a **short** final vowel:

verb	present stem
δείκνυμι *show*	δεικνῡ-/δεικνῠ-
ἵστημι *make stand, set up*	ἱστη-/ἱστᾰ-
τίθημι *put, place*	τιθη-/τιθε-
ἵημι *send, let go*	ἱη-/ἱε-
δίδωμι *give*	διδω-/διδο-
φημί *say, claim*	φη-/φᾰ-

12.38   The **long variant** appears in:

– singular forms of the active indicative (but for thematic forms of the imperfect, →12.53);
– all forms of the subjunctive.

The **short variant** appears in all other forms (including all middle-passive forms except the subjunctive).

Types of -μι Verb; Present Stem Formation

Verbs in -νυμι

12.39   A number of athematic present stems are formed with the nasal infix **-νυ-**. Most of these verbs have a verb stem ending in a velar stop, or in the case of verbs in -ννυμι, a verb stem originally ending in σ (there are some others). E.g.:

verb (present stem)	verb stem	compare
verb stems ending in a velar stop:		
δείκνυμι *show*	δεικ-	aor. ἔδειξα
ζεύγνυμι *yoke*	ζευγ-/ζῠγ-	aor. ἔζευξα
μείγνυμι *mix*	μειγ-/μῐγ-	aor. ἔμειξα
πήγνυμι *affix, fasten*	πηγ-/πᾰγ-	aor. ἔπηξα
ῥήγνυμι *(cause to) break*	ῥηγ-/ῥωγ-/ῥᾰγ-	aor. ἔρρηξα
verb stems originally ending in σ:		
κεράννυμι *mix* (<*κεράσ-νυ-μι)	κερᾰ(σ)-/κρᾱ-	aor. ἐκέρασ(σ)α
κρεμάννυμι *hang up* (<*κρεμάσ-νυ-μι)	κρεμᾰ(σ)-	aor. ἐκρέμασ(σ)α
σβέννυμι *quench, put out* (<*σβέσ-νυ-μι)	σβη-/σβε(σ)-	aor. pass. ἐσβέσθην
χώννυμι *heap up* (<*χώσ-νυ-μι)	χω(σ)-/χο-	aor. pass. ἐχώσθην

other verbs

ὄμνυμι *swear*	ὀμ(ο)-	aor. ὤμοσα
ὄλλυμι *lose* (<*ὄλ-νυ-μι)	ὀλ(ε)-	fut. ὀλῶ

Reduplicated Verbs

12.40 A few important athematic present stems are formed by **reduplication** (→12.32 above):

verb (present stem)	verb stem	compare
ἵ-στημι *make stand, set up* (<*σί-στᾱμι)	στη-/στᾰ-	aor. ἔστησα
δί-δωμι *give*	δω-/δο-	aor. ἔδωκα
τί-θημι *put, place*	θη-/θε-	aor. ἔθηκα
ἵ-ημι *send, let go* (<*yί-yημι)	ἡ-/ἑ-	aor. ἧκα

12.41 More complex is the formation of πίμπλημι, πίμπρημι, and ὀνίνημι, which have a nasal infix in addition to reduplication. They are all conjugated in the present like ἵστημι:

verb (present stem)	verb stem	compare
πί-μ-πλημι *fill*	πλη-/πλᾰ-	aor. ἔπλησα
πί-μ-πρημι *burn*	πρη-/πρᾰ-	aor. ἔπρησα
ὀ-νί-νημι *help, benefit*	ὀνη-/ὀνᾰ-	aor. ὤνησα

Root Presents

12.42 Finally, there are several athematic **root presents** (or 'primitive verbs'), whose present stem is an unelaborated verbal root (→23.2 with n.3):

verb (present stem)	verb stem
εἰμί *be*	ἐσ- (εἰμί = ἐμί <*ἐσμί, →1.68)
εἶμι *go*	εἰ-/ἰ-
φημί *say, claim*	φη-/φᾰ-
ἠμί *say, speak*	ἠ-

Note 1: The verb ἠμί *say* occurs primarily in the past-tense forms ἦν *I said*, ἦ *he/she said*, normally in the speech formulas ἦν δ' ἐγώ *and I said* and ἦ δ' ὅς *and he said*.

12.43 To this category also belong a few verbs with only middle-passive forms (thus only a short-vowel stem is used in the present conjugation, →12.38):

verb (present stem)	verb stem
κεῖμαι *lie*	κει-
(κάθ)ημαι *sit*	ἡ(σ)-
ἄγαμαι *admire, love*	ἀγᾰ-
ἐπίσταμαι *know, be able*	ἐπιστη-/ἐπιστᾰ-
δύναμαι *be able*	δυνη-/δυνᾰ-
κρέμαμαι *hang*	κρεμᾰ(σ)-

Note 1: κεῖμαι is conjugated like middle-passive δείκνυμαι; the subj. and opt. use the stem κε-, e.g. 3 sg. subj. κέηται, 3 pl. opt. κέοιντο.

The present/imperfect forms of κεῖμαι serve as the perfect/pluperfect passive of the verb τίθημι *put, place*, particularly its compounds: e.g. διατίθημι *dispose, put in a certain state*; διάκειμαι *be disposed, be in a certain state*.

Note 2: ἄγαμαι, ἐπίσταμαι, δύναμαι, and κρέμαμαι are conjugated in the present like ἴσταμαι (although there are, with δύναμαι, ἐπίσταμαι and κρέμαμαι, a few differences in accentuation, e.g. 3 pl. opt. δύναιντο/ἰσταῖντο).

Note 3: (κάθ)ημαι is conjugated like middle-passive δείκνυμαι, but with subj. καθῶμαι, καθῇ, etc.; opt. καθοίμην, etc. The original σ of the stem is visible in 3 sg. impf. καθῆστο (next to ἐκάθητο, see below).

The present/imperfect forms of κάθημαι *sit* serve as the perfect/pluperfect of the verb καθέζομαι *sit down*.

It is frequently treated as a simplex verb in the imperfect (augment ἐκαθήμην rather than καθήμην; →11.58).

The simplex (non-compound) verb ἧμαι occurs sometimes in poetry, not in prose.

12.44   Most forms of impersonal **χρή** *it is necessary* derive from combinations of the noun χρή *necessity* and forms of εἰμί *be*: subj. χρῇ (<χρὴ ᾖ), opt. χρείη (<χρὴ εἴη), inf. χρῆναι (<χρὴ εἶναι), part. χρεών (<χρὴ ὄν, →1.71). The imperfect is χρῆν (<χρὴ ἦν) or ἐχρῆν (with an additional augment).

Endings

12.45   The endings of athematic presents are listed in 11.20–33. Present-stem forms of -μι verbs are built as follows.

12.46   **Present indicative**: formed with primary endings. E.g. 1 sg. act. δείκνῡ-μι, τίθη-μι, 2 sg. act. δείκνῡ-ς, τίθη-ς; 1 sg. mp. δείκνῡ-μαι, τίθε-μαι. Note that the σ of the 2 sg. mp. does not disappear: δείκνῡ-σαι, τίθε-σαι. The root presents have several irregular forms (see the overview of forms).

Note 1: Occasionally, the σ of the 2 sg. mp. *does* disappear after α: e.g. δύνᾳ (more regularly δύνασαι), ἐπίστᾳ (ἐπίστασαι).

12.47   **Imperfect**: formed with the augment, and with secondary endings. E.g. 1 sg. act. ἐ-δείκνῡ-ν, 2 sg. act. ἐ-δείκνῡ-ς; 1 sg. mp. ἐ-δεικνῡ-μην. Note that the σ of the 2 sg. mp. does not disappear: ἐ-δείκνῡ-σο. Some singular active forms are thematic, →12.53 below. The root presents have several irregular forms (see the overview of forms).

Note 1: Occasionally, the σ of the 2 sg. mp. *does* disappear after α, followed by contraction: e.g. ἠπίστω (more regularly ἠπίστασο), ἐδύνω (ἐδύνασο), ἴστω (ἴστασο).

12.48   **Imperative**: the 2 sg. act. is usually formed without ending (some are thematic), but the root presents have ἴσ<u>θι</u>, ἴ<u>θι</u>, φά<u>θι</u>. Other imperatives: e.g. 2 pl. act. δείκνῠ-<u>τε</u>, 2 sg. mp. δείκνῠ-<u>σο</u>.

12.49   **Subjunctive**: formed with the long thematic vowel of the subjunctive and primary endings. In reduplicated -μι presents and in κάθημαι, the long thematic vowel contracts with the preceding (long) vowel: e.g. 1 sg. act. διδῶ (<*-<u>ώ</u>-<u>ω</u>), 2 sg. act. διδῷς (<*-ώ-<u>ῃς</u>), 1 sg. mp. διδῶμαι (<*-ώ-<u>ω</u>-<u>μαι</u>), 2 sg. act. ἰῇς (<*ἱή-<u>ῃς</u>), 2 pl. mp. ἱστῆσθε (<*ἱστή-<u>η</u>-<u>σθε</u>).

> **Note 1:** For the forms built on stems ending in η and with subjunctive long thematic vowel ω, which involve quantitative metathesis, →1.71: e.g. 1 sg. act. ἰῶ (<ἱέω <*ἱή-ω), 1 sg. mp. τιθῶμαι (<τιθέωμαι <*τιθή-ω-μαι), 1 pl. act. ἱστῶμεν (<ἱστέωμεν <*ἱστή-ω-μεν).

12.50   **Optative**: the optatives of -νυμι verbs, κάθημαι and κεῖμαι are thematic, →12.53. Others are formed with the optative suffix -ιη- in the singular, with optative suffix -ι- in the plural and all middle-passive forms, and with secondary endings. The iota forms a diphthong with the preceding short stem vowel. E.g. 1 sg. act. διδο<u>ίη</u>-<u>ν</u>, 1 pl. act. διδο<u>ῖ</u>-<u>μεν</u>, 1 sg. mp. διδο<u>ί</u>-<u>μην</u>; 1 sg. act. τιθ<u>είη</u>-<u>ν</u>, 1 pl. act. τιθ<u>εῖ</u>-<u>μεν</u>, 1 sg. mp. τιθ<u>εί</u>-<u>μην</u>.

> **Note 1:** In the optative of εἰμί be and φημί say, plural forms with -ιη- occur frequently, next to forms with ι (e.g. εἴημεν next to εἶμεν, φαίημεν next to φαῖμεν; 2 pl. φαῖτε does not occur in classical Greek, perhaps by chance).
>
> **Note 2:** There is, in classical Greek (as transmitted), one probable case of an athematic optative of a stem in νυ, πηγνῦτο (Pl. *Phd.* 118a, with the optative suffix contracted into υ). Homeric Greek has more υ-optatives, e.g. δῦμεν (1 pl. aor. opt. of δύομαι *dive*).

12.51   **Active infinitive**: formed with -ναι. E.g. act. δεικνύ-<u>ναι</u>. But the inf. of εἶμι *go* ends in -εναι: ἰ-<u>έναι</u>.

      Middle-passive infinitive: formed with -σθαι. E.g. δείκνῠ-<u>σθαι</u>, κεῖ-<u>σθαι</u>

12.52   **Active participle**: formed with -ντ-; for the declension, →5.17–18. E.g. gen. sg. masc. δεικνύ-<u>ντ</u>-ος, nom. sg. fem. δεικνῦσα (<*-ύ<u>ντ</u>γα).

      Middle-passive participle: formed with -μεν-; for the declension, →5.3–4. E.g. nom. sg. masc. δεικνύ-<u>μεν</u>-ος, nom. sg. fem. δεικνῠ-<u>μέν</u>-η.

Thematic Forms

12.53   Some forms of -μι verbs are **regularly thematic**:

    – most forms of the singular impf. act. of τίθημι, ἵημι, and δίδωμι: e.g. ἵε<u>ις</u> (formed like ἐποίεις), ἐδίδ<u>ουν</u> (formed like ἐδήλουν);

- all subjunctives (with long theme vowels): e.g. 1 pl. act. δεικνύ<u>ω</u>μεν, τιθῶμεν (< τιθέωμεν <*τιθή-<u>ω</u>μεν, →1.71), ὦμεν (< ἔ<u>ω</u>μεν);
- all optatives of the verbs in -νυμι, of εἶμι *go*, and of κάθημαι and κεῖμαι: e.g. 2 sg. act. δεικνύ<u>οι</u>ς, 1 pl. δεικνύ<u>οι</u>μεν, 3 pl. ἴ<u>οι</u>εν, 1 sg. καθ<u>οί</u>μην, 3 pl. κέ<u>οι</u>ντο;
- 2 sg. act. imp. of τίθημι, ἵημι, δίδωμι: e.g. τίθ<u>ει</u> (formed like ποίει), δίδ<u>ου</u> (formed like δήλου);
- participles of εἰμί *be* (with no visible stem in Attic) and εἶμι *go*; e.g. with εἰμί, nom. pl. masc. ὄντες, nom./acc. pl. neut. ὄντα; with εἶμι, nom. pl. masc. ἰ<u>ό</u>ντες, nom./ acc. pl. neut. ἰ<u>ό</u>ντα.

Note 1: For the Ionic participle of εἰμί (ἐών, etc.), →25.40.

12.54   In the active of -νυμι verbs, **alternative thematic forms** are found next to the 'regular' athematic forms, especially from the fourth century onwards: e.g. 3 sg. pres. ind. δεικνύ<u>ει</u>, 2 sg. imp. δείκνυ<u>ε</u>, inf. δεικνύ<u>ειν</u>, nom. sg. masc. act. ppl. δεικνύ<u>ων</u>, gen. δεικνύ<u>ο</u>ντος.

Note 1: The thematic forms of these verbs are frequent in Ionic, →25.38.

12.55   Similarly, thematic variants occur of (primarily) second- and third-person forms in the pres. act. ind. of reduplicated athematic verbs: ἱεῖς, ἱεῖ; τιθεῖς, τιθεῖ; διδοῖς, διδοῖ; ἱστᾷς, ἱστᾷ (the thematic alternatives are formed like ποιεῖς, δηλοῖς, τιμᾷς, etc.).

Note 1: These forms occur particularly often in Ionic, →25.38.

12.56   The verb φημί *say* uses some thematic forms built on the stem **φασκ-** (for -σκ-, →12.31):

- in Attic prose, the regular forms of the participle are φάσκων, φάσκοντος, etc. (in poetry and Ionic prose, φάς, φάντος, etc.);
- the imperfect ἔφασκον, etc. occurs regularly;
- some other forms occur, e.g. 1 sg. opt. φάσκοιμι, 3 pl. subj. φάσκωσιν.

13

The Aorist: Active and Middle

Types of Aorist (Active and Middle) Stem

13.1   Aorist (active and middle) stems are formed in one of three different ways:

- **Sigmatic aorists** (the most common type): aorist stems are formed by adding σ (and α, →13.6–7) to the verb stem. E.g. with παιδεύω *educate* (verb stem παιδευ-): aorist stem παιδευσ(α)-, 1 sg. ind. aor. act. ἐπαίδευσα; with δείκνῡμι *show* (verb stem δεικ-): aorist stem δειξ(α)-, 1 sg. ind. aor. act. ἔδειξα.

  With verb stems ending in a resonant the sigma disappeared with compensatory lengthening of the vowel preceding the resonant: the so-called 'pseudo-sigmatic' aorist. E.g. with ἀγγέλλω *report* (verb stem ἀγγελ-): aorist stem ἀγγειλ(α)- (<*ἀγγελσα-), 1 sg. ind. aor. act. ἤγγειλα; with φαίνω *show* (verb stem φᾰν-): aorist stem φην(α)- (<*φανσα-), 1 sg. ind. aor. act. ἔφηνα.

- **Thematic aorists**: a group of aorists is formed by adding a thematic vowel and endings directly to the aorist stem (normally identical to (a variant of) the verb stem), which ends in a consonant. E.g. with λαμβάνω *get, take* (verb stem ληβ-/λᾰβ-): aorist stem λᾰβ-, 1 sg. ind. aor. act. ἔ-λαβ-ο-ν; with λείπω *leave* (verb stem λειπ-/λοιπ-/λῐπ-): aorist stem λῐπ-, 1 sg. ind. aor. act. ἔ-λιπ-ο-ν.

- **Root aorists**: a small number of verbs has aorists formed by directly adding endings to the aorist stem, which always ends in a vowel. E.g. with γιγνώσκω *know, recognize* (verb stem γνω-): aorist stem γνω-, 1 sg. ind. aor. act. ἔ-γνω-ν; with ἵσταμαι *come to stand* (verb stem στη-/στᾰ-): aorist stem στη-, 1 sg. ind. aor. act. ἔ-στη-ν.

Note 1: Thus sigmatic aorist stems are formed by an *addition* (-σα-) to the verb stem, while in the case of both thematic and root aorists, the stem is usually *identical* to (a variant of) the verb stem. The difference between the latter two is that forms of the thematic aorist (stems usually ending in a consonant) are formed using a thematic vowel, whereas root aorists (which have stems ending in a vowel) are not: contrast e.g. ἔ-λιπ-ο-ν with ἔ-γνω-ν.

Note 2: Sigmatic aorists are often called 'first' or 'weak' aorists; thematic and root aorists are often called 'second' or 'strong' aorists. For these distinctions, see the section *On Terminology* at the start of this book.

13.2   The verbs **δίδωμι** *give*, **τίθημι** *put, place* and **ἵημι** *send, let go* have a distinct conjugation in the aorist, mostly of the root type but with some peculiarities. →13.51–62.

13.3   Although most verbs have only one type of aorist, there are a few that have more than one, in some cases with important distinctions of meaning. For these verbs, →13.63–4.

Sigmatic (and Pseudo-Sigmatic) Aorists

Overview of Forms

13.4   **Active** forms:

			verb stems ending in ι, υ or a diphthong	verb stems ending in α, ε, ο or η	verb stems ending in a labial or velar stop	verb stems ending in a dental stop	verb stems ending in a resonant
			παιδεύω *educate* stem παιδευσ(α)-	τιμάω *honour* stem τιμησ(α)-	τρίβω *rub* stem τριψ(α)-	κομίζω *convey* stem κομισ(α)-	ἀγγέλλω *report* stem ἀγγειλ(α)-
ind.	sg.	1	ἐπαίδευσα	ἐτίμησα	ἔτριψα	ἐκόμισα	ἤγγειλα
		2	ἐπαίδευσας	ἐτίμησας	ἔτριψας	ἐκόμισας	ἤγγειλας
		3	ἐπαίδευσε(ν)	ἐτίμησε(ν)	ἔτριψε(ν)	ἐκόμισε(ν)	ἤγγειλε(ν)
	pl.	1	ἐπαιδεύσαμεν	ἐτιμήσαμεν	ἐτρίψαμεν	ἐκομίσαμεν	ἠγγείλαμεν
		2	ἐπαιδεύσατε	ἐτιμήσατε	ἐτρίψατε	ἐκομίσατε	ἠγγείλατε
		3	ἐπαίδευσαν	ἐτίμησαν	ἔτριψαν	ἐκόμισαν	ἤγγειλαν
subj.	sg.	1	παιδεύσω	τιμήσω	τρίψω	κομίσω	ἀγγείλω
		2	παιδεύσῃς	τιμήσῃς	τρίψῃς	κομίσῃς	ἀγγείλῃς
		3	παιδεύσῃ	τιμήσῃ	τρίψῃ	κομίσῃ	ἀγγείλῃ
	pl.	1	παιδεύσωμεν	τιμήσωμεν	τρίψωμεν	κομίσωμεν	ἀγγείλωμεν
		2	παιδεύσητε	τιμήσητε	τρίψητε	κομίσητε	ἀγγείλητε
		3	παιδεύσωσι(ν)	τιμήσωσι(ν)	τρίψωσι(ν)	κομίσωσι(ν)	ἀγγείλωσι(ν)
opt.	sg.	1	παιδεύσαιμι	τιμήσαιμι	τρίψαιμι	κομίσαιμι	ἀγγείλαιμι
		2	παιδεύσειας[1]	τιμήσειας[1]	τρίψειας[1]	κομίσειας[1]	ἀγγείλειας[1]
		3	παιδεύσειε(ν)[2]	τιμήσειε(ν)[2]	τρίψειε(ν)[2]	κομίσειε(ν)[2]	ἀγγείλειε(ν)[2]
	pl.	1	παιδεύσαιμεν	τιμήσαιμεν	τρίψαιμεν	κομίσαιμεν	ἀγγείλαιμεν
		2	παιδεύσαιτε	τιμήσαιτε	τρίψαιτε	κομίσαιτε	ἀγγείλαιτε
		3	παιδεύσειαν[3]	τιμήσειαν[3]	τρίψειαν[3]	κομίσειαν[3]	ἀγγείλειαν[3]
imp.	sg.	2	παίδευσον	τίμησον	τρῖψον	κόμισον	ἄγγειλον
		3	παιδευσάτω	τιμησάτω	τριψάτω	κομισάτω	ἀγγειλάτω
	pl.	2	παιδεύσατε	τιμήσατε	τρίψατε	κομίσατε	ἀγγείλατε
		3	παιδευσάντων	τιμησάντων	τριψάντων	κομισάντων	ἀγγειλάντων
inf.			παιδεῦσαι	τιμῆσαι	τρῖψαι	κομίσαι	ἀγγεῖλαι
ppl.	masc.		παιδεύσας, -αντος	τιμήσας, -αντος	τρίψας, -αντος	κομίσας, -αντος	ἀγγείλας, -αντος
	fem.		παιδεύσασα, -άσης	τιμήσασα, -άσης	τρίψασα, -άσης	κομίσασα, -άσης	ἀγγείλασα, -άσης
	neut.		παιδεῦσαν, -αντος	τιμῆσαν, -αντος	τρῖψαν, -αντος	κομίσαν, -αντος	ἀγγείλαν, -αντος

[1] Also -σαις, e.g. παιδεύσαις, τιμήσαις, etc.

[2] Also -σαι, e.g. παιδεύσαι, τρίψαι, etc.

[3] Also -σαιεν, e.g. παιδεύσαιεν, ἀγγείλαιεν, etc.

13.5 **Middle** forms:

			verb stems ending in ι, υ or a diphthong	verb stems ending in α, ε, o or η	verb stems ending in a labial or velar stop	verb stems ending in a dental stop	verb stems ending in a resonant
			παιδεύω *educate* stem παιδευσ(α)-	τιμάω *honour* stem τιμησ(α)-	τρίβω *rub* stem τριψ(α)-	κομίζω *convey* stem κομισ(α)-	ἀγγέλλω *report* stem ἀγγειλ(α)-
ind.	sg.	1	ἐπαιδευσάμην	ἐτιμησάμην	ἐτριψάμην	ἐκομισάμην	ἠγγειλάμην
		2	ἐπαιδεύσω	ἐτιμήσω	ἐτρίψω	ἐκομίσω	ἠγγείλω
		3	ἐπαιδεύσατο	ἐτιμήσατο	ἐτρίψατο	ἐκομίσατο	ἠγγείλατο
	pl.	1	ἐπαιδευσάμεθα	ἐτιμησάμεθα	ἐτριψάμεθα	ἐκομισάμεθα	ἠγγειλάμεθα
		2	ἐπαιδεύσασθε	ἐτιμήσασθε	ἐτρίψασθε	ἐκομίσασθε	ἠγγείλασθε
		3	ἐπαιδεύσαντο	ἐτιμήσαντο	ἐτρίψαντο	ἐκομίσαντο	ἠγγείλαντο
subj.	sg.	1	παιδεύσωμαι	τιμήσωμαι	τρίψωμαι	κομίσωμαι	ἀγγείλωμαι
		2	παιδεύσῃ	τιμήσῃ	τρίψῃ	κομίσῃ	ἀγγείλῃ
		3	παιδεύσηται	τιμήσηται	τρίψηται	κομίσηται	ἀγγείληται
	pl.	1	παιδευσώμεθα	τιμησώμεθα	τριψώμεθα	κομισώμεθα	ἀγγειλώμεθα
		2	παιδεύσησθε	τιμήσησθε	τρίψησθε	κομίσησθε	ἀγγείλησθε
		3	παιδεύσωνται	τιμήσωνται	τρίψωνται	κομίσωνται	ἀγγείλωνται
opt.	sg.	1	παιδευσαίμην	τιμησαίμην	τριψαίμην	κομισαίμην	ἀγγειλαίμην
		2	παιδεύσαιο	τιμήσαιο	τρίψαιο	κομίσαιο	ἀγγείλαιο
		3	παιδεύσαιτο	τιμήσαιτο	τρίψαιτο	κομίσαιτο	ἀγγείλαιτο
	pl.	1	παιδευσαίμεθα	τιμησαίμεθα	τριψαίμεθα	κομισαίμεθα	ἀγγειλαίμεθα
		2	παιδεύσαισθε	τιμήσαισθε	τρίψαισθε	κομίσαισθε	ἀγγείλαισθε
		3	παιδεύσαιντο	τιμήσαιντο	τρίψαιντο	κομίσαιντο	ἀγγείλαιντο
imp.	sg.	2	παίδευσαι	τίμησαι	τρῖψαι	κόμισαι	ἄγγειλαι
		3	παιδευσάσθω	τιμησάσθω	τριψάσθω	κομισάσθω	ἀγγειλάσθω
	pl.	2	παιδεύσασθε	τιμήσασθε	τρίψασθε	κομίσασθε	ἀγγείλασθε
		3	παιδευσάσθων	τιμησάσθων	τριψάσθων	κομισάσθων	ἀγγειλάσθων
inf.			παιδεύσασθαι	τιμήσασθαι	τρίψασθαι	κομίσασθαι	ἀγγείλασθαι
ppl.	masc.		παιδευσάμενος, -ου	τιμησάμενος, -ου	τριψάμενος, -ου	κομισάμενος, -ου	ἀγγειλάμενος, -ου
	fem.		παιδευσαμένη, -ης	τιμησαμένη, -ης	τριψαμένη, -ης	κομισαμένη, -ης	ἀγγειλαμένη, -ης
	neut.		παιδευσάμενον, -ου	τιμησάμενον, -ου	τριψάμενον, -ου	κομισάμενον, -ου	ἀγγειλάμενον, -ου

Sigma and Alpha

13.6   As the name suggests, sigmatic (and pseudo-sigmatic) aorists feature a **sigma** in the stem (though this σ has disappeared in the case of pseudo-sigmatic aorists, →13.24).

13.7   In addition, nearly all forms of the sigmatic aorist have an **alpha**. This ᾰ goes back to an original 1 sg. ending *-m (final *-m changed to -ᾰ after consonants (→1.86), e.g. ἔ-δειξ-ἄ < *ἔ-δειξ-m̥; it changed to -ν after vowels, →1.73, contrast e.g. ἔ-λαβ-ο-ν < *-ο-m). The alpha was then generalized throughout the conjugation, so that sigmatic aorists in general may be recognized by the combination σἄ (or merely ἄ in the case of pseudo-sigmatic aorists): in essence, the alpha has become part of the aorist stem. Note, however, that the alpha is absent in the 3 sg. act. ind. (e.g. ἐπαίδευσε), the 2 sg. act. imp. (e.g. παίδευσον), all aor. subjunctives (e.g. 1 sg. mid. παιδεύσωμαι), and some optative forms (e.g. 2 sg. act. παιδεύσειας). Below, aorist stems are therefore given with the alpha between parentheses.

Endings

13.8   The endings of (pseudo-)sigmatic aorists differ in some cases from those listed in 11.20–33, particularly in imperative, optative, and infinitive. They are detailed below.

13.9   The aorist **indicative**, as a secondary (past-tense) indicative, is formed with the augment (→11.35). The endings per person are:

- The 1 sg. act. ind. ends in -α as described above (→13.7): e.g. ἐ-παίδευσα, ἤγγειλα.
- All other indicative forms add the regular secondary endings to the stem with the alpha: e.g. 2 sg. act. ind. ἐ-παίδευσα-ς, 1 pl. act. ind. ἠγγείλα-μεν, 1 sg. mid. ind. ἐ-παιδευσά-μην, 3 pl. mid. ind. ἠγγείλα-ντο. The ending of 3 pl. act. ind. is -ν, e.g. ἐ-παίδευσα-ν.

    However, in the 3 sg. act. ind. the alpha is *not* used; it ends in -ε(ν): e.g. ἐ-παίδευσ-ε(ν), ἤγγειλ-ε(ν).
- Note the 2 sg. mid. ind., where the ending -σο has lost its σ, and α and ο have contracted: e.g. ἐ-παιδεύσω (<*ἐ-παιδεύσα-(σ)ο).

Note 1: The 2 sg. mp. does not contract in Ionic, →25.6, 25.32.
Note 2: Note that the augment is used *only* in indicatives (contrast e.g. 1 sg. act. ind. ἐπαίδευσα with 1 sg. act. subj. παιδεύσω, inf. παιδεῦσαι).

13.10   **Imperative**:

- the 2 sg. act. imp. does not have the alpha and ends in -**ον**: e.g. παίδευσον, ἄγγειλον;
- the 2 sg. mid. imp. ends in -**αι**: e.g. παίδευσαι, ἄγγειλαι;
- all other imperative forms add regular imperative endings (→11.29) after the alpha: e.g. 3 sg. act. imp. ἀγγειλά-τω, 2 pl. imp. mid. παιδεύσα-σθε.

13.11 Aorist **subjunctives** do not have α. The long thematic vowel of the subjunctive and primary endings are used. E.g. 1 pl. act. subj. παιδεύσ-ω-μεν, 1 sg. mid. subj. παιδεύσ-ω-μαι, 3 sg. mid. subj. ἀγγείλ-η-ται.

13.12 Aorist **optatives** use the optative suffix -ι-, which forms a diphthong with the preceding alpha of the stem (→11.16); secondary endings are added (→11.22–7). E.g. 1 pl. act. opt. ἀγγείλαι-μεν, 1 sg. mid. opt. παιδευσαί-μην. The 1 sg. act. opt. uses the primary ending -μι, e.g. παιδεύσαι-μι.

More frequent alternative forms exist for the 2 sg. act. opt. (παιδεύσειας next to παιδεύσαι-ς), 3 sg. act. opt. (παιδεύσειε(ν) next to παιδεύσαι) and 3 pl. act. opt. (παιδεύσειαν next to παιδεύσαι-εν).

13.13 The **active infinitive** ends in -αι: e.g. παιδεῦσαι, ἀγγεῖλαι.

The **middle infinitive** ends in -σθαι: e.g. παιδεύσα-σθαι, ἀγγείλα-σθαι.

Note 1: For differences in accentuation between different forms ending in -(σ)αι, →24.20 n.1.

13.14 **Active participles** add -ντ- to the stem: e.g. gen. sg. masc. παιδεύσᾰ-ντ-ος, gen. sg. fem. παιδευσά̆σης (<*-σᾰντγ-). For the entire declension, →5.17–18.

Middle participles add -μεν- to the stem: e.g. nom. sg. masc. ἀγγειλά-μεν-ος, nom. sg. fem. ἀγγειλα-μέν-η. For the entire declension, →5.3–4.

Stem Formation of Sigmatic Aorists

Verb Stems Ending in ι, υ or a Diphthong

13.15 Verb stems ending in ι, υ, or diphthongs stay unchanged before the added σ. Some examples:

verb	verb stem	aorist stem	1 sg. ind.	inf.
χρίω *anoint*	χρῑ-	χρισ(α)-	ἔχρισα	χρῖσαι
κωλύω *hinder*	κωλῡ-	κωλυσ(α)-	ἐκώλυσα	κωλῦσαι
παίω *strike*	παι-	παισ(α)-	ἔπαισα	παῖσαι
παύω *stop*	παυ-	παυσ(α)-	ἔπαυσα	παῦσαι
παιδεύω *educate*	παιδευ-	παιδευσ(α)-	ἐπαίδευσα	παιδεῦσαι
ἀκούω *hear*	ἀκο(υ)(σ)-	ἀκουσ(α)-	ἤκουσα	ἀκοῦσαι

Verb Stems Ending in ε, α or ο (or η or ω)

13.16 With verb stems ending (in the present) in ε, α or ο (i.e. contract verbs), the aorist stem is built on the **long variant** of the verb stem (→11.11):

- pres. stem ε: aor. stem η;
- pres. stem ᾰ (or η): aor. stem η (but ᾱ after ε, ι or ρ);

– pres. stem o: aor. stem ω; a few verbs with a verb stem ending in ω have a similarly formed aorist.

Some examples:

verb	verb stem	aorist stem	1 sg. ind.	inf.
ποιέω *make, do*	ποιη-/ποιε-	ποιησ(α)-	ἐποίησα	ποιῆσαι
ἡγέομαι *lead, consider*	ἡγη-/ἡγε-	ἡγησ(α)-	ἡγησάμην	ἡγήσασθαι
τιμάω *honour*	τιμη-/τιμᾰ-	τιμησ(α)-	ἐτίμησα	τιμῆσαι
κτάομαι *acquire*	κτη-/κτᾰ-	κτησ(α)-	ἐκτησάμην	κτήσασθαι
δράω *do*	δρᾱ-/δρᾰ-	δρᾱσ(α)-	ἔδρᾱσα	δρᾶσαι
δηλόω *make clear*	δηλω-/δηλο-	δηλωσ(α)-	ἐδήλωσα	δηλῶσαι
χρήομαι *use, need*	χρη-	χρησ(α)-	ἐχρησάμην	χρήσασθαι
τιτρώσκω *wound*	τρω-	τρωσ(α)-	ἔτρωσα	τρῶσαι

13.17   Similarly, with -μι verbs that have variant verb stems ending in η/ᾰ (→12.37–8), the long variant of the verb stem is used:

ἵστημι *make stand, set up*	στη-/στᾰ-	στησ(α)-	ἔστησα	στῆσαι
πίμπλημι *fill*	πλη-/πλᾰ-	πλησ(α)-	ἔπλησα	πλῆσαι
ὀνίνημι *benefit*	ὀνη-/ὀνᾰ-	ὀνησ(α)-	ὤνησα	ὀνῆσαι

13.18   Some verbs in -άω and -έω that had a verb stem ending in σ do not have a long vowel in the aorist (the original σ is visible in the Homeric/epic aorist in -σσα, and often in other tense stems):

ζέω *boil* (verb stem ζε(σ)-)   aor. ἔζεσα (<ἔζεσσα, epic)   inf. ζέσαι

τελέω *finish* (verb stem τελε(σ)-)   aor. ἐτέλεσα (<ἐτέλεσσα, epic)   inf. τελέσαι

γελάω *laugh* (verb stem γελᾰ(σ)-)   aor. ἐγέλασα (<ἐγέλᾱσσα, epic) inf. γελάσαι

In some cases such verbs did not originally have a stem in σ, but were absorbed into this type by analogy (→1.49), based on an epic aorist in -σσα:

καλέω *call* (verb stem κᾰλε-/κλη-)   aor. ἐκάλεσα (ἐκάλεσσα, epic)   inf. καλέσαι

Verbs in -άννυμι and -έννυμι also had a stem in σ:

κεράννυμι *mix* (<*κερᾰσ-νυμι)   aor. ἐκέρᾰσα (<ἐκέρᾱσσα, epic) inf. κερᾰσαι

ἀμφι-έννυμι *clothe* (<*-ἕσ-νυμι)   aor. ἠμφίεσα (<-εσσα, epic)   inf. ἀμφιέσαι

13.19   A few other verbs have only a verb stem with a short vowel (and no variant with a long vowel); these verbs thus have a short vowel in the aorist:

(ἐπ)αἰνέω *praise* (verb stem αἰνε-)   aor. ᾔνεσα   inf. αἰνέσαι

ἀρκέω *suffice* (verb stem ἀρκε-)   aor. ἤρκεσα   inf. ἀρκέσαι

13.20   A few verbs in -άω and -έω that originally had a verb stem ending in ϝ (→12.25, 12.29 n.1) have an aorist in -αυσα or -ευσα, respectively:

κά̄ω (also καίω) *set on fire* (<*κάϝγω) aor. ἔκαυσα (<*ἔκαϝσα)   inf. καῦσαι

πλέ̄ω *sail* (<*πλέϝω)   aor. ἔπλευσα (<*ἔπλεϝσα) inf. πλεῦσαι

πνέ̄ω *blow* (<*πνέϝω)   aor. ἔπνευσα (<*ἔπνεϝσα) inf. πνεῦσαι

Verb Stems Ending in a Labial or Velar Stop

13.21 Verb stems ending in a labial stop get an aorist stem in **ψ(α)** (π/β/φ + σ = ψ). Some examples:

verb	verb stem	aorist stem	1 sg. ind.	inf.
πέμπω *send*	πεμπ-/πομπ-	πεμψ(α)-	ἔπεμψα	πέμψαι
τρίβω *rub*	τρῑβ-/τρῐβ-	τριψ(α)-	ἔτριψα	τρῖψαι
γράφω *write*	γρᾰφ-	γραψ(α)-	ἔγραψα	γράψαι

Note especially verbs that have a present in -πτω (→12.27):

| βλάπτω *harm, damage* | βλᾰβ- | βλαψ(α)- | ἔβλαψα | βλάψαι |
| κρύπτω *hide* | κρῠφ-/κρῠβ- | κρυψ(α)- | ἔκρυψα | κρύψαι |

13.22 Verb stems ending in velar stops get an aorist stem in **ξ(α)** (κ/γ/χ + σ = ξ). Some examples:

verb	verb stem	aorist stem	1 sg. ind.	inf.
διώκω *chase*	διωκ-	διωξ(α)-	ἐδίωξα	διῶξαι
λήγω *cease*	ληγ-	ληξ(α)-	ἔληξα	λῆξαι
ἄρχω *rule, begin*	ἀρχ-	ἀρξ(α)-	ἦρξα	ἄρξαι

Note especially verbs that have a present in -ττω, and a few in -ζω (→12.27):

φυλάττω *guard*	φυλᾰκ-	φυλαξ(α)-	ἐφύλαξα	φυλάξαι
τάττω *array, appoint*	τᾰγ-	ταξ(α)-	ἔταξα	τάξαι
οἰμώζω *groan*	οἰμωγ-	οἰμωξ(α)-	ᾤμωξα	οἰμῶξαι

And note that a number of -νυμι verbs have verb stems ending in a velar stop (→12.39). For example:

| δείκνυμι *show* | δεικ- | δειξ(α)- | ἔδειξα | δεῖξαι |
| πήγνυμι *affix, fasten* | πηγ-/πᾰγ- | πηξ(α)- | ἔπηξα | πῆξαι |

Verb Stems Ending in a Dental Stop

13.23 With verb stems ending in a dental stop (τ/δ/θ), that **dental stop disappears before σ** in the aorist:

verb	verb stem	aorist stem	1 sg. ind.	inf.
ἀνύτω *complete*	ἀνῠ(τ)-	ἀνυσ(α)-	ἤνυσα	ἀνύσαι
ψεύδομαι *lie*	ψευδ-	ψευσ(α)-	ἐψευσάμην	ψεύσασθαι
πείθω *persuade*	πειθ-/ποιθ-/πῑθ-	πεισ(α)-	ἔπεισα	πεῖσαι

Note especially verbs that have a present in -ζω, and a few in -ττω (→12.27):

ἁρμόζω/ἁρμόττω *fit together*	ἁρμοδ-/ἁρμοτ-	ἁρμοσ(α)-	ἥρμοσα	ἁρμόσαι
λογίζομαι *count*	λογῐδ-	λογισ(α)-	ἐλογισάμην	λογίσασθαι
κομίζω *convey*	κομῐδ-	κομισ(α)-	ἐκόμισα	κομίσαι
νομίζω *believe*	νομῐδ-	νομισ(α)-	ἐνόμισα	νομίσαι
ἐρέττω *row*	ἐρετ-	ἔρεσ(α)-	ἤρεσα	ἐρέσαι
πλάττω *mould*	πλᾰθ-	πλασ(α)-	ἔπλασα	πλάσαι

The Pseudo-Sigmatic Aorist – Verb Stems Ending in a Resonant

13.24 With verb stems ending in a resonant (nasal (μ, ν) or liquid (λ, ρ)) consonant, the **sigma of the aorist has disappeared** (hence the term 'pseudo-sigmatic' aorist); the alpha remains. The disappearance of the sigma led to **compensatory lengthening** of the vowel preceding the resonant.

E.g. with φαίνω *show* (verb stem φην-/φᾰν-): 1 sg. aor. act. ind. ἔφηνα (<*ἔφᾱνα <*ἔ-φᾰν-σα), aor. act. inf. φῆναι (<*φᾰν-σαι).

E.g. with ἀγγέλλω *report* (verb stem ἀγγελ-): 1 sg. aor. act. ind. ἤγγειλα (<*ἤγγελ-σα), aor. act. inf. ἀγγεῖλαι (<*ἀγγέλ-σαι).

Some other examples:

verb	verb stem	aorist stem	1 sg. ind.	inf.
μένω *stay, (a)wait*	μεν-	μειν(α)-	ἔμεινα	μεῖναι
νέμω *deal out*	νεμ-	νειμ(α)-	ἔνειμα	νεῖμαι
δέμω *build*	δεμ-	δειμ(α)-	ἔδειμα	δεῖμαι

Note especially verbs that have a present in -λλω or in -αίνω/-αίρω, -είνω/-είρω, -ίνω/-ίρω, -ύνω/-ύρω (→12.28):

στέλλω *dispatch*	<u>στελ-</u>/στᾰλ-	στειλ(α)-	ἔστειλα	στεῖλαι
σφάλλω *cause to stumble*	σφᾰλ-	σφηλ(α)-	ἔσφηλα	σφῆλαι
ἀπο-κτείνω *kill*	<u>κτεν-</u>/κτον-/κτᾰν-	κτειν(α)-	ἀπ-έκτεινα	ἀποκτεῖναι
μιαίνω *stain*	μιᾰν-	μιᾱν(α)-	ἐμίανα	μιᾶναι
καθαίρω *cleanse*	καθᾰρ-	καθηρ(α)-	ἐκάθηρα	καθῆραι
ἀμύνω *defend, succour*	ἀμῠν-	ἀμῡν(α)-	ἤμῡνα	ἀμῦναι
κρίνω *decide, judge*	κρῐ(ν)-	κρῑν(α)-	ἔκρῑνα	κρῖναι

But note:

αἴρω *lift*	ἀρ- (<*ἀερ-)	ἀρ(α)-	ἦρα	ἆραι

13.25 The present stem of these verbs is often different from the verb stem as well, usually due to the disappearance of y. In some cases, the present and aorist have the same vowel as a result, e.g. with verb stem κτεν-, pres. ἀποκτείνω (<*ἀποκτέν-yω), aor. ἀπέκτεινα (<*ἀπέκτεν-σα): →1.68–9.

As a result, the 3 sg. impf. act. and 3 sg. aor. act. ind. of some verbs may be identical: cf. e.g. impf. ἀπέκτεινε (<*ἀπ-έ-κτεν-yε) with aor. ἀπέκτεινε (<*ἀπ-έ-κτεν-σε).

13.26 This type of stem is sometimes called 'sigmatic aorist improper', or 'liquid first aorist'.

Thematic Aorists

Overview of Forms

13.27 **Active** forms:

			regular forms	ἔχω	φέρω (mixed thematic/ α-conjugation)
			λαμβάνω *get, take*	*have, hold*	*carry, bring*
			stem λᾰβ-	stem σχ-	stem ἐνεγκ(α)-
ind.	sg.	1	ἔλαβον	ἔσχον	ἤνεγκον *or* ἤνεγκα
		2	ἔλαβες	ἔσχες	ἤνεγκας
		3	ἔλαβε(ν)	ἔσχε(ν)	ἤνεγκε(ν)
	pl.	1	ἐλάβομεν	ἔσχομεν	ἠνέγκαμεν
		2	ἐλάβετε	ἔσχετε	ἠνέγκατε
		3	ἔλαβον	ἔσχον	ἤνεγκαν
subj.	sg.	1	λάβω	σχῶ	ἐνέγκω
		2	λάβῃς	σχῇς	ἐνέγκῃς
		3	λάβῃ	σχῇ	ἐνέγκῃ
	pl.	1	λάβωμεν	σχῶμεν	ἐνέγκωμεν
		2	λάβητε	σχῆτε	ἐνέγκητε
		3	λάβωσι(ν)	σχῶσι(ν)	ἐνέγκωσι(ν)
opt.	sg.	1	λάβοιμι	σχοίην	ἐνέγκαιμι
		2	λάβοις	σχοίης	ἐνέγκοις *or* ἐνέγκαις
		3	λάβοι	σχοίη	ἐνέγκοι *or* ἐνέγκαι
	pl.	1	λάβοιμεν	σχοῖμεν	ἐνέγκοιμεν *or* ἐνέγκαιμεν
		2	λάβοιτε	σχοῖτε	ἐνέγκαιτε
		3	λάβοιεν	σχοῖεν	ἐνέγκοιεν *or* ἐνέγκαιεν
imp.	sg.	2	λαβέ	σχές	ἔνεγκε
		3	λαβέτω	σχέτω	ἐνεγκάτω
	pl.	2	λάβετε	σχέτε	ἐνέγκατε
		3	λαβόντων	σχόντων	ἐνεγκάντων
inf.			λαβεῖν	σχεῖν	ἐνεγκεῖν
ppl.	masc.		λαβών, -όντος	σχών, -όντος	ἐνεγκών, -όντος *or* ἐνέγκας, -αντος
	fem.		λαβοῦσα, -ούσης	σχοῦσα, -ούσης	ἐνεγκοῦσα, -ούσης *or* ἐνέγκασα, -άσης
	neut.		λαβόν, -όντος	σχόν, -όντος	ἐνεγκόν, -όντος *or* ἐνέγκαν, -αντος

13.28   **Middle** forms:

			regular forms	φέρω (α-conjugation)
			λαμβάνω *get, take*	*carry, bring*
			stem λᾰβ-	stem ἐνεγκ(α)-
ind.	sg.	1	ἐλαβόμην	ἠνεγκάμην
		2	ἐλάβου	ἠνέγκω
		3	ἐλάβετο	ἠνέγκατο
	pl.	1	ἐλαβόμεθα	ἠνεγκάμεθα
		2	ἐλάβεσθε	ἠνέγκασθε
		3	ἐλάβοντο	ἠνέγκαντο
subj.	sg.	1	λάβωμαι	ἐνέγκωμαι
		2	λάβῃ	ἐνέγκῃ
		3	λάβηται	ἐνέγκηται
	pl.	1	λαβώμεθα	ἐνεγκώμεθα
		2	λάβησθε	ἐνέγκησθε
		3	λάβωνται	ἐνέγκωνται
opt.	sg.	1	λαβοίμην	ἐνεγκαίμην
		2	λάβοιο	ἐνέγκαιο
		3	λάβοιτο	ἐνέγκαιτο
	pl.	1	λαβοίμεθα	ἐνεγκαίμεθα
		2	λάβοισθε	ἐνέγκαισθε
		3	λάβοιντο	ἐνέγκαιντο
imp.	sg.	2	λαβοῦ	ἐνεγκοῦ
		3	λαβέσθω	ἐνεγκάσθω
	pl.	2	λάβεσθε	ἐνέγκασθε
		3	λαβέσθων	ἐνεγκάσθων
inf.			λαβέσθαι	ἐνέγκασθαι
ppl.	masc.		λαβόμενος, -ου	ἐνεγκάμενος, -ου
	fem.		λαβομένη, -ης	ἐνεγκαμένη, -ης
	neut.		λαβόμενον, -ου	ἐνεγκάμενον, -ου

Stems and Endings

13.29   The aorist stem of verbs with a thematic aorist is always **different from the present stem**, in three possible ways:

- because it has a different variant of the verb stem from the present: e.g. with λείπω (verb stem λειπ-/λοιπ-/λῐπ-): aorist stem λῐπ-;
- because the present stem is the result of changes/additions to the verb stem (→12.30): e.g. with λαμβάνω (verb stem ληβ-/λᾰβ-): aorist stem λᾰβ-;

– in some cases because an entirely different verb stem is used for the aorist than for the present (suppletive verbs, →11.13): e.g. with αἱρέω (verb stem αἱρη-/αἱρε-, ἑλ-): aorist stem ἑλ-.

13.30   The endings and thematic vowels used are those listed in 11.18–34, and are thus exactly the same as those used with the present system of -ω verbs (→12.3–13). Note that the aorist indicative, a past tense, uses secondary endings (these are thus the same as those of the imperfect of -ω verbs).

E.g. λαμβάνω: act: ind. ἔλαβ<u>ον</u> (cf. impf. ἐλάμβαν<u>ον</u>), opt. λάβ<u>οιμι</u> (pres. opt. λαμβάν<u>οιμι</u>), imp. λαβ<u>έ</u> (pres. imp. λάμβαν<u>ε</u>), ppl. λαβ<u>ών</u> (pres. ppl. λαμβάν<u>ων</u>), etc.

Note 1: Since the endings of thematic aorists are identical to those of the present system of -ω verbs, the only difference between present and aorist forms of these verbs is in the **stem** used; this is sometimes only a small difference. Contrast e.g. 1 sg. impf. act. ἔλειπον with 1 sg. aor. act. ind. ἔλιπον, and pres. act. inf. λείπειν with aor. act. inf. λιπεῖν, etc.

Note 2: For differences in accentuation between thematic aorist forms and present-stem participles and infinitives (e.g. aor. act. inf. λιπεῖν vs. pres. act. inf. λείπειν), →24.20. For the accentuation of imperatives such as λαβέ and ἐνεγκοῦ, →24.17.

'Irregular' Forms

13.31   The verb ἔχω *have, hold* has some irregular forms in the aorist (built on the stem σχ-): 2 sg. aor. act. imp. σχ-έ-ς, and sg. aor. opt. σχ-οίη-ν, σχ-οίη-ς, σχ-οίη.

13.32   Several verbs with a thematic aorist nonetheless have **forms with α** (analogous to the sigmatic aorist) in their conjugations:

– The aorist of φέρω *carry, bring* formed with stem **ἐνεγκ**-, has a mixed thematic/ α-conjugation; α predominates, particularly in the middle. E.g. 3 pl. aor. act. ind. ἤνεγκαν, 1 sg. aor. act. opt. ἐνέγκαιμι, etc. See the overview of forms, →13.27–28.

– In the aorist of λέγω *say, speak*, formed with stem **εἰπ**-, several forms with α are found alongside thematic ones. Alongside εἶπον, εἶπες and imp. εἰπέτω, εἴπετε also occur: εἶπα, εἶπας, εἰπάτω and εἴπατε. In Herodotus also alongside inf. εἰπεῖν and ppl. εἰπών: inf. εἶπαι, ppl. εἴπας, -αντος. Over time, the α-forms of this aorist gradually replaced the thematic ones.

– In addition, the verb χέω *pour* has 1 sg. aor. act. ind. ἔχεα, with (in compound forms only) inf. -χέαι, 3 sg. aor. imp. -χεάτω, etc. (These forms derive from a stem *χερ-, e.g. ἔχεα <*ἔχερ-m̥, cf. Homeric ἔχευα).

Note 1: For other aorists with an α-conjugation, e.g. ἐπριάμην, ἐπτάμην, →13.50. The difference with such aorists – root aorists – is that the α in ἐπριάμην, etc., is (considered to be) part of the stem, and used consistently throughout the conjugation.

The Most Common Thematic Aorists

Verbs with Vowel Variations between the Present and Aorist Stems

13.33   A number of verbs show different ablaut grades (→1.51–6) in the present and thematic aorist stems (the zero-grade is normally used in the aorist):

verb	verb stem	aorist stem	1 sg. ind.	inf.
ἕπομαι *follow*	ἑπ-/σπ-	σπ-	ἑσπόμην	σπέσθαι
ἔχω *have, hold*	ἐχ-/σχ-	σχ-	ἔσχον	σχεῖν
λείπω *leave*	λειπ-/λοιπ-/λῐπ-	λιπ-	ἔλιπον	λιπεῖν
πείθομαι *believe, obey*	πειθ-/ποιθ-/πῐθ-	πιθ-	ἐπιθόμην	πιθέσθαι
τρέπομαι *turn around (intr.)*	τρεπ-/τροπ-/τρᾰπ-	τραπ-	ἐτραπόμην	τραπέσθαι
φεύγω *flee*	φευγ-/φῠγ-	φυγ-	ἔφυγον	φυγεῖν

13.34   But several verbs with a reduplicated present stem have the zero-grade in the present stem, and normal e-grade in the aorist stem:

verb	verb stem	aorist stem	1 sg. ind.	inf.
γί-γν-ομαι *become, be born*	γεν(η)-/γον-/γν-	γεν-	ἐγενόμην	γενέσθαι
τίκτω *give birth* (<*τί-τκ-ω)	τεκ-/τοκ-/τκ-	τεκ-	ἔτεκον	τεκεῖν
πί-πτ-ω *fall*	πεσ-/πτ(ω)-	πεσ-	ἔπεσον	πεσεῖν

Other Differences between the Present and Aorist Stems

13.35   Several presents formed with a **nasal infix** (→12.30) have thematic aorists:

–   Verbs ending in -άνω/-άνομαι:

verb	verb stem	aorist stem	1 sg. ind.	inf.
αἰσθάνομαι *perceive*	αἰσθ-	αἰσθ-	ᾐσθόμην	αἰσθέσθαι
ἁμαρτάνω *miss, err*	ἁμαρτ-	ἁμαρτ-	ἥμαρτον	ἁμαρτεῖν
ἀπ-εχθάνομαι *incur hatred*	ἐχθ-	ἐχθ-	ἀπηχθόμην	ἀπεχθέσθαι
λαγχάνω *obtain by lot*	ληχ-/λᾰχ-	λαχ-	ἔλαχον	λαχεῖν
λαμβάνω *get, take*	ληβ-/λᾰβ-	λαβ-	ἔλαβον	λαβεῖν
λανθάνω *go unnoticed*	ληθ-/λᾰθ-	λαθ-	ἔλαθον	λαθεῖν
μανθάνω *learn, understand*	μαθ-	μαθ-	ἔμαθον	μαθεῖν
πυνθάνομαι *inquire, learn*	πευθ-/πῠθ-	πυθ-	ἐπυθόμην	πυθέσθαι
τυγχάνω *hit upon, happen to*	τευχ-/τῠχ-	τυχ-	ἔτυχον	τυχεῖν

–   Other verbs with a nasal infix:

verb	verb stem	aorist stem	1 sg. ind.	inf.
κάμνω *toil, be sick*	κᾰμ-/κμη-	καμ-	ἔκαμον	καμεῖν
πίνω *drink*	πω-/πο-/ πῑ-/πῐ-	πῑ-	ἔπιον	πιεῖν
τέμνω *cut*	τεμ-/τμη-	τεμ-	ἔτεμον	τεμεῖν
ἀφικνέομαι *arrive*	ἱκ-	ἱκ-	ἀφ-ικόμην	ἀφ-ικέσθαι

13.36   A few verbs whose present stem is formed with the suffix -(**ι**)**σκ**- have thematic aorists:

verb	verb stem	aorist stem	1 sg. ind.	inf.
ἀπο-θνήσκω/ -θνῄσκω *die*	θᾰν-/θνη-	θαν-	ἀπέ-θανον	ἀπο- θανεῖν
βλώσκω *come*	μολ-/(μ)βλω-	μολ-	ἔμολον	μολεῖν
εὑρίσκω *find*	εὑρ-	εὑρ-	ηὗρον	εὑρεῖν
πάσχω *suffer* (→1.96)	πενθ-/πονθ-/πᾰθ-	παθ-	ἔπαθον	παθεῖν

13.37   Two verbs show other differences between the present and aorist stems:

verb	verb stem	aorist stem	1 sg. ind.	inf.
ἄγω *lead, bring*	ἀγ-	ἀγαγ- (→11.50)	ἤγαγον	ἀγαγεῖν
βάλλω *throw, hit* (→1.78)	βᾰλ-/βλη-	βαλ-	ἔβαλον	βαλεῖν

Suppletive Verbs

13.38   Finally, a number of verbs have an aorist stem built on an entirely **different verb stem** from the present stem:

verb	verb stem	aorist stem	1 sg. ind.	inf.
αἱρέω *take*	αἱρη-/αἱρε-, ἑλ-	ἑλ-	εἷλον	ἑλεῖν
ἔρχομαι *go, come*	ἐρχ-, ἐλευθ-/ἐλ(ῠ)θ-, εἰ-/ῐ-	ἐλθ-	ἦλθον	ἐλθεῖν
ἐρωτάω *ask*	ἐρ-, ἐρωτη-/ἐρωτᾰ-	ἐρ-	ἠρόμην	ἐρέσθαι
ἐσθίω *eat*	ἐσθῑ-, φᾰγ-, ἐδε-/ἐδο-/ἐδ-	φαγ-	ἔφαγον	φαγεῖν
λέγω *say, speak*	λεγ-/λογ-, εἰπ-, ἐρ-/ρη-	εἰπ- but also: λεξ(α)-	εἶπον/ ἔλεξα	εἰπεῖν/ λέξαι
ὁράω *see*	ὁρᾰ-, ῐδ-, ὀπ-	ἰδ-	εἶδον	ἰδεῖν
τρέχω *run*	τρεχ-, δρᾰμ-	δραμ-	ἔδραμον	δραμεῖν
φέρω *carry, bring*	φερ-, ἐνεκ-/ἐνοκ-/ἐγκ-, οἰτ-	ἐνεγκ- (→13.28)	ἤνεγκον	ἐνεγκεῖν

Note 1: Observe that the aorist stem of λέγω is εἰπ- (cf. inf. εἰπεῖν). In the ind. εἶπον the augment has been absorbed into the opening diphthong. The ει in εἶδον (aor. with ὁράω) and εἷλον (aor. with αἱρέω), however, is different from the stems ἰδ- (cf. inf. ἰδεῖν) and ἑλ- (cf. inf. ἑλεῖν), due to augment ἐ- (→11.40).

Note 2: Of the two aorists of λέγω *say, speak*, εἶπον is more common, while ἔλεξα is in the classical period used especially in contexts in which its proper meaning *argue, explain* has some force (e.g. in the introductions of long directly reported speeches).

In compound verbs the difference between the two aorists is more marked. Compounds with -έλεξα typically belong to λέγω in its meaning *gather*, whereas compounds with -εῖπον have meanings related to *say, speak*. Compounds with the same prefix correspond to different presents: aorists with -εῖπον are suppletive to presents with -αγορεύω or -φημι. For instance:

ἀπέλεξα	with ἀπολέγω *pick out*	ἀπεῖπον	with ἀπαγορεύω *forbid*
ἐξέλεξα	with ἐκλέγω *pick out*	ἐξεῖπον	with ἐξαγορεύω *declare, make known*

κατέλεξα with καταλέγω *reckon* (mid.   κατεῖπον with καταγορεύω *denounce, speak*
            draw up a list)   *against*
συνέλεξα with συλλέγω *collect*   συνεῖπον with συναγορεύω/σύμφημι *agree,*
                                                              speak in support of

For other verbs with more than one type of aorist, →13.63.

Root Aorists

Overview of Forms

13.39   The conjugation of root aorists is as follows:

			stems ending in η	stem ending in ᾱ	stems ending in ω	stems ending in ῡ
			ἵσταμαι *come to stand*	ἀπο-διδράσκω *run away*	γιγνώσκω *know, recognize*	δύομαι *dive*
			aorist stem στη-	aorist stem δρᾱ-	aorist stem γνω-	aorist stem δῡ-
ind.	sg.	1	ἔστην	ἀπ-έδρᾱν	ἔγνων	ἔδῡν
		2	ἔστης	ἀπ-έδρᾱς	ἔγνως	ἔδῡς
		3	ἔστη	ἀπ-έδρᾱ	ἔγνω	ἔδῡ
	pl.	1	ἔστημεν	ἀπ-έδρᾱμεν	ἔγνωμεν	ἔδῡμεν
		2	ἔστητε	ἀπ-έδρᾱτε	ἔγνωτε	ἔδῡτε
		3	ἔστησαν	ἀπ-έδρᾱσαν	ἔγνωσαν	ἔδῡσαν
subj.	sg.	1	στῶ	ἀπο-δρῶ	γνῶ	δύω
		2	στῇς	ἀπο-δρᾷς	γνῷς	δύῃς
		3	στῇ	ἀπο-δρᾷ	γνῷ	δύῃ
	pl.	1	στῶμεν	ἀπο-δρῶμεν	γνῶμεν	δύωμεν
		2	στῆτε	ἀπο-δρᾶτε	γνῶτε	δύητε
		3	στῶσι(ν)	ἀπο-δρῶσι(ν)	γνῶσι(ν)	δύωσι(ν)
opt.	sg.	1	σταίην	ἀπο-δραίην	γνοίην	
		2	σταίης	ἀπο-δραίης	γνοίης	
		3	σταίη	ἀπο-δραίη	γνοίη	
	pl.	1	σταῖμεν[1]	ἀπο-δραῖμεν[1]	γνοῖμεν[1]	
		2	σταῖτε[2]	ἀπο-δραῖτε[2]	γνοῖτε[2]	
		3	σταῖεν	ἀπο-δραῖεν	γνοῖεν[3]	
imp.	sg.	2	στῆθι	ἀπό-δρᾱθι	γνῶθι	δῦθι
		3	στήτω	ἀπό-δρᾱτω	γνώτω	δύτω
	pl.	2	στῆτε	ἀπό-δρᾱτε	γνῶτε	δῦτε
		3	στάντων	ἀπο-δρᾱντων	γνόντων	δύντων
inf.			στῆναι	ἀπο-δρᾶναι	γνῶναι	δῦναι
ppl.	masc.		στάς, -άντος	ἀπο-δράς, -άντος	γνούς, -όντος	δύς, -ύντος
	fem.		στᾶσα, -άσης	ἀπο-δρᾶσα, -άσης	γνοῦσα, -ούσης	δῦσα, -ύσης
	neut.		στάν, -άντος	ἀπο-δράν, -άντος	γνόν, -όντος	δύν, -ύντος

[1] Also -ίημεν, e.g. σταίημεν, ἀποδραίημεν.
[2] Also -ίητε, e.g. σταίητε, γνοίητε.
[3] Also γνοίησαν.

Stems

13.40 The aorist stem of verbs with a root aorist is always an unelaborated verbal root (→23.2 with n.3), usually **different from the present stem**, in one of three ways:

– because a different variant of the verb stem is selected: e.g. with βαίνω *go, walk* (verb stem βη-/βᾰ(ν)-), aorist stem βη-;

– or because the present stem is the result of changes/additions to the verb stem (→12.25): e.g. with γιγνώσκω *know, recognize* (verb stem γνω-), aorist stem γνω-;

– or, in one case, because an entirely different verb stem is used for the aorist than for the present (a suppletive verb, →11.13): ζήω *live* (verb stem ζη-), aorist stem βιω- (verb stem βιω-).

With δύομαι *dive* (verb stem δῡ-/δῠ-) the present stem and aorist stem differ only in vowel length (δύομαι vs. ἔδῡν); with φύομαι *grow* (verb stem φῡ-), the aorist and present stems are identical (φῡ-).

13.41 Only a handful of verbs have a root aorist. Their stems end either in η (ᾱ after ρ), ῡ, or ω. The most frequent verbs and their stems are:

– Stems ending in η (-ᾱ):

verb	verb stem	aorist stem	1 sg. ind.	inf.
ἵσταμαι *come to stand*	στη-/στᾰ-	στη-	ἔστην	στῆναι
ἀπο-διδράσκω *run away*	δρᾱ-	δρᾱ-	ἀπ-έδραν	ἀπο-δρᾶναι
βαίνω *go, walk*	βη-/βᾰ(ν)-	βη-	ἔβην	βῆναι
(τλάω) *endure, dare to*	τλη-/τλᾰ-	τλη-	ἔτλην	τλῆναι

– Stems ending in ω:

ἁλίσκομαι *be captured*	ἁλ(ω)-	ἁλω-	ἑάλων/ἥλων	ἁλῶναι
γιγνώσκω *know, recognize*	γνω-	γνω-	ἔγνων	γνῶναι
ζήω *live*	ζη-, βιω-	βιω-	ἐβίων	βιῶναι

– Stems ending in ῡ:

δύομαι *dive*	δῡ-/δῠ-	δῡ-	ἔδυν	δῦναι
φύομαι *grow*	φῡ-	φῡ-	ἔφυν	φῦναι

Note 1: For a few other, much less frequent root aorists, e.g. ἔσβην (σβέννυμαι *go out, be quenched*), ἔφθην (φθάνω *be first*), →22.9.

Note that ἔσβην is not exactly conjugated as ἔστην, particularly in the opt. and ppl. (opt.: σβείην, etc.; ppl. σβείς, etc.; the η of the stem does not derive from ᾱ, but is the long variant of ε).

Note 2: For aor. ἐπριάμην (suppletive with ὠνέομαι *buy*), →13.50.

Endings

13.42 The endings used in the conjugation of root aorists are those detailed in 11.20–33. Note that **no thematic vowel is used** in conjugating the root aorist. The following additional points should be noted.

13.43 **Indicative**: formed with the augment and secondary endings. The 3 pl. ending is -σαν. E.g. ἔ-βη-<u>ν</u>, ἔ-βη-<u>ς</u>, ἔ-βη, ἔ-βη-<u>μεν</u>, ἔ-βη-<u>τε</u>, ἔ-βη-<u>σαν</u>.

13.44 **Subjunctive**: with aorist stems ending in α, η or ω (but not υ), the subjunctive endings have contracted with the preceding vowel, e.g. 1 sg. βῶ (<*βή-<u>ω</u>), 2 sg. βῇς (<*βή-<u>ης</u>); 1 sg. ἀπο-δρῶ (<*δρά-<u>ω</u>), 2 sg. δρᾷς (<*δρά-<u>ης</u>); 1 sg. γνῶ (<*γνώ-<u>ω</u>), 2 sg. γνῷς (<*γνώ-<u>ης</u>); but δύ-<u>ω</u>, δύ-<u>ης</u>, etc.

13.45 **Optative**: formed in the singular with optative suffix -ιη-, in the plural with optative suffix -ι-. The iota forms a diphthong with a **shortened** stem vowel (→1.70 n.1). Secondary endings are used: e.g. 1 sg. βαίη-<u>ν</u>, 1 pl. βαῖ-<u>μεν</u>; 1 sg. γνοίη-<u>ν</u>, 1 pl. γνοῖ-<u>μεν</u>; etc.

However, in the plural, alternative forms with optative suffix -ιη- are found, e.g. 1 pl. βαίη-<u>μεν</u>, 2 pl. γνοίη-<u>τε</u>.

Note 1: The optative of stems ending in υ appears not to occur, but →12.50 n.2.

13.46 **Imperative**: the 2 sg. imp. ends in -θι: e.g. βῆ-<u>θι</u>, γνῶ-<u>θι</u>, δῦ-<u>θι</u>. Note that the vowel of the stem is shortened in the 3 pl. imp.: e.g. βά-<u>ντων</u>, γνό-<u>ντων</u>, δύ-<u>ντων</u> (→1.70).

13.47 The **infinitive** ends in -ναι: e.g. βῆ-<u>ναι</u>, ἀποδρᾶ-<u>ναι</u>, φῦ-<u>ναι</u>.

13.48 In the **participle** the long stem vowel is **shortened** before -ντ- (→1.70): e.g. gen. sg. masc. βά-<u>ντ</u>-ος, gen. sg. fem. βάσης (<*βά<u>ντy</u>-); gen. sg. masc. γνό-<u>ντ</u>-ος, nom. sg. masc. γνούς (<*γνό<u>ντς</u>). For the entire declension, →5.17–18.

13.49 Apart from the verbs δίδωμι, τίθημι, and ἵημι (treated below, →13.51–2) and ἐπριάμην, ἐπτάμην (→13.50), root aorists use only active endings. Note, however, that the root aorists ἔστην, ἔδυν and ἔφυν go with the middle (senses of the) verbs ἵσταμαι, δύομαι and φύομαι (for details, →13.64), respectively, and that ἑάλων goes with middle-only ἁλίσκομαι. For such voice distinctions more generally, →35.

13.50 A root aorist with only middle forms is **ἐπριάμην**, suppletive aorist with the verb ὠνέομαι *buy*: e.g. 1 sg. ind. ἐπριάμην, 2 sg. ind. ἐπρίω; 1 sg. subj. πρίωμαι, 1 sg. opt. πριαίμην, inf. πρίασθαι, nom. sg. masc. ppl. πριάμενος. Note 2 sg. imp. πρίω (<*πρίασο).

Similarly, the verb πέτομαι *fly* has a middle root aorist ἐπτάμην, next to a thematic aor. ἐπτόμην, as well as a rare (active) root aorist ἔπτην.

δίδωμι, τίθημι **and** ἵημι

Overview of Forms

13.51   **Active** forms:

			δίδωμι	τίθημι	ἵημι
			give	*put, place*	*send, let go*
			stem δω-/δο-	stem θη-/θε-	stem ἡ-/ἑ-
ind.	sg.	1	ἔδωκα	ἔθηκα	ἧκα
		2	ἔδωκας	ἔθηκας	ἧκας
		3	ἔδωκε(ν)	ἔθηκε(ν)	ἧκε(ν)
	pl.	1	ἔδομεν[1]	ἔθεμεν[1]	εἷμεν[1]
		2	ἔδοτε[2]	ἔθετε[2]	εἷτε[2]
		3	ἔδοσαν[3]	ἔθεσαν[3]	εἷσαν[3]
subj.	sg.	1	δῶ	θῶ	ὧ
		2	δῷς	θῇς	ᾗς
		3	δῷ	θῇ	ᾗ
	pl.	1	δῶμεν	θῶμεν	ὧμεν
		2	δῶτε	θῆτε	ἧτε
		3	δῶσι(ν)	θῶσι(ν)	ὧσι(ν)
opt.	sg.	1	δοίην	θείην	εἵην
		2	δοίης	θείης	εἵης
		3	δοίη	θείη	εἵη
	pl.	1	δοῖμεν[4]	θεῖμεν[4]	εἷμεν[4]
		2	δοῖτε[5]	θεῖτε[5]	εἷτε[5]
		3	δοῖεν[6]	θεῖεν[6]	εἷεν[6]
imp.	sg.	2	δός	θές	ἕς
		3	δότω	θέτω	ἕτω
	pl.	2	δότε	θέτε	ἕτε
		3	δόντων	θέντων	ἕντων
inf.			δοῦναι	θεῖναι	εἷναι
ppl.	masc.		δούς, -όντος	θείς, -έντος	εἵς, ἕντος
	fem.		δοῦσα, -ούσης	θεῖσα, -είσης	εἷσα, εἵσης
	neut.		δόν, -όντος	θέν, -έντος	ἕν, ἕντος

[1] Also -καμεν, e.g. ἐδώκαμεν, ἐθήκαμεν.
[2] Also, -κατε, e.g. ἐδώκατε, ἥκατε.
[3] Also -καν, e.g. ἔθηκαν, ἧκαν.
[4] Also -ίημεν, e.g. δοίημεν, θείημεν.
[5] Also -ίητε, e.g. δοίητε, θείητε.
[6] Also -ίησαν, e.g. δοίησαν, εἵησαν.

13.52   **Middle** forms:

			δίδωμι	τίθημι	ἵημι
			give	*put, place*	*send, let go*
			stem δω-/δο-	stem θη-/θε-	stem ἡ-/ἑ-
ind.	sg.	1	ἐδόμην	ἐθέμην	εἵμην
		2	ἔδου	ἔθου	εἷσο
		3	ἔδοτο	ἔθετο	εἷτο
	pl.	1	ἐδόμεθα	ἐθέμεθα	εἵμεθα
		2	ἔδοσθε	ἔθεσθε	εἷσθε
		3	ἔδοντο	ἔθεντο	εἷντο
subj.	sg.	1	δῶμαι	θῶμαι	ὧμαι
		2	δῷ	θῇ	ᾗ
		3	δῶται	θῆται	ἧται
	pl.	1	δώμεθα	θώμεθα	ὥμεθα
		2	δῶσθε	θῆσθε	ἧσθε
		3	δῶνται	θῶνται	ὧνται
opt.	sg.	1	δοίμην	θείμην	εἵμην
		2	δοῖο	θεῖο	εἷο
		3	δοῖτο	θεῖτο	εἷτο
	pl.	1	δοίμεθα	θείμεθα	εἵμεθα
		2	δοῖσθε	θεῖσθε	εἷσθε
		3	δοῖντο	θεῖντο	εἷντο
imp.	sg.	2	δοῦ	θοῦ	οὗ
		3	δόσθω	θέσθω	ἔσθω
	pl.	2	δόσθε	θέσθε	ἔσθε
		3	δόσθων	θέσθων	ἔσθων
inf.			δόσθαι	θέσθαι	ἔσθαι
ppl.	masc.		δόμενος, -ου	θέμενος, -ου	ἔμενος, -ου
	fem.		δομένη, -ης	θεμένη, -ης	ἑμένη, -ης
	neut.		δόμενον, -ου	θέμενον, -ου	ἔμενον, -ου

Stems

13.53   The verbs **δίδωμι** *give* (verb stem δω-/δο-), **τίθημι** *put, place* (verb stem θη-/θε-) and **ἵημι** *send, let go* (verb stem ἡ-/ἑ-) have a distinct conjugation in the aorist:

– Most forms are built on the short variant of the (unelaborated) verb stem, and follow the root aorist pattern.

– However, a number are built on the long variant of the stem, and formed differently.

13.54   Observe that these verbs have a middle conjugation in addition to an active one (unlike the root aorists treated above).

13.55   In prose, the verb τίθημι occurs most often in compound forms (ὑποτίθημι, etc.), the verb ἵημι almost exclusively: their corresponding root aorists, accordingly, also occur most often in compounds.

Endings

13.56   In the **indicative**:

   – The **singular** forms of the active are built on the **long** form of the stem (δω-/θη-/ἡ-), and followed by a **kappa** and alpha-endings -α, -ας, -ε(ν): ἔ-δω-κα, ἔ-δω-κας, ἔ-δω-κε(ν); ἔ-θη-κα, ἔ-θη-κας, ἔ-θη-κε(ν); ἧ-κα, ἧ-κας, ἧ-κε(ν).
   – The **plural** forms of the active and all forms of the middle are built on the **short** form of the stem (δο-/θε-/ἑ-), and are formed like root aorists, e.g. 1 pl. act. ἔ-δο-μεν, 1 sg. mid. ἐ-δό-μην, 1 pl. mid. ἐ-δό-μεθα; 1 pl. act. ἔ-θε-μεν, 1 sg. mid. ἐ-θέ-μην, 1 pl. mid. ἐ-θέ-μεθα; 1 pl. act. εἷ-μεν, 1 sg. mid. εἵ-μην, 1 pl. mid. εἵ-μεθα.
   – However, alternative kappa/alpha-forms are sometimes found for these latter forms as well, e.g. ἐ-δώ-καμεν, ἔ-θη-καν, ἧ-καντο.
   – The second singular middle indicative has lost the σ of the ending -σο (→1.83), and the forms have contracted, in the case of ἔδου (<*ἔ-δο-(σ)ο) and ἔθου (<*ἔ-θε-(σ)ο), but not in εἷσο.

Note 1: Observe the different results of augment + stem with ἵημι: sg. ἧκα (<*ἔ-(y)η-κα) and εἷμεν (<*ἔ-(y)ε-μεν): →11.40.

13.57   The **subjunctive** endings contract with the preceding long vowel, sometimes after quantitative metathesis (→1.71): e.g. 1 sg. act. δῶ (<*δώ-ω), 2 sg. act. δῷς (<*δώ-ης), 1 sg. mid. δῶμαι (<*δώ-ω-μαι); 1 sg. act. ὧ (<ἕω <*ἥ-ω), 2 sg. act. ᾗς (<*ἥ-ης), 1 sg. mid. ὧμαι (<ἕωμαι <*ἥ-ω-μαι).

13.58   **Optatives** are formed with optative suffix -ιη- in the singular, with optative suffix -ι- in the plural and all middle forms. The iota forms a diphthong with the preceding short stem vowel. Secondary endings are used. E.g. 1 sg. act. δοίη-ν, 1 pl. act. δοῖ-μεν, 1 sg. mid. δοί-μην; 1 sg. act. θείη-ν, 1 pl. act. θεῖ-μεν, 1 sg. mid. θεί-μην.

   In the first- and second-person plural active, alternative forms with optative suffix -ιη- are found, e.g. 1 pl. θείη-μεν, 2 pl. θείη-τε. See the overview of forms, →13.51.

Note 1: Isolated thematic optative forms of these verbs occasionally occur, e.g. προοῖτο (3 sg. aor. mid. opt. of προΐημι *send forth*), ἐπιθοῖντο (3 pl. aor. mid. opt. of ἐπιτίθημι *put, place on*).

13.59   The subjunctive and optative forms differ from the corresponding forms of the present (→12.49–50) only by the absence of the present reduplication: compare 2 pl. act. subj. δῶτε, θῆτε, ἧτε with present διδῶτε, τιθῆτε, ἱῆτε; 3 sg. mid. opt. δοῖτο, θεῖτο, εἷτο with present διδοῖτο, τιθεῖτο, ἱεῖτο.

13.60   The **imperative** is built on the short variant of the stem. The second singular active imperative ends in -ς: δό-ς, θέ-ς, ἕ-ς.

   In all three verbs, the second singular middle imperative lost the σ of its ending -σο (→1.83), and the form has contracted: δοῦ (<*δό-(σ)ο), θοῦ (<*θέ-(σ)ο), οὗ (<*ἕ-(σ)ο).

13.61   The **active infinitive** is built on the short variant of the stem, and ends in -εναι, the ε of which contracts with the preceding short vowel: δοῦναι (<*δό-εναι), θεῖναι, εἷναι.

   The **middle infinitive** ends in -σθαι as normal: δό-σθαι, θέ-σθαι, ἕ-σθαι.

13.62   **Active participles** use the short variant of the stem before the suffix -ντ-: e.g. gen. sg. masc. θέ-ντ-ος, gen. sg. fem. θείσης (<*θέντγ-); gen. sg. masc. ἕ-ντ-ος, nom. sg. masc. εἵς (<*ἕντς). For the entire declension, →5.17–18.

   Middle participles also use the short variant of the stem before -μεν-: e.g. nom. sg. masc. θέ-μεν-ος, nom. sg. fem. θε-μέν-η, nom. sg. masc. ἕ-μεν-ος, nom. sg. fem. ἑ-μέν-η. For the entire declension, →5.3–4.

Verbs with More Than One Type of Aorist

13.63   Most verbs have only one type of aorist, but there are a few exceptions. Typically the different types of aorist are built on different variants of the verb stem or different verb stems altogether (suppletion, →11.13):

verb	verb stem	aorists	
ἐρωτάω ask	ἐρ-, ἐρωτη-/ἐρωτᾰ-	sigm.: ἠρώτησα	them.: (mid.) ἠρόμην
λέγω say	λεγ-/λογ-, εἰπ-, ἐρ-/ρη-	sigm.: ἔλεξα	them.: εἷπον (also εἷπα, →13.32)
(ἀπο)κτείνω kill	κτεν-/κτον-/κτᾰν-	pseudo-sigm.: (ἀπ)έκτεινα	them.: ἔκτανον (in poetry)
τρέπω turn	τρεπ-/τροπ-/τρᾰπ-	sigm.: ἔτρεψα	them.: ἔτραπον (in poetry)
πέτομαι fly	πετ-/πτη-/πτ(ᾰ)-	them.: ἐπτόμην	root: ἐπτάμην/ἔπτην

13.64   In several other cases, different aorist stems also represent a significant **difference of meaning**, especially in the middle (for such differences of voice, →35, and observe that similar meanings are also often expressed by θη-/η-aorists; for fuller details on these individual verbs, →22.9):

δύω *submerge* (verb stem δῡ-/δῠ-)

| with act. δύω | sigmatic aor. (act.) ἔδυσα: *submerged X* |
| with mp. δύομαι *dive* | root aor. ἔδυν: *dived* |

ἐγείρω *wake, rouse* (verb stem ἐγερ-/ἐγορ-/ἐγρ-)

| with act. ἐγείρω | pseudo-sigmatic aor. (act.) ἤγειρα: *woke X* |
| with mp. ἐγείρομαι *wake up* | thematic aor. (mid.) ἠγρόμην: *woke up* (also ἠγέρθην, →35.17 with n.2) |

ἵστημι *make stand, set up* (verb stem στη-/στᾰ-)

| with act. ἵστημι | sigmatic aor. (act.) ἔστησα: *made X to stand* |
| with mp. ἵσταμαι *come to stand* | root aor. ἔστην: *came to stand, stood still* |

πείθω *persuade* (verb stem πειθ-/ποιθ-/πῐθ-)

| with act. πείθω | sigmatic aor. (act.) ἔπεισα: *persuaded* |
| with mp. πείθομαι *believe, obey* | thematic aor. (mid.) ἐπιθόμην: *believed, obeyed* (also θη-aor. ἐπείσθην, →35.19 with n.1) |

τρέπω *turn* (verb stem τρεπ-/τροπ-/τρᾰπ-)

| with act. τρέπω | sigmatic/thematic aor. (act.) ἔτρεψα/ἔτραπον: *turned X* |
| with mp. τρέπομαι *turn around* (intr.) | thematic aor. (mid.) ἐτραπόμην: *turned around* (also ἐτράπην/ἐτρέφθην, →35.17 with n.2) |

φύω *cause to grow* (verb stem φῡ-)

| with act. φύω | sigmatic aor. (act.) ἔφυσα: *caused X to grow* |
| with mp. φύομαι *grow (up)* | root aor. ἔφυν: *grew (up), was born* |

14

The Aorist: Passive (θη-/η-)

Types of Aorist Passive Stem

14.1   There are two types of stem which are commonly called 'aorist passive':

– stems formed by adding the suffix -**θη**- to the verb stem, e.g. with παιδεύω *educate* (verb stem παιδευ-), aor. pass. stem παιδευθη-; with δείκνυμι *show* (verb stem δεικ-), aor. pass. stem δειχθη- (for χθ, →14.19 below);

– stems formed by adding the suffix -**η**- to the verb stem, e.g. with γράφω *write* (verb stem γρᾰφ-), aor. pass. stem γραφη-; with βλάπτω *harm, damage* (verb stem βλᾰβ-), aor. pass. stem βλαβη-.

The common element of both stems, then, is the vowel η. Most verbs have only one of the two stems, and the aorist in -θη- is the much more common one. Some verbs have both stems: e.g. with φαίνω *show* (verb stem φην-/φᾰν-), φανθη- and φανη-.

Note 1: The 'passive' aorist has passive meaning only when it is formed from active and some middle verbs which take an object or complement (→26.3): e.g. with παιδεύω *educate*, ἐπαιδεύθην *was educated*; with δείκνυμι *show*, ἐδείχθην *was shown*; with αἰτιάομαι *accuse*, ᾐτιάθην *was accused*. With other verbs, however, the passive aorist does not have (or rarely has) passive meaning. Thus with βούλομαι *want, prefer*, there is nothing semantically passive about the aorist ἐβουλήθην *wanted*. Of the 'passive' aorists formed with -η-, in fact, only a minority (regularly) has passive meaning. Below, therefore, these aorists are called 'θη-aorist' or 'η-aorist', and with several verbs the meaning of the θη-/η-aorist is added for clarity.

For full details about the meanings and forms of the 'passive' aorist, and the development of its use in Greek, →35.

Conjugation of θη-Aorists and η-Aorists

Overview of Forms

14.2   **θη-aorists**:

			verb stems ending in ι, υ or a diphthong	verb stems ending in α, ε, ο or η	verb stems ending in a labial or velar stop	verb stems ending in a dental stop	verb stems ending in a resonant
			παιδεύω *educate* stem παιδευθη-	τιμάω *honour* stem τιμηθη-	δείκνυμι *show* stem δειχθη-	κομίζω *convey* stem κομισθη-	ἀγγέλλω *report* stem ἀγγελθη-
ind.	sg.	1	ἐπαιδεύθην	ἐτιμήθην	ἐδείχθην	ἐκομίσθην	ἠγγέλθην
		2	ἐπαιδεύθης	ἐτιμήθης	ἐδείχθης	ἐκομίσθης	ἠγγέλθης
		3	ἐπαιδεύθη	ἐτιμήθη	ἐδείχθη	ἐκομίσθη	ἠγγέλθη
	pl.	1	ἐπαιδεύθημεν	ἐτιμήθημεν	ἐδείχθημεν	ἐκομίσθημεν	ἠγγέλθημεν
		2	ἐπαιδεύθητε	ἐτιμήθητε	ἐδείχθητε	ἐκομίσθητε	ἠγγέλθητε
		3	ἐπαιδεύθησαν	ἐτιμήθησαν	ἐδείχθησαν	ἐκομίσθησαν	ἠγγέλθησαν
subj.	sg.	1	παιδευθῶ	τιμηθῶ	δειχθῶ	κομισθῶ	ἀγγελθῶ
		2	παιδευθῇς	τιμηθῇς	δειχθῇς	κομισθῇς	ἀγγελθῇς
		3	παιδευθῇ	τιμηθῇ	δειχθῇ	κομισθῇ	ἀγγελθῇ
	pl.	1	παιδευθῶμεν	τιμηθῶμεν	δειχθῶμεν	κομισθῶμεν	ἀγγελθῶμεν
		2	παιδευθῆτε	τιμηθῆτε	δειχθῆτε	κομισθῆτε	ἀγγελθῆτε
		3	παιδευθῶσι(ν)	τιμηθῶσι(ν)	δειχθῶσι(ν)	κομισθῶσι(ν)	ἀγγελθῶσι(ν)
opt.	sg.	1	παιδευθείην	τιμηθείην	δειχθείην	κομισθείην	ἀγγελθείην
		2	παιδευθείης	τιμηθείης	δειχθείης	κομισθείης	ἀγγελθείης
		3	παιδευθείη	τιμηθείη	δειχθείη	κομισθείη	ἀγγελθείη
	pl.	1	παιδευθεῖμεν[1]	τιμηθεῖμεν[1]	δειχθεῖμεν[1]	κομισθεῖμεν[1]	ἀγγελθεῖμεν[1]
		2	παιδευθεῖτε[1]	τιμηθεῖτε[1]	δειχθεῖτε[1]	κομισθεῖτε[1]	ἀγγελθεῖτε[1]
		3	παιδευθεῖεν[1]	τιμηθεῖεν[1]	δειχθεῖεν[1]	κομισθεῖεν[1]	ἀγγελθεῖεν[1]
imp.	sg.	2	παιδεύθητι	τιμήθητι	δείχθητι	κομίσθητι	ἀγγέλθητι
		3	παιδευθήτω	τιμηθήτω	δειχθήτω	κομισθήτω	ἀγγελθήτω
	pl.	2	παιδεύθητε	τιμήθητε	δείχθητε	κομίσθητε	ἀγγέλθητε
		3	παιδευθέντων	τιμηθέντων	δειχθέντων	κομισθέντων	ἀγγελθέντων
inf.			παιδευθῆναι	τιμηθῆναι	δειχθῆναι	κομισθῆναι	ἀγγελθῆναι
ppl.	masc.		παιδευθείς, -θέντος	τιμηθείς, -θέντος	δειχθείς, -θέντος	κομισθείς, -θέντος	ἀγγελθείς, -θέντος
	fem.		παιδευθεῖσα, -θείσης	τιμηθεῖσα, -θείσης	δειχθεῖσα, -θείσης	κομισθεῖσα, -θείσης	ἀγγελθεῖσα, -θείσης
	neut.		παιδευθέν, -θέντος	τιμηθέν, -θέντος	δειχθέν, -θέντος	κομισθέν, -θέντος	ἀγγελθέν, -θέντος

---

[1] Also -θείημεν, -θείητε, -θείησαν, e.g. παιδευθείημεν, παιδευθείητε, παιδευθείησαν.

14.3   **η-aorists**:

			η-aorists φαίνω *show* stem φανη-
ind.	sg.	1	ἐφάνην
		2	ἐφάνης
		3	ἐφάνη
	pl.	1	ἐφάνημεν
		2	ἐφάνητε
		3	ἐφάνησαν
subj.	sg.	1	φανῶ
		2	φανῇς
		3	φανῇ
	pl.	1	φανῶμεν
		2	φανῆτε
		3	φανῶσι(ν)
opt.	sg.	1	φανείην
		2	φανείης
		3	φανείη
	pl.	1	φανεῖμεν[1]
		2	φανεῖτε[1]
		3	φανεῖεν[1]
imp.	sg.	2	φάνηθι
		3	φανήτω
	pl.	2	φάνητε
		3	φανέντων
inf.			φανῆναι
ppl.	masc.		φανείς, -έντος
	fem.		φανεῖσα, -είσης
	neut.		φανέν, -έντος

---

[1] Also -είημεν, -είητε, -είησαν.

Endings

14.4   θη- and η-aorists have **active** personal endings (→11.20).

14.5   **Indicatives** are formed with the **augment** (→11.35–42), and active secondary endings (→11.22–7): e.g. 1 sg. ἐ-παιδεύθη-<u>ν</u>, 2 sg. ἐ-δείχθη-<u>ς</u>, 2 pl. ἐ-γράφη-<u>τε</u>, etc. The ending of 3 pl. ind. is -σαν, e.g. ἐ-παιδεύθη-<u>σαν</u>.

14.6 **Imperative**: the 2 sg. imp. ends in -θι: e.g. 2 sg. imp. φάνη-θι, κατακλίνη-θι. With
       θη-aorists, however, the ending changes to -τι, e.g. παιδεύθη-τι (instead of
       expected †-τηθι <*-θηθι (→1.97), by analogy with e.g. παιδεύθητε, 2 pl.).

       Other imperatives have the regular (active) endings: e.g. 2 pl. παιδεύθη-τε, 3 pl.
       φανέ-ντων (<*-ήντων, →1.70)

14.7 **Subjunctives** are formed with the long thematic vowel of the subjunctive
       (→11.16) and primary endings; these contract with the η of the stem, sometimes
       after quantitative metathesis (→1.71). E.g. 1 pl. δειχθῶμεν (<-θέωμεν <*-θήωμεν), 2
       pl. γραφῆτε (<*-ήητε).

14.8 **Optatives** are formed with the optative suffix -ιη- in the singular, with the optative
       suffix -ι- in the plural (-ιη- is found occasionally also in the plural). The iota forms
       a diphthong with the η of the stem, shortened to ε (→1.70 n.1). Active secondary
       endings are added. E.g. 1 sg. φανείη-ν, 1 pl. παιδευθεῖ-μεν.

14.9 The **infinitive** ends in -ναι: e.g. λειφθῆ-ναι.

14.10 **Participles** add -ντ- to the stem, which is shortened to -(θ)ε- (→1.70): e.g. gen. sg.
       masc. παιδευθέ-ντ-ος, gen. sg. fem. γραφείσης (<*-έντη-). For the entire declension,
       →5.17–18.

θη-Aorist Stems

Formation of θη-Aorist Stems

Verb Stems Ending in υ or a Diphthong

14.11 Verb stems ending in **υ or a diphthong** stay **unchanged** before the added -θη-
       (although there may be variations in vowel length). Some examples:

verb		verb stem	θη-aor. stem	1 sg. ind.	inf.
θύω	*sacrifice*	θῡ-/θῠ-	τῠθη- (→1.97)	ἐτύθην	τυθῆναι
ἱδρύω	*found, establish*	ἱδρυ-	ἱδρυθη-	ἱδρύθην	ἱδρυθῆναι
λύω	*loosen, release*	λῡ-/λῠ-	λῠθη-	ἐλύθην	λυθῆναι
μηνύω	*reveal, make known*	μηνῡ-	μηνυθη-	ἐμηνύθην	μηνυθῆναι
παίω	*strike*	παι-	παιθη-	ἐπαίθην	παιθῆναι
παιδεύω	*educate*	παιδευ-	παιδευθη-	ἐπαιδεύθην	παιδευθῆναι
λούω	*bathe*	λου-	λουθη-	ἐλούθην	λουθῆναι

Note 1: With monosyllabic stems which have long ῡ in the present stem, the θη-aorist has
a short ῠ. See e.g. θύω, λύω.

14.12   The θη-aorist of κάω/καίω *set on fire*, which originally had verb stem *κᾰϝ- (→12.29), is
ἐκαύθην. The θη-aorist of χέω *pour* (original verb stem *χεϝ-/χῠ-) is ἐχύθην.

Verb Stems Ending in Other Vowels

14.13   With verb stems ending in η/ε, η/ᾰ, ω/ο (i.e. contract verbs), -θη- is added to the
long variant of the verb stem (→11.11):

- pres. stem ε: θη-aor. stem η;
- pres. stem ᾰ: θη-aor. stem η (but ᾱ after ε, ι or ρ);
- pres. stem ο: θη-aor. stem ω; a few verbs with a verb stem ending in ω have
  a similarly formed θη-aorist.

Some examples:

verb	verb stem	θη-aor. stem	1 sg. ind.	inf.
ποιέω *make, do*	ποιη-/ποιε-	ποιηθη-	ἐποιήθην	ποιηθῆναι
τιμάω *honour*	τιμη-/τιμᾰ-	τιμηθη-	ἐτιμήθην	τιμηθῆναι
πειράομαι *try*	πειρᾱ-/ πειρᾰ-	πειρᾱθη-	ἐπειρᾱθην *tried*	πειρᾱθῆναι
αἰτιάομαι *accuse*	αἰτιᾱ-/αἰτιᾰ-	αἰτιᾱθη-	ᾐτιᾱθην *was accused*	αἰτιᾱθῆναι
ἀξιόω *deem worthy*	ἀξιω-/ἀξιο-	ἀξιωθη-	ἠξιώθην	ἀξιωθῆναι
σῴζομαι *escape*	σω-	σωθη-	ἐσώθην *escaped*	σωθῆναι
τιτρώσκω *wound*	τρω-	τρωθη-	ἐτρώθην	τρωθῆναι

14.14   The alternation between ᾰ and η also occurs with the passive-only -μι verbs
δύνᾰμαι *have the power (to), be able (to)*, aor. ἐδυνήθην *was able* (also, more rarely,
ἐδυνάσθην, →14.27), and **ἐπίστᾰμαι** *know (how to), understand*, aor. ἠπιστήθην
knew.

14.15   With the verbs **ἵστημι, τίθημι, ἵημι** and **δίδωμι**, the θη-aorist is built on the short
variant of the stem:

verb	verb stem	θη-aor. stem	1 sg. ind.	inf.
ἵστημι *make stand, set up*	στη-/στᾰ-	στᾰθη-	ἐστᾰθην	σταθῆναι
τίθημι *put, place*	θη-/θε-	τεθη- (→1.97)	ἐτέθην	τεθῆναι
ἵημι *send, let go*	ἡ-/ἑ-	ἑθη-	εἵθην (→11.40)	ἑθῆναι
δίδωμι *give*	δω-/δο-	δοθη-	ἐδόθην	δοθῆναι

Note 1: The simplex forms of ἵημι are rare, especially in prose; the verb normally occurs in
compound forms like ἀφείθην, παρείθην.

14.16   Several verbs in -άω and -έω, which have a verb stem ending in a σ (→12.29 n.1), retain that σ before the added θη:

verb	verb stem	θη-aor. stem	1 sg. ind.	inf.
αἰδέομαι *stand in awe*	αἰδε(σ)-	αἰδεσθη-	ἠδέσθην *stood in awe*	αἰδεσθῆναι
ἔραμαι *love*	ἐρᾰ(σ)-	ἐρασθη-	ἠράσθην *fell in love*	ἐρασθῆναι
τελέω *finish*	τελε(σ)-	τελεσθη-	ἐτελέσθην	τελεσθῆναι

Also note verbs in -άννυμι and -έννυμι (which have a stem in σ):

κεράννυμι *mix*	κερᾰ(σ)-/κρᾱ-	κερασθη-	ἐκεράσθην	κερασθῆναι
σβέννυμι *quench, put out*	σβη-/σβε(σ)-	σβεσθη-	ἐσβέσθην	σβεσθῆναι

Some verbs which do not have this σ as part of their stem nevertheless have it in their θη-aorist (a so-called 'parasitic' σ). So e.g. with γιγνώσκω *know, recognize* (verb stem γνω-), ἐγνώσθην. For these verbs, →14.27 below.

14.17   Observe the following further exceptions with verbs in -έω:

verb	verb stem	θη-aor. stem	1 sg. ind.	inf.
αἰνέω *praise*	αἰνε-	αἰνεθη-	ἠνέθην	αἰνεθῆναι
αἱρέω *take*	αἱρη-/αἱρε-, ἑλ-	αἱρεθη-	ᾑρέθην *was taken*	αἱρεθῆναι
also mid. αἱρέομαι *choose*			*was chosen*	
δέω *bind*	δη-/δε-	δεθη-	ἐδέθην	δεθῆναι
καλέω *call, summon*	κᾰλε-/κλη-	κληθη-	ἐκλήθην	κληθῆναι
ὠθέω *thrust, push*	ὠθη-/ὠθ(ε)-	ὠσθη- (→14.20)	ἐώσθην	ὠσθῆναι

Verb Stems Ending in a Labial or Velar Stop

14.18   Stems ending in a labial stop get a θη-aor. stem in **φθη** (π/β/φ + θη > φθη):

verb	verb stem	θη-aor. stem	1 sg. ind.	inf.
λείπω *leave*	λειπ-/λοιπ-/λῐπ-	λειφθη-	ἐλείφθην	λειφθῆναι
πέμπω *send*	πεμπ-/πομπ-	πεμφθη-	ἐπέμφθην	πεμφθῆναι
τρίβω *rub*	τρῑβ-/τρῐβ-	τριφθη-	ἐτρίφθην	τριφθῆναι
λαμβάνω *get, take*	ληβ-/λᾰβ-	ληφθη-	ἐλήφθην	ληφθῆναι

Note especially verbs that have a present in -πτω (→12.27):

ῥίπτω *throw*	ῥῑπ-	ῥιφθη-	ἐρρίφθην	ῥιφθῆναι
βλάπτω *harm, damage*	βλᾰβ-	βλαφθη-	ἐβλάφθην	βλαφθῆναι
κρύπτω *hide*	κρῠφ-/κρῠβ-	κρυφθη-	ἐκρύφθην	κρυφθῆναι

Note 1: For the more common η-aorists (with passive meaning) ἐτρίβην *was rubbed* (τρίβω), ἐβλάβην *was harmed* (βλάπτω), ἐρρίφην *was thrown* (ῥίπτω), →14.30.

14.19   Stems ending in a velar stop get a θη-aor. stem in **χθη** (κ/γ/χ + θη > χθη):

verb	verb stem	θη-aor. stem	1 sg. ind.	inf.
διώκω *chase*	διωκ-	διωχθη-	ἐδιώχθην	διωχθῆναι
ἄγω *lead, bring*	ἀγ-	ἀχθη-	ἤχθην	ἀχθῆναι
λέγω *say, speak*	λεγ-/λογ-,	λεχθη-	ἐλέχθην	λεχθῆναι
διαλέγομαι *converse*	εἰπ-, ἐρ-/ ῥη-		διελέχθην *discussed*	διαλεχθῆναι
συλλέγομαι *come together*			συνελέχθην *came together*	συλλεχθῆναι
ἄρχω *rule, begin*	ἀρχ-	ἀρχθη-	ἤρχθην	ἀρχθῆναι

Note especially (almost all) verbs that have a present in -ττω/-ττομαι (→13.22), a few in -ζω, and several in -νυμι:

ἀπαλλάττομαι *depart*	ἀλλᾰγ-	ἀλλαχθη-	ἀπ-ηλλάχθην *departed*	ἀπαλλαχθῆναι
τάττω *array, appoint*	τᾰγ-	ταχθη-	ἐτάχθην	ταχθῆναι
ὀρύττω *dig*	ὀρῠχ-	ὀρυχθη-	ὠρύχθην	ὀρυχθῆναι
δαΐζω *cleave*	δαϊγ-	δαϊχθη-	ἐδαΐχθην	δαϊχθῆναι
δείκνυμι *show*	δεικ-	δειχθη-	ἐδείχθην	δειχθῆναι
μ(ε)ίγνυμι *mix*	μειγ-/μῑγ-	μ(ε)ιχθη-	ἐμ(ε)ίχθην	μ(ε)ιχθῆναι

Note 1: Besides ἐλέχθην (λέγω), the aorist ἐρρήθην (suppletive, →11.13) occurs frequently (e.g. ἐρρήθη *it was said*).
Note 2: For the more common η-aorists συνελέγην *came together* (συλλέγομαι), ἀπηλλάγην *departed* (ἀπ-αλλάττομαι; -ηλλάγην is more frequent in prose, -ηλλάχθην in poetry), ἐμίγην *was mixed, had intercourse with* (μείγνυμι), →14.30.

Verb Stems Ending in a Dental Stop

14.20   Stems ending in a dental stop get a θη-aor. stem in **σθη** (τ/δ/θ + θη > σθη, →1.89):

verb	verb stem	θη-aor. stem	1 sg. ind.	inf.
ψεύδομαι *err*	ψευδ-	ψευσθη-	ἐψεύσθην *erred*	ψευσθῆναι
ἥδομαι *enjoy*	ἡδ-	ἡσθη-	ἥσθην *enjoyed*	ἡσθῆναι
πείθω *persuade*	πειθ-/ποιθ-/πῐθ-	πεισθη-	ἐπείσθην	πεισθῆναι

Note especially most verbs that have a present in -ζω/-ζομαι, and a few in -ττω (→13.23):

κομίζω *convey*	κομῐδ-	κομισθη-	ἐκομίσθην	κομισθῆναι
νομίζω *believe*	νομῐδ-	νομισθη-	ἐνομίσθην	νομισθῆναι
λογίζομαι *count, reckon*	λογῐδ-	λογισθη-	ἐλογίσθην *was counted*	λογισθῆναι
ἁρμόζω/ἁρμόττω *fit together*	ἁρμοδ-/ἁρμοτ-	ἁρμοσθη-	ἡρμόσθην	ἁρμοσθῆναι
πλάττω *mould*	πλᾰθ-	πλασθη-	ἐπλάσθην	πλασθῆναι

Note 1: With ψεύδω *cheat, deceive*, sigmatic aor. mid. ἐψευσάμην = *lied*; θη-aor. ἐψεύσθην = *was mistaken, was deceived, erred*.

Note 2: Next to ἐπείσθην *was/became persuaded*, there is also a thematic middle aorist ἐπιθόμην *believed, obeyed* (→13.64). ἐπείσθην is more regular in prose, and became progressively more common.

Verb Stems Ending in a Resonant

14.21 Verb stems ending in a resonant (nasal/liquid) **stay unchanged** before -θη-. Note especially verbs that have a present in -λλω in -αίνω/-αίρω, -είνω/-είρω, -ἱνω/-ἱρω, -ὑνω/-ὑρω, (→12.28). Some examples:

verb	verb stem	θη-aor. stem	1 sg. ind.	inf.
αἰσχΰνομαι *be ashamed*	αἰσχῠν-	αἰσχΰνθη-	ᾐσχΰνθην *was ashamed*	αἰσχυνθῆναι
ἀγγέλλω *report*	ἀγγελ-	ἀγγελθη-	ἠγγέλθην	ἀγγελθῆναι
τίλλω *pluck*	τῑλ-	τιλθη-	ἐτίλθην	τιλθῆναι
αἴρω *lift*	ἀρ-	ἀρθη-	ἤρθην	ἀρθῆναι
ἐγείρομαι *wake up*	ἐγερ-/ἐγορ-/ ἐγρ-	ἐγερθη-	ἠγέρθην *woke up*	ἐγερθῆναι
μιαίνω *stain*	μιᾰν-	μιανθη-	ἐμιάνθην	μιανθῆναι
φαίνω *show*	φην-/φᾰν-	φανθη-	ἐφάνθην	φανθῆναι

Note 1: With φαίνω *show*, ἐφάνθην = *was shown* (pass.), η-aor. ἐφάνην = *appeared, seemed* (→14.30).

Note 2: Next to ἠγέρθην (ἐγείρομαι *wake up*), there is also a thematic middle aorist ἠγρόμην *woke up* (→13.64). ἠγέρθην is normal in prose, and on the whole more common.

14.22 Observe the aorist passive of τείνω *stretch*:

τείνω *stretch*	τεν-/τᾰ- (→1.86) τᾰθη-		ἐτάθην	ταθῆναι

14.23 Some verbs with a present stem ending in a nasal do not have that nasal in the aorist passive (it was not originally part of the verb stem, but a suffix added in the present stem (→12.30), even though this was sometimes extended to other stems):

κλίνομαι *lean*	κλῑ(ν)-	κλῑθη-	ἐκλίθην *leaned*	κλίθῆναι
κρίνω *pick out, decide*	κρῑ(ν)-	κρῐθη-	ἐκρίθην	κρίθῆναι

For the more common η-aorist -εκλίνην *leaned* (κλίνω, but only in compounds), →14.30.

14.24 Numerous verbs with a stem in a nasal or liquid have an η-aorist: →14.30. Several other verbs which have a stem in a nasal or liquid form a θη-aorist with an extra η intervening between stem and θη: e.g. with νέμω *deal out* (verb stem νεμ-), ἐνεμήθην. For these verbs, →14.28.

14.25 The θη-aor. of εὑρίσκω *find* (verb stem εὑρ-, cf. inf. aor. act. εὑρ-εῖν), is ηὑρέθην.

Suppletive Stems

14.26   With a few frequently occurring verbs the stem of the θη-aor. is wholly unrelated to that of the present stem (→11.13):

verb	verb stem	θη-aor. stem	1 sg. ind.	inf.
λέγω *say, speak*	λεγ-/λογ-, εἰπ-, ἐρ-/ῥη-	ῥηθη-	ἐρρήθην	ῥηθῆναι
ὁράω *see*	ὁρᾱ-, ἰδ-, ὀπ-	ὀφθη-	ὤφθην	ὀφθῆναι
φέρω *carry, bring*	φερ-, ἐνεκ-/ἐνοκ-/ἐγκ-, οἰτ-	ἐνεχθη-	ἠνέχθην	ἐνεχθῆναι

Note 1: For ἐλέχθην as alternative to ἐρρήθην (λέγω), →14.19 above.

Further Notes and Exceptions

14.27   Numerous verbs with a stem ending in a vowel get a 'parasitic' σ between the verb stem and the θη-suffix (contrast 14.16, verbs with a stem ending in an original σ; this σ spread to other vowel-verbs). For instance:

verb	verb stem	θη-aor. stem	1 sg. ind.	inf.
ἄγαμαι *admire*	ἀγᾰ-	ἀγασθη-	ἠγάσθην *admired*	ἀγασθῆναι
γιγνώσκω *know, recognize*	γνω-	γνωσθη-	ἐγνώσθην	γνωσθῆναι
δράω *do*	δρᾱ-/δρᾰ-	δρασθη-	ἐδράσθην	δρασθῆναι
δύναμαι *be able*	δυνη-/δυνᾰ-	δυνασθη-	ἐδυνάσθην *was able*	δυνασθῆναι
ἕλκω *draw, drag*	ἑλκ(ῠ)-	ἑλκυσθη-	εἱλκύσθην (→11.40)	ἑλκυσθῆναι
ἐσθίω *eat*	ἐσθῐ-, φᾰγ-, ἐδε-/ἐδο-/ἐδ-	ἐδεσθη-	ἠδέσθην	ἐδεσθῆναι
κελεύω *order*	κελευ-	κελευσθη-	ἐκελεύσθην	κελευσθῆναι
κλαίω/κλάω *cry, weep*	κλα(υ)-	κλαυσθη-	ἐκλαύσθην	κλαυσθῆναι
κλῄω/κλείω *close*	κλη-/κλει-	κλησθη-/ κλεισθη-	ἐκλήσθην/ ἐκλείσθην	κλησθῆναι κλεισθῆναι
μιμνῄσκομαι *remember*	μνη-	μνησθη-	ἐμνήσθην *remembered*	μνησθῆναι
ὄμνυμι *swear*	ὀμ(ο)-	ὀμοσθη-	ὠμόσθην, also ὠμόθην	ὀμοσθῆναι
παύω *stop*	παυ-	παυσθη-	ἐπαύσθην, also ἐπαύθην	παυσθῆναι
πίμπλημι *fill*	πλη-/πλᾰ-	πλησθη-	ἐπλήσθην	πλησθῆναι
πίμπρημι *burn*	πρη-/πρᾰ-	πρησθη-	ἐπρήσθην	πρησθῆναι
σπάω *draw, tear*	σπᾰ-	σπασθη-	ἐσπάσθην	σπασθῆναι
χρήομαι *use, need*	χρη-	χρησθη-	ἐχρήσθην	χρησθῆναι
χρίω *anoint*	χρῑ-	χρισθη-	ἐχρίσθην	χρισθῆναι

For ἐδυνήθην, the more frequent alternative to ἐδυνάσθην (δύναμαι), →14.14 above.

14.28   Various verbs with stems ending in a consonant have an additional η between the verb stem and the θη-suffix. For example:

stems ending in a dental stop:

ἁμαρτάνω *miss, err*   ἁμαρτ-   ἁμαρτη̲θη-   ἡμαρτήθην   ἁμαρτηθῆναι

stems ending in a resonant:

βούλομαι *want, prefer*   βουλ-   βουλη̲θη-   ἐβουλήθην *wanted*   βουληθῆναι
νέμω *deal out*   νεμ-   νεμη̲θη-   ἐνεμήθην   νεμηθῆναι

stems ending in ξ or ψ:

αὐξάνω, αὔξω *increase*   αὐξ-   αὐξη̲θη-   ηὐξήθην   αὐξηθῆναι
ἕψω *boil*   ἑψ-   ἑψη̲θη-   ἡψήθην   ἑψηθῆναι

Note 1: With γίγνομαι, thematic aor. mid. ἐγενόμην = *became, was born*; θη-aor. ἐγενήθην = *was born*. ἐγενήθην is much more frequent in later Greek.

η-Aorist Stems

Formation of η-Aorist Stems

14.29   η-aorists occur only with stems ending in a consonant. The suffix -η- is added immediately to the verb stem, which may show a different vowel grade from the present stem (see below).

Verbs without Vowel Differences between the Present and η-Aorist Stem

14.30   The following verbs have the same vowel in the present and η-aorist stems:

verb	*verb stem*	*η-aor. stem*	*1 sg. ind.*	*inf.*
βλάπτω *harm, damage*	βλᾰβ-	βλαβη-	ἐβλάβην	βλαβῆναι
τύπτω *hit*	τῠπ-	τυπη-	ἐτύπην	τυπῆναι
κόπτω *hit*	κοπ-	κοπη-	ἐκόπην	κοπῆναι
γράφω *write*	γρᾰφ-	γραφη-	ἐγράφην	γραφῆναι
ῥίπτω *throw*	ῥῑπ-	ῥῐφη-	ἐρρίφην	ῥιφῆναι
κρύπτω *hide*	κρῠφ-/κρῠβ-	κρυφη-	ἐκρύφην	κρυφῆναι
θάπτω *bury*	θᾰφ-	ταφη- (→1.97)	ἐτάφην	ταφῆναι
(κατ)άγνυμαι *break* (intr.)	ἀγ-/ᾰ̓γ-	ἀγη-	κατ-εάγην *broke* (intr.)	καταγῆναι
ἀπαλλάττομαι *depart*	ἀλλᾰγ-	ἀλλαγη-	ἀπ-ηλλάγην *departed*	ἀπαλλαγῆναι

πλήττω strike	πληγ-/πλᾰγ-	πληγη-	ἐπλήγην	πληγῆναι
σύλλέγομαι come together	λεγ-/λογ-	λεγη-	συν-ελέγην came together	συλλεγῆναι
κατακλίνομαι recline	κλῐ(ν)-	κλινη-	κατ-εκλίνην reclined	κατακλινῆναι
σφάλλομαι stumble	σφᾰλ-	σφαλη-	ἐσφάλην stumbled	σφαλῆναι
μαίνομαι rage	μην-/μᾰν-	μανη-	ἐμάνην raged	μανῆναι
φαίνομαι appear, seem	φην-/φᾰν-	φανη-	ἐφάνην appeared	φανῆναι
χαίρω rejoice	χᾰρ-	χαρη-	ἐχάρην rejoiced	χαρῆναι

Note 1: Many of these verbs also have a θη-aorist: βλάπτω, θάπτω, ῥίπτω, κρύπτω, ἀλλάττω, συλλέγω, κλίνω, φαίνω. →14.18–19.

Verbs with Vowel Differences between the Present and η-Aorist Stems

14.31   Verbs that have vowel-variation (ablaut, →1.51) between the present and η-aorist stems (the η-aorist uses the zero-grade):

verb	verb stem	η-aor. stem	1 sg. ind.	inf.
ζεύγνυμι yoke	ζευγ-/ζῠγ-	ζῠγη-	ἐζύγην	ζυγῆναι
κλέπτω steal	κλεπ-/κλοπ-/ κλᾰπ-	κλᾰπη-	ἐκλάπην	κλαπῆναι
μ(ε)ίγνυμι/μίσγω mix	μειγ-/μῐγ-	μῐγη-	ἐμίγην	μιγῆναι
πήγνυμαι become solid	πηγ-/πᾰγ-	πᾰγη-	ἐπάγην became solid	παγῆναι
ἐκπλήττομαι be panic-stricken	πληγ-/πλᾰγ-	πλᾰγη-	ἐξ-επλάγην lost my wits	ἐκπλαγῆναι
ῥέω flow	ῥε-/ῥῠ-	ῥῠη-	ἐρρύην flowed	ῥυῆναι
ῥήγνυμαι break (intr.)	ῥηγ-/ῥωγ-/ ῥᾰγ-	ῥᾰγη-	ἐρράγην broke (intr.)	ῥαγῆναι
σπείρω sow	σπερ-/σπᾰρ-	σπᾰρη-	ἐσπάρην	σπαρῆναι
στέλλομαι set out	στελ-/στᾰλ-	στᾰλη-	ἐστάλην set out	σταλῆναι
στρέφομαι turn around (intr.)	στρεφ-/στροφ-/ στρᾰφ-	στρᾰφη-	ἐστράφην turned around	στραφῆναι
τήκομαι melt (intr.)	τηκ-/τᾰκ-	τᾰκη-	ἐτάκην melted	τακῆναι
τρέπομαι turn around (intr.)	τρεπ-/τροπ-/ τρᾰπ-	τρᾰπη-	ἐτράπην turned around	τραπῆναι

τρέφομαι *grow (up)*	θρεφ-/θροφ-/ <u>θρᾰφ-</u>	τρᾰφη- (→1.97)	ἐτράφην *grew (up)*	τραφῆναι
δια-φθείρομαι *perish*	φθερ-/φθορ-/ <u>φθᾰρ-</u>	φθᾰρη-	δι-εφθάρην *perished*	φθαρῆναι

Note 1: Some of these verbs also have θη-aorists, e.g. ἐμ(ε)ίχθην (μείγνυμι, →14.19), ἐπήχθην (πήγνυμαι), ἐστρέφθην (στρέφομαι), ἐτρέφθην (τρέπομαι), ἐθρέφθην (τρέφω, instead of expected †ἐτρέφθην, →1.97).

15

The Future: Active and Middle

Types of Future Stem

15.1 The future stem of nearly all verbs is **sigmatic**, i.e. it is formed by adding a σ to the verb stem:

– Most verbs add this σ immediately to the verb stem: e.g. with παιδεύω *educate* (verb stem παιδευ-), fut. stem παιδευσ-; with δείκνυμι *show* (verb stem δεικ-), fut. stem δειξ-.
– However, verbs with a **stem in a resonant**, or with a polysyllabic stem in ιδ- (i.e. most **verbs in -ιζω/-ιζομαι**), have a so-called **Attic future**, formed with an ε and having lost the sigma: e.g. with ἀγγέλλω *report* (verb stem ἀγγελ-), fut. stem ἀγγελε-; with κομίζω *convey* (verb stem κομιδ-), fut. stem. κομιε-.

Note 1: The formation of the sigmatic future stem thus greatly resembles that of the sigmatic aorist stem (→13.15–23). Compare:

verb	*verb stem*	*future stem*	*aorist stem*
παιδεύω *educate*	παιδευ-	παιδευσ-	παιδευσ(α)-
τιμάω *honour*	τιμη-/τιμᾰ-	τιμησ-	τιμησ(α)-
τρίβω *rub*	τρῑβ-/τρῐβ-	τρῑψ-	τρῑψ(α)-
διώκω *chase*	διωκ-	διωξ-	διωξ(α)-
κολάζω *punish*	κολᾰδ-	κολασ-	κολασ(α)-

But the formation of Attic futures diverges from that of (pseudo-)sigmatic aorists:

ἀγγέλλω *report*	ἀγγελ-	ἀγγελε-	ἀγγειλ(α)-
κομίζω *convey*	κομιδ-	κομιε-	κομισ(α)-

Conjugation of the Future

Overview of Forms

Sigmatic Future

15.2   Active forms:

			verb stems ending in ι, υ or a diphthong παιδεύω *educate* stem παιδευσ-	verb stems ending in α, ε, ο or η τιμάω *honour* stem τιμησ-	verb stems ending in a labial or velar stop τρίβω *rub* stem τριψ-	verb stems ending in a dental stop κολάζω *punish* stem κολασ-
ind.	sg.	1	παιδεύσω	τιμήσω	τρίψω	κολάσω
		2	παιδεύσεις	τιμήσεις	τρίψεις	κολάσεις
		3	παιδεύσει	τιμήσει	τρίψει	κολάσει
	pl.	1	παιδεύσομεν	τιμήσομεν	τρίψομεν	κολάσομεν
		2	παιδεύσετε	τιμήσετε	τρίψετε	κολάσετε
		3	παιδεύσουσι(ν)	τιμήσουσι(ν)	τρίψουσι(ν)	κολάσουσι(ν)
opt.	sg.	1	παιδεύσοιμι	τιμήσοιμι	τρίψοιμι	κολάσοιμι
		2	παιδεύσοις	τιμήσοις	τρίψοις	κολάσοις
		3	παιδεύσοι	τιμήσοι	τρίψοι	κολάσοι
	pl.	1	παιδεύσοιμεν	τιμήσοιμεν	τρίψοιμεν	κολάσοιμεν
		2	παιδεύσοιτε	τιμήσοιτε	τρίψοιτε	κολάσοιτε
		3	παιδεύσοιεν	τιμήσοιεν	τρίψοιεν	κολάσοιεν
inf.			παιδεύσειν	τιμήσειν	τρίψειν	κολάσειν
ppl.	masc.		παιδεύσων, -οντος	τιμήσων, -οντος	τρίψων, -οντος	κολάσων, -οντος
	fem.		παιδεύσουσα, -ούσης	τιμήσουσα, -ούσης	τρίψουσα, -ούσης	κολάσουσα, -ούσης
	neut.		παιδεῦσον, -οντος	τιμῆσον, -οντος	τρῖψον, -οντος	κολάσον, -οντος

15.3   Middle forms:

			verb stems ending in ι, υ or a diphthong παιδεύω *educate* stem παιδευσ-	verb stems ending in α, ε, ο or η τιμάω *honour* stem τιμησ-	verb stems ending in a labial or velar stop τρίβω *rub* stem τριψ-	verb stems ending in a dental stop κολάζω *punish* stem κολασ-
ind.	sg.	1	παιδεύσομαι	τιμήσομαι	τρίψομαι	κολάσομαι
		2	παιδεύσει/-ῃ	τιμήσει/-ῃ	τρίψει/-ῃ	κολάσει/-ῃ
		3	παιδεύσεται	τιμήσεται	τρίψεται	κολάσεται
	pl.	1	παιδευσόμεθα	τιμησόμεθα	τριψόμεθα	κολασόμεθα
		2	παιδεύσεσθε	τιμήσεσθε	τρίψεσθε	κολάσεσθε
		3	παιδεύσονται	τιμήσονται	τρίψονται	κολάσονται
opt.	sg.	1	παιδευσοίμην	τιμησοίμην	τριψοίμην	κολασοίμην
		2	παιδεύσοιο (<*-σοι-σο)	τιμήσοιο	τρίψοιο	κολάσοιο
		3	παιδεύσοιτο	τιμήσοιτο	τρίψοιτο	κολάσοιτο
	pl.	1	παιδευσοίμεθα	τιμησοίμεθα	τριψοίμεθα	κολασοίμεθα
		2	παιδεύσοισθε	τιμήσοισθε	τρίψοισθε	κολάσοισθε
		3	παιδεύσοιντο	τιμήσοιντο	τρίψοιντο	κολάσοιντο
inf.			παιδεύσεσθαι	τιμήσεσθαι	τρίψεσθαι	κολάσεσθαι
ppl.	masc.		παιδευσόμενος, -ου	τιμησόμενος, -ου	τριψόμενος, -ου	κολασόμενος, -ου
	fem.		παιδευσομένη, -ης	τιμησομένη, -ης	τριψομένη, -ης	κολασομένη, -ης
	neut.		παιδευσόμενον, -ου	τιμησόμενον, -ου	τριψόμενον, -ου	κολασόμενον, -ου

Attic Future

15.4 **Active** forms:

			verb stems ending in a resonant		polysyllabic verb stems ending in ιδ-	
			ἀγγέλλω *report*		κομίζω *convey*	
			stem ἀγγελε-		stem κομιε-	
ind.	sg.	1	ἀγγελῶ	(<-έω)	κομιῶ	(<-έω)
		2	ἀγγελεῖς	(<-έεις)	κομιεῖς	(<-έεις)
		3	ἀγγελεῖ	(<-έει)	κομιεῖ	(<-έει)
	pl.	1	ἀγγελοῦμεν	(<-έομεν)	κομιοῦμεν	(<-έομεν)
		2	ἀγγελεῖτε	(<-έετε)	κομιεῖτε	(<-έετε)
		3	ἀγγελοῦσι(ν)	(<-έουσιν)	κομιοῦσι(ν)	(<-έουσιν)
opt.	sg.	1	ἀγγελοίην / -οῖμι	(<-εοίην)	κομιοίην	(<-εοίην)
		2	ἀγγελοίης / -οῖς	(<-εοίης)	κομιοίης	(<-εοίης)
		3	ἀγγελοίη / -οῖ	(<-εοίη)	κομιοίη	(<-εοίη)
	pl.	1	ἀγγελοῖμεν	(<-έοιμεν)	κομιοῖμεν	(<-έοιμεν)
		2	ἀγγελοῖτε	(<-έοιτε)	κομιοῖτε	(<-έοιτε)
		3	ἀγγελοῖεν	(<-έοιεν)	κομιοῖεν	(<-έοιεν)
inf.			ἀγγελεῖν	(<-έεεν)	κομιεῖν	(<-έεεν)
ppl.	masc.		ἀγγελῶν,	(<-έων)	κομιῶν,	(<-έων)
			-οῦντος	(<-έοντος)	-οῦντος	(<-έοντος)
	fem.		ἀγγελοῦσα,	(<-έουσα)	κομιοῦσα,	(<-έουσα)
			-ούσης	(<-εούσης)	-ούσης	(<-εούσης)
	neut.		ἀγγελοῦν,	(<-έον)	κομιοῦν,	(<-έον)
			-οῦντος	(<-έοντος)	-οῦντος	(<-έοντος)

15.5 **Middle** forms:

			verb stems ending in a resonant		polysyllabic verb stems ending in ιδ-	
			ἀγγέλλω *report*		κομίζω *convey*	
			stem ἀγγελε-		stem κομιε-	
ind.	sg.	1	ἀγγελοῦμαι	(<-έομαι)	κομιοῦμαι	(<-έομαι)
		2	ἀγγελεῖ / -ῇ	(<-έε(σ)αι)	κομιεῖ / -ῇ	(<-έε(σ)αι)
		3	ἀγγελεῖται	(<-έεται)	κομιεῖται	(<-έεται)
	pl.	1	ἀγγελούμεθα	(<-εόμεθα)	κομιούμεθα	(<-εόμεθα)
		2	ἀγγελεῖσθε	(<-έεσθε)	κομιεῖσθε	(<-έεσθε)
		3	ἀγγελοῦνται	(<-έονται)	κομιοῦνται	(<-έονται)
opt.	sg.	1	ἀγγελοίμην	(<-εοίμην)	κομιοίμην	(<-εοίμην)
		2	ἀγγελοῖο	(<-έοι(σ)ο)	κομιοῖο	(<-έοι(σ)ο)
		3	ἀγγελοῖτο	(<-έοιτο)	κομιοῖτο	(<-έοιτο)
	pl.	1	ἀγγελοίμεθα	(<-εοίμεθα)	κομιοίμεθα	(<-εοίμεθα)
		2	ἀγγελοῖσθε	(<-έοισθε)	κομιοῖσθε	(<-έοισθε)
		3	ἀγγελοῖντο	(<-έοιντο)	κομιοῖντο	(<-έοιντο)
inf.			ἀγγελεῖσθαι	(<-έεσθαι)	κομιεῖσθαι	(<-έεσθαι)
ppl.	masc.		ἀγγελούμενος, -ου	(<-εόμενος)	κομιούμενος, -ου	(<-εόμενος)
	fem.		ἀγγελουμένη, -ης	(<-εομένη)	κομιουμένη, -ης	(<-εομένη)
	neut.		ἀγγελούμενον, -ου	(<-εόμενον)	κομιούμενον, -ου	(<-εόμενον)

Endings

15.6 The active and middle future is **always thematic** (→11.18). The endings are identical to those used in the present of -ω verbs (→12.3–16). This means that the conjugation after the stem is identical to that of the present of παιδεύω; but with Attic futures, the conjugation after the stem is identical to that of the present of ποιέω.

15.7 **Indicatives**: formed with primary endings, e.g. 1 sg. act. παιδεύσ-ω, 2 sg. παιδεύσ-εις, 1 sg. mid. παιδεύσ-ο-μαι; Att.: 1 sg. act. ἀγγελῶ (<-έ-ω), 2 sg. ἀγγελεῖς (<-έ-εις), 1 sg. mid. ἀγγελοῦμαι (<-έ-ο-μαι).

15.8 **Optatives**: formed with the optative suffix -ι-/-ιη- and (mostly) secondary endings, e.g. 2 sg. act. παιδεύσ-οι-ς, 3 pl. mid. παιδεύσ-οι-ντο; Att. 2 sg. act. ἀγγελοίης (<-ε-οίη-ς), 3 pl. mid. ἀγγελοῖντο (<-έ-οι-ντο).

15.9 **Infinitives**: formed in the act. with -εν and in the mid. with -σθαι, e.g. act. παιδεύσ-ειν (<-ε-εν), mid. παιδεύσ-ε-σθαι; Att. ἀγγελεῖν (<-έ-ε-εν), ἀγγελεῖσθαι (<-έ-ε-σθαι).

15.10 **Active participles**: formed with -ντ-; for the declension, →5.17–18. E.g. gen. sg. masc. παιδεύσ-ο-ντ-ος, nom. sg. fem. παιδεύσ-ουσα (<*-οντ-yα); Att. gen. sg. masc. ἀγγελοῦντος (<-έ-ο-ντ-ος), nom. sg. fem. ἀγγελοῦσα.

15.11 **Middle participles**: formed with -μεν-; for the declension, →5.3–4. E.g. nom. sg. masc. παιδευσ-ό-μεν-ος, nom. sg. fem. παιδευσ-ο-μέν-η; Att. nom. sg. masc. ἀγγελούμενος (<-ε-ό-μενος), nom. sg. fem. ἀγγελουμένη (<-ε-ο-μένη).

15.12 There is **no future imperative or subjunctive**.

15.13 A few Attic futures have a conjugation which is identical to that of the present of τιμάω. For these verbs, →15.38.

15.14 Quite a few verbs with an active present have a future with only middle forms. E.g. with ἀκούω *hear*, 1 sg. fut. ind. ἀκούσομαι. For these verbs, →15.40.

Sigmatic Future Stems

Stem Formation

Verb Stems Ending in ι, υ or a Diphthong

15.15 Verb stems ending in ι, υ, or diphthongs stay unchanged before the added σ. Some examples:

verb	verb stem	future stem	1 sg. ind.
χρίω *anoint*	χρῑ-	χρισ-	χρίσω
δύομαι *dive*	δῡ-/δῠ-	δυσ-	δύσομαι
λύω *loosen, release*	λῡ-/λῠ-	λῡσ-	λύσω

κωλύω *hinder*	κωλῡ-	κωλυσ-	κωλύσω
παίω *strike*	παι-	παισ-	παίσω
παύω *stop*	παυ-	παυσ-	παύσω
παιδεύω *educate*	παιδευ-	παιδευσ-	παιδεύσω
λούω *bathe*	λου-	λουσ-	λούσω
ἀκούω *hear*	ἀκο(υ)(σ)-	ἀκουσ-	ἀκούσομαι

Verb Stems Ending in Other Vowels

15.16   With verb stems ending in η/ε, η/ᾰ, ω/ο (i.e. contract verbs), σ is added to the **long variant** of the verb stem (→11.11):

– pres. stem ε: fut. stem η;
– pres. stem ᾰ (or η): fut. stem η (but ᾱ after ε, ι or ρ);
– pres. stem ο: fut. stem ω; a few verbs with a verb stem ending in ω have a similarly formed future.

Some examples:

verb	*verb stem*	*future stem*	*1 sg. ind.*
ποιέω *make, do*	ποιη-/ποιε-	ποιησ-	ποιήσω
ἡγέομαι *lead, consider*	ἡγη-/ἡγε-	ἡγησ-	ἡγήσομαι
τιμάω *honour*	τιμη-/τιμᾰ-	τιμησ-	τιμήσω
κτάομαι *acquire*	κτη-/κτᾰ-	κτησ-	κτήσομαι
δράω *do*	δρᾱ-/δρᾰ-	δρᾱσ-	δρᾱσω
δηλόω *make clear*	δηλω-/δηλο-	δηλωσ-	δηλώσω
χρήομαι *use, need*	χρη-	χρησ-	χρήσομαι
τιτρώσκω *wound*	τρω-	τρωσ-	τρώσω

15.17   Similarly, with **-μι verbs** that have variant verb stems ending in η/ᾰ, η/ε, or ω/ο (→12.37), the **long** variant of the stem is used:

verb	*verb stem*	*future stem*	*1 sg. ind.*
δίδωμι *give*	δω-/δο-	δωσ-	δώσω
δύναμαι *be able*	δυνη-/δυνᾰ-	δυνησ-	δυνήσομαι
ἐπίσταμαι *know, be able*	ἐπιστη-/ἐπιστᾰ-	ἐπιστησ-	ἐπιστήσομαι
ἵημι *send, let go*	ἡ-/ἑ-	ἡσ-	ἥσω
ἵστημι *make stand, set up*	στη-/στᾰ-	στησ-	στήσω
πίμπλημι *fill*	πλη-/πλᾰ-	πλησ-	πλήσω
τίθημι *put, place*	θη-/θε-	θησ-	θήσω

15.18   The verbs **βαίνω** and **φθάνω** also use a stem with long η (as opposed to ᾰ):

verb	*verb stem*	*future stem*	*1 sg. ind.*
βαίνω *go, walk*	βη-/βᾰ(ν)-	βησ-	βήσομαι
φθάνω *be first*	φθη-/φθᾰ-	φθησ-	φθήσω

15.19 A few verbs in -έω and -άω which originally had a verb stem ending in a σ (or were 'absorbed' into that type, →13.18) do not have a long vowel in the future:

verb	verb stem	future stem	1 sg. ind.
ἀρκέω *suffice*	ἀρκε(σ)-	ἀρκεσ-	ἀρκέσω
γελάω *laugh*	γελᾰ(σ)-	γελᾰσ-	γελᾰ́σομαι
ζέω *boil*	ζε(σ)-	ζεσ-	ζέσω
καλέω *call*	κᾰλε-/κλη-	καλεσ-	καλέσω (but for the much more common future καλῶ, →15.35)
τελέω *finish*	τελε(σ)-	τελεσ-	τελέσω (but for the more common future τελῶ, →15.35 n.1)

Also note the short vowel of:

(ἐπ)αἰνέω *praise*	αἰνε-	αἰνεσ-	(ἐπ)αἰνέσω

Similarly formed (i.e. with a short vowel) are the futures of verbs in -άννυμι or -έννυμι (which have a stem in σ), as well as εἰμί *be*:

εἰμί *be*	ἐσ-	ἐσ-	ἔσομαι (3 sg. ind. ἔσται)
ἕννυμι *put on (clothing)*	ἑ(σ)-	ἑσ-	ἕσ(σ)ω
(κατα)σβέννυμι *quench*	σβη-/σβε(σ)-	σβεσ-	(κατα)σβέσ(σ)ω, but also (ἀπο)σβήσομαι

15.20 A few verbs in -άω and -έω that originally had a verb stem ending in ϝ (→12.29 n.1) have a future in -αύσω and -εύσω, respectively:

verb	verb stem	future stem	1 sg. ind.
κᾰ́ω (also καίω) *set on fire*	κα(υ)- (<*κᾰϝ-)	καυσ-	καύσω
κλᾰ́ω (also κλαίω) *cry, weep*	κλα(υ)- (<*κλᾰϝ-)	κλαυσ-	κλαύσομαι
πλέω *sail*	πλε(υ)- (<*πλεϝ-)	πλευσ-	πλεύσομαι
πνέω *blow*	πνε(υ)- (<*πνεϝ-)	πνευσ-	πνεύσομαι

15.21 The future of the -έω verbs δοκέω *seem, think*, and ὠθέω *thrust, push* is built on the stems δοκ- and ὠθ-, respectively: δόξω, ὤσω (→15.27), the latter mostly in ἀπώσω. Occasionally, however, δοκήσω and ὠθήσω are found.

Verb Stems Ending in a Labial Stop

15.22 Stems ending in a **labial stop** get a future stem in **ψ** (π/β/φ + σ = ψ). Some examples:

verb	verb stem	future stem	1 sg. ind.
πέμπω *send*	πεμπ-/πομπ-	πεμψ-	πέμψω
ἕπομαι *follow*	ἑπ-/σπ-	ἑψ-	ἕψομαι
τρῑ́βω *rub*	τρῑβ-/τρῐβ-	τρῑψ-	τρῑ́ψω
γράφω *write*	γρᾰφ-	γραψ-	γράψω

Note especially verbs that have a present in -πτω (→12.27):

κλέπτω *steal*	κλεπ-/κλοπ-/κλᾰπ-	κλεψ-	κλέψω
βλάπτω *harm, damage*	βλᾰβ-	βλαψ-	βλάψω
κρύπτω *hide*	κρῠφ-/κρῠβ-	κρυψ-	κρύψω

15.23   The future of λαμβάνω *get, take* (verb stem ληβ-/λᾰβ-) uses the long variant of the verb stem, and has middle endings (→15.40): future stem ληψ-, 1 sg. ind. λήψομαι.

Verb Stems Ending in a Velar Stop

15.24   Stems ending in a **velar stop** get a future stem in **ξ** (κ/γ/χ + σ = ξ). Some examples:

verb	verb stem	future stem	1 sg. ind.
διώκω *chase*	διωκ-	διωξ-	διώξω
λήγω *cease*	ληγ-	ληξ-	λήξω
ἄγω *lead, bring*	ἀγ-	ἀξ-	ἄξω
φεύγω *flee*	φευγ-/φῠγ-	φευξ-	φεύξομαι
ἄρχω *rule, begin*	ἀρχ-	ἀρξ-	ἄρξω

Note especially verbs that have a present in -ττω (→12.27), and a few in -ζω (→12.27):

φυλάττω *guard*	φυλᾰκ-	φυλαξ-	φυλάξω
τάττω *array, appoint*	τᾰγ-	ταξ-	τάξω
ὀρύττω *dig*	ὀρῠχ-	ὀρυξ-	ὀρύξω
οἰμώζω *groan*	οἰμωγ-	οἰμωξ-	οἰμώξομαι
κλάζω *scream*	κλᾰγγ-	κλαγξ-	κλάγξω

And note that a number of verbs in -νῡμι have a stem ending in a velar stop (→13.22). For example:

δείκνυμι *show*	δεικ-	δειξ-	δείξω
ζεύγνυμι *yoke*	ζευγ-/ζῠγ-	ζευξ-	ζεύξω
πήγνυμι *affix, fasten*	πηγ-/πᾰγ-	πηξ-	πήξω

15.25   ἔχω *have, hold* has two future stems:

ἔχω *have, hold*	ἐχ- (<*(σ)εχ-, →1.97)	ἑξ-	ἕξω
	σχ-	σχησ-	σχήσω (cf. aor. ἔσχον)

For the alternation between rough/smooth breathing, →1.97 n.1. For the added η in σχησ-, →15.30 below.

ἕξω is considerably more common in Attic prose. The difference between the two forms appears to be primarily aspectual: ἕξω *will have/hold*, imperfective aspect; σχήσω *will get* (also *will hold back/restrain*), perfective aspect; for such aspectual distinctions, →33.4–7, 33.43 n.2.

15.26 The future of τυγχάνω *hit upon, happen to* (verb stem τευχ-/τῠχ-) uses the e-grade of the verb stem, and has middle endings (→15.40): future stem τευξ-, 1 sg. ind. τεύξομαι.

Verb Stems Ending in a Dental Stop

15.27 With most stems ending in a **dental stop** the stop disappears before the σ of the future (τ/δ/θ + σ = σ, →1.91); the stems may show vowel and other variations:

verb	verb stem	future stem	1 sg. ind.
ἀνύτω *accomplish*	ἀνῠ(τ)-	ἀνῠσ-	ἀνῠσω
ψεύδομαι *lie, cheat*	ψευδ-	ψευσ-	ψεύσομαι
οἶδα *know*	εἰδ-/οἰδ-/ἰδ-	εἰσ-	εἴσομαι
πάσχω *suffer*	πενθ-/πονθ-/πᾰθ-	πεισ-	πείσομαι (<*πένθσομαι)
πείθω *persuade*	πειθ-/ποιθ-/πῐθ-	πεισ-	πείσω
πυνθάνομαι *inquire, learn*	πευθ-/πῠθ-	πευσ-	πεύσομαι

Note especially verbs that have a present in -ζω (and some in -ττω) (→12.27):

ἁρμόζω/ἁρμόττω *fit together*	ἁρμοδ-/ἁρμοτ-	ἁρμοσ-	ἁρμόσω
παρασκευάζω *prepare, provide*	σκευᾰδ-	σκευασ-	παρασκευάσω
κτίζω *found*	κτῐδ-	κτισ-	κτίσω
σχίζω *split, cleave*	σχῐδ-	σχισ-	σχίσω

Note 1: πείσομαι can be the future both of middle-passive πείθομαι *believe, obey* and of πάσχω *suffer*.

15.28 Verbs in -ίζω with a verb stem with more than one syllable – unlike κτίζω and σχίζω, which have a monosyllabic verb stem – have an Attic future: →15.33 below.

Suppletive Verbs

15.29 In a few cases the future is built on a different stem from that of the present and/or other tenses (suppletive verbs, →13.38):

verb	verb stem	future stem	1 sg. ind.
ἔρχομαι *go, come*	ἐρχ-, ἐλευθ-/ἐλ(ῠ)θ-, εἰ-/ῐ-	ἐλευσ-	ἐλεύσομαι
ὁράω *see*	ὁρᾰ-, ἰδ-, ὀπ-	ὀψ-	ὄψομαι
φέρω *carry, bring*	φερ-, ἐνεκ-/ἐνοκ-/ἐγκ-, οἰτ-	οἰσ-	οἴσω

Further Particulars

15.30 Various verbs with a verb stem ending in a consonant have an additional η between the verb stem and the σ of the future. For example:

verb	verb stem	future stem	1 sg. ind.
ἁμαρτάνω *miss, err*	ἁμᾰρτ-	ἁμαρτησ-	ἁμαρτήσομαι
(ἐ)θέλω *be willing*	(ἐ)θελ-	ἐθελησ-	ἐθελήσω
εὑρίσκω *find*	εὑρ-	εὑρησ-	εὑρήσω
μανθάνω *learn*	μᾰθ-	μαθησ-	μαθήσομαι
αἰσθάνομαι *perceive*	αἰσθ-	αἰσθησ-	αἰσθήσομαι
βούλομαι *want, prefer*	βουλ-	βουλησ-	βουλήσομαι

15.31 The future of ῥέω *flow* (<*ῥέϝω, verb stem ῥε(ϝ)-/ῥŭ-) is built on the zero-grade of the stem + η: ῥῠήσομαι. Cf. aor. ἐρρύην, →14.31.

Attic Future Stems

Stem Formation

Verb Stems Ending in a Resonant

15.32 With most verb stems ending in a resonant (nasal (μ, ν) or liquid (λ, ρ)), an ε is added to the verb stem. Originally, this ε was followed by -σω, -σεις, etc., but in classical Greek the **sigma has disappeared**: *-έσω > -έω, which in Attic contracted to -ῶ. This is called the **Attic future** (or 'contract future'). It is conjugated like the present of contracted verbs in -έω (ποιέω, →12.3–4).

Note 1: The name 'Attic future' derives from antiquity; it does not refer to a dialect phenomenon per se (this type of future also occurs in Ionic), but to the fact that this future is not much used in later Koine Greek.

E.g. with ἀγγέλλω *report* (verb stem ἀγγελ-): future stem ἀγγελε-, 1 sg. fut. act. ind. ἀγγελῶ (<ἀγγελέω <*ἀγγελέσω), 1 pl. ἀγγελοῦμεν (<ἀγγελέομεν), inf. ἀγγελεῖν, (<*ἀγγελέεεν) gen. sg. masc. act. ppl. ἀγγελοῦντος (<ἀγγελέοντος).

E.g. with βάλλω *throw, hit* (verb stem βᾰλ-): future stem βαλε-, 1 sg. fut. act. ind. βαλῶ (<βαλέω <*βαλέσω), 1 pl. βαλοῦμεν (<βαλέομεν), inf. βαλεῖν (<βαλέειν), gen. sg. masc. act. ppl. βαλοῦντος (<βαλέοντος).

Note 2: The origin of the ε in these futures is a matter of controversy. With βάλλω and some other verbs, a variant of the verb stem in ε (i.e. βαλε-) can safely be reconstructed; the use of the ε in the future of this verb may then have been generalized across verb stems ending in a resonant. However, the ε may also have an independent origin.

Other examples:

verb	verb stem	future stem	1 sg. fut. ind.
μένω *stay, (a)wait*	μεν-	μενε-	μενῶ (<-έω)
νέμω *deal out*	νεμ-	νεμε-	νεμῶ (<-έω)
ἀποθνῄσκω *die*	θᾰν-/θνη-	θᾰνε-	ἀποθανοῦμαι (<-έομαι)
ἀπόλλῡμι *destroy*	ὀλ(ε)-	ὀλε-	ἀπολῶ (<-έω)
τέμνω *cut*	τεμ-/τμη-	τεμε-	τεμῶ (<-έω)

Note especially verbs that have a present in -λλω or in -αίνω/-αίρω, -είνω/-είρω, -ίνω/-ίρω, -ύνω/-ύρω (→12.28):

σφάλλω *cause to stumble*	σφαλ-	σφᾰλε-	σφᾰλῶ (<-έω)
στέλλω *dispatch*	στελ-/στᾰλ-	στελε-	στελῶ (<-έω)
φαίνω *show*	φην-/φᾰν-	φᾰνε-	φανῶ (<-έω)
τείνω *stretch*	τεν-/τᾰν-	τενε-	τενῶ (<-έω)
ἀποκτείνω *kill*	κτεν-/κτον-/κτᾰν-	κτενε-	ἀποκτενῶ (<-έω)
διαφθείρω *destroy*	φθερ-/φθορ-/φθᾰρ-	διαφθερε-	διαφθερῶ (<-έω)
σπείρω *sow*	σπερ-/σπᾰρ-	σπερε-	σπερῶ (<-έω)
κρίνω *decide, judge*	κρῑ(ν)-	κρῐνε-	κρῐνῶ (<-έω)

Verb Stems Ending in a Dental Stop

15.33 The future in -έω (-ῶ) is also found with polysyllabic stems in -ιδ- (i.e. most verbs in -ίζω/-ίζομαι), without the δ of the verb stem.

E.g. with κομίζω *convey* (verb stem κομῐδ-): future stem κομιε-, 1 sg. fut. act. ind. κομιῶ (<κομιέω), 1 pl. κομιοῦμεν (<κομιέομεν), inf. κομιεῖν (<κομιέειν), gen. sg. masc. act. ppl. κομιοῦντος (<κομιέοντος).

The future of such verbs was probably regularly sigmatic at an earlier stage (κομίσω, with δ disappearing before σ, →15.27); after the sigma dropped out between vowels (→1.83), the forms were given the same conjugation as other non-sigmatic (Attic) futures like βαλῶ (i.e. as -έω verbs).

Other examples:

verb	verb stem	future stem	1 sg. ind.
νομίζω *believe*	νομῐδ-	νομιε-	νομιῶ (<-έω)
βαδίζω *walk, go*	βαδῐδ-	βαδιε-	βαδιοῦμαι (<-έομαι)
ἀγωνίζομαι *contend*	ἀγωνῐδ-	ἀγωνιε-	ἀγωνιοῦμαι (<-έομαι)
λογίζομαι *reckon*	λογῐδ-	λογιε-	λογιοῦμαι (<-έομαι)

Note 1: 'Regularly' sigmatic forms of (some) of these verbs also occur, especially in later Greek, e.g. with ἐλπίζω *hope, expect*, fut. ἐλπίσω next to ἐλπιῶ.

Note 2: The verb καθίζω *make sit down, sit down* also has a future of the Attic type (καθιῶ <-έω), analogous to other verbs in -ίζω, although its verb stem did not originally end in ιδ (the stem is ἱζ- < reduplicated *σῐ-σδ-).

Other Attic Futures

15.34   In a few cases an Attic future is built on a different stem from the present or other tenses (suppletive verbs, →11.13):

verb	verb stem	future stem	1 sg. ind.
λέγω *say, speak*	λεγ-/λογ-, εἰπ-, <u>ἐρ-</u>/ῥη-	ἐρε-	ἐρῶ (<-έω)
τρέχω *run*	τρεχ-, <u>δρᾰμ-</u>	δραμε-	δραμοῦμαι (<-έομαι)

15.35   There are also a few verbs with a present stem in ε that does not alternate with η, as in ποιέω/ποιήσω/ἐποίησα, but retains the ε in future and aorist active (for these aorists, →13.18). In the future this results in forms that are formally identical with Attic futures, and are usually also called 'Attic':

verb	verb stem	future stem	1 sg. ind.
καλέω *call, summon*	<u>κᾰλε-</u>/κλη-	καλε-	καλῶ (<-έω <*-έσω)
γαμέω *marry*	γᾰμ(ε)-	γαμε-	γαμῶ (<-έω)

Note 1: τελέω *finish* has both a future in -σω (→15.19) and an Attic future, τελῶ. The conjugation of the Attic future τελῶ is identical to the present, as is that of καλῶ and γαμῶ.

Similarly, in addition to καλῶ, the future καλέσω (→15.19) occasionally occurs.

15.36   Some other verbs have an Attic future:

– μάχομαι *fight* (verb stem μᾰχ(ε)-), fut. stem μαχε-, 1 sg. ind. μαχοῦμαι (<-έομαι), cf. aor. ἐμαχεσάμην;

– πίπτω *fall* (verb stem <u>πεσ-</u>/πτ(ω)-), fut. stem πεσε-, 1 sg. ind. πεσοῦμαι (<-έομαι);

– καθ-έζομαι *sit down* (verb stem ἑδ-), fut. stem ἑδε-, 1 sg. ind. καθεδοῦμαι (<-έομαι).

15.37   The future of ὄμνυμι *swear* (verb stem ὀμ(ο)-) is ὀμοῦμαι (<*ὀμόσομαι, cf. aor. ὤμοσα). But this future was reinterpreted as an Attic future in -έομαι: the 3 sg. ind. fut. is ὀμεῖται.

15.38   There are also some verbs with an Attic future in -άω (conjugated like τιμάω, →12.3–4). The most important are:

– ἐλαύνω *drive, ride* (verb stem ἐλᾰ-), fut. stem ἐλᾰ-, ind. ἐλῶ, ἐλᾷς, etc., inf. ἐλᾶν (cf. aor. ἤλασα);

– verbs in -άννυμι (with a verb stem originally in σ, →12.39): e.g. σκεδάννυμι *scatter, disperse* (verb stem σκεδᾰ(σ)-), fut. stem σκεδᾰ-, ind. σκεδῶ, σκεδᾷς, etc., inf. σκεδᾶν (cf. aor. ἐσκέδᾰσα); so too κρεμάννυμι *hang up*, fut. ind. κρεμῶ, κρεμᾷς, etc.; πετάννυμι *spread out*, fut. ind. πετῶ, πετᾷς, etc.

Other Futures

15.39 With the verbs ἐσθίω *eat* and πίνω *drink*, the future is formed without sigma or any other kind of suffix; the future uses a different stem than the present:

verb	verb stem	future stem	1 sg. ind.
ἐσθίω *eat*	ἐσθῑ-, φᾰγ-, ἐδε-/ἐδο-/<u>ἐδ</u>-	ἐδ-	ἔδομαι
πίνω *drink*	πω-/πο-/<u>πῑ</u>-	πῑ-	πίομαι (forms with πῑ- also occur)

These futures are conjugated simply as the present middle-passive παιδεύομαι (→12.4).

Note 1: These were based on an older form of the subjunctive, using short thematic vowels ο/ε.

Verbs with a Middle Future

15.40 There are numerous verbs with an active present which have only or predominantly **middle forms in the future**. These verbs tend to belong to one of a few specific semantic categories: a list of the most frequent verbs with a middle future, arranged according to these semantic categories, is given here.

The list is not exhaustive; information about further individual verbs may be found in dictionaries. Several of the verbs in the list have irregularly formed future stems; some have suppletive stems. These are treated in more detail in the list of principal parts, →22.9.

– Verbs of **uttering sounds/speech** (and their opposites, of **keeping silence**):

verb	future (1 sg. ind.)
ᾄδω *sing*	ᾄσομαι
βοάω *shout, call on*	βοήσομαι
γελάω *laugh*	γελάσομαι
ἐγκωμιάζω *praise*	ἐγκωμιάσομαι (but also ἐγκωμιάσω)
ἐπαινέω *praise*	ἐπαινέσομαι (but also ἐπαινέσω)
ἐρωτάω *ask*	ἐρήσομαι (but also ἐρωτήσω)
οἰμώζω *groan*	οἰμώξομαι
ὄμνυμι *swear*	ὀμοῦμαι, -ῇ
σιγάω *keep silence, be still; keep secret*	σιγήσομαι
σιωπάω *keep silence, be still; keep secret*	σιωπήσομαι

– Verbs of **grasping, taking (in), obtaining**, both mentally and physically (and their opposites, of **missing**):

ἀκούω *hear*	ἀκούσομαι
ἁμαρτάνω *miss, err*	ἁμαρτήσομαι
ἀπολαύω *benefit from, enjoy*	ἀπολαύσομαι
ἁρπάζω *seize, snatch*	ἁρπάσομαι (but also ἁρπάσω)
βλέπω *look, see*	βλέψομαι (but also βλέψω)
γιγνώσκω *know, recognize*	γνώσομαι
δάκνω *bite*	δήξομαι
λαγχάνω *obtain by lot*	λήξομαι
λαμβάνω *get, take*	λήψομαι
μανθάνω *learn*	μαθήσομαι
οἶδα *know*	εἴσομαι
ὁράω *see*	ὄψομαι
σκοπέω/σκέπτομαι *look, examine*	σκέψομαι
τυγχάνω *hit upon, happen to*	τεύξομαι

– Verbs of **taking in food/drink**:

βιβρώσκω *eat*	βρώσομαι
ἐσθίω *eat*	ἔδομαι
πίνω *drink*	πίομαι

– Verbs of **movement**:

ἀπαντάω *meet, oppose*	ἀπαντήσομαι
βαδίζω *walk, go*	βαδιοῦμαι, -ῇ
βαίνω *go, walk*	βήσομαι
βλώσκω *come*	μολοῦμαι, -ῇ
(ἀπο)διδράσκω *run away*	(ἀπο)δράσομαι
διώκω *chase*	διώξομαι (but also διώξω)
πλέω *sail*	πλεύσομαι
πίπτω *fall*	πεσοῦμαι, -ῇ
ῥέω *flow*	ῥυήσομαι
τρέχω *run*	δραμοῦμαι, -ῇ
φεύγω *flee*	φεύξομαι
φθάνω *be first*	φθήσομαι
χωρέω *give way, go*	χωρήσομαι (but also χωρήσω)

– Verbs of **bodily conditions and affections**:

εἰμί *be*	ἔσομαι (3 sg. ἔσται)
ζήω/βιόω *live*	βιώσομαι
(ἀπο)θνῄσκω *die*	(ἀπο)θανοῦμαι, -ῇ
κάμνω *toil, be sick*	καμοῦμαι, -ῇ

πάσχω *suffer*   πείσομαι
πνέω *breathe, blow*   πνεύσομαι
τίκτω *give birth*   τέξομαι (but also τέξω)

– Verbs expressing various **emotions**:

δέδοικα / δείδω (Ion.) *fear*   δείσομαι (not in Attic)
θαυμάζω *wonder, marvel at*   θαυμάσομαι
σπουδάζω *be eager (about)*   σπουδάσομαι

16

The Future: Passive (θη-/η-)

Types of Future Passive Stem

16.1   Based on the aorist passive in -θην or -ην (→14) Greek developed a 'passive' sigmatic future in **-θήσομαι** and **-ήσομαι**, respectively. The stem is formed by adding a sigma to the θη-/η-aorist stem:

- **θη-future** (with verbs with a θη-aorist):

    e.g. with παιδεύω *educate* (verb stem παιδευ-, θη-aor. stem παιδευθη-): θη-future stem παιδευθησ̱-;

    e.g. with δείκνυμι *show* (verb stem δεικ-, θη-aor. stem δειχθη-): θη-future stem δειχθησ̱-.

- **η-future** (with verbs with an η-aorist):

    e.g. with γράφω *write* (verb stem γράφ-, η-aor. stem γραφη-): η-future stem γραφησ̱-;

    e.g. with φαίνω *show* (verb stem φην-/φᾰν-, η-aor. stem φανη-): η-future stem φανησ̱-.

Note 1: The 'passive' future, like the 'passive' aorist, has passive meaning *only* when it is formed from active verbs taking an object: e.g. with παιδεύω *educate*, παιδευθήσομαι *I will be educated*; with δείκνυμι *show*, δειχθήσομαι *I will be shown*. With many other verbs it has a 'change-of-state' meaning: e.g. with φαίνω *show, cause to appear*, φανήσομαι *I will appear*; some other meanings occur with passive-only verbs. For all these features, →35. Below, the meaning of the θη-/η-future is added with several verbs for clarity.

On the whole, the meaning of a future 'passive' stem corresponds to that of the aorist 'passive' stem on which it is built.

Note 2: The middle future (→15) may also express the meanings expressed by the θη-/η-future: e.g. τιμήσομαι *I will be honoured* (passive), φανοῦμαι *I will appear* (change-of-state meaning, →35.17). With η-aorists with change-of-state meaning in particular, the corresponding future is often the middle rather than an η-future: e.g. with τρέπομαι *turn*, aor. ἐτράπην *I turned around*, fut. τρέψομαι *I will turn around*. For details, also on the diachronic development of this phenomenon, →35.30.

16.2   The conjugation is thematic; the indicative uses primary endings: this means that the sigma is followed by the endings that are identical to those of the future middle (→15.3): -σομαι, -σει/-σῃ, -σεται, etc.

As with all future stems, there is **no imperative or subjunctive**.

Conjugation of the Future Passive

Overview of Forms

16.3 **θη-futures** and **η-futures**:

			θη-future	η-future
			παιδεύω *educate* stem παιδευθησ-	φαίνομαι *appear, seem* stem φανησ-
ind.	sg.	1	παιδευθήσομαι	φανήσομαι
		2	παιδευθήσει/-η	φανήσει/-η
		3	παιδευθήσεται	φανήσεται
	pl.	1	παιδευθησόμεθα	φανησόμεθα
		2	παιδευθήσεσθε	φανήσεσθε
		3	παιδευθήσονται	φανήσονται
opt.	sg.	1	παιδευθησοίμην	φανησοίμην
		2	παιδευθήσοιο	φανήσοιο
		3	παιδευθήσοιτο	φανήσοιτο
	pl.	1	παιδευθησοίμεθα	φανησοίμεθα
		2	παιδευθήσοισθε	φανήσοισθε
		3	παιδευθήσοιντο	φανήσοιντο
inf.			παιδευθήσεσθαι	φανήσεσθαι
ppl.	masc.		παιδευθησόμενος, -ου	φανησόμενος, -ου
	fem.		παιδευθησομένη, -ης	φανησομένη, -ης
	neut.		παιδευθησόμενον, -ου	φανησόμενον, -ου

Particulars

16.4 Some further examples of θη-futures:

verb	*θη-aorist*	*θη-future*
λύω *loosen, release*	ἐλύθην	λυθήσομαι
τιμάω *honour*	ἐτιμήθην	τιμηθήσομαι
πολιορκέω *besiege*	ἐπολιορκήθην	πολιορκηθήσομαι
τίθημι *put, place*	ἐτέθην	τεθήσομαι
βάλλω *throw, hit*	ἐβλήθην	βληθήσομαι
ὁράω *see*	ὤφθην	ὀφθήσομαι
λέγω *say, speak*	ἐρρήθην	ῥηθήσομαι

16.5   Some further examples of η-futures:

verb	η-aorist	η-future
βλάπτω *harm, damage*	ἐβλάβην	βλαβήσομαι
πλήττω *strike*	ἐπλήγην	πληγήσομαι
ἐκπλήττομαι *be panic-stricken*	ἐξεπλάγην	ἐκπλαγήσομαι *will be frightened*
σφάλλομαι *stumble*	ἐσφάλην	σφαλήσομαι *will stumble*
δια-φθείρομαι *perish*	δι-εφθάρην	δια-φθαρήσομαι *will perish*

16.6   Not all verbs with θη-/η-aorists form the corresponding futures. Note in particular the following two:

βούλομαι *want, prefer*	ἐβουλήθην	βουλήσομαι (middle) *will want*
πείθομαι *believe, obey*	ἐπείσθην	πείσομαι (middle)
	(older: ἐπιθόμην)	*will believe, obey*

Also →16.1 n.2.

17

The Perfect (and Future Perfect): Introduction

Perfect (and Future Perfect) Stems

Types of Stem

17.1 There are two types of **perfect stem** (many verbs have both, some have only one):

– A **perfect active** stem. There are three types: **κ-perfect, aspirated perfect**, and **stem perfect**. In addition, there are some verbs which have a **mixed perfect**. For details, →18.
– A **perfect middle-passive** stem. For details, →19.

For the meanings of the perfect stem, →33.11–12, 33.34–42.

17.2 There are also two types of **future perfect stem**:

– A **future perfect active** stem, formed by adding σ to the perfect active stem. These forms are very rare, and occur with only a few verbs.
– A **future perfect middle-passive** stem, formed by adding σ to the perfect middle-passive stem. These forms also occur infrequently.

For details, →20. For the meanings of the future perfect stem, →33.46–7.

17.3 All perfect and future perfect stems (except those of οἶδα *know*) include a **reduplication**. For the rules governing the formation of perfect reduplications, →11.43–8.

17.4 Some examples of perfect and future perfect stems:

with παιδεύω *educate* (verb stem παιδευ-):

| pf. act. stem πεπαιδευκ-: | πε- | παιδευ- | κ- |
| | *reduplication* | *verb stem* | *kappa* |

with δείκνυμι *show* (verb stem δεικ-):

| pf. act. stem δεδειχ-: | δε- | δειχ- | |
| | *reduplication* | *verb stem* (δεικ-) + *aspiration* | |

with νικάω *educate* (verb stem νικη-/νικᾱ-):

| pf. mp. stem νενικη-: | νε- | νικη- | |
| | *reduplication* | *verb stem* | |

with λύω *loosen, release* (verb stem λῡ-/λῠ-):

| fut. pf. mp. stem λελῡσ-: | λε- | λῡ- | σ- |
| | *reduplication* | *verb stem* | *sigma* |

Periphrastic Forms

17.5   Perfect forms may also be **periphrastic**: a periphrastic construction consists of a **perfect participle and an auxiliary form of εἰμί** – as opposed to single, 'synthetic' forms. This occurs especially with the perfect middle-passive, where in some cases *only* periphrastic forms occur (→19.8–9); but active periphrastic forms are also found, especially in the subjunctive and the optative.

17.6   The forms of εἰμί (→12.36) used in periphrastic constructions are:

- For the periphrastic **perfect indicative**: the **pres. ind.** of εἰμί: e.g. ἀφιγμένοι εἰσί(ν) 3 pl. pf. mp. ind. of ἀφικνέομαι *arrive*; γεγονυῖά ἐστι(ν) instead of γέγονε(ν), 3 sg. pf. act. ind. of γίγνομαι *become, be born*.
- For the periphrastic **pluperfect**: the **impf.** of εἰμί: e.g. γεγραμμένοι ἦσαν 3 pl. plpf. mp. of γράφω *write*; δεδωκὼς ἦν instead of ἐδεδώκει, 3 sg. plpf. act. of δίδωμι *give*.
- For the periphrastic **future perfect indicative**: the **fut. ind.** of εἰμί: e.g. ἐγνωκὼς ἔσται, 3 sg. fut. pf. act. ind. of γιγνώσκω *know, recognize*.
- For the periphrastic **perfect subjunctive**: the **pres. subj.** of εἰμί: e.g. παρεσκευασμένον ᾖ 3 sg. pf. mp. subj. of παρασκευάζω *prepare*.
- For the periphrastic **perfect optative**: the **pres. opt.** of εἰμί: e.g. πεποιηκὼς εἴη instead of πεποιήκοι, 3 sg. pf. act. opt. of ποιέω *make, do*.
- For the periphrastic **perfect infinitive**: the **pres. inf.** εἶναι: e.g. πεπραγμένα εἶναι instead of πεπρᾶχθαι, pf. mp. inf. of πράττω *do, act*.

17.7   The participle in periphrastic constructions **agrees** in number and gender with the subject (→27.7): e.g. οἱ νόμοι γεγραμμένοι εἰσίν *the laws have been written*, ἡ μίσθωσις ἦν γεγραμμένη *the contract had been written*.

18

The Perfect: Active

Types of Perfect Active Stem

18.1 All perfect stems (except οἶδα *know*) include a **reduplication**, either in the form of a consonant + ε or formed in the same way as the augment; for the rules governing reduplication, →11.43–8.

18.2 Apart from reduplication, **perfect active stems** are formed in one of three different ways:

- **κ-perfects**: with most verb stems ending in a vowel, resonant or dental stop, a κ is added to the verb stem. E.g. with παιδεύω *educate* (verb stem παιδευ-): perfect stem πεπαιδευκ-.
- **Aspirated perfects**: with most verb stems ending in a labial or velar stop, the perfect stem is formed by using the aspirated variant of that stop (φ or χ). E.g. with βλάπτω *harm, damage* (verb stem βλαβ-): perfect stem βεβλαφ-.
- **Stem perfects**: with a number of verbs (whose verb stems always end in a consonant), no additions other than reduplication are made to the verb stem in the perfect stem; in most cases, such perfect stems differ from the present stem because of ablaut (→1.51–6). E.g. with λείπω *leave* (verb stem λειπ-/λοιπ-/λῐπ-): perfect stem λελοιπ-.

  To this category belong also the verbs οἶδα, ἔοικα and εἴωθα, which have some irregular forms.

There are, in addition, a few '**mixed**' perfects, formed partly like κ-perfects, partly like stem perfects: δέδοικα *fear*, ἕστηκα (ἵσταμαι *come to stand*), τέθνηκα ((ἀπο)θνῄσκω *die*), and βέβηκα (βαίνω *go, walk*).

Note 1: κ-perfects and regularly formed aspirated perfects are a relatively late development of the language, and are younger than stem perfects, from which they derive their conjugation. For verbs that formed a κ-perfect in addition to an already existing stem perfect (normally with a distinction in meaning), →18.26.

Note 2: Stem perfects are often called 'second' or 'strong' perfects: for this terminology, see the section *On Terminology* at the start of this book.

κ-Perfects, Aspirated Perfects, Stem Perfects: Conjugation

Overview of Forms

18.3   κ-perfects:

			verb stems ending in ι, υ or α diphthong	verb stems ending in α, ε, ο or η	verb stems ending in a dental stop	verb stems ending in a resonant
			παιδεύω *educate* stem πεπαιδευκ-	τιμάω *honour* stem τετιμηκ-	κομίζω *convey* stem κεκομικ-	ἀγγέλλω *report* stem ἠγγελκ-
prim. ind. (pf.)	sg.	1	πεπαίδευκα	τετίμηκα	κεκόμικα	ἤγγελκα
		2	πεπαίδευκας	τετίμηκας	κεκόμικας	ἤγγελκας
		3	πεπαίδευκε(ν)	τετίμηκε(ν)	κεκόμικε(ν)	ἤγγελκε(ν)
	pl.	1	πεπαιδεύκαμεν	τετιμήκαμεν	κεκομίκαμεν	ἠγγέλκαμεν
		2	πεπαιδεύκατε	τετιμήκατε	κεκομίκατε	ἠγγέλκατε
		3	πεπαιδεύκασι(ν)	τετιμήκασι(ν)	κεκομίκασι(ν)	ἠγγέλκασι(ν)
sec. ind. (plpf.)	sg.	1	ἐπεπαιδεύκειν[1]	ἐτετιμήκειν[1]	ἐκεκομίκειν[1]	ἠγγέλκειν[1]
		2	ἐπεπαιδεύκεις	ἐτετιμήκεις	ἐκεκομίκεις	ἠγγέλκεις
		3	ἐπεπαιδεύκει(ν)	ἐτετιμήκει(ν)	ἐκεκομίκει(ν)	ἠγγέλκει(ν)
	pl.	1	ἐπεπαιδεύκεμεν[2]	ἐτετιμήκεμεν[2]	ἐκεκομίκεμεν[2]	ἠγγέλκεμεν[2]
		2	ἐπεπαιδεύκετε[2]	ἐτετιμήκετε[2]	ἐκεκομίκετε[2]	ἠγγέλκετε[2]
		3	ἐπεπαιδεύκεσαν[2]	ἐτετιμήκεσαν[2]	ἐκεκομίκεσαν[2]	ἠγγέλκεσαν[2]
subj.[3]	sg.	1	πεπαιδεύκω	τετιμήκω	κεκομίκω	ἠγγέλκω
		2	πεπαιδεύκῃς	τετιμήκῃς	κεκομίκῃς	ἠγγέλκῃς
		3	πεπαιδεύκῃ	τετιμήκῃ	κεκομίκῃ	ἠγγέλκῃ
	pl.	1	πεπαιδεύκωμεν	τετιμήκωμεν	κεκομίκωμεν	ἠγγέλκωμεν
		2	πεπαιδεύκητε	τετιμήκητε	κεκομίκητε	ἠγγέλκητε
		3	πεπαιδεύκωσι(ν)	τετιμήκωσι(ν)	κεκομίκωσι(ν)	ἠγγέλκωσι(ν)
opt.[4]	sg.	1	πεπαιδεύκοιμι	τετιμήκοιμι	κεκομίκοιμι	ἠγγέλκοιμι
		2	πεπαιδεύκοις	τετιμήκοις	κεκομίκοις	ἠγγέλκοις
		3	πεπαιδεύκοι	τετιμήκοι	κεκομίκοι	ἠγγέλκοι
	pl.	1	πεπαιδεύκοιμεν	τετιμήκοιμεν	κεκομίκοιμεν	ἠγγέλκοιμεν
		2	πεπαιδεύκοιτε	τετιμήκοιτε	κεκομίκοιτε	ἠγγέλκοιτε
		3	πεπαιδεύκοιεν	τετιμήκοιεν	κεκομίκοιεν	ἠγγέλκοιεν
imp.[5]			✕	✕	✕	✕
inf.			πεπαιδευκέναι	τετιμηκέναι	κεκομικέναι	ἠγγελκέναι
ppl.	masc.		πεπαιδευκώς, -ότος	τετιμηκώς, -ότος	κεκομικώς, -ότος	ἠγγελκώς, -ότος
	fem.		πεπαιδευκυῖα, -υίας	τετιμηκυῖα, -υίας	κεκομικυῖα, -υίας	ἠγγελκυῖα, -υίας
	neut.		πεπαιδευκός, -ότος	τετιμηκός, -ότος	κεκομικός, -ότος	ἠγγελκός, -ότος

[1]   Also (older) -κη, e.g. ἐπεπαιδεύκη.

[2]   Also (newer) -κειμεν, -κειτε, -κεισαν, e.g. ἐπεπαιδεύκειμεν.

[3]   The pf. subj. is very rare: often periphrastic (e.g. πεπαιδευκὼς ὦ)

[4]   The pf. opt. is very rare: often periphrastic (e.g. πεπαιδευκὼς εἴην)

[5]   The pf. act. imp. does not exist: only periphrastic (e.g. πεπαιδευκὼς ἴσθι)

18.4 Aspirated perfects, stem perfects, οἶδα:

			verb stems ending in a labial or velar stop (aspirated perfects)	stem perfects	οἶδα
			τρίβω *rub* stem τετριφ-	φεύγω *flee* stem πεφευγ-	οἶδα *know* stem εἰδ-/οἶδ-/ἰδ-
prim. ind. (pf.)	sg.	1	τέτριφα	πέφευγα	οἶδα
		2	τέτριφας	πέφευγας	οἶσθα
		3	τέτριφε(ν)	πέφευγε(ν)	οἶδε(ν)
	pl.	1	τετρίφαμεν	πεφεύγαμεν	ἴσμεν
		2	τετρίφατε	πεφεύγατε	ἴστε
		3	τετρίφασι(ν)	πεφεύγασι(ν)	ἴσασι(ν)
sec. ind. (plpf.)	sg.	1	ἐτετρίφειν[1]	ἐπεφεύγειν[1]	ἤδη *or* ᾔδειν
		2	ἐτετρίφεις[1]	ἐπεφεύγεις[1]	ᾔδησθα *or* ᾔδεις
		3	ἐτετρίφει(ν)	ἐπεφεύγει(ν)	ᾔδει(ν)
	pl.	1	ἐτετρίφεμεν[2]	ἐπεφεύγεμεν[2]	ᾖσμεν *or* ᾔδεμεν[2]
		2	ἐτετρίφετε[2]	ἐπεφεύγετε[2]	ᾖστε *or* ᾔδετε[2]
		3	ἐτετρίφεσαν[2]	ἐπεφεύγεσαν[2]	ᾖσαν *or* ᾔδεσαν[2]
subj.[3]	sg.	1	τετρίφω	πεφεύγω	εἰδῶ
		2	τετρίφῃς	πεφεύγῃς	εἰδῇς
		3	τετρίφῃ	πεφεύγῃ	εἰδῇ
	pl.	1	τετρίφωμεν	πεφεύγωμεν	εἰδῶμεν
		2	τετρίφητε	πεφεύγητε	εἰδῆτε
		3	τετρίφωσι(ν)	πεφεύγωσι(ν)	εἰδῶσι(ν)
opt.[4]	sg.	1	τετρίφοιμι	πεφεύγοιμι	εἰδείην
		2	τετρίφοις	πεφεύγοις	εἰδείης
		3	τετρίφοι	πεφεύγοι	εἰδείη
	pl.	1	τετρίφοιμεν	πεφεύγοιμεν	εἰδεῖμεν
		2	τετρίφοιτε	πεφεύγοιτε	εἰδεῖτε
		3	τετρίφοιεν	πεφεύγοιεν	εἰδεῖεν
imp.[5]	sg.	2			ἴσθι
		3			ἴστω
	pl.	2			ἴστε
		3			ἴστων
inf.			τετριφέναι	πεφευγέναι	εἰδέναι
ppl.	masc.		τετριφώς, -ότος	πεφευγώς, -ότος	εἰδώς, -ότος
	fem.		τετριφυῖα, -υίας	πεφευγυῖα, -υίας	εἰδυῖα, -υίας
	neut.		τετριφός, -ότος	πεφευγός, -ότος	εἰδός, -ότος

[1] Also (older) -η, -ης e.g. ἐτετρίφη, ἐπεφεύγης, etc.

[2] Also (newer) -ειμεν, -ειτε, -εισαν, e.g. ἐπεφεύγειτε, ᾔδειμεν.

[3] The pf. subj. is very rare: periphrastic forms (e.g. τετριφὼς ὦ) are more common. οἶδα does have regularly used separate forms.

[4] The pf. opt. is very rare: periphrastic forms (e.g. τετριφὼς εἴην) are more common. οἶδα does have regularly used separate forms.

[5] The pf. act. imp. does not exist (except with οἶδα): periphrastic forms do occur (e.g. τετριφὼς ἴσθι).

Note 1: ἴσθι (2 sg. pf. imp. of οἶδα) is identical to the imperative of εἰμί *be* (→12.36); ἦσαν (3 pl. plpf. of οἶδα) is identical to the imperfect of εἶμι *go* (→12.36).

Endings, Periphrastic Forms

18.5   The primary and secondary **indicatives** (i.e. the pf. ind. and plpf.) have different sets of endings from those listed in 11.20–33. They are as follows:

	primary	**secondary**
1 sg.	-ᾰ	-ειν
		(also, older: -η (<-εα))
2 sg.	-ᾰς	-εις
		(also, older: -ης (<-εας))
3 sg.	-ε(**ν**)	-ει(**ν**)
1 pl.	-ᾰμεν	-εμεν
	(mixed: -μεν)	(also, newer: -ειμεν)
		(mixed: -μεν)
2 pl.	-ᾰτε	-ετε
	(mixed: -τε)	(also, newer: -ειτε)
		(mixed: -τε)
3 pl.	-ᾱσι(**ν**)	-εσαν
		(also, newer: -εισαν)
		(mixed: -σαν)

Pluperfects also have an augment (→11.35–42, 11.55).
E.g. 1 pl. pf. act. ind. πεπαιδεύκ-<u>αμεν</u>, 1 pl. pf. act. ind. (mixed): δέδι-<u>μεν</u>; 2 sg. plpf. act. ἐ-πεπαιδεύκ-<u>εις</u> (older ἐπεπαιδεύκης).

18.6   Perfect active **subjunctives and optatives** are **thematic**, and have the usual endings (resulting in subjunctive -ω, -ῃς, -ῃ, etc.; optative -οιμι, -οις, -οι, etc.). E.g. 2 sg. act. subj. πεπαιδεύκ-<u>ῃς</u>, 3 pl. act. opt. πεπαιδεύκ-<u>οιεν</u>. These forms, however, are exceedingly rare: often we find 'periphrastic' forms instead, which use a participle and forms of εἰμί (→17.5–7).

18.7   The perfect active **imperative** occurs only with a few verbs, →18.23, 18.30.

18.8   The ending of the perfect active **infinitive** is **-έναι**, e.g. πεπαιδευκ-έναι.

18.9   Perfect active **participles** follow the pattern masc. -ώς, gen. -ότος; fem. -υῖα, gen. -υίας; neut. -ός, gen. -ότος. E.g. dat. sg. masc. πεπαιδευκότι. For the entire declension, →5.19–20.

κ-Perfects, Aspirated Perfects, Stem Perfects: Stems

Stem Formation

Verb Stems Ending in ι, υ or a Diphthong

18.10 Verb stems ending in ι, υ or a diphthong stay unchanged before the added κ, although the stems may show variations in vowel length. Some examples:

verb	verb stem	perfect stem	1 sg. ind.
χρίω *anoint*	χρῑ-	κεχρικ-	κέχρικα
θύω *sacrifice*	θῡ-/θῠ̆-	τεθῠ̆κ-	τέθυκα
λύω *loosen, release*	λῡ-/λῠ̆-	λελῠ̆κ-	λέλυκα
μηνύω *disclose*	μηνῡ-	μεμηνυκ-	μεμήνυκα
παίω *strike*	παι-	πεπαικ-	πέπαικα
παιδεύω *educate*	παιδευ-	πεπαιδευκ-	πεπαίδευκα
λούω *bathe, wash*	λου-	λελουκ-	λέλουκα

Note 1: With monosyllabic stems that have long ῡ in the present stem, the perfect active has a short ῠ; cf. the θη-aor., →14.11 n.1.

Verb Stems Ending in Other Vowels

18.11 With verb stems ending in η/ε, η/ᾰ, ω/ο (i.e. contract verbs), κ is added to the **long variant** of the verb stem (→11.11):

– pres. stem ε: pf. stem η;
– pres. stem ᾰ (or η): pf. stem η (but ᾱ after ε, ι or ρ);
– pres. stem ο: pf. stem ω; a few verbs with a verb stem ending in ω have a similarly formed perfect.

Some examples:

verb	verb stem	perfect stem	1 sg. ind.
ποιέω *make, do*	ποιη-/ποιε-	πεποιηκ-	πεποίηκα
στρατηγέω *be general*	στρατηγη-/ στρατηγε-	ἐστρατηγηκ-	ἐστρατήγηκα
τιμάω *honour*	τιμη-/τιμᾰ-	τετιμηκ-	τετίμηκα
δράω *do*	δρᾱ-/δρᾰ-	δεδρᾱκ-	δέδρακα
πεινήω *be hungry*	πεινη-	πεπεινηκ-	πεπείνηκα
δηλόω *make clear*	δηλω-/δηλο-	δεδηλωκ-	δεδήλωκα
γιγνώσκω *know, recognize*	γνω-	ἐγνωκ-	ἔγνωκα
σῴζω *save*	σω-	σεσωκ-	σέσωκα

18.12   Similarly, with -μι verbs that have variant verb stems ending in η/ᾰ, η/ε or ω/ο (→12.37), the long variant of the verb stem is used:

verb	verb stem	perfect stem	1 sg. ind.
πίμπλημι *fill*	πλη-/πλᾰ-	πεπληκ-	πέπληκα
τίθημι *put, place*	θη-/θε-	τεθηκ- (also τεθεικ-)	τέθηκα (also τέθεικα)
δίδωμι *give*	δω-/δο-	δεδωκ-	δέδωκα

But the verb ἵημι uses the short verb stem in the perfect:

ἵημι *send, let go*	ἡ-/ἑ-	εἱκ- (→11.47)	εἱκα

18.13   Some other verbs have a short stem-vowel in the perfect (these verbs usually also have a short vowel in the aorist and future stems; →13.18–19, 15.19). For example:

αἰνέω *praise*	pf. ind. ᾔνεκα
τελέω *finish* (verb stem τελε(σ)-)	pf. ind. τετέλεκα (note the loss of σ)
δέω *bind*	pf. ind. δέδεκα (but aor. ind. ἔδησα)

18.14   A few verbs in -άω and -έω that originally had a verb stem ending in ϝ (→13.20, 15.20, 19.17) have a perfect in -αυκα and -ευκα, respectively:

κάω (also καίω) *set on fire* (<*κάϝγω)	pf. ind. κέκαυκα (<*κέκᾰϝκα)
πλέω *sail* (<*πλέϝω)	pf. ind. πέπλευκα (<*πέπλεϝκα)
πνέω *blow* (<*πνέϝω)	pf. ind. πέπνευκα (<*πέπνεϝκα)

Verb Stems Ending in a Dental Stop

18.15   With verb stems ending in a dental stop (τ/δ/θ), that **dental stop disappears before κ** in the perfect:

verb	verb stem	perfect stem	1 sg. ind.
ἀνύτω *complete*	ἀνῠ(τ)-	ἤνυκ-	ἤνυκα
πείθω *persuade*	πειθ-/ποιθ-/πῐθ-	πεπεικ-	πέπεικα

Note especially verbs that have a present in -ζω or -ττω (→12.27):

ἁρμόζω/ἁρμόττω *fit together*	ἁρμοδ-/ἁρμοτ-	ἡρμοκ-	ἥρμοκα
κομίζω *convey*	κομῐδ-	κεκομικ-	κεκόμικα
νομίζω *believe*	νομῐδ-	νενομικ-	νενόμικα
ὀνομάζω *name*	ὀνομᾰδ-	ὠνομακ-	ὠνόμακα
πλάττω *mould*	πλᾰθ-	πεπλακ-	πέπλακα

Verb Stems Ending in a Resonant

18.16   Verb stems ending in a resonant stay unchanged before the added κ. Some examples (note especially verbs that have a present in -λλω or in -αίνω/-αίρω, -είνω/-είρω, -ύνω/-ύρω, →12.28):

verb	verb stem	perfect stem	1 sg. ind.
ἀγγέλλω *report*	ἀγγελ-	ἠγγελκ-	ἤγγελκα
αἴρω *lift*	ἀρ-	ἠρκ-	ἦρκα

Note that *ν* before κ is spelled γ ('angma', →1.29 n.1):

φαίνω *show*	φην-/<u>φᾰν-</u>	πεφᾰγκ-	πέφαγκα

Many liquid-stem verbs use the zero-grade variant of the verb stem in the perfect. This usually results in a stem with ᾰ (→1.53):

δια-φθείρω *destroy*	φθερ-/φθορ-/<u>φθᾰρ-</u>	δι-εφθᾰρκ-	δι-έφθαρκα
στέλλω *dispatch*	στελ-/<u>στᾰλ-</u>	ἐστᾰλκ-	ἔσταλκα

Several other verbs add η between the resonant and κ: for such verbs, →18.24.

18.17   Some verbs with a present stem ending in a nasal do not have that consonant in the perfect (it was not originally part of the verb stem, but a suffix added to the present stem, and then sometimes extended to other stems; →12.30 n.2):

verb	verb stem	perfect stem	1 sg. ind.
κλίνω *cause to lean*	κλῑ(ν)-	κεκλῐκ-	κέκλικα
κρίνω *pick out, decide, judge*	κρῑ(ν)-	κεκρῐκ-	κέκρικα
(ἐκ)τίνω *pay, atone*	<u>τει-/τῑ-</u>	τετεικ-	(ἐκ)τέτεικα

18.18   Observe the perfect of τείνω *stretch*

verb	verb stem	perfect stem	1 sg. ind.
τείνω *stretch*	τεν-/<u>τᾰ-</u> (<*τη̥- →1.86)	τετᾰκ-	τέτακα

The Aspirated Perfect – Verb Stems Ending in a Labial or Velar Stop

18.19   With most verb stems that end in a labial stop (π/β/φ), the perfect stem uses the aspirated version of that labial stop: φ (those with φ remain unchanged). There are often vowel changes between the perfect stem and other tense stems as well. Some examples:

– Without vowel change (between the perfect and present stems):

verb	verb stem	perfect stem	1 sg. ind.
τρίβω *rub*	τρῑβ-/<u>τρῐβ-</u>	τετρῐφ-	τέτρῐφα
γράφω *write*	γρᾰφ-	γεγραφ-	γέγραφα

Note especially verbs that have a present in -πτω (→12.27):

κόπτω *hit*	κοπ-		κεκοφ-	κέκοφα
ῥίπτω *throw*	ῥῑπ-		ἐρριφ-	ἔρριφα

– With vowel change (often with o, →1.56):

κλέπτω *steal*	κλεπ-/<u>κλοπ</u>-/κλᾰπ-	κεκλοφ-	κέκλοφα
λαμβάνω *get, take*	<u>ληβ</u>-/λᾰβ-	εἰληφ- (→11.47)	εἴληφα
πέμπω *send*	πεμπ-/<u>πομπ</u>-	πεπομφ-	πέπομφα
τρέφω *nourish, rear*	τρεφ-/<u>τροφ</u>-/τρᾰφ-	τετροφ-	τέτροφα

18.20 Similarly, with most verb stems that end in a velar stop (κ/γ/χ), the perfect stem uses the aspirated version of that velar stop: χ (those with χ remain unchanged). Again, there are often vowel changes between the perfect stem and other tense stems as well. Some examples:

– Without vowel change (between the perfect and present stems):

verb	*verb stem*	*perfect stem*	*1 sg. ind.*
διώκω *chase*	διωκ-	δεδιωχ-	δεδίωχα
ἄγω *lead, bring*	ἀγ-	ἠχ-	ἦχα
ἄρχω *begin, rule*	ἀρχ-	ἠρχ-	ἦρχα

Note especially verbs that have a present in -ττω (→12.27):

φυλάττω *guard*	φυλᾰκ-	πεφυλαχ-	πεφύλαχα
τάττω *array, appoint*	τᾰγ-	τεταχ-	τέταχα

Of the -νυμι verbs that have verb stems ending in a velar stop (→12.39), only δείκνυμι has a regular aspirated perfect in classical Greek (for (ἀν)οίγνυμι, →18.25):

δείκνυμι *show*	δεικ-	δεδειχ-	δέδειχα

– With vowel change (often with o, →1.56):

λαγχάνω *obtain by lot*	<u>ληχ</u>-/λᾰχ-	εἰληχ- (→11.47)	εἴληχα
φέρω *carry, bring*	φερ-, ἐνεκ-/<u>ἐνοκ</u>-/ἐγκ-, οἰτ-	ἐνηνοχ- (→11.48)	ἐνήνοχα
συλ-λέγω *gather*	λεγ-/<u>λογ</u>-, εἰπ-, ἐρ-/ῥη-	-ειλοχ-	συνείλοχα

Stem Perfects

18.21 Stem perfects have a perfect stem which, apart from the reduplication, is identical to the verb stem. Many of these verbs have vowel change between the perfect stem and other tense stems (ablaut, →1.51–6; the o-grade is frequently used in the perfect stem). Several active stem perfects correspond to a middle-passive present (with a 'change-of-state' meaning, →35.17; the meanings of these perfects are given below).

The most common stem perfects are the following:

– Without vowel change (between the perfect and present stems):

verb	verb stem	perfect stem	1 sg. ind.
ἀπόλλυμαι *perish*	ὀλ(ε)-	ὀλωλ- (→11.48)	(ἀπ)όλωλα *have perished*
πήγνυμαι *become solid*	πηγ-/πᾰγ-	πεπηγ-	πέπηγα *be stuck*
φεύγω *flee*	φευγ-/φῠγ-	πεφευγ-	πέφευγα

– With vowel change (often with ο, →1.56):

ἀκούω *hear*	ἀκο(υ)- (<*ἀκοϝ-)	ἀκήκο- (→11.48)	ἀκήκοα (<*ἀκηκοϝα))
ἀποκτείνω *kill*	κτεν-/κτον-/κτᾰν-	-ἐκτον-	ἀπέκτονα
γίγνομαι *become, be born*	γεν(η)-/γον-/γν-	γεγον-	γέγονα *be (born)*
διαφθείρομαι *perish*	φθερ-/φθορ-/φθᾰρ-	-ἐφθορ-	διέφθορα *have lost one's wits*
ἐγείρομαι *wake up*	ἐγερ-/ἐγορ-/ἐγρ-	ἐγρηγορ- (→11.48)	ἐγρήγορα *be awake*
ἔρχομαι *go, come*	ἐρχ-, ἐλευθ-/ἐλ(ῠ)θ-, εἰ-/ἰ-	ἐληλυθ- (→11.48)	ἐλήλυθα *have come*
λανθάνω *go unnoticed*	ληθ-/λᾰθ-	λεληθ-	λέληθα
λείπω *leave*	λειπ-/λοιπ-/λῐπ-	λελοιπ-	λέλοιπα
μαίνομαι *rage*	μην-/μᾰν-	μεμην-	μέμηνα *be furious*
πάσχω *suffer*	πενθ-/πονθ-/πᾰθ-	πεπονθ-	πέπονθα
πείθομαι *believe, obey*	πειθ-/ποιθ-/πῐθ-	πεποιθ-	πέποιθα *believe, trust*
ῥήγνυμαι *break* (intr.)	ῥηγ-/ῥωγ-/ῥᾰγ-	ἐρρωγ-	ἔρρωγα *be torn*
στρέφομαι *turn around*	στρεφ-/στροφ-/στρᾰφ-	ἐστροφ-	ἔστροφα *have turned around*
τίκτω *give birth*	τεκ-/τοκ-/τκ-	τετοκ-	τέτοκα
φαίνομαι *appear, seem*	φην-/φᾰν-	πεφην-	πέφηνα *have appeared*

Note 1: There is no real difference between aspirated perfects and stem perfects if the verb stem itself ends in a -φ or -χ already. E.g. with γράφω (verb stem γρᾰφ-), pf. ind. γέγραφ-α.

Irregular Stem Perfects: ἔοικα, εἴωθα, οἶδα

18.22   The verbs ἔοικα *be likely* and εἴωθα *be accustomed*, of which no corresponding presents exist, are conjugated like other stem perfects, except for the following points:

– no subjunctive or optative forms of these verbs occur;
– ἔοικα has participle εἰκώς, -ότος (next to ἐοικώς, -ότος); it has infinitive εἰκέναι next to ἐοικέναι;
– the infinitive of εἴωθα (εἰωθέναι) is very rare.

18.23   The verb οἶδα *know*, of which no corresponding present exists, has an irregular conjugation, built on the verb stem εἰδ-/οἰδ-/ἰδ- (<*ϝειδ-/*ϝοιδ-/*ϝῐδ-):

E.g. 1 sg. pf. ind. οἶδ-α, 2 sg. οἶσθα (<*οἶδ-θα, →1.89), 2 pl. ἴστε (<*ῐδ-τε); 2 sg. imp. ἴσθι (<*ῐδ-θι); 1 sg. plpf. ᾔδ-η (εἰδ- with augment); inf. εἰδ-έναι.

Full forms are given in the overview, →18.4. Note that unlike most perfects, οἶδα has imperative forms (as well as subjunctive and optative forms, which are also absent from many perfects). It behaves in all respects like a present.

Further Particulars

18.24   A number of verbs that in other tenses use a verb stem which ends in a consonant, have a perfect stem with an additional η. For example:

verb	*verb stem*	*perfect stem*	*1 sg. ind.*
stems ending in a dental or velar stop:			
ἁμαρτάνω *miss, err*	ἁμαρτ-	ἡμαρτηκ-	ἡμάρτηκα (cf. aor. ἥμαρτ-ον)
ἔχω *have, hold*	ἐχ-/σχ-	ἐσχηκ-	ἔσχηκα (cf. aor. ἔ-σχ-ον)
μανθάνω *learn, understand*	μᾰθ-	μεμαθηκ-	μεμάθηκα (cf. aor. ἔ-μαθ-ον)
stems ending in a resonant:			
εὑρίσκω *find*	εὑρ-	ηὑρηκ-	ηὕρηκα (cf. aor. ηὖρ-ον)
μένω *stay, (a)wait*	μεν-	μεμενηκ-	μεμένηκα (cf. pres. μέν-ω)
νέμω *deal out*	νεμ-	νενεμηκ-	νενέμηκα (cf. pres. νέμ-ω)
stems ending in ξ or ψ:			
αὐξάνω, αὔξω *increase*	αὐξ-	ηὐξηκ-	ηὔξηκα (cf. pres. αὔξ-ω)
ἕψω *boil*	ἑψ-	ἡψηκ-	ἥψηκα (cf. pres. ἕψ-ω)

18.25   The verbs ἀν-οίγω (also: ἀνοίγνυμι) *open* and πράττω *do, act* have both an aspirated perfect (ἀνέῳχα and πέπρᾱχα, respectively), and a stem perfect (ἀνέῳγα and πέπρᾱγα, respectively). πέπρᾱχα is typically construed with an object (*have done something*), πέπρᾱγα with an adverb (*have fared a certain way*).

For the reduplication in ἀνέῳχα/ἀνέῳγα, →11.40.

18.26　Several verbs have both κ-perfect and stem perfect forms. The κ-perfects are a later development, and tend to have a different meaning, especially if the stem perfects correspond to a middle-passive present with a 'change-of-state' meaning (for full discussion, →35.17):

ἀπ-όλλυμι *destroy* (verb stem ὀλ(ε)-)

with act. ἀπόλλυμι	κ-pf. ἀπολώλεκα: *have destroyed X*
with mid. ἀπόλλυμαι *perish*	stem pf. ἀπόλωλα: *be ruined*

δια-φθείρω *destroy* (verb stem φθερ-/φθορ-/φθᾰρ-)

with act. διαφθείρω	κ-pf. διέφθαρκα *and* stem pf. διέφθορα: *have destroyed X*
with mid. διαφθείρομαι *perish*	stem pf. διέφθορα: *have lost one's wits, be corrupted* (Homer and late prose only)

ἐγείρω *wake, rouse* (verb stem ἐγερ-/ἐγορ-/ἐγρ-)

with act. ἐγείρω	(in later Greek:) κ-pf. ἐγήγερκα: *have woken X*
with mid. ἐγείρομαι *wake up* (intr.)	stem pf. ἐγρήγορα: *be awake* (in later Greek also mp. pf. ἐγήγερμαι)

φαίνω *show* (verb stem φην-/φᾰν-)

with act. φαίνω	(rare) κ-pf. πέφαγκα: *have shown, have caused X to appear*
with mid. φαίνομαι *appear, seem*	stem pf. πέφηνα: *have appeared*

Mixed Perfects (δέδοικα, ἕστηκα, τέθνηκα and βέβηκα)

Overview of Forms

18.27　The following perfects have some distinct forms:

- δέδοικα *fear* (verb stem δει-/δοι-/δῐ-; no corresponding present occurs in classical Greek): perfect stems δεδοικ-/δε(ι)δι-;
- (ἀπο)θνῄσκω *die* (verb stem θᾰν-/θνη-): perfect stems τεθνηκ-/τεθνα- *be dead*;
- ἵσταμαι *come to stand* (verb stem στη-/στᾰ-): perfect stems ἑστηκ-/ἑστα- *stand*;
- βαίνω *go, walk* (verb stem βη-/βᾰ(ν)-): perfect stems βεβηκ-/βεβα- *stand (firm)*.

These verbs have regular κ-perfect forms built on the long variant of the stem. Other forms occur, however, which are built on a short variant of the stem, and use slightly different endings. The following tables give the most frequently occurring **short-stem forms** (note that these perfects, unlike most active perfects described above, have imperative forms):

	δέδοικα *fear*	τέθνηκα *be dead*	ἕστηκα *stand*	βέβηκα *stand (firm)*
	(no present) stem δε(ι)δι-	(ἀπο)θνῄσκω *die* stem τεθνα-	ἵσταμαι *come to stand* stem ἑστα-	βαίνω *go, walk* stem βεβα-
prim. ind. (pf.)	1 pl. δέδιμεν, 2 pl. δέδιτε, 3 pl. δεδίασιν *also:* 1 sg. δέδια, 3 sg. δέδιεν	3 pl. τεθνᾶσι(ν)	2 pl. ἕστατε, 3 pl. ἑστᾶσι(ν)	3 pl. βεβᾶσι(ν)
sec. ind. (plpf.)	1 pl. ἐδέδιμεν, 2 pl. ἐδέδιτε, 3 pl. ἐδέδι(ε)σαν *also:* sg. ἐδεδίειν, ἐδεδίεις, ἐδεδίει(ν)	3 pl. ἐτέθνασαν	3 pl. ἕστασαν	—
subj.	3 sg. δεδίῃ, 3 pl. δεδίωσι(ν)	—	—	—
opt.	—	1 sg. τεθναίην, 3pl. τεθναῖεν, etc.	—	—
imp.	2 sg. δέδιθι	2 sg. τέθναθι, 3 sg. τεθνάτω	2 sg. ἕσταθι, 3 sg. ἑστάτω	—
inf.	δεδιέναι	τεθνάναι	ἑστάναι	—
ppl.	δεδιώς, -ότος δεδιυῖα, -υίας δεδιός, -ότος	τεθνεώς, -ῶτος τεθνεῶσα, -ώσης τεθνεός, -ῶτος	ἑστώς, -ῶτος ἑστῶσα, -ώσης ἑστώς, -ῶτος	βεβώς, -ῶτος βεβῶσα, -ώσης βεβώς, -ῶτος

Particulars

18.28   In the **indicative** (perfect and pluperfect):

- Most forms are built on the long form of the stem (δεδοικ-/τεθνηκ-/ἕστηκ-), and conjugated like κ-perfects. Thus pf. ind. δέδοικα, δέδοικας, δέδοικε(ν); τέθνηκα, etc.; ἕστηκα, etc., plpf. ἐδεδοίκειν, ἐδεδοίκεις, ἐδεδοίκειν; ἐτεθνήκειν, etc.; ἑστήκειν, etc.
- Some forms, however, especially 3 pl. forms, are built on the short form of the stem (δεδι-/τεθνα-/ἑστα-): thus. e.g. pf. ind. δέδι-μεν, δέδι-τε, δεδί-ασι(ν); τεθνᾶσι(ν) (<*τεθνά-ασι); ἑστᾶσι(ν) (<*ἑστά-ασι).

However, alternative κ-forms are often found for the short-stem forms as well, e.g. δεδοίκαμεν, τεθνήκασι(ν), etc.

Note 1: In the pluperfect of ἕστηκα, κ-forms regularly begin with εἰ- (with visible augment) rather than ἑ-: for example, εἱστήκη (next to ἑστήκη), εἱστήκεσαν (next to ἑστήκεσαν/ἕστασαν).

18.29   Short-stem forms of the **subjunctive and optative** are rare (the subj. and opt. are rare altogether), although optative τεθναίην (etc.) does occur occasionally.

18.30   **Imperatives** (very infrequent) are built on the short variant of the stem. The second singular active imperative ends in -**θι**: e.g. δέδι-θι, τέθνα-θι, ἕστα-θι.

18.31   The **infinitive** is normally built on the short variant of the stem, and ends in -**έναι** (δεδιέναι) or -**ναι** (τεθνάναι, ἑστάναι). However, κ-forms are also found alongside the short-stem forms, e.g. δεδοικέναι, τεθνηκέναι, ἑστηκέναι, βεβηκέναι.

18.32   The **participle** is normally built on the short variant of the stem (e.g. δεδιώς, -ότος), and has some irregular forms:

- with τέθνηκα: masc. τεθνεώς, -ῶτος; fem. τεθνεῶσα, -ώσης; neut. τεθνεός, -ῶτος;
- with ἕστηκα: masc. ἑστώς, -ῶτος; fem. ἑστῶσα, -ώσης; neut. ἑστώς, -ῶτος;
- with βέβηκα: masc. βεβώς, -ῶτος; fem. βεβῶσα, -ώσης; neut. βεβώς, -ῶτος.

However, alternative κ-forms are also found alongside the short-stem forms, e.g. δεδοικώς, τεθνηκώς, ἑστηκώς, βεβηκώς, etc.

Note 1: The verb γίγνομαι *become, be born* occasionally has a similarly formed pf. ppl. in poetry: γεγώς, fem. γεγῶσα.

19

The Perfect: Middle-Passive

The Perfect Middle-Passive Stem

19.1 All middle-passive perfect stems include a **reduplication** (just like active perfect stems), either in the form of a consonant + ε, or formed in the same way as the augment. For the rules governing reduplication, →11.43–8.

19.2 Apart from reduplication, perfect middle-passive stems have **no additions** to the verb stem. Thus e.g. with the verb παιδεύω *educate* (verb stem παιδευ-), the perfect middle-passive stem is πεπαιδευ-; with δείκνυμι *show* (verb stem δεικ-), the perfect middle-passive stem is δεδεικ-.

19.3 With verb stems that occur in different 'ablaut' vowel-grades, the middle-passive perfect stem normally shows one of the following:

- e-grade, same as the present stem but different from the active perfect stem: e.g. with πέμπω *send*, pf. act. stem πεπομφ-, pf. mp. stem πεπεμπ-; with λείπω *leave*, pf. act. λελοιπ-, pf. mp. stem λελειπ-;
- in some cases, particularly with stems in liquids: zero-grade, normally resulting in a stem with ᾰ (→1.53, 1.87); different from the present stem, but same as the active perfect stem: e.g. with στέλλω, pf. act. stem ἐσταλκ-, pf. mp. stem ἐσταλ-.

Conjugation of the Perfect Middle-Passive

Overview of Forms

19.4 The perfect middle-passive is conjugated as follows:

			verb stems ending in ι, υ, diphthongs or liquids		verb stems ending in α, ε, ο or η		verb stems ending in ν	
			παιδεύω *educate* stem πεπαιδευ-		τιμάω *honour* stem τετιμη-		φαίνομαι *appear, seem* stem πεφαν-	
prim. ind. (pf.)	sg.	1	πεπαίδευμαι		τετίμημαι		πέφασμαι	
		2	πεπαίδευσαι		τετίμησαι		πέφανσαι	
		3	πεπαίδευται		τετίμηται		πέφανται	
	pl.	1	πεπαιδεύμεθα		τετιμήμεθα		πεφάσμεθα	
		2	πεπαίδευσθε		τετίμησθε		πέφανθε	
		3	πεπαίδευνται		τετίμηνται		πεφασμένοι εἰσί(ν)	
sec. ind. (plpf.)	sg.	1	ἐπεπαιδεύμην		ἐτετιμήμην		ἐπεφάσμην	
		2	ἐπεπαίδευσο		ἐτετίμησο		ἐπέφανσο	
		3	ἐπεπαίδευτο		ἐτετίμητο		ἐπέφαντο	
	pl.	1	ἐπεπαιδεύμεθα		ἐτετιμήμεθα		ἐπεφάσμεθα	
		2	ἐπεπαίδευσθε		ἐτετίμησθε		ἐπέφανθε	
		3	ἐπεπαίδευντο		ἐτετίμηντο		πεφασμένοι ἦσαν	
subj.	sg.	1	πεπαιδευμένος	ὦ	τετιμημένος	ὦ	πεφασμένος	ὦ
		2		ᾖς		ᾖς		ᾖς
		3		ᾖ		ᾖ		ᾖ
	pl.	1	πεπαιδευμένοι	ὦμεν	τετιμημένοι	ὦμεν	πεφασμένοι	ὦμεν
		2		ἦτε		ἦτε		ἦτε
		3		ὦσι(ν)		ὦσι(ν)		ὦσι(ν)
opt.	sg.	1	πεπαιδευμένος	εἴην	τετιμημένος	εἴην	πεφασμένος	εἴην
		2		εἴης		εἴης		εἴης
		3		εἴη		εἴη		εἴη
	pl.	1	πεπαιδευμένοι	εἶμεν	τετιμημένοι	εἶμεν	πεφασμένοι	εἶμεν
		2		εἶτε		εἶτε		εἶτε
		3		εἶεν		εἶεν		εἶεν
imp.	sg.	2	πεπαίδευσο		τετίμησο		πέφανσο	
		3	πεπαιδεύσθω		τετιμήσθω		πεφάνθω	
	pl.	2	πεπαίδευσθε		τετίμησθε		πέφανθε	
		3	πεπαιδεύσθων		τετιμήσθων		πεφάνθων	
inf.			πεπαιδεῦσθαι		τετιμῆσθαι		πεφάνθαι	
ppl.	masc.		πεπαιδευμένος, -ου		τετιμημένος, -ου		πεφασμένος, -ου	
	fem.		πεπαιδευμένη, -ης		τετιμημένη, -ης		πεφασμένη, -ης	
	neut.		πεπαιδευμένον, -ου		τετιμημένον, -ου		πεφασμένον, -ου	

			verb stems ending in labial stops	verb stems ending in velar stops	verb stems ending in dental stops
			τρίβω *rub*	δείκνυμι *show*	κομίζω *convey*
			stem τετριβ-	stem δεδεικ-	stem κεκομῐδ-
prim. ind. (pf.)	sg.	1	τέτριμμαι	δέδειγμαι	κεκόμισμαι
		2	τέτριψαι	δέδειξαι	κεκόμισαι
		3	τέτριπται	δέδεικται	κεκόμισται
	pl.	1	τετρίμμεθα	δεδείγμεθα	κεκομίσμεθα
		2	τέτριφθε	δέδειχθε	κεκόμισθε
		3	τετριμμένοι εἰσί(ν)	δεδειγμένοι εἰσί(ν)	κεκομισμένοι εἰσί(ν)
sec. ind. (plpf.)	sg.	1	ἐτετρίμμην	ἐδεδείγμην	ἐκεκομίσμην
		2	ἐτέτριψο	ἐδέδειξο	ἐκεκόμισο
		3	ἐτέτριπτο	ἐδέδεικτο	ἐκεκόμιστο
	pl.	1	ἐτετρίμμεθα	ἐδεδείγμεθα	ἐκεκομίσμεθα
		2	ἐτέτριφθε	ἐδέδειχθε	ἐκεκόμισθε
		3	τετριμμένοι ἦσαν	δεδειγμένοι ἦσαν	κεκομισμένοι ἦσαν
subj.	sg.	1	τετριμμένος ὦ	δεδειγμένος ὦ	κεκομισμένος ὦ
		2	ᾖς	ᾖς	ᾖς
		3	ᾖ	ᾖ	ᾖ
	pl.	1	τετριμμένοι ὦμεν	δεδειγμένοι ὦμεν	κεκομισμένοι ὦμεν
		2	ἦτε	ἦτε	ἦτε
		3	ὦσι(ν)	ὦσι(ν)	ὦσι(ν)
opt.	sg.	1	τετριμμένος εἴην	δεδειγμένος εἴην	κεκομισμένος εἴην
		2	εἴης	εἴης	εἴης
		3	εἴη	εἴη	εἴη
	pl.	1	τετριμμένοι εἶμεν	δεδειγμένοι εἶμεν	κεκομισμένοι εἶμεν
		2	εἶτε	εἶτε	εἶτε
		3	εἶεν	εἶεν	εἶεν
imp.	sg.	2	τέτριψο	δέδειξο	κεκόμισο
		3	τετρίφθω	δεδείχθω	κεκομίσθω
	pl.	2	τέτριφθε	δέδειχθε	κεκόμισθε
		3	τετρίφθων	δεδείχθων	κεκομίσθων
inf.			τετρῖφθαι	δεδεῖχθαι	κεκομίσθαι
ppl.	masc.		τετριμμένος, -ου	δεδειγμένος, -ου	κεκομισμένος, -ου
	fem.		τετριμμένη, -ης	δεδειγμένη, -ης	κεκομισμένη, -ης
	neut.		τετριμμένον, -ου	δεδειγμένον, -ου	κεκομισμένον, -ου

Endings

19.5   All perfect middle-passive forms are **athematic**: endings follow immediately upon the stem. The regular endings listed in 11.20–33 are used in the perfect middle-passive, but the following points should be noted.

19.6   Endings beginning with **σθ** (e.g. second person plural -σθε or infinitive -σθαι) lose their σ with all perfect middle-passive stems except those ending in a vowel or diphthong (→1.94): e.g. πεπαίδευ-σθε but ἔρριφ-θε (for this latter form, also →19.7).

19.7   The final sound of perfect middle-passive stems **ending in a consonant** often changes by **assimilation** (→1.88–93) to the ending: e.g. βέβλαμ-μαι, βέβλαπ-ται with stem βεβλαβ-. For an overview of such changes, →19.10.

19.8   The **third person plural indicative** exists as a 'synthetic' (single) form only with perfect middle-passive stems ending in a vowel/diphthong (e.g. ἐπεπαίδευντο); with all other verbs, 'periphrastic' forms are used (the perfect middle-passive participle and a form of εἰμί *be*, →17.5–7), e.g. δεδειγμένοι εἰσί(ν).

Note 1: For the Ionic 3 pl. ind. endings -αται (pf.) and -ατο (plpf.), →25.39.

19.9   Middle-passive **subjunctives and optatives** do not exist as synthetic (single) forms: in their place periphrastic forms are used (→17.5–7).

Overview of Middle-Passive Perfect Stem Changes Before Different Endings

19.10   The following table presents an overview of the changes of the final sound of a verb stem before different perfect middle-passive endings:

verb stems ending with	endings beginning with			
	μ	σ	τ	(σ)θ
vowels/diphthongs/liquids	*no change*	*no change*	*no change*	*no change*
e.g. παιδευ-	πεπαίδευμαι	πεπαίδευσαι	πεπαίδευται	πεπαίδευσθε
ν	(-μμ- or) -σμ-	*no change*	*no change*	-νθ-
e.g. φᾰν-	πέφασμαι	πέφανσαι	πέφανται	πέφανθε
labial stops	-μμ-	-ψ-	-πτ-	-φθ-
e.g. τριβ-	τέτριμμαι	τέτριψαι	τέτριπται	τέτριφθε
velar stops	-γμ-	-ξ-	-κτ-	-χθ-
e.g. δεικ-	δέδειγμαι	δέδειξαι	δέδεικται	δέδειχθε
dental stops	-σμ-	-σ-	-στ-	-σθ-
e.g. ψευδ-	ἔψευσμαι	ἔψευσαι	ἔψευσται	ἔψευσθε

Perfect Middle-Passive Stems

Stem Formation

Verb Stems Ending in ι, υ or a Diphthong

19.11   Verb stems ending in ι, υ, or a diphthong do not change. Some examples:

verb	verb stem	perfect mp. stem	1 sg. ind.
παιδεύω *educate*	παιδευ-	πεπαιδευ-	πεπαίδευμαι
χρίω *anoint*	χρῑ-	κεχρι-	κέχριμαι (also κέχρισμαι, →19.32)
λύω *loosen, release*	λῡ-/λῠ-	λελῠ-	λέλῠμαι
κλῄω/κλείω *close*	κλη-/κλει-	κεκλει-	κέκλειμαι (also κέκλεισμαι, →19.32)
παύω *stop*	παυ-	πεπαυ-	πέπαυμαι
κρούω *strike*	κρου(σ)-	κεκρου(σ)-	κέκρουμαι, also κέκρουσμαι

Note 1: With monosyllabic stems which have long ῡ in the present stem, the perfect middle-passive has a stem with short ῠ; also →14.11 n.1, 18.10 n.1.

19.12   These verbs add all the endings as normal, including -σθε and -σθαι. There are 'synthetic' forms (→17.5) for the whole conjugation except subjunctives and optatives (where periphrastic forms are always used).

Verb Stems Ending in Other Vowels

19.13   With verb stems ending in η/ε, η/ᾰ, ω/ο (i.e. contract verbs), the **long variant** of the verb stem is used (→11.11):

– pres. stem ε: pf. mp. stem η;
– pres. stem ᾰ (or η): pf. mp. stem η (but ᾱ after ε, ι or ρ);
– pres. stem ο: aor. stem ω; a few verbs with a verb stem ending in ω have a similarly formed perfect middle-passive.

Some examples:

verb	verb stem	perfect mp. stem	1 sg. ind.
ποιέω *make, do*	ποιη-/ποιε-	πεποιη-	πεποίημαι
ἡγέομαι *lead, consider*	ἡγη-/ἡγε-	ἡγη-	ἥγημαι
τιμάω *honour*	τιμη-/τιμᾰ-	τετιμη-	τετίμημαι
νικάω *win*	νικη-/νικᾰ-	νενικη-	νενίκημαι
αἰτιάομαι *accuse*	αἰτιᾱ-/αἰτιᾰ-	ᾐτιᾱ-	ᾐτίᾱμαι
δηλόω *make clear*	δηλω-/δηλο-	δεδηλω-	δεδήλωμαι
ἐναντιόομαι *oppose*	ἐναντιω-/ἐναντιο-	ἠναντιω-	ἠναντίωμαι
χρήομαι *use, need*	χρη-	κεχρη-	κέχρημαι
τιτρώσκω *wound*	τρω-	τετρω-	τέτρωμαι

19.14   With several -μι verbs that have variant verb stems ending in η/ᾰ, η/ε or ω/ο (→12.37), the **short variant** of the verb stem is used in the perfect middle-passive:

verb	verb stem	perfect mp. stem	1 sg. ind.
ἵστημι *make stand, set up*	στη-/στᾰ-	ἑστα- (→11.48)	ἕσταμαι
ἵημι *send, let go*	ἡ-/ἑ-	εἱ- (→11.47)	εἷμαι
δίδωμι *give*	δω-/δο-	δεδο-	δέδομαι

But πίμπρημι uses the long verb stem in the perfect middle-passive:

| πίμπρημι *burn* | πρη-/πρᾰ- | πεπρη- | πέπρημαι |

And τίθημι has the irregular perfect middle-passive stem τεθει- (cf. pf. act. τέθεικα, →18.12; note, however, that forms of κεῖμαι are often used as the perfect passive of τίθημι, →12.43 n.1):

| τίθημι *put, place* | θη-/θε- | τεθει- | τέθειμαι |

19.15   A few verbs in -άω and -έω that originally had a verb stem ending in σ (or were treated as such, →13.18) have that σ in the middle-passive perfect (except before endings which themselves begin with σ):

αἰδέομαι *fear* (<*αἰδέσ̲-(y)ομαι, →12.29 n.1)   pf. mp. ind. ᾔδεσμαι

τελέω *finish* (<*τελέσ̲-(y)ω, →12.29 n.1)   pf. mp. ind. τετέλεσμαι (but τετέλεσαι <*-εσ-σαι)

Also note verbs in -έννυμι and -άννυμι (which have a stem in σ):

ἀμφιέννυμαι *dress oneself* (<*-έσ̲νυμαι)   pf. mp. ind. ἠμφίεσμαι (for the reduplication, →11.57)

For ἔγνωσμαι, πέπρησμαι, etc., which have a 'parasitic' σ, →19.32 below.

19.16   (ἐπ)αινέω *praise*, which in all other stems uses a short vowel (e.g. aor. ᾔνε̲σα, pf. act. ᾔνε̲κα, →15.19, 18.13), has a long stem vowel in the middle-passive perfect: (ἐπ)ῄνη̲μαι.

19.17   A few verbs in -άω (also -αίω) and -έω that originally had a verb stem ending in ϝ (→13.20, 15.20, 18.14) have a middle-passive perfect in -αυμαι and -ευμαι, respectively:

κάω (also καίω) *set on fire* (<*κάϝyω)   pf. mp. ind. κέκαυμαι (<*κέκᾰϝμαι)

πλέω *sail* (<*πλέϝω)   pf. mp. ind. πέπλευμαι (<*πέπλεϝμαι)

πνέω *blow* (<*πνέϝω)   pf. mp. ind. πέπνευμαι (<*πέπνεϝμαι)

19.18   These verbs add all the endings as normal, including -σθε and -σθαι. There are synthetic forms (→17.5) for the whole conjugation except subjunctives and optatives (where periphrastic forms are always used).

Verb Stems Ending in a Labial Stop

19.19   With most verb stems that end in a labial stop (π/β/φ), that stop changes before the first sound of the ending, in the following way:

- **labial + μ > μμ**: e.g. with τρίβω, verb stem τρῑβ-/τρῐβ-, pf. mp. stem τετριβ- (both ῑ and ῐ are found), 1 sg. pf. mp. ind. τέτριμμαι (<*τέτριβ-μαι), nom. sg. masc. ppl. τετριμμένος (<*τετριβ-μένος);
- **labial + σ > ψ** (only -σαι and -σο, for -(σ)θε and -(σ)θαι see below): e.g. 2 sg. pf. mp. ind. τέτριψαι, 2 sg. plpf. mp. ἐτέτριψο;
- **labial + τ > πτ**: 3 sg. pf. mp. ind. τέτριπται (<*τέτριβ-ται);
- **labial + θ > φθ** (-σθε and -σθαι lose σ): e.g. pf. mp. inf. τετρῖφθαι/τετρῖφθαι (<*τετριβ-(σ)θαι).

Some examples:

verb	verb stem	perfect mp. stem	1 sg. ind.
τρίβω *rub*	τρῑβ-/τρῐβ-	τετρῑβ-/τετρῐβ-	τέτριμμαι
γράφω *write*	γρᾰφ-	γεγραφ-	γέγραμμαι
λείπω *leave*	λειπ-/λοιπ-/λῐπ-	λελειπ-	λέλειμμαι

Note especially verbs that have a present in -πτω (→12.27):

βλάπτω *harm, damage*	βλᾰβ-	βεβλαβ-	βέβλαμμαι
ῥίπτω *throw*	ῥῑπ-	ἐρριπ-	ἔρριμμαι
θάπτω *bury*	θᾰφ-	τεθαφ-	τέθαμμαι

19.20   If a stem has a μ preceding the labial consonant, and the ending starts with μ, the resulting combination μμμ is simplified to μμ: e.g. with πέμπω, pf. mp. stem πεπεμπ-, 1 sg. pf. mp. ind. πέπεμμαι.

19.21   These verbs always use a periphrastic form in the third person plural indicative and all subjunctives and optatives, e.g. τετριμμένοι εἰσίν 3 pl. pf. mp. ind.

Verb Stems Ending in a Velar Stop

19.22   With verb stems that end in a velar stop (κ/γ/χ), that stop changes before the first sound of the ending, in the following ways:

– **velar + μ > γμ**: e.g. with δείκνυμι, verb stem δεικ-, 1 sg. pf. mp. inf. δέδειγμαι (<*δέδεικ-μαι), nom. sg. masc. ppl. pf. mp. δεδειγμένος (<*δεδεικ-μένος);
– **velar + σ > ξ** (only -σαι and -σο, for -(σ)θε and -(σ)θαι see below): e.g. 2 sg. pf. mp. ind. δέδειξαι, 2 sg. plpf. mp. ἐδέδειξο;
– **velar + τ > κτ**: e.g. with τάττω, verb stem τᾰγ-, 3 sg. pf. mp. ind. τέτακται (<*τέταγ-ται);
– **velar + θ > χθ** (σ is lost from -σθε and -σθαι): e.g. pf. mp. inf. δεδεῖχθαι (<*δέδεικ-(σ)θαι).

Some examples:

verb	verb stem	perfect mp. stem	1 sg. ind.
ἄγω *lead, bring*	ἀγ-	ἠγ-	ἦγμαι
ἄρχω *begin, rule*	ἀρχ-	ἠρχ-	ἦργμαι
πλέκω *plait, weave*	πλεκ-	πεπλεκ-	πέπλεγμαι

Note especially (almost all) verbs that have a present in -ττω/-ττομαι (→12.27), a few in -ζω, and several in -νυμι:

τάττω *array, appoint*	τᾰγ-	τεταγ-	τέταγμαι
φυλάττω *guard*	φυλᾰκ-	πεφυλακ-	πεφύλαγμαι
αἰνίττομαι *speak in riddles*	αἰνῐγ-	ἠνιγ-	ἤνιγμαι
δείκνυμι *show*	δεικ-	δεδειγ-	δέδειγμαι

19.23   If a stem has a γ preceding the velar consonant, and the ending starts with μ, the resulting combination γγμ is simplified to γμ: e.g. with ἐλέγχω *test, prove*, pf. mp. stem ἐληλεγχ- (→11.48), 1 sg. pf. mp. ind. ἐλήλεγμαι.

19.24   These verbs always use a periphrastic form in the third person plural indicative and all subjunctives and optatives, e.g. δεδειγμένοι εἰσίν 3 pl. pf. mp. ind.

Verb Stems Ending in a Dental Stop

19.25   With verb stems ending in a dental stop (τ/δ/θ):

- **dental disappears before** σ, e.g. 2 sg. pf. mp. ind. ἔψευσαι (<*ἔψευδ-σαι), 2 sg. pf. imp. mp. ἔψευσο (<*ἔψευδ-σο);
- or **becomes** σ **itself before other sounds**, e.g. 1 sg. pf. mp. ind. ἔψευσμαι (<*ἔψευδ-μαι), 3 sg. ἔψευσται (<*ἔψευδ-ται).

Some examples:

verb	verb stem	perfect stem	1 sg. ind.
ψεύδομαι *lie*	ψευδ-	ἐψευδ-	ἔψευσμαι
πείθω *persuade*	πειθ-/ποιθ-/πῐθ-	πεπειθ-	πέπεισμαι

Note especially most verbs that have a present in -ζω/-ζομαι, and a few in -ττω (→12.27):

ἀγωνίζομαι *contend, fight*	ἀγωνῐδ-	ἠγωνιδ-	ἠγώνισμαι
κομίζω *convey*	κομῐδ-	κεκομιδ-	κεκόμισμαι
ἁρμόζω/ἁρμόττω *fit together*	ἁρμοδ-/ἁρμοτ-	ἡρμοτ-	ἥρμοσμαι
πλάττω *mould, shape*	πλᾱθ-	πεπλαθ-	πέπλασμαι

19.26   These verbs always use a periphrastic form in the third person plural indicative and all subjunctives and optatives, e.g. ἐψευσμένοι εἰσίν 3 pl. pf. mp. ind.

Verb Stems Ending in a Resonant

19.27   Verb stems **ending in a liquid consonant** (λ/ρ) stay unchanged (except for reduplication) before the endings (e.g. with ἀγγέλλω, verb stem ἀγγελ-, 1 sg. pf. mp. ind. ἤγγελ-μαι). Note that σ is lost from the endings -σθε and -σθαι (e.g. with ἀγγέλλω, pf. mp. inf. ἠγγέλθαι). Note especially verbs that have a present in -λλω or in -αίρω/-είρω (→12.28).

Some examples:

verb	verb stem	perfect mp. stem	1 sg. ind.
φύρω *mix, defile*	φῠρ-	πεφυρ-	πέφυρμαι
ἀγγέλλω *report*	ἀγγελ-	ἠγγελ-	ἤγγελμαι
ποικίλλω *embroider*	ποικῐλ-	πεποικιλ-	πεποίκιλμαι
καθαίρω *cleanse*	καθᾰρ-	κεκαθαρ-	κεκάθαρμαι
αἴρω *lift*	ἀρ-	ἠρ-	ἦρμαι

Many liquid-stem verbs use the zero-grade variant of the verb stem in the perfect middle-passive. This usually results in a stem with ᾰ (→1.56):

δια-φθείρω *destroy*	φθερ-/φθορ-/ φθᾰρ-	δι-εφθαρ-	δι-έφθαρμαι
σπείρω *sow*	σπερ-/<u>σπᾰρ-</u>	ἐσπαρ-	ἔσπαρμαι
στέλλω *dispatch*	στελ-/<u>στᾰλ-</u>	ἐσταλ-	ἔσταλμαι

19.28   With verb stems **ending in ν**:

– **ν + μ > μμ**: e.g. with ὀξύνω *sharpen* (verb stem ὀξῡν-) 1 sg. pf. mp. ind. ὤξυμμαι (<*ὤξυν-μαι), nom. sg. masc. ppl. pf. mp. ὠξυμμένος (<*ὠξυν-μένος). Most of these verbs, however, get an irregular perfect mp. stem ending in σ before μ (i.e. **ν + μ gives σμ**), notably φαίνω (verb stem φην-/φᾰν-): 1 sg. pf. mp. ind. πέφασμαι, nom. sg. masc. ppl. pf. mp. πεφασμένος (σμ was probably imported from dental stems by analogy, →19.25).

– ν stays **unchanged before other sounds**: e.g. 2 sg. pf. mp. ind. πέφανσαι, pf. mp. inf. πεφάνθαι. (Note that σ is lost from the endings -σθε and -σθαι.)

Some examples:

verb	verb stem	pf. mp. stem	1 sg. ind.
αἰσχύνομαι *be ashamed*	αἰσχῡν-	ᾐσχυν-	ᾔσχυμμαι
φαίνω *show*	φην-/<u>φᾰν-</u>	πεφαν-	πέφασμαι
ἡδύνω *make pleasant*	ἡδῡν-	ἡδυν-	ἥδυσμαι
σημαίνω *signify*	σημᾰν-	σεσημαν-	σεσήμασμαι

19.29   Verbs with a stem ending in a resonant always use a periphrastic form in the third person plural indicative, and all subjunctives and optatives, e.g. ἠγγελμένοι εἰσίν, πεφασμένοι εἰσίν 3 pl. pf. mp. ind.

19.30   Some verbs with a present stem ending in ν do not have the nasal in the perfect (it was not originally part of the verb stem, but a suffix added to the present stem, and then extended to some other stems; →12.30 n.2):

verb	verb stem	pf. mp. stem	1 sg. ind.
κλίνω *cause to lean*	κλῑ(ν)-	κεκλι-	κέκλιμαι
κρίνω *pick out, decide, judge*	κρῑ(ν)-	κεκρι-	κέκριμαι

19.31   Observe the perfect middle-passive of τείνω *stretch*:

τείνω *stretch*	τεν-/<u>τᾰ-</u>	τετα-	τέταμαι
	(<*τη̥- →1.86)		

Further Notes and Exceptions

19.32 Several verbs with verb stems ending in a vowel may get a 'parasitic' σ between stem and ending in the perfect middle-passive (also often in the aorist passive, →14.27). Whether this parasitic σ is used in a particular verb may vary from author to author, although some verbs always have it. For example:

verb	verb stem	pf. mp. stem.	1 sg. ind.
γιγνώσκω *know, recognize*	γνω-	ἐγνωσ-	ἔγνωσμαι
ἕλκω *draw, drag*	ἑλκ(ῠ)-	εἱλκυσ-	εἵλκυσμαι
κλῄω/κλείω *close*	κλη-/κλει-	κεκλει(σ)-	κέκλειμαι *or* κέκλεισμαι
πίμπρημι *burn*	πρη-/πρᾰ-	πεπρη(σ)-	πέπρημαι *or* πέπρησμαι
σῴζω *save*	σω-	σεσω(σ)-	σέσωμαι *or* σέσωσμαι

19.33 A number of verbs that in other tenses use a verb stem which ends in a consonant have a middle-passive perfect stem with an additional η (these verbs also have this η in the perfect active, →18.24). For example:

stems ending in a dental or velar stop:

ἁμαρτάνω *miss, err*	ἁμᾱρτ-	ἡμαρτη-	ἡμάρτημαι (cf. act. ἡμάρτηκα)
ἔχω *have, hold*	ἐχ-/σχ-	ἐσχη-	ἔσχημαι (cf. act. ἔσχηκα)
μανθάνω *learn, understand*	μᾰθ-	μεμαθη-	μεμάθημαι (cf. act. μεμάθηκα)

stems ending in a resonant:

βούλομαι *want, prefer*	βουλ-	βεβουλη-	βεβούλημαι
νέμω *deal out*	νεμ-	νενεμη-	νενέμημαι (cf. act. νενέμηκα)

stems ending in ξ or ψ:

αὐξάνω, αὔξω *increase*	αὐξ-	ηὐξη-	ηὔξημαι (cf. act. ηὔξηκα)
ἕψω *boil*	ἑψ-	ἡψη-	ἥψημαι (cf. act. ἥψηκα)

20

The Future Perfect

Formation of the Future Perfect

General

20.1   The **future perfect stems** (active and middle-passive) are formed by adding σ to the relevant perfect stem:

  – **active**: e.g. with (ἀπο)θνῄσκω *die* (verb stem θᾰν-/θνη-), perfect active stem τεθνηκ-: future perfect active stem τεθνηξ-;
  – **middle-passive**: e.g. with γράφω *write* (verb stem γρᾰφ-), perfect middle-passive stem γεγραφ-: future perfect middle-passive stem γεγραψ-.

20.2   **Active future perfects** are conjugated like active futures, e.g. 1 sg. ind. τεθνήξω *I will be dead*, 2 sg. τεθνήξεις, inf. τεθνήξειν, etc. However, more often a periphrastic construction is used (→20.5 below).

  Middle-passive future perfects are conjugated like middle futures, e.g. 1 sg. ind. γεγράψομαι, 2 sg. γεγράψει/-ῃ, inf. γεγράψεσθαι, etc. They normally have passive meaning (γεγράψεται *it will have been written*).

20.3   For the meanings and uses of the future perfect, →33.46–7.

Future Perfect Active: Particulars

20.4   The **active** future perfect is **very rare**. Regularly formed future perfects are practically confined to:

  – ἵσταμαι *come to stand*, pf. ἕστηκα *stand*, future perfect ἑστήξω *will stand*;
  – and (ἀπο)θνῄσκω *die, be killed*, pf. τέθνηκα *be dead*, future perfect τεθνήξω *I will be dead*.

20.5   More often the active future perfect is expressed by a **periphrastic construction** (→17.5–7), which combines the forms of the active perfect participle with forms of the future of εἰμί *be* (ἔσομαι, ἔσει/-ῃ, ἔσται, etc.). For instance:

  with γιγνώσκω *know, recognize* (pf. ἔγνωκα): 3 sg. fut. pf. act. ind. ἐγνωκὼς ἔσται *he will have recognized*;

with ἀφαιρέω *take away* (pf. ἀφῄρηκα): 1 pl. fut. pf. act. ind. ἀφῃρηκότες ἐσόμεθα *we will have taken away*;

with γίγνομαι *become, be born* (pf. γέγονα): 3 sg. fut. pf. act. ind. γεγονὼς ἔσται *he will have become*;

with δίδωμι *give* (pf. δέδωκα): fut. pf. act. inf. ἔσεσθαι δεδωκώς *to be going to have given*.

Future Perfect Middle-Passive: Particulars

20.6 The **middle-passive** future perfect is more common than the active, although still rare. Some examples:

verb	*pf. mp. stem*	*fut. pf. mp. stem*	*1 sg. ind.*
τιμάω *honour*	τετιμη-	τετιμησ-	τετιμήσομαι *will have been honoured*
αἱρέω *take*	ᾑρη-	ᾑρησ-	ᾑρήσομαι *will have been chosen* (→35.9)
λείπω *leave*	λελειπ-	λελειψ-	λελείψομαι *will have been left*
κτάομαι *acquire*	(κ)εκτη-	(κ)εκτησ-	κεκτήσομαι, ἐκτήσομαι *will possess*
μιμνήσκομαι *remember*	μεμνη-	μεμνησ-	μεμνήσομαι *will remember*
παύω *stop*	πεπαυ-	πεπαυσ-	πεπαύσομαι *will have stopped*
λέγω *say, speak*	εἰρη-/λελεγ-	εἰρησ-/λελεξ-	εἰρήσομαι/λελέξομαι *will have been said*

Note 1: Perfect middle-passive stems ending in a short vowel lengthen that vowel in the future perfect, just as in the future active and middle:

δέω *bind*	δεδε̱-	δεδησ-	δεδήσομαι

20.7 The middle-passive future perfect may also be expressed by a **periphrastic construction** (→17.5–7), which combines the forms of the middle-passive perfect participle with forms of the future of εἰμί *be* (ἔσομαι, ἔσει/-ῃ, ἔσται, etc.). For instance:

with ψεύδομαι *lie, be mistaken* (pf. ἔψευσμαι): 3 pl. fut. pf. ind. ἐψευσμένοι ἔσονται *they will have lied*;

with καταστρέφομαι *subdue* (pf. κατέστραμμαι): 2 sg. fut. pf. ind. κατεστραμμένος ἔσει *you will have subdued*;

with τάττω *array, appoint* (pf. mp. τέταγμαι): 3 sg. fut. pf. mp. opt. ἔσοιτο τεταγμένη *(that) it would have been appointed*.

21

The Dual: Verb Forms

Endings

21.1 Dual verb forms (verb forms whose subject is a group of exactly two) are formed in exactly the same way as verb forms treated in the preceding chapters: they use the same stems, thematic vowels, augment, optative/subjunctive markers, etc. The only respect in which they differ is their **endings**.

Like the other endings of the verb (→11.20–34), dual endings may be divided between:

- **primary endings** (used in the indicative present, future and perfect, and in the subjunctive), **secondary endings** (used in secondary indicatives – imperfect, aorist and pluperfect – and in the optative), and **imperative endings**;
- **active endings** (used in active forms and forms of the θη-/η-aorist) and **middle-passive endings** (used in middle-passive forms).

21.2 Overview of endings:

	active			middle-passive		
	primary	secondary	imperative	primary	secondary	imperative
1 du.	—	—	—	(-μεθον)[1]	—	—
2 du.	-τον[2]	-τον[2]	-τον[2]	-σθον[2]	-σθον[2]	-σθον[2]
3 du.	-τον	-την[3]	-των	-σθον	-σθην	-σθων[4]

[1] The 1 du. middle-passive ending -μεθον is exceedingly rare, e.g. λελείμμεθον (1 du. pf. pass. ind. λείπω, *the two of us have been left*; Soph. *El.* 950).

[2] In the second person, the primary, secondary and imperative endings are identical.

[3] -την is also, but rarely and only in poetry, used as a second-person secondary ending.

[4] Note that in the third person middle-passive, the imperative ending of the dual is identical to that of the plural (→11.29)

21.3 Some further points:

- **Thematic** dual forms always use the thematic vowel ε or (subj.) η, except in the optative (always ο before the ι of the opt.);
- **Present-stem** dual forms of -μι verbs are built on the short variant (→12.37) of the stem (e.g. δίδο-τον, not διδω-).

21.4 For the endings of **dual participles**, →10.1.

Examples of Dual Forms

21.5   Examples of dual forms in each of the tense-aspect stems are given below.

21.6   **Present** stem (→12):

-ω verbs

φυλάττετον	2/3 du. pres. act. ind. φυλάττω	*the two of you/them guard*
	2 du. pres. act. imp.	*guard (you two)!*
ἐπραττέτην	3 du. impf. act. πράττω	*the two of them did, acted*
ἀνῃρεῖσθον	2 du. impf. mid. ἀναιρέω	*the two of you took up for yourselves*
ὁπόταν γίγνησθον	2/3 du. pres. mid. subj. γίγνομαι	*when the two of you/them become*
εὐδαιμονοῖτον	2 du. pres. act. opt. εὐδαιμονέω	*may you two be happy*
εὐτυχοίτην	3 du. pres. act. opt. εὐτυχέω	*may the two of them be successful*
χαίρετον ἄμφω	2 du. pres. act. imp. χαίρω	*greetings to both of you*
ἑπέσθων	3 du. pres. mid. imp. ἕπομαι	*the two of them must follow*
ζῶντε	nom./acc. du. masc./neut. pres. act. ppl. ζήω	*living*
ἡγουμένω	nom./acc. du. masc./neut. pres. mid. ppl. ἡγέομαι	*leading, considering*
γιγνομέναιν	gen./dat. du. fem. pres. mid. ppl. γίγνομαι	*becoming*

-μι verbs

προδίδοτον	2/3 du. pres. act. ind. προδίδωμι	*the two of you/them betray*
	2 du. pres. act. imp.	*betray (you two)!*
ἔστων	3 du. pres. act. imp. εἰμί	*the two of them must be*
παρόντοιν	gen./dat. du. masc./neut. pres. act. ppl. πάρειμι	*being present*

Note 1: ἔστων and ἑπέσθων are also 3 pl. imp.: *they must be, they must follow* (→21.2 n.3).

21.7   **Aorist** stem (active and middle, →13):

(pseudo-)sigmatic:

ἠρκέσατον	2 du. aor. act. ind. ἀρκέω	*the two of you sufficed*
ἠθελησάτην	3 du. aor. act. ind. ἐθέλω	*the two of them were willing*
ἐνειμάσθην	3 du. aor. mid. ind. νέμω	*the two of them divided between them*
φιλήσατόν με	2 du. aor. act. imp. φιλέω	*kiss me (you two)!*
παύσασθον	2 du. aor. mid. imp. παύομαι	*stop (you two)!*
ἀποκτείναντε	nom./acc. du. masc./neut. aor. act. ppl. ἀποκτείνω	*having killed*

thematic:

ἀπεφύγετον	2 du. aor. act. ind. ἀποφεύγω	*the two of you escaped*
εἱλέσθην	3 du. aor. mid. ind. αἱρέω	*the two of them chose*
ὁπόταν ἀγάγησθον	2/3 du. aor. mid. subj. ἄγω	*when the two of you/them lead (in your/their own interest)*
οὐκ ἂν γενοίσθην	3 du. aor. mid. opt. γίγνομαι	*the two of them could not become*
ἔλθετον	2 du. aor. act. imp. ἔρχομαι	*come (you two)!*
λαβομένω	nom./acc. du. masc./neut. aor. mid. ppl. λαμβάνω	*having taken for themselves*

root:

ἐθέσθην	3 du. aor. mid. ind. τίθημι	*the two of them placed in their own interest*
ἀνταποδοῖτον	2. du. aor. act. opt. ἀνταποδίδωμι	*may you two return the favour*
μέθετόν με	2. du. aor. act. imp. μεθίημι	*let me go (you two)!*
διαδύντε	nom./acc. du. masc./neut. aor. act. ppl. διαδύομαι	*having slipped through*

21.8   Aorist passive stem (θη-/η-aorist, →14):

θη-aorist:

ὅταν συμμιχθῆτον	2/3 du. aor. pass. subj. συμμείγνυμαι	*whenever the two of you/them are mixed together*
διαλέχθητον	2 du. aor. pass. imp. διαλέγομαι	*converse (you two)!*
βασανισθέντοιν	gen./dat. du. masc./neut. aor. pass. ppl. βασανίζω	*having been put to the test*

η-aorist:

ὅταν συμπαγῆτον	2/3 du. aor. pass. subj. συμπήγνυμι	*when the two of you/them are formed*
τραφέντε	nom./acc. du. masc./neut. aor. pass. ppl. τρέφω	*having been reared*

21.9   Future stem (active and middle, →15):

sigmatic:

συνοίσετον	2/3 du. fut. act. ind. συμφέρω	*the two of you/them will bring together, benefit*
προστήσεσθον	2/3 du. fut. mid. ind. προΐσταμαι	*the two of you/them will stand up before*
ἐπιδείξοντε	nom./acc. du. masc./neut. fut. act. ppl. ἐπιδείκνυμι	*about to/in order to display*

Attic:

ἀπολεῖσθον	2/3 du. fut. mid. ind. ἀπόλλυμαι	*the two of you/them will perish, go to ground*
ἀποθανεῖσθον	2/3 du. fut. mid. ind. ἀποθνῄσκω	*the two of you/them will die*

21.10 **Perfect active** stem (→18):

κ-perfect:

δεδράκατον	2/3 du. pf. act. ind. δράω	*the two of you/them have done*

aspirated perfect:

μετειλήφατον	2/3 du. pf. act. ind. μεταλαμβάνω	*the two of you/them have acquired a share of*

stem perfect:

ἴστον	2/3 du. pf. act. ind. οἶδα	*the two of you/them know*
	2 du. pf. act. imp.	*know (you two)!*

mixed perfect:

τέθνατον	2/3 du. pf. act. ind. (ἀπο)θνῄσκω	*the two of you/them are dead*
ἑστάτην	3 du. plpf. act. ἵσταμαι	*the two of them stood*
δεδιότε	nom./acc. du. masc./neut. pf. act. ppl. δέδοικα	*being afraid*

21.11 **Perfect middle-passive** stem (→19):

γεγένησθον	2/3 du. pf. mid. ind. γίγνομαι	*the two of you/them have become/been born*
ἀφιγμένω ἐσμέν	1 du. pf. mid. ind. (periphrastic) ἀφικνέομαι	*the two of us have arrived*
ἀπεστερημένοιν	gen./dat. du. masc./neut. pf. pass. ppl. ἀποστερέω	*having been robbed of*

Note 1: As with the endings -σθε and -σθαι, the σ of the dual ending -σθον drops out in forms of perfect middle-passive stems ending in a consonant (→19.6), e.g. ἀφῖχθον (<*-ῑγ-σθον) 2/3 du. pf. mid. ind. *the two of you/them have arrived.*

21.12 **Future perfect** stem (→20):

ἐκτετμήσεσθον	2/3 du. fut. pf. pass. ind. ἐκτέμνω	*the two of you/them will have been cut out*

22

Principal Parts

22.1   The **principal parts** are divided into two lists (numbered consecutively):

– the first contains the principal parts of verbs without irregularities; the listed verbs may serve as examples of specific types of verb stem;
– the second list contains principal parts with irregularities/peculiarities.

Both lists give the 1 sg. ind. active of the present, aorist, future and perfect stems, followed by the 1 sg. ind. aorist and perfect passive. Some verbs (as a whole or their individual tense stems), however, only occur in one voice (*e.g.* βούλομαι *want, prefer*, which is a passive-only verb, →35.6, 35.26), whereas other verbs are not found in all tense stems (*e.g.* ἀρκέω *suffice*, which does not occur in the perfect tense in classical Greek). The future passive is omitted unless it cannot be derived from the aorist passive.

The lists also include the meaning(s) of the verb, the verb stem(s), and, under 'particulars', additional information about irregularities and, where useful, alternative forms that are found in poetry and/or Ionic prose. Indications of vowel length (˘ or ¯) are given for α, ι and υ in the verb stems, and for other verb forms only if variations in vowel length occur.

A dash (—) indicates that the verb form is very rare or not found in classical Greek, and therefore not included in the list.

Regular Principal Parts

22.2   The overview below (→22.3) gives the principal parts of examples of 'regular' verbs, with verb stems ending in:

– υ or a diphthong;
– η/ᾰ (or ᾱ/ᾰ), η/ε, ω/ο: 'contract verbs' (→12.3–5, 12.15–21);
– labial or velar stops (π, β, φ; κ, γ, χ);
– dental stops (τ, δ, θ);
– resonants (λ, ρ; μ, ν).

Note 1: The present stem of these verbs was usually formed with a yod (e.g. κρύπτω <*κρύφ-yω, φυλάττω <*φυλάκ-yω, καθαίρω <*καθάρ-yω; for details →12.26–9); such formations are considered regular below.

The verbs in the list share the following characteristics:

- a sigmatic aorist in -σα, or, in the case of verb stems ending in a resonant, a pseudo-sigmatic aorist in -α;
- an aorist passive in -θην (θη-aorist);
- a sigmatic future active in -σω, or, in the case of verbs ending in resonants and in -ίζω, an Attic future with contracted endings (-ῶ, -εῖς, etc.);
- a κ-perfect (active) in -κα, or, in the case of verbs ending in labial or velar stops, an aspirated perfect in -φα or -χα;
- a perfect middle/passive in -μαι.

22.3   **Verb stems ending in υ or a diphthong:**

verb (present)	verb stem	aorist	future	perfect
παιδεύω	παιδευ-	ἐπαίδευσα	παιδεύσω	πεπαίδευκα
educate		ἐπαιδεύθην		πεπαίδευμαι
λύω	λῡ-/λῠ-	ἔλῡσα	λύσω	λέλῠκα
loosen, release		ἐλύθην		λέλῠμαι

22.4   **Verb stems ending in η/ᾰ (or ᾱ/ᾰ), η/ε or ω/ο:**

verb (present)	verb stem	aorist	future	perfect
τῑμάω	τῑμη-/τῑμᾰ-	ἐτίμησα	τιμήσω	τετίμηκα
honour		ἐτιμήθην		τετίμημαι
ποιέω	ποιη-/ποιε-	ἐποίησα	ποιήσω	πεποίηκα
make, do		ἐποιήθην		πεποίημαι
δηλόω	δηλω-/δηλο-	ἐδήλωσα	δηλώσω	δεδήλωκα
make clear		ἐδηλώθην		δεδήλωμαι

All stems except the present stem are built on the **long** variant of the verb stem (→1.11).

    Observe that verb stems ending in εα, ια and ρα have long ᾱ in all stems (→1.57), e.g. θεᾱ́ομαι *gaze, view*, fut. θεᾱ́σομαι, ἀνιᾱ́ω *grieve*, aor. ἠνῑ́ᾱσα, δρᾱ́ω *do*, pf. δέδρᾱκα.

Note 1: For regular η-contract verbs (e.g. χρήομαι, διψήω, πεινήω) and ω-contract verbs (e.g. ἱδρώω), →12.19–20.

22.5   **Verb stems ending in a labial or velar stop:**

verb (present)	verb stem	aorist	future	perfect	particulars
τρῑ́βω	τρῑβ-/τρῐβ-	ἔτρῑψα	τρῑ́ψω	τέτρῑφα	also (more frequent)
rub		ἐτρίφθην		τέτριμμαι	η-aor. ἐτρῐ́βην; both
					ῑ and ῐ found in
					pf. mp.

κρύπτω *hide*	κρῠφ-/κρῠβ-	ἔκρυψα ἐκρύφθην	κρύψω	— κέκρυμμαι	pres. <*κρύφ-yω; also η-aor. ἐκρύφην (rare; in later Gk. frequently ἐκρύβην); pf. κέκρυφα only in later Gk.
ἄρχω *rule, begin*	ἀρχ-	ἦρξα ἤρχθην	ἄρξω	ἦρχα ἦργμαι	
φυλάττω *guard*	φυλᾰκ-	ἐφύλαξα ἐφυλάχθην	φυλάξω	πεφύλαχα πεφύλαγμαι	pres. <*φυλάκ-yω

22.6 Verb stems ending in a dental stop:

verb (present)	verb stem	aorist	future	perfect	particulars
ὀνομάζω *name*	ὀνομᾰδ-	ὠνόμασα ὠνομάσθην	ὀνομάσω	ὠνόμακα ὠνόμασμαι	for -άζω, →23.48
νομίζω *believe*	νομῐδ-	ἐνόμισα ἐνομίσθην	νομιῶ, -εῖς	νενόμικα νενόμισμαι	pres. <*νομίδ-yω

22.7 Verb stems ending in a resonant:

verb (present)	verb stem	aorist	future	perfect	particulars
ἀγγέλλω *report*	ἀγγελ-	ἤγγειλα ἠγγέλθην	ἀγγελῶ, -εῖς	ἤγγελκα ἤγγελμαι	pres. <*ἀγγέλ-yω
καθαίρω *cleanse*	καθᾰρ-	ἐκάθηρα ἐκαθάρθην	καθαρῶ, -εῖς	— κεκάθαρμαι	pres. <*καθάρ-yω; pf. act. κεκάθαρκα only in later Gk.
αἰσχύνω *disgrace* mp. *be ashamed*	αἰσχῠν-	ᾔσχῡνα ᾐσχύνθην	αἰσχυνῶ, -εῖς	— ᾔσχυμμαι	pres. <*αἰσχύν-yω; pf. act. ᾔσχυγκα only in later Gk.
μιαίνω *stain*	μιᾰν-	ἐμίᾱνα ἐμιάνθην	μιανῶ, -εῖς	— μεμίασμαι	pres. <*μιάν-yω; pf. act. μεμίαγκα only in later Gk.

Principal Parts with Peculiarities

22.8 The principal parts of the most common verbs with peculiarities are listed below (→22.9) in alphabetical order.

Note 1: Verbs which rarely occur as simplex (uncompounded) forms are listed alphabetically under the simplex form, but with the most common prefix added in parentheses (e.g. (ἐπ)αινέω *praise*; simplex αἰνέω is rare). If the simplex form does not occur at all, the verb is listed as a compound (e.g. ἀπ-εχθάνομαι *incur hatred*; simplex ἐχθάνομαι does not occur).

Typical peculiarities are the following:

- changes in vowels between the tense stems due to ablaut, e.g. pres. πέμπω *send*, pf. πέπομφα (→1.51–6);
- tense stems have different etymological derivations (suppletive verbs), e.g. pres. ὁράω *see*, aor. εἶδον (stems ὁρᾰ- and ἰδ-) (→11.13);
- an athematic (-μι) present, e.g. ζεύγνυμι *yoke* (→12.33–56);
- a thematic aorist, e.g. aor. ἔβαλον with pres. βάλλω *throw, hit* (→13.27–38);
- a root aorist, e.g. aor. ἔγνων with pres. γιγνώσκω *know, recognize* (→13.39–50); also aorists in -κα, e.g. ἔδωκα with δίδωμι *give* (→13.51–62);
- an aorist passive in -ην (η-aorist), e.g. aor. ἐγράφην with γράφω *write* (→14.29–31);
- an unexpected Attic future, e.g. fut. γαμῶ, -εῖς with pres. γαμέω *marry* (→15.34–7);
- an Attic future in -άω, e.g. fut. ἐλῶ, -ᾷς with pres. ἐλαύνω *drive, ride* (→15.38);
- a stem perfect, e.g. pf. ἀπέκτονα with pres. ἀποκτείνω *kill* (→18.21–3);
- a mixed perfect, e.g. pf. τέθνηκα, pl. τέθναμεν with (ἀπο)θνῄσκω *die* (→18.27–32);
- the verb is passive-only, e.g. aor. ἥσθην, fut. ἡσθήσομαι with ἥδομαι *enjoy* (→35.6, 35.21–9);
- tense stems are different in voice but not in meaning, e.g. pres. ἀκούω *hear*, fut. ἀκούσομαι (future middle) *I will hear*; verbs that have a middle future but no other anomalies (*e.g.* διώκω *chase*, fut. διώξομαι) are not included in the list (for an overview of the most frequent of these verbs, →15.40);
- an (original) stem ending in σ (→12.29 n.1) as well as some verbs which were 'absorbed' into this type (→13.18); the σ is indicated within brackets: e.g. pres. τελέω *finish*, verb stem τελε(σ)-;
- a 'parasitic' σ added to certain tense stems: e.g. pres. μιμνῄσκω *remind* (verb stem μνη-), θη-aor. ἐμνήσθην; the parasitic σ is not indicated in the verb stem; verbs that in one or more stems have a 'parasitic' σ but no other anomalies (*e.g.* κελεύω *order*, θη-aor. pass. ἐκελεύσθην, pf. mp. κεκέλευσμαι) are not included in the list (for more examples of verbs that have a 'parasitic' σ, →14.27, 19.23);
- vowels are added to certain tense stems, e.g. pres. ὀφείλω *owe, be bound to* (verb stem ὀφε(ι)λ-), fut. ὀφειλήσω (→12.29 n.2, 14.28, 15.30, 18.24, 19.33);
- 'irregular' formation of the augment or reduplication due to disappearing consonants, e.g. aor. εἴᾱσα (<*ἐσέϝα-, from ἐάω *allow*) (→11.40);
- a perfect with Attic reduplication, e.g. pf. ὀμώμοκα (ὄμνῡμι *swear*) (→11.48).

Note 2: Verbs whose active forms have a 'causative' sense, and whose middle-passive forms (may) express a change of state or a (change of) mental state, are given a separate middle-passive entry in the list when the latter meaning is expressed by *separate* aorist, future and/or perfect forms. Thus e.g. with causative ἵστημι *make stand, set up*, there is a separate entry for (change-of-state) ἵσταμαι *come to stand*, because a separate aorist (ἔστην *I came to stand*) and perfect (ἕστηκα *I stand*) express the change-of-state sense. For details on such verbs, →35.4, 35.17–20.

22.9 **List of principal parts:**

	verb (present)	verb stem	aorist	future	perfect	particulars
1	ἄγαμαι *admire*	ἀγᾰ-	ἠγάσθην	ἀγάσομαι	—	pass. only; athem. pres.; parasitic σ in θη-aor.
2a	(κατ)άγνυμι *(cause to) break*	ἆγ-/ᾰγ-	(κατ)έαξα/-ῆξα	(κατ)άξω	—	augm./redupl. ἐα- (verb stem <*ϝαγ-); athem. pres.
2b	(κατ)άγνυμαι *break (intr.)*	ἆγ-/ᾰγ-	(κατ)εάγην		(κατ)έᾱγα	η-aor.; act. stem pf. (κατέαγα *be broken*); Ion. pf. -έηγα
•	(ἀπ)αγορεύω →λέγω					
3	ἄγω *lead, bring*	ἀγ-	ἤγαγον / ἤχθην	ἄξω	ἦχα / ἦγμαι	them. aor. with redupl. →11.50
4	αἰδέομαι *be ashamed, fear*	αἰδε(σ)-	ᾐδεσάμην/ᾐδέσθην	αἰδέσομαι	ᾔδεσμαι	pass. only, but also occasionally mid. aor.; fut. mid.; verb stem in σ (hence short ε outside pres.)
5	(ἐπ)αινέω *praise*	αἰνε-	(ἐπ)ῄνεσα / (ἐπ)ῃνέθην	(ἐπ)αινέσω	(ἐπ)ῄνεκα / (ἐπ)ῄνημαι	in Att., short ε outside pres., except in pf. mp.; simplex verb rare in Att. prose
6	αἱρέω *take;* mid.: *choose*	αἱρη-/αἱρε-, ἑλ-	εἷλον / ᾑρέθην	αἱρήσω	ᾕρηκα / ᾕρημαι	suppletive; them. aor.; augm. in aor. εἱ- (verb stem <*σελ-); short ε in θη-aor.; Ion. pf. ᾁραίρηκα, ᾁραίρημαι
7	αἴρω *lift*	ἀρ-	ἦρα / ἤρθην	ἀρῶ, -εῖς	ἦρκα / ἦρμαι	verb stem <*ἀερ-; pres. ἀείρω and θη-aor. ἠέρθην in Ion. and poetry
8	αἰσθάνομαι *perceive*	αἰσθ-	ᾐσθόμην	αἰσθήσομαι	ᾔσθημαι	them. aor.; η added in fut. and pf.

No.		Verb stem				
9	ἀκούω *hear*	ἀκο(υ)(σ)-	ἤκουσα ἠκούσθην	ἀκούσομαι	ἀκήκοα	verb stem <*ἀκοϝ(σ)-; fut. mid.; stem pf. (-κοα <*-κοϝα); Att. redupl.; pf. mp. ἤκουσμαι only in later Gk.
10	ἀλείφω *anoint*	ἀλειφ-/ἀλῑφ-	ἤλειψα ἠλείφθην	ἀλείψω	ἀλήλιφα ἀλήλιμμαι	mostly in direct-refl. mid. ἀλείφομαι *anoint oneself* →35.11; stem pf.; Att. redupl.
11	ἀλέξω *ward off*	ἀλεκ-/ἀλεξ-	ἤλεξα/ἠλέξησα	ἀλέξω/ἀλεξήσω	—	η added in aor. ἠλέξησα and fut. ἀλεξήσω
12a	ἁλίσκομαι *be captured*	ἁλ(ω)-/ἁλο-	ἑάλων/ἥλων	ἁλώσομαι	ἑάλωκα/ἥλωκα	pres. with suffix -ισκ-; augm./redupl. ἑα- (verb stem <*ϝαλ(ω)-); act. root aor. and pf. (ἑάλων *was captured*, ἑάλωκα *have been captured*)
12b	ἀν-ἁλίσκω/ἀν-ᾱλόω *spend*		ἀνήλωσα ἀνηλώθην	ἀνᾱλώσω	ἀνήλωκα ἀνήλωμαι	
13a	ἀλλάττω *(ex)change*	ἀλλᾱγ-	ἤλλαξα ἠλλάγην/ἠλλάχθην	ἀλλάξω	ἤλλαχα ἤλλαγμαι	η-aor. more frequent in prose; θη-aor. mostly in Ion. and poetry
13b	ἀπ-αλλάττω *remove;* *mp.: depart*		ἀπήλλαξα ἀπηλλάγην/ ἀπηλλάχθην	ἀπαλλάξω	ἀπήλλαχα ἀπήλλαγμαι	
14	ἅλλομαι *leap*	ἁλ-	ἡλάμην/ἡλόμην	ἁλοῦμαι, -ῇ	—	them. aor. (next to pseudo-sigm. aor.)

(Continued)

	verb (present)	verb stem	aorist	future	perfect	particulars
15	ἁμαρτάνω *miss, err*	ἁμἄρτ-	ἥμαρτον / ἡμαρτήθην	ἁμαρτήσομαι	ἡμάρτηκα / ἡμάρτημαι	fut. mid.; them. aor.; η added in θη-aor., fut, and pf. stems
16	ἁνδάνω *please*	ἁδ-	ἔαδον/ἧσα	ἁδήσω	—	augm. ἔα- (verb stem <*σϝαδ-); them. aor.
17	ἀνώγω/ἄνωγα *command*	ἀνωγ-	—	—	ἄνωγα	poetic; all other tenses derived from pf.; aor. ἤνωξα and fut. ἀνώξω in epic Gk.
18	ἀπ-εχθάνομαι *incur hatred*	ἐχθ-	ἀπηχθόμην	ἀπεχθήσομαι	ἀπήχθημαι	them. aor.; η added in fut. and pf; in poetry occasionally ἔχθω *hate*
19	ἀραρίσκω *fit together*	ἀρ-	ἤραρον/ἧρσα	—	ἄρᾱρα	redupl. in them. aor.; pres. stem based on aor., with suffix -ισκ-; aor. ppl. ἄρμενος; stem pf. with Att. redupl.; mostly in poetry
20	ἀρέσκω *please*	ἀρε-	ἤρεσα	ἀρέσω	—	pres. with suffix -σκ-; short ε in aor. and fut.; θη-aor. opt. ἀρεσθείη in Soph.
21	ἀρκέω *suffice*	ἀρκε-	ἤρκεσα	ἀρκέσω	—	short ε in aor. and fut.
22	ἁρμόζω/ἁρμόττω *fit together*	ἁρμοδ-/ἁρμοτ-	ἥρμοσα / ἡρμόσθην	ἁρμόσω	ἥρμοκα / ἥρμοσμαι	pres. ἁρμόττω regular in prose, ἁρμόζω more frequent in poetry

No.	Present & meaning	Stem	Aorist	Future	Perfect	Notes
23	αὐξάνω/αὔξω *increase*; mp.: *grow*	αὐξ-	ηὔξησα / ηὐξήθην	αὐξήσω	ηὔξηκα / ηὔξημαι	pres. with nasal suffix -αν-; η added in stems outside pres.
24	ἄχθομαι *be angry*	ἀχθ-/ἀχθε(σ)-	ἠχθέσθην	ἀχθέσομαι	—	pass. only; verb stem in σ used outside pres; fut. also ἀχθεσθήσομαι
25	βαίνω *go, walk*	βη-/βᾰ(ν)-	ἔβην	βήσομαι	βέβηκα	pres. <*βάν-yω; root aor.; mixed pf.; causative (→35.4) aor. ἔβησα *made go* and fut. βήσω *will make go*
26	βάλλω *throw, hit*	βᾰλ-/βλη-	ἔβαλον / ἐβλήθην	βαλῶ, -εῖς	βέβληκα / βέβλημαι	pres. <*βάλ-yω; them. aor.
27	βάπτω *dip*	βᾰφ-	ἔβαψα / ἐβάφην	βάψομαι	—	η-aor.; fut. mid.
28	βιβάζω *cause to go*	βιβᾰδ-	ἐβίβασα / ἐβιβάσθην	βιβῶ, -ᾷς	βέβασμαι	Att. fut. in -άω; causative (→35.4) of βαίνω
29	βιβρώσκω *eat*	βρω-	ἐβρώθην	—	βέβρωκα	pres. with redupl. and suffix -σκ-; mostly Ion. (Att. uses ἐσθίω); aor. ἔβρωσα and fut. βρώσω in epic Gk; root aor. ἔβρων and pf. ppl. βεβρώς, -ῶτος in poetry
30	βλάπτω *harm, damage*	βλᾰβ-	ἔβλαψα / ἐβλάβην/ἐβλάφθην	βλάψω	βέβλαφα / βέβλαμμαι	η-aor. and θη-aor. both used

(*Continued*)

	verb (present)	verb stem	aorist	future	perfect	particulars
31	βλαστάνω *sprout*	βλᾰστ-	ἔβλαστον	βλαστήσω	βεβλάστηκα	pres. with nasal suffix -αν-; them. aor.; η added in fut. and pf. stems
32	βλώσκω *come, go*	μολ-/(μ)βλω-	ἔμολον	μολοῦμαι, -ῇ	μέμβλωκα	βλ- < *μλ- →1.93; pres. with suffix -σκ; them. aor.; fut. mid.; only in poetry
33	βούλομαι *want, prefer*	βουλ-	ἐβουλήθην	βουλήσομαι	βεβούλημαι	pass. only; fut. mid.; impf. ἠβουλόμην →11.41
34	γαμέω *marry (a woman)*; mid: *marry (a man)*	γᾰμ(ε)-	ἔγημα	γαμῶ, -εῖς	γεγάμηκα γεγάμημαι	Att. fut. (identical to pres.)
35	γελάω *laugh*	γελᾰ(σ)-	ἐγέλασα ἐγελάσθην	γελάσομαι	—	fut. mid.; verb stem in σ (hence short ᾰ in aor. and fut.)
36	γηθέω *rejoice*	γηθ(ε)-	ἐγήθησα	γηθήσω	γέγηθα	nearly exclusively pf. (*be glad,* →33.37) in class. Gk.
37	γίγνομαι *become, be born*	γεν(η)-/γον-/γν-	ἐγενόμην/ἐγενήθην	γενήσομαι	γέγονα/γεγένημαι	pres. redupl.; them. aor.; θη-aor. and act. pf. (ἐγενήθην *was born,* γέγονα *be, have been born*); pf. ppl. γεγώς in poetry →18.32 n.1; Ion. γίνομαι →25.14
38	γιγνώσκω *know, recognize*	γνω-	ἔγνων ἐγνώσθην	γνώσομαι	ἔγνωκα ἔγνωσμαι	pres. with redupl. and suffix -σκ; root aor.; fut. mid.; parasitic σ in θη-aor. and pf. mp.; Ion. γῑνώσκω →25.14

#	Present / meaning	Stem	Aorist	Future	Perfect	Notes
39	γράφω *write*	γράφ-	ἔγραψα / ἐγράφην	γράψω	γέγραφα / γέγραμμαι	η-aor.
40	δάκνω *bite*	δηκ-/δᾱκ-	ἔδακον / ἐδήχθην	δήξομαι	— / δέδηγμαι	pres. with nasal suffix -ν-; them. aor.; fut. mid.
41	(δέδοικα) *fear*	δει-/δοι-/δι-	ἔδεισα	—	δέδοικα	mixed pf.; forms, →18.27; fut. δείσομαι not found in classical Gk.
42	δέρω *skin*	δερ-/δᾰρ-	ἔδειρα / ἐδάρην	δερῶ, -εῖς	— / δέδαρμαι	η-aor.; δᾰρ- <*δρ̥-
43	δέω (*i*) *bind*	δη-/δε-	ἔδησα / ἐδέθην	δήσω	δέδεκα / δέδεμαι	pres. <*δέ-γω; short ε in θη-aor. and pf. stems
44a	δέω (*ii*) *lack*	δε-	ἐδέησα	δεήσω	δεδέηκα	pres. <*δέϝ-ω; η added outside pres.
44b	δεῖ *it is necessary*		ἐδέησε(ν)	δεήσει	δεδέηκε(ν)	impers. →36.3
44c	δέομαι *ask, need*		ἐδεήθην	δεήσομαι	δεδέημαι	
45	διδάσκω *teach*	διδᾰ(σ)κ-	ἐδίδαξα / ἐδιδάχθην	διδάξω	δεδίδαχα / δεδίδαγμαι	pres. redupl. δι- and suffix -σκ- generalized throughout other stems
46	(ἀπο)διδράσκω *run away*	δρᾱ-	(ἀπ)έδρᾱν	(ἀπο)δρᾱ́σομαι	(ἀπο)δέδρᾱκα	pres. with redupl. and suffix -σκ-; root aor.; fut. mid.; stem in ᾱ after ρ; simplex διδρᾱ́σκω very rare

(*Continued*)

	verb (present)	verb stem	aorist	future	perfect	particulars
47	δίδωμι *give*	δω-/δο-	ἔδωκα ἐδόθην	δώσω	δέδωκα δέδομαι	pres. redupl.; athem. pres.; κα-aor.
48a	δοκέω *seem, think*	δοκ(ε)-	ἔδοξα	δόξω	δέδοχα δέδογμαι	stem δοκε- used only in pres.; in poetry sometimes aor. ἐδόκησα, fut. δοκήσω, pf. δεδόκηκα
48b	δοκεῖ *it seems (right)*		ἔδοξε(ν)	δόξει	δέδοκται	impers. (for uses →36.4)
49	δύναμαι *be able*	δυνη-/δυνᾰ-	ἐδυνήθην (ἐδυνάσθην)	δυνήσομαι	δεδύνημαι	pass. only; fut. mid.; athem. pres.; impf. ἠδυνάμην, aor. ἠδυνήθην →11.41
50a	δύω *submerge*	δῡ-/δῠ-	ἔδῡσα ἐδύθην	δύσω	— δέδῡμαι	δύνω also used
50b	δύομαι *dive*		ἔδῡν	δύσομαι	δέδῠκα	act. root aor. and pf. ἔδυν *dived*, δέδυκα *be under*
51	ἐάω *allow*	ἐᾱ-/ἐᾰ-	εἴᾱσα εἰάθην	ἐᾱσω	εἴᾱκα εἴᾱμαι	augm./redupl. εἰ- (verb stem <*σεϝα-)
52a	ἐγείρω *wake, rouse*	ἐγερ-/ἐγορ-/ἐγρ-	ἤγειρα ἠγέρθην	ἐγερῶ, -εῖς	—	Att. redupl.; act. pf. ἐγήγερκα only in later Gk.
52b	ἐγείρομαι *wake up*		ἠγέρθην/ἠγρόμην	—	ἐγρήγορα	them. aor.; act. stem pf. ἐγρήγορα *be awake*; Att. redupl.; pf. mp. ἐγήγερμαι only in later Gk.; ἠγρόμην rare

- ἔδω →ἐσθίω

53a	(καθ)έζομαι *sit (down)*	-έδ-/-ίζ-	(ἐκαθ)εζόμην/(καθ)εζόμην	(καθ)εζοῦμαι, -ῆ	(κάθημαι)	<*σεδ-, pres. <*σεδγ-<*σε-σδ-; them. aor.; pres. κάθημαι used as pf.; simplex not in prose; for the augm. →11.57
53b	(καθ)ίζω *make sit down, sit down* (intr.)		ἐκάθισα/-εισα	καθιῶ, -εῖς	—	redupl. pres. <*σι-σδ-, with aor. ἐκάθισα and fut. derived from the pres.; for the augm. →11.57; simplex ἵζω mainly in poetry, ἵζομαι in Ion. prose
54	(ἐ)θέλω *be willing*	(ἐ)θελ-	ἠθέλησα	ἐθελήσω	ἠθέληκα	η added outside pres.
55a	εἰμί *be*	ἐσ-	—	ἔσομαι 3 sg. ἔσται	—	for the conjugation of pres. and impf., →12.36
55b	ἔξεστι(ν)/ἔστι(ν) *it is possible, it is permitted*		—	ἐξέσται/ἔσται	—	impers. →36.4
56	εἶμι *go*	εἰ-/ἰ-	—	—	—	for the conjugation of pres. and impf., →12.36; →ἔρχομαι; pres. with fut. value
57	(εἴωθα) *be accustomed*	ὠθ-	—	—	εἴωθα	Ion. ἔωθα; stem pf.; no pres.; →18.22

(Continued)

	verb (present)	verb stem	aorist	future	perfect	particulars
58	ἐλαύνω *drive, ride*	ἐλᾰ-	ἤλασα / ἠλάθην	ἐλῶ, -ᾷς	ἐλήλακα / ἐλήλαμαι	pres. with -υν-; Att. fut. in -άσω; Att. redupl.; pf. mp. ἐλήλασμαι rare
59	ἐλέγχω *test, prove*	ἐλεγχ-	ἤλεγξα / ἠλέγχθην	ἐλέγξω	—	Att. redupl.
60	ἕλκω *draw, drag*	ἑλκ(ῠ)-	εἵλκυσα / εἱλκύσθην	ἕλξω	εἵλκυκα / εἵλκυσμαι	augm./redupl. εἱ- (verb stem <*σελκ-); stems outside pres. and fut. add υ (Ion. fut. ἑλκύσω); parasitic σ in θη-aor. and pf. mp.
61a	ἀμφι-έννυμι *clothe with*	ἑ(σ)-	ἠμφίεσα	ἀμφιῶ, -εῖς	—	verb stem <*Ϝεσ-; athem. pres.; augm./redupl. before prefix →11.57; simplex only in poetry, with fut. ἕσ(σ)ω
61b	ἀμφι-έννυμαι *dress oneself in*		ἠμφιεσάμην	ἀμφιέσομαι	ἠμφίεσμαι	
62	(ἔοικα) *be like(ly)*	εἰκ-/οἰκ-	—	(εἴξω)	ἔοικα	<*ϜέϜοικα; stem pf, no pres.; plpf. ἐῴκη; ppl. εἰκώς, Ion. οἶκα (without redupl.) →25.43; often impers. ἔοικε(ν) *it seems, it is reasonable*
63	ἐπίσταμαι *know, be able*	ἐπιστη-/ἐπιστᾰ-	ἠπιστήθην	ἐπιστήσομαι	—	pass. only; athem. pres.
64	ἕπομαι *follow*	ἑπ-/σπ-	ἑσπόμην	ἕψομαι	—	middle only; impf. εἱπόμην with augm. εἱ- (<*ἑσε-)

No.	Present / meaning	Stem	Aorist	Future	Perfect	Notes
65	ἕρπω *walk, go*	ἑρπ-/ἕρπυδ-	εἵρπυσα/ἥρψα	ἕρψω	—	augm. εἱ- (verb stem <*σερπ-); Att. forms in -υσ- based on pres. ἑρπύζω (only in Hom.); mainly in poetry
66	ἔρχομαι *go, come*	ἐρχ-, ἐλευθ-/ ἐλ(ὐ)θ-, εἰ-/ἰ-	ἦλθον	ἐλεύσομαι/εἶμι	ἐλήλυθα	suppletive; them. aor. (in poetry sometimes ἤλυθον); stem pf.; ἔρχομαι mainly in pres. indicative, for other forms →εἶμι go, 12.36
67	ἐρωτάω *ask*	ἐρ-, ἐρωτη-/ ἐρωτᾰ-	ἠρώτησα/ἠρόμην ἠρωτήθην	ἐρωτήσω/ ἐρήσομαι	ἠρώτηκα ἠρώτημαι	suppletive; them. aor.; Ion. pres. εἴρομαι, impf. and aor. εἰρόμην
68	ἐσθίω *eat*	ἐσθῐ-, φᾰγ-, ἐδε-/ ἐδο-/ἐδ-	ἔφαγον / ἠδέσθην	ἔδομαι	ἐδήδοκα ἐδήδεσμαι	suppletive; them. aor.; fut. mid. Att. redupl; act. ἔδω rare; in poetry and Ion. prose pf. βέβρωκα, βέβρωμαι
69	(καθ)εύδω *(go to) sleep*	εὐδ-	(ἐκαθ)εύδησα	(καθ)ευδήσω	—	impf. ἐκάθευδον and καθηῦδον; η added in aor. and fut.; aor. rare in Att.; simplex mainly in poetry and Ion. prose
70	εὑρίσκω *find*	εὑρ-	ηὗρον ηὑρέθην	εὑρήσω	ηὕρηκα ηὕρημαι	pres. with suffix -ισκ-; them. aor.; aor. and pf. also εὑ- (without augm./redupl.; εὕρηκα, etc.)

(Continued)

verb (present)	verb stem	aorist	future	perfect	particulars
71a ἔχω have, hold; aor.: get; mid: be held	ἔχ-/σχ-	ἔσχον ἐσχέθην	ἕξω/σχήσω	ἔσχηκα ἔσχημαι	verb stem <*σ(ε)χ; pres. ἔχ- <*ἔχ- →1.97; them. aor.; impf. εἶχον (<*ἔ-σεχον) →11.40; aor. imp. σχές
71b ἀν-έχομαι endure, bear		ἠνεσχόμην	ἀνέξομαι	—	them. aor.; double augm. and redupl. →11.58; impf. ἠνειχόμην
71c ὑπισχνέομαι promise		ὑπεσχόμην	ὑποσχήσομαι	ὑπέσχημαι	them. aor.; pres. with suffix -νε- (hence ε-contract)
72 ζεύγνυμι yoke	ζευγ-/ζῠγ-	ἔζευξα ἐζύγην	ζεύξω	— ἔζευγμαι	athem. pres.; occasionally θη-aor. ἐξεύχθην
73 ζέω boil	ζε(σ)-	ἔζεσα	ζέσω	—	verb stem in σ (hence short ε outside pres.); θη-aor. ἐξέσθην and pf. pass. ἔξεσμαι in later Gk.
74 ζήω live	ζη-, βῐω-	ἐβίων/ἐβίωσα	βιώσομαι	βεβίωκα βεβίωμαι	suppletive; pres. βιόω gradually more frequent; ζήω η-contract; root aor. ἐβίων; fut. mid., but occasionally act. βιώσω
75 ζώννυμι gird	ζω(σ)-	ἔζωσα ἐζώσθην	ζώσω	— ἔζωσμαι	athem. pres.; verb stem in σ
76 ἥδομαι enjoy	ἡδ-	ἥσθην	ἡσθήσομαι	—	pass. only
77 (κάθ)ημαι sit	-ἡ(σ)-	—	—	—	athem. pres.; used as pf. to καθέζομαι; impf. ἐκαθήμην, →11.57

No.	Present & meaning	Stem	Future	Aorist	Perfect	Notes
78	θάπτω bury	θαφ-	θάψω	ἔθαψα / ἐτάφην	— / τέθαμμαι	pres. <*θάφ-yω; ταφ- <*θαφ, →1.97; θη-aor. ἐθάφθην rare
•	θέλω → ἐθέλω					
79	θέω run	θε(υ)-	θεύσομαι	ἔθευσα	—	verb stem <*θεϝ-; fut. mid.
80	θιγγάνω touch	θιγ-	θίξομαι	ἔθιγον	—	them. aor.; fut. mid.; mainly in poetry
81	(ἀπο)θνῄσκω/-θνῇσκω die	θᾰν-/θνη-	(ἀπο)θανοῦμαι, -ῇ	(ἀπ)έθανον	τέθνηκα	θνῄσκω <*θνη-ίσκ-ω; fut. mid.; τέθνηκα be dead; simplex θνῄσκω/θνῇσκω only in poetry
82	θύω sacrifice	θῠ-/θῡ-	θύσω	ἔθῡσα / ἐτύθην	τέθῠκα / τέθῠμαι	τυθη- <*θυθη- →1.97
•	(καθ)ίζω → (καθ)έζομαι					
83	ἵημι send, let go	ἡ-/ἑ-	ἥσω	ἧκα / εἵθην	εἷκα / εἷμαι	verb stem <*yη-/*yε- (pres. redupl.); athem. pres.; κα-aor.; augm./redupl. εἱ-; in prose mostly in compounds
84	ἱλάσκομαι appease	ἱλᾰ(σ)-	ἱλάσομαι	ἱλασάμην	—	pres. ἱλ- <*σῐσλ- (pres. redupl.) and with suffix -σκ-; long ῑ generalized in other tenses

(*Continued*)

	verb (present)	verb stem	aorist	future	perfect	particulars
85	(ἀφ)ικνέομαι *arrive*	ἵκ-	(ἀφ)ῑκόμην	(ἀφ)ίξομαι	(ἀφ)ῖγμαι	them. aor.; pres. with suffix -νε- (hence ε-contract); simplex ἱκνέομαι mainly in poetry
86a	ἵστημι *make stand, set up*	στη-/στᾰ-	ἔστησα ἐστάθην	στήσω σταθήσομαι	— ἕσταμαι	pres. <*σί-στ- (redupl.), pf. <*σέ-στ-; athem. pres.; in prose mostly in compounds
86b	ἵσταμαι *come to stand*		ἔστην	στήσομαι	ἕστηκα	act. root aor. and pf. ἔστην *came to stand, ἕστηκα stand*
87	(κατα)καίνω *kill*	κον-/κᾰν-	(κατ)έκανον	(κατα)κανῶ, -εῖς	(κατα)κέκονα	them. aor.; stem pf.; καίνω mainly in poetry; κατακαίνω Doric for Att. ἀποκτείνω (adopted by Xen.)
88	καίω/κάω *set on fire*	κα(υ)-	ἔκαυσα ἐκαύθην/ἐκάην	καύσω	κέκαυκα κέκαυμαι	pres. <*κᾰϝ-yω; κάω does not contract; η-aor. ἐκάην rare, mainly in poetry
89	καλέω *call, summon*	κᾰλε-/κλη-	ἐκάλεσα ἐκλήθην	καλῶ, -εῖς/καλέσω	κέκληκα κέκλημαι	pres. and Att. fut. are identical; aor. and fut. καλέσω analogous to verbs with stem in σ →13.18
90	κάμνω *toil, be sick*	κᾰμ-/κμη-	ἔκαμον	καμοῦμαι, -ῇ	κέκμηκα	pres. with nasal suffix -ν-; them. aor.; fut. mid.

#	Present / meaning	Stem	Future	Aorist	Perfect act.	Perfect m-p	Notes
91	κεῖμαι *lie, be put*	κει-	κεῖσομαι	—	—	—	athem. pres.; used as pf. pass. of τίθημι →12.43 n.1
92	κεράννυμι *mix*	κερᾰ(σ)-/κρᾱ-	—	ἐκέρᾱσα / ἐκεράσθην/ἐκρᾱ́θην	—	κέκρᾱμαι/ κεκρᾱ́σμαι	verb stem in σ; athem. pres.
93	κλαίω/κλάω *cry, weep*	κλα(υ)-	κλαύσομαι/ κλαήσω	ἔκλαυσα / ἐκλαύσθην	κέκλαυκα	κέκλαυ(σ)μαι	pres. <*κλάϝ-γω; pres. κλάω does not contract; fut. mid.; parasitic σ in θη-aor.
94	κλέπτω *steal*	κλεπ-/κλοπ-/ κλᾰπ-	κλέψω	ἔκλεψα / ἐκλάπην	κέκλοφα	κέκλεμμαι	η-aor., in poetry and Ion. occasionally ἐκλέφθην; stem pf.; *κλᾰπ- <*κλ̥π-
95a	κλῑνω *cause to lean;* mp.: *lean*	κλῐ(ν)-	κλῐνῶ, -εῖς	ἔκλῑνα / ἐκλῐ́θην	κέκλῐκα	κέκλῐμαι	pres. (<*κλῐν-γω) with nasal suffix -ν, extended to aor., fut.; in poetry also θη-aor. ἐκλίνθην
95b	κατακλῑνομαι *recline*		κατακλῐνήσομαι	κατεκλῐ́νην		κατακέκλῐμαι	η-aor.; θη-aor. κατεκλίθην also found
96	κόπτω *hit*	κοπ-	κόψω	ἔκοψα / ἐκόπην	κέκοφα	κέκομμαι	η-aor.
97	(ἀνα)κράζω *shout*	κρᾱγ-/κρᾰγ-	κεκράξομαι	(ἀν)έκρᾰγον	(ἀνα)κέκρᾱγα	—	them. aor.; stem pf. κέκρᾱγα *scream*, fut. pf. κεκράξομαι used as regular fut.; pres. rare until later Gk., which also has aor. (ἀνα)κράξω

(Continued)

	verb (present)	verb stem	aorist	future	perfect	particulars
98a	κρεμάννυμι *hang up*	κρεμᾰ(σ)-	ἐκρέμασα	κρεμῶ, -ᾷς	—	verb stem in σ; athem. pres.; Att. fut. in -άω; mostly in compounds
98b	κρέμαμαι *hang*			κρεμήσομαι	ἐκρεμάσθην / κεκρέμασμαι	athem. pres. (conjugation analogous to ἵσταμαι)
99	κρίνω *decide, judge*	κρῐ(ν)-	ἔκρῑνα / ἐκρίθην	κρῐνῶ, -εῖς	κέκρῐκα / κέκρῐμαι	pres. (<*κρίν-γω) with nasal suffix -ν-, extended to aor., fut.
100	κτάομαι *acquire*	κτη-/κτᾰ-	ἐκτησάμην	κτήσομαι	ἔκτημαι / κέκτημαι	pf. ἔκτημαι mainly Ion. and Pl.
101	(ἀπο)κτείνω *kill*	κτεν-/κτον-/κτᾰν-	(ἀπ)έκτεινα / (ἀπ)έκτανον	(ἀπο)κτενῶ, -εῖς	(ἀπ)έκτονα	stem pf.; them. aor. (ἀπ)έκτανον in poetry; also athem. ἀποκτίννυμι in prose
102	λαγχάνω *obtain by lot*	λαχ-/λᾰχ-	ἔλαχον	λήξομαι	εἴληχα / εἴληγμαι	pres. with nasal suffix -γ-αν-; them. aor.; fut. mid.; pf. with redupl. εἰ-; in poetry occasionally pf. λέλογχα
103	λαμβάνω *get, take*	ληβ-/λᾰβ-	ἔλαβον / ἐλήφθην	λήψομαι	εἴληφα / εἴλημμαι	pres. with nasal suffix -μ-αν-; them. aor.; fut. mid.; redupl. εἰ-; pf. mp. λέλημμαι in tragedy; in Hdt. θη-aor. ἐλάμφθην and pf. act. λελάβηκα
104a	λανθάνω *go unnoticed*	ληθ-/λᾰθ-	ἔλαθον / ἐλήσθην	λήσω	λέληθα / λέλησμαι	pres. with nasal suffix -ν-αν-; them. aor.; stem pf.; in poetry also pres. λήθω, λήθομαι
104b	ἐπιλανθάνομαι *forget*		ἐπελαθόμην	ἐπιλήσομαι	ἐπιλέλησμαι	

105a λέγω *say, speak*	λεγ-/λογ-, εἰπ-, ἐρ-/ῥη-	ἔλεξα/εἶπον ἐλέχθην/ἐρρήθην	λέξω/ἐρῶ, -εῖς	εἴρηκα εἴρημαι/λέλεγμαι	suppletive; them. aor. (for εἶπα/εἶπον →13.32; for ἔλεξα vs. εἶπον, →13.38 n.2); redupl. εἰ- <*ϝεϝρ-
105b δια-λέγομαι *converse*		δι-ελέχθην/ δι-ελέγην	διαλέξομαι	δι-είλεγμαι	fut. mid.; fut. διαλεχθήσομαι is occasionally found
105c συλ-λέγω *collect; mp: come together*		συνέλεξα συνελέγην/ συνελέχθην	συλλέξω	συνείλοχα συνείλεγμαι	η-aor.
105d ἀπ-αγορεύω *forbid, give up*	ἀγορευ-, εἰπ-, ἐρ-/ῥη-	ἀπεῖπον ἀπερρήθην	ἀπερῶ, -εῖς	ἀπείρηκα ἀπείρημαι	them. aor.; occasionally aor. ἀπηγόρευσα; simplex verb ἀγορεύω *proclaim* only in pres./impf. in Att.
106 λείπω *leave*	λειπ-/λοιπ-/λῐπ-	ἔλιπον ἐλείφθην	λείψω	λέλοιπα λέλειμμαι	them. aor.; stem pf.
107 μαίνομαι *rage*	μην-/μᾰν-	ἐμάνην	μανοῦμαι, -ῇ	μέμηνα	η-aor.; in poetry causative (→35.4) aor. ἔμηνα *made mad* occasionally; act. stem pf. (μέμηνα *be furious*)
108 μανθάνω *learn, understand*	μαθ-	ἔμαθον	μαθήσομαι	μεμάθηκα	pres. with nasal suffix -ν-αν-; them. aor.; fut. mid.

(Continued)

	verb (present)	verb stem	aorist	future	perfect	particulars
109	μάχομαι *fight*	μᾰχ(ε)-	ἐμαχεσάμην	μαχοῦμαι, -ῇ	μεμάχημαι	aor. with short ε; Att. fut.; η added in pf. stem; Ion. fut. μαχήσομαι
110	μ(ε)ίγνυμι/μίσγω *mix*	μειγ-/μῖγ-	ἔμ(ε)ιξα ἐμίγην/ἐμ(ε)ίχθην	μείξω	—	athem. pres.; η-aor.; Homeric pres. μίσγω sometimes also in Att.
111a	(ἐπι)μέλομαι/ (ἐπι)μελέομαι *take care*	μελη-/μελ(ε)-	(ἐπ)εμελήθην	(ἐπι)μελήσομαι	(ἐπι)μεμέλημαι	pres. -έομαι more common than -ομαι
111b	μέλει *it is of concern*		ἐμέλησε(ν)	μελήσει	μεμέληκε(ν)	impers. →36.15
112	μέλλω *be about to, delay*	μελλ-	ἐμέλλησα	μελλήσω	—	impf. ἤμελλον →11.41; η added outside pres.
113	μένω *stay, (a)wait*	μεν-	ἔμεινα	μενῶ, -εῖς	μεμένηκα	η added in pf.; in poetry also pres. μίμνω (with redupl.)
114	μιμνῄσκω *remind;* *mp.: remember*	μνη-	ἔμνησα ἐμνήσθην	μνήσω	μέμνημαι	pres. redupl. and suffix -(ι)σκ-; act. mostly in compounds; parasitic σ in θη-aor.
115	νέμω *deal out*	νεμ-	ἔνειμα ἐνεμήθην	νεμῶ, -εῖς	νενέμηκα νενέμημαι	η added in θη-aor. and pf. stems
116	νέω *swim*	νε-	ἔνευσα	νεύσομαι	νένευκα	ευ-forms possibly by analogy with πλέω; fut. mid.
117	(νίπτω/)νίζω *wash*	νῑπ-	ἔνιψα ἐνιψάμην	νίψω	— νένιμμαι	pres. νίζω <*νίγ-yω; other stems (and newer pres. νίπτω) built on νιπ-

	Stem	Aorist	Future	Perfect	
118 (ἀν)οίγνυμι/(ἀν)οίγω *open*	οἰγ-	(ἀν)έῳξα / (ἀν)εῴχθην	(ἀν)οίξω	(ἀν)έῳχα/ (ἀν)έῳγα (ἀν)έῳγμαι	athem. pres.; stem pf. →18.25; augm./redupl. →11.40
119 (οἶδα) *know*	εἰδ-/οἰδ-/ῐδ-	—	εἴσομαι	οἶδα	verb stem <*ϝειδ-/*ϝοιδ-/*ϝῐδ-; no pres.; for conjugation →18.4; fut. mid.
120 οἴομαι/οἶμαι *think*	οἰ-	ᾠήθην	οἰήσομαι	—	pass. only; fut. mid.; οἶμαι and ᾤμην without thematic vowel; η added in θη-aor. and fut.
121 οἴχομαι *depart, be gone*	οἰχ-	—	οἰχήσομαι	ὤχωκα/οἴχωκα	no aor.; η added in fut.; act. pf. οἴχωκα in Ion. and poetry, but also διοίχημαι in Hdt.
122a (ἀπ)όλλυμι *destroy*	ὀλ(ε)-	(ἀπ)ώλεσα	(ἀπ)ολῶ, -εῖς	(ἀπ)ολώλεκα	stem with ε in sigm. aor., pf. (and Att. fut.); athem. pres.; Att. redupl.
122b (ἀπ)όλλυμαι *perish*		(ἀπ)ωλόμην	(ἀπ)ολοῦμαι, -ῇ	(ἀπ)όλωλα	them. aor.; act. stem pf. ὄλωλα *be ruined*
123 ὄμνυμι *swear*	ὀμ(ο)-	ὤμοσα / ὠμό(σ)θην	ὀμοῦμαι, -ῇ	ὀμώμοκα ὀμώμομαι	athem. pres., but also them. forms (ὀμνύω, etc.); fut. mid.; Att. redupl. →11.48; occasionally pf. mp. ὀμώμοσμαι

(*Continued*)

	verb (present)	verb stem	aorist	future	perfect	particulars
124	ὀνίνημι benefit; mid. benefit from	ὀνη-/ὀνᾰ-	ὤνησα ὠνήθην	ὀνήσω	—	athem. pres.; root mid. aor. ὠνήμην/ὠνάμην; impf. supplied by ὠφελέω benefit, help; mostly in poetry
125	ὁράω see	ὁρᾰ-, ἰδ-, ὀπ-	εἶδον ὤφθην	ὄψομαι	ἑόρᾱκα/ἑώρᾱκα/ ὄπωπα ἑόρᾱμαι/ἑώρᾱμαι/ ὦμμαι	suppletive; ὁρᾰ- <*Ϝορᾰ-; ἰδ- <*Ϝιδ- (cf. οἶδα); impf. ἑώρων (augm. →11.40), also ὥρων; fut. mid.; stem pf. ὄπωπα
126	ὀρύττω dig	ὀρῠχ-	ὤρυξα ὠρύχθην	ὀρύξω	ὀρώρυγμαι	Att. redupl.; η-fut. -ορυχησ- in Ar.
127	ὀφείλω owe, be bound to	ὀφε(ι)λ-	ὠφείλησα/ὤφελον	ὀφειλήσω	ὠφείληκα	pres. ὀφέλλω in poetry; them. aor.; also impf. and aor. ὄφελ(λ)ον, η added in various stems
128	ὀφλισκάνω incur a charge, lose (a case)	ὀφλ-	ὤφλησα/ὦφλον	ὀφλήσω	ὤφληκα ὤφλημαι	pres. with suffixes -ισκ- and -αν-; them. aor.; η added in various stems
129	πάσχω suffer	πενθ-/πονθ-/ πᾰθ-	ἔπαθον	πείσομαι	πέπονθα	pres. <*πηθ-σκ-ω →1.96; fut. <*πένθσομαι; them. aor.; mid.; stem pf.
130a	πείθω persuade	πειθ-/ποιθ-/πῐθ-	ἔπεισα ἐπείσθην	πείσω	πέπεικα πέπεισμαι	in poetry occasionally aor. ἔπιθον
130b	πείθομαι believe, obey		ἐπιθόμην/ἐπείσθην	πείσομαι	πέποιθα	them. aor.; act. stem pf. (πέποιθα trust)

No.	Present / gloss	Stem	Aorist	Future	Perfect	Notes
131	πέμπω *send*	πεμπ-/πομπ-	ἔπεμψα / ἐπέμφθην	πέμψω	πέπομφα / πέπεμμαι	athem. pres.; poetic alternatives πίτνημι, πίτνάω; verb stem in σ; Att. fut. in -ἀω (-ἀσσω found in poetry); mostly in compounds
132	πετάννυμι *spread out*	πετᾰ(σ)-	ἐπέτασα / ἐπετάσθην	πετῶ, -ᾷς	—	occasionally athem. pres. πέτᾰμαι; them. aor.; in poetry also root aor. ἐπτάμην (→13.32 n.1, 13.50, 13.63); root aor. ἔπτην (rare)
133	πέτομαι *fly*	πετ-/πτη-/πτ(ᾰ)-	ἐπτόμην/ἐπττάμην/ ἔπτην	πτήσομαι/ πετήσομαι	πέπταμαι	athem. pres.
134a	πήγνυμι *affix, fasten*	πηγ-/πᾰγ-	ἔπηξα	πήξω	—	act. stem pf. (πέπηγα *be set, fixed*)
134b	πήγνυμαι *become solid*		ἐπάγην/ἐπήχθην	παγήσομαι	πέπηγα	
135	πίμπλημι *fill*	πλη-/πλᾰ-	ἔπλησα / ἐπλήσθην	πλήσω	πέπληκα / πέπλη(σ)μαι	pres. redupl.; athem. pres.; in poetry occasionally mid. root aor. ἐπλήμην *I filled myself*; parasitic σ in θη-aor.
136	(ἐμ)πίμπρημι *burn*	πρη-/πρᾰ-	(ἐν)έπρησα / (ἐν)επρήσθην	(ἐμ)πρήσω	(ἐμ)πέπρηκα / (ἐμ)πέπρη(σ)μαι	pres. redupl.; athem. pres.
137	πίνω *drink*	πω-/πο-/πῑ-/πῐ-	ἔπῐον / ἐπόθην	πίομαι	πέπωκα / πέπομαι	pres. with nasal suffix -ν; them. aor. with short ῐ, but imp. πῖθι; fut. mid.
138	πιπράσκω *sell*	πρᾰ-	— / ἐπράθην	—	πέπρᾱκα / πέπρᾱμαι	pres. with redupl. and suffix -σκ-; pres. and aor. usually supplied by ἀποδίδομαι, pres. and fut. also by πωλέω

(Continued)

	verb (present)	verb stem	aorist	future	perfect	particulars
139	πίπτω *fall*	πεσ-/πτ(ω)-	ἔπεσον	πεσοῦμαι, -ῇ	πέπτωκα	pres. redupl. (πι-πτ-); in poetry occasionally pres. πίτνω; them. aor.; fut. mid.
140	πλέκω *plait, devise*	πλεκ-/πλᾰκ-	ἔπλεξα ἐπλάκην/ἐπλέχθην	πλέξω	— πέπλεγμαι	η-aor. (in Ion. also ἐπλέκην)
141	πλέω *sail*	πλε(υ)-	ἔπλευσα	πλεύσομαι	πέπλευκα	pres. <*πλέϝω; fut. mid.; Ion. πλώω
142a	πλήττω *strike*	πληγ-/πλᾱγ-	ἔπληξα ἐπλήγην	πλήξω πληγήσομαι	πέπληγα πέπληγμαι	η-aor.; stem pf.
142b	(ἐκ)πλήττω *frighten; mp.: be frightened*		(ἐξ)έπληξα (ἐξ)επλάγην	(ἐκ)πλήξω	(ἐκ)πέπληγα (ἐκ)πέπληγμαι	η-aor. with short stem (πλᾰγ-); θη-aor. ἐξεπλήχθην rare
143	πνέω *blow*	πνε(υ)-	ἔπνευσα	πνεύσομαι	πέπνευκα	pres. <*πνέϝω; fut. mid.; occasionally fut. πνεύσω and πνευσοῦμαι, -ῇ
144	(ἔπορον) *give; pf. pass. it is destined*	πορ-/πρω-	ἔπορον	—	πέπρωται	them. aor.; aor. and pf. only; poetry only
145	πράττω *do, act*	πρᾱγ-	ἔπραξα	πράξω	πέπρᾱχα/ πέπρᾱγα πέπραγμαι	stem pf. πέπρᾱγα; Ion. πρήσσω

	Present	Verb stem	Aorist	Future	Perfect	Notes
146	πυνθάνομαι *inquire, learn*	πευθ-/πῠθ-	ἐπυθόμην	πεύσομαι	πέπυσμαι	pres. with nasal suffix -ν-αν-; them. aor.
147	ῥέω *flow*	ῥε(υ)-/ῥῠ-	ἐρρύην	ῥυήσομαι	ἐρρύηκα	pres. <*ῥέϝω; impf. ἔρρεον; η-aor./fut.; aor. ἔρρευσα and fut. ῥεύσομαι/-έομαι rare; η added in pf.
148a	ῥήγνυμι *cause to break*	ῥηγ-/ῥωγ-/ῥᾱγ-	ἔρρηξα	ῥήξω	—	athem. pres.
148b	ῥήγνυμαι *break (intr.)*		ἐρράγην		ἔρρωγα	η-aor.; act. stem pf. (ἔρρωγα *be torn*)
149	ῥίπτω *throw*	ῥῑπ-	ἔρριψα / ἐρρίφθην/ἐρρίφην	ῥίψω	ἔρριφα / ἔρριμμαι	η-aor. (with short ῐ and φ)
150	ῥώννυμι *strengthen; mp.: have strength*	ῥω(σ)-	ἔρρωσα / ἐρρώσθην	—	ἔρρωμαι	athem. pres.; verb stem in σ; fut. ῥώσω in later Gk.
151a	σβέννυμι *quench, put out*	σβη-/σβε(σ)-	ἔσβεσα / ἐσβέσθην	σβέσω / σβεσθήσομαι	ἔσβεσμαι	athem. pres.; verb stem in σ; usually in compounds
151b	σβέννυμαι *go out, be quenched*		ἔσβην	σβήσομαι	ἔσβηκα	act. root aor. and stem pf. (ἔσβην *went out*, ἔσβηκα *be out*)

(Continued)

	verb (present)	verb stem	aorist	future	perfect	particulars
152a	σήπω *make rotten*	σηπ-/σᾰπ-	ἔσηψα	σήψω	—	act. forms very rare
152b	σήπομαι *rot*		ἐσάπην	σαπήσομαι	σέσηπα	η-aor.; act. stem pf. (σέσηπα *be rotten*)
153	σκάπτω *dig*	σκᾰφ-	ἔσκαψα / ἐσκάφην	σκάψω	ἔσκαφα / ἔσκαμμαι	η-aor.
154	σκεδάννυμι *disperse; mp.: spread out (intr.)*	σκεδᾰ(σ)-	ἐσκέδασα / ἐσκεδάσθην	σκεδῶ, -ᾷς	— / ἐσκέδασμαι	athem. pres.; verb stem in σ; Att. fut. in -άω; poetic alternative σκίδνημι; often in compounds
155	σκοπέω/σκέπτομαι *look, examine*	σκεπ-/σκοπε-	ἐσκεψάμην	σκέψομαι	ἔσκεμμαι	later Gk. has tense stems derived from σκοπέω
156	σπάω *draw, tear*	σπᾰ(σ)-	ἔσπασα / ἐσπάσθην	σπάσω	ἔσπακα / ἔσπασμαι	verb stem in σ (hence short ᾰ in aor. and fut.)
157	σπείρω *sow*	σπερ-/σπᾰρ-	ἔσπειρα / ἐσπάρην	σπερῶ, -εῖς	ἔσπαρκα / ἔσπαρμαι	η-aor.; σπᾰρ- <*σπῐ̥ρ-
158	σπένδω *pour liquid, libate; mid.: make a treaty*	σπενδ-	ἔσπεισα	σπείσω	— / ἔσπεισμαι	σπεισ- <*σπενδσ-
159	στέλλω *dispatch; mp.: journey*	στελ-/στᾰλ-	ἔστειλα / ἐστάλην	στελῶ, -εῖς	ἔσταλκα / ἔσταλμαι	η-aor., στᾰλ- <*στῐ̥λ-
160	στόρνυμι/στρώννυμι *cover, make level*	στορ(εσ)-/στρω-	ἐστόρεσα/ἔστρωσα / ἐστορέσθην/ἐστρώθην	στορῶ/στρώσω	— / ἐστόρεσμαι/ἔστρωμαι	athem. pres.; also στορέννυμι

		stem	aorist	future	perfect	notes
161	στρέφω turn (around); mp.: turn around (intr.)	στρεφ-/στροφ-/στρᾰφ-	ἔστρεψα/ἐστράφην/ἐστρέφθην	στρέψω	ἔστροφα/ἔστραμμαι	η-aor.; stem pf. ἔστροφα rare; στρᾰφ- <*στρᵒφ-
162	σφάλλω cause to stumble; mp.: stumble	σφᾰλ-	ἔσφηλα/ἐσφάλην	σφαλῶ, -εῖς	ἔσφαλκα/ἔσφαλμαι	η-aor.
163	σφάττω/σφάζω slaughter	σφᾰγ-	ἔσφαξα/ἐσφάγην/ἐσφάχθην	σφάξω	—/ἔσφαγμαι	η-aor; σφάττω Att., σφάζω Ion. and in poetry; pf. ἔσφακα in later Gk.
164a	σῴζω save	σω-	ἔσωσα	σώσω	σέσωκα	pres. <*σω-ίζω; aor./fut. also sometimes written σῳσ-
164b	σῴζομαι escape		ἐσώθην		σέσω(σ)μαι	σέσωσμαι regular in poetry, σέσωσμαι in prose
165	τείνω stretch	τεν-/τᾰ-	ἔτεινα/ἐτάθην	τενῶ, -εῖς	τέτακα/τέταμαι	τᾰ- <*τη-
166	τελέω finish	τελε(σ)-	ἐτέλεσα/ἐτελέσθην	τελέσω/τελῶ, -εῖς	τετέλεκα/τετέλεσμαι	stem in σ (hence short ε outside pres.); Att. fut. identical to pres.
167	(ἀνα)τέλλω (cause to) rise	τελ-/τᾰλ-	(ἀν)έτειλα	(ἀνα)τελῶ, -εῖς	(ἀνα)τέταλκα/(ἀνα)τέταλμαι	τᾰλ- <*τ̥l-
168	τέμνω cut	τεμ-/τμη-	ἔτεμον/ἐτμήθην	τεμῶ, -εῖς	τέτμηκα/τέτμημαι	them. aor.; Ion. τάμνω, them. aor. ἔταμον

(Continued)

	verb (present)	verb stem	aorist	future	perfect	particulars
169a	τήκω *cause to melt*	τηκ-/τᾰκ-	ἔτηξα	τήξω	—	
169b	τήκομαι *melt*		ἐτάκην	—	τέτηκα	η-aor.; act. stem pf. (τέτηκα *be melted*)
170	τίθημι *put, place*	θη-/θε-	ἔθηκα ἐτέθην	θήσω	τέθηκα/τέθεικα τέθειμαι/κεῖμαι	athem. pres.; pres. redupl.; κα-aor.; τιθ-/τε θ- < *θιθ-/*θεθ- →1.97; κεῖμαι used as pf. pass.; often in compounds
171	τίκτω *give birth*	τεκ-/τοκ-/τκ-	ἔτεκον	τέξομαι	τέτοκα	pres. <*τί-τκω (redupl.); them. aor.; fut. mid.; in poetry occasionally θη-aor. ἐτέχθην and fut. τέξω
172	τίνω *pay, atone; mid.: make pay, avenge*	τει-/τῐ-	ἔτεισα	τείσω	τέτεικα τέτεισμαι	pres. with nasal suffix -ν-; pf. only found in compound ἐκτίνω *pay off*
173	(ἔτλην) *endure, dare to*	τλη-/τλᾰ-	ἔτλην	τλήσομαι	τέτληκα	pres. τλάω not found (τολμάω is used); root aor.; mostly in poetry
174	πιτρώσκω *wound*	τρω-	ἔτρωσα ἐτρώθην	τρώσω	τέτρωκα τέτρωμαι	pres. with redupl. and suffix -σκ-

	Stems	Aorist	Future/Present	Perfect	Notes
175a τρέπω *turn*	τρεπ-/τροπ-/ τρᾰπ-	ἔτρεψα/ἔτρᾰπον/ ἐτράφθην/	τρέψω	τέτροφα	them. aor. ἔτρᾰπον mostly in poetry; stem pf.; τρᾰπ- <*τρᾰπ-
175b τρέπομαι *turn around (intr.)*		ἐτράπην/ ἐτραπόμην	τρέψομαι	τέτραμμαι	η-aor. and them. aor.
176 τρέφω *nourish, rear; mp.: grow (up)*	θρεφ-/θροφ-/ θρᾰφ-	ἔθρεψα/ ἐτράφην	θρέψω	τέτροφα τέθραμμαι	τρεφ- <*θρεφ-, τροφ- <*θροφ- →1.97; η-aor.; ἐθρέφθην rare; θρᾰφ- <*θρᾰφ-; stem pf.
177 τρέχω *run*	τρεχ-, δρᾰμ-	ἔδραμον	δραμοῦμαι, -ῇ	δεδράμηκα	suppletive; them. aor.; in poetry also rarely aor. ἔθρεξα; fut. mid.
178 τυγχάνω *hit upon, happen to*	τευχ-/τῠχ-	ἔτυχον	τεύξομαι	τετύχηκα	pres. with nasal suffix -γ-αν-; them. aor.; fut. mid.
179 τύπτω *hit*	τῠπ-	ἔτυψα/ ἐτύπην	τύψω/τυπτήσω	— τέτυμμαι	η-aor.; occasionally them. aor. ἔτυπτον for ἔτυψα
180a φαίνω *show*	φην-/φᾰν-	ἔφηνα/ ἐφάνθην	φανῶ, -εῖς	πέφαγκα πέφασμαι	pf. act. and mp. rare and mostly in compounds
180b φαίνομαι *appear, seem*		ἐφάνην	φανήσομαι/ φανοῦμαι, -ῇ	πέφηνα	η-aor.; act. stem pf. (πέφηνα *have appeared*)
181 φέρω *carry, bring*	φερ-, ἐνεκ-/ἐνοκ-/ ἐγκ-, οἰτ-	ἤνεγκον/ἤνεγκα/ ἠνέχθην	οἴσω	ἐνήνοχα ἐνήνεγμαι	suppletive; them. aor.; for aor. ἤνεγκα →13.27, 13.32; Ion. aor. ἤνεικα; stem pf. with Attic reduplication

(Continued)

	verb (present)	verb stem	aorist	future	perfect	particulars
182	φεύγω *flee*	φευγ-/φῠγ-	ἔφυγον	φεύξομαι	πέφευγα	them. aor.; fut. mid.; fut. φευξοῦμαι, -ῇ occasionally in poetry
183	φημί/φάσκω *say, claim*	φη-/φᾰ-	ἔφησα	φήσω	—	athem. pres.; impf. ἔφην →12.36, 12.42; φάσκω not found in pres. ind, but supplies ppl. φάσκων, impf. ἔφασκον, etc. (→12.56)
184	φθάνω *be first*	φθη-/φθᾰ-	ἔφθασα	φθήσομαι	ἔφθακα	pres. with nasal suffix -ν-; also root aor. ἔφθην; fut. mid.
185a	(δια)φθείρω *destroy*	φθερ-/φθορ-/φθᾰρ-	(δι)έφθειρα	(δια)φθερῶ, -εῖς	(δι)έφθαρκα	φθᾰρ- < *φθr̥-
185b	(δια)φθείρομαι *perish*		(δι)εφθάρην		(δι)έφθορα/ (δι)έφθαρμαι	η-aor.; act. stem pf. (διέφθορα *have lost one's wits*)
186a	φύω *cause to grow*	φῡ-	ἔφῡσα	φύσω	—	usually φῠ- before vowels, φῡ- before consonants
186b	φύομαι *grow (up)*		ἔφῡν	φύσομαι	πέφῡκα	act. root aor. and pf. (ἔφυν *grew*, πέφυκα *be (by nature)*)

187	χαίρω *rejoice*	χᾰρ-	ἐχάρην	χαιρήσω	κεχάρηκα	η-aor. (with act. sense); fut. built on pres. stem, with added η; in poetry occasionally η; mp. pf. κεχάρημαι, κεχάρμαι
188	χέω *pour*	χε(υ)-/χῠ-	ἔχεα ἐχύθην	χέω	κέχυκα κέχυμαι	pres. <*χέϝω; in poetry also rarely aor. ἔχευα and ἐχύμην
189	χώννυμι/χόω *heap up*	χω(σ)-/-χο-	ἔχωσα ἐχώ(σ)θην	χώσω	κέχωκα κέχωσμαι	athem. pres.; verb stem in σ; pres. χόω occasionally in Att., Hdt.
190	ὠθέω *thrust, push*	ὠθη-/ὠθ(ε)-	ἔωσα/ὦσα ἐώσθην, ὤσθην	ὠθήσω/ὤσω	— ἔωσμαι	augm./redupl. ἐω- (verb stem <*ϝωθ-)
191	ὠνέομαι *buy*	ὠνη-/ὠνε-, πρῐ-	ἐπριάμην ἐωνήθην	ὠνήσομαι	ἐώνημαι	augm./redupl. usually ἐω- (verb stem <*ϝων-); for suppletive ἐπριάμην <*ϝρων-); →13.32 n.1, 13.50

23

Word Formation

Introduction

23.1   Ancient Greek had a wide variety of means to form new words. Two main processes of word formation may be distinguished:

- **Derivation**: the addition of **suffixes** to a root (→23.2) to derive a new nominal or verbal form. In English, cf. e.g. *singer, writer, driver*, formed with the suffix *-er* added to a verbal root (*sing, write, drive*) to form nouns indicating 'someone (habitually) performing the activity of . . .' (so-called 'agent nouns', see below); *childish, foolish*, formed with the suffix *-ish* added to nouns (*child, fool*) to form adjectives; *childishly, foolishly*, with *-ly* to form adverbs from adjectives; *child-ishness, foolishness*, with *-ness* to form nouns from adjectives indicating 'the condition of being . . .'; etc.
- **Composition**: the combination of two (or more) nominal or verbal roots to form a new nominal or verbal form. **Compound** forms are opposed to **simplex** (non-compound) forms.
  In English, cf. e.g. *sunrise* (*sun* + *rise*), *headache* (*head* + *ache*); *washing machine, car radio*, etc.

23.2   The basis for word-forming processes are not words as such, but **roots**. Thus, the Greek root κρι- (signifying 'decision', 'judgement') is the base of the derived nouns ἡ κρίσις *judgement, decisive moment*, ὁ κριτής *judge*, τὸ κριτήριον *means for judging, court*; of the adjective κριτικός, -ή, -όν *critical, judging*; and of the verb κρίνω *decide, judge* (<*κρῐ-ν-yω, →12.28, 12.30 n.2).

Similarly, the compound noun ὁ ναυπηγός *shipbuilder* is composed of the two roots ναυ- and πηγ-, also present in the noun ἡ ναῦς *ship* and the verb πήγνυμι *affix, fasten*.

Note 1: Strictly speaking, nouns such as κρίσις and κριτής combine the root κρι- with the suffixes -σι-/-σε(y)- and -τᾱ-, respectively, followed by the nominal case *ending* -ς (itself originally a suffix). The parts κρισι-/κρισε(y)- and κριτᾱ- are (nominal) *stems*. Below, endings are treated as part of derivational suffixes. For nominal stems and endings, →2.

Note 2: In addition to derivation and composition (and the introduction of entirely new words, i.e. new roots), the vocabulary of a language also changes by the addition of new *uses* and/or *meanings* to existing words; these are not discussed here.

Note 3: Although they often overlap, roots may be distinguished from nominal or verbal stems in that the latter can have elaborations. Thus, the verb stem παιδευ- which serves as the basis for all forms of the verb παιδεύω *educate*, and which itself is elaborated in specific tense-aspect stems, such as aor. παιδευσ(α)-, aor. pass. παιδευθη-, pf. act. πεπαιδευκ-, etc., derives from the root παιδ- ('child') and an elaboration -ευ-. In the case of certain types of verbal conjugation, such as the present of 'primitive' verbs (→12.24 n.1, 12.42) and root aorists (→13.40–1), the stem used is an unelaborated root without any kind of suffix (e.g. root aorist ἔ-στη-ν, using the root στη- as aorist stem).

23.3   The greater part of the Greek vocabulary consists of words that are in one way or another the product of word formation along the lines discussed above. Few words, in fact, consist of just a root (and case endings, where applicable). Examples of such **root nouns** are: ἡ χείρ *hand, arm*, τὸ πῦρ *fire*, ἡ γῆ *land, earth*, ὁ ἰχθῦς *fish* (with nom. sg. ending -ς), ὁ γύψ *vulture* (with nom. sg. ending -ς).

The main suffixes and principles involved in Greek word formation are treated below. For fuller treatments, the works referenced in the Bibliography at the end of this book may be consulted.

Nominal Word Formation

Nominal Word Formation by Means of Derivation

23.4   The following sections deal with the **derivation of nouns and adjectives**: some specific terminology concerning different kinds of nouns is treated first.

Some Terminology Concerning Nouns

23.5   **Abstract nouns** refer to ideas, emotions, concepts, etc., not to physical entities; in English e.g. *love, justice, kingship*.

Concrete nouns refer to specific entities (typically, but not necessarily, physical entities which can be observed by the senses), in English e.g. *lover, judge, kingdom*.

23.6   **(De)verbal nouns** are nouns that are derived from a verbal root. Such nouns may refer, among other things:

– to an action, process or event itself: **action/event nouns**, in English e.g. *investigation* (from the verbal root *investigat-*), the *building* of the wall (from the root *build-*);
– to the entity performing an action: **agent nouns**, e.g. *investigator, builder*;
– to the result or effect of an action: **result/effect/object nouns**, e.g. *dent, scratch, a stone building*.

List of Derivational Suffixes

23.7   Below follows a list, in alphabetical order, of the most common suffixes that are involved in the derivation of nouns and adjectives. The list predominantly contains suffixes that are found in classical Attic prose and in Herodotus. Some less frequent suffixes are printed in smaller type.

Note 1: If the accentuation of a particular type of (simplex, i.e. non-compound) derived noun or adjective is regular (and persistent, →24.21), this is usually indicated below (on the suffix itself or in the accompanying explanation).

Note 2: The suffixes of participles and infinitives are not included systematically in this list; for their formation, →11.16, 11.31–3. Verbal adjectives in -τέος and -τός, however, are treated in this chapter: →23.29, 23.34.

23.8   -ᾰ̆/-ή (accentuation varies): forms feminine action nouns:

ἀρχή *reign; beginning*	(ἄρχω *reign, rule; begin*)
γραφή *writing, indictment*	(γράφω *write*, γράφομαι *indict*)
μάχη *fight(ing)*	(μάχομαι *fight*)
θέᾱ *seeing, sight*	(θεάομαι *gaze, view*)

If the corresponding verb shows e-grade ablaut in the present stem, the noun usually shows the o-grade (→1.55):

(δια)φθορά *destruction*	((δια)φθείρω *destroy*)
πομπή *escort, procession*	(πέμπω *send, conduct*)
σπουδή *haste, speed*	(σπεύδω *make haste*)
τροφή *nurture, rearing; nourishment*	(τρέφω *nurture, rear, cause to grow*)
but φυγή *flight, exile* (zero grade)	(φεύγω *flee, escape*)

23.9   *-yᾰ̆: frequent suffix forming **feminine** forms of the following types of adjectives and participles:

- adjectives in -υς (→5.21–2): e.g. ἡδεῖα *sweet* (<*ἡδέϝ-yα; with masc. ἡδύς, -έος);
- ν-stem adjectives (→5.23–4): e.g. μέλαινα *dark* (<*μέλαν-yα; with masc. μέλας, -ανος); also with the adjective μάκαρ *blessed* (stem in ρ), poetic μάκαιρα (<*μάκαρ-yα; →5.32);
- ντ-stem adjectives/participles (→5.15–18): πᾶσα *every, all* (<*πάντ-yα; with masc. πᾶς, παντός);
- perfect active participles (→5.20 n.1).

*-yᾰ̆ also forms feminine counterparts to masculine agent nouns, of different types (these nouns are all recessive, →24.27):

- consonant stems: e.g. ἄνασσα *queen, lady* (<*ἄνακ(τ)-yα, cf. masc. ἄναξ *lord*), Φοίνισσα *Phoenician woman* (cf. masc. Φοῖνιξ *Phoenician*; in later

Greek -ισσα became a frequent suffix in its own right, e.g. βασίλισσα *queen*);

- nouns ending in -εύς (→23.15): e.g. βασίλειᾰ *queen* (<*βασίληϝ-yα, cf. βασιλεύς *king*), ἱέρεια *priestess* (cf. ἱερεύς *priest*);
- nouns ending in -τήρ (→23.30): e.g. σώτειρα *(female) saviour* (<*σώτερ-yα, cf. σωτήρ *saviour*).

23.10 **-ᾱς, -ᾰδος**: forms masculine and feminine agent nouns, e.g. φυγάς *fugitive, exile* (φεύγω *flee, escape*), αἱ Κυκλάδες (νῆσοι) *the Cyclades* ('the encircling islands').

23.11 **-ειᾱ (Ion. -είη)**:

- This suffix forms (mostly abstract) action nouns, alongside verbs in -εύω:

παιδείᾱ *training and teaching, education* (παιδεύω *educate*)
πολιτείᾱ *administration, (form of) government* (πολιτεύω, -ομαι *be a citizen, govern*)
βασιλείᾱ *kingdom, monarchy* (βασιλεύω *be king, rule*)

- Also, feminine abstract nouns from third-declension adjectives in -ής were formed originally in -ειᾰ: in Ionic this changed to -είη (→25.15 n.1), but in Attic these nouns end in -ειᾰ (they were analogically assimilated to fem. forms such as ἡδεῖᾰ, βασίλειᾰ):

ἀλήθειᾰ *truth(fulness)*, Ion. ἀληθείη (ἀληθής *true*)
ἀσέβειᾰ *impiety*, Ion. ἀσεβείη (ἀσεβής *impious*)

These nouns are recessive (→24.13, 24.27).

23.12 **-εῖον**: forms neuter nouns denoting a *location*, from nominal stems:

καπηλεῖον *shop, tavern* (κάπηλος *dealer*)
χαλκεῖον *forge, smithy* (χαλκεύς *(copper)smith*)

23.13 **-εις, -εσσα, -εν** (declension →5.25): suffix forming adjectives expressing 'rich in …' or '…-ful'; mainly poetic: e.g. δακρυόεις *tearful* (δάκρυ/δάκρυον *tear*), τιμήεις *honoured* (τιμή *honour*).

23.14 **-εος, -εᾱ, -εον**: see -οῦς, →23.26.

23.15 **-εύς, -έως** (declension →4.84–5): forms masculine agent nouns, from nominal stems; the general meaning of -εύς is '(professionally) occupies himself with …':

ἱερεύς *priest* (ἱερά *offerings*)
συγγραφεύς *prose writer* (συγγραφή *prose writing*)
χαλκεύς *(copper)smith* (χαλκός *copper*)

Note 1: A few nouns in -εύς are 'primitive', i.e. non-derived agent nouns, e.g. βασιλεύς *king*, ἑρμηνεύς *interpreter*.

Note 2: The suffix -εύς is also found in proper names: Ἀτρεύς, Ἀχιλλεύς, Ὀδυσσεύς, Τυδεύς, etc., and in adjectives indicating geographical origin: Ἁλικαρνασσεύς *from Halicarnassus*, Μεγαρεύς *from Megara*, Ἀχαρνεύς *from (the deme of) Acharnae*.

23.16   **-ίᾱ:** forms abstract nouns denoting qualities or properties, from other nouns or from adjectives:

ἐλευθερία *freedom, liberty*	(ἐλεύθερος *free*)
ἡγεμονία *leadership, authority, supremacy*	(ἡγεμών *ruler, guide*)
σοφία *cleverness, wisdom*	(σοφός *wise*)

Note 1: Where a corresponding verb exists, forms in -ίᾱ may also have action noun or result noun meaning, e.g. in ἀδικία *unjust act* (as well as *injustice*) (ἀδικέω *act unjustly*).

23.17   **-ικός, -ή, -όν:** productive suffix used to form adjectives from nouns, with the general meaning 'pertaining to . . .', often 'skilled in . . .', 'occupying oneself with . . .':

γραμματικός *expert in letters; grammarian*	(γράμμα *letter*)
ἱππικός *of a horse; skilled in riding*	(ἵππος *horse*)
ποιητικός *capable of making, creative*	(ποιητής *maker, poet*)
φυσικός *natural, concerning nature, physical*	(φύσις *nature*)

Feminine forms (in -ική) often have the meaning 'the art of . . .', with or without τέχνη added: ἡ γραμματική (τέχνη) *(the art of) grammar*, ἡ ἱππική (τέχνη) *the art of horse riding*, ἡ ποιητική (τέχνη) *the art of poetry*, etc.

23.18   **-ιον:** forms neuter nouns from nominal roots, with various meanings: 'place where', 'part of', 'made of'. The general meaning is: 'denotes an object or action related to . . .' (cf. -ιος below). These nouns are recessive if they have more than three syllables (accentuation varies in trisyllabic nouns):

τὰ Διονύσια *festival of Dionysus*	(Διόνυσος *Dionysus*)
ἀργύριον *silver coin, money*	(ἄργυρος *silver*)
χρυσίον *piece of gold*	(χρυσός *gold*)
γυμνάσιον *exercise; (gymnastic) school*	(γυμναστής *trainer*)
συμπόσιον *drinking-party*	(συμπότης *fellow-drinker*)

-ιον is also used as a **diminutive** suffix: alone, or with enlargements (-άριον, -ίδιον, -ύλλιον), the suffix forms diminutive nouns, denoting a small specimen or used as a term of affection or depreciation:

ληκύθιον *small oil-flask* (λήκυθος *oil-flask*)

οἰκίδιον *small house* (οἰκία *house*)

παιδίον *small or young child* (παῖς *child*)

παιδάριον *small child* (παῖς *child*)

ἐπύλλιον *short (epic) poem* (ἔπος *word, epic poem*)

23.19 **-ιος, -ιᾱ, -ιον** (also -αιος; -ειος, Ion. -ῆιος): forms adjectives from a variety of nominal roots. The general meaning of the suffix is: 'belonging to . . .', 'pertaining to . . .':

πάτριος *derived from one's fathers, hereditary* (πατήρ *father*)

ἀναγκαῖος *necessary, inevitable* (ἀνάγκη *necessity*)

δίκαιος *lawful, just* (δίκη *justice*)

ὁμοῖος *like, resembling* (ὁμός *one and the same*)

οἰκεῖος *of the house, personal, private* (οἶκος *house*)

23.20 **-ισκος, -ισκη:** forms diminutive nouns (cf. -ιον, →23.18), e.g. ἀνθρωπίσκος *little person* (ἄνθρωπος *person*), νεανίσκος *youth, young man* (νεανίας *young man*), παιδίσκη *young girl, young female slave* (παῖς *child, slave*).

23.21 **-μα, -ματος** (declension →4.40): a frequent suffix which forms neuter effect/result nouns; often in the form -ημα. As neuter third-declension nouns, they are recessive (→24.28):

γράμμα *line (drawn), (written) character, letter* (γράφω *write*)

μάθημα *(what is learnt) lesson* (μανθάνω *learn*)

πρᾶγμα *deed, thing, affair* (πράττω *do*)

χρῆμα *thing (used); esp. pl. χρήματα* (χρήομαι *use*)
   property, goods, money

23.22 **-μός, -μοῦ:** forms masculine action nouns, particularly from verbs with a stem in a velar consonant:

διωγμός *chase, pursuit* (διώκω *chase, pursue*)

ὀλολυγμός *loud cry* (ὀλολύζω *cry out*)

The suffix also occurs frequently in the form **-σμός** with nouns derived from verbs in -άζω or -ίζω (i.e. with a stem in δ: -δμός > -σμός, →1.90):

ἐνθουσιασμός *inspiration, frenzy,* (ἐνθουσιάζω *be inspired/inspire*)
   enthusiasm

λογισμός *counting, calculation;* (λογίζομαι *calculate*)
   reasoning

μηδισμός *conspiracy/sympathy* (μηδίζω *conspire/sym-*
   with the Persians *pathize with the Persians*)

From the late fifth century onward it was especially frequent in the form -ισμός (corresponding to verbs in -ίζω), notably in technical terms (from medicine, philosophy, linguistics, literary and historical studies, etc.):

ἀττικισμός *loyalty to Athens*; later: *Attic style*	(ἀττικίζω *side with the Athenians*; later: *use Attic*)
βαρβαρισμός *use of a foreign language*	(βαρβαρίζω *use a foreign language*)
(ἐξ)ὀστρακισμός *ostracism*	(ὀστρακίζω *ostracize*)

23.23   **-ος, -ου**: forms masculine action nouns. These nouns are normally paroxytone (→24.5). If the corresponding verb shows e-grade ablaut in the present stem, the noun usually shows the o-grade (→1.55):

λόγος *reckoning, account; reasoning, speech*	(λέγω *say*)
πλοῦς/πλόος *sailing, voyage*	(πλέω *sail*)
πόνος *toil, labour*	(πένομαι *toil, work*)
στόλος *equipment; journey*	(στέλλω *fit out, dispatch*)
τόκος *childbirth; offspring*	(τίκτω, ἔτεκον *give birth*)
τρόπος *direction, way (of acting, behaving)*	(τρέπω, -ομαι *turn around*)
φόρος *payment, tribute*	(φέρω *bear, offer, present*)
ψόγος *blame, censure*	(ψέγω *blame, censure*)

23.24   **-ός, -οῦ**: forms masculine agent nouns. If the corresponding verb shows e-grade ablaut in the present stem, the noun usually shows the o-grade (→1.55):

ἀοιδός *singer*	(ἀείδω *sing*)
σκοπός *spy, lookout*	(σκέπτομαι *look, examine*)
τροφός *feeder, rearer*; esp. ἡ τροφός *wet-nurse*	(τρέφω *feed, nourish*)

In compounds (also →23.37–40, and →24.29 for accentuation):

οἰκοδόμος *architect* ('house-builder')   (οἶκος *house* + δέμω *build, construct*)

23.25   **-ος, -ους** (σ-stem nouns, declension →4.65): this suffix forms neuter nouns:

– Nouns in -ος are often deverbal, denoting an object or condition involved in the verbal action:

βέλος *missile, arrow* (what is thrown)	(βάλλω *throw*)
γένος *race, offspring; class*	(γίγνομαι *become, be born*)
εἶδος *form* (what is seen)	(εἶδον (aor.) *saw*)
ἔπος *word* (what is said)	(εἶπον (aor.) *said*)
θέρος *summer* (<heat)	(θέρομαι *become hot*)
πάθος *suffering, experience* (what is suffered)	(πάσχω, aor. ἔπαθον *suffer, experience*)
ψεῦδος *lie, falsehood*	(ψεύδομαι *lie*)

Note 1: In principle, these nouns do not denote a result, which is rather expressed by nouns in -μα (→23.21). But the distinction should not be pressed: thus, both πάθος and πάθημα are used for 'what one suffers' (πάθημα is preferred in technical prose writing, πάθος in poetry).

– -ος is also used in the formation of various other neuter nouns:

αἶσχος *disgrace, ugliness*	(cf. αἰσχρός *disgraceful, ugly*)
ἔχθος *hate*	(cf. ἐχθρός *hated*)
κάλλος *beauty*	(cf. καλός *beautiful*)
μέγεθος *greatness, magnitude*	(cf. μέγας *great, large*)
τάχος *speed, velocity*	(cf. ταχύς *quick*)

These nouns are all recessive, as are all neuter third-declension nouns (→24.28).

23.26 **-οῦς, -ᾶ, -οῦν** (contracted from -έος, etc., declension →5.5; Ion. -έος, -έη, -έον): forms adjectives of material, e.g. ἀργυροῦς (*of*) *silver* (ἄργυρος *silver*), χρυσοῦς *gold(en)* (χρυσός *gold*).

23.27 **-σις, -εως** (declension →4.74): the most productive action noun suffix: it could be added to virtually any verbal root, especially in the formation of a technical or scientific vocabulary. Such nouns are feminine, and recessive:

ἀκρόασις *the listening to; also lecture*	(ἀκροάομαι *listen*)
γένεσις *generation, coming into being*	(γίγνομαι *become, be born*)
κρίσις *decision, judgement; critical point*	(κρίνω *decide*)
λύσις *releasing, solution*	(λύω *release, loosen*)
μάθησις (the act of) *learning*	(μανθάνω *learn*)
ποίησις *fabrication, production; poetry*	(ποιέω *make, do*)
πρᾶξις *doing, act(ion), performance*	(πράττω *make, do, act*)
σκέψις *examination, consideration*	(σκέπτομαι *look, examine*)

Note 1: In principle, these words do not denote a result, which is rather expressed by nouns in -μα (see above). But the distinction should not be pressed: thus, both ποίησις ('a(n) act of) producing') and ποίημα ('a production') may be used for 'what is made' (there is nonetheless a difference: ποίημα is a countable noun (cf. Engl. *a poem*), whereas ποίησις is a mass noun (cf. Engl. *poetry*).

23.28 **-σύνη**: forms a small number of abstract nouns, mostly from adjectives in -ων, -ονος, especially -φρων and -μων:

σωφροσύνη *prudence, self-control*	(σώφρων *prudent*)
ἀπραγμοσύνη *easy-goingness*	(ἀπράγμων *easy-going*)
μνημοσύνη *mindfulness, memory*	(μνήμων *mindful*)

Other nouns were formed by analogy, e.g. δικαιο-σύνη *righteousness* (δικαιός *just*).

23.29 **-τέος, -τέᾱ, -τέον:** forms verbal adjectives expressing passive necessity (for the use of these adjectives, →37.2–3). The suffix is added directly to the verb stem:

παιδευτέος *to be educated*   (παιδεύω *educate*, verb stem παιδευ-)

γραπτέος *to be written*   (γράφω *write*, verb stem γραφ-; for πτ (assimilation), →1.89)

φυλακτέος *to be guarded*   (φυλάττω *guard*, verb stem φυλακ-)

κομιστέος *to be brought*   (κομίζω *bring*, verb stem κομιδ-; for στ, →1.89)

With verb stems that have ablaut variants, the full e-grade is typically used; with verb stems alternating between a long and a short final stem vowel, the long vowel is used (→11.11):

φευκτέος *to be fled*   (φεύγω *flee*, verb stem φευγ-/φῠγ-)

λειπτέος *to be left*   (λείπω *leave*, verb stem λειπ-/λοιπ-/λῐπ-)

ποιητέος *to be done, made*   (ποιέω *do, make*, verb stem ποιη-/ποιε-)

τιμητέος *to be honoured*   (τιμάω *honour*, verb stem τιμη-/τιμᾰ-)

23.30 **-τήρ, -τῆρος** (declension, →4.55–7): forms masculine agent nouns, especially in dialects other than Attic. In Attic, -τής is preferred, and -τήρ is virtually confined to tragedy, predominantly in words borrowed from Homer. Some examples are ἀροτήρ *ploughman* (ἀρόω *plough*), δοτήρ *giver, dispenser* (δίδωμι *give*), σωτήρ *saviour* (σῴζω *save*). Also in κρατήρ *mixing vessel, bowl* (κεράννυμι *mix*).

23.31 **-τήριον, -ου:** forms concrete nouns denoting instruments and locations; originally formed from agent nouns in -τήρ and the suffix -ιον (for both, see above); in Attic frequently corresponding to an agent noun in -τής:

ποτήριον *drinking cup*   (πίνω, θη-aor. ἐπόθην *drink*)

δικαστήριον *court (of justice)*   (δικαστής *judge, member of jury;*, cf. δικάζω *be a judge*)

χρηστήριον *oracle*   (cf. χρήω *give an oracle*)

23.32 **-της, -ου** (declension, →4.8–10; accentuation varies): forms masculine agent nouns:

θεᾱτής *spectator*   (θεάομαι *gaze, view*)

κριτής *judge*   (κρίνω *decide*)

ποιητής *maker, poet*   (ποιέω *make*)

σοφιστής *expert, wise man, sophist*   (σοφίζομαι *be wise, be clever*)

ὑφάντης *weaver*   (ὑφαίνω *weave*)

23.33 **-της, -τητος** (declension, →4.40–1; accentuation varies): forms feminine abstract nouns denoting qualities or properties, from adjectives in -ος or -υς; the general meaning is 'the quality/property of being . . .':

κακότης *badness, wickedness*   (κακός *bad, wicked*)

λευκότης *whiteness*   (λευκός *white*)

ταὐτότης *identity*   (τὸ αὐτό *the same*)

ταχυτής *quickness, velocity*   (ταχύς *quick*)

23.34   **-τός, -τή, -τόν**: forms verbal adjectives expressing a passive state or passive possibility (for the use of these adjectives, →37.4). The formation is directly analogous to that of adjectives in -τέος (→23.29 above), with the suffix added directly to the verb stem:

παιδευτός *teachable*   (παιδεύω *educate*, verb stem παιδευ-)

φευκτός *avoidable*   (φεύγω *flee*, verb stem <u>φευγ</u>-/<u>φῠγ</u>-)

ποιητός *done, made*   (ποιέω *do, make*, verb stem <u>ποιη</u>-/ποιε-)

Note 1: When such adjectives are built on a compound stem, accentuation can vary, sometimes with a corresponding difference of meaning: e.g. διαλυτός *capable of dissolution*, διάλυτος *relaxed* (δια-λύω *dissolve*). For accentuation of compound adjectives more generally, →24.29.

23.35   **-τρον, -ου** (accentuation varies): forms concrete deverbal neuter nouns denoting instruments and locations:

κάτοπτρον *mirror*   (καθοράω *spot, see*)

σκῆπτρον *staff*   (σκήπτομαι *lean on*)

θέατρον *theatre* ('viewer-place')   (θεάομαι *gaze, view*)

λουτρόν *bath*   (λούω *wash, bathe*)

23.36   **-ών, -ῶνος** (declension →4.49; Ion. -εών, -εῶνος): forms masculine nouns denoting locations from nominal roots, e.g. ἀνδρών, -ῶνος *men's apartment* (ἀνήρ *man*), παρθενών, -ῶνος *maiden's apartment* (παρθένος *maiden*).

Nominal Word Formation by Means of Composition

Compound Adjectives with Nominal/Adverbial Element + Nominal Element

23.37   The first member in these compounds qualifies the second. The first member may be the root of a noun or adjective, a numeral, a preposition, or an adverbial prefix (e.g. δυσ-, εὐ-). Some examples:

μεγαλόψυχος *high-souled, generous*   (μέγας *great, large*, ψυχή *soul*)

Πολυκράτης *Polycrates* ('having much power')   (πολύς *much, great*, κράτος *power*)

πενταέτης *five-year-long*   (πέντε *five*, ἔτος *year*)

ἔνθεος *inspired* ('having a god within')   (ἐν *in*, θεός *god*)

περίφοβος *very frightened* ('having exceeding   (περί *exceeding*, φόβος *fear*)
fear')

δυστυχής *unfortunate* ('with a bad fate')   (δυσ- *bad-, ill-*, τύχη *fate*)

εὐμενής *well-disposed, kind* ('with a good   (εὖ *well*, μένος *purpose, force*)
temper')

To this category belong also adjectives with so-called **privative ἀ-** (before consonant) or **ἀν-** (before vowel), with the general meaning 'not' (cf. Engl. *un-, a-, im-*):

ἄδικος *unjust*   (ἀ-, δίκη *justice*)

ἀθάνατος *immortal*   (ἀ-, θάνατος *death*)

ἀνάξιος *unworthy*   (ἀν-, ἀξία *worth, value*)

Note 1: δυσ- and ἀ-/ἀν- do not exist outside compounds.

Note 2: There are also compound nouns in which the first member qualifies the second member in this way: ἀκρόπολις, ἡ *citadel* (the highest part of the city; ἀκρός, πόλις); σύνδουλος *fellow-slave* (σύν, δοῦλος); τρίπους *tripod* (τρεῖς, πούς).

A few compound nouns have a nominal case form as first member, e.g. Διόσκουροι *Zeus' sons* (Διός gen. sg. of Ζεύς), Ἑλλήσποντος *Hellespont* ('Helle's sea'; Ἕλλης gen. sg. of Ἕλλη).

23.38   A special case is that of compound adjectives, and some nouns, of the type **παράδοξος**. These compounds can be considered nominalizations of prepositional phrases: παράδοξος *incredible, unexpected* is the adjectival form of the preposi-tional phrase παρὰ δόξαν *contrary to expectation*. Some further examples:

ἐγκέφαλος, ὁ *brain*   (ἐν κεφαλῇ *in the head*)

ἐκποδών (adverb) *out of the way, away*   (ἐκ ποδῶν *away from the feet*)

ἐπιχώριος *(being) in* or *of the country, local*   (ἐπὶ χώρᾳ *in the country*)

σύμφωνος *agreeing in sound, harmonious*   (σὺν φωνῇ *together with the sound*)

φροῦδος *gone, vanished*   (πρὸ ὁδοῦ *in front of the way*)

Note 1: Such adjectives may also be based on noun phrases, e.g. πολυχρόνιος *long lasting*, based on πολὺν χρόνον *for a long time*.

Compound Forms with Verbal Element + Nominal Element

23.39   In these compounds the second (nominal) member fulfils the role of object to the first (verbal) member. The first member ends in:

– ο:

λιποτάξιον, τό *desertion*   (λείπω *leave*, τάξις *position*)

φιλόσοφος *loving wisdom*   (φιλέω *love*, σοφία *wisdom*)

φιλότιμος *loving honour, ambitious*   (φιλέω *love*, τιμή *honour*)

Also with elision of o:

μισ-/φιλάνθρωπος *hating/loving*   (μισέω *hate* / φιλέω *love*, ἄνθρωπος
   mankind   *man, person*)

– ε (mainly poetic):

ἐλέπ(τ)ολις *city-destroying*   (αἱρέω, aor. εἷλον *take*, πόλις *city*)

– σι (cf. action nouns in -σις, →23.27):

λυσιτελής *profitable* ('paying expenses')   (λύω *loosen, resolve* τέλος *payment*)
Πεισίστρατος *Pisistratus*   (πείθω *persuade*, στρατός *army*)

Compound Forms with Nominal/Adverbial Element + Verbal Element

23.40   To this category belong several groups of nouns and adjectives:

– Agent nouns, and adjectives referring to either the agent or the object of an
action. When such nouns or adjectives refer to the agent, the first (nominal) part fulfils the role of object or instrument to the second (verbal) part.
The verbal root occurs in the o-grade if it has different ablaut variants
(→1.55):

δορυφόρος *spear-bearer, bodyguard*   (δόρυ *spear*, φέρω *bear*)
οἰκοδόμος *(house)builder, architect*   (οἶκος *house*, δέμω *build, construct*)
στρατηγός *commander of an army,*   (στρατός *army*, ἄγω *lead*)
   general
λιθοβόλος *throwing stones*, λιθόβολος   (λίθος *stone*, βάλλω *throw, hit*)
   hit by stones
Ὀλυμπιονίκης *conqueror in the*   (Ὀλύμπια *Olympia*, νικάω *win*)
   Olympic games

Note 1: Compound nouns and adjectives in -ος of this type normally have the accent
on the verbal part (i.e. they are oxytone or paroxytone) when they refer to the agent:
e.g. λιθοβόλος *throwing stones*, ψυχοπομπός *guide of souls*, λαιμοτόμος *throat-cutting*
(but note exceptions such as ἡνίοχος *rein-holder*, ἵππαρχος *commander of horses*); they
are recessive when they refer to the object: λιθόβολος *hit by stones, stoned*, λαιμότομος
with throat cut.

– Agent nouns, with a second member formed with the suffix -της (→23.32):

ἐπιστάτης *overseer, one who is set over*   (ἐφίσταμαι *come to stand over*)
νομοθέτης *lawgiver*   (νόμος *law*, τίθημι *put in place*)
προδότης *traitor*   (προδίδωμι *betray*)

– Adjectives with passive meaning, from verbal adjectives in -τος (for such adjectives, →23.34):

δοριάλωτος *taken by the spear, taken in war*   (δόρυ *spear*, ἁλίσκομαι *be taken*)

περίρρυτος *surrounded with water*   (περί *around*, ῥέω *flow*)

σύμμεικτος *commingled*   (σύν *together*, μείγνυμι *mix*)

εὔγνωστος *well-known; easily known, easy to know*   (εὖ *well*, γιγνώσκω *know, recognize*)

ἄβατος *impassable; not to be trodden*   (ἀ-, βαίνω *go*)

Verbal Word Formation

23.41   Many of the suffixes involved in the formation of Greek verbs are treated in the chapters on verbal morphology (→11 for thematic vowels, the optative suffix, the augment, reduplication, endings, etc.; and the relevant chapters for suffixes marking tense-aspect). Below, some further details are given on the processes involved in the formation of **denominative verbs** (verbs derived from nominal stems), and on **compound verbs**.

Denominative Verbs Formed with *-yω

23.42   The suffix *-yω was used to derive many (present stems of) denominative verbs:

– verbs derived from a nominal stem ending in a vowel (i.e. contract verbs in -έω, -άω, -όω and -ήω); these verbs were contracted in Attic after the disappearance of y (→1.76, 12.29);

– verbs derived from a nominal stem ending in a consonant.

Note 1: -ω verbs like λέγω, λείπω, πείθω, πέμπω, τρέχω, and many other so-called 'non-derived' or 'primitive' verbs, are formed without a suffix: thematic vowels/endings follow directly after the root (→12.24 n.1).

Verbs Formed with *-yω from Nominal Stems Ending in a Vowel

23.43   -άω/-άομαι: from nominal stems in ā/η (i.e. first-declension nouns): e.g. τιμάω *honour* (<*-άγω; cf. τιμή *honour*); the ā was shortened in the formation of the present stem (not elsewhere: e.g. aor. ἐτίμησα, fut. τιμήσω, pf. τετίμηκα; all with Att. ā > η, →1.57). Other examples:

νικάω *win, be victorious*   (νίκη *victory*)

μηχανάομαι *contrive by design*   (μηχανή *contrivance, scheme*)

θηράω *hunt, chase*   (θήρα *hunting, chase*)

αἰτιάομαι *accuse*   (αἰτία *cause*)

Note 1: There are also a few primitive presents in -άω, where the endings follow directly after the root e.g. δράω *do*.
Note 2: A few verbs in -άω derive from σ-stems rather than a stem ending in ᾱ/η, e.g. γελάω *laugh* <*γελάσ-yω (→12.29 n.1). The σ of the stem has, with such verbs, usually left traces in other tense stems: e.g. aor. ἐγέλασα (epic aor. ἐγέλασσα, →13.18), fut. γελάσομαι (→15.19), etc.

23.44   **-έω/-έομαι:**

- <*-έγω, from the e-grade of thematic nominal stems (i.e. second-declension nouns in ος): e.g. οἰκέω *inhabit* (<*(ϝ)οικέγω, cf. οἶκος *house*); the stem was lengthened in other tenses (e.g. aor. ᾤκησα, fut. οἰκήσω), by analogy with the -άω type and verbs such as φιλέω (→n.1 below). Some further examples:

κοσμέω *order, arrange, adorn*	(κόσμος *order*)
νοσέω *be ill*	(νόσος *illness*)
ἀριθμέω *count*	(ἀριθμός *number*)

There are, however, also numerous denominative verbs in -έω/-έομαι deriving from other nominal stems, including stems ending in a consonant:

- -έω<*-έσγω, from the stem in εσ of neuter nouns in ος: e.g. τελέω *finish* (<*τελέσγω, cf. τέλος *end*); for such verbs, also →12.29 n.1;
- other stems: e.g. μαρτυρέω *bear witness, give evidence* (cf. μάρτυς *witness*, gen. μάρτυρ-ος).

Further examples:

μισέω *hate*	(μῖσος, -ους *hatred*)
εὐδαιμονέω *be prosperous, be happy*	(εὐδαίμων, -ονος *happy*)
ὑπηρετέω *serve*	(ὑπηρέτης *servant*)
φωνέω *speak out*	(φωνή *voice*)

Note 1: Numerous verbs in -έω probably derive from original stative verbs in *-ήγω, built on the suffix -η- (cf. η-aorists, →14): e.g. φιλέω *love* (<*φιλ-ήγω), ἀλγέω *feel pain* (<*ἀλγ-ήγω); the 'original' η is still visible in aor. ἐφίλησα, fut. φιλήσω, pf. πεφίληκα, etc. (it was shortened in the present stem).
Note 2: With a few verbs in -έω deriving from a stem in εσ, such as τελέω *finish*, the σ of the original stem has left traces in other tense stems: e.g. aor. ἐτέλεσα (epic aor. ἐτέλεσσα, →13.18), θη-aor. ἐτελέσθην (→14.16), Attic fut. τελῶ (sometimes τελέσω; →15.19), etc. But with other such verbs the conjugation is fully like that of the standard -έω type, e.g. μισέω, aor. ἐμίσησα, etc.
Note 3: There are also some verbs in -έω that are derived from other verbs; they show o-ablaut in their stem and have intensive-frequentative meaning: e.g. σκοπέω, -ομαι *behold, consider* (σκέπτομαι *look, examine*), and φορέω *carry habitually* (φέρω *carry*).
Note 4: A few verbs in -έω are primitive (i.e. non-derived); these have always lost ϝ, σ, or y after ε: e.g. ῥέω *flow* (<*ῥέϝω), πλέω *sail* (<*πλέϝω), δέω *bind* (<*δέyω).
Note 5: For -έω forming compound verbs, →23.50.

23.45   **-όω/-όομαι**: from nominal stems in o. These verbs generally have **factitive** meaning (*make . . .*), and are mostly built on (second-declension) **adjectives** in -ος; e.g. δηλόω *make clear, show, make manifest* (<*δηλόγω, cf. δῆλος *manifest*). Some other examples:

ἀξιόω *think worthy, claim*	(ἄξιος *worthy*)
ἐλευθερόω *set free*	(ἐλεύθερος *free*)

Some are built on **nouns** in -ος:

δουλόω *enslave*	(δοῦλος *slave*, possibly originally an adj.)
στεφανόω *(give a) crown*	(στέφανος *crown, garland*)

Note 1: Note pairs like factitive δουλόω *enslave* as against stative δουλεύω *be a slave*.

23.46   Verbs in **-εύω** were originally the result of denominative formations in based on nouns in -εύς (→4.84–5); later -εύω became a productive suffix in its own right, used also to form verbs from other noun types. Verbs in -εύω often have stative meaning:

βασιλεύω *be king*	(βασιλεύς *king*)
ἀγορεύω *speak in public*	(ἀγορά *marketplace*)
δουλεύω *be a slave*	(δοῦλος *slave*)
παιδεύω *educate*	(παῖς *child*)

Verbs Formed with *-yω from Nominal Stems Ending in a Consonant

23.47   When combined with a nominal stem ending in other consonants, the y of the suffix *-yω led to varying results, for instance:

ἁρπάζω *snatch away, seize*	<*ἁρπάγ-yω	(cf. ἁρπαγ-ή *seizure*)
ἐλπίζω *expect, hope*	<*ἐλπίδ-yω	(ἐλπίς, -ίδος *hope*)
ἀγγέλλω *report, bear a message*	<*ἀγγέλ-yω	(cf. ἄγγελ-ος *messenger*)
παίζω *play*	<*παίδ-yω	(παῖς, παιδός *child*)
ταράττω *stir, trouble*	<*ταράχ-yω	(cf. ταραχή *disturbance*)

For the sound changes involved, →1.77–8; for a fuller overview of these present stems, →12.27–8.

Note 1: There are also verbs in this group which are not denominative, e.g. φράζω *point out, explain* (<*φράδ-yω), βαίνω *go, walk* (<*βάν-yω), φαίνω *show* (<*φάν-yω).

23.48   Several of these formations resulted in newly productive suffixes:

– The formations in -άζω and -ίζω were the basis for the development of **-άζω** and **-ίζω** as suffixes in their own right, which were used to form a large number of denominative verbs:

ἀναγκάζω *force*	(ἀνάγκη *necessity*)
γυμνάζω *exercise*	(γυμνός *naked*)
θαυμάζω *marvel at, admire*	(θαῦμα *wonder*)
εὐδαιμονίζω *call/consider happy*	(εὐδαίμων *happy*)
κουφίζω *make light, lighten*	(κοῦφος *light*)
λογίζομαι *count, reckon; consider*	(λόγος *reckoning*)
ἑλληνίζω *speak/write pure Greek*	(Ἕλλην *Greek*)
νομίζω *believe; have as a custom*	(νόμος *law, custom*)
ὑβρίζω *abuse, maltreat*	(ὕβρις *abuse, brutality*)

Note 1: Verbs in -ίζω generally have either 'factitive' meaning ('make X Y'; e.g. κουφίζω), or meanings having to do with types of behaviour (e.g. ἑλληνίζω, ὑβρίζω).

Note 2: Other stems of these verbs are formed as if derived from stems in -ιδ- and -αδ- (that is to say, the pattern of -ίζω/-άζω verbs was highly regularized): e.g. aor. ἐθαύμασα, fut. λογιοῦμαι, pf. mp. ἠνάγκασμαι, etc. (for these regular principal parts, →22.6).

– **-αίνω:** this suffix – originally the result of *-ανγω, e.g. εὐφραίνω *make glad* (<*εὐφράνγω, cf. εὔφρων) – forms verbs derived from nouns in -μα and certain adjectives in -ος and -ης:

ὀνομαίνω *name, call by name*	(ὄνομα *name*)
σημαίνω *show by a sign, indicate*	(σῆμα *sign*)
χαλεπαίνω *be angry* ('make difficulties')	(χαλεπός *difficult*)
ὑγιαίνω *be sound, be healthy*	(ὑγιής *healthy*)

– **-ύνω:** used to form verbs from adjectives in -ύς:

θρασύνω *embolden, encourage*	(θρασύς *bold*)
ἰθύνω *make straight, straighten*	(ἰθύς *straight*)
ὀξύνω *sharpen*	(ὀξύς *sharp*)

Note 3: -ύνω is also found with some nouns in -ος, e.g. αἰσχύνω *disgrace, disfigure* (αἶσχος *disgrace, disfigurement*).

Compound Verbs

23.49   There are two ways of forming compound verbs:

– by forming **denominative** verbs **from compound nouns and adjectives;**
– by **prefixation** of simplex verbs.

Denominative Compound Verbs from Compound Nouns/Adjectives

23.50   Several verbs are formed **from compound nouns and adjectives** (→23.37–40), with the suffix -έω:

οἰκοδομέω *build*	(οἰκοδόμος *architect, builder*)
στρατηγέω *be general*	(στρατηγός *general*)
ἐπιστατέω *preside, be in charge*	(ἐπιστάτης *president, commander*)
δυστυχέω *be unfortunate*	(δυστυχής *unfortunate*)
φιλοσοφέω *love/pursue knowledge*	(φιλόσοφος *lover of knowledge*)

Note 1: Some verbs of this type may be construed with a direct object and can also be passivized: e.g. οἰκοδομέω γέφυραν *build a bridge*, οἰκοδομέομαι *be built*. This shows that the nominal stem of the first member (οἰκο-), which denotes the object of the verbal action (δέμω), was no longer felt as such in compounds such as οἰκοδομέω.

Compound Verbs Formed by Prefixation

23.51   A very large number of compound verbs are formed by **prefixation**, i.e. by prefixing one or more prepositions (preverbs) to a simplex verb or a denominative verb:

ἐκ-βαίνω *go out of*	συν-εκ-βαίνω *go out together*	(βαίνω *go, walk*)
ἐμ-βιβάζω *put on board a ship*	μετ-εμ-βιβάζω *transfer to another ship*	(βιβάζω *cause to go*)
κατα-τίθεμαι *deposit for oneself*	παρα-κατα-τίθεμαι *deposit one's property with another*	(τίθεμαι *lay down for oneself*)
παρ-οικοδομέω *build across*		(οἰκοδομέω *build*)

Note 1: Prefixation is the only way in which simplex verbs are compounded.
Note 2: Only compound verbs formed by prefixation are separable by an augment or reduplication: κατ-ε-τιθέμην, συν-εκ-βέ-βηκα, but ἐ-φιλοσόφουν, πε-φιλοσόφηκα (denominative compounds); also →11.56. However, when a denominative verb is formed from a compound noun which itself includes a preposition (e.g. ἐπιστατέω *preside* formed from ἐπιστάτης *president*), it is sometimes treated as if it were formed by prefixation (impf. ἐπεστάτει).

24

Accentuation

Introduction

24.1 Some familiarity with the basic rules of Ancient Greek accentuation is invaluable in distinguishing between different grammatical forms (e.g. ποιεῖ 3 sg. pres. act. ind., but ποίει 2 sg. pres. act. imp.), or between different words (e.g. ἤ *or, than*, but ἦ *truly, really* or 1 sg. impf. of εἰμί *be*; νόμος *law, custom* but νομός *pasture, province*). Below, an overview of the basic rules of Greek accentuation is given. For more comprehensive studies, see the Bibliography at the end of this book.

> **Note 1:** For conventions regarding the placement of accents on diphthongs and capitals, →1.8.

24.2 Ancient Greek was a pitch-accent language. Unlike English or Modern Greek, words were not pronounced with fixed emphasis (or stress) on one syllable, but with a variation in pitch (or tone) that was partially fixed and partially dependent on a word's position in its clause. Written Greek uses three accent signs to indicate these variations. Two of them are placed on the vowel of a syllable that is marked for its high pitch:

– The **acute accent**, e.g. ά, οί (Greek: ὀξεῖα προσῳδία) marks the syllable with the highest pitch of the word. It can be written on all short and long vowels and on diphthongs, e.g. ὄψ *voice*, ἄρα *then*, γένος *race*, ὁδός *road*, ἀλήθεια *truth*, ἥδομαι *I enjoy*, πορεύομαι *I march*.
– The **circumflex accent**, e.g. ᾶ, οῖ (Greek: περισπωμένη προσῳδία) also marks the syllable with the highest pitch in the word, but it is only written on long vowels and diphthongs and indicates that the highest pitch falls on the first part of the long vowel or diphthong and that the pitch lowers in the second part, e.g. παῖς *child, slave*, ὧδε *thus*, πνεῦμα *breath*, Περικλῆς *Pericles*, κακοῦργος *villain*, εἶμι *I will go*.

> **Note 1:** If the highest pitch falls on the second part of the long vowel or diphthong, an acute accent is used, e.g. πορευώμεθα *let us march*, ηὕρομεν *we found*. The circumflex accent is always placed on the second letter of the diphthong, although it marks the high pitch of its first part. As a sign, the circumflex results from a fusion of acute and grave accent. Thus εῦ < έὐ.

– The third accent sign, the **grave accent**, e.g. ὰ, οὶ (Greek: βαρεῖα προσῳδία), is conventionally written in continuous texts to replace an acute accent on the final syllable of a word if it is followed by a non-enclitic word (for enclitic words and their accentuation → 24.34, 24.38 below) without intervening punctuation, e.g. αὐτὸ τὸ θηρίον ἀγαθὸν καὶ καλόν ἐστι *the wild beast itself is noble and beautiful* (observe that καλόν keeps the acute accent as it is followed by enclitic ἐστι). The grave is not used on interrogative τίς and τί, even if followed by a non-enclitic word.

Note 2: There is no conclusive evidence about the pitch that is indicated by the grave accent on the last syllable; the most likely possibility is that it indicates that a syllable is pronounced on a higher pitch than the unaccented syllables of the word, but on a lower pitch than other accented syllables.

24.3   Greek also has unaccented words (**enclitics** and **proclitics**). For the specific rules applying to their accentuation, →24.33–9 below.

General Rules of Accentuation

Possible Positions of the Accent; 'Long' and 'Short' Syllables

24.4   Accents can only fall on one of the last three syllables of a word:
– the **ultima**: the final syllable of a word ($x \cdot x \cdot \underline{x}$);
– the **penult**: the second-to-last syllable of a word ($x \cdot \underline{x} \cdot x$);
– the **antepenult**: the third-to-last syllable of a word ($\underline{x} \cdot x \cdot x$).

24.5   The acute may fall on any of the last three syllables of a word. The circumflex accent may fall only on the ultima or the penult. Thus the following five positions of the accent are distinguished:
– **oxytone**: an acute accent on the ultima ($x \cdot x \cdot \underline{\acute{x}}$), e.g. ἀνήρ, ὀξύς, ἐπί, τιθείς, ἀγαγών, αὐτός, οὐδείς;
  when the accent changes to a grave (→24.2 above), such words are also called **barytone**;
– **paroxytone**: an acute accent on the penult ($x \cdot \underline{\acute{x}} \cdot x$), e.g. τύχη, παρθένος, Εὐριπίδης, λελειμμένος, δεικνύναι, ἐνθάδε;
– **proparoxytone**: an acute accent on the antepenult ($\underline{\acute{x}} \cdot x \cdot x$), e.g. ἄγαλμα, ὅσιος, δίκαιος, βασίλεια, φυόμενος, τέθνηκα, πεντήκοντα, μακρότερος;
– **perispomenon**: a circumflex accent on the ultima ($x \cdot x \cdot \underline{\tilde{x}}$), e.g. Σοφοκλῆς, ἀργυροῦς, ἀληθῶς, τιμῶ, ποιεῖν, ἐμαυτῷ, οὐκοῦν;
– **properispomenon**: a circumflex accent on the penult ($x \cdot \underline{\tilde{x}} \cdot x$), e.g. σῆμα, νῆες, πολῖται, τοιοῦτος, ἀπῆγε, δηλοῦμεν, ἐκεῖθεν.

24.6   The positions on which the accent *can* **fall** are further limited by the **rule of limitation** (→24.8–10) and the **σωτῆρᾰ-rule** (→24.11).

The position on which the accent *does* **actually fall** depends on whether a word is a verbal form or a nominal form, and is then conditioned by further rules (for verbs, →24.16–20; for nominal forms, →24.21–32).

24.7   Accentuation is determined strongly by the **length** of the last two syllables of a word. For the purposes of accentuation:

- a syllable is **long** if it contains a **long vowel** or a **diphthong**;
- a syllable is **short** if it contains a **short vowel** (or, in the case of the ultima, -οι or -αι, →24.10).

For vowel quantity (long/short), →1.18. The quantity of vowels in nominal and verbal endings is given in the relevant sections of the morphology (particularly the tables of endings, →2.6, 11.22–30). Vowel quantity is also normally given in dictionaries.

Note 1: The length of a syllable for the purposes of accentuation is not the same as its metrical quantity or 'weight'. For instance, the first syllables of νύκτα, ἔργον and τύπτε are short for the purposes of accentuation because they have a short vowel, but they count as 'heavy' (or 'long') for metrical purposes because the vowels are followed by a double consonant (meaning that the syllables end in a consonant: νύκ·τα, ἔρ·γον, τύπ·τε).

The Rule of Limitation

24.8   The syllables that can be accented are *limited* to:

- the **last three** of a word in the case of the **acute** accent;
- the **last two** in the case of the **circumflex** accent.

Thus †παιδευόμενος, †ἤγαγες and †τῑμᾱτε are impossible (correct: παιδευόμενος, ἤγαγες and τιμᾱτε).

24.9   If the **ultima** of a word is **long**:

- the **acute** accent is limited to the **last two syllables**: †παιδευόμενης, †πόλιτου are impossible (correct: παιδευομένης, πολίτου);
- the **circumflex** accent can fall **only on the last**, long syllable: †σκῆνης, †αὖτοις are impossible (correct: σκηνῆς, αὐτοῖς).

24.10   If a word **ends in -οι or -αι**, however, the ultima counts as **short**. Thus the acute may fall on the antepenult and the circumflex on the penult, e.g. παιδευόμενοι, ἐπιτήδειαι, ἑκοῦσαι, οἷοι.

But optative endings -οι and -αι are long. Thus παιδεύοι (not †παίδευοι), βουλεύσαι (aor. opt., →13.12).

Note 1: Also long are the endings -οι and -αι of some old locative forms such as οἴκοι *at home*, and interjections such as αἰαῖ *oh!*

Note 2: When ω in an ultima results from quantitative metathesis (→1.71), the accentuation reflects the state prior to quantitative metathesis (and therefore sometimes appears to violate the rule of limitation): e.g. πόλεως (gen. sg.) <*πόληος, Μενέλεως (nom. sg.) <*Μενέλᾱ(Ϝ)ος. The gen. pl. πόλεων is analogous to πόλεως.

Several υ-stem nouns (→4.79–83) received accentuation analogous to the πόλις-type, e.g. with πῆχυς *forearm*, gen. sg. πήχεως, gen. pl. πήχεων; with ἄστυ *city*, gen. sg. ἄστεως (gen. pl. ἀστέων in (texts of) Pindar; ἄστεων in later Greek).

The σωτῆρᾰ-Rule

24.11   If the following three conditions hold:

- the **ultima** is **short**,
- the **penult** is **long**, and
- the accent falls on the **penult**,

then this accent is **always circumflex** (i.e. the word is properispomenon):

e.g. σωτῆρᾰ (contrast σωτήρων), λῦε (contrast λύου), ἦγες (contrast ἤγου), πολῖτᾰ (contrast πολίτης), βασιλεῦσιν (contrast βασιλεύσᾱς), τοσοῦτος (contrast τοσούτῳ).

Note 1: The σωτῆρᾰ-rule applies *only* if it is the penult that carries the accent. Thus, e.g. οἶκος *house* (gen. sg. οἴκου), but ἄποικος *colony* (gen. sg. ἀποίκου).

Note 2: Since final -αι and -οι (except optative endings, →24.10) count as short, the σωτῆρᾰ-rule also applies with these endings, e.g. πολῖται (nom. pl.), δοῦλοι (nom. pl.).

Note 3: The σωτῆρᾰ-rule is also sometimes called the 'properispomenon rule'.

Contraction

24.12   The accentuation of words that contain a long vowel or diphthong which results from contraction (→1.58–66) is determined by the position of the accent **before the contraction took place**. The following rules apply:

(i)   If the accent originally fell on the **first vowel involved in the contraction**, the resulting vowel or diphthong is accented with a **circumflex**: e.g. άε > ᾶ, έα > ῆ, έο > οῦ, άο > ῶ.

(ii)   If the accent originally fell on the **second vowel involved in the contraction**, the resulting vowel or diphthong has the **same accent**, e.g. αέ > ά, εά > ή, εό > ού, αό > ώ, εῶ > ῶ.

(iii)   If **neither vowel** involved in the contraction contained an accent the resulting contracted vowel or diphthong is not accented.

These rules may be illustrated by the sg. of νοῦς *mind* and the impf. act. and mp. of the contract verb ποιέω *make, do*:

uncontracted		*contracted*
νό-ος	>	νοῦς (i)
νό-ου	>	νοῦ (i)
νό-ῳ	>	νῷ (i)
νό-ον	>	νοῦν (i)

impf. act.			*impf. mp.*		
uncontracted		*contracted*	*uncontracted*		*contracted*
ἐ-ποίε-ον	>	ἐ-ποίουν (iii)	ἐ-ποιε-όμην	>	ἐ-ποιούμην (ii)
ἐ-ποίε-ες	>	ἐ-ποίεις (iii)	ἐ-ποιέ-ου	>	ἐ-ποιοῦ (i)
ἐ-ποίε-ε	>	ἐ-ποίει (iii)	ἐ-ποιέ-ετο	>	ἐ-ποιεῖτο (i)
ἐ-ποιέ-ομεν	>	ἐ-ποιοῦμεν (i)	ἐ-ποιε-όμεθα	>	ἐ-ποιούμεθα (ii)
ἐ-ποιέ-ετε	>	ἐ-ποιεῖτε (i)	ἐ-ποιέ-εσθε	>	ἐ-ποιεῖσθε (i)
ἐ-ποίε-ον	>	ἐ-ποίουν (iii)	ἐ-ποιέ-οντο	>	ἐ-ποιοῦντο (i)

Note 1: The σωτῆρᾰ-rule (as applied to the resulting form) takes precedence over these rules, e.g. κληδοῦχος, *not* †κληδούχος (although <*κληδο-όχος).

Note 2: In compound adjectives ending in -νους (<-νοος; εὔνους *favourable*, κακόνους *ill-disposed*) these rules are disregarded, e.g. εὔνου (gen. sg.; *not* †εὐνοῦ <*εὐνό-ου), εὔνων (gen. pl.; *not* †εὐνῶν <*εὐνό-ων).

Note 3: If the nominative and accusative dual ending -ω is accented, it is always accented with an acute/grave, regardless of contraction, e.g. νώ (*two minds*; <*νόω), εὐνώ *favourable* (nom./acc. du.).

Note 4: For contraction in optative forms, →24.18 below.

Recessive, Persistent, and Mobile Accentuation

24.13   Many Greek words, including nearly all finite verb forms, have an accent which falls on ('recedes to') the earliest syllable possible within the confinements of the rule of limitation and the rules of contraction. This is called **recessive accentuation** (for details, →24.16 below).

24.14   Non-finite verb forms (participles and infinitives), and many nominal forms (nouns, adjectives, pronouns, etc.), have a **persistent accent**, which remains in place when these words are declined unless it is affected by the rule of limitation, the σωτῆρᾰ-rule or the rules of contraction.

Here, a distinction may be made between **base accent** and **case accent**:

–   The **base accent** is provided by the nom. sg. of nouns, and the nom. sg. masc. of adjectives/participles/pronouns. For instance, base accents are provided by nom. sg. ἄνθρωπος *man*, nom. sg. παρθένος *maiden*, and nom. sg. masc. δεινός *impressive*. The base accent is placed according to regular patterns in the case of non-finite verb forms (participles and infinitives, →24.20 below). For nouns, adjectives and pronouns some patterns can be identified in words of similar morphological or semantic categories (→24.25–32 below), but there are many exceptions;

- In the other grammatical cases of these words the accent (**case accent**) stays on the same syllable (counted from the beginning of the word) as the base accent, unless this is prohibited by the rule of limitation, the σωτῆρᾰ-rule or the rules of contraction. For instance, nom. pl. ἄνθρωποι (same syllable as base accent), but gen. pl. ἀνθρώπων (not †ἄνθρωπων, prohibited by the law of limitation, as final -ων is long).

Note 1: There is no practical difference between recessive accentuation and persistent accentuation with words such as ἄνθρωπος whose base form is proparoxytone.

24.15   Some third-declension nouns have a **mobile accent**, which alternates between falling on the ultima and the penult, depending on the case. For details, →24.23.

Finite Verbs: Recessive Accentuation

24.16   Nearly all **finite verb forms** are **recessive**: the accent recedes to the earliest syllable possible, given the rule of limitation (marked (i) below), the σωτῆρᾰ-rule (ii) and the rules of contraction (iii).

Note 1: For uncontracted forms, this gives the following possibilities (syllable divisions are indicated by dots):

- Forms with **three syllables or more**:

short ultima	proparoxytone	e.g. λυ·ό·με·θα, λέ·γω·μαι, ἐ·μεί·να·μεν
long ultima (i)	paroxytone	e.g. λυ·οί·μην, κω·λύ·ω, δεικ·νύ·οις

- Forms with **two syllables**:

short penult	paroxytone	e.g. τύπ·τει, τύπ·τε
long penult, long ultima	paroxytone	e.g. λύ·ω, κλῖ·νεις, κλαύ·σαι
		(aor. opt. act.; opt. -αι = long)
long penult, short ultima (ii)	properispomenon	e.g. λῦ·ε, κλῖ·νον, κλαῦ·σαι
		(aor. inf. act.; inf. -αι = short)

- Forms with **one syllable** (the accent can, of course, fall only on that syllable):

short	oxytone	e.g. θές, δός
long	perispomenon	e.g. εἶ

The following examples illustrate these principles. Given are the pres. mp. ind. of παιδεύω *educate*, the impf. act. of ἄγω *lead, bring*, and the pres. mp. ind. of τιμάω *honour*:

παιδεύ·ο·μαι (i)   ἦ·γον (i, ii)   τιμῶμαι (<*τιμά·ο·μαι) (i, ii, iii)

παιδεύ·ῃ (<*παιδεύ·ε·αι,   ἦ·γες (i, ii)   τιμᾷ (<*τιμά·ει) (i, iii)
  →1.83, 11.23) (i, iii)

παιδεύ·ε·ται (i)   ἦ·γε (i, ii)   τιμᾶται (<*τιμά·ε·ται) (i, ii, iii)

παιδευ·ό·με·θᾰ (i)   ἤ·γο·μεν (i)   τιμώμεθᾰ (<*τιμα·ό·με·θᾰ) (i, iii)

παιδεύ·εσ·θε (i)   ἤ·γε·τε (i)   τιμᾶσθε (<*τιμά·εσ·θε) (i, ii, iii)

παιδεύ·ον·ται (i)   ἦ·γον (i, ii)   τιμῶνται (<*τιμά·ον·ται) (i, ii, iii)

24.17   The following finite verbs, by way of exception, are **not recessive**:

- 2 sg. pres. ind. φής/φῄς (→12.36);
- the following five 2 sg. act. imp. forms of thematic aorists: εἰπέ say!, ἐλθέ come!, εὑρέ find!, ἰδέ see!, λαβέ take!;
- all 2 sg. imp. mid. forms of thematic aorists (in -οῦ), e.g. ἀπολοῦ perish!, ἀφικοῦ arrive!, γενοῦ become!, ἑλοῦ choose!, ἐροῦ ask!;
- χρή it is necessary, impf. (ἐ)χρῆν (not originally verb forms, →11.41, 12.44).

24.18   The following **subjunctive** and **optative** forms are **contracted**, and are accented accordingly:

- present of contract verbs, e.g. subj. ποιῶμεν < ποιέ·ω·μεν, opt. ποιοῖο < ποιέ·οι·ο; δουλοῖντο < δουλό·οι·ντο;
- present of -μι verbs, e.g. subj. ἱστῶμαι <*ἱστή·ω·μαι, τιθῇς <*τιθή·ης, ὦσι <*ἔ·ω·σι; opt. διδοῖμεν <*διδό·ι·μεν, τιθεῖσθε <*τιθέ·ι·σθε;
- root aorists, e.g. subj. μεθῆσθε <*μεθή·η·σθε, γνῶμεν <*γνώ·ω·μεν, δώμεθα <*δω·ώ·μεθα; opt. ἀφεῖεν <*ἀφέ·ι·εν;
- θη-/η-aorists, e.g. subj. λυθῶ <*λυθή·ω, φανῇς <*φανή·ης; opt. λυθεῖτε <*λυθέ·ι·τε;
- mixed perfects, e.g. subj. ἑστῶ <*ἑστέ·ω (ἵσταμαι), and οἶδα know, e.g. subj. εἰδῶ <*εἰδέ·ω, opt. εἰδεῖεν <*εἰδέ·ι·εν.

But no contraction takes place in the case of athematic stems ending in ι/υ, e.g. ἴω (εἶμι go), δεικνύω (δείκνυμι), δύωμεν (root aor. of δύομαι dive, →13.39–41, 13.44), φύωμεν (root aor. of φύομαι grow (up), →13.39–41, 13.44). Present subjunctives and optatives of the (middle-only) -μι verbs δύναμαι be able, ἐπίσταμαι know, and κρέμαμαι hang are also treated as uncontracted: e.g. δύνωμαι, ἐπίσταιντο.

In other optative forms than those listed above, the diphthong formed with the optative suffix -ι- counts as uncontracted: e.g. παιδεύ·οι·μεν (contrast διδοῖμεν above), τιμή·σαι·σθε (contrast τιθεῖσθε above).

24.19   **Compound** verbs are recessive, but the accent cannot fall earlier than a syllable containing an augment or reduplication:

ἀπ-άγω carry away   e.g. ἀπῆγε (impf.), ἀπῆχε (pf.); contrast pres. imp. ἄπαγε

παρ-έχω provide   e.g. παρεῖχε (impf.) and παρέσχε (aor.); contrast pres. imp. πάρεχε

If a prefix has two syllables, the accent never recedes before the last syllable of the prefix: e.g. περίθες (aor. imp. περι-τίθημι put around), ἀπόδος (aor. imp. ἀπο-δίδωμι give away).

Non-Finite Verb Forms: Participles and Infinitives

24.20   The overview below details the accentuation of **participles** and **infinitives**:

– **Participles** have a **persistent** accent (→24.14). The base accent is provided by the nom. sg. masc. form: other cases (and genders) keep the *same accent* on the *same syllable* (counted from the front of the word), as long as this is not prohibited by the rule of limitation (marked (i) below), the σωτῆρᾰ-rule (ii) and the rules of contraction (iii).

– **Infinitives** (indeclinable forms) normally have the accent on the same syllable as the base accent of corresponding *active* participles (this often, but not always, holds for middle-passive infinitives as well); for details see the table.

		active	middle-passive
thematic present and future			
		base accent: paroxytone	*base accent: proparoxytone*
ppl.	nom. sg. masc. (base)	παιδεύ(σ)ων	παιδευ(σ)όμενος
	gen. sg. masc./neut.	παιδεύ(σ)οντος	παιδευ(σ)ομένου (i)
	dat. pl. masc./neut.	παιδεύ(σ)ουσι	παιδευ(σ)ομένοις (i)
	nom. sg. fem.	παιδεύ(σ)ουσᾰ	παιδευ(σ)ομένη (i)
	gen. sg. fem.	παιδευ(σ)ούσης (i)	παιδευ(σ)ομένης (i)
	gen. pl. fem.	παιδευ(σ)ουσῶν (<*-ᾱων) (i, iii)	παιδευ(σ)ομένων (i)
	nom./acc. sg. neut.	παιδεῦ(σ)ον (ii)	παιδευ(σ)όμενον
inf.		παιδεύ(σ)ειν	παιδεύ(σ)εσθαι
contract verbs (present)			
ppl.	nom. sg. masc. (base)	τιμῶν (<*-ᾱων) (iii)	τιμώμενος (<*-αόμενος)
	nom. sg. fem.	τιμῶσᾰ (<*-ᾱουσᾰ) (ii, iii)	τιμωμένη (i)
	nom./acc. sg. neut.	τιμῶν (<*-ᾱον) (iii)	τιμώμενον
inf.		τιμᾶν (<*-ᾱειν) (iii)	τιμᾶσθαι (<*-ᾱεσθαι) (ii, iii)
thematic aorist			
		base accent: oxytone	*base accent: proparoxytone*
ppl.	nom. sg. masc. (base)	λαβών	λαβόμενος
	gen. sg. masc./neut.	λαβόντος	λαβομένου (i)
	dat. pl. masc./neut.	λαβοῦσι (ii)	λαβομένοις (i)
	nom. sg. fem.	λαβοῦσᾰ (ii)	λαβομένη (i)
	gen. sg. fem.	λαβούσης	λαβομένης (i)
	gen. pl. fem.	λαβουσῶν (i, iii)	λαβομένων (i)
	nom./acc. sg. neut.	λαβόν	λαβόμενον
inf.		λαβεῖν (perispomenon)	λαβέσθαι
sigmatic aorist			
		base accent: paroxytone	*base accent: proparoxytone*
ppl.	nom. sg. masc. (base)	παιδεύσᾱς	παιδευσάμενος
	gen. sg. masc./neut.	παιδεύσαντος	παιδευσαμένου (i)
	dat. pl. masc./neut.	παιδεύσασι	παιδευσαμένοις (i)
	nom. sg. fem.	παιδεύσασᾰ	παιδευσαμένη (i)

		active	middle-passive
	gen. sg. fem.	παιδευσᾱ́σης (i)	παιδευσαμένης (i)
	gen. pl. fem.	παιδευσασῶν (i, iii)	παιδευσαμένων (i)
	nom./acc. sg. neut.	παιδεῦσᾰν (ii)	παιδευσάμενον
inf.		παιδεῦσαι (ii)	παιδεύσασθαι
		τρέψαι	τρέψασθαι

athematic stems (present of -μι verbs, root aorist, θη-/η-aorist)

		-μι verbs *base accent: oxytone*	*base accent: proparoxytone*
ppl.	nom. sg. masc. (base)	δεικνῡ́ς	δεικνύμενος
	gen. sg. masc./neut.	δεικνῡ́ντος	δεικνυμένου (i)
	dat. pl. masc./neut.	δεικνῦσι (ii)	δεικνυμένοις (i)
	nom. sg. fem.	δεικνῦσᾰ (ii)	δεικνυμένη (i)
	gen. sg. fem.	δεικνῡ́σης	δεικνυμένης (i)
	gen. pl. fem.	δεικνυσῶν (i, iii)	δεικνυμένων (i)
	nom./acc. sg. neut.	δεικνῡ́ν	δεικνύμενον
inf.		δεικνῦναι	δείκνυσθαι

		root aorists *base accent: oxytone*	*base accent: proparoxytone*
ppl.	nom. sg. masc. (base)	δούς	δόμενος
	gen. sg. masc./neut.	δόντος	δομένου (i)
	nom. sg. fem.	δοῦσᾰ (ii)	δομένη (i)
	gen. sg. fem.	δούσης	δομένης (i)
	nom./acc. sg. neut.	δόν	δόμενον
inf.		δοῦναι (ii)	δόσθαι

		θη-/η-aorists *base accent: oxytone*	
ppl.	nom. sg. masc. (base)	παιδευθείς	
	gen. sg. masc./neut.	παιδευθέντος	
	nom. sg. fem.	παιδευθεῖσᾰ (ii)	
	gen. sg. fem.	παιδευθείσης	
	nom./acc. sg.	παιδευθέν	
inf.		παιδευθῆναι (ii)	

perfect

		base accent: oxytone	*base accent: paroxytone*
ppl.	nom. sg. masc. (base)	πεπαιδευκώς	πεπαιδευμένος
	gen. sg. masc./neut.	πεπαιδευκότος	πεπαιδευμένου
	dat. pl. masc./neut.	πεπαιδευκόσι	πεπαιδευμένοις
	nom. sg. fem.	πεπαιδευκυῖᾰ (ii)	πεπαιδευμένη
	gen. sg. fem.	πεπαιδευκυίᾱς	πεπαιδευμένης
	gen. pl. fem.	πεπαιδευκυιῶν (i, iii)	πεπαιδευμένων
	nom./acc. sg. neut.	πεπαιδευκός	πεπαιδευμένον
inf.		πεπαιδευκέναι	πεπαιδεῦσθαι (ii)
		λελυκέναι	λελύσθαι

Note 1: Observe the differences in accent between several (pseudo-)sigmatic aorist forms ending in -σαι:

	verb stem ending in a long vowel/diphthong		verb stem ending in a short vowel	
	two or more syllables	*one syllable*	*two or more syllables*	*one syllable*
2 sg. aor. mid. imp. (recessive; -αι = short)	βούλευσαι	λῦσαι	κάλεσαι	τρέψαι
3 sg. aor. act. opt. (recessive; -αι = long)	βουλεύσαι	λύσαι	καλέσαι	τρέψαι
aor. act. inf. (not recessive)	βουλεῦσαι	λῦσαι	καλέσαι	τρέψαι

Nominal Forms: Nouns, Adjectives, Pronouns, Numerals

General Rules

24.21   Almost all nouns, adjectives and pronouns have a **persistent** accent (→24.14). The nom. sg. provides the (position of the) base accent of nouns; the nom. sg. masc. form provides the base accent of adjectives. Other cases (and genders) keep the accent on the same syllable, as long as this is not prohibited by the rule of limitation (marked (i) below), the σωτῆρᾰ-rule (ii) and the rules of contraction (iii).

This principle may be illustrated by the declensions of ὁ ἄνθρωπος *man*, ἡ θάλαττᾰ *sea*, ἡ χώρᾱ *place*, and τὸ ῥεῦμᾰ *current*:

		ὁ ἄνθρωπος	ἡ θάλαττᾰ	ἡ χώρᾱ	τὸ ῥεῦμᾰ
		man	*sea*	*place*	*current*
sg.	nom.	ἄνθρωπος	θάλαττᾰ	χώρᾱ	ῥεῦμᾰ (ii)
	gen.	ἀνθρώπου (i)	θαλάττης (i)	χώρᾱς	ῥεύματος
	dat.	ἀνθρώπῳ (i)	θαλάττῃ (i)	χώρᾳ	ῥεύματι
	acc.	ἄνθρωπον	θάλαττᾰν	χώρᾱν	ῥεῦμα (ii)
	voc.	ἄνθρωπε	θάλαττᾰ	χώρᾱ	ῥεῦμα (ii)
pl.	nom.	ἄνθρωποι	θάλατται	χῶραι (ii)	ῥεύματα
	gen.	ἀνθρώπων (i)	θαλαττῶν (<*-άων) (i, iii)	χωρῶν (<*-άων) (i, iii)	ῥευμάτων (i)
	dat.	ἀνθρώποις (i)	θαλάτταις (i)	χώραις	ῥεύμασι
	acc.	ἀνθρώπους (i)	θαλάττᾱς (i)	χώρᾱς	ῥεύματα

24.22   An additional rule affects nominal forms of the **first and second declensions** with a base accent on the **ultima**: the genitive and dative singular and plural forms of such words **always** have a **circumflex** accent.

This may be illustrated by the declensions of θεός *god(dess)*, the adjectives ἱερός *holy* and πολύς *much* and the article ὁ, ἡ, τό:

		θεός *god(dess)*	ἱερός *holy*		
			masc.	fem.	neut.
sg.	nom.	θεός	ἱερός	ἱερά	ἱερόν
	gen.	θεοῦ	ἱεροῦ	ἱερᾶς	ἱεροῦ
	dat.	θεῷ	ἱερῷ	ἱερᾷ	ἱερῷ
	acc.	θεόν	ἱερόν	ἱεράν	ἱερόν
pl.	nom.	θεοί	ἱεροί	ἱεραί	ἱερά
	gen.	θεῶν	ἱερῶν	ἱερῶν	ἱερῶν
	dat.	θεοῖς	ἱεροῖς	ἱεραῖς	ἱεροῖς
	acc.	θεούς	ἱερούς	ἱεράς	ἱερά

		πολύς *much*			ὁ, ἡ, τό		
		masc.	fem.	neut.	masc.	fem.	neut.
sg.	nom.	πολύς	πολλή	πολύ	ὁ	ἡ	τό
	gen.	πολλοῦ	πολλῆς	πολλοῦ	τοῦ	τῆς	τοῦ
	dat.	πολλῷ	πολλῇ	πολλῷ	τῷ	τῇ	τῷ
	acc.	πολύν	πολλήν	πολύ	τόν	τήν	τό
pl.	nom.	πολλοί	πολλαί	πολλά	οἱ	αἱ	τά
	gen.	πολλῶν	πολλῶν	πολλῶν	τῶν	τῶν	τῶν
	dat.	πολλοῖς	πολλαῖς	πολλοῖς	τοῖς	ταῖς	τοῖς
	acc.	πολλούς	πολλάς	πολλά	τούς	τάς	τά

Note 1: First-declension gen. pl. forms are (in Attic) contracted from -έων (<-ήων <-άων, →1.57), and are accordingly always accented -ῶν (cf. e.g. θαλαττῶν next to θάλαττα, θαλάττης; χωρῶν next to χώρα, etc).

This also holds for the feminine declension of many adjectives and participles, except when the gen. pl. fem. is *identical* in form to the masc. and neut.: in such cases, the accentuation of the masc./neut. is used in the fem. as well: so, e.g. masc./neut. μελάνων and fem. μελαινῶν (distinct forms, fem. accented -ῶν), but masc./fem./neut. μεγάλων (form and accent identical in all three genders); participles: masc./neut. παιδευόντων, fem. παιδευουσῶν, but masc./fem./neut. παιδευομένων.

Mobile Accentuation of Some Third-Declension Nouns

24.23   With **third-declension** nominal forms with a **monosyllabic stem**, the accent of the **genitive and dative** falls on the ending (an acute if the ending has a short vowel, a circumflex if it has a long vowel): so, e.g. the nouns μήν *month*, χείρ *hand*, πούς *foot*. This rule also applies to the inflected cardinals εἷς *one*, δύο *two* and τρεῖς *three*:

		μήν *month*	χείρ *hand*	πούς *foot*
sg.	nom.	μήν	χείρ	πούς
	gen.	μηνός	χειρός	ποδός
	dat.	μηνί	χειρί	ποδί
	acc.	μῆνᾰ	χεῖρᾰ	πόδᾰ
pl.	nom.	μῆνες	χεῖρες	πόδες
	gen.	μηνῶν	χειρῶν	ποδῶν
	dat.	μησί(ν)	χερσί(ν)	ποσί(ν)
	acc.	μῆνᾱς	χεῖρᾱς	πόδᾱς

		εἷς *one*			δύο *two*	τρεῖς *three*	
		masc.	fem.	neut.		masc./fem.	neut.
sg.	nom.	εἷς	μία	ἕν	δύο	τρεῖς	τρία
	gen.	ἑνός	μιᾶς	ἑνός	δυοῖν	τριῶν	τριῶν
	dat.	ἑνί	μιᾷ	ἑνί	δυοῖν	τρισί(ν)	τρισί(ν)
	acc.	ἕνα	μίαν	ἕν	δύο	τρεῖς	τρία

Note 1: Exceptions to this rule are the gen. pl. of παῖς *child, slave* (παίδων) and the gen. and dat. pl. masc./neut. of πᾶς, πᾶν *every, all* (πάντων, πᾶσιν, but παντός, παντί).

24.24   The noun ἀνήρ *man* also has mobile accentuation: ἀνήρ, ἀνδρός, ἀνδρί, ἄνδρα; ἄνδρες, ἀνδρῶν, ἀνδράσι, ἄνδρας. With the nouns πατήρ *father*, μήτηρ *mother*, γαστήρ *stomach*, θυγάτηρ *daughter*, the accent falls on the ending in the gen. and dat. sg, but not in the gen. pl. and dat. pl. Thus e.g. πατήρ, πατρός, πατρί, πατέρα; πατέρες, πατέρων, πατράσι, πατέρας. For these nouns, →4.62–4.

Some Rules for the Placement of Base Accents on Nominal Forms

24.25   The rules that determine the placement of the base accent on nouns and adjectives with persistent accentuation are complex. Only very limited guidance is given in the sections below; for more information, specialized reference works may be consulted (see the Bibliography at the end of this book); the accentuation of some types of regularly formed nouns and adjectives is also treated in 23.

24.26   Most proper names are recessive, e.g. Πεισίστρατος, Νικίας, Μυρρίνη, Νέαιρᾰ, Πλάτων, Ἀριστοτέλης, Διογένης. Note that names in -κλῆς (Ἡρακλῆς, Σοφοκλῆς) owe their perispomenon accent to contraction -κλῆς < -κλέης.

Exceptions are names ending in -εύς (Ἀχιλλεύς, Περσεύς, Ζεύς) and in -ώ (Καλυψώ, Σαπφώ, Λαμπιτώ), which have acute in nominative and circumflex in vocative (Ζεῦ, Σαπφοῖ).

24.27   Nouns ending in short -ᾰ are recessive: ἀλήθειᾰ *truth*, γαῖᾰ *earth*, θάλαττᾰ *sea*, δόξᾰ *opinion*.

24.28   Neuter third-declension nouns are recessive: ὄνειδος *rebuke*, ὄνομα *name*, πρᾶγμα *affair, deed*.

24.29 Most compound nouns and adjectives are recessive, e.g. σύμβολον *symbol, token*; περίπατος *a walk*; ἄμορφος *misshapen, shapeless*; πρόδρομος *running ahead*.

Exceptions are compound adjectives ending in -ής, which are mostly oxytone, e.g. ἀκλεής *without fame*; συμπρεπής *befitting*; εὐτυχής *successful*.

For the difference in accentuation between such forms as λιθόβολος *struck with stones* and λιθοβόλος *throwing stones*, →23.40 n.1.

24.30 Many adjectives have an oxytone base accent:

- nearly all non-compound adjectives in -υς, e.g. ταχύς *quick*, ὀξύς *sharp*, ἡδύς *sweet*, βραχύς *short*; exceptions are θῆλυς *feminine* and ἥμισυς *half*;
- most adjectives in -ης, many of which are compounds (→24.29), e.g. ἀληθής *true*, ὑγιής *healthy*, εὐτυχής *successful*, ἀσθενής *weak*; there are several exceptions, however (e.g. πλήρης *full*, εὐήθης *good-hearted*);
- a large number of adjectives in -ος, e.g. ἀγαθός *good, noble*, καλός *fine, beautiful*, ξενικός *foreign* (so all adjectives in -ικός), δεινός *impressive*, αἰσχρός *shameful, ugly* (and most other adjectives in -νος or -ρος); but there are numerous exceptions (e.g. γνώριμος *familiar*, πλούσιος *rich*, δύστηνος *wretched*, ἐλεύθερος *free*; also →24.32).

24.31 Adverbs ending in -ως are accented in the same way as the corresponding adjective's genitive masculine plural: e.g. ἀληθῶς *truly* (gen. pl. masc. ἀληθῶν), ὀξέως *sharply* (gen. pl. masc. ὀξέων); for details, →6.3.

24.32 Comparatives and superlatives are properly recessive in all their forms (there is no base accent, meaning that the accent may fall further from the end of a form than in the corresponding nom. sg. masc.): e.g. δεινότερος *more impressive*, δεινότατος *most impressive*; ἀληθέστερος *more truthful*, ἀληθέστατος *most truthful*; ἀμείνων *better* (note neut. ἄμεινον), ἄριστος *best*; κακίων *worse* (note neut. κάκιον), κάκιστος *worst*; μείζων *greater* (neut. μεῖζον), μέγιστος *greatest*.

Enclitics and Proclitics

Introduction

24.33 Two groups of words do not have an accent of their own (though they may acquire one in a sentence):

- **enclitics**: unaccented words that 'lean back on' (cf. ἐγκλίνομαι) the preceding word and together with this word form a single unit in pronunciation;
- **proclitics**: words that 'lean towards' (cf. προκλίνομαι) the following word and together with this word form a single unit in pronunciation.

Note 1: Enclitics and (unaccented) proclitics were pronounced with a lower pitch than the accented syllable of the word on which they 'leaned'.

24.34   The following words are **enclitic**:

- the indefinite pronoun τις and all its forms (τινος/του, τινι/τῳ, τινα, τινων, etc.), except ἄττα (→7.24);
- indefinite adverbs such as πω, που, ποι, πῃ, ποτε, ποθεν, ποθι (→8.2);
- unaccented forms of the personal pronoun (→7.1–2): μου, μοι, με, σου, σοι, σε, ἑ, οὑ, οἱ, μιν, νιν, σφε, etc.;
- the particles γε, τε, νυ(ν) (not the adverb νῦν), τοι, περ;
- present indicative forms of εἰμι *be* and φημι *say, claim* except the 2 sg. forms εἶ and φής/φῄς (note that this last form is not recessive, →24.17).

Note 1: Alongside enclitic 3 sg. ἐστι *he/she/it is*, there is a recessive form ἔστι, used at the start of the clause, in the 'existential' use *there is* (→26.10), *it is possible* (= ἔξεστι), and when it follows οὐκ, μή, εἰ, ὡς, καί, ἀλλά or τοῦτο.

24.35   The following words are **proclitic**:

- the forms of the article that begin with a vowel: ὁ, ἡ, οἱ, αἱ;
- the prepositions ἐν, εἰς/ἐς, ἐκ/ἐξ, ὡς;
- the conjunctions εἰ and ὡς;
- the negative οὐ/οὐκ/οὐχ.

The following also behave like proclitics, but are always written with an accent; they are often called **prepositives** to distinguish them from the proper proclitics:

- other forms of the article: τοῦ, τῆς, τοῖς, ταῖς, τά, etc.;
- other prepositions: ἀνά, ἀπό, διά, ἐπί, πρός, σύν/ξύν, ὑπό, etc.;
- the conjunctions/particles ἀλλά, καί, οὐδέ, μηδέ, ἐπεί, ἤ;
- the negative μή.

24.36   The negative οὐ/οὐκ/οὐχ has an accented counterpart (οὔ/οὔκ/οὔχ) which serves as an emphatic negative, used when it stands before punctuation, as in πῶς γὰρ οὔ; *of course*; this occurs especially in answers (→38.21).

24.37   Two-syllable prepositions have the accent on the ultima; this normally changes to a grave, e.g. ἀπὸ τῶν νεῶν *away from the ships*, περὶ παίδων *about children*. However, when the preposition is placed after the noun which it governs (anastrophe, →60.14) the accent recedes to the first syllable, e.g. νεῶν ἄπο *away from the ships*, παίδων πέρι *about the children*.

The accent also recedes to the first syllable when a preposition is used instead of a compound form with ἐστι or εἰσι, e.g. πάρα = πάρεστι/πάρεισι, ἔνι = ἔνεστι/ἔνεισι, ἔπι = ἔπεστι/ἔπεισι, μέτα = μέτεστι/μέτεισι. This occurs mainly in poetry, and particularly frequently with the impersonal use of πάρεστι, ἔνεστι, μέτεστι (→36.6).

Accentuation of Enclitics and Proclitics

24.38   The following rules apply to enclitics and the words they follow:

- **oxytone word + enclitic**: the acute on the preceding word remains in place and does not change into a grave (*x·x·x́ e*), e.g. ποιμήν τις *a certain shepherd* (but ποιμὴν εἷς *one shepherd*), οὐ γάρ που *for not, I think* (but οὐ γὰρ δή *for not, indeed*);

- **perispomenon word + enclitic**: no change (*x·x·x̂ e*), e.g. ἦν τις ἀνήρ *there was a certain man*, ἐμοῦ γε ὄντος *at least while I am alive*;

- **proparoxytone word + enclitic**: a second acute is added to the ultima of the preceding word (*x́·x·x́ e*), e.g. λέαινά τις *a certain lioness*; ἄνθρωπός τε *and a man*, παιδεύουσί τινες *some people educate*;

- **properispomenon word + enclitic**: an acute is added to the ultima of the preceding word (*x·x̂·x́ e*), e.g. οἶκός τις *a (certain) house*; δῶρόν τε *and a gift*, σωτῆρά τινα *a certain saviour*;

- **paroxytone word + monosyllabic enclitic**: no change (*x·x́·x e*), e.g. παρθένος τις *a certain maiden*, πολέμου γε ὄντος *at least at a time of war*;

- **paroxytone word + two-syllable enclitic**: an acute/grave is added to the second syllable of the enclitic (*x·x́·x e·é*; τινων gets a circumflex), e.g. παρθένοι τινές *certain maidens*, ἄλλων τινῶν *some others*, ὅστις ἐστὶ μὴ κακός *whoever is not base*;

- if an **enclitic** is **followed by another enclitic**, an auxiliary accent is placed on the (last syllable of the) first enclitic, e.g. ἦσάν τινές ποτε παρθένοι *once there were certain maidens*; τοῦτό γέ μοι δοκεῖ καλὸν εἶναι *this, I think, is beautiful*.

Note 1: As these rules show, forms of indefinite (enclitic) τις *a certain, some(one)* with two syllables are accented, if at all, on the second syllable (e.g. τινά, τινές, τινῶν): this allows easy distinction from two-syllable forms of interrogative τίς *who?, which?* (e.g. τίνα, τίνες, τίνων). Similarly, when accented at all, indefinite πού *somewhere* (or the particle πού *I suppose*), ποτέ *sometime*, πή *somehow*, etc., are always distinct from interrogative ποῦ *where?*, πότε *when?*, πῇ *how?*, etc.

Only when monosyllabic enclitic τις or τι receive an acute do these forms overlap with interrogative τίς/τί (always with acute, →24.2), but context then allows distinction between the two.

24.39   Proclitics do not affect the accentuation of other words. However, if an unaccented **proclitic is followed by an enclitic**, the proclitic gets an acute: e.g. οἵ τε ἄνδρες καὶ γυναῖκες *the men and women*.

Observe that οὔτε/μήτε *neither*, εἴτε *or*, εἴπερ *if indeed*, ὥστε *so that, so as to*, ὥσπερ *as if*, which are accented according to this rule, are written as one word. Note that these words appear to violate the σωτῆρᾰ-rule; so too certain forms of ὅδε: τήνδε, τούσδε, τάσδε.

Elision and Crasis

24.40   **Elision** (→1.34–8): if a vowel which would be accented is elided, the accent recedes to the previous syllable as an acute, e.g. σόφ᾽ εἰδέναι *to know wise things* (= σοφὰ εἰδέναι), λάβ᾽ ἄλλα *take other things* (= λαβὲ ἄλλα), αὔτ᾽ ἐάσω *I will let these things lie* (= αὐτὰ ἐάσω).

However, this does not happen with most elided prepositions or particles, e.g. ἀλλ᾽ εἶπε *but he said* (= ἀλλὰ εἶπε); οὐδ᾽ εἶπε *and/but he did not say* (= οὐδὲ εἶπε); παρ᾽ αὐτῶν *from them* (= παρὰ αὐτῶν).

24.41   If a two-syllable enclitic follows an elided word (this happens particularly with forms of εἰμί), an acute or grave is added to the second syllable of the enclitic, e.g. οὐχ ὑγιεία μεγάλη τοῦτ᾽ ἐστί; *Is this not a very healthy thing?*, ἄτιμοι δ᾽ ἐσμὲν οἱ πρὸ τοῦ φίλοι *We who were previously friends are held in disregard.*

24.42   **Crasis** (→1.43–5): the first word of two that merge in crasis loses its accent; the accentuation of the second word remains unchanged: e.g. ὦνθρωπε (= ὦ ἄνθρωπε), τοὐρανοῦ (= τοῦ οὐρανοῦ), τἀν (= τὰ ἐν). But the σωτῆρᾱ-rule takes precedence: τοὔργον (= τὸ ἔργον, not †τοῦργον).

25

Ionic and Other Dialects

Introduction

25.1   Different dialects of Greek were spoken throughout Greece: the Spartans, for example, spoke Laconian, the Thebans Boeotian, and the Milesians Ionic. Until the third century BCE, our written sources attest about thirty such dialects apart from (and different to a greater or smaller extent from) Attic, the dialect used in Athens in the classical period, which this grammar primarily treats.

The attested dialects are usually classified as belonging to the following four groups:

- **Attic**-**Ionic** dialects (Attica, Euboea, the Cyclades and Ionia);
- **Arcado**-**Cypriot** dialects (Arcadia in the Peloponnese, and Cyprus);
- **Aeolic** dialects (Thessaly, Boeotia and the north-eastern Aegean; Lesbian, the dialect of the lyric poetry of Sappho and Alcaeus, belongs to this category);
- **West Greek** dialects (also sometimes called 'Doric' dialects; north-western and central Greece, most parts of the Peloponnese, and many colonies across the Mediterranean, e.g. Syracuse on Sicily).

25.2   Alongside the dialects of everyday and official language, **literary dialects** developed within Greek literature. These were based on the spoken dialects, but came to be identified with specific genres of Greek literature to such an extent that in the course of time it was primarily the choice of genre (not the origin of the author) that determined the literary dialect used.

The four main literary dialects that are distinguished until the end of the fourth century are the following:

- **Attic**:

    Tragedy and comedy (spoken parts): e.g. Aeschylus, Sophocles, Euripides, Aristophanes (fifth century)
    Historiography: e.g. Thucydides (fifth century), Xenophon (fourth century)
    Oratory: e.g. Lysias, Demosthenes, Isocrates (fourth century)
    Philosophical dialogue: e.g. Plato, Xenophon (fourth century)

- **Ionic**:

    Epic: e.g. Homer, Hesiod (eighth century) (but see n.1)
    Elegiac: e.g. Archilochus, Tyrtaeus, Solon (seventh–sixth century)
    Historiography: e.g. Herodotus (fifth century)
    Medical writings: Hippocratic corpus (fifth century and later)

– **Aeolic/Lesbian:**

Lyric: Alcaeus and Sappho (seventh–sixth century)

– **Doric:**

Choral lyric: e.g. Alcman, Stesichorus, Bacchylides, Pindar (sixth–fifth century)
Tragedy and comedy (choral parts have a superficial Doric 'colouring'):
e.g. Aeschylus, Sophocles, Euripides, Aristophanes (fifth century)

Note 1: All literary dialects are to a certain extent artificial constructs, only partially representing spoken language. The language of the Homeric epics is a special case – a blend of forms from different dialects (primarily Ionic, with older Aeolic elements and some traces of a dialect that was in use during the Mycenaean era), and wholly artificial forms created for metrical convenience. The language of Homeric epic greatly influenced later Greek poetry throughout antiquity. In the Hellenistic period it was studied in depth at the Library of Alexandria, and affiliated third-century poets like Theocritus (who wrote a highly stylized form of Doric), Callimachus and Apollonius modelled their own poetry on it.

25.3   Already in the classical period a version of Attic with several Ionic features was adopted as a common language for commerce, diplomacy and officialdom. In the Hellenistic period this formed the basis for the **Koine** (κοινή, 'common') dialect that came to be used across the Mediterranean and the Near East for (administrative and literary) writing and increasingly also as spoken language (presumably still with regional variations). The Koine was used, among others, by Polybius (second century BCE), Josephus (first century CE), Arrian and Plutarch (second century CE), by the translators of the *Septuagint* (third century BCE) and by the authors of the *New Testament* (first century CE). It is the basis of all later forms of Greek, including present-day Modern Greek.

25.4   This chapter is confined to a summary of the characteristics of the main non-Attic dialect of the classical period, the **Ionic literary prose** dialect of the historian Herodotus (→25.5–45). A few observations about the 'Doric' ᾱ in the dialect of choral lyric (→25.46–7) are given at the end of the chapter. For more extensive treatments of the different Greek dialects, specialized works may be consulted (see the Bibliography at the end of this book).

Note 1: Some Attic authors use certain forms which are Ionic rather than strictly Attic. Thus, for instance, Thucydides and the tragedians write -σσ- rather than -ττ- (→1.77) and -ρσ- rather than -ρρ- (→1.84 n.1); Thucydides has ἐς (→25.14) rather than εἰς (the two alternate in tragedy), etc.

Ionic Literary Prose

Phonology

25.5 Original ᾱ **always changed to η**, also after ε, ι and ρ (for Attic, →1.57):

e.g. γενεή *generation*, οἰκίη *house*, χώρη *land*, πρῆγμα *thing*, κρητήρ *mixing bowl*, νεηνίης *young man* (Att. γενεά, οἰκίᾱ, χώρᾱ, πρᾶγμα, κρᾱτήρ, νεᾱνίᾱς)

Note 1: ᾱ resulting from (second stage) compensatory lengthening (→1.57 n.2) has not changed: πᾶσα <*πάντ-yα (not: †πῆσα), acc. pl. δόξᾱς <*δόξανς (not: †δόξης).

25.6 Ionic has the following rules of **contraction** (→1.58–66):

- εα, εε, εει, εη, εω and οο are often left uncontracted: e.g. nom./acc. pl. γένεα *races*, mp. inf. ποιέεσθαι *do, make*, act. inf. ποιέειν *do*, Ἡρακλέης *Heracles*, Ποσειδέων *Poseidon*, νόος *mind* (Att. γένη, ποιεῖσθαι, ποιεῖν, Ἡρακλῆς, Ποσειδῶν, νοῦς).
- εο is either left uncontracted or made into a diphthong ευ: e.g. 1 pl. mp. ind. ποιεόμεθα, ποιεύμεθα *we do*, gen. ἐμέο, ἐμεῦ (Att. ποιούμεθα, ἐμοῦ).
- οη is more often contracted to ω than in Attic, where it is sometimes left uncontracted: e.g. 1 sg. aor. ind. ἐβῶσα *cried* (Att. ἐβόησα).
- when uncontracted εε is followed by a vowel, one ε has disappeared; this is called **hyphaeresis** (ὑφαιρέω *take out*): e.g. 2 sg. imp. ἡγέο *lead, consider* (<*ἡγέεο), gen. sg. Ἡρακλέος (<Ἡρακλέεος), 2 sg. ind. φοβέαι *you fear* (<*φοβέ-εαι) (Att. ἡγοῦ, Ἡρακλέους, φοβεῖ/-ῇ).

25.7 In both Attic and Ionic the rules of **quantitative metathesis** apply (→1.71), but in Ionic no subsequent contraction has taken place: e.g. 1st decl. gen. pl. ending -έων (<-ήων <-άων), χρέωμαι *use* (<*χρήομαι), aor. subj. θέω *put, place* (<*θήω), pl. θέωμεν (<*θήομεν) (Att. -ῶν, χρῶμαι, θῶ, θῶμεν).

25.8 For Att. ει(ο), Ionic has ηϊ(ο) in many nouns (e.g. μαντήϊον *oracle*, χαλκήϊον *cauldron*) and adjectives (e.g. βασιλήϊος *royal*, γυναικήϊος *of a woman*) and in some verbs (e.g. οἰκηϊόω *appropriate*, κληΐω *shut*) (Att. μαντεῖον, χαλκεῖον, βασίλειος, γυναικεῖος, οἰκειόω, κλείω).

Exceptions are θεῖος *divine*, proper names like Δαρεῖος *Darius* and ethnic adjectives (Ἀργεῖος *Argive*, Ἠλεῖος *Elean*).

25.9 Ionic has lost the aspirate [h] (→1.7) at the beginning of words/stems: this is called **psilosis** ('baring', 'stripping'). The rough breathing is however written in Ionic texts by convention. As a result, psilosis can only be observed in the case of elision (→1.34) and compounds (→1.35):

e.g. ἀπ' οὗ *since*, κάτημαι *be seated*, ἀπαιρέω *remove*, μετίημι *abandon*, κάτοδος *return* (Att. ἀφ' οὗ, κάθημαι, ἀφαιρέω, μεθίημι, κάθοδος).

Note 1: The aspirated stops (θ, φ, χ) have *not* lost aspiration: χώρη (not: †κώρη).
Note 2: Because of psilosis, the form κατά can be both conjunction (Att. καθά/καθ᾽ ἅ *just as*) and preposition (Att. κατά)

25.10   Ionic has σσ (<*κy/*τy, →1.77) where Attic has ττ:

e.g. φυλάσσω *guard* (<*φυλάκ-yω), ἥσσων *worse* (<*ἧκ-yων), μέλισσᾰ *bee* (<*μέλιτ-yᾰ) (Att. φυλάττω, ἥττων, μέλιττᾰ).

Note 1: If Att. ττ is not the result of *κy/*τy, Ionic has ττ as well: e.g. in toponyms such as Ἀττική *Attica*, proper names such as Ἀλυάττης *Alyattes*, and the loanword ἀττέλεβος *locust*.

25.11   The loss of ϝ after most consonants (→1.80–2) has normally led to compensatory lengthening (→1.68–9) of a preceding vowel:

e.g. ξεῖνος *stranger, guest-friend* (<*ξένϝος), μοῦνος *alone* (<*μόνϝος) (Att. ξένος, μόνος).

25.12   Indefinite, interrogative and indefinite relative pronouns have κ- instead of π-:

e.g. κοῦ *where?*, κου *somewhere*, ὅκου *where*; κότε *when?*, κοτε *once*, ὁκότε *when*, etc. (Att. ποῦ, που, ὅπου; πότε, ποτε, ὁπότε)

But τίς *who?*, τις *someone* and ὅστις *whoever* have τ-.

25.13   Assimilation of ρσ to ρρ (→1.84 n.1) has not taken place in Ionic: e.g. ἄρσην *male, masculine*, θάρσος *courage* (Att. ἄρρην, θάρρος).

25.14   Observe the following further phonological particulars:

- τωὐτό *the same*, ἑωυτοῦ, -τῷ *himself*, etc. (Att. ταὐτό, ἑαυτοῦ, -τῷ, etc.);
- τρῶμα *disaster*, θῶμα *(object of) admiration*, θωμάζω *admire* (Att. τραῦμα, θαῦμα, θαυμάζω);
- gen. sg. βασιλέος *king* (Att. βασιλέως, →4.84–5);
- comparatives μέζων *bigger*, κρέσσων *better, stronger* (Att., irregularly: μείζων, κρείττων);
- 1 pl. ind. of οἶδα *know*: ἴδμεν (Att. ἴσμεν);
- γίνομαι *become, be born*, γινώσκω *(get to) know* (γ lost with compensatory lengthening; Att. γίγνομαι, γιγνώσκω);
- ὦν (Att. οὖν);
- the ppl. of εἰμί *be* is ἐών (Att. ὤν), →25.40 below;
- ἐς *(in)to* (Att. normally: εἰς);
- οὔνομα *name*, εἵνεκα/εἵνεκεν *because, due to* (Att. ὄνομα, ἕνεκα);
- ἐπεάν/ἐπήν (ἐπεί + ἄν; Att. normally ἐπάν);
- ἤν *if* (εἰ + ἄν; Att. ἐάν/ἄν/ἤν).

Note 1: Editions of Herodotus do not normally print movable ν (→1.39) except in quoted hexameter poetry: e.g. ἔδοξε αὐτοῖσι (not ἔδοξεν), ἐστι ἄνθρωπος (not ἐστιν). Whether or not Herodotus actually used movable ν is unclear; in any case it is left out in the tables below.

Morphology: Nominal Forms

First Declension

25.15   Feminine words (→4.3–7):

– type φυγή *flight*, χώρη *land* (Att. φυγή, χώρᾱ):

	sg.	pl.
nom. = voc.	χώρη	χῶραι
gen.	χώρης	χωρέων (<*-ήων, Att. -ῶν)
dat.	χώρῃ	χώρῃσι (Att. -αις)
acc.	χώρην	χώρᾱς

– type δόξᾰ *opinion*:

	sg.	pl.
nom. = voc.	δόξᾰ	δόξαι
gen.	δόξης	δοξέων (<*-ήων, Att. -ῶν)
dat.	δόξῃ	δόξῃσι (Att. -αις)
acc.	δόξᾰν	δόξᾱς

Note 1: Some abstract nouns of the Att. διάνοιᾰ type are in Ionic declined like χώρη: e.g. ἀληθείη *truth*, εὐνοίη *good will* (Att. ἀλήθειᾰ, εὔνοιᾰ). Also →23.11.

25.16   Masculine words, type δεσπότης *master* (→4.8–12):

	sg.	pl.
nom.	δεσπότης	δεσπόται
gen.	δεσπότεω (<*-ηο, Att. -ου)	δεσποτέων (<*-ήων, Att. -ῶν)
dat.	δεσπότῃ	δεσπότῃσι (Att. -αις)
acc.	δεσπότην	δεσπότᾱς
voc.	δέσποτᾰ	= nom.

In Ionic -ης, etc. are also used after ε, ι, ρ (→25.5): hence ὁ νεηνίης *young man* (Att. νεᾱνίᾱς), ὁ ταμίης *treasurer* (Att. ταμίᾱς).

Note 1: Some proper names of this category occasionally have a genitive in -εος (Ὀτάνεος *Otanes*) and/or an accusative in -εα (Γύγεα *Gyges*, Ξέρξεα *Xerxes*), imported from the third declension. These forms occur alongside those given above (e.g. Ξέρξην).
Note 2: Ionic uses ὁ πολιήτης *citizen* (Att. πολίτης).

Second Declension

25.17   Types δοῦλος *slave*, δῶρον *gift* (→4.19–26): the **dat. pl.** ends in **-οισι** (Att. -οις).

25.18   Types νόος *mind*, ὀστέον *bone* (Att. νοῦς, ὀστοῦν, →4.19-26): forms are uncontracted (→25.6 above). E.g.:

	sg.	pl.
nom.	ν<u>όο</u>ς (Att. νοῦς)	ν<u>όο</u>ι (Att. νοῖ)
gen.	ν<u>όο</u>υ (Att. νοῦ)	ν<u>όω</u>ν (Att. νῶν)
dat.	ν<u>όῳ</u> (Att. νῷ)	ν<u>όο</u>ισι (Att. νοῖς)
acc.	ν<u>όο</u>ν (Att. νοῦν)	ν<u>όο</u>υς (Att. νοῦς)
voc.	ν<u>όε</u> (Att. νοῦ)	

25.19   The Attic second declension (→4.27) is not consistently used. Both λεώς *band, army* and older λᾱός are found in Herodotus (possibly owing to confusion in the manuscript tradition); νηός *temple* is generally preferred over νεώς.

Third Declension

25.20   **Stems ending in labial** (π, β, φ), **velar** (κ, γ, χ) and **dental stops** (τ, δ, θ), and stems ending in ντ, ν, λ, ρ and (ε)ρ (πατήρ *father*, ἀνήρ *man*) display no differences between Attic and Ionic. For their declensions, →4.35, 4.40, 4.45, 4.49, 4.55, 4.62. Observe that instead of φύλαξ Ionic uses second-declension ὁ φύλακος *guard*.

Note 1: χάρις *favour, gratitude* (χαριτ-) and ὄρνις *bird* (ὀρνιθ-) have acc. sg. forms ending in -ν and -α: χάριν and χάριτα; ὄρνιν and ὄρνιθα.

25.21   **Stems ending in σ** (→4.65–73); type γένος *race*, Πολυκράτης *Polycrates*, Ἡρακλέης *Heracles*; the endings are uncontracted (→25.6).

	sg.	pl.
nom.	γέν<u>ος</u>	γέν<u>εα</u> (Att. γένη)
gen.	γέν<u>εος</u> (Att. γένους)	γεν<u>έων</u> (Att. γενῶν)
dat.	γέν<u>εϊ</u> (Att. γένει)	γέν<u>ε</u>σι
acc.	γέν<u>ος</u>	γέν<u>εα</u> (Att. γένη)
nom.	Πολυκράτης	Θεμιστοκλ<u>έης</u> (Att. -κλῆς)
gen.	Πολυκράτ<u>εος</u> (Att. -κράτους)	Θεμιστοκλ<u>έος</u> (<*-κλέεος, *hyphaeresis*, →25.6; Att. -κλέους)
dat.	Πολυκράτ<u>εϊ</u> (Att. -κράτει)	Θεμιστοκλ<u>έϊ</u> (<*-κλέεϊ; Att. -κλεῖ)
acc.	Πολυκράτ<u>εα</u> (Att. -κράτη, -ην)	Θεμιστοκλ<u>έ</u>ᾱ (<*-κλέεα; Att. -κλέᾱ)
voc.	Πολύκρατες	Θεμιστόκλ<u>εες</u> (Att. -κλεις)

25.22 **Stems ending in ι** (→4.74–6); type πόλις *city*; there is no ablaut variation (cf. Att. οἶς *sheep* →4.77):

	sg.	pl.
nom.	πόλῐς	πόλῐες (Att. πόλεις)
gen.	πόλῐος (Att. πόλεως)	πολί̄ων (Att. πόλεων)
dat.	πόλῑ (Att. πόλει)	πόλῐσι (Att. πόλεσι(ν))
acc.	πόλῐν	πόλῑς (<*-ινς, Att. πόλεις)
voc.	πόλῐ	= nom.

Note 1: πόλις in modern editions of prose texts (without indication of vowel length) can be both nom. sg. and acc. pl.

25.23 **Stems ending in υ** (→4.79–83); the type without ablaut (ἰσχύς *strength*) is declined as in Attic; the type *with* ablaut (πῆχυς *forearm*, ἄστυ *town*) has uncontracted endings:

	sg.	pl.
nom.	πῆχυς	πήχεες (Att. πήχεις)
gen.	πήχεος (Att. πήχεως)	πήχεων
dat.	πήχεϊ (Att. πήχει)	πήχεσι
acc.	πῆχυν	πήχεας (Att. πήχεις)
nom.	ἄστυ	ἄστεα (Att. ἄστη)
gen.	ἄστεος (Att. ἄστεως)	ἄστεων
dat.	ἄστεϊ (Att. ἄστει)	ἄστεσι
acc.	ἄστυ	ἄστεα (Att. ἄστη)

25.24 **Stems ending in ευ** (type βασιλεύς *king*, →4.84–5):

	sg.	pl.
nom.	βασιλεύς	βασιλέες (Att. βασιλεῖς/-ῆς)
gen.	βασιλέος (Att. βασιλέως)	βασιλέων
dat.	βασιλέϊ (Att. βασιλεῖ)	βασιλεῦσι
acc.	βασιλέα (Att. βασιλέᾱ)	βασιλέᾱς (Att. βασιλέᾱς, βασιλεῖς)
voc.	βασιλεῦ	= voc.

25.25 **ναῦς** *ship* (→4.86–7):

	sg.	pl.
nom.	νηῦς (Att. ναῦς)	νέες (Att. νῆες)
gen.	νεός (Att. νεώς)	νεῶν
dat.	νηΐ	νηυσί (Att. ναυσί(ν))
acc.	νέᾱ (Att. ναῦν)	νέᾱς (Att. ναῦς)

Ζεύς *Zeus* and **βοῦς** *ox* are declined as in Attic (→4.86–7).

The Article, Adjectives

25.26   The **article** is declined in accordance with the rules given for the first and second declensions above (→25.15–18), but the gen. pl. fem. is identical to the masc./neut. (τῶν). Forms different from the Attic declension (→3.1) are underlined:

	sg.			*pl.*		
	masc.	*fem.*	*neut.*	*masc.*	*fem.*	*neut.*
nom.	ὁ	ἡ	τό	οἱ	αἱ	τά
gen.	τοῦ	τῆς	τοῦ	τῶν	τῶν	τῶν
dat.	τῷ	τῇ	τῷ	<u>τοῖσι</u>	<u>τῇσι</u>	<u>τοῖσι</u>
acc.	τόν	τήν	τό	τούς	τάς	τά

25.27   **Adjectives** follow, depending on their patterns of declension (for which, →5), the paradigms given above. Some specific points:

- first-and-second-declension adjectives which are contracted in Attic (type χρυσοῦς *gold(en)*, →5.5) are not contracted in Ionic, e.g. dat. pl. masc./neut. χρυσέοισι (Att. χρυσοῖς), dat. sg. fem. σιδερέη *iron* (Att. σιδηρᾷ);
- πλέος, πλέη, πλέον *full* (Att. πλέως, πλέα, πλέων, →5.12);
- πολλός, πολλή, πολλόν *large, many*, declined regularly (Att. πολύς, →5.13–14);
- adjectives ending in -ης (type ἀληθής *true*, with a stem in εσ, →5.28–30) have uncontracted forms: e.g. ἀληθέος (Att. ἀληθοῦς), ἀληθέες (Att. ἀληθεῖς), etc.;
- adjectives ending in -υς (type ἡδύς *sweet*, with a stem in υ/εϝ, →5.21–2) have uncontracted forms in the masc. and neut., e.g. ἡδέες (Att. ἡδεῖς), and the feminine is declined ἡδέα, ἡδέης, etc. (Att. ἡδεῖα, ἡδείας, etc.).

Pronouns

25.28   **Personal pronouns** (accented and unaccented, →7.1–2); forms different from Attic are underlined:

		first person	*second person*	*third person (for Att., →7.2)*
sg.	*nom.*	ἐγώ	σύ	—
	gen.	<u>ἐμέο</u> (Att. ἐμοῦ); <u>μευ</u>, μου	<u>σέο</u>; <u>σεο, σευ</u> (Att. σοῦ; σου)	<u>εὔ</u>
	dat.	ἐμοί; μοι	σοί; σοι, <u>τοι</u>	οἷ; οἱ
	acc.	ἐμέ; με	σέ; σε	<u>μιν</u>
pl.	*nom.*	ἡμεῖς, <u>ἡμέες</u>	ὑμεῖς, <u>ὑμέες</u>	(σφεῖς)
	gen.	<u>ἡμέων</u> (Att. ἡμῶν)	<u>ὑμέων</u> (Att. ὑμῶν)	<u>σφέων</u> (Att. σφῶν); <u>σφεων</u>
	dat.	ἡμῖν	ὑμῖν	σφίσι; σφισι; σφι
	acc.	<u>ἡμέας</u> (Att. ἡμᾶς)	<u>ὑμέας</u> (Att. ὑμᾶς)	<u>σφέας</u> (Att. σφᾶς); <u>σφεας</u>; neut. <u>σφέα</u>; <u>σφε, σφεα</u> (no Att. equivalents)

Note 1: ἑ (3 sg. acc., →7.2) is used in Herodotus only in quoted hexameter poetry.
Note 2: τοι is also used in Herodotus with the force of an attitudinal particle, for which →59.51.

25.29   For **forms of αὐτός in crasis** (τωὐτά = τὰ αὐτά; reflexive pronoun ἑωυτοῦ), →25.14.

25.30   **Interrogative and indefinite pronouns**: apart from the regular third-declension forms (→7.24), some second-declension forms are used: gen. sg. τέο/τεῦ, dat. τέῳ, gen. pl. τέων, dat. τέοισι.

       Hence also indefinite relative pronouns such as ὅτεο, ὁτέοισι, etc.

25.31   **Relative pronouns**: the form of the relative pronoun is identical with the article in all cases except the nom. sg. masc. ὅς, and with respect to accentuation, the nom. sg. fem. ἥ and the nom. pl. masc./fem. οἵ and αἵ:

	sg.			pl.		
	masc.	fem.	neut.	masc.	fem.	neut.
nom.	ὅς	ἥ	τό	οἵ	αἵ	τά
gen.	τοῦ	τῆς	τοῦ	τῶν	τῶν	τῶν
dat.	τῷ	τῇ	τῷ	τοῖσι	τῇσι	τοῖσι
acc.	τόν	τήν	τό	τούς	τάς	τά

Example: δοῦναι τὸ ἀνθρώπῳ τυχεῖν ἄριστόν ἐστι *to give what is best for a man to get*
(Hdt. 1.31.4)

But when they follow a preposition that can be elided the relative pronouns are used as in Attic: ἀντ᾽ ὧν (note psilosis: Att. ἀνθ᾽ ὧν), ἐπ᾽ οἷσι (Att. ἐφ᾽ οἷσι), παρ᾽ ἥν.

Morphology: Verbal Forms

Thematic Conjugations

25.32   **Thematic conjugations** do not differ much from Attic (παιδεύω, παιδεύεις, etc.). The 2 sg. middle-passive endings are not contracted: -εαι (<*-εσαι; Att. -ει/ῃ) and -εο (<*-εσο):

       e.g. pres. ind. βούλεαι *you want*, impf. ἐπηγγέλλεο *you offered*, aor. ind. εἴρεο *you asked*, aor. ind. ἐγένεο *you became*, pres. imp. αἰτέο *ask!* (<αἰτέεο, →25.6) (Att. βούλει, ἐπηγγέλλου, ἤρου, ἐγένου, αἰτοῦ).

25.33   **α-stem contract verbs** (Att. type τιμάω *honour*): usually contracted as in Attic. Before an ο/ω an uncontracted form may be used with an ε as substitute for α:

       e.g. τολμέω *I dare* (Att. τολμῶ <-άω), ἐφοίτεον *they visited* (next to ἐφοίτων <-αον; so in Att.), ἐπιτιμέων *honouring* (Att. ἐπιτιμῶν <-άων).

25.34   **ε-stem contract verbs** (type ποιέω *make, do*) are generally left uncontracted (→25.6 above), but εο can be contracted to ευ:

		present active	*present middle-passive*
sg.	*1*	ποιέω (Att. ποιῶ)	ποιέομαι/ποιεῦμαι (Att. ποιοῦμαι)
	2	ποιέεις (Att. ποιεῖς)	ποιέαι (with *hyphaeresis*, →25.6; Att. ποιεῖ/-ῇ)
	3	ποιέει (Att. ποιεῖ)	ποιέεται (Att. ποιεῖται)
pl.	*1*	ποιέομεν/ποιεῦμεν (Att. ποιοῦμεν)	ποιεόμεθα/ποιεύμεθα (Att. ποιούμεθα)
	2	ποιέετε (Att. ποιεῖτε)	ποιέεσθε (Att. ποιεῖσθε)
	3	ποιέουσι/ποιεῦσι (Att. ποιοῦσι)	ποιέονται/ποιεῦνται (Att. ποιοῦνται)

		imperfect active	*imperfect middle-passive*
sg.	*1*	ἐποίεον/ἐποίευν (Att. ἐποίουν)	ἐποιεόμην/ἐποιεύμην (Att. ἐποιούμην)
	2	ἐποίεες (Att. ἐποίεις)	ἐποιέο (with *hyphaeresis*; Att. ἐποιοῦ)
	3	ἐποίεε (Att. ἐποίει)	ἐποιέετο (Att. ἐποιεῖτο)
pl.	*1*	ἐποιέομεν/ἐποιεῦμεν (Att. ἐποιοῦμεν)	ἐποιεόμεθα/ἐποιεύμεθα (Att. ἐποιούμεθα)
	2	ἐποιέετε (Att. ἐποιεῖτε)	ἐποιέεσθε (Att. ἐποιεῖσθε)
	3	ἐποίεον/ἐποίευν (Att. ἐποίουν)	ἐποιέοντο/ἐποιεῦντο (Att. ἐποιοῦντο)

Also note:

– optatives sometimes contract after diphthongs: e.g. 1 sg. ποιοῖμι, 3 sg. ποιοῖ (but uncontracted 3 pl. ποιέοιεν; Att. ποιοῖεν);

– optatives are always uncontracted after consonants: καλέοι, φρονέοιεν (Att. καλοίη/καλοῖ, φρονοῖεν);

– infinitive: ποιέειν, ποιέεσθαι (Att. ποιεῖν, ποιεῖσθαι);

– participle: ποιέων, ποιέουσα, ποιέον, etc. (Att. ποιῶν, ποιοῦσα, ποιοῦν, etc.); also attested are forms such as ποιεῦντα, ποιεῦσα.

25.35   **ο-stem contract verbs** (type δηλόω *make clear*): contracted as in Attic. In some editions spurious forms like ἐδικαίευν (= ἐδικαίουν *I thought it right to*) and ἀξιεῦμαι (= ἀξιοῦμαι *I deem worthy*) are found.

25.36   Observe quantitative metathesis (→1.71, 25.7) and the absence of contraction (→25.6) in η-stem contract verb forms like χρέωμαι *use* (<*χρήομαι, Att. χρῶμαι).

Athematic Conjugations

25.37   The **2 sg. middle** ending of the *sigmatic aorist* is **not contracted**: -αο (<*-ασο, Att. -ω): e.g. ἐδέξαο *you received* (δέχομαι), ἐφθέγξαο *you uttered* (φθέγγομαι) (Att. ἐδέξω, ἐφθέγξω).

25.38 **Thematic forms** are found in the present and imperfect conjugations of -μι verbs (for similar forms in Attic, →12.53–6):

τίθημι *put, place*: 3 sg. pres. act. ind. τιθεῖ (Att. τίθησι)

δίδωμι *give*: 2 sg. pres. act. ind. διδοῖς, 3 sg. διδοῖ (also δίδωσι), 3 pl. διδοῦσι (Att. δίδως, δίδωσι, διδόασι)

ἵστημι *make stand, set up*: 3 sg. pres. act. ind. ἱστᾷ, 2 sg. pres. act. imp. ἵστᾱ (Att. ἵστησι, ἵστη)

ἵημι *send, let go*: 3 sg. pres. act. ind. ἐξιεῖ (Att. ἐξίησι)

-νυμι verbs (e.g. δείκνυμι *show*, ὄμνυμι *swear*, ζεύγνυμι *yoke*): 3 sg. pres. act. ind. δεικνύει, 3 pl. ὀμνύουσι, 1 sg. impf. ἐζεύγνυον, 3 sg. ἐζεύγνυε (Att. δείκνυσι, ὀμνύᾱσι, ἐζεύγνυν, ἐζεύγνυ)

25.39 Instead of the 3 pl. middle-passive endings -νται and -ντο, **-ᾰται** and **-ᾰτο** (with vocalized ν, →1.86) are generally used in athematic conjugations (this includes pf. and plpf. forms which in Attic occur only as periphrastic forms, →17.5–7, 19.8):

e.g. τιθέαται, κέαται, κεχωρίδαται, κατέαται, ἠπιστέατο (Att. τίθενται, κεῖνται, κεχωρισμένοι/-αι εἰσί, κάθηνται, ἠπίσταντο).

Note 1: These endings are also used in the optative: βουλοίατο, γενοίατο (Att. βούλοιντο, γένοιντο).

25.40 **εἰμί** *be*:

	present	*imperfect*
1 sg.	εἰμί	ἔα (Att. ἦ(ν))
2	εἶς (Att. εἶ)	ἔας (Att. ἦσθα)
3	ἐστί	ἦν
1 pl.	εἰμέν (Att. ἐσμέν)	ἔαμεν (Att. ἦμεν)
2	ἐστέ	ἔατε (Att. ἦτε)
3	εἰσί	ἦσαν

subj. 1 sg. ἔω, 3 pl. ἔωσι (Att. ὦ, ὦσι(ν))

ppl. ἐών, ἐοῦσα, ἐόν, etc. (Att. ὤν, οὖσα, ὄν)

25.41 The endings of the aorist passive subjunctive are uncontracted (→25.6 above): e.g. ἀπαιρεθέω *I am robbed of* (subj.) (<*-θη-ω, →14.7; Att. ἀφαιρεθῶ).

Similarly, note e.g. aor. subj. θέωμεν *let us place* (<θήομεν, Att. θῶμεν).

Further Points on Verbal Morphology

25.42 Herodotus uses imperfects with the **iterative suffix -σκ-**, always without the augment: ἔσκε *he was*, διαφθείρεσκε *he kept destroying*, ποιέεσκον *I/they kept doing*.

25.43   The so-called temporal augment (with stems that begin with a vowel or diphthong, →11.37–8, with n.1) is often lacking: ἀμείβετο *he replied* (impf. of ἀμείβομαι, instead of ἠμείβετο), διαιτώμην *I dwelt* (impf. of διαιτάομαι, instead of διῃτώμην), οἴκητο *it was inhabited* (plpf. of οἰκέω, instead of ᾤκητο).

Observe also the absence of reduplication in the case of the irregular perfect οῖκα *be likely* (Att. ἔοικα, →18.22), ppl. οἰκός, οἰκός (ἐστι) (*it is*) *likely*.

25.44   In a compound verb a postpositive particle (such as τε, δέ, μέν, ὦν) may separate the prefix from the verb: e.g. κατ᾽ ὦν ἐκάλυψε *he buried* (Hdt. 2.47.3): this is called **tmesis**.

Further Particulars

25.45   Observe the following further uses which diverge from Attic:

- ἐπείτε *when* alongside ἐπεί, and ἔπειτε *thereupon* occasionally, alongside more frequent ἔπειτα (note the difference in accentuation between ἐπείτε and ἔπειτε);
- ἐς ὅ and ἐς οὖ *until* (conjunctions; Att. ἕως);
- μετά *after* is also used in adverbial sense *afterwards*;
- ὥστε + ppl. and οἶα + ppl. are used in the same sense as ἅτε + ppl. (→52.39);
- οὐδαμά, μηδαμά *never*.

The 'Doric' ᾱ in Choral Lyric

25.46   A particular feature of the choral lyric of the Attic dramatists, which has a superficial 'Doric' colouring (→25.2), is the **use of original long ᾱ** rather than the Attic-Ionic η (→1.57, 25.5).

Note 1: This use of ᾱ is therefore often called 'Doric', even though long ᾱ was used in all dialects apart from Attic-Ionic.

25.47   Long ᾱ for Attic η is found in lyrics in drama under the following circumstances:

- in **first declension endings**: γᾶ *land*, βιοτᾶ *living*, πταμένᾱς βροντᾶς (gen.) *when the thunder flies*, Κρονίδᾱς *son of Cronus* (Att. γῆ, βιοτή, πταμένης βροντῆς, Κρονίδης);
   'Doric' long ᾱ + ο/ω contracts to ᾱ (not ω): thus, gen. sg. of masculine first-declension nouns in ᾱ (<-ᾱο, Att. -ου), and gen. pl. of all first-declension nouns in ᾶν (<-άων, Att. -ῶν): νεανίᾱ *young man*, βακχᾶν *bacchants*, μελισσᾶν *bees* (Att. νεανίου, βακχῶν, μελιττῶν);
- 1 sg. middle-passive forms with secondary ending **-μᾱν**: e.g. ἀνειλόμᾱν *I killed* (Att. ἀνειλόμην);
- in **augmented** forms of ἄγω *lead, bring*, e.g. ᾶγες (Att. ἦγες);
- in other individual words like μάτηρ *mother*, Ἅλιος *sun*, etc.

Note 1: The use of the 'Doric' ᾱ in choral lyric is not consistent. In the lyrical parodos to the *Bacchae*, for example, Euripides uses ἡδύν *sweet* (Eur. *Bacch.* 66) and ἡδύς (135), but ᾱδυβόᾳ *sweet-sounding* (127).

Part II

Syntax

26

Introduction to Simple Sentences

26.1 Below, the basic syntactic principles and concepts that will be relevant in chapters 27 to 38 are discussed. All examples in this chapter are taken from Xenophon's *Anabasis*, unless otherwise indicated.

26.2 Chapters 40 to 52 deal with the various types of subordinate constructions found in complex sentences (subordinate clauses, participles, infinitives, and verbal adjectives): these will be separately introduced in chapter 39.

The Sentence Core

Predicate, Subject, Object, Complement

26.3 Most sentences (for the exceptions, →26.13) contain at least a **predicate** (nearly always a finite verb) and one or more **obligatory constituents** that belong to that predicate; together these make up the **sentence core**.

– Nearly all verbs take at least one obligatory constituent, a **subject**. Subjects are marked by the nominative case (→30.2), and agree in person and number with the predicate (→27.1). Some verbs take only a subject:

(1) Κῦρος_{SUBJECT} . . . ἐτελεύτησεν_{PREDICATE}. (1.9.1)
Cyrus came to his end.

(2) ἀπέθανον_{PREDICATE} δὲ ὀλίγοι_{SUBJECT}. (6.5.29)
And a few died.

(3) ὑμεῖς_{SUBJECT} δὲ εὐτυχοῖτε_{PREDICATE}. (Xen. *Hell.* 7.1.11)
May you be fortunate.

– Many verbs take both a subject and another obligatory constituent. With a majority of such verbs, this second obligatory constituent is the (**direct**) **object**, which is marked by the accusative case (→30.8); some verbs take second obligatory constituents in a different case (such constituents are called **complements**):

(4) στρουθὸν_{OBJECT} δὲ οὐδεὶς_{SUBJECT} ἔλαβεν_{PREDICATE}. (1.5.3)
No one caught an ostrich.

(5) ἐγὼ_{SUBJECT} . . . ὑμᾶς_{OBJECT} ἐπαινῶ_{PREDICATE}. (1.4.16)
I commend you.

(6) πάντες οἱ πολῖται_SUBJECT . . . μετεῖχον_PREDICATE τῆς ἑορτῆς_COMPLEMENT. (5.3.9)
All the citizens took part in the festival.

(7) οἱ δὲ στρατιῶται_SUBJECT ἐχαλέπαινον_PREDICATE τοῖς στρατηγοῖς_COMPLEMENT.
(1.4.12)
The soldiers were angry at the generals.

– Some verbs take more than two obligatory constituents: a subject, an object, and one (or more) further complements. Often the third obligatory constituent is the **indirect object**, which is marked by the dative case (→30.37); other verbs take a second complement in the accusative or genitive:

(8) Συέννεσις_SUBJECT μὲν ἔδωκε_PREDICATE Κύρῳ_INDIRECT OBJECT χρήματα πολλά_OBJECT. (1.2.27)
Syennesis gave Cyrus much money.

(9) Ἀρίστιππος δὲ ὁ Θετταλὸς_SUBJECT . . . αἰτεῖ_PREDICATE αὐτὸν_OBJECT . . . δισχιλίους ξένους_COMPLEMENT. (1.1.10)
Aristippus the Thessalian asked him for two thousand mercenaries.

26.4   In the examples above, the obligatory constituents of a verb are expressed by a **noun phrase or a pronoun** (these are treated more fully below, →26.16–23).
Such obligatory constituents may also take other forms, however. The most important of these are:

– **prepositional phrases** (consisting of a preposition and its complement):

(10) ἀφικνοῦνται_PREDICATE πρὸς Ἀριαῖον COMPLEMENT . . . οἱ ἀδελφοί_SUBJECT. (2.4.1)
To Ariaeus came his brothers.

– **adverbs**:

(11) ἐνταῦθα_COMPLEMENT ἀφικνεῖται_PREDICATE Ἐπύαξα_SUBJECT. (1.2.12)
Epyaxa came there.

– **subordinate clauses**:

(12) οὗτοι_SUBJECT ἔλεγον_PREDICATE ὅτι Κῦρος . . . τέθνηκεν_OBJECT. (2.1.3)
These men said that Cyrus was dead. *The declarative subordinate clause (→41) fulfils the role of object with the predicate ἔλεγον: compare ταῦτα in ἔλεγον ταῦτα 'They said those things.'*

– **infinitive constructions**:

(13) ἐγώ_SUBJECT φημι_PREDICATE ταῦτα . . . φλυαρίας εἶναι_OBJECT. (1.3.18)
I say that that is nonsense. *The accusative-and-infinitive construction (→51.21) fulfils the role of object with the predicate φημί: compare ταῦτα in φημὶ ταῦτα 'I say those things.'*

– **participle constructions**:

(14) ἐγώ_{SUBJECT} ... <u>οἶδα</u>_{PREDICATE} ... ἡμῖν ὅρκους γεγενημένους_{OBJECT} (2.5.3)

I know that there are oaths between us. *The accusative-and-participle construction (→52.13) fulfils the role of object with the predicate* οἶδα: *compare* ταῦτα *in* οἶδα ταῦτα *'I know those things.'*

When a constituent is expressed in the form of a subordinate clause or a construction with an infinitive or participle, this is called a **complex sentence**. For complex sentences, →39.

Note 1: The number of obligatory constituents that accompany a verb is called the 'valency' of that verb: thus ἀποθνῄσκω *die* (2) has a valency of one (or: is 'one-place'), δίδωμι *give* (8) has a valency of three (or: is 'three-place').

Some verbs have different valencies in different meanings. For instance, the verb φεύγω, when it takes only a subject, means *run away, flee, be in exile*, but may also take an object and then means *flee (someone), be chased by someone*:

(15) οἱ βάρβαροι_{SUBJECT} ... <u>φεύγουσι</u>_{PREDICATE}. (1.8.19)

The barbarians fled.

(16) οἱ δειλοὶ κύνες_{SUBJECT} ... <u>τοὺς</u> ... <u>διώκοντας</u>_{OBJECT} <u>φεύγουσιν</u>_{PREDICATE}. (3.2.35)

Cowardly dogs run away from those who chase them.

Note 2: The subject, object and other obligatory constituents that belong to the predicate are also called 'arguments'. The sentence core is also called the 'nucleus' of a sentence.

Note 3: It is sometimes difficult to assess whether a constituent should be considered 'obligatory' in the sense given above (i.e. whether they are required with a predicate to form a grammatically correct core sentence). This is true particularly of adverbial complements such as ἐνταῦθα in (11), and with verbs which may have different valencies (cf. n.1 above). In reality, syntactic 'obligatoriness' is better seen as a scale, with constituents being *more* or *less* obligatory depending on the verb and construction used.

26.5   There are a few verbs which do not have a subject ('impersonal' verbs, →36), and very few of these take no other obligatory constituents (i.e. are 'zero-place'). The sentence core then consists of nothing but the verb: e.g. ὕει *it is raining*.

'Omission' of the Subject and Other Constituents

26.6   That a verb takes a certain number of obligatory constituents does not mean that all those constituents are necessarily expressed every single time that verb is used. A constituent may be omitted if it is sufficiently **clear from the context** who or what is meant:

(17) ταύτην τὴν ἐπιστολήν_{OBJECT} <u>δίδωσι</u>_{PREDICATE} πιστῷ ἀνδρί_{INDIRECT OBJECT} ... ὁ δέ_{SUBJECT} ... Κύρῳ_{INDIRECT OBJECT} <u>δίδωσιν</u>_{PREDICATE}. (1.6.3)

He (*Orontas*) gave that letter to a trustworthy man ... But he gave it to Cyrus. *The first sentence has no explicit subject – Orontas has been the subject of the previous few sentences and need not be mentioned explicitly again. The second sentence has no explicit object – it is clear that the letter is meant. Note that these constituents have to be supplied in translation ('he', 'it').*

26.7   The lack of an explicit, separately expressed **subject** is particularly frequent in Greek, and constitutes a regular feature of the language. Information about the subject of a verb is often expressed only by the **personal ending** of that verb:

(18) λέγει Σεύθης· Ἀργύριον μὲν οὐκ ἔχω. (7.7.53)

Seuthes said: 'I do not have silver.' *The subject ('I') is expressed by the first-person singular ending.*

(19) θέσθε τὰ ὅπλα ἐν τάξει. (7.1.22)

Position your weapons in battle order. *The subject is expressed by the second-person plural ending. Note that English, too, normally omits the subject with imperatives.*

(20) Κῦρος δὲ ... ὡρμᾶτο ἀπὸ Σάρδεων· καὶ ἐξελαύνει διὰ τῆς Λυδίας. (1.2.5)

Cyrus set off from Sardis. And he marched through Lydia. *The subject of ἐξελαύνει is expressed by the third-person singular ending; the identity of the subject, Cyrus, is clear from the preceding context.*

In the third person, the omission of the subject is regular if the subject of the previous sentence is continued, as in (20). If the subject changes, as in (17), an explicitly expressed subject is normally required.

In the first and second person, explicitly expressed subjects (in the form of the personal pronouns ἐγώ, σύ, ἡμεῖς, ὑμεῖς) are used only for emphasis or contrast. For such 'contrastive' pronouns, →29.1–4.

Note 1: The omission of other elements than the subject (such as the object in (17)) is much more restricted and infrequent than the lack of an explicitly expressed subject.

Linking Verb, Predicative Complement

26.8   A **linking verb** (or **copulative/copular verb, copula**) 'links' a subject to a nominal constituent, the so-called **predicative complement**, which identifies the subject or assigns a property to it. The predicative complement is usually an **adjective** which agrees in case, number and gender with the subject, or a **noun** which agrees with the subject in case (→27.7, 30.3).

Examples of verbs that can function as linking verbs are εἰμί *be*, γίγνομαι *become*, καθίσταμαι *become*, μένω *remain, stay*, φαίνομαι *seem, appear to be, prove to be*, etc.

(21) τὸ στράτευμα_{SUBJECT} πάμπολυ_{PREDICATIVE ADJECTIVE} ἐφάνη_{LINKING VERB} _{PREDICATE}· (3.4.13)

The army appeared to be very large. *πάμπολυ agrees with τὸ στράτευμα in case, number and gender.*

(22) μεγάλα_{PREDICATIVE ADJECTIVE} ... τόξα τὰ Περσικά_{SUBJECT} ἐστιν_{LINKING VERB} _{PREDICATE}· (3.4.17)

The Persian bows are large. *μεγάλα agrees with τόξα in case, number and gender.*

(23) τὰ δὲ ἆθλα_{SUBJECT} [ἦσαν_{LINKING VERB} στλεγγίδες χρυσαῖ_{PREDICATIVE NOUN}]_{PREDICATE}. (1.2.10)

The prizes were golden strigils. *στλεγγίδες χρυσαῖ agrees with τὰ ἆθλα in case. For the plural ἦσαν with a neut. pl. subject, →27.2.*

Note 1: Predicative nouns or adjectives are sometimes called 'predicate nouns/adjectives'. Predicative complements agreeing with a subject are also sometimes called 'subject(ive) complements'.

26.9 Many linking verbs also occur with an adverbial expression of place or circumstance as their complement: e.g. εἰμί *be (somewhere), find oneself (somewhere)*, γίγνομαι *get somewhere*, μένω *stay somewhere*. In many grammatical treatments, such complements are also seen as predicative complements:

(24) ἐνθάδε_{COMPLEMENT} δ' εἰμί_{LINKING VERB}. (3.3.2)
I am here.

(25) Πρόξενος δὲ καὶ Μένων_{SUBJECT} . . . ἐν μεγάλῃ τιμῇ_{COMPLEMENT} εἰσιν_{LINKING VERB}. (2.5.38)
And Proxenus and Meno are (held) in great esteem.

26.10 The verb εἰμί also occurs with only a subject in the meaning *exist*. In this '**existential**' use, the verb usually stands before its subject (→60.30, cf. 50.12, 50.35). Such cases can be translated with *there is* (ἔστι(ν), so accented, →24.34 n.1), *there are* (εἰσί(ν)), 'there was' (ἦν), 'there were' (ἦσαν). The verb γίγνομαι also has an existential use, and then means *exist* or *happen*:

(26) ἔστι_{PREDICATE} χωρίον χρημάτων πολλῶν μεστόν_{SUBJECT}. (5.2.7)
There is a place filled with many riches.

(27) ἀγαθὸν_{SUBJECT} . . . γεγένηται_{PREDICATE}. (5.4.19)
A good thing has happened.

26.11 As an alternative for the linking verb εἰμί + adjective classical Greek frequently uses **ἔχω + adverb** in the meaning *to be (in a . . . state)*, e.g.:

(28) χαλεπῶς δὲ ἔχει ἡμῖν πρὸς τοῖς ἄλλοις καὶ ἡ πειθώ. (Thuc. 3.53.4)
In addition to the other things persuading is difficult for us as well.

(29) ΔΗ. ὦ κακόδαιμον, πῶς ἔχεις; :: ΝΙ. κακῶς, καθάπερ σύ. (Ar. *Eq.* 7–8)
(Demos:) you wretched one, how are you? :: (Nicias:) I'm not doing well, just like you.

26.12 Some other verbs link an **object** to a predicative complement that agrees with that object (both are accusative). Examples of such verbs are νομίζω *consider X (to be) Y*, ἡγέομαι *consider X (to be) Y*, ποιέω *make X Y*, αἱρέομαι *appoint X as Y* (for more details, →30.10):

(30) [σχολαίαν_{PREDICATIVE ADJECTIVE} . . . ἐποίουν_{VERB}]_{PREDICATE} τὴν πορείαν_{OBJECT} . . . τὰ ὑποζύγια_{SUBJECT}. (4.1.13)
The baggage animals made the journey slow. *σχολαίαν agrees with τὴν πορείαν in case, number, and gender.*

(31) | δικαστάς PREDICATIVE NOUN | δὲ τοὺς λοχαγούς OBJECT | ἐποιήσαντο VERB |PREDICATE.
(5.7.34)

As judges they appointed the captains. *δικαστὰς agrees with τοὺς λοχαγοὺς in case.*

(32) μηκέτι με OBJECT | Κῦρον PREDICATIVE NOUN νομίζετε VERB |PREDICATE. (1.4.16)

You must no longer consider me (to be) Cyrus. *Κῦρον agrees with με in case.*

Note 1: Predicative complements agreeing with an object are sometimes called 'object(ive) complements'.

Omission of a Linking Verb: Nominal Sentences

26.13   Frequently, a linking verb such as **ἐστί(ν) or εἰσί(ν)** is lacking in a sentence, whose core then contains only nominal elements. This occurs especially in the following cases:

– with evaluative words, such as χαλεπόν *(it is) difficult*, ἀνάγκη *(it is) necessary*, εἰκός *(it is) likely, proper*, etc.:

(33) Ἀναμιμνῄσκονται ἄρα ἅ ποτε ἔμαθον; :: Ἀνάγκη PREDICATE. (Pl. *Phd.* 76c)
(Socrates:) Then they recollect the things they once learned? :: (Simmias:) Necessarily. *Lit.: '<it is> a necessity'.*

(34) Σω. σὺ δὲ αὐτός ... Μένων, τί φῂς ἀρετὴν εἶναι; ... :: ΜΕ. ἀλλ' οὐ χαλεπόν PREDICATE, ὦ Σώκρατες, εἰπεῖν SUBJECT. (Pl. *Men.* 71d–e)
(Socrates:) But you yourself, Meno, what do you say virtue is? :: (Meno:) Why, it is not hard to say, Socrates.

– with verbal adjectives in -τέος, -τέα, -τέον (especially in the impersonal use of the neuter, →37.3):

(35) ἡ δ' ὁδός SUBJECT πορευτέα PREDICATE. (Soph. *Phil.* 993)
The road must be travelled. *(lit. 'the road <is> to be travelled')*

(36) πορευτέον PREDICATE δ' ἡμῖν τοὺς πρώτους σταθμούς. (2.2.12)
We must make the first marches. *Impersonal use (lit. 'There <is> to be travelled by us the first marches'); for this construction, →37.3.*

– in so-called gnomic utterances (proverbs, maxims, etc.), general statements and exclamations:

(37) δυσάρεστος ἡμῶν καὶ φιλόψογος PREDICATIVE ADJECTIVE πόλις SUBJECT. (Eur. *El.* 904)
Our city is peevish and inclined to criticize.

(38) οἷον PREDICATIVE ADJECTIVE τὸ τεκεῖν SUBJECT. (Ar. *Lys.* 884)
How momentous is motherhood! *Lit.: 'What a thing <is> bearing <children>!'*

– in formulaic questions and answers:

(39) εἶτα τί_{PREDICATE} τοῦτο_{SUBJECT}; (Ar. *Nub.* 347)

So what? *Lit.: 'What <is> this, then?'*

– and sometimes more freely:

(40) καλὸς_{PREDICATE} Ἀρχίας_{SUBJECT}. (*IG* I³ 1405)

Archias is handsome.

Only the present indicative of εἰμί *be* is regularly omitted as linking verb in this way: other forms such as imperfect ἦν or potential optative εἴη ἄν (→34.13) are not normally omitted.

Optional Constituents

Adverbial Modifiers and Other Optional Constituents

26.14   Many core sentences are elaborated by one or more **optional (non-obligatory) constituents**, which can be left out without making the sentence ungrammatical, and which supplement the sentence core in various ways. Most often such constituents are **adverbial modifiers**.

Such optional constituents can be expressed by:

– **adverbs**:

(41) Τισσαφέρνης_{SUBJECT} ... ἐκεῖ_{ADVERBIAL MODIFIER} συντυγχάνει_{PREDICATE} βασιλεῖ_{COMPLEMENT}. (1.10.8)

Tissaphernes met the king there. *Adverbial modifier of place.*

– **noun phrases** and **pronouns** (in the accusative, genitive or dative, →29, 30):

(42) Ξενοφῶν_{SUBJECT} ... ᾤχετο_{PREDICATE} τῆς νυκτός_{ADVERBIAL MODIFIER}. (7.2.17)

Xenophon departed during the night. *Adverbial modifier of time, expressed by the genitive, →30.32.*

(43) ἄλλο δὲ στράτευμα_{SUBJECT} αὐτῷ_{OPTIONAL CONSTITUENT} συνελέγετο_{PREDICATE} ἐν Χερρονήσῳ. (1.1.9)

Another army was being assembled for him in the Chersonese. *Constituent representing the beneficiary/interested party, expressed by the dative, →30.49. Such constituents are often taken as indirect objects, but unlike indirect objects with verbs of giving, etc. (for which →26.3), they are optional.*

– **prepositional phrases**:

(44) ἐπὶ τούτῳ_{ADVERBIAL MODIFIER} Κλεάνωρ ὁ Ὀρχομένιος_{SUBJECT} ἀνέστη_{PREDICATE}. (3.2.4)

Thereupon, Cleanor the Orchomenian stood up. *Adverbial modifier of time.*

And in the case of complex sentences, by:

– **subordinate clauses**:

(45) ἐπεὶ δὲ καὶ οἱ ἄλλοι στρατιῶται συνῆλθον_{ADVERBIAL MODIFIER} ἀνέστη_{PREDICATE} ···
Χειρίσοφος ὁ Λακεδαιμόνιος_{SUBJECT}. (3.2.1)
When the other soldiers too had assembled, Chirisophus the Spartan stood up.
The temporal subordinate clause (→47) serves as an adverbial modifier of time.

– **participle constructions** (also →26.26):

(46) καὶ ἅμα ταῦτα ποιούντων ἡμῶν_{ADVERBIAL MODIFIER} ··· Ἀριαῖος_{SUBJECT}
ἀφεστήξει_{PREDICATE}. (2.4.5)
And while we are doing that, Ariaeus will have abandoned us. *The genitive absolute construction serves as an adverbial modifier of time.*

26.15   Adverbial modifiers operate on different 'levels' of the sentence:

– The adverbial modifiers in examples (41)–(46) express such semantic categories as the place where, the time when, the circumstance(s) under which, the manner in which, the reasons because of which, etc., the action expressed by a predicate takes place. Adverbial modifiers functioning at this level (i.e. those which have scope over (the verb in) the core sentence) are often called **adjuncts**.

– Adverbial modifiers may also have scope over a constituent only, modifying nouns, attributive modifiers, other adverbial modifiers, etc. (such adverbial modifiers are called **subjuncts**):

(47) τοὺς ··· λοχαγοὺς_{HEAD} ⌈τοὺς μάλιστα_{ADVERBIAL MODIFIER} φίλους⌉_{ATTRIBUTIVE MODIFIER}
(7.8.11)
the captains who were his most intimate friends ... *μάλιστα, a so-called 'intensifier', modifies φίλους, which itself is an attributive modifier with λοχαγούς.*

(48) ἐκλώπευον_{PREDICATE} ··· οἱ Παφλαγόνες_{SUBJECT} ⌈εὖ μάλα_{ADVERBIAL MODIFIER}⌉ τοὺς
ἀποσκεδαννυμένους_{OBJECT}. (6.1.1)
The Paphlagonians very easily kidnapped the stragglers. *The intensifier μάλα modifies εὖ, which itself is an adverbial modifier of manner.*

(49) ἐξεπλάγη_{PREDICATE} δέ ··· ⌈καὶ_{ADVERBIAL MODIFIER} βασιλεύς⌉_{SUBJECT}. (2.2.18)
And even the king was terrified. *καί, a marker of 'scope' (→59.56), modifies βασιλεύς, which is the subject of ἐξεπλάγη.*

– Some other adverbial modifiers are, syntactically speaking, more detached, and have scope over the sentence as a whole, expressing the attitude of the speaker towards the reality or desirability of the *content* of his sentence, or his attitude towards the *form* or *style* of the sentence (such modifiers are often called **disjuncts**):

(50) ἴσως_{ADVERBIAL MODIFIER} δὲ καὶ τῶν ἐπιτηδείων σπανιεῖ. (2.2.12)
Perhaps he will lack supplies as well. *The adverb ἴσως expresses the speaker's attitude towards the reality of the content of the sentence.*

(51) ἀληθές γε ὡς ἔπος εἰπεῖν_{ADVERBIAL MODIFIER} οὐδὲν εἰρήκασιν. (Pl. *Ap.* 17a)

They have said not a single thing, so to say, which is true. *The idiomatic phrase ὡς ἔπος εἰπεῖν (→51.49) expresses the speaker's (Socrates') attitude towards the form of his utterance – Socrates signals that his words (specifically οὐδέν) should not be taken too literally.*

– Finally, grammars typically recognize a fourth type of adverbial modifier, that of **conjuncts**, which indicate how one sentence or larger unit of text relates to its surrounding context, i.e. which play a role in structuring a text; such forms are treated in this grammar as **connective discourse particles**, →59.7–39:

(52) ἐνταῦθα ἔμεινεν ὁ Κῦρος καὶ ἡ στρατιὰ ἡμέρας εἴκοσιν· οἱ γὰρ στρατιῶται οὐκ ἔφασαν ἰέναι τοῦ πρόσω· ὑπώπτευον γὰρ ἤδη ἐπὶ βασιλέα ἰέναι· μισθωθῆναι δὲ οὐκ ἐπὶ τούτῳ ἔφασαν. (1.3.1)

There Cyrus and the army stayed for twenty days, for the soldiers said that they would not go on. For they already suspected that they were moving on the king, and they said that they had not enlisted with that in mind.

Noun Phrases

Elements of the Noun Phrase

26.16 In most of the examples above, constituents take the form of a noun phrase. A **noun phrase** consists of (at least) a **head**, and (possibly) various kinds of **modifiers** which are added to the head.

For example, in each of the examples below, a noun phrase with ἄνδρα as its head serves as object to a form of ὁράω *see*:

(53) ἄνδρα_{HEAD}|_{OBJECT} ὁρῶ_{PREDICATE}.
I see a man.

(54) τὸν_{MODIFIER} ἄνδρα_{HEAD}|_{OBJECT} ὁρῶ_{PREDICATE}. (1.8.26)
I see the man.

(55) ἐν πολέμῳ δὲ ἤδη εἶδες_{PREDICATE} ἄνδρα_{HEAD} δειλόν_{MODIFIER}|_{OBJECT}; (Pl. *Grg.* 498a)
And in war, have you ever seen a cowardly man?

(56) ὁρᾷ_{PREDICATE} τὸν_{MODIFIER} ἄνδρα_{HEAD} τῆς γυναικός_{MODIFIER}|_{OBJECT}. (Ar. *Av.* 794)
He sees the woman's husband.

(57) οὐκ εἶδον_{PREDICATE} οὕτως ἄνδρ'_{HEAD} ἄγροικον … | οὐδ' ἄπορον οὐδὲ σκαιὸν οὐδ' ἐπιλήσμονα | ὅστις σκαλαθυρμάτι' ἄττα μικρὰ μανθάνων | ταῦτ' ἐπιλέλησται πρὶν μαθεῖν_{OBJECT}. (Ar. *Nub.* 628–31)
I have seen no man so boorish, so incapable, so dimwitted, so forgetful that when he learns petty quibbles he has forgotten them before he has learnt them. *All of the adjectives and the ὅστις-clause may be seen as modifiers of ἄνδρα in a long noun phrase (for this kind of ὅστις-clause, however, →50.25).*

Types of Modifier

26.17   The following types of modifier **agree** with the head in case, number and gender
(→27.7):

– the **definite article** (for a full treatment, →28);

– **demonstrative, indefinite, interrogative**, and **possessive pronouns** (for details,
→29):

(58)   ταύτης_{MODIFIER} ··· τῆς_{MODIFIER} ἡμέρας_{HEAD} | τοῦτο_{MODIFIER} τὸ_{MODIFIER}
τέλος_{HEAD} ἐγένετο. (1.10.18)
Such was the ending of this day. *ταύτης agrees with ἡμέρας, τοῦτο with τέλος.*

(59)   τίνα_{MODIFIER} γνώμην_{HEAD} ἔχεις περὶ τῆς πορείας; (2.2.10)
What opinion do you have concerning the expedition? *τίνα agrees with
γνώμην.*

– **numerals**: cardinal numerals such as εἷς *one*, δύο *two*, ordinal numerals such as
πρῶτος *first*, δεύτερος *second* (for details, →9); among the ordinals may also be
reckoned adjectives such as ἄλλος *other* and ἕτερος *other* (for details, →29.48–
52), λοῖπος *further, remaining*, and several others:

(60)   αἰτεῖ αὐτὸν ... δισχιλίους_{MODIFIER} ξένους_{HEAD}. (1.1.10)
He asked him for two thousand mercenaries. *δισχιλίους agrees with ξένους.*

(61)   ἀφικνοῦνται ἐπὶ τὸ ὄρος τῇ_{MODIFIER} πέμπτῃ_{MODIFIER} ἡμέρᾳ_{HEAD} (4.7.21)
They reached the mountain on the fifth day. *πέμπτη agrees with ἡμέρᾳ.*

– **quantifiers**: certain adjectives indicating quantity, such as πολύς *much, many*,
ὀλίγος *little, few*, πᾶς *all, every*, ἕκαστος *every, each*:

(62)   ἦρχον δὲ τότε πάντων_{MODIFIER} τῶν_{MODIFIER} Ἑλλήνων_{HEAD} οἱ Λακεδαιμόνιοι.
(6.6.9)
The Spartans ruled over all the Greeks at that time. *πάντων agrees with
Ἑλλήνων.*

– (other) **adjectives** and **participles** (→52):

(63)   τὴν_{MODIFIER} δὲ Ἑλληνικὴν_{MODIFIER} δύναμιν_{HEAD} ἤθροιζεν. (1.1.6)
He gathered the Greek force. *Adjective; Ἑλληνικήν agrees with δύναμιν.*

(64)   ἧκον_{PREDICATE} ... οἱ_{MODIFIER} προπεμφθέντες_{MODIFIER} σκοποί_{HEAD}. (2.2.15)
The scouts who had been sent ahead arrived. *Participle; προπεμφθέντες agrees
with σκοποί.*

Note 1: For the relative ordering of such modifiers, particularly with respect to the article,
→28.11.

Note 2: Most of these pronouns, numerals and adjectives/participles may also have
a predicative relationship with a noun, either as predicative complement (→26.8 above) or
as predicative modifier (→26.26 below).

26.18   The following types of modifier do not agree with their head:

– **attributive genitives**: noun phrases/pronouns in the genitive very frequently serve as modifier in a noun phrase (for details, →30.28–9):

(65)   τὸ~MODIFIER~ Μένωνος~MODIFIER~ στράτευμα~HEAD~ . . . ἐν Κιλικίᾳ ἦν. (1.2.21)
Menon's army was in Cilicia.

(66)   ἐστεφανωμένους τοῦ ξηροῦ χιλοῦ~MODIFIER~ στεφάνοις~HEAD~ (4.5.33)
crowned with wreaths of hay . . . *Observe that τοῦ ξηροῦ χιλοῦ, as a noun phrase, has its own internal structure, with a head (χιλοῦ) and modifiers (τοῦ, ξηροῦ).*

(67)   ᾤχοντο ἀπελαύνοντες εἰς τὸ~MODIFIER~ ἑαυτῶν~MODIFIER~ στρατόπεδον~HEAD~ (7.6.42)
They rode into their (own) camp.

Note 1: For the relative ordering of such genitives and the article (if present), →28.15.
Note 2: In several uses, the attributive genitive may also be used as predicative complement; for details, →30.26.

– **adverbs** or **prepositional phrases**:

(68)   παίουσιν . . . τοὺς ἔνδον~MODIFIER~ ἀνθρώπους~HEAD~ (5.2.17)
They struck the people (who were) inside.

(69)   ὁρῶσι τὰ ἐπὶ ταῖς πύλαις~MODIFIER~ πράγματα~HEAD~. (7.1.17)
They saw the things (that were happening) at the gates.

– **relative clauses** (for a full treatment, →50).

Types of Head

26.19   The **head** of a noun phrase is typically a **noun**, such as ἄνδρα in (53)–(57); proper names also belong to this class:

(70)   εἶδε τὸν~MODIFIER~ Κῦρον~HEAD~. (Xen. *Cyr.* 3.2.15)
He saw Cyrus.

(71)   πικρὰν~MODIFIER~ Ἑλένην~HEAD~ ὄψει. (Ar. *Thesm.* 853)
You will see a bitter Helen.

26.20   Most of the kinds of modifiers listed above (→26.17–18) may also serve as head, however, particularly when they are modified by the article (→28.23):

– **adjectives** and **participles**; normally with the article, sometimes with other modifiers as well:

(72)   τοιγαροῦν αὐτῷ οἱ~MODIFIER~ μὲν καλοί τε καὶ ἀγαθοί~HEAD~ τῶν συνόντων~MODIFIER~ εὖνοι ἦσαν, οἱ~MODIFIER~ δὲ ἄδικοι~HEAD~ ἐπεβούλευον. (2.6.20)
For that reason, the good and brave among those in his company were well-disposed to him, while the unjust plotted against him. *Adjectives as head.*

(73) πολλοὶ . . . ἦσαν οἱ_MODIFIER τετρωμένοι_HEAD. (3.4.30)
    The wounded were many. *Participle as head.*

– **attributive genitives, adverbs** and **prepositional phrases**; always with the article:

(74) τὰ_MODIFIER τῶν θεῶν_HEAD καλῶς εἶχεν. (3.2.9)
    The affairs of the gods were in good order.

(75) εἶχε δὲ τὸ μὲν δεξιὸν Μένων καὶ οἱ_MODIFIER σὺν αὐτῷ_HEAD. (1.2.15)
    Menon and those with him occupied the right flank.

26.21 In these uses masculine forms/forms with the masculine article refer to men or mixed groups of people, feminine forms to women, neuter forms to objects, concepts, etc.:

οἱ ἀγαθοί	the good men
αἱ ἀγαθαί	the good women
τὰ ἀγαθά	the good things, benefits

Pronominal and Adnominal Use of Pronouns, Quantifiers and Cardinal Numerals

26.22 In addition to the types of head treated above, various **pronouns** and **quantifiers** and (occasionally) **cardinal numerals** can serve as head. For these forms, a distinction is made between:

– the **pronominal use**, when the pronoun/quantifier serves as head;
– the **adnominal use**, when the pronoun/quantifier serves as modifier.

In the pronominal use, such forms typically cannot be modified by the article or other modifiers (there are exceptions, however); in other words, such pronouns/quantifiers then function as noun phrases **by themselves**:

(76) οὗτοι_HEAD . . . βαρβάρους ἀνθρώπους ἔχουσιν. (Xen. *Mem.* 2.7.6)
    These people keep foreign men (as slaves). *Pronominal use.*

(77) ἔχουσι δὲ οὗτοι_MODIFIER οἱ_MODIFIER ἄνθρωποι_HEAD ἀνὰ ὀκτὼ δακτύλους ἐφ᾽ ἑκατέρᾳ χειρί. (Ctes. fr. 45.561–2 Lenfant)
    These people have up to eight fingers on each hand. *Adnominal use.*

(78) καὶ ἅμα ἐφθέγξαντο πάντες_HEAD . . . καὶ πάντες_HEAD δὲ ἔθεον. (1.8.18)
    And at the same time, everyone struck up the war cry . . . and next, everyone was running. *Pronominal use.*

(79) πάντες_MODIFIER οἱ_MODIFIER περὶ αὐτὸν_MODIFIER φίλοι_HEAD καὶ συντράπεζοι_HEAD ἀπέθανον. (1.9.31)
    All his bodyguard of friends and table companions perished. *Adnominal use.*

Note 1: Personal, reflexive and reciprocal pronouns are used only pronominally (→29).
Note 2: For so-called 'autonomous' relative clauses (i.e. relative clauses serving as noun phrases by themselves), →50.7.

26.23   In the pronominal use, masculine forms refer to men or mixed groups of people, feminine forms to women, neuter forms to objects, concepts, etc.:

οἵδε	these men, these people	εἷς	one man
αἵδε	these women	μία	one woman
τάδε	these things, this	ἕν	one thing

Apposition

26.24   **Apposition** is the placement of two words or word groups parallel to each other without any coordinating particle (τε or καί, →59.20–2, 59.37), with one, the 'appositive' defining or modifying the other. In this way, two noun phrases (each with their own head), may together serve as a single constituent:

(80) ⌈ἡ δ' ἡμετέρα πόλις_{HEAD}⌉ ⌈ἡ κοινὴ καταφυγὴ_{HEAD} τῶν Ἑλλήνων⌉ . . . νῦν οὐκέτι περὶ τῆς τῶν Ἑλλήνων ἡγεμονίας ἀγωνίζεται. (Aeschin. 3.134)
Our city, the shared safe haven for the Greeks, is now no longer contending for the leadership of the Greeks. *The combined phrase ἡ δ' ἡμετέρα . . . Ἑλλήνων is subject of ἀγωνίζεται.*

(81) ⌈τὴν θυγατέρα_{HEAD}⌉, ⌈δεινόν_{HEAD} τι κάλλος καὶ μέγεθος⌉ . . . ἐξάγων ὧδ' εἶπεν· . . . (Xen. *Cyr.* 5.2.7)
He brought out his daughter, an impressive creature in beauty and stature, and spoke as follows: . . . *The combined phrase τὴν . . . μέγεθος is object of ἐξάγων.*

For agreement in apposition, →27.13–14.

26.25   Certain nouns denoting age, gender, occupation, status or geographical origin are used in apposition particularly often in Greek. Among them are ἀνήρ *man*, ἄνθρωπος *man/woman*, γυνή *woman*, Ἕλλην *Greek*, etc.:

(82) ἀπόκριναί μοι, τίνος οὕνεκα χρὴ θαυμάζειν ἄνδρα ποιητήν; (Ar. *Ran.* 1008)
Answer me: why ought someone to be impressed by a poet? *ἀνήρ in such cases does not permit easy translation.*

(83) ἀλαλάξαντες οἱ Ἕλληνες πελτασταὶ ἔθεον. (6.5.26)
Raising a shout, the Greek peltasts ran forward.

Vocative forms of ἀνήρ are frequently so used in (respectful) forms of address (ὦ) ἄνδρες δικασταί *gentlemen of the jury*, (ὦ) ἄνδρες πολῖται *citizens*.

Predicative Modifiers

26.26   Some constituents simultaneously serve as adverbial modifier and to modify the head of a noun phrase. Such constituents are called **predicative modifiers**: they occur in the form of adjectives and especially participles, which agree with their noun in case, number and gender. For example:

(84) ἀναστάς_{PREDICATIVE MODIFIER} ... εἶπε_{PREDICATE} Ξενοφῶν_{SUBJECT} · ... (3.2.34)

Having stood up, Xenophon said: ... *The participle ἀναστάς agrees with the subject Ξενοφῶν in case, number and gender: it describes Xenophon. At the same time, it serves as an adverbial modifier, describing the circumstances/time of Xenophon's speech.*

(85) οἱ Ἕλληνες_{SUBJECT} ἔθεον_{PREDICATE} ἐπὶ τὰ ὅπλα ... ἐκπεπληγμένοι_{PREDICATIVE} _{MODIFIER.} (2.5.34)

The Greeks ran to their weapons panic-stricken. *The participle ἐκπεπληγμένοι agrees with the subject οἱ Ἕλληνες: it describes the Greeks. At the same time, it serves as an adverbial modifier, describing the manner/circumstances of the Greeks' running.*

(86) προσβάλλουσι_{PREDICATE} πρὸς τὸν λόφον ὀρθίοις_{PREDICATIVE MODIFIER} τοῖς λόχοις_{ADVERBIAL MODIFIER.} (4.2.11)

They attacked the hill, with their companies in column. *The adjective ὀρθίοις agrees with τοῖς λόχοις: it describes the companies. At the same time, it serves as an adverbial modifier, describing the manner of the attack.*

Note 1: For this so-called 'circumstantial' use of the participle in (84) and (85) (by far its most frequent use), →52.29–45.

Note 2: For the position of predicative modifiers relative to their head and the article (if present), →28.11.

Elements Interrupting or Outside the Syntax of a Sentence

Parentheses

26.27   Sentences may be interrupted by other sentences – **parentheses**. These are often relatively short, and frequently contain some form of comment, as in:

(87) ἃ πρέπει, οἶμαι ἔγωγε, ἀνδρὶ εἰπεῖν καὶ ὁποῖα γυναικί ... (Pl. *Ion* 540b)

The things, I imagine, that it befits a man to say, and a woman, ...

(88) ἆρα ὁποῖα ἄρχοντι, λέγεις, ἐν θαλάττῃ χειμαζομένου πλοίου πρέπει εἰπεῖν, ὁ ῥαψῳδὸς γνώσεται κάλλιον ἢ ὁ κυβερνήτης; (Pl. *Ion* 540b)

So what sort of thing someone in charge of a storm-tossed vessel at sea should say the rhapsode, you mean, will know better than the pilot?

Parenthetical sentences or clauses are also used to introduce, beforehand, important information which relates to the host sentence that is still to come, as in:

(89) ταῦτα νομίζων, ἦν γὰρ οἱ τῶν αἰχμοφόρων Γύγης ... ἀρεσκόμενος μάλιστα, τούτῳ τῷ Γύγῃ ... τὰ σπουδαιέστερα τῶν πρηγμάτων ὑπερετίθετο ὁ Κανδαύλης. (Hdt. 1.8.1)

(*Lit.*) (Candaules,) believing this – there was among his bodyguard a certain Gyges, who was his favourite – to this Gyges Candaules entrusted all his most important secrets. *Such preposed parentheses usually do not permit easy 'literal' translation into English.* For this use of γάρ, →59.15.

Elements 'Outside' the Syntax of a Sentence

26.28   Some elements stand 'outside' the sentence, i.e. they are not part of the syntactic structure of predicates, complements and modifiers. The most important of these are:

– **forms of address** (→30.55):

(90) φιλοσόφῳ μὲν ἔοικας, <u>ὦ νεανίσκε</u>. (2.1.13)
You resemble a philosopher, young man.

– **exclamations, interjections**, etc. (also, in answers, **ναί** *yes*):

(91) ἀλλὰ <u>μὰ τοὺς θεούς</u> οὐκ ἔγωγε αὐτοὺς διώξω. (1.4.8)
But, by the gods, I will not pursue them.

(92) <u>παπαῖ, φεῦ. παπαῖ μάλ᾽</u>, ὦ πούς, οἷά μ᾽ ἐργάσῃ κακά. (Soph. *Phil.* 785–6)
Aiai! Alas! Aiaiai! Oh foot, what evils will you inflict on me!

(93) <u>φεῦ τοῦ ἀνδρός</u>. (Xen. *Cyr.* 3.1.39)
Alas for the man! *For this use of the genitive,* →30.30.

(94) ἐνταῦθα δὴ ἀναγιγνώσκει αὐτὸν καὶ ἤρετο· Ἦ σὺ εἶ ὁ τὸν κάμνοντα ἀγαγών; <u>Ναὶ μὰ Δί᾽</u>, ἔφη· Σὺ γὰρ ἠνάγκαζες. (5.8.6)
At that he recognized him, and asked: 'Are you the one who carried the sick man?' 'Yes, by Zeus,' he said, 'for you forced me to do so.'

26.29   Some other elements which stand outside the syntactic structure (or rather: have no syntactic structure) are:

– list entries:

(95) Σπαρτόλιοι : ΗΗ Αἰραῖοι : ΗΗΗ (IG I^3 259, col. III, 24–5)
Spartolians: 200; Aeraeans: 300. *A 'tribute list', inscribed on a stone found in Athens; for these numerals,* →9.13.

– headings/titles:

(96) <u>Ξενοφῶντος Κύρου Ἀναβάσεως λόγος πρῶτος</u>. Δαρείου καὶ Παρυσάτιδος γίγνονται παῖδες δύο... (1.1)
Xenophon's *Expedition of Cyrus*, Book One. Darius and Parysatis had two children...

Such elements normally appear in the nominative case (however, in (95) the nominatives could also be interpreted as subjects with an implied verb; *give, pay*, or the like; note that the genitives Ξενοφῶντος Κύρου Ἀναβάσεως in (96) are all attributive (Ἀναβάσεως modifying λόγος; Κύρου modifying Ἀναβάσεως; Ξενοφῶντος modifying the combined Κύρου Ἀναβάσεως).

27

Agreement

Subject – Finite Verb

Basic Rule

27.1   Basic rule: a finite verb agrees in **person and number** with its subject:

ἡ ναῦς ἀνάγεται   the ship is setting out (*third person singular*)
αἱ νῆες ἀνάγονται   the ships are setting out (*third person plural*)
ἡμεῖς ἀναγόμεθα   we are setting out (*first person plural*)

Exceptions

27.2   When a subject is **neuter plural**, the verb is normally singular:

(1) τὰ ἔθνη ταῦτα τῇ πόλει πολέμια ἦν. (Thuc. 5.51.2)
    These tribes were hostile to the city.

(2) οὐ καθεῖτο τείχη ὥσπερ νῦν. (Thuc. 4.103.5)
    The walls did not reach down as they do now.

The plural form of the verb may, however, be used to emphasize that the subject consists of various individual members:

(3) τοσάδε μὲν μετὰ Ἀθηναίων ἔθνη ἐστράτευον. (Thuc. 7.57.11)
    So many tribes fought on the side of Athens. *This is the conclusion of a catalogue that mentions each individual tribe.*

(4) ἦσαν δὲ ταῦτα δύο τείχη, καὶ τὸ μὲν ... , τὸ δὲ ... (Xen. *An.* 1.4.4)
    These were two walls, and the first ... , whereas the second ... *Note the numeral.*

27.3   When the subject is **dual**, the verb may be either dual or plural. When the subject consists of a pair, but is grammatically plural, the verb sometimes appears in the dual:

(5) τὼ ἄνδρε ... ἐγενέσθην φύλακε. (Xen. *Hell.* 4.4.8)
    Both men became guards. *Dual subject, dual verb.*

(6) ἔλεξαν γὰρ ... ὅτι αὐτὼ με τὼ θεὼ παραγάγοιεν. (Andoc. 1.113)
    For they said that the Two Goddesses themselves led me astray. *Dual subject, plural verb.*

(7) τῶν δὲ Ἀργείων <u>δύο ἄνδρες</u>, Θράσυλός τε . . . καὶ Ἀλκίφρων . . . , Ἄγιδι <u>διελεγέσθην</u> μὴ ποιεῖν μάχην. (Thuc. 5.59.5)

Two men belonging to the Argive army, Thrasylus and Alciphron, urged Agis in a conversation not to bring on a battle. *Plural subject, dual verb.*

27.4   When there are **multiple subjects**, the verb will normally be plural. Sometimes, however, especially when the verb precedes a first singular subject, it may be singular:

(8) <u>Εὐρυμέδων καὶ Σοφοκλῆς</u> . . . ἀφικόμενοι ἐς Κέρκυραν <u>ἐστράτευσαν</u> . . . (Thuc. 4.46.1)

After their arrival in Corcyra, Eurymedon and Sophocles made an attack . . . *Multiple subjects, plural verb.*

(9) <u>ἔλεγε</u> δὲ <u>ὁ Στύφων</u> καὶ <u>οἱ μετ' αὐτοῦ</u> ὅτι . . . (Thuc. 4.38.2)

Styphon said, as did his company, that . . . *The verb agrees merely with ὁ Στύφων, not with the other subject.*

(10) <u>πάρειμι</u> καὶ <u>ἐγὼ</u> καὶ <u>οὗτος Φρυνίσκος</u> . . . καὶ <u>Πολυκράτης</u>. (Xen. An. 7.2.29)

I am present, and so are this man Phryniscus and Polycrates. *The verb agrees merely with ἐγώ, not with the other subjects (note that πάρειμι also agrees only with ἐγώ in person.*

27.5   When there are **multiple subjects of different persons** and the verb is plural, the verb will normally be in the first person if a first-person subject is present and combined with a second- and/or third-person subject, and in the second person if a second-person subject combines with a third-person subject. Exceptions to this general rule are, however, fairly frequent:

(11) ἀεὶ γὰρ <u>ἐγὼ</u> καὶ <u>ὁ σὸς πατὴρ</u> ἑταίρω τε καὶ φίλω <u>ἦμεν</u>. (Pl. *La.* 180e)

For your father and I always were comrades and friends.

(12) οὐ <u>σὺ</u> μόνος οὐδὲ <u>οἱ σοὶ φίλοι</u> πρῶτοι καὶ πρῶτον ταύτην δόξαν <u>ἔσχετε</u> . . . (Pl. *Leg.* 888b)

You and your friends are not the first and foremost to have taken this as their view . . .

(13) ἐὰν <u>ὑμεῖς</u> τε καὶ <u>οἱ θεοὶ</u> <u>θέλωσιν</u> (Antiph. 1.20)

if you and the gods wish it so . . . *One of the subjects is second-person, yet the verb is third-person.*

27.6   The verb may agree in number with the subject in meaning rather than in grammatical form: this is called the **sense construction** (Lat. *constructio ad sensum*, Gr. κατὰ σύνεσιν, 'according to sense'); for example, when the subject is singular but refers to a collective, the verb may be plural in form:

(14) τοιαῦτα δὲ ἀκούσασα ἡ πόλις ... Ἀγησίλαον εἵλοντο βασιλέα. (Xen. *Hell.* 3.3.4)
The city, when it had heard such arguments, elected Agesilaus king.

(15) φρουρὰ μία τῶν περὶ τὴν χώραν ... ξυνεσελθεῖν μὲν ἐς τὸ τεῖχος οὐκ ἠθέλησαν.
(Thuc. 4.57.1)
One of the district garrisons refused to accompany them inside the city
walls.

Head – Modifier (in Noun Phrases); Predicative Modifiers and Complements

Basic Rule

27.7   Basic rule: an article, adjective, participle, adnominal pronoun or numeral agrees in
case, **number** and **gender** with the head it modifies:

ὁ σοφὸς ἀνήρ	the wise man (*nom. sg. masc.*)
τοῖς σοφοῖς ἀνδράσιν	the wise men (*dat. pl. masc.*)
ἡ γυνὴ ἡ σοφή	the wise woman (*nom. sg. fem*)
τούτων τῶν γυναικῶν	those wise women (*gen. pl. fem.*)
εἷς ἀνήρ	one man (*nom. sg. masc.*)
μία γυνή	one woman (*nom. sg. fem.*)

An adjective, pronoun, etc., functioning as predicative modifier (→26.26) or
predicative complement (→26.8–12) similarly agrees with its head/subject in
case, number and gender:

ἡ γυνὴ σοφή	the woman is wise / the woman, being wise, ... (*nom. sg. fem., adjective in predicative position*)

Note 1: Not all adjectives/pronouns have separate masculine and feminine forms (for
adjectives 'of two endings', →5.7–11); this does not mean that the basic rule does not
apply (in ἄδικος γυνή *unjust woman*, ἄδικος is feminine).
Note 2: Only some numerals decline: for indeclinable numerals, →9.2–5.
Note 3: Other types of modifiers do not agree with their head, particularly attributive
genitives, adverbs and prepositional phrases. For examples, →26.20.

Exceptions

27.8   A masculine or feminine abstract noun is often construed with a **neuter adjective
used as predicative complement** ('X is a Y thing'). This occurs especially in
generalizations, gnomic statements, etc.:

(16) <u>σοφὸν</u> ... <u>ἡ προμηθίη</u>. (Hdt. 3.36.1)

Foresight is a sensible thing.

(17) <u>καλὸν</u> μὲν <u>ἡ σωφροσύνη</u> τε καὶ <u>δικαιοσύνη</u>, <u>χαλεπὸν</u> μέντοι καὶ <u>ἐπίπονον</u>. (Pl. *Resp.* 364a)

Temperance and justness are a beautiful thing, yet difficult and laborious.

27.9 A demonstrative pronoun which serves as subject to a linking verb and predicative noun ('this is X', 'that is X') may either agree with that noun, or appear in the neuter:

(18) παρὰ τῶν προγεγενημένων μανθάνετε· <u>αὕτη</u> γὰρ <u>ἀρίστη</u> <u>διδασκαλία</u>. (Xen. *Cyr.* 8.7.24)

Learn from what happened before, for that is the best source of teaching.

(19) εἰ δέ τις <u>ταύτην</u> <u>εἰρήνην</u> ὑπολαμβάνει ... (Dem. 9.9)

But if anyone considers that to be peace ...

(20) <u>τοῦτ'</u> ἐστὶν <u>ἡ δικαιοσύνη</u>. (Pl. *Resp.* 432b)

This is what we call justice. *Neuter subject ('this thing is ...').*

Antecedent – Relative Pronoun

Basic Rule

27.10 Basic rule: a relative pronoun **agrees in number and gender** with its antecedent, but its **case** is determined by its syntactical function in the relative clause (for details, →50.8):

ἡ ναῦς <u>ἣ</u> ἀνάγεται   the ship which is putting out to sea

singular and feminine as the antecedent, nominative as subject in the relative clause

ἡ ναῦς <u>ἣν</u> ὁρᾷς   the ship which you see

singular and feminine as the antecedent, accusative as object in the relative clause

Exceptions

27.11 The **sense construction** (→27.6) is frequent with relative pronouns:

(21) ... ἀπὸ <u>Πελοποννήσου</u> παρεσομένης ὠφελίας, <u>οἳ</u> τῶνδε κρείσσους εἰσί (Thuc. 6.80.1)

... as help will come from the Peloponnesians (*lit.* 'from the Peloponnese'), who are stronger than these men.

27.12 For other exceptions, especially 'relative attraction', →50.13–14.

Apposition

27.13   An appositive (→26.24–5) **agrees in case** with the word it belongs to, but has **its own number and gender**:

(22)   Θῆβαι, πόλις ἀστυγείτων (Aeschin. 3.133)
        Thebes, our neighbouring city

(23)   τὴν θυγατέρα, δεινόν τι κάλλος καὶ μέγεθος . . . ἐξάγων ὧδ᾽ εἶπεν· . . . (Xen. *Cyr.* 5.2.7)
        He brought out his daughter, an impressive creature in beauty and stature, and spoke as follows: . . .

27.14   Note a few special cases with respect to agreement:

– An appositive to a **possessive pronoun** (or an adjective equivalent to a possessive) may stand in the **genitive**:

(24)   τὸν ἐμὸν . . . τοῦ ταλαιπώρου . . . βίον (Ar. *Plut.* 33–4)
        the life of me, miserable me

(25)   Ἀθηναῖος ὤν, πόλεως τῆς μεγίστης (Pl. *Ap.* 29d)
        being a citizen of Athens (*lit.* 'an Athenian'), the greatest city

– An appositive to a **whole clause or sentence** usually stands in the **accusative** (→30.19), occasionally in the **nominative**:

(26)   εὐδαιμονοίης μισθὸν ἡδίστων λόγων. (Eur. *El.* 231)
        May you fare well – a payment for your most pleasing message. *Accusative.*

(27)   τὸ λοίσθιον δέ, θριγκὸς ἀθλίων κακῶν, | δούλη γυνὴ γραῦς Ἑλλάδ᾽ εἰσαφίξομαι. (Eur. *Tro.* 489–90)
        And finally – to cap my miserable suffering – I will come to Greece, a slave in my old age. *Nominative (lit. 'a capstone of . . .').*

The nominative in apposition to clauses is especially frequent in phrases with a neuter (superlative) adjective such as τὸ λοίσθιον *the last thing, finally* (as in (27)), τὸ μέγιστον *the greatest thing, most significant of all*, τὸ δεινότατον *the worst thing of all*, τὸ κεφάλαιον *the main point, to sum up*, etc. Such appositions introduce and qualify the sentence that follows them:

(28)   καὶ τὸ πάντων δεινότατον, ὑμεῖς μὲν τοῦτον οὐ προΰδοτε, . . . οὗτος δ᾽ ὑμᾶς νυνὶ προδέδωκεν. (Aeschin. 3.161)
        And worst of all, you did not betray him, but he has now betrayed you.

Note 1: The clause following such appositions in the nominative is sometimes introduced by the particle γάρ (which may be translated in such instances by *namely*, or left untranslated, →59.14):

(29) τὸ δὲ μέγιστον τῶν κακῶν· δεδιότες <u>γὰρ</u> διατελοῦσιν μὴ Θηβαῖοι ... μείζοσιν αὐτοὺς συμφοραῖς περιβάλωσιν τῶν πρότερον γεγενημένων. (Isoc. 5.50)

And the greatest of their ills (is this), namely (that) they are continually afraid that the Thebans will involve them in greater calamities than those that have happened before. *Note, apart from γάρ, the use of a high dot in most text editions to punctuate between the appositive and the main sentence.*

Note 2: A closely parallel construction is the use of a relative clause with neuter ὅ in apposition to a sentence, e.g. ὃ δὲ μέγιστον *and what is most significant:* ..., καὶ ὃ πάντων θαυμαστότατον *and what is the most amazing thing of all:* ... For this construction, →50.12.

28

The Article

Meaning of the Definite Article

Basic Meaning

28.1 Greek has a **definite article** (ὁ, ἡ, τό *the*), but no indefinite article (Engl. singular *a(n)*). The Greek equivalent of an indefinite article is the **lack of an article**:

(1) πρῶτον μὲν ἠρεμεῖν δεῖ διδάσκειν <u>τὸν ἵππον</u>. (Xen. *Eq.* 7.8)
First it is necessary to teach the horse to stay still.

(2) οὐ γὰρ πώποτε ἐκτήσω <u>ἵππον</u> πλείονος ἄξιον ἢ τριῶν μνῶν. (Isae. 5.43)
For you have never had a horse worth more than three minae.

The article is 'definite' because it refers to someone/something that is **identifiable**: the article expresses that it is clear who/what is meant, and that it can be distinguished from other people/things.

Note 1: Greek often uses the definite article where English would not (see examples below).
Note 2: For the indefinite pronoun τις (which can in some cases be translated as *a(n)*) →29.38–42.

28.2 The lack of an article in prose is normally significant, but in poetry the article is omitted much more freely:

(3) χολωθεὶς <u>τέκτονας</u> Δίου <u>πυρὸς</u> | κτείνω <u>Κύκλωπας</u>· καί με θητεύειν <u>πατὴρ</u> | θνητῷ παρ᾽ ἀνδρὶ τῶνδ᾽ ἄποιν᾽ ἠνάγκασεν. (Eur. *Alc.* 5–7)
In anger, I slew the Cyclopes, makers of Zeus' fire: and in punishment for this, my father forced me to work as servant for a mortal man. *τέκτονας ... Κύκλωπας, πυρός and πατήρ are all identifiable, and in prose would probably have been given an article (θνητῷ ... ἀνδρί would probably be without article in prose).*

Reasons for Identifiability of a Referent

28.3 The referent of a noun is usually identifiable when it has been **mentioned before**:

(4) κἂν ἄρα γέ τις <u>ἵππον</u> πριάμενος μὴ ἐπίστηται αὐτῷ χρῆσθαι, ἀλλὰ καταπίπτων ἀπ᾽ αὐτοῦ κακὰ λαμβάνῃ, οὐ χρήματα αὐτῷ ἐστιν <u>ὁ ἵππος</u>; (Xen. *Oec.* 1.8)
And so when someone buys a horse and does not know how to manage it, but keeps falling off of it and getting injured, the horse is not wealth for him, is it? *When the horse is first introduced it is not yet identifiable and has no article. The next time it is mentioned, it is identifiable and therefore has the article.*

28.4   A referent is identifiable when it is **obvious from the context** or **made specific by the immediate context**:

(5) ἱππεύς τις προσήλαυνε καὶ μάλα ἰσχυρῶς ἱδρῶντι τῷ ἵππῳ. (Xen. *Hell.* 4.5.7)
A horseman rode up, with his horse sweating profusely. *A rider implies the presence of a horse, so the horse is identifiable at first mention. For the translation 'his', see n.1 below.*

(6) τῷ ἀνδρὶ ὃν ἂν ἕλησθε πείσομαι ᾗ δυνατὸν μάλιστα. (Xen. *An.* 1.3.15)
I will obey the man you choose as best I can. *The relative clause provides the information needed to make the man identifiable.*

Note 1: In many cases, if a noun with article refers to something whose possessor or origin is obvious (usually the subject), Greek uses only the article where English would use a possessive pronoun (→29.24), as in (5) and in:

(7) περὶ τούτων γὰρ ὑμεῖς νυνὶ τὴν ψῆφον οἴσετε. (Dem. 40.60)
For you will now cast your vote about these matters.

28.5   A referent is identifiable when it is considered **generally well-known**:

(8) ὁ δὲ κολωνός ἐστι ἐν τῇ ἐσόδῳ, ὅκου νῦν ὁ λίθινος λέων ἕστηκε ἐπὶ Λεωνίδῃ. (Hdt. 7.225.2)
The hill is at the mouth of the pass, where the stone lion dedicated to Leonidas now stands. *The lion-statue is a famous monument.*

28.6   A referent is identifiable when it is a **species or class in its entirety** (in this use the article is called **generic** – note that English does not use the definite article in many such cases):

(9) οὐκ ἐκβάλλει δ᾽ ἔνια αὐτῶν πλὴν τοὺς κυνόδοντας, οἷον οἱ λέοντες. (Arist. *Gen. an.* 788b16–17)
Some of them do not shed any (teeth) except the canine teeth, for example lions.

(10) πονηρόν, ἄνδρες Ἀθηναῖοι, πονηρὸν ὁ συκοφάντης ἀεί. (Dem. 18.242)
An informant is a vile creature, men of Athens, a vile creature always.

(11) ὁ ἀγαθὸς ἀνὴρ πάντας τοὺς φίλους εὖ ποιεῖ. (Arist. *Rh.* 1402b5)
The good man treats all his friends well.

28.7   A noun usually also has the article when it refers to an **abstract concept** (note that English does not use the article in such cases):

(12) ἡ σωφροσύνη . . . καὶ αὐτὴ ἡ φρόνησις μὴ καθαρμός τις ᾖ. (Pl. *Phd.* 69c)
Restraint and wisdom itself may well be some form of purification. *For μή . . . ᾖ, →34.10.*

(13) ἡ ἀρετὴ μᾶλλον ἢ ἡ φυγὴ σῴζει τὰς ψυχάς. (Xen. *Cyr.* 4.1.5)
Valour rather than flight saves lives.

28.8   **Proper names** often have an article, especially when the person or place is generally well-known or prominent in the context:

(14) τοσαῦτα εἰπών ... ὁ Ἀρχίδαμος Μελήσιππον πρῶτον ἀποστέλλει ἐς τὰς Ἀθήνας. (Thuc. 2.12.1)

Having said this much, Archidamus first sent Melesippus to Athens. *Archidamus has been a major focus of attention in this part of the narrative, while Athens is generally well-known; Melesippus, by contrast, is here mentioned for the first time, and is not very famous.*

Note 1: In many cases, however, the lack of the article with proper names is difficult to account for, and depends on idiom and the preferences of individual authors.
Note 2: βασιλεύς (*the*) *King* is regularly used without an article to refer to the Persian king, even if he is clearly identifiable. In this use βασιλεύς is much like a proper name or title.

28.9   A **predicative complement** (→26.8–12) normally does not have the article, as it generally introduces new information. However, it has the article when it is identifiable for one of the reasons given above (e.g. because the concept has been mentioned before, or because it refers to an entire class):

(15) ὁ ἐρῶν τῶν καλῶν ἐραστὴς καλεῖται. (Pl. *Phdr.* 249e)

He who loves beautiful things is called a lover.

(16) οἱ τιθέμενοι τοὺς νόμους οἱ ἀσθενεῖς ἄνθρωποί εἰσιν. (Pl. *Grg.* 483b)

The people who institute laws are the weak sort. *The article is used because the noun refers to a class.*

For the articles in ὁ ἐρῶν, τῶν καλῶν and οἱ τιθέμενοι, →28.23.

28.10   The principle that the article indicates identifiability is also valid for words that are in **apposition** (→26.24–5). If an appositive has the article, it means that the word(s) to which it is appended is/are identifiable through the information added in the apposition:

(17) Ἑκαταῖος δ' ὁ λογοποιός ... οὐκ ἔα πόλεμον βασιλέϊ τῶν Περσέων ἀναιρέεσθαι. (Hdt. 5.36.2)

But Hecataeus the historian advised them not to start a war against the king of Persia. *The addition of ὁ λογοποιός helps to identify Hecataeus by his profession as a historian. For βασιλέϊ, →28.8 n.2.*

(18) Θουκυδίδης Ἀθηναῖος ξυνέγραψε τὸν πόλεμον τῶν Πελοποννησίων καὶ Ἀθηναίων. (Thuc. 1.1.1)

Thucydides, an Athenian, has recorded the war between the Peloponnesians and the Athenians. *Thucydides introduces himself for the first time to his readers; Θουκυδίδης ὁ Ἀθηναῖος would have meant 'Thucydides the Athenian' (already known as such).*

Relative Position of Article, Head and Modifiers in a Noun Phrase

Attributive and Predicative Position

28.11 When the head of a noun phrase is modified by the article and one or more other modifiers (adjectives, pronouns, numerals, participles, →26.17–18), two different orderings of article, head and modifier can be distinguished:

- so-called **attributive position** of the modifier (the modifier is preceded directly by the article):

ὁ <u>ἀγαθὸς</u> ἀνήρ
ὁ ἀνὴρ ὁ <u>ἀγαθός</u>   } the good man
ἀνὴρ ὁ <u>ἀγαθός</u> (*less frequent*)

- so-called **predicative position** of the modifier (the modifier is not preceded directly by the article):

<u>ἀγαθὸς</u> (. . .) ὁ ἀνήρ
ὁ ἀνὴρ (. . .) <u>ἀγαθός</u>   } the man, being good, . . . (*or*: the man is good)

Note 1: For the difference between the different possible orderings of head and modifier (head–modifier vs. modifier–head), →60.15–16.
Note 2: The difference between the pattern ὁ ἀνὴρ ὁ ἀγαθός and ἀνὴρ ὁ ἀγαθός resides in the identifiability of the head: in the article–head–article–modifier configuration, the head is identifiable on its own, and the modifier is added to confirm that this is the intended referent, or to specify a subgroup; in the less frequent head–article–modifier configuration, the head is typically not identifiable without the information provided by the modifier.

28.12 The general difference between attributive and predicative position may be described as follows:

- A modifier in **attributive position** describes an **attribute/characteristic** of the referent, or describes its **origin/possessor/target** etc. Modifiers so used typically serve to **identify** the referent of the head noun (cf. e.g. Engl. *the good man*, as opposed to any other man):

(19) ταῦτα . . . πράττειν, Αἰσχίνη, <u>τὸν καλὸν κἀγαθὸν πολίτην</u> ἔδει. (Dem. 18.306)
These things, Aeschines, are what a good and right citizen ought to do.

(20) <u>τὸν χρυσοῦν στέφανον</u> . . . ἱερὸν εἶναι . . . ὁ νόμος κελεύει. (Aeschin. 3.46)
The law ordains that the golden crown is sacred.

(21) ἐγὼ μὲν καὶ ἐτράφην καὶ ἐπαιδεύθην . . . ἐν <u>τῇ τοῦ πατρὸς οἰκίᾳ</u>. (Dem. 40.50)
I was raised and brought up in my father's house.

(22) συνέβη γὰρ αὐτῷ διὰ <u>τὴν ἄφιξιν τὴν εἰς Κύπρον</u> καὶ ποιῆσαι καὶ παθεῖν πλεῖστ᾽ ἀγαθά. (Isoc. 9.53)
Because of his arrival on Cyprus, he chanced to do and experience very many good things.

(23) ἄν τις Ἀθηναίων . . . ἑταιρήσῃ, μὴ ἐξέστω αὐτῷ <u>τῶν ἐννέα ἀρχόντων</u> γενέσθαι.
(Aeschin. 1.19)

If an Athenian has prostituted himself, let it not be permitted for him to become one of the nine archons.

– A modifier in **predicative position** is not used to identify the referent. Rather, adjectives and participles in predicative position say something about the **condition** the referent is in (cf. Engl. *I drink my coffee black, They found the premises deserted*):

(24) ἐπὶ <u>ψυχρὸν</u> τὸν ἰπνὸν Περίανδρος τοὺς ἄρτους ἐπέβαλε. (Hdt. 5.92η.2)

Periander put the loaves in the oven when it was cold.

(25) <u>ἀθάνατον</u> τὴν περὶ αὐτῶν μνήμην καταλείψουσιν. (Isoc. 9.3)

They will leave their memory behind to be immortal.

(26) <u>τὰς τριήρεις</u> ἀφείλκυσαν <u>κενάς</u>. (Thuc. 2.93.4)

They towed the triremes without their crews (*lit.* 'empty').

(27) οὐχ . . . <u>ἕνα</u> τὸν ἀγῶνα περὶ τοῦ πράγματος ἐποιήσω, ἀλλὰ ἀμφισβήτησιν καὶ λόγον ὑπελείπου. (Antiph. 5.16)

You have not arraigned the case concerning this matter to be tried once, but you left room for argument and discussion.

28.13   The predicative position is always used for **predicative complements** with linking verbs (→26.8–9):

(28) <u>κοινή</u> . . . ἡ τύχη καὶ <u>τὸ μέλλον</u> ἀόρατον. ([Isoc.] 1.29)

Fate is common to all, and the future is invisible. *For the omission of ἐστί,* →*26.13.*

(29) πάντα . . . τἄλλ' <u>εὐτυχῆ</u> τὴν πόλιν κρίνων, ἐν οὐδέποτ' εὐτυχῆσαι τοῦτο <u>νομίζω</u>. (Dem. 62.55.1)

Although I consider the city fortunate in every other respect, in this one respect I believe that it has never been fortunate.

28.14   However, there are various kinds of modifiers which can occur only in attributive or only in predicative position: in such cases the distinction between the positions outlined above does not hold. These are treated below, →28.15–22.

Attributive Genitives

28.15   Most **attributive genitives** (→30.28–9; e.g. 'possessive', 'subjective', 'objective' genitives) can occur in both positions:

ὁ δῆμος ὁ <u>τῶν Ἀθηναίων</u> ὁ δῆμος <u>τῶν Ἀθηναίων</u> }	the Athenian people
τὸ <u>Παυσανίου</u> μῖσος	the hatred of Pausanias
τὸ μῖσος <u>τῶν Λακεδαιμονίων</u>	the hatred of the Spartans

Note 1: The difference between the two constructions appears to be that in attributive position, the genitive is presented as (more) vital for the identification of the head noun (for example, when the Athenian people are contrasted with another people, the attributive position will be used). But often the distinction is slight. Also →60.15.

28.16 Some types of attributive genitive, however, only occur in one of the two positions:

- **Partitive genitives** (→30.25, 30.29) stand in predicative position:

οἱ πλούσιοι <u>τῶν πολιτῶν</u>	the rich among the citizens
<u>τούτων</u> οἱ πλεῖστοι	the majority of them

- Genitives of **personal pronouns** (μου, σου, etc., →7.1, 29.1) and genitives of αὐτός used as a personal pronoun (→7.2, 7.10, 29.7) always follow the head in predicative position when used attributively:

ἡ οἰκία <u>αὐτοῦ</u>	his house
τὸν πατέρα <u>μου</u> διαβάλλοντες	slandering my father

- But attributive genitives of **demonstrative pronouns** (τοῦδε, etc., →7.13–15), of the **reflexive pronoun** (ἐμαυτοῦ, etc., →7.3) and of the **reciprocal pronoun** (ἀλλήλων, →7.6) all stand in attributive position:

τὸ <u>ταύτης</u> βιβλίον	her book
τὸ <u>ἑαυτοῦ</u> βιβλίον	his (own) book

(30) χαίρουσιν ἐπὶ τοῖς <u>ἀλλήλων</u> κακοῖς. (Isoc. 4.168)
    They take pleasure in each other's troubles.

Note 1: In each of these uses, modifiers in 'predicative' position actually do not have predicative function (for predicative function, →26.8–12, 28.12). The terminology is therefore somewhat misleading, and should be taken to refer merely to word order.

Demonstrative and Possessive Pronouns

28.17 The **demonstrative pronouns** ὅδε *this*, οὗτος *this/that* and ἐκεῖνος *that*, when used adnominally, always stand **in predicative position**. In prose, heads modified by these pronouns nearly always have the article:

ὁ πόλεμος <u>ὅδε</u>	this war
ἐν <u>ταύτῃ</u> τῇ πόλει	in that city
<u>ἐκεῖνο</u> τὸ πάγκαλον ἔργον	that very beautiful work

Note 1: With these pronouns, 'predicative' position should again not be taken to imply predicative function (cf. 28.16 n.1 above).

Note 2: Particularly in prose, when a noun is modified by a demonstrative pronoun but does not have the article, this indicates that the noun has predicative function:

(31) <u>ταύτην</u> γὰρ <u>τέχνην</u> ἔχει. (Lys. 1.16)
    He has this as a profession. (<u>ταύτην</u> <u>τὴν</u> <u>τέχνην</u> ἔχει would have meant 'he has this profession'. Also →29.34).

28.18   The **possessive adjectives** ἐμός *my*, ἡμέτερος *our*, etc., normally stand **in attributive position**:

ἡ ἐμὴ μήτηρ	my mother
πρὸς τοὺς σφετέρους συμμάχους	against their allies
συμφέρει τῇ πόλει τῇ ὑμετέρᾳ	it benefits your city

Note 1: These pronouns may also be used as predicative complements with linking verbs (→26.8–10), and then of course stand in predicative position:

(32) καὶ ἕως μὲν ἂν ἐγὼ ζῶ, ἐμὴ γίγνεται ἡ ἐν Πέρσαις βασιλεία. (Xen. *Cyr.* 8.5.26)
     As long as I live, the Persian throne is mine.

αὐτός

28.19   When used as an adjective, **αὐτός** differs in meaning depending on whether it stands in attributive or predicative position:

ὁ ἀνὴρ αὐτός / αὐτὸς ὁ ἀνήρ	the man himself
ὁ αὐτὸς ἀνήρ	the same man

For details, →29.7–13.

Quantifiers

28.20   Many quantifiers, such as πᾶς *every, all, whole*, ὅλος *whole, in its entirety*, etc. may appear either in attributive or predicative position, with a distinction in meaning. For details, →29.45–52.

28.21   The following quantifiers always take predicative position when combined with the article: **ἕκαστος** *each, every*, **ἑκάτερος** *each (of two), either*, **ἄμφω/ἀμφότερος** *both*:

ἑκάτερον τὸ πάθος	either of the two affections
ἑκάστη ἡ παρ᾽ ἡμῖν ἐπιστήμη	each form of knowledge available to us
ἄμφω τὼ πόλεε	both cities

Adjectives Determining Position (μέσος, ἄκρος, ἔσχατος etc.)

28.22   **Adjectives that determine a position**, such as μέσος *middle*, ἄκρος *high*, ἔσχατος *utmost, extreme*, have different meanings when in attributive or predicative position:

ἐν τῇ μέσῃ ἀγορᾷ	in the middle marketplace (*of three or more*)
ἐν μέσῃ τῇ ἀγορᾷ	in the middle of the marketplace
εἰς τὸ ὄρος τὸ ἄκρον	to the high mountain
εἰς ἄκρον τὸ ὄρος	to the top of the mountain
ἐν τῇ ἐσχάτῃ νήσῳ	on the last island
ἐν ἐσχάτῃ τῇ νήσῳ	at the edge of the island

The Article as Substantivizer

28.23 When a word (group) other than a noun is modified by the definite article, it is 'substantivized' (i.e. 'turned into a noun'), and **serves as head of a noun phrase** (→26.16, 26.20–1).

28.24 Depending on the gender of the article, such constructions may refer to men or people **in general** (masculine article), to women (feminine article), or to things/concepts (neuter article):

ὁ ἀγαθός	the good man	οἱ ἀγαθοί	good men
ἡ ἀγαθή	the good woman	αἱ ἀγαθαί	good women
τὸ ἀγαθόν	the good thing, goodness	τὰ ἀγαθά	good things, benefits

Alternatively, such constructions may identify **a subset from a larger group**; the group may be expressed in the form of a partitive genitive (→30.25, 30.29) or supplied from the context:

(33) τοὺς μὲν δὴ ἱππέας ἐδέξαντο <u>οἱ ἀγαθοὶ τῶν Περσῶν</u>. (Xen. *Ages.* 1.32)
The elite forces of the Persians stood to face the (charge of) the riders.

(34) ... οἱ τὰς πολιτείας καθιστάντες, <u>οἵ τε τὰς ἀριστοκρατικὰς</u> καὶ <u>οἱ τὰς ὀλιγαρχικὰς</u> καὶ πάλιν <u>οἱ τὰς δημοκρατικὰς</u> ... (Arist. *Pol.* 1288a21–2)
... those who introduce forms of government, be they those who introduce aristocratic ones, oligarchic ones, or, again, democratic ones ...
The article functions as substantivizer in all instances in this example except the first τάς (which modifies πολιτείας).

Note 1: In translation, a relative clause often conveys such senses well: e.g. τὰ ἀγαθά *the things that are good*, οἱ σοφοί *men who are wise*. Also note the translation of οἱ ... καθιστάντες in (34).

28.25 The following types of word or phrase are frequently substantivized in this way:

– **Adjectives** (the article is often generic, →28.6):

τὸ κακόν	evil
τὸ δίκαιον	justice
οἱ πολλοί	the many, the masses, the majority
ἡ δύστηνος	the wretched woman

– **Participles** (in any tense and voice; the article is often generic, →28.6):

ὁ ἐρῶν	the man who loves, the lover
ὁ βουλόμενος	anyone who likes
οἱ τεθνηκότες	the dead
τὰ γενόμενα	the things which have happened, the events

(35) ... ὅπως ὦσι καὶ <u>οἱ ποιήσοντες</u> ἡμῖν τὰ ἐπιτήδεια. (Xen. *Cyr.* 4.2.40)

... so that we have people to provide for us as well (*lit.* 'who will make provisions').

(36) μετέγνων καὶ <u>τὰ πρόσθ᾽ εἰρημένα.</u> (Eur. *Med.* 64)

I regret what I have said already (*lit.* 'what has already been said').

- **Adverbs:**

οἱ ἔνδον	the people inside
οἱ πέλας	those nearby, the neighbours
οἱ νῦν	those living today
οἱ πάλαι	the people of long ago, our forebears
τὸ νῦν, τὰ νῦν	the present moment/period (*often used adverbially,* 'now')
τὸ πρότερον	the last time, the earlier period, (*often used adverbially,* 'previously', →6.13)

- **Prepositional phrases:**

οἱ ἐν τέλει	those in charge, the authorities
οἱ ἐπὶ τῶν πραγμάτων	those in power (the government)
οἱ ἐπ᾽ ἐμοῦ	those in my lifetime, the people of my generation
οἱ ἐν τῇ ἡλικίᾳ	those in the prime of their youth

- **Attributive genitives** (frequently with a neuter article to indicate 'the affairs of ...'):

οἱ Ξέρξου	the soldiers/men of Xerxes
τὸ τῶν Ἑρμῶν	the affair of the Hermae
τὰ τοῦ γήρως	the lot of old age

(37) <u>τὰ τοῦ δήμου</u> φρονεῖ. (Ar. *Eq.* 1216)

He favours the people's side.

(38) ἄδηλα ... <u>τὰ τῶν πολέμων.</u> (Thuc. 2.11.4)

The events of wars are unpredictable.

- **Infinitives**, with the neuter article ('articular' infinitive, →51.38–46):

τὸ ὑπὸ ἡδονῶν ἄρχεσθαι	(the) being led by pleasures, to be led by pleasures
ἐνικήσαμεν τῷ λέγειν	we have conquered by speaking

- Whole **word groups, clauses** or **sentences**, with the neuter article:

(39) λέγω δὲ δεδημοσιευμένα οἷον <u>τὸ γνῶθι σαυτὸν</u> καὶ <u>τὸ μηδὲν ἄγαν</u>. (Arist. *Rh.* 1395a21–2)

I am referring to sayings which have become popularized, such as 'Know thyself' and 'Nothing in excess'.

Note 1: The negative with substantivized adjectives, participles, adverbs and prepositional phrases is μή when the noun phrase has a generic sense: e.g. ὁ μὴ εἰδώς *whoever does not know*, but ὁ οὐκ εἰδώς *the (specific) man who does not know:* →56.16 n.1.

Pronominal Uses of the Article

28.26   In a few highly specific uses the article has a pronominal function (i.e. serves as a noun phrase by itself, →26.16).

> **Note 1:** These uses are remnants from earlier Greek, in which the article had a largely pronominal function. In Homer, forms of the article are still used nearly exclusively as a demonstrative pronoun:
>
> (40) τὴν μὲν ἐγώ ... πέμψω. (Hom. *Il.* 1.183–4)
>   I will send her away.
>
> This use has largely disappeared from classical Greek, but is retained in the specific expressions treated below.

28.27   Parallel articles combined with the particles μέν and δέ (e.g. **ὁ μέν ... ὁ δέ**; →59.24) are used to contrast individuals, groups, etc.:

ὁ μέν ... ὁ δέ	the one (man) ... the other (man) ... ; someone ... someone else ...; the former ... the latter
οἱ μέν ... οἱ δέ	some ... others ... ; a few ... others ...; the former ... the latter
τὸ μέν ... τὸ δέ	on the one hand ... on the other hand ... ; partly ... partly ... (*also:* τοῦτο μέν ... τοῦτο δέ)

(41) καὶ οἱ μὲν ὕπνον ᾑροῦντο κατὰ μέρος, οἱ δὲ ἤλαυνον. (Thuc. 3.49.3)
     And taking turns, one group went to sleep and the other rowed.

(42) σοφὴ γὰρ οὖσα, τοῖς μέν εἰμ' ἐπίφθονος, ... τοῖς δ' αὖ προσάντης. (Eur. *Med.* 303–5)
     Because I am wise, I am enviable to some, and despicable to others.

(43) ἆρ' οὖν ἐθελήσαις ἄν ... διατελέσαι τὸ μὲν ἐρωτῶν, τὸ δ' ἀποκρινόμενος; (Pl. *Grg.* 449b)
     Would you be willing, then, to keep going, partly by asking questions, partly by answering them?

(44) τοῦτο μὲν δή, εἰ νικήσεις, τί σφεας ἀπαιρήσεαι, τοῖσί γε μὴ ἔστι μηδέν; τοῦτο δέ, ἢν νικηθῇς, μάθε ὅσα ἀγαθὰ ἀποβαλέεις. (Hdt. 1.71.3)
     If, on the one hand, you conquer them, what will you take from them, who have nothing? But if, on the other hand, you are defeated, discover how many good things you will lose. *For εἰ νικήσεις ... ἢν νικηθῇς →49.5–6.*

28.28   An article combined with δέ (**ὁ δέ, ἡ δέ**, etc.) at the start of a clause or sentence indicates a shift from one 'topic' (the person or thing spoken about, usually the subject, →59.16) to the next. Usually, the new topic is present in the preceding sentence. In such cases, ὁ δέ may be translated by *and he, but he,* or *he, however:*

(45) Σίμων δὲ οὑτοσὶ καὶ Θεόφιλος ... εἷλκον τὸ μειράκιον. ὁ δὲ ῥίψας τὸ ἱμάτιον ᾤχετο φεύγων. (Lys. 3.12)
     Simon here and Theophilus were dragging the boy along. He, however, flung off his cloak and ran away. *The first sentence is about the men*

dragging the boy along; it does mention that boy, who is then taken up as the topic of the new sentence, and referred to by ὁ δέ.

(46) ἐγὼ τὴν γυναῖκα ἀπιέναι ἐκέλευον . . . <u>ἡ δὲ</u> τὸ μὲν πρῶτον οὐκ ἤθελεν. (Lys. 1.12)

I was telling my wife to go away, but she, at first, did not want to. *The wife, mentioned in the first sentence, is the topic of the second.*

28.29   Much less frequently, topic shift is indicated by καὶ ὅς (acc. καὶ τόν, fem. καὶ ἥ, etc.; ὅς is the article expanded with -ς characteristic of the nom. sg. masc.).

28.30   The article is used similarly in the phrases ὅς καὶ ὅς (acc. τὸν καὶ τόν, neut. τὸ καὶ τό, etc.) *so and so, this and that*, and in πρὸ τοῦ *previously*.

28.31   The article is sometimes used in poetry as a relative pronoun:

(47) OP. ἦ καὶ μετ᾽ αὐτοῦ μητέρ᾽ ἂν τλαίης κτανεῖν; | :: ΗΛ. ταὐτῷ γε πελέκει <u>τῷ</u> πατὴρ ἀπώλετο. (Eur. *El.* 278–9)

(Orestes:) Would you really dare to kill your mother with him? :: (Electra:) Yes, with the same axe by which my father perished.

29

Pronouns and Quantifiers

Personal Pronouns

Contrastive and Non-Contrastive Personal Pronouns

29.1   Personal pronouns are used only pronominally (→26.22–3). They are either accented or non-accented (for details, →7.1–2): to an extent, this distinction corresponds to a **contrastive** (or: 'emphatic') and a **non-contrastive** (or: 'unemphatic') function. The distinctions between these functions are treated below, →29.4–5, 29.7.

Contrastive: first person: ἐγώ, ἐμοῦ, ἐμοί, ἐμέ *I, me*; pl. ἡμεῖς, ἡμῶν, ἡμῖν, ἡμᾶς *we, us*
second person: σύ, σοῦ, σοί, σέ *you*; pl. ὑμεῖς, ὑμῶν, ὑμῖν, ὑμᾶς *you*
Non-contrastive: first person: μου, μοι, με *me*; ἡμῶν, ἡμῖν, ἡμᾶς *us*
second person: σου, σοι, σε *you*; ὑμῶν, ὑμῖν, ὑμᾶς *you*

Attic prose does not use separate personal pronouns of the third person (*he, him; she, her; it*), but the oblique cases of αὐτός are used as non-contrastive pronouns (→7.10, 29.5, 29.7).

Note 1: The oblique cases of the plural do not have distinct forms for non-contrastive functions. But in poetry some editors follow the ancient grammatical tradition of distinguishing non-contrastive forms of the oblique cases of the plural: for these forms →7.1 n.2.
Note 2: The unaccented personal pronouns (μου, etc.) are enclitic (→24.34). Non-contrastive plural forms (ἡμῶν, etc.) and forms of αὐτός used as personal pronoun behave like enclitics for the purposes of word order (→60.5).

29.2   The old forms of the third-person personal pronoun (e.g. οὗ/οὑ, οἷ/οἱ; for these forms, →7.2) are not used in Attic prose as personal pronouns (they are so used in Herodotus, →25.28). These forms do occur as indirect reflexive pronouns (→29.18 below).

29.3   In tragedy and Herodotus μιν is frequently used as accusative singular personal pronoun of the third person, →25.28. νιν is also used in tragedy as accusative, singular and plural.

First and Second Person

29.4   For the **first-** and **second-person personal pronouns**, the following rules apply:

- When describing the subject: the **nominative** forms of the personal pronouns (ἐγώ, ἡμεῖς; σύ, ὑμεῖς) are mostly used when some form of (contrastive) emphasis is placed on the subject – i.e. to distinguish it from a different subject, to clarify the identity of the subject, to emphasize responsibility, etc. When no (contrastive) emphasis is needed, the personal endings of the verb form suffice:

(1) ἐπεὶ ὑμεῖς ἐμοὶ οὐ θέλετε πείθεσθαι, ἐγὼ σὺν ὑμῖν ἔψομαι. (Xen. *An.* 1.3.6)
   Since you do not wish to obey me, I will follow you. *Contrastive emphasis.*

(2) οὐδένες ὑμῶν . . . μᾶλλόν εἰσιν αἴτιοι. οὐδὲ γὰρ δίκην ἔτι λαμβάνειν ἐθέλετε παρὰ τῶν ἀδικούντων. (Dem. 23.204)
   No one is more to blame than you. For you no longer wish to punish criminals. *Personal ending only: the subject 'you' is taken from the previous sentence, and requires no emphasis.*

- The **oblique cases** of accented pronouns are used in cases of (contrastive) emphasis, and **after prepositions**. The unaccented pronouns are used when there is no specific emphasis on the pronoun:

(3) τί μᾶλλον ἐμοῦ σὺ ταῦτα κατηγορεῖς ἢ ἐγὼ σοῦ; (Dem. 18.196)
   Why do you accuse me of these things rather than I you?

(4) καὶ πείσας ἐμὲ πιστὰ . . . ἔδωκάς μοι καὶ ἔλαβες παρ᾽ ἐμοῦ; (Xen. *An.* 1.6.7)
   And after you persuaded *me*, did you pledge me your faith and did you receive it from me?

(5) οὕτω μὲν ἃ κατηγόρηταί μου, πάντα ἄπιστά ἐστιν. (Antiph. 2.2.10)
   As such, the things of which I stand accused are all unreliable.

Note 1: For the use of the oblique cases of personal pronouns as reflexives (i.e. to refer back to the subject), →29.17–18 below.

Third Person

29.5   For **third-person pronouns**, the following rules apply:

- When describing the **subject**: a demonstrative pronoun or a nominative of αὐτός (emphatic use, →29.9) can be used to clarify the identity of the subject or to provide (contrastive) emphasis. In other cases personal endings suffice:

(6) αὕτη δὲ ὀργιζομένη . . . ὅτι οὐκέτι ὁμοίως ἐφοίτα . . . ἐφύλαττεν ἕως ἐξηῦρεν ὅ τι εἴη τὸ αἴτιον. (Lys. 1.15)
   This woman, angry because (her lover) no longer visited as frequently, waited until she discovered what the reason for this was. αὕτη (*a form of demonstrative* οὗτος) *is used to clarify the subject.*

(7) ἔλεξεν . . . ὅτι καὶ αὐτὴ ἀδικοῖτο ὑπὸ τοῦ πατρὸς τοῦ ἡμετέρου. (Antiph. 1.15)
   She said (*personal ending only*) that she herself (*emphatic use of* αὐτός, →29.9) too was being treated unjustly by our father.

– In the **oblique cases**, forms of αὐτός are used as non-contrastive third-person pronouns (→29.7); also after prepositions (9). If (contrastive) emphasis is required, an oblique case of a **demonstrative pronoun** is used (10):

(8) ἐκέλευον αὐτὴν ἀπιέναι. (Lys. 1.12)
   I told her to go away.

(9) ἦ καὶ μετ᾽ αὐτοῦ μητέρ᾽ ἂν τλαίης κτανεῖν; (Eur. *El.* 278)
   Would you truly dare to kill your mother together with him?

(10) πότερον ἐκείνῳ παῖδες οὐκ ἦσαν διπλοῖ, | οὓς τῆσδε μᾶλλον εἰκὸς ἦν θνῄσκειν; (Soph. *El.* 539–40)
   Did *he* (*Menelaus*) not have two children, who should in fairness have died instead of *her* (*Iphigenia*)?

29.6   In Herodotus, and very rarely in Attic (only in the plural), oblique cases of an old third-person personal pronoun are used (for these forms, →7.2, 25.28):

(11) εἰ νικήσεις, τί σφεας ἀπαιρήσεαι, τοῖσί γε μὴ ἔστι μηδέν; (Hdt. 1.71.3)
   If you are victorious, of what will you deprive them – they who have nothing?

(12) χερσί τἂν θιγὼν | δοκοῖμ᾽ ἔχειν σφας. (Soph. *OT* 1469–70)
   When I touch them with my hands, I might seem to have them with me.

αὐτός

As Third-Person Personal Pronoun

29.7   The oblique cases of αὐτός (αὐτοῦ, αὐτῷ, αὐτόν, αὐτῆς, etc.) are used as **non-contrastive personal pronouns of the third person** (*him, her, it; them*; etc.; →29.5); in this use αὐτός is purely pronominal (→26.22–3).

When used as a third-person pronoun, αὐτός always refers back to someone or something introduced before (anaphoric use):

(13) τί ποτε λέγει ὁ θεός, καὶ τί ποτε αἰνίττεται; . . . οὐ γὰρ δήπου ψεύδεταί γε· οὐ γὰρ θέμις αὐτῷ. (Pl. *Ap.* 21b)
   What on earth is the god saying, and what do his riddles mean? For at any rate he is not lying, I think, since that is not allowed to him.

(14) καὶ ἡμεῖς ἐκελεύομεν αὐτὸν πείθειν αὐτὴν περὶ τούτων. (Isae. 2.8)
   And we told him to persuade her with regard to those matters. αὐτόν *refers to Menecles, the accused, and* αὐτήν *to the sister of the plaintiff.*

(15) ἄρχει τις αὐτῶν, ἢ ᾽πὶ τῷ πλήθει λόγος; (Soph. *OC* 66)
   Does someone govern them, or does authority rest with the masses? αὐτῶν *refers to the Athenians, the topic of discussion.*

(16) καὶ εἰς τὴν οἰκίαν <u>αὐτοῦ</u> εἰσεφόρησαν ὡς ἐδύναντο πλεῖστα. (Xen. *An.* 4.6.1)

And they carried as much as they could into his house. *The attributive genitive αὐτοῦ here expresses possession, →30.28.*

Note 1: Nominative forms of αὐτός are not used as a personal pronoun (non-contrastive third-person *he, she, it* are typically expressed by the verbal endings, →29.5).

Note 2: The oblique cases of αὐτός normally do not refer back to the subject of the clause (in that case, a form of the reflexive pronoun is more often used; for full details and exceptions, →29.14–20).

As an Adjective, Expressing Identicalness: *The Same*

29.8   αὐτός (in any case) is used as an attributive adjective expressing identicalness: *(the) same.* In this use αὐτός is always **directly preceded by the article**, and thus stands in attributive position (→28.11–12):

(17) γέγραφε δὲ καὶ ταῦτα ὁ <u>αὐτὸς Θουκυδίδης</u> Ἀθηναῖος. (Thuc. 5.26.1)

Of this, too, the same Thucydides of Athens is the author.

(18) καὶ τριήρης <u>τῇ αὐτῇ ἡμέρᾳ</u> ἁλίσκεται τῶν Ἀθηναίων ὑπὸ τῶν Συρακοσίων. (Thuc. 7.3.5)

And on the same day, a trireme of the Athenians was captured by the Syracusans.

(19) πάλιν δὴ ἐπὶ <u>τῶν αὐτῶν τεχνῶν</u> λέγωμεν ὧνπερ νυνδή. (Pl. *Grg.* 453e)

Let us, then, resume our discussion concerning the same arts we spoke of just now.

Forms of αὐτός in this use frequently serve as head of their noun phrase (→26.22), e.g. ὁ αὐτός *the same man*, οἱ αὐτοί *the same men/people*, τὰ αὐτά *the same things*, etc.:

(20) σὺ δ' ἴσως διὰ τὸ πολυμαθὴς εἶναι περὶ <u>τῶν αὐτῶν</u> οὐδέποτε <u>τὰ αὐτὰ</u> λέγεις. (Xen. *Mem.* 4.4.6)

And perhaps it is on account of the fact that you are so learned that you never say the same things about the same things.

Note 1: To express the person or entity to which someone or something is identical, Greek uses the dative, καί, or a relative clause introduced by a form of ὅσπερ (as in (19) above). For details, →32.14–15.

Note 2: In this use, particularly when αὐτός is the head of the noun phrase, the article often coalesces with the form of αὐτός (crasis, →1.43–5): αὐτός (= ὁ αὐτός), αὕτή (= ἡ αὐτή), ταὐτά ταῦτα (= τὰ αὐτὰ ταῦτα):

(21) καὶ νῦν ἔθ' <u>αὐτός</u> εἰμι τῷ βουλεύματι. (Soph. *OT* 557)

And even now, I am still of the same mind. *Lit. 'the same man in mind'.*

As an Adjective, Emphatic Use: *Self*

29.9   Finally, αὐτός (in any case) is used as a predicative adjective stressing the identity of a person or thing, in opposition to other persons or things: *self*. In such cases αὐτός always stands in **predicative position** (i.e. not preceded directly by the article, →28.11–12):

(22) ἀκούσας δὲ καὶ <u>αὐτὸς ὁ Ψαμμήτιχος</u> ἐπυνθάνετο οἵτινες ἀνθρώπων Βεκός τι καλέουσι. (Hdt. 2.2.4)
When Psammetichus himself had been told as well, he inquired which people have a word 'bekos'.

(23) ἀνατείνας τὼ σκέλει διαμηριῶ | <u>τὴν Ἶριν αὐτήν</u>. (Ar. *Av.* 1254–5)
I'll spread her two legs and screw Iris herself.

(24) ὡς δὲ ἀληθῆ λέγω, <u>αὐτὸ</u> ὑμῖν <u>τὸ ψήφισμα</u> δηλώσει. (Lys. 13.71)
That I am speaking the truth, the decree itself will make clear to you.

αὐτός *self* also frequently stands on its own in the nominative, agreeing with the (unexpressed) subject of a verb:

(25) ΕΧ. <u>αὐτός</u>, ὦ Φαίδων, παρεγένου Σωκράτει ἐκείνῃ τῇ ἡμέρᾳ ᾗ τὸ φάρμακον ἔπιεν . . . ἢ ἄλλου του ἤκουσας; :: ΦΑ. <u>αὐτός</u>, ὦ Ἐχέκρατες. (Pl. *Phd.* 57a).
(Echecrates:) Were you with Socrates yourself, Phaedo, on that day when he drank the poison . . . or did you hear about it from someone else? :: (Phaedo:) I was there myself, Echecrates.

(26) <u>αὐτός</u> σοι ἡγήσομαι. (Xen. *Hell.* 5.2.28)
I will act as your guide myself.

29.10   In some cases personal pronouns in the nominative are strengthened by αὐτός:

(27) τοῦτο . . . οὐκ ἐπεχείρησα ποιεῖν, ὡς <u>αὐτοὶ ὑμεῖς</u> ἐπίστασθε. (Xen. *An.* 7.6.12)
I did not try to do that, as you know for yourselves.

29.11   Forms of αὐτός are often combined with reflexive pronouns to emphasize a direct reflexive relationship (→29.17):

(28) οὕτω μεῖζον ἂν καὶ ἔλαττον εἴη <u>αὐτὸ ἑαυτοῦ</u> τὸ ἕν. (Pl. *Prm.* 151a)
In this way, the one thing would be both greater and smaller than itself (*lit.* 'the one thing itself . . . than itself').

29.12   Some further **idiomatic uses** of αὐτός:

– *by itself, in itself, unaided, alone, bare, very*:

(29) ἥξει γὰρ <u>αὐτά</u>. (Soph. *OT* 341)
For it will happen on its own accord.

– *just, merely*:

(30) λεγόντων ἄλλο μὲν οὐδὲν ὧν πρότερον εἰώθεσαν, <u>αὐτὰ</u> δὲ <u>τάδε</u> ὅτι . . . (Thuc. 1.139.3)
saying nothing of what they previously used to say, but merely this, that . . .

– *exactly, precisely* (with expressions of time or place):

(31) φυλάξαντες . . . <u>αὐτὸ</u> τὸ περίορθρον (Thuc. 2.3.4)
waiting for the exact moment of dawn

– *with . . . and all* (with the dative of accompaniment, →30.51):

(32) εἶπεν . . . ἥκειν εἰς τὰς τάξεις <u>αὐτοῖς</u> στεφάνοις. (Xen. *Cyr.* 3.3.40)
He told them to come to their posts with crowns and all.

– *with/and . . . others* (with ordinals):

(33) τεσσαράκοντα δὲ ναυσὶ καὶ τέσσαρσι Περικλέους δεκάτου <u>αὐτοῦ</u> στρατηγοῦντος
ἐναυμάχησαν. (Thuc. 1.116.1)
They gave battle with forty-four ships, under the command of Pericles (himself) and nine
others (*lit. 'himself the tenth'*).

Summary of the Uses of αὐτός

29.13   The following overview lists the main differences between the three basic uses of
αὐτός:

as third-person personal pronoun: *him, her, it*, etc.	expressing identicalness: *the same*	emphatic use: *self*
oblique cases only	all cases	all cases
used pronominally (i.e. as a noun phrase by itself)	used adnominally, with the article often as head of a noun phrase: e.g. τὰ αὐτά *the same things*	used adnominally, as predicative modifier
	attributive position, always directly preceded by the article: ὁ αὐτὸς ἀνὴρ τοῦτο ποιεῖ *the same man does this*	predicative position: ὁ ἀνὴρ αὐτὸς τοῦτο ποιεῖ *the man does this himself*
		often by itself in the nom., agreeing with an unexpressed subject: e.g. αὐτὸς ποιεῖ ταῦτα *he himself does these things*

Reflexive Pronouns and Other Reflexive Expressions

Introduction; Pronouns Used as Reflexives; Direct and Indirect Reflexives

29.14 **Reflexivity** is the phenomenon whereby a pronoun is used to 'reflect' (i.e. refer back or forwards to) another constituent of the sentence or clause, nearly always the **subject**:

(34) ἐκεῖνον μὲν οὐδὲν ἐπαινῶ, ἐμαυτὸν δὲ ψέγω. (Xen. *Ages.* 5.7)

I am in no way praising him, I am censuring myself. *ἐμαυτόν refers to the (unexpressed) first-person subject of ψέγω.*

(35) οἱ δὲ ἡττώμενοι ἅμα ἑαυτούς τε καὶ τὰ ἑαυτῶν πάντα ἀποβάλλουσιν. (Xen. *Cyr.* 3.3.45)

The vanquished throw both themselves and all their possessions away. *ἑαυτούς and ἑαυτῶν refer back to οἱ ἡττώμενοι.*

Note 1: Rarely, reflexives refer back to a constituent other than the subject, e.g. the object:

(36) τοὺς μὲν Σπαρτιάτας ἀπέλυσεν οἴκαδε, τοὺς δὲ περιοίκους ἀφῆκεν ἐπὶ τὰς ἑαυτῶν πόλεις. (Xen. *Hell.* 6.5.21)

He let the Spartiates go home, and sent the Perioeci to their respective cities. *ἑαυτῶν refers back to the object τοὺς περιοίκους.*

29.15 A distinction is made between:

- **direct reflexivity**: pronouns which refer back to an element within the same clause/construction;
- **indirect reflexivity**: pronouns in a subordinate construction (subordinate clauses, infinitive or participle constructions), which refer back to an element in the main/matrix clause (for subordination, →39.2, 39.5):

(37) γνῶθι σαυτόν.

Know thyself. *Direct reflexive: σαυτόν is object of γνῶθι, and refers to its (unexpressed) subject.*

(38) οὐδέν σε κωλύσει σεαυ|τὸν ἐμβαλεῖν εἰς τὸ βάραθρον. (Ar. *Nub.* 1448–9)

Nothing will prevent you from throwing yourself into the pit. *Direct reflexive: σεαυτόν is object of ἐμβαλεῖν, and refers to its subject (2 sg. taken from σε).*

(39) τοιοῦτος γίγνου περὶ τοὺς γονεῖς, οἵους ἂν εὔξαιο περὶ σεαυτὸν γενέσθαι τοὺς σεαυτοῦ παῖδας. ([Isoc.] 1.14)

Behave yourself towards your parents such as you would wish your children to behave themselves towards you. *Lit. 'be(come) such as …'. Indirect reflexives: σεαυτόν and σεαυτοῦ refer back to the subject of εὔξαιο, but syntactically are part of the accusative-and-infinitive construction γενέσθαι … παῖδας.*

Note 1: Direct reflexive actions can also be expressed by the middle voice, but only with certain verbs ('verbs of grooming', →35.11). In other cases a pronoun is required.

The term 'indirect reflexive' is also used for a different phenomenon in connection with the middle voice, for which →35.8–9.

29.16   The following pronouns are used in reflexive constructions:

- most widely: the reflexive pronoun (ἐμαυτοῦ, σεαυτοῦ, ἑαυτοῦ, ἡμῶν αὐτῶν, etc., →7.3);
- forms of the obsolete third-person personal pronoun (οὗ/οὑ, οἷ/οἱ, ἕ/ἑ; σφεῖς, σφῶν/σφων, etc., →7.2);
- (oblique cases of) the personal pronoun (μου/ἐμοῦ, σου/σοῦ, ἡμῶν, etc.);
- (oblique cases of) αὐτός (αὐτοῦ, etc.).

Note 1: A distinction should thus be maintained between 'reflexive pronouns' (a morphological category, referring to a specific type of pronoun, ἐμαυτοῦ, etc.) and 'pronouns used in reflexive constructions' (a syntactic phenomenon). While reflexive pronouns always express reflexivity, reflexivity is not always necessarily marked by the use of a reflexive pronoun.

Note 2: Reflexive pronouns are frequently used in contexts where English does not use *myself, yourself*, etc. or *my own, his own*, etc., especially in the case of attributive genitives (cf. (35) and (36) above) and indirect reflexives (cf. (39)).

Pronouns Used as Direct and Indirect Reflexives

Direct Reflexivity

29.17   In the direct reflexive use, the **reflexive pronoun** (ἐμαυτοῦ, σεαυτοῦ, ἑαυτοῦ, etc., →7.3) is normally required:

(40) οἱ δὲ ... τὰ ὅπλα παρέδοσαν καὶ <u>σφᾶς αὐτούς</u>. (Thuc. 4.38.3)

And they gave up their weapons and surrendered (*lit. 'gave up ... themselves'*). σφᾶς αὐτούς, *object of* παρέδοσαν, *refers back to its subject* οἱ δέ.

(41) ἐκεῖνο <u>ἐμαυτῷ</u> σύνοιδα, ὅτι περὶ Ὁμήρου κάλλιστ' ἀνθρώπων λέγω. (Pl. *Ion* 533c)

This one thing I know of myself: that I excel all men in speaking on Homer. ἐμαυτῷ *refers to the (unexpressed) first-person subject of* σύνοιδα.

(42) αἰσχρὰ μὲν <u>σαυτῷ</u> λέγεις. (Eur. *Andr.* 648)

You say things which are shameful to yourself. *Reflexive pronoun* σαυτῷ *refers to the (unexpressed) subject of* λέγεις.

(43) ὑμεῖς οὖν, ἐὰν σωφρονῆτε, οὐ τούτου ἀλλ' <u>ὑμῶν αὐτῶν</u> φείσεσθε. (Xen. *Hell.* 2.3.34)

If you are wise, you will not spare this man, but rather yourselves. ὑμῶν αὐτῶν *refers to the subject of* φείσεσθε, ὑμεῖς.

However, in the first and second person, and in poetry much more freely than in prose, **personal pronouns** can be used as direct reflexives:

(44) ὡς ἐγὼ δοκῶ <u>μοι</u> τῶν σοφῶν τινος ἀκηκοέναι (Pl. *Resp.* 583b)

as I think I have heard from some wise man (*lit.* '*I seem to me to have heard*'). *Personal pronoun μοι refers to the subject of δοκῶ. δοκῶ ἐμαυτῷ is rare, and used particularly in cases of contrastive emphasis.*

(45) φονέας ἔτικτες ἆρά <u>σοι</u>. (Eur. *El.* 1229)

Apparently you bore your own killers. *Personal pronoun σοι refers to the subject of ἔτικτες. Contrast (42) above.*

Note 1: In tragedy, manuscript evidence provides several instances of αὐτός being used as a third-person direct reflexive: these are usually corrected in modern editions to contracted forms of ἑαυτοῦ (the difference between e.g. αὐτοῦ and αὑτοῦ resides only in the breathing mark (→7.26), and manuscript evidence is not reliable when it comes to breathings, →1.7, 1.12). It is possible, however, that such examples are authentic.
Note 2: For combinations of αὐτός and ἑαυτοῦ in direct reflexive contexts: →29.11, 29.19.

Indirect Reflexivity

29.18   In indirect reflexive contexts, the following pronouns are used:

– In the **first** and **second person**, personal pronouns are typically used (the reflexive pronoun is relatively rare):

(46) οὐ λόγῳ ἀλλ᾽ ἔργῳ … ἐνεδειξάμην ὅτι <u>ἐμοὶ</u> θανάτου μὲν μέλει … οὐδ᾽ ὁτιοῦν. (Pl. *Ap.* 32d)

I have shown, not only in word but in deed, that I am not in the least concerned about death. *Personal pronoun.*

(47) ὦ τέκν᾽, ἀκούεθ᾽ οἷος εἰς <u>ὑμᾶς</u> πατήρ; (Eur. *Med.* 82)

O children, do you hear what kind of man your father is toward you? *Personal pronoun.*

(48) οὐ τοῖς εἰσηγησαμένοις ταῦτ᾽ ἐπιτιμῶ … ἀλλ᾽ ὑμῖν, εἰ ταῦθ᾽ ἱκανὰ <u>ὑμῖν αὐτοῖς</u> ὑπολαμβάνετ᾽ εἶναι. (Dem. 13.30)

I do not blame those who have introduced these measures, but you, if you think that these things are sufficient for you. *Reflexive pronoun.*

– In the **third person**, the reflexive pronoun occurs regularly:

(49) παρεκελεύοντο δὲ αὐτῷ πάντες … μὴ μάχεσθαι, ἀλλ᾽ ὄπισθεν <u>ἑαυτῶν</u> τάττεσθαι. (Xen. *An.* 1.7.9)

All urged him not to take part in the fighting, but to take position behind them. *ἑαυτῶν refers back to πάντες.*

(50) τούτους δ᾽ ἐάσω, μή με φῶσιν κακῶς <u>αὐτούς</u> λέγειν. (Dem. 38.26)

I shall leave them unmentioned, so that they may not say that I am slandering them. *αὐτούς refers back to the subject of φῶσιν.*

In addition, the forms οὖ, οἶ, ἕ, σφῶν, etc. (contrastive) and οὐ, οἱ, ἑ, σφων (non-contrastive) are regularly used as indirect reflexives:

(51) ἐς τὴν Ἔγεσταν πέμψαντες ἐκέλευον ἵππους <u>σφίσιν</u> ὡς πλείστους πέμπειν. (Thuc. 6.88.6)

They sent to Egesta and asked that they send them as many horses as possible. *σφίσιν refers back to the subject of ἐκέλευον.*

(52) κατιδὼν ... ἡμᾶς ... Πολέμαρχος ... ἐκέλευσε δραμόντα τὸν παῖδα περιμεῖναί <u>ἑ</u> κελεῦσαι. (Pl. *Resp.* 327b)

Catching sight of us, Polemarchus ... ordered his boy to run and bid us to wait for him. *ἑ refers back to Πολέμαρχος; strictly speaking it could also have referred back to the boy, although the context leaves no doubt about who is meant.*

Finally, oblique cases of αὐτός are frequently used as third-person indirect reflexives:

(53) οἱ δ᾽ ... εὐθὺς ἀφήσουσι τὴν λείαν, ἐπειδὰν ἴδωσί τινας ἐπ᾽ <u>αὐτοὺς</u> ἐλαύνοντας. (Xen. *Cyr.* 1.4.19)

They will drop their booty as soon as they see anyone charging them. *αὐτοὺς refers back to the subject of ἴδωσι.*

Note 1: It is difficult to account fully for the difference between the use of these pronouns in the third-person indirect reflexive. Reflexive pronouns (ἑαυτοῦ, etc.) are consistently used, even in the first and second person, when they function as attributive genitives; otherwise, the use of reflexive pronouns and forms of οὖ, etc., is particularly prevalent in those cases where the subordinate construction represents the thoughts, words or intentions of the subject of the matrix clause (nom. σφεῖς can also be so used; for examples of indirect reflexives in indirect speech/thought, →41.9 (16), 41.20 (46)).

After the fifth century αὐτός appears to gain ground as a standard form for indirect reflexives (but for problems of manuscript transmission, →29.17 n.1).

Further Particulars

29.19   The third-person reflexive pronoun is not infrequently used instead of a first- or second-person pronoun:

(54) ἀμ|φὶ δ᾽ <u>αὑτᾶς</u> θροεῖς | νόμον ἄνομον. (Aesch. *Ag.* 1140–2)

You cry a lawless strain about yourself. *αὑτ- instead of σ(ε)αυτ-. For ᾶ in αὑτᾶς,* →25.46–7.

This occurs regularly in fixed phrases such as αὐτὸς καθ᾽ αὑτόν *by myself/yourself/himself,* αὐτὸς ἐφ᾽ αὑτοῦ *by myself/yourself/himself* and superlative + αὐτὸς αὑτοῦ *at his/her/its -est* (for which, →32.10):

(55) ὅσας ... ναυμαχίας <u>αὐτοὶ καθ᾽ αὑτοὺς</u> νενικήκατε ... (Xen. *Hell.* 1.1.28)

All the naval battles that you have won by yourselves ...

Again, such instances are sometimes emended in modern text editions: many instances are probably authentic, however. Especially from the fourth century onwards, the third-person reflexive pronoun seems to have gradually supplanted the first-person and second-person reflexive pronouns.

29.20 Reflexive pronouns are not infrequently used to express reciprocal relationships, where one might expect the reciprocal pronoun ἀλλήλων (for which →29.26):

(56) οἱ συγγενεῖς σύνεισι σφίσιν αὐτοῖς. (Xen. *Hell.* 1.7.8)
Kinsmen join with each other.

The two pronouns may be combined, however, to express a contrast between reflexive and reciprocal actions:

(57) ἀμφισβητοῦμεν ἀλλήλοις τε καὶ ἡμῖν αὐτοῖς; (Pl. *Phdr.* 263b)
Do we disagree with each other as well as with ourselves?

Possessive Pronouns and Other Expressions of Possession

Introduction; Pronouns Used as Possessives

29.21 Greek uses the following pronouns to express **possession, belonging, descent, origin**, etc.:

– possessive pronouns (ἐμός, -ή, -όν *my*; σός, -ή, -όν *your* (sg.); ἡμέτερος, -α, -ον *our*; ὑμέτερος, -α, -ον *your* (pl.); these are properly adjectives, and thus always agree with their head noun); the plural forms in particular are sometimes combined with the genitive of αὐτός: e.g. ἡμέτερος αὐτῶν *our (own)*, σφετέρας αὐτῶν *their (own)*, →7.7–9;
– the genitive of the non-contrastive personal pronoun (μου, σου, ἡμῶν, ὑμῶν), and the genitive of αὐτός (αὐτοῦ, αὐτῆς, αὐτῶν, used as a non-contrastive third-person personal pronoun);
– the genitive of the reflexive pronoun (ἐμαυτοῦ, σεαυτοῦ, ἑαυτοῦ);
– the genitive of demonstrative pronouns (τούτου, ἐκείνης, etc.).

Note 1: For the position of each of these pronouns relative to noun and article, →28.16, 28.18.

Pronouns Used in Different Constructions

First and Second Person

29.22 For the **first** and **second person**, the following pronouns are used:

- If the possessor is also the **subject** of the sentence, the possessive pronoun (ἐμός, etc.) is used, or, with emphasis, the genitive of the reflexive pronoun (ἐμαυτοῦ, etc.). In the plural, the emphatic combinations ἡμέτερος αὐτῶν, ὑμέτερος αὐτῶν occur:

(58) τόν ... παῖδα τὸν ἐμὸν παρέδωκα βασανίσαι. (Andoc. 1.64)
     I gave up my slave to be tortured.

(59) αἰτιασάμενος ... με ... , τὸν πατέρα ὡς ἀπέκτονα ἐγώ τὸν ἐμαυτοῦ ... , εἰς ἀγῶνα κατέστησεν. (Dem. 22.2)
     Bringing the accusation against me that I have killed my own father, he has taken me to court. *For the word order, with* τὸν πατέρα *preceding its clause,* →60.33.

(60) διδάσκετε τοὺς παῖδας τοὺς ὑμετέρους αὐτῶν. (Isoc. 3.57)
     Teach your (own) children.

- If the possessor is **not the subject** of the sentence, the genitive of the non-contrastive personal pronoun (μου, etc.) or the possessive pronoun (ἐμός, etc., especially when with emphasis) is used:

(61) πλείω χρόνον διατρίβουσι τὸν πατέρα μου διαβάλλοντες. (Isoc. 16.2)
     They spend more time slandering my father.

(62) διῃτᾶτο παρ᾽ ἡμῖν τὸν ἅπαντα χρόνον ὁ Ἀστύφιλος καὶ ἐπαιδεύθη ὑπὸ τοῦ πατρὸς τοῦ ἐμοῦ. (Isae. 9.27)
     Astyphilus lived in our house the whole time, and was brought up by my father.

Third Person

29.23   For the **third person**, the following pronouns are used:

- If the possessor is also the **subject** of the sentence, the genitive of the reflexive pronoun is used (ἑαυτοῦ, -ῆς; αὑτοῦ, αὑτῆς). In the plural the form is either ἑαυτῶν or (less commonly) σφέτερος αὐτῶν:

(63) Περδίκκας δὲ ὕστερον Στρατονίκην τὴν ἑαυτοῦ ἀδελφὴν δίδωσι Σεύθῃ. (Thuc. 2.101.6)
     Afterwards Perdiccas gave his sister Stratonice to Seuthes.

(64) οἰκέτας τοὺς σφετέρους αὐτῶν ἐπικαλοῦνται μάρτυρας. (Antiph. 1.30)
     They call their slaves to witness.

- If the possessor is **not the subject** of the sentence, the genitive of αὐτός is used, or (less commonly, with emphasis) the genitive of demonstrative pronouns (ἐκείνου, etc.):

(65) ὁ γὰρ πατὴρ αὐτῆς Ἱππόνικος ... τὸν πατέρα τὸν ἐμὸν ... κηδεστὴν ἐπεθύμησε ποιήσασθαι. (Isoc. 16.31)
     For her father Hipponicus set his heart upon making my father related to him by marriage.

(66) τὸ <u>ταύτης</u> σῶμα τιμᾶσθαι χρεών. (Eur. *Alc.* 619)

We must honour her body.

Further Particulars

29.24 When the possessor is beyond doubt, Greek often uses no more than the **article** (which may then be translated as a possessive pronoun, →28.4 n.1). This is especially frequent in cases of 'inalienable' possession:

(67) πρῶτον μὲν σεαυτὸν σῷσον, εἶτα δὲ <u>τὸν</u> πατέρα. (Andoc. 1.50)

Save yourself first, and next your father.

29.25 All the possessive expressions treated above may be used with the force of a **subjective** or **objective genitive** (→30.28):

φιλίᾳ τῇ <u>ἐμῇ</u>   out of my friendship (for someone else) / friendship for me

διὰ τὴν <u>ἐκείνων</u> ἀπιστίαν   on account of mistrust for them / their mistrust

Reciprocal Pronouns

29.26 The **reciprocal pronoun**, used only pronominally, expresses the idea that two or more persons are **simultaneously involved** in one and the same action, like English *each other, one another*:

(68) ὡς δὲ κατεῖδον <u>ἀλλήλους</u>, ἀντιπαρετάσσοντο. (Thuc. 1.48.3)

As soon as they got sight of each other, they arrayed themselves against each other.

(69) λυσιτελεῖ γὰρ οἶμαι ἡμῖν ἡ <u>ἀλλήλων</u> δικαιοσύνη καὶ ἀρετή. (Pl. *Prt.* 327b)

For we profit, I think, from each other's justice and virtue.

Note 1: The reciprocal pronoun does not have a nominative and is always plural. As appears from example (69), the genitive ἀλλήλων may also be used as a possessive, in attributive position (→28.16).

Note 2: Reciprocal actions can also be expressed in Greek by the middle voice (e.g. διελέγοντο *they conversed with each other*; cf. also ἀντιπαρετάσσοντο in (68); →35.24), by the reflexive pronoun (ἔκοπτον αὑτούς *they hit themselves/each other*; →29.20 above) and by the repetition of nouns:

(70) <u>τάξις</u> δὲ <u>τάξιν</u> παρεκάλει. (Aesch. *Pers.* 380)

Line cheered on line.

Demonstrative Pronouns

Pronominal and Adnominal Use; Pointing Outside or Inside the Text

29.27   The three demonstrative pronouns (ὅδε, οὗτος, ἐκεῖνος) may be used pronominally or adnominally. In the latter case, they normally take the article (in prose), and
stand in predicative position (→28.17):

ὅδε / ὅδε ὁ ἀνήρ	this man (here)
οὗτος / οὗτος ὁ ἀνήρ	this man
ἐκεῖνος / ἐκεῖνος ὁ ἀνήρ	that man (there)

Note 1: Predicative position is in this case not indicative of predicative function.

29.28   Demonstratives have a pointing or **deictic** function (from δείκνυμι *point*). They may
either point to someone/thing in the world **outside the text**, or to a single word or
larger segment of **the text itself**. When a demonstrative refers to an element in the
text itself it may refer backward to something introduced before (**anaphoric** use) or
point forward in the text to something about to be introduced (**cataphoric** use):

(71) καὶ οὕτω καταφρονεῖς <u>τῶνδε</u> καὶ οἴει αὐτοὺς ἀπείρους γραμμάτων εἶναι
ὥστε . . .; (Pl. *Ap.* 26d)
Do you so despise these gentlemen (here) and think that they are so unversed
in letters that . . .? *τῶνδε refers to the judges, men actually present for Socrates'*
speech – we might imagine Socrates pointing at them.

(72) ὁ δὲ Ἀριαῖος εἶπε· . . . ἐπὶ <u>τούτοις</u> Ξενοφῶν <u>τάδε</u> εἶπε· . . . (Xen. *An.* 2.5.40)
And Ariaeus said: . . . In reaction to these words Xenophon spoke as follows: . . .
The pronouns refer to elements in the text – τούτοις anaphorically to Ariaeus'
speech, and τάδε cataphorically to Xenophon's speech which is to follow.

General Differences between ὅδε, οὗτος and ἐκεῖνος

29.29   ὅδε refers to something **immediately near/present to the speaker** (physically or
mentally). Often one may imagine the speaker pointing at something or someone
nearby: it is used in drama to announce characters coming onstage (73), and can
even refer to the speaker himself (74). When it points to an element within the text,
ὅδε normally serves to announce something that will follow immediately (cataphoric use, (75)), or refers to something prominent in the speaker's mind (76):

(73) ἀλλ' <u>ὅδε</u> . . . βασιλεὺς . . . χωρεῖ. (Soph. *Ant.* 155–8)
But here comes the king.

(74) <u>τῆσδέ</u> γε ζώσης ἔτι (Soph. *Trach.* 305)
while this women still lives (*i.e. 'while I still live'*)

(75) καὶ τόδε ἕτερον συνέπεσε γενόμενον … (Hdt. 9.101.1)

And in addition the following coincidence occurred: … *Cataphoric.*

(76) ὁ μέντοι μῦθος εἰ σαφὴς ὅδε | οὐκ οἶδα· βουλοίμην δ᾽ ἂν οὐκ εἶναι τόδε. (Eur. *Med.* 72–3)

Yet if this story is true I do not know, but I would wish that this is not the case.

29.30 **οὗτος** refers to something **within the reach of the speaker and/or addressee** (physically or mentally), but not specifically near to the speaker. The reference may be to something within reach of the addressee, or even to the addressee him/ herself. In oratory, it is often used to point to accusers or defendants present in the court (77). It is occasionally used in dialogue to address someone ('hey there', (78)). οὗτος very frequently points in the text, and is then used most often to refer to something mentioned previously (anaphoric use, (79)):

(77) ἔπειτά εἰσιν οὗτοι οἱ κατήγοροι πολλοὶ καὶ πολὺν χρόνον ἤδη κατηγορηκότες. (Pl. *Ap.* 18c)

Moreover, these accusers are many and have been making their accusations already for a long time.

(78) οὗτος, τί ποιεῖς; (Ar. *Ran.* 198)

Hey there, what are you doing?

(79) ταύτην … τὴν ἡμέραν καὶ τῆς ὑστεραίας μέρος τι προσβολὰς ποιησάμενοι ἐπέπαυντο. (Thuc. 4.13.1)

Having continued their efforts for that day (*just described*) and part of the next, they were now quiet. *Anaphoric.*

(80) Γοργίας … οὗτος ὁ Λεοντῖνος σοφιστής … (Pl. *Hp. mai.* 282b)

Gorgias, that sophist from Leontini … *A recognisable figure to both speaker and addressee: the use of* οὗτος *may indicate that the speaker suggests some 'distance' between himself and Gorgias.*

29.31 **ἐκεῖνος** refers to something **beyond the reach of the speaker and addressee** (physically or mentally). It may refer to something physically far away (or out of sight) from both speaker and addressee (81). When ἐκεῖνος points within the text, it usually refers anaphorically to something which has not been mentioned for a while (or it is used to pick up something which was mentioned before a form of οὗτος or ὅδε 'intervened') (82). It may also refer to something that is 'distant' in other ways: because it is special or unexpected, because it lies in distant memory, etc. (83):

(81) τοῖς δὲ Κερκυραίοις … οὐχ ἑωρῶντο … πρίν τινες ἰδόντες εἶπον ὅτι νῆες ἐκεῖναι ἐπιπλέουσιν. (Thuc. 1.51.2)

They went unseen by the Corcyraeans, until a few noticed them and said that there in the distance ships were approaching.

(82) (ἔδοξέ μοι) αὐτῶν αὕτη ἡ πλημμέλεια <u>ἐκείνην</u> τὴν σοφίαν ἀποκρύπτειν. (Pl. *Ap.* 22d)

This folly (*just mentioned*) of theirs seemed to me to obscure that wisdom (*mentioned further back in the text*). *Anaphoric.*

(83) γραφὴν σέ τις, ὡς ἔοικε, γέγραπται· οὐ γὰρ <u>ἐκεῖνό</u> γε καταγνώσομαι, ὡς σὺ ἕτερον. (Pl. *Euthphr.* 2b)

It seems that someone has brought a suit against you. For of one thing I will not accuse you, that you have done so against someone else. *Cataphoric; ἐκεῖνο appears to emphasize that the content of the ὡς-clause (Socrates bringing a suit against someone else) is unimaginable.*

29.32   As a general rule, when referring within the text, **οὗτος** is the pronoun used anaphorically (pointing backwards), and **ὅδε** the pronoun used cataphorically (pointing forwards):

ταῦτα εἰπών . . .   having said these things . . .

. . . εἶπε τάδε·   . . . he said the following: . . .

Note 1: There are, however, many exceptions to this rule: οὗτος may refer forward (especially when it introduces a relative clause); ὅδε may refer backward:

(84) καὶ φιλόπολις <u>οὗτος</u> ὀρθῶς . . . <u>ὃς</u> ἂν ἐκ παντὸς τρόπου . . . πειραθῇ αὐτὴν ἀναλαβεῖν. (Thuc. 6.92.4)

That man is truly a patriot, who seeks to recover it (*his country*) by all means.

(85) <u>τάδε</u> μὲν ἡμῖν πατέρες οἱ ὑμέτεροι ἔδοσαν. (Thuc. 2.71.3)

These are the things (*just described*) your ancestors passed on to us. *The use of τάδε rather than ταῦτα may emphasize that the things passed on are still relevant for the speaker and his audience.*

29.33   When referring back to two persons/groups/things just mentioned, '**the former** . . . **the latter**' in Greek is represented by '**ἐκεῖνος** . . . **οὗτος/ὅδε**' (but also frequently by ὁ μέν . . . ὁ δέ, →28.27):

(86) πολὺ ἂν δικαιότερον <u>ἐκείνοις</u> τοῖς γράμμασιν ἢ <u>τούτοις</u> πιστεύοιτε. (Lys. 16.7)

You would be far more justified relying on the former lists than the latter.

(87) ὑμεῖς <u>ἐκείνων</u> πρότερον ἠκούσατε κατηγορούντων καὶ πολὺ μᾶλλον ἢ <u>τῶνδε</u> τῶν ὕστερον. (Pl. *Ap.* 18e)

You have heard the former make their accusations earlier and with much more vehemence than these men here who came later. *Socrates has just distinguished two groups among his accusers.*

Further Particulars

29.34   The demonstrative pronouns are often used with a noun in a predicative relationship. In such cases, the noun usually does not have the article; the demonstrative pronoun is used pronominally and functions as subject/object of the verb. Contrast:

(88) Ἁρπάγῳ μὲν Ἀστυάγης <u>δίκην ταύτην</u> ἐπέθηκε. (Hdt. 1.120.1)

This was the punishment which Astyages inflicted on Harpagus. *Predicative use. More literally, 'Astyages inflicted this as punishment on Harpagus'; ταύτην refers anaphorically to the preceding context, in which Astyages' treatment of Harpagus was described.*

(89) οὐδεμιᾷ φιλοπραγμοσύνῃ . . . <u>τὴν δίκην ταύτην</u> ἔλαχον Βοιωτῷ. (Dem. 39.1)

It was not through any love of litigation that I brought this suit against Boeotus. *Adnominal use. ταύτην expresses the nuance 'just mentioned'.*

For the agreement between the pronoun and the noun in such cases, also →27.9.

29.35   There are also groups of **demonstrative adjectives** and **adverbs** which correspond, in the ways in which they 'point', to ὅδε and οὗτος (and sometimes ἐκεῖνος):

Used like ὅδε	Used like οὗτος	Used like ἐκεῖνος	Meaning
τοιόσδε	τοιοῦτος		such, of such a kind
τοσόσδε	τοσοῦτος		so great (sg.), so many (pl.)
ὧδε	οὕτω(ς)		in this way, so, such
ἐνθένδε	ἐντεῦθεν	ἐκεῖθεν	from here/there
etc. (→8)			

> **Note 1:** The placement of τοιοῦτος and τοσοῦτος is different from that of οὗτος: when they are used adnominally, they stand in attributive position: e.g. οἱ τοιοῦτοι ἄνδρες *such men*, τὰ τοσαῦτα καὶ τοιαῦτα ἀγαθά *so many and such blessings*.

These adjectives and adverbs often anticipate or pick up a correlative relative clause (e.g. τοσοῦτος . . . ὅσος *so large . . . as*; ὅσοι . . . τοσοῦτοι *so many as . . . , so many (too)*; →50.5) or anticipate a result clause (e.g. τοιοῦτος . . . ὥστε *such . . . that*; →46.2).

29.36   Forms of demonstrative pronouns, adjectives or adverbs are sometimes expanded with the **deictic suffix** -ί (→7.18). In such cases the demonstrative nearly always refers to something in the world outside the text: deictic iota appears to emphasize the 'pointing' effect of the pronoun. It is especially frequent in comedy:

(90) <u>ὁδὶ</u> δὲ τίς ποτ' ἐστίν; οὐ δήπου Στράτων; (Ar. *Ach.* 122)

And this guy here, who's he? Can't be Straton, can he?

(91) καὶ μὴν ὁρῶ καὶ Βλεψίδημον <u>τουτονὶ</u> | προσιόντα. (Ar. *Plut.* 332–3)

And look, there I see Blepsidemus approaching too.

(92) ΠΕ. <u>οὑτοσὶ</u> δὲ πηνέλοψ. :: ΕΥ. <u>ἐκεινηὶ</u> δέ γ' ἀλκυών. (Ar. *Av.* 298)

(Pisetaerus:) And that one is a wigeon. :: (Euelpides:) And that one a halcyon.

(93) τοιουτοσὶ τοίνυν με δαρδάπτει πόθος | Εὐριπίδου. (Ar. *Ran.* 66–7)

Such, I tell you, is the desire for Euripides which is devouring me.

29.37   A relatively frequent idiomatic use of anaphoric οὗτος is in the fixed expression καὶ ταῦτά (γε) *and . . . at that, and . . . to boot, and what's more: . . .* , modifying a participle, noun phrase or adjective:

(94) Οὐκοῦν καὶ χρυσίον, ἦ δ' ὅς, ἀγαθὸν δοκεῖ σοι εἶναι ἔχειν; :: Πάνυ, καὶ ταῦτά γε πολύ, ἔφη ὁ Κτήσιππος. (Pl. *Euthd.* 299d)

'Don't you think,' he said, 'that it is a good thing to have gold?' :: 'Certainly,' said Ctesippus, 'and a lot of it at that.' *ταῦτα picks up the idea 'it is good to have gold', to which Ctesippus adds the additional and specific proviso (for καί and γε, →59.20, 59.53) that it should be a lot of gold.*

Indefinite Pronouns

29.38   The **indefinite pronoun** τις *any, some, a(n), (a) certain*, can be used pronominally or adnominally. It refers to someone/something that is not identifiable as a specific individual:

– Normally, τις is used to refer to any of a number of individuals whose specific identity is **unknown** or **irrelevant**:

(95) ἡμῶν . . . ἔχει τις κατηγορῆσαι ἢ ὡς ἐπὶ πόλιν τινὰ ἐστρατεύσαμεν ἢ ὡς χρήματά τινων ἐλάβομεν; (Xen. *Hell.* 6.5.37)

Can anyone accuse us of attacking some city or taking anyone's possessions?

(96) εἴ τις ἐπιβουλεύει τι τῷ δήμῳ κακὸν | τῷ τῶν γυναικῶν . . . κακῶς ἀπολέσθαι τοῦτον αὐτὸν κᾠκίαν | ἀρᾶσθε. (Ar. *Thesm.* 335–6, 349–50)

If anyone plans to do any harm to the Women's Commonwealth, pray that he himself and his house may perish miserably.

(97) εἰ δή τῳ σοφώτερός του φαίην εἶναι, τούτῳ ἄν . . . (Pl. *Ap.* 29b)

If I were to claim that I am wiser than anyone in any respect, it would be in this respect, that . . . *For the forms τῳ and του, →7.24.*

– Sometimes, τις is used when **the speaker does not wish to reveal**, or **pay attention to**, the identity of a specific individual:

(98) δώσει τις δίκην. (Ar. *Ran.* 554)

Someone is going to pay for this! *The speaker means: 'you're going to pay for this'.*

(99) ἴθ', ὦ γύναι, δήλωσον εἰσελθοῦσ' ὅτι | Φωκῆς ματεύουσ' ἄνδρες Αἴγισθόν τινες. (Soph. *El.* 1106–7)

Go on, woman, go inside and let it be known that there are certain Phocians here looking for Aegisthus.

29.39   The indefinite pronoun can convey a **collective** sense, where *someone* is short for *every someone* (cf. Germ. *man*, Fr. *on*). The combinations πᾶς τις and ἕκαστός τις in particular are used with this meaning:

(100) γαστρὶ δὲ <u>πᾶς τις</u> ἀμύνων λιμὸν αἰανῆ τέταται. (Pind. *Isthm.* 1.49)
        Everyone is intent on warding off persistent hunger from his belly.

29.40   Forms of τις may be added to **adverbs and numerals** to weaken their force or make them less specific:

| σχεδόν <u>τι</u> | pretty nearly, virtually |
| ὀγδοήκοντά <u>τινες</u> | roughly/around/some eighty |

29.41   The **acc. sg. neut. τι** is frequently used in the meaning *somehow, somewhat, in some way*:

(101) παρεθάρρυνε μέν <u>τι</u> αὐτοὺς καὶ ὁ χρησμὸς ὁ λεγόμενος ὡς . . . (Xen. *Hell.* 6.4.7)
        They were also somewhat encouraged by the oracle which was given, that . . .
(102) διαλεγομένῳ τε οὔ <u>τι</u> προσδιελέγετο. (Hdt. 3.50.3)
        When spoken to he would not reply in any way.

29.42   Also note the following idiomatic uses:

λέγειν <u>τι</u>	to make sense, have a point (*lit. 'to say something'*)
εἶναί <u>τις</u>	to be someone (of worth, to be reckoned with)
εἴ <u>τις</u> ἄλλος	if any, if at all; as . . . as any

(103) νῦν δ᾽, <u>εἴ τις ἄλλη</u>, δυστυχεστάτη γυνή. (Eur. *Andr.* 6)
        But as it is I am, if any woman ever was, the most unfortunate woman of all.

Interrogative Pronouns

29.43   The **interrogative pronoun** τίς *who?, which?* can be used pronominally or adnominally:

| <u>τίς</u> λέγει τοῦτο; | Who says that? |
| <u>τίς ἀνὴρ</u> λέγει τοῦτο; | Which man says that? |

For its use in direct and indirect questions, →38.11–14 and 42.5–6.

Relative Pronouns

29.44   For the use of relative pronouns, →50.8–16.

Quantifiers

πᾶς

29.45   The quantifier **πᾶς** (also ἅπας, σύμπας) in the singular means *(as a) whole, in its entirety* when it stands with the article (usually in predicative position). Without the article, it usually means *each, every*:

πᾶσα ἡ πόλις / ἡ πόλις πᾶσα   the city as a whole, the entire city

πᾶσα πόλις   each/every city (*sometimes:* an entire city)

In the plural, it means *each, every, all*. The form of πᾶς usually stands in predicative position, but sometimes in attributive position to emphasize the collective nature of the group:

πᾶσαι πόλεις   each/every city, all cities

πᾶσαι αἱ πόλεις/αἱ πόλεις πᾶσαι   all the cities

αἱ πᾶσαι πόλεις   the whole group of cities, the cities collectively

ὅλος

29.46   **ὅλος** means *in its entirety, as a whole* in predicative position, and *whole, entire* in attributive position:

(104) περὶ τὸ πρᾶγμα ὅλον ἄδικός ἐστιν ἄνθρωπος. ([Dem.] 48.36)
He acts as an unlawful fellow in the case as a whole. *Predicative.*

(105) ὑμεῖς τὸ ὅλον πρᾶγμα συνίδετε. (Aeschin. 1.46)
Look at the entire matter. *Attributive.*

μόνος

29.47   **μόνος** means *by itself, alone, (as the) only* in predicative position, and *the only* in attributive position:

(106) τῇμῇ δὲ παιδὶ στέφανος εἷς μιᾷ μόνῃ | πόλεως θανούσῃ τῇσδ᾽ ὕπερ δοθήσεται. (Eur. fr. 360.34–5 Kannicht)
To my single child shall be given a single crown, since she alone shall have died for this city. *Predicative; for τῇμῇ (crasis),* →1.43–5, *for ὕπερ (anastrophe),* →24.37, 60.14.

(107) παίσας εἰς τὰ στέρνα τὸν μόνον μοι καὶ φίλον παῖδα ἀφείλετο τὴν ψυχήν. (Xen. Cyr. 4.6.4)
He struck my only and beloved child in the chest, and took his life. *Attributive.*

ἄλλος and ἕτερος

29.48   The basic meaning of **ἄλλος** is *other (out of many)*, stressing **similarity**. The basic meaning of **ἕτερος** is *other (than something else)*, stressing **difference**:

ἡ ῥητορικὴ καὶ αἱ <u>ἄλλαι</u> τέχναι   rhetoric and the other arts

ἡ ῥητορικὴ <u>ἑτέρα</u> τέχνη τῆς γραμματικῆς ἐστίν   rhetoric is an art different from
                                                        grammar

Often, however, ἕτερος alternates with ἄλλος without a discernible difference in meaning.

29.49   With the article, **ὁ ἕτερος** (ἅτερος in crasis, →1.45 n.3) means 'the other' of a pair:

ὁ <u>ἕτερος</u> ποῦς   the other foot

29.50   With the article, **ὁ ἄλλος** means 'the rest', 'the other(s)':

ἡ <u>ἄλλη</u> Ἑλλάς   the rest of Greece

οἱ <u>ἄλλοι</u> διδάσκαλοι   the other teachers / the rest
                                                     of the teachers

Sometimes ἄλλος with the article is found with a noun that has to be interpreted as an appositive, in which case ἄλλος has the meaning *besides, moreover*:

(108)   παρεκάλεσαν τοὺς ἐν τῷ καταλόγῳ ὁπλίτας καὶ τοὺς <u>ἄλλους</u> ἱππέας. (Xen. Hell. 2.4.9)
         They summoned the hoplites on the roll and the cavalry besides (*'and the others, namely the cavalry'*).

29.51   **A form of ἄλλος followed by another form of ἄλλος** (or adverbial ἄλλως, ἄλλῃ) expresses the same as English *different . . . different*, or a twofold statement *one . . . one, another . . . another*:

(109)   οὗτοι μέν, ὦ Κλέαρχε, <u>ἄλλος ἄλλα</u> λέγει. σὺ δ' ἡμῖν εἰπὲ τί λέγεις. (Xen. An. 2.1.15–16)
         As for them, Clearchus, one says one thing and another says something else. But you must tell us what your opinion is. *Note that ἄλλος (ἄλλα) stands in apposition (→26.24–5) to οὗτοι (for the position of οὗτοι as 'theme', →60.33–4).*

(110)   ἐντεῦθεν πλὴν τετταράκοντα νεῶν <u>ἄλλαι ἄλλῃ</u> ᾤχοντο. (Xen. Hell. 1.1.8)
         From there, all but forty ships departed, each in a different direction. *For ἄλλῃ, →8.2.*

Similarly, **a form of ἕτερος followed by another form of ἕτερος** in another case is used when comparison is made between two members of a pair:

(111)   τί οὖν ἂν . . . <u>ἕτερος ἑτέρου</u> διαφέροι ἡμῶν πλὴν τόλμῃ; (Xen. Cyr. 2.1.17)
         How might the one of us differ from the other except in courage?

29.52   For the idiomatic use of a form of **ἄλλος** followed by (**καὶ δὴ**) **καὶ** (*among other . . . , in particular; particularly*), →59.70.

30

Cases

Functions, Meanings and Labels

30.1   The four main cases of Greek (nominative, genitive, dative, accusative) are used in different syntactic functions (for the vocative, →30.55):

- to mark **obligatory constituents** with verbs and adjectives (subject, object, complement; here belong also certain uses in constructions like the accusative-and-infinitive, accusative-and-participle, etc.);
- to complement **prepositions**;
- to mark **attributive modifiers** (the main function of the genitive);
- to mark various **adverbial modifiers** (here belong also certain uses in constructions like the genitive absolute and accusative absolute);
- a few other, idiomatic uses.

In the overview below, the most important uses of each of the cases are listed, organized by syntactic function. The prepositions are treated separately, →31.

Note 1: The uses of Greek cases in attributive and adverbial modifiers are commonly distinguished by the use of certain semantic 'labels', like *of quantity, of respect, of place,* etc. While such labels are helpful, they often do not distinguish between intrinsically different uses, but between different nuances of a general syntactic function. For example, the genitive is often used to express a close relationship between two nouns (as attributive modifier, →30.28–9 below), without expressing the precise nature of that relationship. Which label applies (and how to translate the genitive) depends on the meanings of the nouns involved and on the context:

ἡ οἰκία ἡ τοῦ ἀνδρός	the man's house (*genitive of possession*)
ἡ φιλία ἡ τοῦ ἀνδρός	the love for the man (*genitive of the object*)
ἡ φιλία ἡ τοῦ ἀνδρός	the man's love (for someone else) (*genitive of the subject*)

Note 2: As regards the use of cases to mark (obligatory) complements to verbs (and prepositions), although there are often historical reasons why particular verbs came to be construed with particular cases, there may no longer be a detectable 'meaning' to the use of a case in classical Greek. For instance, the verb βοηθέω *aid* takes a complement in the dative, a use which probably arose from the dative's use to express benefiting or interested parties ('dative of interest', →30.48–53); yet in classical Greek this use of the case has little meaning: it is the only possible case to go with this particular verb (note also that verbs with a similar meaning, such as ὠφελέω *benefit*, take a direct object in the accusative).

Things are different with individual verbs that can be construed with different cases, with a distinction in meaning. For example, the verb ἡγέομαι may be construed with a dative to mean *lead, guide*, with a genitive to mean *lead, command*, and with a 'double accusative' or with an (accusative and) infinitive to mean *believe, think*. (Note that in some other cases, however, there appears to be very little difference between alternating constructions with the same verb: for instance, πείθομαι *believe, obey* is usually construed with a complement in the dative, but is also sometimes found with a complement in the genitive.)

It is also often possible to group together verbs which are related in meaning and construed with the same case. For instance, verbs and adjectives which mean 'filling', 'emptying', '(being) full/empty' normally take a direct object in the accusative for the thing filled/emptied, and a complement in the genitive for the substance →(30.22). Verbs in such related spheres of meaning are listed together below.

Nominative

As Obligatory Constituent with Verbs

30.2   The nominative is the case used for the **subject** of a finite verb (and any modifiers that agree with it, →27.7).

(1)   μετὰ δὲ ταῦτα οὐ πολλαῖς ἡμέραις ὕστερον ἦλθεν ἐξ Ἀθηνῶν <u>Θυμοχάρης</u> ἔχων ναῦς ὀλίγας· καὶ εὐθὺς ἐναυμάχησαν αὖθις <u>Λακεδαιμόνιοι</u> καὶ <u>Ἀθηναῖοι</u>, ἐνίκησαν δὲ <u>Λακεδαιμόνιοι</u> ἡγουμένου Ἀγησανδρίδου. μετ' ὀλίγον δὲ τούτων <u>Δωριεὺς</u> ὁ Διαγόρου ἐκ Ῥόδου εἰς Ἑλλήσποντον εἰσέπλει ἀρχομένου χειμῶνος τέτταρσι καὶ δέκα ναυσὶν ἅμα ἡμέρᾳ. <u>κατιδὼν</u> δὲ <u>ὁ</u> τῶν Ἀθηναίων <u>ἡμεροσκόπος</u> ἐσήμηνε τοῖς στρατηγοῖς. (Xen. *Hell.* 1.1.1–2)

After these events, not many days later, Thymochares came from Athens with a few ships. And promptly the Spartans and Athenians fought another naval battle, and the Spartans, led by Agesandridas, were victorious. Shortly after this, as winter was setting in, Dorieus the son of Diagoras sailed from Rhodes into the Hellespont with fourteen ships, at daybreak. And when the day-scout of the Athenians spotted him, he signalled to the generals.

(2)   ὅτι μὲν <u>ὑμεῖς</u>, ὦ ἄνδρες Ἀθηναῖοι, πεπόνθατε ὑπὸ τῶν ἐμῶν κατηγόρων, οὐκ οἶδα· ἐγὼ δ' οὖν καὶ <u>αὐτὸς</u> ὑπ' αὐτῶν ὀλίγου ἐμαυτοῦ ἐπελαθόμην, οὕτω πιθανῶς ἔλεγον. καίτοι ἀληθές γε ὡς ἔπος εἰπεῖν οὐδὲν εἰρήκασιν. (Pl. *Ap.* 17a)

How you, men of Athens, have been affected by my accusers, I do not know. I, for my part, however, almost forgot who I was because of them, so convincingly did they speak. And yet they have said not a single thing, so to say, which is true.

Note 1: The subject of Greek finite verbs is very often not explicitly expressed, when the context and the personal ending of the verb make it sufficiently clear who or what is meant (→26.7). In such cases, no subject constituent in the nominative is present; cf. οἶδα, ἔλεγον and εἰρήκασιν in (2), which have no explicit subjects (the translation 'adds' *I, they*).

30.3 **Predicative complements** with **linking verbs** (→26.8) agree with their subject (→27.7), and thus also stand in the nominative:

(3) πᾶν ἐστι <u>ἄνθρωπος συμφορή</u>. (Hdt. 1.32.4)
   A human being is in every way (a victim of) chance.

Note that adjectives, participles and some numerals agree not only in case (nominative), but also in number and gender:

(4) ἡ δ᾽ ἀρετὴ ... οὐ πάνυ <u>δεινή</u> ἐστιν ἐν τῷ παραυτίκα εἰκῇ συνεπισπᾶσθαι. (Xen. Cyr. 2.2.24)
   Virtue is not very clever at drawing people in at first appearance and at random. *Nom. sg. fem.*

(5) αἱ μὲν <u>μηνύσεις</u> ... περὶ τῶν μυστηρίων ... ἐγένοντο <u>τέτταρες</u>. (Andoc. 1.25)
   The reports regarding the mysteries were four in number. *Nom. pl. fem.*

Note 1: In the accusative-and-infinitive construction (→51.11–12, 51.21, 51.41), and in various constructions with participles (→52.13–15, 52.32), such predicative complements may of course take other cases than the nominative.

Other Uses

30.4 The nominative is also used in bare **lists** (→26.29), including entries in dictionaries.

30.5 For the nominative used in **apposition to a sentence**, →27.14.

30.6 For the use of the nominative as a vocative, →30.55 n.1.

Accusative

30.7 The accusative is used to complement verbs (its most frequent function), as well as in various adverbial expressions.

As Obligatory Constituent (to Complement Verbs)

30.8 The accusative is the standard case for the **direct object** with verbs which take an object (→26.3):

(6) <u>γυναῖκα</u> ἠγαγόμην εἰς τὴν οἰκίαν. (Lys. 1.6)
   I brought a wife into my house.

(7) πάντες <u>τὸν ἄνδρα</u> ἐπαινοῦσιν. (Pl. *Prt.* 310e)
   Everyone praises the man.

Note 1: Often, a construction with a Greek verb taking a direct object in the accusative is best rendered into English by means of a prepositional phrase. A few examples:

αἰσχύνομαι   be ashamed of, feel shame for (*sometimes + dat.*)

λανθάνω	go unnoticed by (→52.11)
φοβέομαι	be afraid of
φυλάττομαι	be on guard against

30.9 Several verbs take a '**double accusative**' – a direct object (X) and a complement (Y) in the accusative:

- verbs meaning 'treat', 'do':

ποιέω	do X to Y (*also with adverbs: 'treat X in a . . . way'*)
δράω	do X to Y (*also with adverbs: 'treat X in a . . . way'*)

- some verbs meaning 'ask', 'demand':

αἰτέω	ask, demand X from Y
ἐρωτάω	ask X Y (*also with indirect questions, →42.2*)

- some other verbs:

ἀφαιρέομαι	take X from Y (*also + gen.: 'to take away X (acc.) from Y (gen.)'*)
διδάσκω	teach X Y, teach Y to X
κρύπτω	hide X from Y

(8) ἔλεγε ὅσα ἀγαθὰ Κῦρος Πέρσας πεποιήκοι. (Hdt. 3.75.1)
He recounted how many good things Cyrus had done to the Persians.

(9) ὁ Ἡριππίδας . . . αἰτεῖ τὸν Ἀγησίλαον ὁπλίτας . . . εἰς δισχιλίους. (Xen. *Hell.* 4.1.21)
Herippidas asked Agesilaus for up to two thousand hoplites.

(10) πολλὰ διδάσκει μ' ὁ πολὺς βίοτος. (Eur. *Hipp.* 252)
My long life teaches me many lessons.

(11) Διογείτων τὴν μὲν θυγατέρα ἔκρυπτε τὸν θάνατον τοῦ ἀνδρός. (Lys. 32.7)
Diogiton kept the death of her husband hidden from his daughter.

Note 1: When such verbs appear in the passive, the object of the active construction is used as the subject of the passive verb, while the complement (Y) still stands in the accusative; for details, →35.15.

30.10 The following **verbs** (→26.12) take a **direct object** (X) and **a predicative complement** (Y) that agrees with that object (and thus also stands in the accusative; this, too, is often called a '**double accusative**'):

αἱρέομαι	appoint/select X to be Y
ἡγέομαι	think/consider X to be Y (*+ gen. = 'lead', 'rule'; + dat. = 'guide'; + inf. = 'believe'*)
τίθημι	turn X into Y, make X Y
καθίστημι	install, appoint X as Y
καλέω	name/call X Y
λέγω	name/call X Y

νομίζω   think/consider X to be Y (+ *inf.* = 'think', 'believe')

ποιέω   appoint X as Y, make X into Y

(12) ἐκείνη γάρ, ὅταν μὲν πόλεμος ᾖ, <u>στρατηγοὺς</u> <u>ἡμᾶς</u> αἱρεῖται. (Xen. *Hell.* 6.3.4)
     For whenever there is war, it (*the state*) appoints us as generals.

(13) ἕνα ἕκαστον <u>λέγω</u> <u>αὐτὸν</u> ἑαυτοῦ <u>ἄρχοντα</u>. (Pl. *Grg.* 491d)
     I call every individual man his own ruler.

(14) τοῦτον <u>νόμιζε</u> Ζῆνα, τόνδ' <u>ἡγοῦ</u> θεόν. (Eur. fr. 941.3 Kannicht)
     Consider that to be Zeus, and this to be a god.

Note 1: When these verbs are passive, both the subject and the predicative complement stand in the nominative; for details, →35.15.

30.11   The accusative is also used in the **accusative-and-infinitive** (→51.11–12, 51.21, 51.41), the **accusative absolute** (→52.33) and **accusative-and-participle** constructions (→52.13).

Internal Object

30.12   With verbs that normally do not take a direct object (→26.3), an '**internal**' or '**cognate**' object in the accusative can be added to specify the nature of the action. This accusative is often related in meaning and lexical origin to the verb, and is usually plural and/or modified by an adjective or pronoun:

(15) πέντε τριήρεις ἐθελοντὴς ἐπιδοὺς ... <u>ἐτριηράρχησε</u> <u>τριηραρχίας</u>. (Dem. 45.85)
     He performed his duties as trierarch by contributing five ships willingly.

(16) ἑωρᾶτε ... Σωκράτη τινὰ ... <u>πολλὴν φλυαρίαν</u> <u>φλυαροῦντα</u>. (Pl. *Ap.* 19c)
     You have seen that a certain Socrates talks a lot of nonsense (*lit.* 'drivels a lot of drivel').

The accusative can be 'cognate' to the verb only in meaning (and not in lexical origin):

(17) εἰς Αἴγιναν κατοικισάμενος <u>ἠσθένησεν</u> <u>ταύτην τὴν νόσον</u> ἐξ ἧσπερ ἀπέθανεν. (Isoc. 19.24)
     When he had settled in Aegina he fell ill with this disease which resulted in his death.

Note 1: Occasionally, the noun in the accusative is omitted, in which case only an adjective or pronoun serves as internal object:

(18) τοῦτον μὲν ἀνέκραγον ὡς <u>ὀλίγας</u> παίσειεν. (Xen. *An.* 5.8.12)
     They shouted that he had given that man too few blows. *ὀλίγας agrees with an omitted πληγάς, 'blows'; note that παίσειεν also has a direct object, τοῦτον; for the position of τοῦτον, →60.33.*

30.13 Observe the following idioms, in which κακά/ἀγαθά is an internal object (and X marks a direct object, also in the accusative):

κακά/ἀγαθὰ λέγω X   speak ill of X

κακά/ἀγαθὰ ἀκούω   be spoken ill of

(19) ὁ Θεμιστοκλέης κεῖνόν τε καὶ τοὺς Κορινθίους ... κακὰ ἔλεγε. (Hdt. 8.61.2)
Themistocles spoke ill of him and of the Corinthians.

Note 1: Similarly, κακῶς/εὖ λέγω τινά and κακῶς/εὖ ἀκούω (with adverbs) mean *speak ill/well of, be spoken ill/well of:*

(20) οὐ προδώσω τὸν πατέρα κακῶς ἀκούοντα ἐν ὑμῖν ἀδίκως. (Antiph. 5.75)
I will not betray my father, who has a bad reputation among you, undeservedly.

As an Optional Constituent (Adverbial Modifier)

30.14 With active and middle verbs which do not take an object, with passive verbs, and with adjectives, an **accusative of respect** or **limitation** may be added to specify to which particular element the action or adjective applies ('as concerns ...', 'with respect to'):

ἀλγεῖ τοὺς πόδας   his feet hurt (*lit. 'he has a pain with respect to his feet'*)

(21) διαφέρει γυνὴ ἀνδρὸς τὴν φύσιν. (Pl. *Resp.* 453b)
Man and woman differ by nature.

(22) τρίτον δὲ σχῆμα πολιτείας οὐχ ἡ τοῦ πλήθους ἀρχή, δημοκρατία τοὔνομα κληθεῖσα; (Pl. *Plt.* 291d)
Isn't the third form of government the rule of the many, called 'democracy' by name? τοὔνομα = τὸ ὄνομα, *with crasis,* →1.43–5.

The accusative of respect is also used with nouns, especially in measurements:

ποταμὸς εὖρος δύο πλέθρων   a river two plethra wide (*lit. 'in width'*)

30.15 The **accusative of (duration of) time** expresses the length of time taken up by an action. Usually, such accusatives are accompanied by a numeral or an adjective of quantity (e.g. πολύς, ὀλίγος):

(23) ἀπέπλεε ... πολιορκήσας ... ἓξ καὶ εἴκοσι ἡμέρας ... τὴν νῆσον. (Hdt. 6.135.1)
He sailed away after having laid siege to the island for twenty-six days.

(24) νύμφη μὲν ἦν τρεῖς ἡμέρας (Ar. *Thesm.* 478)
I had been married for three days.

With an ordinal number (without the article), and often with a form of οὑτοσί (→29.36), this accusative expresses 'how long (since)':

(25) τὴν δὲ μητέρα τελευτήσασαν πέπαυμαι τρέφων τρίτον ἔτος τουτί. (Lys. 24.6)
I have not been supporting my mother only since her death two years ago (*lit. 'this (as) the third year'; note that Greek counts 'inclusively',* →9.10).

(26) ΕΤ. ὦ τί λέγεις; Πρωταγόρας ἐπιδεδήμηκεν; :: ΣΩ. τρίτην γε ἤδη ἡμέραν. (Pl. *Prt.* 309d)

(Friend:) What news! Protagoras is in town? :: (Socrates:) Yes, already since the day before yesterday.

30.16   Similarly, the **accusative of space** is used to express the extent of space or distance traversed in an action; this accusative is again often accompanied by a numeral (compare the accusative of duration above):

(27) Μενέλαε, . . . σε κιγχάνω μόλις, | πᾶσαν πλανηθεὶς τήνδε βάρβαρον χθόνα. (Eur. *Hel.* 597–8)

Menelaus, I come to you at last, having wandered through all of this barbarian country.

(28) ἐπορεύθησαν διὰ τῆς Ἀρμενίας πεδίον ἅπαν καὶ λείους γηλόφους οὐ μεῖον ἢ πέντε παρασάγγας. (Xen. *An.* 4.4.1)

They journeyed through Armenia across entirely level country and sloping hills, no less than five parasangs.

30.17   In poetry only, the bare **accusative of direction** is sometimes used to express the place 'to where':

(29) ἐπεὶ . . . ἦλθον πατρὸς ἀρχαῖον τάφον. (Soph. *El.* 893)

When I had come to my father's old grave, . . .

30.18   Many **adverbs** derive their form from the neuter accusative of corresponding adjectives: this is often called the **adverbial accusative**:

οὐδέν	in no way
μέγα	greatly, loudly
πολύ	very, highly, much
πολλά	often, frequently

Note 1: These forms are usually best seen as actual adverbs in their own right, not as (e.g.) modifiers in a noun phrase with the head left implicit. Alongside adverbial accusatives, some such adjectives (but not e.g. πολύ) also have adverbs formed regularly with the suffix -ως (→6.3–4), e.g. μεγάλως.

Note 2: This is the regular process by which adverbs of comparatives and superlatives are formed: →6.13–14.

Apposition to a Sentence

30.19   When an **appositive** is added to an entire sentence or clause, it normally stands in the accusative (→27.14):

(30) ἄλλαι δὲ θύρσους ἵεσαν δι' αἰθέρος | Πενθέως, στόχον δύστηνον. (Eur. *Bacch.* 1099–1100)

And other women threw their thyrsus staves through the air at Pentheus, a woeful aiming.

(31) Ἑλένην κτάνωμεν, <u>Μενέλεῳ λύπην πικράν</u>. (Eur. *Or.* 1105)
Let us slay Helen; a sore grief to Menelaus!

Genitive

30.20   The main function of the genitive is at the level of the noun phrase, to mark attributive modifiers (i.e. expressing various relations between (pro)nouns/noun phrases). It is also used to mark some required constituents (complements) with verbs/adjectives, and functions in a few adverbial expressions.

As Obligatory Constituent (to Complement Verbs/Adjectives)

Verbs Taking the Genitive

30.21   The genitive is used to complement, among others, the following **verbs**:

– some verbs meaning 'begin' or 'end':

ἄρχω/ἄρχομαι	begin (*sometimes + acc.; also + ppl. or inf.,* →52.27)
λήγω	cease from (*also + ppl.,* →52.9)
παύομαι	cease from (*also + ppl.,* →52.9)

– many verbs expressing sensorial or mental processes:

αἰσθάνομαι	perceive (*by ear, the gen. marks the source of sound;* αἰσθάνομαι *+ acc. = 'become aware of', 'learn'; combinations of gen./acc. occur*)
ἀκούω	hear (*the gen. marks the source of sound;* ἀκούω *+ acc. = 'be told', 'hear', e.g.* ἀκούω λόγον *'hear a story'; combinations of gen./acc. occur*)
ἀκροάομαι	listen to, hear (*in combinations gen./acc., the gen. marks the speaking person (i.e. the source of sound), the acc. the thing said*)
ἅπτομαι	grab hold of, touch
γεύομαι	taste
ἐπιθυμέω	long for, desire
ἐπιλανθάνομαι	forget (*sometimes + acc.*)
ἐπιμελ(έ)ομαι	take care of, ensure (*also + inf. or effort-clause = 'ensure that',* →44.1)
ἐφίεμαι	strive, long for (*also + inf. = 'strive to'*)
μιμνήσκομαι	remember (*sometimes + acc.*)
μέλει μοι (impers.)	. . . is of concern to me, I care for
μεταμέλει μοι (impers.)	I am sorry about, I regret
πείθομαι	obey, listen to (*rare; much more frequently + dat.*)
φροντίζω	be concerned about (*sometimes + acc.*)

– many verbs expressing leading, difference or superiority:

ἄρχω	lead, rule over (*sometimes + dat.*)
διαφέρω	differ from, excel, surpass
ἡγέομαι	lead (*also + dat. = 'guide'; + 2x acc. = 'consider'; + inf. = 'believe'*)
κρατέω	rule, be master of (*also + acc. = 'defeat'*)
περιγίγνομαι	be superior to, overcome
προέχω	be ahead of, beat, surpass

– many verbs meaning 'take part in', 'meet', 'strive for', and their opposites:

ἁμαρτάνω	miss, mistake, fail (*also + ppl. = 'err in'*)
ἀπέχω	be distant from
δεῖ (impers.)	there is a lack of, . . . is needed
δέομαι	require, lack, need (*also + 2x gen. = 'ask for X from Y'*)
ἔχομαι	cling to, border on, pertain to
κυρέω	hit upon, meet, get, achieve (*also + ppl. = 'happen to'*, →cf. 52.11)
μετέχω	take part in (*sometimes + acc. for the part itself*)
μέτεστί μοι (impers.)	I have a share in something
τυγχάνω	hit upon, meet, get, achieve (*also + ppl. = 'happen to'*, →52.11)

(32) ἀλλ' οὐ μὲν δὴ | λήξω θρήνων στυγερῶν τε γόων. (Soph. *El.* 103–4)
But I will not quit my lamentations and wretched wails.

(33) καὶ μὴν αἰσθάνομαι ψόφου τινός. (Ar. *Ran.* 285)
Hang on, I'm noticing some sort of sound.

(34) ταῦτα δὲ ἀσμένως τινὲς ἤκουον αὐτοῦ. (Dem. 18.36)
Some of them were relieved to hear this from him. *Note the combination of* ταῦτα *(acc.) and* αὐτοῦ *(gen.).*

(35) εἶναι γὰρ ὁμολογεῖται σωφροσύνη τὸ κρατεῖν ἡδονῶν καὶ ἐπιθυμιῶν. (Pl. *Symp.* 196c)
It is agreed that self-control is to have control over pleasures and desires.

(36) ἐμοὶ ἐφαίνετο οὐδεμιᾶς παιδείας μετεσχηκώς. (Aeschin. 3.117)
It was clear to me that he had had no share of any education.

30.22   The following verbs take an **object in the accusative** (X) **and a complement in the genitive** (Y):

– verbs meaning 'accuse', 'convict', etc. (acc. for the person accused, etc.; gen. for the crime or punishment):

αἰτιάομαι	accuse X of Y
διώκω	accuse X of Y, charge X with Y

Note also:

ἁλίσκομαι	be convicted of Y

But if the verb begins with κατα- or ἀπο- the genitive, which syntactically depends on the preverb, usually expresses the person accused, the acc. expresses the crime/punishment:

ἀπογιγνώσκω	acquit Y of X (*'adjudicate an accusation (X) away from Y'*)
ἀποψηφίζομαι	acquit Y of X, reject the punishment of X for Y (*'vote an accusation/punishment (X) away from Y'*)
καταγιγνώσκω	condemn, convict Y of X (*'adjudicate an accusation/punishment (X) against Y'*)
καταψηφίζομαι	condemn, convict Y of X (*'vote an accusation/punishment (X) against Y'*)
κατηγορέω	accuse Y of X, bring the charge of X against Y

- verbs meaning 'remove from', 'rob of', 'free from' etc.:

ἀπαλλάττω	remove/release X from Y
ἀποστερέω	rob X of Y
ἐλευθερόω	free X from Y
παύω	make X stop from Y

- verbs meaning 'fill', 'empty', etc.:

κενόω	empty X of Y
πίμπλημι	fill X with Y
πληρόω	fill X with Y

(37) εἰ γὰρ ἀποψηφιεῖσθε <u>Ἀγοράτου τουτουί</u> ... καὶ <u>ἐκείνων τῶν ἀνδρῶν</u> ... τῇ αὐτῇ ψήφῳ ταύτῃ <u>θάνατον</u> <u>καταψηφίζεσθε</u>. (Lys. 13.93)
For if you acquit this man Agoratus, you also, by that same vote, are condemning those men to death.

(38) οὐ δῆτ', ἐπεί σε <u>τοῦδ'</u> <u>ἐλευθερῶ</u> <u>φόνου</u>. (Eur. *Hipp.* 1449)
Not at all, since I absolve you from this murder.

(39) οὗτος δὲ ἡμᾶς <u>ἀλλοτριότητος</u> μὲν <u>κενοῖ</u>, <u>οἰκειότητος</u> δὲ <u>πληροῖ</u>. (Pl. *Symp.* 197d)
He (*Love*) rids us of estrangement, and fills us with intimacy.

30.23   The following **adjectives** (often related in meaning to the verbs above) are complemented by a genitive:

ἄξιος	worth(y of), deserving of
ἐλεύθερος	free from
ἔμπειρος	experienced in
ἐνδεής	lacking in
ἐπιστήμων	knowledgeable about
ἔρημος	deserted by, lacking in

ἱερός	consecrated to
μεστός	filled with
μέτοχος	(taking/having) part of
πλήρης	filled with

(40) ΑΔ. αἰαί. :: ΧΟ. πέπονθας ἄξι’ αἰαγμάτων. (Eur. *Alc.* 872–3)

(Admetus:) Ai! :: (Chorus:) You have suffered things that are worthy of shouts of 'Ai!'

(41) οἱ παρόντες <u>σπουδῆς</u> μέν, ὡς ὁρᾷς, <u>μεστοί</u>, <u>γέλωτος</u> δὲ ἴσως <u>ἐνδεέστεροι</u>. (Xen. *Symp.* 1.13)

The guests, as you can see, are full of seriousness, but perhaps rather lacking in laughter.

Genitive of Comparison

30.24   The **genitive of comparison** is used to complement comparatives:

(42) (φῂς) Σιμμίαν <u>Σωκράτους</u> . . . <u>μείζω</u> εἶναι, <u>Φαίδωνος</u> δὲ <u>ἐλάττω</u>. (Pl. *Phd.* 102b)
You say that Simmias is taller than Socrates, but shorter than Phaedo.

For more details on comparatives and their constructions, →32.

Attributive Genitives as Object, Predicative Complement, or Prepositional Complement

30.25   The **partitive genitive** (→30.29) is sometimes used **in place of a direct object**, and then implies that the action concerns only part of something larger, or a subsection from a larger group:

(43) Χειρίσοφος <u>πέμπει</u> <u>τῶν ἐκ τῆς κώμης</u> σκεψομένους πῶς ἔχοιεν οἱ τελευταῖοι. (Xen. *An.* 4.5.22)

Chirisophus sent some of the people from the village, to see how those in the rear were faring. *Note that the participle σκεψομένους agrees with the implied partial object (one might supply τινας with τῶν ἐκ τῆς κώμης). τοὺς ἐκ τῆς κώμης would have meant '(all) the men from the village'.*

(44) <u>τῆς τε γῆς</u> ἔτεμον καὶ αὐτὸ τὸ πόλισμα εἷλον. (Thuc. 2.56.6)
They ravaged part of the land and captured the settlement itself.

30.26   Many of the **attributive uses** of the genitive (→30.28–9) also occur **as predicative complement** with linking verbs:

(45) Ἱπποκράτης ὅδε <u>ἐστὶν</u> μὲν <u>τῶν ἐπιχωρίων</u>, <u>Ἀπολλοδώρου</u> υἱός, <u>οἰκίας μεγάλης</u> τε καὶ <u>εὐδαίμονος</u>. (Pl. *Prt.* 316b)

This man Hippocrates is one of the locals, a son of Apollodorus, and belongs to a great and prosperous house. *Partitive genitive and genitive of belonging.*

(46) ἐντεῦθεν ἐξελαύνει ... ἐπὶ τὸν Εὐφράτην ποταμόν, <u>ὄντα</u> τὸ εὖρος <u>τεττάρων</u>
<u>σταδίων</u>. (Xen. *An.* 1.4.11)
From there he marched to the river Euphrates, which is four stades in width.
Genitive of quantity.

(47) τὸν καθ᾽ ἡμέραν | βίον <u>λογίζου</u> σόν, τὰ δ᾽ ἄλλα <u>τῆς τύχης</u>. (Eur. *Alc.* 788–9)
Regard this day's life as your own, but the rest as belonging to fate.
*Genitive of possession. Note that the possessive pronoun σόν is functionally
equivalent to the genitive τῆς τύχης.*

The **genitive of quality**, used to express a certain characteristic or manner of being,
occurs exclusively in this way:

(48) ἐγὼ δὲ <u>τούτου τοῦ τρόπου</u> πώς <u>εἰμ᾽</u> ἀεί. (Ar. *Plut.* 246)
I am always somehow of that disposition.

(49) ὅσοι <u>τῆς αὐτῆς γνώμης</u> <u>ἦσαν</u> (Thuc. 1.113.2)
all who were of the same opinion

30.27   Similarly, attributive uses of the genitive may occur instead of other cases after
certain **prepositions** (→31.8 εἰς, ἐν); this occurs regularly with ἐν, εἰς or ἐκ + proper
name (in the genitive) to express 'in/to/from someone's house' (frequently with
Ἅϊδου *the house of Hades*, i.e. the Underworld):

(50) ἐκέλευον ... ἐμὲ ... μεθ᾽ αὑτῶν ἀκολουθεῖν <u>εἰς Δαμνίππου</u>. (Lys. 12.12)
They commanded me to follow them to Damnippus' house.

As Modifier in a Noun Phrase: the Attributive Genitive

30.28   The genitive is used particularly within noun phrases, to mark a noun phrase or
pronoun as modifier of a head (→26.18). Traditionally, many different categories
within this **attributive genitive** use are distinguished; the most important of these
are given below:

- The **genitive of possession** or **belonging** denotes ownership, belonging, possession, etc.:
ἡ <u>τοῦ πατρὸς</u> οἰκία   his father's house/the house belonging to his father
τὴν ψυχὴν <u>τὴν Σόλωνος</u> Solon's soul

- The **genitive of origin** denotes the origin, offspring, source, etc. of the head:
ἡ <u>τῆς Νεαίρας</u> θυγάτηρ Neaera's daughter
τὰ <u>τοῦ Σόλωνος</u> ἐλεγεῖα Solon's elegies/the elegies authored by Solon

- With nouns that express an action ('action nouns', →23.6), the genitive is used
for the subject or object of that action – **genitive of the subject** (or 'subjective'
genitive) or **of the object** (or 'objective' genitive):

ἡ μάχη ἡ <u>τῶν στρατιωτῶν</u>	the soldiers' battle/the battle fought by the soldiers (*of the subject*)
ἡ <u>τοῦ τείχους</u> ποίησις	the building of the wall (*of the object*)
ὁ <u>τῶν πολεμίων</u> φόβος	the enemies' fear/the fear felt by the enemies (*of the subject*) *or* the fear for/inspired by the enemies (*of the object*) (*ambiguous, the interpretation depends on the context*)

– To measure time, space, degree, age, the genitive of **quantity** or **measure** can be used (usually with a numeral):

<u>ὀκτὼ σταδίων</u> τεῖχος	a wall eight stades in length
ἀνὴρ <u>εἴκοσιν ἐτῶν</u>	a man twenty years of age

Note 1: For expressions of age, a construction with γεγονώς (pf. ppl. of γίγνομαι) and the accusative of duration (→30.15) is more common: e.g. εἴκοσιν ἔτη γεγονώς *twenty years old* (lit. 'having been in existence twenty years').

– Other relations between nouns: **material/contents, price/value, elaboration**, etc.:

(51) δῶρα … <u>χρυσοῦ τε καὶ ἀργύρου</u> προσεφέρετο. (Thuc. 2.97.3)
   Gifts of gold and silver were added.

<u>χιλίων δραχμῶν</u> δίκην φεύγω	I am defendant in a lawsuit involving a thousand drachmas.
τὸ <u>τῶν Ἑρμῶν</u>	the affair of the Hermae/concerning the Hermae
γραφὴ <u>κλοπῆς</u>	a charge of theft
ἡ <u>Σόλωνος</u> εἰκών	the statue of Solon
τὸ <u>τῆς ἀρετῆς</u> ὄνομα	the word 'virtue'

Note 2: Attributive genitives are frequently used as predicative complement (→26.8).
Note 3: For the position of attributive genitives relative to the head noun and the article, →28.15.

30.29   The **partitive genitive** (also 'of the divided whole') denotes a whole to which the head belongs as a part:

οἱ χρηστοὶ <u>τῶν ἀνθρώπων</u>	the good people (*lit.* 'the good among the people')
πολλοὶ <u>τῶν λόγων</u>	many of the words

(52) τούτῳ τῷ ἀνδρὶ ἐτύγχανε ἐοῦσα γυνὴ καλλίστη μακρῷ <u>τῶν ἐν Σπάρτῃ γυναικῶν</u>. (Hdt. 6.61.2)
   This man happened to have by far the most beautiful wife of all women in Sparta.

Note 1: The partitive genitive is frequently used as predicative complement (→26.8).
Note 2: For the position of partitive genitives relative to the head noun and the article, →28.16.

The partitive genitive is often used with the interrogative pronouns ποῦ, ποῖ, πόθεν, and with neuter forms of the demonstrative pronoun οὗτος and the demonstrative adjective τοσοῦτος:

(53) τίς τε ἐὼν καὶ κόθεν τῆς Φρυγίης ἥκων ἐπίστιός μοι ἐγένεο; (Hdt. 1.35.3)

Who are you, where in Phrygia did you come from, that you are now my suppliant?

(54) εἰς τοσοῦτον ὕβρεως καὶ ἀναιδείας ἦλθεν Στέφανος οὑτοσὶ ... , ὥστε ... ([Dem.] 59.72)

This fellow Stephanus reached such a state of brutality and shamelessness, that he ...

As an Optional Constituent (Adverbial Modifier)

30.30 In sentences which have a verb or other expression of emotion (e.g. admiration, sorrow, anger, envy, etc.), the **genitive of cause** or **source of emotion** may express the reason for that emotion:

(55) στένω σε ... τῆς ἁμαρτίας. (Eur. *Hipp.* 1409)

I bewail you for your error.

This genitive is also used in **exclamations** (→38.50), without a verb of emotion:

(56) ἀλλὰ τῆς ἐμῆς κάκης, | τὸ καὶ προσέσθαι μαλθακοὺς λόγους φρενί. (Eur. *Med.* 1051–2)

But oh, what cowardice on my part, even to let soft words into my heart.

30.31 In sentences which have a verb meaning 'sell' or 'buy', the price of something bought or sold may be expressed in the genitive – **genitive of price/value**:

(57) τῇ σάλπιγγι τῇδε ... | ἣν ἐπριάμην δραχμῶν ποθ' ἑξήκοντ' ἐγώ (Ar. *Pax.* 1240–1)

this bugle, which I once bought for 60 drachmas

Note 1: This genitive is also used, but normally with the preposition περί added, in the fixed expressions περὶ πολλοῦ (πλείονος, πλείστου, etc.) ποιέομαι/τιμάομαι/ἡγέομαι *value highly (more highly, most highly)* and περὶ ὀλίγου (ἐλάττονος, ἐλαχίστου, etc.) ποιέομαι/τιμάομαι/ ἡγέομαι *value lightly (more lightly, most lightly)*:

(58) ἀποκτιννύναι μὲν γὰρ ἀνθρώπους περὶ οὐδενὸς ἡγοῦντο, λαμβάνειν δὲ χρήματα περὶ πολλοῦ ἐποιοῦντο. (Lys. 12.7)

For they thought nothing of killing men, but placed a premium on getting money.

(59) πολλοῦ γὰρ ποιοῦμαι ἀκηκοέναι ἃ ἀκήκοα Πρωταγόρου. (Pl. *Prt.* 328d)

For I consider it a treat to have heard what I have heard from Protagoras.

30.32 The **genitive of time** expresses the time within which something takes place; with some specific nouns, notably νύξ *night*, θέρος *summer* and χειμών *winter*, it can also express the time when:

(60) βασιλεὺς οὐ μαχεῖται <u>δέκα ἡμερῶν</u>. (Xen. *An.* 1.7.18)
   The king will not fight within the next ten days.

(61) ἀποδράντες <u>νυκτὸς</u> ᾤχοντο εἰς Δεκέλειαν. (Xen. *Hell.* 1.2.14)
   Running off in the night, they headed for Decelea.

(62) οἱ δ᾽ ἐν τῇ Σικελίᾳ Ἀθηναῖοι <u>τοῦ αὐτοῦ χειμῶνος</u> ἔς τε τὴν Ἱμεραίαν ἀπόβασιν
   ἐποιήσαντο. (Thuc. 3.115.1)
   The same winter, the Athenians in Sicily made landing at Himera.

With the article, this genitive can be used **distributively** to mean 'once per . . .',
'every . . .':

(63) δραχμὴν ἐλάμβανε <u>τῆς ἡμέρας</u>. (Thuc. 3.17.4)
   He earned a drachma per day.

30.33   The **genitive of space** is sometimes used to express the space within which an
   action takes place. This occurs primarily in poetry:

(64) <u>λαιᾶς δὲ χειρὸς</u> . . . | οἰκοῦσι Χάλυβες. (Aesch. *PV* 714–15)
   And on the left hand dwell the Chalubes.

30.34   The **genitive of separation** is used with verbs of motion to express the place or
   entity from which the motion takes place. This use is rare in prose:

(65) ἀλλ᾽ ὡς τάχιστα, παῖδες, ὑμεῖς μὲν <u>βάθρων</u> | ἵστασθε. (Soph. *OT* 142–3)
   But, children, get up from the steps as quickly as possible.

30.35   The genitive is also used in the **genitive absolute** construction (→52.32) and the
   genitive and participle construction (→52.14).

Dative

30.36   The main function of the dative is to mark non-obligatory (adverbial) modifiers.
   It is also used to mark some required complements with verbs/adjectives.

As Obligatory Constituent (to Complement Verbs/Adjectives)
As Indirect Object

30.37   The dative is used to express the **indirect object** (Y) with the following types of
   verbs (X indicates a direct object in the accusative, where present):

   – verbs meaning 'give', 'entrust', etc.:

δίδωμι	give X to Y
ἐπιτρέπω	entrust X to Y
παρέχω	entrust X to Y/furnish Y with X

- verbs meaning 'say', 'tell', 'report', etc. (usually with direct or indirect statement, →41.3):

| λέγω | tell/say to Y |
| ἀγγέλλω | convey/report to Y |

- most verbs meaning 'command', 'order', 'advise' etc. (usually together with an infinitive, →51.8):

ἐπιτάττω	order/command Y (to do something)
λέγω	tell/command Y (to do something)
παραγγέλλω	convey an order to Y (to do something)
παραινέω	recommend to Y (to do something)

- most verbs meaning 'seem', 'appear', etc.:

| δοκέω | seem (*also + inf. (without dat.) = 'think'; for the possible constructions,* →51.30) |
| φαίνομαι | appear, seem (*for the possible constructions,* →52.24) |

(66) ἔπρασσε δὲ ταῦτα μετὰ Γογγύλου τοῦ Ἐρετριῶς, ᾧπερ ἐπέτρεψε τό τε Βυζάντιον καὶ τοὺς αἰχμαλώτους. (Thuc. 1.128.6)

He did this together with Gongylus of Eretria, to whom he had entrusted Byzantium and the prisoners.

(67) εἰπέ μοι, τουτὶ τί ἦν; (Ar. *Ach.* 157)

Tell me, what was that?

(68) εἶπεν αὐτοῖς ἀπιέναι ἐκ τοῦ στρατεύματος ὡς τάχιστα. (Xen. *Cyr.* 7.2.5)

He told them to leave the army as soon as possible.

(69) καλῶς γέ μοι, ὦ Εὐθύφρων, φαίνῃ λέγειν. (Pl. *Euthphr.* 12e)

You seem to me to be speaking well, Euthyphro.

Note 1: For verbs of speech used as verbs of commanding, →51.32. Note that κελεύω takes an accusative-and-infinitive (→51.11–12), not a dative.

30.38   The dative as indirect object complements the following **impersonal verbs** (→36.4–5), usually together with an infinitive (→51.8) (Y marks the dative):

δοκεῖ	it seems (right) to Y (to do something), Y decides (to do something)
συμφέρει	it profits Y (to do something)
λυσιτελεῖ	it profits Y (to do something), it is best for Y (to do something)
μέλει	it is of concern to Y (to do something), Y cares for (*frequently + gen.,* →36.15)
ἔξεστι	it is possible for Y (to do something)
πρέπει	it is fitting for Y (to do something)

(70) ἔδοξεν τῷ δήμῳ ... ἐπαινέσαι ... (inscriptions)

The people have resolved to praise ...

(71) κάλει δὴ καὶ τὸν Στράτωνα αὐτὸν τὸν τὰ τοιαῦτα πεπονθότα· ἑστάναι γὰρ
ἐξέσται δήπουθεν αὐτῷ. (Dem. 21.95)

Also call Straton himself, the man who has endured such things. For no doubt
he will be allowed to stand up in court.

With Other Verbs and Adjectives

30.39   The dative is used as first complement with the following **verbs** (among others):

ἀπειλέω	threaten
ἀρέσκω	please, satisfy (*sometimes + acc.*)
βοηθέω	help, come to the aid of
διαλέγομαι	converse with
εἴκω	yield, give way to (*sometimes combined with gen. of separation,* →30.34)
ἐπιτίθεμαι	apply oneself to, attack
ἕπομαι	follow (*also often with prepositions, especially* σύν *+ dat. and* μετά *+ gen.*)
ἡγέομαι	guide (*also + gen. =* 'lead', 'rule'; *+ 2x acc. =* 'consider'; *+ inf. =* 'believe')
μάχομαι	fight against
ὀργίζομαι	get angry at
πείθομαι	listen to, believe, obey (*rarely + gen.*)
πελάζω	approach (*sometimes + gen.*)
πιστεύω	trust, believe
πολεμέω	make war against
συγγιγνώσκω	forgive, pardon (*also + acc. =* 'acknowledge', 'confess')
συμβουλεύω	advise, counsel
φθονέω	be envious of, bear ill will to (*sometimes combined with gen. of cause,* →30.30)
χαλεπαίνω	be angry at (*sometimes with gen. of cause,* →30.30)
χρήομαι	use, treat with, be intimate with

(72) τοῖς δὲ ἀποψηφισαμένοις ἡδέως ἂν διαλεχθείην ὑπὲρ τοῦ γεγονότος τουτουὶ
πράγματος. (Pl. *Ap.* 39e)

I would be happy to discuss this thing that has happened with those who
voted for my acquittal.

(73) νομίζοντες ἀδυνάτους ἔσεσθαι Ἀθηναίους βοηθεῖν τοῖς Μεγαρεῦσιν (Thuc.
1.105.3)

thinking that the Athenians would be unable to come to the Megarians' aid

(74) Βοιωτοὶ Ἀθηναίοισι ἐμαχέσαντο χρόνον ἐπὶ συχνόν. (Hdt. 9.67)

The Boeotians fought against the Athenians for a long time.

(75) οὐδενὶ χρῇ τῶν οἰκείων οὐδὲ πιστεύεις τῶν σαυτοῦ οὐδενί. ([Dem.] 49.41)

You are on good terms with none of your relatives, and trust none of your friends.

Note 1: There are also verbs with similar meanings which take a direct object in the accusative: e.g. ὠφελέω *benefit*, βλάπτω *harm, damage*, μισέω *hate*, ζηλόω *envy*.

30.40 The following **adjectives** are complemented by a dative:

ἐναντίος	opposite, contrary to
εὔνους	well-disposed towards
ἐχθρός	hostile to, hated by
ἴσος	equal to, the same as
κοινός	shared with
ὅμοιος	similar to, equal to
φίλος	friendly with, loved by
also: ὁ αὐτός	the same as

(76) κοινὸς ... δὴ ἔστω ὑμῖν ὁ λόγος. (Pl. *Prt.* 358a)
Let our conversation be shared with you.

(77) καὶ ἐάν τινα αἰσθανώμεθα ἐναντίον τῇ ὀλιγαρχίᾳ, ὅσον δυνάμεθα ἐκποδὼν ποιούμεθα. (Xen. *Hell.* 2.3.26)
And if we discover someone opposed to the oligarchy, we get rid of him, so far as we have the power.

Note 1: For the constructions of ὅμοιος, ἴσος and ὁ αὐτός, →32.14–15.

Dative of the Possessor

30.41 The **dative of the possessor** is used to complement 'existential' εἰμί and γίγνομαι (*there is, there (be)comes*, →26.10), denoting possession, belonging, or interest:

(78) ... εἰρομένου Ξέρξεω εἰ ἔστι ἄλλη ἔξοδος ἐς θάλασσαν τῷ Πηνειῷ ... (Hdt. 7.130.1)
... when Xerxes asked if the (river) Peneus had any other outlet into the sea ...

(79) τοῖς ... πλουσίοις πολλὰ παραμύθιά φασιν εἶναι. (Pl. *Resp.* 329e)
It is said that rich people have much comfort (*lit. 'that there are many comforts for rich people'*).

As an Optional Constituent (Adverbial Modifier)

Referring to Things or Abstract Entities

30.42 The dative is very frequently used to express optional adverbial modifiers (→26.14). It marks **nouns referring to things or abstract entities** in various kinds of adverbial modifiers.

30.43   The **dative of instrument** expresses the instrument used in an action.

λίθοις ἔβαλλον   they were pelting with rocks

οὐδὲν ἤνυε <u>τούτοις</u>   he accomplished nothing by this

(80)   μητέρα κατειργάσαντο <u>κοινωνῷ ξίφει</u>. (Eur. *IT* 1173)
They killed their mother with one common sword.

30.44   The **dative of means, manner** or **circumstance** expresses the method by which or the circumstances under which an action takes place:

(81)   <u>κραυγῇ πολλῇ</u> ἐπίασιν. (Xen. *An.* 1.7.4)
They will attack shouting loudly / with loud shouting.

(82)   ταῦτα ἔπρηξα τῇ σῇ μὲν <u>εὐδαιμονίῃ</u>, τῇ ἐμεωυτοῦ δὲ <u>κακοδαιμονίῃ</u>. (Hdt. 1.87.3)
I have done these things for your good fortune, but to my own detriment.

Note 1: In some cases it is difficult to distinguish between instrument and means :

(83)   βούλονται δὲ <u>πολέμῳ</u> μᾶλλον ἢ <u>λόγοις</u> τὰ ἐγκλήματα διαλύεσθαι. (Thuc. 1.140.2)
They prefer to resolve complaints with war rather than with words.

But this is a 'problem' of classification rather than of case meaning (for the value of labels, →30.1 n.1).

Note 2: The dative of manner underlies the use of the ending -ῃ in various pronominal forms meaning 'in a certain manner', 'via a certain route': e.g. ταύτῃ *that way*, πῇ *how?*, πῃ *somehow*, etc. For these forms, also →8.2.

30.45   The **dative of cause** expresses reason or cause:

(84)   ἔφερον … οἱ ὁπλῖται … αὐτοὶ τὰ σφέτερα αὐτῶν σιτία, οἱ μὲν <u>ἀπορίᾳ</u> ἀκολούθων, οἱ δὲ <u>ἀπιστίᾳ</u>. (Thuc. 7.75.5)
The hoplites carried their own food themselves, some for lack of servants, others from mistrust of them.

(85)   <u>ὕβρει</u> καὶ οὐκ <u>οἴνῳ</u> τοῦτο ποιοῦντος (Dem. 21.74)
doing this out of insolence, and not because he was drunk

30.46   The **dative of time** expresses the time when the action takes place (it refers to a specific moment or period). It is often accompanied by a numeral:

τρίτῳ ἔτει   in the third year / after two years (→9.10)

τῇ ὑστεραίᾳ   (on) the following day

(86)   … δεδόχθαι τῇ βουλῇ … στεφανῶσαι Χαρίδημον … καὶ ἀναγορεῦσαι <u>Παναθηναίοις τοῖς μεγάλοις</u> ἐν τῷ γυμνικῷ ἀγῶνι καὶ <u>Διονυσίοις τραγῳδοῖς καινοῖς</u>. (Dem. 18.116)
(A decree) that it be resolved by the Council to crown Charidemus and to proclaim this at the Great Panathenaea at the gymnastic contest, and at the Dionysia at the performance of new tragedies.

30.47 In poetry, the bare **dative of place** may be used to express the place where an action takes place. In prose, this dative occurs only with a limited number of place names (in other cases a preposition is normally required, →31.4):

(87) ἐπεὶ δὲ γῇ | ἔκειτο τλήμων, δεινά γ᾽ ἦν τἀνθένδ᾽ ὁρᾶν. (Soph. *OT* 1266–7)
And when the hapless woman lay on the ground, what happened next was horrible to see.

(88) (ἐπαιδεύθησαν ὑπὸ) τῶν τε Μαραθῶνι μαχεσαμένων καὶ τῶν ἐν Σαλαμῖνι ναυμαχησάντων. (Pl. *Menex.* 241b)
(They have been educated by) those who fought at Marathon and those who were in the naval battle at Salamis.

Referring to Persons

30.48 The dative may also mark **nouns referring to persons**, to indicate individuals or groups who are in some way closely involved in the action expressed by the verb (these uses may be gathered under the general heading **dative of interest**).

30.49 The **dative of advantage** and **dative of disadvantage** are used to indicate the beneficiary (or opposite) of an action; they express in or against whose interest an action is performed:

(89) ἐπειδὴ αὐτοῖς οἱ βάρβαροι ἐκ τῆς χώρας ἀπῆλθον, ... (Thuc. 1.89.3)
When the barbarians had departed their country for them (*for their benefit*), ...

(90) ἥδε ἡ ἡμέρα τοῖς Ἕλλησι μεγάλων κακῶν ἄρξει. (Thuc. 2.12.3)
This day will spell for the Greeks the beginning of great evils.

30.50 With verbs in the passive, the **dative of agent** can be used to express the agent of the action. This occurs in prose almost exclusively with passive verbs in the (plu)perfect (91) and with verbal adjectives in -τέος (92), but in poetry sometimes also with other passive verb forms (93):

(91) ἐπειδὴ αὐτοῖς παρεσκεύαστο ... (Thuc. 1.46.1)
When preparations had been made by them ...

(92) οὔ σφι περιοπτέη ἐστὶ ἡ Ἑλλὰς ἀπολλυμένη. (Hdt. 7.168.1)
It is not to be endured by them that Greece is being destroyed.

(93) οἶδά σοι στυγουμένη. (Eur. *Tro.* 898)
I know that I am hated by you.

30.51 The **dative of accompaniment**, without preposition, is used almost exclusively with military terminology to denote accompaniment (in other cases, a preposition is normally used):

(94) πέντε δὲ ἔλαβον, καὶ μίαν τούτων αὐτοῖς ἀνδράσιν. (Thuc. 4.14.1)
They captured five (ships), one of them with crew and all. *For this use of αὐτός, →29.12.*

(95) οἱ . . . Ἀθηναῖοι ἀπίκοντο εἴκοσι νηυσί. (Hdt. 5.99.1)

The Athenians arrived with twenty ships.

30.52 The dative also marks the person **from whose perspective or vantage point** the action is perceived:

(96) ὁ μὲν χρύσεος ἔκειτο ἐπὶ δεξιὰ ἐσιόντι ἐς τὸν νηόν. (Hdt. 1.51.1)

The golden (bowl) stood on the right for someone entering the temple.

(97) οἴκτιρον . . . με | πολλοῖσιν οἰκτρόν. (Soph. *Trach.* 1070–1)

Take pity on me, who am pitiable in the eyes of many.

30.53 Difficult to translate is the use of the so-called **ethical dative** ('of feeling'): personal pronouns of the first or second person (μοι, ἡμῖν, σοι, ὑμῖν) can loosely express the involvement of the speaker or addressee in the action:

(98) ὦ μῆτερ, ὡς καλός μοι ὁ πάππος. (Xen. *Cyr.* 1.3.2)

Mother, how handsome is my grandfather!

(99) τοιοῦτο . . . ὑμῖν ἐστι ἡ τυραννίς. (Hdt. 5.92η.4)

There's tyranny for you.

(100) σύντεμνέ μοι τὰς ἀποκρίσεις καὶ βραχυτέρας ποίει. (Pl. *Prt.* 334d)

Please cut your answers short, and make them more succinct. *With an imperative, μοι may often appropriately be translated 'please'.*

With Expressions of Comparison

30.54 With comparatives, superlatives and other expressions of comparison, the **dative of measure of difference** expresses the degree to which one entity differs from another:

κεφαλῇ ἐλάττων	a head shorter
πολλῷ τε κάλλιστα καὶ	by far the most beautiful and by far the
πολλῷ μέγιστα	greatest things
οὐ πολλαῖς ἡμέραις ὕστερον	not many days later

For the possible constructions of comparatives and superlatives with this dative, →32.11.

Vocative

30.55 The vocative case is used:

– in **calls** or **summonses**, always at the beginning of a sentence, to attract the attention of a person nearby, or of a god;

– in **addresses**, to acknowledge or maintain contact with some person nearby.

Vocatives are often, but not always, preceded by the word ὦ:

(101) Εὐριπίδη, Εὐριπίδιον, | ὑπάκουσον, εἴπερ πώποτ' ἀνθρώπων τινί. (Ar. *Ach.* 404–5)

Euripides, my little Euripides, listen, if you've ever listened to anyone. *Call/ summons.*

(102) ὁ δὲ Κῦρος . . . ἐπηύξατο· Ἀλλ', ὦ Ζεῦ μέγιστε, αἰτοῦμαί σε, δός . . . (Xen. *Cyr.* 5.1.29)

Cyrus uttered this prayer: 'Zeus almighty, I beseech thee, grant that . . .' *Call/ summons.*

(103) καλῶς ἔλεξας, ὦ γύναι. (Eur. *Hel.* 158)

Well said, my lady! *Address.*

Note 1: In a few cases, the nominative is used instead of the vocative in calls/summonses, e.g. ὁ παῖς (rather than ὦ παῖ) used by masters to call their slaves (*boy!*), and οὗτος *hey there!* (→29.30).

Observe that in many further cases (and always in the plural), the vocative is morphologically identical to the nominative, as Εὐριπίδιον in (101).

Cases and the Expression of Time and Space

30.56   For the different uses of the cases in expressions of time and space, →30.15–16, 30.17, 30.28, 30.32–3, 30.46. For the uses of these cases with prepositions to indicate time and space, →31.4, 31.8-9. Whether they are used with a preposition or not, the following generalizations about the various cases can be made:

– In spatial **expressions** (with or without a preposition), the genitive tends to express **place from which** or **space within which**; the **dative** tends to express the **place where**, and the **accusative** the **place to which** or the **distance traversed**:

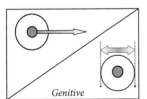
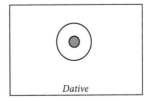
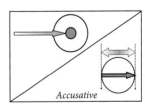

Figure 30.1: The use of cases in spatial expressions

– In temporal expressions (with or without a preposition), the **genitive** tends to express **time within which**, the **dative time when**, and the **accusative time during which**:

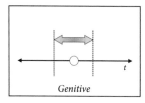 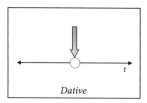 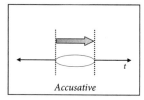

Figure 30.2: The use of cases in temporal expressions

30.57   Apart from the genitive, dative and accusative, Greek also uses various **fossilized forms** (originally case forms) in spatial (and sometimes temporal) expressions: e.g. οἶκοι *at home*, Ἀθήνησι *in Athens*, Ἀθήνηθεν *from Athens*, Ἀθήναζε *to Athens*. For details on such forms, →6.7–11.

30.58   For **measurements**, Greek normally uses a combination of genitive of measurement (→30.28) and accusative of respect (→30.14), usually with article:

(104) κρηπὶς . . . τὸ εὖρος πεντήκοντα ποδῶν καὶ τὸ ὕψος πεντήκοντα (Xen. *An.* 3.4.11)
a foundation fifty feet wide and fifty feet high

31

Prepositions

Introduction

31.1 Greek **prepositions** can be accompanied by (pro)nominal constituents in the genitive, dative or accusative. Together with this constituent they form a **prepositional phrase** (e.g. εἰς τὴν πόλιν *into the city*). These can be used to indicate spatial, temporal or other, more abstract relationships:

(1) τὴν γὰρ ἄνθρωπον ἀποπέμψω ἐκ τῆς οἰκίας. ([Dem.] 59.82)
For I will send the woman away, out of my house. *Spatial.*

(2) ὑμᾶς δέ, ὦ παῖδες, οὕτως ἐξ ἀρχῆς ἐπαίδευον. (Xen. *Cyr.* 8.7.10)
And in this way I educated you, my children, from the beginning. *Temporal.*

(3) ταῦτα γὰρ οἱ ἐνετέταλτο ἐκ Δαρείου, Θρηίκην καταστρέφεσθαι. (Hdt. 5.2.2)
For this had been ordered to him by Darius, to conquer Thrace. *Abstract, the prepositional phrase indicates the source/origin of the order expressed by ἐνετέταλτο ('by' in the Engl. translation somewhat obscures this relationship).*

31.2 Distinction is made between

– **'proper'** prepositions: prepositions that also appear in compound verbs, such as ἐκ (cf. e.g. ἐκβαίνω, ἐξέρχομαι) and ἀπό (cf. e.g. ἀποβαίνω, ἀπαγγέλλω, ἀφίστημι): →31.8;

– **'improper'** prepositions: prepositions that are not used in compound verbs, such as χωρίς + gen., ἅμα + dat., ὡς + acc.: these also appear regularly as adverbs without accompanying constituent: →31.9.

31.3 Some prepositions are always accompanied by constituents in a single fixed case (e.g. ἐκ + gen., ἐν + dat., εἰς + acc.), whereas others allow a choice between two or three cases (e.g. διά + gen./acc., παρά + gen./dat./acc.) and differ in meaning accordingly (→31.8). Improper prepositions are always accompanied by one fixed case.

31.4   With the spatial senses of prepositions:

- the **genitive** is frequently used for motion away from something (e.g. ἐκ + gen. *away from*, παρά + gen. *from the side of*);
- the **dative** is frequently used for stationary position (e.g. ἐν + dat. *in, at*, παρά + dat. *at the side of*);
- the **accusative** is normally used for motion towards something (e.g. εἰς + acc. *to(wards)*, παρά + acc. *to the side of*), or motion through a larger area or stretch of space (e.g. παρά + acc. *alongside*).

For these values, cf. also the 'genitive of separation' (→30.34), the 'dative of place' (→30.47), and the 'accusative of direction' and the 'accusative of space' (→30.16–17); also →30.56.

In the other senses of prepositions the contribution of an individual case to the meaning of a preposition–case combination is frequently more difficult to determine. In some cases the distinction between the use of one case and another with the same preposition is very slight.

31.5   Prepositional phrases can be substantivized by the addition of an article, e.g. τὰ περὶ Κύρου *the events concerning Cyrus*; →28.25, cf. 26.19–20.

31.6   Many prepositions can also occur without an accompanying constituent, as adverbs; this is, however, relatively rare in prose, apart from πρός *furthermore, besides*, and μετά *thereafter*.

31.7   For the accentuation of the proper prepositions, →24.37; note especially that prepositions with two syllables have their accent on the ultima, unless they follow their accompanying constituent ('anastrophe', →60.14), are used adverbially, or are used instead of a compound with ἐστί(ν)/εἰσί(ν) (e.g. πάρα = πάρεστι/πάρεισι, ἔνι = ἔνεστι/ἔνεισι).

Common Uses of the Prepositions

Proper Prepositions

31.8   The table below gives the most frequent uses of prepositions in classical Greek. Only 'proper' prepositions are included in the table, listed alphabetically. Some deviating uses in Ionic (Herodotus) and poetry have been left out.

	spatial	temporal	abstract/metaphorical
ἀμφί (ἀμφ')			
+ genitive			concerning, about
			ἡ δίκη ἀμφὶ τοῦ πατρός
			the trial concerning the father
+ dative (poetry and Ion.)			(*cause*) **about, for the sake of**
			φοβεῖται ἀμφὶ τῇ γυναικί
			he is afraid for the sake of his wife
+ accusative	**around**	**around, about**	concerning, about
	ἀμφὶ πῦρ καθήμενοι	ἀμφὶ μέσας νύκτας	εἶναι/ἔχειν ἀμφί τι
	sitting around the fire	around midnight	be occupied /concerned with something
	(*with people*)		(*with numerals*) **about**
	οἱ ἀμφὶ Κῦρον		ἀμφὶ τοὺς δισχιλίους
	Cyrus and his followers		about two thousand
ἀνά (ἀν')			
+ dative (poetry)	(*position*) **on, upon**		
	ἀνὰ ναυσίν		
	on their ships		
+ accusative	(*vertical*) **up along**	(*distributively*)	(*to express proportion*)
	ἀνὰ τὸν ποταμόν	ἀν' ἕκαστον ἔτος	ἀνὰ λόγον
	up along the river, upstream	year by year, yearly	proportionately
	ἀνὰ τὸ ὄρος		ἀνὰ κράτος
	up the mountain	ἀνὰ χρόνον	with all his might (= 'proportionate to his strength')
		over time	
	(*horizontal*) **spread out over, across**		
	ἀνὰ τὴν χώραν		
	spread across the country		
ἀντί (ἀντ', ἀνθ')			
+ genitive			**in exchange for, instead of**
			ἀντὶ χρημάτων
			(in exchange) for money
			πολέμιος ἀντὶ φίλου
			enemy instead of friend
			on account of, because of
			ἀντὶ τοῦ;
			because of what?, why?

	spatial	temporal	abstract/metaphorical
		ἀπό (ἀπ', ἀφ')	
+ genitive	(away/originating) **from**	**since, from**	*(separation)*
	ἀπὸ τῶν νεῶν	ἀπ' ἀρχῆς	οὐκ ἀπὸ τρόπου
	from the ships	since the beginning	true to character
	ἀπὸ τῆς θαλάττης	ἀφ' οὗ (*conjunction*)	*(origin)*
	at a distance from the sea	since	καλεῖσθαι ἀπό τινος
			be named after
	ἀφ' ἵππου μάχεσθαι		ἀπὸ τῶν παρόντων
	fight on horseback		based on the available means
			ἐπράχθη ἀπ' αὐτῶν οὐδέν
			nothing was done on their part
		διά (δι')	
+ genitive	**through**	**through(out), . . . long**	**through, via, by means of**
	διὰ τοῦ θώρακος	διὰ νυκτός	δι' ἑρμηνέως λέγειν
	(clean) through the breastplate	throughout the night, all night long	speak via an interpreter
		διὰ βίου	δι' ἑαυτοῦ
		his whole life long	on his own strength
			διὰ τάχους
			with speed
		διὰ χρόνου	δι' ὀργῆς εἶναι
		after (a period of) time	be furious
+ accusative			*(causal)* **thanks to, on account of, because of**
			δι' ἀρετὴν ἐνίκησαν
			they won because of their valour
			διὰ ταῦτα
			because of this
		εἰς (Ion. ἐς)	
+ accusative	**into, to, towards, against**	**up to, until**	*(goal)*
	εἰς ὕδωρ βάλλειν	εἰς τὴν τελευτήν	εἰς Ἀθηναίους ἀγορεύειν
	throw in(to) the water	up to the end	speak to Athenians
	εἰς τὴν πόλιν	ἐς ὅ (*Ionic conjunction*)	ἁμαρτάνειν εἰς τοὺς θεούς
	into the city	until	err against the gods
	εἰς οἰκίαν εἰσιέναι		
	to go into a house	**towards**	*(specification)* **as far as . . . is concerned, in**
	εἰς Αἴγυπτον	εἰς ἑσπέραν	πρῶτος εἰς πάντα
	to/against Egypt	towards the evening, at dusk	first in everything

	spatial	temporal	abstract/metaphorical
		(*with a limited period*) **for**	ἐς τὰ ἄλλα
	εἰς Ἅιδου	εἰς ἐνιαυτόν	in other respects
	to the house of Hades	for a year	
	(*i.e. to the Underworld; for the gen.,* →30.27)		(*with numerals*) **up to, as many as, close on**
			εἰς τριάκοντα
			as many as thirty

ἐκ (ἐξ before a vowel)			
+ genitive	**(away) from, out (of)**	**from, since**	(*origin*) **from, (out) of, from within**
	ἐκ τῆς μάχης ἔφυγεν	ἐξ ἀρχῆς	ἐκ πατρὸς ἀγαθοῦ
	he fled from the battle	from/since the beginning	from a good father
			ἐκ ξύλου
	ἐκ δεξιᾶς / ἐξ ἀριστερᾶς	ἐκ τούτου	(made) from wood
	on the right / on the left	after that, since that time	ἐκ τῶν δυνάτων
		ἐξ οὗ (*conjunction*)	judging from the possibilities
		since	
			(*cause, instrument*) **on the basis of, through, by means of, via**
			ἐκ θεοπροπίου
			on the basis of an oracle
			προστέτακται ἐκ μαντείων
			it is commanded by way of oracles
			(*with passives*) **by**
			τὰ λεχθέντα ἐξ Ἀλεξάνδρου
			the things said by Alexander
			ἐξ ἴσου
			equally

ἐν (Ion./poetry also ἐνί)			
+ dative	(*usually stationary*) **in, on, among**	**in, during, on, at**	(*circumstances, manner*)
	ἐν τῇ οἰκίᾳ	ἐν μιᾷ νυκτί	ἐν τάχει
	in the house	in one night	quickly, in a hurry
	ἐν πᾶσιν ἀνθρώποις	ἐν τούτῳ τῷ καιρῷ	ἐν μέρει
	in the presence of all	at that crucial moment	taking turns
	ἐν νήσῳ	ἐν τούτῳ	ἐν ἀπορίᾳ εἶναι
	on an island	meanwhile	be at a loss
	ἐν τοῖς ὅπλοις	ἐν ᾧ (*conjunction*)	ἐν σοί ἐστιν
	armed	while	it depends on you
	ἐν Ἅιδου		οἱ ἐν τέλει
	in the house of Hades (*i.e. in the Underworld; for the gen.,* →30.27)		those in power

	spatial	temporal	abstract/metaphorical
	(*with motion, emphasizing the end point*) ἐν τῇ θαλάττῃ πίπτειν fall into the sea		

ἐπί (ἐπ', ἐφ')			
+ genitive	(*stationary*) **on (top of)** ἔχειν τι ἐπὶ τῶν ὤμων have something on one's shoulders	**during, in the time of** ἐπ' εἰρήνης in peacetime τὰ ἐπ' ἐμοῦ the events of my lifetime	(*in various expressions*) ἐπ' ἐμαυτοῦ on my own, by myself, independently οἱ ἐπὶ τῶν πραγμάτων those in power ἐπὶ τεττάρων ταχθῆναι be drawn up four deep
	(*motion*) **heading for, in the direction of** ἐπ' Αἰγύπτου ἀποπλεῖν sail off heading for Egypt		(*judicial*) ἐπὶ πάντων before all, in the presence of all
+ dative	**(near)by, on** ἐπὶ ποταμῷ οἰκεῖν live on a river τὸ ἐπὶ θαλάσσῃ τεῖχος the wall by the sea	(*directly*) **following on** ἐπὶ τούτῳ after that, subsequently	(*addition*) ἐπὶ τούτοις moreover, in addition
			(*cause*) θαυμάζειν τινὰ ἐπὶ σοφίᾳ to admire someone for their wisdom γελᾶν ἐπί τινι to laugh at/over someone
			(*motive, reason, goal*) ἐπ' ἐλευθερώσει τῶν Ἑλλήνων in order to free the Greeks
			(*condition*) ἐπὶ τούτῳ on that condition ἐφ' ᾧ (*conjunction*) on the condition that (→49.26)
			(*sphere of influence*) ἐφ' ὑμῖν ἐστιν it is in your power, it is up to you

	spatial	temporal	abstract/metaphorical
+ accusative	(*end point*) **up to, on(to)**	**during, for**	(*purpose*) **for**
	ἐπὶ τοὺς ἵππους ἀναβῆναι	ἐπὶ πολὺν χρόνον	ἐπὶ τί . . . ;
	climb on the horses, mount the horses	for a long time	with what purpose?, why?
			(*in various expressions*)
	(*goal*) **towards, against**		τὸ ἐπ' ἐμέ
	ἐπ' Ἀθήνας		as far as I am concerned
	towards Athens		ὡς ἐπὶ τὸ πολύ
	ἐφ' ὕδωρ πέμπειν		in general, normally
	send to get water		
	ἐπὶ τοὺς πολεμίους ἰέναι		
	move against the enemies		
	(*with surfaces*) **extended over**		
	ἐπὶ πᾶσαν Εὐρώπην		
	(extended) all over Europe		

κατά (κατ', καθ')			
+ genitive	**down from, down toward**		**against, to the detriment of**
	κατὰ τοῦ ὄρους		λέγειν κατά τινος
	down from the mountain		speak against someone
	under		(*in a weakened sense*) **with respect to, concerning**
	κατὰ γῆς κρύπτειν		καθ' ἁπάντων
	hide under the ground		with respect to everyone
	κατὰ νώτου εἶναι τοῦ πολεμίου		
	be in the enemy's rear		
+ accusative	(*motion*) **following, with**	(*distributively*) **per, every**	(*manner*) **conforming to, according to**
	κατ' οὖρον	καθ' ἡμέραν	κατὰ τοὺς νόμους
	following the wind	per day, every day	according to the laws
	(*downwards motion*)	**at the time of**	κατὰ δόξαν
	κατὰ τὸν ποταμόν	κατ' ἀρχάς	as expected
	downstream	in the beginning	κατὰ δύναμιν
		κατ' ἐκεῖνον τὸν χρόνον	according to one's means, as much as possible
		(roughly) at/during that time	κατὰ κράτος
	(*with surfaces*) **spread out over, everywhere on, across**		by force
	κατὰ τὴν ἀγοράν		καθ' ἑαυτόν
	in various places across the market		on his own, by himself

	spatial	temporal	abstract/metaphorical
	(*with fixed points*) **off, near, opposite** κατὰ τοὺς Ἕλληνας τάττειν position opposite the Greeks		(*distributively*) κατ' ἔθνη nation by nation, per nation καθ' ἕκαστον point by point, in detail κατὰ μικρόν little by little (*relation*) **with respect to, as to** τὸ κατ' ἐμέ as to me, as far as it concerns me
μετά (μετ', μεθ')			
+ genitive	**together with, accompanied by** μετὰ τῶν συμμάχων together with the allies		(*accompanying circumstances*) μετὰ σπουδῆς with haste, hastily μετὰ τοῦ νόμου with the law on my side
+ dative (poetry)	(*usually with people*) **among** μετὰ μαινάσι among the maenads		
+ accusative		**after** μετὰ τὰ Μηδικά after the Persian wars μετὰ ταῦτα afterwards, after that μεθ' ἡμέραν by day, during the day (*orig. 'after day (break)'*)	(*of rank*) **after** ἄριστος μετά τινα the best after someone
παρά (παρ')			
+ genitive	(*origin, with motion, usually with people*) **from (the side/ quarter of)** ἄγγελος παρὰ βασιλέως ἥκει a messenger has come from the Persian King		(*origin, usually with people*) **from (the side/quarter of)** λαμβάνειν τι παρά τινος get something from someone μανθάνειν τι παρά τινος hear/learn something from someone

	spatial	temporal	abstract/metaphorical
			(*with passives*) **by**
			τὰ λεγόμενα παρά τινος
			the things said by someone
+ dative	(*usually with people*) **with, at, in the presence of**		**in the eyes of**
	οἱ παρὰ σοί		παρ᾽ ἐμοί
	those with you		in my opinion
	παρὰ δικασταῖς		**at the side of, in the service of**
	before the jury		στρατηγεῖν παρὰ Κύρῳ
			be a general in the service of Cyrus
+ accusative	(*end point, usually with people*) **to, at (the side of)**	**during, throughout**	(*in comparisons*) **next to, compared to**
	ἀφικνεῖσθαι παρά τινα	παρὰ πάντα τὸν χρόνον	γελοῖος παρ᾽ αὐτὸν
	arrive at someone's side	all the time, throughout time	laughable as compared to him
	πέμπειν παρά τινα		
	send to someone		(*exclusion*) **next to, apart from**
			οὐδὲν ἄλλο παρὰ ταῦτα
			nothing other than that
	(*with verbs meaning 'put', 'position'*) **next to, with**		**contrary to, against, in violation of**
	καθέζεσθαι παρά τινα		παρὰ τοὺς νόμους
	sit down next to someone		in violation of the laws
	(*of parallel extent*) **along, alongside, beside**		
	παρὰ τὴν ἤπειρον πλεῖν		
	sail alongside the mainland		

περί (*never elided*)

	spatial	temporal	abstract/metaphorical
+ genitive			(*with verbs of competition, strife, etc.*) **about, for, over**
			μάχεσθαι περὶ πατρίδος
			fight for one's home country
			(*with verbs of fearing and concern*) **of, concerning, about**
			φοβεῖσθαι περί τινος
			be concerned about someone/something

	spatial	temporal	abstract/metaphorical
			(*with verbs of speaking, etc.*) **about, over**
			βουλεύεσθαι περὶ τῆς εἰρήνης deliberate about the peace
			ἀκούειν περί τινος hear about someone
			(*relations*) **in relation to, concerning**
			τὰ περὶ τῆς ἀρετῆς that which concerns virtue
			περὶ πολλοῦ/ὀλίγου ποιεῖσθαι consider of great/little importance
+ dative	(*with weapons and clothing*) **around**		(*with verbs of fearing and concern*) **for, concerning**
	ἃ περὶ τοῖς σώμασιν ἔχουσιν the clothes they have on their bodies		δεδιότες περὶ τῷ χωρίῳ afraid for their land
+ accusative	**around**	**around**	**about, with respect to**
	περὶ τὴν Ἀττικὴν περιέρχεται he goes around Attica	περὶ τούτους τοὺς χρόνους around that time	γνώμην ἔχειν περί τι/τινα have an opinion about something/someone
	περὶ τὸ στρατόπεδον φυλακαὶ ἦσαν around the camp there were sentries		ἁμαρτάνειν περί τινα err with respect to someone
			εἶναι περί τι be occupied/concerned with something
	οἱ περὶ Κῦρον Cyrus and his followers		

		πρό (never elided)	
+ genitive	**in front of**	**before**	**in defence of, on behalf of, for**
	πρὸ τῶν ἁμαξῶν in front of the wagons	πρὸ τῶν Μηδικῶν before the Persian wars	πρὸ τῶν πολιτῶν μάχεσθαι fight for the citizens
	πρὸ ποδῶν at one's feet	πρὸ τοῦ previously, earlier	
			in preference to
			αἱρεῖσθαί τι πρό τινος prefer something over something

	spatial	temporal	abstract/metaphorical
		πρός	
+ genitive	**on the side of, facing** τὸ πρὸς ἑσπέρας τεῖχος the wall facing the west		**from the side of, at the hands of** πάσχειν πρός τινος suffer at the hands of someone ἀκούειν πρός τινος hear from someone **on the side of** πρὸς ἡμῶν ἐστιν he is on our side (*with passives*) **by** τὸ ποιούμενον πρός τινος the thing done by someone (*in exclamations*) **by** πρὸς θεῶν by the gods!
+ dative	**at, near** πρὸς αὐτῇ τῇ πόλει καθίστανται they position themselves near the city itself /right near the city		(*addition*) **with** πρὸς τούτῳ, πρὸς τούτοις moreover, on top of that εἶναι πρός τινι be occupied with something
+ accusative	(*motion*) **towards, facing towards** ἄγειν πρός τινα bring to someone ἀποβλέπειν πρός τινα look at someone (*hostile*) **against** πορεύεσθαι, πολεμεῖν πρός τινα march against, wage war against	**by, towards** πρὸς ἑσπέραν towards dusk	(*with verbs of speaking, etc.*) **to, addressing** λέγειν πρὸς τὸ πλῆθος speak to the multitude (*relations*) **concerning, with regard to** πρὸς ταῦτα in view of that, with regard to that χρήσιμος πρός τι useful with regard to something

	spatial	temporal	abstract/metaphorical
			(*direction, goal*) **towards, to**
			πρὸς ἀνδρείαν παιδεύεσθαι
			be educated/raised to bravery
			λέγειν τι πρὸς χάριν τινός
			say something to oblige someone
			(*comparison*) **in comparison to, according to**
			πρὸς τὴν δύναμιν
			according to one's means/ability
			κρίνειν πρός τι
			judge by something
			πρὸς βίαν
			violently

σύν/ξύν

+ dative	(together) **with, accompanied by** (*rare in Att.; usually* μετά + *gen.*)		**including**
	πολεμεῖν σὺν τοῖς φυγάσι		δισχίλιαι δραχμαὶ σὺν ταῖς Νικίου
	wage war together with the exiles		two thousand drachmas including those of Nicias
			(*accompanying circumstances*)
			σὺν κραυγῇ
			with a loud scream
			σὺν θεῷ
			with god's help

ὑπέρ

+ genitive	(*stationary*) **above**		**in defence of, to protect . . . , on behalf of**
	ὑπὲρ τῶν γονάτων		ὑπὲρ τῆς πατρίδος
	above the knees		in defence of (his) home country
	ὑπὲρ Ἁλικαρνησσοῦ μεσόγαια		ἀποκρίνεσθαι ὑπέρ τινος
	the hinterland of Halicarnassus		answer on someone's behalf
	(*relative geographical position: inland from*)		
	(*motion*) **over**		(*cause*) **about, in order to**
	ὑπὲρ τῶν ἄκρων κατέβαινον		χάριν ἔχειν ὑπέρ τινος
	they came down over the hilltops		be grateful about something
			ὑπὲρ τοῦ ταῦτα λαβεῖν
			in order to get this

	spatial	temporal	abstract/metaphorical
+ accusative	**above, beyond** οἱ ὑπὲρ τὸν Ἑλλήσποντον οἰκούμενοι those who live beyond the Hellespont		**beyond** ὑπὲρ δύναμιν beyond one's means ὑπὲρ ἐλπίδα beyond expectation
ὑπό (ὑπ', ὑφ')			
+ genitive	(*motion away from*) **out from under** λαβὼν βοῦν ὑπὸ ἁμάξης taking an ox from a wagon **under** τὰ ὑπὸ γῆς the things under the earth		(*with passives and verbs with passive meaning, expressing the agent*) **by** παιδεύεσθαι ὑπό τινος be raised by someone πάσχειν τι ὑπό τινος suffer something at the hands of someone (*with causes*) ὑπὸ λιμοῦ ἀπόλλυσθαι perish from hunger (*accompanying circumstance*) ὑπὸ σάλπιγγος at the sound of a trumpet
+ dative	**at the foot of, under** ὑπ' Ἰλίῳ under the walls of Troy (*rare in prose*)		(*subjection, dependence, influence*) ὑφ' ἑαυτῷ εἶναι be in his power ὑπὸ παιδοτρίβῃ ἀγαθῷ πεπαιδευμένος educated under a good master
+ accusative	(*end point*) **at/to the foot of, to under** ἔστησε τὸ στράτευμα ὑπὸ τὸν λόφον he made the army halt at the foot of the hill	**in the course of, during** ὑπὸ τὴν νύκτα ταύτην in the course of that night ὑπὸ τὴν εἰρήνην under peacetime conditions ὑπὸ νύκτα under cover of night	(*subjection, dependence, influence*) ὑπὸ σφᾶς ποιεῖσθαι bring under their power (*accompaniment*) ὑπὸ ὄρχησίν τε καὶ ᾠδήν acompanied by dance and song

Improper Prepositions

31.9   Unlike the 'proper' prepositions (→31.2, 31.8), the following 'improper' prepositions are not used in compound verbs:

ἅμα + dat.	together with (*also temporal*: 'at the same time with', ἅμ' ἕῳ, ἅμ' ἡμέρᾳ = 'at daybreak')
ἄνευ + gen.	without, apart from
δίκην + gen.	in the way of, like
ἐγγύς + gen.	near, close to
εἴσω, ἔσω + gen.	inside
ἐναντίον + gen.	opposite, in the presence of
gen. + ἕνεκα (*also οὕνεκα; usually a postposition, but →41.4 n.1, 48.2*)	because of, owing to, on account of, for the sake of
ἐκτός + gen.	outside of, apart from
ἐντός + gen.	within (*also temporal*)
ἔξω + gen.	outside of, out (*also abstract*: ἔξω φρενῶν = 'beside his wits')
ἐπίπροσθεν + gen.	in the way of (*especially with* γίγνομαι, 'get in the way of')
μεταξύ + gen.	between (*also temporal*)
μέχρι + gen.	up to (*also temporal*: 'up until', μέχρι οὗ = 'until the moment that')
ὁμοῦ + dat.	together with (*also temporal*: 'at the same time as')
ὄπισθεν + gen.	behind, at the rear of
πάροιθε + gen.	in front of, before (*also temporal*)
gen. + πέλας (*commonly a postposition*)	near to, alongside
πέρα(ν) + gen.	further than, beyond, on the other side of (*also abstract*: πέρα τοῦ μετρίου = 'beyond measure')
πλήν + gen.	except (*also with subordinate clauses*: πλὴν ὅτι = 'except that'; πλὴν εἰ = 'except if')
πλησίον + gen.	near to
πόρρω, πρόσω + gen.	far from, far in (*also abstract*: πόρρω σοφίας ἥκειν = 'to come far in wisdom')

πρόσθεν, ἔμπροσθεν + gen.	at the front of, before (*also temporal*)
gen. + χάριν (*postposition*)	for the sake of
χωρίς + gen.	apart from (*also abstract: 'not considering'*)
ὡς + acc.	to (*only with persons, e.g.* ὡς Ἀλέξανδρον *to Alexander*)

32

Comparison

Meaning of Comparatives and Superlatives

32.1   The **comparative** (formed with -τερος or -(ί)ων, →5.34, 5.36, 5.38–40, 5.41, 5.43–4) expresses the **higher degree** of the meaning of an adjective, the **superlative** (formed with -τατος or -ιστος, →5.34, 5.37–40, 5.42–4) the **highest degree**:

οὗτος <u>σοφώτερος</u> Σωκράτους | That man is wiser than Socrates (*with genitive of comparison, →32.6 below*)
Σωκράτης <u>σοφώτατος</u> πάντων | Socrates is wisest of all (*with partitive genitive, →32.8 below*)

When two entities are compared, the **comparative** expresses the higher and thereby automatically the **highest degree**:

Σωκράτης <u>σοφώτερος</u> ἡμῶν δυοῖν | Socrates is the wisest of the two of us (*with partitive genitive, →32.9 below*)

32.2   When an element of comparison is absent, the **superlative** may express a **very high degree** (sometimes called the 'elative' use):

Σωκράτης <u>σοφώτατος</u> | Socrates is very wise

32.3   The comparative suffix **-τερος** often expresses a **contrast** between two concepts, persons, entities or groups, as can be seen in δεξίτερος *right* vs. ἀρίστερος *left*, or in an example like

(1) οὕτως ... ἐπαίδευον, τοὺς μὲν <u>γεραιτέρους</u> προτιμᾶν, τῶν δὲ <u>νεωτέρων</u> προτετιμῆσθαι. (Xen. *Cyr.* 8.7.10)
     This is how I raised you, to give preference in honour to the old, and to be honoured above those who are young.

32.4   When the **superlative** is **preceded by** ὡς (sometimes ὅπως) or **ὅτι** it means *as ... as possible*:

(2) εἰ μὴ θήσομαι | τἄμ' <u>ὡς ἄριστα</u>, φαῦλός εἰμι κοὐ σοφός. (Eur. *Andr.* 378–9)
     If I shall not put my things in order as well as possible, I am worthless and not smart.

Comparison

32.5 Greek has various constructions that can be used to express the entity to which someone or something is compared. Distinction should be made between:

- constructions that **follow a comparative** (cf. e.g. Engl.: *better than* ... , *more than* ...): →32.6–7;
- constructions that are used to indicate that something is **identical, similar** or **equal** to something else (cf. e.g. Engl.: *like* ... , *just as, similar to*): →32.14–15.

Note 1: For clauses of comparison (ὡς-clauses) →50.37; for comparative temporal and conditional clauses (ὡς ὅτε-clauses and ὡσ(περ) εἰ-clauses), →47.17, 49.22–4; for participles of comparison (with ὥσπερ), →52.43.

Constructions of Comparison that Follow a Comparative or Superlative

32.6 **Comparatives** are usually construed with a **genitive of comparison** (→30.24) or with ἤ; in the latter case, the second member of the comparison (after ἤ) stands in the same case as the first:

(3) πόλεμος ἔνδοξος εἰρήνης αἰσχρᾶς αἱρετώτερος. (Dem. fr. 13.26 Baiter-Sauppe)
A glorious war is preferable to a shameful peace. *Genitive of comparison.*

(4) ἀνδρὸς ... ἑνὸς τοῦ ἀρίστου οὐδὲν ἄμεινον ἂν φανείη. (Hdt. 3.82.2)
Nothing would appear better than the rule of one man, the best one. *Genitive of comparison.*

(5) οὗτος ὁ Ἡγήσανδρος ἀφικνεῖται, ὃν ὑμεῖς ἴστε κάλλιον ἢ ἐγώ. (Aeschin. 1.56)
This fellow Hegesandrus arrives, whom you know better than I.

(6) οὐ πολλῷ τινὶ ὑποδεέστερον πόλεμον ἀνῃροῦντο ἢ τὸν πρὸς Πελοποννησίους. (Thuc. 6.1.1)
They undertook a war not much inferior to that against the Peloponnesians. *For πολλῷ, →32.11.*

A construction with ἤ is normally used when the first and second member of the comparison stand in the **genitive** or **dative** (the genitive of comparison is rare in such cases):

(7) ἐγὼ ... οὔτ’ ἂν μίλτου ἁπτοίμην ἥδιον ἢ σοῦ. (Xen. *Oec.* 10.6)
I would not touch red lead with more pleasure than (I would touch) you.

(8) σοί τε νῦν ἔτι ἐχθίονές εἰσιν ἢ ἐμοί. (Xen. *Cyr.* 4.5.23)
They are now even more hostile to you than to me.

32.7 The same constructions are used when the comparative is expressed by way of **μᾶλλον (ἤ)** *more (than), rather (than)*:

(9) τὸ θῆλυ γάρ πως μᾶλλον οἰκτρὸν ἀρσένων. (Eur. *Her.* 536)

For the female sex is in a way more emotional than men. *Genitive of comparison.*

(10) οἱ Λακεδαιμόνιοι πάσῃ πολιτείᾳ μᾶλλον ἂν ἢ δημοκρατίᾳ πιστεύσειαν. (Xen. *Hell.* 2.3.45)

The Spartans would trust any constitution more than a democracy. *Comparative with ἤ.*

Note 1: The genitive (of comparison) is also found with verbs that are derived from comparatives, such as ὑστερέω *to be later* (cf. ὕστερος *later*), πλεονεκτέω *have a larger share* (cf. πλείων *more*), ἡττάομαι *to be weaker than, be defeated by* (cf. ἥττων *weaker*) – for the genitive as complement with verbs, →30.21–2:

(11) ἡττώμεθα ... ἀμφότεροι τοῦ ταῦτα ἔχοντος βεβαίως βίου. (Pl. *Phlb.* 11e)

We are both defeated by the life that has firm possession of that.

32.8   **Superlatives** are often combined with a **partitive genitive** (→30.29) to express the group or class within which something is marked as the highest:

εὐδαιμονέστατοι τῶν Ἑλλήνων   the most fortunate people of the Greeks
πάντων μέγιστον ἄλγος   the greatest ill of all

Note 1: This use occasionally occurs when the superlative refers to an entity which is not itself part of the group indicated by the partitive genitive; the genitive is in such cases also often called 'comparative':

(12) Θουκυδίδης Ἀθηναῖος ξυνέγραψε τὸν πόλεμον ... ἐλπίσας ... ἔσεσθαι ... ἀξιολογώτατον τῶν προγεγενημένων. (Thuc. 1.1.1)

Thucydides from Athens has written a book about the war, as he expected it to be most noteworthy, more than any of the wars that preceded. *The war that Thucydides describes is not one of those that came before.*

32.9   The partitive genitive is also sometimes used with **comparatives**, especially when two entities are compared (in which case the comparative marks the highest degree, →32.1 above).

(13) δυοῖν γὰρ ἀθλίοιν εὐδαιμονέστερος μὲν οὐκ ἂν εἴη. (Pl. *Grg.* 473d)

For among two wretched men there could not be a most fortunate one. *ἀθλίοιν is dual, →10.1–5.*

32.10   Other constructions with superlatives:

– superlatives may be strengthened by 'adverbial' καί (→59.56):

(14) οἶμαι δ' αὐτὸ καὶ σοφώτατον | θνητοῖσιν εἶναι κτῆμα τοῖσι χρωμένοις. (Eur. *Bacch.* 1151–2)

And I think that this is the very most sensible possession for mortals who use it.

– superlatives may be modified by the fixed expression αὐτὸς (ἑ)αυτοῦ *at his/her/its -est*, indicating that the feature denoted by the adjective is or has been present in the same entity to various degrees; the superlative then refers to the highest of those degrees:

(15) . . . ἡ λίμνη . . . ἐοῦσα βάθος, τῇ <u>βαθυτάτη αὐτὴ ἑωυτῆς</u>, πεντηκοντόργυιος. (Hdt. 2.149.1)
. . . the lake, being, at the point where it is at its deepest, fifty fathoms deep. *The lake is less deep elsewhere.*

– in prose (particularly Herodotus, Thucydides and Plato) superlatives are sometimes combined with the idiomatic expression ἐν τοῖς:

(16) <u>ἐν τοῖς</u> πρῶτοι δὲ Ἀθηναῖοι τὸν . . . σίδηρον κατέθεντο. (Thuc. 1.6.3)
The Athenians were the first to lay down their sword. *ἐν τοῖς (lit. 'among them/some') appears to make explicit that the Athenians were not the only ones to stop carrying weapons, but that, of those who did, they were the first.*

32.11   Both the comparative and the superlative may be modified by an expression of degree in the dative (**dative of measure**, →30.54):

<u>πολλῷ</u> ἀμείνων   much better
σωφρονέστατα καὶ ἀσφαλέστατα <u>μακρῷ</u>   most sensible and safest by far

Note the frequent use of this dative in correlative clauses with (τοσούτῳ and) ὅσῳ (→50.5), to express *the more . . . the more . . .* :

(17) <u>ὅσῳ</u> ἂν μείζω τούτῳ δωρήσῃ, <u>τοσούτῳ</u> μείζω ὑπὸ τούτου ἀγαθὰ πείσῃ. (Xen. *An.* 7.3.20)
The greater the gifts you bestow on him, the greater good will you experience at his hands.

32.12   When **two adjectives or adverbs** that refer to the same subject or predicate are compared to each other, they are **both comparative**, or the first is modified by μᾶλλον ἤ, and the second comparative:

(18) ἐποίησα <u>ταχύτερα ἢ σοφώτερα</u>. (Hdt. 3.65.3)
I acted more quickly than wisely.

(19) εἰς Ἰωλκὸν ἱκόμην | σὺν σοί, <u>πρόθυμος μᾶλλον ἢ σοφωτέρα</u>. (Eur. *Med.* 484–5)
I came to Iolcus with you, eager rather than wise.

32.13   Note the following **fixed expressions with comparatives**:

– comparative with ἤ ὥστε + **infinitive** (→46.8), or with ἢ κατά + **accusative**: *too . . . to . . .* :

(20) σοφώτερ' ἢ κατ' ἄνδρα συμβαλεῖν ἔπη (Eur. *Med.* 675)
words too wise for a man to understand

(21) <u>νεώτεροί</u> εἰσιν <u>ἢ ὥστε</u> εἰδέναι οἵων πατέρων ἐστέρηνται. (Lys. 2.72)

They are too young to know of what kind of fathers they have been deprived.

– comparative with **ἤ** + **comparative ὡς-clause** (→50.37): *too … to …* (this occurs particularly when the ὡς-clause has a potential optative or counterfactual secondary indicative):

(22) ἔστι γὰρ <u>μείζω</u> τἀκείνων ἔργα <u>ἢ ὡς</u> τῷ λόγῳ τις <u>ἂν εἴποι</u>. (Dem. 6.11)

For their achievements are too great for anyone to put them in words (*lit. 'greater than that anyone could somehow …'*).

(23) εἰσπηδήσαντες εἰς τὸν πηλὸν <u>θᾶττον ἢ ὡς</u> τις <u>ἂν ᾤετο</u> μετεώρους ἐξεκόμισαν τὰς ἁμάξας. (Xen. *An.* 1.5.8)

They jumped into the mud and lifted the wagons on dry land more quickly than anyone could have thought possible.

– **οὐδενὸς ἐλάττων** (also χείρων, ὕστερος, etc.), lit. 'inferior to no one' = *better than all, the best by far*:

(24) ὃ κἀμοὶ δοκεῖ <u>οὐδενὸς ἔλαττον</u> εἶναι τεκμήριον τῆς ἀπογραφῆς ὅτι ἀληθὴς οὖσα τυγχάνει. (Lys. 29.1)

This seems also to me to be the clearest evidence by far that the declaration happens to be true.

Constructions of Comparison that Express Identicalness, Similarity or Equality: ὁ αὐτός, ὅμοιος and ἴσος

32.14   The most common adjectives or pronouns that express identicalness, similarity or equality are:

– ὁ αὐτός (often with crasis: αὑτός, αὑτή, ταὐτά, →7.11) *the same as*
– ὅμοιος *similar to, like*
– ἴσος *like, equal to*

Each of these may be followed by a complement in the **dative** (→30.40) or by **καί**:

(25) φαίνεται γὰρ τῷ δήμῳ βοηθῶν, <u>τῆς αὐτῆς</u> πολιτείας <u>ὑμῖν</u> ἐπιθυμῶν. (Isoc. 16.41)

He is evidently supporting the people, desiring the same constitution as you.

(26) οὐκ, ἐπειδὰν <u>ταὐτὸν</u> γένηταί <u>τῳ</u> τι, ἓν γίγνεται. (Pl. *Prm.* 139d)

Whenever a thing becomes the same as any thing, it does not become one.

(27) κλίμακας ἐποιήσαντο <u>ἴσας τῷ τείχει</u> τῶν πολεμίων. (Thuc. 3.20.3)

They made ladders for themselves that were equal (in height) to the wall of the enemy.

(28) <u>ταὐτὰ</u> ὑμῖν συνέφερε <u>καὶ</u> τοῖς ἐκεῖ. (Lys. 20.27)

The same happened to you as to the people there.

(29) οἷον δὲ πνεῖς ... | :: μῶν οὖν <u>ὅμοιον καὶ</u> γυλιοῦ στρατιωτικοῦ; (Ar. *Pax* 525–7)
How wonderful do you smell! :: Not then, I take it, like the smell of a soldier's
knapsack? *γυλιοῦ στρατιωτικοῦ is genitive of belonging (→30.28) with an
omitted 'smell'.*

(30) οὐ δῆθ᾽ ὅτῳ γε νοῦς <u>ἴσος καὶ</u> σοὶ πάρα. (Soph. *OC* 810)
Certainly not for a man who has a mind equal to yours. *For the accentuation
and position of πάρα, →24.37, 36.6.*

32.15 After the same expressions (especially after ὁ αὐτός) a relative clause with -περ (e.g.
ὅσπερ) is also regularly found, sometimes with 'adverbial' καί *also, too* following
the relative pronoun:

(31) ἡ γὰρ πάλαι ἡμῶν φύσις οὐχ <u>αὐτὴ</u> ἦν <u>ἥπερ</u> νῦν. (Pl. *Symp.* 189d)
For our original nature was not the same as our present one.

(32) ἐκ <u>τοῦ αὐτοῦ</u> ... <u>χωρίου</u> ἡ ὁρμὴ ἔσται <u>ὅθενπερ καὶ</u> ἐκεῖνος ἐμὲ ἐπεδέξατο
γυμνήν. (Hdt. 1.11.5)
The attack will take place from the same spot as the one from which that man
displayed me naked.

(33) μόνοι τε ὄντες <u>ὅμοια</u> ἔπραττον <u>ἅπερ</u> ἂν μετ᾽ ἄλλων ὄντες. (Xen. *An.* 5.4.34)
When they were alone, they behaved just as if they were with others (*lit.* 'they
did similar things as (they would do) if they had been with others').

33

The Verb: Tense and Aspect

Basic Notions and Terminology

Tense

33.1   **Tense** concerns the location of an action in time relative to some other moment. A distinction can be made between absolute tense and relative tense:

– **Absolute tense** concerns the location of an action in the past, present or future, **relative to the moment of speaking**:

The Greeks <u>burned</u> Troy.	past
The Greeks <u>are burning</u> Troy.	present
The Greeks <u>will burn</u> Troy.	future

– **Relative tense** concerns the location of an action in time **relative to another temporal reference point given in the context**, either prior to that reference point (**anteriority**), at the same time as that reference point (**simultaneity**), or after it (**posteriority**):

We arrived when the Greeks <u>had burned</u> Troy.	*anterior* to a moment in the past
We arrived when the Greeks <u>were burning</u> Troy.	*simultaneous* with a moment in the past
By the time we arrive, the Greeks <u>will have burned</u> Troy.	*anterior* to a moment in the future
The Greeks said that they <u>would burn</u> Troy.	*posterior* to a moment in the past

33.2   The **indicatives** of the Greek verb, when used in main clauses, express absolute tense:

– the **present indicative** and **perfect indicative** refer to the **present** (i.e. the moment of speaking);
– the **imperfect, aorist indicative** and **pluperfect** refer to the **past** (these are 'secondary' indicatives (→11.7), and have secondary endings (→11.20–7) and an augment (→11.35–42));
– the **future indicative** and **future perfect indicative** refer to the **future**:

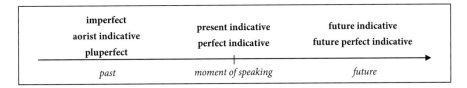

Figure 33.1: Absolute tense expressed by indicatives

(1) οἱ Ἀριαίου πρόσθεν σὺν ἡμῖν ταττόμενοι νῦν ἀφεστήκασιν. (Xen. *An.* 3.2.17)
Ariaeus' men, although they previously used to line up alongside us, have now
deserted us. *Pf. ind. referring to the present; note* νῦν.

(2) τότε . . . πεδία πλήρη γῆς πιείρας ἐκέκτητο, καὶ πολλὴν ἐν τοῖς ὄρεσιν ὕλην εἶχεν.
(Pl. *Criti.* 111c)
At that time, (the country) possessed plains full of rich soil, and had much
forestland in the mountains. *Plpf. and impf. referring to the past; note* τότε.

(3) ἦ μὴν σὺ δώσεις αὔριον τούτων δίκην. (Ar. *Vesp.* 1331)
I swear, you'll pay for this tomorrow. *Fut. ind., referring to the future; note*
αὔριον.

33.3   Outside main clauses, indicatives frequently receive a relative-tense interpretation
in addition to, or instead of, an absolute-tense interpretation (→33.57–62 below).

Moods other than the indicative (i.e. the subjunctive, optative and imperative)
and **non-finite forms of the verb** (infinitives, participles and verbal adjectives), **do
not inherently express tense**, but only aspect. Their aspectual value, however, may
lead to a relative-tense interpretation (→33.57–62 below).

Aspect

Grammatical Aspect

33.4   **Grammatical aspect** (usually simply called 'aspect') concerns the way in which
an action is presented or regarded, particularly with respect to its internal
composition: it can be presented as a single and **complete** whole (an action in
its entirety), without any separate component parts of the action being envisaged, or as **incomplete** (an action that is ongoing or repeated, that can
conceivably be interrupted), with several component parts being envisaged.
Note that what matters is not whether an action *has* component parts, but
whether the speaker is interested in presenting these component parts as
relevant.

33.5   With the exception of the future-tense forms (see below) **all Greek verb forms
express aspect**.

33.6   The tense-aspect **stems** of the Greek verb express three different aspectual values:

– The **present stem** presents an action as **incomplete**, focusing on one or more of its intermediate stages, but leaving its boundaries (beginning and end) out of focus. It thus normally signifies that an action is **ongoing** or **repeated**. This is called **imperfective aspect**.

– The **aorist stems** (aorist stem, aorist passive stem) present an action as **complete**, as a **single** (uninterruptable) **whole**: it ignores any component parts by looking only at the boundaries of the action, rolling beginning, middle and end into one. This is called **perfective aspect**.

– The **perfect stems** (perfect active stem, perfect middle-passive stem, future perfect stem) present an action as a **state** resulting from a preceding completed action, or it signifies that the **effects** of the completed action are somehow still **relevant**.

The future stems (future stem, future passive stem) have a temporal value (they express futurity/posteriority) but no aspectual one: they are aspectually neutral, and make no formal distinction between an imperfective or perfective presentation of actions.

Note 1: Note that 'perfective' aspect is expressed by the aorist stem: this is not to be confused with the Greek perfect, which does not express perfective aspect.

Other terms found for the aspect expressed by the present stem are 'durative', 'progressive', 'iterative', 'habitual', 'unbounded'; other terms found for the aspect expressed by the aorist stem are 'aoristic', 'confective', 'semelfactive', 'punctual', 'bounded', 'simple'. These terms do not always overlap entirely, and there is some disagreement (and much confusion) in scholarly views concerning the precise values of the Greek aspect stems.

33.7   As the above definitions indicate, the selection of a specific stem (grammatical aspect) depends not so much on any objective properties of the action itself (for such objective properties, →33.8–9), but on a speaker's (subjective) needs and choices in presenting an action in a certain way. What matters most is whether a speaker is interested in drawing attention to any component parts (or conversely, the boundaries) of an action. This crucial feature will become fully apparent in the sections below, but a few initial examples may illustrate the point:

(4) οἱ δὲ Ὀλύνθιοι ὡς εἶδον προθέοντας τοὺς πελταστάς, ἀναστρέψαντες ... <u>διέβησαν</u> πάλιν τὸν ποταμόν. οἱ δ᾽ ἠκολούθουν μάλα θρασέως, καὶ ὡς φεύγουσι διώξοντες <u>ἐπιδιέβαινον</u>. ἔνθα δὴ οἱ Ὀλύνθιοι ἱππεῖς, ἡνίκα ἔτι εὐχείρωτοι αὐτοῖς ἐδόκουν εἶναι οἱ <u>διαβεβηκότες</u>, ἀναστρέψαντες ἐμβάλλουσιν αὐτοῖς, καὶ ... ἀπέκτειναν ... πλείους ἢ ἑκατόν. (Xen. *Hell.* 5.3.4)

The Olynthians, when they saw the peltasts running forward, turned around and crossed the river again. The peltasts followed them very rashly, and, convinced that they were fleeing, proceeded to cross so as to give chase.

Then the Olynthian horsemen, at a moment when those who had crossed still seemed to them to be easy to overcome, wheeled about and attacked them, and they killed more than a hundred. *The narrator uses the aorist indicative διέβησαν to describe the Olynthians' crossing in its entirety (perfective aspect): he is interested in the simple fact that it happened, not in its process; further events which took place during their crossing are not referred to. When the peltasts cross, however, he uses present-stem (impf.) ἐπιδιέβαινον to describe the crossing in process (i.e. before its end-point was reached; imperfective aspect), because he is interested in other events that happened during it (the attack). The perfect participle διαβεβηκότες, finally, refers to men who are in the state of having successfully crossed the river. Observe that the killing of these men is expressed by means of aorist ἀπέκτειναν (even though it will have taken quite some time to kill over a hundred men), because the narrator is interested in the simple fact that it happened; again, further events which took place during the killing spree (individual killings, resistance, etc.) are not referred to. For this kind of alternation between imperfects and aorists in narrative texts, →33.48–9. For the historical present ἐμβάλλουσιν, →33.54–5.*

(5) Πρωταγόρας μὲν . . . τοιαῦτα ἐπιδειξάμενος <u>ἀπεπαύσατο</u> τοῦ λόγου. καὶ ἐγὼ ἐπὶ μὲν πολὺν χρόνον . . . πρὸς αὐτὸν <u>ἔβλεπον</u> ὡς ἐροῦντά τι, ἐπιθυμῶν ἀκούειν· ἐπεὶ δὲ δὴ ᾐσθόμην ὅτι τῷ ὄντι <u>πεπαυμένος εἴη</u>, . . . εἶπον, <u>βλέψας</u> πρὸς τὸν Ἱπποκράτη· . . . (Pl. *Prt.* 328d)

Protagoras, having made such a performance, stopped speaking. And for a long time, I kept looking at him as if he was going to say something else, desirous to hear it. But when I realized that he was truly done, I said, casting my glance towards Hippocrates: . . . *The aorist indicative ἀπεπαύσατο presents Protagoras' falling quiet after a long speech, without any reference to component parts of the action of finishing; it is picked up later by the perfect-stem form πεπαυμένος εἴη (for the optative, →40.12, 41.15), which emphasizes that Protagoras had not simply paused, but finished altogether, resulting in a new state (that of 'being done'). The example also features a contrast between present-stem (impf.) ἔβλεπον, used to refer to an ongoing gaze, and the aorist participle βλέψας, which is used to refer to the single moment that Socrates shifted his gaze towards another participant in the conversation (for this 'ingressive' interpretation of the aorist, →33.29).*

(6) τοῖσι ὑπολειπομένοισι <u>ἔδοξε</u> <u>πλανᾶν</u> μὲν μηκέτι Πέρσας, σῖτα δὲ ἑκάστοτε ἀναιρεομένοισι <u>ἐπιτίθεσθαι</u>. νωμῶντες ὦν σῖτα ἀναιρεομένους τοὺς Δαρείου ἐποίευν τὰ βεβουλευμένα. (Hdt. 4.128.2)

Those (Scythians) who remained behind decided to lead the Persians astray no longer, but to attack them wherever they were foraging for provision. So, observing the men of Darius as they were foraging, they carried out their plans.

(7) ὁ δὲ Ἀρκεσίλεως εἵπετο φεύγουσι, ἐς οὗ ἐν Λεύκωνί τε τῆς Λιβύης ἐγίνετο ἐπιδιώκων καὶ ἔδοξε τοῖσι Λίβυσι ἐπιθέσθαι οἱ. συμβαλόντες δὲ ἐνίκησαν τοὺς Κυρηναίους. (Hdt. 4.160.3)

Arcesilaus pursued them as they fled, until he came in his pursuit to Leucon in Libya and the Libyans decided to attack him. They engaged and overcame the Cyrenaeans.

The present infinitive ἐπιτίθεσθαι in (6) refers to a composite campaign, which is to consist of repeated attacks made on different occasions (interest in the component parts: imperfective aspect). The aorist infinitive ἐπιθέσθαι in (7), by contrast, refers to a single attack to be made on a particular occasion. What is also relevant for the choice of the aorist stem is that the narrator immediately moves from the moment of attack to their victory (ἐνίκησαν): he is not interested in the component parts of the attack (perfective aspect). The present infinitive πλανᾶν in (6), finally, expresses an action currently still in process, which the Scythians now decide to stop.

Lexical Aspect

33.8   **Lexical aspect** refers to the temporal structure of a specific action **inherent in the verb's meaning**: does it have duration, and is it directed towards an end-point? As opposed to grammatical aspect, lexical aspect thus has to do with the **objective** properties of an action, rather than with subjective ways of presenting that action.

For instance, inherent in the meaning of the verb διαβαίνω *cross* is that it has an end-point, namely the moment at which someone reaches the other side. The simplex verb βαίνω *go, walk*, on the other hand, has no natural end-point which is part of the inherent meaning of the verb (in principle, one can walk for as long as one likes). The following categories of lexical aspect are important for the interpretation of Greek verb forms:

- **Telic verbs**: verbs which, inherent in their meaning, are directed towards an end-point: e.g. διαβαίνω *cross*, πείθω *persuade*, δίδωμι *give*, κατεργάζομαι *achieve, make an end of*, τήκομαι *melt*;
- **Atelic verbs**: verbs which are not inherently directed towards an end-point: e.g. βαίνω *go, walk*, γελάω *laugh*, θαυμάζω *admire*, θεάομαι *gaze at*. A subset of this class consists of so-called **stative verbs**, verbs which normally have a prolonged duration and in which no change takes place over time: e.g. βασιλεύω *be king*, φιλέω *love*, νοσέω *be ill*, εἰμί *be*, ἔχω *have*.

Note 1: Lexical aspect is frequently referred to by the German term *Aktionsart*, sometimes also by the terms 'actionality' or 'situation type'. Other terminology commonly found for telic verbs is 'terminative' and 'bounded', and for atelic verbs 'non-terminative' and 'unbounded'. Again, the terminology does not always overlap entirely.

Below, when the bare term 'aspect' is used, it refers to grammatical aspect.

33.9   Lexical aspect depends not only on the verb itself, but also on the context/construction in which that verb is used. For instance, the verb τρέχω *run* has a different lexical aspect in the following two examples:

(8) οἷα πιππίζουσι καὶ <u>τρέχουσι</u> διακεκραγότες. (Ar. *Av.* 306)

How they chirp and run around screeching! *Atelic: not directed towards an end-point: one can run around for as long as one likes.*

(9) ἦ πρός τε μαστοῖς εἰσι χὑπὸ μητέρων | πλευρὰς <u>τρέχουσι</u>; (Eur. *Cyc.* 207–8)

Are they at the teat and running to their mothers' sides? *Telic: directed towards an end-point, the moment of arrival at the mother's side.*

Factors Influencing Interpretation

33.10   The interpretation of tense and aspect in any specific verb form depends on a variety of factors:

– the nature of the verb form used (finite or non-finite; with finite forms, mood – note that absolute tense is expressed only by indicatives) and the construction in which it is used (main clauses, various kinds of subordinate clauses, various uses of the participle and infinitive);
– the interaction between grammatical and lexical aspect;
– the type of text in which the form is used (see especially below on narrative vs. non-narrative texts, →33.13).

The remainder of this chapter first treats the uses of the indicative in main clauses, followed by a discussion of the possible interpretations of aspect outside the indicative.

Tense and Aspect Combined: The Indicative in Main Clauses

Basic Values of the Indicative; Narrative and Non-Narrative Text

The Seven Indicatives of Greek: Basic Values

33.11   Sections 33.14–55 give an overview of the use of **indicatives in main clauses** (for indicatives in subordinate clauses, →40.5–11 and chapters 41–5). The interpretation of indicatives depends in the first place on the **interaction between tense and grammatical aspect**. Combining the aspectual and temporal values described above, the Greek indicative expresses the following tense/aspect-distinctions (using the verbs κτάομαι *acquire* and παιδεύω *educate* as examples):

- The **present indicative** expresses an action, located at the moment of speaking (i.e. in the present), that is presented as **ongoing or repeated**:

  κτῶμαι   I am acquiring / I (habitually) acquire

  παιδεύω   I am educating / I (habitually) educate

- The **imperfect** (or 'secondary present indicative') expresses an action, located in the **past**, that is presented as **ongoing or repeated**:

  ἐκτώμην   I was acquiring / I (habitually) acquired

  ἐπαίδευον   I was educating / I (habitually) educated

- The **aorist indicative** expresses an action, located in the **past**, presented as a **complete** whole:

  ἐκτησάμην   I acquired / I have acquired (for these translations,
                 →33.28 with n.1)

  ἐπαίδευσα   I educated/ I have educated

- The **future indicative** expresses an action (either as a single occurrence or as ongoing/repeated), located in the **future**:

  κτήσομαι   I will acquire / I will be acquiring

  παιδεύσω   I will educate / I will be educating

- The **perfect indicative** expresses a **state**, located at the **present**, that is the result of a completed action; or it expresses that the effects of the completed action are still in some way relevant at the present:

  κέκτημαι   I possess (< *I have acquired*)

  πεπαίδευκα   I have educated / I am responsible for the education of
                 (→33.34–5 below)

- The **pluperfect** (or 'secondary perfect indicative') expresses a **state**, located in the **past**, that is the result of a completed action; or it expresses that the effects of the completed action are in some way relevant at the moment in the past:

  ἐκεκτήμην   I possessed (< *I had acquired*)

  ἐπεπαιδεύκειν I had educated / I was responsible for the education of

- The (rare) **future perfect indicative** expresses a **state**, located in the **future**, that is the result of a completed action; or it expresses that the effects of the completed action are in some way relevant at the moment in the future:

  κεκτήσομαι   I will possess (< *I will have acquired*)

33.12   The following table provides an overview of the seven indicatives:

	imperfective aspect (present stem)	perfective aspect (aorist stem)	perfect-stem aspect
present	*present indicative* ΚΤῶμαι	—	*perfect indicative* ΚέΚΤημαι
past	*imperfect* ἐΚΤώμην	*aorist indicative* ἐΚΤησάμην	*pluperfect* ἐΚεΚΤήμην
future	*future indicative* ΚΤήσομαι		*future perfect indicative* ΚεΚΤήσομαι

Note 1: As this table shows, there is no designated form referring to the present which expresses perfective aspect. The need for such a form is in fact limited, since speakers normally refer to actions occurring in the present only when they are (still) ongoing at the moment of speaking. There are, however, exceptions in highly specific kinds of context: for these exceptions, →33.20, 33.32–3, 33.54–6.

Narrative and Non-Narrative Text

33.13   The **type of text** in which an indicative (in a main clause) is used is often significant in interpretation. A (rough) distinction may be drawn here between **narrative** and **non-narrative** text:

- **Narrative text** is storytelling: it relates (usually in chronological order) a sequence of actions that took place in the (real or fictive) past, and how they are related to each other. It normally contains a mix of imperfects/pluperfects and aorist indicatives together with less frequent historical presents. Examples: historical accounts, mythological tales, *narrationes* in oratory, messenger speeches in tragedy, etc.
- **Non-narrative text** is everything else. Main verbs will normally be indicatives of the present, aorist, perfect and future stems, with other moods used apart from the indicative. Examples: most dialogue in tragedy/comedy, philosophical discussions, arguments, general descriptions of habits and customs, etc.

Note 1: Narrative and non-narrative passages can come in quick succession or mixed together. A clear distinction between the two is not always possible. For further discussion of 'text types' and more extensive examples, →58.7–10, 61.

The use of indicatives in narrative is treated in detail in 33.48–55, including some phenomena which are peculiar to narrative contexts.

Present Indicative

Basic Uses

33.14   The present indicative refers to actions that occur at the **moment of speaking**. By virtue of its imperfective aspect (incomplete), it is used by default to refer to actions which are **ongoing** at the moment of speaking:

(10)   τί κάτησθε, ὦ Πέρσαι, ἐνθαῦτα; (Hdt. 3.151.2)
         Why are you sitting there, Persians?

(11)   παραβοηθεῖθ᾽, ὡς ὑπ᾽ ἀνδρῶν τύπτομαι ξυνωμοτῶν. (Ar. *Eq.* 257)
         Help me: I'm being roughed up by conspirators!

Note 1: The ongoing action referred to by the present indicative may have begun long before the moment of speaking, and an expression of duration is sometimes added:

(12)   εἰ διδακτόν ἐστιν ἀρετὴ πάλαι σκοποῦμεν. (Pl. *Men.* 93b)
         We have long been investigating whether virtue is something that can be taught. *Observe that Engl. here prefers a present perfect ('have been investigating').*

33.15   The present indicative is also used to refer to **repeated** or **habitual actions**; the habit is in effect at the moment of speaking:

(13)   οὗτος μὲν γὰρ ὕδωρ, ἐγὼ δὲ οἶνον πίνω. (Dem. 19.46)
         For this man tends to drink water, whereas I normally drink wine.

(14)   πάντες γὰρ οἱ τῶν ἀρίστων Περσῶν παῖδες ἐπὶ ταῖς βασιλέως θύραις παιδεύονται. (Xen. *An.* 1.9.3)
         For all the sons of the Persian aristocracy are educated at the King's palace.

33.16   The present indicative may be used to refer to **general** or **timeless truths** which are continuously in effect (also →33.31 for the 'gnomic' aorist):

(15)   ἄγει δὲ πρὸς φῶς τὴν ἀλήθειαν χρόνος. (Men. *Sent.* 11)
         Time brings the truth to light.

(16)   τὰ δὶς πέντε δέκα ἐστίν. (Xen. *Mem.* 4.4.7)
         Two times five is ten.

Specific Interpretations

33.17   With **telic** verbs such as πείθω *persuade*, δίδωμι *give*, βάλλω *throw, hit*, the present stem may refer to an (unsuccessful) attempt, because it indicates that the end-point of the action has so far not been reached (imperfective aspect). This is called the **conative** interpretation of the present:

(17) ταῦτ᾽ ἐστίν, ὦ Λάκριτε, ἃ τουτουσὶ <u>πείθεις</u>. (Dem. 35.47)

This is the opinion, Lacritus, of which you are trying to persuade these men. *Present indicative.*

Note 1: The notion of 'attempt' is an *interpretation* (rather than an inherent feature of the present), relying on context and the combination of imperfective grammatical aspect and telic lexical aspect. As such, it is not limited to the present indicative, but available for any present-stem form of the relevant verbs. For the conative imperfect, →33.25. For other forms, →33.60.

33.18   With a number of specific verbs (all telic), the present stem may refer to the **ongoing result** of an action as well as to the action itself. This **resultative** use occurs particularly with the following verbs:

ἀδικέω	be unjust, treat unjustly / have treated unjustly
δίδωμι	give / have given
γίγνομαι	be born / be a descendant
ἥκω	arrive / have arrived, be present
ἡττάομαι	suffer a defeat / be vanquished
νικάω	defeat / be victorious, have defeated
οἴχομαι	depart / be gone
τίκτω	give birth / be parent
φεύγω	flee / be in exile

(18)   <u>ἥκω</u> Διὸς παῖς τήνδε Θηβαίαν χθόνα | Διόνυσος. (Eur. *Bacch.* 1–2)

I, Dionysus, son of Zeus, have come to this Theban land. *Dionysus is already in Thebes, so 'am arriving' is not a possible translation for* ἥκω.

(19)   λέγει Κάλχας τάδε· ... Ἀγάμεμνον, ... παῖδ᾽ ... σῇ Κλυταιμήστρα δάμαρ | <u>τίκτει</u> ... ἣν χρή σε θῦσαι. (Eur. *IT* 16–24)

Calchas spoke as follows: 'Agamemnon, your wife Clytaemestra has borne a child, whom you must sacrifice.' *Interpreting* τίκτει *as 'is giving birth' is impossible (Iphigenia was clearly already born).* λέγει *is historical present,* →33.54–5.

Note 1: This use is sometimes called 'present for perfect' or 'perfective present', as the present stem resembles the perfect stem in this use (this 'perfective' label should not be confused with perfective aspect).

Other present-stem forms of these specific verbs may also be resultative: for the imperfect, →33.26; for other forms, →33.60.

Note 2: οἴχομαι *depart, be gone*, when used with resultative meaning, is often combined with a participle expressing the manner of departure: →52.42 n.3.

Note 3: Similar, but not exactly the same, is the use of the present indicative of some verbs of hearing, learning, saying, etc., to refer to the content of an earlier speech or message. For instance:

ἀκούω	hear / have heard (cf. Engl. *I hear that*)
λέγω	say / have said (cf. Engl. *John here says that …*)
πυνθάνομαι	inquire, learn / have learned

33.19   The present indicative of **εἶμι** *go* normally refers to the future: e.g. εἶμι *I will go*, εἶσι(ν) *he will go*, ἴασι(ν) *they will go*. Observe that this does not normally hold for forms other than the present indicative (impf. ᾖα *I went*, ppl. ἰών *going*, etc.).

33.20   In certain highly specific contexts, speakers can refer to a single action *begun and completed* at (approximately) the moment of speaking — the **instantaneous present**. In such cases the present-tense value of the present indicative is more important for its selection than the imperfective aspect expressed by its stem.

A frequent context for this use is that of **performatives**, first-person indicatives which describe the speech act of which they are part (and thus refer to actions that are completed as soon as the utterance is completed):

(20)   νῦν οὖν σὺ μὲν φύλασσε τἀν οἴκωι καλῶς, | … | ὑμῖν δ' ἐπαινῶ γλῶσσαν εὔφημον φέρειν | … | τὰ δ' ἄλλα τούτωι δεῦρ' ἐποπτεῦσαι λέγω. (Aesch. *Cho.* 579–83)

So now you (*Electra*) must watch what happens in the house carefully, and you (*Chorus*) I advise to keep silent; as for the rest, I call upon him (*Apollo*) to cast his glance this way. *With ἐπαινῶ and λέγω, the speaker (Orestes) describes the speech acts he is performing.*

The instantaneous present also occurs, rarely, in 'simultaneous narration', i.e. when a speaker narrates a sequence of actions as they occur in the present. This in fact occurs much more frequently when speakers present actions in the past *as if* they occur in the present — the 'historical present'. This use is treated separately in 33.54–5 (cf. also the 'present for the future', →33.56).

Note 1: For performatives expressed by an aorist indicative (the 'tragic aorist'), →33.32.

33.21   Questions with **(τί) οὐ + first- or second-person present indicative** are sometimes used as **requests** or **suggestions** (also →38.33):

(21)   Τί οὖν, ἦ δ' ὅς, οὐκ ἐρωτᾷς; :: Ἀλλ' ἐρήσομαι, ἦν δ' ἐγώ. (Pl. *Ly.* 211d)

'Why not ask him, then?', he said. 'Indeed I will ask', I said.

The speaker observes, with such questions, that the action is not being carried out, and implies that it should be.

Note 1: For such questions with an aorist indicative, →33.33.

Imperfect

33.22   The imperfect, being built on the same stem, has the same basic values as the present indicative, but refers to the past. It is primarily used in narrative texts to provide background information; in this use it alternates with the aorist as one of the main ingredients of narration. This alternation is treated more fully below (→33.48–53), and some specifically narrative interpretations of the imperfect are treated there as well.

For the 'modal' use of the imperfect (in counterfactual statements, unrealizable wishes, and with verbs of possibility/necessity), →34.15–18.

Basic Uses

33.23   The imperfect is used to refer to actions which are presented as **ongoing** in the past:

(22)   καὶ ταῦτα πολὺν χρόνον οὕτως ἐγίγνετο, καὶ ἐγὼ οὐδέποτε ὑπώπτευσα, ἀλλ᾽ οὕτως ἠλιθίως διεκείμην, ὥστε ᾤμην τὴν ἑαυτοῦ γυναῖκα πασῶν σωφρονεστάτην εἶναι τῶν ἐν τῇ πόλει. (Lys. 1.10)
   The situation was like this for a long time, and I never got suspicious, but I was so naive that I supposed that my wife was the most chaste of all in the city. *Each of the imperfects expresses ongoing actions (ἐγίγνετο may also be interpreted as referring to repeated actions, →33.24). Contrast aorist ὑπώπτευσα, referring to (the absence of) a single action within the ongoing period referred to by the imperfects.*

33.24   The imperfect is also used to refer to **repeated actions** in the past:

(23)   οἵπερ πρόσθεν προσεκύνουν, καὶ τότε προσεκύνησαν. (Xen. An. 1.6.10)
   The very men who earlier used to prostrate themselves before him, prostrated themselves on that occasion too. *Note the aorist προσεκύνησαν, expressing a single action.*

(24)   σὺ δ᾽ αὐτὸν καὶ ζῶντα ἔλεγες κακῶς καὶ νῦν γράφεις κακῶς. (Unknown origin, cited at Arist. Rh. 1410a35–6)
   You used to speak ill about him while he was alive, and now (that he is dead) you write ill about him as well.

Note 1: To express emphatically that an action occurred **on repeated occasions,** ἄν is sometimes added to the imperfect or aorist indicative. In this use, ἄν is called **iterative**:

(25)   ὁ δὲ χορός γ᾽ ἤρειδεν ὁρμαθοὺς ἄν | μελῶν ἐφεξῆς τέτταρας. (Ar. Ran. 914)
   And the chorus would hurl forth four strings of lyrics, one after the other.

(26)   σαφὲς δ᾽ ἂν εἶπεν οὐδὲ ἕν. (Ar. Ran. 927)
   And he would not say a single thing that was intelligible.

In this scene of the Frogs, Euripides is discussing dramatic techniques that Aeschylus used time and time again in his plays. The difference between the imperfect (ἤρειδεν) and aorist indicative (εἶπεν) in these cases is purely aspectual (note ἐφεξῆς in (25), referring to repeated actions, and ἕν in (26), referring to (the absence of) a single action).

The combination of a secondary indicative (i.e. impf. or aor. ind.) with ἄν occurs much more frequently in the counterfactual use, for which →34.16.

Specific Interpretations

33.25   Like the present indicative (→33.17), and more often than it, the imperfect of telic verbs may refer to an (unsuccessful) attempt, thus eliciting a **conative** interpretation:

(27) Νέων δὲ καὶ παρ' Ἀριστάρχου ἄλλοι <u>ἔπειθον</u> ἀποτρέπεσθαι· οἱ δ' οὐχ ὑπήκουον. (Xen. *An.* 7.3.7)
Neon and others from Aristarchus tried to persuade them to turn back, but they would not listen.

(28) ἡ Ἀβουλία ἀτυχία δοκεῖ εἶναι, ὡς οὐ βαλόντος οὐδὲ τυχόντος οὗ τ' <u>ἔβαλλε</u>. (Pl. *Cra.* 420c)
The word ἀβουλία seems to refer to a failure to hit, as if someone missed and did not hit the target which he aimed for (*tried to hit*).

Note 1: Related to the conative use is the use of the imperfect of telic verbs to refer to actions which were **likely** or **about** to happen, but in the end did not:

(29) μετάρσια ληφθεῖσ' <u>ἐκαινόμην</u> ξίφει. | ἀλλ' ἐξέκλεψεν . . . | Ἄρτεμις (Eur. *IT* 27–8)
I was lifted high in the air and about to be killed by the sword. But Artemis stole me away.

33.26   Verbs whose present stem may have a **resultative** sense (→33.18) can also be so used in the imperfect; with several such verbs, such as ἥκω *arrive/have arrived*, νικάω *defeat/be victorious*, the resultative sense is, in fact, the default interpretation of the imperfect:

(30) περὶ αὐτῶν ὁ Θεμιστοκλῆς τοῖς Ἀθηναίοις κρύφα πέμπει κελεύων . . . μὴ ἀφεῖναι πρὶν ἂν αὐτοὶ πάλιν κομισθῶσιν (ἤδη γὰρ καὶ <u>ἧκον</u> αὐτῷ οἱ ξυμπρέσβεις). (Thuc. 1.91.3)
Concerning these men, Themistocles sent a secret message to the Athenians not to let them go before they themselves had returned (for his fellow ambassadors had now also arrived). *ἤδη and the wider context make it clear that ἧκον cannot be interpreted as 'were arriving'. πέμπει is historical present,* →33.54–5.

Aorist Indicative

33.27 The aorist indicative is used very often in narrative texts (for details on its use there, →33.48–9); however, it also has a few specific uses outside narrative.

For the 'modal' use of the aorist (in counterfactual statements, unrealizable wishes, etc.), →34.15–18.

Basic Uses

33.28 The aorist indicative is used to present the occurrence of an action in the past, without reference to its duration or process, but presenting the action as a single, uninterruptable whole. As such, the aorist is the default tense **in narrative texts** to record **single, complete actions**:

(31) σκοποὺς δὲ καταστήσας <u>συνέλεξε</u> τοὺς στρατιώτας καὶ <u>ἔλεξεν·</u> ... (Xen. *An.* 6.3.11)
He posted watchmen, called his troops together, and spoke as follows: ...

(32) ἅμα δὲ τῇ ἡμέρᾳ συνελθόντες οἱ στρατηγοὶ ἐθαύμαζον ὅτι Κῦρος οὔτε ἄλλον πέμπει ... οὔτε αὐτὸς φαίνοιτο. <u>ἔδοξεν</u> οὖν αὐτοῖς ... ἐξοπλισαμένοις προϊέναι εἰς τὸ πρόσθεν. (Xen. *An.* 2.1.2)
At daybreak the generals gathered, and wondered why Cyrus neither sent anyone else nor appeared himself. They resolved, then, to arm themselves and push forward. *For the alternation with the imperfect ἐθαύμαζον, →33.49.*

In **non-narrative text**, the aorist is typically used to observe or conclude that an action has been completed by the moment of speaking. This is sometimes called the **constative aorist**:

(33) ἔλεγε Ξέρξης τάδε· ... ὑμέας νῦν ἐγὼ <u>συνέλεξα</u>, ἵνα ... (Hdt. 7.8–8α.2)
Xerxes spoke as follows: 'I have now called you together, in order that ...'
Aorist indicative συνέλεξα, used in a speech by Xerxes (non-narrative text). Note νῦν, which locates the completion of the 'calling together' in the very immediate past.

(34) <u>ἔδοξε</u> τῇ βουλῇ ... (decrees)
The Council has resolved ...

Note 1: Observe the different translations in (31)/(33) and (32)/(34): whereas the English present perfect (*I have called, the Council has resolved*) is often the most suitable translation for the constative use, the simple past (*he called, they resolved*) is the most suitable translation of aorist indicatives in narrative.

Specific Interpretations

33.29 With **atelic** verbs (→33.8) such as γελάω *laugh*, βλέπω *gaze*, and particularly with **stative** verbs, such as πλουτέω *be rich*, βασιλεύω *rule*, ἐράω *love*, νοσέω *be sick*, ἔχω *have*, the aorist stem often leads to an **ingressive** interpretation (referring to the beginning of a state; observe that perfective aspect is concerned with the 'boundaries' of an action, →33.4–6):

(35) καὶ οἱ πάντα τε ἐκεῖνα διδοῖ καὶ πρὸς ἑτέροισί μιν δωρέεται ... οὕτω μὲν ἐπλούτησε ἡ οἰκίη αὕτη μεγάλως. (Hdt. 6.125.5)

And he gave all those things to him and in addition gifted him with others. In this way, that family became very wealthy. *διδοῖ and δωρέεται are historical presents, →33.54–5 below; for πρός, →31.6.*

(36) ἀποβάντες τοὺς ἀντιστάντας μάχῃ νικήσαντες τὴν πόλιν ἔσχον. (Thuc. 8.23.3)

They disembarked, defeated those who met them in battle, and gained possession of the city.

Note 1: The ingressive interpretation is not limited to the indicative, but available for any aorist-stem form of the relevant verbs. For non-indicative forms, →33.59; cf. also βλέψας in (5).

33.30   The aorist of such verbs can, however, also be used as an expression of an entire period (viewed as a complete whole from beginning to end, without any interest in its component parts). This is the so-called **complexive** (or 'concentrating') use of the aorist. Typically, an **expression of the duration** of the action is included:

(37) Ἄρδυος δὲ βασιλεύσαντος ἑνὸς δέοντα πεντήκοντα ἔτεα ἐξεδέξατο Σαδυάττης ὁ Ἄρδυος, καὶ ἐβασίλευσε ἔτεα δυώδεκα, Σαδυάττεω δὲ Ἀλυάττης. οὗτος δὲ Κυαξάρῃ τε τῷ Δηιόκεω ἀπογόνῳ ἐπολέμησε. (Hdt. 1.16.1–2)

When Ardys had ruled for forty-nine years, his son Sadyattes assumed the throne, and he ruled for twelve years. Alyattes then took over the throne from Sadyattes. He made war against Cyaxares, the descendent of Deioces. *Herodotus details a succession of rulers, presenting some basic narrative facts about their exploits. In the case of Sadyattes, Herodotus uses the aorist ἐβασίλευσε to relate the simple fact of his kingship (with its duration), without going into any of the events that occurred during that period.*

(38) αὐτοὶ δὲ Κυδωνίην τὴν ἐν Κρήτῃ ἔκτισαν ... ἔμειναν δ' ἐν ταύτῃ καὶ εὐδαιμόνησαν ἐπ' ἔτεα πέντε. (Hdt. 3.59.1–2)

They themselves settled in Cydonia on Crete. They stayed there and prospered for five years.

Note 1: The complexive interpretation is, again, not limited to the indicative, but available for any aorist-stem form (for instance, βασιλεύσαντος in (37) is an example of a complexive aorist participle).

Non-Past Uses of the Aorist

33.31   The aorist is sometimes used in non-narrative text to express general tendencies, habits, procedures, etc. In this use the aorist does not seem to refer to the
past: it is called the **gnomic aorist** (γνώμη *saying, maxim*; also 'generic'
aorist):

(39) καὶ σώφρων ἥμαρτε. (Thgn. 665)
       Even a wise man makes mistakes.

(40) ἐν δὲ ὀλιγαρχίη ... στάσιες ἐγγίνονται, ἐκ δὲ τῶν στασίων φόνος· ἐκ δὲ τοῦ
       φόνου ἀπέβη ἐς μουναρχίην. (Hdt. 3.82.3)
       In an oligarchy, factions tend to occur, and from these factions arises
       bloodshed; and from the bloodshed, the result is a shift towards
       monarchy.

Note 1: The gnomic aorist occurs with telic verbs (→33.8); it is not normally used with
stative verbs, like ἔχω *have*, βασιλεύω *be king*, etc. For truly 'timeless' truths the present
indicative is used (→33.16).

33.32   In answers and reactions in tragic and comic dialogue, the **first-person aorist indicative** is
sometimes used with verbs that refer to the performance of speech acts, such as ὄμνυμι *swear*,
ἐπαινέω *praise*, οἰμώζω *bewail, lament*. This use of the aorist indicative in **performatives** is
known as the **tragic aorist** (or 'dramatic aorist', 'instantaneous aorist'):

(41) ἐγημάμεσθ᾽, ὦ ξεῖνε, θανάσιμον γάμον. | :: ὤμωξ᾽ ἀδελφὸν σόν. (Eur. *El.* 247–8)
       I have entered into a deathly marriage, stranger. :: I lament your brother!

Note 1: The use of the aorist indicative for performatives, which are by definition
perfective (by uttering the act, it is complete), makes sense given the lack of a present-
tense perfective form in the tense/aspect framework of classical Greek (→33.12 n.1):
the aorist is chosen for its aspectual value, in spite of its tense. Performatives may,
however, also be expressed by the present indicative (→33.20). The co-existence of
these two uses suggests that either tense (pres. ind.) or aspect (aor. ind.) could be
emphasized. Note, however, that the tragic aorist is confined to a few specific genres
(tragedy and comedy): variables such as register and metre may also have played
a role.

33.33   **Questions introduced by τί οὐ and with a first- or second-person aorist indicative** are
sometimes used as requests or suggestions (also →38.33):

(42) ΕΤ. τί οὖν οὐ διηγήσω ἡμῖν τὴν συνουσίαν, εἰ μή σέ τι κωλύει ... ; :: ΣΩ. πάνυ μὲν οὖν. (Pl.
       Prt. 310a)
       (Friend:) Let me have the story of your gathering, then, if nothing prevents you. ::
       (Socrates:) Certainly.

Note 1: For such questions expressed by the present indicative, →33.21. The aorist indicative in this use may suggest that the action should already have been carried out ('Why haven't you . . . ?'), in which case it is not really a non-past use. Alternatively, as with the tragic aorist (→33.32 n.1), the aorist may be used purely for its aspectual value and in spite of its tense.

Perfect Indicative

Basic Uses; Active versus Passive

33.34   The **perfect indicative** signifies that an action has been completed in the past and that the effects of that action are in some way **relevant in the present**; frequently it expresses a more or less **permanent state in the present** which exists as the result of a completed action in the past:

(43) ἔτι δὲ χρήματα μὲν ὀλίγα, φίλους δὲ πολλοὺς <u>κέκτηται</u>. (Isoc. 21.9)
As of now he possesses little money, but many friends (< *has acquired*).

(44) κεῖνος μὲν οὖν <u>δέδωκε</u> σὺν θεοῖς δίκην. (Eur. *Tro.* 867)
That man, with the gods' help, has paid the penalty. *κεῖνος refers to Paris, who is now dead – his punishment for taking Helen.*

(45) οἱ νόμοι . . . περὶ . . . τῶν δωροδοκούντων δύο μόνον τιμήματα <u>πεποιήκασιν</u>, ἢ θάνατον . . . ἢ δεκαπλοῦν . . . τὸ τίμημα τῶν δώρων. (Din. 1.60)
The laws have prescribed only two forms of punishment concerning those involved with bribery: either the death penalty, or a fine amounting to the bribe tenfold. *The penalties prescribed by law have relevance to the case in hand.*

33.35   Especially with telic verbs, **active forms** of the perfect are often used to emphasize the **responsibility** of the subject for the state that has resulted from a past action (they are particularly frequent in oratory):

(46) <u>γέγραφε</u> δὲ καὶ ταῦτα ὁ αὐτὸς Θουκυδίδης Ἀθηναῖος. (Thuc. 5.26.1)
Of this, too, the same Thucydides of Athens is the author (< *has written*).

(47) ὃ δὲ πάντων δεινότατον οἱ συνεστηκότες <u>πεποιήκασιν</u> (καί . . . μηδεὶς ὑπολάβῃ δυσκόλως, ἐὰν τοὺς ἠδικηκότας ἐμαυτὸν πονηροὺς ὄντας ἐπιδεικνύω) . . . (Dem. 57.59)
And the worst of all things that the conspirators have on their conscience (< *have done*) (and let no one be offended if I show that the people who have done me wrong are villains) . . .

Passive forms of the perfect stem, on the other hand, usually indicate that the subject is in the state resulting from the action completed upon it. The emphasis in such cases is not so much on the responsibility of the agent of the action, but on the current state of the subject:

(48) τὸν Ὀλυμπιονίκαν ἀνάγνωτέ μοι | Ἀρχεστράτου παῖδα, πόθι φρενός | ἐμᾶς γέγραπται. (Pind. *Ol.* 10.1–3)
Read me the name of the Olympic champion, the son of Archestratus, where it is etched firmly in my heart (< *has been written*).

(49) μῦ μῦ. :: τί μύζεις; πάντα <u>πεποίηται</u> καλῶς. (Ar. *Thesm.* 231)
Muuh! muuh! :: What are you muuh-ing about? It's all done, well and good (< *everything has been done nicely*).

Note 1: The perfect indicative is a **present tense**, referring to the moment of speaking (→33.2). Note that it has no augment, it uses primary endings (in the middle passive e.g. -μαι, -σαι, etc.; for the active endings, →18.5), and, if followed by subordinate clauses, these are not in secondary sequence (→40.12, cf. (45)). The balance between these two components (present and past reference) varies: while a resulting state in the present is often the main focus, in other cases there is greater focus on the past action, the completion of which is presented as particularly relevant at the moment of speaking – the so-called 'current-relevance perfect'. Examples such as (44), (45) and (47) are sometimes classed under this heading.
Note 2: Differences of nuance between active and passive perfects are, of course, not restricted to the indicative. Observe, for instance, the implication of responsibility present in active ἠδικηκότας in (47).

Specific Interpretations

33.36   A number of specific Greek verbs, when they occur in the perfect stem, express an ongoing state without any clear reference to an (inferable) preceding action, and therefore function much like present-stem forms. These are sometimes called **perfects with present meaning** (but they do not differ in a real sense from other perfects). For instance:

πέφυκα	be (by nature)	(φύομαι *grow, be born*)
μέμνημαι	remember	(μιμνήσκομαι *call to mind*; the present is rare until later Greek)
πέποιθα	trust, have confidence in	(πείθομαι *obey, believe*)
εἴθισμαι	be accustomed to	(ἐθίζομαι *become accustomed to*)
βέβηκα	stand (firm)	(βαίνω *go, walk*)
ἕστηκα	stand	(ἵσταμαι *come to stand*)

A number of verbs occur (at least in classical Greek) **only in the perfect stem**, and do not have a corresponding present stem. Such verbs may be considered functionally equivalent to presents in nearly all respects:

οἶδα	know
δέδοικα	fear

ἔοικα   be likely, be proper, appear

εἴωθα   be used to, be accustomed to

These normally have the pluperfect as their only past indicative (but note aor. ἔδεισα with δέδοικα).

(50) γυνή . . . οὐκ ἂν ἐξαπατηθείη ποτέ· | αὐταὶ γάρ <u>εἰσιν</u> ἐξαπατᾶν <u>εἰθισμέναι</u>. (Ar. *Eccl.* 236–8)

A woman will not easily be deceived: they themselves are used to deceiving.

(51) τῆς δὴ ταλασιουργικῆς δύο τμήματά ἐστον, καὶ τούτοιν ἑκάτερον ἅμα δυοῖν <u>πεφύκατον</u> τέχναιν μέρη. (Pl. *Plt.* 282b)

There are two parts to woolworking, and of these each is a part of two arts at once. *Note that* πεφύκατον *is coordinated with pres. ind.* ἐστον *(duals, →21)*.

(52) οἱ μὲν γὰρ εἰδότες ἑαυτοὺς τά τε ἐπιτήδεια ἑαυτοῖς <u>ἴσασι</u> καὶ διαγιγνώσκουσιν ἅ τε δύνανται καὶ ἃ μή. (Xen. *Mem.* 4.2.26)

For those who know themselves, know what things are good for them and recognize what they can and cannot do. *Note that* ἴσασιν *is coordinated with pres. ind.* διαγιγνώσκουσιν.

Note 1: The 'present-like' sense of these perfects is not limited to perfect indicatives: cf. e.g. εἰδότες in (52), which similarly expresses a state without reference to an (inferable) preceding action. For pluperfects, →33.41. For other forms, →33.61.

The four verbs δέδοικα, ἔοικα, εἴωθα and (especially) οἶδα, occur with some frequency in the subjunctive, optative, and imperative. With other verbs, forms of these moods of the perfect stem are typically very rare (except the somewhat more frequent pf. imp. pass., →34.21). With these four verbs, such forms are functionally equivalent to present-stem subjunctives, optatives, and imperatives.

33.37   With **atelic** verbs (→33.8), such as φοβέομαι *be afraid*, θαυμάζω *be in awe, admire*, νομίζω *believe*, the perfect stem often gives rise to a so-called **intensive** interpretation (marking an extreme degree of the state). Again, there seems to be no clear reference to an (inferable) preceding action with these perfects. For instance:

γέγηθα   be delighted   (γηθέω *be pleased*; rare in the present)

μέμηνα   be raging mad   (μαίνομαι *rage*)

νενόμικα   be convinced   (νομίζω *believe*)

πεφόβημαι be terrified   (φοβέομαι *be afraid*)

σεσιώπηκα maintain complete silence   (σιωπάω *be silent*)

τεθαύμακα be very surprised, admire   (θαυμάζω *wonder, admire*)
                     greatly

The perfect is also so used with some verbs that refer to various ways of **making sound**:

λέληκα	shriek	(λάσκω *cry*)
κέκραγα	scream	(κράζω *shout*, rare in the present)

(53) πολλὰ δὲ θαυμάζων τῶν εἰωθότων λέγεσθαι παρ᾽ ὑμῖν, οὐδενὸς ἧττον, ὦ ἄνδρες Ἀθηναῖοι, τεθαύμακα, ὃ καὶ πρώην τινὸς ἤκουσα εἰπόντος ἐν τῇ βουλῇ. (Dem. 8.4)

Although I am often surprised about the speeches that are usually delivered before you, men of Athens, I am positively astounded, more than at anything else, at what I heard someone say in the Council the other day.

(54) τί κέκραγας; ἐμβαλῶ σοι πάτταλον, | ἢν μὴ σιωπᾷς. (Ar. *Thesm.* 222–3)

What are you screaming about? I'll put a peg in you, if you don't shut up.

Note 1: The intensive interpretation is, again, not limited to the perfect indicative, but available for any perfect-stem form. For intensive pluperfects, →33.42; for other forms, →33.61.

33.38   The perfect indicative is occasionally used, especially after conditional clauses, for actions that have not actually occurred yet: these are thereby presented as already having had effect. This is sometimes referred to as the **rhetorical** (use of the) perfect, or the 'perfect for future perfect':

(55) τοὺς νόμους οὖν δεῖ τηρεῖν . . . ποιεῖν τοὺς ἀεὶ δικάζοντας ὑμῶν . . . εἰ δὲ μή, λέλυται πάντα, ἀνέῳκται, συγκέχυται. (Dem. 25.24–5)

It is necessary that those of you who sit on a jury, protect the laws. If you don't, everything is dissolved, broken up, thrown into confusion (< *has been dissolved, has been opened, has been mixed together*).

Pluperfect

33.39   The pluperfect is used primarily in narrative text, where (like the imperfect) it serves to provide background information (→33.50). Being built on the same stem as the perfect indicative, it has the same basic values, but refers to the past rather than the present.

Basic Uses

33.40   The **pluperfect** expresses that at a moment in the past a state existed as the result of a previous action, or that the effects of a previous action were still in force and relevant at that moment in the past:

(56) λογίσασθαι δ' ἤθελον αὐτῷ καθ' ἕκαστον ... οὕτω γάρ μοι ἀκριβῶς ἐγέγραπτο, ὥστ' οὐ μόνον αὐτά μοι τἀναλώματα ἐγέγραπτο, ἀλλὰ καὶ ὅποι ἀνηλώθη. (Dem. 50.30)

I was ready to reckon everything up for him item by item. For I had such an accurate account to hand that not only the expenditures themselves stood recorded, but also what they had been spent on. *The pluperfects refer to the state of being written down, and provide relevant background information. Note the contrast with the aorist ἀνηλώθη, which does not refer to a state resulting from the expenditure.*

(57) ὁ Δαρεῖός τε ἤσχαλλε καὶ ἡ στρατιὴ πᾶσα οὐ δυνατὴ ἐοῦσα ἑλεῖν τοὺς Βαβυλωνίους. καίτοι πάντα σοφίσματα καὶ πάσας μηχανὰς ἐπεποιήκεε ἐς αὐτοὺς Δαρεῖος. (Hdt. 3.152)

Darius was bitter, as was his entire army, about being unable to seize Babylon. And yet Darius had tried every possible trick and device against them. *The pluperfect emphasizes the ongoing effects for Darius of his previous failed attempts.*

Note 1: Unlike the English (and Latin) pluperfect, the Greek pluperfect does not necessarily express a 'past in the past' ('John came back to class. He *had been ill* the week before': the Engl. pluperfect here is a relative tense, expressing anteriority to 'came'). This is because the pluperfect, like other Greek indicatives in main clauses, expresses absolute tense. To express past in the past, Greek can use any of the three past tenses (aorist, imperfect and pluperfect), with their normal aspectual values: it is the context which warrants an interpretation as past in the past:

(58) ἐνταῦθα πόλις ἦν ἐρήμη ... · ᾤκουν δ' αὐτὴν τὸ παλαιὸν Μῆδοι. (Xen. *An.* 3.4.7)

There lay an abandoned city: in the past, Medes had lived/used to live there. *The impf. expresses an ongoing action in the past; the adverb τὸ παλαιόν locates it in a more remote past than that of the previous sentence (ἦν).*

(59) τοὺς ... Ἱμεραίους ἔπεισαν ... τοῖς ἐκ τῶν νεῶν τῶν σφετέρων ναύταις ... ὅπλα παρασχεῖν. τὰς γὰρ ναῦς ἀνείλκυσαν ἐν Ἱμέρᾳ. (Thuc. 7.1.3)

They persuaded the Himeraeans to supply weapons for the seamen from their vessels. For they had beached their ships at Himera. *The aor. ind. expresses a complete action anterior to the action of the preceding sentence (ἔπεισαν); note the particle γάρ which signals that the new sentence provides explanatory information (taking a step back in the historical chronology), →59.14.*

(60) σπανιώτερα τὰ ἐπιτήδεια ἦν· τὰ μὲν γὰρ ἀνήλωτο, τὰ δὲ διήρπαστο. (Xen. *Hell.* 6.5.50)

The supplies were more scarce: some of them had been consumed, others had been plundered. *The plpf. forms express states in the past resulting from a previously completed action (the states themselves are in fact simultaneous with ἦν); note again the particle γάρ.*

Specific Interpretations

33.41 Perfects with a '**present-like**' sense normally use the pluperfect as their regular past tense ('pluperfect for imperfect'):

(61) ἐφύλαττον αὐτὸν εἰ καὶ τὴν νύκτα ἑστήξοι. ὁ δὲ εἱστήκει μέχρι ἕως ἐγένετο καὶ ἥλιος ἀνέσχεν. (Pl. *Symp.* 220d)

They watched him to see if he would actually stay standing through the night, too. And he stood there until dawn came and the sun came up. *εἱστήκει expresses the state of standing in the past, without reference to a preceding 'coming to stand'. For the fut. pf. opt. ἑστήξοι, →20.4 (form), 42.7 (use of the opt.).*

(62) ἰδὼν δ' ὁ κῆρυξ τὰ ὅπλα ... ἐθαύμαζε τὸ πλῆθος· οὐ γὰρ ᾔδει τὸ πάθος. (Thuc. 3.113.2)

When the herald saw the arms, he was amazed at their number. For he did not know about the disaster. *οἶδα has no present-stem forms.*

33.42 Like the perfect indicative (→33.37), pluperfects of certain atelic verbs may also be **intensive**:

(63) ἔξω ... οἱ τῶν Ἀρκάδων ὁπλῖται παντάπασιν οὐκ ἀντεξῇσαν· οὕτω τοὺς πελταστὰς ἐπεφόβηντο. (Xen. *Hell.* 4.4.16)

The Arcadian hoplites did not come out to meet them at all. Such overwhelming fear did they feel for the peltasts. *Intensive pluperfect.*

Future Indicative

33.43 The **future indicative** presents the realization of some action in the future as (virtually) certain (more so than, for example, the 'potential' optative, →34.13). Depending on the context, the future indicative can be used for various communicative purposes, such as predictions, statements of intention, announcements, promises, threats, suggestions, etc.:

(64) τήνδε δείξω μὴ λέγουσαν ἔνδικα. (Eur. *Tro.* 970)

I will show that this woman is not speaking justly. *Announcement.*

(65) οὔτοι καταπροίξει ... τοῦτο δρῶν. (Ar. *Vesp.* 1366)

You won't get away with this behaviour. *Threat.*

(66) Θηβαῖοι δ' ἔχουσι μέν ... ἀπεχθῶς, ἔτι δ' ἐχθροτέρως σχήσουσιν. (Dem. 5.18)

The Thebans are hostile, and will become more hostile still. *Prediction. For ἔχω + adv., →26.11. For σχήσω vs. ἕξω, →15.25.*

Note 1: Future actions may also be expressed by μέλλω + infinitive: →51.33.

Note 2: The future indicative is normally aspect-neutral, i.e. it may refer both to a single action seen as an uninterruptable whole, or to an action presented as ongoing or repeated in the future. For exceptions, →15.25, 35.30.

33.44   The second-person future indicative may be used in **questions introduced by** οὐ, with the force of an **urgent command**; prohibitions have οὐ μή:

(67) οὐ μὴ φρενώσεις μ', ἀλλὰ δέσμιος φυγὼν | σώσῃ τόδ'; (Eur. *Bacch.* 792)

Do not lecture me; rather, now that you have escaped from prison, hold on to that.

For this use, also →38.32.

Note 1: To express a strong command or exhortation, the future indicative is also sometimes used with ὅπως (μή). This is the construction of 'effort clauses' (→44), but used in main clauses. For this use, →38.34.

33.45   The future indicative predominantly refers to an action that is situated in the 'actual' future relative to some other moment (in main clauses, the moment of speaking), as in (64)–(67). The future indicative may, however, also be used to express:

- **hypothetical scenarios** and **general truths** (cf. Engl. *If A is larger than B, B will be smaller than A; Oil will float on water*);
- **inferences** (cf. Engl. *That'll be the postman*).

In such cases the realization of the action does not necessarily lie in the future; rather, the sense underlying the use of the future indicative is that the truth of the statement will be ascertainable at some future moment (if reasoning is followed to its logical conclusion, or if evidence becomes available):

(68) λείπεται δὴ ἐκεῖνος μόνος ... φίλος τῷ τοιούτῳ, ὃς ἂν ὁμοήθης ὢν ... οὗτος μέγα ἐν ταύτῃ τῇ πόλει δυνήσεται, τοῦτον οὐδεὶς χαίρων ἀδικήσει. οὐχ οὕτως ἔχει; (Pl. *Grg.* 510c)

The only possible friend that remains for such a man (*a tyrant*) is whoever shares his temper. That man will have great power in that city, and no one will wrong him with impunity. Isn't that right? *This passage concludes a section of a (hypothetical) argument about how someone can avoid being wronged. The future indicative presents the conclusion as the logical outcome of the argument. Note the assent-seeking question* οὐχ οὕτως ἔχει; *(with a present indicative), by which Socrates asks his interlocutor to confirm that the reasoning holds.*

(69) Ἄκουε δή, ἦ δ' ὅς. Φημὶ γὰρ ἐγὼ εἶναι τὸ δίκαιον οὐκ ἄλλο τι ἢ τὸ τοῦ κρείττονος συμφέρον. ἀλλὰ τί οὐκ ἐπαινεῖς; ἀλλ' οὐκ ἐθελήσεις. Ἐὰν μάθω γε πρῶτον, ἔφην, τί λέγεις· νῦν γὰρ οὔπω οἶδα. (Pl. *Resp.* 338c)

'So listen', he said. 'I claim that justice is nothing other than what is beneficial for the stronger. Why aren't you applauding my claim? Well, I suppose you won't want to.' 'Yes I do', I said, 'if only I learn first what it is that you mean. For I don't know that yet now.' *On the basis of their preceding conversation, Thrasymachus draws an inference about Socrates' unwillingness to agree with him. Socrates challenges that inference in his reply.*

Future Perfect Indicative

33.46   The (rare) **future perfect indicative** serves as the future tense of the perfect stem, and expresses that a resulting state will exist, or that the effects of a completed action will be relevant at some point in the future:

(70)   σὲ δ' ἄλλη τις γυνὴ κεκτήσεται. (Eur. *Alc.* 181)
         Some other woman will have you (< *will have acquired*).

(71)   ταῦτα ὅκως σοι πρὸ τῶν ἐπιμηνίων ἡμέρῃ μιῇ πρόσθεν πεποιήσεται. (Hippoc. *Mul.* 37.30)
         Make sure that you have completed this treatment one day before menstruation (< *will have been done by you*). *For strong commands expressed by* ὅπως *(Ion.* ὅκως, →*25.12) + fut. (pf.) ind.,* →*38.34.*

33.47   Specific interpretations of the perfect stem ('present-like', intensive, →33.36–7) may also be attached to the future perfect (in any of its forms, not only the indicative):

(72)   ἤν τ' ἴδῃ λύκον, | κεκράξεται. (Eup. fr. 1.2–3 Kock)
         When he sees a wolf, he will cry out. *Intensive with a verb of making sound (*κράζω, →*33.37).*

The Alternation of Tenses in Narrative Text

33.48   Narrative text normally consists of a mix of aorist indicatives, imperfects, pluperfects and historical present indicatives, and within narrative each of these tenses performs specific roles. The following sections discuss this division of labour. For an extended example of narrative with discussion, →61.1–3.

Aorist versus Imperfect (and Pluperfect)

33.49   **Aorist indicatives** and **imperfects** are the main tenses of Greek narrative; both tenses locate an action in the past, but they differ aspectually. Imperfects, by suggesting that the actions they express are incomplete (imperfective aspect), typically do not 'push a story forward': rather they are used to 'set the stage' or to create a **background/framework** in which main events take place which do move the story forward. These **main events**, in turn, appear in the **aorist** indicative:

(73) καὶ ὅτε δὴ ἦν δεκαέτης ὁ παῖς, πρῆγμα ἐς αὐτὸν τοιόνδε γενόμενον ἐξέφηνέ μιν· <u>ἔπαιζε</u> ἐν τῇ κώμῃ ... μετ᾽ ἄλλων ἡλίκων ἐν ὁδῷ. καὶ οἱ παῖδες παίζοντες <u>εἵλοντο</u> ἑωυτῶν βασιλέα εἶναι τοῦτον δὴ τὸν τοῦ βουκόλου ἐπίκλησιν παῖδα. ὁ δὲ αὐτῶν <u>διέταξε</u> τοὺς μὲν οἰκίας οἰκοδομέειν ... (Hdt. 1.114.1–2)

Now when the boy (*Cyrus*) was ten years old, the following occurrence revealed him for what he was. He was playing outdoors in the village with others of his age. The boys in their games chose to be their king this one who was supposed to be the son of the cowherd. Then he assigned some of them to the building of houses. *The imperfect ἔπαιζε 'sets the stage' for the events that take place (it forms the background against which the rest of the story is presented). The aorists εἵλοντο and διέταξε are used to narrate the events that move the story along, while the children were playing (note the present participle παίζοντες 'while they were playing', implying simultaneity with εἵλοντο; →33.57). Note further the aorist ἐξέφηνε, which summarizes the entire story by way of announcement (an imperfect here would have suggested that the 'revealing' served as background to other actions).*

(74) δμῶες πρὸς ἔργον πάντες <u>ἵεσαν</u> χέρας. | οἱ μὲν σφαγεῖον <u>ἔφερον</u>, οἱ δ᾽ <u>ᾖρον</u> κανᾶ, | ἄλλοι δὲ πῦρ <u>ἀνῆπτον</u> ἀμφί τ᾽ ἐσχάραις | λέβητας <u>ὤρθουν</u>· πᾶσα δ᾽ <u>ἐκτύπει</u> στέγη. | ... ἐκ κανοῦ δ᾽ ἑλὼν | Αἴγισθος ὀρθὴν σφαγίδα, μοσχείαν τρίχα | τεμὼν ἐφ᾽ ἁγνὸν πῦρ <u>ἔθηκε</u> δεξιᾷ. (Eur. *El.* 799–812)

The slaves all applied their hands to the work. Some brought a sacrificial bowl, others took up baskets, while others kindled fire and set cauldrons around the hearth: the whole house was clattering with the sound. And Aegisthus took from a basket a long straight knife, and cutting off some of the calf's hair laid it with his right hand on the sacred fire. *A long series of imperfects (here abbreviated) paints a scene which forms the background against which the main events of the sacrifice, starting with the aorist ἔθηκε, take place.*

33.50   Like the imperfect, the **pluperfect** often sketches the **background** circumstances under which main actions take place:

(75) φθάνουσι τῶν Πλαταιῶν καὶ οἱ ὕστατοι διαβάντες τὴν τάφρον, χαλεπῶς δὲ καὶ βιαίως· κρύσταλλός τε γὰρ <u>ἐπεπήγει</u> οὐ βέβαιος ἐν αὐτῇ ὥστ᾽ ἐπελθεῖν, ... καὶ ἡ νὺξ ... ὑπονειφομένη πολὺ τὸ ὕδωρ ... <u>ἐπεποιήκει</u>. (Thuc. 3.23.4–5)

Even the last of the Plataeans managed to cross the ditch in time, although with difficulty and effort. For ice had formed on it, not firm enough to walk on, and the snow that had fallen in the night had made the water deep. *φθάνουσι is historical present, →33.54–5.*

Special Uses of the Imperfect in Narrative

33.51   In its 'stage-setting' use, the **imperfect** of **telic** verbs may refer to actions which have clearly reached their end-point by the time the next action in a narrative occurs. In such cases, the aspect of the present stem suggests that the action and its effects are not yet complete, and the imperfect thus **directs attention towards the consequences** of the action. This occurs particularly often with verbs of speech and verbs of commanding, when a reaction to a speech or command is expected:

(76) ὁ μὲν δή σφι τὰ ἐντεταλμένα ἀπήγγελλε, τοῖσι δὲ ἕαδε μὲν βοηθέειν Ἀθηναίοισι ... (Hdt. 6.106.3)

So he delivered the message with which he had been charged, and they decided to come to the Athenians' aid. *The reason for the use of the impf. is obviously not that the narrator is interested in something else that happened during the delivery of the message, and the narrator immediately moves on to what happened after it (contrast (4) and (73)–(74)); rather, the imperfect suggests that with ἀπήγγελλε, this 'episode' of the narrative is not yet complete, and focuses attention on the reaction to the message.*

(77) ἐκεῖθεν δὲ τῇ ὑστεραίᾳ ἔπλεον οἱ Ἀθηναῖοι ἐπὶ Κύζικον. οἱ δὲ Κυζικηνοὶ τῶν Πελοποννησίων καὶ Φαρναβάζου ἐκλιπόντων αὐτὴν ἐδέχοντο τοὺς Ἀθηναίους· Ἀλκιβιάδης δὲ μείνας αὐτοῦ εἴκοσιν ἡμέρας καὶ χρήματα πολλὰ λαβὼν παρὰ τῶν Κυζικηνῶν, οὐδὲν ἄλλο κακὸν ἐργασάμενος ἐν τῇ πόλει ἀπέπλευσεν εἰς Προκόννησον. (Xen. *Hell.* 1.1.18–20)

From there (*Proconnesus*) the Athenians (*with Alcibiades*) sailed on the next day against Cyzicus. The Cyzicenes, now that the Peloponnesians and Pharnabazus had evacuated the city, admitted them. There Alcibiades stayed for twenty days, and obtained a great deal of money from the Cyzicenes, but without doing any further harm in the city, he sailed back to Proconnesus. *The use of the imperfects ἔπλεον and ἐδέχοντο each direct the reader's attention to the sequel: what happened at Cyzicus? What happened when the Cyzicenes admitted the Athenians? The aorist ἀπέπλευσεν rounds off the episode. The value 'incomplete' of the imperfect and the value 'complete' of the aorist in such a case pertain to a unit of discourse rather than to a single action.*

33.52   With **atelic** verbs, the imperfect in narrative may refer to an action in process immediately following on another action; this use is sometimes called **immediative** (or the 'imperfect of consecutive action'):

(78) καὶ τάχα δὴ ἀκούουσι βοώντων τῶν στρατιωτῶν Θάλαττα θάλαττα καὶ παρεγγυώντων. ἔνθα δὴ ἔθεον πάντες. (Xen. *An.* 4.7.24)

And soon they heard the soldiers shouting 'The sea! The sea!', and passing the word around. And then everyone was running.

Note 1: The terms 'inceptive' or 'inchoative' are sometimes used in grammars for this use of the imperfect, but they are misleading. Although the beginning of the action is implied (and the translation *began to/proceeded to* ... sometimes works), the imperfect expresses the action *in process* rather than its starting point: indeed, the use of the imperfect implies that there was no clear dividing line between this and the preceding action (cf. Engl. *no sooner had . . . than . . .*). To refer to the beginning of an action, Greek may use ἄρχομαι + ppl./inf. (→52.27) or the ingressive aorist (→33.29). The difference between such uses is clear in the following example:

(79)   ὡς δὲ πορευομένων ἐξεκύμαινέ τι τῆς φάλαγγος, τὸ ὑπολειπόμενον ἤρξατο δρόμῳ θεῖν· καὶ ἅμα ἐφθέγξαντο πάντες οἷον τῷ Ἐνυαλίῳ ἐλελίζουσι, καὶ πάντες δὲ ἔθεον. (Xen. *An.* 1.8.18)

When a part of the phalanx swerved out as they went, the part that was left behind began to run. And at the same time, everyone struck up the war cry which they raise to Enyalius. And next, they were all running. *ἄρχομαι + inf. explicitly indicates that one part of the phalanx began (i.e. was the first) to run; the ingressive aorist ἐφθέγξαντο refers to the initial onset of the Greeks' war cry; next, the immediative imperfect ἔθεον puts the reader in the middle of the all-out charge that followed.*

33.53   The **pluperfect** may be similarly used, even to refer to main events in a narrative. It then suggests that an action was accomplished completely in a very brief period, as if the resulting state existed almost immediately:

(80)   ἐπεὶ δ᾽ ἅπαξ ἤρξαντο ὑπείκειν, ταχὺ δὴ πᾶσα ἡ ἀκρόπολις ἔρημος τῶν πολεμίων ἐγεγένητο. (Xen. *Hell.* 7.2.9)

Once they had begun to give way, the whole acropolis had before long become free of enemies.

Historical Present

33.54   The **present indicative** is used occasionally to highlight **decisive or crucial events** in a narrative, often those that definitively change the situation in the narrated world; in effect, this so-called **historic(al) present** (or 'narrative present') makes it seem as if an action that occurred in the past occurs in the present and is, therefore, all the more urgent. It occurs nearly exclusively with telic verbs (thus verbs such as εἰμί *be*, κεῖμαι *lie*, are not normally used as historical presents):

(81)   παρῆν καὶ ἡ γυνή. ἐσελθοῦσαν δὲ καὶ τιθεῖσαν τὰ εἵματα ἐθηεῖτο ὁ Γύγης. ὡς δὲ κατὰ νώτου ἐγένετο ἰούσης τῆς γυναικὸς ἐς τὴν κοίτην, ὑπεκδὺς ἐχώρεε ἔξω. καὶ ἡ γυνὴ ἐπορᾷ μιν ἐξιόντα. (Hdt. 1.10.1–2)

The woman appeared as well. Gyges saw her come in and undress. And, as the woman was getting into bed and her back was turned to him, he slipped away and was on his way out. And the woman spotted him leaving. *The historical present ἐπορᾷ marks the pivotal moment in the story that will have dramatic consequences for the woman, her husband the king, and his bodyguard Gyges.*

(82) ὤσαντες δὲ τὴν θύραν τοῦ δωματίου οἱ μὲν πρῶτοι εἰσιόντες ἔτι εἴδομεν αὐτὸν κατακείμενον παρὰ τῇ γυναικί, οἱ δ᾽ ὕστερον ἐν τῇ κλίνῃ γυμνὸν ἑστηκότα. ἐγὼ δ᾽, ὦ ἄνδρες, πατάξας <u>καταβάλλω</u> αὐτόν. (Lys. 1.24–5)

And pushing in the door of the bedroom, the first of us to go in saw him still lying with my wife, and those who came in later saw him standing naked on the bed. And I, gentlemen, gave him a blow and struck him down. *The speaker's violent reaction to the man he catches in bed with his wife is expressed in the historical present.*

Note 1: The imperfective aspect of the present stem appears to play no role in the historical present, which usually presents actions as complete. For this, →33.20.

For other examples of the historical present cf. (4), (19), (30), (35), (75), (85), and especially →61.1–3.

33.55   Authors make a fairly individual use of the historical present. In some texts it is not so much used at dramatic turns, but rather to '**punctuate**' a narrative, dividing it up into separate sections by highlighting each new step:

(83) Κῦρος ... ὡρμᾶτο ἀπὸ Σάρδεων· καὶ <u>ἐξελαύνει</u> διὰ τῆς Λυδίας. ... <u>ἐξελαύνει</u> διὰ Φρυγίας ... ἐντεῦθεν <u>ἐξελαύνει</u> ... εἰς Κελαινάς (Xen. *An.* 1.2.5, 1.2.6, 1.2.7, etc.)

Cyrus set forth from Sardis; and he marched through Lydia ... He marched through Phrygia ... From there he marched to Celaena. *The historical present* ἐξελαύνει *here introduces each successive new stage in Cyrus' march.*

Note 1: This use may be similar to the use of the English simple present in summaries and chapter headings (e.g. Henry Fielding, *Tom Jones*, Book 5, chapter 7, *In which Mr Allworthy appears on a Sick-Bed*). The reason for the use of a present tense in such cases appears to be that the information is presented as accessible at any time. On this analysis, this use is in fact closer to the 'timeless' use of the present indicative (→33.16) than to the historical present of 33.54.

33.56   Just as the present indicative may be used to present past actions as if they occur in the present, it may also be used to present actions **in the future** as if they take place in the present. This **present for the future** occurs particularly in the language of oracles and prophecies: the future is seen as taking place in front of the prophet's eyes:

(84) τότ᾽ ἐλεύθερον Ἑλλάδος ἦμαρ | εὐρύοπα Κρονίδης <u>ἐπάγει</u> καὶ πότνια Νίκη. (Hdt. 8.77.2)

At that time, far-seeing Zeus and mighty Victory shall bring the day of freedom for Greece. *The conclusion of an oracle, as reported by Herodotus.*

Aspect Outside the Indicative in Main Clauses

Aspect and Relative Tense

33.57   Greek verb forms, other than those of the future stem, **do not inherently express relative tense**. However, in a number of subordinate constructions, **anteriority or simultaneity is conventionally implied** by the use of a form of a certain tense-aspect stem, by virtue of the aspect expressed by that form. Aspect tends to lead to a relative-tense interpretation when there is a clear, fixed point of reference given by the verb in the matrix clause:

- with finite verb forms (indicatives, subjunctives and optatives) in **temporal clauses** (→47), **causal clauses** (→48), **conditional clauses** (→49), **and relative clauses** (→50);
- with the **oblique optative in indirect speech and thought** (→41.9); time relative to the moment of speech/thought);
- with the **declarative infinitive** (→51.25–6; time relative to the moment of speech/thought);
- with **participles** (→52.4).

In such cases:

- **present**-stem forms, by virtue of their imperfective aspect ('not-complete'), tend to suggest that the action is not-complete *relative to the action in the matrix clause* (normally the main verb, →39.2–4), i.e. they imply **simultaneity**;
- **perfect**-stem forms, too, by referring to an ongoing state or ongoing effects (resulting from a preceding action), imply **simultaneity**;
- **aorist**-stem forms, by virtue of their perfective aspect ('complete'), tend to suggest that the action is complete *relative to the action in the matrix clause*, i.e. they imply **anteriority**;
- **future** forms always express **posteriority**.

Note 1: For the temporal interpretation of the indicative in indirect speech/thought and indirect perception/knowledge/emotion, →41.8, 41.10, 41.14, 41.15.

Some examples:

(85) ἐπεὶ δὲ πορευόμενοι ἐκ τοῦ πεδίου <u>ἀνέβησαν</u> ἐπὶ τὸν πρῶτον γήλοφον καὶ <u>κατέβαινον</u> . . . , ἐνταῦθα ἐπιγίγνονται οἱ βάρβαροι. (Xen. *An.* 3.4.25)
And when, during their march out of the plain, they had ascended onto the first hill and were descending it, at that moment the foreigners attacked them. *The main verb ἐπιγίγνονται (a historical present, →33.54) refers to an action in the past; in the temporal clause introduced by ἐπεί, aor. ind. ἀνέβησαν is anterior to that action, impf. (i.e. present-stem) κατέβαινον is simultaneous with it.*

(86) χρὴ δέ, ὅταν μὲν <u>τιθῆσθε</u> τοὺς νόμους, ὁποῖοί τινές εἰσιν σκοπεῖν, ἐπειδὰν δὲ <u>θῆσθε</u>, φυλάττειν καὶ χρῆσθαι. (Dem. 21.34)

When you are instituting the laws, you should carefully look at what sort of laws they are, but once you have instituted them, you should safeguard them and abide by them. *The present subjunctive* τιθῆσθε *expresses the institution of the laws in process, i.e. as an action simultaneous with* σκοπεῖν; *the aorist subjunctive* θῆσθε *in the second temporal clause is anterior to* φυλάττειν *and* χρῆσθαι *(procedures to be followed once the laws have been put in place).*

(87) <u>ὀμόσας</u> μὴ <u>λαβεῖν</u> δῶρα μηδὲ <u>λήψεσθαι</u> . . . εἰληφὼς ἠλέγχθη . . . εἴκοσι μνᾶς. (Aeschin. 1.114–15)

Although he had sworn that he neither had taken bribes nor would take them, it was proven that he was guilty of accepting twenty minae. *The declarative infinitives* λαβεῖν *(aor.) and* λήψεσθαι *(fut.) refer to actions which are anterior and posterior, respectively, to the moment of swearing* (ὀμόσας). *The aor. ppl.* ὀμόσας *itself implies that the action of promising took place before* ἠλέγχθη.

(88) (ἀδικοῦσι) τοὺς ἢ <u>πεποιηκότας</u> κακῶς ἢ <u>βουληθέντας</u> ἢ <u>βουλομένους</u> ἢ <u>ποιήσοντας</u>. (Arist. *Rh.* 1373a13–14)

They commit crimes against those who are responsible for mistreating them, or those who have intended to do so, or those who are intending to do so, or who are about to do so. *The participles all refer to actions whose time is relative to that of* ἀδικοῦσι: *respectively simultaneous* (πεποιηκότας; *for the translation,* →33.35), *anterior (aor.* βουληθέντας), *simultaneous (pres.* βουλομένους) *and posterior (fut.* ποιήσοντας).

Further Interpretations; Exceptions

33.58 The relative-tense interpretation which attaches to the forms listed above is a conventional one, but not a necessary one. In many cases, a choice of a specific tense stem leads to interpretations in addition to, or other than, that of a relative-tense relationship to the matrix verb. Some examples of such 'exceptions' are given below; for further discussion and examples, →51.26 with n.1 (declarative infinitives) and 52.4–5 (participles).

33.59 Rather than implying anteriority (only), **aorist-stem forms** may be **ingressive** (→33.29) or **complexive** (→33.30):

(89) ἐπειδὴ δὲ Θησεὺς <u>ἐβασίλευσε</u>, . . . διεκόσμησε τὴν χώραν. (Thuc. 2.15.2)

When Theseus had become king, he organized the country. *Aorist indicative in temporal clause with ingressive interpretation; note that the implication of anteriority still holds.*

(90) πολλοὶ γὰρ καὶ χρημάτων δυνάμενοι φείδεσθαι πρὶν ἐρᾶν, <u>ἐρασθέντες</u> οὐκέτι δύνανται. (Xen. *Mem.* 1.2.22)

Many, after all, who are able to be careful with their money before they love, after falling in love are no longer able to do so. *Ingressive aorist participle. Again, the implication of anteriority still holds.*

Participles, in particular, sometimes express an action which is not anterior to that of the matrix verb, but overlaps with it entirely (from beginning to end). This is called the **coincident** use of the aorist participle:

(91) ἀπώλεσέν μ' <u>εἰποῦσα</u> συμφορὰς ἐμάς. (Eur. *Hipp.* 596)

She has destroyed me by speaking of my troubles. *Both actions (ἀπώλεσεν and εἰποῦσα) coincide and are presented in their entirety.*

For more examples of coincident aorist participles, →52.5.

33.60   **Present-stem forms** may, rather than being simultaneous (only), refer to actions which are presented as **ongoing or repeated**, invite a **conative** interpretation (→33.17) or, with certain verbs, be **resultative** (→33.18):

(92) πρότερον γὰρ οὐκ <u>ἔχων</u> πρόφασιν ἐφ' ἧς τοῦ βίου λόγον δοίην, νυνὶ διὰ τοῦτον εἴληφα. (Lys. 24.1)

For although in the past I had no excuse on account of which I could give an account of my life, I have got one now, because of this man. *Present participle referring to an ongoing action anterior to the matrix verb (note πρότερον, which rules out a simultaneous interpretation, and νῦν). The participle in such cases is sometimes called an 'imperfect participle'.*

(93) τίνας οὖν εὐχὰς ὑπολαμβάνετ' <u>εὔχεσθαι</u> τοῖς θεοῖς τὸν Φίλιππον, ὅτ' ἔσπενδεν, ἢ τοὺς Θηβαίους; (Dem. 19.130)

What prayers do you suppose Philip made to the gods, when he made his libation, or the Thebans? *The present infinitive presents an action which is anterior to the matrix verb ὑπολαμβάνετε, as is shown by ὅτ' ἔσπενδεν. It presents the action of praying as a process (note that Demosthenes, through τίνας εὐχάς, appears to ask about its constituent parts). A corresponding direct speech would have impf. ηὔχετο.*

(94) ὅστις δ' ἀφικνεῖτο τῶν παρὰ βασιλέως πρὸς αὐτὸν πάντας οὕτω <u>διατιθεὶς</u> ἀπεπέμπετο ὥστε αὐτῷ μᾶλλον φίλους εἶναι ἢ βασιλεῖ. (Xen. *An.* 1.1.5)

Whoever came to him from the king, he always treated all of them in such a way that they were more devoted to him than to the king, and then sent them away. *Present participle referring to a repeated action. διατιθείς is not necessarily simultaneous with ἀπεπέμπετο.*

(95) οὕτω μὲν ἑκάτεροι <u>νικᾶν</u> ἠξίουν. (Thuc. 1.55.1)

In this way, both sides claimed victory. *Declarative infinitive with resultative meaning ('that they had won'), specific to the verb νικάω.*

33.61 **Perfect-stem forms** of some verbs may be '**present-like**' (→33.36) or **intensive** (→33.37), in addition to indicating simultaneity:

(96) ὁ δὲ Σιλανὸς <u>δεδιὼς</u> μὴ γένηται ταῦτα . . . ἐκφέρει εἰς τὸ στράτευμα λόγον ὅτι . . . (Xen. *An.* 5.6.17)

Silanus, afraid that this might happen, carried a report to the camp, that . . . *'Present-like' perfect participle.*

(97) ΣΩ. οὐκοῦν ἐὰν μὲν οὗτος ἐμμένῃ, <u>γεγηθὼς</u> ἀπέρχεται ἐκ τοῦ θεάτρου ὁ ποιητής· ἐὰν δὲ ἐξαλειφθῇ . . . πενθεῖ αὐτός τε καὶ οἱ ἑταῖροι. :: ΦΑ. καὶ μάλα. :: ΣΩ. δῆλόν γε ὅτι οὐχ ὡς ὑπερφρονοῦντες τοῦ ἐπιτηδεύματος, ἀλλ᾽ ὡς <u>τεθαυμακότες</u>. (Pl. *Phdr.* 258b)

(Socrates:) Isn't it the case that if this motion is carried, the author leaves the theatre greatly pleased, but if it is stricken, he himself and his friends are aggrieved? :: (Phaedrus:) Certainly :: (Socrates:) Obviously not because they look down on the pursuit, but because they greatly admire it. *Intensive perfect participles.*

33.62 Finally, **future-stem forms always express posteriority**, but may have additional nuances such as **result, purpose**, or **likelihood**, particularly in relative clauses and participles (also →50.24–5, 52.41, 52.49 n.1):

(98) καὶ αὐτῶν μία μὲν ἐς Πελοπόννησον ᾤχετο, πρέσβεις ἄγουσα οἵπερ τὰ . . . σφέτερα <u>φράσουσιν</u> ὅτι ἐν ἐλπίσιν εἰσί. (Thuc. 7.25.1)

One of these (*ships*) went to the Peloponnese, carrying ambassadors who were to describe the hopeful state of their affairs. *The future indicative in a relative clause expresses purpose.*

(99) τοῖς στρατηγοῖς τὸ μὲν ἐνθύμημα χαρίεν ἐδόκει εἶναι, τὸ δ᾽ ἔργον ἀδύνατον· ἦσαν γὰρ <u>οἱ κωλύσοντες</u> πέραν πολλοὶ ἱππεῖς, οἳ εὐθὺς τοῖς πρώτοις οὐδὲν ἂν ἐπέτρεπον τούτων ποιεῖν. (Xen. *An.* 3.5.12)

It seemed to the generals that the plan was appealing but impossible in practice; for there were people on the other side (*of the river*) who would stop them, many horsemen, who would immediately prevent even the first comers from carrying out any part of the plan. *The future participle (with article) expresses likelihood/ability.*

Aspectual Interpretation in Temporally Fixed Contexts

33.63 There are many constructions, both in main and subordinate clauses, which have a **fixed temporal reference**, in particular an **absolute or relative future reference**. For instance, an imperative like '*Close the door*' necessarily expresses an action which is located in the future (the door is not closed yet at the moment of speech). An expression of purpose such as 'He closed the door in order to *have privacy*' necessarily refers to a situation (having privacy) which is located after the action expressed in the matrix verb (closing the door; for the term 'matrix verb', →39.2–4).

33.64   In Greek, the following constructions necessarily refer to the **future**:

- the imperative (→34.19);
- hortatory subjunctive, prohibitive subjunctive, and deliberative subjunctive (→34.6–8);
- the optative in realizable wishes (→34.14);
- (usually) the potential optative (→34.13).

The following subordinate constructions refer to actions which are for the most part **posterior** to that of the matrix verb:

- (most) fear clauses (→43);
- effort clauses (→44);
- purpose clauses (→45);
- (most) result clauses (→46);
- most dynamic infinitives (after verbs meaning 'command', 'want', etc., →51.8–17).

33.65   In each of these constructions, both present-stem and aorist-stem forms may be used (perfect-stem forms are considerably more rare). As the temporal reference of the verb form used in such constructions is predetermined by the construction itself, the different stems are in **aspectual opposition only**. The choice for one form or the other depends on the speaker's subjective choices in presenting an action as complete or incomplete, given various possible connotations of these two aspects (repeated vs. single actions, general procedures vs. specific instances, ongoing/interruptable processes vs. uninterruptable actions, etc., as well as interpretations such as 'conative', 'ingressive', 'complexive', etc.):

(100)   σκοπεῖτε δὴ καὶ λογίσασθ' ἐν ὑμῖν αὐτοῖς, εἰ ... (Dem. 20.87)
         Consider the case and decide for yourselves, whether ... *The jurors are invited to engage in a process of deliberation (present imperative) and then to reach a single, definitive conclusion (aorist imperative).*

(101)   εἴπωμεν ἢ σιγῶμεν; (Eur. *Ion* 757)
         Should we speak up or keep quiet? *Deliberative subjunctives, both referring to a possible action in the future: the aorist subjunctive εἴπωμεν expresses a single action presented as a complete whole, namely a single utterance the speaker could make which would irrevocably interrupt the continuous silence (present subjunctive σιγῶμεν).*

(102) δεήσεται δ' ὑμῶν οὗτος μὲν ὑπὲρ τῆς μητρός ... ὅπως δίκην μὴ <u>δῷ</u> ... · ἐγὼ δ' ὑμᾶς ὑπὲρ τοῦ πατρὸς τοὐμοῦ τεθνεῶτος αἰτοῦμαι, ὅπως παντὶ τρόπῳ <u>δῷ</u>· ὑμεῖς δέ, ὅπως <u>διδῷ</u> δίκην οἱ ἀδικοῦντες, τούτου γε ἕνεκα καὶ δικασταὶ ἐγένεσθε καὶ ἐκλήθητε. (Antiph. 1.23)

This man will plead with you, on behalf of his mother, so that she may not be punished. But I ask you, for the sake of my dead father, that she may by all means be punished. And you have become and been called judges for this very reason: so that wrongdoers may be punished. *Subjunctives in purpose clauses (introduced by ὅπως, →45.2–3). The speaker twice uses the aorist subjunctive (δίκην) δῷ to refer to a single, concrete instance of punishment, without regard for the process or duration of these instances. However, he uses the present subjunctive διδῷ δίκην to refer to the punishment that criminals should face in general (as a repeated procedure, with no regard to its end-point).*

(103) καὶ δὴ σφι πρὸς ταῦτα <u>ἔδοξε</u> τῷ κήρυκι τῶν πολεμίων <u>χρᾶσθαι</u>, δόξαν δέ σφι ἐποίευν τοιόνδε· ὅκως ὁ Σπαρτιήτης κῆρυξ προσημαίνοι τι Λακεδαιμονίοισι, ἐποίευν καὶ οἱ Ἀργεῖοι τὠυτὸ τοῦτο. (Hdt. 6.77.3)

Therefore, in the face of this they decided to make use of the enemies' herald, and they carried out their decision in the following way: whenever the Spartiate herald signalled anything to the Spartans, the Argives did the same.

(104) ἅμα ἡμέρῃ δὲ ἐς λόγους προεκαλέετο τοὺς Βαρκαίους. οἱ δὲ ἀσπαστῶς ὑπήκουσαν, ἐς ὃ σφι <u>ἕαδε</u> ὁμολογίη <u>χρήσασθαι</u>. τὴν δὲ ὁμολογίην ἐποιεῦντο τοιήνδε τινά, ... (Hdt. 4.201.2)

When day came, he invited the Barcaeans to talks. They readily consented, (and they talked) until they decided to come to an agreement. The agreement they made was something like this, ...

The present infinitive χρᾶσθαι in (103) refers to a line of conduct, to be carried out in repeated actions. The aorist infinitive χρήσασθαι in (104) by contrast, receives an ingressive interpretation, in that it refers to the reaching of an agreement.

Also cf. (6)–(7) above.

Note 1: Observe that, despite the fact that these constructions normally have a future/ posterior reference, future stem forms are not used. The main exception are 'effort clauses', which also necessarily have a posterior time reference, but are construed with a future indicative (or optative); →44. For the use of the future infinitive after ἐλπίζω *hope, expect*, ὑπισχνέομαι *promise*, and ὄμνυμι *swear, state under oath*, →51.31.

Note 2: Perfect-stem forms are rare in each of these constructions, apart from forms of verbs which typically occur only in the perfect stem (such as οἶδα; →33.36). When perfect forms do appear, the stem has its typical aspectual value(s), for which →33.6–7, 33.34–5. For the perfect imperative, also →34.21.

33.66 For further discussion and examples, →38.30 (imperatives and subjunctives in commands), 38.41 (wishes), 51.15 (dynamic infinitives).

34

The Verb: Mood

Introduction to Moods

34.1 A distinction should be drawn between moods as they are **used in main clauses** and moods which are grammatically required in various types of subordinate clause. The moods used in subordinate clauses are treated in 40.5–16 and in the relevant chapters, 41–50. An overview of all uses of moods is provided in 54.

34.2 The various moods of the Greek verb are used **in main clauses** to express different **communicative functions** (for more on this, →38) and different **attitudes** on the part of the speaker towards an action, in terms of its reality or desirability. For example:

(1) καλὸν τὸ πῶμα δαιτὶ πρὸς καλῇ <u>δίδως</u>. (Eur. *Cyc.* 419)
 You offer me a fine drink on top of a fine meal. *δίδως = 2 sg. pres.* <u>*indicative*</u> *act.: the speaker* <u>*states*</u>, *asserts that the addressee is giving.*

(2) πλέων δὲ τὸν σκύφον <u>δίδου</u> μόνον. (Eur. *Cyc.* 556)
 Just give me the cup when it is full. *δίδου = 2 sg. pres.* <u>*imperative*</u> *act.: the speaker* <u>*orders*</u> *the addressee to give.*

(3) ὦ Ζεῦ, <u>διδοίης</u> τοῖσι τοιούτοισιν εὖ. (Soph. *OC* 642)
 Zeus, may you provide such men well. *διδοίης = 2 sg. pres.* <u>*optative*</u> *act.: the speaker* <u>*wishes*</u>, *hopes that the addressee may give.*

34.3 The nuances expressed by an individual mood in a main clause depend on various factors:

  – the **type of sentence** in which the verb stands (declarative, interrogative, directive, →38.1);
  – the presence of the **modal particle** ἄν (→34.4);
  – the presence of a **negative** (οὐ, μή);
  – the **person** of the verb (first, second, third);
  – the **tense/aspect** of the verb;
  – other **contextual** factors.

34.4 Several of the Greek moods may be combined with the **modal particle** ἄν. The precise function of this particle varies depending on the mood with which it is combined (for an overview, →55). **In main clauses**, the basic function of constructions with ἄν is to qualify the **likelihood** of the realization of the action. For example:

(4) τοσούτῳ δ' ἂν δικαιότερον οὗτος ἀποθάνοι τῶν ἐκ τῶν στρατοπέδων φευγόντων. (Lycurg. 1.131)

This man would die that much more justly than those who have deserted the camp. *Optative + ἄν; potential construction, →34.13; it is (still) possible that the action will occur.*

(5) εἰ τὸ καὶ τὸ ἐποίησεν ἄνθρωπος οὑτοσί, οὐκ ἂν ἀπέθανεν. (Dem. 18.243)

If this man had done this or that, he would not have died. *Indicative + ἄν; counterfactual construction, →34.16; it is no longer possible for the action to be undone, i.e. not to occur.*

Note 1: ἄν is not combined with the primary indicative, imperative, or future optative. For subj. + ἄν in subordinate clauses, →40.7–9; for inf. + ἄν, →51.27; for ppl. + ἄν, →52.7.

Indicative in Main Clauses

34.5 The **indicative** is used in **statements and assertions of fact** (or expressions of belief presented as fact), and **questions about facts**, concerning actions in the past, present or future. For details of the use of the different tenses of the indicative, →33.11–55. For the indicative used in interrogatives to express requests, commands or suggestions (οὐ + second-person fut. ind.; (τί) οὐ + first- or second-person pres./aor. ind.), →38.32–3.

For the 'modal indicative' (in counterfactual statements and unrealizable wishes), →34.15–18.

Subjunctive in Main Clauses

Hortatory and Prohibitive Subjunctive (in Commands/Requests)

34.6 **Hortatory subjunctive:** in the **first person** (usually plural), the subjunctive is used both in positive commands and negative commands (with μή):

(6) ἀλλ' ἴωμεν ἐς δόμους. (Eur. *El.* 787)
But let us go into the palace.

(7) ἴδωμεν δὴ εἴ τι λέγουσιν. (Pl. *Chrm.* 159b)
Let us see if there is something in what they say.

(8) καὶ μὴ περιίδωμεν ὑβρισθεῖσαν τὴν Λακεδαίμονα. (Isoc. 6.108)
And let us not overlook the fact that Sparta has been humiliated.

34.7 **Prohibitive subjunctive:** in the second, and occasionally the third, person, to express a prohibition the **aorist subjunctive** with μή is used (not the aor. imp.; in the present stem prohibitions are expressed by μή + imp., →38.26):

(9) μὴ οὖν προδόται γένησθε ὑμῶν αὐτῶν. (Thuc. 3.40.7)
Do not, then, become traitors to your own cause.

(10) ἀλλὰ μή μ' ἀφῇς | ἐρῆμον. (Soph. Phil. 486–7)

No, don't leave me behind alone.

Deliberative Subjunctive (in Questions)

34.8   The **deliberative** (or 'dubitative') **subjunctive**: first-person subjunctives are used in questions, to express doubt about what action to take (in specifying questions, →38.4), or whether or not to proceed with a certain action (in yes/no-questions and alternative questions, →38.4). The negative is μή:

(11) οἴμοι, τί δράσω; ποῖ φύγω μητρὸς χέρας; (Eur. Med. 1271)

Woe, what should I do? Where should I flee from my mother's hands?

(12) πότερον βίαν φῶμεν ἢ μὴ φῶμεν εἶναι; (Xen. Mem. 1.2.45)

Are we to call this violence, or aren't we?

Note 1: The deliberative subjunctive is also used in indirect questions, →42.8.

Note 2: In dialogue, deliberative subjunctives are sometimes introduced by βούλει/βούλεσθε or θέλεις do you want . . . ; in such cases the speaker asks the addressee whether he/she should do something:

(13) βούλεσθε δῆτα κοινῇ | σκώψωμεν Ἀρχέδημον; (Ar. Ran. 416–17)

If you want, shall we make fun of Archedemus together?

Further Particulars

34.9   The combination **οὐ μή + subjunctive** expresses an **emphatic denial**, a strong belief that something will not be the case:

(14) κοὐ μή ποτέ σου παρὰ τὰς κάννας οὐρήσω μηδ' ἀποπάρδω. (Ar. Vesp. 394)

And I'll never ever piss or fart on your fence.

(15) οὐ μὴ πίθηται. (Soph. Phil. 103)

He will certainly not obey.

34.10   The combination **μή + subjunctive** (the construction of fear clauses, →43) is sometimes used in independent sentences to express an anxious, cautious or **tentative assertion** (negative μὴ οὐ). This occurs primarily in Plato:

(16) μὴ ἀγροικότερον ᾖ τὸ ἀληθὲς εἰπεῖν. (Pl. Grg. 462e)

I suspect it's too rude to tell the truth.

(17) ἀλλὰ μὴ οὐ τοῦτ' ᾖ χαλεπόν, ὦ ἄνδρες, θάνατον ἐκφυγεῖν, ἀλλὰ πολὺ χαλεπώτερον πονηρίαν. (Pl. Ap. 39a)

But, gentlemen, the difficult thing is perhaps not to escape death; rather it may be much more difficult to escape wickedness.

34.11   The difference between the use of present and aorist subjunctives in each of the constructions above is purely one of aspect, →33.63–5, 38.30. The perfect subjunctive is rarely used in these constructions (but the perfect has its normal aspectual value(s) when it is, e.g. μεμνώμεθα *let us remember*, hortatory pf. subj.).

34.12 In classical Greek (unlike in Homer) the subjunctive is not used together with ἄν in main clauses, only in subordinate clauses. For the uses of ἄν + subjunctive in subordinate clauses, →40.7–9.

Optative in Main Clauses

Potential Optative with ἄν (in Statements/Questions)

34.13 The **optative with ἄν** is used to indicate that the realization of an action is possible: the **potential construction**. This construction is used to express a range of nuances:

- to describe actions that **might hypothetically occur**, or to make a **weak assertion** (i.e. to state something more cautiously than with the indicative):

(18) εἰ δοίητε ὑμέας αὐτοὺς βασιλέϊ . . . ἕκαστος ἂν ὑμέων ἄρχοι γῆς Ἑλλάδος δόντος βασιλέος. (Hdt. 7.135.2)
Should you deliver yourselves to the king, each of you would rule over land in Greece at the bequest of the king. *For the combination with εἰ + opt.* →49.8–9.

(19) ἀρετὴ μὲν ἄρα, ὡς ἔοικεν, ὑγίειά τέ τις ἂν εἴη καὶ κάλλος καὶ εὐεξία ψυχῆς. (Pl. *Resp.* 444d)
Virtue, then, would – as it appears – be a kind of health and beauty and good condition of the soul.

(20) γνοίης δ' ἂν ὅτι τοῦθ' οὕτως ἔχει. (Xen. *Cyr.* 1.6.21)
You might/could/may acknowledge that this is so.

- the negative potential optative (with οὐ) expresses an **emphatic negation**: it is not even possible that the action could occur:

(21) πρὸς βίαν δ' οὐκ ἂν λάβοις. (Soph. *Phil.* 103)
You can never take him by force.

- the second-person potential optative can express a **cautious command or request**; the first-person potential optative can indicate that someone cautiously takes **permission** to do something, or complies with an order or request:

(22) λέγοις ἂν εἴ τι τῶνδ' ἔχεις ὑπέρτερον. | :: . . . | λέξω, κελεύεις γάρ, τὸν ἐκ φρενὸς λόγον. (Aesch. *Cho.* 105–7)
If you have a better way than this, please explain it (*lit. 'you might say it'*). :: I will voice my inmost thoughts, since you bid me to. *Note κελεύεις, which makes clear that the potential optative is felt to be a request.*

(23) ΜΕ. λέγ'· . . . . :: ΟΡ. λέγοιμ' ἂν ἤδη. (Eur. *Or.* 638–40)
(Menelaus:) Speak . . . :: (Orestes:) I will go ahead and speak, then. *Note imperative λέγ', to which λέγοιμ' ἂν is a reaction.*

Note 1: The difference between the use of present, aorist and (much less frequently) perfect optatives in the potential construction is purely aspectual, →33.63–5.

Cupitive Optative (in Wishes)

34.14   The **optative without ἄν** is used in wishes (**cupitive optative**), often with εἴθε, εἰ γάρ or ὡς. The negative is μή:

(24) εἰ γὰρ γενοίμην, τέκνον, ἀντὶ σοῦ νεκρός. (Eur. *Hipp.* 1410)
        May I die (*lit. 'become a corpse'*) in your place, child.

(25) ὦ παῖ, γένοιο πατρὸς εὐτυχέστερος, | τὰ δ' ἄλλ' ὁμοῖος. (Soph. *Aj.* 550–1)
        Child, I wish that you become more fortunate than your father, but equal in all other respects.

(26) μὴ πλείω κακὰ | πάθοιεν. (Soph. *Ant.* 928–9)
        May they suffer no more evil.

Note 1: For an overview of constructions used to express various kinds of wishes, →38.38–42.
Note 2: The difference between the use of present and aorist optatives in wishes is purely aspectual, →33.63–5.
   The perfect optative is rarely used in wishes, but has its normal aspectual value(s) when it is (e.g. τεθναίην *I wish I were dead*).

'Modal' (Secondary) Indicative in Main Clauses

34.15   The **secondary indicative** – i.e. the indicative of past tenses (with an augment): imperfect, aorist or pluperfect – is used in various constructions, some with ἄν and some without, to express **counterfactual** actions (or 'contrary-to-fact', 'unreal'). The indicative in these uses is called **modal**.

In Statements/Questions

34.16   The secondary **indicative with ἄν** is used in statements or questions to indicate that an action would occur or would have occurred under certain conditions which are/were *not* met. The conditions may be expressed by a conditional εἰ-clause (→49.10), a participle (→52.40), an adverb, or left unexpressed:

(27) ἔπραξαν ἄν ταῦτα, εἰ μὴ ὑπ' Ἀγοράτου τουτουὶ ἀπώλοντο. (Lys. 13.16)
        They would have done these things, if they had not been destroyed by this man Agoratus (*but they have been*).

(28) εἰ μὴ πατὴρ ἦσθ', εἶπον ἄν σ' οὐκ εὖ φρονεῖν. (Soph. *Ant.* 755)
        If you were not my father (*but you are*), I would say that you are out of your mind.

(29) καὶ μὴ γενομένης μὲν κρίσεως περὶ τοῦ πράγματος ἑάλω ἄν. (Aeschin. 1.85)
        Even if there had not been a trial about the matter (*but there is a trial*), he would have been convicted.

(30) τότε δὲ αὐτὸ τὸ πρᾶγμα ἄν ἐκρίνετο ἐφ' αὑτοῦ. (Dem. 18.224)
        At that time, the matter would be judged on its own merits.

With a negative (οὐ), this construction expresses that (even) if certain conditions were/had been met, the action would *not* occur/have occurred:

(31) μὴ κατηγορήσαντος Αἰσχίνου μηδὲν ἔξω τῆς γραφῆς <u>οὐδ' ἂν</u> ἐγὼ λόγον <u>οὐδένα</u> ἐποιούμην ἕτερον. (Dem. 18.34)

If Aeschines had not gone beyond the written indictment in his accusation (*but he has*), I would not be making a single other argument.

(32) σίγησε δ' αἰθήρ ... θηρῶν δ' <u>οὐκ ἂν ἤκουσας</u> βοήν. (Eur. *Bacch.* 1084–5)

The air fell silent, and you would not have heard the shout of wild animals (*if you had been there, but you weren't*).

Note 1: The term 'counterfactual' should not be taken to mean that the action expressed by the indicative + ἄν is itself necessarily contrary to reality: in the case of (29), for instance, the accused does in fact get convicted; in (32), the addressee in fact did not hear the shouts of animals. Rather, the *conditions under which* the action would have occurred are contrary to fact.

In most cases, however, it is *implied* that the action expressed by indicative + ἄν is itself also contrary to fact: this is the case, for instance, in (27) (they did in fact not succeed), (30) (the matter was in fact not decided on its own merits), and (31) (Demosthenes is in fact digressing). In some cases, by extension, the counterfactual construction is used *to argue that* the conditions under which the action would have occurred must be contrary to fact, since the action expressed by the indicative + ἄν did not occur:

(33) καίτοι οὗτοι, εἰ ἦσαν ἄνδρες ἀγαθοί, ὡς σὺ φής, οὐκ <u>ἂν</u> ποτε ταῦτα <u>ἔπασχον</u>. (Pl. *Grg.* 516e)

And yet these men, if they had been good men – as you claim – would never have suffered these things (*but they did suffer those things, so they cannot have been good men*).

Note 2: Examples such as (32) are often considered a distinct type (the so-called 'past potential') in grammars – a translation with 'could/might (not)' is possible. This occurs most often in cases with a generic or second-person subject, and in questions (e.g. τί ἂν ἐποίησεν; *what could he have done?*). There is no real difference between such cases and other counterfactual statements: the conditions under which a certain action would *or could* occur are not realized.

Note 3: The difference between the imperfect and the aorist indicative in this construction is one of aspect. In practice, the aorist indicative usually refers to something which would have happened in the past (cf. (27), (29), (32), but contrast (28)), while the imperfect usually refers to something which would be occurring in the present (cf. (31)), less frequently in the past (cf. (30), (33)).

The pluperfect indicative is much less frequently used, but tends to refer to a state which would exist in the present under certain counterfactual conditions:

(34) μὴ γὰρ ὁμολογούντων τῶν ἀνδραπόδων οὗτός τ' εὖ εἰδὼς ἂν ἀπελογεῖτο ... καὶ ἡ μήτηρ αὐτοῦ <u>ἀπήλλακτο ἂν</u> ταύτης τῆς αἰτίας. (Antiph. 1.8)

If the slaves had denied this, he would be mounting his defence based on sure knowledge, and his mother would be clear (*would (already) have been cleared*) of this charge.

34.17   In some types of statement with a counterfactual nuance, ἄν is omitted:

– The **imperfect** of **impersonal verbs** expressing **necessity, obligation**, or **appropriateness** (e.g. ἔδει, (ἐ)χρῆν, καλῶς εἶχε, etc.) can be used **without ἄν** to indicate that an action contrary to the one occurring is or was required:

(35) ἔδει τὰ ἐνέχυρα τότε λαβεῖν. (Xen. *An.* 7.6.23)

We ought to have taken the fortified positions then (*but we didn't*).

(36) εἶεν, τί σιγᾷς; οὐκ ἐχρῆν σιγᾶν, τέκνον. (Eur. *Hipp.* 297)

Well now, why do you keep silent? You shouldn't be silent, my child (*but you are*).

- The first-person imperfect **ἐβουλόμην** *I would want/would have wanted* is normally used **without ἄν**, referring to a desire for an action which does not/did not occur:

(37) ἐβουλόμην ... τὴν βουλὴν τοὺς πεντακοσίους ... ὑπὸ τῶν ἐφεστηκότων ὀρθῶς διοικεῖσθαι· (Aeschin. 3.2)

I would wish that the Council of the Five Hundred were properly conducted by those who preside over them (*but it isn't*).

- The **imperfect of μέλλω** *be about/going to* (+ inf., →51.33) can be used **without ἄν** to refer to an action bound or likely to happen in a given counterfactual scenario:

(38) ἔτι δὲ καὶ ἡ ἑτέρα θυγάτηρ ἀνέκδοτος ἔμελλεν ἔσεσθαι· τίς γὰρ ἄν ποτε ... ἔλαβεν ἄπροικον; ([Dem.] 59.8)

Moreover, his other daughter would have been likely to remain unmarried. For who would ever have taken a woman without a dowry?

Note 1: In the first two of these uses, the necessity/obligation (ἔδει, (ἐ)χρῆν, etc.) or desire (ἐβουλόμην) itself does/did exist, but its 'target' is/was not realized: in (35) the fortified positions were not taken, in (36) Phaedra is silent; in (37) the Council is not properly presided over.

When imperfects such as ἔδει are themselves combined with ἄν, this indicates that the necessity or obligation *itself* does/did not exist (i.e. these are 'regular' counterfactuals):

(39) εἰ μέν που ἦσαν πεπαιδευμένοι, ἔδει ἄν τὸν ἐπιχειροῦντα αὐτοῖς ἀνταγωνίζεσθαι ... ἰέναι ὡς ἐπ' ἀθλητάς. (Pl. *Alc.* 1.119b)

I suppose that if they were well-educated, anyone attempting to contend against them would need to go as if against athletes (*but they aren't well-educated, so there's no need*).

Note 2: Observe that these uses may refer to counterfactual scenarios either in the present, as in (36)–(37), or the past, as in (35) and (38).

In Unrealizable Wishes

34.18   The secondary indicative is used **without ἄν**, but always together with either **εἴθε** or **εἰ γάρ**, to express **unrealizable wishes** (for something desirable that can no longer occur, also →38.39, with n.1). The negative is μή:

(40) εἰ γὰρ τοσαύτην δύναμιν εἶχον. (Eur. *Alc.* 1072)

Would that I had such power (*but I don't*).

(41) εἴθε σοι, ὦ Περίκλεις, τότε συνεγενόμην. (Xen. *Mem.* 1.2.46)

If only, Pericles, I had met you then (*but I didn't*).

(42) εἴθε σ᾽ εἴθε σε | μήποτ᾽ εἰδόμαν. (Soph. *OT* 1217–18)

Would, would that I had never seen you (*but I did*). For εἰδόμαν (= εἰδόμην),
→*25.46–7*.

Note 1: The distinction between aorist indicatives and imperfects in such wishes is one of
aspect. In practice, the aorist indicative is used in unrealizable wishes about the past, as in
(41)–(42), the imperfect usually in wishes about the present, as in (40), sometimes in wishes
about the past. The pluperfect seems not to be used in unrealizable wishes.

Note 2: Unrealizable wishes may also be expressed by a form of ὤφελον + inf. For this
construction and all other possible constructions of wishes, →*38.38–42*.

Imperative

34.19   The imperative mood is used in **second- or third-person directives** (commands,
requests, etc.). The negative (for **prohibitions**) is μή:

(43) ταῦτά μοι <u>πρᾶξον</u>, τέκνον, | καὶ <u>μὴ βράδυνε</u>. (Soph. *Phil.* 1399–1400)

Do this for me, child, and do not delay.

(44) <u>λεγέτω</u> εἴ τι ἔχει τοιοῦτον. (Pl. *Ap.* 34a)

Let him say if he has something of that nature.

In second-person prohibitions, the imperative is used only in the present stem (the
prohibitive subjunctive is used for prohibitions with the aorist stem, →*38.26*): thus
†μὴ ποίησον (with aor. imp.) is not used.

34.20   The imperative can express a variety of nuances: peremptory commands, polite
requests, suggestions, etc. Such nuances depend on the content of the directive and
on the context in which it is uttered (the relative authority/status of the speaker
and addressee, their relationship, the level of imposition on the addressee inherent
in the requested action, etc.). The Greek imperative is thus not inherently impolite.

In some cases, the nuance expressed by an imperative is not properly directive:

– in expressions of (often sarcastic) **concession** or **resignation**:

(45) ἐξημπόλημαι κἀκπεφόρτισμαι πάλαι. | <u>κερδαίνετ᾽</u> . . . εἰ βούλεσθε . . . | τάφῳ δ᾽
ἐκεῖνον οὐχὶ κρύψετε. (Soph. *Ant.* 1036–9)

I have long been sold out and traded away. Well, go on making your profit, if
you want: you will not bury him!

– in **greetings** (specifically imperatives of χαίρω: χαῖρε/χαίρετε *hello/goodbye*,
χαιρέτω *farewell to him*, etc.) and **curses** (e.g. βάλλ᾽ ἐς κόρακας *go to hell!*).

Also →*38.2*.

Note 1: For an overview of constructions used to express commands, directions,
exhortations, etc., and for the differences between such constructions, →*38.25–37*.

34.21   The difference between present and aorist imperatives is purely one of aspect, →33.63–5, 38.30.

The perfect imperative occurs infrequently, except with a few isolated verbs (ἴσθι with οἶδα *know*, μέμνησο with μέμνημαι *remember*), and in the third person passive. The perfect has its normal aspectual value(s) in the imperative:

(46) ἀλλὰ περὶ μὲν τούτων τοσαῦτά μοι εἰρήσθω· πάλιν δ' ἐπάνειμι ὅθεν ἀπέλιπον. (Isae. 5.12)
But concerning these topics, this much must suffice (*let this much have been said*): I will now return to where I left off. *The perfect refers to a completed state.*

Overview of the Uses of Moods in Main Clauses

34.22   The following table gives a summary of the uses described above:

mood		meanings / uses	negative
indicative		statements and questions about present, past and future	οὐ
subjunctive		'hortatory': first person exhortations	μή
		'prohibitive': second person prohibitions, with μή, aorist only	
		'deliberative': first person doubtful questions	
		emphatic denials with οὐ μή	
		doubtful assertions with μή	
optative	– ἄν	'cupitive' in wishes	μή
	+ ἄν	'potential' in statements and questions of possibility, cautious assertions	οὐ
modal (secondary) indicative	– ἄν	unrealizable wishes (with εἴθε or εἰ γάρ)	οὐ
	+ ἄν	'counterfactual' statements and questions	οὐ
	– ἄν	impf. of impersonal verbs (ἔδει, etc.): unfulfilled necessity, etc.	
		ἐβουλόμην *I would (have) want(ed)*	
		ἔμελλον *I would (have) be(en) going/likely to*	
imperative		second and third person commands and prohibitions	μή
		(second person prohibitions: pres. imp. only)	

35

The Verb: Voice

Introduction

Basic Terminology

Voice: Active and Middle-Passive Meanings

35.1 The category of **voice** pertains to **different ways in which the subject** of a verb form is **affected** by the action. The Greek voice-system derives from a basic two-way distinction:

- A voice which is traditionally called **active**: this voice may be considered semantically **neutral**, in that it does not inherently say anything about the affectedness of the subject:

  παρασκευάζει   he makes (something) ready, he prepares (something)

- The so-called **middle-passive** voice, which expresses that the subject is somehow **affected** by the action; the precise way in which the subject is affected may vary, so that a range of different meanings may be expressed by this voice, for example:

  παρασκευάζεται he makes (something) ready for himself (*the subject benefits from the action: indirect-reflexive meaning*);

  he gets ready, he prepares himself (*the subject performs the action on himself: direct-reflexive meaning*);

  he is made ready, he is being prepared (*the action is performed on the subject by someone else: passive meaning*).

The different possible meanings of the middle-passive voice are treated below, →35.8–29.

Note 1: That the active voice is 'neutral' means that the subject of an active verb *can* be affected by the action: in fact, some active verbs express actions in which the subject is very clearly affected, e.g. ἀποθνῄσκει *he dies*, πάσχει κακά *he suffers evil*.

When there is an opposition between active and middle-passive forms of the same verb (e.g. παρασκευάζει vs. παρασκευάζεται), the active verb nearly always takes an object or other complement (→35.8–16).

Active, Middle and Passive Forms

35.2   In the **present** and **perfect** stems, all different possible meanings of the middle-passive voice are expressed by a single set of forms (middle-passive forms).

However, in the **aorist** and **future** stems, different possible meanings of the middle-passive voice are realized by different forms. Traditionally, a distinction is then made between **middle** forms and **passive** forms:

παρεσκεύασε(ν) (3 sg. aor. ind. <u>active form</u>)	he made (something) ready (*active meaning: no indication of the affectedness of the subject*);
παρεσκευάσατο (3 sg. aor. ind. <u>middle form</u>)	he made (something) ready for himself (*indirect-reflexive meaning*), →35.8–10;
	he made himself ready (*direct-reflexive meaning*), →35.11–12;
παρεσκευάσθη (3 sg. aor. ind. <u>passive form</u>)	he was made ready (*passive meaning*), →35.13–16.

Since no morphological distinction exists between middle and passive forms in the present and perfect stems, how to interpret them depends on the context, e.g.:

(1) οἱ Κορίνθιοι . . . <u>παρεσκευάζοντο</u> . . . νεῶν στόλον. (Thuc. 1.31.1)
The Corinthians prepared an expeditionary force of ships for themselves. *Indirect-reflexive meaning: the equivalent form of the aorist would be middle.*

(2) Κορινθίων νῆες <u>παρεσκευάζοντο</u> τριάκοντα. (Thuc. 1.27.2)
Thirty ships of the Corinthians were prepared. *Passive meaning: the equivalent form of the aorist would be passive.*

For more details on the different forms expressing voice, →35.5–7 below.

Note 1: The terms 'active', 'middle' and 'passive' are used traditionally to describe both morphological distinctions and distinctions of meaning. This is often unfortunate, since, for example, not all 'passive' forms express passive meaning (e.g. ἠγέρθην *I woke up*, ἐβουλήθην *I preferred*; for these verbs, →35.17 and 35.26, respectively), and because some verbs have distinct forms expressing distinct meanings which nonetheless belong to the same morphological category (e.g. ἔστησα *I made stand* and ἔστην *I came to stand*, both morphologically 'active'; for an overview of this verb, →35.35).

Another term for the meaning of a particular voice is **diathesis** (ἐβουλήθην then has passive 'voice' morphologically, but no passive diathesis).

Below, several different meanings of the middle-passive voice are distinguished, and these are linked to the forms that may express them.

Verbs with and without an Object; Causative Verbs

35.3 A useful distinction for the interpretation of Greek verbs with respect to voice is that between verbs which normally take an object or complement, and those which do not:

- **Verbs that take an object** in the accusative, or a **complement** in the genitive or dative, express actions in which two (or more) entities are involved, usually because one somehow affects the other. These verbs may appear in the passive (→35.13–15 below): e.g. τύπτω *hit*, παρασκευάζω *make ready*, γράφω *write*, φιλέω *love*, δείκνυμι *show, display*, ἐπιβουλεύω + dat. *plot against*, κατεργάζομαι *finish, achieve*.
- **Verbs that do not take an object or complement** express actions in which only one entity is involved; they take only a subject, and cannot normally appear in the passive: e.g. ἀποθνῄσκω *die*, νοσέω *be sick*, βασιλεύω *be king*, βαίνω *go, walk*, εἰμί *be*, ἔρχομαι *go, come*, γίγνομαι *become, be born*.

Note 1: This distinction is traditionally described as one between 'transitive' and 'intransitive' verbs. In many current linguistic treatments, however, 'transitivity' is viewed as a scale rather than a binary opposition, and there are other reasons why the terminology is not always helpful in describing Greek verbs:

- 'transitive' is a term often reserved for verbs which take a direct object in the accusative, which wrongly suggests that Greek verbs taking a complement in the genitive or dative are intransitive;
- there are some Greek verbs, such as φοβέομαι *fear*, which do take an object in the accusative but which should not be seen as properly transitive (for this verb, →35.19; note that 'passive' aorist ἐφοβήθην means *I feared*, never *I was feared*).

In this grammar, we use 'intransitive' (intr.) only to clarify the sense of some English verbs used as translations of Greek ones, e.g. τήκω *(cause to) melt* vs. τήκομαι *melt* (intr.). For the difference between τήκω and τήκομαι, →35.17 (and the next section).

35.4 Numerous middle-passive verbs which do not take an object or complement, and which express a change of physical or mental state, have an active counterpart which does take an object; this counterpart expresses that an entity brings about that change in another entity. Such active counterparts are called **causative verbs**. For example:

ἐγείρομαι *wake up*	causative ἐγείρω *cause to wake up, wake, rouse*
ἵσταμαι *come to stand*	causative ἵστημι *make stand, set up*
τήκομαι *melt*	causative τήκω *cause to melt, melt something*
φύομαι *grow (up)*	causative φύω *cause to grow*
φαίνομαι *appear, seem*	causative φαίνω *cause to appear, show*

There are also some causative verbs whose middle-passive counterpart does take an object or complement:

φοβέομαι + acc. *be afraid of*   causative φοβέω *make afraid, terrify*
μιμνῄσκομαι + gen. *remember*   causative μιμνῄσκω *cause to remember, remind*

Note 1: The middle-passive forms of all these verbs tend to occur more frequently than the causative active ones.

The Morphology of Voice

Voice Distinctions in the Different Tense Stems

35.5   Each of the different tense-aspect stems has two or more distinct conjugations that differ in their expression of voice:

– **present stem** (→12):

active	conjugations in -ω (thematic) and -μι (athematic)	e.g. παρασκευάζω, ἄγω, γράφω, φαίνω, ἵστημι, δίδωμι
middle-passive	conjugations in -μαι (thematic and athematic)	e.g. παρασκευάζομαι, ἄγομαι, γράφομαι, φαίνομαι, ἵσταμαι, δίδομαι

– **aorist stems** (→13–14):

active	conjugations in -(σ)α ((pseudo-)sigmatic) and -ν or -κα (thematic and root)	e.g. παρεσκεύασα, ἤγαγον, ἔγραψα, ἔφηνα, ἔστησα and ἔστην, ἔδωκα
middle	conjugations in -μην ((pseudo-)sigmatic, thematic and root)	e.g. παρεσκευασάμην, ἠγαγόμην, ἐγραψάμην, ἐφηνάμην, ἐστησάμην, ἐδόμην
passive	conjugations in -θην and -ην (θη-aorists and η-aorists)	e.g. παρεσκευάσθην, ἤχθην, ἐγράφην, ἐφάνθην and ἐφάνην, ἐστάθην, ἐδόθην

– **future stems** (→15–16):

active	conjugations in -σω/-ῶ (sigmatic and Attic)	e.g. παρασκευάσω, ἄξω, γράψω, φανῶ, δείξω, στήσω, δώσω
middle	conjugations in -σομαι/-οῦμαι (sigmatic and Attic)	e.g. παρασκευάσομαι, ἄξομαι, γράψομαι, φανοῦμαι, δείξομαι, στήσομαι, δώσομαι
passive	conjugations in -θήσομαι and -ήσομαι	e.g. παρασκευασθήσομαι, γραφήσομαι, φανήσομαι, σταθήσομαι, δοθήσομαι

– **perfect stems** (→18–19):

active   conjugations in -α (kappa,   e.g. παρεσκεύακα, ἦχα, γέγραφα, πέφηνα
                    aspirated, mixed)   and πέφαγκα, δέδειχα, ἕστηκα, δέδωκα

middle-passive conjugation in -μαι   e.g. παρεσκεύασμαι, ἦγμαι, γέγραμμαι,
                                                πέφασμαι, δέδειγμαι, ἕσταμαι, δέδομαι

Note 1: As these examples show, the voice system of some verbs is very complex: ἵστημι has two morphologically 'active' aorists and a total of four different aorists (ἔστησα, ἔστην, ἐστησάμην, ἐστάθην); φαίνω has four different aorists too (ἔφηνα, ἐφηνάμην, ἐφάνην, ἐφάνθην), as well as two morphologically 'active' perfects (πέφαγκα, πέφηνα). For an overview of these specific verbs, →35.35.

Verbs with Only One Voice; Verbs Switching Voice between Tense Stems

35.6   Some verbs have only one morphological voice: for instance, ἀσθενέω *be weak*, ἐθέλω *be willing*, have only active forms.

Verbs with only middle-passive forms (much more frequent than verbs with only active forms) may be further distinguished with respect to the type of conjugation they have in the aorist (and future):

– **Middle-only verbs** (*media tantum*): verbs that have middle forms in the aorist (and future), e.g. ἡγέομαι *lead, guide, consider* (aor. ἡγησάμην), κτάομαι *acquire* (aor. ἐκτησάμην), μηχανάομαι *contrive* (aor. ἐμηχανησάμην).
– **Passive-only verbs** (*passiva tantum*): verbs that have only passive forms in the aorist (and future), e.g. βούλομαι *want, prefer* (aor. ἐβουλήθην), δύναμαι *be able* (aor. ἐδυνήθην), φοβέομαι *be afraid* (aor. ἐφοβήθην).

For more details on middle-only verbs and passive-only verbs, →35.21–9 below.

Note 1: Middle-only and passive-only verbs are often grouped together and then called 'deponent' verbs (a term borrowed from Latin grammar): it is useful, however, to distinguish between the two categories, since they tend to express different kinds of meanings.
Note 2: Several passive-only verbs do have middle forms in the future (but are still referred to in this grammar as 'passive-only'): for examples, →35.31

35.7   Many verbs **switch voice between tense stems**. Note in particular the following groups:

– A large number of active verbs of moving, acquiring, perceiving and saying have a corresponding **middle future**, e.g. βαίνω *go, walk* (fut. βήσομαι), φεύγω *flee* (fut. φεύξομαι), λαμβάνω *get, take* (fut. λήψομαι), ὁράω *see* (fut. ὄψομαι); cf. also εἰμί *be* (fut. ἔσομαι). For a fuller list of such verbs, →15.40.
– The verbs **ἁλίσκομαι** *be captured*, **φύομαι** *grow*, **ἵσταμαι** *come to stand* and **δύομαι** *dive* have corresponding active root aorists (→13.39–50) ἑάλων *was captured*, ἔφυν

grew, ἔστην *came to stand*, and ἔδυν *dived*. These verbs also have corresponding active perfects ἥλωκα, πέφυκα, ἕστηκα, and δέδυκα. For details, →35.17, 35.28.

Note 1: Apart from ἁλίσκομαι, each of these verbs has an active causative counterpart: φύω *cause to grow*, ἵστημι *make stand, set up*, δύ(ν)ω *submerge*, with a corresponding sigmatic aorist: ἔφυσα, ἔστησα, ἔδυσα.

- Several other **active perfects** (usually of the 'stem' type, →18.21) correspond to middle-passive forms in other tenses: e.g. pf. πέφηνα (φαίνομαι *appear, seem*), pf. ἀπόλωλα (ἀπόλλυμαι *perish*), pf. πέποιθα (πείθομαι *believe, obey*), pf. γέγονα (γίγνομαι *become, be born*). For details, →35.17 with n.3.
- Some **suppletive verbs** (→11.13) use different voices in their different verb stems: thus e.g. middle-passive ἔρχομαι *go, come* has active aorist ἦλθον, active ἐρωτάω *ask* has middle aorist ἠρόμην (in Attic), etc.

Middle-Passive Meanings

Indirect-Reflexive Meaning

35.8   With most verbs whose active forms take an object, middle-passive forms can be used – also with an object – to indicate that the subject has a special interest in (i.e. benefits from) the action expressed by the verb. This meaning is called **indirect-reflexive**.

Indirect-reflexive meaning is expressed in the aorist and future by **middle forms** (i.e. aorist -μην, future -μαι).

Contrast the following pairs of examples:

(3) πλοῖα καὶ ἐπικούρους παρασκευασάμενοι διέβησαν ἐς τὴν νῆσον. (Thuc. 3.85.3)
Having procured ships and allies they crossed over to the island. *Middle.*

(4) ναυτικὸν παρεσκεύαζον ὅτι πέμψουσιν ἐς τὴν Λέσβον. (Thuc. 3.16.3)
They prepared a fleet to send it to Lesbos. *Active.*

The middle παρασκευασάμενοι in (3) indicates that the subject has prepared the ships and allies for their own benefit – they will use them; the active παρεσκεύαζον in (4) does not express whether the subject especially benefited or not (the subject is here preparing the fleet for someone else).

(5) οὐ γάρ κώ τοί ἐστι υἱὸς οἷον σὲ ἐκεῖνος κατελίπετο. (Hdt. 3.34.5)
For you do not have a son yet such as he has left you. *Middle.*

(6) κατέλιπε δὲ τούς τε ὄνους καὶ τοὺς ἀσθενέας τῆς στρατιῆς. (Hdt. 4.135.2)
He left behind the asses and those of the army who were weakened. *Active.*

The middle καταλείπομαι is used in the context of dynastic succession, as in (5). The royal family benefits from the birth of a son which may guarantee its continuation. In other contexts active καταλείπω is used, as in (6).

(7) ἀπὸ ὀλυρέων <u>ποιεῦνται</u> σιτία. (Hdt. 2.36.2)

They make food from a coarse grain. *Middle.*

(8) οἱ ἀστοὶ ἄλευρά τε καὶ ἄλφιτα <u>ἐποίευν</u>. (Hdt. 7.119.2)

The townspeople made wheat and barley meal. *Active.*

The food prepared in (7) is used by the subject of ποιεῦνται themselves; the food in (8) is made by the townspeople for the Persian king.

Note 1: Indirect-reflexive meaning is usually easily recognizable by the presence of a direct object, as in (3), (5) and (7).

35.9   Observe the specific meaning of the indirect-reflexive middle with verbs such as:

active	*middle*
αἱρέω *take*	αἱρέομαι *choose*
αἰτέω *ask, demand*	αἰτέομαι *beg*
ἀποδίδωμι *give back*	ἀποδίδομαι *sell*
γράφω *write*	γράφομαι *indict*
μισθόω *let, hire out*	μισθόομαι *rent (for oneself)*
τιμωρέω *avenge, help* (+ dat.)	τιμωρέομαι *take revenge on* (+ acc.)
τίνω *pay, atone*	τίνομαι *make pay, avenge, punish*
χράω *give an oracle*	χράομαι *consult an oracle*

Note also that compounds of τίθημι and ἵημι occur frequently in the indirect-reflexive middle, often with specific meanings: e.g. κατατίθεμαι *deposit, lay aside* (κατατίθημι *put down*), προσίεμαι *admit, accept, allow* (προσίημι *let near*). For other compounds of ἵημι, τίθημι and ἵστημι, →35.17 nn.1–2, 35.27 n.3.

35.10   Passive forms of these verbs normally have passive meaning: e.g. ἐποιήθην *was done*, ἐφυλάχθην *was guarded*. In some cases, passive forms express the passive variant of a particular indirect-reflexive meaning: note particularly αἱρέω *take*, middle αἱρέομαι *choose* (aor. εἱλόμην), passive αἱρέομαι *be taken* or (more often) *be chosen* (aor. ᾑρέθην).

The perfect middle-passive of these verbs may, like the present, express both indirect-reflexive and passive meaning: e.g. πεποίημαι *have done for one's own benefit* (indirect-reflexive) or *have been done* (passive): the passive sense is much more common.

Direct-Reflexive Meaning

35.11   Primarily with verbs that denote a habitual physical treatment, like λούω *bathe*, κείρω *cut hair*, κοσμέω *adorn*, ἀλείφω *anoint* – so-called **verbs of grooming** – the middle-passive voice may indicate that the subject applies the action to himself: **direct-reflexive meaning**. A few other verbs whose middle-passive voice may have direct-reflexive meaning are παρασκευάζω *prepare*, γυμνάζω *train*, στεφανόω *crown*, τάττω *array*, δέφω *knead* (the middle δέφομαι means *masturbate*).

Direct-reflexive meaning is expressed in the aorist and future by **middle forms** (i.e. aorist -(σ)αμην, future -σομαι/-οὖμαι).

(9) οὐκ ἐλούσατ' ἐξ ὅτουπερ ἐγένετο. (Ar. *Plut.* 85)
He hasn't bathed since he was born.

(10) ὑπὸ ταῖς μορίαις ἀποθρέξει | στεφανωσάμενος καλάμῳ λεπτῷ. (Ar. *Nub.* 1005–6)
You'll run races beneath the olive trees, having crowned yourself with fine reeds.

(11) μετὰ τοῦ γυμνάζεσθαι ἠλείψαντο. (Thuc. 1.6.5)
In the course of their exercise they anointed themselves.

(12) τοῖς αἰσχροῖς | ἐψήφισται προτέροις βινεῖν, | ὑμᾶς δὲ τέως . . . ἐν τοῖς προθύροισι δέφεσθαι. (Ar. *Eccl.* 705–9)
It's been decreed that the ugly ones get to fuck first, while you have to jerk off in the doorway in the meantime.

Active forms of these verbs (which take an object) indicate that the action is performed on someone other than the subject:

(13) πρῶτον μὲν αὐτὸν ἐπὶ θάλατταν ἤγομεν, | ἔπειτ' ἐλοῦμεν. (Ar. *Plut.* 656–7)
First we took him to the sea, then we bathed him.

Note 1: The middle of verbs that do not belong to this limited set of verbs cannot normally express direct-reflexive meaning: when the subject performs the action on himself this is expressed by means of a reflexive pronoun (ἐμαυτόν, etc.). Thus παιδεύεται cannot mean *he educates himself*, λύεται cannot mean *he releases himself* (instead, this would be παιδεύει ἑαυτόν, λύει ἑαυτόν). For example:

(14) ῥίπτει αὐτὸν εἰς τὴν θάλατταν. (Dem. 32.6)
He throws himself into the sea.

35.12   Middles such as κείρομαι, παρασκευάζομαι, etc. may also have indirect-reflexive meaning, for which →35.8 above; this is the only possible interpretation when these verbs are construed with a direct object, as e.g. in (1) and (3). Passive forms of these verbs express passive meaning: e.g. ἐλούθην *was bathed*, ἐκοσμήθην *was adorned*, παρεσκευάσθην *was made ready*, ἐστεφανώθην *was crowned*. The perfect middle-passive of these verbs may, like the present, express all three meanings, e.g. παρεσκεύασμαι *have prepared X (for one's own benefit)* (indirect-reflexive), *have prepared oneself* (direct-reflexive), *have been prepared* (passive).

Passive Meaning

35.13   **Passive** meaning occurs only with verbs which take an object in the accusative, or sometimes with verbs that take a complement in the genitive or dative, →30.21, 30.39. The middle-passive voice in this case expresses that an action is performed on the subject by someone else. The object/complement in an active construction serves as subject in the passive construction.

Passive meaning is expressed in the aorist and future by **passive** forms, usually by θη-aorists, sometimes by η-aorists.

(15) καὶ διητᾶτο παρ' ἡμῖν τὸν ἅπαντα χρόνον ὁ Ἀστύφιλος καὶ <u>ἐπαιδεύθη</u> ὑπὸ τοῦ πατρὸς τοῦ ἐμοῦ. (Isae. 9.27)

Astyphilus lived in our house the whole time, and was brought up by my father. παιδεύω *takes a direct object in the accusative: compare* ὁ πατὴρ ὁ ἐμὸς ἐπαίδευσε τὸν Ἀστύφιλον *'my father educated Astyphilus'*.

(16) αἱ δὲ κῶμαι αὗται <u>ἦσαν δεδομέναι</u> ὑπὸ Σεύθου Μηδοσάδῃ. (Xen. *An.* 7.7.1)

These villages had been given to Medosades by Seuthes. δίδωμι *takes a direct object in the accusative: compare* ταύτας τὰς κώμας ἐδεδώκει Σεύθης Μηδοσάδῃ *'Seuthes had given these villages to Medosades'*.

(17) <u>ἐπιβουλευόμενοι</u> διάξουσι πάντα τὸν βίον. (Pl. *Resp.* 417b)

They will pass their entire life being plotted against. ἐπιβουλεύω *takes a complement in the dative: compare* ἐπιβουλεύει αὐτοῖς *'he plots against them'*.

Note 1: η-aorists with passive meaning include ἀπηλλάγην *was removed* (ἀπαλλάττω *remove*; ἀπηλλάχθην also occurs, →35.17), ἐβλάβην *was damaged* (βλάπτω *harm, damage*), ἐγράφην *was written* (γράφω *write*), ἐδάρην *was flayed* (δέρω *skin*), ἐκόπην *was struck* (κόπτω *hit*), ἐρρίφην *was thrown* (ῥίπτω *throw*; ἐρρίφθην also occurs), ἐτύπην *was hit* (τύπτω *hit*).

The vast majority of passive aorists are θη-aorists.

Note 2: The middle aorist of ἔχω *have, hold* and its compounds may also have passive meaning:

(18) οἱ νεηνίαι οὐκέτι ἀνέστησαν, ἀλλ' ἐν τέλεϊ τούτῳ <u>ἔσχοντο</u>. (Hdt. 1.31.5)

The young men did not rise again, but ended their lives like this (*lit. 'were held in this end'*).

35.14   The **agent** (the entity controlling the action) of a passive verb is often not expressed; it may, however, be expressed by:

– ὑπό (sometimes παρά, πρός or ἐκ) + **genitive**:

(19) ἦ δεινὸν ... ἐλεύθερον ὄντα <u>ὑπὸ δούλου</u> ἄρχεσθαι. (Pl. *Ly.* 208c)

It is really terrible as a free man to be commanded by a slave. *Also cf.* (15)–(16).

– a **dative of agent** (→30.50), usually with perfect passives and adjectives in -τέος:

(20) ἀναμνήσω ὑμᾶς τὰ <u>τούτῳ</u> πεπραγμένα. (Xen. *Hell.* 2.3.30)

I will remind you of the things that have been done by him.

35.15   Some active verbs take both an object and another complement in the accusative ('double accusative', →30.9), e.g. ἐρωτάω τινά τι *ask something of someone*, αἰτέω τινά τι *demand something of someone*. When such verbs are put in the passive, the object ('someone') is used as the subject of the passive verb, the second complement still stands in the accusative:

(21)   ἐτελεύτησεν οὐ . . . τὸν δῆμον <u>αἰτήσας</u> δωρεάς. (Din. 1.17)
He died without having asked the people for gifts. *Active, object and complement in the accusative.*

(22)   ἓν <u>αἰτηθεὶς</u> πολλὰ δίδως. (Pl. *Tht.* 146d)
Although you were asked for one thing, you give many. *Passive, with ἕν as complement in the accusative.*

However, with verbs that take an object and a predicative complement (→30.10), both constituents are put in the nominative when the verb is passive:

(23)   Ἰφικράτην στρατηγὸν <u>εἵλοντο</u>. (Xen. *An.* 6.5.49)
They appointed Iphicrates general. *Active, object and predicative complement in the accusative.*

(24)   ἡγεμὼν δὲ καὶ κύριος <u>ᾑρέθη</u> Φίλιππος ἁπάντων. (Dem. 18.201)
Philip was appointed leader and master of all. *Passive, subject and predicative complement in the nominative.*

35.16   A few active verbs which do not take an object may also serve as the passive to different verbs (suppletion, →11.13): ἀποθνῄσκω *die, be killed* (passive of ἀποκτείνω *kill*); φεύγω *flee, be prosecuted* (passive of διώκω *prosecute*); ἐκπίπτω *fall out, be banished* (passive of ἐκβάλλω *throw out, banish*). Note also middle-only ἁλίσκομαι *be captured* (passive of e.g. αἱρέω *take*). These verbs are construed as other passives (e.g. with ὑπό + gen. to express the agent).

Change-of-State Verbs

Change of Physical State or Position

35.17   Verbs that express a **change of (physical) state** by a spontaneous process, a **change of body position** or **change of position of a group** are often middle-passive. These verbs usually have active **causative** counterparts. The most common verbs of this type are:

Middle-passive		*Active causative*	
ἀθροίζομαι	gather, get together	ἀθροίζω	gather someone/thing
ἀπαλλάττομαι	depart	ἀπαλλάττω	remove
δύομαι	dive	δύ(ν)ω	cause to dive, submerge
ἐγείρομαι	wake up	ἐγείρω	wake, rouse
ἵσταμαι	come to stand	ἵστημι	make stand, set up
κλίνομαι	lean, recline	κλίνω	cause to lean
κομίζομαι	journey, travel	κομίζω	convey

(ἀπ)όλλυμαι	perish	(ἀπ)όλλυμι	destroy, lose
πήγνυμαι	be fixed, become solid	πήγνυμι	affix, fasten
πορεύομαι	travel	πορεύω	make go, convey
ῥήγνυμαι	burst, break	ῥήγνυμι	(cause to) break, shatter
στέλλομαι	set out, journey	στέλλω	dispatch, send
στρέφομαι	turn around	στρέφω	turn someone/thing around
συλλέγομαι	gather, come together	συλλέγω	gather someone/thing, collect
σφάλλομαι	stumble, err	σφάλλω	cause to stumble
σῴζομαι	get to safety, escape	σῴζω	save, make safe
τήκομαι	melt	τήκω	cause to melt
τρέπομαι	turn around (intr.)	τρέπω	turn someone/thing around
τρέφομαι	grow (up)	τρέφω	cause to grow, nourish, rear
φαίνομαι	appear, seem	φαίνω	cause to appear, show
φύομαι	grow (up)	φύω	cause to grow, bring forth, beget

Note 1: Observe the specific meaning of various compounds of ἵστημι: ἀνίσταμαι *stand up (to speak)* (ἀνίστημι *make stand up*), ἀφίσταμαι *come to stand at a remove, revolt* (ἀφίστημι *set at a remove, incite to revolt*), καθίσταμαι *acquire a position* (καθίστημι *install, set down*), ἐφίσταμαι *come to stand at, gain charge of* (ἐφίστημι *make stand at, put in charge of*), etc.

Change-of-state verbs usually have **passive forms** in the aorist (θη-/η-aorists) and future. A significant number of η-aorists belongs to this category. E.g. ἀπηλλάγην *departed* (also ἀπηλλάχθην), ἐπορεύθην *travelled*, ἐστάλην *set out*, συνελέγην *gathered*, ἐσφάλην *stumbled*, ἐσώθην *escaped*, ἐτάκην *melted*, ἐφάνην *appeared, seemed*.

However, the verbs ἵσταμαι *come to stand* (ἵστημι), δύομαι *dive* (δύ(ν)ω) and φύομαι *grow (up)* (φύω) have corresponding **active root aorists**: ἔστην *came to stand*, ἔδυν *dived*, ἔφυν *grew (up)*.

Note 2: In some cases a thematic middle aorist occurs to express this meaning: e.g. ἀπωλόμην *perished* (ἀπόλλυμαι), ἠγρόμην *woke up* (ἐγείρομαι; next to ἠγέρθην), ἐτραπόμην *turned around* (τρέπομαι; next to ἐτράπην/ἐτρέφθην).

To this category also belong compounds such as ἐπιτίθεμαι *attack, apply oneself to* (ἐπιτίθημι *set against, impose*) and (ἐφ)ίεμαι *hasten towards, long for* ((ἐφ)ίημι *let go towards*): these have middle root aorist forms, e.g. ἐπεθέμην *attacked*.

Some of these verbs have corresponding **active perfects** (normally of the 'stem' type, →18.21): e.g. ἐγρήγορα *be awake*, ἕστηκα *stand*, ὄλωλα *have perished, be dead*, πέφηνα *have appeared*.

Note 3: Such perfect forms express the state resulting from the spontaneous process, change of (body) position, etc.: for instance, being awake (ἐγρήγορα) is the state resulting from waking up (ἐγείρομαι), standing (ἕστηκα) is the state resulting from coming to stand (ἵσταμαι).

(25) οὐδέτεροι οὐδὲν πλέον ἔχοντες <u>ἐφάνησαν</u> ἢ πρὶν τὴν μάχην γενέσθαι. (Xen. *Hell.* 7.5.27)

Neither party turned out to have anything more than before the battle occurred. *For φαίνομαι + ppl.,* →52.10; *for οὐδέτεροι οὐδέν,* →56.4.

(26) οἱ Χῖοι καὶ οἱ ἄλλοι σύμμαχοι <u>συλλεγέντες</u> εἰς Ἔφεσον ἐβουλεύσαντο . . . πέμπειν εἰς Λακεδαίμονα πρέσβεις. (Xen. *Hell.* 2.1.6)

The Chians and other allies, having gathered in Ephesus, resolved to send emissaries to Sparta.

(27) ἐκ δὲ τούτου <u>ἀνίσταντο</u> οἱ μὲν ἐκ τοῦ αὐτομάτου, λέξοντες ἃ ἐγίγνωσκον. (Xen. *An.* 1.3.13)

After this some stood up on their own initiative, in order to say what they were thinking.

(28) καὶ τῆς ἀρχῆς ἀπόδειξιν ἔχει τῆς τῶν Ἀθηναίων ἐν οἵῳ τρόπῳ <u>κατέστη</u>. (Thuc. 1.97.2)

And (my discussion) can show of the empire of the Athenians in what way it acquired its power.

(29) Ὦ Σώκρατες, ἔφη, <u>ἐγρήγορας</u> ἢ καθεύδεις; (Pl. *Prt.* 310b)

'Socrates,' he said, 'are you awake or are you sleeping?'

35.18   The active (causative) counterparts of most of these verbs may themselves have middle-passive forms which express indirect-reflexive or passive meaning. This results in highly complex voice systems: thus ἀθροίζομαι may mean *get together* (change-of-state, aor. ἠθροίσθην) but also either *gather for oneself* (indirect-reflexive, aor. ἠθροισάμην) or *be gathered together* (passive, aor. ἠθροίσθην). For the cases of ἵσταμαι *come to stand* and φαίνομαι *appear, seem* →35.35 below.

(Change of) Mental State

35.19   To the category of change-of-state verbs also belong several verbs which express a (change of a) certain mental state. These verbs tend to take an object or complement in the middle-passive; they also have active causative counterparts. Examples are:

Middle-passive		*Active causative*	
μιμνήσκομαι + *gen.*	call to mind, remember	μιμνήσκω	remind, call to mind
ὀργίζομαι + *dat.*	be(come) angry	ὀργίζω	make angry
πείθομαι + *dat.*	believe, obey	πείθω	convince, persuade
φοβέομαι + *acc.*	be(come) afraid	φοβέω	make afraid, terrify

These verbs have **passive aorists**: ἐμνήσθην *remembered*, ὠργίσθην *was angry*, ἐπείσθην *believed, obeyed*, ἐφοβήθην *was afraid*.

(30) τίνι τρόπῳ | Χρεμύλος πεπλούτηκ' ἐξαπίνης; οὐ <u>πείθομαι</u>. (Ar. *Plut.* 335–6)

How has Chremulus got rich all of a sudden? I don't believe it.

(31) καί μοι μηδὲν <u>ὀργισθῇς</u>· οὐδὲν γὰρ φλαῦρον ἐρῶ σε. (Dem. 20.102)

And don't get angry with me: for I will not say anything offensive about you.

(32) τίς δὲ οὐκ ἂν πολέμιος <u>φοβηθείη</u> ἰδὼν διηυκρινημένους ὁπλίτας; (Xen. *Oec.* 8.6)

And what enemy would not be afraid on seeing carefully arranged hoplites?

Note 1: πείθομαι also has a thematic middle aorist which expresses this meaning: ἐπιθόμην *believed, obeyed* (next to ἐπείσθην, which is more frequent in later Greek). In addition, it has an active perfect, πέποιθα *believe* (next to πέπεισμαι, more frequent in prose).

35.20   The passive forms of these verbs may also express passive meaning: e.g. aor. ἐπείσθην *was persuaded*, ἐφοβήθην *was made afraid*; pf. πέπεισμαι *be convinced/persuaded*.

Middle-Only Verbs and Passive-Only Verbs

35.21   Middle-only verbs and passive-only verbs can express any of the meanings treated above, as well as various similar meanings (the basic meaning of 'subject-affectedness' is relevant in each case).

Middle-only verbs belong to categories which use middle aorist and future forms (e.g. indirect-reflexive meaning, →35.8 above), passive-only verbs mostly belong to categories which use passive aorist and future forms (e.g. change-of-state verbs, →35.17–19 above).

Indirect-Reflexive Meaning

35.22   Some **middle-only** verbs express **indirect-reflexive meaning** (the subject benefits from the action). Examples are:

δέχομαι - ἐδεξάμην	accept
ἐργάζομαι - εἰργασάμην	achieve, work
κτάομαι - ἐκτησάμην	acquire
ὠνέομαι	buy (*with suppletive aor.* ἐπριάμην)

35.23   These middle-only verbs may also get passive forms to express passive meaning: ἐκτήθην *was acquired*, εἰργάσθην *was achieved*, ἐωνήθην *was bought*. The perfect middle-passive may have both senses: e.g. εἴργασμαι *have achieved/be achieved*, ἐώνημαι *have bought/be bought*.

Reciprocal Meaning

35.24   Some **middle-only** verbs indicate that the subject is (part of) a group of which the members perform an action on each other: **reciprocal meaning** (this is similar to direct-reflexive meaning, →35.11). Some of these verbs take a complement in the dative. Examples are:

ἀγωνίζομαι - ἠγωνισάμην   fight, struggle
μάχομαι - ἐμαχεσάμην   fight against (+ *dat.*)
ἁμιλλάομαι - ἡμιλλησάμην   contend with (+ *dat.*), strive

Note 1: The verb ἁμιλλάομαι *strive, contend* also has passive aorist ἡμιλλήθην *strove* (more frequent in classical Greek). The verb διαλέγομαι *converse*, which can be grouped under this header, uses only passive aorists διελέχθην/διελέγην *conversed*.

Change-of-State; Mental State

35.25   Some **middle-only verbs** express a **change of state or position** (→35.17):

ἀφικνέομαι - ἀφικόμην   arrive
γίγνομαι - ἐγενόμην   become, be born (*later also aor.* ἐγενήθην 'was born'; *act. stem pf.* γέγονα, *later also mid. pf.* γεγένημαι)
ἕπομαι - ἑσπόμην   follow
ἔρχομαι   go, come (*with suppletive active aor.* ἦλθον)
οἴχομαι   depart (*no aor., fut.* οἰχήσομαι)
πέτομαι - ἐπτόμην   fly

35.26   **Passive-only verbs** usually belong to the category of **mental (change-of-)state verbs** (→35.19). Examples are:

αἰδέομαι - ᾐδέσθην   be ashamed, respect (+ *acc.*)
ἄχθομαι - ἠχθέσθην   be angry with/about (+ *dat., also with ppl.*)
βούλομαι - ἐβουλήθην   want, prefer
διανοέομαι - διενοήθην   think, suppose, intend
ἐνθυμέομαι - ἐνεθυμήθην   ponder (+ *acc.*)
ἐπιμελ(έ)ομαι - ἐπεμελήθην   take care of (+ *gen., also with effort clause*)
ἐπίσταμαι - ἠπιστήθην   know, be able
ἥδομαι - ἥσθην   be glad, be happy about (+ *dat.*)
οἴ(ο)μαι - ᾠήθην   think

Note 1: Classical Greek also has an active causative counterpart ἥδω *make glad* corresponding to ἥδομαι, developed in post-Homeric Greek, but never widely used.

Other Middle-Only and Passive-Only Verbs

35.27   Remaining verbs generally belong to one of the following groups:

- Verbs of **intentional or unintentional mental activity** (the subject is affected mentally or emotionally), notably verbs of perception: e.g. (intentional) ἀκροάομαι *listen to*, ἡγέομαι *believe, consider*, θεάομαι *gaze at, view admiringly*, λογίζομαι *reckon, calculate*, μηχανάομαι *devise, plan*, σκέπτομαι *look, examine*, τεκμαίρομαι *judge from signs*; (unintentional) αἰσθάνομαι *perceive, notice*, ὀσφραίνομαι *smell*;
- Verbs that express certain **types of speech**: ἀράομαι *pray*, αἰτιάομαι *accuse*, ἀρνέομαι *refuse, deny*, δέομαι *ask, beg*, εὔχομαι *pray*, μέμφομαι *censure*, ὀλοφύρομαι *lament*, ὑπισχνέομαι *promise*.

These verbs are nearly all middle-only (i.e. have (sigmatic) middle aorist and future forms: e.g. ἐσκεψάμην *examined*, ἐθεασάμην *viewed*, ἐλογισάμην *calculated*, ᾐτιασάμην *accused*, ἐμεμψάμην *censured*). The verbs δέομαι and ἀρνέομαι, however, are passive-only (with θη-aorists ἐδεήθην *asked*, ἠρνήθην *refused*).

Note 1: From the fourth century onwards, more passive forms are found in these meanings (the θη-aorist was 'gaining ground' in the development of the language): e.g. ὠσφράνθην *smelled*, ἐλογίσθην *calculated*.

Note 2: μέμφομαι also occurs as a verb expressing a mental state in the meaning *blame, be angry at*, and then takes the corresponding passive aorist ἐμέμφθην *blamed*.

Note 3: There are also some active verbs whose middle-passive counterparts express these types of meaning: e.g. γεύω *have (someone) taste (something)*, γεύομαι *taste* (perception); τίθημι *make X into Y*, τίθεμαι *regard X as Y* (mental activity); with ποιέω *make*, the idiom περὶ πολλοῦ/ὀλίγου ποιέομαι *value highly/little* (mental activity); συμβουλεύω *give counsel*, συμβουλεύομαι *ask counsel* (type of speech).

In some cases an active causative verb was developed in a later period to correspond to one of these middle-only or passive-only verbs, e.g. ὀσφραίνω *cause to smell*, θεάω *cause to see*; these are rare.

35.28 The verb **ἁλίσκομαι** *be captured* (with active root aorist ἑάλων, and active perfect ἑάλωκα/ἥλωκα) is passive in meaning.

35.29 The passive-only verb **δύναμαι** *be able* (aor. ἐδυνήθην, ἐδυνάσθην) is difficult to classify.

Further Particulars

Middle Future Forms with Passive Meaning

35.30 In classical Greek (especially in poetry), **middle future forms** frequently have passive or change-of-state/mental state meaning. In these meanings, there is sometimes an aspectual distinction between the use of the future middle and the future passive: the future middle (built on the aspect-neutral future stem, →33.6), can be used for ongoing or repeated actions, whereas the future passive (built on an aorist stem in θη/η (+ σ, →16.1) is used for actions presented as a complete whole.

(33) ἢν δέ τις ἄρα καὶ βουληθῇ, κολασθήσεται τῇ πρεπούσῃ ζημίᾳ, οἱ δὲ ἀγαθοὶ τιμήσονται τοῖς προσήκουσιν ἄθλοις τῆς ἀρετῆς. (Thuc. 2.87.9)

Should, then, someone choose to go on doing so (misbehaving), he shall be punished with the appropriate penalty, while the brave shall be honoured with the appropriate rewards of valour. *The ἀγαθοί will be continuously (or each individually) held in esteem, as opposed to the wrongdoers who will be punished once.*

(34) καὶ εἰ καταστρέψονται ἡμᾶς Ἀθηναῖοι, ταῖς μὲν ὑμετέραις γνώμαις κρατήσουσι, τῷ δ᾽ αὐτῶν ὀνόματι τιμηθήσονται. (Thuc. 6.80.4)

And if the Athenians subdue us, they will be victorious due to your decisions, but they will meet with honour in their own name. *The bestowing of honour on the Athenians for their putative victory is presented as a single, complete whole.*

(35) ἐν τοῖς γὰρ οἰκείοισιν ὅστις ἔστ᾽ ἀνὴρ | χρηστός, φανεῖται κἀν πόλει δίκαιος ὤν. (Soph. *Ant.* 661–2)

The man who is good in family matters, will be seen to be just in the city as well. *A generic/repeated action.*

(36) φανήσεται δὲ παισὶ τοῖς αὑτοῦ ξυνὼν | ἀδελφὸς αὑτὸς καὶ πατήρ. (Soph. *OT* 457–8)

He (*Oedipus*) will turn out to live together with his own children, the same man both as brother and as father. *A single moment will bring the truth to light.*

This aspectual difference apparently disappeared in about the fourth century, when futures in -(θ)ησομαι became more prominent.

35.31   Similarly, many passive-only verbs have (only) middle futures until (at least) the fourth century: e.g. βούλομαι *want, prefer*, aor. ἐβουλήθην, fut. βουλήσομαι; ἐπίσταμαι *know, be able*, aor. ἠπιστήθην, fut. ἐπιστήσομαι; δέομαι *ask, need*, aor. ἐδεήθην, fut. δεήσομαι; ἄχθομαι *be angry*, aor. ἠχθέσθην, fut. ἀχθέσομαι (also ἀχθεσθήσομαι); etc.

'Synonymous' Active and Middle Verbs

35.32   A few verbs have approximately the same meaning in the active and middle voice: e.g. βουλεύω/βουλεύομαι *consider, deliberate*, ὁρμάω/ὁρμάομαι *set out, start, get in motion* (but ὁρμάω can also be causative, *cause to move*), πολιτεύω/πολιτεύομαι *be/ act as a citizen*. In some cases which form is chosen depends on the individual preference of an author.

Overviews

Overview of the Middle-Passive Meanings and Forms of Some Important Types of Verbs

(Active) Verbs which Take an Object/Complement

35.33   Examples include παιδεύω, λύω, τιμάω, δηλόω, ποιέω, and most other verbs taking an object.

	present	aorist	future	perfect
active *educate*	παιδεύω	ἐπαίδευσα	παιδεύσω	πεπαίδευκα
indirect-reflexive *educate for oneself*	παιδεύομαι	ἐπαιδευσάμην	παιδεύσομαι	πεπαίδευμαι
passive *be educated*	παιδεύομαι	ἐπαιδεύθην	παιδευθήσομαι	πεπαίδευμαι

Verbs Whose Middle-Passive May Have a Direct-Reflexive Meaning

35.34 Examples include παρασκευάζω, κοσμέω, κείρω, γυμνάζω, στεφανόω, etc.:

	present	aorist	future	perfect
active *prepare, make ready*	παρασκευάζω	παρεσκεύασα	παρασκευάσω	παρεσκεύακα
indirect-reflexive *prepare for oneself*	παρασκευάζομαι	παρεσκευασάμην	παρασκευάσομαι	παρεσκεύασμαι
direct-reflexive *prepare oneself*	παρασκευάζομαι	παρεσκευασάμην	παρασκευάσομαι	παρεσκεύασμαι
passive *be prepared, be made ready*	παρασκευάζομαι	παρεσκευάσθην	παρασκευασθήσομαι	παρεσκεύασμαι

Verbs Whose Middle-Passive May Have a Change-of-State Meaning

35.35 Examples include φαίνω, ἵστημι, ἀθροίζω, ἀπόλλυμι, σφάλλω, φοβέομαι, etc.:

	present	aorist	future	perfect
active *show*	φαίνω	ἔφηνα	φανῶ	πέφαγκα (*rare*)
indirect-reflexive *show for oneself*	φαίνομαι	ἐφηνάμην	φανοῦμαι	πέφασμαι
change-of-state *appear, seem*[1]	φαίνομαι	ἐφάνην	φανήσομαι/φανοῦμαι	πέφηνα
passive *be shown*	φαίνομαι	ἐφάνθην	φανθήσομαι	πέφασμαι

[1] In the meaning *seem*, φαίνομαι (+ inf.) need not denote a *change* of state ('become visible') but may refer to a state proper ('be visible'). This sense is probably derived from the change-of-state meaning. The perfect πέφηνα inherently expresses a state ('have appeared', 'be visible').

	present	aorist	future	perfect
active *make stand, set up*	ἵστημι	ἔστησα	στήσω	—
indirect-reflexive *make stand for oneself*	ἵσταμαι	ἐστησάμην	στήσομαι	ἕσταμαι
change-of-state *come to stand*	ἵσταμαι	ἔστην	στήσομαι	ἕστηκα
passive *be made to stand*	ἵσταμαι	ἐστάθην	σταθήσομαι	ἕσταμαι

Overview of the Meanings Expressed by Aorist and Future Conjugations

35.36   The figure below details the meanings which different types of aorist and future forms can express (blocks indicate types which consistently express a certain meaning; more sporadic cases are listed separately):

	aorist				future	
	(pseudo-) sigmatic	thematic	root	θη/η-aorist	sigmatic/ Attic	θη/η-future
active	-(σ)α	-ον	-ν/-κα		-σω -ῶ	
indirect- reflexive (→35.8–10)		-όμην	ἐδόμην ἐθέμην εἵμην			
direct- reflexive (→35.11–12)	-(σ)άμην				-σομαι -οῦμαι	
reciprocity, mental activity, etc. (→35.24, 35.27)		e.g. ᾐσθόμην	e.g. ἐθέμην			
change-of- state, etc. (→35.17–19, 35.25–6)		e.g. ἀφικόμην ἐπιθόμην ἀπωλόμην	e.g. ἔστην ἔδυν	-(θ)ην	→35.30–1	-(θ)ήσομαι
passive (→35.13)		ἐσχόμην	ἑάλων			

36

Impersonal Constructions

Introduction

36.1   Impersonal verbs have no subject in the normal sense. Such verbs always appear in the **third person singular** (and, if marked for gender, **neuter**). They can be further divided in the following categories:

- '**Quasi-impersonal**' verbs, for which an (accusative and) infinitive or subordinate clause functions as the subject; for details, →36.3–10 below. For example:

    (1) δεῖ με γίγνεσθ' Ἀνδρομέδαν. (Ar. *Thesm.* 1012)

    I must become Andromeda (lit. *'It is necessary that I become Andromeda'*). *The accusative-and-infinitive construction με γίγνεσθαι Ἀνδρομέδαν serves as subject of δεῖ.*

    (2) πρόδηλόν ἐστιν ὅτι παῖδες ὄντες καλῶς ἐπαιδεύθησαν. (Hyp. *Epit.* 4.27)

    It is evidently clear that when they were children they were well educated. *The ὅτι-clause serves as subject of πρόδηλόν ἐστιν; note that πρόδηλον is neuter.*

- '**Proper**' impersonal verbs, which have no subject at all. This group is virtually limited to weather terms, expressions of time, and 'impersonal passive' constructions; for details, →36.11–15 below. For example:

    (3) νείφει. βαβαιάξ. (Ar. *Ach.* 1141)

    It's snowing. Blast! *Weather term.*

    (4) ἤδη δὲ ἦν ὀψὲ καὶ ἐπεπαιάνιστο αὐτοῖς ὡς ἐς ἐπίπλουν. (Thuc. 1.50.5)

    It was already late and the paean had been sung by them as if for the attack. *Time expression and impersonal passive; lit. 'there had been paean-singing'.*

Some proper impersonal verbs do not have a subject, but do take other obligatory constituents:

    (5) καὶ πάνυ γ' . . . μέλει μοι τούτων ὧν ἐρωτᾷς. (Xen. *Oec.* 11.9)

    I am indeed very concerned about the things about which you ask. *Impersonal μέλει 'there is concern' takes complements in the dative (person to whom there is concern) and in the genitive (thing about which there is concern).*

Note 1: English impersonal verbs use the so-called 'dummy pronoun' *it*, e.g. *It is raining*. With English quasi-impersonal verbs *it* 'anticipates' the subordinate construction, e.g. *It is clear that he is coming* (cf. *That he is coming is clear.*)

36.2   For infinitives of impersonal constructions, →51.10 n.1, 51.20 n.1. For participles of impersonal constructions (especially the accusative absolute construction), →52.16, 52.33.

Quasi-Impersonal Verbs and Constructions

Verbs

36.3   The following common quasi-impersonal verbs take an (**accusative-and-**) **infinitive** construction as their subject (→51.11):

δεῖ (με) + inf.	it is necessary (for me) to, I must/ought
χρή (με) + inf.	it is necessary (for me) to, I must/ought

(6) τί δεῖ ἡμᾶς, ὦ ἄνδρες, μάχεσθαι; (Xen. *Hell.* 7.4.25)
     Why, men, must we fight?

(7) γυναῖκα γὰρ χρὴ πάντα συγχωρεῖν πόσει. (Eur. *El.* 1052)
     A woman must accede to her husband in everything.

Note 1: δεῖ is also construed (as a proper impersonal verb) with a genitive in the meaning *there is a need for (something)*; →36.15 below.

36.4   The following quasi-impersonal verbs take an (accusative and) **infinitive** as subject, and frequently also a complement in the **dative**:

δοκεῖ (μοι) + inf.	it seems a good idea (to me), I decide
ἔξεστί/πάρεστί (μοι) + inf.	it is possible/permitted (for me), I can
μέτεστί (μοι) + inf.	it is my nature, I am capable
πρέπει (μοι) + inf.	it is fitting/becoming (for me), it suits (me)
προσήκει (μοι) + inf.	it is fitting/becoming (for me), it suits (me)
συμβαίνει (μοι) + inf.	it happens (to me)
συμφέρει (μοι) + inf.	it is of use (to me), it is advantageous (for me)
λυσιτελεῖ (μοι) + inf.	it is profitable (for me)
ἔνεστί (μοι) + inf.	it is in my power, I am able

(8) καὶ ἔδοξεν αὐτοῖς ἐπὶ τῆς Ἱμέρας πλεῖν. (Thuc. 7.1.2)
     They decided to sail for Himera.

(9) μὴ σκυθρώπαζ᾽, ὦ τέκνον. | οὐ γὰρ <u>πρέπει</u> <u>σοι</u> <u>τοξοποιεῖν</u> τὰς ὀφρῦς. (Ar. *Lys.* 7–8)

Don't frown, child. It doesn't suit you to knit your eyebrows.

The simplex ἔστι (so accented) is often used instead of ἔξεστι *it is possible*:

(10) καὶ ταῦτα ... <u>ἔστι</u> μοι | κομπεῖν. (Soph. *OC* 1344–5)

And I can boast these things.

36.5   With some of these verbs, there sometimes appears to be little difference between their construction with a dative complement and the construction with an accusative-and-infinitive:

(11) ἀγαθοῖς τε <u>ὑμῖν</u> <u>προσήκει</u> εἶναι. (Xen. *An.* 3.2.11)

It is fitting for you to be brave.

(12) <u>ὑμᾶς</u> <u>προσήκει</u> ... ἀμείνονας ... εἶναι. (Xen. *An.* 3.2.15)

It is fitting for you to be braver *(more literally: 'it is fitting that you be braver')*.

36.6   Especially in poetry, bare prepositions are sometimes used instead of forms compounded with impersonal ἐστί: thus e.g. πάρα (so accented, →24.37) for πάρεστι, μέτα for μέτεστι, ἔνι for ἔνεστι:

(13) τί γὰρ οὐ <u>πάρα</u> μοι μελέα στενάχειν; (Eur. *Tro.* 106)

For why is it not permitted for me, unhappy one, to wail?

36.7   In poetry, the form λύει is sometimes used instead of λυσιτελεῖ.

Neuter Adjectives; Nouns

36.8   The **neuter singular** of many **adjectives** is used with a third-person singular form of εἰμί *be* in quasi-impersonal constructions, taking an (accusative-and-)infinitive construction or ὅτι-clause. For example:

αἰσχρόν ἐστι	it is shameful
ἀναγκαῖόν ἐστι	it is necessary
δῆλόν ἐστι	it is clear
δυνατόν ἐστι	it is possible
καλόν ἐστι	it is good, honourable
οἷόν τέ ἐστι	it is possible
φανερόν ἐστι	it is clear
χαλεπόν ἐστι	it is difficult

Some **nouns** are similarly used in quasi-impersonal constructions. For example:

ἀνάγκη ἐστί	it is necessary
θέμις ἐστί	it is right, proper

(14) <u>χαλεπόν ἐστι</u> περὶ τὴν αὐτὴν ὑπόθεσιν δύο λόγους ἀνεκτῶς εἰπεῖν. (Isoc. 5.11)

It is difficult to make two speeches about the same topic in a tolerable fashion.

(15) πολὺ γὰρ οὐχ <u>οἷόν τε ἦν</u> ἀπὸ τοῦ ἄλλου στρατεύματος διώκειν. (Xen. *An.* 3.3.9)

For it was not possible to make a pursuit far away from the rest of the army. *For ἄλλος meaning 'rest (of)', →29.50.*

(16) ἐμοὶ <u>ἀνάγκη ἐστὶ</u> πολλὴ βοηθεῖν τῷ . . . πατρί. (Isae. 2.1)

It is absolutely necessary for me to help my father.

36.9   With such adjectives and nouns **ἐστί** is very often **omitted** (→26.13):

(17) <u>δῆλον</u> ὅτι τῶν χρηστῶν τις . . . εἶ. (Ar. *Plut.* 826)

It is clear that you are one of the good men.

(18) οὐ <u>θέμις</u> εἰσορᾶν | ὄργια σεμνά. (Ar. *Thesm.* 1150–1)

It is not proper to look on the holy rites.

36.10   The adverb corresponding to these adjectives may be used in the impersonal construction **ἔχει + adverb** *it is . . .*, the impersonal counterpart of the construction ἔχω + adv. (for which →26.11). For example:

(19) <u>ἀναγκαίως</u> ἡμῖν <u>ἔχει</u> δηλῶσαι πρὸς ὑμέας . . . (Hdt. 9.27.1)

It is necessary for us to make clear to you . . .

Proper Impersonal Verbs and Constructions

Weather and Time Expressions

36.11   Weather verbs such as the following are used impersonally:

ὕει	it rains / it is raining
ἀστράπτει	there is lightning
νείφει	it snows / it is snowing
χειμάζει	there is a storm
βροντᾷ	there is a thunderstorm
σείει	there is an earthquake

(20) ἡμέρας . . . <u>ἐχείμαζε</u> τρεῖς. (Hdt. 7.191.2)

It stormed for three days.

(21) τοῦ αὐτοῦ μηνὸς ἱσταμένου <u>ἔσεισεν</u>. (Thuc. 4.52.1)

In the early part of the same month there was an earthquake.

Note 1: Such verbs also appear with a god as subject: ὕει ὁ θεός *the god sends rain/it rains*, ἔσεισεν ὁ θεός *the god shook the earth/there was an earthquake*.

Note 2: These verbs sometimes take the place where it rains, snows, etc. as their object. This construction may, in turn, be put in the passive, with the place as subject:

(22) ἑπτὰ δὲ ἐτέων μετὰ ταῦτα οὐκ <u>ὗε</u> <u>τὴν Θήρην</u>. (Hdt. 4.151.1)

For seven years after this there was no rain in Thera.

(23) <u>ὕεται</u> πᾶσα <u>ἡ χώρη</u> τῶν Ἑλλήνων. (Hdt. 2.13.3)

There is rain everywhere in the land of the Greeks (*lit.* 'the entire Greek land is rained upon').

Note 3: Somewhat similar to weather verbs (and regularly treated as impersonal verbs) are some instances of third-person verbs referring to procedural actions whose subject is an unspecified person to be supplied from the context, e.g. σαλπίζει *the trumpet sounds* (lit. '(the trumpeter) sounds the trumpet'), ἐκήρυξε *a proclamation was made* (lit. '(the herald) proclaimed'), ἐσήμηνε *the signal was given* (lit. '(the appointed person) gave the signal').

36.12   Some expressions of time use an impersonal form of εἰμί *be*:

ὀψέ ἐστι   it is late

(24)   ἤδη ... ἀμφὶ ἡλίου δυσμὰς ἦν. (Xen. *An.* 6.4.26)

It was already around sunset.

Impersonal Passives and the Impersonal Use of Verbal Adjectives in -τέον

36.13   Occasionally, a third-person singular passive form without a subject is used of verbs which do not take an object (→35.3) or which take a complement in the genitive or dative. Such **impersonal passives** occur particularly with the perfect passive; the agent may be expressed in the dative (→30.50):

(25)   οὐκ ἄλλως αὐτοῖς πεπόνηται. (Pl. *Phdr.* 232a)

Their labour has not been in vain (*lit. 'there has been laboured by them'*).

(26)   ἐμοὶ ... βεβοήθηται τῷ τεθνεῶτι καὶ τῷ νόμῳ. (Antiph. 1.31)

I have lent my aid to the dead man and to the law (*lit. 'there has been given aid by me'*). βοηθέω *takes a complement in the dative* (→30.39).

Note 1: More commonly (with verbs that do take an object), a subject for such passive forms can be supplied from the context, or occurs in the form of a subordinate construction:

(27)   κατὰ δὲ τοῦτο τοῦ ὄρεος ἐφύλασσον, ὡς καὶ πρότερόν μοι δεδήλωται, Φωκέων χίλιοι ὁπλῖται. (Hdt. 7.217.2)

At that part of the mountain, as I have said before, a thousand Phocian hoplites stood guard (*lit. 'as (it) has been made clear by me'*).

(28)   ἐψήφισται τοὺς ἀδικοῦντας τοῖσι δικασταῖς παραδοῦναι. (Ar. *Vesp.* 591)

It has been decided to hand over the culprits to the judges. *The infinitive* παραδοῦναι *serves as subject to* ἐψήφισται.

36.14   To this category belongs also the **impersonal use of neuter adjectives in** -τέον:

(29)   οὐκ ἀποστατέον ἔτι τοῦ πολέμου ... ἀλλ' ἐθελοντὶ ἰτέον ἐπὶ τοὺς Ἀθηναίους. (Thuc. 8.2.1)

We should no longer stand aside from the war, but willingly go against the Athenians (*lit. 'there should no longer be stood aside', 'there should be gone'*).

For details on this construction, →37.3.

Proper Impersonal Verbs with a (Dative and) Genitive

36.15   The following impersonal verbs take a complement in the genitive (→30.21), usually combined with a complement in the dative for the person involved:

δεῖ (μοί) τινος	there is a need (for me) for something, I need
μέτεστί μοί τινος	I have a share in something
μέλει μοί τινος	I care for something, something is of concern to me
μεταμέλει μοί τινος	I am sorry about something, I regret
προσήκει μοί τινος	something pertains/belongs to me, I have something to do with something

(30)   τῶν γὰρ πατρῴων οὐδ' ἀκαρῆ μέτεστί σοι. (Ar. *Av.* 1649)
You have not even the smallest claim to your father's possessions.

(31)   νῦν τοίνυν ὑμῖν μεταμελησάτω τῶν πεπραγμένων. (Lys. 30.30)
So now you ought to regret the things you have done.

(32)   πάνυ ἁπλοῦν ἐστιν διαγνῶναι ὑμῖν ὑπὲρ ταύτης τῆς δίκης, καὶ οὐδὲν δεῖ λόγων πολλῶν. (Dem. 56.37)
It is very simple for you to come to a verdict concerning this suit, and there is no need for a long exposition. *Note that οὐδέν is an adverbial accusative (→30.18, lit. 'there is in no way a need'); it is often so used with δεῖ (similarly δεῖ τι, 'there is in some way a need').*

Note 1: δεῖ is also construed with an (accusative and) infinitive, →36.3 above.

Note 2: μέλει μοι is also construed with an effort clause (ὅπως + fut. ind.), →44.

Note 3: μεταμέλει + dat. is also construed with a participle (dative-and-participle construction, →52.15), sometimes with a ὅτι-clause (→41.3–15).

37

Verbal Adjectives

Types of Verbal Adjectives

37.1 Greek has two types of **verbal adjectives** (adjectives formed from verb stems):

- adjectives in -τέος, -τέα, -τέον;
- adjectives in -τός, -τή, -τόν (the accent varies: sometimes, in compounds, -τος, -τη, -τον).

For the formation of these adjectives, →23.29, 23.34. For the use of participles (which are also a kind of verbal adjective), →52.

Adjectives in -τέος, -τέα, -τέον

As Predicative Complement

37.2 Verbal adjectives **in -τέος, -τέα, -τέον** (also called **gerundives**) express a **passive necessity**: the word or phrase with which the adjective agrees is to undergo a certain action, e.g. παιδευτέος (ἐστί) *(he is) to be educated*, τὰ πρακτέα *the things which must be done* (substantivized, →28.23).

Such adjectives are used as predicative complement with the linking verb εἰμί *be* (though the linking verb is in fact often omitted, →26.13):

(1) ἐὰν δέ τις κατά τι κακὸς γίγνηται, <u>κολαστέος ἐστί</u>. (Pl. *Grg.* 527b)
    If someone becomes bad in some respect, he ought to be punished. (*κολάζω*)

(2) οὐκοῦν αὗται (ἁρμονίαι), ἦν δ' ἐγώ, <u>ἀφαιρετέαι</u>; (Pl. *Resp.* 398e)
    'Aren't these modes of music,' I said, 'to be done away with?' (*ἀφαιρέω*)

If expressed, the **agent** appears in the **dative** (→30.50):

(3) ταῦτα μὲν οὖν, ὦ ἄνδρες δικασταί, <u>τούτοις</u> <u>ποιητέα ἦν</u>. (Andoc. 1.136)
    These are the things, men of the jury, that had to be done by these men. (*ποιέω*)

(4) <u>νουθετητέος</u> δέ <u>μοι</u> | Φοῖβος. (Eur. *Ion* 436–7)
    I must rebuke Phoebus. (*νουθετέω*)

Impersonal Use

37.3   The neuter singular form in -τέον (rarely the plural -τέα) may be used **impersonally** (→36) to indicate that an action ought to be performed. The **dative** is used to
express the agent (→30.50), if present. This construction is used:

– with **verbs that do not take an object/complement** (these cannot otherwise be
used in the passive, →35.3):

(5) εἰσιτέον εἴσω δ᾽ ἐστίν. (Men. *Cith.* 63)
    I should go inside *(lit. 'there is to be gone inside'). εἴσειμι cannot normally be used
    in the passive.*

(6) ἐν ἀσπίσιν σοι πρῶτα κινδυνευτέον. (Eur. *Supp.* 572)
    First, you must run a risk behind your shields *(lit. 'there is to be run a risk by
    you'). (κινδυνεύω)*

– with verbs that take **an object or complement**; in this case such objects or
complements are expressed in the case-form required by the verb:

(7) πᾶσαν κολακείαν ... φευκτέον. (Pl. *Grg.* 527c)
    Every kind of flattery must be avoided. *φεύγω takes a direct object in the
    accusative.*

(8) ἀκροατέον ὑμῖν ἐν μέρει τῶν κρειττόνων. (Ar. *Av.* 1228)
    It's now your turn to obey your superiors. *ἀκροάομαι takes a complement in the
    genitive, →30.21.*

(9) τί ταῦτ᾽ ἀλύω; πειστέον πατρὸς λόγοις. (Eur. *Hipp.* 1182)
    Why should I be distraught at this? The words of a father must be obeyed.
    πείθομαι takes a complement in the dative, →30.39.

Note 1: Such expressions may be seen as roughly equivalent to δεῖ/χρή + inf.; for (7), for
instance, cf. δεῖ φεύγειν πᾶσαν κολακείαν. This similarity was clearly felt by Attic authors,
who sometimes express the agent with an accusative (the case to complement δεῖ/χρή) rather
than a dative:

(10) οὐ μὴν δουλευτέον τοὺς νοῦν ἔχοντας τοῖς οὕτω κακῶς φρονοῦσιν. (Isoc. 9.7)
     Men of intelligence should not serve as slaves to those who are perverted in this way.

Note 2: With verbs which have a different meaning in the active and middle-passive (e.g.
πείθω *persuade, convince* and πείθομαι *obey, believe,* →35.19), the impersonal verbal
adjective in -τέον is ambiguous, and may correspond to either meaning. The construction
or context makes clear which meaning is intended. For example, with (9), compare:

(11) τοὺς φύλακας ἐκεῖνο ἀναγκαστέον ποιεῖν καὶ πειστέον. (Pl. *Resp.* 421b)
     The guardians must be forced and persuaded to do this. *πειστέον corresponds to active
     πείθω, which takes a direct object in the accusative.*

Adjectives in -τός, -τή, -τόν

37.4   The adjectives in **-τός, -τή, -τόν** either express a **passive state** (like a perfect passive participle) or express **passive possibility**:

κρυπτός   hidden (*passive state; κρύπτω*)

πόλις ἀφύλακτος   an unguarded city (*passive state; φυλάττω*)

πιστός   reliable (= '*who can/may be trusted*', *passive possibility; πείθομαι*)

ποταμὸς διαβατός   a fordable river (*passive possibility; διαβαίνω*)

(12) δίδαξον, εἰ <u>διδακτόν</u>, ἐξ ὅτου φοβῇ. (Soph. *Trach.* 671)
       Explain to me, if it may be explained, the cause of your fear.

Note 1: 'Passive possibility' should here be taken to include a range of nuances, such as 'permission' (as in (12)), 'right', 'appropriateness', etc.

Several adjectives have **both meanings**, e.g.:

ἄγνωστος   unknown; unknowable (*γιγνώσκω*)

ἀόρατος   unseen; invisible (*ὁράω*)

Note 2: A few of these adjectives have both passive and active meaning:

δυνατός   which can/may be done (*passive*); capable, powerful (*active*) (*δύναμαι*)

ἄπρακτος   intractable, unprofitable, not to be done (*passive*); unsuccessful (*active*)
            (*πράττω*)

38

Questions, Directives, Wishes, Exclamations

Introduction: Sentence Types and Communicative Functions

38.1   In principle, utterances belong to one of three different **sentence types**:

– **declarative:** e.g.

(1) ὦ ξέν’, οὐ δίκαια δρᾷς. (Soph. *OC* 831)

Stranger, what you are doing is wrong.

– **interrogative:** e.g.

(2) οὗτος, τί δρᾷς; (Ar. *Av.* 1567)

Hey there, what are you doing?

– **imperative:** e.g.

(3) μὴ δρᾶ τάδε. (Soph. *OT* 1064)

Do not do this.

Sentence type is determined principally by the mood of the main verb (→34) and by the intonation of the utterance.

Note 1: It is sometimes not straightforward to determine the sentence type of an individual utterance: our knowledge about the intonation of Greek utterances is limited, and written punctuation and accents were added only after the classical period (→1.12–13). Modern editions of texts are typically based on the evidence provided in medieval manuscripts.

Note 2: 'Desideratives' (wishes) and 'exclamatives' (exclamations) are sometimes distinguished as additional, separate sentence types. For wishes and exclamations, →38.38–42 and 38.43–51.

38.2   Although there is a correlation between the sentence type of an utterance and the **communicative functions** that may be performed by that utterance (such functions include 'request', 'wish', 'command', 'assertion', 'question'), one and the same linguistic form may (in different contexts) serve various communicative functions. For instance, each of the following examples is in the interrogative form, but the communicative functions they perform are different:

(4) ΕΥ. τί οὖν; ποιήσεις ταῦτα; :: ΑΓ. μὴ δόκει γε σύ. (Ar. *Thesm.* 208)

(Euripides:) So what's your answer? Will you do this? :: (Agathon:) Don't you count on it. *Interrogative ποιήσεις ταῦτα; is used in a question, a genuine request for information, which is answered by Agathon.*

(5) οὐ μὴ ... ποιήσεις ἅπερ οἱ τρυγοδαίμονες οὗτοι; | ἀλλ' εὐφήμει. (Ar. *Nub.* 296–7)

Don't do what these poor-devil poets do, but speak words of good omen. *Interrogative οὐ μή ... ποιήσεις ...; (lit. 'won't you refrain from doing ...?') expresses a command; →38.32.*

(6) ἴσως καὶ μάλιστα πρέπει μέλλοντα ἐκεῖσε ἀποδημεῖν διασκοπεῖν ... περὶ τῆς ἀποδημίας τῆς ἐκεῖ .... · τί γὰρ ἄν τις καὶ ποιοῖ ἄλλο ἐν τῷ μέχρι ἡλίου δυσμῶν χρόνῳ; (Pl. *Phd.* 61d–e)

Perhaps, in fact, it is most fitting to investigate living there (*in the Underworld*), since I am about to go and live there. For what else might someone do in the time until sunset? *τί ἄν τις ποιοῖ is phrased as a question, but used to assert something ('there is nothing else that we can do') – this is a 'rhetorical' question (→38.19).*

Conversely, different linguistic forms may serve similar communicative functions. For instance, each of the following examples serves as a request or command to someone to speak (for the different nuances of each of these constructions, →38.31–7):

(7) λέγε, πέραινε σοὺς λόγους. (Eur. *Ion* 1348)

Speak, finish what you were saying. *Present imperative.*

(8) φέρε τοῦτό μοι ἀτρεκέως εἰπέ. (Hdt. 7.47.1)

Come, tell me this truthfully. *Aorist imperative.*

(9) τί σοί ποτ' ἔστ' ὄνομ'; οὐκ ἐρεῖς; (Ar. *Pax* 185)

What on earth is your name? Won't you speak? *Interrogative with οὐ + future indicative.*

(10) λέγοις ἄν· εὔνους δ' οὖσ' ἐρεῖς ὅσ' ἄν λέγῃς. (Eur. *Ion* 1336)

Please speak: you will say whatever you say kindly. *Potential optative.*

(11) εἰπεῖν μοι πρὸς βασιλέα, Μαρδόνιε, ὡς ἐγὼ τάδε λέγω. (Hdt. 8.68α.1)

Tell the king for me, Mardonius, these things as I say them. *Imperatival infinitive.*

(12) δεῖ σε λέγειν τι καινόν. (Ar. *Nub.* 1032)

You must say something new. *δεῖ + accusative + infinitive (declarative sentence type).*

(13) αὐτοῖς ... ὑμᾶς κελεύω λέγειν. (Xen. *Cyr.* 3.3.39)

I bid you to speak to them. *κελεύω + accusative + infinitive (declarative sentence type).*

(14) τί σιγᾷς; οὐκ ἐχρῆν σιγᾶν, τέκνον. (Eur. *Hipp.* 297)

Why are you silent? You shouldn't be silent, child. *Interrogative, followed by 'modal' ἐχρῆν (→34.17; declarative sentence type).*

Note 1: The technical term for the communicative function of an utterance (as distinct from sentence type) is 'illocution' or 'illocutionary force'.

Note 2: For examples of the imperative mood used to express non-directive communicative functions, →34.20.

38.3   This chapter treats:

- the basic forms of **questions**, and some of the communicative uses to which the Greek interrogative sentence type may be put (→38.4–24);
- the basic constructions used for **directives** (commands, requests, exhortations, etc.), and some other constructions used to perform similar communicative functions (→38.25–37);
- the different constructions used in **wishes** (→38.38–42);
- some points about **exclamations** (→38.43–51).

Questions

Introduction: Basic Terminology

38.4   There are two main types of questions:

- Questions that are answered by yes or no: '**yes/no-questions**' – cf. *Are whales fish?* A subset of this type consists of questions that give two (or more) alternatives to choose from: '**alternative questions**' or 'double questions' – cf. *Are whales fish or mammals?*
- Questions that are answered by specifying one or more persons, things, places, etc. (or 'no one', 'nothing', etc.). Such questions are commonly known as 'wh-questions' (as they are, in English, usually introduced by a 'wh-word', such as *who?, when?, why?* etc.), or as '**specifying questions**': cf. *What kind of animal are whales?*

38.5   For indirect/dependent questions, i.e. the representation of questions in indirect speech/thought (cf. Engl. *He asked what kind of animal whales are*), →42.1–8.

Yes/No-Questions and Alternative Questions

38.6   Questions may be introduced by various particles. Yes/no-questions introduced by ἆρα (→59.43) or ἦ (→59.48) are **neutral**: they do not explicitly expect or desire a particular answer:

(15) ΣΩ. ἆρα ἐρωτᾷς ἥντινα τέχνην φημὶ εἶναι; :: ΠΩ. ἔγωγε. (Pl. *Grg.* 462b)
      (Socrates:) Do you ask me what kind of art I claim it (*rhetoric*) to be? :: (Polus:) Yes, I do.

(16) ΟΙ. ἦ κἄν δόμοισι τυγχάνει τανῦν παρών; | :: ΙΩ. οὐ δῆτ'. (Soph. *OT* 757–8)

 (Oedipus:) Does he happen to be in the house now? :: (Iocasta:) Certainly not.

Frequently, no particle at all is used to introduce a neutral yes/no-question:

(17) Θησεύς τιν' ἡμάρτηκεν ἐς σ' ἁμαρτίαν; (Eur. *Hipp.* 320)

 Has Theseus committed some wrong against you?

38.7 By using a question introduced by **οὐ, ἆρ' οὐ**, or **οὐκοῦν** (→59.33), a speaker signals that he **expects** or **desires the answer to be** 'yes' (cf. in English the similar use of the negative, of a negative 'tag question', or *surely*):

(18) οὐχὶ ξυνῆκας πρόσθεν; (Soph. *OT* 360)

 Did you not understand me before? / You understood me before, didn't you? / Surely you understood me before?

(19) Πρῶτον μὲν αὐτῶν τούτων, καίπερ ὄντων γενναίων, ἆρ' οὐκ εἰσί τινες ... ἄριστοι; :: Εἰσίν. (Pl. *Resp.* 459a)

 (Socrates:) In the first place, among these men themselves, even though they are noble, are there not some who are the best? :: (Glaucon:) Indeed there are.

38.8 By starting a question with **μή** (seldom ἆρα μή) or **μῶν**, a speaker signals that he is **reluctant to accept a positive answer as true**, often to convey apprehension or surprise (cf. Engl. *really?, surely not?*, or the use of a positive 'tag question'):

(20) Ἀλλὰ μὴ ἀρχιτέκτων βούλει γενέσθαι; ... Οὔκουν ἔγωγ', ἔφη. (Xen. *Mem.* 4.2.10)

 'But you don't want to become an architect, do you?' / 'But surely you don't want to become an architect?' 'Indeed I don't,' he said.

(21) ἰδού, πάρειμι. μῶν ἐπισχεῖν σοι δοκῶ; (Ar. *Pax* 1042)

 Look, here I am. You don't think I've taken long, do you?

38.9 Occasionally, questions are introduced by **μῶν οὐ**, indicating that the speaker is **reluctant to accept a negative answer as true**:

(22) ΑΙ. μῶν οὐ πέποιθας; ἢ τί σοι τὸ δυσχερές; | :: ΜΗ. πέποιθα. (Eur. *Med.* 733–4)

 (Aegeus:) Surely you do not distrust me? Or what is your difficulty? :: (Medea:) I do trust you.

38.10 Alternative questions in Greek have **ἤ** *or* between the parts that make up the question. They can be (but do not have to be) introduced by **πότερον/πότερα** (which marks the question as an alternative one, and cannot be translated):

(23) πότερα δ' ἐν οἴκοις, ἢ 'ν ἀγροῖς ὁ Λάϊος, | ἢ γῆς ἐπ' ἄλλης τῷδε συμπίπτει φόνῳ; (Soph. *OT* 112)

 Did Laius fall to this murder in the house, in the fields, or on other ground?

(24) ΟΔ. ἄνωθεν ἢ κάτωθεν; ... :: ΝΕ. τόδ' ἐξύπερθε. (Soph. *Phil.* 28–9)

 (Odysseus:) Above you, or beneath you? :: (Neoptolemus:) Here, above me.

Specifying Questions

38.11   Specifying questions in Greek are introduced by a **question word** – an interrogative pronoun, adjective or adverb (these begin with τ- or π-, →8.1–2). The most common are:

τίς; / τί;	who?, what?; which?
τί; / διὰ τί;	why?
πότερος;	who of the two?; which . . . of the two?
πόσος;	how large? (sg.); how many? (pl.)
ποῖος;	what sort of?
ποῦ;	where?
ποῖ;	to where?
πόθεν;	from where?
πότε;	when?
πῶς;	how?
πῇ;	along which route?, in what way?, how?

Note 1: Observe the accentuation of these question words: τίς *who?, what?; which?* (always with acute, →24.2) as opposed to indefinite τις *some(one), a(n), (a) certain*, πότε *when?* as opposed to indefinite ποτε *sometime*, etc. For details, →24.38 n.1.

Note 2: Ionic forms begin with κ- rather than π-: κῶς, κότε, etc. (→25.12).

38.12   Interrogative pronouns and adjectives can be used **pronominally** (independently, as a noun) or **adnominally** (modifying a noun): →26.22–3.

(25)   κᾆτα <u>τίς</u> γαμεῖ; (Soph. *OT* 1500)
         And then who will marry you? *Pronominal.*

(26)   <u>τίς</u> με <u>πότμος</u> ἔτι περιμένει; (Soph. *Ant.* 1296)
         What fate still awaits me? *Adnominal: τίς modifies πότμος, agreeing with it in case, number and gender.*

(27)   Οὐ πάνυ, ἦν δ' ἐγώ, ἔτυχες οὗ λέγω. <u>Ποῖα</u> μήν, ἔφη, λέγεις; (Pl. *Resp.* 523b)
         'You have quite missed my meaning,' I said. 'What kind of things *do* you mean?', he asked. *Pronominal.*

(28)   καὶ <u>ποῖ'</u> <u>ἀδικήματα</u> ζητεῖτ' ἕτερα μείζω τῶν εἰρημένων ἀκοῦσαι; (Din. 3.17)
         And what kind of other injustices, greater still than those which have already been said, are you seeking to hear about? *Adnominal: ποῖ(α) modifies ἀδικήματα.*

38.13   Interrogative pronouns and adjectives also frequently occur in a predicative relationship with a noun (cf. the similar use of demonstrative pronouns, →29.34):

(29)   ἀλλὰ <u>ποῖα</u> <u>ταῦτα</u> λέγεις; (Pl. *Cra.* 391e)
         But what sort of instances are you referring to? *ποῖα is predicative with ταῦτα: lit. 'you are referring to these instances (being) of what sort?'.*

38.14 In Greek, question words may function as obligatory constituents and modifiers not only of the main verb (as in the examples above), but also of subordinate constructions such as participles:

(30) ὁ δὲ Καλλίας τί βουλόμενος ἐτίθει τὴν ἱκετηρίαν; (Andoc. 1.117)

With what motive (*lit.* 'wanting what') did Callias place the bough (on the altar)? *τί is object of βουλόμενος: note that such examples often do not permit literal translation into English.*

The Use of Moods in Questions

38.15 Most direct questions have the indicative (cf. (15)–(30) above). However, other moods occur, particularly the potential optative (→34.13) and counterfactual indicative (→34.16):

(31) πῶς δ’, ὦ Σώκρατες, ἂν εἶεν ψευδεῖς ἡδοναὶ ἢ λῦπαι; (Pl. *Phlb.* 36c)

But, Socrates, how could there be false pleasures or pains? *Potential optative.*

(32) τί ἂν ἀπεκρίνω μοι, εἴ σε ἠρόμην· . . . εἰπέ, τί ἂν ἀπεκρίνω οὕτως ἐρωτηθείς; (Pl. *Men.* 72b)

What would have been your answer to me, if I had asked you: ' . . . '; tell me, what would you have answered if asked such questions? *Counterfactual indicative.*

38.16 The (first-person) **subjunctive** is used in **deliberative questions** (→34.8):

(33) τί δρῶμεν; ἀγγέλλωμεν ἐς πόλιν τάδε | ἢ σῖγ’ ἔχωμεν; (Eur. *Or.* 1539–40)

What must we do? Should we report this to the city? Or should we keep quiet?

(34) ἀλλ’ ἐκδιδαχθῶ δῆτα δυσσεβεῖν, πάτερ; (Soph. *Trach.* 1245)

Am I to be taught, then, father, to be ungodly?

38.17 Deliberative questions are sometimes introduced by **βούλει/βούλεσθε** *do you want*, or (in poetry) θέλεις/θέλετε:

(35) θέλεις | μείνωμεν αὐτοῦ; (Soph. *El.* 80–1)

Would you like us to stay here?

Further Particulars

Is That a Question? – 'Non-Standard' Communicative Functions of the Interrogative Sentence Type

38.18 Many expressions in the interrogative sentence type are not used by speakers to elicit information, but perform other communicative functions (→38.2 above), e.g. assertions, commands/requests, etc.

38.19   Any type of interrogative may be used in **rhetorical questions**, i.e. interrogatives which (although they have the appearance of a 'genuine' question) actually have **the force of a (strong) assertion**. Cf. e.g. (25) above: Oedipus' question κᾆτα τίς γαμεῖ; does not really invite his children to come up with the names of future husbands, but asserts that they will never marry (Oedipus makes this implicit assertion explicit in his next line: οὐκ ἔστιν οὐδείς, ὦ τέκν' *there is no one, my children*). In (28), ποῖα ἀδικήματα ζητεῖτε implies 'there are no greater injustices'.

   Rhetorical questions are very frequent in Greek literature, particularly in oratory.

Note 1: When used rhetorically:

– yes/no-questions with οὐ/ἆρ' οὐ imply that the answer is 'yes' (→38.7); neutral questions imply that the answer is 'no';
– specifying questions imply that the answer is an 'empty set': τίς in (25) implies 'no one'; ποῖα in (28) implies 'of no kind'; specifying questions with a negative imply the answer 'all' (e.g. τίς οὐ . . . ; *who not?* implies 'everyone'); cf. also next note.

Note 2: Observe the following idiomatic expressions (these are in essence rhetorical questions):

– πῶς γὰρ οὔ; *certainly, of course* (lit. 'for how not?'); πῶς γάρ; *certainly not* (lit. 'for how?');
– τί γὰρ οὔ; *certainly, of course* (lit. 'for why not?'); τί γάρ; *certainly not* (lit. 'for why?').

For γάρ in these expressions, →59.14.

38.20   The following types of interrogative are regularly used to express commands/requests (**directives**):

– Questions with **οὐ + second person future indicative** (neg. οὐ μή): →38.32.
– Questions with **(τί) οὐ + first-** or **second-person present/aorist indicative**: →38.33.

Answers

38.21   To answer yes/no-questions:

Affirmative answers ('yes') may be expressed by:

– the repetition of the focus (→60.20–4) of a question in the answer: cf. (19) above, εἰσί *yes, there are* answering ἆρ' οὐκ εἰσί; *are there not?*;
– a personal pronoun reinforced by γε (especially ἔγωγε), when the question asks whether a person is doing something: cf. (15) above, ἔγωγε *I am*, answering ἐρωτᾷς *are you asking?*;
– first-person verbs expressing affirmation or agreement: φημί *I say so*, ὁμολογῶ *I agree*;
– various expressions of likelihood and truth: ἀνάγκη *(that's) inevitable*, φαίνεται *(so) it seems*, εἰκός (γε) *(that's) likely*; ἔστι ταῦτα *that is the case*, ἀληθῆ *true*; πῶς δ' οὔ;/πῶς γὰρ οὔ;/τί γὰρ οὔ; (→38.19 n.2);

– affirmative adverbs and adverbial phrases (the Greek equivalents of *yes, certainly, by all means, of course*, etc.): ναί, μάλα, μάλα γε, μάλιστα, πάνυ γε, παντάπασί γε, παντάπασι μὲν οὖν, etc.

Negative answers may be expressed by:

– οὔ *not* (so accented; a verb has to be supplied from the question), e.g.:

(36) ΝΕ. οὐκ αἰσχρὸν ἡγῇ δῆτα τὸ ψευδῆ λέγειν; | :: ΟΔ. <u>οὔκ</u>, εἰ τὸ σωθῆναί γε τὸ ψεῦδος φέρει. (Soph. *Phil.* 108–9)

(Neoptolemus:) Do you not think it disgraceful to tell lies? :: (Odysseus:) Not *(i.e. 'I do not think it disgraceful')* if the lie brings us salvation.

A translation *no* will often be preferred for οὔ. It may be reinforced by particles (e.g. οὖν in (20) above, οὔκουν ἔγωγε *indeed I don't*, δῆτα in (16) *certainly not*).

– ἥκιστα *not at all*, οὐδαμῶς *certainly not*, and πῶς γάρ;/τί γάρ; *certainly not*.

Note 1: For the use of γάρ and γε in answers to yes/no-questions, →59.14, 59.53.

38.22 **Alternative questions**, which present a choice between two possibilities, are normally answered by one of these possibilities: cf. (24) above.

38.23 **Specifying questions** will naturally be answered by an item that satisfies the information asked for, e.g.:

(37) ΣΩ. ὦ φίλε Φαῖδρε, <u>ποῖ</u> δὴ καὶ <u>πόθεν</u>; :: ΦΑ. <u>παρὰ Λυσίου</u> . . . <u>τοῦ Κεφάλου</u>· πορεύομαι δὲ πρὸς περίπατον ἔξω τείχους. (Pl. *Phdr.* 227a)

(Socrates:) My dear Phaedrus, where are you going, and where are you coming from? :: (Phaedrus:) From Lysias, the son of Cephalus; and I am going for a walk outside the wall.

38.24 Speakers may, of course, also provide 'non-answers' to any type of question (e.g. οὐκ οἶδα *I don't know*), or no answer at all.

Directives

Basic Constructions

38.25 Commands, suggestions, requests, exhortations (etc.) in the **second or third person** are regularly expressed by the **imperative**:

(38) σὺ οὖν ἐκείναις <u>λέγε</u> ὅτι ἀντὶ κυνὸς εἶ φύλαξ. (Xen. *Mem.* 2.7.14)

You must tell those women, then, that you are their guardian in place of a dog.

(39) <u>λεγέτω</u> δ' ὑπὲρ ὑμῶν μί' ἅπερ ἂν κἀγὼ λέγω. (Ar. *Lys.* 210)

Let one woman, on behalf of all of you, repeat exactly what I say.

For self-exhortations in the **first person** (most often plural), the **hortatory subjunctive** is used:

(40) ἴωμεν ἐπὶ τοὺς πολεμίους. (Xen. *Cyr.* 1.5.11)
Let us move against our enemies.

38.26   Negative commands and requests (**prohibitions**) in the **second person** are formed with **μή** and either the **present imperative** or the **aorist subjunctive** (μή + second-person aorist imperative and μή + second-person present subjunctive do not occur):

(41) πιστοὺς δὲ μὴ νόμιζε φύσει φύεσθαι ἀνθρώπους. (Xen. *Cyr.* 8.7.13)
Don't think that men are born trustworthy by nature.

(42) μὴ γὰρ ἄλλο τι νομίσητε τὴν γῆν αὐτῶν ἢ ὅμηρον. (Thuc. 1.82.4)
Don't consider their land to be anything other than a hostage.

In the **third person**, μή is most commonly used with the imperative (either aorist or present), but the subjunctive (most often aorist, seldom present) also occurs:

(43) καὶ μηδεὶς αὐτὰ φαῦλα νομισάτω εἶναι. (Xen. *Cyn.* 2.2)
And let no one think that these things are meaningless. *Aorist imperative.*

(44) ὑπολάβῃ δὲ μηδεὶς ὡς οὐδὲν προσῆκον ὑμῶν κηδόμεθα. (Thuc. 6.84.1)
And let no one suppose that we are concerned for you when we have nothing to do with you. *Aorist subjunctive.*

In the **first person**, the **hortatory subjunctive + μή** is used:

(45) μὴ μέλλωμεν ἤδη τώδε τίλλειν καὶ δάκνειν. (Ar. *Av.* 352)
Let's not wait any longer to pluck and bite these two.

38.27   Each of these constructions may be preceded by interjections like ἄγε(τε), φέρε(τε), ἴθι (often with δή): *come (on), go ahead*:

(46) ἄγε δή, ὦ Ἀριαῖε, . . . εἰπὲ τίνα γνώμην ἔχεις. (Xen. *An.* 2.2.10)
Come now, Ariaeus, say what your opinion is.

(47) φέρετε, τοῦ λοιποῦ μὴ πειθώμεθα αὐτοῦ. (Hdt. 6.12.3)
Come, let us not listen to him in the future. *For the infrequent construction of πείθομαι with the genitive, →30.21.*

38.28   **Indirect directives**, i.e. the representation of a command/request in indirect speech/thought (→41.1–2; cf. Engl. *He told him to leave* (indirect) as opposed to *Leave!* (direct)), are expressed in Greek by means of a 'manipulative' verb (verbs meaning 'command', 'request', 'beg', etc.) followed by a dynamic infinitive. For details, →51.8–15.

38.29   Overview of basic directive constructions:

	first person	second person	third person
positive (commands, exhortations, suggestions, etc.)	subjunctive	imperative	imperative
negative (prohibitions, warnings, etc.)	μή + subjunctive	μή + present imperative *or* μή + aorist subjunctive	μή + imperative (or subjunctive)

Difference between Present-Stem and Aorist-Stem Imperatives/Subjunctives

38.30   The difference between present and aorist imperatives/subjunctives in these constructions is **purely aspectual** (→33.63–5): present-stem forms (with imperfective aspect) present the action to be carried out as a process, i.e. as ongoing or repeated; aorist-stem forms (with perfective aspect) present an action as a single complete whole:

(48)   ΣΩ. καὶ νῦν δὴ τούτων ὁπότερον βούλει ποίει, ἐρώτα ἢ ἀποκρίνου. :: ΠΩΛ. ἀλλὰ ποιήσω ταῦτα. καί μοι ἀπόκριναι, ὦ Σώκρατες· ἐπειδὴ Γοργίας ἀπορεῖν σοι δοκεῖ περὶ τῆς ῥητορικῆς, σὺ αὐτὴν τίνα φὴς εἶναι; (Pl. *Grg.* 462b)

(Socrates:) So now please do whichever of these you like, either ask the questions or answer them. :: (Polus:) All right, I will do so. So, answer me, Socrates: Since you think Gorgias is confused about oratory, which craft do you say it is? *Socrates uses the present imperatives* ἐρώτα *and* ἀποκρίνου *to press Polus to undertake a certain process (the pres. imp. is often so used in 'procedural' commands: Polus is to act either as 'questioner' or as 'answerer'). Polus' aorist imperative* ἀπόκριναι *is a request to answer a single question.*

The present imperative/subjunctive may also function as a request to get an action underway (this is sometimes called the **immediative** use of the present imperative):

(49)   ἀνάγνωθι δέ μοι λαβὼν τουτονὶ ... τὸν νόμον, ὃς διαρρήδην οὐκ ἐᾷ ... ἀναγίγνωσκε. (Dem. 24.32)

Take up and read aloud for me this law, which plainly forbids ... Go on, read it out. *The aorist imperative refers to the reading out in its entirety (a command to do something), whereas the 'immediative' present imperative refers to the process of reading out (a command to be doing something).*

(50) καί μοι, ὦ ἄνδρες Ἀθηναῖοι, μὴ θορυβήσητε, μηδ' ἐὰν δόξω τι ὑμῖν μέγα λέγειν . . .
εἰς Δελφοὺς ἐλθὼν ἐτόλμησε τοῦτο μαντεύσασθαι – καί, ὅπερ λέγω, μὴ
θορυβεῖτε, ὦ ἄνδρες – ἤρετο γὰρ δὴ εἴ τις ἐμοῦ εἴη σοφώτερος. (Pl. *Ap.* 20e–21a)
And please, Athenians, do not interrupt me, not even if I shall seem to be
saying something outrageous to you. . . When he arrived at Delphi, he dared to
put the following matter to the oracle – and as I have said, gentlemen, please do
not interrupt me – he asked whether there was someone wiser than myself.
With the aorist subjunctive (μὴ) θορυβήσητε, Socrates formulates his request as
a simple instruction not to perform a certain action. He is not (yet) interested in
the 'process' of not-disturbing, only in the basic fact of non-disturbance. Later,
when the possibility that the audience will cause an uproar is at its peak (Socrates
is about to say something outrageous, μέγα λέγειν), he reformulates the request
using the present imperative (μὴ) θορυβεῖτε: the process is now relevant, as the
previously stated request (note ὅπερ λέγω) becomes 'operational'.

The present imperative/subjunctive is also used to command someone to continue
or (with μή) cease doing something (**continuative** use):

(51) ἔστιν οὖν ὅστις βούλεται ὑπὸ τῶν συνόντων βλάπτεσθαι μᾶλλον ἢ ὠφελεῖσθαι;
ἀποκρίνου, ὦ ἀγαθέ· καὶ γὰρ ὁ νόμος κελεύει ἀποκρίνεσθαι. (Pl. *Ap.* 25d)
Is there anyone who wishes to be harmed by those around him rather than be
helped? Keep answering, good man, for the law demands that one keeps
answering. *Socrates' question is part of an ongoing series of questions.*

(52) γυναικὶ δὴ ταύτῃ τῇ νῦν συνοικέεις μὴ συνοίκεε. (Hdt. 9.111.2)
Stop living with this woman with whom you are living now.

Note 1: Perfect imperatives and subjunctives are rarely used, but have their normal aspectual
value(s) when they are. For the use of the third-person passive perfect imperative, →34.21.

Other Expressions Used as Directives; Differences between These Expressions

38.31   There are several other idiomatic ways to express commands and requests in
Greek (cf. also (7)–(14) above). The reasons why a speaker may select one directive
expression over another are complex, having to do with differences of social status
between speaker and addressee, the urgency and severity of the directive, the desire
to be polite, etc.
The most frequent alternative expressions with directive force are listed below.

38.32   Interrogatives with **οὐ** + **second-person future indicative** function as **urgent
commands** or **requests**, or (with οὐ μή) as urgent prohibitions (also →33.44):

(53) οὐ καὶ σὺ αὖ ὁμολογήσεις μηδὲν ὑπ' ἐμοῦ ἀδικεῖσθαι; (Xen. *Cyr.* 5.5.13)
Will you not for your part also agree that you have in no way been wronged
by me? (= *'agree that . . . !'*)

38.33   Interrogatives with (τί) οὐ + **first-** or **second-person present/aorist indicative** are
used to express a **request** or **suggestion** (also →33.21, 33.33):

(54) ΑΘ. <u>τί οὐ καλοῦμεν</u> δῆτα τὴν Λυσιστράτην, | ἥπερ διαλλάξειεν ἡμᾶς ἂν μόνη; | ::
ΛΑ. ναὶ τὼ σιώ. (Ar. *Lys.* 1103–5)
(Athenian:) Let's call Lysistrata, then, since she's the only one who can reconcile
us. :: (Spartan:) By the two gods, let's. σιώ *is Laconian* (→25.1) *for* θεώ *(dual).*

(55) <u>Τί</u> οὖν, ἔφην ἐγώ, <u>οὐ</u> καὶ Πρόδικον καὶ Ἱππίαν <u>ἐκαλέσαμεν</u> καὶ τοὺς μετ' αὐτῶν,
ἵνα ἐπακούσωσιν ἡμῶν; :: Πάνυ μὲν οὖν, ἔφη ὁ Πρωταγόρας. (Pl. *Prt.* 317d)
'Let's call', said I, 'Prodicus and Hippias and those with them as well, so they
can listen to us.' 'Absolutely', said Protagoras.

Note 1: The difference between present and aorist indicatives in such questions may be
purely aspectual (and not temporal): →33.33 n.1 (and cf. 38.30).

38.34   ὅπως (neg. ὅπως μή) + **second/third person future indicative** (the construction of
effort clauses, →44) can be used independently to express an **emphatic exhorta-
tion/warning**. ὅπως is not a conjunction in these cases:

(56) <u>ὅπως</u> οὖν <u>ἔσεσθε</u> ἄνδρες ἄξιοι τῆς ἐλευθερίας ἧς κέκτησθε. (Xen. *An.* 1.7.3)
You must, then, be men worthy of the freedom which you possess. *For the
case of* ἧς, →50.13.

38.35   The second-person **potential optative** (with ἄν) may have the force of a **cautious
command or request** (→34.13):

(57) τῷδ' <u>ἂν</u> μὴ προέσθαι ἡμᾶς <u>μάθοιτε</u>. (Thuc. 1.36.3)
You should learn from this not to betray us.

Similarly, the **first-person potential optative** may be used to express a **cautious
self-exhortation**: this is often found when the speaker has been invited to do
something:

(58) ΙΦ. οὐκοῦν λέγειν μὲν χρὴ σέ, μανθάνειν δ' ἐμέ; | :: ΟΡ. <u>λέγοιμ' ἄν</u>. (Eur.
IT 810–11)
(Iphigenia:) Isn't it proper for you to speak, then, and for me to be informed? ::
(Orestes:) I shall speak.

38.36   Especially in circumstances where a speaker wishes not to be too direct (for
instance in addressing a superior), he or she may use an impersonal construction
such as δεῖ/χρή:

(59) <u>δεῖ</u> δ' οὐ τοιούτων, ἀλλ' ὅπως τὰ τοῦ θεοῦ | μαντεῖ' ἄριστα λύσομεν, τόδε
σκοπεῖν. (Soph. *OT* 406–7)
There is no need for such things, but to examine how we may best resolve the
oracles of the god. *The chorus advises Oedipus, its king.*

38.37   The infinitive is sometimes used in directives – the **imperatival infinitive** (Lat. *infinitivus pro imperativo*), to express the **proper procedure** to be followed in a specific type of, mostly conventional, situation:

(60)   εἰ μὲν γὰρ ἀξιόχρεος δοκέεις εἶναι σεωυτῷ τοῖσι ἐμοῖσι πρήγμασιν ἀντιωθῆναι, σὺ δὲ ... μάχεσθαι· εἰ δὲ συγγινώσκεαι εἶναι ἥσσων, σὺ δὲ ... δεσπότῃ τῷ σῷ ... ἐλθὲ ἐς λόγους. (Hdt. 4.126)

For if you think yourself capable of opposing my power, then you must fight. But if you admit you are weaker, then come to terms with your master. *The infinitive μάχεσθαι expresses the proper procedure to follow in war if one party thinks it has a chance of winning. The imperative ἐλθέ is what the speaker (Darius) actually wants the addressee to do. For 'apodotic' δέ (twice with σὺ δέ), →59.17.*

(61)   σύ νυν τοῦτον τὸν ἄνδρα παῦσον ταῦτα ποιεῦντα, ἵνα μὴ οἰκηίῳ πολέμῳ συνέχῃ... ἐπεὰν δὲ αὐτὸν περιλάβῃς, ποιέειν ὅκως μηκέτι κεῖνος ἐς Ἕλληνας ἀπίξεται. (Hdt. 5.23.3)

Stop this man, then, from doing this, so that you may not be embroiled in a civil war. And when you have him in your grasp, proceed to take measures so that he never returns to Greece. *ποιέειν expresses the procedure to follow in dealing with the threat posed by Histiaeus (τοῦτον τὸν ἄνδρα).*

Note 1: The imperatival infinitive is a 'dynamic' infinitive (the negative is μή, and the difference between present and aorist infinitives is purely aspectual; →51.4).

Wishes

Realizable and Unrealizable Wishes

38.38   In wishes that a speaker considers **realizable** the **cupitive optative** without ἄν is used (→34.14), sometimes introduced by εἴθε, εἰ γάρ or ὡς (poetic): 'would that', 'if only', 'may ...', 'I wish that ...'. The negative is μή:

(62)   γένοιτο ... κατὰ νόον τοι, βασιλεῦ. (Hdt. 7.104.5)
    May it go according to plan for you, sire.

(63)   εἴθ', ὦ λῷστε, σύ τοιοῦτος ὢν φίλος ἡμῖν γένοιο. (Xen. *Hell.* 4.1.38)
    May you, my dearest man, being such as you are, become our friend.

38.39   In wishes that (the speaker thinks) can no longer come true – **unrealizable wishes** – the **modal (secondary) indicative** (aorist, imperfect, or pluperfect) is used, always introduced by εἴθε or εἰ γάρ (→34.18). The negative is μή:

(64)   εἴθ' ἦν Ὀρέστης πλησίον κλύων τάδε. (Eur. *El.* 282)
    If only Orestes were nearby to hear these things!

(65) εἴθε με Καδμείων ἔναρον στίχες ἐν κονίαισιν. (Eur. *Supp.* 821)

Would that the ranks of the Cadmeans had laid me in the dust. ἔναρον *is an unaugmented aorist (of* ἐναίρω '*slay*').

Note 1: Unrealizable wishes do not express hope for the realization of an action, but rather serve as a regretful or resigned comment on a situation which can no longer be altered.

38.40   Unrealizable wishes may also be expressed by a form of the imperfect **ὤφελον + infinitive** (lit: *I ought to have, I owed* . . .).

(66) ὤφελε . . . Κῦρος ζῆν. (Xen. *An.* 2.1.4)

If only Cyrus were alive.

(67) ὀλέσθαι δ' ὤφελον τῇδ' ἡμέρᾳ. (Soph. *OT* 1157)

Would that I had perished that day.

Note 1: εἰ γὰρ ὤφελον/ὤφελεν can stand on its own, meaning *If only!*; the thing longed for in such instances is clear from the context.

Difference between Present-Stem and Aorist-Stem Forms

38.41   The difference between aorist and present optatives in realizable wishes is one of **aspect** (→33.63–5): present-stem optatives (with imperfective aspect) regard an action as ongoing/repeated, aorist optatives (with perfective aspect) regard an action in completion, as a single whole.

(68) ληφθείς γ' ὑπὸ λῃστῶν ἐσθίοι κριθὰς μόνας. (Ar. *Pax* 449)

May he be captured by bandits and eat only barley.

(69) καὶ μήποτ' αὐτῆς μᾶζαν ἡδίω φάγοι. (Ar. *Pax* 3)

And may it never eat a tastier cake than that one.

In (68), the chorus use a present optative to emphasize the habitual/ongoing duress that they wish the subject to suffer from. In (69), the speaker is talking about a single and discrete action of cake-eating, as appears from the use of the aorist.

Note 1: The perfect optative is very rarely used in wishes, but has its normal aspectual value(s) when it is (e.g. τεθναίην *I wish I were dead*).
Note 2: The 'immediative' and 'continuative' nuances described above for the present imperative (→38.30) may occasionally be detected in the present optative.

38.42   Similarly, in unrealizable wishes, the difference between imperfects and aorist indicatives (or with ὤφελον, present and aorist infinitives) is aspectual. In practice, unrealizable wishes about the present use present-stem forms (impf., pres. inf.: cf. (64) and (66) above), while unrealizable wishes referring to the past normally use aorist-stem forms (aor. ind., aor. inf.: cf. (65) and (67)). Also →34.18 n. 1.

Exclamations

Introduction: Basic Terminology

38.43 **Exclamatory sentences** express a speaker's strong emotion (surprise, indignation, anger, happiness, etc.) towards an action, person or thing. In principle, any sentence can be an exclamation (this is signalled in English by an exclamation mark – e.g. *Alice did a great job!* – but no exclamation mark is used in standard Greek texts). However, special sentence types, whose **form** indicates that an exclamation is being expressed, can also be used (in English, for instance, by means of an inverted word order: *Did Alice ever do a great job!*).

38.44 Several types of exclamation need to be distinguished:

- **Exclamations of degree** or ***wh*-exclamations** (cf. Engl. *What a great job!*): In Greek, such exclamations are expressed by means of the definite relative adjectives and adverbs (οἷος, ὅσος, ὡς, etc.);
- **Nominal exclamations** (cf. Engl. *Great job!*): In Greek, such exclamations are expressed by means of the nominative or genitive case;
- **Sentence exclamations** (cf. Engl. *Did Alice do a great job!*): To the extent that such exclamations are expressed through a special construction in Greek, the infinitive is used (→38.51).

38.45 Exclamatory sentences in Greek are often accompanied by vocatives and/or interjections (φεῦ, οἴμοι, etc.).

38.46 For indirect exclamations, i.e. the representation of exclamations in indirect discourse (cf. Engl. *He was amazed at what a cool car John drove*), →42.9–11.

Exclamations of Degree

38.47 With **exclamations of degree**, the speaker expresses his/her surprise or emotion at the fact that a situation or thing has in some respect (quality, quantity, etc.) exceeded his expectations. To express this type of exclamation, Greek uses the **definite relative adjectives** (οἷος, ὅσος, etc.; →8.1). The adjective may modify a noun (adnominal use) or be used pronominally (→26.22–3):

(70) ὦ πάππε, <u>ὅσα πράγματα</u> ἔχεις ἐν τῷ δείπνῳ, εἰ ἀνάγκη σοι ἐπὶ πάντα τὰ λεκάρια ταῦτα διατείνειν τὰς χεῖρας καὶ ἀπογεύεσθαι τούτων τῶν παντοδαπῶν βρωμάτων. (Xen. *Cyr.* 1.3.4)
Oh grandfather, how many troubles you have at dinner, if you have to stretch out your arms to all those dishes and have to taste of all those different kinds of food! *ὅσα modifies πράγματα, agreeing with it in case, number and gender.*

(71) ὦ δύσδαιμον, οἷα πάσχομεν. (Eur. *Alc.* 258)

My unhappy wife, what (*lit. 'what kind of'*) things we suffer! *οἷα is used pronominally, as the object of* πάσχομεν.

The **relative manner adverb ὡς** *how* is used to qualify either adjectives (or adverbs) or verbs (with the latter it expresses the remarkable degree to which an action is carried out):

(72) παπαιάξ, ὡς καλὴν ὀσμὴν ἔχει. (Eur. *Cyc.* 153)

My oh my! What a beautiful smell it has!

(73) ὦ φίλταθ' Αἷμον, ὡς σ' ἀτιμάζει πατήρ. (Soph. *Ant.* 572)

My dearest Haemon, how your father dishonours you!

38.48   The definite relative adjectives may be used predicatively (cf. the similar use of interrogative adjectives and demonstrative pronouns, →38.13, 29.34):

(74) ὅσην ἔχεις τὴν δύναμιν, ὦναξ δέσποτα. (Ar. *Plut.* 748)

How great is the power you wield, lord my master! *ὅσην is used predicatively with* τὴν δύναμιν *(note the article), the object of* ἔχεις.

(75) οἵαν ἔχιδναν τήνδ' ἔφυσας. (Eur. *Ion* 1262)

What a viper is this woman you have begotten! *οἵαν ἔχιδναν is used predicatively with* τήνδ', *the object of* ἔφυσας.

These examples differ subtly from (70)–(71). In (74), for instance, the exclamation only concerns the predicative part; one could paraphrase the sentence as 'you wield power and how great is it!' By contrast, in (70) the exclamation concerns the whole expression ὅσα πράγματα ἔχεις.

38.49   Exclamations of degree frequently omit a verb:

(76) ὦ Ζεῦ πολυτίμηθ', ὡς καλαί. (Ar. *Eq.* 1390)

O much-honoured Zeus, what beautiful women!

Nominal Exclamations

38.50   **Nominal exclamations** express a speaker's surprise or emotion about a person or thing. They can be expressed by the **nominative case** (often with the interjection ὦ added) or by the **genitive of cause** (→30.30). With the latter construction an interjection (such as φεῦ, οἴμοι or ὤμοι) is virtually always present (interjections are a direct expression of grief/indignation/etc., to which the genitive is then added to convey the cause of that grief/indignation/etc.):

(77) ΦΑ. γέγραφε γὰρ δὴ ὁ Λυσίας πειρώμενόν τινα τῶν καλῶν, οὐχ ὑπ' ἐραστοῦ δέ, ἀλλ' αὐτὸ δὴ τοῦτο καὶ κεκόμψευται . . . :: ΣΩ. ὦ γενναῖος. (Pl. *Phdr.* 227c)

(Phaedrus:) For Lysias represents one of the beautiful boys as being seduced, but not by a lover. That's the clever thing about it. :: (Socrates:) O, noble man! *Note the accentuation of the interjection* ὦ *(not 'vocative'* ὦ).

(78) οἴμοι <u>ταλαίνης</u> ἄρα <u>τῆσδε συμφορᾶς</u>. (Soph. *El.* 1179)

Ah, so sad, then, is this misfortune! *More literally 'Alas, then, for this misfortune.'*

Note 1: With interjections such as οἴμοι, the genitive of cause is used to refer to the second and third person; to refer to him/herself, the speaker uses the nominative:

(79) οἴμοι <u>τάλαινα</u>. (Soph. *Ant.* 554)

Ah, poor me!

The Exclamatory Infinitive

38.51   The **infinitive** is used in exclamations to express surprise or indignation at **the very fact that a certain situation obtains**. The subject, if present, is expressed in the accusative (accusative-and-infinitive construction, →51.21):

(80) βάλλ’ ἐς κόρακας. τοιουτονὶ <u>τρέφειν</u> κύνα. (Ar. *Vesp.* 835)

Damn it to hell! Oh that anyone would keep such a dog!

(81) <u>ἐμὲ</u> <u>παθεῖν</u> τάδε, | φεῦ, <u>ἐμὲ</u> παλαιόφρονα κατά τε γᾶν <u>οἰκεῖν</u>. (Aesch. *Eum.* 837–8)

That I should have been treated so – ah! – and that I, old and wise as I am, should live under the earth!

39

Introduction to Complex Sentences

Definitions; Functions of Subordinate Clauses

39.1 In chapter 26, an account was given of simple sentences, which are structured around a single predicate and several obligatory and optional constituents. When a sentence contains more than one predicate, we speak of **complex sentences**.

39.2 Predicates can combine to form complex sentences either

 – by **co-ordination** (also 'parataxis', lit.: 'placement next to');
 – or by **subordination** (also 'hypotaxis', lit.: 'placement under').

In subordination, one predicate is 'superior' to another in the structure of the sentence, in that the subordinate predicate fulfils a syntactic role with its superordinate predicate:

(1) τότε μὲν οὖν . . . ἐδειπνηποιήσαντο καὶ ἐκοιμήθησαν. (Xen. *Ages.* 2.15)
 Then they took dinner and went to sleep. *Co-ordination – two main clauses are co-ordinated by καί.*

(2) τότε μὲν οὖν . . . δειπνηποιησάμενοι ἐκοιμήθησαν. (Xen. *Hell.* 4.3.20)
 Then, having taken dinner, they went to sleep. *Subordination – the subordinate predicate, which here takes the form of a participle (δειπνηποιησάμενοι), fulfils the role of predicative modifier (→26.26) with the superordinate predicate ἐκοιμήθησαν.*

Superordinate predicates such as ἐκοιμήθησαν in (2) will be called **matrix predicates** below; the clauses in which such predicates stand will be called **matrix clauses**.

39.3 Subordinate predicates may fulfil all syntactic roles which nominal elements can fulfil. Thus they may be an **obligatory constituent** of the matrix predicate (subject, object, complement), an **optional constituent** with that predicate (adverbial modifier, predicative modifier) or, in the case of many relative clauses and participles, a **modifier within a noun phrase**.

(3) πόλεμον . . . οἶμαι προσήκειν ἡμῖν ὑπομένειν. (Isoc. 6.89)
 I think that it is fitting for us to endure war. *The infinitive construction consisting of προσήκειν and everything that depends on it fulfils the role of object*

(an obligatory constituent) with the main predicate οἶμαι; *in turn, the infinitive construction* πόλεμον ὑπομένειν *fulfils the role of subject (again an obligatory constituent) with* προσήκειν.

(4) καλλίστην γὰρ μάχην <u>νικήσαντες</u> καὶ δόξαν ἐξ αὐτῆς μεγίστην <u>λαβόντες</u> . . . οὐδὲν βέλτιον <u>πράττουσιν</u>. (Isoc. 5.53)

For although they won a splendid victory and acquired a very great reputation from it, they are no better off. *The two co-ordinated participle constructions fulfil the role of predicative modifiers in the clause centred around* πράττουσιν.

(5) <u>ἐκεῖνοι</u> δέ, <u>οὓς</u> οὗτοι <u>ἀπώλεσαν</u>, . . . πέρας <u>ἔχουσι</u> τῆς παρὰ τῶν ἐχθρῶν τιμωρίας. (Lys. 12.88)

But those men, whom these men have killed, are beyond getting satisfaction from their enemies. *The relative clause* οὓς . . . ἀπώλεσαν *fulfils the role of attributive modifier with* ἐκεῖνοι, *a constituent of the matrix clause centred around the predicate* ἔχουσι.

39.4   Examples (3) and (4) make clear that co-ordination and subordination are **recursive processes**: subordinate predicates can themselves have further subordinate predicates, or be co-ordinated with other subordinate predicates. Schematically, the hierarchical structure of the examples can be rendered as follows:

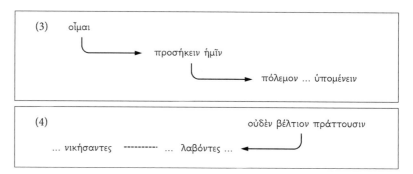

Note that in (3) προσήκειν is the matrix predicate of the infinitive construction πόλεμον ὑπομένειν. Thus there is a difference between the terms 'matrix predicate/clause' and '**main predicate/clause**': the latter term refers only to the 'outermost' matrix clause, in which all subordinate constructions are embedded (e.g. οἶμαι in (3)).

Types of Subordinate Constructions

39.5   As the examples given above show, Greek displays three major types of subordination, defined in terms of the verb form of the subordinate predicate:

- **infinitives** (e.g. (3));
- **participles** (e.g. (2) and (4));
- **finite clauses** (e.g. (5)), which contain a **subordinator** (conjunction, relative pronoun, etc.) and **finite verb** (with a personal ending).

Note 1: Just as predicates may determine the case of the nominal constituents in a simple sentence (e.g. παιδεύω *educate* takes an object in the accusative, but βοηθέω *aid* takes a complement in the dative), so matrix predicates often pose constraints on the expression of tense, mood and other features of the subordinate predicate.

In (4), for instance, a choice of οἶμαι *think* predetermines the selection of an infinitive for the object, because this verb always takes an infinitive (and not a ὅτι/ὡς-clause or participle, →51.19 with n.1); the same restriction exists for προσήκειν (→51.8).

In (2), the participle is built on the aorist stem, implying that the 'taking dinner' temporally preceded the 'going to sleep': the matrix predicate functions as the temporal anchor for the subordinate predicate (→33.57). Furthermore, the participle agrees with the subject of the matrix predicate.

Although all these forms involve strategies of subordination, the term **subordinate clause** is usually reserved for the last category. In the structure of this book, too, we first treat different kinds of finite subordinate clauses (40–50), while the syntax of the infinitive and of the participle are treated separately in 51 and 52.

An overview of the various subordinate constructions is given in 53.

40

Introduction to Finite Subordinate Clauses

Subordinators

40.1 The following types of **subordinators** introduce Greek finite subordinate clauses:

- **conjunctions** (ὅτι, ὡς, εἰ, ὅτε, ἐπεί, διότι, μή, etc.);
- **relative pronouns** (ὅς, ἥ, ὅ; ὅστις, etc.), **relative adjectives** (οἷος, ὅσος; ὁποῖος, ὁπόσος, etc.), or **relative adverbs** (ἔνθα, ὡς; ὅπως, etc.);
- in indirect questions, **interrogative pronouns** (τίς, etc.), or **indefinite relative pronouns** (ὅστις, etc.).

Note 1: Greek finite subordinate clauses **always** have a subordinator, in contrast to English, where such subordinators may sometimes be left out (contrast *He said that I was clever* with *He said I was clever*; *The man that/whom I saw was ugly* with *The man I saw was ugly*).

The only exception in Greek is the use of the subjunctive after second-person βούλει/βούλεσθε or θέλεις/θέλετε, for which →34.8 n.2, 38.17. (This is perhaps best seen as a case of co-ordination, rather than subordination, however.)

Functions and Types of Finite Subordinate Clauses

40.2 The following types of subordinate clause function as **obligatory constituents** with certain kinds of matrix predicates: the subordinate clause functions as subject or object with the matrix predicate (and the subordinate clause therefore cannot be left out). Such clauses are called **complement clauses**:

- **declarative** subordinate clauses (indirect statement), introduced by ὅτι or ὡς (→41);
- **indirect questions**, introduced by εἰ / πότερον ... ἤ / εἴτε ... εἴτε, interrogative pronouns/adjectives/adverbs (τίς, πόσος, ποῦ, etc.), or indefinite relative pronouns/adjectives/adverbs (ὅστις, ὁπόσος, ὅπου, etc.); and **indirect exclamations**, introduced by definite relative adjectives or adverbs (ὅσος, ὡς, etc.) (→42);
- **fear clauses**, introduced by μή (→43);
- **effort clauses**, introduced by ὅπως (→44).

Note 1: These clauses are also often called 'substantival clauses' (because they fulfil the same syntactic role that may be fulfilled by noun phrases, i.e. substantives) or 'object clauses'. Note that, in spite of the terms 'complement clause' and 'object clause', such clauses may also function as subject, e.g. in ἐλέγετο ὅτι ... *it was reported that* ..., where the ὅτι-clause is subject of ἐλέγετο.

40.3   The following types of subordinate clause can be added to a matrix clause optionally; the subordinate clause functions as an **optional adverbial modifier** with the matrix predicate. Such clauses are called **adverbial clauses**:

- **purpose clauses**, introduced by ἵνα, ὅπως, ὡς, or μή (→45);
- **result clauses**, introduced by ὥστε (→46);
- **temporal clauses**, introduced by ὅτε, ἐπεί, πρίν, ἕως, etc. (→47);
- **causal clauses**, introduced by ὅτι or διότι (→48);
- **conditional clauses**, introduced by εἰ (also concessive clauses introduced by εἰ καί/καὶ εἰ) (→49).

40.4   Finally, **relative clauses** (→50), introduced by the relative pronouns ὅς, ὅστις, etc. or by relative adjectives such as οἷος, ὅσος, etc., typically function as an (attributive) **modifier** of a head (pro)noun in the matrix clause (the antecedent). However, there are also 'autonomous' relative clauses, which lack a nominal antecedent in the matrix clause (→50.7) and function as constituents in the matrix clause by themselves. Such clauses can or cannot be omitted depending on their function in the sentence.

Note 1: Because they usually modify an antecedent noun, relative clauses are often called 'adjectival clauses'. But autonomous relative clauses are not properly 'adjectival'.

Other **relative clauses** function as optional adverbial modifiers (particularly those introduced by relative adverbs such as ἔνθα, ὡς: →50.34–40).

Moods in Subordinate Clauses

Subordinate Clauses Which Use the Same Moods as Independent Sentences

40.5   Several types of subordinate clause use the **same moods as are used in independent sentences** (→34):

- declarative ὅτι/ὡς-clauses (→41);
- indirect questions (→42; the same moods are used as in direct questions, for which →38.15–17);
- causal clauses (→48);

– some result clauses with ὥστε (→46.4–5);
– 'digressive' relative clauses (→50.6, 50.17).

In the first three of these (ὅτι/ὡς-clauses, indirect questions and in causal clauses introduced by ὅτι), an oblique optative may 'replace' the mood used in historic sequence (→40.12–14).

Note 1: The main moods used in all these clauses are the indicative, 'potential' optative (+ ἄν) and 'counterfactual' modal (secondary) indicative (+ ἄν). The optative and modal indicative in wishes and the imperative and subjunctive in commands are all very rare in subordinate clauses.

Subordinate Clauses with Required Moods

40.6   Several types of subordinate clause grammatically **require the use of a certain mood**:

– fear clauses (fear for the future): the subjunctive (clauses expressing concern about the past or present use the indicative) (→43);
– effort clauses: the future indicative, sometimes the subjunctive (→44);
– purpose clauses: the subjunctive (→45).

In each of these types, an oblique optative may 'replace' the mood used in historic sequence (→40.12–14).

Moods and the Use of ἄν in Temporal, Conditional and Relative Clauses

40.7   In **temporal clauses** (→47), **conditional clauses** (→49) and 'restrictive' **relative clauses** (→50.6, 50.18–22) a speaker may use different moods and/or the particle ἄν to express differences with respect to the time, reality or likelihood of the action in the subordinate clause. These constructions are discussed in detail in the relevant chapters; since these types share certain features, however, some general points may be made here.

40.8   Various factors play a role in the choice of moods in temporal, conditional and relative clauses:

– whether the action referred to is in the **past**, **present** or **future**;
– whether the speaker refers to a **single action** or a **repeated/habitual action**;
– in conditional and some relative clauses, in addition, whether it is considered **likely**, (remotely) **possible**, or **no longer possible** that an action will take place (or is taking place/has taken place), or if no such attitude about the likelihood of the action is adopted (i.e. a **neutral** attitude).

Note 1: Temporal clauses always present an action as taking place: no distinctions between different degrees of likelihood are expressed by such clauses.

40.9   The following constructions are commonly used in **temporal, conditional, and relative clauses**:

- **Indicative**: used by a speaker (in temporal clauses and relative clauses) to refer to actions which **factually** took place in the past or are taking place in the present, or used (in conditional and certain relative clauses) when a speaker adopts a **neutral** attitude towards the reality/likelihood of a past, present or future action:

(1) ἐπειδὴ δὲ Θησεὺς ... δημοκρατίαν ἐποίησεν ..., τὸν ... βασιλέα οὐδὲν ἧττον ὁ δῆμος ᾑρεῖτο ἐκ προκρίτων. ([Dem.] 59.75)
     And when Theseus had established a democracy, the people nonetheless chose their king from a select few. *Temporal clause with aor. ind.; the narrator presents the establishment of the democracy as a factual event in the past.*

(2) ... περὶ Ὑπερβορέων εἰρημένα ... ἔστι ... Ὁμήρῳ ἐν Ἐπιγόνοισι, εἰ δὴ τῷ ἐόντι γε Ὅμηρος ταῦτα τὰ ἔπεα ἐποίησε. (Hdt. 4.32)
     There is discussion of the Hyperboreans by Homer in his *Epigoni*, if indeed Homer did write that work. *Conditional clause with aor. ind.; the narrator expresses a neutral stance: he gives no verdict on whether Homer wrote the* Epigoni *or not (though a degree of scepticism is expressed by* τῷ ἐόντι γε; *for such scepticism in neutral conditional clauses,* →49.4).

- **'Prospective' subjunctive + ἄν**: to refer to actions which the speaker presents as occurring (temporal clauses) or probably occurring (conditional/relative clauses) **in the future**; the main clause normally has a verb form with future reference (e.g. a future indicative, imperative, hortatory subjunctive, etc.; →33.63–4):

(3) ὁπότερος ἂν σφῷν ... με μᾶλλον εὖ ποιῇ, | τούτῳ παραδώσω τῆς Πυκνὸς τὰς ἡνίας. (Ar. *Eq.* 1108–9)
     Whichever one of you two treats me better, to him I will return the reins of the state. *Relative clause with* ἄν + *subj., main clause with fut. ind.; the speaker refers to good treatment in the future, which he considers very likely.*

- **'Indefinite' subjunctive + ἄν**: to refer to actions which occur habitually (repeatedly, typically, generically) in or up to the present; the main clause normally has a present indicative referring to an habitual action (→33.15):

(4) ὃς ἂν δακρῦσαι μάλιστα ... ποιήσῃ πόλιν, οὗτος τὰ νικητήρια φέρει. (Pl. *Leg.* 800d)

Whoever best succeeds at making the city cry, that man (always) carries off the palm of victory. *Relative clause with ἄν + subj., main clause with pres. ind.; the speaker refers to a recurring situation in the city.*

In historic sequence, the **indefinite** construction (referring to actions which took place repeatedly in the past) is expressed by '**iterative' optative** without ἄν (→40.13); the main clause usually has an imperfect referring to a habitual action in the past (→33.24):

(5) ὅκως γὰρ τειχήρεας ποιήσειε, τὸ ἐνθεῦτεν χώματα χῶν πρὸς τὰ τείχεα ἐπόρθεε. (Hdt. 1.162.2)

Whenever he had locked them up inside their walls, he would next heap up mounds against the walls and destroy the city. *Temporal clause with opt., main clause with impf.: the narrator refers to repeated build-ups to sieges.*

Note 1: The prospective construction (sometimes called 'anticipatory') is the default construction for temporal/conditional/relative clauses referring to the future; in temporal clauses it is the only possible construction (→47.8). Note that English in such cases uses present-tense forms (the so-called 'concealed' future, cf. 'treats' in the translation of (3)).

Note 2: Different labels such as 'prospective' and 'indefinite' for subjunctive + ἄν are traditional, but the distinction between the two types should not be pressed too hard: both constructions refer to an *unspecified* time. Whether ἄν + subjunctive is to be called prospective or indefinite depends on the verb used in the matrix clause: if the matrix clause has a verb with future reference (fut. ind., imp., etc.), a subordinate clause with ἄν + subj. is 'prospective'; if the matrix clause has a pres. ind. expressing a repeated action or general truth, ἄν + subj. in the subordinate clause is 'indefinite'.

Even so, the distinction is sometimes irrelevant:

(6) τοῦτο ὑμῶν δέομαι ... · ἐὰν διὰ τῶν αὐτῶν λόγων ἀκούητέ μου ἀπολογουμένου δι᾽ ὧνπερ εἴωθα λέγειν ... μήτε θαυμάζειν μήτε θορυβεῖν τούτου ἕνεκα. (Pl. *Ap.* 17c–d)

This thing I ask of you: if/whenever you hear me defend myself using the same words which I am accustomed to speak, not to be surprised or to make a disturbance on that account. *The dynamic infinitives in the matrix clause (θαυμάζειν and θορυβεῖν, dependent on δέομαι) have future reference, and ἄν + subj. could therefore be seen as 'prospective'; at the same time, the sentence refers to a general prescription, so an 'indefinite' reading is equally valid.*

40.10   In **conditional and some relative clauses** (but *not* temporal clauses), the following additional constructions are possible:

– '**Potential' optative:** to refer to actions in the future (or a different reality), of which the speaker considers it **possible** (but no more than that) that they will occur; the main clause normally has potential optative + ἄν (→34.13):

(7) εἰ μέν τις τῶν τραγικῶν ποιητῶν ... ποιήσειεν ἐν τραγῳδίᾳ τὸν Θερσίτην ὑπὸ τῶν Ἑλλήνων στεφανούμενον, οὐδεὶς ἂν ὑμῶν ὑπομείνειεν. (Aeschin. 3.231)

If some tragic poet should portray Thersites in a tragedy being crowned by the Greeks, none of you would abide it. *Conditional clause with opt., main clause with ἄν + opt.; the speaker refers to a possible (but not very likely) plot of a tragedy.*

– **'Counterfactual' modal** (secondary) **indicative**: to refer to actions in the present or past, which the speaker considers **no longer possible**; the main clause normally has counterfactual modal indicative + ἄν (→34.16):

(8) εἰ τὸ καὶ τὸ ἐποίησεν ἄνθρωπος οὑτοσί, οὐκ ἂν ἀπέθανεν. (Dem. 18.243)

If this man had done this or that, he would not have died. *Conditional clause with secondary ind., main clause with ἄν + secondary ind.: the doing of 'this or that' is presented as no longer possible. For τὸ καὶ τό, →28.30.*

40.11 The following table summarizes the possible constructions:

Temporal, Conditional and Relative Clauses		
construction/meaning	subordinate clause	matrix clause
factual/neutral:	indicative	any tense/mood
prospective:	subjunctive + ἄν	future indicative, etc.
indefinite:	subjunctive + ἄν	present indicative, etc.
(*in historic sequence:*)	'iterative' optative without ἄν	imperfect
Conditional and Relative Clauses (only)		
construction/meaning	subordinate clause	matrix clause
potential:	optative (without ἄν)	optative + ἄν
counterfactual:	secondary indicative (without ἄν)	secondary indicative + ἄν

Sequence of Moods; the Oblique Optative

40.12 In many (but not all) types of subordinate clause, the use of moods may be affected by the **tense** (→33.1–2) of the matrix clause:

– if the verb in the matrix clause is in a **non**-past tense (present, perfect, future) – this is called **primary sequence** – the use of moods is normally not affected;

– if the verb in the matrix clause is in a **past tense** (imperfect, aorist, pluperfect) – this is called **historic** (or **secondary**) **sequence** – a so-called **oblique optative** is regularly used in the subordinate clause, 'replacing' the mood that would be used in primary sequence, although that 'original' mood may also be 'retained'; the **tense stem** is always unchanged.

For example:

(9)   ... ὃ ... δέδοικ' ἐγὼ μὴ πάθηθ' ὑμεῖς. (Dem. 9.65)
      ... which I am afraid you might suffer.

(10) ἔδεισα μὴ ... πάθοιτέ τι. (Xen. *Cyr.* 2.1.11)
      I was afraid that you might suffer something.

(11) πολὺν μὲν φόβον ἡμῖν παρείχετε μή τι πάθητε. (Xen. *Cyr.* 4.5.48)
      You gave us much fear that you might suffer something.

> *In (9), in primary sequence (after pf. ind. δέδοικ(α)), the subjunctive πάθητ(ε) is used in a fear clause (→43.3). In (10), in historic sequence (after aor. ind. ἔδεισα), the oblique aor. optative πάθοιτε replaces an aor. subj. Finally, in (11), in historic sequence (after impf. παρείχετε), the aor. subj. πάθητε is retained.*

(12) λέγει ὅτι παρὰ τοῦ αὑτοῦ ἀνθρώπου ἔχει τὸ ἀργύριον. ([Dem.] 48.37)
      He says that he has got the money from his own slave.

(13) εἶπε ... ὅτι παρασπόνδους ὑμᾶς ἔχοι. (Lys. 12.74)
      He said that he held you to be oathbreakers.

> *In (12), in primary sequence (after pres. ind. λέγει), the indicative ἔχει is a standard mood in a declarative ὅτι-clause (→41.7); in (13), in historic sequence (after aor. ind. εἶπε), the oblique pres. optative ἔχοι replaces a pres. ind.*

Note 1: Thus, unlike English, Greek does not normally have a sequence of tenses with 'back-shifting' (compare *He says that he has*, *He said that he had*; for fuller discussion, →41.1), only a sequence of moods. For exceptions, →41.15.

Note 2: It is often said that in historic sequence the 'original' tense or mood is either 'retained' or 'replaced' by an oblique optative of the same tense stem. Such formulations are a didactic convenience and occasionally used in this grammar. However, they should not be taken to reflect what speakers actually consciously do, nor should it be inferred that the oblique optative is a more marked or unexpected construction. In most contexts, the oblique optative is the more common, even default, option (→41.13 n.1, 45.3).

In historic sequence, there is a nuanced difference between retaining the original mood and using the oblique optative. For detailed discussion and examples of this difference in various types of subordinate clause, →41.13–14, 43.3 n.2, 45.3 n.1, 48.2.

40.13   **Indefinite** subordinate clauses (→40.9) in historic sequence **always** use the **iterative optative** (without ἄν; in primary sequence, they have ἄν + subjunctive): thus there is no choice in such cases between using the optative and retaining an original mood.

40.14   If a subordinate clause in historic sequence that may take the oblique optative **itself has another subordinate clause**, that subordinate clause too *may* (but does not have to) take the optative:

(14) ἐσκόπει ὁ Μενεκλῆς ὅπως ... ἔσοιτο αὐτῷ ὅστις ζῶντα ... <u>γηροτροφήσοι</u>. (Isae. 2.10)

Menecles wondered how he might have someone to attend to him while still alive. *Relative clause (ὅστις ... γηροτροφήσοι) subordinate to an indirect question (ὅπως ... αὐτῷ), which is itself subordinate to ἐσκόπει; fut. opt. ἔσοιτο 'replaces' fut. ind. ἔσται; fut. opt. γηροτροφήσοι replaces fut. ind. γηροτροφήσει. For relative clauses with a fut. ind., →50.24.*

In such clauses, prospective/indefinite ἄν + subjunctive is replaced (if not retained) by optative without ἄν:

(15) ἠπείλησε τῇ γυναικὶ ὅτι εἰ μὴ <u>βούλοιτο</u> ἑκοῦσα, ἄκουσα ποιήσοι ταῦτα. (Xen. Cyr. 6.1.33)

He threatened the woman that if she did not choose it willingly, she would do these things against her will. *Conditional clause (εἰ ... ἑκοῦσα) subordinate to a declarative ὅτι-clause (ὅτι ... ταῦτα), itself subordinate to ἠπείλησε: fut. opt. ποιήσοι replaces fut. ind. ποιήσει; pres. opt. βούλοιτο replaces pres. subj. βούληται + ἄν.*

Attraction of Mood

40.15   In subordinate clauses modifying a matrix clause with a **potential optative + ἄν** (→34.13) or a **cupitive optative** (→34.14), the finite verb in the subordinate clause sometimes also appears in the optative (rather than in another, 'expected' mood): the action is thus presented as part of the possible or wished-for scenario. This phenomenon is known as **attraction of mood**. For example:

(16) <u>βούλοιντ'</u> ἄν ἡμᾶς πάντας ἐξολωλέναι, | ἵνα τὰς τελετὰς <u>λάβοιεν</u> αὐτοὶ τῶν θεῶν. (Ar. *Pax* 412–13)

They'd want us all annihilated, so they could take over the rites of the gods themselves. *Purpose clauses with ἵνα normally take the subjunctive (→45.3); here, the optative λάβοιεν is used instead, as the mood attracts to that of potential βούλοιντ' ἄν.*

(17) <u>ἔρδοι</u> τις ἣν ἕκαστος <u>εἰδείη</u> τέχνην. (Ar. *Vesp.* 1431)

May everyone perform the craft that he is knowledgeable of. *The optative εἰδείη is attracted to cupitive ἔρδοι: the relative clause introduced by ἣν would otherwise have taken indefinite ἄν + subj.*

Attraction of mood also occurs in subordinate clauses modifying matrix clauses with a **counterfactual modal (secondary) indicative** (→34.15–18). In such clauses the verb in the subordinate clause is a secondary indicative. For example:

(18) <u>ἐβουλόμην</u> δ' ἄν, ὦ βουλή, Σίμωνα τὴν αὐτὴν γνώμην ἐμοὶ ἔχειν, ἵν' ἀμφοτέρων ἡμῶν ἀκούσαντες τἀληθῆ ῥᾳδίως <u>ἔγνωτε</u> τὰ δίκαια. (Lys. 3.21)

I would have preferred, Council, for Simon to have the same intention as myself, so that you might have easily come to a just verdict after hearing the truth from both sides. *Purpose clauses with ἵνα take the subjunctive (or optative in historic sequence): in this case the secondary indicative is found, attracted to counterfactual ἐβουλόμην ἄν.*

41

Indirect Statements

Introduction: Indirect Speech

Direct versus Indirect Speech

41.1   A reporter may represent speech (or thought) in one of two forms:

- **Direct**: 'John said to Jane: "I want to see you."'
- **Indirect**: 'John said to Jane that he wanted to see her.'

Direct speech conveys the impression that John's words are reported in the same form in which he spoke them (whether John *actually* said anything of the sort is an open question). Indirect speech conveys the impression that the reported words are given from the perspective of the reporter, necessitating certain changes to their original form. These changes include:

- Indications of **grammatical person**: in direct speech, person indications (*I*, *you*, *he*) are oriented on the perspective (or 'deictic centre') of the person whose words are reported. In the first example John and Jane are referred to by first-person *I* and second-person *you* respectively, evoking the roles of speaker and addressee which John and Jane fulfilled in the reported speech situation. In indirect speech, such indications are oriented on the reporter's perspective. In the second example both John and Jane are referred to by third-person pronouns (*he*, *her*) from the perspective of the reporter, as John and Jane are not the speaker and addressee of the current speech situation.
- **Tense**: in direct speech tense is oriented on the temporal perspective of the person whose words are reported. In the first example, the present tense *want* is used, expressing the idea that the moment of 'wanting (to see Jane)' was in the present for John when he spoke. In indirect speech tense is oriented on the temporal perspective of the reporting speaker: in the second example, the past tense *wanted* expresses the idea that the moment of 'wanting to see Jane' is in the reporter's past. This operation is called the **back-shifting** of tense.
- **Subordination vs. co-ordination**: direct speech is not explicitly subordinated to a verb of 'speaking' or 'thinking': the syntactic relationship between the two clauses is best thought of as paratactic (→39.2). By contrast, indirect speech is

explicitly subordinated to a verb of 'speaking' or 'thinking', in the example above through the conjunction *that*.

The first two changes are not mechanical, but depend on the relationship of the participants and time in the reported and in the current speech situation. For instance, if the reporter reports John's utterance to Jane (who was also the addressee in the reported speech situation), the appropriate indirect report is *John said to you that he wanted to see you*. Furthermore, some languages (including Greek) may use paratactic indirect speech and subordinated direct speech (→41.16 and 41.5).

Types of Indirect Speech

41.2   Different types of utterances (→38.1) are subordinated to a matrix verb in different ways when they are indirectly reported:

- Indirect declarative clauses, called **indirect statements** or *that*-clauses: these are regularly introduced by ὅτι or ὡς *that*; this chapter is concerned with such **ὅτι/ὡς-clauses**.

    Depending on the matrix verb, indirect declarative constructions may also take the form of a declarative infinitive or participle: for these constructions, →51.19–27 and 52.8, 52.10.

Note 1: For the differences between declarative infinitives and ὅτι/ὡς-clauses, →51.19 n.1; for the differences between declarative participles and ὅτι/ὡς-clauses, →52.28. For an overview, also →53.1–4.

- Indirect interrogative clauses, called **indirect questions**; →42:

(1)   νῦν ἐρωτᾷς εἰ ἔχω σε διδάξαι. (Pl. *Men.* 82a)
      Now you are asking whether I am capable of teaching you.

- **Indirect exclamations**; →42:

(2)   τὸν λόγον δέ σου πάλαι θαυμάσας ἔχω, ὅσῳ καλλίω τοῦ προτέρου ἀπηργάσω. (Pl. *Phdr.* 257c)
      As for your speech, I have all this time been surprised how much more beautifully you managed it than your earlier one.

- **Indirect commands**; Greek uses the dynamic infinitive for these, →51.2–4, 51.8–15:

(3)   πέμπειν οὖν ἐκέλευεν αὐτοὺς ναῦς. (Thuc. 7.31.4)
      So he ordered them to send ships.

Indirect Statements

Verbs Introducing Indirect Statements

41.3   There are many verbs which may take ὅτι/ὡς-clauses. Some of the most frequent are:

αἰσθάνομαι	learn that, hear that
ἀκούω	hear, be told that
ἄχθομαι	be angry that
γιγνώσκω	realize that, recognize that
δείκνυμι	point out that
δῆλόν (ἐστι)	it is clear that
διδάσκω	teach that
λέγω/εἶπον	say that
μανθάνω	learn that
οἶδα	know that
ὁράω	see that
πυνθάνομαι	learn that
φαίνεται	it is clear that
φράζω	say that
χαίρω	be glad that

Note 1: Many verbs which take indirect statements do not involve speech, but rather knowledge, (mental) perception, or emotion (these verbs are also regularly construed with a participle, →52.10). In the case of impersonal expressions like δῆλόν ἐστι and φαίνεται, there is not even a clearly defined reported 'speaker'. In such cases, it is perhaps not quite appropriate to speak of 'indirect speech' and a corresponding 'direct speech', but the term is a convenient shorthand.

Subordinators Introducing Indirect Statements

41.4   Indirect statements (*that*-clauses) are introduced by **ὅτι** or **ὡς**.

Note 1: Alternative subordinators for indirect statements are ὅπως (next to ὡς), διότι (next to ὅτι; διότι usually introduces causal clauses, →48.2), οὕνεκα and ὁθούνεκα (both confined to poetry).

41.5   ὅτι, but not on the whole ὡς, is sometimes used to introduce direct speech; this use is known as **ὅτι** *recitativum*:

(4)   ἐπεὶ δὲ Πρόξενος εἶπεν <u>ὅτι</u> αὐτός εἰμι ὃν ζητεῖς, εἶπεν ὁ ἄνθρωπος τάδε· . . . (Xen. *An.* 2.4.16)
        When Proxenus said (that) 'I am the very man you are looking for', the man said the following: . . .

41.6   In classical Attic ὅτι is the default conjunction (and ὡς becomes progressively rarer over time). ὡς is mostly used if the reporter expressly wishes to convey that the truth of the reported statement is open to doubt. But ὡς is also used to give the meaning 'how' or 'how it can be said that' (compare πῶς λέγεις; 'What do you mean?'/'How is it that you say … ?'), and so is often employed in (factual) summaries:

(5) λέγουσιν <u>ὡς</u> οὐδὲν κακὸν οὐδ' αἰσχρὸν εἰργασμένοι εἰσίν. ἐγὼ δ' ἐβουλόμην ἂν αὐτοὺς ἀληθῆ λέγειν. (Lys. 12.22)

They say that they have not perpetrated any wicked or disgraceful act. I would wish they speak the truth. *Through the use of ὡς the reporter indicates that he believes the reported speakers' statement to be false.*

(6) κατηγόρει πρῶτον μὲν <u>ὡς</u> μετὰ τὴν ἐκφορὰν αὐτῇ προσίοι, ἔπειτα <u>ὡς</u> αὐτὴ τελευτῶσα εἰσαγγείλειε καὶ <u>ὡς</u> ἐκείνη τῷ χρόνῳ πεισθείη, καὶ τὰς εἰσόδους οἷς τρόποις προσιεῖτο … καὶ τἆλλα τὰ γενόμενα πάντα ἀκριβῶς διηγήσατο. (Lys. 1.20)

She accused him, telling first how after the funeral he had approached her, then how she ended up acting as his messenger and how my wife in time was persuaded, and the ways in which she used to let him into the house … And all the other things that had happened she told me in detail. *The use of ὡς 'how' suggests that the reported speaker focused in a detailed way on how the reported states of affairs came about; ὅτι 'that' would not carry the same suggestion: compare 'She told me how he had approached her' to 'She told me that he had approached her'. The reported speaker said more than is reported in the ὡς-clauses, so that the report only presents a summary of what originally was a much lengthier story. Note, too, the co-ordination of ὡς with οἷς τρόποις.*

(7) ἡγοῦμαι τοίνυν, ὦ βουλή, ἐμὸν ἔργον ἀποδεῖξαι, ὡς, ἐπειδὴ τὸ χωρίον ἐκτησάμην, οὔτ' ἐλάα οὔτε σηκὸς ἐνῆν ἐν αὐτῷ. (Lys. 7.5)

I believe therefore, members of the Council, that it is my task to prove (how it can be) that when I acquired the estate, there was neither an olive tree nor a stump on it. *The speaker summarizes beforehand the points which he will go on to present in greater detail.*

Tense and Mood in ὅτι/ὡς-Clauses

In Primary Sequence

41.7   In **primary sequence** (→40.12) – i.e. after verbs in a **primary tense** (present, future, perfect), and also after imperatives, potential optatives and modal indicatives – the tense stem and mood of the corresponding direct speech are retained:

(8) <u>λέγει</u> δ' ὡς ἡμεῖς <u>ἤλθομεν</u> ἐπὶ τὴν οἰκίαν τὴν τούτου ὄστρακον ἔχοντες, καὶ ὡς <u>ἠπείλουν</u> αὐτῷ ἐγὼ ἀποκτενεῖν, καὶ ὡς τοῦτό <u>ἐστιν</u> ἡ πρόνοια. (Lys. 3.28)

He says that we came to his house carrying pieces of broken pottery and that I threatened to kill him, and that this constitutes 'premeditation'. *Direct speech: ἦλθον, ἠπείλει, ἐστίν.*

(9) καὶ ἐμοὶ οὐδεὶς <u>λόγος ἔσται</u> ἔτι, ἐάν τι πάσχω, ὡς παρανόμως <u>ἀπωλόμην</u>. (Antiph. 5.96)

And I will have no reason left for complaining, if I am convicted, that I have been destroyed illegally. *Direct speech: ἀπωλόμην. Note that the 'destroying' may take place in the reporter's future, but by the time he will speak about it, it will be in the past.*

(10) ἀλλ' <u>εἴποι ἄν</u> τις ὅτι παῖδες ὄντες <u>ἐμάνθανον</u>. (Xen. *Cyr.* 4.3.10)

But perhaps someone will say that they learned when they were boys. *Direct speech: ἐμάνθανον.*

(11) παρελθών τις ... <u>δειξάτω</u> ... ὡς οἱ ... δεδουλωμένοι νῦν οὐκ <u>ἂν</u> ἐλεύθεροι <u>γένοιντο</u> ἄσμενοι. (Dem. 2.8)

Let someone come forward and show that those who have been reduced to slavery would not now welcome their freedom. *Direct speech: οὐκ ἂν γένοιντο.*

In Historic Sequence

With Verbs of Speaking

41.8   In historic sequence (→40.12) – i.e. after a verb in a **secondary tense** (imperfect, aorist, pluperfect, and after historical presents) – the tense stem and mood may be the same as that of the corresponding direct speech (in contrast to English, then, Greek does not 'back-shift' tense):

(12) αὐτίκα δὲ ἔς τε τοὺς δήμους <u>φάτις ἀπίκετο</u> ὡς Ἀθηναίη Πεισίστρατον <u>κατάγει</u>. (Hdt. 1.60.5)

Word soon reached the demes that Athena was bringing Pisistratus back. *Direct speech: κατάγει. Note back-shifted 'was bringing' in the translation. Note also ὡς (→41.6): as the reader already knows from the preceding context, it is in fact not Athena who is bringing back Pisistratus.*

(13) <u>ἀπεκρίνατο</u> ... ὅτι πειθομένοις αὐτοῖς οὐ <u>μεταμελήσει</u>. (Xen. *An.* 7.1.34)

He replied that they would not regret obeying. *Direct speech: ὑμῖν οὐ μεταμελήσει. Note back-shifted 'would ... regret' in the translation.*

(14) Κροῖσος δέ οἱ <u>ἐπαλιλλόγησε</u> ... ὡς ἐπαρθεὶς τῷ μαντηίῳ <u>ἐστρατεύσατο</u> ἐπὶ Πέρσας. (Hdt. 1.90.3)

Croesus recapitulated for him ... how, encouraged by the oracle, he had gone to war against the Persians. *Direct speech: ἐστρατευσάμην. Note back-shifted 'had gone to war' in the translation.*

(15) Εὐφίλητος ... <u>λέγει</u> πρὸς αὐτοὺς ὅτι <u>πέπεισμαι</u> ταῦτα συμποιεῖν καὶ <u>ὡμολόγηκα</u> αὐτῷ μεθέξειν τοῦ ἔργου. (Andoc. 1.62)

Euphiletus said to them that I had consented to join them and had agreed to help him in carrying out the crime. *Direct speech: πέπεισται, ὡμολόγηκε. λέγει is historical present (→33.54); note back-shifted 'had consented' and 'had agreed' in the translation.*

41.9 Alternatively, the **oblique optative** is used instead of the indicative mood of the verb in direct speech; the tense-aspect stem stays the same:

(16) εἶπον ὅτι σφίσι μὲν δοκοῖεν ἀδικεῖν οἱ Ἀθηναῖοι. (Thuc. 1.87.4)

They said that they thought the Athenians did them wrong. *Direct speech: ἡμῖν δοκοῦσι. The present indicative is replaced by a present optative. Note that first-person ἡμῖν is replaced by the indirect reflexive third-person pronoun σφίσι (→29.18).*

(17) ἔλεγεν ὅτι πεισθείη ὑπὸ τούτων ἐμοῦ καταψεύδεσθαι. (Antiph. 5.33)

He said that he had been persuaded by these men to lie about me. *Direct speech: ἐπείσθην. The aorist indicative is replaced by an aorist optative.*

(18) εἶπεν ὡς τὸν Παφλαγόνα φίλον ποιήσοιντο. (Xen. An. 5.6.3)

He said that they would make the Paphlagonian their friend. *Direct speech: ποιησόμεθα. The future indicative is replaced by a future optative.*

(19) ἐπέστελλον . . . καὶ ἄλλοι πολλοὶ τῷ Ξενοφῶντι ὡς διαβεβλημένος εἴη. (Xen. An. 7.6.44)

Many others also sent word to Xenophon, that he had been slandered. *Direct speech: διαβέβλησαι. The perfect indicative is replaced by a perfect optative (in the usual periphrastic form, →19.9).*

41.10 In principle, the present optative replaces both the present indicative and imperfect, and the perfect optative both the perfect indicative and pluperfect. In practice, however, the confusion which this could cause is avoided, in that the **imperfect and pluperfect are only very occasionally replaced** by an optative:

(20) εἶχε γὰρ λέγειν καὶ ὅτι μόνοι τῶν Ἑλλήνων βασιλεῖ συνεμάχοντο ἐν Πλαταιαῖς, καὶ ὅτι ὕστερον οὐδεπώποτε στρατεύσαιντο ἐπὶ βασιλέα. (Xen. Hell. 7.1.34)

For he could state both that they alone among the Greeks had fought on the side of the king at Plataea, and that they had never since undertaken a campaign against the king. *Direct speech: καὶ συνεμαχόμεθα . . . καὶ . . . οὐδεπώποτε ἐστρατευσάμεθα. Note that while the imperfect is retained, the aorist indicative is replaced by an aorist optative.*

(21) ταῦτα μὲν τοῦ Ὀρχομενίου Θερσάνδρου ἤκουον, καὶ τάδε πρὸς τούτοισι, ὡς αὐτὸς αὐτίκα λέγοι ταῦτα πρὸς ἀνθρώπους πρότερον ἢ γενέσθαι ἐν Πλαταιῇσι τὴν μάχην. (Hdt. 9.16.5)

This is what I heard from Thersander of Orchomenus, and he added to it that he himself had immediately told the story to others, before the battle of Plataea took place. *Direct speech ἔλεγον, not λέγω (the optative, unusually, replaces an imperfect). Note πρότερον ἢ γενέσθαι ἐν Πλαταιῇσι τὴν μάχην, which shows that the whole clause belongs to the past with respect to ἤκουον.*

41.11   Potential optatives (+ ἄν, →34.13) and counterfactual modal indicatives (+ ἄν, →34.16–17) are **always retained** in indirect speech:

(22) ἀπελογοῦντο ὡς οὐκ <u>ἄν</u> ποτε οὕτω μῶροι <u>ἦσαν</u> ὡς . . . (Xen. *Hell.* 5.4.22)
They pleaded that they would never have been so foolish as to . . . *Direct speech: οὐκ ἄν ἦμεν.*

(23) πέμψας πρὸς τὸν Δερκυλίδαν εἶπεν ὅτι <u>ἔλθοι ἄν</u> εἰς λόγους, εἰ ὁμήρους λάβοι. (Xen. *Hell.* 3.1.20)
He (*Midias*) sent to Dercylidas and said that he would meet to negotiate with him, if he could first take hostages. *Direct speech: ἔλθοιμι ἄν.*

41.12   The possibilities for tense and mood in indirect statements in ὅτι/ὡς-clauses after a secondary tense are set out in the following table:

Tense/Mood Direct Speech	Direct	Indirect
pres. ind.	ὁ Σωκράτης ἐπιστολὴν <u>γράφει</u> Socrates is writing a letter	εἶπεν ὅτι ὁ Σωκράτης ἐπιστολὴν <u>γράφει</u> / <u>γράφοι</u> (*pres. ind./opt.*) He said that Socrates was writing a letter (*Socrates was writing while the reported speaker spoke*)
impf.	ὁ Σωκράτης ἐπιστολὴν <u>ἔγραφε</u> Socrates was writing a letter	εἶπεν ὅτι ὁ Σωκράτης ἐπιστολὴν <u>ἔγραφε</u> (/<u>γράφοι</u>) (*impf. / pres. opt. (rarely)*) He said that Socrates had been writing a letter (*Socrates was writing before the reported speaker spoke*)
fut. ind.	ὁ Σωκράτης ἐπιστολὴν <u>γράψει</u> Socrates will write a letter	εἶπεν ὅτι ὁ Σωκράτης ἐπιστολὴν <u>γράψει</u> / <u>γράψοι</u> (*fut. ind./opt.*) He said that Socrates would write a letter
aor. ind.	ὁ Σωκράτης ἐπιστολὴν <u>ἔγραψε</u> Socrates wrote a letter	εἶπεν ὅτι ὁ Σωκράτης ἐπιστολὴν <u>ἔγραψε</u> /<u>γράψειε</u> (*aor. ind./opt.*) He said that Socrates had written a letter
pf. ind.	ὁ Σωκράτης ἐπιστολὴν <u>γέγραφε</u> Socrates is the writer of a letter	εἶπεν ὅτι ὁ Σωκράτης ἐπιστολὴν <u>γέγραφε</u> / <u>γεγράφοι</u> (*pf. ind. /opt.*) He said that Socrates was the writer of a letter
plpf.	ὁ Σωκράτης ἐπιστολὴν <u>ἐγεγράφει</u> Socrates was the writer of a letter	εἶπεν ὅτι ὁ Σωκράτης ἐπιστολὴν <u>ἐγεγράφει</u> (/<u>γεγράφοι</u>) (*plpf. / pf. opt. (rarely)*) He said that Socrates had been the writer of a letter
opt. + ἄν	ὁ Σωκράτης ἐπιστολὴν <u>γράψειεν ἄν</u> Socrates may write a letter	εἶπεν ὅτι ὁ Σωκράτης ἐπιστολὴν <u>γράψειεν ἄν</u> (*opt. + ἄν*) He said that Socrates might write a letter
ind. + ἄν	ὁ Σωκράτης ἐπιστολὴν <u>ἔγραψεν ἄν</u> Socrates would have written a letter	εἶπεν ὅτι ὁ Σωκράτης ἐπιστολὴν <u>ἔγραψεν ἄν</u> (*ind. + ἄν*) He said that Socrates would have written a letter

41.13 In those cases in which the reporter has a choice, there is a nuanced difference between retaining the mood of direct speech in historic sequence and using the oblique optative:

- The **oblique optative** signals that the reporter presents everything from his own temporal perspective: he puts himself between the original speaker and the addressee, emphasizing his role as mediator.
- The use of the **mood of the corresponding direct speech** presents the content of the speech emphatically from the **perspective of the reported speaker**. As such, the construction functions as a distancing device: it may suggest that the reporter believes the reported words to be false or otherwise inappropriate, or that the reported words were of particular importance in the reported speech situation (crucial to the reported speaker and to the addressee) and less important in the current speech situation.

Such nuances are especially clear in instances in which both constructions are used in single reports:

(24) ἔτι δὲ ἀμφὶ δείλην ἔδοξαν πολεμίους ὁρᾶν ἱππέας ... ἐν ᾧ δὲ ὡπλίζοντο ἧκον λέγοντες οἱ προπεμφθέντες σκοποὶ ὅτι οὐχ ἱππεῖς <u>εἰσιν</u>, ἀλλ᾽ ὑποζύγια <u>νέμοιντο</u>. (Xen. An. 2.2.14–15)

While it was still late in the afternoon, they thought they saw enemy horsemen ... While they were arming themselves, the scouts who had been sent ahead said that they were not enemy horsemen, but yoke-animals grazing there. *The part of the message of particular importance to the soldiers is that which corrects their expectations: contrary to what they believed, the animals they saw were not enemy horsemen (but yoke-animals).*

(25) ὁ δ᾽ ἑρμηνεὺς εἶπε περσιστὶ ὅτι παρὰ βασιλέως <u>πορεύονται</u> πρὸς τὸν σατράπην. αἱ δὲ ἀπεκρίναντο ὅτι οὐκ ἐνταῦθα <u>εἴη</u>, ἀλλ᾽ <u>ἀπέχει</u> ὅσον παρασάγγην. (Xen. An. 4.5.10)

The interpreter said in Persian that they (*the Greeks*) were on their way from the king to the satrap. The women answered that he wasn't there, but was about a parasang away. *The interpreter tells a 'white lie' to some local women to find out the satrap's whereabouts (the Greeks are not actually on their way to him, but trying to avoid him) – the reporter does not take responsibility for* πορεύονται πρὸς τὸν σατράπην. *The most salient part of the women's answer is not their assertion about where he is not (the Greeks had suspected that he was not there; hence they took this route), but their assertion that he is only a parasang away.*

Note 1: The optative is the more common construction throughout classical prose (discounting indicatives which cannot easily be replaced by the optative; →41.14), although there are differences between individual authors. However, the future and perfect optative are both rare forms and the indicative of these tenses is more often retained than that of the present and aorist. Furthermore, the oblique optative rapidly disappeared from common use after ca. 300 BCE.

Note 2: The future optative is used almost exclusively as oblique optative in indirect speech contexts (although it also occurs in effort clauses, →44.2).

41.14   Not all present indicatives in historic sequence are readily replaced by the optative. If the speaker/narrator wishes to stress that a reported state of affairs obtained in the reported speaker's past **and continues to obtain in the present**, the **optative is not usually found**. For such indirect statements, it is not quite correct to say that the present indicative from the corresponding direct speech has been retained: tense is oriented on the reporter's 'now'. Note that in English, too, the tense is normally not 'back-shifted' under these circumstances (cf. the translations of (26)–(27)):

(26) κἀγὼ ἔγνων αὐτὸν ὅτι μοι χαλεπαίνοι διαστέλλοντι τὰ λεγόμενα ... ἀνεμνήσθην οὖν τοῦ Κόννου, ὅτι μοι κἀκεῖνος χαλεπαίνει ἑκάστοτε ὅταν αὐτῷ μὴ ὑπείκω, ἔπειτά μου ἧττον ἐπιμελεῖται ὡς ἀμαθοῦς ὄντος. (Pl. *Euthd.* 295d)

I realized that he (*Euthydemus*) was angry with me for making distinctions in his phrases ... I remembered that Connus, too, becomes angry with me every time I do not give in to him and that afterwards he devotes less attention to me because he believes that I am stupid. *Euthydemus is no longer angry with Socrates when the latter reports his anger. By contrast, Connus' getting angry and (not) paying attention are habitual actions (note ἑκάστοτε and the indefinite), which continue to the present time. Note that the reason for the alternation of the indicative and optative in this example is different from that in examples such as (24)–(25).*

(27) ταῦτα ... ἐποίεε, ἐπιστάμενος ὅτι τῷ δικαίῳ τὸ ἄδικον πολέμιόν ἐστι. (Hdt. 1.96.2)

These things ... he did, understanding that injustice is the enemy of justice. *The ὅτι-clause contains a generalization which is always valid, including at the reporter's time; for this use of the present indicative, →33.16.*

The future indicative also occasionally pertains to the reporter's future, and not only to that of the reported speaker:

(28) τοῦτο ... ὁ τιθεὶς τὸν νόμον εἶδεν, ὅτι τούτων μὲν οὐδεὶς εἴσεται τὸν ἑαυτῷ κεχαρισμένον ὑμῶν, οἱ θεοὶ δὲ εἴσονται καὶ τὸ δαιμόνιον τὸν μὴ τὰ δίκαια ψηφισάμενον. (Dem. 19.239)

This ... is what the legislator saw, that not one of these men will know which one of you has done him a favour, but that the gods and the divine will know whoever casts an unrighteous vote. *The procedure under discussion (secret voting) is still in place and, as τούτων shows (→29.30), what matters to Demosthenes is the current trial, the outcome of which depends on the jurors' future voting.*

With Verbs of Perception, Knowledge and Emotion

41.15   With verbs of perception, knowledge and emotion in a **secondary tense**, Greek on the whole uses the same constructions of ὅτι/ὡς-clauses as after verbs of speaking: either the tense stem and mood of the corresponding direct speech are used, or the oblique optative:

(29)   οὗτος ὁ Κόμων ἐτελεύτησεν ἄπαις ... καὶ ἦν πρεσβύτερος ὅτε ἐτελεύτα. καὶ ἐγὼ ἐπειδὴ ᾐσθόμην ὅτι οὐχ οἷός τέ ἐστιν περιγενέσθαι ... ([Dem.] 48.5)

This man Comon died childless and was quite old when he died. And when I became aware that he was not able to recover, ... *Pres. ind. retained* ('direct speech': οὐχ οἷός τέ ἐστιν περιγενέσθαι).

(30)   ἐπεὶ δ' ᾔσθοντο οἱ μὲν Ἕλληνες ὅτι βασιλεὺς σὺν τῷ στρατεύματι ἐν τοῖς σκευοφόροις εἴη ... (Xen. An. 1.10.5)

When the Greeks became aware that the king was in their baggage train with his forces, ... *Oblique optative* ('direct speech': βασιλεὺς ἐν τοῖς σκευοφόροις ἐστί).

However, a third construction is also possible, which resembles the 'back-shifting' of tenses found in English: present and perfect indicatives of the original direct speech are represented by imperfects and pluperfects, and future indicatives are represented by ἔμελλον + future infinitive. This construction is *not* used after verbs of speaking, but it is the *only* construction of ὅτι/ὡς-clauses after ὁράω/εἶδον 'see':

(31)   καὶ εὐθὺς ἔγνωσαν πάντες ὅτι ἐγγύς που ἐστρατοπεδεύετο βασιλεύς. (Xen. An. 2.2.15)

And immediately everybody realized that the king was camping somewhere nearby. *'Direct speech'*: στρατοπεδεύεται 'he is camping'.

(32)   ἐν πολλῇ δὴ ἀπορίᾳ ἦσαν οἱ Ἕλληνες, ἐννοούμενοι ... ὅτι ἐπὶ ταῖς βασιλέως θύραις ἦσαν, ... ἀγορὰν δὲ οὐδεὶς ἔτι παρέξειν ἔμελλεν ... προυδεδώκεσαν δὲ αὐτοὺς καὶ οἱ σὺν Κύρῳ ἀναβάντες βάρβαροι, μόνοι δὲ καταλελειμμένοι ἦσαν. (Xen. An. 3.1.2)

The Greeks were naturally in great perplexity, reflecting that they were at the King's gates, that no one would provide them with a market any longer, that the barbarians who had made the upward march with Cyrus had also betrayed them, and that they were left on their own. *'Direct speech'*: ἦσαν for ἐσμέν 'we are', παρέξειν ἔμελλεν for παρέξει 'he will provide', προυδεδώκεσαν for προδεδώκασιν 'they are traitors', καταλελειμμένοι ἦσαν for καταλελείμμεθα 'we are left'.

Note 1: In this construction, the indirect statements are not presented as thoughts of the subject of the main clause, but as independent facts from the reporter's temporal perspective, on which the subject of the matrix verb reflects. By contrast, the use of the indicative of the corresponding 'direct speech' (29) or of the optative (30) after verbs of perception, knowledge and emotion has the effect that the reported statement is presented as a mental content which occurred to the subject of the matrix clause in the past.

Note 2: For the use of participles with verbs of perception, knowledge and emotion, →52.10, with further discussion at 52.17–28.

The Continuation of Indirect Speech

41.16   Indirect speech often consists of more than one sentence. Reporters have several ways of indicating that the indirect speech extends over more than one statement:

- To each new sentence a new verb of speaking can be added; forms of φημί with a declarative infinitive (→51.19–27) are particularly frequent:

(33) οἱ δὲ στρατιῶται ἔκοπτον τὰς πύλας καὶ ἔλεγον ὅτι ἀδικώτατα πάσχοιεν ἐκβαλλόμενοι εἰς τοὺς πολεμίους· κατασχίσειν τε τὰς πύλας ἔφασαν, εἰ μὴ ἑκόντες ἀνοίξουσιν. (Xen. An. 7.1.16)
The soldiers were beating on the gates and kept saying that it was most unjust that they were being thrown out into enemy territory. And they said that they would smash down the gates, if they would not voluntarily open them.

- A shift from a ὅτι/ὡς-clause to a declarative infinitive can also take place without an inserted ἔφη:

(34) ἡ δὲ ἀπεκρίνατο ὅτι βούλοιτο μὲν ἅπαντα τῷ πατρὶ χαρίζεσθαι, ἄκοντα μέντοι τὸν παῖδα χαλεπὸν εἶναι νομίζειν καταλιπεῖν. (Xen. Cyr. 1.3.13)
She answered that she wished to please her father in everything, but that she believed it was difficult to leave her son behind if he did not want her to.

- Since the oblique optative is a clear marker of indirect speech, its use can indicate that a report continues beyond a single sentence:

(35) ἔλεξα ὅτι τὸν μὲν νόμον οὐ δικαίως μου προκαθισταίη Φιλοκράτης ... διαβάλλων εἰς τὸ δικαστήριον ... ἃ μέντοι ... διαβάλλοι, ῥᾳδίως ἐξελεγχθήσοιτο ψευδόμενος· εἶεν γὰρ οἱ συνειδότες πολλοί ... καὶ εἶπόν ... ταῦτα ἐν τῷ δικαστηρίῳ. (Antiph. 6.21–3)
I said that Philocrates had no right to place legal impediments in my way, by slandering me before the court; that, however, concerning the content of his slander, it would be easy to prove that he was lying. After all, there were many witnesses. This was what I told the court.

- Another frequent way of continuing reported speech is by switching from indirect to direct speech, with or without an inserted ἔφη:

(36) ἔλεγον ὅτι ἐγὼ πάντα εἴην πεπυσμένος τὰ γιγνόμενα ἐν τῇ οἰκίᾳ· Σοὶ οὖν, ἔφην, ἔξεστι δυοῖν ὁπότερον βούλει ἑλέσθαι, ... (Lys. 1.18)
I said that I had heard all about what was happening in my home. 'Therefore', I continued, 'two options are open to you, whichever you want, ...'.

(37) ἐπεὶ δὲ ἀφίκοντο ἐπὶ σταθμόν, εὐθὺς ὥσπερ εἶχεν ὁ Ξενοφῶν ἐλθὼν πρὸς τὸν Χειρίσοφον ᾐτιᾶτο αὐτὸν ὅτι οὐχ ὑπέμεινεν, ἀλλ᾽ ἠναγκάζοντο φεύγοντες ἅμα μάχεσθαι. <u>Καὶ νῦν δύο καλώ τε κἀγαθὼ ἄνδρε τέθνατον καὶ οὔτε ἀνελέσθαι οὔτε θάψαι ἐδυνάμεθα.</u> (Xen. *An.* 4.1.19)

When they reached a staging area, Xenophon immediately went, without further ado, to Chirisophus and reproached him for not waiting, but forcing them to fight and retreat at the same time. 'And now, two great men are dead and we could not collect their bodies and bury them.'

Subordinate Clauses in Indirect Speech

41.17 Reported sentences in indirect speech (whether they are statements, interrogatives, commands or exclamations) can have their own subordinate clauses. In the corresponding direct speech, these would be subordinate clauses to the main clause. In English, cf.:

- Direct: 'John said to Jane: "I want to see you <u>as soon as I arrive</u>."'
- Indirect: 'John said to Jane that he wanted to see her <u>as soon as he arrived</u>.'

In Greek, the use of moods in such subordinate clauses is largely similar to that described above (→41.7–15), with a few further points of note.

41.18 In **primary sequence**, all subordinate verbs retain the tense stem and mood of the corresponding direct speech (→41.7):

(38) λέγουσιν ὡς, <u>ἐπειδάν</u> τις ἀγαθὸς ὢν <u>τελευτήσῃ</u>, μεγάλην μοῖραν καὶ τιμὴν <u>ἔχει</u>. (Pl. *Cra.* 398b)

They say that, when someone who is good dies, he enjoys great esteem and honour. *Direct speech: ἐπειδάν ... τελευτήσῃ, ... ἔχει (habitual temporal clause with ἄν + subjunctive, →47.9).*

(39) λέγουσιν, ὅτι εἰ σαρκώδης <u>ἦν</u>, μακροβιώτερον <u>ἂν ἦν</u> τὸ γένος. (Arist. *Part. an.* 656a16–17)

They say that, if it were more fleshy, the species would live longer. *Direct speech: εἰ ... ἦν, ... ἂν ἦν (counterfactual conditional clause with a modal secondary indicative, →49.10).*

41.19 In **historic sequence**, all tense stems and moods may be retained (→41.8). Alternatively, **indicatives** may be replaced by an oblique optative of the same tense stem (→41.9), with the exception of the imperfect and pluperfect (→41.10).

(40) ἀπεκρίνατο ὅτι μανθάνοιεν οἱ μανθάνοντες ἃ οὐκ <u>ἐπίσταιντο</u>. (Pl. *Euthd.* 276e)

He answered that learners learned things which they did not understand. *Direct speech: μανθάνουσι . . . ἃ οὐκ ἐπίστανται. The present indicative in the relative clause is replaced by a present optative.*

(41) εἶχε γὰρ λέγειν . . . ὡς Λακεδαιμόνιοι διὰ τοῦτο πολεμήσειαν αὐτοῖς, ὅτι οὐκ <u>ἐθελήσαιεν</u> μετ' Ἀγησιλάου ἐλθεῖν ἐπ' αὐτὸν οὐδὲ θῦσαι <u>ἐάσαιεν</u> αὐτὸν ἐν Αὐλίδι τῇ Ἀρτέμιδι. (Xen. *Hell.* 7.1.34)

For he (*Pelopidas*) was able to explain how the Spartans had waged war against them, because they had not been prepared to go with Agesilaus against him and had refused to let him make sacrifices to Artemis in Aulis. *Direct speech: ἐπολέμησαν ἡμῖν, ὅτι οὐκ ἠθελήσαμεν . . . οὐδὲ . . . εἰάσαμεν. The aorist indicatives of the causal clause are replaced by aorist optatives.*

41.20   In historic sequence, modal secondary indicatives and all optatives remain unchanged (→41.11). But **subjunctives** (in any use) may be replaced by the optative; if ἄν was required for the subjunctive, it disappears:

(43) ἐδόκει . . . εἰ μὴ <u>ἔφθασαν</u> δὴ αὐτοὶ . . . ξυλλαβόντες τοὺς ἄνδρας, προδοθῆναι ἄν ἡ πόλις. (Thuc. 6.61.2)

It seemed that, if they themselves had not first arrested the men, the city would have been betrayed. *Direct speech: εἰ μὴ ἐφθάσαμεν . . . προυδόθη ἄν. The aorist indicative, required by the counterfactual conditional (→49.10), is retained.*

(43) εἶπον ὅτι ἀπίοιεν ἄν, εἰ σφίσιν ἀσφάλειαν μετὰ τῶν ὅπλων ἀπιοῦσι <u>διδοῖεν</u>. (Xen. *Hell.* 5.4.11)

They said that they would withdraw, if they (*the Thebans*) were to allow them safe passage with their weapons while withdrawing. *Direct speech: ἀπίοιμεν ἄν εἰ ἀσφάλειαν διδοῖτε. The optative required by the potential conditional (→49.8) is retained in indirect speech.*

(44) ἤλπιζον ὑπὸ τῶν σφετέρων αὐτῶν παίδων γηροτροφηθέντες, ἐπειδὴ <u>τελευτήσειαν</u> τὸν βίον, ταφήσεσθαι. (Lys. 13.45)

They imagined that they would be taken care of by their own children in their old age and, when they died, that they would be buried by them. *Direct speech: ἐπειδὰν τελευτήσωμεν . . . , ταφησόμεθα. ἄν + aorist subjunctive, required by the temporal clause referring to the future (→47.8), is replaced by an aorist optative, without ἄν.*

(45) Κίμωνος εἰπόντος ὅτι φοβοῖτο μὴ δικαιολογούμενος <u>περιγένοιτο</u> ἡμῶν ὁ Φίλιππος . . . (Aeschin. 2.21)

And when Cimon said that he was afraid that Philip would get the better of us in pleading his cause . . . *Direct speech: φοβοῦμαι μὴ περιγένηται. The aorist subjunctive, required by the construction of verbs of fearing in primary sequence (→43.3) is replaced by an optative.*

Note 1: Since it is potentially unclear whether an aorist optative represents an original aorist indicative or subjunctive, aorist indicatives are often retained in subordinate clauses in indirect speech, while aorist subjunctives are more readily replaced by the optative.

Note 2: Some cases allow for more than one feasible interpretation of an optative, typically either as replacing original subjunctive + ἄν, or retaining an original optative:

(46) οἱ δὲ πεμφθέντες λέγουσι Κύρῳ ὅτι μισοῖέν τε τοὺς Ἀσσυρίους δικαίως, νῦν τ᾽, εἰ <u>βούλοιτο</u> ἰέναι ἐπ᾽ αὐτούς, καὶ σφεῖς σύμμαχοι <u>ὑπάρξοιεν</u> καὶ <u>ἡγήσοιντο</u>. (Xen. Cyr. 4.2.4)

Those who were sent told Cyrus that they had good grounds for hating the Assyrians and that now, if he wished to march against them, they themselves would, in fact, be his allies and his guides. *Direct speech: μισοῦμέν τε ... νῦν τ᾽, ἐὰν βούλῃ/εἰ βούλοιο ... καὶ αὐτοὶ σύμμαχοι ὑπάρξομεν καὶ ἡγησόμεθα. Pres. opt. βούλοιτο may represent either ἄν + pres. subj. (prospective conditional clause; direct speech: 'if you wish') or pres. opt. (potential conditional clause; direct speech: 'if you should wish'). Both options are compatible with the future optatives of the apodosis, replacing future indicatives (the option with an original optative would represent a common type of 'mixed' conditional, →49.17; this would add a note of politeness). Note further the emphatic indirect reflexive pronoun σφεῖς (equivalent to αὐτοί in direct speech), and the use of νῦν to refer to the present moment of the reported speech.*

41.21 Subordinate clauses which are not part of the reported words, but which are inserted as a comment by the reporter, are presented from the temporal perspective of the reporter: the oblique optative is then not used, and imperfects and pluperfects can be used in a manner similar to English 'back-shifting' (cf. 41.15 with n.1):

(47) ᾔδει δὴ σαφῶς, οἶμαι, τοῦτο ὅτι νῦν, ἡνίκ᾽ <u>ἐστασίαζε</u> μὲν αὐτῷ τὰ Θετταλῶν, καὶ Φεραῖοι πρῶτον οὐ <u>συνηκολούθουν</u>, <u>ἐκρατοῦντο</u> δὲ Θηβαῖοι καὶ μάχην <u>ἥττηντο</u> καὶ τρόπαιον ἀπ᾽ αὐτῶν <u>εἱστήκει</u>, οὐκ ἔνεστι παρελθεῖν, εἰ <u>βοηθήσεσθ᾽</u> ὑμεῖς. (Dem. 19.320)

For he (*Philip*) knew perfectly well, I suppose, that now, when things in Thessaly were at variance with him, and the Pheraeans, for one, were refusing to join him, and the Thebans were being beaten and losing in battle and had a trophy erected over them, it would be impossible to force the passage if you would come to the rescue. *The temporal clause is an additional comment by the reporter, Demosthenes. Had the clause been presented from Philip's perspective, στασιάζει, συνακολουθοῦσιν, etc. would have been expected. Observe that the other subordinate clause, εἰ βοηθήσεσθ᾽, does represent Philip's temporal perspective: this is clear from the retained future indicative βοηθήσεσθ᾽ (for which, →49.5).*

41.22 These rules also apply in subordinate clauses which are subordinated to a declarative (accusative and) infinitive (→51.19–27) in historic sequence:

(48) οὐδεὶς ἦν ὅστις οὐκ ᾤετο, εἰ μάχη <u>ἔσοιτο</u>, τοὺς ... κρατήσαντας ἄρξειν. (Xen. Hell. 7.5.26)

There was no one who did not think that, if a battle were to happen, the victors would rule. *Conditional clause (εἰ ... ἔσοιτο) subordinate to the accusative-and-infinitive construction τοὺς κρατήσαντας ἄρξειν. Fut. opt. ἔσοιτο replaces fut. ind. ἔσται.*

41.23   Occasionally, the declarative infinitive is used in subordinate clauses in indirect speech, when the matrix clause is also reported in the infinitive:

(49) λέγεται . . . ἐπειδὴ ἐκ τῆς Ὀάσιος ταύτης <u>ἰέναι</u> . . . ἐπιπνεῦσαι νότον μέγαν τε καὶ ἐξαίσιον. (Hdt. 3.26.3)

It is said that when they were crossing (the desert) from that city Oasis, a strong and violent southern wind blew upon them. *Direct speech: ἐπειδὴ ἦσαν . . . ἐπέπνευσε νότος; the indicative in the ἐπειδή-clause is replaced by an infinitive.*

42

Indirect Questions and Indirect Exclamations

Indirect Questions

Introduction: Direct versus Indirect Questions

42.1 Indirect (or 'dependent') questions are the counterpart in indirect speech/thought of direct questions:

– **direct**: e.g. τίς εἶ; *who are you?*; (ἦ/ἆρα) ἐποίησε τοῦτο; *has he done that?*
– **indirect**: e.g. ἐρωτᾷ τίς εἰμι *he asks who I am*; οὐκ ᾔδη εἰ τοῦτο ἐποίησεν *I didn't know whether he had done that.*

For direct questions (types, use of moods, etc.), →38.4–24. For indirect speech/thought in general, →41.1–2.

Verbs Introducing Indirect Questions

42.2 Indirect questions can be introduced by verbs of asking, wondering, learning, telling, showing, knowing, etc. Some examples of such verbs are:

ἀγγέλλω	report, announce
ἀπορέω	be at a loss
γιγνώσκω	(come to) know, recognize
δείκνυμι	show
ἐρωτάω	ask
θαυμάζω	wonder
μανθάνω	learn
οἶδα	know
πυνθάνομαι	learn
ὁράω	see

Verbs which refer to knowledge or (mental) perception may take indirect questions when the matrix clause expresses a **lack of knowledge**, as in 'I don't know if . . .', 'Do you know if . . . ?', 'Who knows if . . . ?' (cf. (2)–(3), (13)–(15), (18) below).

Subordinators Introducing Indirect Questions

Yes/No-Questions and Alternative Questions

42.3 **Indirect yes/no-questions** are introduced by εἰ *whether, if*:

(1) νῦν ἐρωτᾷς εἰ ἔχω σε διδάξαι. (Pl. *Men.* 82a)
Now you are asking if I am capable of teaching you.

(2) τίς οἶδεν εἰ κάτω 'στιν εὐαγῆ τάδε; (Soph. *Ant.* 521)
Who knows if below these things are free from blame?

(3) τίς οὖν ὁ γνωσόμενος εἰ τὸ προσῆκον εἶδος κερκίδος ἐν ὁποιῳοῦν ξύλῳ κεῖται; (Pl. *Cra.* 390b)
Who is likely to know whether the correct form of a shuttle resides in a certain piece of wood?

42.4 **Indirect alternative questions** are introduced by one of the combinations πότερον/α ... ἤ, εἰ ... ἤ, εἰ ... εἴτε or εἴτε ... εἴτε *whether/if ... or*. The negative in the second member is μή:

(4) ἐρωτᾷ πότερον βούλεται εἰρήνην ἢ πόλεμον ἔχειν. (Xen. *Hell.* 3.2.1)
He asked if he wanted to have peace or war.

(5) ἀθρήσατ' ... εἰ τὸν Αἵμονος | φθόγγον συνίημ', ἢ θεοῖσι κλέπτομαι. (Soph. *Ant.* 1216–18)
Observe whether it is Haemon's voice that I recognize, or if I am being deceived by the gods.

(6) καὶ δείξεις τάχα | εἴτ' εὐγενὴς πέφυκας εἴτ' ... κακή. (Soph. *Ant.* 37–8)
And you will soon show whether you are noble by nature or cowardly.

(7) σκοπεῖτε εἴτ' ὀρθῶς λογίζομαι ταῦτ' εἴτε μή. (Dem. 15.11)
Consider whether I reason rightly or not.

Specifying Questions

42.5 **Indirect specifying questions** can be introduced either by the regular **interrogative pronouns/adjectives/adverbs** (τίς, πόσος, ποῦ, etc.; →8.1–2, 38.11), or by the corresponding **indefinite relative pronouns/adjectives/adverbs** (beginning with ὁ-: ὅστις, ὁπόσος, ὅπου, etc.; →8.1–2).

(8) ὅταν σ' ἐρωτᾷ τίς τε καὶ πόθεν πάρει ... (Soph. *Phil.* 56)
When he asks you who and from where you are ...

(9) ἐρωτῶντος γὰρ Στρατοκλέους ὅστις αὐτῷ ἀποδώσει τὰ χρήματα ... (Isoc. 17.37)
For when Stratocles asked who would give him the money ...

(10) ἐλθὼν δέ σ' ἠρώτησα πῶς τροχηλάτου | μανίας ἂν ἔλθοιμ' ἐς τέλος πόνων τ' ἐμῶν. (Eur. *IT* 82)
I came and asked you how I might reach the end of this whirlwind of madness and of my troubles.

(11) τοῦτο δὴ ἄρτι ἠρώτων, <u>ὅπως</u> χρὴ τοῖς ὀνόμασι χρώμενον λέγειν περὶ αὐτῶν. (Pl. *Tht.* 198e)

This, then, was my question just now, in what terms one should speak about them (*lit. 'using terms in which way it is necessary to speak about them'*).

42.6 As in direct questions (→38.14), question words may function as obligatory constituents and modifiers not only of the finite verb, but also of subordinate constructions such as participles:

(12) ἐλθὼν δ' ὁ Ξενοφῶν ἐπήρετο τὸν Ἀπόλλω <u>τίνι</u> ἂν θεῶν θύων καὶ εὐχόμενος κάλλιστα καὶ ἄριστα ἔλθοι τὴν ὁδόν. (Xen. *An.* 3.1.6)

Xenophon went and asked Apollo to which of the gods he should offer and pray in order to best and most successfully complete the journey (*lit. 'offering and praying to which of the gods'*). τίνι is indirect object with θύων and εὐχόμενος.

The Use of Moods in Indirect Questions

42.7 In indirect questions, the same **sequence of moods** is used as in ὅτι/ὡς-clauses of indirect statement (→41.7–14): tense and mood are unchanged (relative to the corresponding direct question) with a matrix clause which has a non-past tense (primary sequence):

(13) κεῖνος δ' <u>ὅπου</u> | <u>βέβηκεν</u> οὐδεὶς οἶδε. (Soph. *Trach.* 40–1)

No one knows where that man has gone. *Direct question: ποῦ βέβηκεν;*

(14) ἐγὼ μὲν οὐκ οἶδ' <u>ὅπως</u> <u>ἄν</u> τις σαφέστερον <u>ἐπιδείξειεν</u>. (Dem. 27.48)

I for my part do not know how someone could show it more clearly. *Direct question: πῶς ἂν ἐπιδείξειεν;*

The oblique optative of the same tense stem may (but does not have to) be used in a past-tense environment (historic sequence):

(15) τὸν Μιλύαν δ' οὐδ' <u>ὅστις</u> <u>ἔστιν</u> οὐδεὶς ᾔδει. (Dem. 29.29)

As for Milyas, not a single person even knew who he was. *Original mood retained; direct question: τίς ἔστιν; For the double negative οὐδ'... οὐδείς, →56.4.*

(16) ἔφη... παραγενέσθαι ἐρωτωμένῳ ἑτέρῳ ὑπὸ ἑτέρου <u>ὅπου</u> <u>εἴη</u> Ἀρδιαῖος ὁ μέγας. (Pl. *Resp.* 615c)

He said that he had been present when one was asked by another where Ardiaeus the Great was. *Oblique optative; direct question: ποῦ ἔστιν;*

Note 1: For the difference between the use of the oblique optative as opposed to retaining the original mood, →41.13–14.

42.8 The exact same rules hold for **deliberative questions** (→34.8, 38.16): in primary sequence, the deliberative subjunctive is retained, in historic sequence the optative may be used:

(17) καὶ ἐρωτᾷ δὴ πῶς με θάπτῃ. (Pl. *Phd.* 115d)

And he asks how he is to bury me. *Primary sequence; direct question:* πῶς σε θάπτω;

(18) ὁ Ἀριστεὺς . . . ἠπόρησε . . . ὁποτέρωσε διακινδυνεύσῃ χωρήσας. (Thuc. 1.63.1)

Aristeus was at a loss as to which direction he should risk taking. *Historic sequence, with retained subjunctive; direct question:* ποτέρωσε διακινδυνεύσω;

(19) οὐχ ὡς ἐπιθυμοῦντες τῆς ἐξόδου ἠρωτήσατε εἰ ἐξίοιτε. (Xen. *Cyr.* 4.5.21)

It was not out of desire for the expedition that you asked whether you should go on the expedition. *Historic sequence, with oblique optative; direct question:* ἐξίωμεν;

Indirect Exclamations

Introduction: Direct versus Indirect Exclamations

42.9   Indirect (or 'dependent') exclamations are the counterpart in indirect speech/ thought of direct exclamations:

– **direct**: e.g. οἷός ἐστι *What a man he is!*
– **indirect**: e.g. θαυμάζω οἷός ἐστι *I am amazed at what a man he is.*

For direct exclamations, →38.43–51. For indirect speech/thought in general, →41.1.

Note 1: Only exclamations of degree have an identifiable construction in indirect speech/ thought – there is no separate construction for nominal exclamations and sentence exclamations (for these categories, →38.44).

Verbs Introducing Indirect Exclamations

42.10   Indirect exclamations are used in particular to complement verbs which refer to the **expression of emotions**, such as θαυμάζω *express surprise/admiration* and κατοικτείρω/-ίρω *feel/show pity*, and after verbs which refer to a process of **reflection**, such as ἐνθυμέομαι *reflect*.

Construction of Indirect Exclamations

42.11   Indirect exclamations of degree are introduced in the same way as their direct counterparts, by the **definite relative adjectives or adverbs** (οἷος, ὅσος, etc.; ὡς).

They follow the constructions of indirect statements (→41.7–14): in primary sequence, tenses and moods of the corresponding direct exclamations are used; in historic sequence the optative may be used. The negative is οὐ:

(20) ἐννοηθέντες δὲ οἷά τε πάσχουσιν ὑπὸ τῶν Ἀσσυρίων . . . ταῦτα ἐνθυμουμένοις
ἔδοξεν αὐτοῖς νῦν καλὸν εἶναι ἀποστῆναι. (Xen. Cyr. 4.2.3)

But as they reflected what (terrible) things they suffered at the hands of the
Assyrians . . . – when they reflected on these matters, they thought now was
the right time to revolt. *Direct exclamation: οἷα πάσχομεν.*

(21) ὁ μὲν δὴ ταῦτ᾽ εἰπὼν ἀπῄει, κατοικτίρων τήν τε γυναῖκα οἵου ἀνδρὸς στέροιτο
καὶ τὸν ἄνδρα οἵαν γυναῖκα καταλιπὼν οὐκέτ᾽ ὄψοιτο. (Xen. Cyr. 7.3.14)

When he had said this, he left, feeling pity for the woman, thinking of what
a husband she was robbed, and for the man, reflecting what a woman he left
and would never see again. *Direct exclamation: οἵου ἀνδρὸς στερεῖται . . . οἵαν
γυναῖκα καταλιπὼν οὐκέτ᾽ ὄψεται.*

(22) ἐθαύμαζεν . . . ὁ Λύσανδρος ὡς καλὰ μὲν τὰ δένδρα εἴη. (Xen. Oec. 4.21)

Lysander expressed his admiration at how beautiful the trees were. *Direct
exclamation: ὡς καλὰ τὰ δένδρα ἐστί.*

Note 1: Indirect exclamations should be distinguished from indirect questions (→42.1–8
above), introduced by the interrogative pronouns/adverbs (πῶς, etc.) or the indefinite
relative pronouns/adverbs (ὅπως, etc.). Compare to (22):

(23) ἴσως . . . θαυμάζεις σὺ πῶς ἐγὼ ἀνήλωκα σοῦ αὐτοὺς τρέφοντος. (Xen. Cyr. 2.4.9)

Perhaps you wonder how I have spent money on them while you maintained them.

*In (22), θαυμάζω is followed by an indirect exclamation and means 'express admiration
at something'; in (23), it is followed by an indirect question and means 'wonder about
something'.*

43

Fear Clauses

Introduction; Verbs of Fearing and Apprehension

43.1   Subordinate **fear clauses**, introduced by **μή** *that* (negative μὴ οὐ), may complement verbs of fearing, apprehension, anxiety, suspicion, etc. Some examples of such verbs are:

δέδοικα	fear, be afraid that
φοβέομαι	be afraid that
δέος ἐστί	there is a fear that
κίνδυνός ἐστι	there is danger/risk that
φόβος ἐστί	there is a fear that
ἀθυμέω	be anxious that
φροντίζω	be worried that
ὑποπτεύω	suspect that, be concerned that

43.2   In combination with a fear clause, these verbs may express:

- fear/apprehension that an action will **occur in the future**: μή (οὐ) is followed by an aor./pres. **subjunctive** or, in historic sequence, optative; e.g. φοβοῦμαι μὴ τοῦτο ποιήσῃ *I am afraid that he may do that*;

- fear/apprehension that **it will prove in the future** that an action is currently taking place or has already taken place: μή (οὐ) is followed by a pres./pf. **subjunctive** or, in historic sequence, **optative**; e.g. φοβοῦμαι μὴ τοῦτο ποιῇ *I am afraid that he may (prove to) be doing that*;

- disappointment/apprehension concerning (the consequences of) an action whose reality has already been ascertained (i.e. **about facts**): μή (οὐ) is followed by a pf./pres. **indicative**; e.g. φοβοῦμαι μὴ τοῦτο ποιεῖ *I am afraid that he is doing that* (i.e. *he is, I fear, doing that*).

Note that, in these constructions, μή should generally be translated *that* (i.e. not with a negative).

Note 1: Several of the verbs listed above also have different senses in combination with different constructions. For instance, φοβοῦμαι *fear* may, with varying senses, be followed by a dynamic infinitive ('be afraid to do something'), indirect questions (e.g. 'doubt whether'), prepositional phrases (e.g. with περί 'be afraid for'), a direct object ('be afraid of'), etc.

There is, in particular, a great deal of overlap between verbs of fearing and verbs of effort (→44.6–7, also for the use of verbs of effort with fear clauses).

Construction and Meaning of Fear Clauses

Fear for Possible Future Actions

43.3 When the subject's fear or apprehension concerns an action **which may possibly occur in the future**, the fear clause has **μή (οὐ) + aorist or present subjunctive**:

(1) ταῦτ' οὖν περί μου δέδοικε μὴ διαφθαρῶ. (Ar. *Vesp.* 1358)
So that's his worry about me, that I'll be corrupted.

(2) οἱ Περσέων στρατηγοὶ πυθόμενοι τὸ πλῆθος τῶν Ἰάδων νεῶν κατταρρώδησαν μὴ οὐ δυνατοὶ γένωνται ὑπερβαλέσθαι. (Hdt. 6.9.1)
The Persian generals, upon learning the number of Ionic ships, feared that they would not be able to defeat it.

(3) οἱ μέγιστον δυνάμενοι ... αἰσχύνονται ... καταλείπειν συγγράμματα ἑαυτῶν, δόξαν φοβούμενοι τοῦ ἔπειτα χρόνου, μὴ σοφισταὶ καλῶνται. (Pl. *Phdr.* 257d)
The most influential men are ashamed to leave their writings behind, afraid that they will, in the opinion of posterity, be known as sophists. *Observe that φοβούμενοι is construed here with a direct object (δόξαν; lit. 'afraid of the opinion of posterity'), which is then elaborated by the fearing clause. Such elaborating fearing clauses are not uncommon.*

In **historic sequence**, such fear clauses frequently have an oblique **optative**, although the subjunctive may also be retained:

(4) οἱ πρὸς τοῖς Κερκυραίοις ... δείσαντες μὴ ὅπερ ἐν Ναυπάκτῳ γένοιτο, ἐπιβοηθοῦσι. (Thuc. 3.78.2)
The (Peloponnesian) division facing off against the Corcyraeans, fearing that exactly what happened at Naupactus would happen (again), sent a relief-party. *Optative; note that ἐπιβοηθοῦσι is historic present.*

(5) οἱ δὲ Λακεδαιμόνιοι ... ἐν φυλακῇ πολλῇ ἦσαν, φοβούμενοι μὴ σφίσι νεώτερόν τι γένηται. (Thuc. 4.55.1)
The Spartans were very much on the defensive, afraid that some unexpected ill would befall them. *Subjunctive retained.*

Note 1: The difference between the use of present and aorist subjunctives/optatives in such fear clauses is purely one of aspect (→33.63–5). Aorist subjunctives/optatives are the most common (so in (1)–(2) and (4)–(5)), since the action feared is usually presented as a complete whole. By contrast, in (3), pres. subj. καλῶνται is used to refer to an ongoing reputation.

Note 2: For the difference between the oblique optative and retaining the subjunctive, →41.13. The difference between γένοιτο in (4) and γένηται in (5) appears to be that subjunctive γένηται presents the fear from the perspective of the Spartans, whereas the optative γένοιτο presents the Peloponnesians' fear as 'moderated' by the narrator.

Fear for (Uncertain) Present or Past Actions

43.4   When the subject's fear or apprehension concerns an action which **may possibly be occurring** in the present or **may already have occurred**, but whose certainty has not been ascertained yet, the fear clause is construed with a **present or perfect subjunctive**:

(6) δεινῶς ἀθυμῶ μὴ βλέπων ὁ μάντις ᾖ. (Soph. *OT* 747)
    I am very worried that the seer can see. *For* βλέπων ᾖ, →52.51.

(7) γυναῖκες, ὡς δέδοικα μὴ περαιτέρω | πεπραγμέν' ᾖ μοι πάνθ' ὅσ' ἀρτίως ἔδρων.
    (Soph. *Trach.* 663–4)
    Friends, how I fear that I have gone too far in everything that I have just been doing!

In **historic sequence**, such fear clauses may again get the oblique **optative**:

(8) τὰ περὶ τοῦ Μνασίππου αὐτόπτου μὲν οὐδενὸς ἠκηκόει, ὑπώπτευε δὲ μὴ ἀπάτης
    ἕνεκα λέγοιτο. (Xen. *Hell.* 6.2.31)
    He had not heard the news about Mnasippus from any eye-witness, and he suspected that it was being told to deceive him.

Note 1: Observe that present subjunctives/optatives are also used in fear clauses concerning future actions (e.g. (3) above). Perfect-stem subjunctives/optatives are, on the whole, relatively rare in fear clauses.

Use of Fear Clauses to Express Disappointment

43.5   Fearing verbs (normally in the first person) may also be used to express the subject's regret, disappointment or apprehension about (the consequences of) an action which has been ascertained to be true: in such cases **μή (οὐ)** is followed by a **perfect or present indicative**:

(9) νῦν δὲ φοβούμεθα μὴ ἀμφοτέρων ἅμα ἡμαρτήκαμεν. (Thuc. 3.53.2)
    As matters stand, we must, we fear, conclude that we have been deceived in both regards.

(10) δέδοικά σ', ὦ πρεσβῦτα, μὴ πληγῶν δέει. (Ar. *Nub.* 493)
     I'm afraid, old man, that you need some blows.

In such cases the fearing construction does not express an actual fear as such, but is rather used as a 'hedge', i.e. to assert the content of the fear clause in a polite or careful fashion (this device may also be used ironically, as in (10)).

Note 1: The perfect indicative is especially common in such clauses (signifying that an undesired state exists as the result of a completed action). The aorist indicative is not normally so used in classical Greek, although it is found in Homer:

(11) δείδω μὴ δὴ πάντα θεὰ νημερτέα εἶπεν. (Hom. *Od.* 5.300)
    I am afraid that the goddess has said everything truthfully.

Independent Use of μή + Subjunctive

43.6   For the independent use of μή (οὐ) + subj. (the construction of fear clauses) to express a cautious or anxious statement, →34.10.

44

Effort Clauses

Introduction; Verbs of Effort, (Pre)caution and Contriving

44.1   **Effort clauses** (introduced by ὅπως *that*, sometimes ὡς) are used to complement verbs of effort, (pre)caution, contriving, etc.; some examples of such verbs are:

ἐπιμέλομαι	take care that, ensure that
εὐλαβέομαι	take care that, ensure that
μέλει μοι	I take care that (*lit. 'it is of concern to me that'*)
μηχανάομαι	contrive that, devise that
ὁράω	see to it that
παρασκευάζομαι	make preparations in order that
ποιέω	make, ensure that
σκοπέω	see to it that
σπεύδω	strive to
φροντίζω	take care that
φυλάττω/-ομαι	be on one's guard (in order) that

In combination with a ὅπως-clause (or ὡς-clause), these verbs express an effort or precaution which ensures that a certain action will or will not take place in the future: e.g. μηχανῶνται ὅπως τοῦτο γενήσεται *they contrive that this will happen.*

Note 1: Many of the verbs listed above also have different senses in combination with different constructions; for instance, ὁράω is most often used as a verb of perception (*see*); φροντίζω is also used as a verb of fearing (*be concerned that*, with fear clauses, →43.1).

In particular, effort verbs are also often construed with purpose clauses (→44.3 below), and with dynamic (accusative-and-)infinitive constructions (→51.8, including as verbs of hindering, →51.34). There is, finally, a great deal of overlap between verbs of effort and verbs of fearing (→44.6–7).

Construction of Effort Clauses

44.2   Effort clauses are introduced by **ὅπως** (sometimes ὡς) (*so*) *that* and followed by a **future indicative**; the negative is ὅπως μή:

(1)   τοῦτο δεῖ <u>παρασκευάσασθαι</u>, ὅπως ὡς κράτιστα <u>μαχούμεθα</u>. (Xen. *An.* 4.6.10)
        We must prepare to this end, that we fight as well as possible.

(2) ὅρα δ' ὅπως ὠθήσομεν τούσδε . . . ἐξ ἄστεως. (Ar. *Eccl.* 300)

See to it that we expel these men from the city.

(3) φύλαττέ θ' ὅπως μὴ τὴν βάλανον ἐκτρώξεται. (Ar. *Vesp.* 155)

And take care that he doesn't eat the bolt-pin.

The future indicative is normally **retained in historic sequence** (→40.12), although the future optative also occurs (rarely):

(4) ἔπρασσον ὅπως τις βοήθεια ἥξει. (Thuc. 3.4.6)

They were trying to ensure that some form of help would come.

(5) ἐπεμελεῖτο δὲ ὅπως μήτε ἄσιτοι μήτε ἄποτοί ποτε ἔσοιντο. (Xen. *Cyr.* 8.1.43)

He took care that they would never be without food or drink.

44.3   Effort clauses are similar in sense to purpose clauses (with ὅπως/ὡς/ἵνα + subj./opt.; →45.2–3). Indeed, verbs of effort are fairly often **construed with a purpose clause** with ὅπως/ὡς (but not ἵνα), i.e. followed by a **subjunctive** rather than a future indicative. This is especially frequent in Xenophon:

(6) ἐπιμελητέον . . . ὅπως τρέφωνται οἱ ἵπποι. (Xen. *Eq. mag.* 1.3)

Care must be taken that the horses are fed.

44.4   Occasionally, such clauses are construed with **ὅπως (μή) ἄν + subjunctive**; the use of ἄν + subjunctive (prospective, →40.9, cf. 45.4) may suggest that it is considered very likely that the objective aimed at will occur:

(7) καὶ αὐτός τε θηρᾷ καὶ τῶν ἄλλων ἐπιμελεῖται ὅπως ἂν θηρῶσιν. (Xen. *Cyr.* 1.2.10)

He takes part in the hunt himself and ensures that the others hunt as well.

44.5   After verbs such as σκοπέω and φροντίζω, it is sometimes difficult to distinguish effort clauses from indirect questions (ὅπως may then also be the counterpart of πῶς *how?*; →42.5):

(8) ἡμεῖς . . . οὐδὲν φροντίζομεν, οὐδὲ σκοποῦμεν ὅπως ἐπανορθώσομεν αὐτήν. (Isoc. 7.15)

We do not give it any thought, nor do we see to it that we put it (the city) right. *Or, as an indirect question: 'consider how we will put the city right'.*

Further Particulars

'Interference' between Fear and Effort Clauses

44.6   Not infrequently, **verbs of effort are construed with fear clauses** (with μή + subjunctive/optative). The fear or apprehension concerning a future or present action expressed by such fear clauses (→43.3) is combined with the matrix predicate's meaning, i.e. 'strive to ensure that something feared may not happen' or 'strive to ascertain that something feared is not happening'. In such cases μή may be translated *that not, for fear that, lest*:

(9) ... ἵνα | σκοπῆτε ... μὴ καὶ προσπέσῃ | ὑμῖν ... πρᾶγμα δεινὸν καὶ μέγα. (Ar. *Thesm.* 579–81)

... so that you watch out that some great danger doesn't actually happen to you. *Aor. subj.: fear for a future action.*

(10) φύλαξαι μὴ θράσος τέκῃ φόβον. (Aesch. *Supp.* 498)

Be on your guard lest audacity breed fear. *Aor. subj.: fear for a future action.*

(11) ὑποβλέπουσ᾽ ἡμᾶς σκοποῦνταί τ᾽ εὐθέως | μὴ μοιχὸς ἔνδον ᾖ τις ἀποκεκρυμμένος. (Ar. *Thesm.* 396–7)

They look at us suspiciously, and right away start checking to make sure that there isn't a lover hidden inside. *Pf. subj.: fear for a present state.*

Note 1: In examples such as (9) and (10) it is sometimes also possible to interpret the construction as a purpose clause (with μή + subj.), for which →44.3.

44.7   Conversely, verbs of fearing are occasionally construed with effort clauses (with ὅπως μή + fut. ind.):

(12) δέδοιχ᾽ ὅπως | μὴ ᾽κ τῆς σιωπῆς τῆσδ᾽ ἀναρρήξει κακά. (Soph. *OT* 1074–5)

I fear that sorrows will break forth from this silence.

Note 1: This construction may imply that the subject of the fearing verb intends to make an effort to avert the thing feared.

Independent Use of ὅπως + Future Indicative

44.8   For the independent use of ὅπως (μή) + fut. ind. (the construction of effort clauses) to express a strong command, →38.34.

45

Purpose Clauses

Introduction

45.1   To communicate the (intentional) **purpose** of an action, Greek can use the following expressions:

- a **purpose clause** (also called 'final' clause), treated below;
- a future participle, frequently combined with ὡς (→52.41);
- a relative clause with a future indicative (→50.24);
- certain prepositional phrases (e.g. ἐπί + dat.; →31).

> **Note 1:** Greek, unlike English, does not normally use the infinitive to express purpose. However, an infinitive with purpose-value may occur after verbs of going, giving or taking: →51.16–17.
>
> For ἐάν + subj. or εἰ + opt. expressing purpose (*in the hope that*), →49.25. For ὥστε-clauses expressing an intended result, →46.9.

Construction of Purpose Clauses

45.2   Greek purpose clauses are introduced by **ἵνα, ὅπως** and sometimes **ὡς** *in order that, in order to, so that, (so as) to.*

Negative purpose clauses are introduced by ἵνα μή, ὅπως μή, ὡς μή and occasionally by μή alone: *in order that not*, etc., *to prevent/avoid that.*

> **Note 1:** In poetry, the conjunction ὄφρα is occasionally used in purpose clauses.

45.3   In **primary sequence**, the mood in purpose clauses is the **subjunctive**:

(1)   τῶν παίδων ἕνεκα βούλει ζῆν, ἵνα αὐτοὺς ἐκθρέψῃς καὶ παιδεύσῃς; (Pl. *Cri.* 54a)
       Do you wish to live for the children's sake, so that you may raise and educate them?

(2)   πορεύεσθε ἔμπροσθεν, ὅπως ... λανθάνωμεν ὅτι πλεῖστον χρόνον. (Xen. *Cyr.* 4.2.23)
       You must march in front of us, in order that we may go undetected for as long as possible.

(3)   διενοοῦντο τὰς προσβάσεις ... φυλάσσειν, ὅπως μή ... λάθωσι σφᾶς ἀναβάντες οἱ πολέμιοι. (Thuc. 6.96.1)
       They decided to guard the access routes (of the mountain), to prevent the enemy from ascending it unnoticed by them.

In **historic sequence**, purpose clauses frequently use the **oblique optative** (→40.12), although the subjunctive may also be retained:

(4) ἐπρεσβεύοντο . . . πρὸς τοὺς Ἀθηναίους ἐγκλήματα ποιούμενοι, <u>ὅπως</u> σφίσιν ὅτι μεγίστη πρόφασις <u>εἴη</u> τοῦ πολεμεῖν. (Thuc. 1.126.1)

Making complaints, they sent messengers to the Athenians, in order to have as great an excuse for waging war as possible. *Oblique optative.*

(5) οἱ πλείους αὐτῶν, <u>ἵνα μὴ</u> ἀπ’ οἴκου <u>ὦσι</u>, χρήματα ἐτάξαντο ἀντὶ τῶν νεῶν. (Thuc. 1.99.3)

The majority of them, to avoid being away from home, furnished money instead of ships. *Retained subjunctive.*

Note 1: For the difference between the optative and the retained subjunctive, →41.13. The difference between εἴη in (4) and ὦσι in (5) appears to be that the subjunctive ὦσι presents the intention from the perspective of the subject of the matrix clause (the narrator takes no responsibility for their motives), whereas the optative εἴη presents the purpose of an action as 'moderated' by the narrator.

In examples where the subjunctive and optative are used next to each other, the subjunctive tends to highlight the purpose more immediately relevant for the subject of the verb:

(6) τῶνδε δὲ εἵνεκα ἀνῆγον τὰς νέας, <u>ἵνα</u> δὴ τοῖσι Ἕλλησι μηδὲ φυγεῖν <u>ἐξῇ</u>, ἀλλ’ . . . <u>δοῖεν</u> τίσιν τῶν ἐπ’ Ἀρτεμισίῳ ἀγωνισμάτων. (Hdt. 8.76.2)

They put out their ships for the following reason, that it would not be possible for the Greeks to escape, but that they would be punished for their achievements off Artemisium. *The 'retained' subjunctive ἐξῇ presents the purpose which is most immediately relevant for the subject; the optative δοῖεν presents a secondary purpose.*

The subjunctive is also used in cases where the original purpose is still valid at the moment of speaking (→41.14):

(7) τούτων ἕνεκα ἐγεννήθη τῶν ἄστρων ὅσα . . . ἔσχεν τροπάς, <u>ἵνα</u> τόδε ὡς ὁμοιότατον <u>ᾖ</u> τῷ τελέῳ . . . ζῴῳ. (Pl. *Ti.* 39d–e)

For these reasons were generated all those stars which turned themselves around, in order that this (universe) would be as similar as possible to the perfect creature. *The purpose for the design of the universe is still valid in the speaker's present.*

Note 2: The difference between the use of present and aorist subjunctives/optatives in purpose clauses is one of aspect (→33.63–5). For instance, in (3) the aor. subj. λάθωσι expresses an action *in its entirety* (the enemy is not to escape notice at all), whereas the pres. subj. λανθάνωμεν in (2) expresses an action *in process* (note ὅτι πλεῖστον χρόνον).

45.4   After ὅπως or ὡς (but not ἵνα), purpose clauses sometimes have **ἄν + subjunctive**:

(8) δεῦρ’ ἔλθ’, <u>ὅπως ἄν</u> καὶ σοφώτερος <u>γένῃ</u>. (Eur. *Alc.* 779)

Come here, so that you may become wiser still.

(9) <u>ὡς</u> δ’ <u>ἄν μάθῃς</u> . . . ἀντάκουσον. (Xen. *An.* 2.5.16)

So that you might learn, listen to me in turn.

Note 1: This is the prospective use of ἄν + subj. (→40.9), and a prospective nuance may be present: the purpose is presented as something which very likely will occur.

46

Result Clauses

Introduction

46.1 To communicate the (intentional or unintentional) **result** of an action, Greek uses the following expressions:

- a **result clause** (also called 'consecutive' clause) with ὥστε, treated below;
- a relative clause, often with ὅστις or with οἷος, etc. (→50.25); for the infinitive after οἷος, etc., →46.10.

46.2 Result clauses in Greek are introduced by **ὥστε** (infrequently by ὡς) *(so) that, (so as) to*. In the matrix clause, there is often a 'signpost' anticipating the result clause. Such signposts are words like (also →8.1–2):

οὕτω(ς)	so, in such a way
τοιοῦτος, τοιαύτη, τοιοῦτο	such, of this kind
τοσοῦτος, τοσαύτη, τοσοῦτο	so great, so much, so many (pl.)
εἰς τοῦτο + gen.	to such a degree of . . .
εἰς τοσοῦτο(ν) + gen.	so far in . . ., to such an extent of . . .

46.3 There are two possible constructions for result clauses:

- **ὥστε + the moods of independent sentences** (normally the indicative): expressing an actual result (→46.4–6);
- **ὥστε + infinitive** (or acc.-and-inf. construction): expressing a potential (natural, inevitable) result (→46.7–11).

Construction of Result Clauses

With the Moods of Independent Sentences

46.4 When ὥστε is used with an **indicative**, the result is presented as **fact**, i.e. actually taking place at a particular point in time. The negative is οὐ:

(1) <u>οὕτω</u> πονηρός ἐστι . . . <u>ὥστε</u> . . . ποιησαμένων αὐτὸν Τροιζηνίων πολίτην . . . κατα-σταθεὶς ἄρχων <u>ἐξέβαλεν</u> τοὺς πολίτας ἐκ τῆς πόλεως. (Hyp. *Ath.* 15.5–11)
He is so vile that, after the Troezenians had given him citizenship, when he had been installed as magistrate, he expelled the citizens from the city.

(2) ἡ τῶν ἰδίων ἐπιμέλεια … τοὺς … πλουσίους ἐμποδίζει, <u>ὥστε</u> πολλάκις <u>οὐ</u> <u>κοινωνοῦσι</u> τῆς ἐκκλησίας. (Arist. *Pol.* 1293a7–9)

The care of their private affairs hinders the rich, so that they often do not take part in the assembly.

(3) αὐτοὺς … ἐς κίνδυνον καθίστασαν, <u>ὥστε</u> τέλος ἡσυχίαν <u>ἦγον</u>. (Thuc. 2.100.5)

They put themselves at risk, so that in the end they desisted.

46.5   **Other moods** of independent sentences may also be used:

- ὥστε + ἄν + optative (potential, →34.13) indicates that a possibility (actually) results from an action;

- ὥστε + ἄν + modal indicative (counterfactual, →34.16) indicates that as the result of an action, another action would (have) come about if certain conditions had been met (but they are/were actually not met):

(4) οὕτω γὰρ ἀμφοτέρων σφόδρα πεπείρασθε, <u>ὥστε</u> καὶ τοὺς ἄλλους ὑμεῖς ἄριστ' <u>ἂν</u> <u>διδάξαιτε</u> περὶ αὐτῶν. (Isoc. 18.44)

You are so very experienced in both things, that it is you who might best teach the others about them.

(5) τοὺς στρατιώτας τὸν μισθὸν ἀπεστέρησεν, <u>ὥστε</u> τὸ μὲν ἐπ' ἐκείνῳ πολλάκις <u>ἂν</u> <u>διελύθησαν</u>, διὰ δὲ τὸν ἐφεστῶτα … ναυμαχοῦντες ἐνίκησαν. (Isoc. 4.142)

He deprived the soldiers of their pay, so that, had it been up to him (*τὸ μὲν ἐπ' ἐκείνῳ; but it wasn't up to him*), they would have been disbanded more than once; but thanks to their commander, they won a naval battle.

ὥστε Introducing a New Sentence

46.6   Frequently, ὥστε occurs **at the start of a new sentence** (as printed in modern editions). In such cases, ὥστε may be translated *the result was that …, as a result,* or *therefore, so*:

(6) βασιλεὺς … ἔδοξε … Κύρῳ … ἀπεγνωκέναι τοῦ μάχεσθαι· <u>ὥστε</u> τῇ ὑστεραίᾳ Κῦρος ἐπορεύετο ἠμελημένως μᾶλλον. (Xen. *An.* 1.7.19)

It seemed to Cyrus that the king had decided against offering battle. As a result Cyrus proceeded more carelessly the next day.

(7) τίνες ἂν τούτοις τῶν ἄλλων Ἑλλήνων ἤρισαν … ἀρετῇ; <u>ὥστε</u> δικαίως … τἀριστεῖα τῆς ναυμαχίας ἔλαβον παρὰ τῆς Ἑλλάδος. (Lys. 2.42–3)

Who among the other Greeks could have vied with these men in valour? So it was just that they received from Greece prize of prowess in the sea-fight. *ὥστε indicates the result of the Athenians' superlative valour, which Lysias asserts by way of a rhetorical question (→38.19).*

This occurs frequently when ὥστε introduces a command or a direct question:

(8) θνητοῦ πέφυκας πατρός, Ἠλέκτρα, φρόνει, | θνητὸς δ' Ὀρέστης· <u>ὥστε</u> μὴ λίαν <u>στένε</u>. (Soph. *El.* 1171–2)

You are sprung from a mortal father, Electra, keep that in mind, and Orestes is mortal. So do not wail excessively.

(9) προσήκει δήπου ... χάριν αὐτοὺς ἔχειν ... <u>ὥστε</u> <u>πῶς</u> οὐ βοηθήσουσιν ἡμῖν ἐπ' Ὠρωπόν; (Dem. 16.13)

Surely, I think, they ought to be grateful ... How, therefore, can they refuse to help us at Oropus?

With the Infinitive

46.7 When **ὥστε/ὡς** is used with the (accusative and) **infinitive**, the speaker presents the result as one which **naturally or inevitably results** from the action in the matrix clause. It is not specified whether or not the result actually occurs or has occurred, merely that the **action in the matrix clause is of a kind which enables or favours** the bringing about of the result. The negative is μή:

(10) ἔχει γὰρ οὕτως <u>ὥστε</u> <u>μὴ</u> σιγᾶν <u>πρέπειν</u>. (Soph. *Trach.* 1126)

The situation is such that it is not right to keep silent.

(11) πειράσομαι οὕτω ποιεῖν <u>ὥστε</u> καὶ ὑμᾶς ἐμὲ <u>ἐπαινεῖν</u>. (Xen. *Cyr.* 5.1.21)

I will try to act in such a way that you praise me as well.

(12) τὸν μὲν ἄλλον χρόνον οὕτω διεκείμην <u>ὥστε</u> <u>μήτε</u> <u>λυπεῖν</u> <u>μήτε</u> λίαν ἐπ' ἐκείνῃ <u>εἶναι</u> ὅ τι ἂν ἐθέλῃ ποιεῖν. (Lys. 1.6)

For some time I behaved towards her in such a way as not to harass her, nor to have it be too much up to her to do whatever she wanted.

Note 1: The difference between ὥστε + the moods of independent sentences and ὥστε + infinitive may be illustrated from examples such as the following:

(13) εἰς τοῦτ' ἀφικνεῖται βδελυρίας <u>ὥστε</u> τύπτειν <u>ἐπεχείρησε</u> τὸν ἄνθρωπον. (Dem. 25.60)
He came to such a level of disgrace that he tried to strike the man.

(14) ἀλλὰ ξυνέπεσεν ἐς τοῦτο ἀνάγκης <u>ὥστε</u> <u>ἐπιχειρῆσαι</u> ἀλλήλοις <u>τοὺς Κορινθίους καὶ Ἀθηναίους</u>. (Thuc. 1.49.7)
But it came to the point of necessity for the Corinthians and Athenians to attack each other.

In (13) – part of a forensic speech – the attack itself is presented as a relevant fact which has taken place at a certain point in time: that fact is presented as the result of poor character. In (14) – part of a narrative description of a naval battle, in which the Athenian fleet is gradually drawn into a fight in which it wanted no active part – the principal import of the sentence is that the (climactic) point of the battle was reached where the two sides had no option but to engage; that they did in fact fight is implied (and clear from the surrounding context).

Note 2: The difference between ὥστε + present infinitive and ὥστε + aorist infinitive is one of aspect: →33.63–5.

46.8   The infinitive is used by default:

- after a **negative matrix clause** (e.g. (15));
- after a **comparative with ἢ ὥστε** ('more X than to' = 'too X to'; e.g. (16));
- when the matrix clause is a **conditional clause** (e.g. (17)):

(15) οὐ γὰρ ἀλκὴν ἔχομεν <u>ὥστε μὴ θανεῖν</u>. (Eur. *Her.* 326)
      We do not have a defence against death (*lit. 'so as not to die'*).

(16) <u>καταφανέστερον ἢ ὥστε λανθάνειν</u> οὐ προθύμως ξυνεπολέμει. (Thuc. 8.46.5)
      (Tissaphernes) engaged in war with a lack of zeal that was too clear to escape notice (*lit. 'clearer than so as to escape notice'*).

(17) εἰ οὖν μηχανή τις γένοιτο <u>ὥστε πόλιν γενέσθαι</u> . . . ἐραστῶν τε καὶ παιδικῶν . . . (Pl. *Symp.* 178e)
      If, then, there were some method so that a city of lovers and their favourites might exist . . .

Note 1: In each of these cases the use of the infinitive rather than the moods of independent sentences is expected: there is no question of an *actual* result: in (15) and (17) the action leading to the result is itself not presented as actually taking place; in (16) the construction indicates that the actual situation is in conflict with the result (Tissaphernes' lack of zeal was so obvious that it was not possible for it to go unnoticed).

46.9   The infinitive is also used when the ὥστε-clause refers to an **intended result**:

(18) πᾶν ποιοῦσιν <u>ὥστε</u> δίκην μὴ <u>διδόναι</u>. (Pl. *Grg.* 479c)
      They do everything so as to avoid being punished.

Note 1: Again, the use of the infinitive is expected in such cases: the matrix clause expresses an action which is performed *in such a way* that it (naturally) leads to the intended result. Herein also lies the difference between ὥστε-clauses referring to an intended result and purpose clauses (→45; purpose clauses do not specify the nature of consequence between the matrix clause and the subordinate clause). These clauses are, however, similar in sense to effort clauses (→44).

46.10 When the matrix clause has a signpost like τοιοῦτος, τοσοῦτος (→46.2), a result clause may also be formed using the **correlative adjectives οἷος, ὅσος** (→8.1) with the **infinitive** (the sense is similar to the construction with ὥστε + infinitive described above):

(19) ἐγώ . . . <u>τοιοῦτος οἷος</u> . . . μηδενὶ ἄλλῳ <u>πείθεσθαι</u> ἢ τῷ λόγῳ ὃς . . . (Pl. *Cri.* 46b)
      I am the type of man who follows nothing but the reasoning which . . .

This sometimes occurs without a preceding form of τοιοῦτος, etc.:

(20) ἐλείπετο τῆς νυκτὸς ὅσον σκοταίους διελθεῖν τὸ πεδίον. (Xen. *An.* 4.1.5)

So much of the night remained that they could cross the plain in the dark.

The use of the infinitive distinguishes such result clauses from correlative clauses introduced by οἷος, ὅσος with a finite verb (for which →50.28), giving them an unambiguous result meaning.

46.11   For the redundant use of ὥστε with obligatory infinitives after verbs such as πείθω, →51.17.

47

Temporal Clauses

Introduction

Expressions of 'Time When'

47.1 To communicate **when** an action takes place, Greek can use the following expressions:

- a prepositional phrase with temporal meaning (→31):
  - (1) μετὰ ταῦτα ... οἱ Θηβαῖοι ... ἀπῆλθον οἴκαδε. (Xen. *Hell.* 7.1.22)
    After this, the Thebans went home.
- a temporal adverb;
- a dative or genitive used as an adverbial modifier of time (→30.32, 30.46, 30.56):
  - (2) καὶ δὴ καὶ τότε πρωαίτερον συνελέγημεν· τῇ γὰρ προτεραίᾳ ἐπειδὴ ἐξήλθομεν ἐκ τοῦ δεσμωτηρίου ἑσπέρας, ... (Pl. *Phd.* 59d–e)
    And on that occasion we gathered at an earlier hour. For on the day before, when we had left the prison in the evening, ...
- a connected participle or genitive absolute expressing a temporal relation (→52.35–7)
  - (3) ταῦτ' ἀκούσαντες οἱ στρατηγοὶ ... ἀπῆλθον. (Xen. *An.* 2.2.5)
    Having heard this, the generals left.
- a **subordinate temporal clause** (treated below):
  - (4) ἐπεὶ κατεστρατοπεδεύοντο οἱ Ἕλληνες ... , ἀπῆλθον οἱ βάρβαροι. (Xen. *An.* 3.4.18)
    When the Greeks were setting up camp, the foreigners withdrew.

Note 1: For impersonal expressions of time, e.g. ὀψέ ἐστι *it is late*, →36.12.

Conjunctions Used in Temporal Clauses

47.2 Temporal clauses are introduced by one of the following subordinating **conjunctions**:

ἐπεί, ἐπειδή (Ion. ἐπείτε)	after, when; now that
ὡς	after, when

ὅτε	when, after; now that
ὁπότε	when(ever); now that
ἐπεί/ὡς τάχιστα	as soon as
ἡνίκα	at the moment that, (exactly) when
ἕως	so long as *or* until
μέχρι (οὗ)	so long as *or* until
ἔστε	so long as *or* until
πρίν (ἤ)	before *or* until
πρότερον ἤ	before
ἐν ᾧ	while
ἐς ὅ	until
ἐξ/ἀφ’ οὗ	since

When followed by ἄν, the conjunctions ἐπεί, ἐπειδή, ὅτε and ὁπότε become, by crasis (→1.43–5), ἐπήν/ἐπεάν/ἐπάν, ἐπειδάν, ὅταν and ὁπόταν.

Note 1: Combinations such as ἐν ᾧ, consisting of a preposition and a relative pronoun ('while' < 'during (the time) that') were fossilized to such an extent that they may be seen as individual conjunctions (note that they are never separated: we find e.g. ἐν ᾧ δέ, not ἐν δὲ ᾧ).

Moods and Tenses Used in Temporal Clauses

47.3 Different kinds of temporal relations are expressed in Greek not only by the selection of different conjunctions, but also by the **selection of different tense-aspect stems** for the verb in the temporal clause. For instance:

ἐπεί + impf. *when*	but	ἐπεί + aor. ind. *after, when* (→47.7)
ἕως ἄν + pres. subj. *so long as*	but	ἕως ἄν + aor. subj. *until* (→47.12)

47.4 The **use of moods** (and the negative) in temporal clauses varies according to the nature of the temporal relationship between the subordinate and matrix clause. There are three main types:

- temporal clauses referring to (a single action in) the **past**, with a secondary (i.e. past-tense) **indicative**, negative οὐ; →47.7;
- temporal clauses referring to the **future**, with **subjunctive + ἄν** (**prospective**), negative μή; →47.8;
- temporal clauses referring to a **repeated/habitual** action: such clauses have **subjunctive + ἄν** (**indefinite**) if the temporal clause refers to the present or future, or an **iterative optative** (without ἄν) if the temporal clause refers to the past; the negative is μή; →47.9–11.

47.5 The conjunction **πρίν** can be followed both by finite verb forms in various moods and by an infinitive; →47.14–16 below.

'Temporal' Clauses with Causal Force

47.6   In non-narrative contexts (→33.13), clauses introduced by ἐπεί, ἐπειδή, ἐπείτε, ὅτε and (more rarely) ὁπότε and ὡς are also used with **causal** meaning: *now that, as, since.*

   When they are so used, the moods and tenses used are those of independent sentences. The negative is οὐ. These clauses are treated separately in 48.3–5.

Note 1: The use of an indicative with present reference (pres. ind., pf. ind.) with any of these conjunctions generally indicates that the clause has a causal sense. Such clauses are thus not treated in this chapter.

Temporal Clauses Referring to a Single Action in the Past

47.7   Temporal clauses referring to a single action in the **past** use a secondary (i.e. past-tense) indicative: **aorist, imperfect**, or **pluperfect**; the negative is οὐ. The matrix clause may have any past tense or, rarely, a present tense. The difference between the tenses of the subordinate clause is aspectual; in temporal clauses, there is nearly always an implication of relative tense (→33.57). Generally:

- the **imperfect**, by presenting the action of the subordinate clause as incomplete, suggests that the action of the subordinate clause is going on at the same time as that of the matrix clause (**simultaneity**);
- (more rarely) the **pluperfect**, by referring to an ongoing state (resulting from a previously completed action), suggests that that state exists at the same time as the action of the matrix clause (**simultaneity**);
- the **aorist indicative**, by presenting the action of the subordinate clause as complete, suggests that the action of the subordinate clause precedes that of the matrix clause (**anteriority**):

(5) ὡς ἐγεωργοῦμεν ἐν τῇ Νάξῳ, ἐθήτευεν ἐκεῖ παρ᾽ ἡμῖν. (Pl. *Euthphr.* 4c)
   When we were farmers on Naxos, he was a labourer for us there. *Imperfect, simultaneous.*

(6) Ἀριαῖος ... ἐθωρακίζετο καὶ οἱ σὺν αὐτῷ. ἐν ᾧ δὲ ὡπλίζοντο ἧκον ... οἱ προπεμφθέντες σκοποί. (Xen. *An.* 2.2.14–15)
   Ariaeus put on his breastplate and so did those who were with him. While they were arming themselves, however, the scouts returned. *Imperfect, simultaneous.*

(7) ἐπειδὴ οὐ προυχώρει ᾗ προσεδέχοντο, ἀπῆλθον ἐπ᾽ Ἀντίσσης. (Thuc. 3.18.1)
   When it was not turning out for them as they expected, they left for Antissa. *Imperfect, simultaneous.*

(8) ἑβδομαῖος ἀφ᾽ οὗ ἔκαμεν ἔξω τοῦ ἱεροῦ ἐτελεύτησε. (Xen. *Hell.* 5.3.19)

On the seventh day after he had fallen sick, he died outside the sanctuary. *Aorist, anterior.*

(9) ἐπεὶ δὲ παρεσκεύαστο ἀμφοτέροις, ἦσαν ἐς χεῖρας. (Thuc. 3.107.4)

As soon as everything was prepared on both sides, they were locked in battle. *Pluperfect ('had been prepared by both sides'); the resulting state is presented as simultaneous with ἦσαν (for the 'immediative' interpretation of this impf., →33.52).*

Note 1: Temporal clauses with a negative (such as (7)) often have a causal connotation.

Note 2: In narrative texts, clauses with conjunctions meaning *when, after* (ἐπεί, ἐπειδή, ἐπείτε, ὡς, ὅτε, ὁπότε, ἡνίκα) or *while* (ἐν ᾧ) usually precede the matrix clause (as in (5)–(9)), whereas clauses with ἐς ὅ *until* follow the matrix clause. Such sentences exhibit a so-called 'iconic' ordering: what came first is presented first, what came last, last. (Another factor influencing initial placement is the frequent function of temporal clauses as 'setting', for which →60.32).

Particularly ἡνίκα-clauses, however, may also follow the matrix clause, in which case the temporal clause generally expresses the more important action, and often includes an idea of delay or surprise:

(10) καὶ ἤδη ... ἦν ἀμφὶ ἀγορὰν πλήθουσαν ..., ἡνίκα Πατηγύας ... προφαίνεται. (Xen. *An.* 1.8.1)

It was already about full-market time, when Pategyas appeared. *Note that the ἡνίκα-clause is construed, unusually, with the historical present (προφαίνεται); the historical present is rare in subordinate clauses.*

Temporal Clauses Referring to the Future

47.8   Temporal clauses referring to the **future** always have ἄν + **subjunctive** (prospective, →40.9); the negative is μή. The matrix clause has either a future indicative or another verb with future reference (e.g. imperative, hortatory subjunctive, etc.; →33.63–4).

The difference between the use of present and aorist subjunctives is aspectual, typically implying relative tense (as above in 47.7):

– ἄν + **present subjunctive** (imperfective aspect) normally suggests that the action in the temporal clause is situated at the same time as the action in the main/matrix clause (**simultaneity**);

– ἄν + **aorist subjunctive** (perfective aspect) normally suggests that the action in the temporal clause is situated before the action in the main/matrix clause (**anteriority**):

(11) καὶ ἐν ᾧ ἂν ζῶμεν, οὕτως, ὡς ἔοικεν, ἐγγυτάτω ἐσόμεθα τοῦ εἰδέναι . . . (Pl. *Phd.* 67a)

And while we live, we will, it seems, be nearest to knowing in the following way . . . *Future indicative in the matrix clause; the present subjunctive implies simultaneity.*

(12) ἐξάρξω μὲν οὖν ἐγὼ ἡνίκ᾽ ἂν καιρὸς ᾖ παιᾶνα. (Xen. *Hell.* 2.4.17)

I will strike up the paean when the time is right. *Future indicative in the matrix clause; the present subjunctive implies simultaneity.*

(13) τοὺς ὑεῖς μου, ἐπειδὰν ἡβήσωσι, τιμωρήσασθε, ὦ ἄνδρες. (Pl. *Ap.* 41e)

Gentlemen, you must punish my sons when they have grown up. *Imperative in the matrix clause; the aorist subjunctive implies anteriority.*

(14) νῦν ὦν μοι δοκέει, ἐπεὰν τάχιστα νὺξ ἐπέλθῃ . . . ἀπαλλάσσεσθαι. (Hdt. 4.134.3)

So now it seems best to me to depart as soon as night has fallen. *The dynamic infinitive ἀπαλλάσσεσθαι has future reference; the aorist subjunctive implies anteriority.*

Note 1: Perfect-stem subjunctives (other than of οἶδα) are infrequently used in such clauses; when they do occur the perfect has its normal aspectual value (→33.6, 33.34–7), which in temporal clauses typically implies simultaneity:

(15) ὅταν γὰρ ἐν κακοῖς | ἤδη βεβήκῃς, τἄμ᾽ ἐπαινέσεις ἔπη. (Soph. *El.* 1056–7)

Eventually, when you find yourself in trouble, you will approve of my words. *Future indicative in the matrix clause; the perfect subjunctive (referring to an ongoing state) implies simultaneity.*

Note 2: Greek does not normally use a future indicative in temporal clauses referring to the future (for causal clauses with fut. ind., →48.3 with n.1; for conditional clauses, →49.5).

Note 3: Observe that English typically uses a present-stem form (a 'concealed future') in temporal clauses referring to the future (e.g. *live* in the translation of (11), *is* in (12)).

Temporal Clauses Referring to a Repeated or Habitual Action

47.9   Temporal clauses referring to a **repeated** or **habitual** action **in the present or future** have **ἄν + subjunctive** (indefinite, →40.9); the negative is μή. The matrix clause contains a generalized statement, usually in the present indicative.

The difference between aorist and present subjunctives is aspectual, normally with an implication of relative tense (as above):

(16) οἱ γὰρ ἀδικούμενοι πάντες εἰσίν, ὁπόταν τις τὴν πόλιν ἀδικῇ. (Pl. *Leg.* 768a)

Everyone is being wronged whenever someone wrongs the city. *Present indicative in the matrix clause; the present subjunctive implies simultaneity.*

(17) μεγίστη <u>γίγνεται</u> σωτηρία, | <u>ὅταν</u> γυνὴ πρὸς ἄνδρα <u>μὴ</u> <u>διχοστατῇ</u>. (Eur. *Med.* 14–15)

It is the greatest source of safety, when a woman is not at odds with her husband. *Present indicative in the matrix clause; the present subjunctive implies simultaneity.*

(18) <u>ἡνίκ᾽</u> ἂν οὖν ὁ ἀγὼν <u>ἔλθῃ</u> τοῦ πολέμου, πᾶς τις εὐχερῶς ἑαυτὸν <u>σῴζει</u>. (Dem. 60.25)

Whenever, then, the test of war has arrived, everyone handily saves himself. *Present indicative in the matrix clause; the aorist subjunctive implies anteriority.*

47.10   When the temporal clause refers to the **past**, it has an **iterative optative** (without ἄν). The matrix clause normally has an imperfect, sometimes a pluperfect.

The difference between the aorist and present optatives is aspectual, normally with an implication of relative tense (as above):

(19) ἐθήρευεν ἀπὸ ἵππου, <u>ὁπότε</u> γυμνάσαι <u>βούλοιτο</u> ἑαυτόν τε καὶ τοὺς ἵππους. (Xen. *An.* 1.2.7)

He used to hunt on horseback whenever he wanted to give himself and his horses exercise. *Imperfect in the matrix clause; the present optative implies simultaneity.*

(20) ἐπὶ τῷ λιμένι, <u>ὁπότε</u> <u>μὴ</u> χειμὼν <u>κωλύοι</u>, ἐφώρμει. (Xen. *Hell.* 6.2.7)

He put up a blockade (*lit. 'anchored'*) at the mouth of the harbour, whenever a storm did not prevent it. *Imperfect in the matrix clause; the present optative implies simultaneity.*

(21) <u>ἐπειδὴ</u> γὰρ <u>προσβάλοιεν</u> ἀλλήλοις, οὐ ῥαδίως ἀπελύοντο ὑπό τε τοῦ πλήθους καὶ ὄχλου τῶν νεῶν. (Thuc. 1.49.3)

Each time they had charged each other, it was not easy to untangle them, due to the multitude and throng of ships. *Imperfect in the matrix clause; the aorist optative implies anteriority.*

Note 1: Perfect subjunctives/optatives (other than of οἶδα) are not frequently used in such clauses; when they do occur the perfect stem has its normal aspectual value, which in temporal clauses typically implies simultaneity:

(22) τοὺς δὲ παραδιδομένους νόμους δοκιμασάτω πρότερον ἡ βουλὴ καὶ οἱ νομοθέται οἱ πεντακόσιοι οὓς οἱ δημόται εἵλοντο, <u>ἐπειδὰν</u> <u>ὀμωμόκωσιν</u>. (Andoc. 1.84)
The laws which are handed over shall be scrutinized beforehand by the Council and the five hundred Lawgivers elected by the Demes, when they are under oath. *The imperative δοκιμασάτω is a general instruction: the condition of being sworn in (ἐπειδὰν ὀμωμόκωσιν, perfect subjunctive) is simultaneous with δοκιμασάτω.*

47.11   In general statements, the optative (without ἄν) is infrequently used in temporal clauses which do not refer to the past:

(23) ὁ . . . ἑκὼν πεινῶν φάγοι ἂν ὁπότε βούλοιτο. (Xen. *Mem.* 2.1.18)
He who is hungry willingly may eat whenever he wants.

This occurs especially when the main clause has a potential optative with ἄν, as in (23) (cf. 'potential' conditional clauses, →49.8; such cases may be seen as instances of attraction of mood, →40.15).

ἕως

47.12   The conjunction ἕως can mean either **as long as** or **until**. The interpretation depends on the aspectual value of the (subordinate) verb it is found with:

– With a verb form expressing **incompleteness** (present indicative, imperfect/ pluperfect, ἄν + present subjunctive, present optative), ἕως = **as long as**, indicating that the action of the matrix clause is simultaneous with, and conditional upon, the action in the temporal clause;
– With a verb form expressing **completeness** (aorist indicative, ἄν + aorist subjunctive, aorist optative), ἕως = **until**, expressing that the action of the matrix clause reaches its end when the action in the subordinate clause takes place. The ἕως-clause typically follows the matrix clause.

Some examples:

(24) οὐδὲν γὰρ κωλύει διαμυθολογῆσαι πρὸς ἀλλήλους ἕως ἔξεστιν. (Pl. *Ap.* 39e)
For nothing prevents us from chatting with each other as long as it is possible. *ἕως + present indicative: 'as long as'; single present action.*
(25) ἕως δὲ ἀφειστήκη πόρρωθεν, ἐφαίνετό τί μοι λέγεσθαι. (Pl. *Tht.* 208e)
As long as I was standing at a distance, it seemed to me that there was something in the discussion. *ἕως + pluperfect: 'as long as'; single past action; for the idiom λέγω τι, →29.42.*
(26) ἐφίει τὸ δόρυ διὰ τῆς χειρός, ἕως ἄκρου τοῦ στύρακος ἀντελάβετο. (Pl. *La.* 184a)
He let the spear slip through his hand until he gripped it by the butt-end of the shaft. *ἕως + aorist indicative: 'until'; single past action.*
(27) ἕωσπερ ἂν ἐμπνέω καὶ οἷός τε ὦ, οὐ μὴ παύσωμαι φιλοσοφῶν. (Pl. *Ap.* 29d)
As long as I am breathing and able, I will certainly not stop practising philosophy. *ἕως ἄν + present subjunctive (prospective): 'as long as'; action (continuing) in the future; for οὐ μή + subj., →34.9.*

(28) ἀλλὰ χρή, ἔφη ὁ Σωκράτης, ἐπᾴδειν αὐτῷ ἑκάστης ἡμέρας <u>ἕως ἂν ἐξεπᾴσητε</u>. (Pl. *Phd.* 77e)

'Ah,' said Socrates, 'you must sing charms to him every day until you have charmed away his fear.' *ἕως ἄν* + *aorist subjunctive (prospective): 'until'; action in the future.*

(29) περιεμένομεν οὖν ἑκάστοτε <u>ἕως ἀνοιχθείη</u> τὸ δεσμωτήριον … ἐπειδὴ δὲ ἀνοιχθείη, εἰσῆμεν παρὰ τὸν Σωκράτη. (Pl. *Phd.* 59d)

So we would wait, every time, until the jail was opened; and when it was opened, we would go to see Socrates. *ἕως* + *aorist optative: 'until'; repeated action in the past.*

47.13   The rarer conjunctions <u>ἔστε</u> and μέχρι (οὗ) function in the same way as ἕως. Two examples are:

(30) ἐγὼ μὲν οὖν <u>ἔστε</u> μὲν αἱ σπονδαὶ ἦσαν οὔποτε ἐπαυόμην ἡμᾶς … οἰκτίρων. (Xen. *An.* 3.1.19)

As for me, then, as long as the treaty was in effect I never ceased pitying us.

(31) ἐμάχοντο ἀπό τε τῶν νεῶν καὶ τῆς γῆς <u>μέχρι</u> οἱ Ἀθηναῖοι ἀπέπλευσαν εἰς Μάδυτον. (Xen. *Hell.* 1.1.3)

They fought in naval and land battles until the Athenians sailed away to Madytus.

πρίν

47.14   The conjunction **πρίν** (also **πρὶν ἤ**, and sometimes πρότερον ἤ), which expresses that the action of the subordinate clause is **posterior** to that of the matrix clause, is construed in two ways:

– When the **matrix clause is negative** (or has an intrinsically negative verb like ἀπαγορεύω *forbid*, ἀδύνατόν (ἐστι) *it is impossible*, etc.), πρίν is usually followed by a finite aorist-stem form. In such cases, πρίν can be translated with *before* or *until* (or, leaving the negative in the matrix clause untranslated, *only when*). The πρίν-clause typically follows the matrix clause:

(32) πρότερον δ' <u>οὐκ</u> ἦν γένος ἀθανάτων, <u>πρὶν</u> Ἔρως <u>ξυνέμειξεν</u> ἅπαντα. (Ar. *Av.* 700)

And there was no race of immortals before Eros mixed everything together. *Aorist indicative; single past action.*

(33) <u>οὐ</u> πρότερον κακῶν παύσονται αἱ πόλεις, <u>πρὶν ἂν</u> ἐν αὐταῖς οἱ φιλόσοφοι <u>ἄρξωσιν</u>. (Pl. *Resp.* 487e)

The cities will cease their wrongdoings only when the philosophers assume power in them. *ἄν* + *aorist subjunctive (prospective); future action.*

(34) ἀπηγόρευε μηδένα βάλλειν, πρὶν Κῦρος ἐμπλησθείη θηρῶν. (Xen. *Cyr.* 1.4.14)

He forbade anyone from throwing a spear until Cyrus had gotten his fill of hunting. *For the construction after verbs of preventing, →51.35; the aorist optative ἐμπλησθείη is oblique, replacing prospective ἄν + subjunctive (→40.14); the 'direct command' would have been e.g. μὴ βάλλετε πρὶν ἄν Κῦρος ἐμπλησθῇ θηρῶν.*

– When the **matrix clause is affirmative** (not-negative), πρίν is normally followed by the (accusative and) **infinitive**. In such cases, πρίν can be translated only with *before*, not with *until*:

(35) λέγοιμ' ἄν ἤδη. πρὶν λέγειν δ', ὑμᾶς τοδὶ | ἐπερήσομαί τι μικρόν. (Ar. *Lys.* 97–8)

I'll make my speech momentarily. But before making it, I'll ask you this, a small issue.

(36) ὀλίγον δὲ πρὶν ἡμᾶς ἀπιέναι μάχη ἐγεγόνει ἐν τῇ Ποτειδαίᾳ. (Pl. *Chrm.* 153b)

Not long before we went back, a battle had taken place in Potidaea.

(37) ἦν ἡμίν, ὦναξ, Λάϊός ποθ' ἡγεμὼν | γῆς τῆσδε, πρὶν σὲ τήνδ' ἀπευθύνειν πόλιν. (Soph. *OT* 103–4)

Once, my lord, Laius was the king of this land, before you had control of this city.

Note 1: πρίν-clauses, either with finite verbs or with infinitives, cannot normally themselves be negated.

Note 2: Posteriority may also be expressed by ἕως, →47.12.

47.15   Occasionally in poetry, and rarely in prose, πρίν with a finite aorist-stem form occurs after an affirmative main clause (and may in such cases be translated with either *before* or *until*):

(38) ἡγόμην δ' ἀνὴρ | ἀστῶν μέγιστος τῶν ἐκεῖ, πρὶν μοι τύχη | τοιάδ' ἐπέστη ... (Soph. *OT* 775–7)

I was considered to be foremost among the citizens there, until the following chance event befell me: ...

47.16   In poetry and Herodotus (and, according to the manuscript tradition, Thucydides), ἄν is occasionally omitted in πρίν-clauses referring to the future or a habitual action:

(39) οὐκ ἔστιν ὅστις αὐτὸν ἐξαιρήσεται | ..., πρὶν γυναῖκ' ἐμοὶ μεθῇ. (Eur. *Alc.* 848–9)

No one will free him until he releases the woman to me. *For οὐκ ἔστιν ὅστις, →50.12.*

Note 1: πρὶν ἤ is never followed by ἄν, taking only the subjunctive when referring to the future or a habitual action.

Comparative Temporal Clauses (ὡς ὅτε/ὡς ὁπότε)

47.17 ὅτε and ὁπότε are sometimes combined in poetry with ὡς (**ὡς ὅτε/ὡς ὁπότε** *as when*), in **comparisons** and similes, comparing one situation to another. The verb in such clauses is regularly omitted (in such cases ὡς ὅτε may be translated with *like, as it were*):

(40) χρυσέας ὑποστάσαντες ... | κίονας, <u>ὡς ὅτε θαητὸν μέγαρον</u> | πάξομεν. (Pind. *Ol.* 6.1–3)
Putting up golden columns, we will build, as it were, a marvellous hall.

48

Causal Clauses

Introduction

48.1   To communicate for what **reason, motive** or **cause** the action expressed by a verb takes place, the following expressions are regularly used in Greek:

 – modifiers in the dative (→30.45), or, with verbs of emotion, in the genitive (→30.30);
 – preposition phrases, especially with διά and ἕνεκα (→31);
 – circumstantial participles, especially when modified by ὡς or ἅτε (→52.38–9);
 – certain types of relative clauses (→50.23);
 – **causal clauses**, introduced by ὅτι or διότι, or by one of the conjunctions used in temporal clauses (ἐπεί, etc.); these are treated below.

Note 1: Reason, motivation and cause are also frequently expressed in sentences introduced by the particle γάρ (→59.14–15). There is a significant difference, however, between causal clauses (adverbial subordinate clauses), which are syntactically integrated in a complex sentence (→39), and explanatory γάρ-clauses, which form new independent sentences. Compare the two constructions in:

(1) ταῦτα ἐς τοὺς πάντας Ἕλληνας ἀπέρριψε ὁ Κῦρος τὰ ἔπεα, ὅτι ἀγορὰς στησάμενοι ὠνῇ τε καὶ πρήσι χρέωνται· αὐτοὶ γὰρ οἱ Πέρσαι ἀγορῇσι οὐδὲν ἐώθασι χρᾶσθαι, οὐδέ σφι ἐστὶ τὸ παράπαν ἀγορή. (Hdt. 1.153.2)

These words Cyrus meant as an insult against the whole Greek nation, because they set up market-places and buy and sell there; for the Persians themselves do not tend to use markets, and in fact have no market-place at all. *In the ὅτι-clause Herodotus ascribes to Cyrus a reason for his (unfriendly) words to the Greeks (ἀπέρριψε), while in the γάρ-clause Herodotus explains why Cyrus specifically mentioned markets to the Greeks.*

Note also that only ὅτι/διότι-clauses (not γάρ-clauses) can answer a question expressed by τί; and διὰ τί; *why?, for what reason?* (cf. e.g. examples (2) and (5) below).

Construction of Causal Clauses

ὅτι and διότι

48.2   In causal clauses introduced by the conjunctions **ὅτι** and **διότι** (in poetry also ὁθούνεκα and οὕνεκα), the moods and tenses used are those of independent declarative sentences (→34). The indicative is by far the most common mood; counterfactual indicatives (+ ἄν) and potential optatives (+ ἄν) also occur. The negative is οὐ:

(2) ΘΕ. διὰ τί δῆτα κλαύσομαι; | :: ΣΤ. <u>ὅτι</u> τῶν παχειῶν <u>ἐνετίθεις</u> θρυαλλίδων. (Ar. *Nub.* 58–9)

Servant:) Why then will I be punished? :: (Strepsiades:) Because you were putting in one of the thick wicks.

(3) ὀκνῶ εἰπεῖν ὅτι οὐκ ἔχω τί λέγω, <u>διότι</u> μοι νυνδὴ <u>ἐπέπληξας</u> εἰπόντι αὐτό. (Pl. *Tht.* 158a)

I hesitate to admit that I don't know what to say, because you've scolded me just now when I said that.

(4) οἵ τ' Ἀθηναῖοι ἐνόμιζον ἡσσᾶσθαι <u>ὅτι</u> οὐ πολὺ <u>ἐνίκων</u>. (Thuc. 7.34.7)

The Athenians thought themselves vanquished, because they were not decidedly victorious. *Note that in this example it is the narrator who provides, as an independent fact, the reason for the Athenians' thinking, i.e. the ὅτι-clause does not present the Athenians' own explanation for the loss they believed themselves to have suffered (contrast (6) below, and →41.21). For the translation of present-stem ἡσσᾶσθαι and ἐνίκων, →33.18.*

(5) τί ποτ' οὖν ... τῶν ἐμοὶ πεπραγμένων οὐχὶ μέμνηται; <u>ὅτι</u> τῶν ἀδικημάτων <u>ἄν</u> <u>ἐμέμνητο</u> τῶν αὐτοῦ. (Dem. 18.79)

Why on earth, then, doesn't he mention the things done by me? Because he would have been reminded of his own unlawful deeds (*if he had mentioned them, but he didn't*).

In historic sequence (when the verb in the main clause is imperfect, aorist or pluperfect) the **oblique optative** (→40.12) may also be used in a causal clause, **when the reason is reported or alleged**:

(6) τὸν Περικλέα ... ἐκάκιζον <u>ὅτι</u> στρατηγὸς ὢν οὐκ <u>ἐπεξάγοι</u>. (Thuc. 2.21.3)

They abused Pericles on the ground that, although he was their general, he did not lead them out.

'Temporal' Conjunctions with Causal Force

48.3   The temporal conjunctions ἐπεί, ἐπειδή, ὅτε and (less frequently) ὁπότε are also used with **causal force**. This occurs specifically in **non-narrative text** (→33.13). The subordinate clause most often refers to the present: moods used are those of independent sentences, i.e. present indicative, perfect indicative, 'constative' aorist indicative, but also future indicative, potential optative (+ ἄν) and counterfactual modal (secondary) indicative (+ ἄν).

Note 1: Observe that the moods used in such clauses do not normally occur in 'proper' temporal clauses (→47.4), but are the same as those used in ὅτι/διότι-clauses treated above.

48.4   When such a clause **precedes its matrix clause**, it expresses **cause or reason**; the matrix clause regularly has a form with future reference (fut. ind., imp., etc.; →33.63–4):

(7)   ἐπεί με ἀναγκάζεις δεσπότεα τὸν ἐμὸν κτείνειν οὐκ ἐθέλοντα, φέρε ἀκούσω . . .
(Hdt. 1.11.4)
Now that you are compelling me to slay my master against my will, please let me hear . . . *Pres. ind. in the ἐπεί-clause; hortatory subj. in the main clause.*

(8)   νῦν δὲ ἐπειδὴ οὐκ ἐθέλεις καὶ ἐμοί τις ἀσχολία ἐστὶν . . . εἶμι. (Pl. Prt. 335c)
But now, since you do not want to and I have an obligation, I'm off. *Pres. ind. in the ἐπειδή-clause; εἶμι in the main clause has future reference (→33.19).*

(9)   ὅτε . . . διακεκρίμεθα χωρὶς τάς τε καθαρὰς ἡδονὰς καὶ τὰς . . . ἀκαθάρτους . . . ,
προσθῶμεν . . . (Pl. Phlb. 52c)
Now that we have a distinction between the pure and the impure pleasures, let us add . . . *Pf. ind. in the ὅτε-clause; hortatory subj. in the main clause.*

(10)   ἐπεὶ δὲ τάδε ἀκινδυνότερα ἔδοξεν εἶναι, ἡμῖν . . . ἀπολογητέον. (Antiph. 4.4.1)
But since we have decided that this is the safer course of action, we must conduct the defence. *'Constative' aor. ind. (→33.28) in the ἐπεί-clause; ἀπολογητέον in the main clause has future reference.*

When such a clause with ἐπεί or ἐπειδή **follows its matrix clause**, it nearly always expresses the **motivation** for making the preceding utterance. ὡς is also so used:

(11)   ἀλλ' ἐμοῦ μὲν οὐ τυραννεύσουσ', ἐπεὶ φυλάξομαι | καὶ φορήσω τὸ ξίφος. (Ar. Lys.
631–2)
But they won't control me, since I'll be on guard and bear my sword. *Fut. ind.*

(12)   Λακεδαιμόνιοί . . . ἄκοντας προσάγουσι τοὺς πολλοὺς ἐς τὸν κίνδυνον, ἐπεὶ οὐκ
ἂν ποτε ἐνεχείρησαν ἡσσηθέντες παρὰ πολὺ αὖθις ναυμαχεῖν. (Thuc. 2.89.4)
The Spartans lead the majority into danger against their will, since they would never have ventured to fight at sea again after having been defeated very severely (*if they hadn't been forced, but they were*). *Counterfactual modal secondary ind. + ἄν.*

(13)   προϊέναι βέλτιστα νῷν, | ὡς οὗτος ὁ τόπος ἐστὶν οὗ τὰ θηρία | τὰ δείν' ἔφασκ'
ἐκεῖνος. (Ar. Ran. 277–9)
We'd better move on, as this is the place where that man said there are terrifying creatures. *Pres. ind.*

ἐπεί/ὡς Introducing a New Sentence

48.5   When used to provide a motivation for the preceding utterance, ἐπεί and ὡς
        regularly **introduce a new sentence** (as printed in modern editions), and may
        occur after a change of speaker:

(14) τί ποτε λέγεις, ὦ τέκνον; <u>ὡς</u> οὐ μανθάνω (Soph. *Phil.* 914)
     What on earth are you saying, child? For I do not understand.

(15) Ἰω. μητρὸς τάδ᾽ ἡμῖν ἐκφέρεις ζητήματα; | :: ΠΡ. <u>ἐπεί</u> γ᾽ ὁ δαίμων βούλεται. (Eur.
     Ion 1352–3)
     (Ion:) Are you laying out the means to find my mother here? :: (Priestess:)
     Yes, since the god wants it.

49

Conditional Clauses

Introduction

49.1   A **conditional sentence** consists of:

- a subordinate conditional clause (the **protasis**): 'If Achilles is shot in the heel, . . .';
- a matrix clause (the **apodosis**): ' . . . (then) he will die.'

The whole of the conditional sentence expresses that the realization of the action in the matrix clause depends on the realization of the action in the subordinate clause.

By using different types of conditional sentences, speakers can indicate their assessment of the **likelihood/factuality of the condition's fulfilment**. In English, cf. e.g.:

(1) 'If Achilles has (in fact) been shot in the heel, he will die.' *A 'neutral' or 'open' condition: no indication of likelihood/factuality.*

(2) 'If Achilles were to be shot in the heel, he would die.' *A 'remote' or 'future hypothetical' condition: fulfilment is possible (in the future), but no more than that.*

(3) 'If Achilles had been shot in the heel, he would have died.' *A 'counterfactual', 'unfulfilled', or 'past hypothetical' condition: fulfilment is no longer possible.*

Along such lines, Greek has a complex system of five basic types of conditional clauses: **neutral, prospective, potential, counterfactual** and **habitual** conditions. Each type expresses a different attitude of the speaker towards the likelihood of the condition in the protasis being fulfilled. Different moods and tenses are used in each of the different types.

49.2   Greek conditional clauses are introduced by εἰ. If εἰ is joined with ἄν, it becomes ἐάν, ἤν or ἄν through crasis (→1.43–5). The negative in the protasis is nearly always μή.

49.3   The definition of conditional sentences given above, that the realization of the action in the apodosis depends on the realization of the action in the protasis, holds for a majority of conditional sentences, but not for all. In some conditional sentences, the protasis specifies a condition on the *truth* or *relevance* of (putting forward) the apodosis:

– truth: e.g. *If my sources are correct, Achilles has died.* Achilles' death does not depend on the correctness of the speaker's sources; the truth of the statement *Achilles has died*, however, does (and Achilles may still be alive);

– relevance: e.g. *If you're interested: Achilles has died.* Again, Achilles' death does not depend on the addressee's interest, nor does the truth of the statement *Achilles has died* (Achilles is in fact dead); the condition pertains to whether or not the utterance of that statement is itself relevant or of interest to the addressee.

The latter type of conditional clause is often called an 'illocutionary condition'; such conditions function as an adverbial disjunct (→26.15).

An example in Greek of the former type (truth) is (9) below; examples of the latter type (relevance) are (7) and (37).

Neutral Conditions

49.4   In **neutral conditions**, the speaker gives no indication of the likelihood of the realization of the action in the protasis. The speaker simply puts forward that 'if it is true that X' or 'if it is the case that X', 'then Y'.

Neutral conditions have εἰ + **indicative** in the protasis; **any mood and tense** may be used in the apodosis.

(4) ἀξιῶ δέ, ὦ βουλή, <u>εἰ</u> μὲν <u>ἀδικῶ</u>, μηδεμιᾶς συγγνώμης τυγχάνειν. (Lys. 3.4)
    I do not ask, Council, to meet with any forgiveness if I am guilty.

(5) <u>εἰ</u> ... ὑμᾶς <u>οἴονται</u> ... ὑπὸ τῶν διαβολῶν πεισθέντας καταψηφιεῖσθαί μου, οὐκ ἂν θαυμάσαιμι. (Lys. 9.2)
    If they think that you, having been persuaded by slander, will convict me, that would not surprise me.

(6) <u>εἰ</u> μεγάλ' ἐγκαλῶν ὀλίγ' <u>ἐπράξατο</u>, οὐ ... τοῦτο τεκμήριόν ἐστιν ὡς ἡ δίαιτα οὐ γέγονεν. (Isoc. 18.14)
    If, when he was making enormous demands he exacted only little, this is not evidence that there was no arbitration.

(7) μέλλω κτενεῖν σου θυγατέρ', <u>εἰ βούλῃ</u> μαθεῖν. (Eur. *Or.* 1578)
    I intend to kill your daughter, if you care to know.

The use of a neutral condition often implies a degree of **scepticism** on the speaker's part, which may be made explicit by adding a phrase like (ὡς) ἀληθῶς *really, truly*:

(8) <u>εἰ</u> γάρ τις <u>ὡς ἀληθῶς χαίρει</u> τῇ εἰρήνῃ, τοῖς στρατηγοῖς, ὧν κατηγοροῦσιν ἅπαντες, χάριν αὐτῆς ἐχέτω. (Dem. 19.96)
    For if anyone is truly pleased with the peace, let him be thankful for it to the generals whom everyone is accusing.

(9) Ἀλκμεωνίδαι δὲ ἐμφανέως ἠλευθέρωσαν, <u>εἰ</u> δὴ οὗτοί γε <u>ἀληθέως</u> <u>ἦσαν</u> οἱ τὴν Πυθίην ἀναπείσαντες προσημαίνειν Λακεδαιμονίοισι ἐλευθεροῦν τὰς Ἀθήνας. (Hdt. 6.123.2)

Clearly the Alcmeonids set (the city) free, if it is in fact true that they were the ones who persuaded the Pythia to indicate to the Spartans that they should free Athens.

Neutral Conditions with a Future Indicative in the Protasis

49.5   In the case of a neutral condition with a **future indicative**, the apodosis often carries a connotation of unpleasantness, undesirability, etc. Conditionals with the future indicative are therefore often found in **threats, appeals, warnings**, etc.:

(10) <u>εἰ</u> δ' αὐτὸν εἴσω τῆσδε <u>λήψομαι</u> χθονός, | παύσω κτυποῦντα θύρσον ἀνασείοντά τε | κόμας, τράχηλον σώματος χωρὶς τεμών. (Eur. *Bacch.* 239–41)

But if I catch him within this land, I will make him stop making noise with the thyrsus and shaking his hair by severing his head from his body.

(11) ὅτι γε οὐ στήσεται, δῆλον, <u>εἰ</u> μή τις <u>κωλύσει</u>. (Dem. 4.43)

That he will not desist unless someone stops him, that much is clear.

Note 1: In many grammars, conditions with εἰ + future indicative in the protasis are called 'future most vivid' conditions or 'emotional future' conditions, because they are often found in threats, etc. Such terms are not always applicable, however: the value of the indicative is really no different than in other neutral conditions, although this value lends itself well for contexts of scepticism, threat, etc. (the speaker indicates simply that the action in the apodosis (e.g. punishment, destruction) will follow if the condition in the protasis is fulfilled, leaving it to the addressee to assess the likelihood of that fulfilment). For other 'loaded' uses of the future indicative, →33.43.

Prospective Conditions

49.6   **Prospective conditions** are by far the most common type of conditionals referring to the future. By using this type of condition, the speaker presents fulfilment of the condition as very well possible/likely: 'If X happens – and I consider it very well possible that it will, then Y will happen.'

Note 1: This type of condition is often called 'future more vivid' or 'future open' in grammars.

Prospective conditions in Greek have **ἐάν** + **subjunctive** (**prospective**, →40.9) in
the protasis, and a verb form with **future reference** (e.g. future indicative, imperative, hortatory subjunctive; →33.63–4) in the apodosis.

(12) ἐὰν δὲ νῦν καταληφθεὶς ἀποθάνω, ἀνόσια ὀνείδη τοῖς παισὶν ὑπολείψω.
(Antiph. 2.2.9)
If I am now taken into custody and die, I will leave shameful disgrace to my
children. *Future indicative in the apodosis.*

(13) Τεύκρῳ . . . , ἢν μόλῃ, σημήνατε | μέλειν μὲν ἡμῶν. (Soph. *Aj.* 688–9)
If Teucer comes, tell him to take care of me. *Imperative in the apodosis.*

(14) καί με μηδεὶς ὑπολάβῃ ἀπαρτᾶν τὸν λόγον τῆς γραφῆς, ἐὰν εἰς Ἑλληνικὰς
πράξεις . . . ἐμπέσω. (Dem. 18.59)
And let no one suppose that I am separating my argument from the indictment, if I touch upon Greek affairs. *Prohibitive subjunctive in the apodosis.*
In this example ἄν + subj. might also be taken as indefinite, →40.9 n.2.

(15) ἂν σοι πειθώμεθα, οὔτε ὁ γεωργὸς γεωργὸς ἔσται οὔτε ὁ κεραμεὺς κεραμεύς. (Pl.
Resp. 420e)
If we obey you, the farmer will not be a farmer, nor the potter a potter. *Future
indicative in the apodosis.*

(16) ἢν . . . χρόνον τινὰ μέλλῃς ἐν τῷ αὐτῷ μένειν, ὑγιεινοῦ πρῶτον δεῖ στρατοπέδου
μὴ ἀμελῆσαι. (Xen. *Cyr.* 1.6.16)
If you are going to remain in the same place for some time, your first concern
must be a clean place to camp. *δεῖ + inf. has future reference.*

Note 2: Note that in the translations above, the English conditional clauses typically have
a simple present (a so-called 'concealed' future).

49.7   The difference between the use of present and aorist subjunctives is aspectual,
typically implying relative tense relationships (→33.57). As a rule:

– ἄν + aorist subjunctive implies anteriority, as in (12)–(13);
– ἄν + present subjunctive implies simultaneity, as in (15)–(16).

Note 1: As always, such implications of relative tense are typical (holding in a majority of
cases), but not necessary. For instance, in examples such as (14), and perhaps also (12), the
aorist subjunctive seems to refer to a 'coincident' action. For discussion, →33.58–62.

Potential Conditions

49.8   **Potential conditions** also refer to the future (although a future which is considered less likely to occur), or refer to a hypothetical possibility. The speaker considers fulfilment of the condition possible, but no more than that. It is usually

implied that the condition is only remotely relevant: 'If X should/were to happen, Y would happen,' 'If X happened, Y would happen.'

Note 1: This type of condition is variously called 'future less vivid', 'should-would' or 'future remote' condition in grammars.

Potential conditions have **εἰ + optative** in the protasis and **ἄν + optative** (potential construction, →34.13) in the apodosis.

(17) παραχθεὶς δὲ ὑπὸ τῶνδε εἰ ἀδίκως ἁλοίην, ἀποδραίην ἄν. (Lys. 9.21)

But if, summoned by them, I were to be unjustly convicted, I would run away.

(18) θέλοις ἄν, εἰ σώσαιμί σ’, ἀγγεῖλαί τί μοι | πρὸς Ἄργος ἐλθὼν τοῖς ἐμοῖς ἐκεῖ φίλοις; (Eur. *IT* 582–3)

Would you be willing, if I saved you, to go to Argos and convey a message to my friends there?

(19) ὑμᾶς γὰρ ἄν αὐτοὺς ἀτιμάζοιτ’ εἰ τοιαῦτα γιγνώσκοιτε περὶ τῶν πολιτῶν. (Isoc. 20.19)

For you would be paying disrespect to yourselves, should you have such an opinion about the citizen population.

(20) εἰ δὲ ὑπ’ ἑνὸς ἄρχοιτο ἢ φρονέοι κατὰ τὠυτό, ἄμαχόν τ’ ἄν εἴη καὶ πολλῷ κράτιστον πάντων ἐθνέων κατὰ γνώμην τὴν ἐμήν. (Hdt. 5.3.1)

If they were ruled by one man, or united in purpose, they would be invincible and by far the strongest of all races, in my opinion.

49.9   The difference between the use of present and aorist optatives is aspectual; typically relative-tense relationships are implied. As a rule:

- εἰ + aorist optative implies anteriority, as in (17)–(18);
- εἰ + present optative implies simultaneity, as in (19)–(20).

Counterfactual Conditions

49.10   **Counterfactual conditions** indicate that the speaker considers the fulfilment of a present or past condition impossible or no longer possible: 'If X were true, Y would be true (but X isn't true)' or 'If X had happened, Y would have happened (but X didn't happen).'

Note 1: This type of condition is variously called 'unfulfilled', 'unreal' or 'hypothetical' in grammars.

Counterfactual conditions have **εἰ + modal (secondary) indicative** in the protasis and **modal (secondary) indicative + ἄν** (→34.16) or a counterfactual construction without ἄν (→34.17) in the apodosis.

(21) ἴσαι αἱ ψῆφοι αὐτῷ ἐγένοντο· εἰ δὲ μία ψῆφος μετέπεσεν, ὑπερώριστ᾽ ἄν. (Aeschin. 3.252)

The votes cast over him were tied; and if a single vote had gone the other way, he would now be banished (*but it didn't go the other way*).

(22) καὶ ταῦτα εἰ μὲν ἠπίστουν, ἐξελέγχειν ἂν ἐζήτουν. ([Lys.] 8.9)

And if I disbelieved these things, I would seek to test them (*but I don't disbelieve them*).

(23) εἰ . . . ὁ Καμβύσης ἐγνωσιμάχεε καὶ ἀπῆγε ὀπίσω τὸν στρατόν, . . . ἦν ἂν ἀνὴρ σοφός· (Hdt. 3.25.5)

If Cambyses had relented and led his army back, he would have been a wise man (*but he didn't give up*).

(24) οὐ γὰρ ἔσθ᾽ ὅπως οὐκ ἠναντιώθη ἄν μοι τὸ εἰωθὸς σημεῖον, εἰ μή τι ἔμελλον ἐγὼ ἀγαθὸν πράξειν. (Pl. *Ap.* 40c)

For the familiar sign would absolutely have stopped me, if something good were not about to happen to me (*but it is about to*). For οὐ γὰρ ἔσθ᾽ ὅπως οὐκ, →50.39.

(25) εἰ γάρ με τότε ἤρου, εἶπον ἂν ὅτι . . . (Pl. *Prt.* 350c)

If you had asked me then, I would have said that . . .

(26) ἀλλ᾽ εἴ σ᾽ ἐγὼ ἠρόμην· . . . τί ἄν μοι ἀπεκρίνω; (Pl. *Ion* 540e)

But if I asked you . . . ; how would you answer me?

49.11   The difference between modal imperfects, pluperfects and aorist indicatives is aspectual. In practice, however:

- the aorist indicative usually refers to something which would have happened in the past, as in (21), (24) and (25); but contrast (26), where aor. ἠρόμην and ἀπεκρίνω are used to refer to a single question-and-answer pair in a hypothetical (unreal) scenario;
- the imperfect usually refers to a something which would be occurring in the present, as in (22); so too the (rare) pluperfect, as in (21); less frequently they refer to the past, as in (23); imperfect ἔμελλον, together with the infinitive (→51.33), may also refer to a counterfactual future scenario, as in (24);
- observe that the protasis and apodosis may refer to different times, as in (21) and (24).

For further examples, →34.16 n.3.

Habitual Conditions

49.12   Using a **habitual condition**, speakers indicate that a recurring action is dependent on something else happening, in other words, that one repeated or habitual action leads to another: 'If ever (≈ whenever) X happens, then Y happens.' Different constructions are used for present and past habitual conditions.

Note 1: This type of condition is variously called 'indefinite', 'generic' or 'general'.

49.13   Habitual conditions referring to the **present** have ἄν + **subjunctive** (**indefinite**, →40.9) in the protasis and typically have a **present indicative** (expressing a repeated action or a general fact) in the apodosis:

(27) ἐάν ... νουθετῇ τις εὐνοίᾳ λέγων, | στυγεῖς. (Soph. *Phil.* 1322–3)
      If someone admonishes you, speaking with good intentions, you detest him.

(28) αἰτιᾶσθε δὲ πολλάκις ἐξαπατᾶν ὑμᾶς αὐτούς, ἐὰν μὴ πάνθ᾽ ὃν ἂν ὑμεῖς τρόπον βούλησθε γένηται. (Dem. 62.25.1)
      But you often accuse someone of deceiving you, whenever everything does not go the way you want.

Habitual conditions referring to the **past** have **(iterative) optative without** ἄν in the protasis and an **imperfect** (or pluperfect) in the apodosis:

(29) τῶν δὲ πολλῶν εἴ τις αἴσθοιτο, ἐσίγα καὶ κατεπέπληκτο. (Dem. 9.61)
      And if ever anyone among the common people learned of it, he would keep silent and be in terror.

(30) ὑμῖν δέ, εἴ τι δέοισθε, χρήματα ὑπῆρχε κοινῇ πλεῖστα τῶν πάντων Ἑλλήνων. (Dem. 23.209)
      And you had, if ever you lacked something, funds surpassing all Greeks in your treasury.

Note 1: Observe that the construction of habitual conditional clauses is, in the subordinate clause, identical to that of prospective conditions (ἐάν + subj.; →49.6) or, when referring to the past, to potential conditions (εἰ + opt., →49.8). It is only with reference to the matrix clause that it is possible to determine which type of subordinate clause is at issue.

49.14   The difference between the use of present and aorist subjunctives/optatives is aspectual, typically implying relative tense relationships:

– ἄν + aorist subjunctive/optative implies anteriority, as in (28) and (29);
– ἄν + present subjunctive/optative implies simultaneity, as in (27) and (30).

49.15   In poetry and Herodotus, ἄν is sometimes omitted (εἰ + subj. is used):

(31) ἀλλ᾽ ἄνδρα, κεἴ τις ᾖ σοφός, τὸ μανθάνειν | πόλλ᾽ αἰσχρὸν οὐδέν. (Soph. *Ant.* 710–11)
      But there is no shame in a man learning much, even if he is someone wise. *For καὶ εἰ (κεῖ by crasis), →49.19–21. ἄνδρα is subject with (τὸ) μανθάνειν, →51.41.*

49.16   The difference between habitual conditional clauses and habitual temporal clauses (→47.9–10) is sometimes difficult to grasp. The protasis of a habitual condition refers to something that sometimes occurs and other times does not occur (the apodosis applies only in the cases that it does occur); habitual temporal clauses, on the other hand, refer simply to something which takes place more than once. In general, both may be translated with *whenever*:

(32) ἐπειδὴ δὲ <u>προσμείξειαν</u>, οἱ ἐπιβάται … ἐπειρῶντο ταῖς ἀλλήλων ναυσὶν ἐπιβαίνειν. (Thuc. 7.70.5)

And whenever they (*the ships*) came close the marines tried to board each other's ships.

(33) <u>εἰ</u> μὲν <u>ἐπίοιεν</u> οἱ Ἀθηναῖοι, ὑπεχώρουν, <u>εἰ</u> δ' <u>ἀναχωροῖεν</u>, ἐπέκειντο. (Thuc. 7.79.5)

If the Athenians attacked, they (*the Syracusans*) would retreat, and if they (*the Athenians*) withdrew from battle, they (*the Syracusans*) would press upon them.

The habitual temporal clause in (32) refers to a type of fighting that took place more than once during the naval battle between Athenians and Syracusans. The habitual conditional clauses in (33) refer to Athenian actions in battle that cannot take place simultaneously: if the one action (attacking) occurs, the other (withdrawing) does not. The apodosis in each case describes the Syracusan military response depending on the action undertaken by the Athenians.

Further Particulars

Mixed Conditionals

49.17 Although most examples from Greek texts follow the prototypes above, there are also many **mixed conditionals** where a protasis and an apodosis from different types are used together. The protasis and apodosis separately have the senses outlined above. Some possible combinations are:

– Neutral protasis with future indicative, potential apodosis:

(34) πάντων γὰρ ἀθλιώτατος <u>ἂν</u> <u>γενοίμην</u>, εἰ φυγὰς ἀδίκως <u>καταστήσομαι</u>. (Lys. 7.41)

I would become the most unfortunate of all men, if I am to be driven into exile unjustly

– Potential protasis, future indicative in the apodosis:

(35) ὅλως γὰρ <u>εἰ</u> ᾿<u>θέλοιμεν</u> σκοπεῖν τὰς φύσεις τὰς τῶν ἀνθρώπων, <u>εὑρήσομεν</u> τοὺς πολλοὺς αὐτῶν οὔτε τῶν σιτίων χαίροντας. (Isoc. 2.45)

For should we wish to examine the nature of men as a whole, we shall find that most of them do not take pleasure in food.

– Potential protasis, non-future indicative in the apodosis:

(36) εἰ γὰρ σύ μοι <u>ἐθέλοις</u> συνεῖναι, <u>ἐξαρκεῖ</u> καὶ οὐδένα ἄλλον <u>ζητῶ</u>. ([Pl.] *Thg.* 127a)

For should you be willing to take me on, that is enough, and I seek no other.

(37) ὁ χρυσός, <u>εἰ</u> <u>βούλοιο</u> τἀληθῆ λέγειν, | <u>ἔκτεινε</u> τὸν ἐμὸν παῖδα καὶ κέρδη τὰ σά. (Eur. *Hec.* 1206–7)

For if you were willing to speak the truth: it was gold, and your profit, that killed my child. *On this example, also →49.3.*

Various other combinations occur.

49.18   Occasionally, two different types of protasis are found in quick succession, referring to different possible outcomes which are presented with different degrees of likelihood:

(38) εἰ μὲν οὖν πρὸς ἕκαστον αὐτῶν τὰς πράξεις τὰς Εὐαγόρου <u>παραβάλλοιμεν</u> . . . , οὔτ’ ἂν ὁ χρόνος τοῖς λεγομένοις ἀρκέσειεν· <u>ἢν</u> δὲ προελόμενοι τοὺς εὐδοκιμωτάτους . . . <u>σκοπῶμεν</u> . . . , πολὺ . . . συντομώτερον διαλεχθησόμεθα περὶ αὐτῶν. (Isoc. 9.34)

If we were to compare the deeds of Evagoras with those of each of them, the time would not suffice for the telling. But if we select the most illustrious of these rulers and perform our examination, our discussion will be much more brief. *Potential condition (εἰ + optative), referring to the less likely (and by implication less desirable) course of action, followed by a prospective condition (ἢν + subj.), referring to the more likely one.*

(39) ὥστ’ <u>εἰ</u> μὲν <u>ἀποψηφιεῖσθε</u> τούτων, οὐδὲν δεινὸν δόξει αὐτοῖς εἶναι . . . ἐκ τῶν ὑμετέρων ὠφελεῖσθαι· <u>ἐὰν</u> δὲ καταψηφισάμενοι θανάτου <u>τιμήσητε</u>, . . . τούς . . . ἄλλους κοσμιωτέρους ποιήσετε ἢ νῦν εἰσι. (Lys. 27.7)

Therefore, if you acquit these men, they will think that making a profit at your expense is in no way dangerous; but if you condemn them and sentence them to death, you will make the rest more orderly than they are now. *Neutral condition (with a connotation of undesirability: εἰ + fut. ind.) referring to the verdict the speaker does not hope for, followed by a prospective condition (ἐάν + subj.) referring to the verdict the speaker wants.*

Concessive Clauses: εἰ καί and καὶ εἰ

49.19   Conditional clauses introduced by **καὶ εἰ** or **εἰ** (. . .) **καί** *even if* are known as **concessive clauses**, and express an exceptional or unlikely condition. The realization of the action of the apodosis is presented as contrary to expectation given the realization of the action in the protasis, yet in the end not affected by that realization.

All types of conditional occur, and the use of moods and tenses is as described above. The negative counterpart of such clauses is expressed by οὐδ’ εἰ/μηδ’ εἰ *not even if*. The apodosis may have ὅμως *all the same, nevertheless*, to emphasize the contrast between protasis and apodosis.

(40) ἀλλά τοι <u>εἰ καί</u> πάντα ταῦτα πεποίηκε καὶ ἄλλα τούτων πολλαπλάσια, οὐδεὶς ἂν δύναιτο αὐτῆς ἀνασχέσθαι τὴν χαλεπότητα. (Xen. *Mem.* 2.2.7)

Yet let me tell you: even if she has done all these things, and far more besides, still no one could put up with her vile temper. *Neutral condition.*

(41) τοῦτο μέν, | <u>οὐδ’ ἢν</u> θέλῃ, δράσει ποτ’. (Soph. *Phil.* 981–2)

That he will never do, even if he wishes to. *Prospective condition.*

(42) <u>εἰ καί</u> τὸν ἄλλον χρόνον εἴθιστο συκοφαντεῖν, τότ’ ἂν ἐπαύσατο. (Isoc. 21.11)

Even if he had been accustomed to bring slanderous accusations in former times, he would have given up the practice then. *Counterfactual condition.*

(43) τῆς γῆς κρατοῦντες <u>καὶ εἰ</u> θαλάττης εἴργοιντο, δύναιντ' ἂν καλῶς διαζῆν. (Xen. *Hell.* 7.1.8)

With control over the land, they could live comfortably even if they should be cut off from the sea. *Potential condition.*

Note 1: For this adverbial use of καί, and οὐδέ as its negative counterpart, →59.56.

Note 2: Not all instances of καὶ εἰ or εἰ καί are concessive: in some cases of καὶ εἰ, καί is simply a coordinating conjunction: *and if*;

(44) οὕτω γὰρ ἂν πονεῖν τε ἔτι μᾶλλον δύναιτο <u>καὶ εἰ</u> ἕλκοι τις αὐτὸν ἢ ὠθοίη ἧττον ἂν σφάλλοιτο. (Xen. *Eq.* 7.7)

For in this way, (the horse) will be able to last longer, and if someone drags or pushes it, he will stumble less quickly.

And in some cases of εἰ (...) καί, καί has narrow scope over a single element of the subordinate clause: *if ... as well; if also ... ; if, in fact ...* :

(45) ΑΝ. ἀλλ' οἶδ' ἀρέσκουσ' οἷς μάλισθ' ἁδεῖν με χρή. | :: ΙΣ. <u>εἰ</u> <u>καὶ</u> δυνήσῃ γ'. (Soph. *Ant.* 89–90)

(Antigone:) But I know that I am pleasing those whom I must please above all. :: (Ismene:) If you will in fact be able to. *καί has scope over δυνήσῃ only.*

49.20 The difference between καὶ εἰ and εἰ καί may be described as follows:

- καὶ εἰ (where καί has scope over the entire εἰ-clause) tends to emphasize that the action in the apodosis will be realized, may be realized, would have been realized (etc.), in spite of *any* unfavourable conditions, *including* the (extreme) one given in the protasis – thus, (43) could be paraphrased 'They will live comfortably – EVEN if they are cut off from the sea.'

- εἰ καί (where καί has scope over the predicate or another element *within* the εἰ-clause) puts focus on the action in the protasis, often to emphasize its unlikely nature – thus, example (40) could be paraphrased 'Even if she HAS done all those things (which is unusual/unlikely/exceptional), no one could stand her.'

In practice, however, the difference is often very slight. καὶ εἰ is, on the whole, the more frequent of the two combinations.

49.21 In some cases an indicative in the protasis expresses an action whose realization is presupposed – i.e. that action is not presented as in doubt. In such cases εἰ καί and καὶ εἰ may be translated *although, even though*:

(46) <u>καὶ γὰρ εἰ</u> πένης ἔφυν, | οὔτοι τό γ' ἦθος δυσγενὲς παρέξομαι. (Eur. *El.* 362–3)

Even though I am poor, I will show that my character is not ill-bred. *The speaker is poor.*

Such concessive relationships are more commonly expressed by καίπερ + ppl., for which →52.44.

Comparative Conditional Clauses: ὡς εἰ, ὥσπερ εἰ and ὥσπερ ἂν εἰ *as if*

49.22   To compare an action with another, hypothetical one (cf. Engl. *as if, like*), Greek may combine εἰ with comparative ὡς or ὥσπερ (for which, →50.37), often with ἄν added: ὡς εἰ, ὥσπερ εἰ, ὥσπερ ἂν εἰ.

Such clauses normally take an optative (potential conditional clauses, →49.8) or a modal (secondary) indicative (counterfactual conditional clauses, →49.10):

(47)   ὦ Ἀγησίλαε, ὥσπερ εἰ ἐν αὐτοῖς εἴημεν τοῖς πολεμίοις, οὕτω μοι σημαίνεται. (Xen. *Hell.* 3.3.4)
Agesilaus, it is as if we were in the very midst of the enemies that a sign is given to me.

(48)   πρὸς μόνους τοὺς προγόνους τοὺς ἡμετέρους συμβαλόντες ὁμοίως διεφθάρησαν ὥσπερ ἂν εἰ πρὸς ἅπαντας ἀνθρώπους ἐπολέμησαν. (Isoc. 4.69)
Fighting against only our forefathers, they perished as if they had waged war against all of mankind.

Note 1: For participles with ὥσπερ (with a comparative interpretation), →52.43.

49.23   ὡς εἰ, ὥσπερ εἰ and ὥσπερ ἂν εἰ are often written as one word: ὡσεί, ὡσπερεί, ὡσπερανεί.

49.24   ὡσεί, ὡσπερεί and ὡσπερανεί (written together or apart) are frequently found without a finite verb in the conditional clause:

(49)   ἀλλ’ οὖν εὐνοίᾳ γ’ αὐδῶ, | μάτηρ ὡσεί τις πιστά. (Soph. *Ant.* 233–4)
Well, I speak with good intent, like a mother whom you can trust.

(50)   χὠ κολοιὸς οὑτοσὶ | ἄνω κέχηνεν ὡσπερεὶ δεικνύς τί μοι. (Ar. *Av.* 50–1)
And the jay here is craning its neck and opening its beak as if showing me something or other. χὠ = καὶ ὁ *by crasis*, →1.43–5.

εἰ/ἐάν *in case, in the hope that*

49.25   Clauses with **ἐάν + subjunctive** or (in past contexts) with **εἰ + (oblique) optative** sometimes have a force similar to that of purpose clauses, best translated ***in the hope that***. Such clauses normally follow their main clause:

(51)   ἴθ’, ἀντιβολῶ σ’, ἢν πως κομίσωμαι τὼ βόε. (Ar. *Ach.* 1031)
Come, I’m begging you, in the hope that I may retrieve my two oxen.

(52)   ἐπέπλει οὖν ... πρὸς τὴν Σύμην ..., εἴ πως περιλάβοι ... τὰς ναῦς. (Thuc. 8.42.1)
So he sailed in the direction of Syme, in the hope that he might in some way intercept the ships.

Such instances cannot really be called ‘conditional’ clauses: the fulfilment, truth or appropriateness of the main clause does not depend on the fulfilment of the action in the subordinate clause.

Note 1: This fact (that there is no relation of dependence between main clause and subordinate clause) makes it relatively straightforward to distinguish this type of εἰ-clause from 'genuine' conditional clauses. Note that example (52), in a narrative past tense, can easily be distinguished as well from conditions on the truth or appropriateness of the matrix clause (for which →49.3 above), although it is feasible that this use is an extension of the latter type.

Note 2: The use of moods in such clauses is fundamentally the same as in purpose clauses (→45.3–4; subjunctive or, in past contexts, optative). The difference between purpose clauses with ἵνα/ὅπως/ὡς and this type appears to be that the use of the conditional conjunction (εἰ/ἐάν) explicitly indicates that the realization of the action hoped for is uncertain, and not controlled by the subject of the verb in the matrix clause.

ἐφ' ᾧ(τε) *on the condition that*

49.26   A separate type of clause expressing conditionality is introduced by **ἐφ' ᾧ** or **ἐφ' ᾧτε** *on the condition that* (for ἐπί + dat. with conditional force, →31.8). Such clauses usually have an **infinitive** (sometimes the future indicative). The negative is μή.

(53) ἀφίεμέν σε, ἐπὶ τούτῳ μέντοι, ἐφ' ᾧτε μηκέτι ... φιλοσοφεῖν (Pl. *Ap.* 29c)
We are letting you go; on the condition, however, that you will no longer be a philosopher.

(54) ξυνέβησαν ... ἐφ' ᾧ ἐξίασιν ἐκ Πελοποννήσου ὑπόσπονδοι καὶ μηδέποτε ἐπιβήσονται αὐτῆς. (Thuc. 1.103.1)
They made an agreement on the condition that they would leave the Peloponnese bound by a treaty and never enter it again. *ἐξίασιν, formally a present-tense form, is functionally a future indicative, →33.19.*

Conditional Clauses in Indirect Discourse

49.27   When an entire conditional sentence is reported as indirect speech or thought after a verb of speaking/thinking/etc. in a past tense (historic sequence), the oblique optative may be used, both in the protasis and in the apodosis; if the optative replaces subjunctive + ἄν in the protasis, ἄν is dropped:

(55) ἡγεῖτ' οὖν, εἰ μὲν ὑμᾶς ἕλοιτο, φίλους ἐπὶ τοῖς δικαίοις αἱρήσεσθαι. (Dem. 6.12)
So he thought that if he chose you, he would choose friends, based on justice.
Direct speech: ἐὰν αὐτοὺς ἕλωμαι, φίλους ἐπὶ τοῖς δικαίοις αἱρήσομαι.

The oblique optative is not used in the case of counterfactual conditionals or potential conditionals. For further details, →41.19–22.

Overview of Conditional Sentences (Basic Types)

49.28   The following overview lists the basic types of conditional sentence described above:

	past protasis	apodosis	present protasis	apodosis	future protasis	apodosis
neutral	**εἰ + past ind.**	**any tense/ mood**	**εἰ + pres. ind.**	**any tense/ mood**	**εἰ + fut. ind.**	**any tense/ mood**
	εἰ τοῦτο ἐποίησε	κολασθήσε-ται	εἰ τοῦτο ποιεῖ	κολασθήσε-ται	εἰ τοῦτο ποιήσει	κολασθήσε-ται
	If he has done that	*he will be punished.*	*If he is doing that*	*he will be punished.*	*If he is to do that*	*he will be punished.*
						Often used in threats, warnings, etc.
prospective					**ἐάν + subj.**	**fut. ind./ etc.**
					ἐάν τοῦτο ποιήσῃ	κολασθήσε-ται
					If he does that	*he will be punished.*
potential					**εἰ + opt.**	**ἄν + opt.**
					εἰ τοῦτο ποιήσειε	κολασθείη ἄν
					If he were to do that	*he would be punished.*
counter-factual	**εἰ + aor. ind.**	**ἄν + aor. ind.**	**εἰ + impf.**	**ἄν + impf.**		
	εἰ τοῦτο ἐποίησεν	ἐκολάσθη ἄν	εἰ τοῦτο ἐποίει	ἐκολάζετο ἄν		
	If he had done that	*he would have been punished.*	*If he were doing that*	*he would be punished.*		
	The difference between aor. ind. and impf. is aspectual: the past–present distinction indicated here is a rule of thumb only.					
habitual	**εἰ + opt.**	**impf.**	**ἐάν + subj.**	**pres. ind.**		
	εἰ τοῦτο ποιήσειεν	ἐκολάζετο	ἐάν τοῦτο ποιήσῃ	κολάζεται		
	If he did that	*he would always be punished.*	*If he does that*	*he is punished.*		

50

Relative Clauses

Introduction

Relative Pronouns, Adjectives and Adverbs; Definite and Indefinite Relatives

50.1   **Relative clauses** are introduced by one of the following relative pronouns/adjectives/adverbs:

Definite	Indefinite	
Pronouns		
ὅς	ὅστις	who(m), which, that
Adjectives		
οἷος	ὁποῖος	such as, of the kind that
ὅσος	ὁπόσος	as great, much (*sg.*)/many (*pl.*) as (*often best translated by 'all who(m)'*)
Adverbs		
ἔνθα, οὗ	ὅπου	where
ἔνθεν, ὅθεν	ὁπόθεν	from where
ἔνθα, οἷ	ὅποι	to where
ᾗ	ὅπῃ	along which/where, by which/where, as, like, in the way of
ὡς	ὅπως	as, like, in the way of

Note 1: For the forms of the relative pronoun in Ionic, →25.31. For the use of the article as relative pronoun in poetry, →28.31.

   Note 2: The indefinite pronouns, adjectives and adverbs are also used in indirect questions (→42.5); οἷος and ὅσος are also used in direct and indirect exclamations (→38.47–9, 42.9–11) and in result clauses (→46.10). ὅπως is also used in effort clauses (→44) and purpose clauses (→45). For other uses of ὡς, →57.

50.2   As a general rule:

   – the **definite relative** is used when the relative clause refers to a specific (identifiable) entity; when there is an antecedent (a word or phrase in the matrix clause to which the relative refers) it will often have the article;

– the **indefinite relative** is used when the relative clause refers to an unspecific (unidentifiable, generic) entity, i.e. when the relative could refer to any of a number of entities or when the precise referent is unknown; when there is an antecedent it will usually not have the article.

(1) τίς ἡ γυνὴ δῆτ᾿ ἐστὶν ἣν ἥκεις ἄγων; (Soph. *Trach.* 400)

Who, then, is the woman with whom you have come here? *A specific woman is meant; note the use of the article with the antecedent,* →28.1.

(2) γυνὴ δ᾿ ἀπόντος ἀνδρὸς ἥτις ἐκ δόμων | ἐς κάλλος ἀσκεῖ, διάγραφ᾿ ὡς οὖσαν κακήν. (Eur. *El.* 1072–3)

A woman who, when her husband is away from home, concerns herself with beauty, write her off as no good. *A certain type of woman, not a specific woman is meant; note the lack of article with the antecedent. For the theme construction (nominative absolute),* →60.34.

50.3   The distribution between ὅς and ὅστις is, however, not always easy to account for:

– Note particularly that in relative constructions with indefinite subjunctive + ἄν or iterative optative (→50.21 below), the definite relative is more common:

(3) ἐπειδὰν δὲ κρύψωσι γῇ, ἀνὴρ ᾑρημένος ὑπὸ τῆς πόλεως, ὃς ἄν ... ἀξιώσει προήκῃ, λέγει ἐπ᾿ αὐτοῖς ἔπαινον τὸν πρέποντα. (Thuc. 2.34.6).

After they have buried (the fallen), a man elected by the state, who is pre-eminent in reputation, pronounces the appropriate eulogy over them. *The relative pronoun does not refer to a specific person (the speaker changes yearly), and the antecedent has no article, yet the definite relative pronoun is used.*

Indefinite ὅστις ἄν + subj. does occur, suggesting that even extreme cases should be taken into account (*whoever at all ...*):

(4) καὶ ἢν τινες ἐς τὴν Ἀθηναίων γῆν ἴωσι πολέμιοι ... , ὠφελεῖν Λακεδαιμονίους Ἀθηναίους τρόπῳ ὅτῳ ἄν δύνωνται ἰσχυροτάτῳ. (Thuc. 5.23.2)

And if enemy forces invade Athenian territory, (the treaty states that) the Spartans must come to the Athenians' aid in whatever most effective manner they can.

– Conversely, ὅστις is sometimes used to refer to a very specific person or thing, with a definite antecedent:

(5) ἐγώ ... | μαίνομαι; σὺ μᾶλλον, ὅστις ἀπολέσας κακὸν λέχος | ἀναλαβεῖν θέλεις. (Eur. *IA* 388–90)

Am I mad? No, you are, who after losing an evil wife are seeking to take her back.

For the nuances that ὅστις-clauses typically have in such cases, →50.6 n.2 and 50.23.

50.4 The definite relative may be compounded with **περ** (ὅσπερ *exactly who*), expressing identity. The 'indefiniteness' of an indefinite relative may be emphasized by adding **ποτε** (ὅστις ποτέ *whoever*).

Note 1: For οὖν added to indefinite relatives to express universality, →59.35.

Correlative Clauses

50.5 Relative pronouns, adjectives and adverbs are frequently anticipated or followed by a demonstrative pronoun, adjective or adverb in the matrix clause. For instance:

Matrix clause	*Relative clause*	
οὗτος	ὅσ(τις)	that man ... who
τοιοῦτος	οἷος	such ... as
τοσοῦτος	ὅσος	so great/many ... as
ἐνταῦθα	ἔνθα	there ... where
οὕτω(ς)	ὡς	such ... as

Such clauses are called **correlative clauses**. For the full system of correlative pronouns, adjectives and adverbs, →8.

Clauses introduced by relative adjectives and adverbs (where correlation is particularly frequent) are treated more fully below, →50.27–40.

Digressive, Restrictive and Autonomous Relative Clauses

50.6 Two types of relative clause may be distinguished:

– **Restrictive** (or 'determinative') relative clauses: the information in the relative clause serves to identify the antecedent, or limit it to a certain subset:

(6) τῷ Φιλοκτήμονι ἐκ μὲν τῆς γυναικὸς <u>ᾗ συνῴκει</u> οὐκ ἦν παιδίον οὐδέν. (Isae. 6.5)
Philoctemon had no child by the woman he was living with. *The relative clause helps to identify the antecedent: without it, it is unclear to which woman the speaker refers.*

(7) πότερ' ἂν βούλοιο τούτους τοὺς στρατιώτας <u>οὓς Διοπείθης νῦν ἔχει</u> ...
εὐθενεῖν ..., ἢ ... διαφθαρῆναι; (Dem. 8.20)
Would you want those soldiers that Diopithes now has to thrive, or to be destroyed? *The relative clause limits the group of soldiers to a specific subset.*

The use of moods and tenses in restrictive relative clauses is similar to that in temporal/conditional clauses (→50.18–22 below).

– **Digressive** (or 'non-restrictive', 'explanatory') relative clauses: the relative clause gives additional information that is not required to identify or specify the antecedent. In other words, the antecedent still refers to the same entity if the relative clause is left out:

(8) ... ἐξῃρηκότες ... τὴν Σουσίδα γυναῖκα, <u>ἣ καλλίστη δὴ λέγεται ἐν τῇ Ἀσίᾳ γυνὴ γενέσθαι</u>, ... (Xen. *Cyr.* 4.6.11)

... having selected the lady of Susa, who is said to have been the most beautiful woman in Asia, ... *The relative clause is not required to identify the – apparently well-known – lady of Susa, but provides additional information about her.*

(9) στέγαι ... εἰσιν ... οὐδὲ τῷ δήμῳ τῶν στρατιωτῶν, <u>ὧν ἄνευ ἡμεῖς οὐκ ἂν δυναίμεθα στρατεύεσθαι</u>. (Xen. *Cyr.* 6.1.14)

There is also no shelter for the rank and file of the soldiers, without whom we would not be able to wage war. *The relative clause does not identify, or determine a subset of, the soldiers.*

Digressive relative clauses are particularly common with proper names. The use of moods and tenses in digressive relative clauses is similar to that of independent sentences (→50.17 below).

Note 1: In English, restrictive relative clauses normally do not stand between commas; digressive clauses normally do (contrast the two relative clauses in *The animal <u>that you see here</u> is a whale, <u>which is a kind of mammal</u>*). Only restrictive clauses can use *that* as a relative pronoun (cf. 'the soldiers that Diopithes has' in the translation of (7)) or omit a pronoun altogether (cf. 'the woman he was living with' in (6)).

Note 2: As it is a defining feature of digressive relative clauses that they refer to an identifiable entity (in that the antecedent of the clause is identifiable even without the relative clause), the indefinite relatives ὅστις, ὁποῖος, etc. are in principle not suitable to be used in digressive clauses. Nevertheless, they do occasionally occur in such clauses, and then nearly always have a causal nuance (for details, →50.23).

50.7   A special type of restrictive relative clause is the so-called **autonomous** relative clause, which has no antecedent:

(10) ΙΩ. ἣ δ᾽ ἔθρεψέ με :: ΚΡ. τίς; ... :: ΙΩ. Φοίβου προφῆτιν μητέρ᾽ ὣς νομίζομεν. (Eur. *Ion* 319–21)

(Ion:) The woman who raised me – :: (Creusa:) Who was she? :: (Ion:) A prophetess of Phoebus; I regard her as my mother.

Note 1: In translation, an antecedent (e.g. 'the woman' in (10)) often needs to be supplied for autonomous relative clauses; grammars often treat autonomous relative clauses as instances of the 'omission' of an antecedent.

Antecedent, Agreement, Attraction and Connection

Basic Principles of Agreement

50.8   The relative pronoun ὅσ(τις) and the relative adjectives (ὁπ)όσος and (ὁπ)οῖος:

- **agree** in **gender and number** with their antecedent,
- but their **case** is determined by their **syntactic function** in the relative clause:

(11) ὅδ' ἐστὶν ἀνὴρ <u>ὃν</u> λέγεις. (Ar. *Thesm.* 635)

This is the man to whom you are referring. *Masc. sg. in agreement with ἀνήρ, acc. as object of λέγεις. ἀνήρ = ὁ ἀνήρ (crasis, →1.45 n.1).*

(12) ἀνὴρ παρ' ἡμῖν ἐστιν, . . . | Ἕλενος ἀριστόμαντις, <u>ὃς</u> λέγει . . . (Soph. *Phil.* 1337–8)

There is a man with us, Helenus, an exceptionally gifted prophet, who says . . . *Masc. sg. in agreement with ἀνήρ, nom. as subject of λέγει.*

Note 1: The relative pronoun is sometimes formed according to the meaning rather than the grammatical form of its antecedent. For this construction 'according to sense' (Gr. κατὰ σύνεσιν), →27.11 (also cf. 27.6).

50.9   Greek generally **avoids the use of repeated relative pronouns** in successive clauses referring to the same antecedent, especially if the case of the relative pronoun would be different in the different clauses. Instead, subsequent clauses referring to the same antecedent either have no relative pronoun of their own, or use a form of αὐτός or a demonstrative pronoun in the appropriate case:

(13) Ἀριαῖος δέ, <u>ὃν</u> ἡμεῖς ἠθέλομεν βασιλέα καθιστάναι, καὶ ἐδώκαμεν καὶ ἐλάβομεν πιστὰ . . . , καὶ οὗτος . . . ἡμᾶς . . . κακῶς ποιεῖν πειρᾶται. (Xen. *An.* 3.2.5.)

And Ariaeus, whom we were willing to install as king and with whom we exchanged pledges, even he is trying to cause us harm. *Only the single relative pronoun ὅν (acc.; object of καθιστάναι) is used; the following clause ἐδώκαμεν καὶ ἐλάβομεν πιστὰ is not given one of its own (something like μεθ' οὗ may be supplied; observe the translation 'with whom'). Also note that Ἀριαῖος δέ . . . is a theme constituent (→60.33), picked up by 'resumptive' οὗτος (cf. (29) below and 59.15 (14)); this makes it clear that the main clause proper begins only with καθὶ οὗτος.*

(14) ποῦ δὴ ἐκεῖνός ἐστιν ὁ ἀνὴρ <u>ὃς</u> συνεθήρα ἡμῖν καὶ σύ μοι μάλα ἐδόκεις θαυμάζειν <u>αὐτόν</u>. (Xen. *Cyr.* 3.1.38)

Where, then, is that man, who used to hunt with us and whom, I think, you admired greatly? *'The man' is subject in the relative clause (nom. ὅς), but would be object in the subsequent clause (dependent on θαυμάζειν): instead of a second relative pronoun, αὐτόν is used.*

50.10   In the case of autonomous relative clauses, masculine (or feminine) relatives usually refer to individuals or groups of people, neuter pronouns to 'things'; the case is again determined by the function in the relative clause:

(15) <u>οἳ</u> τὰς πόλεις ἔχουσι . . . | τοῖς ἀνθαμίλλοις εἰσὶ πολεμιώτατοι. (Eur. *Ion* 605–6)

Those who hold cities are most hostile to their competitors. *Masc. pronoun, referring to people; nom. as subject of ἔχουσι; the clause as a whole is subject of εἰσί.*

(16) σὺ μὲν βίᾳ | πράξεις <u>ἃ</u> βούλει. (Eur. fr. 953.42–3 Kannicht)

You will do what you want by force. *Neut. pronoun, referring to things or actions.*

50.11   Autonomous relative clauses occur particularly frequently after prepositions. The preposition
may then function either in the relative clause, or in the matrix clause:

(17) οὐκ ἔχω, ὦ Σώκρατες, ὅπως χρὴ <u>πρὸς</u> <u>ἃ</u> λέγεις ἐναντιοῦσθαι. (Pl. *Cra.* 390e)

I don't know how to argue against what you are saying, Socrates. *πρός functions in the*
matrix clause (i.e. depends on ἐναντιοῦσθαι), while the autonomous relative clause comple-
ments πρός: cf. ἐναντιοῦσθαι πρὸς ταῦτα ἃ λέγεις 'argue with the things that you are
saying'.

(18) καὶ κάλει <u>πρὸς</u> <u>οὓς</u> ἐξεμαρτύρησεν. (Aeschin. 2.19)

And call those before whom he made the deposition. *πρός functions in the relative*
clause (i.e. depends on ἐξεμαρτύρησεν); the autonomous relative clause, including the
preposition, serves as object: cf. κάλει τούτους, πρὸς οὓς ἐξεμαρτύρησεν 'call those
before whom he made the deposition'.

50.12   Observe the following idiomatic uses of autonomous relative clauses:

– Autonomous relative clauses with the neuter pronoun ὅ, and typically with
a superlative adjective, can stand in apposition to an entire clause or sentence, e.g.
ὃ δὲ πάντων δεινότατον *and what is the worst thing of all:* ..., καὶ ὃ πάντων
θαυμαστότατον *and the thing that is most amazing of all:* ...; ἐστί is nearly always
omitted from such clauses (cf. 'what *is* the worst thing'). For this use, compare the
closely parallel use of phrases with the neuter article, e.g. τὸ δεινότατον (→27.14):

(19) ὃ δὲ μέγιστον τεκμήριον· Δῆμος γὰρ ὁ Πυριλάμπους ... (Lys. 19.25)

But the strongest piece of evidence is this: Demus, son of Pyrilampes, ... *Lit. 'but what is*
the strongest evidence, ...'. Note the use of γάρ (for which →27.14 n.1), which cannot easily
be translated.

– Autonomous relative clauses are sometimes used in combination with a third-person form
of 'existential' εἰμί (→26.10): ἔστιν ὅστις *someone (there is someone who)*, εἰσὶν οἵ *some (there*
are some who), etc., and with the negative οὐκ ἔστιν ὅστις *no one (there is no one who)*:

(20) οὐκ ἂν εἴη <u>ὅστις</u> οὐκ ἐπὶ τοῖς γεγενημένοις ἀγανακτοίη. (Lys. 1.1)

Everyone would be angry (*lit. 'there would not be anyone who would not be angry'*) at what
has happened. *For the use of the optative, →50.22.*

The construction was heavily fossilized, so that ἔστι could be used even with the
plural (ἔστιν οἵ, ἔστιν ὧν, etc., *some*), and even in past or future contexts (in spite of
present-tense ἔστιν):

(21) ... αἰσθανόμενοι δὲ τοὺς συμμάχους πάντας μὲν ἀθύμως ἔχοντας πρὸς τὸ μάχεσθαι, <u>ἔστι δὲ</u>
<u>οὓς</u> αὐτῶν οὐδὲ ἀχθομένους τῷ γεγενημένῳ ... (Xen. *Hell.* 6.4.15)

... and observing that all the allies were unenthusiastic about fighting, and that some of
them were not even displeased about what had happened ... *ἔστι ... οὕς does not refer to*
the present (this example comes from a stretch of narrative); the accusative is due to the
accusative-and-participle construction following αἰσθανόμενοι, →52.13; note also how the
phrase as a whole has its own attributive genitive αὐτῶν.

Relative Attraction

50.13   An exception to the rules of agreement is the so-called **attraction** of the relative. The relative nearly always takes on the same case as its antecedent if (and only if):

- the relative clause is **restrictive**;
- a form of ὅς, οἷος or ὅσος (but not their indefinite forms) is object in its relative clause, internal object, or subject of an infinitive, i.e. when an **accusative is expected**;
- the **antecedent is in the genitive or dative**:

(22) ὅπως οὖν ἔσεσθε ἄνδρες ἄξιοι τῆς ἐλευθερίας <u>ἧς</u> κέκτησθε. (Xen. *An.* 1.7.3)
    You must, then, be men worthy of the freedom which you possess. *Object of* κέκτησθε, *but genitive under the influence of* τῆς ἐλευθερίας *which is genitive complement with* ἄξιοι.

Attraction also occurs in autonomous relative clauses, i.e. when the genitive or dative antecedent is not expressed:

(23) ἢν δ᾽ ἐπιδειχθῇ . . . πολίτης ὤν . . . τοιοῦτος οἷος οὐδεὶς ἄλλος <u>ὧν</u> ἡμεῖς ἴσμεν, . . . (Isoc. 15.106)
    If he is shown to be a citizen such as no other of the men (that) we know, . . . *Object with* ἴσμεν, *but genitive under the influence of the construction of the matrix clause:* οὐδεὶς ἄλλος *is construed with a partitive genitive. The relative clause is autonomous.*

(24) τίνα γὰρ εἰκὸς ἦν ἧττον ταῦτα ὑπηρετῆσαι ἢ τὸν ἀντειπόντα <u>οἷς</u> ἐκεῖνοι ἐβούλοντο πραχθῆναι; (Lys. 12.27)
    For who was less likely to receive such orders than the man who had spoken against what they wanted to be done? *Subject of the infinitive* πραχθῆναι *(accusative-and-infinitive construction expected with* ἐβούλοντο*), but dative under the influence of* ἀντειπόντα *(which takes a dative complement). The relative clause is, again, autonomous.*

Relative attraction occurs particularly frequently after prepositions, often in autonomous clauses:

(25) ἐπαινῶ σε ἐφ᾽ <u>οἷς</u> λέγεις. (Xen. *An.* 3.1.45)
    I praise you for what you say. *Object of* λέγεις, *but dative after* ἐπί.

(26) ταῦτα μὲν οὖν ἐάσω, ἀπ᾽ αὐτῶν δὲ <u>ὧν</u> αὐτὸς βεβίωκεν ἄρξομαι. (Dem. 18.130)
    Those things, then, I will leave alone, but I will begin with precisely the ways in which he himself has conducted his life. *Internal object (→30.12) of* βεβίωκεν, *but genitive after* ἀπό; αὐτῶν *modifies the entire relative clause.*

Note 1: Very rarely, relative attraction occurs when a nominative or dative (rather than an accusative) is 'expected' in the relative clause:

(27) ὀλίγοι <u>ὧν</u> ἐγὼ ἐντετύχηκα (Pl. *Resp.* 531e)

> a few of those that I have encountered; *a dative is 'expected' with ἐντετύχηκα, but a genitive is used under the influence of the construction of the matrix clause (partitive genitive modifying ὀλίγοι).*

Inverse Relative Attraction

50.14   In some cases an antecedent **preceding** its relative clause attracts to the case of the relative following it (rather than appearing in the case expected for its syntactic function). This is known as **inverse attraction**:

(28) <u>πολιτείαν</u> δ᾽ <u>οἵαν</u> εἶναι χρὴ παρὰ μόνοις ἡμῖν ἐστιν. (Isoc. 6.48)

> And a form of government such as it ought to be exists only with us. *πολιτείαν is subject of ἐστιν, so the expected case for it would be nominative; instead, it attracts to the accusative case of οἵαν (acc. with εἶναι χρή).*

(29) <u>τὸν ἄνδρα τοῦτον</u>, <u>ὃν</u> πάλαι | ζητεῖς . . . | . . ., οὗτός ἐστιν ἐνθάδε. (Soph. *OT* 449–51)

> This man, for whom you have long been looking, is here. *τὸν ἄνδρα τοῦτον is subject of ἐστιν, but attracts to accusative ὅν (object of ζητεῖς). Note the resumptive pronoun οὗτος, which picks up τὸν ἄνδρα τοῦτον and is in the expected case.*

Note 1: Inverse attraction occurs only with nouns whose expected case is nominative (primarily with subjects of passive verbs, verbs which do not take an object, or with εἰμί *be*, as in (28)–(29)) or accusative. It occurs only with constituents functioning as 'theme' or 'topic' in their clause (→60.25–9, 60.33); the rest of the clause always follows the relative clause.

Incorporation of the Antecedent in the Relative Clause

50.15   Sometimes the word that 'should' be antecedent is **incorporated** into a relative clause. The case of this 'antecedent' is identical to that of the relative pronoun (as determined by the rules above; attraction is not unusual):

(30) εἰ δέ τινα ὁρῴη . . . κατασκευάζοντα . . . <u>ἧς</u> ἄρχοι <u>χώρας</u> . . . (Xen. *An.* 1.9.19)

> If he saw that a man was organizing the country over which he ruled . . . *The relative clause is object with κατασκευάζοντα; the genitive is complement with ἄρχοι.*

(31) τούτους . . . ἄρχοντας ἐποίει <u>ἧς</u> κατεστρέφετο <u>χώρας</u>. (Xen. *An.* 1.9.14)

> He appointed them as rulers of the territory which he was subduing. *With relative attraction: object with κατεστρέφετο, but genitive as attributive modifier of ἄρχοντας.*

(32) Ἱπποκράτης ὅδε Πρωταγόρᾳ συγγενόμενος, ᾗ ἂν αὐτῷ ἡμέρᾳ συγγένηται, βελτίων ἄπεισι. (Pl. *Prt.* 318d)

Hippocrates here, upon coming under Protagoras' tutelage, will go away a better man on the day that he has come under his tutelage. *ἡμέρᾳ, with its relative clause, is an adverbial modifier of time with ἄπεισι.*

Incorporated 'antecedents' do not have the article. They may be seen as the head of a noun phrase, with the relative clause as a modifier (→26.16–18). This construction occurs particularly when the relative clause expresses salient information that identifies the 'antecedent'.

Note 1: For this construction, cf. e.g. Engl. *I took what books she gave me.*

Relative Connection

50.16 The relative pronoun is occasionally used to introduce a new independent sentence (the antecedent stands in a previous sentence). This is called **relative connection**. The relative in such cases has a function similar to that of a demonstrative or personal pronoun (and may be translated as such):

(33) ἀνδρῶν γὰρ ἐπιφανῶν πᾶσα γῆ τάφος ... οὓς νῦν ὑμεῖς ζηλώσαντες ... μὴ περιορᾶσθε τοὺς πολεμικοὺς κινδύνους. (Thuc. 2.43.3–4)

For men of renown all the earth is a grave-monument. These men you should now emulate in your turn and not stay aloof from the dangers of war. *For the translation of the participle ζηλώσαντες, →52.6.*

(34) ἡμῖν δὲ δὴ δίδωσιν Ἠλέκτραν ἔχειν | δάμαρτα ... ἣν οὔποθ' ἀνὴρ ὅδε ... | ᾔσχυν' ἐν εὐνῇ. (Eur. *El.* 34–44)

To me he gave Electra, to have as my wife. This woman I have never brought dishonour in bed. *For 'I' as translation of ἀνὴρ ὅδε, →29.29.*

Moods and Tenses in Relative Clauses

In Digressive Clauses

50.17 In **digressive** relative clauses, the **use of moods and tenses is identical to that of independent sentences** (→34). The indicative is by far the most common; the potential optative and modal indicative occur regularly; very rarely also the imperative, hortatory subjunctive, or cupitive optative, etc. The negative is normally οὐ, unless μή is required (e.g. in a wish with the optative).

(35) ἀπῆλθεν εἰς Ἔφεσον, ᾗ ἀπέχει ἀπὸ Σάρδεων τριῶν ἡμερῶν ὁδόν. (Xen. *Hell.* 3.2.11)

He left for Ephesus, which is a three-day journey from Sardis. *Indicative.*

(36) Ἅλυν ..., ὃν οὐκ ἂν δύναισθε ἄνευ πλοίων διαβῆναι (Xen. *An.* 5.6.9)

the Halys, which you could not cross without boats ... *Potential optative.*

(37) κρατῆρές εἰσιν ... ὧν κρᾶτ' ἔρεψον. (Soph. *OC* 472–3)

There are mixing-bowls, the brims of which you must cover. *Imperative.*

(38) τοιαῦτ' ἐβούλευσ'· ὧν ἐμοὶ δοίη δίκην. (Eur. *El.* 269)

Such were his schemes: may he requite me for them. *Cupitive optative; note the relative connection (→50.16).*

In Restrictive Clauses

50.18   In most **restrictive** relative clauses, the **use of moods and tenses is very much like that of temporal/conditional clauses**; thus, the following can be found in restrictive relative clauses.

50.19   **Indicative**; the negative is either οὐ or μή – the latter with a conditional or generic nuance:

(39) ..., ἵν' εἴπω παρθένου χωρὶς λόγους | οὓς οὐκ ἀκούειν τὰς γαμουμένας πρέπει. (Eur. *IA* 1107–8)

... in order that I may, away from the maiden, speak words which are not fit for girls who are getting married to hear.

(40) ὃν μὴ σὺ φράζεις πῶς ὑπολάβοιμ' ἂν λόγον; (Eur. *IA* 523)

How can I understand your meaning if you do not make it clear to me? (*lit. 'which you do not make clear').*

In (39), with negative οὐ, the relative clause refers to specific words which Agamemnon is planning to say, which marrying girls should not hear. In (40), with negative μή, the relative clause has a conditional nuance (note the translation 'if you do not make it clear').

(41) ὑμεῖς ἄρα μανθάνοντες ἃ οὐκ ἠπίστασθε, ἀμαθεῖς ὄντες ἐμανθάνετε. (Pl. *Euthd.* 276b)

So when you learned the things which you did not know, you were ignorant when you learned them.

(42) πότερον γὰρ οἱ μανθάνοντες μανθάνουσιν ἃ ἐπίστανται ἢ ἃ μὴ ἐπίστανται; (Pl. *Euthd.* 276d)

Do learners learn things they know or things they don't know?

In (41), with οὐ, the relative clause refers to the set of specific things which learners did not know but then learned. In (42), with μή, the relative clause refers generically to whatever things the learners do not know.

Note 1: For the conditional/generic force of μή, cf. μή + participle: →52.40, 52.48.

50.20 **Prospective**: in restrictive relative clauses referring to the future, **ἄν + subjunctive** (prospective, →40.9) is regularly used; the negative is μή. The matrix clause has a form with future reference, e.g. future indicative, imperative, etc. (→33.63–4):

(43) τῷ ἀνδρὶ <u>ὃν ἂν ἕλησθε</u> πείσομαι. (Xen. *An.* 1.3.15)
      I will obey the man whom you choose.

(44) ἀκούοντες καὶ σοῦ καὶ τῶν τοῦ Λακωνικοῦ αἱρησόμεθα <u>ἃ ἂν</u> κράτιστα <u>δοκῇ</u> εἶναι. (Xen. *An.* 7.3.8)
      We will, listening to both you and the Spartan's messengers, choose the option which seems best to us.

50.21 **Habitual**: in restrictive relative clauses referring to an habitual or repeated action, **ἄν + subjunctive** (indefinite, →40.9) is used in clauses referring to the present, and **iterative optative** without ἄν is used in clauses referring to the past; the negative is μή. The matrix clause normally has a present indicative or imperfect, respectively:

(45) ἀποτίνει ζημίην <u>τὴν ἂν</u> οἱ ἱρέες <u>τάξωνται</u>. (Hdt. 2.65.5)
      He pays whatever penalty the priests determine. *For the Ionic relative pronoun τήν, →25.31.*

(46) καὶ <u>οὓς</u> μὲν <u>ἴδοι</u> εὐτάκτως καὶ σιωπῇ ἰόντας, προσελαύνων αὐτοῖς ... ἐπῄνει. (Xen. *Cyr.* 5.3.55)
      And whomever he saw moving in an orderly fashion and in silence, he approached and praised.

Note 1: In poetry and Herodotus, ἄν is sometimes omitted from the indefinite construction with subjunctive: →49.15.

50.22 The following (less frequent) types normally have a strong **conditional** nuance (for the use of moods, →49.8–11):

– **Potential**: in restrictive relative clauses referring to a (remotely) possible action, an **optative without ἄν** is used in the relative clause (negative μή). The matrix clause has a potential optative with ἄν:

(47) ἐγὼ γὰρ <u>ὀκνοίην</u> μὲν ἂν εἰς τὰ πλοῖα ἐμβαίνειν <u>ἃ</u> ἡμῖν <u>δοίη</u>. (Xen. *An.* 1.3.17)
      For I would hesitate to embark in the vessels that he might give us (= '*if he were to give us any*').

– **Counterfactual**: in restrictive relative clauses referring to an action which can no longer be realized, a **modal (secondary) indicative without ἄν** is used in the relative clause (negative μή). The matrix clause has a modal secondary indicative + ἄν:

(48) οὔτε γὰρ ἂν αὐτοὶ ἐπεχειροῦμεν πράττειν ἃ μὴ ἠπιστάμεθα, . . . οὔτε τοῖς ἄλλοις ἐπετρέπομεν . . . ἄλλο τι πράττειν ἢ ὅ τι πράττοντες ὀρθῶς ἔμελλον πράξειν. (Pl. *Chrm.* 171e)

For (*in the hypothetical scenario under consideration*) neither would we ourselves undertake to do anything that we did not understand (= '*if we did not understand it*'), nor would we entrust to the others to do anything other than what they were likely to do well when doing it (= '*if they were likely . . .*').

Note 1: In both these constructions, the use of moods is perhaps best seen as an instance of attraction of mood (→40.15).

Further Particulars

Relative Clauses Expressing Cause, Purpose, or Result

50.23   Relative clauses may have a **causal nuance**; this nuance occurs primarily with digressive clauses (since these are not needed to identify the antecedent, they come to express other meanings). Causal relative clauses usually have the **indicative** (negative οὐ):

(49) θαυμαστὸν ποιεῖς, ὃς ἡμῖν . . . οὐδὲν δίδως. (Xen. *Mem.* 2.7.13)

You do a strange thing, you who have given us nothing (= '*because you have . . .*').

The use of the indefinite relative ὅστις in digressive relative clauses (→50.6 n.2) often expresses such a causal nuance:

(50) Λοξίᾳ δὲ μέμφομαι, | ὅστις μ᾽ ἐπάρας ἔργον ἀνοσιώτατον, | τοῖς μὲν λόγοις ηὔφρανε, τοῖς δ᾽ ἔργοισιν οὔ. (Eur. *Or.* 285–7)

I blame Loxias, who drove me to do a most unholy deed and then cheered me with words, but not in deed (= '*because he drove me . . .*').

(51) οἴκτιρόν τέ με | . . . , ὅστις ὥστε παρθένος | βέβρυχα κλαίων. (Soph. *Trach.* 1070–2)

Have pity on me, who am crying loudly like a girl (= '*because I am . . .*').

50.24   Relative clauses with the **future indicative** (digressive or restrictive) often express a nuance of **purpose** (negative μή):

(52) ἀλλ᾽ εἶμ᾽ ἐπὶ τὸν Κλέων᾽, ὃς αὐτοῦ τήμερον | ἐκπηνιεῖται ταῦτα. (Ar. *Ran.* 577–8)

I'm going to get Cleon, who'll wind this out of him today (= '*so that he'll . . .*'). *Digressive.*

(53) ἀποκρύπτεσθαι γὰρ καὶ διαδύεσθαι καὶ πάντα ποιεῖν ἐξ ὧν μὴ λειτουργήσεις τουτοισὶ μεμάθηκας. (Dem. 42.23)

For you have learned how to be secret, how to evade, and how to do everything which will permit you to avoid rendering public service to these men here. *Restrictive.*

Note 1: The future indicative may be used even after a past tense matrix verb: this construction is similar to indirect statement, suggesting that the relative clause expresses the intentions/thoughts underlying the action of the matrix clause; indeed, the oblique future optative typical of indirect statement (→41.13 n.2) is sometimes found in this type of relative clause.

(54) ἔδοξε τῷ δήμῳ τριάκοντα ἄνδρας ἑλέσθαι, οἳ τοὺς ... νόμους συγγράψουσι, καθ' οὓς πολιτεύσουσι. (Xen. Hell. 2.3.2)

The people decided to elect thirty men to codify the laws according to which they were to govern. *Future indicatives after a past tense (ἔδοξε).*

(55) οἱ δὲ τριάκοντα ᾑρέθησαν ... ἐφ' ᾧτε συγγράψαι νόμους, καθ' οὕστινας πολιτεύσοιντο. (Xen. Hell. 2.3.11)

And the thirty were elected on the condition that they would codify laws according to which they were to govern. *Oblique future optative.*

50.25   Relative clauses with the **indicative** which follow their matrix clause may also have the nuance of a **result clause**; such clauses are often anticipated by οὕτως, τοιοῦτος etc. in the matrix clause (cf. result clauses, →46.2). The indefinite relative ὅστις occurs frequently in such clauses; the negative is οὐ:

(56) τίς οὕτω μαίνεται ὅστις οὐ βούλεταί σοι φίλος εἶναι; (Xen. An. 2.5.12)

Who is so mad that he doesn't wish to be your friend?

(57) τί οὐκ ἂν πράξειεν ὁ τοιοῦτος, ὅστις γράμματα λαβὼν μὴ ἀπέδωκεν ὀρθῶς καὶ δικαίως; (Dem. 34.29)

What would he not do, the kind of man that has taken letters and not related them in due and proper course?

Nuances of purpose and result may be combined when a matrix clause with τοιοῦτος, etc. is followed by a relative clause with a future indicative:

(58) κρεῖττόν ἐστιν ... τοῖς τοιούτοις τῶν ἔργων ἐπιτίθεσθαι, ἃ καὶ πρεσβυτέρῳ γενομένῳ ἐπαρκέσει. (Xen. Mem. 2.8.3)

It is better to take up such types of work as will sustain you even after you have grown older (= 'to sustain ...').

Note 1: For the use of οἷος, ὅσος, etc. with an infinitive in result clauses, →46.10.

Potential and Counterfactual Constructions in Restrictive Clauses

50.26   As well as in digressive clauses (→50.17 above), **potential optative + ἄν** (negative οὐ) and **counterfactual modal indicative + ἄν** (negative οὐ) also occur in restrictive relative clauses:

(59) οὐκ ἔσθ' ὅτου θίγοιμ' ἂν ἐνδικώτερον. (Eur. *El.* 224)

There is no one whom I might touch with more right. *Autonomous (i.e. restrictive), potential optative + ἄν.*

(60) πρὸς ταῦτα δὴ ἀκούσατε ἃ ἐγὼ οὐκ ἂν ποτε εἶπον τούτου ἐναντίον, εἰ μή μοι παντάπασιν ἀγνώμονες ἐδοκεῖτε εἶναι. (Xen. *An.* 7.6.23)

In reply to this, listen to words which I would never have spoken to that man's face, if you did not seem to me to be utterly senseless. *Autonomous (i.e. restrictive), counterfactual ind. + ἄν.*

(Cor)relative Clauses with Relative Adjectives or Adverbs

50.27   The use of moods and tenses in (cor)relative clauses introduced by relative adjectives or adverbs is identical to that in relative clauses introduced by relative pronouns, as described above.

With Relative Adjectives (οἷος, ὁποῖος, ὅσος, ὁπόσος)

50.28   The relative adjectives οἷος, ὅποιος, ὅσος, and ὁπόσος are frequently anticipated (or followed) in the matrix clause by an 'antecedent' in the form of a demonstrative adjective (τοιοῦτος, τοσοῦτος, etc.):

(61) οὐδεὶς τοσαῦτα ἀγαθὰ πεποίηκε τὴν πόλιν ὅσα οὗτος ἠδίκηκεν. (Lys. 30.33)

No one has done so much good for the city as this man has done it harm.

(62) δίκαιοί ἐστε καὶ ὑμεῖς περὶ τούτων τοιαύτην ἔχειν τὴν γνώμην οἷάνπερ καὶ αὐτοὶ περὶ αὐτῶν ἔσχον. (Andoc. 1.3)

You too are right to pass such a verdict on them as they passed on themselves.

However, such clauses are also frequently **reduced** (i.e. autonomous), occurring without a demonstrative in the matrix clause:

(63) οὕτω δὴ ἐξῆλθον σχεδὸν ἅπαντες καὶ οἱ Μῆδοι πλὴν ὅσοι σὺν Κυαξάρῃ ἔτυχον σκηνοῦντες. (Xen. *Cyr.* 4.2.11)

The result was that nearly all came out, even the Medes, except all those who (*as many as*) happened to be encamped together with Cyaxares.

(64) ἔκαιον οἷς τοῦτο ἔργον ἦν ὁπόσων μὴ αὐτοὶ ἐδέοντο. (Xen. *Cyr.* 4.5.36)

Those whose task this was burned whatever (*as many things as*) they did not need themselves. *Both the subject and object of ἔκαιον are expressed by autonomous relative clauses (subject: οἷς ... ἦν, object: ὁπόσων ἐδέοντο).*

Note 1: Only when they are preceded by a demonstrative, as in (61)–(62) can the relative adjectives οἷος/ὅσος be translated with *as* (with the demonstratives being translated with *such ... , as much ... , as many ...*, etc.): in other cases the translation required for the relative is respectively *such as, as much as, as many as*, etc., as in (63)–(64).

50.29 Clauses with a relative adjective also frequently stand **in apposition** (→26.24) to a noun, which serves as its antecedent:

(65) καὶ ἐκ μὲν τοῦ πρώτου ἁλόντος χαλεπῶς <u>οἱ ἄνθρωποι</u>, <u>ὅσοι</u> καὶ ἐς τὰ πλοῖα καὶ ὁλκάδα τινὰ κατέφυγον, ἐς τὸ στρατόπεδον ἐξεκομίζοντο. (Thuc. 7.23.2)

The men from the first (fort) that was taken, as many of them as had been able to take flight on board boats and merchant ships, had difficulty reaching the camp. *The ὅσοι-clause stands in apposition to οἱ ἄνθρωποι.*

(66) ... <u>ἆθλ᾽</u>, <u>οἷα</u> μηδεὶς τῶν ἐμῶν τύχοι φίλων. (Soph. *Phil.* 509)

... pains, such as none of my friends may suffer. *Note the cupitive optative in a digressive relative clause.*

50.30 Plural forms of ὅσος and ὁπόσος are frequently anticipated by a form of πᾶς:

(67) στρατηγὸν δὲ αὐτὸν ἀπέδειξε <u>πάντων</u> <u>ὅσοι</u> ἐς Καστωλοῦ πεδίον ἀθροίζονται. (Xen. *An.* 1.1.2)

He appointed him commander of all those who gather in the plain of Castolus.

Note 1: These forms (with or without an anticipating form of πᾶς) are often best translated with *all who*, *everything that*, etc. – cf. also the translations of (63)–(64) above.

50.31 Relative attraction (→50.13) occurs in correlative clauses with relative adjectives as well:

(68) Μήδων ... <u>ὅσων</u> ἑώρακα ... ὁ ἐμὸς πάππος κάλλιστος. (Xen. *Cyr.* 1.3.2)

Of all the Medes that I have seen, my grandfather is the most handsome. *Object of ἑώρακα, but genitive under the influence of Μήδων.*

50.32 The neuter forms οἷον and οἷα are often used adverbially, in which case they can well be translated with *for example, for instance, such as*:

(69) νῦν δὲ περὶ ὀλίγας οἰκίας αἱ κάλλισται τραγῳδίαι συντίθενται, <u>οἷον</u> περὶ Ἀλκμέωνα καὶ Οἰδίπουν καὶ Ὀρέστην ... (Arist. *Poet.* 1453a18–20)

But as it is, the best tragedies are composed about only a few families; for example about Alcmeon, Oedipus, Orestes, ...

50.33 For the use of (τοσούτῳ ...) ὅσῳ, as a dative of measure with comparatives, to express *the more ... the more*, →32.11. For the use of οἷος, ὅσος, etc. with an infinitive in result clauses, →46.10.

With Relative Adverbs

Relative Adverbs of Place (and Time)

50.34 Correlative clauses introduced by adverbs of place (οὗ, ἔνθα, οἷ, ὅθεν, ᾗ, etc.; ὅπου, ὅποι, etc. →8) may be anticipated or followed by a demonstrative adverb:

(70) τί οὖν ἐγὼ <u>ἐνταῦθα</u> ἠδίκησα ἀγαγὼν ὑμᾶς <u>ἔνθα</u> πᾶσιν ὑμῖν ἐδόκει; (Xen. *An.* 7.6.14)

What injustice, then, did I commit by leading you where (*there, where*) you all decided to go?

But such clauses are more often **reduced** (i.e. autonomous, without a preceding demonstrative adverb):

(71) ἄξω ὑμᾶς <u>ἔνθα</u> τὸ πρᾶγμα ἐγένετο. (Xen. *Cyr.* 5.4.21)

I will take you to (*the place*) where the event took place.

(72) ἐθήρα <u>ὅπουπερ</u> ἐπιτυγχάνοιεν θηρίοις. (Xen. *Cyr.* 3.3.5)

He hunted wheresoever they came upon animals. *Note the iterative optative,* →*50.12.*

50.35   Autonomous correlative clauses of this type can be used together with 'existential' ἔστιν (→50.12 above): ἔστιν οὗ *there is a place where, somewhere*, ἔστιν ὅτε *there is a time when, sometimes.*

50.36   Temporal clauses introduced by ὅτε/ὁπότε (→47) are in essence also adverbial correlative clauses of time, usually 'reduced'. Their correlative nature may be seen most clearly in cases where they are anticipated or followed by τότε, for instance:

(73) εἴθε σοι, ὦ Περίκλεις, <u>τότε</u> συνεγενόμην <u>ὅτε</u> δεινότατος ἑαυτοῦ ἦσθα. (Xen. *Mem.* 1.2.46)

Ah, Pericles, if only I had met you at the time when you were at your cleverest. *For ἑαυτοῦ,* →*29.19.*

Relative Adverbs of Manner: Clauses of Comparison

50.37   **Clauses of comparison** are introduced by the relative adverbs ὡς, ὅπως, ὥσπερ, and καθάπερ (*just*) *as,* (*in such a way*) *as.* They are sometimes preceded or followed by οὕτω(ς) (καί) *thus, in this/that/such a way (also), so (too)*:

(74) Πάνυ, ἔφη, ἔχει <u>οὕτως</u> <u>ὡς</u> λέγεις. (Pl. *Phd.* 68c)

'It is indeed just as you say,' he said. *For ἔχει + adv.,* →*26.11 and 36.10.*

(75) <u>οὕτω</u> γὰρ ποιήσω <u>ὅπως</u> ἂν σὺ κελεύῃς. (Pl. *Euthd.* 295b)

I will act in such a way as you command. *Prospective subjunctive + ἄν.*

(76) <u>ὥσπερ</u> οἶνος κιρνᾶται τοῖς τῶν πινόντων τρόποις, <u>οὕτω</u> καὶ φιλία τοῖς τῶν χρωμένων ἤθεσιν. (Dem. fr. 13.27 Baiter-Sauppe)

Just as wine is mixed with the customs of those who drink it, thus also friendship is mixed with the characters of those who enjoy it.

However, most clauses of comparison are **reduced** (i.e. autonomous, without a preceding οὕτω(ς)): only the entity with which someone or something is compared is expressed. The relative adverbs can in such cases also be translated with *as, like*:

(77) ποίει ὅπως ἄριστόν σοι δοκεῖ εἶναι. (Xen. *Cyr.* 4.5.50)

Do as it seems to be best to you.

(78) καί μ' ἀφείλεθ' ἡ τύχη | ὥσπερ πτερὸν πρὸς αἰθέρ' ἡμέρᾳ μιᾷ. (Eur. *Her.* 509–10)

And fate took it away from me in a single day like a feather into the sky.

(79) περιιστώμεθα δὴ καθάπερ ἀθληταὶ πρὸς τοῦτον αὖ τὸν λόγον. (Pl. *Phlb.* 41b)

Let us then like athletes position ourselves around this argument, in turn.

Note that in (78) and (79), the comparative clauses have no finite verb: this occurs frequently with comparative clauses.

50.38   The relative ᾗ may also have this sense (→8.2), and may be anticipated by ταύτῃ:

(80) θεοὺς ... μάρτυρας ποιούμενοι πειρασόμεθα ἀμύνεσθαι πολέμου ἄρχοντας ταύτῃ ᾗ ἂν ὑφηγῆσθε. (Thuc. 1.78.4)

Taking the gods as our witness, we will attempt to ward you off, if you begin hostilities, in whatever manner (*in that way which*) you choose.

50.39   Observe the idioms ἔστιν ὅπως *there is a way in which; it is possible that*, οὐκ ἔστιν ὅπως *there is no way in which; it is impossible that*; →50.12 and 50.35 above.

50.40   For comparative ὥσπερ εἰ and ὥσπερ ἂν εἰ, →49.22–4. For comparative participles with ὥσπερ, →52.43.

51

The Infinitive

Introduction

Basic Properties

51.1   Infinitives are **verbal nouns**:

- they are like nouns in that they may fulfil syntactic roles which are typically fulfilled by noun phrases (subject, object, complement; →26.3), and in that they may be modified by the article;
- they are like verbs in that they are marked for tense-aspect and voice; may be construed with an object, complement, etc.; modified by adverbs; etc.

Overview of Uses: Dynamic and Declarative Infinitives, Articular Infinitives, Other Uses

Without the Article: Dynamic and Declarative Infinitive

51.2   The use of the infinitive **without the article** can be broadly divided into two categories:

- the **dynamic infinitive**: to complement verbs meaning 'must', 'can', 'be able', etc. (modal verbs); 'want', 'desire', 'dare', 'try', etc. (desiderative/volitional verbs); 'be good at', 'teach how to', 'learn how to', etc. (practical knowledge verbs); 'command', 'suggest', 'compel', etc. (manipulative verbs); 'begin', 'stop', etc. (phase verbs); and certain adjectives and nouns with similar meanings; for details, →51.8–18;
- the **declarative infinitive**: to complement certain verbs of speech and verbs of belief and opinion, introducing a form of indirect statement (→41.1–2); for details, →51.19–27;

51.3   As complements, the dynamic and declarative infinitive are different in nature:

- The dynamic infinitive expresses an **action**, the realization of which is enabled, attempted, desired, forced, necessitated, asked for, etc. The action **may or may not be realized**.

– The declarative infinitive expresses the **content** of someone's **speech or belief about an action**. This content (so-called 'propositional' content) **may or may not be true**.

(1) ἡ δὲ Παρύσατις . . . ἐκέλευσε . . . τὴν . . . Ῥωξάνην ζῶσαν κατατεμεῖν· καὶ ἐγένετο. (Ctes. fr. 15.56 Lenfant)

Parysatis ordered Roxane to be cut up alive. And so it happened. *κατατεμεῖν, complementing κελεύω 'command', is a dynamic infinitive. Parysatis asks for a gruesome execution. The narrator then continues to say that this execution was actually carried out.*

(2) φημὶ τοίνυν ἐγώ (καὶ . . . μηδεὶς φθόνῳ τὸ μέλλον ἀκούσῃ, ἀλλ᾽ ἂν ἀληθὲς ᾖ σκοπείτω), . . . κάλλιον Κόνωνα τὰ τείχη στῆσαι Θεμιστοκλέους. (Dem. 20.74)

Now I maintain (and let no one take offence at what is coming, but consider whether it is true) that Conon has put up the walls in a more laudable manner than Themistocles. *στῆσαι, complementing φημί 'say', is a declarative infinitive. Demosthenes puts forward his opinion and asks his audience to consider whether that opinion is true or false.*

(3) ἔδοξε δὲ καὶ τοῖς τῶν Ἀθηναίων στρατηγοῖς . . . πλεῖν . . . ταῦτα δὲ βουλομένους ποιεῖν ἄνεμος καὶ χειμὼν διεκώλυσεν αὐτούς. (Xen. *Hell.* 1.6.35)

The generals of the Athenians also decided to sail. But although they wanted to do this, the wintry, stormy weather prevented them. *ποιεῖν is a dynamic infinitive, complementing βουλομένους, a verb of wanting (so too πλεῖν, after a verb of deciding, impers. ἔδοξε). The Athenian generals want to go ahead with the expedition; the narrator goes on to say that the expedition is in fact not realized.*

(4) οὔ φημι ποιεῖν αὐτοὺς ἃ βούλονται· ἀλλά μ᾽ ἔλεγχε. (Pl. *Grg.* 467b)

I claim that they are not doing what they want: refute me if you can. *ποιεῖν is a declarative infinitive, complementing a verb of speech/opinion (φημί). Socrates puts forward his own opinion and challenges his addressee to prove that opinion false.*

The dynamic infinitive and the declarative infinitive have in common that they do not in themselves specify whether the action is or is not realized or whether the propositional content is or is not true.

Note 1: The infinitive differs in this respect from the supplementary participle, which on the whole specifies the action it expresses as realized or the propositional content as true (→52.8).

Note 2: The 'dynamic' infinitive is so called because it refers to actions which exist 'potentially' (Gk. ἐν δυνάμει). This infinitive is in some works called 'prolative'.

Note 3: With a few verbs taking a dynamic infinitive, notably those meaning 'force' or 'compel' (e.g. ἀναγκάζω, βιάζομαι), but also τολμάω *dare* and ἄρχομαι *begin*, the *full realization* of the matrix verb entails the realization of the action expressed by the infinitive as well:

(5) πρῶτα μὲν τοὺς Λυδοὺς <u>ἠνάγκασε</u> τὰς Κύρου ἐντολὰς <u>ἐπιτελέειν</u>· ἐκ τούτου δὲ κελευσμοσύνης Λυδοὶ τὴν πᾶσαν δίαιταν τῆς ζόης μετέβαλον. (Hdt. 1.157.2)

He first compelled the Lydians to carry out Cyrus' instructions. And because of his order the Lydians changed their whole way of life. *The compelling of the Lydians is carried out and completed. As the subsequent sentence shows, their 'following Cyrus' orders' is realized as well.*

(6) πρῶτος δὲ Κλέαρχος τοὺς αὐτοῦ στρατιώτας <u>ἐβιάζετο</u> ἰέναι· οἱ δ᾽ αὐτόν τε ἔβαλλον καὶ τὰ ὑποζύγια τὰ ἐκείνου, ἐπεὶ ἄρξαιντο προϊέναι. (Xen. *An.* 1.3.1)

Clearchus was the first who tried to compel his own troops to march on. But they pelted him and his pack-animals with stones, every time they began to move forward. *ἐβιάζετο is a conative imperfect, which suggests that the action was never fully realized (→33.25). As the subsequent sentence shows, the soldiers in fact do not 'march on'.*

Note 4: Some verbs may be complemented either by a dynamic infinitive or by a declarative infinitive; the difference in complement corresponds to a difference in meaning of the matrix verb. For full details on these verbs, →51.28–33. Some verbs may also be construed with a participle, →52.22–7.

51.4   The differences detailed above correspond to several crucial **differences of construction** between dynamic and declarative infinitives:

 – The **negative** with dynamic infinitives is μή (→51.13), with declarative infinitives nearly always οὐ (→51.22–3);
 – The dynamic infinitive is never **modified by ἄν**, whereas the declarative infinitive may be modified by ἄν (→51.27);
 – The future infinitive is never used as dynamic infinitive, the perfect infinitive rarely; infinitives of all tense-aspect stems are used as declarative infinitives. For full details on the **interpretation of the tense-aspect stems** in infinitives, →51.15 (dynamic) and 51.25–6 (declarative).

With the Article; Other Uses

51.5   A neuter article (in any case, always singular) may be added to an infinitive to turn it into (the head of) a noun phrase. The infinitive itself never declines: τὸ παιδεύειν, τοῦ παιδεύειν, etc. For full details on this use, the **articular infinitive**, →51.38–45.

51.6   Some remaining uses of the infinitive are treated in 51.47–9.

51.7   For the infinitive with ὥστε (or οἷος, etc.) in result clauses, →46.7–11. For the infinitive with ἐφ᾽ ᾧ(τε) *on the condition that*, →49.26. For the infinitive with πρίν, →47.14.

The Dynamic Infinitive

Verbs Taking a Dynamic Infinitive

51.8   The following classes of verbs take a dynamic infinitive as their complement:

> **Note 1:** Many of the verbs below also have different constructions, in which case they no longer belong to the specific class under which they are listed below. For instance, the verb μανθάνω is used as a verb of practical knowledge (*learn (how) to*) taking a dynamic infinitive, but also as a verb of intellectual knowledge (*learn that*), in which case it takes a supplementary participle (→52.10) or a ὅτι/ὡς-clause (→41.3).
>
> For an overview of verbs belonging to different classes taking either a dynamic or a declarative infinitive, →51.28–32. For verbs taking either an infinitive or a participle, →52. 22–7. For a complete overview of different classes of verb and the type of complements they take, →53.

- **Modal verbs** – the verb expresses the need or possibility of an action taking place, e.g.:

δεῖ	it is necessary to
δύναμαι	be able to
ἔξεστι	it is possible to, it is permitted to (+ *dat.*)
ἔχω	can, be able to
προσήκει	it is fitting to
χρή	it is necessary to

(7) σκοπέειν δὲ χρὴ παντὸς χρήματος τὴν τελευτήν. (Hdt. 1.32.9)
    It is necessary to examine the end of every thing.

(8) οὐδ' ... νόμον ἕξουσι δεῖξαι καθ' ὃν ἐξῆν αὐτῷ ταῦτα πρᾶξαι. (Isae. 10.11)
    And they will not be able to produce a law according to which it was allowed for him to do these things.

- **Verbs of practical knowledge** – the subject learns, teaches, or knows how to do something, e.g.:

διδάσκω	teach (how) to, instruct how to
ἐπίσταμαι	know how to
μανθάνω	learn (how) to

(9) παίδευσις ... καλὴ διδάσκει χρῆσθαι νόμοις καὶ λέγειν περὶ τῶν δικαίων. (Xen. Cyn. 12.14)
    A good education teaches (a man) to observe laws and to speak about what is right.

– **Desiderative/volitional verbs** – the subject intends, wishes or resolves that an action should be realized, e.g.:

αἱρέομαι	choose to
βουλεύω/βουλεύομαι	deliberate, resolve to
βούλομαι	want to, prefer to
διανοέομαι	decide to, intend to
δοκεῖ	it seems right to, it is decided to (+ *dat.*; →36.4, 51.30)
ἐθέλω	be willing to, wish to
σπουδάζω	make haste to, strive to

(10) πρῶτον δὲ <u>διηγήσασθαι</u> <u>βούλομαι</u> τὰ πραχθέντα τῇ τελευταίᾳ ἡμέρᾳ. (Lys. 1.22)

First I want to go through the things which happened on the last day.

(11) οὐ γὰρ λόγοισι τὸν βίον <u>σπουδάζομεν</u> | λαμπρὸν <u>ποεῖσθαι</u> μᾶλλον ἢ τοῖς δρωμένοις. (Soph. *OC* 1143–4)

It is not in words that I strive to give my life renown, so much as it is by my deeds.

– **Verbs of ordering, forcing, manipulating** – the subject forces, tells or asks someone else to do something, e.g.:

αἰτέω	ask to, require to
ἀναγκάζω	force to, compel to
δέομαι	ask to, require to
κελεύω	command to, bid to
πείθω	persuade to

(12) <u>κελεύει</u> με Μαρδόνιος μένοντα αὐτοῦ <u>πειρᾶσθαι</u> τῆς Πελοποννήσου. (Hdt. 8.101.2)

Mardonius commands me to stay here and make an attempt on the Peloponnese.

Note 2: To this category belong also verbs of preventing, hindering, etc.; for these, →51.34–7.
Note 3: For verbs of speaking (e.g. λέγω) used as verbs of ordering, →51.32.

– Some **phase verbs** – the verb expresses some phase of the action (beginning or end), e.g.:

ἄρχομαι	begin to, be the first to
παύω	stop/prevent (someone from doing something)

(13) ἐκ τῶν δὲ πρώτων πρῶτον <u>ἄρξομαι</u> λέγειν. (Eur. *Med.* 475)

I will begin my speech at the very beginning.

Note 4: These and other phase verbs are (more) regularly construed with a participle (→52.9); for the difference between the two constructions, →52.27.

51.9 The dynamic infinitive is also used to complement certain **adjectives and nouns** with meanings similar to those listed above, i.e. expressing ability, possibility, need, desire, etc. Some examples:

Adjectives

ἄξιος	worth(y)
δεινός	good at, skilful, impressive
ἐπιτήδειος	suitable
ἱκανός	competent, adequate, capable
οἷός τε	capable
ῥᾴδιος	easy to

Nouns

ὥρα (ἐστί)	it is time to (+ *pres. inf.*)
ἵμερος	a desire to
σχολή	leisure to, the opportunity to
νόμος	the law (commands that), it is customary to

(14) ἐξ αὐτῶν δὲ τούτων ἐπιδείξω αὐτὸν ἐπιτηδειότερον τεθνάναι μᾶλλον ἢ σῴζεσθαι. ([Andoc.] 4.25)

Based on these very things, I will show that he is more fit to be dead than to survive.

(15) ὥρα προβαίνειν, ὦνδρες, ἡμῖν ἐστι. (Ar. *Eccl.* 285)

It is time, gentlemen, for us to come forward.

Note 1: The constituent to which such an adjective belongs can be supplied with the infinitive as its subject (as in (14), where 'he' is subject of τεθνάναι/σῴζεσθαι) or as its object (as in (16)). In either case, the infinitive tends to be active:

(16) ἦν . . . ὁ Θεμιστοκλῆς . . . ἄξιος θαυμάσαι. (Thuc. 1.138.3)

Themistocles was worthy of admiration (*i.e.* 'to be admired'). *Themistocles can be supplied as object to θαυμάσαι.*

Expression of the Subject of Dynamic Infinitives

51.10 The subject of a dynamic infinitive is **not separately expressed** when it is already given as an obligatory constituent of the matrix verb governing the infinitive:

– as its **subject** (when the subjects of the infinitive and its matrix-verb are **'co-referential'**):

(17) καὶ τέσσερας ἵππους συζευγνύναι παρὰ Λιβύων οἱ Ἕλληνες μεμαθήκασι. (Hdt. 4.189.3)

And the Greeks have learned how to yoke four horses from the Libyans. *The subject of the infinitive is the same as that of μεμαθήκασι, i.e. οἱ Ἕλληνες.*

This is always the case with verbs meaning 'begin to', 'be able to', 'know how to', 'be willing/strive to', or with passive forms of verbs meaning 'force', 'command', etc.:

(18) πῶς γὰρ οὐχὶ γεννάδας, | ὅστις γε πίνειν οἶδε καὶ βινεῖν μόνον; (Ar. *Ran.* 739–40)

Of course he's a gentleman: all he knows is how to drink and fuck. *The subject of the infinitives is co-referential with the subject of οἶδε (ὅστις).*

(19) ἠναγκάσθησαν ... ναυμαχῆσαι πρὸς Φορμίωνα. (Thuc. 2.83.1)

They were compelled to make a naval attack upon Phormio. *The subject of ναυμαχῆσαι is co-referential with the subject of passive ἠναγκάσθησαν.*

– as its **object** or **complement**:

(20) ἔπεισε μὲν Τισσαφέρνην μὴ παρέχειν χρήματα Λακεδαιμονίοις. (Isoc. 16.20)

He persuaded Tissaphernes not to give money to the Spartans. *Τισσαφέρνην is object of ἔπεισε, and serves as subject of παρέχειν.*

(21) ἐδέοντο αὐτοῦ παντὶ τρόπῳ ἀπελθεῖν Ἀθήνηθεν. (Lys. 13.25)

They asked him to leave Athens at all costs. *αὐτοῦ is a complement in the genitive with ἐδέοντο (→30.21); it serves as subject of the infinitive ἀπελθεῖν.*

(22) βασιλεὺς ὁ Αἰθιόπων συμβουλεύει τῷ Περσέων βασιλέϊ ... ἐπ' Αἰθίοπας ... στρατεύεσθαι. (Hdt. 3.21.3)

The king of the Ethiopians counsels the king of the Persians to attack the Ethiopians. *τῷ ... βασιλέϊ is a complement in the dative with συμβουλεύει (→30.39); it serves as subject of στρατεύεσθαι.*

Note 1: Naturally, dynamic infinitives of **impersonal verbs** (→36) also do not have an explicitly expressed subject (as they have no subject at all):

(23) πολλάκις ἐξεργάζεται ὧν μεταμέλειν ἀνάγκη. (Xen. *Eq.* 6.13)

He often does what it is necessary to regret. *μεταμέλειν is a dynamic infinitive representing impersonal μεταμέλει + gen. (→36.15); the inf. depends on ἀνάγκη.*

51.11 If the subject of the dynamic infinitive is not expressed as an obligatory constituent of the matrix verb, it is **separately expressed in the accusative**: this is called the **accusative-and-infinitive construction** (or 'accusative plus infinitive', 'accusative with infinitive'; Lat. *accusativus cum infinitivo*, AcI):

(24) ἅμα δ' ἐκέλευεν ἀναγνωσθῆναι τὸ ψήφισμα τοῦ δήμου. (Aeschin. 2.50)

At the same time he called for the decree of the people to be read. *τὸ ψήφισμα is subject of ἀναγνωσθῆναι, the entire accusative-and-infinitive construction is object of ἐκέλευεν; note that it is impossible in this case to take τὸ ψήφισμα as object of ἐκέλευεν (one cannot give instructions to a decree).*

This occurs frequently with impersonal expressions, such as δεῖ *it is necessary*, χρή *it is necessary*, ἔδοξε *it was decided*, πρέπει *it is fitting*, οἷόν τέ (ἐστι) *it is possible*, etc. (→36.3–5):

(25) δεῖ σε καθεύδειν | . . . παρ᾽ ἐμοί. (Ar. *Eccl.* 700–1)
You must sleep with me (*lit. 'it is necessary that you . . .'). σε is the subject of καθεύδειν; the entire construction σε καθεύδειν παρ᾽ ἐμοί is subject of δεῖ (→36.3).*

(26) ἔδοξε πλεῖν τὸν Ἀλκιβιάδην. (Thuc. 6.29.3)
It was decided that Alcibiades should sail. *τὸν Ἀλκιβιάδην is the subject of πλεῖν; the entire construction πλεῖν τὸν Ἀλκιβιάδην is subject of ἔδοξε (→36.4).*

(27) ὑμᾶς δὲ πρέπει συνεπαινεῖν . . . τοιούτους ἄνδρας. (Pl. *Menex.* 246a)
It is fitting that you should join in praising such men. *ὑμᾶς is subject of συνεπαινεῖν; the entire accusative-and-infinitive construction is subject of πρέπει (→36.4).*

51.12 **Predicative complements** (→26.8) **and predicative modifiers** (→26.26) **of the subject of an infinitive** agree with that subject:

– In the accusative-and-infinitive construction, predicative complements/modifiers agree with the accusative subject (the subject may be implied):

(28) δεῖ με γίγνεσθ᾽ Ἀνδρομέδαν (Ar. *Thesm.* 1012)
I must become Andromeda. *Ἀνδρομέδαν is predicative complement agreeing with με (subject of γίγνεσθ(αι)), and thus accusative.*

(29) χρὴ μικρὰν καὶ ἀσθενῆ γενέσθαι τὴν πόλιν. (Lys. 12.70)
The city must become small and weak. *μικρὰν and ἀσθενῆ agree in case, number and gender with τὴν πόλιν (subject of γενέσθαι).*

(30) καὶ τί δεῖ καθ᾽ ἓν ἕκαστον λέγοντα διατρίβειν; (Isoc. 2.45)
Why should one waste one's time on talking about every single instance? *λέγοντα agrees with the subject of διατρίβειν, which is not expressed; a generalizing subject in the accusative is implied.*

– When the subject of the infinitive is taken from the matrix clause, predicative complements/modifiers typically agree with the relevant constituent in the matrix clause:

(31) ἄλλα τε πάμπολλα ἀγαθὰ γίγνοιτ᾽ ἄν, εἰ τοῦ νόμου τις τούτου δύναιτο ἐγκρατὴς εἶναι. (Pl. *Leg.* 839b)
Many other good things might happen, if someone were able to be in control of this law. *The predicative complement ἐγκρατής agrees with τις, the subject of δύναιτο . . . εἶναι (the subjects are co-referential).*

(32) νῦν σοι ἔξεστιν, ὦ Ξενοφῶν, ἀνδρὶ γενέσθαι. (Xen. *An.* 7.1.21)

Now, Xenophon, it is possible for you to become a man. *The predicative complement ἀνδρί agrees with σοι, the dative complement of ἔξεστιν and the subject of γενέσθαι.*

Note 1: However, such predicative modifiers/complements also sometimes appear in the accusative, as this is the case typically associated with infinitive-subjects (and anything agreeing with them):

(33) Λακεδαιμονίοις ἔξεστιν ὑμῖν φίλους γενέσθαι. (Thuc. 4.20.3)

It is possible for you to become friends to the Spartans. *The predicative complement φίλους appears in the accusative, even though the dat. ὑμῖν is taken as subject for γενέσθαι. Contrast (32).*

(34) ὁ Σωκράτης ... συμβουλεύει τῷ Ξενοφῶντι ἐλθόντα εἰς Δελφοὺς ἀνακοινῶσαι τῷ θεῷ. (Xen. *An.* 3.1.5)

Socrates advised Xenophon to go to Delphi and consult the god. *ἐλθόντα is accusative, even though the subject for ἀνακοινῶσαι is taken from dative τῷ Ξενοφῶντι.*

Negatives with Dynamic Infinitives

51.13   The **negative** with the dynamic infinitive is **μή**:

(35) ἀπιέναι δ' ἐκέλευεν καὶ μὴ ἐρεθίζειν, ἵνα σῶς οἴκαδε ἔλθοι. (Pl. *Resp.* 394a)

He ordered him to go away and not to trouble him, so that he might come home in one piece.

(36) μάλιστα μὲν οὖν ἂν ἠβουλόμην μὴ ἔχειν πράγματα. ([Dem.] 47.4)

I would much have preferred not to have proceedings.

51.14   For μὴ οὐ, τὸ μὴ οὐ, etc., particularly with verbs of forbidding, hindering, preventing, abstaining, etc. →51.34–7.

Tense and Aspect of Dynamic Infinitives

51.15   The dynamic infinitive is limited almost exclusively to the **present and aorist stems** (the perfect is rare; the future infinitive is never dynamic). Both refer to actions which may or may not occur, normally posterior to the matrix verb; the difference between the stems is purely **aspectual** (→33.63–5):

– the **present infinitive** refers to actions **as a process** (ongoing or repeated; imperfective aspect);

– the **aorist infinitive** refers to actions presented as **complete** and therefore **in their entirety** (perfective aspect).

(37) κεῖνον ... ἐκέλευον ἀναβάντα ἐπὶ πύργον ἀγορεῦσαι ὡς ... (Hdt. 3.74.3)

They ordered him to go up on a tower and declare that ... *For the translation of the ppl. ἀναβάντα, →52.6.*

(38) ἀνεβίβασαν αὐτὸν ἐπὶ πύργον καὶ <u>ἀγορεύειν</u> ἐκέλευον. (Hdt. 3.75.1)
They brought him up on a tower and ordered him to (start) speak(ing).

Herodotus twice narrates how Prexaspes is ordered to speak. The aorist infinitive ἀγορεῦσαι in (37) looks at the speech that he has to make as a whole (note that the content of that speech is given by the ὡς-clause that will follow). The present infinitive ἀγορεύειν in (38) is used to refer to the actual process of speaking, which Prexaspes is ordered to get underway. Note that the action expressed by both infinitives is necessarily posterior to ἐκέλευον (one cannot command someone to already be doing or have done something).

(39) δεῖ . . . τὸν βουλόμενόν τι <u>ποιῆσαι</u> τὴν πόλιν ἡμῶν ἀγαθὸν τὰ ὦτα πρῶτον ὑμῶν ἰάσασθαι· διέφθαρται γάρ. (Dem. 13.13)
Whoever wants to do our city a good turn must first cleanse your ears. For they have been corrupted.

(40) ὡρμηκότα νῦν τὸν ἄνθρωπον φίλον εἶναι καὶ βουλόμενόν τι <u>ποιεῖν</u> ἀγαθὸν τὴν πόλιν εἰς ἀθυμίαν τρέψομεν, εἰ καταψηφιούμεθα. (Dem. 23.194)
The man (*Chersobleptes*), who has now embarked on a course of friendship, and who wants to (be) do(ing) the city a good turn, we will cause to be disheartened, if we are to vote down the decree.

In (39) the aorist inf. ποιῆσαι indicates that the speaker is not interested in the process of providing benefit to the city, but in anyone's aspiration towards the simple fact of it. Example (40), on the other hand, concerns a type of behaviour (present inf. ποιεῖν) which Chersobleptes has already begun (ὡρμηκότα) to display: he wants to provide some benefit to the city, but this provision might be interrupted if the Athenians vote the 'wrong' way.

Note 1: The interpretation attached to the present infinitive in (38) is similar to the 'immediative' nuance of the present imperative, for which →38.30.

Further Particulars

Dynamic Infinitives Expressing Purpose or Result

51.16   A dynamic infinitive is added regularly to verbs meaning 'give', 'entrust', 'take', 'receive', etc., or verbs meaning 'have (at one's disposal)', to express **purpose or result** (without ὥστε or ὡς). This use of the infinitive is usually called **final-consecutive**:

(41) ταύτην τὴν χώραν <u>ἐπέτρεψε</u> <u>διαρπάσαι</u> τοῖς Ἕλλησιν. (Xen. *An.* 1.2.19)
That country he left to the Greeks to plunder.

(42) οἱ στρατιῶται ἤχθοντο, ὅτι <u>οὐκ εἶχον</u> ἀργύριον <u>ἐπισιτίζεσθαι</u> εἰς τὴν πορείαν. (Xen. *An.* 7.1.7)
The soldiers were angry, because they did not have money to provision themselves for the journey.

Note 1: This use may be seen – rather than as a special use of the infinitive – as a special construction of the relevant verbs of giving, entrusting, etc. Thus, for instance, in (41) ἐπέτρεψε is construed with a subject ('he'), object (ταύτην τὴν χώραν), indirect object (τοῖς Ἕλλησιν) and a fourth obligatory constituent in the infinitive (διαρπάσαι).

Note 2: Especially in poetry, final-consecutive infinitives are sometimes added more freely – i.e. after other kinds of verbs (and adjectives/nouns):

(43) ἀρχόμεσθ' ἐκ κρεισσόνων | καὶ ταῦτ' <u>ἀκούειν</u> κἄτι τῶνδ' ἀλγίονα. (Soph. *Ant.* 63–4)

We are ruled by men who are more powerful, so that we (must) obey in these things and things more painful than these still. *The infinitive expresses the result of the men's superior power (κρεισσόνων).*

Note 3: The final-consecutive infinitive is sometimes called 'epexegetical' ('added to explain'): however, this term, if used at all, is best reserved for the infinitive limiting the meaning of adverbs and nouns, for which →51.18.

51.17   Sometimes, ὥστε is added to make explicit the consecutive value of a dynamic infinitive although it follows a verb belonging to one of the classes listed in 51.8. In such cases ὥστε is redundant (and need not be translated):

(44) ὁ Πειθίας ... <u>πείθει</u> ὥστε τῷ νόμῳ <u>χρήσασθαι</u>. (Thuc. 3.70.5)

Pithias persuades (them) to use the law. *πείθω is regularly followed by a 'bare' infinitive.*

Dynamic Infinitives Specifying Adjectives and Nouns

51.18   Especially in poetry, the dynamic infinitive is sometimes used to **limit or specify** the meaning of an adjective or noun (other than those with the types of meaning listed in 51.9); the infinitive in this use is often called **epexegetic(al)**:

(45) λευκόπωλος ἡμέρα | πᾶσαν κατέσχε γαῖαν <u>εὐφεγγὴς</u> <u>ἰδεῖν</u>. (Aesch. *Pers.* 386–7)

White-horsed day, bright to see, covered the entire earth.

(46) ΚΛ. ἐν Αἰγύπτῳ δὲ δὴ πῶς τὸ τοιοῦτον φῂς νενομοθετῆσθαι; :: ΑΘ. <u>θαῦμα</u> καὶ <u>ἀκοῦσαι</u>. (Pl. *Leg.* 656d)

(Clinias:) How then do you say that this matter is legislated in Egypt? :: (Athenian:) It is a wonder even to hear it.

In such cases the infinitive does not express purpose or result; in sense this use is similar to the accusative of respect, for which →30.14.

Note 1: Such infinitives tend to be active in form, even though they typically depend on a noun or adjective referring to the 'object' of the infinitive (note the translation 'hear *it*' in (46)); also →51.9 n.1 above.

The Declarative Infinitive

Verbs Taking a Declarative Infinitive

51.19   The declarative (accusative and) infinitive is used in indirect discourse (→41.1) after **verbs of opinion** and **verbs of believing**, and after certain **verbs of speech**:

– **verbs of opinion and believing**, e.g.:

γιγνώσκω	judge that
λογίζομαι	reckon that, guess that
νομίζω	believe that
ἡγέομαι	believe that, be of the opinion that
οἴομαι/οἶμαι	think that
πιστεύω	believe that, trust that
ὑπολαμβάνω	assume that, grasp that
ὑποπτεύω	suspect that

To this group belong also verbs meaning 'seem', i.e. verbs relating to the belief or opinion of someone other than the subject:

φαίνομαι	seem (+ *dat.; for the difference with* φαίνομαι + *ppl.,* →52.24)
δοκέω	seem (+ *dat.; for other constructions of* δοκέω/δοκεῖ, →51.30)

– **declarative utterance verbs, i.e. verbs of speech**, e.g.:

ἀγγέλλω	report that, announce that
ἀκούω	hear (*in the sense* be told that)
δηλόω	make clear that
λέγω	say that
φημί	say that, claim that

For verbs of denying, →51.34–6.

Note 1: Verbs of speech, apart from φημί, more regularly take a ὅτι/ὡς-clause. The declarative infinitive occurs for the most part when it does not represent an actual utterance, but an opinion or a rumour (in other words, when the verb is used more as a verb of opinion). The infinitive frequently occurs in this way with ἀκούω (in the sense *be told*) and λέγω (especially with the forms λέγουσι *they say* and λέγεται *it is said*), but much less frequently with εἶπον. The infinitive is the standard construction with φημί (ὅτι/ὡς-clauses are very rare with this verb), because the verb usually means *claim* (rather than *utter*), and with πείθω *convince* (for this verb, →51.32):

(47) Κριτίαν ... ἀπέτρεπε φάσκων ἀνελεύθερόν τε εἶναι καὶ οὐ πρέπον ... τὸν ἐρώμενον ... προσαιτεῖν ὥσπερ τοὺς πτωχούς ... τοῦ δὲ Κριτίου τοῖς τοιούτοις οὐχ ὑπακούοντος οὐδὲ ἀποτρεπομένου, λέγεται τὸν Σωκράτην ἄλλων τε πολλῶν παρόντων καὶ τοῦ Εὐθυδήμου εἰπεῖν ὅτι ὑικὸν αὐτῷ δοκοίη πάσχειν ὁ Κριτίας. (Xen. *Mem.* 1.2.29–30)

He tried to restrain Critias by saying that it was mean and unbecoming to approach one's beloved like a beggar. But when Critias paid no heed to such words and was not restrained, it is said that Socrates said, in the presence of

Euthydemus and many others, that he thought that Critias had the sentiments of a pig. φάσκων, *followed (as almost always) by an infinitive, refers to a general claim Socrates made about what is and what is not fitting;* λέγεται, *followed by an infinitive* (εἰπεῖν), *refers to a rumour about Socrates;* εἰπεῖν *itself, followed by a* ὅτι-*clause, refers to a single utterance made by Socrates.*

Expression of the Subject with Declarative Infinitives

51.20   When the subject of the infinitive and the matrix verb governing it are the same (when they are **co-referential**), the subject of the infinitive is **not separately expressed**:

(48) ὑπώπτευον γὰρ ἤδη ἐπὶ βασιλέα <u>ἰέναι</u>. (Xen. *An.* 1.3.1)
For they already suspected that they were on their way to attack the king.

(49) ὁ Ἀσσύριος εἰς τὴν χώραν . . . <u>ἐμβαλεῖν</u> ἀγγέλλεται. (Xen. *Cyr.* 5.3.30)
It is reported that the Assyrian will invade the country. *Note the passive: lit. 'The Assyrian is reported . . .'.*

Any predicative complements or modifiers with the subject (which must agree with the subject) naturally also occur in the nominative (the **nominative-and-infinitive** construction):

(50) ἀλλὰ <u>φημὶ</u> μὲν ἔγωγε, ὦ Σώκρατες, καὶ αὐτὸς <u>τοιοῦτος εἶναι</u> οἷον σὺ ὑφηγῇ. (Pl. *Grg.* 458b)
But, Socrates, I myself too claim that I am the sort of man you are suggesting.

Note 1: Naturally, declarative infinitives of **impersonal verbs** (→36) also do not have an explicitly expressed subject (as they have no subject at all): so e.g. the frequent phrase οἶμαι δεῖν (+ accusative-and-infinitive) *I think that it is necessary . . .*, with δεῖν representing impersonal δεῖ in the indirect discourse construction dependent on οἶμαι.

51.21   In the vast majority of cases, the subject of a declarative infinitive is not the same as that of the matrix verb: in this case, the subject is **separately expressed in the accusative** (**accusative-and-infinitive** construction):

(51) ἐκ τούτων δὲ τῶν λίθων ἔφασαν <u>τὴν πυραμίδα</u> <u>οἰκοδομηθῆναι</u> <u>τὴν ἐν μέσῳ τῶν τριῶν ἑστηκυῖαν</u>. (Hdt. 2.126.2)
They said that the pyramid standing in the middle of the three had been built from these stones. τὴν πυραμίδα . . . τὴν . . . ἑστηκυῖαν *is subject of* οἰκοδομηθῆναι; *the entire accusative-and-infinitive construction complements* ἔφασαν.

(52) <u>ἥξειν</u> νομίζεις <u>παῖδα σὸν</u> γαίας ὕπο; (Eur. *Her.* 296)
Do you think your son will return from beneath the earth? παῖδα σόν *is subject of* ἥξειν; *the entire accusative-and-infinitive construction complements* νομίζεις.

Any predicative complements or modifiers with the subject of the infinitive (which must agree with the subject) naturally also occur in the accusative:

(53) πονηρὰν μὲν φήσομεν οὕτω γίγνεσθαι δόξαν, πονηρὰν δὲ καὶ ἡδονήν; (Pl. *Phlb.* 37d)

Shall we say that in this way opinion becomes bad, and that pleasure becomes bad as well? *πονηρὰν agrees with δόξαν and ἡδονήν, respectively, the subjects of γίγνεσθαι.*

Negatives with the Declarative Infinitive

51.22   The **negative** with the declarative infinitive is normally **οὐ** (as it would be in corresponding direct statements):

(54) κυάμους . . . οἱ . . . ἱρέες οὐδὲ ὁρέοντες ἀνέχονται, νομίζοντες οὐ καθαρὸν εἶναί μιν ὄσπριον. (Hdt. 2.37.5)

The priests cannot bear even to see beans, believing that it is not a clean kind of legume. *Corresponding direct speech: οὐ καθαρόν ἐστι.*

(55) καὶ νῦν ἤδη τινές λέγουσιν οὐ γιγνώσκειν τὰς διαλλαγὰς αἵτινές εἰσι. (Andoc. 3.36)

And now already, some are saying that they do not understand what the point of the treaty is. *Corresponding direct speech: οὐ γιγνώσκομεν.*

51.23   However, **μή** is sometimes used with the declarative infinitive when it corresponds to an **emphatic declaration** (often in oracles):

(56) πάντες ἐροῦσι τὸ λοιπὸν μηδὲν εἶναι κερδαλεώτερον ἀρετῆς. (Xen. *Cyr.* 7.1.18)

Everyone will say in the future that *nothing* is more profitable than valour.

(57) ἤρετο γὰρ δὴ εἴ τις ἐμοῦ εἴη σοφώτερος. ἀνεῖλεν οὖν ἡ Πυθία μηδένα σοφώτερον εἶναι. (Pl. *Ap.* 21a)

So he asked if anyone was wiser than I am. The Pythia responded that no one was wiser.

This use of μή is fully regular with verbs such as ἐλπίζω *expect*, ὑπισχνέομαι *promise* and ὄμνυμι *swear*, →51.31.

51.24   For μὴ οὐ, τὸ μὴ οὐ, etc. with verbs of denying, →51.34–6.

Note 1: With φημί, when the verb is used to refer to an opinion/claim that something is *not* the case, the negative most often is attached to the matrix verb (φημί) rather than the infinitive. In other words: οὔ φημι = *claim that not, deny that.*

Tense and Aspect of Declarative Infinitives

51.25   The infinitive of **all tense-aspect stems** can be used as declarative infinitive: which stem is used depends on the tense-aspect of the form that would have been used in a corresponding direct statement (i.e. the speech or thought which the infinitive construction represents, →41.1):

(58) ἔφασαν <u>ἐκβάλλειν</u> τοὺς ξεινικοὺς θεούς. (Hdt. 1.172.2)

They said that they were expelling the foreign gods. *Present infinitive* ἐκβάλλειν *represents present indicative* ἐκβάλλομεν *('we are expelling') from a corresponding direct speech.*

(59) τούτους δέ <u>φασιν</u> . . . τοὺς Πεισιστράτου παῖδας <u>ἐκβαλεῖν</u>. (Dem. 21.144)

They say that it is these men who expelled the sons of Pisistratus. *Aorist infinitive* ἐκβαλεῖν *represents aorist indicative* ἐξέβαλον *('they expelled') in a corresponding direct speech.*

51.26   In practice, this means that the various tense-aspect stems typically get a relative-tense interpretation (→33.57):

– The **present infinitive** typically expresses an action which is **simultaneous** with that of the verb of speech/belief/opinion:

(60) οἱ ἄλλοι τοῦτον τὸν χρόνον . . . <u>ἐδόκουν</u> . . . <u>προσκτᾶσθαί</u> τι. (Xen. *Cyr.* 4.3.3)

During that period the others seemed to be gaining something. *Corresponding 'direct speech': pres. ind.* προσκτῶνται.

– The **future infinitive** always expresses an action which is **posterior** to that of the verb of speech/belief/opinion:

(61) . . . ἔχοντες . . . ἔπιπλα καὶ ἱμάτια γυναικεῖα ὅσα οὐδεπώποτε <u>ᾤοντο</u> <u>κτήσεσθαι</u>. (Lys. 12.19)

. . . having more furniture and women's clothing than they ever thought they would get. *Corresponding direct speech: fut. ind.* κτησόμεθα.

– The **aorist infinitive** typically expresses an action which is **anterior** to that of the verb of speech/belief/opinion:

(62) τολμᾷ . . . <u>λέγειν</u> . . . ὑμᾶς . . . ταῦτα ποιήσαντας . . . τιμὴν παρὰ πᾶσιν ἀνθρώποις <u>κτήσασθαι</u>. (Lys. 14.32–3)

He has the temerity to claim that you, by doing these things, have won recognition among all men. *Corresponding direct speech: aor. ind.* ἐκτήσαντο/ἐκτήσασθε.

– The **perfect infinitive** typically expresses a **state** (or lasting effects), **simultaneous** with that of the verb of speech/belief/opinion, resulting from a previous, completed action:

(63) καὶ γὰρ τὰ Ὁμήρου σέ <u>φασιν</u> ἔπη πάντα <u>κεκτῆσθαι</u>. (Xen. *Mem.* 4.2.10)

And in fact, they tell me that you possess a complete copy of Homer. *Corresponding direct speech: pf. ind.* κέκτησαι.

Note 1: There are occasional exceptions to the relative-tense interpretation outlined above (also →33.58–62): in particular, the present declarative infinitive is sometimes used to refer to *habitual* actions preceding the verb of speech/belief/opinion – i.e. when direct speech would have the imperfect:

(64) καὶ τοὺς ἐπὶ τῶν προγόνων ἡμῶν λέγοντας <u>ἀκούω</u> . . . τούτῳ τῷ ἔθει . . . <u>χρῆσθαι</u>. (Dem. 3.21)

And as a matter of fact, I hear that speakers who lived at the time of our forebears used this custom. *Corresponding direct speech: impf. ἐχρῶντο; the action referred to by χρῆσθαι is anterior to that of ἀκούω. This interpretation is required given the presence of the temporal modifier ἐπὶ τῶν προγόνων, which refers to the past.*

Similarly, the perfect infinitive may be used when direct speech would have the pluperfect.

ἄν with the Declarative Infinitive

51.27 The declarative infinitive **may be modified by ἄν**, and then has a **potential** sense (corresponding to a potential optative, →34.13) or a **counterfactual** sense (corresponding to a counterfactual modal indicative, →34.16):

(65) οἶμαι <u>ἄν</u> σε ταῦτα διαπραξάμενον <u>ἀποπλεῖν</u>, εἰ βούλοιο. (Xen. *Hell.* 3.4.5.)

I think that you could sail off having accomplished these things, should you want to. *ἄν . . . ἀποπλεῖν represents ἀποπλέοις ἄν (potential opt. + ἄν) in direct speech (note the 'potential' conditional clause εἰ βούλοιο).*

(66) καὶ πόσα <u>ἄν</u> ἤδη οἴει μοι χρήματα <u>εἶναι</u>, εἰ συνέλεγον χρυσίον ὥσπερ σὺ κελεύεις; (Xen. *Cyr.* 8.2.16)

And how much money do you think I would have already, if I were amassing gold as you're telling me to do? *(But I'm not.) ἄν . . . εἶναι represents ἦν ἄν (counterfactual ind. + ἄν) in direct speech (note the counterfactual conditional clause εἰ συνέλεγον).*

Note 1: In the absence of explicit clues like the conditional clauses in (65) and (66), context must determine whether ἄν + declarative inf. represents a potential or a counterfactual construction:

(67) οἱ δὲ Ἀκαρνᾶνες ἠξίουν Δημοσθένη . . . ἀποτειχίζειν αὐτούς, νομίζοντες ῥᾳδίως γ' <u>ἄν</u> <u>ἐκπολιορκῆσαι</u> καὶ πόλεως αἰεὶ σφίσι πολεμίας <u>ἀπαλλαγῆναι</u>. (Thuc. 3.94.2)

The Acarnanians urged Demosthenes to build a wall around them (*the Leucadians*), believing that they might easily win the place by siege, and be rid of a city continually hostile to them. *ἄν ἐκπολιορκῆσαι καὶ . . . ἀπαλλαγῆναι can in this case only represent potential ἐκπολιορκήσαιμεν ἄν and ἀπαλλαγεῖμεν ἄν 'we may easily win the city by siege', 'we may be rid'; a counterfactual interpretation is impossible.*

Note 2: Note that the tense-aspect stem of the infinitive is identical to that of the direct speech it represents: in (65) present-stem ἀποπλεῖν represents present optative ἀποπλέοις, in (66) present-stem εἶναι represents imperfect (i.e. present-stem) ἦν, in (67) the aorist infinitives ἐκπολιορκῆσαι and ἀπαλλαγῆναι represent aorist optatives ἐκπολιορκήσαιμεν and ἀπαλλαγεῖμεν.

Verbs Taking Both Constructions

51.28   A number of verbs can be followed **either by a dynamic or by a declarative infinitive**. With such verbs, there is a distinction in meaning between the two constructions (the verbs belong to different classes depending on how they are construed). The most important ones are given below.

Note 1: For verbs which may be construed with an infinitive or a participle, →52.22–7.

51.29   **γιγνώσκω:**
- with a declarative inf. = *judge that* (verb of opinion);
- with a dynamic inf. = *resolve to, decide to* (desiderative verb):

(68)   ἔγνωσαν οἱ παραγενόμενοι Σπαρτιητέων Ἀριστόδημον ... ἔργα ἀποδέξασθαι μεγάλα. (Hdt. 9.71.3)
The Spartiates that were there judged that Aristodemus had achieved great feats. *Declarative aorist infinitive; corresponding direct speech: ἀπεδέξατο.*

(69)   οἱ δὲ Κυμαῖοι ἔγνωσαν συμβουλῆς πέρι ἐς θεὸν ἀνοῖσαι τὸν ἐν Βραγχίδῃσι. (Hdt. 1.157.3)
The Cymaeans resolved to appeal to the god at Branchidae as to what counsel they should take. *Dynamic aorist infinitive.*

Note 1: For γιγνώσκω + ppl. *realize that* (and other possible constructions), →52.24 n.2.

51.30   **δοκέω:**
- as an impersonal verb (δοκεῖ/ἔδοξε/δέδοκται), with a dynamic infinitive (and a dative complement) = *it seems good to (someone) to (do something)* > *it is resolved/decided; someone* (dat.) *decides to (do something)* (desiderative verb);
- as a verb with personal forms (e.g. δοκῶ), with a declarative infinitive (and a dative complement) = *seem (to someone) to* > *someone thinks that ...* (verb of (engendering) belief);
- as a verb with personal forms (e.g. δοκῶ), with a declarative (accusative and) infinitive = *think, deem* (verb of belief):

(70)   τοῖσι δὲ στρατηγοῖσι ἐπιλεξαμένοισι τὸ βυβλίον ... ἔδοξε μὴ καταπλῆξαι Τιμόξεινον προδοσίῃ. (Hdt. 8.128.3)
The generals, having read the letter, decided not to condemn Timoxenus with the charge of treason. *Impersonal verb with dative complement (τοῖσι στρατηγοῖσι) and a dynamic infinitive (καταπλῆξαι): note the negative μή and the aspectual interpretation of the aorist stem.*

(71) εἰ μὲν ὅσιά <u>σοι</u> <u>παθεῖν</u> δοκῶ ... (Eur. *Hec.* 788)

If you think that I (*lit. 'if I seem to you to'*) have experienced things that are sanctioned by the gods ... *Personal form with a dative complement and a declarative infinitive. Corresponding direct speech:* ἔπαθον.

(72) ... , <u>τὴν</u> ἐγώ ... | οὐκ <u>ἄν</u> ποτ' ἐς τοσοῦτον αἰκίας <u>πεσεῖν</u> | <u>ἔδοξ</u>'. (Soph. *OC* 747–9)

... , of whom I thought that she could never fall to such a depth of misery. ἔδοξ(α) *is a personal form with a declarative accusative-and-infinitive. Corresponding direct speech:* οὐκ ἂν πέσοι. *Note the negative* οὐκ *and the use of* ἄν (*potential*). *For the relative pronoun* τήν, →28.31.

51.31   **ἐλπίζω** *hope, expect,* **ὑπισχνέομαι** *promise and* **ὄμνυμι** *swear, state under oath* are followed:

– regularly, by a declarative infinitive – most often with the future infinitive: ἐλπίζω = *expect that* (verb of belief), ὑπισχνέομαι = *promise that* (declarative utterance verb), ὄμνυμι = *swear that* (declarative utterance verb);
– sometimes, by a dynamic infinitive – only when the subjects of the infinitive and matrix verb are co-referential (→51.10): ἐλπίζω = *expect, plan to* (desiderative verb), ὑπισχνέομαι = *promise to* (desiderative/manipulative verb), ὄμνυμι = *swear to* (desiderative/manipulative verb).

Either way, the infinitive with these verbs **always has negative μή**:

(73) ... <u>ἐλπίζων</u> τὸν θεὸν μᾶλλόν τι τούτοισι <u>ἀνακτήσεσθαι</u>. (Hdt. 1.50.1)

... expecting that with such things he would win the god over even more. *Declarative future infinitive.*

(74) τὸ Ῥήγιον <u>ἤλπιζον</u> πεζῇ τε καὶ ναυσὶν ἐφορμοῦντες ῥᾳδίως <u>χειρώσασθαι</u>. (Thuc. 4.24.4)

They expected to capture Rhegium without difficulty, investing it both by land and by sea. *Dynamic aorist infinitive.*

(75) <u>ὑπισχνοῦντο</u> μηδὲν χαλεπὸν αὐτοὺς <u>πείσεσθαι</u>. (Xen. *Hell.* 4.4.5)

They promised that they would suffer no harm. *Declarative future infinitive; note the negative.*

Note 1: Observe that if such a verb is followed by an accusative-and-infinitive construction, it must be interpreted as a declarative infinitive:

(76) <u>ὄμνυσιν</u> ... | <u>μὴ</u> πώποτ' ἀμείνον' ἔπη τούτων κωμῳδικὰ <u>μηδέν'</u> <u>ἀκοῦσαι</u> (Ar. *Vesp.* 1046–7)

He swears ... that no one has ever heard any comic poetry better than that. *Declarative aorist infinitive.*

51.32   Several **verbs of speaking** (i.e. declarative utterance verbs), especially λέγω/εἶπον, but normally not φημί, can also be construed as **verbs of commanding** (i.e.

manipulative verbs) with a dynamic infinitive: thus λέγω + declarative inf. or ὅτι/ ὡς-clause = *say that*; λέγω + dat. + dynamic inf. = *tell (someone) to*.

(77) τούτοις ἔλεγον πλεῖν τὴν ταχίστην ἐφ᾽ Ἑλλησπόντου. (Dem. 19.150)
I told them to sail for the Hellespont as quickly as possible.

(78) εἶπον μηδένα τῶν ὄπισθεν κινεῖσθαι. (Xen. *Cyr.* 2.2.8)
I gave instructions that no one of those behind should make a move. *μηδένα (note the negative with a dynamic infinitive) is subject-accusative of κινεῖσθαι (the person to whom the command was addressed would have been expressed in the dative).*

To this group also belongs πείθω + acc. + declarative (accusative and) infinitive = *convince someone that (something is the case)* (declarative utterance verb); πείθω + acc. + dynamic infinitive = *persuade someone to (do something)* (manipulative verb):

(79) οἱ δὲ τοῦ δήμου προστάται πείθουσιν αὐτὸν πέντε μὲν ναῦς τῶν αὐτοῦ σφίσι καταλιπεῖν . . . , ἴσας δὲ αὐτοὶ πληρώσαντες ἐκ σφῶν αὐτῶν ξυμπέμψειν. (Thuc. 3.75.2)
The leaders of the people persuaded him to leave them five of his ships and they convinced him that they on their part would man and send with him an equal number of their own ships. *In this unusual example, πείθουσιν is followed first by a dynamic infinitive (καταλιπεῖν), and then immediately by a declarative (nominative-plus-)infinitive (αὐτοὶ . . . ξυμπέμψειν; corresponding direct speech: ξυμπέμψομεν).*

51.33   **μέλλω** *be about/going/likely to, plan to, wait to, delay* may be construed with:

– a future infinitive (very regularly):

(80) μέλλω . . . ὑμᾶς διδάξειν ὅθεν μοι ἡ διαβολὴ γέγονεν. (Pl. *Ap.* 21b)
I am going to tell you what the source of the prejudice against me is.

(81) Σοφοκλέα δὲ . . . ἐπὶ τῶν πλειόνων νεῶν ἀποπέμψειν ἔμελλον. (Thuc. 3.115.5)
As for Sophocles, they were going to send him out with the main body of the fleet.

– a dynamic infinitive (μέλλω + pres. inf. is common, and means *be about to*; μέλλω + aor. inf. is rare, and normally has a connotation of inevitability – *be doomed to*):

(82) Σκόπει δὲ ὃ μέλλω λέγειν. :: Λέγε, ἔφη. (Pl. *Resp.* 473c)
'Examine what I am about to say.' :: 'Go ahead and speak,' he said.

(83) καὶ ἐν τῷ παρόντι καιρῷ, ὡς ἤδη ἔμελλον μετὰ κινδύνων ἀλλήλους ἀπολιπεῖν, μᾶλλον αὐτοὺς ἐσῄει τὰ δεινὰ ἢ ὅτε ἐψηφίζοντο πλεῖν. (Thuc. 6.31.1)
And in the present moment, when they were set to leave each other amidst their dangers, the magnitude of it entered upon them more than when they had been voting to sail.

The Infinitive with Verbs of Preventing and Denying

51.34   Some common verbs meaning 'prevent', 'hinder', 'forbid', 'abstain from', etc. and verbs meaning 'dispute', 'deny', etc. are:

Preventing/hindering/abstaining/etc.		*Denying/disputing/etc.*	
ἀναβάλλομαι	*delay*	ἀντιλέγω/ἀντεῖπον	*contradict, dispute*
ἀπαγορεύω	*forbid*	ἀμφισβητέω	*dispute*
ἀπεῖπον (*no present*)	*forbid*	(ἀπ-/ἐξ-/κατ-)ἀρνέομαι	*deny*
ἀπέχομαι	*refrain/abstain from*	ἔξαρνός εἰμι	*deny*
ἀπέχω	*prevent*		
εἴργω	*prevent, cut off from*		
οὐκ ἐάω	*forbid*		
φυλάττομαι	*beware of*		

Note 1: For κωλύω *prevent, hinder* and παύω *prevent, hinder*, →51.36 n.1.
Note 2: Another common construction meaning 'deny' is οὔ φημι *say that not, deny that* (→51.24 n.1); this is, however, not construed according to the rules given below, but always with a declarative (accusative and) infinitive.

51.35   The most common construction with such verbs is **μή + infinitive** (verbs of preventing, hindering, etc.: + dynamic infinitive; verbs of denying, etc.: + declarative infinitive). The negative in Greek conveys the 'not-occurring' of the action (in being prevented or denied); in English translation, μή normally cannot be translated as a negative:

(84)   ἀλλ' ἀπαγορεύω μὴ ποιεῖν ἐκκλησίαν | τοῖς Θραξὶ περὶ μισθοῦ. (Ar. *Ach.* 169–70)
        But I forbid having a meeting of parliament about paying wages to the Thracians. *Dynamic infinitive.*

(85)   τὸν νοῦν τ' ἀπείργει μὴ λέγειν ἃ βούλεται. (Eur. fr. 88a Kannicht)
        He prevents his mind from speaking what it wants. *Dynamic infinitive.*

(86)   φῄς, ἢ καταρνῇ μὴ δεδρακέναι τάδε; (Soph. *Ant.* 442)
        Do you admit or do you deny that you are responsible for these acts? *Declarative infinitive.*

When a verb of preventing, hindering or denying **is itself negated**, it is followed by **μὴ οὐ** (neither negative can be translated as such):

(87)   οὐκ ἄν ποτ' ἔσχον μὴ οὐ τάδ' ἐξειπεῖν πατρί. (Eur. *Hipp.* 658)
        I would never have refrained from divulging this to my father. *Dynamic infinitive; negated verb of preventing.*

(88)   τῶν δὲ φρατέρων οὐδεὶς ἀντεῖπεν οὐδ' ἠμφεσβήτησε μὴ οὐκ ἀληθῆ ταῦτα εἶναι. (Isae. 8.19)
        No one of the phratry denied or disputed that these things were true. *Declarative infinitive; negated verb of denying.*

51.36   Some other constructions that are more or less common with such verbs:

- **τὸ μή** + **infinitive**, or, when the matrix verb itself is negated, τὸ μὴ οὐ + inf. (for the article, →51.38–9):

(89) καὶ ἡμῶν οἱ πολλοὶ . . . οἷοί τε ἦσαν <u>κατέχειν</u> <u>τὸ μὴ</u> <u>δακρύειν</u>, ὡς δὲ . . . (Pl. *Phd.* 117c)

And most of us had been able to refrain from crying, but when . . .

(90) ἐκόμπασε, | <u>μηδ</u>’ ἂν τὸ σεμνὸν πῦρ νιν <u>εἰργαθεῖν</u> Διὸς | <u>τὸ μὴ οὐ</u> . . . <u>ἐλεῖν</u> πόλιν. (Eur. *Phoen.* 1174–6)

He boasted that not even the holy flame of Zeus could prevent him from taking the city.

- similarly, in the genitive, **τοῦ μή** or **τοῦ μὴ οὐ** + **inf.**:

(91) πᾶς γὰρ ἀσκὸς δύ’ ἄνδρας ἕξει <u>τοῦ μὴ</u> <u>καταδῦναι</u>. (Xen. *An.* 3.5.11)

For each wineskin will prevent two men from going under.

- sometimes, with **ὥστε μή** + **inf.**:

(92) εἰ μέλλοιμεν τούτους <u>εἴργειν</u> <u>ὥστε μὴ</u> <u>δύνασθαι</u> βλάπτειν ἡμᾶς πορευομένους . . . (Xen. *An.* 3.3.16)

If we should plan to prevent them from being able (*lit.* ‘so that they are unable’) to harm us on our way . . . *For the redundant use of ὥστε,* →51.17.

- sometimes, with a **bare infinitive** (i.e. without μή):

(93) ὀλίγους ἐπὶ Ὀλύνθου ἀποπέμπουσιν, ὅπως <u>εἴργωσι</u> τοὺς ἐκεῖθεν <u>ἐπιβοηθεῖν</u>. (Thuc. 1.62.4)

They sent a few men to Olynthus, to prevent the people there from coming to aid.

Note 1: The verbs κωλύω *prevent, hinder* and παύω *prevent, hinder* are usually construed with a bare infinitive – observe that παύω is much more frequently construed as a ‘phase’ verb with a participle (*make someone stop doing something*; →52.9):

(94) χάριν δὲ <u>δοῦναι</u> τήνδε <u>κωλύει</u> τί σε; (Eur. *IT* 507)

What hinders you from giving me this favour?

(95) ῥαψῳδοὺς <u>ἔπαυσε</u> ἐν Σικυῶνι <u>ἀγωνίζεσθαι</u> τῶν Ὁμηρείων ἐπέων εἵνεκα. (Hdt. 5.67.1)

He prevented rhapsodes from holding contests at Sicyon because of the Homeric poems.

The Construction of Verbs of Hindering/Preventing with Other Verbs

51.37   Several verbs (or nouns/adjectives), which are by themselves **not verbs of hindering or preventing**, have meanings very similar to such verbs when followed by μή + dynamic infinitive: e.g. δύναμαι μή + inf. *be able not to* is similar in sense to *abstain from*. Accordingly, there is a great deal of overlap between the construction of verbs of hindering/denying and other verbs followed by μή.

In particular, when such a matrix verb is itself **negated**, the negative with the dynamic infinitive is frequently **μὴ οὐ** (one of these negatives must often be translated):

(96) οὐδεὶς οἷός τ' ἐστὶν ἄλλως λέγων μὴ οὐ καταγέλαστος εἶναι. (Pl. *Grg.* 509a)
No one is able not to sound ridiculous when claiming otherwise.

(97) ἐγὼ μὲν δὴ κατανοῶν τοῦ ἀνδρὸς τήν τε σοφίαν καὶ τὴν γενναιότητα οὔτε μὴ μεμνῆσθαι δύναμαι αὐτοῦ οὔτε μεμνημένος μὴ οὐκ ἐπαινεῖν. (Xen. *Ap.* 34)
When I consider the man's wisdom and nobility, I cannot help but remember him, and praise him when I remember him (*lit.* 'I am not able not to praise him').

Note 1: The use of μὴ οὐ in such cases is by no means consistent: bare μή is often found after a negated matrix verb:

(98) οὔτοι μὰ τὴν Δήμητρα δύναμαι μὴ γελᾶν. (Ar. *Ran.* 42)
By Demeter, I can't help laughing (*lit.* 'I am not able not to laugh')!

Also note μὴ μεμνῆσθαι (not μὴ οὐ μεμνῆσθαι) in (97).

Note 2: The alternative constructions given above also occur, e.g. τὸ μὴ οὐ:

(99) κοὐδείς γέ μ' ἂν πείσειεν ἀνθρώπων τὸ μὴ οὐκ | ἐλθεῖν ἐπ' ἐκεῖνον. (Ar. *Ran.* 68–9)
And no one could persuade me not to go to him.

The Articular Infinitive

Introduction

51.38 The neuter singular article, functioning as a 'substantivizer' (→28.23–5), may be added to an infinitive, turning it, together with its complements/modifiers, into (the head of) a noun phrase. This is called the **articular infinitive**.

The articular infinitive can appear in any case, but only the article changes form: e.g. τὸ παιδεύειν, τοῦ παιδεύειν, τῷ παιδεύειν, τὸ παιδεύειν.

Note 1: The articular infinitive is often best translated into English by a gerund, e.g. τὸ παιδεύειν *educating*. For other possible translations, see of the examples below.
Note 2: Articular infinitives, although substantivized, retain all their **verbal characteristics**. For instance:

- they have voice and tense-aspect; for details, →51.44–5;
- they can take objects/complements in the case normally required by the verb: contrast e.g. τὸ παῖδας παιδεύειν *educating children* (object, acc.) with ἡ παίδων παίδευσις *the education of children* (objective gen.); for the expression of subjects with articular infinitives, →51. 40–1;
- they can be modified by adverbs: e.g. τὸ καλῶς παιδεύειν *educating well*.

51.39   The articular infinitive can be used like any other noun phrase, i.e. as a subject, object, or complement of verbs; as an attributive modifier (in the genitive); to complement prepositions; etc. For example:

(100)   οὐκ ἄρα <u>τὸ χαίρειν</u> ἐστὶν εὖ πράττειν. (Pl. *Grg.* 497a)
So enjoying oneself is not to fare well. *Nominative as subject of ἐστιν.*

(101)   . . . <u>τὸ ζῆν</u> περὶ πλείονος ποιησάμενοι <u>τοῦ καλῶς ἀποθανεῖν</u>. (Andoc. 1.57)
. . . placing a higher value on living than on dying well. *τὸ ζῆν is accusative as object of ποιησάμενοι, τοῦ . . . ἀποθανεῖν genitive of comparison after πλείονος.*

(102)   πολλὰ δ᾿ ἄν τις ἔχοι . . . ἐπιδεικνύναι σημεῖα <u>τοῦ τοῦτον συκοφαντεῖν</u>. (Dem. 36.12)
One could show many proofs that this man is committing slander. *Accusative-and-infinitive construction (→51.41) in the genitive, as attributive modifier of σημεῖα.*

(103)   οὐ λίαν ἔγωγε μέγα ἔργον εἶναι νομίζω <u>τὸ κατηγορεῖν</u>. (Aeschin. 1.44)
I do not consider the accusation to be too great a task. *Accusative as subject of εἶναι.*

For an overview of some particularly frequent uses of the articular infinitive, →51.46.

Expression of Subjects with Articular Infinitives

51.40   Articular infinitives are regularly expressed **without a subject**:

– to refer to an action in general (i.e. when no specific subject is intended): cf. examples (100), (101) and (103) above;
– when the subject of the infinitive is identical to a constituent of the matrix clause (typically the subject):

(104)   καὶ τὴν Θέτιν γ᾿ ἔγημε διὰ <u>τὸ σωφρονεῖν</u> ὁ Πηλεύς. (Ar. *Nub.* 1067)
And Peleus married Thetis on account of his being prudent. *Peleus (the subject of the matrix clause) is understood as the subject of σωφρονεῖν.*

In this case any predicative modifiers/complements take the case of the relevant constituent in the matrix clause (typically the nominative):

(105)   ἐκ <u>τοῦ πρότερος λέγειν</u> ὁ διώκων ἰσχύει. (Dem. 18.7)
The prosecutor is strong due to his being the first to speak. *Nominative πρότερος agrees with ὁ διώκων.*

51.41   In some cases the **infinitive has its own subject**, which is expressed in the accusative (**accusative-and-infinitive construction**); any predicative modifiers/complements naturally also occur in the accusative:

(106) ηὕρισκον οὐδὲν μεῖον Λακεδαιμονίοις ἢ σφίσιν ἀγαθὸν <u>τὸ Ἀρκάδας μὴ</u>
<u>προσδεῖσθαι Θηβαίων</u>. (Xen. *Hell.* 7.4.2)
They found that it was no less a benefit for the Spartans than for themselves
that the Arcadians should not require the help of the Thebans. *The*
accusative Ἀρκάδας is subject of προσδεῖσθαι. For σφίσιν, →29.18.

(107) καὶ ἐπιδεδείχθω ... χαλεπὸν ὂν <u>τὸ πόλιν εὔνομον γίγνεσθαι</u>. (Pl. *Leg.* 712a)
And let it count as proven that it is difficult for a city to become well-
governed. *The accusative πόλιν is subject of γίγνεσθαι, the predicative com-*
plement εὔνομον agrees with πόλιν (εὔνομος is of two endings, →5.7–10).

Negative with the Articular Infinitive

51.42 The **negative** with the articular infinitive is **μή**:

(108) <u>τὸ μὴ κακῶς φρονεῖν</u> | θεοῦ μέγιστον δῶρον. (Aesch. *Ag.* 927–8)
Not to have one's mind go astray is the greatest gift from the god.

(109) ... <u>τοῦ μὴ λύειν</u> ἕνεκα τὰς σπονδάς. (Thuc. 1.45.3)
... for the sake of not breaking the treaty.

51.43 For τὸ μή (οὐ) + inf. and τοῦ μή (οὐ) + inf. after verbs of preventing, hindering or
denying, →51.36.

Tense and Aspect of Articular Infinitives

51.44 In the articular use, like in the dynamic use, the difference between present and
aorist infinitives is often **purely aspectual**:

(110) ... εἰδότες ... ἐν <u>τῷ ποιῆσαι</u> τὴν πόλιν εὐδαίμονα τοὺς χρηστοὺς τῶν
πονηρῶν διαφέροντας ... (Isoc. 8.122)
... knowing that good (leaders) differ from bad ones in making the city
prosperous ...

(111) τίς οὐκ οἶδε ... τοὺς μὲν δημοτικοὺς καλουμένους ἑτοίμους ὄντας ὁτιοῦν
πάσχειν ὑπὲρ <u>τοῦ μὴ ποιεῖν</u> τὸ προσταττόμενον. (Isoc. 7.64)
Who is unaware that 'the people's party', as it was called, was ready to suffer
anything for the sake of not doing what was ordered?

In (110), τῷ ποιῆσαι (aor.) expresses the action of making the city prosperous as
a complete whole (i.e. without reference to its process); the overall evaluation of
good leadership depends on leaders having this trait or not. In (111), ὑπὲρ τοῦ ...
ποιεῖν (pres.) expresses an ongoing, consistent posture of defiance.

51.45 However, when an articular infinitive is used to refer to an action which is actually
taking place or has actually taken place (at a specific time and place), the tense-aspect
stem of the infinitive often also leads to an interpretation of **relative tense** (→33.57):

- the aorist infinitive typically expresses actions anterior to the action of the matrix clause;
- the present infinitive typically expresses actions simultaneous with the matrix clause:

(112) ... τὸ τῶν παρθένων ... μνῆμα, αἲ λέγονται διὰ <u>τὸ βιασθῆναι</u> ὑπὸ Λακεδαιμονίων τινῶν ἀποκτεῖναι ἑαυτάς. (Xen. *Hell.* 6.4.7)

... the memorial for the maidens, of whom it is said that they killed themselves on account of their having been raped by some Spartans. *The aorist infinitive in* τὸ βιασθῆναι *refers to an action preceding the maidens' suicide.*

(113) οὐχ οἷόν τ᾽ ἐστὶν εἰπεῖν τοῦτον τὸν λόγον, ὡς ἡμεῖς μὲν διὰ <u>τὸ δημοκρατεῖσθαι</u> κακῶς ἐχρησάμεθα τοῖς πράγμασιν. (Isoc. 8.95)

The following claim cannot be made, that we managed our affairs poorly on account of our having a democratic constitution. *The present infinitive in* τὸ δημοκρατεῖσθαι *refers to an ongoing form of government, simultaneous with* ἐχρησάμεθα.

Frequent Uses of the Articular Infinitive

51.46   The articular infinitive, as noted above, can be used like any other noun phrase (as subject, object, etc.). It occurs particularly often in the following uses:

- the **dative of the articular infinitive** and **διὰ τό + infinitive** are frequently used as instrumental or causal modifiers:

(114) τὴν ἄνοιαν εὖ φέρειν | <u>τῷ σωφρονεῖν</u> νικῶσα προυνοησάμην. (Eur. *Hipp.* 398–9)

My intention was to bear this madness nobly, overcoming it by means of self-control.

(115) χαλεπῶς δὲ αὐτοῖς <u>διὰ τὸ αἰεὶ εἰωθέναι τοὺς πολλοὺς</u> ἐν τοῖς ἀγροῖς διαιτᾶσθαι ἡ ἀνάστασις ἐγίγνετο. (Thuc. 2.14.2)

But because most of them had been used to living in the fields, their evacuation grieved them.

- the **genitive** of the articular infinitive, especially with the negative (i.e. **τοῦ μή + inf.**), is sometimes used with **purpose** value:

(116) ἐτειχίσθη δὲ καὶ Ἀταλάντη ... <u>τοῦ μὴ λῃστὰς</u> ... <u>κακουργεῖν</u> τὴν Εὔβοιαν. (Thuc. 2.32)

Atalanta, too, was fortified, so that pirates could not plunder Euboea.

- for τὸ μή (οὐ) + inf. and τοῦ μή (οὐ) + inf. after verbs of preventing, hindering or denying, →51.36.

Other Uses of the Infinitive

51.47 The infinitive is occasionally used independently in **commands** (the **imperatival infinitive**):

> (117) σὺ δέ μοι ἐπὶ τὴν Ἑλλάδα στρατεύεσθαι. (Hdt. 3.134.5)
> You must undertake an expedition against Greece.

For details, →38.37.

51.48 The infinitive is infrequently used in **exclamations**:

> (118) τῆς μωρίας, | τὸν Δία νομίζειν ὄντα τηλικουτονί. (Ar. *Nub.* 818–19)
> What madness! To believe in Zeus, at your age!

For details, →38.51.

51.49 Finally, the infinitive is used in some **idiomatic expressions**, for instance:

ὡς (ἔπος) εἰπεῖν	so to say, if I may use this expression, as it were, practically (*often with forms of* πᾶς, '*practically everyone*', οὐδείς, '*practically no one*')
(ὡς) συνελόντι εἰπεῖν	in short, to be brief, to cut to the chase, if I may be brief
τὸ σύμπαν εἰπεῖν	in short, in any case
ὀλίγου δεῖν	almost, practically
ἐμοὶ δοκεῖν	it seems to me
ὡς εἰκάσαι	it seems/appears, so far as one might guess
ἑκὼν εἶναι	voluntarily, willingly, intentionally
τὸ νῦν εἶναι	for the time being

In each of these expressions, the infinitive is used absolutely, i.e. not dependent on a verb, adjective, etc.:

> (119) ἔλαβε ἐκ θεοῦ νέμεσις μεγάλη Κροῖσον, ὡς εἰκάσαι, ὅτι ἐνόμισε ἑωυτὸν εἶναι ἀνθρώπων ἀπάντων ὀλβιώτατον. (Hdt. 1.34.1)
> A great vengeance from the god fell on Croesus, so far as one might guess, because he considered himself to be most blessed of all men.

> (120) πέπεισμαι ἐγὼ ἑκὼν εἶναι μηδένα ἀδικεῖν ἀνθρώπων. (Pl. *Ap.* 37a)
> I am convinced that I do not wrong anyone intentionally.

52

The Participle

Introduction

Basic Properties; Main Uses

52.1   Participles are **verbal adjectives**:

- they are like adjectives in that they are marked for case, number and gender, and follow the rules of agreement (→27.7);
- they are like verbs in that they are marked for tense-aspect and voice, and may be construed with an object, complement, etc.; modified by adverbs; etc.

Note 1: For verbal adjectives in -τός or -τέος, →37.

52.2   The uses of participles may be grouped under three headings:

- **Supplementary** (→52.8–28): the participle is used as an obligatory constituent with verbs:

  (1) ὅλην ἀδικῶν φανήσεται τὴν πόλιν. (Dem. 24.29)
      He will prove to be doing wrong to the city as a whole. *ὅλην ἀδικῶν ... τὴν πόλιν is a complement of φανήσεται.*

- **Circumstantial** (→52.29–45): the participle is added as an optional constituent to clauses to express a circumstance, cause, condition, motivation, purpose, etc. It either agrees with a constituent of the clause (**connected** use) or is added with its own subject in the genitive (**genitive absolute**):

  (2) φίλος ... ἐβούλετο εἶναι τοῖς μέγιστα δυναμένοις, ἵνα ἀδικῶν μὴ διδοίη δίκην. (Xen. *An.* 2.6.26)
      He wanted to befriend those who yielded most power, so that he would not be punished if he did wrong. *ἀδικῶν is a predicative modifier agreeing with the subject of διδοίη ('he'): it can be left out without making the clause ἵνα μὴ διδοίη δίκην ungrammatical. It expresses a condition ('if').*

  (3) αὐτοὶ δ' οὐ δύνανται ... ἡσυχίαν ἄγειν οὐδενὸς αὐτοὺς ἀδικοῦντος. (Dem. 8.67)
      They themselves cannot keep quiet, even though no one is wronging them. *οὐδενὸς αὐτοὺς ἀδικοῦντος is an optional constituent added in the genitive absolute construction (for details, →52.32), expressing a concession ('even though').*

- **Attributive/substantival** (→52.46–50): the participle is used, normally with the article, in noun phrases, as modifier (attributive use) or head (substantival use):

(4) ... βοηθεῖν <u>ταῖς ἀδικουμέναις πόλεσι</u>. (Xen. *Hell.* 6.3.18)

... to help the cities that were being wronged. *Attributive: modifier with* ταῖς πόλεσι.

(5) τίμιος ... <u>ὁ μηδὲν ἀδικῶν</u> (Pl. *Leg.* 730d)

The man who does no wrong is honourable. *Substantival: used as head of a noun phrase.*

Additionally, the participle is used in various **periphrastic constructions**. For these, →52.51–3 below.

Placement of Participles

52.3   Both **circumstantial participles** and **supplementary participles** occur in **predicative position** relative to any (head) noun with which they agree; **attributive participles** naturally occur in **attributive position** (→28.11):

(6) ὁρῶντες ... <u>τοὺς ἑαυτῶν ἱππέας φεύγοντας</u> (Xen. *An.* 4.3.23)

seeing that their own cavalry was fleeing ... *Supplementary participle, predicative position.*

(7) οὔτε οἱ πεζοὶ <u>τοὺς πεζοὺς</u> ἐκ πολλοῦ <u>φεύγοντας</u> ἐδύναντο καταλαμβάνειν. (Xen. *An.* 3.3.9)

The infantry could not overtake the (enemy's) infantry either, because it had a head start in their flight. *Circumstantial participle, predicative position.*

(8) <u>τοὺς δούλους</u> παρέλυσεν | <u>τοὺς φεύγοντας</u>. (Ar. *Pax* 742–3)

He cut loose the slaves who run away. *Attributive participle, attributive position.*

Tense/Aspect and 'Mood' of Participles

52.4   Each of the **tense-aspect stems** has its own participle: the difference between the stems is **aspectual** (except for the future stem). In the case of the participle, these aspectual differences lead to a **relative-tense interpretation** in a large majority of cases (→33.57):

- The **present participle** typically expresses an action **simultaneous** with that of the matrix verb:

(9) ταῦτα <u>γράφων</u> ἔννομα ... ἔγραψα. (Dem. 7.25)

In writing those things I wrote things that were lawful.

- The **aorist participle** usually expresses an action **anterior** to that of the matrix verb:

(10) κἂν δέλτου πτυχαῖς | γράψας ἔπεμψα πρὸς δάμαρτα τὴν ἐμήν. (Eur. *IA* 98–9)
After writing (a message) on a folded tablet, I sent it to my wife.

- The **perfect participle** typically refers to a **state** (or lasting effects), **simultaneous** with the matrix verb, resulting from a previously completed action:

(11) ὑπανέγνω τὸ ψήφισμα ὃ γεγραφὼς αὐτὸς ἦν. (Aeschin. 2.109)
He read aloud the motion of which he himself was the author. *Being the author of something is the state that results from writing it.*

- The **future participle** always has a relative-tense interpretation, referring to an action **posterior** to that of the matrix verb:

(12) οὐδέπω ... δῆλος ἦν ... ἐκεῖνος τοιαῦτα γράψων. (Dem. 19.236)
It was not yet clear that that man was going to draft such proposals.

For the use of the future participle to express purpose, →52.41.

52.5   Although the relative-tense interpretation of the stems of the participle outlined above is usually valid, there are numerous exceptions. In such cases, a different interpretation of a certain tense-aspect stem takes precedence over (or is present in addition to) the conventional relative-tense interpretation:

- The **aorist participle** is not infrequently used to refer to an action which does not precede, but coincides with the action of the matrix verb (so-called **coincident** aorist participle); the aorist is then used to refer to the action in its entirety (→33.6). This is especially frequent with circumstantial participles used as a modifier of manner (→52.42):

(13) Σόλων δὲ οὐδὲν ὑποθωπεύσας, ἀλλὰ τῷ ἐόντι χρησάμενος λέγει· ... (Hdt. 1.30.3)
But Solon, not flattering him in any way, but relying on the truth, said: ...
The 'flattering' and 'truth-using' have not ended before Solon's utterance, but coincide with it.

(14) δοκεῖ μοί τις οὐκ ἂν ἁμαρτεῖν εἰπὼν ὅτι ... (Dem. 25.6)
It seems to me that someone would not be mistaken in saying that ... *εἰπών and (ἂν) ἁμαρτεῖν coincide.*

(15) κτενῶ γὰρ αὐτὸν ... | ποινὰς ἀδελφῶν καὶ πατρὸς λαβοῦσ᾽ ἐμοῦ. (Eur. *Tro.* 359–60)
For I shall kill him, exacting revenge for my brothers and my father. *λαβοῦσ(α) coincides with κτενῶ; the aorist participle here expresses the effect of the matrix verb.*

- The **aorist participle** of atelic verbs may also have an **ingressive** or **complexive** interpretation (→33.29–30):

(16) καὶ ὁ Ἰσχόμαχος γελάσας εἶπεν· Ἀλλὰ παίζεις μὲν σύγε, ἔφη, ὦ Σώκρατες. (Xen. *Oec.* 17.10)
And Ischomachus burst out laughing and said: 'But you're being playful, Socrates.' *Ingressive interpretation.*

(17) τῶν δ᾽ ἐμῶν προγόνων ἀκούω <u>τὸν πρῶτον βασιλεύσαντα</u> ἅμα τε βασιλέα καὶ ἐλεύθερον γενέσθαι. (Xen. *Cyr.* 7.2.24)

I am told that the first of my ancestors to have been king was both a king and a free man. *Complexive interpretation: βασιλεύσαντα refers to the kingship in its entirety. An ingressive interpretation ('the first . . . to have become king') would also be possible.*

- A **present participle** may be used to refer to an ongoing, habitual or repeated action (→33.11) preceding the action of the matrix verb; the present participle in such cases is sometimes called an 'imperfect participle'. An explicit indication of anteriority is usually present:

(18) . . . ὥστε φίλος ἡμῖν οὐδεὶς λελείψεται, ἀλλὰ καὶ <u>οἱ πρόσθεν ὄντες</u> πολέμιοι ἡμῖν ἔσονται. (Xen. *An.* 2.4.5)

. . . so that we will have no friend left, but even those who were our friends before will be hostile to us. *Attributive ὄντες is anterior to ἔσονται; this interpretation is forced by πρόσθεν.*

(19) οἱ Κορίνθιοι <u>μέχρι τούτου</u> προθύμως <u>πράσσοντες</u> ἀνεῖσαν τῆς φιλονικίας καὶ ὡρρώδησαν. (Thuc. 5.32.4)

The Corinthians, although they had acted with zeal up to this point, now slackened in their desire for victory and became anxious. *πράσσοντες is anterior to ἀνεῖσαν and ὡρρώδησαν, as is made clear by μέχρι τούτου.*

(20) τὴν γὰρ χώραν οἱ αὐτοὶ αἰεὶ <u>οἰκοῦντες</u> διαδοχῇ τῶν ἐπιγιγνομένων <u>μέχρι τοῦδε</u> ἐλευθέραν δι᾽ ἀρετὴν παρέδοσαν. (Thuc. 2.36.1)

For those same people, who dwelt in the country continuously, passed it on in freedom, on account of their valour, handing it over from generation to generation until the present time. *μέχρι τοῦδε makes it clear that οἱ οἰκοῦντες refers to several generations in the past; note the distributive use of αἰεί, referring to those who dwelt in the land on each given occasion.*

- **Present participles** of telic verbs may also have a **conative** interpretation, or an interpretation as a **resultative** present (→33.17–18):

(21) ἐμοῦ τ᾽ <u>ἐκδιδόντος</u> τὸν παῖδα . . . βασανίζειν . . . οὐκ ἠθέλησε παραλαβεῖν. (Dem. 29.18)

And when I offered my slave for torture, he did not want to accept him. *Conative interpretation: the speaker attempts to give up his slave but is rebuffed.*

(22) ἐπειδὴ ἔμαθε ἀπολωλότας τοὺς Πέρσας καὶ <u>νικῶντας</u> τοὺς Ἕλληνας, . . . (Hdt. 9.76.1)

When she learned that the Persians had perished and that the Greeks had won, . . . *Resultative present; note that νικῶντας is used in conjunction with the perfect participle ἀπολωλότας.*

- For the aspectual values of supplementary participles following verbs of perception, →52.18–21.

52.6   Just as the tense expressed by a participle is, as outlined above, normally relative to the matrix verb, the **modality** (in a broad sense) of a participle is also usually (if not always) relative to the matrix verb:

(23) ἰδού· λαβὼν ἔκπιθι καὶ μηδὲν λίπῃς. (Eur. *Cyc.* 570)

Here you go: take it and drink up, and don't leave anything. *The matrix verb is an imperative, and the 'mood' expressed by the circumstantial participle λαβών depends on it: λαβών is part of the command. For the translation with a main verb (in this case an imperative), cf. (99) below.*

(24) μὴ οὖν ὕστερον τοῦτο γνῶτε, ἀναίτιόν με ὄντα <u>ἀπολέσαντες</u>. (Antiph. 5.71)

Do not, then, discover later that you have destroyed me even though I was innocent. *ἀπολέσαντες is supplementary to μὴ γνῶτε, and as such expresses a hypothetical discovery, one which the speaker implores the judges not to have to make. When he says this, the judges have obviously not 'destroyed' him yet by returning a guilty verdict.*

Also cf. (29) and (109) below.

ἄν with Participles

52.7   The participle (in any of its uses) may be **joined with ἄν**, and then has the force either of a potential optative (→34.13) or a counterfactual indicative (→34.16):

(25) καὶ <u>ὁρῶν</u> τὸ παρατείχισμα τῶν Συρακοσίων ... ῥᾳδίως <u>ἄν</u> ... <u>ληφθέν</u> ... (Thuc. 7.42.4)

And seeing that the fortification of the Syracusans might easily be taken ... *ἄν ληφθέν is supplementary with ὁρῶν, and represents ληφθείη ἄν (potential opt. + ἄν). For more on supplementary participles + ἄν, → 52.10 n.1.*

(26) Ποτείδαιαν ... ἑλὼν καὶ <u>δυνηθεὶς</u> <u>ἄν</u> αὐτὸς ἔχειν, εἴπερ ἐβουλήθη, παρέδωκεν. (Dem. 23.107)

Having taken Potidaea, and even though he would have been able to keep it by himself, had he wanted to, he gave it up. *δυνηθεὶς ἄν is circumstantial, and represents ἐδυνήθη ἄν (counterfactual ind. + ἄν).*

The Supplementary Participle

Introduction; Verbs Taking a Supplementary Participle

52.8   The use of the supplementary participle can be broadly divided into three categories:

- to complement verbs expressing direct sensory perception ('see', 'hear'), verbs expressing some phase of an action ('begin', 'continue', 'stop') and verbs meaning to 'endure', 'persist', etc.;
- to complement verbs meaning 'know', 'recognize', 'make clear', etc. and verbs that express an emotional state ('be glad', 'regret', etc.);
- to complement a few verbs that express a certain manner of being or acting (τυγχάνω *happen to*, λανθάνω *be hidden*, φθάνω *anticipate*).

The supplementary participles with the first and second of these groups are different in nature (→51.3 for a similar distinction between the dynamic and declarative infinitive):

- with the first group, the participle expresses an **action**, the realization of which is seen, heard, stopped, begun, endured, etc.;
- with the second group, the participle expresses the **propositional content** of someone's **knowledge of, or emotional response to, an action**.

All supplementary participles have in common that they specify that the action is actually realized or that the propositional content is true:

(27) καὶ τῶν τις Σκυθέων . . . ἐσήμηνε τῷ βασιλέϊ Σαυλίῳ· ὁ δὲ καὶ αὐτὸς ἀπικόμενος ὡς <u>εἶδε</u> τὸν Ἀνάχαρσιν <u>ποιεῦντα</u> ταῦτα, τοξεύσας αὐτὸν ἀπέκτεινε. (Hdt. 4.76.5)

One of the Scythians told the king, Saulius. And when he came to the scene in person and saw Anacharsis doing this, he shot and killed him. *ποιεῦντα refers to an action actually taking place, which is perceived visually by Saulius when he arrives on the scene.*

(28) μάγους μὲν γὰρ ἀτρεκέως <u>οἶδα</u> ταῦτα <u>ποιέοντας</u>· ἐμφανέως γὰρ δὴ ποιεῦσι. (Hdt. 1.140.2)

I know with certainty that the Magi do this. For they do it out in the open. *ποιέοντας expresses the content of Herodotus' knowledge, which he presents as fact.*

Note 1: The participle differs in this respect from dynamic and declarative infinitives, which do not specify the actions they express as realized or the propositional content they express as true (→51.3).

Note 2: Some verbs may be complemented by both kinds of participle; the difference in complement corresponds to a difference in meaning of the matrix verb. For details, →52.18–20.

Note 3: The factuality expressed by a participle may (but need not) be cancelled if the matrix verb itself is not realized, counterfactual, etc. (for this modal dependency, →52.6):

(29) καὶ ἡμῖν γ᾿ ἂν οἶδ᾿ ὅτι τρισάσμενος ταῦτ᾿ ἐποίει, εἰ <u>ἑώρα</u> ἡμᾶς μένειν <u>κατασκευαζομένους</u>. (Xen. *An.* 3.2.24)

And, surely, he would be three times more willing to do these things for us, if he saw us make preparations to stay. *The speaker, using a counterfactual conditional (→49.10), imagines what would happen if the Persian king saw the Greeks making preparations to settle in the king's country. The king is not described as actually seeing anything, nor, as the previous context shows, are the Greeks actually making preparations to stay.*

(30) Κῦρος δὲ αὐτός . . . ἀπέθανε . . . οὐ . . . <u>ᾔδεσαν</u> αὐτὸν <u>τεθνηκότα</u>. (Xen. *An.* 1.8.27, 1.10.16)

And Cyrus himself perished . . . They did not know that he was dead. *Xenophon first reports that Cyrus is among the fallen of the battle of Cunaxa; several sections later he mentions that some of his soldiers did not know that Cyrus had died. The factuality of the participle τεθνηκότα is not affected by the negation of ᾔδεσαν.*

Verbs Taking a Supplementary Participle which Expresses an Action which is Realized

52.9   With the following verbs, a supplementary participle expresses an action which is realized:

- verbs of direct **sensory perception** – the subject perceives an action occurring (almost exclusively with pres. ppl.):

αἰσθάνομαι	perceive, hear (+ *gen.*), see (+ *acc.*; →52.20)
ἀκούω	hear (+ *gen.*; →52.14)
ὁράω	see
πυνθάνομαι	perceive, hear, see

- so-called **phase verbs** – the verb expresses some phase of the action (beginning, continuation or end), e.g. (only with pres. ppl.):

ἄρχομαι	begin
διατελέω	continue, go on
λήγω	stop, cease
παύω	stop (someone (*acc.*) from doing something)
παύομαι	stop, cease

To this category also belong verbs meaning **endure, persist, allow, give up**:

ἀνέχομαι	endure, bear
ἀπαγορεύω	give up
ἀπεῖπον (*no present*)	get tired of, fail to
περιοράω	allow, permit, stand idly by while

(31) ὁρῶ γὰρ αὐτὸν πρὸς δόμους <u>στείχοντ'</u> ἐμούς. (Eur. *Phoen.* 696)
For I see him coming to my halls. *Verb of sensory perception.*

(32) ὁ νόμος οὗτος <u>διατελέει ἐὼν</u> ὅμοιος τὸ μέχρι ἐμεῦ ἀπ' ἀρχῆς. (Hdt. 2.113.3)
This law has continued to be the same from its beginning to my time. *Phase verb.*

(33) μόνον δὴ τὸ αὐτὸ κινοῦν, ἅτε οὐκ ἀπολεῖπον ἑαυτό, οὔποτε <u>λήγει κινούμενον</u>. (Pl. *Phdr.* 245c)
Only that which moves itself, given that it never leaves itself, never ceases to move. *Phase verb.*

(34) νῦν δ' οὖν οὔ σε <u>περιόψομαι</u> | γυμνὸν <u>ὄνθ'</u> οὕτως. (Ar. *Lys.* 1019–20)
But right now, I won't permit you to be naked like this. *Verb in the group 'endure', etc.*

Note 1: Verbs of perception are also often used as verbs of knowledge: →52.18–19.

Verbs Taking a Supplementary Participle which Expresses Propositional Content

52.10   With the following verbs, the supplementary participle expresses the propositional content of someone's knowledge of, or emotional reaction to, an action:

– verbs of **intellectual knowledge** – the subject learns, discovers, knows or understands that something is the case:

οἶδα	know that
ἐπίσταμαι	understand that
γιγνώσκω	know that, recognize that, realize that, find that
μανθάνω	learn that
μέμνημαι	remember that
αἰσθάνομαι	learn that, find that, become aware of the fact that (+ *acc.*, →52.20)
ἀκούω	learn (by being told) that (+ *acc.*, →52.19)
ὁράω	see that, acknowledge that
πυνθάνομαι	learn that, realize that, be told that

To this category also belong verbs meaning **make it clear that, it is clear that, be clear**: the subject in this case conveys knowledge that something is the case:

ἀγγέλλω	report that (*for* ἀγγέλλω + *inf.*, →52.25)
δείκνυμι	make it clear that
δῆλός εἰμι	be clearly, it is clear that I am (doing something)
φαίνομαι	be clearly, be obviously, prove/turn out to be (doing something)
φανερός εἰμι	be clearly, it is clear that I am (doing something)

– Verbs expressing an **emotional state** – the subject has a certain emotional attitude to the fact that something is the case:

αἰσχύνομαι	be ashamed that
ἄχθομαι	be displeased that, be annoyed that
ἥδομαι	enjoy, be pleased that
μεταμέλομαι	regret that
μεταμέλει μοι	regret that (*impers.*)
χαίρω	rejoice, enjoy, be pleased that

(35) Χαρμίδην δὲ τόνδε <u>οἶδα</u> πολλοὺς μὲν ἐραστὰς <u>κτησάμενον</u>. (Xen. *Symp.* 8.2)
I know that Charmides here has won many lovers. *Verb of intellectual knowledge.*

(36) ὡς ἥ τε ἡμέρα ἐγένετο καὶ <u>ἔγνωσαν</u> τοὺς Ἀθηναίους <u>ἀπεληλυθότας</u>, . . . (Thuc. 7.81.1)
When day broke and they found that the Athenians had gone, . . . *Verb of intellectual knowledge.*

(37) πῶς ἂν φανερώτερον ἢ οὕτως <u>ψευδομένους</u> <u>ἀποδείξαιμι</u> τοὺς κατηγόρους; (Lys. 25.14)

How might I prove more clearly than this that the claimants are lying? *Verb of intellectual knowledge ('make clear that').*

(38) ἀριστοκρατεῖσθαι <u>δῆλος εἶ</u> <u>ζητῶν</u>. (Ar. *Av.* 125)

You're obviously / it's clear that you're looking to live in an aristocracy. *Verb of intellectual knowledge ('be clear').*

(39) οὔτε νῦν <u>μοι</u> <u>μεταμέλει</u> οὕτως <u>ἀπολογησαμένῳ</u>. (Pl. *Ap.* 38e)

And I do not now regret having defended myself this way. *Verb expressing an emotional state.*

(40) ΧΟ. καὶ δέδρακας τοῦτο τοὔργον; :: ΕΠ. καὶ <u>δεδρακώς</u> γ᾽ <u>ἥδομαι</u>. (Ar. *Av.* 325)

(Chorus:) And have you done this? :: (Hoopoe:) Yes, and I'm pleased I have. *Verb expressing an emotional state.*

Note 1: Of the verbs that can take a supplementary participle, only this group can take a participle with ἄν (ἄν + ppl. in such cases represents a potential or counterfactual construction, →52.7):

(41) πάντ᾽ ἂν <u>φοβηθεῖσ᾽</u> <u>ἴσθι</u>. (Eur. *Hipp.* 519)

Know that you would be afraid of anything. *ἂν φοβηθεῖσ(α) is supplementary with ἴσθι, and represents potential φοβηθείης ἄν, 'you would be afraid'.*

For a similar distinction between verbs which can and cannot take an infinitive with ἄν, →51.4. ἄν occurs more often with circumstantial than with supplementary participles.

Note 2: Many of these verbs may also be followed by different constructions, e.g. a ὅτι/ὡς-clause or an infinitive. For the differences between these constructions, →52.22–8.

Note 3: With verbs expressing an emotional state, it is sometimes difficult to assess whether one is dealing with a supplementary participle or a circumstantial participle; thus, in (40), for instance, we could also translate *having done it, I am happy* (with δεδρακώς taken as a circumstantial participle).

Verbs Taking a Supplementary Participle which Expresses a Way of Being

52.11   The following three verbs express a certain **way of being or acting** and are complemented by a participle:

τυγχάνω   happen to (do something), (do) as it happens

λανθάνω   go unnoticed (by someone (*acc.*) in doing something), be hidden

φθάνω   be earlier (than someone (*acc.*) in doing something), anticipate

(42) ὅτε δ᾽ αὕτη ἡ μάχη ἐγένετο, Τισσαφέρνης ἐν Σάρδεσιν <u>ἔτυχεν ὤν</u>. (Xen. *Hell.* 3.4.25)

And when this battle occurred, Tissaphernes happened to be in Sardis.

(43) οὐ φοβῇ δικαζόμενος τῷ πατρὶ ὅπως μὴ αὖ σὺ ἀνόσιον πρᾶγμα <u>τυγχάνῃς</u> <u>πράττων</u>; (Pl. *Euthphr.* 4e)

Are you not afraid that you are the one who, as it happens, is behaving impiously by prosecuting your father? *For ὅπως μή in fear clauses,* →*44.7.*

(44) παρεσκευάζοντο εὐθὺς ὅπως μὴ <u>λήσουσιν</u> <u>αὐτοὺς</u> αἱ νῆες ... <u>ἀφορμηθεῖσαι</u>. (Thuc. 8.10.1)

Straight away they made preparations so that the ships would not set out without their notice.

(45) περιέπλεον Σούνιον, βουλόμενοι <u>φθῆναι</u> <u>τοὺς Ἀθηναίους</u> <u>ἀπικόμενοι</u> ἐς τὸ ἄστυ. (Hdt. 6.115)

They sailed around Sunium, because they wanted to arrive at the city before the Athenians.

When these verbs are construed with a participle, they may be seen as a kind of auxiliary verb: the participle expresses the main action, while the -άνω verb qualifies the action in some way.

Note 1: Observe that with λανθάνω, the participle is commonly translated as a main verb, with λανθάνω + acc. translated with *unnoticed by X, with X unawares*, etc. (or alternatively, the object may be translated as subject: *X does not notice that Y . . .*).

With φθάνω, too, the participle is commonly translated as main verb, and φθάνω + acc. with *before X*: note the translation *arrive before the Athenians* in (45).

Note 2: For οἴχομαι + ppl. (a construction also commonly listed under this heading), →52.42 n.3.

The Case Form of Supplementary Participles and their Subjects

52.12   If the **subjects of the matrix verb and the supplementary participle are the same** (i.e. are **co-referential**), the participle (and any predicative complement or modifier) agrees with the subject, and therefore typically stands in the nominative (**nominative-and-participle construction**):

(46) ἐγὼ ... <u>ἀπείρηκα</u> ... <u>συσκευαζόμενος</u> καὶ <u>βαδίζων</u> καὶ ... (Xen. *An.* 5.1.2)

I, for my part, am tired of packing up and walking, and . . .

(47) ἐπειδὴ ... <u>ἀδύνατοι</u> <u>ὁρῶμεν</u> <u>ὄντες</u> ... περιγενέσθαι ... (Thuc. 1.32.5)

Now that we see that we are unable to prevail . . .

(48) <u>ἔτυχον</u> ... ἐν τῇ ἀγορᾷ ὁπλῖται <u>καθεύδοντες</u>. (Thuc. 4.113.2)

Hoplites happened to be sleeping in the marketplace.

Note 1: This is always the case with phase verbs (except παύω when it takes an object), with φαίνομαι, δῆλός εἰμι, etc., and with λανθάνω, τυγχάνω, and φθάνω.

52.13   If the **subjects of the participle and the matrix verb are different**, the subject of the participle is generally expressed separately in the accusative, and the participle – agreeing with its subject – also appears in the accusative (**accusative-and-participle construction**):

(49) βούλομαι δεῖξαι αὐτὸν ψευδόμενον. (Dem. 37.21)
I propose to demonstrate that he is lying.

(50) ἀλλ' ἐπεὶ ἤκουσε Κῦρον ἐν Κιλικίᾳ ὄντα, . . . (Xen. *An.* 1.4.5)
But when he learned that Cyrus was in Cilicia, . . .

(51) τοὺς ξυμμάχους . . . οὐ περιοψόμεθα ἀδικουμένους. (Thuc. 1.86.2)
We will not tolerate our allies being wronged.

Any predicative complements or modifiers with the subject of the participle (i.e. words which agree with the subject) naturally also occur in the accusative:

(52) πάντες δέ σ' ᾔσθοντ' οὖσαν Ἕλληνες σοφήν (Eur. *Med.* 539)
All the Greeks have learned that you are clever. *σοφήν agrees with σ(ε), subject of οὖσαν.*

52.14   But when **verbs of hearing** (ἀκούω, αἰσθάνομαι) are used to express **direct auditory perception**, a supplementary participle and its subject are expressed in the genitive (**genitive-and-participle** construction):

(53) ἤκουσα . . . αὐτοῦ καὶ περὶ φίλων διαλεγομένου. (Xen. *Mem.* 2.4.1)
I heard him have a conversation about friendship as well.

(54) ὅστις . . . σ' ἐξέθρεψα, | αἰσθανόμενός σου πάντα τραυλίζοντος . . . (Ar. *Nub.* 1380–1)
I, the one who raised you, listening to all your baby-talk . . .

Note 1: Contrast the uses of ἀκούω in (53) (direct perception) and (50) (intellectual knowledge) above. For this difference, also →52.19.

52.15   Finally, with some verbs, a supplementary participle and its subject are expressed in the dative (**dative-and-participle** construction): this occurs with χαίρω *enjoy*, and with certain impersonal verbs: e.g. μεταμέλει μοι + ppl. *I regret* (cf. (39) above), φίλον ἐστί μοι + ppl. *it is pleasing for me that I*, etc.

(55) χαίρουσιν ἐξεταζομένοις τοῖς οἰομένοις μὲν εἶναι σοφοῖς, οὖσι δ' οὔ. (Pl. *Ap.* 33c)
They enjoy it when those who think they are wise, but are not, are examined. *The participle ἐξεταζόμενοις and its subject (the entire phrase τοῖς . . . οὔ) are in the dative; note that the subject consists of two contrasting substantivally used participles (οἰομένοις and οὖσι, both modified by τοῖς); the predicative complement (εἶναι) σοφοῖς also agrees with these datives. χαίρω is more commonly construed with ἐπί + dat. + ppl.*

(56) Ζεύς, ὅστις ποτ' ἐστίν, εἰ τόδ' αὐ|τῷ φίλον κεκλημένῳ, . . . (Aesch. *Ag.* 160–1)
Zeus, whoever he is, if in fact it is pleasing for him to be called that, . . .

52.16 The **supplementary participle of impersonal verbs** takes the form of the accusative neuter singular (cf. the 'accusative absolute', →52.33):

(57) Εὐρύλοχος δὲ καὶ οἱ μετ' αὐτοῦ ὡς <u>ᾔσθοντο</u> ... <u>ἀδύνατον ὂν</u> τὴν πόλιν βίᾳ ἑλεῖν, ἀνεχώρησαν ... ἐς τὴν Αἰολίδα. (Thuc. 3.102.5)
When Eurylochus and those in his company found that it was impossible to capture the city by force, they withdrew to Aeolis. *ἀδύνατον ὂν is the participle of impersonal ἀδύνατόν ἐστι; it is a complement of ᾔσθοντο.*

Supplementary Participles and Other Complement Constructions

52.17 A number of verbs which can be complemented by a certain type of supplementary participle can also take various other kinds of complement constructions.

Verbs of Perception Taking More Than One Type of Supplementary Participle

52.18 **Verbs of visual perception**, such as ὁράω *see*, are not only used to refer to the visual perception of an action, but are also frequently used to refer to intellectual knowledge/understanding (cf. Engl. *I see your point*, in which no actual visual perception is involved):

– when used as verbs of visual perception, such verbs are complemented by a participle expressing the action perceived; the participle occurs almost exclusively in the present stem (because the action is necessarily ongoing when it is perceived);
– when used as verbs of intellectual knowledge, they are complemented by a participle expressing the propositional content of the knowledge; the participle occurs in any stem (with the usual relative-tense implication; →52.4):

(58) <u>εἶδε</u> Κλέαρχον <u>διελαύνοντα</u>. (Xen. *An.* 1.5.12)
He saw Clearchus riding through. *Present participle; εἶδε denotes visual perception.*

(59) <u>ὁρῶ</u> δὲ καὶ τὴν τύχην ἡμῖν <u>συλλαμβάνουσαν</u> καὶ τὸν παρόντα καιρὸν <u>συναγωνιζόμενον</u>. ([Isoc.] 1.3)
And I see that luck is on our side, too, and that the present circumstances are in league with us. *Present participles (simultaneous with ὁρῶ); ὁρῶ denotes intellectual understanding.*

(60) ἐπειδὴ δ' οὐδ' ὣς ἄνευ ἀγῶνος <u>ἑώρα ἐσόμενα</u> τὰ πράγματα, ... (Andoc. 1.122)
But when he realized that even so matters would not be settled without a trial, ... *Future participle (posterior to ἑώρα); ἑώρα denotes intellectual understanding.*

Note 1: With examples of visual perception, such as (58), the subject of the participle is always an entity which can itself be visually perceived. This makes it possible to interpret the participle as circumstantial: 'He saw Clearchus, while he was riding.' With examples of intellectual knowledge, this is not necessarily the case: note that one cannot actually visually perceive 'luck' or 'the present circumstances' in (59) or 'the matters' in (60).

Note 2: When used in their 'intellectual knowledge' sense, verbs of visual perception can also be complemented by a ὅτι/ὡς-clause (→52.28).

52.19   Similarly, **verbs of auditory perception**, such as ἀκούω *hear*, can be used not only to refer to the actual auditory perception of an action, but also to refer to the transmission of factual information, and then means 'learn', 'be told (a fact)' (cf. Engl. *I hear that Julia has performed well in her job*, in which no auditory perception of Julia working is involved):

 – when used as verbs of auditory perception, such verbs are complemented by a genitive-and-participle construction (→52.14); the participle occurs nearly exclusively in the present (because the perceived action is necessarily ongoing when it is perceived);
 – when used as verbs of (acquiring) knowledge, they are complemented by an accusative-and-participle construction expressing the propositional content of the information; all tenses of the participle are used, with the usual relative-tense implication (→52.4):

(61) καὶ ταῦτα πολλοὶ ἡμῶν ἤκουον τοῦ ἱεροφάντου λέγοντος. (Lys. 6.1)
      And many of us heard the priest say these things. *Present participle in the genitive; ἤκουον denotes auditive perception.*

(62) Ἀβροκόμας δὲ ... ἐπεὶ ἤκουσε Κῦρον ἐν Κιλικίᾳ ὄντα, ἀναστρέψας ἐκ Φοινίκης παρὰ βασιλέα ἀπήλαυνεν (Xen. *An.* 1.4.5)
      When it was made known to Abrocomas that Cyrus was in Cilicia, he turned about from his journey from Phoenicia and marched off to the king. *Present participle (simultaneous with ἤκουσε) in the accusative; ἤκουσε means 'learn (from being told)'.*

(63) προειδότες καὶ προακηκοότες παρὰ τούτων καὶ τοὺς συμμάχους ἀπολουμένους καὶ Θηβαίους ἰσχυροὺς γενησομένους ... (Dem. 19.219)
      Having foreknowledge and having been warned by these men that your allies would be ruined and that the Thebans would gain strength, ... *Future participles (posterior to προακηκοότες) in the accusative; προακηκοότες means to 'be reliably informed' (note its coordination with a verb of knowledge, προειδότες).*

Note 1: With examples of actual auditory perception, it is possible to interpret the participle as circumstantial: e.g. in (61) 'We heard the priest (genitive of the source of sound), while he was speaking.' With examples of the acquisition of knowledge, such as (62), this is impossible: it is not suggested that Cyrus makes any audible noise in Cilicia.

Note 2: ἀκούω can also be construed as a declarative utterance verb, taking a declarative infinitive or ὅτι/ὡς-clause (for the difference between the two, →51.19 n.1), or an indirect question (→41.3: for the difference between the construction as a verb of knowledge (with participle) or a declarative utterance verb, →52.25.

52.20   **αἰσθάνομαι** *perceive* is used as a verb of auditory perception (+gen. and pres. ppl., *hear*), a verb of visual perception (+acc. and pres. ppl., *see*) and as a verb of intellectual knowledge (+acc. and ppl., *perceive, see*).

πυνθάνομαι *perceive, enquire* has all these same constructions, and is additionally construed with a declarative infinitive, ὅτι/ὡς-clause or indirect question: for details, →52.25.

With αἰσθάνομαι and πυνθάνομαι, there is some interference between the genitive-and-participle and the accusative-and-participle constructions (the one sometimes being used where one would expect the other).

52.21   Infrequently, participles complementing a verb of **actual visual or auditory perception** occur in the **aorist**, which is in aspectual opposition to the present (the action is of necessity simultaneous with the matrix verb; compare the aspectual difference between the present and aorist dynamic infinitive; →51.15).

(64)   τοσαῦτα φωνήσαντος εἰσηκούσαμεν. (Soph. *OC* 1645)
That much we heard him say. *The aorist participle refers to the speech as a whole: 'this much', and nothing more or less, was said.*

(65)   ὡς δὲ εἶδεν ἔλαφον ἐκπηδήσασαν, ... (Xen. *Cyr.* 1.4.8)
When he (Cyrus) saw a deer spring out from under cover, ... *The aorist participle indicates that Cyrus perceived the deer's jumping in its entirety, i.e. until the deer had completely appeared. As above (→52.18 n.1), it is also possible in such cases to interpret the participle as circumstantial: 'a deer, after it had sprung out'.*

Verbs Taking a Participle or an Infinitive: Verbs of Knowledge

52.22   The main characteristic of the participial complement is that it refers to actions which **actually occur**, or expresses propositional content which is **actually true** (→52.8). These values become particularly clear in the case of verbs which may be construed with either a participle or an infinitive: infinitives with such verbs express actions which **may or may not occur** or propositional content which **may or may not be true** (→51.3).

52.23   Many **verbs of knowledge** take either a participle to express **intellectual knowledge** ('know that something is the case'), or a dynamic infinitive to express **practical knowledge** ('know how to do something', →51.8): examples are οἶδα *know that* (+ ppl.)/*know how to* (+ inf.), ἐπίσταμαι *understand that* (+ ppl.)/*know how to* (+ inf.), μανθάνω *learn that* (+ ppl.)/*learn how to* (+ inf.):

(66) τά τε κατὰ τὴν θάλασσαν συντυχόντα σφι παθήματα <u>κατεργασαμένους</u>
μάλιστα Ἀθηναίους <u>ἐπίστατο</u>. (Hdt. 8.136.2)
And he understood that the Athenians in particular had wrought the calamities that had befallen them at sea.

(67) νῦν δ᾽ ἅπας τις τῶν ποιμένων <u>ἐπίσταται</u> <u>ξυλουργέειν</u> (Hdt. 3.113.2)
But now every single shepherd knows how to do carpentry.

Note 1: When these verbs are used as verbs of intellectual knowledge, they can also be
construed with ὅτι/ὡς-clauses (for the difference, →52.28), and especially when negated,
with indirect questions (→42.2).

52.24   Some verbs are used either as a **verb of intellectual knowledge** (with a participle)
or as a **verb of opinion** (with a declarative infinitive): the difference is one of
degree in certainty. Examples are ὑπολαμβάνω *assume that* (+ inf.) / *grasp that* (+
ppl.); εὑρίσκω *think (upon reflection) that* (+ inf.) / *find that* (+ ppl.), αἰσθάνομαι
believe that (+ inf.) / *perceive that* (+ ppl.).

(68) ἱστορέων δὲ <u>εὕρισκε</u> Λακεδαιμονίους τε καὶ Ἀθηναίους <u>προέχοντας</u>, τοὺς μὲν τοῦ
Δωρικοῦ γένεος, τοὺς δὲ τοῦ Ἰωνικοῦ. (Hdt. 1.56.2)
When he inquired he found that the Spartans and Athenians were the
outstanding people, the former among the Dorian race, the latter among
the Ionian. *The participle refers to knowledge regarded as certain by
Herodotus.*

(69) φροντίζων δὲ <u>εὕρισκέ</u> τε ταῦτα καιριώτατα <u>εἶναι</u>. (Hdt. 1.125.1)
On reflection, he found that the following measures might be most effective.
*The declarative infinitive expresses the subject's opinion (just how effective the
proposed measures are remains to be seen).*

To this group also belongs **φαίνομαι** *seem* (+ inf.) / *appear, prove to* (+ ppl.):

(70) καὶ οἱ κατήγοροι . . . οὐδαμῇ εὖνοι <u>ὄντες</u> <u>ἐφαίνοντο</u> τῷ δήμῳ. (Lys. 20.17)
And the accusers proved to be in no way well-intentioned towards the people.
ἐφαίνοντο + ppl. refers to a fact which is now known.

(71) οἱ . . . χῶροι οὗτοι τοῖσι Ἕλλησι <u>εἶναι</u> <u>ἐφαίνοντο</u> ἐπιτήδεοι. (Hdt. 7.177.1)
These lands seemed to the Greeks to be suitable. *ἐφαίνοντο + inf. expresses the
impression/opinion which Herodotus ascribes to the Greeks.*

Note 1: When these verbs are used as verbs of knowledge, they can also be construed with
ὅτι/ὡς-clauses (for the difference, →52.28), and especially when negated, with indirect
questions (→42.2).

Note 2: The verb γιγνώσκω belongs to this category, but has an additional use as
a desiderative verb (→51.29):

– as a verb of knowledge: γιγνώσκω + ppl. or ὅτι/ὡς-clause = *find, notice, realize, know that*;
– as a verb of opinion: γιγνώσκω + declarative inf. = *judge*;
– as a desiderative verb: γιγνώσκω + dynamic inf. = *decide, resolve to*.

(72) καὶ ὃς ἐθαύμασεν ... κἀγὼ <u>γνοὺς</u> αὐτὸν <u>θαυμάζοντα</u> ... ἔφην ... (Pl. *Euthd.* 279d)

He was puzzled ... and when I noticed his puzzlement, I said ... *Participle. For* καὶ ὅς, →28.29.

(73) Τελμησσέες μέντοι τάδε <u>ἔγνωσαν</u>, στρατὸν ἀλλόθροον προσδόκιμον <u>εἶναι</u> Κροίσῳ ἐπὶ τὴν χώρην. (Hdt. 1.78.3)

However, the Telmessians' interpretation was that Croesus should expect a foreign army to invade his land. *Declarative infinitive.*

(74) ὁ Ἀγησίλαος ... <u>ἔγνω</u> <u>διώκειν</u> τοὺς ἐκ τῶν εὐωνύμων προσκειμένους. (Xen. *Hell.* 4.6.9)

Agesilaus decided to pursue those who were attacking from the left. *Dynamic infinitive.*

52.25 Similarly, a few verbs are used either as a **verb of (conveying) intellectual knowledge** (with a participle) or as a **declarative utterance verb** (with a declarative infinitive). Again, the difference resides in the degree of certainty. The most important of these are ἀγγέλλω *relay (the fact) that* (+ ppl.)/*report (the rumour) that* (+ inf.), ἀκούω *be informed (of the fact) that* (+ ppl.)/*be told (the rumour) that* (+ inf.), and πυνθάνομαι (same senses as ἀκούω):

(75) ἐπειδὴ τάχιστα <u>ἠγγέλθη</u> Ἀστύφιλος <u>τετελευτηκώς</u> ... (Isae. 9.3)

As soon as it was reported that Astyphilus was dead, ... *Astyphilus' death is presented as fact.*

(76) μετὰ δὲ τοῦτο ... <u>ἠγγέλλετο</u> βασιλεὺς <u>διανοεῖσθαι</u> ὡς ἐπιχειρήσων πάλιν ἐπὶ τοὺς Ἕλληνας. (Pl. *Menex.* 241d)

After this (the victory at Plataea) there were reports that the King was planning another assault on the Greeks. *Xerxes' plans were rumoured only: a further invasion never took place.*

Note 1: ἀκούω and πυνθάνομαι are also used as verbs of direct sensory perception, →52.19.

Verbs Taking a Participle or an Infinitive: Other Verbs

52.26 **αἰσχύνομαι** is used in two senses, with different types of complement:

– αἰσχύνομαι + dynamic inf. = *be ashamed to, be hesitant to, do not want to* (as a kind of desiderative verb);

– αἰσχύνομαι + ppl. (or ὅτι/ὡς-clause) = *be ashamed that* (as a verb expressing an emotional state):

(77) <u>αἰσχύνομαι</u> οὖν ὑμῖν <u>εἰπεῖν</u>, ὦ ἄνδρες, τἀληθῆ. (Pl. *Ap.* 22b)

So I hesitate, gentlemen, to tell you the truth.

(78) οὐκ <u>αἰσχύνῃ</u> εἰς τοιαῦτα <u>ἄγων</u>, ὦ Σώκρατες, τοὺς λόγους; (Pl. *Grg.* 494e)

Are you not ashamed, Socrates, to be taking the discussion to such topics?

52.27   The phase verbs ἄρχομαι and παύω may be construed either with a dynamic infinitive or with a (present) participle:

- ἄρχομαι + infinitive = *undertake to do something, begin to do something* (for the first time), *be the first to do something*;
- ἄρχομαι + participle = *begin doing something* (perform the first stage of an action):

(79)   ἤρξαντο δὲ κατὰ τοὺς χρόνους τούτους καὶ τὰ μακρὰ τείχη Ἀθηναῖοι ἐς θάλασσαν <u>οἰκοδομεῖν</u>. (Thuc. 1.107.1)
Around this time, the Athenians began to construct the Long Walls towards the sea.

(80)   εἰ τοίνυν ἐχιόνιζε … ταύτην τὴν χώρην … ἐκ τῆς <u>ἄρχεται</u> <u>ῥέων</u> ὁ Νεῖλος, … (Hdt. 2.22.4)
Now if it snowed in this land from where the Nile starts flowing, …

- παύω + dynamic infinitive = *prevent* (*someone from doing something*) – the action that is prevented has not actually started yet;
- παύω + participle = *stop* (*someone doing something*) – the subject stops or interrupts an action that has already begun:

(81)   εὔχετο … μηδεμίαν οἱ συντυχίην τοιαύτην γενέσθαι ἥ μιν <u>παύσει</u> <u>καταστρέψασθαι</u> τὴν Εὐρώπην πρότερον ἢ ἐπὶ τέρμασι τοῖσι ἐκείνης γένηται. (Hdt. 7.54.2)
He prayed that no accident might befall him of such a kind that it would prevent him from subduing Europe before he reached its borders.

(82)   λέγει γὰρ τὰ γεγραμμένα ὅσην ἡ πόλις ὑμῶν <u>ἔπαυσέν</u> ποτε δύναμιν ὕβρει <u>πορευομένην</u> ἅμα ἐπὶ πᾶσαν Εὐρώπην καὶ Ἀσίαν. (Pl. *Ti.* 24e)
For our records state what a great power your city once stopped marching in insolence against the whole of Europe and Asia.

Note 1: Middle παύομαι *stop (doing something)* only takes a (present) participle, as it always expresses the interruption of an ongoing action.

Verbs Taking Both Participles and ὅτι/ὡς-Clauses

52.28   **Verbs of intellectual knowledge** and **verbs of emotion** may be construed with a ὅτι/ὡς-clause as well as a supplementary participle. The difference between the two constructions is subtle:

- if a participle is used, this generally suggests that the information presented in the complement is considered to be already known and not in itself salient;
- if a ὅτι/ὡς-clause is used, this generally suggests that the information presented in the complement is new ('asserted', →60.20) and therefore salient:

(83) λέγει ὁ Κλέαρχος τάδε· Ἐγώ, ὦ Τισσαφέρνη, <u>οἶδα</u> μὲν ἡμῖν ὅρκους <u>γεγενημένους</u> καὶ
δεξιὰς <u>δεδομένας</u> μὴ ἀδικήσειν ἀλλήλους· φυλαττόμενον δὲ σέ τε ὁρῶ ὡς πολεμίους ἡμᾶς
. . . ἐπεὶ δὲ σκοπῶν οὐ δύναμαι οὔτε σὲ αἰσθέσθαι πειρώμενον ἡμᾶς κακῶς ποιεῖν ἐγώ τε
σαφῶς <u>οἶδα</u> ὅτι ἡμεῖς γε οὐδὲ <u>ἐπινοοῦμεν</u> τοιοῦτον οὐδέν, ἔδοξέ μοι εἰς λόγους σοι ἐλθεῖν.
(Xen. *An.* 2.5.3–4)

Clearchus said the following: 'Tissaphernes, I am well aware that we have sworn under
oath and pledged that neither of us will initiate hostilities against the other, but I see that
you are taking the kinds of precautions against us that you would against enemies.
However, my investigations have produced no evidence that you are trying to injure us
and I know for sure that we have no such scheme in mind either. So I wanted to talk things
over with you.' *Clearchus first reminds Tissaphernes of the oaths they have sworn (ppl.); this
is but a preliminary point, and one with which Tissaphernes is, of course, familiar. Next,
Clearchus assures Tissaphernes that the Greeks are not plotting against him (ὅτι-clause): this
is the main point Clearchus wishes to make, and it is newsworthy for Tissaphernes.*

(84) τί οὖν . . . ἔτι ἀπιστεῖς, ἐπειδὴ <u>ὁρᾷς</u> ἀποθανόντος τοῦ ἀνθρώπου τό γε ἀσθενέστερον ἔτι <u>ὄν</u>;
(Pl. *Phd.* 87a)

Why, then, do you still disbelieve, when you see that after a man has died, the weaker
part (*the soul*) still exists?

(85) καὶ ὅταν γέ τις αἵρεσις ᾖ . . . <u>ὁρᾷς</u> <u>ὅτι</u> οἱ ῥήτορές <u>εἰσιν</u> οἱ συμβουλεύοντες καὶ οἱ νικῶντες τὰς
γνώμας. (Pl. *Grg.* 456a)

And when there is an election, you see that it is the orators who offer the advice and
whose advice carries the day.

*In (84), the fact that the soul continues its existence after the body dies has been established
in the preceding discussion (ὁράω + ppl.). In (85), the speaker wishes, at this point in the
discussion, to establish it as a fact that orators are influential in elections (ὁράω + ὅτι-
clause).*

The Circumstantial Participle

Introduction

52.29   The circumstantial participle is an optional constituent, added to a clause to
express time, cause, motivation, condition, purpose, etc. (which interpretation is
relevant depends on context and the use of certain adverbs, →52.34–44).

The Case Form of Circumstantial Participles and their Subjects

52.30   The **subject** of a circumstantial participle is:

- either identical to a constituent of the matrix clause: the participle is then
connected to that constituent (agreeing with it in case, number and gender);

– or not a constituent of the matrix clause: the subject is then added separately, and together with the participle stands in the genitive case – the so-called **genitive absolute** construction.

Circumstantial participles of impersonal verbs appear in the accusative singular neuter: the **accusative absolute** construction.

Connected Participles

52.31   When the **subject of the participle is a constituent of the matrix clause**, the participle is connected to that constituent as a predicative modifier (→26.26), **agreeing with it in case, number and gender**:

(86) ὁ δὲ Κῦρος ταῦτα ἀκούσας ἐπηύξατο· ... (Xen. *Cyr.* 5.1.29)
Cyrus, upon hearing these things, uttered this prayer: ... *ὁ Κῦρος is nominative as subject of ἐπηύξατο; ἀκούσας agrees with it in case, number and gender.*

(87) ἀκούσαντι ταῦτα τῷ Κύρῳ ἔδοξεν ἄξια ἐπιμελείας λέγειν. (Xen. *Cyr.* 5.4.37)
Upon hearing these things, it seemed to Cyrus that he (Gadatas) was saying things worthy of consideration. *τῷ Κύρῳ is dative complement of ἔδοξεν; ἀκούσαντι agrees with it in case, number and gender.*

(88) (λέγεται) ... ἀκούσαντα ... ταῦτα τὸν Κῦρον ἡσθῆναί τε καὶ εἰπεῖν ... (Xen. *Oec.* 4.22)
It is said that Cyrus, upon hearing these things, was glad, and said ... *τὸν Κῦρον is accusative as subject of ἡσθῆναι (accusative and infinitive); ἀκούσαντα agrees with it in case, number and gender.*

Note 1: Participles may agree with a subject which is not explicitly expressed (→26.7):

(89) ἀκούσας δὲ τοῦ ἰατροῦ ὅτι οὐδὲν ἔτι εἴη ἡ ἄνθρωπος, πάλιν ἑτέρους μάρτυρας παραλαβὼν τήν τε ἄνθρωπον ἐπέδειξα ὡς εἶχεν. ([Dem.] 47.67)
Upon hearing from the doctor that the woman's condition was hopeless, I again gathered further witnesses and showed them what condition she was in. *Both ἀκούσας and παραλαβών agree with the first-person subject of ἐπέδειξα.*

(90) ἀκούσας δὲ οὗ ἕνεκα ἤλθομεν, αὐτὸς σκέψαι. (Pl. *Prt.* 316b)
Hear why we have come and then decide for yourself. *ἀκούσας agrees with the second-person subject of the imperative σκέψαι. For the translation of the aorist participle preceding an imperative, →52.6.*

Genitive Absolute

52.32   When the **subject of the participle is not a constituent of the matrix clause**, it must be expressed separately. In this case, both the participle and its subject are added in the **genitive** case. This is called the **genitive absolute** construction:

(91) τὰ δ' ἐκ τῆς ἄλλης οἰκίας ἐξέφερον σκεύη, <u>ἀπαγορευούσης τῆς γυναικὸς</u> μὴ ἅπτεσθαι αὐτοῖς. ([Dem.] 47.56–7)

They carried away the furniture from the rest of the house, even though my wife forbade them to touch it. *Since the wife is not a constituent of the clause* τὰ δ' ἐκ τῆς ἄλλης οἰκίας ἐξέφερον σκεύη, *the participle 'forbidding' cannot be connected to a form of* γυνή *already present in that clause. Instead, both are added in the genitive case.*

(92) προθύμως ... ἐλευκοῦντο οἱ ἱππεῖς τὰ κράνη <u>κελεύοντος ἐκείνου</u>. (Xen. *Hell.* 7.5.20)

The horsemen eagerly painted their helmets white at his (*Epaminondas'*) command. *Epaminondas is not a constituent of the clause* ἐλευκοῦντο οἱ ἱππεῖς τὰ κράνη: *the pronoun referring to him and the participle are added in the genitive.*

(93) οὕτως οὖν <u>ἐχόντων τούτων</u> τῇ φύσει, πρὸς τοὺς πρὸ ἐμαυτοῦ νῦν ἐγὼ κρίνωμαι καὶ θεωρῶμαι; μηδαμῶς. (Dem. 18.315)

Given, then, that these things are so by nature, am I now to be judged and examined in comparison to my predecessors? Certainly not! *The subject of the initial genitive absolute ('these things') is not a constituent of the remainder of the sentence.*

Note 1: Observe the following exceptions and special cases:

– Occasionally, when the subject of a genitive absolute may be easily supplied from the context, it is not expressed:

   (94) εἵποντο δ' αὐτοῖς καὶ τῶν Ἑλλήνων τινές ... οἱ δὲ πολέμιοι <u>προσιόντων</u> τέως μὲν ἡσύχαζον. (Xen. *An.* 5.4.16)

   Some Greeks were following them. And the enemy forces kept quiet for a while as they (*the Greeks*) were drawing near. *The subject of* προσιόντων *is the Greeks, but this is not separately expressed by a genitive noun (e.g.* τῶν Ἑλλήνων) *or pronoun (e.g.* αὐτῶν).

– Infrequently, the subject of a genitive absolute *is* used as a constituent of the matrix clause; this occurs primarily when the genitive absolute precedes that clause (in essence, the construction begins one way, and is modified midway through the sentence):

   (95) οὕτω δὴ <u>δεξαμένου τοῦ Κύρου</u> οἱ ... γεραίτεροι αἱροῦνται <u>αὐτὸν</u> ἄρχοντα. (Xen. *Cyr.* 1.5.5)

   When Cyrus had accepted (the invitation) in this way, the elders elected him general. *Since Cyrus (*αὐτόν) *is object of* αἱροῦνται, *the genitive absolute construction is, strictly speaking, ungrammatical (the construction* δεξάμενον τὸν Κῦρον αἱροῦνται ἄρχοντα *is possible). The use of the genitive absolute suggests that it is a separate unit.*

Accusative Absolute

52.33   Circumstantial participles of **impersonal verbs** cannot agree with a subject (since they have no subject, →36.1). Such participles are expressed in the accusative singular neuter form: this is called the **accusative absolute** construction:

(96) τί δὴ ὑμᾶς <u>ἐξὸν</u> ἀπολέσαι οὐκ ἐπὶ τοῦτο ἤλθομεν; (Xen. *An.* 2.5.22)
Why then, when it was possible to kill you, did we not proceed to do so? *ἐξόν is accusative absolute of impersonal ἔξεστι 'it is possible'.*

(97) καὶ δὴ σφι πρὸς ταῦτα ἔδοξε τῷ κήρυκι τῶν πολεμίων χρᾶσθαι, <u>δόξαν</u> δέ σφι ἐποίεον τοιόνδε· (Hdt. 6.77.3)
In reaction to this, they decided to use the enemies' herald; and when they had reached this decision, they went about it in the following way: . . . *δόξαν is (aorist) accusative absolute of impersonal ἔδοξε 'it was decided' (→51.30) and it takes its regular dative complement (σφι). δόξαν picks up the preceding ἔδοξε.*

Note 1: But impersonal weather terms which can take a god as subject (→36.11 n.1) sometimes occur in the genitive absolute, without an explicitly expressed subject: e.g. ὕοντος *when it is/was raining*, βροντήσαντος *when a thunderstorm has come on*.

Interpretation of Circumstantial Participles

52.34   How a circumstantial participle should be interpreted (as expressing time, cause, motivation, etc.) depends on the context, and on certain adverbs and/or particles which may appear with the participle. It is not always possible, and certainly not necessary, to limit the interpretation of a circumstantial participle to one of the possibilities outlined below.

Time, Circumstance

52.35   Circumstantial participles are often naturally interpreted as expressing the **time** when (or **circumstances** under which) the action in the matrix clause takes place. This is especially the case when the participle **precedes the matrix verb** (often as 'setting', →60.32):

(98) οὓς δ' ἐν τῷ πολέμῳ συμμάχους ἐκτησάμεθα, <u>εἰρήνης οὔσης</u> ἀπολωλέκασιν οὗτοι. (Dem. 3.28)
Those whom we gained as allies during the war, these men have lost in peacetime. *The parallelism with ἐν τῷ πολέμῳ encourages the temporal interpretation.*

52.36   An **aorist participle** preceding a finite verb is very often used to express a sequence of actions (particularly in narrative text, →58.9; the order ppl.–verb is 'iconic', →47.7 n.2):

(99) <u>συλλέξας</u> στράτευμα ἐπολιόρκει Μίλητον. (Xen. *An.* 1.1.7)

He collected an army and laid siege to Miletus. *Note that the sequence of events may be conveyed in translation by two co-ordinated main verbs ('collected', 'laid siege').*

(100) ἐξ Ἐρετρίης δὲ <u>ὁρμηθέντες</u> διὰ ἐνδεκάτου ἔτεος ἀπίκοντο ὀπίσω. (Hdt. 1.62.1)

After ten years they set out from Eretria and returned home. *For 'inclusive' counting (διὰ ἐνδεκάτου ἔτεος = 'after ten years'), →9.10.*

52.37 The temporal relationship between the participle and the matrix verb may be made explicit by temporal adverbs such as ἅμα *while, at the same time*, ἤδη *already*, αὐτίκα *immediately*, etc.

(101) ἐπαιάνιζον ... <u>ἅμα</u> ... <u>πλέοντες</u>. (Thuc. 2.91.2)

They were singing a paean while rowing.

Note 1: Circumstantial participles of τελευτάω *finish* should normally be interpreted as adverbial expressions of time, with the sense *finally, eventually, in the end, at last*:

(102) πολλὰ ἂν εἴη λέγειν, ὅσον πένθος ἐν τῇ ἐμῇ οἰκίᾳ ἦν ἐν ἐκείνῳ τῷ χρόνῳ. <u>τελευτῶσα</u> δὲ ἡ μήτηρ αὐτῶν ἠντεβόλει με καὶ ἱκέτευε ... (Lys. 32.11)

It would take long to tell how much mourning there was in my house in that period. In the end, their mother beseeched and begged me ...

Cause, Motivation

52.38 Circumstantial participles often express the **cause or motivation** for an action or statement, especially when they **follow the matrix verb**:

(103) Παρύσατις μὲν δὴ ἡ μήτηρ ὑπῆρχε τῷ Κύρῳ, <u>φιλοῦσα</u> αὐτὸν μᾶλλον ἢ τὸν βασιλεύοντα Ἀρταξέρξην. (Xen. *An.* 1.1.4)

Parysatis, the mother, was on the side of Cyrus, as she loved him more than Artaxerxes, who ruled as king.

52.39 The relationship between participle and matrix verb may be made explicit by:

– ὡς to give a 'subjective' reason or motivation, for which responsibility lies with the subject of the matrix verb (*because, thinking that, in the conviction that, as*);

– ἅτε (sometimes οἷα, οἷον) to give an 'objective' reason, for which the speaker/narrator takes responsibility (*because, given the fact that, (inasmuch) as*).

(104) αὐτοὶ ἐνταῦθ᾽ ἔμενον <u>ὡς</u> τὸ ἄκρον <u>κατέχοντες</u>. οἱ δ᾽ οὐ κατεῖχον. (Xen. *An.* 4.2.5)

There they remained thinking that they held the summit. But they did not hold it. *Subjective reason. The narrator does not share the subjects' reasoning, as οἱ δ᾽ οὐ κατεῖχον makes clear.*

(105) λέξατε οὖν πρός με τί ἐν νῷ ἔχετε <u>ὡς</u> . . . <u>βουλόμενον</u> κοινῇ σὺν ὑμῖν τὸν στόλον ποιεῖσθαι. (Xen. *An.* 3.3.2).

So, tell me what your plans are, in the conviction that I wish to make the journey together with you. *The speaker (Mithradates) provides the addressees (Greek commanders) with certain assumptions about him on which they should base the answer which he wants them to give.*

(106) καὶ τὸ μειράκιον, <u>ἅτε</u> μεγάλου <u>ὄντος</u> τοῦ ἐρωτήματος, ἠρυθρίασέν τε καὶ ἀπορήσας ἐνέβλεψεν εἰς ἐμέ. (Pl. *Euthd.* 275d)

And since the question was a big one, the young man blushed and glanced at me in his helplessness. *The speaker gives the reason for the young man's reaction.*

(107) καὶ <u>οἷα</u> δὴ <u>ἀπιόντων</u> πρὸς δεῖπνον . . . τῶν πελταστῶν . . . ἐπελαύνουσι. (Xen. *Hell.* 5.4.39)

And since the peltasts were going away to dinner, they (*the Thebans*) charged upon them. *The genitive absolute with οἷα explains why the Thebans could attack easily.*

Condition

52.40   A participle may express the **condition** under which the action in the main clause may occur:

(108) σὺ δὲ <u>κλύων</u> εἴσει τάχα. (Ar. *Av.* 1390)

If you listen, you will soon find out.

If the matrix clause has a potential optative (→34.13) or a counterfactual indicative (→34.16), the participle may have the force of the corresponding potential or counterfactual conditional clause:

(109) νῦν δὲ Ἀθηναίους ἄν τις <u>λέγων</u> σωτῆρας γενέσθαι τῆς Ἑλλάδος <u>οὐκ ἂν ἁμαρτάνοι</u> τἀληθές. (Hdt. 7.139.5)

As it is, if anyone were to say that the Athenians were the saviours of Greece, he would not be wrong. *Given the potential optative (οὐκ ἂν ἁμαρτάνοι) in the matrix clause, the participle has the force of a potential conditional clause (→49.8). For the repetition of ἄν, →60.12.*

(110) ἀκρίτου μὲν γὰρ <u>ὄντος</u> τοῦ πράγματος <u>οὐκ ἂν ἠπίστασθ'</u> . . . (Isoc. 19.2)

For if the case had not gone to trial, you would not have known . . . *The genitive absolute has counterfactual force, given the counterfactual matrix clause (οὐκ ἂν ἠπίστασθ(ε)).*

The **negative** with the participle in the conditional use is **μή** (μή + circumstantial participle is nearly always conditional):

(111) . . . ὃ νῦν ὑμεῖς <u>μὴ πειθόμενοι</u> ἡμῖν πάθοιτε ἄν. (Thuc. 1.40.2)

. . . which might well happen to you now if you do not listen to us.

Purpose

52.41 The **future participle** usually expresses **purpose**, often in combination with ὡς, which expresses the intention of the subject:

(112) παρεσκευάζοντο ὡς πολεμήσοντες. (Thuc. 2.7.1)
They prepared in order to wage war.

(113) δεξιᾷ δὲ λαμπάδα | Τιτὰν Προμηθεὺς ἔφερεν ὡς πρήσων πόλιν. (Eur. *Phoen.* 1121–2)
The Titan Prometheus carried a torch in his right hand to burn the city.

But ὡς is frequently omitted, especially after verbs of sending and going:

(114) αὖθις ὁ βάρβαρος ... ἐπὶ τὴν Ἑλλάδα δουλωσόμενος ἦλθεν. (Thuc. 1.18.2)
The barbarian returned to Greece in order to enslave it.

Note 1: Observe the idiomatic expression ἔρχομαι + fut. ppl. *be about to, be going to*, especially with participles of verbs of speech:

(115) ἐγὼ δὲ περὶ μὲν τούτων οὐκ ἔρχομαι ἐρέων ὡς ... (Hdt. 1.5.3)
I am not going to say about these things, that ...

Manner, Means

52.42 A present participle or 'coincident' aorist participle (→52.5) is sometimes used to express **manner or means** :

(116) ληζόμενοι ζῶσι. (Xen. *Cyr.* 3.2.25)
They live by pillaging.

(117) ἀπώλεσέν μ᾽ εἰποῦσα συμφορὰς ἐμάς. (Eur. *Hipp.* 596)
She has destroyed me by revealing my misfortunes. *Coincident aorist participle.*

Note 1: Circumstantial participles of verbs meaning 'have', 'take', 'use', etc. (e.g. ἔχων, χρώμενος (+ dat.), φέρων, ἄγων, λαβών) often express little more than Engl. *with*:

(118) ἔρχεται ... τὸν υἱὸν ἔχουσα. (Xen. *Cyr.* 1.3.1)
She came with her son.

Note 2: The participle ἔχων may be combined with a present indicative with the sense *continually, unceasingly*:

(119) ΣΩ. τὸν σκυτοτόμον ἴσως μέγιστα δεῖ ὑποδήματα καὶ πλεῖστα ὑποδεδεμένον περιπατεῖν. :: ΚΑ. ποῖα ὑποδήματα; φλυαρεῖς ἔχων. (Pl. *Grg.* 490e)
(Socrates:) Perhaps the shoemaker should walk around wearing the largest and the most shoes. :: (Callicles:) Shoes? What shoes? You keep talking nonsense.

Note 3: The verb οἴχομαι *depart, be gone* (→33.18) is often combined with a participle, usually of a verb of motion, to express the manner of departure: e.g. οἴχεται φεύγων *he has fled*, ᾤχετο ἀπελαύνων *he rode off*, ᾤχοντο ἀπιόντες *they left*.

Comparison

52.43   A participle may be combined with **ὥσπερ** (sometimes ὡς) *like, as (if)* to express comparison:

> (120) αὖθις γὰρ δή, <u>ὥσπερ</u> ἑτέρων τούτων <u>ὄντων</u> κατηγόρων, λάβωμεν αὖ τὴν τούτων ἀντωμοσίαν. (Pl. *Ap.* 24b)
>
> Let us then again, as if they are other plaintiffs, take up in turn their sworn statement.

Note that ὥσπερ can be accompanied by ὁμοίως *in a similar way as (if), just as though*:

> (121) κείνη δ', <u>ὁμοίως ὥσπερ</u> οὐκ ἰδοῦσα φῶς, | τέθνηκε κοὐδὲν οἶδε τῶν αὑτῆς κακῶν (Eur. *Tro.* 641–2)
>
> But she is dead, just as though she has never seen light, and she knows nothing of her own misfortunes.

Note 1: Comparison may also be expressed by **ὡσπερανεί** (ὥσπερ ἂν εἰ) + participle. This construction may be seen as a case of a comparative conditional clause without a verb (→49.24):

> (122) κραυγὴ καὶ βοὴ τῶν γυναικῶν τοσαύτη ... ἦν <u>ὡσπερανεὶ</u> <u>τεθνεῶτός</u> τινος, ὥστε ... (Dem. 54.20)
>
> There was so much wailing and shouting of the women as if someone had died, that ...

Concession

52.44   To express concession, a participle is usually combined with **καίπερ, καί** (*even though, although, even if*) or **καὶ ταῦτα** (*and that even though, regardless of the fact that*) preceding the participle:

> (123) Ἄδρηστον κατοικτίρει, <u>καίπερ ἐὼν</u> ἐν κακῷ ... τοσούτῳ. (Hdt. 1.45.2)
>
> He took pity on Adrastus, although he found himself in so much agony.

> (124) πῶς οὐκ ἂν ἄθλιοι γεγονότες εἶεν ... μηδὲν πλέον νέμοντες τοῖς φίλοις ... ἢ τοῖς ἐχθροῖς, <u>καὶ ταῦτα</u> <u>ἄρχοντες</u> ἐν τῇ ἑαυτῶν πόλει; (Pl. *Grg.* 492b–c)
>
> How could they fail to be wretched, if they did not give a larger portion to their friends than to their enemies, and that even though they ruled in their own city?

Note 1: In poetry περ (→59.55) is sometimes used to give concessive force to the participle:

> (125) χώρει σύ· μὴ πρόσλευσσε, γενναῖός <u>περ</u> ὤν. (Soph. *Phil.* 1068)
>
> Go. Don't look at him, noble though you are.

Dominant Use of Circumstantial Participles

52.45   Occasionally, a circumstantial participle is indispensable for the correct interpretation of a sentence, providing more relevant information than the head noun it modifies (syntactically speaking). The participle, together with its noun, serves as obligatory constituent (and as such, the participle is not syntactically 'optional'). This is called the **dominant** use of the participle:

(126) ἐλύπει αὐτὸν ἡ χώρα πορθουμένη. (Xen. *An.* 7.7.12)

> The fact that the country was being ravaged grieved him (*lit. 'the country being ravaged grieved him'*). *The entirety of ἡ χώρα πορθουμένη, not merely ἡ χώρα, is subject of ἐλύπει. The interpretation as a dominant participle is facilitated by the fact that a country cannot normally cause grief.*

In essence, such constructions are nominalized clauses: ἡ χώρα πορθουμένη in (126) represents ἡ χώρα πορθεῖται *the country is being ravaged* in nominal form (in the nom. as subject of ἐλύπει).

Dominant participle constructions are also often used to complement prepositions:

μετὰ <u>Σόλωνα οἰχόμενον</u>	after Solon's departure
ἐπὶ <u>Θεοφίλου ἄρχοντος</u>	during the archonship of Theophilus

(127) ἐς μὲν γὰρ <u>ἄνδρα</u> σκῆψιν εἶχ' <u>ὀλωλότα</u>, | παίδων δ' ἔδεισε μὴ φθονηθείη φόνῳ. (Eur. *El.* 29–30)

> For with respect to the death of her husband she had an excuse (*lit. 'with respect to her husband, being dead, she had an excuse'*), but she feared that she would be despised for the murder of her children.

Note 1: The construction is also sometimes called the *ab urbe condita* construction, after the comparable Latin construction (*ab urbe condita* = 'from the founding of the city').

The Participle in Noun Phrases

Attributive Use (as Modifier) and Substantival Use (as Head)

52.46   The participle can be used with an article in noun phrases, either as a modifier (attributive use) or as head (substantival use):

οἱ νόμοι οἱ <u>κείμενοι</u>	the standing laws (*attributive, modifier with νόμοι*)
τὰ <u>παρόντα</u> πράγματα	the present circumstances (*attributive, modifier with πράγματα*)
οἱ <u>ἀπόντες</u>	the absent ones, absentees, those who are/were absent (*substantival, used as head*)
τὰ ἀεὶ <u>παρόντα</u>	the circumstances at any given time (*substantival, used as head*)

(128) ἐν ᾧ δὲ ὡπλίζοντο ἧκον ... οἱ <u>προπεμφθέντες</u> σκοποί. (Xen. *An.* 2.2.15)

While they were arming, the scouts who had been sent ahead returned. *Attributive, modifier with* σκοποί.

(129) ἔλεγον ὡς εἴη τὰ ἔργα τὰ <u>γεγενημένα</u> οὐκ ὀλίγων ἀνδρῶν ἀλλ' ἐπὶ τῇ τοῦ δήμου καταλύσει. (Andoc. 1.36)

They claimed that the acts which had been committed were not those of a few men, but were intended to overthrow the democracy. *Attributive, modifier with* ἔργα.

(130) ΚΑ. τίνος πρόσωπον δῆτ' ἐν ἀγκάλαις ἔχεις; | :: ΑΓ. λέοντος, ὥς γ' ἔφασκον αἱ <u>θηρώμεναι</u>. (Eur. *Bacch.* 1277–8)

(Cadmus:) Whose head, then, are you carrying in your arms? :: (Agaue:) That of a lion, or so the hunting women said, at least. *Substantival*.

(131) ... ἀναλαβὼν ... τοὺς ἐν τῇ μάχῃ πρὸς τοὺς Ἕλληνας <u>αὐτομολήσαντας</u>. (Xen. *An.* 1.10.6)

... having picked up those who had defected to the Greeks during the battle. *Substantival. Observe that the participle is itself modified by* ἐν τῇ μάχῃ πρὸς τοὺς Ἕλληνας.

Note 1: For the position of the participle relative to the article (and the head noun), →28.11–12, 28.25.

Note 2: Some substantivally used participles developed into nouns: e.g. ὁ ἄρχων *chief, magistrate* (cf. ἄρχω *rule*).

52.47   Occasionally, attributive/substantival participles occur without an article:

(132) ... φαμένη τὸν Νεῖλον ῥέειν ἀπὸ <u>τηκομένης</u> χιόνος. (Hdt. 2.22.1)

... claiming that the Nile flows from melting snow. *Attributive, modifier with* χιόνος.

(133) ἔπλει δώδεκα τριήρεις ἔχων ἐπὶ πολλὰς ναῦς <u>κεκτημένους</u>. (Xen. *Hell.* 5.1.19)

He sailed with twelve triremes against men who had many ships. *Substantival*.

Generic Use

52.48   When the article is used with a participle (especially with present participles), it often has **generic value** (→28.6), with the sense 'whoever . . .'. The **negative** in this case is **μή**:

(134) πῶς ἂν γένοιντο πονηρότεροι ἄνθρωποι ... <u>τοῦ παιδεύοντος</u> τὰ τοιαῦτα; (Dem. 35.42)

How could there be men more wicked than whoever teaches such things?

(135) ὁ <u>μὴ γαμῶν</u> ἄνθρωπος οὐκ ἔχει κακά. (Men. *Sent.* 437)

An unmarried man has no troubles.

Note 1: The participle of βούλομαι *want* is used generically particularly often: ὁ βουλόμενος *anyone who likes, any chance person*:

(136) ΣΥ. κατηγορεῖ δὲ τίς; | :: ΔΙ. ὁ βουλόμενος. :: ΣΥ. οὔκουν ἐκεῖνός εἰμ' ἐγώ; (Ar. *Plut.*
    917–18)
    (Sycophant:) And who's the accuser? :: (Just Man:) Any volunteer. :: (Sycophant:) I'm it!

Tense/Aspect of Attributive and Substantival Participles

52.49   The **aspectual distinctions** between different tense stems (→52.4–5) are fully
    relevant for attributive and substantival participles.

- Such distinctions typically result in an interpretation of relative tense (→33.57);
    for instance, προπεμφθέντες in (128) above is anterior to ἧκον, θηρώμεναι in
    (130) is simultaneous with ἔφασκον, γεγενημένα in (129) refers to a state simul-
    taneous with εἴη;
- Not infrequently, however, other connotations of aspect are equally or more
    relevant (also →33.58):

(137) Τραυσοὶ ... κατὰ δὲ τὸν γινόμενόν σφι καὶ ἀπογινόμενον ποιεῦσι τοιάδε· τὸν
    μὲν γενόμενον ... ὀλοφύρονται, ... τὸν δ' ἀπογενόμενον παίζοντές τε καὶ
    ἡδόμενοι γῇ κρύπτουσι. (Hdt. 5.4.1)
    The Trausi behave as follows with respect to those who are born and those
    who die. When a child is born they lament it, but when someone dies they
    bury him with celebration and gladness. *The present participles γινόμενον
    and ἀπογινόμενον refer to repeated births and deaths ('every time someone is
    born/dies'), while the aorist participles γενόμενον and ἀπογενόμενον single out
    an individual birth or death to discuss what happens in such cases ('the one
    who is born/who has died').*

Note 1: The future participle with the article can be used to refer to an identifiable
group or class of people who intend, are intended and/or are able and likely to carry
out an action:

(138) τίς οὖν ὁ γνωσόμενος εἰ τὸ προσῆκον εἶδος κερκίδος ἐν ὁποιῳοῦν ξύλῳ κεῖται; ὁ
    ποιήσας, ὁ τέκτων, ἢ ὁ χρησόμενος ὁ ὑφάντης; (Pl. *Cra.* 390b)
    Who is likely to know whether the correct form of a shuttle resides in a certain piece
    of wood? The person who made it, the carpenter, or the one who is to use it, the
    weaver?

Participles in Apposition

52.50   Attributive participles may also occur **in apposition** to a noun (phrase). This
    occurs particularly frequently with the participle of εἰμί *be*, often in apposition to
    a proper name.

(139) ἦγον δὲ καὶ ἄλλοι Θεσσαλῶν αὐτὸν καὶ ἐκ Λαρίσης Νικονίδας Περδίκκᾳ ἐπιτήδειος <u>ὤν</u>. (Thuc. 4.78.2)

Other Thessalians escorted him as well, among them Niconidas from Larissa, who was a friend of Perdiccas. *Περδίκκᾳ ἐπιτήδειος ὤν stands in apposition to Νικονίδας.*

Note 1: As the participle in such cases does not stand in attributive position relative to the head noun and the article, context must determine whether a participle is to be interpreted as being in apposition or as a circumstantial participle (i.e. as standing in predicative position). In some cases both interpretations are possible:

(140) Ἐριχθόνιος ... παρὰ Κέκροπος ἄπαιδος <u>ὄντος</u> ἀρρένων παίδων ... τὴν βασιλείαν παρέλαβεν. (Isoc. 12.126)

Erichthonius took over the kingship from Cecrops, who was without male children. *As translated, the participle is interpreted as being in apposition; it is also possible to translate 'because he was without male children' (circumstantial participle).*

Periphrastic Uses of the Participle

εἰμί + Participle

52.51   In **εἰμί + participle** (usually present or perfect, less frequently aorist), the combined phrase is roughly equivalent to a finite form of the same verb (and in the same tense-aspect stem):

(141) ... ὅπως, ἂν μὲν ὑμῖν ἑκατὸν δέῃ τριήρων, τὴν ... δαπάνην ἑξήκοντα τάλαντα συντελῇ ... ἂν δὲ διακοσίων, τριάκοντα ... <u>ᾖ</u> τάλαντα τὴν δαπάνην <u>συντελοῦντα</u>. (Dem. 14.20)

... so that, if you need a hundred triremes, sixty talents will cover the cost, but if you need two hundred, thirty talents will cover the cost. *ᾖ συντελοῦντα corresponds roughly to pres. subj. συντελῇ, which is in fact used earlier in the sentence.*

(142) οἱ δὲ Αἰτωλοὶ (<u>βεβοηθηκότες</u> γὰρ ἤδη <u>ἦσαν</u> ἐπὶ τὸ Αἰγίτιον) προσέβαλλον τοῖς Ἀθηναίοις. (Thuc. 3.97.3)

But the Aetolians (since by this time they had come to the rescue of Aegition), attacked the Athenians. *βεβοηθηκότες ἦσαν corresponds to ἐβεβοηθήκεσαν.*

Note 1: There are various reasons why authors may have used a periphrastic construction with εἰμί instead of a synthetic form, including possible slight differences of meaning, considerations of word order, metrical constraints (in poetry), register, variation, etc.

The considerations involved were probably not consistent over time, nor across tense stems or types of verb used for the participle.

52.52 Various **perfect middle-passive forms** occur **only in periphrastic form** with forms of εἰμί. For details, →19.8.

ἔχω + Participle

52.53 **ἔχω + participle** (nearly always with an aorist participle) – a construction known as the σχῆμα Ἀττικόν or σχῆμα Σοφόκλειον – is roughly equivalent to a perfect indicative:

(143) καὶ νῦν ἀδελφὰ τῶνδε <u>κηρύξας ἔχω</u> | ἀστοῖσι παίδων τῶν ἀπ' Οἰδίπου πέρι. (Soph. *Ant.* 192–3)
And now I have proclaimed things akin to these to the citizens, concerning the sons of Oedipus. *κηρύξας ἔχω is roughly equivalent to κεκήρυχα.*

(144) τὸν λόγον δέ σου πάλαι <u>θαυμάσας ἔχω</u> ... (Pl. *Phdr.* 257c)
For a long time I have wondered about your speech ... *θαυμάσας ἔχω corresponds to τεθαύμακα.*

Note 1: ἔχω + participle occurs primarily in Sophocles and, less frequently, in Euripides and Herodotus. It occurs only rarely in later prose authors.

Note 2: The difference between ἔχω + aorist participle and a perfect indicative (e.g. τεθαύμακα) is not always clear, and (as with εἰμί + ppl., →52.51 n.1) various considerations may have played a role in the choice of one over the other. The connotations of the periphrastic construction also were probably not consistent over time, nor across various types of verb used as the participle.

53

Overview of Subordinate Constructions

Complements

53.1 Complement clauses fulfil the role of an obligatory constituent of the main predicate, usually subject or object (→39.3). Such complements can take the form of:

- a dynamic or declarative infinitive;
- a supplementary participle;
- a ὅτι/ὡς-clause;
- an indirect question;
- a fear clause with μή;
- or an effort clause with ὅπως.

The following overview lists a number of semantically determined classes of verbs, together with the complements they take.

Verb Class	Meaning	Complement	→
Phase ἄρχομαι *begin* παύομαι *stop* παύω *stop (someone)*	The verb expresses some phase of the action (beginning, continuation or end)	Present participle; Dynamic infinitive	51.8, 52.9
Modal δύναμαι *be able* δεῖ *it is necessary*	The verb expresses the need or possibility of an action taking place	Dynamic infinitive	51.8
Manipulative ἀναγκάζω *force* κελεύω *order*	The subject forces, tells or asks someone else to do something	Dynamic infinitive	51.8
Desiderative/Volitional βούλομαι *want to* αἱρέομαι *choose to* γιγνώσκω *resolve to, decide to*	The subject wishes or decides that something should happen	Dynamic infinitive	51.8
Practical knowledge ἐπίσταμαι *know (how to)* διδάσκω *teach (how to)*	The subject knows how to do something or teaches others how to do something	Dynamic infinitive	51.8
Direct perception ὁράω *see* ἀκούω *hear*	The subject perceives an action occurring by (one of) the senses	Present participle	52.9, 52.14
Fearing φοβέομαι *fear* φόβος ἐστί *there is a fear*	The subject fears the (future) realization of an action	μή + subjunctive[1] (for μή + ind., →43.5)	43

Verb Class	Meaning	Complement	→
Effort φροντίζω *take care* σπεύδω *strive*	The subject makes an effort to realize an action	ὅπως + future indicative[1] (for other constructions, →44.6–7)	44
Opinion νομίζω *believe* οἴομαι *think* γιγνώσκω *judge*	The subject believes the action expressed in the complement to be true	Declarative infinitive	51.19
Intellectual knowledge and emotion ἐπίσταμαι *understand* γιγνώσκω *know, realize* ἥδομαι *be pleased, enjoy*	The subject knows, or emotionally responds to, the action expressed in the complement	Participle; ὅτι + any tense/mood[1] (for these verbs with indirect questions, →42.2)	41.3, 41.15, 52.10
Declarative utterance (verbs of speech) λέγω *say* φημί *say, claim*	The subjects asserts the action expressed in the complement	Declarative infinitive; ὅτι + any tense/mood[1] (φημί very rarely with ὅτι/ὡς-clause)	41.3, 51.19
Interrogative utterance ἐρωτάω *ask* βουλεύομαι *deliberate*	The subject is uncertain about (an aspect of) the action expressed in the complement	(*yes/no-questions*) εἰ, πότερον . . . ἤ . . . , εἰ . . . εἴτε . . . ; (*specifying questions*) τίς/ὅστις, πόσος/ὁπόσος, etc. + tense/mood of direct questions[1]	42

[1] Or oblique optative in historic sequence (after past-tense matrix verbs, →40.12).

Further Particulars

53.2 There are numerous verbs which – depending on their complement – may belong to more than one type: for example γιγνώσκω + declarative inf. = *judge* (verb of opinion), γιγνώσκω + dynamic inf. = *resolve to, decide to* (desiderative verb), γιγνώσκω + ppl. or ὅτι/ὡς-clause = *realize* (intellectual knowledge). For overviews of such verbs, →51.28–33 and 52.17–28.

53.3 Some classes in the overview may be construed with more than one type of complement, with a distinction of meaning between the use of one complement or the other. For details, →52.27 (phase verbs), →52.28 (verbs of intellectual knowledge and emotion), and →51.19 n.1 (declarative utterance verbs).

53.4 For the difference between the use of an oblique optative and 'retaining' the original mood in historic sequence, →41.13–14.

Adverbial and Adjectival Subordinate Clauses

53.5   The following overview lists the different adverbial and adjectival (i.e. relative) subordinate clauses of Greek, together with the conjunction(s) and mood(s) used for each type; if the use of a particular mood is dependent on (or strongly corresponds to) the use of a particular tense/mood in the matrix clause, this is given as well:

	Mood/tense in subordinate clause	Mood/tense in matrix clause	→
Purpose: ἵνα, ὅπως, ὡς, μή (neg.)			45
	subjunctive (tense stem according to aspect); oblique optative frequent with past-tense matrix clauses		
Result: ὥστε			46
actual result	moods/tenses as in independent sentences		
natural/inevitable result	infinitive (tense stem according to aspect)		
Temporal: ὅτε, ὡς, ἐπεί, ἐπειδή, ἐν ᾧ, ἕως, πρίν, etc.			47
referring to the past	past indicative		
referring to the future	ἄν + subjunctive (tense stem according to aspect)	form with future reference	
referring to habitual occurrence	ἄν + subjunctive (tense stem according to aspect)	present indicative	
	optative without ἄν (tense stem according to aspect)	imperfect	
πρίν	as above (with aor.-stem finite verb)	negative main clause, any tense/mood	
	infinitive (tense stem according to aspect)	non-negative main clause, any tense/mood	
Causal: ὅτι, διότι and ἐπεί, ὡς			48
	moods/tenses as in independent sentences	any tense/mood	
	oblique optative with past-tense matrix clauses (with reported or alleged reason)		
Conditional: εἰ (concessive with καὶ εἰ / εἰ καί)			49
neutral	indicative (present or past tense)	any tense/mood	
	future indicative (often in threats, warnings, etc.)	form with future reference	

	Mood/tense in subordinate clause	Mood/tense in matrix clause →
prospective	ἄν + subjunctive (tense stem according to aspect)	form with future reference
potential	optative without ἄν (tense stem according to aspect)	ἄν + optative (tense stem according to aspect)
counterfactual	modal (secondary) indicative without ἄν (aor./impf./plpf. according to aspect)	ἄν + modal (secondary) indicative (aor./impf./plpf. according to aspect)
habitual	ἄν + subjunctive (tense stem according to aspect)	present indicative
	optative without ἄν (tense stem according to aspect)	imperfect, pluperfect

A protasis (subordinate clause) and apodosis (main clause) from two different types are often combined ('mixed conditionals').

(Cor)relative: ὅς (etc.), ὅστις (etc.), ἔνθα, ὡς, etc.		50
digressive	moods/tenses as in independent sentences	
restrictive	moods/tenses as in temporal and conditional clauses; counterfactual ἄν + sec. ind. and potential ἄν + opt. are possible	

The future indicative can be used in relative clauses with purpose value; past or present indicatives are used with causal value or result value (often after ὅστις).

Further Particulars

53.6 For the difference between the use of an oblique optative and 'retaining' the subjunctive in purpose clauses, →45.3 n.1.

53.7 For attraction of mood (i.e. subordinate clauses taking on the mood of their matrix clauses), overriding the use of moods as detailed in the table, →40.15.

54

Overview of Moods

Indicative

54.1   Indicative in **main clauses**:

use	negative	→
in **statements and questions** about present, past and future ποιοῦσι ταῦτα *they are doing that* τί ποιοῦσιν; *what are they doing?*	οὐ	34.5
οὐ + second-person fut. ind. expressing an **urgent command** οὐ ποιήσεις ταῦτα; *won't you do that? / do that!*	(οὐ) μή	38.32
(τί) οὐ + first- or second-person pres./aor. ind. expressing a **request** or **suggestion** τί οὐκ ἐποιήσαμεν ταῦτα; *why don't we do that?*	(οὐ)	38.33
ὅπως + fut. ind. expressing a **strong command** ὅπως ποιήσεις ταῦτα *(make sure you) do that!*	μή	38.34

54.2   Indicative in **subordinate clauses**:

use	negative	→
in **fear clauses** expressing disappointment about a present or past fact, with **μή + pres. or pf. ind.** δέδοικα μὴ πεποιήκασι ταῦτα *I fear that they have done that*	οὐ	43.5
in **effort clauses** (depending on a verb of effort), with **ὅπως (ὡς) + fut. ind.** ὅρα ὅπως ποιήσουσι ταῦτα *see to it that they do that*	μή	44.2
in **temporal clauses** to refer to a single action in the past ὅτε ταῦτα ἐποίησαν, ηὐτύχουν *when they had done that, they prospered*	οὐ	47.7
in **neutral conditional clauses**, with εἰ εἰ ταῦτα ποιοῦσιν εὐτυχοῦσιν *if they do that they prosper*	μή	49.4
in **neutral conditional clauses**, with **εἰ + fut. ind.** (esp. in threats, warnings, etc.) εἰ ταῦτα ποιήσουσιν ἀποθανοῦνται *if they do that they will die*	μή	49.5
in **restrictive relative clauses** ἐπαινῶ ταῦτα ἃ ποιοῦσιν *I praise the things which they are doing*	οὐ/μή	50.19
in (digressive) **relative clauses** with **causal force**	οὐ	50.23

use	negative →	
μὴ θορυβήσητε, οἳ οὐδὲν λέγουσιν *don't make noise, you who speak nonsense*		
in **relative clauses** with **purpose force**, with **fut. ind.**	οὐ	50.24
σύλλεγε ἄνδρας οἳ ταῦτα ποιήσουσιν *gather men to do that (who will do that)*		
in **relative clauses** with **result force**	οὐ	50.25
οὐδεὶς οὕτω μάχεται ὅστις οὐκ ἀποθανεῖν ἐθέλει *no one fights in such a way that he is not willing to die*		

for indirect statements, indirect questions, result clauses, causal clauses, digressive relative clauses, →54.11

Modal (Secondary) Indicative

54.3   Modal indicative in **main clauses**:

ἄν	use	negative →	
+ ἄν	in **counterfactual statements and questions**	οὐ	34.16
	ἐποίησαν ἄν ταῦτα *they would (have) do(ne) that* (but didn't)		
- ἄν	in **unrealizable wishes**, with εἴθε, εἰ γάρ	μή	34.18
	εἴθε ἐποίησαν ταῦτα *would that they had done that* (but they haven't)		
	imperfect of impersonal verbs expressing unfulfilled necessity	οὐ	34.17
	ἔδει αὐτοὺς ποιεῖν/ποιῆσαι ταῦτα *they should do/have done that* (but don't/didn't)		
	imperfect ἐβουλόμην *I would (have) like(d)*, ἔμελλον *I would (have) be(en) likely to*	οὐ	34.17

54.4   Modal indicative in **subordinate clauses**:

ἄν	use	negative →	
+ ἄν	in **relative clauses** referring to a **counterfactual action**	οὐ	50.17, 50.26
	ἐπαινῶ ταῦτα ἃ ἄν ἐποίησαν *I praise the things which they would have done* (but didn't)		
	for indirect statements, indirect questions, result clauses, causal clauses, digressive relative clauses, →54.11		
- ἄν	in **counterfactual conditional clauses** (main clause: modal (secondary) indicative with ἄν)	μή	49.10
	εἰ ταῦτα ἐποίησαν ηὐτύχουν ἄν *if they had done that they would prosper* (but they didn't)		
	in **restrictive relative clauses** with a **counterfactual conditional force** (main clause: modal (secondary) indicative with ἄν)	μή	50.22
	ἐπῄνεσεν ἄν ταῦτα ἃ ἐποίησαν *he would have praised the things they would have done* (i.e. if they had done them, but they didn't)		
	through **attraction of mood**	μή	40.15

Subjunctive

54.5   Subjunctive in **main clauses**:

use		negative →
in first-person exhortations (**hortatory**) ποιῶμεν ταῦτα *let us do that*	μή	34.6
in second-person prohibitions, (**prohibitive**) with μή, aor. subj. only μὴ ποιήσῃς ταῦτα *don't do that*	μή	34.7
in first-person doubtful questions (**deliberative**) τί ποιῶμεν; *what should we do?*	μή	34.8
in emphatic denials with **οὐ μή** οὐ μὴ ποιήσω ταῦτα *I will certainly not do that*	οὐ μή	34.9
in doubtful assertions with **μή** μὴ οὐχ οὕτως ἔχῃ *I suspect that is not the case*	(μή) οὐ	34.10

54.6   Subjunctive in **subordinate clauses**:

ἄν	use		negative →
- ἄν	in **fear clauses** (depending on a verb of fearing) referring to the future, with μή δέδοικα μὴ ποιήσωσι ταῦτα *I fear that they do that*	οὐ	43.3
	in **fear clauses** (depending on a verb of fearing) referring to an uncertain present or past action, with μή δέδοικα μὴ πεποιήκωσι ταῦτα *I fear that they may have done that*	οὐ	43.4
	in **purpose clauses**, with ἵνα, ὅπως, ὡς (also sometimes in effort clauses with ὅπως, ὡς) ἀπέρχονται ἵνα ποιήσωσιν ταῦτα *they are leaving in order to do that*	μή	45.3, 44.3
+ ἄν	in **prospective temporal, conditional** and **restrictive relative clauses** referring to (single) actions **in the future** (main clause: fut. ind., imp., etc.) ὅταν/ἐὰν ταῦτα ποιήσωσιν εὐτυχήσουσιν *when/if they do that they will prosper* ἐπαινέσω ταῦτα ἃ ἂν ποιήσωσιν *I will praise the things which they do* (i.e. if they do them)	μή	40.9, 47.8, 49.6, 50.20
	in **indefinite temporal, conditional** and **restrictive relative clauses** referring to a non-past **habitual/repeated action** (main clause: pres. ind.) ὅταν/ἐὰν ταῦτα ποιήσωσιν εὐτυχοῦσιν *whenever/if ever they do that they prosper* ὃς ἂν ταῦτα ποιῇ εὐτυχεῖ *whoever does that prospers*	μή	40.9, 47.9, 49.13, 50.21

ἄν	use	negative →
	occasionally in **purpose clauses** (also in effort clauses) with ὅπως, ὡς; prospective ἄν + subj.	μή 45.5, 44.4
	ἀπέρχονται ὅπως ἄν ποιήσωσι ταῦτα *they are leaving in order to do that*	

Optative

54.7 Optative in **main clauses**:

ἄν	use	negative →
- ἄν	in **realizable wishes** ('cupitive'), often with εἴθε, εἰ γάρ, ὡς (εἴθε) ποιοίης ταῦτα *may you do that*	μή **34.14**
+ ἄν	**potential optative:**	οὐ **34.13**
	- in statements and questions about possible actions ποιοῖεν ἄν ταῦτα *they may/might/could do that*	
	- (with a negative) in emphatic negations οὐ ποιοῖεν ἄν ταῦτα *they could/would not do that*	
	- in cautious commands, permissions, etc. ποιοίης ἄν ταῦτα *please, do that*	

54.8 Optative in **subordinate clauses**:

ἄν	use	negative →
- ἄν	**iterative optative:** in **temporal, conditional and restrictive relative clauses** referring to a **habitual/repeated action in the past** (main clause: imperfect)	μή 40.9, 47.10, 49.13, 50.21
	ὅτε/εἰ ταῦτα ποιήσειαν ηὐτύχουν *whenever/if ever they did that they prospered*	
	ὅς ταῦτα ποιοίη ηὐτύχει *whoever did that prospered*	
	in **potential conditional clauses** (main clause: potential optative with ἄν)	μή 49.8
	εἰ ταῦτα ποιοῖεν εὐτυχοῖεν ἄν *if they were to do that they may/could/might prosper*	
	in **restrictive relative clauses** with a **potential conditional value** (main clause: potential optative with ἄν)	μή 50.22
	ἐπαινέσαιμ' ἄν ταῦτα ἅ ποιήσειαν *I would praise the things which they do* (i.e. if they should do them)	

ἄν	use		negative →
	in historic sequence an **oblique optative** _can_ be used in:		40.12
	- **indirect statements** (ὅτι/ὡς)	οὐ	41.9
	ἔλεγον ὅτι <u>ποιοῖεν</u> ταῦτα _they said that they were doing that_		
	- **indirect questions** (also to replace deliberative subj.)	οὐ	42.7
	ἤροντο τί <u>ποιοῖεν</u> _they asked what they did/should do_		
	- **fear clauses** (frequently)	(μή) οὐ	43.3
	ἐφοβούμην <u>μὴ</u> <u>ποιήσειαν</u> ταῦτα _I feared that they would do that_		
	- **effort clauses** (rarely) with fut. opt.	μή	44.2
	ἐπεμέλοντο <u>ὅπως</u> <u>ποιήσοιεν</u> ταῦτα _they took care that they did that_		
	- **purpose clauses** (frequently)	μή	45.3
	ἀπῆλθον <u>ἵνα</u> <u>ποιοῖεν</u> ταῦτα _they left in order to do that_		
	- **causal clauses**, to refer to an alleged/reported reason	οὐ	48.2
	ἐγράφοντο αὐτὸν <u>διότι</u> τοὺς νέους <u>διαφθείρειε</u> _they sued him on the grounds that he spoilt the youth_		
	- also in **subordinate clauses within subordinate clauses** (where ἄν + subj. is replaced by opt. without ἄν), particularly subordinate clauses within indirect speech		40.14, 41.19
	ἔλεγον ὅτι εὐτυχήσοιεν <u>ὅτε/εἰ</u> ταῦτα <u>ποιήσειαν</u> _they said that they would prosper when/if they did that_		
	through **attraction of mood**	μή	40.15
	for the (rare) use of the cupitive optative in subordinate clauses, →54.11		
+ ἄν	in **relative clauses** referring to a **possible action**	οὐ	50.17, 50.26
	ἐπαινῶ ταῦτα <u>ἃ</u> ἂν <u>ποιήσειαν</u> _I praise the things which they might do_		
	for indirect statements, indirect questions, result clauses, causal clauses, digressive relative clauses, →54.11		

Imperative

54.9   Imperative in **main clauses**:

use	negative →
in second- and third-person **commands, requests**, etc.	34.19–20
<u>ποίει</u> ταῦτα _do that_	
<u>ποιείτω</u> ταῦτα _let him do that_	
in second-person **prohibitions** with μή, (pres. imp. only)	μή 34.19–20
<u>μὴ ποίει</u> ταῦτα _don't do that / stop doing that_	

54.10   For the (rare) use of the imperative in subordinate clauses, →54.11.

Moods of Independent Sentences in Subordinate Clauses

54.11   In indirect statements (ὅτι/ὡς-clauses; →41.7–15), indirect questions (→42.7–8), result clauses (not with the inf., →46.4–6), causal clauses (→48.2–3), and in digressive relative clauses (→50.17) the **moods of independent sentences are used** (although imperatives, hortatory/prohibitive subjunctives and cupitive optatives are all rare).

The oblique optative can be used in historic sequence in some of these types (indirect speech, indirect questions, causal clauses).

55

Overview of the Uses of ἄν

In Independent Sentences

55.1 The uses of ἄν in independent sentences:

	main clause	(corresponding subordinate clause)
with optative (pres./aor./pf.)	**potential construction** (→34.13): in statements/questions about a possible action, cautious requests, etc.	corresponding conditional/relative clauses usually have optative without ἄν (→40.10)
	ποιήσειαν ἄν ταῦτα *They would/might/could do that*	εἰ πλούσιοι γένοιντο. *if they should become rich.*
with secondary indicative (impf./aor./plpf.)	**counterfactual construction** (→34.15–17): in statements/questions about an action that would have occurred under certain circumstances which were/are not realized	corresponding conditional/relative clauses usually have secondary indicative without ἄν (→40.10)
	ἐποίησαν ἄν ταῦτα *They would have done that*	εἰ πλούσιοι ἦσαν *if they were rich* (but they were not).
	iterative ἄν (→33.24 n.1): referring to repeated actions in the past ἐποίησαν ἄν ταῦτα *They used to do that.*	

In Finite Subordinate Clauses

55.2 The uses of ἄν in subordinate clauses:

	subordinate clause	corresponding matrix clause
with subjunctive (pres./aor./pf.)	**prospective construction** (→40.9): in temporal, conditional and relative clauses referring to the future	verb form with future reference (fut. ind., imp., subj., →33.63–4)

	subordinate clause	corresponding matrix clause
	ἐὰν ποιήσωσι ταῦτα *If they (will) do that*	πλούσιοι γενήσονται *they will become rich.*
	the prospective construction is sometimes used in purpose clauses (→45.4), and in effort clauses (→44.4)	
	indefinite construction (→40.9): in temporal, conditional and relative clauses referring to a repeated, typical action	present indicative (or other verb form referring to a repeated, typical action)
	ἐὰν ποιήσωσι ταῦτα *Whenever they do that*	πλούσιοι γίγνονται *they become rich.*
with optative (pres./aor./pf.)	**potential construction**: in subordinate clauses that use the moods of main clauses (→40.5), and sometimes in restrictive relative clauses (→50.26)	
with secondary indicative (impf./aor./plpf.)	**counterfactual construction**: in subordinate clauses that use the moods of main clauses (→40.5), and sometimes in restrictive relative clauses (→50.26)	

With Infinitives and Participles

55.3   The uses of ἄν with infinitives and participles:

with infinitive (pres./aor./pf.)	with **declarative infinitives** (in indirect speech/thought, →51.27), representing either: – a **potential** construction: οἴει αὐτοὺς τοῦτο ἂν ποιῆσαι, εἰ πλούσιοι γένοιντο; *Do you think that they could/might/would do that, if they should become rich?* – or a **counterfactual** construction: οἴει αὐτοὺς τοῦτο ἂν ποιῆσαι, εἰ πλούσιοι ἦσαν; *Do you think that they would have done that, if they had been rich?*
with participle (pres./aor./pf.)	with the participle in any use (but not with all types of supplementary participle, and only sometimes with circumstantial participles), representing either a potential optative or a counterfactual indicative (→52.7, 52.10 n.1)

56

Overview of Negatives

General Points

οὐ versus μή

56.1   The distinction between two different negatives in Greek, **οὐ** and **μή**, extends throughout their use in various compound forms:

οὐ	μή	not
οὔτε . . . οὔτε	μήτε . . . μήτε	neither . . . nor; not . . . and not
οὐδέ	μηδέ	and not; but not; not even
οὐδείς	μηδείς	no one / nothing
οὐδαμοῦ	μηδαμοῦ	nowhere
οὔποτε / οὐ . . . ποτε	μήποτε / μή . . . ποτε	never
οὔπω / οὐ . . . πω	μήπω / μή . . . πω	not yet (in poetry also: in no way)
οὐκέτι / οὐ . . . ἔτι	μηκέτι / μή . . . ἔτι	no longer

Before vowels, οὐ takes the form οὐ<u>κ</u>; before vowels with rough breathing, οὐ<u>χ</u> (→1.42). The form οὔ/οὔκ/οὔχ (with accent) is used primarily in answers (→38.21). There is also an intensive, emphatic form, οὐχί.

56.2   The distinction between the two negatives is, broadly speaking, as follows:

- **οὐ** is the **neutral negative**, expressing that something is factually not the case (or, in questions, asking whether it is not). It contradicts or denies: οὐκ ἔστι ταῦτα *that is not true*.
- **μή** is the **subjective negative**, expressing something about what is desired or hoped. It rejects and deprecates: μὴ ἔστω ταῦτα *let that not be true*.

There are, however, several specific uses of μή which do not easily fall under this definition (→56.6–17).

Multiple Negatives

56.3   If there are two or more negatives in one clause, they **cancel** each other if (and only if):

- the second negative is simple, i.e. not a compound form;
- both negatives belong to the same predicate:

(1) οὐδεὶς ἀνθρώπων ἀδικῶν τίσιν οὐκ ἀποτίσει. (Hdt. 5.56.1)

No man will not get punishment for being unjust. (= *'Everyone who is unjust will be punished.'; the second negative is simple and both negatives belong to the same predicate, so they cancel each other.*)

56.4   If the second negative is a compound, it **intensifies** the first (only one should be translated as negative):

(2) οὐκ ἔστιν ἀνδρὶ ἀγαθῷ κακὸν οὐδέν. (Pl. *Ap.* 41d)

Nothing evil (at all) happens to a good man. *The second negative is a compound form, so it strengthens the first.*

56.5   Negatives belonging to different predicates or phrases keep their force:

(3) οὐ διὰ τὸ μὴ ἀκοντίζειν οὐκ ἔβαλον αὐτόν. (Antiph. 3.4.6)

It was not because they did not throw (*lit.* 'not because of the not-throwing') that they did not hit him. *The first* οὐ *modifies the prepositional phrase* διὰ ... ἀκοντίζειν, μή *modifies* ἀκοντίζειν, *the second* οὐκ *modifies* ἔβαλον: *the suggestion is 'it was not for a lack of trying that they missed him'.*

In Independent Sentences

56.6   In **statements, οὐ** and its compounds are used with:

– the indicative;
– the potential optative with ἄν (→34.13);
– the modal (secondary) indicative with ἄν (counterfactual, →34.16); also the 'modal' use of imperfects like ἔδει/(ἐ)χρῆν (→34.17).

Note 1: The combination οὐ μή + (aor.) subj. expresses an emphatic denial, a strong belief that something will not be the case (→34.9).
Note 2: The combination μή (οὐ) + subj. expresses a doubtful assertion (→34.10).

56.7   In negative **wishes**, negative **adhortations, prohibitions**, etc., **μή** and its compounds are used with:

– the imperative or aorist subjunctive (in prohibitions) (→34.19, 34.7);
– the first-person (or third-person) subjunctive (in negative adhortations) (→34.6);
– the cupitive optative without ἄν (in negative wishes) (→34.14).

56.8   In **questions**:

– when introducing a yes/no-question, **οὐ/οὐκοῦν** signals that the answer **yes** is expected: 'isn't it the case that ... ?', 'it is the case that ... , isn't it?', 'surely ... ?' (→38.7);

– **μή/μῶν** is used in yes/no-questions to indicate that the speaker is reluctant to accept a positive answer as true: 'is it really the case that . . . ?', 'it isn't the case that . . . , is it?', 'surely not . . . ?' (→38.8);
– in specifying questions (→38.11–14), **οὐ** is used.

In Subordinate Clauses

56.9   In the following types of subordinate clause, **οὐ** is used:

– **declarative** ὡς/ὅτι-clauses (indirect speech) (→41) and **indirect questions/ exclamations** (→42);
– **fear clauses** (note that the subordinator in these clauses is μή *that*) (→43);
– **result clauses** (ὥστε) with the **moods of independent sentences** (actual result) (→46.4–6);
– **temporal clauses** referring to the past (ἐπεί, ὅτε, etc.) (→47.7);
– **causal** clauses (ὅτι, διότι; ἐπεί, etc.) (→48);
– digressive **relative clauses** (ὅς, etc.), some restrictive relative clauses, relative clauses with causal or result force, relative clauses with potential opt. + ἄν or counterfactual modal ind. + ἄν (→50.17, 50.19, 50.23, 50.25–6).

56.10   In the following types of subordinate clause, **μή** is used:

– **effort clauses** (ὅπως) (→44);
– **purpose clauses** (ἵνα, ὅπως, ὡς; μή is also used on its own) (→45);
– **result clauses** (ὥστε) with the **infinitive** (likely/natural result) (→46.7–11);
– **temporal clauses** referring to the future or to repeated/habitual occurrences (→47.8–11);
– **conditional clauses** (εἰ) and **concessive** clauses (εἰ καί/καὶ εἰ) (→49);
– most restrictive **relative clauses** (ὅς, etc.), relative clauses with the force of purpose-clauses (→50.18–22, 50.24).

> **Note 1:** Restrictive relative clauses with the indicative have μή when the clause has conditional or generic force: →50.19.

With Infinitives

56.11   The negative with the **dynamic infinitive** (to complement verbs) is **μή** (→51.13).

> **Note 1:** When a verb that takes a dynamic infinitive is itself negated, the negative with the infinitive is often μὴ οὐ, →51.37.

56.12   The negative with the **declarative infinitive** (used in indirect speech) is nearly
         always οὐ (→51.22; for exceptions, →51.23).

56.13   μή is always used with verbs of denying (+ decl. inf.) and verbs of preventing,
         forbidding, etc. (+ dyn. inf.). When a verb of denying or preventing, etc. is itself
         negated, it is followed by μὴ οὐ (→51.34–6).

56.14   The **articular** infinitive (with the article) has negative μή (→51.42).

With Participles

56.15   With the **supplementary** participle (used to complement verbs, e.g. τυγχάνω,
         οἶδα, χαίρω), the negative is οὐ.

56.16   The participle **in noun phrases** has:

         – οὐ when it refers to a specific entity: ὁ οὐ βαίνων *the* (specific) *man who is not*
           walking;
         – μή when it refers to an entire species or class ('generic', →52.48): ὁ μὴ βαίνων =
           whatever man is not walking.

         Note 1: This same 'generic' use of μή is also common with nouns and with substantivized
         adjectives: οἱ μὴ πλούσιοι *whoever are not rich* (i.e. *the non-rich*); ὁ μὴ ἰατρός *whoever is not*
         a doctor; and with restrictive relative clauses with the indicative, →50.19.

56.17   The **circumstantial** participle (connected/genitive absolute) usually has οὐ, but μή
         when the participle has a conditional nuance (→52.40).

57

Overview of the Uses of ὡς

As a Conjunction

57.1 The word ὡς functions as a **conjunction** in the following cases:

- as a relative adverb in **clauses of comparison** (*such as, like*; also ὅπως, ὥσπερ and καθάπερ), either with or without οὕτω(ς) in the matrix clause, →50.37:

ὡς ἔοικε	as it appears
ὡς ἐμοὶ δοκεῖ	as it seems to me

(1) ἐκέλευσε δὲ τοὺς Ἕλληνας, <u>ὡς</u> νόμος αὐτοῖς εἰς μάχην, <u>οὕτω</u> ταχθῆναι. (Xen. *An.* 1.2.15)

He ordered that the Greeks be stationed as was their custom in battle.

Also in answers to questions with πῶς (more frequently ὥσπερ):

(2) ΘΕ. πῶς τοὺς θανόντας θάπτετ᾽ ἐν πόντῳ νεκρούς; | :: ΜΕ. <u>ὡς</u> ἂν παρούσης οὐσίας ἕκαστος ᾖ (Eur. *Hel.* 1252–3)

(Theoclymenus:) How do you bury those who die at sea? :: (Menelaus:) As well as each man's wealth allows.

Note 1: For comparative temporal clauses (ὡς ὅτε *as when, like*), →47.17; for comparative conditional clauses (ὡσ(περ) (ἂν) εἰ *as if, like*), →49.22–4.

- in **indirect statement** after verbs of speech, etc. (*that, how*), →41.4–6:

λέγει <u>ὡς</u> . . .   he says that . . .

- in **indirect exclamations** (*what, how*), →42.9–11:

θαυμάζει <u>ὡς</u> . . .   he is amazed at how . . .

- to complement verbs of **effort**, with the future indicative (more frequently ὅπως) (*that*), →44;
- in **purpose clauses** with the subjunctive (or optative in historic sequence), sometimes with ἂν (*so as to, in order to*), →45:

(3) καὶ ἅμα ταῦτ᾽ εἰπὼν ἀνέστη, ὡς μὴ μέλλοιτο . . . τὰ δέοντα. (Xen. *An.* 3.1.47)

And as soon as he had said these things, he stood up, so that what was required would not be delayed.

– in **result clauses** (more frequently ὥστε), with the infinitive or with the moods of independent sentences (*so that, with the result that*), →46:

(4) . . . ὑψηλὸν δὲ οὕτω . . . ὡς τὰς κορυφὰς οὐκ οἷά τε εἶναι ἰδέσθαι. (Hdt. 4.184.3)

. . . but so high that it was impossible to see the mountaintops.

– in **temporal clauses** (*when, after, as soon as*, especially in the form ὡς (. . .) τάχιστα), →47:

(5) ὡς τάχιστα ἕως ὑπέφαινεν, ἐθύοντο. (Xen. *An.* 4.3.9)

As soon as a shimmer of daylight was breaking through, they sacrificed.

(6) ὡς διαβαίνειν ἐπειρᾶτο ὁ Κῦρος . . . , ἐνθαῦτα . . . (Hdt. 1.189.1)

When Cyrus tried to cross, at that moment . . .

– introducing **new sentences**, with **causal** force, expressing a motivation for the previous utterance (*because, as*), →48.5.

As an Adverb

57.2   In the following constructions, ὡς is an **adverb**:

– in **direct exclamations** (*how!*), modifying an adjective, adverb or verb, →38.47:

(7) ὡς πολλὸν ἀλλήλων κεχωρισμένα ἐργάσαο. (Hdt. 7.46.1)

How different from each other the things that you have done!

– with a **superlative** (*as . . . as possible*):

ὡς κράτιστα   as strong as possible

– with a **participle**, giving a subjective reason or motivation (*because, on the grounds that, thinking that*), purpose (with the future participle, *so as to, in order to*) or to express comparison (*as (if), just like*), →52.39, 52.41, 52.43:

(8) ταύτην τὴν χώραν ἐπέτρεψε διαρπάσαι τοῖς Ἕλλησιν ὡς πολεμίαν οὖσαν. (Xen. *An.* 1.2.19)

He turned this country over to the Greeks to ravage, on the grounds that it was hostile.

(9) παρεσκευάζοντο ὡς πολεμήσοντες. (Thuc. 2.7.1)

They made preparations to go to war.

(10) λέγουσιν ἡμᾶς ὡς ὀλωλότας. (Aesch. *Ag.* 672)

They speak of us as dead.

– in various **idiomatic expressions** with the **infinitive**, e.g. ὡς εἰπεῖν *as it were, if I may use this expression*, →51.49;

– in **wishes** (in poetry) (*would that, if only*), →38.38;

– with **numerals** and **words indicating degree** (*roughly, about*):

(11) ὁπλίτας ἔχων <u>ὡς</u> πεντακοσίους (Xen. *An.* 1.2.3)
        having about five hundred hoplites

Note 1: ὥς (so accented) is a **demonstrative adverb** (*so, thus, in this way*):

καὶ ὥς	even so
οὐδ' ὥς	not even in that case
Similarly:	
ὡσαύτως	in the same way

As a Preposition

57.3 ὡς functions as a **preposition** with the accusative meaning *to(wards)*, used only with motion to people, →31.9:

ὡς Σωκράτη   to Socrates

Part III

Textual Coherence

58

Introduction to Textual Coherence

Coherence

Sentences versus Texts

58.1 Almost all of the grammatical phenomena discussed in part II of this book operate at the level of individual **sentences**. However, when people communicate in speech or writing, they usually do not stop at a single sentence. Rather, their sentences combine to form a larger whole: a speaker may relate a series of separate events to tell an overarching story, or make a claim and back it up with proofs and explanations, or describe a person or thing, commenting on various relevant aspects, and so forth. In short, when people communicate with each other, they usually speak or write entire **texts**, which may vary in length from a few sentences to entire speeches or books.

58.2 Texts do not consist of sentences which are randomly placed together: a text is always more than the sum of its parts. In fact, when people hear or read a text, they intuitively look for relationships between the individual sentences: they look for **textual coherence**.

By way of example, the following two English sentences may, at first sight, be nothing more than two assertions randomly put together:

(1) It was raining.
(2) Mary stayed at home.

However, it is rather difficult to resist the urge to regard these two sentences together, as a coherent and meaningful text. When we do, it is easy to find a relationship between the sentences. If we read the sentences together,

(3) It was raining. Mary stayed at home.

we will interpret the first sentence as providing the reason for the second: *It was raining* explains why *Mary stayed at home*.

The coherence between the two sentences may be made explicit by adding a word which connects them:

(4) It was raining. <u>Therefore</u> Mary stayed at home.

In this new text, the word *therefore* is an explicit signal that there is a causal connection between the two sentences. The addition of *therefore* is not necessary to establish that causal connection, but it is a way for the speaker/writer to make interpreting the text easier for the addressee.

Relations between Text Segments; Hierarchy; Interactional Relations

58.3   In the following two examples, as in (4), the word *therefore* indicates a connection between two segments of text:

(5) It is raining. Therefore (=that is why) the streets are wet.

(6) The streets are wet. Therefore (≠that is why) it is raining.

In (5) it is possible to speak of a 'real-world' causal connection between the two sentences: the fact that it is raining causes the streets to be wet. But in (6), a different kind of causal relationship exists: the fact that the streets are wet is not the cause of rain, but rather, the speaker of (6) uses *therefore* to explain why he can say that it is raining. Note that here *is* might be paraphrased as *must be*.

Often, textual devices which indicate coherence relations in texts function specifically on this latter level: they do not refer to relations or entities in the world described by the text, but to **relationships between text segments**. Such relations include 'explanation', 'justification', 'conclusion', 'elaboration', etc. Greek connective particles (→59.7–39) function to indicate such relations particularly often.

58.4   It is often useful to think of the relations between text segments in terms of **hierarchy**: one text segment may be more 'central' than, or 'superior' to, another text segment which serves to explain, support, elaborate, etc. the former. Many indicators of coherence relations have a rather abstract function indicating hierarchy, with different individual 'effects' in different contexts:

(7) Two times two equals four. So four divided by two equals two. *The first sentence logically entails and thus supports the second: 'so' indicates the transition to the conclusion, which is the hierarchically 'superior' text segment.*

(8) John left home late. So he missed his train. *The main 'point' of this bit of story is that John missed his train; the fact that he left home late is information needed to understand that point; 'so' indicates the transition to the more central text segment.*

(9) That is what he said about that. So let us examine if what he said was true. *The first sentence appears to round off a previous text segment, after which the speaker turns to the now more relevant part of what he wants to do; 'so' marks the transition.*

Note 1: There is, of course, a causal relationship between (e.g.) 'leaving home late' and 'missing one's train' in (8), but this relationship of causality, although very frequently present with *so*, may be seen as only one possible instantiation of a more basic function, indicating certain kinds of (hierarchical) textual relations.

Thus, meanings such as 'cause', 'explanation', 'justification', etc. may sometimes be seen as side effects of more abstract, basic textual functions. An additional complication is that devices often change their function over time: words which originally had a very specific meaning (e.g. cause) may develop into an indicator of more abstract textual relationships (e.g. indicating hierarchical relationships), while maintaining its original function in some instances.

58.5   In addition to relations between text segments, some indicators of coherence operate on the level of **interaction between speaker, addressee and text**:

(10)   It is raining. <u>After all</u>, the streets are wet.

Just like in (6), *after all* serves to explain why the speaker can say that it is raining. But it also appears to do something else: *after all* appeals to the knowledge of the addressee, or at least to the addressee's willingness to accept that the streets are wet. Apart from appealing to addressees' knowledge, speakers may also use such **interactional** devices to indicate their own commitment to a point, forestall any doubt or objections an addressee may have, etc.

Devices Indicating Coherence

58.6   The chapters in part III are about various kinds of linguistic clues in Greek which establish coherence between sentences. A great number of aspects of the grammar of Greek cannot be completely understood without widening the level of analysis from sentences to larger units of texts. These aspects include:

– **Pronouns**: in 29.28 we discussed the 'cataphoric' and 'anaphoric' uses of the demonstrative pronouns ὅδε, οὗτος and ἐκεῖνος and of non-nominative forms of αὐτός. Whether or not a person can be referred to by these pronouns, and which one should be used, is determined in large part by the extent to which that person is already familiar from the previous context. This is true for English pronouns as well:

(11) Jane celebrated her birthday. <u>She</u> got a lot of presents.

In (11), it is clear that *she* refers to Jane. But we can only ascertain this by looking at the surrounding context (without the first sentence, we would not know who is meant by *she*). The context is similarly important for distinguishing between the uses of 'contrastive' and 'non-contrastive' personal pronouns (→29.1), as well as several other uses of pronouns.

- **Tenses**: in 33.49–51 we looked at the way in which the imperfect tense in narratives can create a framework, in which other events, expressed by the aorist (which pushes the story forward), occur. The imperfect raises the question 'What else happened?', and the subsequent context answers that question. We also saw that the historical present is used to mark 'decisive' events in a story (→33.54). Tenses are therefore of vital importance in recognizing how a speaker or writer organizes his text hierarchically (→58.4). As we will show in chapter 61, the use of tenses also varies significantly according to the specific communicative purpose a speaker has in formulating his text. Tenses are thus also important for understanding what it is a speaker is trying to accomplish.

- **Particles**: many Greek particles (indeclinable, small words) establish relationships of all kinds between sentences, similar to 'therefore' and 'so' in English (see examples above). These are called 'connective' (or 'text-structuring') particles. Another set of particles allows speakers to provide their addressees with an indication of how a piece of information is to be considered: as a fact or not, as important, as something that the addressee is expected to agree with, etc. These are called 'attitudinal' (or 'interactional') particles. A third group of particles is used to specify the extent to which (parts of) utterances are applicable: we call these particles of 'scope'. Particles will be treated in detail in chapter 59.

- **Word order**: the order of constituents in a Greek sentence is often determined by the importance and the 'newness' of the information each constituent contributes to the text. Therefore, when describing the word order of a sentence, it is crucial to look at the context surrounding that sentence. Word order is discussed in chapter 60.

As noted above, how these aspects work together to establish textual coherence cannot be fully understood unless they are studied at the level of larger sections of text. For that reason, four case studies are provided in chapter 61: these are analyses of longer passages in which all of the factors mentioned above, and many more, are at work.

Text Types

58.7   The excerpts in chapter 61 have been selected as representative of various **text types**. It was mentioned in 33.13 that there is an important difference between narrative and non-narrative text, but it is useful to draw finer distinctions still: someone who relates a story will structure his text in different ways from someone who is describing a landscape, and this is different again from someone who is defending a certain claim in a debate. The differences between these text types lie, among others, in how they progress through time, how they refer to the entities which they speak about, and in the ways speakers and addressees are 'visible' in the text.

58.8   A first important distinction that may be made between various kinds of texts is
        that between **monological texts** and **dialogical texts**:

        – In **monological texts**, a single speaker/writer controls the 'flow' of the text,
          stringing together sentences to construct a longer story, argument, etc.
        – In **dialogical texts**, two or more interlocutors together build a text, exchanging
          facts, opinions and instructions and often trying to convince or persuade each
          other. Dialogical texts are often characterized (at least more so than monological
          texts) by a wide variety of moods and tenses, by the frequent occurrence of
          attitudinal particles (→59.40), and by the use of the first and second person.

        Although the distinction monologue vs. dialogue appears straightforward, it is
        actually better to see 'monological' and 'dialogical' as opposite ends on a scale.
        In dialogues, individual speakers may expand in long speeches which seem almost
        monological; conversely, even a very long speech or treatise by a single speaker or
        author can show the presence of an addressee (e.g. a speech addressed to a specific
        audience, a letter to a friend), which can influence how a text is constructed and
        presented.

58.9   Secondly, we can distinguish between various uses to which a text can be put: to
        tell a story, to describe an object or characterize a person, to provide information,
        to persuade, etc. More or less in line with such functions, we discuss here three
        text types that occur frequently in Greek literature: **narrative, description**
        and **argument** (the list is not exhaustive; various other text types may be
        distinguished):

        – In a **narrative**, a speaker relates a series of successive events, typically in the past.
          Normally (excepting flashbacks and flash-forwards), the events are related in
          chronological order, which means that many finite verbs in main clauses push
          the narrative forward in time, although through the choice of tenses and the
          frequent use of subordinate clauses a speaker may also indicate background
          events. Usually, a narrative features a limited number of characters, who
          are referred to repeatedly, but in different ways. The speaker may or may
          not be a participant in the story: narratives can be told in the first or the third
          person.
        – A **description** of a person or thing, by contrast, does not usually progress
          through time; rather, the speaker discusses several aspects of the person/thing
          in turn, resulting in an enumeration of these aspects. Although descriptions may
          be set either in the present or the past, the flow of time plays no part in them,
          which normally results in the consistent use of the same tense (present or
          imperfect) throughout a descriptive passage. The order in which the individual
          items are treated often depends on spatial considerations (e.g. a description may
          'zoom in', getting ever more detailed, or describe an object from top to bottom,

or vice versa). Because various aspects are discussed, new entities are often introduced throughout the text.

- In an **argumentative text**, a speaker makes one or more claims which he backs up with proofs, explanations, etc. Often, claims in arguments are meant to have a general validity, resulting in the frequent use of the present tense. An argument often has a complex hierarchical structure, which involves a varied set of connective particles. Since arguments are meant to convince or persuade some-one, there may be frequent signs of the addressee to whom the argument is directed, e.g. in the form of second-person verbs and attitudinal particles.

58.10   The four passages treated in chapter 61 exemplify some of the many different possible combinations of forms (monological, dialogical) and functions (narrative, descriptive, argumentative, etc.) that are found in texts. It should be observed that texts seldom correspond simply to the generalizations made above, and that they are very often mixed. Descriptions, for example, are often part of a larger narrative; a narrative, in turn, may support a claim by providing an example of the applic-ability of that claim, and thus be rather argumentative; and so forth. The four 'representative' samples discussed in 61 are, as such, by no means examples of 'pure' narrative, description, etc.

Note 1: The notions of different text types presented above should be seen as distinct from, but not wholly unrelated to, **genres** (epic, tragedy, comedy, lyric, historiography, philosophical dialogue, etc.). Any genre may feature various different text types, although certain types tend to proliferate in certain genres: historiography primarily consists of narrative and descriptive material, philosophical dialogues are rich in argumentative text, etc.

58.11   In chapter 61, we attempt to elucidate the manifold factors which are at work in making our four sample passages into organized, meaningful texts: an interplay between not only the features mentioned above (pronouns, tenses, word order and particles), but many other grammatical features as well. Cross-references to the relevant sections of the grammar will be made throughout.

59

Particles

Introduction

Meanings and Functions; Types of Particle

59.1   **Particles** are usually considered a class separate from adverbs, conjunctions and interjections (οἴμοι, ἔα, ἒ ἔ, etc.), even though there is a considerable overlap between these classes. It is indeed almost impossible to draw clear boundaries between particles and adverbs, or between particles and conjunctions.

> **Note 1:** The connective particles καί, ἀλλά, τε and ἤ are, in fact, often unambiguously used as co-ordinating conjunctions.
>
> The dividing line between particles and adverbs is particularly blurry since particles can typically be described, in terms of their syntactic function, as adverbial modifiers operating on different levels of the sentence, i.e. as disjuncts, conjuncts and occasionally as subjuncts; for these terms, →26.15.
>
> In some treatments, certain lexical items are considered to belong in some of their uses to one class, and in others to another (e.g. αὖ, which is sometimes treated as an adverb, sometimes as a connective particle).

The words classed as particles do share some formal characteristics:

- they are **short words** (mostly one or two syllables) that are **never declined**, and normally not derived (→23.1);
- they are either **postpositive** or **prepositive** (→60.5–6).

59.2   Particles often have no 'meaning' in the same way that words like οἰκία *house*, σοφία *wisdom*, βαίνειν *walk*, or ἀνδρεῖος *courageous* have meaning. Such words refer to entities, actions, relationships or properties *in the world* described by a text ('referential meaning'). Particles, rather, have a **functional meaning**: they indicate how certain parts *of the text itself* relate to each other, or how the text relates to the attitudes and expectations of the speaker and the addressee (→58.3–5).

> **Note 1:** Because they have a (often rather abstract) functional meaning rather than a referential meaning, and because there is not always an English word with the exact same function, there is often no one-to-one equivalent for a particular Greek particle in English translation. The same basic function of a particle may, in different contexts and/or text types (→58.7–11), lead to different interpretations, which in turn lead to different possible translations.

It is sometimes difficult to determine what the exact function of a Greek particle is, especially because such functions may also change and become more diffuse over time. Furthermore, there is not always scholarly consensus about the function of an individual particle.

59.3   Particles may be subdivided among the following categories, each treated separately below:

- **connective** (or 'text-structuring') particles, which function (primarily) to indicate relationships between (the content of) text segments: ἀλλά, αὖ, γάρ, δέ, ἤ, καί, καίτοι, μέν, μέντοι, νυν, οὐδέ/μηδέ, οὔκουν/οὐκοῦν, οὖν, οὔτε/μήτε, τε, τοιγάρ, τοιγαροῦν, τοιγάρτοι and τοίνυν (→59.7–39);

- **attitudinal** (also: 'modal' or 'interactional') particles, which function (primarily) to indicate a speaker's attitude towards the content of his/her utterance, or his/her anticipation of the addressee's attitude towards that content: ἄρα, ἆρα, δή, δήπου, ἦ, μήν, που, and τοι (→59.40–51);

- **particles of scope**, which determine the applicability of an utterance's content to a particular element: γε, γοῦν, so-called 'adverbial' καί, and περ (→59.52–6).

Note 1: In several cases particles (may) have both a connective and an attitudinal function, and sometimes it is difficult to draw a clear distinction between the two: such particles are discussed under the heading of 'connective particles' below if their use is considered to prevent asyndeton (for which →59.9; connective δή and μήν are, however, treated together with their attitudinal uses: →59.44, 59.49). Connective particles and attitudinal particles together are often called 'discourse particles'.

Note 2: This chapter does not treat the particle ἄν, for which →55.

Particle Combinations

59.4   Particles very frequently occur in **combinations**: e.g. ἀλλὰ μήν, μὲν οὖν, καὶ δή, ἦ μήν. It is not always possible to reduce the function of these particle combinations to the sum of their individual parts, as certain (relatively) fixed combinations have acquired specific uses. Such particle combinations are treated separately below, →59.57–76.

Some particle combinations are so fixed that they were probably not 'felt' as separate particles in their use, and are indeed conventionally written as one word, e.g. καίτοι (καί + τοι), μέντοι (μέν + τοι), τοίνυν (τοι + νυν), δήπου (δή + που): these are treated below as single particles; all others are treated as combinations.

There are also frequent combinations of particles with negatives, also traditionally written as one word: e.g. οὐδέ, οὔτε, οὐκοῦν. These are also treated as single particles below.

The Position of Particles

59.5 Many particles cannot occur in the first position of a clause but are **postpositives**, i.e. they stand in 'second position' of the clause or word group that they modify (for details, →60.7–12). These postpositive particles are: ἄρα, αὖ, γάρ, γε, γοῦν, δέ, δή, δήπου, μέν, μέντοι, μήν, νυν, οὖν, περ, που, τε, τοι, τοίνυν.

59.6 Other particles are **prepositives**, i.e. they normally stand in front of the clause or word group that they modify (for details, →60.13). These prepositive particles are: ἀλλά, ἄρα, ἤ, ἦ, καί, καίτοι, and οὐδέ/μηδέ, οὔκουν/οὐκοῦν, οὔτε/μήτε, τοιγάρ, τοιγαροῦν, τοιγάρτοι.

Connective Particles

Introduction

59.7 The vast majority of Greek sentences are 'connected' in some way to their surrounding context, in most cases by a **connective particle**. Different connective particles establish different kinds of coherence relationships between the text segment they stand in and the preceding and/or following context (segments may have more than one connective particle to indicate complex relationships, and there are several common combinations).

59.8 Connective particles are used to connect individual sentences, but they can also function to link various clauses within a sentence, various elements within a clause, or (very frequently) to indicate relationships between larger sections of text.

59.9 The lack of any particle to connect sentences is relatively rare in Greek texts. It is called **asyndeton**, and occurs only in certain circumstances (→61 for several examples).

Note 1: This characterization ('relatively rare') holds for transitions between sentences uttered by a single speaker: the use of particles by one speaker to connect a sentence to that of another speaker is much less regular, although not uncommon.

59.10 Most connective particles have a rather abstract function, indicating general (often hierarchical, →58.4) relations between text segments. In different contexts, such general functions may result in different specific interpretations (and translations).

For instance, the particle ἀλλά has as its basic general function **substitution** or **correction**: (an element of) the new text segment introduced by ἀλλά – the 'host' segment – replaces (an element of) the preceding text segment. This basic function has a wide range of specific instantiations in different contexts:

(1) δοκεῖτε ... μοι νήφειν. οὐκ ἐπιτρεπτέον οὖν ὑμῖν, <u>ἀλλὰ</u> ποτέον. (Pl. *Symp.* 213e)

You seem to me to be sober. You must not be allowed this: rather you must drink. *Substitution of an explicit element: ἀλλά replaces one explicit alternative (ἐπιτρεπτέον) with another (ποτέον); it is frequently so used in the formula 'οὐ X, ἀλλά Y' (= 'not X, but (rather) Y'), in which case ἀλλά is a co-ordinating conjunction.*

(2) ΦΙ. διατρώξομαι τοίνυν ὀδὰξ τὸ δίκτυον. :: ΒΔ. <u>ἀλλ'</u> οὐκ ἔχεις ὀδόντας. (Ar. *Vesp.* 164–5)

(Philocleon:) Then I'll gnaw through the net with my teeth. :: (Bdelycleon:) But you don't have any teeth! *Substitution of a presupposed element: Philocleon's assertion that he will use his teeth presupposes that he has any to begin with; ἀλλά corrects this presupposition.*

(3) Εἰπέ, ὠγαθέ, τίς αὐτοὺς ἀμείνους ποιεῖ; :: Οἱ νόμοι. :: Ἀλλ' οὐ τοῦτο ἐρωτῶ, ὦ βέλτιστε, <u>ἀλλὰ</u> τίς ἄνθρωπος; (Pl. *Ap.* 24d–e)

(Socrates:) Tell me, sir, who makes them better? :: (Meletus:) The laws do. :: (Socrates:) But that's not what I'm asking, my dear sir: which man makes them better? *Substitution of an implicit element: ἀλλά corrects the notion (implicit in Meletus' reply) that Socrates' question has been satisfactorily answered. The second ἀλλά replaces an explicit element, as in (1).*

(4) ΣΩ. πειρῶ ἀποκρίνεσθαι τὸ ἐρωτώμενον ᾗ ἂν μάλιστα οἴῃ. :: ΚΡ. <u>ἀλλὰ</u> πειράσομαι. (Pl. *Cri.* 49a)

(Socrates:) Try to answer what I ask you in the way you deem best. :: (Crito:) Of course I'll try. *In this case, ἀλλά 'replaces' the implicit possibility that Crito will not comply with Socrates' request (which is still open) with the assurance that that request will be fulfilled. Thus Crito implies that he is ready to move on to the questions, and that there was no need for Socrates to worry about his preliminary request.*

(5) οὐκ ἀντέτεινον <u>ἀλλ'</u> εἶκον, μέχρι ὅσου κάρτα ἐδέοντο αὐτῶν ... · ὡς γὰρ δὴ διωσάμενοι τὸν Πέρσην περὶ τῆς ἐκείνου ἤδη τὸν ἀγῶνα ἐποιεῦντο ... ἀπείλοντο τὴν ἡγεμονίην τοὺς Λακεδαιμονίους. <u>ἀλλὰ</u> ταῦτα μὲν ὕστερον ἐγένετο. τότε δὲ ... (Hdt. 8.3.2–4.1)

(The Athenians) did not resist but waived (their claim to the command), as long as (the Greeks) desperately needed them; for when they had driven the Persians out and brought the battle to their territory, they deprived the Spartans of the command. That, however, happened later; presently, ... *Substitution of a discourse topic: ἀλλά breaks off the story about the Athenians' later action, as Herodotus wants to return to the storyline he left behind earlier. The first ἀλλά replaces an explicit element.*

Note 1: Depending on the specific context, ἀλλά may thus receive very different translations into English e.g. *but, no, rather, however, on the contrary* and in some cases as *well, anyway; of course, all right,* etc. As noted above (→59.2 n. 1), there is often no single equivalent in English for a Greek particle: translation often depends on an analysis of the specific context (including text type, →58.7–11) of a particle's use, as well as that particle's basic function.

The descriptions of connective particles below concern both their abstract general function and certain common types of specific contexts in which the particle is found. Suggested possible translations are given in parentheses (these are not exhaustive).

List of Connective Particles

ἀλλά

59.11   Basic function: **substitution/correction/elimination** – ἀλλά corrects one explicit or implicit element and replaces it with another:

- (as a co-ordinating conjunction within sentences:) correcting explicit elements: οὐ A, ἀλλά B = 'not A but B' (*but, rather, no, on the contrary*);
- correcting implicit or presupposed elements from the preceding contexts (*but, on the contrary*);
- to break off a certain topic of discourse and replace it with a new one (*well, however, anyway, so much for that*);
- in dialogue frequently in commands/requests, suggesting that the preceding line of conversation is broken off and that the addressee should turn to the new matter at hand (*but, well, now, so much for that*);
- in dialogue also frequent in answers, suggesting that no more attention needs to be paid to (an element of) the context eliciting the answer (*but, all right, of course*).

For examples →59.10.

59.12   ἀλλά is sometimes used in a main clause 'correcting' or 'substituting' (an element from) a preceding subordinate clause – so-called **apodotic ἀλλά**:

(6)   νῦν ὦν ἐπειδὴ οὐκ ὑμεῖς ἤρξατε τούτου τοῦ λόγου, ἀλλ' ἡμεῖς ἄρξομεν. (Hdt. 9.48.3)
      Well then, since you did not start this conversation, we will rather start it. *Picking up οὐκ (ὑμεῖς), ἀλλά dismisses 'you' in the subordinate ἐπειδή-clause, and replaces it with 'we' as the initiator of the conversation in the main clause.*

As apodotic ἀλλά syntactically has no connective function (it could be left out without disrupting the syntax), it is often called 'adverbial'; its basic function (substitution, etc.) is not fundamentally different, however.

ἀτάρ

→δέ 59.18.

αὖ and αὖτε

59.13   Postpositive. Basic function: indicates a shift to a **different topic** – αὖ(τε) signals that the speaker is moving on to another, related discourse topic (for 'topic', →60.25; e.g. a second, third, etc. member of a larger group; an opposing idea, etc.); the particle is often combined with δέ:

- in argumentative and descriptive texts (infrequently in narrative), moving to a different, related topic (*in turn, again, on the other hand, then, as for, furthermore*);
- in questions introducing a different, related topic (*and what about X, then?, again, in turn, on the other hand, as for*).

(7) τὰ μὲν καθ' Ἑλένην ὧδ' ἔχει· σὲ δ' <u>αὖ</u> χρεών, | Ὀρέστα, . . . Παρράσιον οἰκεῖν δάπεδον. (Eur. *Or.* 1643–5)

This is how things stand with Helen. As for you, in turn, Orestes, you must live on Parrhasian soil.

(8) Τὸ ἐπιμελεῖσθαι καὶ ἄρχειν . . . καὶ τὰ τοιαῦτα πάντα, ἔσθ' ὅτῳ ἄλλῳ ἢ ψυχῇ δικαίως ἂν αὐτὰ ἀποδοῖμεν . . . ; :: Οὐδενὶ ἄλλῳ. :: Τί δ' <u>αὖ</u> τὸ ζῆν; οὐ ψυχῆς φήσομεν ἔργον εἶναι; (Pl. *Resp.* 353d)

(Socrates:) Concerning management, and rule, and all such things, is there anything else than the soul to which we could rightly assign these? :: (Thrasymachus:) Nothing else. :: (Socrates:) And what about life, in turn? Shall we not say that it is a function of the soul?

Note 1: αὖτε is used only in (early) poetry, αὖ elsewhere.
Note 2: αὖ and αὖτε also have 'purely' adverbial uses, meaning *again* (i.e. for a second time), *once more*.

γάρ

59.14   Postpositive. Basic function: introduces a subsidiary text segment – the segment containing γάρ serves as **explanation, motivation, elaboration** or **exemplification** for the surrounding context; the information provided by the γάρ segment helps to interpret the information in the preceding (or, much more rarely, the following) segment:

- in argumentative texts: to provide supporting arguments, explanations, etc. (*for, after all, for example*, sometimes best left untranslated or 'translated' by a colon);
- in narrative texts: to provide explanatory background information about certain characters, entities or events, motivations for certain actions, etc. (*for*, sometimes best left untranslated or 'translated' by a colon);

- in dialogue, γάρ can be used by one speaker to connect his/her utterance to that of another (especially in answers to questions: the answer 'yes' or 'no' is often implicit in the use of γάρ, which then provides an explanation for that answer) (*yes/no, for; (you say that) because*);
- in dialogue also often in certain short idiomatic questions:

πῶς γὰρ οὔ; / τί γὰρ οὔ;	*of course, naturally, how could it not?*
πῶς γάρ; / τί γάρ;	*of course not, how could that be?*
οὐ γάρ;	*isn't that the case?*

Examples:

(9) οὐ περὶ τῶν ἴσων ἀγωνίζομαι· οὐ γάρ ἐστιν ἴσον νῦν ἐμοὶ τῆς παρ᾽ ὑμῶν εὐνοίας διαμαρτεῖν καὶ τούτῳ μὴ ἑλεῖν τὴν γραφήν. (Dem. 18.3)

I am not contesting this suit on equal footing. For at present it is not the same for me to lose your goodwill as it is for him not to win the verdict. *The γάρ-clause explains the preceding claim.*

(10) τὸν μὲν ἀμφὶ τὸν χειμῶνα χρόνον διῆγεν ἐν Βαβυλῶνι ἑπτὰ μῆνας· αὕτη γὰρ ἀλεεινὴ ἡ χώρα. (Xen. *Cyr.* 8.6.22)

In the winter season he spent seven months in Babylon, for that country has a warm climate. *Explanatory background information in a narrative.*

(11) ἀλλ᾽ ὁ μέν, ὡς καὶ πρότερόν μοι εἴρηται, ὁδῷ χρεώμενος ἅμα τῷ ἄλλῳ στρατῷ ἀπενόστησε ἐς τὴν Ἀσίην. μέγα δὲ καὶ τόδε μαρτύριον· φαίνεται γὰρ Ξέρξης ἐν τῇ ὀπίσω κομιδῇ ἀπικόμενος ἐς Ἄβδηρα. (Hdt. 8.119–20)

No, as I have said before, he travelled back to Asia via the road, together with the rest of his army. And the following is convincing proof for this: it turns out that Xerxes visited Abdera during his retreat. *γάρ introduces information (Xerxes' visit to Abdera, which is on the land route, not the sea route, to Persia) which functions as the supporting evidence which Herodotus has announced (τόδε μαρτύριον). Note that γάρ is 'translated' with a colon here.*

(12) ΧΟ. ἀλλὰ κτανεῖν σὸν σπέρμα τολμήσεις, γύναι; | :: ΜΗ. οὕτω γὰρ ἂν μάλιστα δηχθείη πόσις. (Eur. *Med.* 816–17)

(Chorus:) But will you dare to kill your offspring, woman? :: (Medea:) Yes, as that way my husband may be injured most severely. *Medea gives an affirmative answer and provides an explanation for it.*

59.15   Although γάρ typically introduces a segment which supports or explains (only) the preceding text (as in each of the examples above), γάρ is also sometimes used **in anticipation** of information still to come. The speaker breaks off a line of reasoning or narrative in order to provide information which will be required to understand what follows. In this use, the γάρ-segment in fact sometimes interrupts a sentence (**parenthesis**, →26.27):

(13) ἔτι τοίνυν ἀκούσατε καὶ τάδε. ἐπὶ λείαν γὰρ ὑμῶν ἐκπορεύσονταί τινες. οἴομαι οὖν
βέλτιστον εἶναι ... (Xen. *An.* 5.1.8)

Now, listen as well to this further advice. Some of you will go out to plunder.
I think, then, that this is our best course of action: ... *Before proceeding to give
the advice he has announced, the speaker provides background information in the
light of which the advice is to be seen as relevant. Note that when he resumes his
'main' line of reasoning, i.e. the advice itself, he marks the transition with* οὖν *(for
which* →59.34*).*

(14) ὁ Κανδαύλης ... ἐνόμιζέ οἱ εἶναι γυναῖκα πολλὸν πασέων καλλίστην. ὥστε δὲ ταῦτα
νομίζων – ἦν γὰρ οἱ τῶν αἰχμοφόρων Γύγης ... ἀρεσκόμενος μάλιστα – τούτῳ τῷ Γύγῃ
καὶ τὰ σπουδαιέστερα τῶν πρηγμάτων ὑπερετίθετο ὁ Κανδαύλης καὶ δὴ καὶ τὸ εἶδος τῆς
γυναικὸς ὑπερεπαινέων. (Hdt. 1.8.1)

Candaules believed that his wife was the most beautiful of all by far. So as he believed
this – and here I should add that there was among his bodyguard a certain Gyges, who
was his favourite – to this Gyges, Candaules entrusted his most intimate secrets, including praising his wife's beauty. *The* γάρ*-segment introduces Gyges, who will be one of the
main figures in the following narrative. The* γάρ*-segment is used parenthetically, intervening between* ὥστε δὲ ταῦτα νομίζων *and* τούτῳ τῷ Γύγῃ*, which picks up the interrupted
sentence and the narrative where it left off (observe the 'resumptive' use of* τούτῳ*, and the
repeated subject* ὁ Κανδαύλης*).*

In some cases in narrative texts γάρ introduces an entire embedded narrative which serves as
background information:

(15) τὸ μὲν Ἀττικὸν κατεχόμενον ... ἐπυνθάνετο ὁ Κροῖσος ὑπὸ Πεισιστράτου τοῦ Ἱπποκράτεος
τοῦτον τὸν χρόνον τυραννεύοντος Ἀθηναίων. Ἱπποκράτεϊ γὰρ ἐόντι ἰδιώτῃ καὶ θεωρέοντι
τὰ Ὀλύμπια τέρας ἐγένετο μέγα. (Hdt. 1.59.1)

Croesus learned that the Attic people were held subjugated by Pisistratus, son of
Hippocrates, who at that time ruled the Athenians. A great marvel had befallen
Hippocrates when he was a private citizen visiting the Olympic games. γάρ *introduces
an embedded narrative which provides the necessary background information about
Hippocrates and Pisistratus; it will go on for five chapters, after which the main story
about Croesus is picked up again.*

Parenthetical γάρ is also regularly used after forms of address (vocatives), intervening
between the addressee and the remainder of an utterance to explain why that utterance
is directed at that particular addressee, or why that particular form of address has been
chosen:

(16) ὦ δέσποτ' – ἤδη γὰρ τόδ' ὀνομάζω σ' ἔπος – | ὄλωλα. (Eur. *Hel.* 1193–4)

Lord, for by this name I address you now, I am destroyed! *Note that* γάρ *is not really
anticipatory in this case (it explains the form of address, not* ὄλωλα*); the degree to which*
γάρ *following a form of address is anticipatory varies.*

δέ

59.16 Postpositive. Basic function: δέ indicates a **shift to a new, distinct, text segment**, often with a change of topic (for 'topic', →60.25); δέ is one of the commonest particles in Greek texts to connect clauses and/or sentences:

- in moving to a new point, a new argument, a new topic for discussion, or another aspect of a certain larger topic (*and, now, next*; with a new topic: *as for ..., as regards ...*; in contrasts: *but*; often best left untranslated);
- in narrative: in moving to a new step in the story, shifting to a different character, etc. (*and, now, next; and as for ..., and as regards ...*; in contrasts: *but*; often best left untranslated);
- frequently in combination with a preceding μέν (→59.24; for ὁ μέν ... ὁ δέ, τό μέν ... τό δέ, etc., →28.27);
- in dialogue, idiomatic τί δέ; *what now?, how so?*; also τί δέ X; *and what of X?*;
- for ὁ δέ resuming a topic, →28.28.

(17) τὸν βίον οὐκ ἐκ τῶν ἰδίων προσόδων πορίζεται, ἀλλ' ἐκ τῶν ὑμετέρων κινδύνων. πρὸς δ' εὐγνωμοσύνην καὶ λόγου δύναμιν πῶς πέφυκε; δεινὸς λέγειν, κακὸς βιῶναι. (Aeschin. 3.173–4)

He provides for himself not from his private means but from your risk. Now as for his good judgement and his power of speech, what kind of man is he? Impressive in words, infamous in life! *Aeschines moves on to a new topic for discussion:* δέ *marks the shift.*

(18) κατὰ δὲ τὸν αὐτὸν χρόνον ... Εὐρυμέδων καὶ Σοφοκλῆς ... ἀφικόμενοι ἐς Κέρκυραν ἐστράτευσαν ... ἐπὶ τοὺς ἐν τῷ ὄρει τῆς Ἰστώνης Κερκυραίων καθιδρυμένους ... προσβαλόντες δὲ τὸ μὲν τείχισμα εἷλον, οἱ δὲ ἄνδρες καταπεφευγότες ... ξυνέβησαν. (Thuc. 4.46.1–2)

In the same period Eurymedon and Sophocles, having arrived at Corcyra, attacked the Corcyraeans established on mount Istone. They attacked the fortification and captured it; the men, having escaped, accepted terms. *The first* δέ *marks a shift in the narrative to another episode in Thucydides' narrative about the year 425 BCE; the next stage in that episode, the capture of the fortification, is again indicated by* δέ; *the topic of the narrative then shifts (with* δέ*) to the Corcyraeans who flee and surrender.*

(19) ἐς δὲ Προιτίδας | πύλας ἐχώρει ... | ὁ μάντις Ἀμφιάραος ... Ὠγύγια δ' ἐς πυλώμαθ' Ἱππομέδων ἄναξ | ἔστειχ' ... Ὁμολώσιν δὲ τάξιν εἶχε πρὸς πύλαις | Τυδεύς. (Eur. *Phoen.* 1109–20)

Towards the Proetean gates came the prophet Amphiaraus. To the Ogygian gates marched lord Hippomedon ... At the Homoloean gates

Tydeus had his post. *A messenger relates which attacker attacked which Theban gate: each new section about a gate/attacker is marked by δέ.*

(20) ΑΝ. νέα πέφυκας καὶ λέγεις αἰσχρῶν πέρι. | :: ΕΡ. σὺ δ' οὐ λέγεις γε, δρᾷς δέ μ' εἰς ὅσον δύνᾳ. | :: ΑΝ. οὐκ αὖ σιωπῇ Κύπριδος ἀλγήσεις πέρι; | :: ΕΡ. τί δ'; οὐ γυναιξὶ ταῦτα πρῶτα πανταχοῦ; (Eur. *Andr.* 238–41)

(Andromache:) You are young and speak of shameful things. :: (Hermione:) And you do not *speak* of them, but you *do* them to me as much as you can. :: (Andromache:) Will you not suffer over your marriage in silence? :: (Hermione:) What? Are these things not of principal importance to women everywhere? *The first δ' marks a shift from Hermione to Andromache; the second from speaking to doing. τί δ' is a surprised question, normally immediately followed by another question. For δύνᾳ (an alternative form for δύνασαι), →12.46 n.1.*

Note 1: For the difference between δέ and καί, →59.21.

59.17   Similarly to ἀλλά (→59.12), δέ is sometimes used to set off a main clause from a subordinate clause which precedes it – so-called **apodotic δέ**:

(21) εἰ δὲ συγγινώσκεαι εἶναι ἥσσων, σὺ δὲ ... δεσπότη τῷ σῷ ... ἐλθὲ ἐς λόγους. (Hdt. 4.126)

But if you admit that you are weaker, then come to terms with your master. *The second δέ marks the main clause as 'distinct' from the subordinate conditional clause, emphasizing its importance. Note that unlike the first δέ (following εἰ), the second δέ does not connect sentences, and could easily be left out without disrupting the syntax.*

As with apodotic ἀλλά, the particle syntactically has no connective function in this use, and is therefore often called 'adverbial'; its basic function (introducing a distinct segment of text) is not fundamentally different, however.

59.18   The particle **ἀτάρ** is very similar in function to δέ, although the 'break' suggested by ἀτάρ is often a bit stronger than by δέ. It is usually found in contexts where δέ cannot be used, e.g. together with vocatives (often at the beginning of a new speaking turn). It may have been colloquial in tone:

(22) ἀτάρ, ὦ φίλε Φαῖδρε, δοκῶ τι σοί ... θεῖον πάθος πεπονθέναι; (Pl. *Phdr.* 238c)

Well, my dear Phaedrus, do I seem to you to be divinely inspired? *Socrates has just finished a speech meant to surpass the eloquence of Lysias. ἀτάρ is used (together with the vocative) to signal the break from the speech itself to its evaluation.*

ἤ

59.19   Basic function: indicates **disjunction** – ἤ connects two alternatives:

– as a co-ordinating conjunction within sentences: connecting two alternative clauses or phrases (*or, or else*); often with ἤ also preceding the first alternative (ἤ ... ἤ *either ... or*); so also in alternative questions (→38.10): the first alternative is often preceded by πότερον (in indirect alternative questions also by εἰ, →42.4);

– at the beginning of questions providing a self-correction and/or alternative suggestion (*or rather ... ?*);

– after comparatives, μᾶλλον and forms of ἄλλος to introduce the second element of a comparison (*than*) (→32.6–7).

(23)   ἀμαθής τις εἶ θεός ἤ δίκαιος οὐκ ἔφυς. (Eur. *Her.* 347)
You are an unwise god, or else you are not just.

(24)   πρὸς ἕκαστα δὲ δεῖ ἤ ἐχθρὸν ἤ φίλον μετὰ καιροῦ γίγνεσθαι. (Thuc. 6.85.1)
One must in every case become either an enemy or a friend according to circumstances.

(25)   πότερον συνηγόρευες τοῖς κελεύουσιν ἀποκτεῖναι ἤ ἀντέλεγες; (Lys. 12.25)
Did you agree with those who were giving the order to kill, or did you oppose them?

(26)   τίς αὐτὸν τῶν ἐπιστημῶν ποιεῖ εὐδαίμονα; ἤ ἅπασαι ὁμοίως; (Pl. *Chrm.* 174a)
Which of the sciences makes him happy? Or do all in equal measure?

(27)   τούς γε μὴν διαβόλους μᾶλλον ἤ τοὺς κλέπτας ἐμίσει, μείζω ζημίαν ἡγούμενος φίλων ἤ χρημάτων στερίσκεσθαι. (Xen. *Ages.* 11.5)
He hated slanderers more than thieves, thinking it a graver loss to be robbed of friends than of money.

Note 1: For πρὶν ἤ, →47.14, 47.16 n.1. For ἤ, →59.48.

καί

59.20   Basic function: indicates **addition** – καί connects two elements, adding the second to the first:

– as a co-ordinating conjunction within sentences: to connect two words or word groups, or two clauses (*and*); the first of two connected elements is sometimes preceded by καί, signalling that another καί will follow (the first καί is adverbial, →59.56): καί A καί B = 'both A and B' (*both ... and, as well as, and also*);

– connecting sentences (i.e. beginning a sentence), indicating that the new sentence is closely linked to the previous one; for instance in narratives to indicate that one action closely follows upon, or is the direct consequence of, another (*and, also, and so, and then*); in this use καί is often combined with other particles (e.g. καὶ γάρ, καὶ δή, καὶ μήν; for these combinations, →59.66–71);

– for combinations of καί and τε, →59.37.

(28) ταῦθ᾽ ὑμεῖς, ὦ ἄνδρες δικασταί, ὀρθῶς <u>καὶ</u> καλῶς πᾶσιν Ἕλλησι <u>καὶ</u> βαρβάροις δοκεῖτε ἐψηφίσθαι κατ᾽ ἀνδρῶν προδοτῶν <u>καὶ</u> θεοῖς ἐχθρῶν. (Dem. 19.268)

It seems to all the Greeks and foreigners, gentlemen of the jury, that you have acted righteously and properly in passing this vote against traitors and enemies of the gods. *καί connects ὀρθῶς and καλῶς, Ἕλλησι and βαρβάροις, and ἀνδρῶν προδοτῶν and θεοῖς ἐχθρῶν, respectively.*

(29) πολλάκις ἡ γυνὴ ἀπῄει κάτω καθευδήσουσα ὡς τὸ παιδίον, ἵνα τὸν τιτθὸν αὐτῷ διδῷ <u>καὶ</u> μὴ βοᾷ. <u>καὶ</u> ταῦτα πολὺν χρόνον οὕτως ἐγίγνετο, <u>καὶ</u> ἐγὼ οὐδέποτε ὑπώπτευσα. (Lys. 1.10)

Often my wife would go down to sleep, to the baby, so that she could breastfeed it and it wouldn't cry. And things went on like this for a long time, and I never even got suspicious of anything. *καί connects clauses (διδῷ and βοᾷ) and sentences. The quick succession of instances of καί in the narrative portion of this speech may suggest a 'simple' style of narration.*

(30) καὶ μὴν ὁρῶ <u>καὶ</u> Κλειναρέτην <u>καὶ</u> Σωστράτην | προσιοῦσαν ἤδη τήνδε <u>καὶ</u> Φιλαινέτην. (Ar. *Eccl.* 41–2)

Look, I see Clinarete coming, as well as Sostrate here, and also Philaenete. *Adverbial καί precedes the first of the listed names, the next two instances of καί connect the other names. For καὶ μήν marking entrances in drama, →59.71.*

Note 1: For 'adverbial' καί *also, even*, →59.56.

59.21   Although both δέ and καί (and τε, →59.37) may be translated with *and*, these particles operate on different levels: whereas δέ serves to indicate shifts from one text segment/topic to another (→59.16), καί connects several things said about a topic, linking several elements *within* a larger text segment. For the difference between καί/τε and δέ, compare also the following example:

(31) οὗτος ὢν ὁ Ὀτάνης ... Βυζαντίους <u>τε</u> εἷλε <u>καὶ</u> Καλχηδονίους, εἷλε <u>δὲ</u> Ἄντανδρον τὴν ἐν τῇ Τρῳάδι γῇ, εἷλε <u>δὲ</u> Λαμπώνιον, λαβὼν <u>δὲ</u> παρὰ Λεσβίων νέας εἷλε Λῆμνόν <u>τε καὶ</u> Ἴμβρον. (Hdt. 5.26)

This Otanes, then, captured Byzantium and Calchedon; next he captured Antandrus in the Troad, and next Lamponius; and having taken some ships from the Lesbians he captured Lemnus and Imbrus. *Some of the captured cities are connected by (τε) καί, others by δέ: this suggests several distinct campaigns of conquest, with Byzantium and Calchedon being captured in the one campaign, and Lemnus and Imbrus in another.*

59.22 The particle ἠδέ (*and*) connects only elements within sentences; in the classical period it is found only in tragic and lyric poetry.

καίτοι

59.23 Basic function: indicates a transition to a text segment which adds information (καί) which is worthy of note (τοι) in light of the preceding context – καίτοι invites a **reconsideration** of what the speaker has just said:

- introducing objections (often in the form of a rhetorical question); the καίτοι-segment shows that (an element in) the preceding context is to be rejected (*but, and yet, (al)though*);
- introducing background information in narrative or argumentative texts: the information in the καίτοι-segment gives rise to expectations which are contradicted by the preceding information (cf. Engl. 'he is unhappy, even though he is rich'; this is the inverse of 'denial of expectation', for which cf. μέντοι, →59.27) (*and yet, even though, (al)though, and that despite the fact that*):

(32) εἰς τοῦτ' ἀναισχυντίας ἐληλύθασιν, ὥστε . . . τῆς . . . τῶν ἄλλων δουλείας αὑτοὺς κυρίους καθιστᾶσιν. <u>καίτοι</u> τίς οὐκ ἂν μισήσειε τὴν τούτων πλεονεξίαν, οἳ τῶν μὲν ἀσθενεστέρων ἄρχειν ζητοῦσι; (Isoc. 14.19–20)
They (*the Thebans*) have reached such a point of shamelessness that they give themselves the right to impose slavery upon everybody else. And yet who would not detest the greed of these people, who seek to rule the weaker? *The rhetorical question (implying 'everyone detests the Thebans' greed') formulates an objection to the Thebans' behaviour.*

(33) καί μοι χέρ', ὦναξ, δεξιὰν ὄρεξον, ὡς | ψαύσω . . . | <u>καίτοι</u> τί φωνῶ; πῶς σ' ἂν ἄθλιος γεγὼς | θιγεῖν θελήσαιμ' ἀνδρὸς ᾧ τίς οὐκ ἔνι | κηλίς; (Soph. *OC* 1130–4)
Give me your right hand, lord, so I may touch it. Yet what am I saying? How could I, wretch that I've become, want you to touch a man in whom every defilement is found? *Oedipus raises an objection to his own request: given his state, that request seems misguided. For the accentuation of ἔνι (=ἔνεστι), →24.37; for τίς οὐκ ἔνι κηλίς;, →38.19 n.1.*

(34) ὁ Δαρεῖός τε ἤσχαλλε καὶ ἡ στρατιὴ πᾶσα οὐ δυνατὴ ἐοῦσα ἑλεῖν τοὺς Βαβυλωνίους. <u>καίτοι</u> πάντα σοφίσματα καὶ πάσας μηχανὰς ἐπεποιήκεε ἐς αὐτοὺς Δαρεῖος· ἀλλ' οὐδ' ὣς ἐδύνατο ἑλεῖν σφεας. (Hdt. 3.152)
Darius and the entire army were upset because they were incapable of conquering the Babylonians. This despite the fact that Darius had tried every trick and every device against them; but even so, he could not conquer them. *καίτοι introduces background information which stands in contrast to*

*the preceding point: Darius' intensive efforts to capture Babylon would nor-
mally give rise to the expectation that he would succeed, but in fact he has
failed. Darius' failure is restated (ἀλλ' οὐδ' ὥς) after the καίτοι-segment.*

μέν

59.24   Postpositive. Basic function: indicates **incompleteness** or **open-endedness** – μέν
signals that its host segment in itself does not provide all the necessary information; it raises the expectation that another text segment will follow to provide an
addition or contrast:

- the expectation raised by μέν is nearly always resolved by δέ: μέν ... δέ is
  a very common way in Greek to mark contrasts (e.g. 'A did X, but B did
  Y'), or more neutral enumerations ('A did X, B did Y, C did Z') (μέν is
  usually best left untranslated, the corresponding δέ translated with *but* or
  and; in contrasts, μέν or δέ may also be translated with *while, whereas*, with
  the other particle left untranslated); μέν ... δέ may balance phrases, clauses
  or larger segments of text; often the words immediately preceding the
  particles are the 'contrastive topics' (→60.28) forming the basis for the
  contrast or enumeration;
- for ὁ μέν ... ὁ δέ, τὸ μέν ... τὸ δέ, etc., →28.27;
- particles other than δέ that may be co-ordinated with μέν are ἀλλά, μέντοι,
  ἀτάρ (each of these suggests a stronger contrast than μέν ... δέ), and καί
  and τε;
- in some cases μέν is not followed by another particle (so-called μέν *solitarium*):
  usually this means that the segment or element contrasting with/adding to the
  μέν-segment is left implicit (*at least, for one, as for ...*).

(35) ὡς δὲ δῆλον ἐγένετο ὅτι οὐκ ἐξίοιεν οἱ πολέμιοι ... ὁ μὲν Κυαξάρης καλέσας τὸν
      Κῦρον ... ἔλεξε τοιάδε· Δοκεῖ μοι, ἔφη, ... δηλοῦν ὅτι θέλομεν μάχεσθαι. οὕτω
      γάρ, ἔφη, ἐὰν μὴ ἀντεπεξίωσιν ἐκεῖνοι, οἱ μὲν ἡμέτεροι μᾶλλον θαρρήσαντες
      ἀπίασιν, οἱ δὲ πολέμιοι ... μᾶλλον φοβήσονται. τούτῳ μὲν οὕτως ἐδόκει. ὁ δὲ
      Κῦρος, Μηδαμῶς, ἔφη, ... (Xen. *Cyr.* 3.3.29–31)
      When it became clear that the enemy would not come out, Cyaxares called
      Cyrus and spoke as follows: 'I propose', he said, 'to show them that we are
      eager to fight. That way,' he went on, 'if they don't come out to meet us,
      our men will come back to camp with more courage, whereas the enemy
      will be more frightened.' Such was his proposal, but Cyrus said: 'In no
      way ...' *The first* μέν *suggests that Cyaxares' speech will not be the whole
      story, but will receive a reaction; when his speech is complete,* μέν *is repeated
      in the summarizing phrase* τούτῳ ... ἐδόκει, *and then picked up by* ὁ δὲ
      Κῦρος. *Within the speech, there is a* μέν/δέ-*pair balancing* οἱ ἡμέτεροι *and* οἱ
      πολέμιοι.

(36) ἐγὼ δὲ λέξω δεινὰ μὲν, δίκαια δέ. (Ar. *Ach.* 501)

I will say things which are terrifying, but right. *μέν . . . δέ balances individual words, both object of λέξω.*

(37) πολλοὺς μὲν . . . | ξένους μολόντας οἶδ' ἐς Ἀδμήτου δόμους, | . . . ἀλλὰ τοῦδ' οὔπω ξένου | κακίον' . . . ἐδεξάμην. (Eur. *Alc.* 747–50)

I know of many guests who have come to Admetus' palace; but I have not yet received a guest more evil than this one. *μέν is 'completed' by ἀλλά, whose corrective force (→59.11) suggests that the μέν-clause is as good as irrelevant: the servant's previous experience with guests good and bad could not prepare him for this one.*

(38) πρῶτα μὲν σκοποὺς | πέμψω . . . μάντεις τ' ἀθροίσας θύσομαι. (Eur. *Heracl.* 337–40)

First, I will send scouts, and then I will gather seers and sacrifice. *μέν is 'completed' by τε.*

(39) φασὶ δὲ οἱ αὐτοὶ οὗτοι, ἐμοὶ μὲν οὐ πιστὰ λέγοντες, τὸν θεὸν αὐτὸν φοιτᾶν . . . ἐς τὸν νηόν. (Hdt. 1.182.1)

And these same men say – though I for one do not believe them – that the god himself frequents the shrine. *μέν solitarium: there is no particle in the following context which is paired with μέν, but a contrast is still implied: Herodotus suggests that, while others may believe the story about the god, he at least doesn't.*

59.25   In certain particle combinations, especially in Ionic, μέν has the force of μήν (→59.49): so, in Herodotus, in the particle combinations οὐ μὲν οὐδέ, γε μέν (δή), καὶ μέν (δή); for most of these combinations, →59.71–6 below. In Attic writers, the same holds for ἀλλὰ μέν (δή), some cases of μὲν οὖν (→59.72), for μέντοι (→59.26–8), and occasionally for μέν alone.

μέντοι

59.26   Postpositive. Two different uses of this particle may be distinguished, as an 'adversative' connective particle, and as an 'emphasizer' (in answers).

59.27   **Adversative μέντοι.** Basic function: **denial of expectation** or **modification** – μέντοι indicates a transition to a text-segment which contradicts or modifies the expectations raised by the preceding context (cf. Engl. 'he is rich, but he is unhappy'):

 – contrasting explicit statements: statement A gives rise to a certain expectation, which statement B (with μέντοι) contradicts (*nevertheless, however, still, but, be that as it may, mind you*);
 – modifying textual relationships: (especially in dialogue) to indicate that a speaker makes a different kind of contribution than might be expected given the preceding context (*however, but*; often difficult to translate):

(40) καὶ εὐθὺς . . . ἐς Οἰνιάδας ἐστράτευσαν καὶ ἐπολιόρκουν, οὐ μέντοι εἷλόν γε, ἀλλ' ἀπεχώρησαν ἐπ' οἴκου. (Thuc. 1.111.3)

And straight away they attacked Oeniadae and besieged it; they did not, however, capture it, but departed for home. *The mention of a siege gives rise to the expectation that the city will be captured; the μέντοι-segment explicitly denies that expectation.*

(41) ἀπικόμενοι παρὰ τὸν Κροῖσον . . . ἄγγελοι ἔλεγον τάδε· Ὦ βασιλεῦ, . . . προσδεόμεθά σευ τὸν παῖδα καὶ λογάδας νεηνίας καὶ κύνας συμπέμψαι ἡμῖν . . . Κροῖσος δὲ . . . ἔλεγέ σφι τάδε· Παιδὸς μὲν πέρι τοῦ ἐμοῦ μὴ μνησθῆτε ἔτι· οὐ γὰρ ἂν ὑμῖν συμπέμψαιμι· . . . Λυδῶν μέντοι λογάδας καὶ τὸ κυνηγέσιον πᾶν συμπέμψω. (Hdt. 1.36.2–3)

Messengers came to Croesus and said: 'Sire, we beg you to send your son and a hunting party with dogs to accompany us.' But Croesus said to them: 'Do not mention my son again: I will not send him with you. But as for Lydian huntsmen, I will send you some, together with a complete hunting outfit.' *Croesus' first rejection may have given rise to the expectation that he would reject the entire request: μέντοι contradicts this. Note that in this example (παιδός) μέν is 'completed' by μέντοι.*

(42) ΚΡ. μεῖνον, τί φεύγεις; :: ΤΕ. ἡ τύχη σ', ἀλλ' οὐκ ἐγώ. | :: ΚΡ. φράσον πολίταις καὶ πόλει σωτηρίαν. | :: ΤΕ. βούλῃ σὺ μέντοι κοὐχὶ βουλήσῃ τάχα. (Eur. *Phoen.* 897–9)

(Creon:) Wait, why are you fleeing? :: (Tiresias:) Fortune is fleeing you, not I. :: (Creon:) Tell me what can save the citizens and their city. :: (Tiresias:) You want this now; soon enough you will not want it. *Creon's request to Tiresias to explain what might save the city raises the expectation of an answer. Tiresias circumvents that expectation (μέντοι) and enigmatically states that Creon will not want to know about σωτηρία at all.*

Note 1: Although ἀλλά, καίτοι and μέντοι are all three 'adversative', there is a difference between them: whereas, in 'A ἀλλά B', B *replaces* A (A is falsified, →59.11–12), in 'A καίτοι B' (→59.23) as well as in 'A B μέντοι', both A and B are valid, but one counters expectations raised by the other.

59.28   **Emphasizing μέντοι.** Basic function: indicates that the speaker is committed to the truth or relevance of his statement, no matter what the addressee might expect (→59.49, μήν) and brings that commitment home to the addressee (→59.51, τοι) – this use of μέντοι is virtually confined to answers, usually assenting:

(43) Λέγεται ψυχὴ ἡ μὲν νοῦν τε ἔχειν . . . , ἡ δὲ ἄνοιαν . . . καὶ ταῦτα ἀληθῶς λέγεται; :: Ἀληθῶς μέντοι. (Pl. *Phd.* 93b–c)

(Socrates:) It is said that one soul possesses sense, another folly . . . And is it true what they say? :: (Simmias:) Most certainly it is. *Simmias confirms the correctness of ἀληθῶς in Socrates' question.*

νυν

59.29 Basic function: indicates a transition to a new text segment which proceeds from the preceding text segment (cf. οὖν below): in Attic νυν is used almost exclusively in commands and requests in dialogue, where it **indicates that the directive flows naturally from the preceding context** (*then, so*):

(44) ΠΥ. ἐς κοινοὺς λόγους | ἔλθωμεν, ὡς ἂν Μενέλεως συνδυστυχῇ. | :: ΟΡ. ὦ φίλτατ᾽, εἰ γὰρ τοῦτο κατθάνοιμ᾽ ἰδών. | :: ΠΥ. πιθοῦ <u>νυν</u>, ἀνάμεινον δὲ φασγάνου τομάς. | :: ΟΡ. μενῶ, τὸν ἐχθρὸν εἴ τι τιμωρήσομαι. | :: ΠΥ. σίγα <u>νυν</u>· ὡς γυναιξὶ πιστεύω βραχύ. (Eur. *Or.* 1098–1103)

(Pylades:) Let us agree on a plan for how Menelaus may share in suffering. :: (Orestes:) Dearest friend, would that I might die having seen that. :: (Pylades:) Listen to me then, and delay the strokes of your sword. :: (Orestes:) I will wait to see if I can take revenge on my enemy in some way. :: (Pylades:) Hush then! I do not have much confidence in women. *In both instances, νυν indicates that Pylades' instructions follow from Orestes' preceding utterances.*

Note 1: The postpositive (→60.5) particle νῦν (with short ῠ) is to be distinguished from the adverb νῦν *now* (with long ῡ). In some cases in poetry, enclitic νυν has a long ῡ for metrical reasons (it is then accented νῦν in some editions). The enclitic particle is found as νυ in epic and in dialect inscriptions.

59.30 In Herodotus, νυν is often used in contexts where Attic would use οὖν, especially in the combination μέν νυν … δέ (for μὲν οὖν … δέ, →59.73):

(45) ταῦτα <u>μέν νυν</u> Πέρσαι τε καὶ Φοίνικες λέγουσι. ἐγὼ <u>δὲ</u> περὶ μὲν τούτων οὐκ ἔρχομαι ἐρέων ὡς οὕτως ἢ ἄλλως κως ταῦτα ἐγένετο. (Hdt. 1.5.3)

This, then, is what the Persians and Phoenicians say. As for me, I will not venture to say about these things that they happened this way or that. *For ἔρχομαι + fut. ppl., →52.41 n.1.*

οὐδέ/μηδέ and οὔτε/μήτε

59.31 οὐδέ/μηδέ is the negative of καί (→59.20); it is used only after a preceding negative: οὐ X οὐδὲ Y = 'not X; and not Y' (*and not, but not, nor*), but also →59.32 n.1.

59.32 οὔτε/μήτε is the negative of τε (→59.37): οὔτε X οὔτε Y = 'neither X nor Y' (*neither … nor, and not*).

(46) … μυρίους ἔδωκε δαρεικούς· οὓς ἐγὼ λαβὼν οὐκ εἰς τὸ ἴδιον κατεθέμην ἐμοὶ <u>οὐδὲ</u> καθηδυπάθησα, ἀλλ᾽ εἰς ὑμᾶς ἐδαπάνησα. (Xen. *An.* 1.3.3)

He gave me ten thousand darics. Having received them, I did not set them aside for private use, nor did I squander them, but I spent them on you.

(47) ... <u>οὔτε</u> σίδηρον <u>οὔτε</u> ξύλον <u>οὔτε</u> ἄλλο οὐδὲν ἔχων, ᾧ τοὺς εἰσελθόντας ἂν ἠμύνατο. (Lys. 1.27)

... having neither a sword, nor a stick, nor anything else, with which he could have defended himself against those who came in.

Note 1: For οὐδέ/μηδέ *not even* (as the negative of adverbial καί), →59.56 below; in this use, οὐδέ/μηδέ need not be preceded by another negative.

Note 2: For the contexts in which οὐ and μή are used, →56.

οὐκοῦν and οὔκουν

59.33   Both these particles combine the negative οὐ with the connective particle οὖν (→59.34): the difference between the two is that in οὔκουν the negative has its normal negative force, whereas in οὐκοῦν it functions as a question word, the emphasis being on οὖν:

– οὐκοῦν introduces yes/no questions; the negative has its usual force of indicating that a positive answer is expected (→38.7), and οὖν serves its regular function of 'getting to the point' (*isn't it the case, then?; not, therefore?*);

– οὐκοῦν is also occasionally used in statements and directives (this use probably derives from its use in questions); the negative here has no force, and the particle is very similar to simple οὖν (*then, so, well, therefore*);

– οὔκουν is used in questions, with emphasis on the negative, expressing doubt that the addressee will really answer 'no' to the question (*is it really the case that not ... , then?; so ... not?*);

– οὔκουν is also, but infrequently, used in statements (particularly in negative answers), again with emphasis on the negative (*not ... , then*); typically combined with γε (*not ... at any rate*).

(48) Τοὐναντίον ἄρα ἐστὶν τὸ ἀφρόνως πράττειν τῷ σωφρόνως; :: ἔφη. :: <u>Οὐκοῦν</u> τὰ μὲν ἀφρόνως πραττόμενα ἀφροσύνῃ πράττεται, τὰ δὲ σωφρόνως σωφροσύνῃ; :: ὡμολόγει. (Pl. *Prt.* 332b)

'Acting immoderately, then, is the opposite of acting wisely?' :: He said that it was. :: 'Isn't it the case, then, that immoderate acts are performed due to a lack of moderation, and moderate acts due to moderation?' :: He agreed. *οὐκοῦν introducing a yes/no question.*

(49) τίνας οὖν εὐχὰς ὑπολαμβάνετ' εὔχεσθαι τοῖς θεοῖς τὸν Φίλιππον ... ; ἆρ' οὐ κράτος πολέμου ... διδόναι ... ; <u>οὐκοῦν</u> ταῦτα συνηύχετο οὗτος καὶ κατηρᾶτο τῇ πατρίδι. (Dem. 19.130)

What prayers do you suppose Philip made to the gods? For them to give him victory in war, wouldn't you think? Well, this man joined in this prayer, and cursed his fatherland. *οὐκοῦν in a statement, indicating a transition to Demosthenes' central point: Aeschines was ill-intentioned towards Athens. For ἆρ' οὐ, →38.7.*

(50) ΣΩ. ὅρα οὖν εἰ ἐθελήσεις ... διδόναι ἔλεγχον ἀποκρινόμενος τὰ ἐρωτώμενα. ἐγὼ
γὰρ δὴ οἶμαι καὶ ἐμὲ καὶ σὲ καὶ τοὺς ἄλλους ἀνθρώπους τὸ ἀδικεῖν τοῦ
ἀδικεῖσθαι κάκιον ἡγεῖσθαι ... :: ΠΩ. πολλοῦ γε δεῖ, ἀλλ' οὔτ' ἐγὼ οὔτε σὺ
οὔτ' ἄλλος οὐδείς. :: ΣΩ. <u>οὔκουν</u> ἀποκρινῇ; :: ΠΩ. πάνυ μὲν οὖν. (Pl. *Grg.* 474b–c)
(Socrates:) See if you want to be examined by answering my questions.
I believe that both I and you and everyone else thinks that it is worse to
commit an injustice than it is to suffer one. :: (Polus:) Far from it: on the
contrary, that isn't true for me, for you, or for anyone else. :: (Socrates:)
So you *won't* answer? :: (Polus:) To be sure I will. *Polus' answer leads Socrates*
to surmise (-ουν) that he does not (οὔκ-) want to answer his questions: he asks if
that is really the case.

(51) ΧΟ. τούτων ἄρα Ζεύς ἐστιν ἀσθενέστερος; | :: ΠΡ. <u>οὔκουν</u> ἂν ἐκφύγοι <u>γε</u> τὴν
πεπρωμένην. (Aesch. *PV.* 517–18)
(Chorus:) Are you saying that Zeus is weaker than they? :: (Prometheus:)
There is no way, at any rate, in which he may escape what has been fated.
Emphatic οὔκουν ... γε in a negative answer.

Note 1: Editors vary greatly in printing οὐκοῦν or οὔκουν, and in punctuating sentences with
οὐκοῦν as questions or statements. As accents are later additions (→1.12), there is no sure
way of knowing which variant is authentic in each case.

οὖν

59.34   Ion. ὦν. Postpositive. Basic function: οὖν indicates a **transition to more to-the-**
point, crucial or relevant information, and indicates that the preceding context
should be seen as preliminary/explanatory to its host segment:

– in argumentative texts: indicating a transition from arguments/premises to
a conclusion or summary (*so, then, therefore; the point is that*);
– in narratives: indicating a transition to the main, foregrounded storyline after
a segment with background narrative (*now, so, then, well*);
– in dialogue (often in questions), to indicate that the point the speaker makes, the
question the speaker asks, etc., is the main thing the speaker wants to convey or
ask, given the preceding context (*so, now, well then, therefore*);
– in dialogue: τί οὖν; *so what?, what, then?*

(52) καὶ ... παμπόλλους ἔχω λέγειν, οἳ αὐτοὶ ἀγαθοὶ ὄντες οὐδένα πώποτε βελτίω
ἐποίησαν ... ἐγὼ <u>οὖν</u>, ὦ Πρωταγόρα, εἰς ταῦτα ἀποβλέπων οὐχ ἡγοῦμαι
διδακτὸν εἶναι ἀρετήν. (Pl. *Prt.* 320b)
And I can tell you of many, who, although they were themselves good, never
made anyone any better. Therefore, Protagoras, considering these matters
I do not think that virtue is something that can be taught. *οὖν marks the*

transition from Socrates' arguments (of which only one is printed in the example) to the conclusion validated by those arguments.

(53) οἱ τριάκοντα ... φάσκοντες χρῆναι τῶν ἀδίκων καθαρὰν ποιῆσαι τὴν πόλιν ... οὐ τοιαῦτα ποιεῖν ἐτόλμων ... Θέογνις γὰρ καὶ Πείσων ἔλεγον ... περὶ τῶν μετοίκων, ὡς εἶέν τινες τῇ πολιτείᾳ ἀχθόμενοι· καλλίστην <u>οὖν</u> εἶναι πρόφασιν τιμωρεῖσθαι μὲν δοκεῖν, τῷ δ' ἔργῳ χρηματίζεσθαι· ... ἔδοξεν <u>οὖν</u> αὐτοῖς δέκα συλλαβεῖν. (Lys. 12.5–7)

The Thirty, although they said that they needed to cleanse the city of criminals, dared to behave in a very different fashion. For Theognis and Pison said concerning the metics, that there were some who were disgruntled with the regime; so that there was an excellent pretext to appear to exact punishment, but in reality to acquire funds. So they decided to arrest ten of them. *The second* οὖν *marks a transition (back) to the main narrative line, rounding off a stretch of explanatory background material (introduced by* γάρ*) which details the deliberations leading up to the Thirty's decision. The first* οὖν *connects two parts of Theognis' and Pison's argument: the preliminary assertion that they have opposition among the resident aliens leads up to the relevant point – their proposal to use them as an excuse for income-gathering. For this passage, also* →61.1–3.

(54) ΕΥ. Ἀγάθωνά μοι δεῦρ' ἐκκάλεσον ... | :: ΘΕ. μηδὲν ἱκέτευ· αὐτὸς γὰρ ἔξεισιν τάχα· | καὶ γὰρ μελοποιεῖν ἄρχεται· χειμῶνος <u>οὖν</u> | ὄντος κατακάμπτειν τὰς στροφὰς οὐ ῥᾴδιον, | ἢν μὴ προΐῃ θύρασι ... | :: ΕΥ. τί <u>οὖν</u> ἐγὼ δρῶ; :: ΘΕ. περίμεν', ὡς ἐξέρχεται. (Ar. *Thesm.* 65–70)

(Euripides:) Call out Agathon for me. :: (Servant:) No need to beg: he'll come out himself soon enough. In fact, he's beginning to compose – the point being that since it's winter, it's not easy for him to mould his couplets unless he comes outside. :: (Euripides:) So what should I do? :: (Servant:) Wait here: he's coming out. *The servant's point that Agathon is beginning to compose is not very helpful in itself; the transition to the relevant point (that this means that he will come out) is indicated by* οὖν. *Euripides then wants the servant to answer the point which matters for him (what he should do in order to speak to Agathon);* οὖν *marks the relevant question.*

59.35   οὖν is sometimes added to indefinite relative pronouns/adjectives to express universality; such pronouns/adjectives usually do *not* introduce (cor)relative clauses, but are used as indefinite pronouns: ὁστισοῦν *anybody who(so)ever*, ὁτιοῦν *anything whatsoever*, ὁποσοιοῦν *however many*, etc.

59.36   For the use of **μῶν** (= μὴ οὖν), →38.8.

τε

59.37   Postpositive. Basic function: indicates **addition** (cf. καί above):

– as a co-ordinating conjunction within sentences: τε follows the word it connects
to the preceding context: X Y τε = 'X and Y' (*and, as well as*);

– τε is also very commonly used to signal that something is the first in an
enumeration, in which case καί or another τε follows it: X τε καὶ Y = 'X and
Y'; X τε Y τε = 'X and Y' (the first τε is typically not translated; *and, both . . . and,
as well as*).

(55) ἐν ἐκείνῃ τῇ νυκτὶ ἐψόφει ἡ μέταυλος θύρα . . . , ὃ οὐδέποτε ἐγένετο, ἔδοξέ τέ μοι
ἡ γυνὴ ἐπιμυθιῶσθαι. (Lys. 1.17)
That night the inner doors made a sound, which had never happened, and
my wife seemed to me to have put on make-up.

(56) ἰὼ μέλαθρα βασιλέων, φίλαι στέγαι, | σεμνοί τε θᾶκοι, δαίμονές τ᾽ ἀντήλιοι . . .
(Aesch. *Ag.* 518–19)
Hail, halls of kings – dear roofs, and blessed thrones, and gods who face the
sun . . .

(57) ἄξιον ἐπαινέσαι τήν τε πατρίδα καὶ τὸ γένος αὐτοῦ. (Xen. *Ages.* 1.4)
It is worth praising his fatherland and descent.

Note 1: In tragic and lyric poetry only (in the classical period), τε is sometimes used to
introduce a general truth. In this use the particle is called **epic τε**; it is especially found in
digressive relative clauses (→50.6):

(58) παῖ Ῥέας, ἅ τε πρυτανεῖα λέλογχας, Ἑστία, . . . (Pind. *Nem.* 11.1)
Daughter of Rhea, to whom city halls have been allotted, Hestia, . . .

Note 2: Observe the idiom οἷός τέ (εἰμι) (*be*) *able to,* (*be*) *capable of.*

τοιγάρ, τοιγαροῦν, *and* τοιγάρτοι

59.38   Basic function: indicates **consequence** – these (infrequent) particles combine
a demonstrative element τοι- (cf. τοιόσδε, τοιοῦτος) with γάρ (whose meaning here is
unclear); their function is to indicate a transition to a text segment whose content follows
from the preceding context.

τοιγάρ typically occurs in answers, τοιγαροῦν and τοιγάρτοι usually in continuous argumentative or narrative texts (*therefore, hence, thus, that is why*).

(59) ΣΙ. Βρομίου δὲ πῶμ᾽ ἔχουσιν, ἀμπέλου ῥοάς; | :: ΟΔ. ἥκιστα· τοιγάρ ἄχορον οἰκοῦσι χθόνα.
(Eur. *Cyc.* 124–5)
(Silenus:) Do they possess Dionysus' drink, that flows from the vine? :: (Odysseus:) Not at
all! Hence the land they dwell in knows no dancing.

(60) ἐξ ὧν αὐτοὶ συνίσασι καὶ ἐξητάκασι, τὴν ψῆφον φέρουσι. <u>τοιγάρτοι</u> διατελεῖ τοῦτο τὸ
συνέδριον εὐδοκιμοῦν ἐν τῇ πόλει. (Aeschin. 1.92)

They cast their verdict based upon what they themselves know and have examined. That
is why this court continues to be reputable in the city.

Note 1: τοιγάρ is mainly found in epic and tragedy, never in Attic prose, which rather uses
(more forceful) τοιγαροῦν and τοιγάρτοι.

τοίνυν

59.39   Postpositive. Basic function: indicates a **transition to a newly relevant, to-the-
point text segment** (νυν, cf. οὖν, →59.29–30, 59.34), and stresses **the importance
or relevance for the addressee** of that new point (τοι, →59.51):

- in argumentative texts, in transitions to an important new point or an important
conclusion (*well, then, so, now; I'll have you know, then*);
- in dialogue, indicating that the statement, question or command uttered by the
speaker is to the point and should be of particular note to the addressee (*then, so,
well*); the reasons why the addressee should take note vary: e.g. because he/she
has asked for it (*very well, then*), because it implies a criticism of him/her (*might
I point out, then*), etc.;
- τοίνυν is rare in narrative.

(61) νῦν δ᾽ οὕνεχ᾽ Ἑλένη μάργος ἦν ... | τούτων ἕκατι παῖδ᾽ ἐμὴν διώλεσεν. | ἐπὶ
τοῖσδε <u>τοίνυν</u> καίπερ ἠδικημένη | οὐκ ἠγριώμην οὐδ᾽ ἂν ἔκτανον πόσιν. (Eur. *El.*
1027–31)

As it was, because Helen was lewd, for that reason he killed my child. Now, in
response to this, although I had been wronged, I was not spiteful, nor would
I have killed my husband. *Clytaemestra moves on to a new point in her argument:
she was initially forgiving towards Agamemnon; this is something she particularly
wants to point out to her addressee, her vindictive daughter Electra.*

(62) ΧΟ. τὴν σαυτοῦ φύσιν εἰπέ. | :: ΚΡ. λέξω <u>τοίνυν</u>. (Ar. *Nub.* 960–1)

(Chorus:) Tell us about your nature. :: (Better Argument:) Very well then,
I will speak. *Since the Chorus has asked for the exposition, Better Argument
implies that his speech is of particular interest to them.*

Note 1: The difference between τοίνυν and the more neutral οὖν is the former's attitudinal
nuance: τοίνυν, in addition to indicating that its host segment presents to-the-point
information, also conveys the notion that this information is of particular interest or
importance for the addressee.

Attitudinal Particles

Introduction

59.40 The particles ἄρα, ἆρα, δή, δήπου, ἦ, μήν, τοι and που (also μέντοι, καίτοι and τοίνυν described above) play a role in managing the attitudes and beliefs that speaker and addressee have towards what is said. By using these particles, speakers can signal that their utterance should be interpreted in a specific way, or they can anticipate what the addressee might or should think about it. These particles are by far the hardest to translate, and the 'definitions' below are by no means certain.

Note 1: Similar devices in English are *perhaps, surely, really, apparently, you know, obviously,* etc.

59.41 These particles normally have no connective function, but there are some exceptions (notably ἄρα and δή).

List of Attitudinal Particles

ἄρα

59.42 Postpositive. Basic function: indicates that the speaker, in view of the preceding context, **cannot but make the contribution** he/she is making (often to his/her surprise or displeasure):

– in statements (*apparently, it seems, then, so, in that case, if this is granted*); often in conclusions, signalling that the conclusion follows necessarily (often surprisingly) from the preceding context;

– commonly with the imperfect or aorist when a speaker retrospectively realizes that something was the case (*apparently, it seems, then, so, as it turns out*);

– in questions, to indicate that the question is necessarily brought on by the context (*so, then, in that case*);

– in later usage, the particle occasionally appears to develop a connective function, linking sentences.

(63) βαρέως δὲ φέρων τῇ ἀτιμίᾳ ... εἶπεν· Ὦ Ἀγησίλαε, μειοῦν μὲν <u>ἄρα</u> σύγε τοὺς φίλους ἠπίστω. (Xen. *Hell.* 3.4.9)

And not bearing his disgrace well, he said: 'It seems that you, at any rate, Agesilaus, knew how to humiliate your friends.' *ἄρα + imperfect to mark a surprising realization in hindsight.*

(64) ΣΩ. τί ... ἂν εἴη ... τὰ παρ' ἡμῶν δῶρα τοῖς θεοῖς; :: ΕΥ. τί ... ἄλλο ἢ τιμή τε καὶ γέρα καὶ ... χάρις; :: ΣΩ. κεχαρισμένον <u>ἄρα</u> ἐστίν, ὦ Εὐθύφρων, τὸ ὅσιον, ἀλλ' οὐχὶ ὠφέλιμον οὐδὲ φίλον τοῖς θεοῖς; :: ΕΥ. οἶμαι ἔγωγε πάντων γε μάλιστα

φίλον. :: ΣΩ. τοῦτο <u>ἄρ’</u> ἐστὶν αὖ, ὡς ἔοικε, τὸ ὅσιον, τὸ τοῖς θεοῖς φίλον. (Pl. *Euthphr.* 15a–b)

(Socrates:) What would our gifts to the gods be? (Euthyphro:) What else than honour and praise and gratitude? :: (Socrates:) So holiness is gratifying, but not beneficial or precious to the gods? :: (Euthyphro:) I do think that it is, above all, precious. :: (Socrates:) In that case, again, it would seem that holiness is what is precious to the gods. *The first ἄρα introduces a question which suggests the inevitable conclusion of the preceding discussion. The second similarly introduces a hypothesis which is inescapable given the preceding line of thought (note ὡς ἔοικε).*

(65) δῆλον ... τῆς ἀρετῆς ἐνέργειαν τῆς ψυχῆς ἄριστον εἶναι. ἣν δὲ καὶ ἡ εὐδαιμονία τὸ ἄριστον. ἔστιν <u>ἄρα</u> ἡ εὐδαιμονία ψυχῆς ἀγαθῆς ἐνέργεια. (Arist. *Eth. Eud.* 1219a28–35)

It is clear that the activity of excellence is the greatest good of the spirit. And happiness was also the greatest good: so happiness is the activity of a good spirit. *ἄρα here also appears to have developed a connective function, as no other connective is present.*

ἄρα

59.43   ἦ (→59.48) + ἄρα (→59.42), used specifically in yes/no-questions. For its use, →38.6.

δαί

→δή 59.46.

δή

Note 1: δή has a particularly wide range of uses. Its basic function is difficult to ascertain, and the subject of considerable scholarly debate.

59.44   Postpositive. Basic function: δή indicates that the speaker considers (and invites the addressee to consider) the text segment or word (group) which it modifies as **evident, clear** or **precise**:

– following individual words or word groups: δή in such cases indicates that the word or word group in question is entirely or evidently applicable (*in fact, actually, very, precisely, indeed*, or translated by emphasis); the particle is so used particularly with adjectives/adverbs expressing quantity, size, frequency, intensity, etc.; with super-latives; with δῆλος; and with certain types of pronouns (in this use δή might more properly be considered a particle of scope, for which →59.52);

- modifying entire clauses, to present the content of the clause as clearly true or relevant (*certainly, indeed*; often with a nuance of obviousness: *obviously, of course, clearly*);
- in many such cases, δή appears to have developed a connective function, indicating a transition to a new, obviously relevant segment (*then, well, now, so*);
- in causal clauses (→48), purpose clauses (→45), comparative clauses (→50.37), and with ὡς + participle (→52.39), the sense 'evidently' is often used with an ironic or sarcastic nuance (*I'm sure, obviously, apparently, no doubt*).

(66) κίνησις γὰρ αὕτη μεγίστη <u>δὴ</u> τοῖς Ἕλλησιν ἐγένετο καὶ μέρει τινὶ τῶν βαρβάρων. (Thuc. 1.1.2)

For this was indeed the greatest movement to occur, for the Greeks as well as a part of the barbarian world. *δή modifies the superlative μεγίστη, underlining that the expedition was undeniably the largest ever.*

(67) σὲ <u>δή</u>, σὲ τὴν νεύουσαν εἰς πέδον κάρα, | φὴς ἢ καταρνεῖ μὴ δεδρακέναι τάδε; (Soph. *Ant.* 441–2)

You, you with your head bowing towards the ground: do you affirm or deny that you have done this? *δή highlights the personal pronoun σέ, with a note of contempt; it is also possible to read δή as indicating that Creon's questioning of Antigone is expected given the preceding context ('you then').*

(68) ἔστι δὲ οὗτος Ἀξιόχου μὲν ὑός ... ὄνομα δ' αὐτῷ Κλεινίας. ἔστι δὲ νέος· φοβούμεθα <u>δὴ</u> περὶ αὐτῷ, οἷον εἰκὸς περὶ νέῳ. (Pl. *Euthd.* 275a–b)

This is the son of Axiochus; his name is Clinias; he's young, and so of course we're concerned for him, as is to be expected with a young man. *Concern is predictable given Clinias' youth; the particle here also appears to have a connective function, connecting the φοβούμεθα-sentence to the preceding one (note that no other connective is present).*

(69) ἐγὼ δ' οὐκ ἀγνοῶ ... ὅτι πολλάκις ... τοὺς ὑστάτους περὶ τῶν πραγμάτων εἰπόντας ἐν ὀργῇ ποιεῖσθε, ἄν τι μὴ κατὰ γνώμην ἐκβῇ· οὐ μὴν οἶμαι δεῖν τὴν ἰδίαν ἀσφάλειαν σκοποῦνθ' ὑποστείλασθαι ... φημὶ <u>δὴ</u> διχῆ βοηθητέον εἶναι ... · εἰ δὲ θατέρου τούτων ὀλιγωρήσετε, ὀκνῶ μὴ μάταιος ἡμῖν ἡ στρατεία γένηται. εἴτε γὰρ ... εἴτε ... δεῖ <u>δὴ</u> πολλὴν καὶ διχῆ τὴν βοήθειαν εἶναι. (Dem. 1.16–18)

And I am well aware that you often get angry at the most recent speakers concerning an affair, if something goes against plan. Yet I believe that I must not, looking at my personal safety, keep quiet. I argue, then, that there must be two relief expeditions. And if you neglect either of them, I worry that our campaign will prove fruitless. *For if . . . or if . . . So our expedition must be on a large scale and twofold.* δή *is used twice with a connective function (note that no other connectives are present in the relevant clauses). In both cases, it marks a transition to an obviously relevant next step in the argument (in the first, Demosthenes proceeds, after having explained why he should not withhold his opinion, actually to give it; in the second, he restates that opinion as a conclusion to the preceding argumentation). In this use,* δή *somewhat resembles* οὖν *(for which,* →59.34*). For* θατέρου, →1.45 *n.3.*

(70) Πολυνείκης πίτνει. | ὃ δ', ὡς κρατῶν δὴ καὶ νενικηκὼς μάχῃ, | ξίφος δικὼν ἐς γαῖαν ἐσκύλευέ νιν. (Eur. *Phoen.* 1415–17)

Polynices fell. And he (*Eteocles*), believing, no doubt, that he had defeated him and won the battle, put his sword down on the ground and proceeded to strip his body. *With an ironic nuance: the 'subjective' motivation given by* ὡς κρατῶν (→52.39) *will prove to be tragically misguided: Polynices is still alive, and will kill Eteocles.*

Note 1: δή is sometimes written as one word with a following indefinite pronoun or adverb which it modifies: e.g. δήποτε; for δήπου, →59.47.

59.45   The particle **δῆτα** (postpositive) is a stronger form of δή, used primarily in answers and questions:

(71) ΗΤ. οὐδὲ γὰρ εἶναι πάνυ φημὶ δίκην. . . ποῦ 'στιν; :: ΚΡ. παρὰ τοῖσι θεοῖς. :: ΗΤ. πῶς δῆτα δίκης οὔσης ὁ Ζεὺς οὐκ ἀπόλωλεν, τὸν πατέρ' αὑτοῦ δήσας; (Ar. *Nub.* 902–6)

(Weaker Argument:) I say that there is no justice at all; where is it? :: (Stronger Argument:) With the gods. :: (Weaker Argument:) How is it possible, then, if there is justice, that Zeus didn't perish when he bound his own father?

59.46   The particle **δαί** (postpositive) is a – probably colloquial – variant of δή, used specifically in questions.

The particle **δῆθε(ν)** appears to be synonymous with δή, although it is found primarily in the 'ironic' contexts described above.

δήπου

59.47   Postpositive. Basic function: combines the 'evidential' force of δή (→59.44) with the uncertainty of που (→59.50) – δήπου tentatively suggests that something ought to be as clear or obvious to the addressee as it is to the speaker (for possible translations →που, 59.50):

(72) ἀναμνήσθητε ὅτι καὶ ἐψηφίσασθε δήπου τοὺς φυγάδας ἀγωγίμους εἶναι ἐκ πασῶν τῶν συμμαχίδων. (Xen. *Hell.* 7.3.11)

Remember: you voted, if I'm not mistaken, that exiles can be extradited from all of our allies.

δῆτα

→δή, 59.45.

ἦ

59.48 Basic function: **'objective' emphasizer** – ἦ indicates a high level of commitment on the part of the speaker to the truth of the content of an utterance, which is considered to be *objectively* true:

– in statements, to underline that the speaker considers his/her statement or a part of it objectively true (*really, truly, certainly*);
– in questions (for ἆρα (= ἦ + ἄρα) →59.43), to ask whether the addressee really considers something the case (*really, truly*); often to introduce a suggested answer to a previous question (*I suppose, is it the case that*).

(73) ἦ πολὺ πλεῖστον ἐκεῖνοι κατὰ τὴν ἀρετὴν ἁπάντων ἀνθρώπων διήνεγκαν. (Lys. 2.40)
These men truly surpassed all men in valour by a great deal.

(74) ἦ κἀν θεοῖσι ταὐτὸν ἐλπίζεις τόδε; (Eur. *Hipp.* 97)
Do you really expect that this same principle is true among the gods as well?

(75) τίνες δ' ἔχουσι γαῖαν; ἦ θηρῶν γένος; (Eur. *Cyc.* 117)
Who lives here? Wild beasts, I suppose?

Note 1: ἦ may be seen as a positive counterpart to the negation οὐ: whereas οὐ expresses that something is *not* the case, ἦ expresses emphatically that it *is*.

μήν

59.49 Postpositive. Basic function: **'subjective' emphasizer** – μήν indicates that the speaker is committed to the truth or relevance of his/her utterance, and anticipates or assumes a possible lack of commitment on the part of the addressee.

– in statements, μήν signals that the speaker vouches for the truth or relevance of his/her statement, no matter what the addressee may believe (it anticipates disbelief or scepticism) (*I assure you, really, truly, certainly, in fact, know that, let me tell you that*);
– in questions, typically after a previous answer has been rejected, to indicate that the speaker wants the addressee to give an answer which *is* true or relevant (translation other than by stress is difficult); so frequently with question words, e.g. ποῦ μήν . . . ; *where is . . . ?*, τί μήν; *then what is . . . ?*; τί μήν is also used 'elliptically', with the sense *what of it? yes, but what is your point?*;
– μήν also appears to have developed a connective force, indicating a transition to a point which is somehow unexpected (*however, be that as it may, yet*; in this use μήν is very similar to adversative μέντοι, →59.27; it is often anticipated by μέν);

– μήν is frequently combined with negatives: οὐ μήν (*truly not, not however; well, . . . not*) (this use is normally combined with γε).

(76) ΓΟ. εἰσὶ μέν . . . ἔνιαι τῶν ἀποκρίσεων ἀναγκαῖαι διὰ μακρῶν τοὺς λόγους ποιεῖσθαι· οὐ μὴν ἀλλὰ πειράσομαί γε ὡς διὰ βραχυτάτων. . . :: ΣΩ. τούτου μὴν δεῖ, ὦ Γοργία· καί μοι ἐπίδειξιν . . . ποίησαι τῆς βραχυλογίας . . . :: ΓΟ. ἀλλὰ ποιήσω. (Pl. *Grg.* 449b–c)

(Gorgias:) Some answers, Socrates, need to be made with long expositions; nevertheless I will try, at least, to make mine as short as possible. :: (Socrates:) That is in fact what is needed, Gorgias; give me a display of your brevity. :: (Gorgias:) I will. *Socrates affirms that he really does want a short explanation (possibly to avoid the impression that he would like Gorgias to make one of his famed longer speeches.) For* οὐ μὴν ἀλλά, →59.75.

(77) ΤΕ. ἐθαύμαζον ὅτι οὐχ οἷός τ’ ἦ εὑρεῖν. :: ΕΥ. οὐ γὰρ ἦ κατὰ πόλιν. :: ΤΕ. ποῦ μήν; (Pl. *Tht.* 142a)

(Terpsion:) I was surprised that I couldn’t find you. :: (Euclides:) You couldn’t because I wasn’t in the city. :: (Terpsion:) Then where *were* you?

(78) καλὸν μὲν ἡ ἀλήθεια, ὦ ξένε, καὶ μόνιμον· ἔοικε μὴν οὐ ῥᾴδιον εἶναι πείθειν. (Pl. *Leg.* 663e)

The truth is a noble thing, stranger, and an enduring one. Yet to convince men of it appears to be no easy matter. *The* μήν-*clause is unexpected given the preceding* μέν *clause.*

(79) διπλοῖς κέντροισί μου καθίκετο. | οὐ μὴν ἴσην γ’ ἔτεισεν . . . κτείνω δὲ τοὺς ξύμπαντας. (Soph. *OT* 809–13)

He struck me with his double whip. Well, he did *not* pay an equal price . . . I killed them all. μήν *underlines the (unexpected) disparity between the attack on Oedipus and his violent reaction to it.*

Note 1: μήν most frequently occurs in combinations, e.g. ἀλλὰ μήν (→59.60), ἦ μήν (59.65), καὶ μήν (59.71), οὐ μὴν ἀλλά (59.75–6).

που

59.50   Ion. κου. Postpositive. Basic function: indicates **uncertainty** – by using που a speaker signals that he/she is not entirely sure about what he/she is saying (the uncertainty may be feigned to convey irony or politeness).

που is used almost always in statements, as a hedging device (*perhaps, possibly, somehow, I suppose, I think, I believe, if I’m not mistaken*):

(80) εἶπον δέ που, πρὶν ἀναγιγνώσκεσθαι τούτους, ὡς . . . (Isoc. 15.75)
I said, I believe, before these words were read, that . . .

(81) ἀλλὰ ταῦτα δαίμονί κου φίλον ἦν οὕτω γενέσθαι. (Hdt. 1.87.4)
No, it was perhaps the desire of a god that it happened in that way.

Note 1: This use of που probably derives from its meaning as an indefinite adverb *somewhere*.

Note 2: που is sometimes used in questions, particularly in certain combinations: οὐ που; (*don't tell me that* ... ; questions about things which the speaker hopes are not true), οὔ τί που; (*surely* ... *not* ... *?*; questions about things which the speaker cannot believe are true), and ἦ που (*I suppose that* ... *?*; questions about things which the speaker believes are true, but does not want to state too firmly).

ΤΟΙ

59.51   Postpositive. Basic function: serves to bring an utterance **to the specific attention of the addressee** (τοι was originally a dative of the second-person pronoun):

– most often in statements, especially in dialogue (*mark you, note, I'll have you know, you know, know that*; sometimes best translated only by emphasis); the reasons why a point is brought to the specific attention of the addressee vary greatly: e.g. to boast, to threaten, correct or criticize, to compliment, to persuade, to point out that a generalization is specifically applicable to the addressee, etc.);

– often with the negative, οὔτοι;

– sometimes in a command, wish or question, to point out that it has specific relevance for the addressee.

(82)   ΚΛ. κτενεῖν ἔοικας, ὦ τέκνον, τὴν μητέρα. | :: ΟΡ. σύ <u>τοι</u> σεαυτήν, οὐκ ἐγώ, κατακτενεῖς. (Aesch. *Cho.* 922–3)

(Clytaemestra:) It appears, child, that you are about to kill your mother. :: (Orestes:) It is *you* who will kill yourself, not I. *Orestes uses τοι to drive home the point that Clytaemestra is responsible for her own demise (correcting her preceding utterance).*

(83)   ΟΔ. μὴ χαῖρ', Ἀτρείδη, κέρδεσιν τοῖς μὴ καλοῖς. | :: ΑΓ. τόν <u>τοι</u> τύραννον εὐσεβεῖν οὐ ῥᾴδιον. | :: ΟΔ. ἀλλ' εὖ λέγουσι τοῖς φίλοις τιμὰς νέμειν. | :: ΑΓ. κλύειν τὸν ἐσθλὸν ἄνδρα χρὴ τῶν ἐν τέλει. | :: ΟΔ. παῦσαι· κρατεῖς <u>τοι</u> τῶν φίλων νικώμενος. (Soph. *Aj.* 1349–53)

(Odysseus:) Do not, son of Atreus, take pleasure in unjust profits. :: (Agamemnon:) It is not easy, I'll have you know, for a ruler to behave piously. :: (Odysseus:) But easy enough to treat friends who give good advice with respect. :: (Agamemnon:) A good man should listen to those in power. :: (Odysseus:) Give up: you still have power, you know, when you surrender to friends. *Agamemnon's τοι points out that the generalization about kings and good behaviour is relevant here, and that Odysseus' request is thus unreasonable. Odysseus' τοι is designed to help persuade Agamemnon that he can accede to it anyway.*

Particles of Scope

Introduction

59.52   The particles γε, γοῦν, καί (negative οὐδέ) and περ are particles that delimit the **scope** or applicability of a certain statement. A speaker can use these particles to signal that what he/she says is applicable 'at least in the case of X', 'even in the case of X' or 'precisely in the case of X'.

List of Scope Particles

γε

59.53   Postpositive. Basic function: expresses **concentration/limitation** – γε focuses attention on the word or phrase it follows (or sometimes the clause as a whole), and limits the applicability of the content of the utterance to *at least* or (*more*) *precisely* that specific element:

- emphasizing words, phrases or clauses (*at least, when it comes to, to be precise*, often best translated by means of stress);
- in dialogue, at the beginning of a speaking turn, γε is used to pick up the previous speaker's syntax but focus it on a specific element (*to be precise*); in answers to yes/no questions, the answer *yes* or *no* is often implied.

(84) οὐκ ἔφη ἑαυτοῦ γε ἄρχοντος οὐδέν᾽ ἂν Ἑλλήνων εἰς τὸ ἐκείνου δυνατὸν ἀνδραποδισθῆναι. (Xen. *Hell.* 1.6.14)
He said that, at least while he was commander, no Greek would be reduced to slavery, as far as was in his power.

(85) καὶ μὲν δὴ τοῦτό γε ἐπίστασθε πάντες, ὅτι ἐσώθην καὶ ἐγὼ καὶ ὁ ἐμὸς πατήρ. (Andoc. 1.20)
And if there is one thing which you all know, it is that I and my father survived.

(86) ΚΡ. δοκεῖ παρεικαθεῖν; :: ΧΟ. ὅσον γ᾽, ἄναξ, τάχιστα. (Soph. *Ant.* 1102–3)
(Creon:) Do you think that I should give way? :: (Chorus:) Yes, my lord, with all speed.

Note 1: Certain combinations with γε are sometimes written as one word (e.g. σύγε, καίτοιγε); this is regularly the case with ἔγωγε *I (at least)*, (ἐγώ + γε; note the shift of accent; dat. ἔμοιγε, also with accent shift).

γοῦν

59.54   Ion. γῶν. Postpositive. A combination of γε and οὖν, γοῦν modifies an utterance which elaborates (οὖν, →59.34) upon (part of) the preceding utterance by restricting its applicability (γε, →59.53) (*at least, at any rate*). It is often used in sentences which provide the 'minimal evidence' or the 'minimal applicability' for a preceding statement:

(87) παρὰ μὲν γὰρ ἐκείνοις μείζων ἐστὶν ὁ τοῦ μέλλοντος φόβος τῆς παρούσης χάριτος, παρὰ δ᾽ ὑμῖν ἀδεῶς ἂν λάβῃ τις ἔχειν ὑπῆρχε τὸν <u>γοῦν</u> ἄλλον χρόνον. (Dem. 20.16)

For in those communities the fear of tomorrow outweighs the favour of today, but in your city it was possible for a man to keep what he wins without fear of loss, at any rate in time past. *τὸν γοῦν ἄλλον χρόνον limits the applicability of the positive description of the city at least to 'time past'.*

Note 1: The negative counterpart of γοῦν is οὔκουν . . . γε, for which →59.33.

περ

59.55 Postpositive. Basic function: expresses **exclusive limitation** – περ limits the applicability of an utterance's content to exactly and only the word (group) it follows.

– in classical Greek περ is common only in combination with relatives (ὅσπερ *precisely who*), with εἰ (*if and only if, precisely if*), and in the combination καίπερ (used with participles→52.44);

– in earlier Greek poetry (e.g. Homer, Hesiod, Aeschylus), περ is used on its own, with concessive force (especially with predicative modifiers (→26.26), particularly participles) (*even though, even if*).

(88) Πάντ᾽, ἔφη, λέγεις οἷα<u>περ</u> ἂν γένοιτο. (Pl. *Resp.* 538c)

He said: 'You describe everything exactly as it may occur.'

(89) μένει τὸ θεῖον δουλίᾳ <u>περ</u> ἐν φρενί. (Aesch. *Ag.* 1084)

The divine power remains in the mind, even though it (*the mind*) is enslaved. *δουλίᾳ (adj.) is a predicative modifier with φρενί.*

'Adverbial' καί

59.56 Basic function: expresses **addition/extension** – καί signals that the applicability of an utterance also extends to the word or phrase following it:

– marking additions which exceed a certain comparable or expected level (*also, too, even, as well*);

– marking the highest point on a scale (*even, also, indeed, too*); for this use with participles (*even though*), →52.44; or marking the lowest point on a scale (*at all, even, so much as*).

(90) βουλόμενος δὲ <u>καὶ</u> αὐτὸς λαμπρόν τι ποιῆσαι . . . καταθεῖ. (Xen. *Cyr.* 5.4.15)

And wanting also himself to do something illustrious, he ran off.

(91) ἐρρήθη γάρ που οὕτως ἡμῶν εἶναι ἡ ψυχὴ <u>καὶ</u> πρὶν εἰς σῶμα ἀφικέσθαι . . . (Pl. *Phd.* 92d)

For it was said, I think, that our soul, even before it enters the body, is of the following nature . . .

(92) τίς δὲ <u>καὶ</u> προσβλέψεται | παίδων σ᾽, ἵν᾽ αὐτῶν προσέμενος κτάνῃς τινά; (Eur. *IA* 1192–3)

Which of your children will so much as look at you, when you've conceded to killing one of them?

The negative is οὐδέ/μηδέ (*also not, not even, not so much as, not at all*):

(93) τούτῳ μὲν <u>οὐδὲ</u> διελέγετο, ἀλλ᾽ ἐμίσει πάντων ἀνθρώπων μάλιστα. (Lys. 3.31)

He did not even exchange words with that man, but hated him above all.

Particle Combinations

List of Particle Combinations

ἀλλὰ γάρ and ἀλλὰ . . . γάρ

59.57   A speaker breaks off (ἀλλά, →59.11) a line of reasoning or narrative, often in mid-speech, and explains why (γάρ, →59.14) (*but enough about this, for . . . ; but why go on? for . . . ; but as a matter of fact . . .*):

(94) ΠΡ. δοκοῦσί γε οὐ φαύλως λέγειν. :: ΣΩ. πῶς γὰρ ἄν, μὴ φαῦλοί γε ὄντες; <u>ἀλλὰ γὰρ</u> ὑπεκστῆναι τὸν λόγον ἐπιφερόμενον τοῦτον βούλομαι. (Pl. *Phlb.* 43a)

(Protarchus:) They appear to speak with some weight. :: (Socrates:) Of course, they are weighty persons. But as a matter of fact I would prefer to dodge this line of reasoning that is advancing upon us. *For πῶς γάρ, →38.19 n.2; 59.14.*

(95) <u>ἀλλ᾽</u> εἰσορῶ <u>γὰρ</u> . . . | Πυλάδην δρομῷ στείχοντα, Φωκέων ἄπο, | ἡδεῖαν ὄψιν. (Eur. *Or.* 725)

But I must stop, for I see Pylades . . . coming at a run from Phocis, a welcome sight. *For the appositive ἡδεῖαν ὄψιν, →27.14.*

59.58   Observe that in the examples above, ἀλλὰ γάρ and ἀλλὰ . . . γάρ are combinations used in a single clause (i.e. with a single predicate). Next to this 'simple' use, the particles also occur, with the same general sense, in 'complex' form, i.e. separately in two clauses, each with their own predicate. In such cases the γάρ-clause is parenthetical:

(96) Φοῖβος δέ, Φοῖβος – <u>ἀλλ᾽</u>, ἄναξ <u>γάρ</u> ἐστ᾽ ἐμός, | σιγῶ. (Eur. *El.* 1245–6)

And Phoebus, Phoebus . . . No, I hold my tongue, for he is my lord. *ἀλλ᾽ introduces the σιγῶ-clause, γάρ introduces the clause with ἐστ᾽.*

Occasionally, in poetry, the particles are not separated when ἀλλὰ γάρ is so used (i.e. each with their own clause):

(97) ἀλλὰ γὰρ Κρέοντα λεύσσω . . . | πρὸς δόμους στείχοντα, παύσω . . . γόους. (Eur. *Phoen.* 1307–8)

But I see Creon coming to the palace, so I will cease from my laments. *Strictly speaking, ἀλλά introduces the παύσω-clause and γάρ the λεύσσω-clause; this use may be seen as a contamination of the 'simple' and the 'complex' uses.*

ἀλλὰ (. . .) δή

59.59   Introduces a text-segment that corrects or replaces an element of the preceding discourse (ἀλλά, →59.11), while indicating that the new utterance is plainly relevant or obvious (δή, →59.44):

(98) οὐκ ἐννοῶ, ὦ Σώκρατες· ἀλλὰ δὴ τίνα γραφήν σε γέγραπται; (Pl. *Euthphr.* 2b–c)

I don't remember him, Socrates; but which indictment has he brought against you then? *The identity of the accuser having turned out to be a dead end, Euthyphro breaks off that line of discussion and naturally passes on to the indictment.*

ἀλλὰ μήν

59.60   Introduces a text-segment that corrects (implications of) earlier information (ἀλλά, →59.11), while the speaker vouches for the correctness and relevance of his/her utterance (μήν, →59.49) (*but, I can assure you; yet it is clear that; well, don't worry;* etc.):

(99) ΣΩ. οὐκοῦν τὸ μετὰ τοῦτο χρὴ ζητεῖν, εἴπερ ἐπιθυμεῖς εἰδέναι, ἥτις ποτ' αὖ ἐστιν αὐτοῦ ἡ ὀρθότης. :: ΕΡ. ἀλλὰ μὴν ἐπιθυμῶ γε εἰδέναι. :: ΣΩ. Σκόπει τοίνυν. (Pl. *Cra.* 391b)

(Socrates:) Then our next task is to try to find out, if you care to know, what kind of correctness, in turn, that is. :: (Hermogenes:) To be sure I care to know. :: (Socrates:) Then investigate. *ἀλλά reacts to the εἴπερ-clause, and corrects the implication that Hermogenes might be unwilling; μήν underlines his commitment.*

ἀλλ' οὖν

59.61   Corrects or dismisses the preceding information (ἀλλά, →59.11) in favour of information which is considered more relevant (οὖν, →59.34) (*be that as it may, anyhow, at any rate*); frequently 'apodotic' (→59.12, ἀλλά) after a conditional clause:

(100) ἔπειτ' εἰ καὶ τυγχάνομεν ἀμφότεροι ψευδῆ λέγοντες, ἀλλ' οὖν ἐγὼ μὲν τούτοις κέχρημαι τοῖς λόγοις, οἷσπερ χρὴ τοὺς ἐπαινοῦντας. (Isoc. 11.33)

Further, even if both of us happen to be wrong, I, at any rate, have used only such arguments as authors of eulogies must use.

γὰρ δή

59.62   δή (→59.44) may lend a nuance of certainty or obviousness to the explanation/motivation given by γάρ (→59.14):

(101) Μάγους . . . ἀτρεκέως οἶδα ταῦτα ποιέοντας· ἐμφανέως <u>γὰρ δὴ</u> ποιεῦσι. (Hdt. 1.140.2)

I know with certainty that this is the practice of the Magi, since they do this where all can see it. δή *expresses the idea that the explanation of the statement 'I know with certainty' is uncontroversial.*

γὰρ οὖν

59.63   Offers an explanation/motivation of the preceding text segment (γάρ, →59.14) in more relevant terms (οὖν, →59.34) (*actually, as a matter of fact, that is to say, what I mean by that is*):

(102) οἴμοι, τόδ᾽ οἷον εἶπας· αἴσθησις <u>γὰρ οὖν</u> | καὶ τῶν θυραίων πημάτων δάκνει βροτούς. (Eur. *El.* 290–1)

Ah, what a thing you have said! I mean, knowing about afflictions, even those of outsiders, is hurtful for mortals.

Note 1: Sometimes, οὖν in this combination seems merely to indicate that the information in the explanation is inferable from the preceding context; with this use of οὖν, the combination occurs frequently as a formula in answers:

(103) ΞΕ. καὶ τοῦ πτηνοῦ μὲν γένους πᾶσα ἡμῖν ἡ θήρα λέγεταί πού τις ὀρνιθευτική. :: ΘΕ. Λέγεται <u>γὰρ οὖν</u>. (Pl. *Soph.* 220b)

(Stranger:) And as for the hunting of winged creatures, as a whole we call it fowling, I suppose. :: (Theaetetus) Yes, as a matter of fact, we do.

δ᾽ οὖν

59.64   The preceding information is abandoned (δέ, indicating a shift, →59.16) in favour of a point which is considered more relevant (οὖν, →59.34) at the particular juncture (*be that as it may, however that may be, anyhow*) (cf. ἀλλ᾽ οὖν, →59.61):

(104) τότε <u>δ᾽ οὖν</u> παρελθὼν τοῖς Ἀθηναίοις παρῄνει τοιάδε. (Thuc. 6.15.5)

However that may be, he now came forward and gave the following advice to the Athenians. *This follows on a digression about Alcibiades and the Athenians' prior views of him.*

(105) οὐκ ἠξίωσε τοῦ θεοῦ προλαμβάνειν | μαντεύμαθ᾽· ἐν <u>δ᾽ οὖν</u> εἶπεν· . . . (Eur. *Ion* 407–8)

He did not think it right to anticipate the god's prophecies. Be that as it may, one thing he did say: . . .

ἦ μήν

59.65   Very strong emphasizer, used by the speaker to affirm both the objective (ἦ, →59.48) and subjective (μήν, →59.49) truth of the utterance; it is used especially in oaths, strong predictions, etc. (*truly, most certainly, I affirm that*):

(106) λαβόμενος τοῦ βωμοῦ ὤμοσεν ἦ μὴν μὴ εἶναί οἱ υἱὸν ἄλλον μηδὲ γενέσθαι πώποτε, εἰ μὴ Ἱππόνικον ἐκ τῆς Γλαύκωνος θυγατρός. (Andoc. 1.126)

Taking hold of the altar he swore that he most certainly had no son, nor had he ever had one, other than Hipponicus, by the daughter of Glaucon.

καὶ γάρ

59.66 The values of καί (→59.20, 59.56) and γάρ (→59.14) may be combined in various ways:

- most often, in continuous discourse, introducing additional information (καί) which has explanatory force (γάρ) (*and as matter of fact, in point of fact, indeed*):

(107) τὸ δὲ δὴ μετὰ τοῦτο ἐπιθυμῶ ὑμῖν χρησμῳδῆσαι, ὦ καταψηφισάμενοί μου· καὶ γάρ εἰμι ἤδη ἐνταῦθα ἐν ᾧ μάλιστα ἄνθρωποι χρησμῳδοῦσιν, ... (Pl. *Ap.* 39c)

And as for the next point, I wish to prophesy to you, you who have condemned me; and as a matter of fact I am now at the time in which men most prophesy, ...

- in continuous discourse, with γάρ introducing an explanation/motivation, and 'adverbial' καί (*for also, for even*):

(108) θάρσει, παρέσται· καὶ γάρ εἰ γέρων ἐγώ, | τὸ τῆσδε χώρας οὐ γεγήρακε σθένος. (Soph. *OC* 726–7)

Do not be afraid, it shall be there! For even if I am old, the strength of this land has not grown aged. *For καὶ εἰ, →49.19–20.*

- in answers in dialogues, with γάρ expressing assent, and 'adverbial' καί (*yes, ... too*):

(109) ΠΩ. οὐκ ἄρτι ὡμολόγεις ποιεῖν ἃ δοκεῖ αὐτοῖς βέλτιστα εἶναι ... ; :: ΣΩ. καὶ γάρ νῦν ὁμολογῶ. (Pl. *Grg.* 467b)

(Polus:) Did you not admit just now that they do what they think best? :: (Socrates:) Yes, and I admit it now too.

καὶ ... δέ

59.67 Introduces new, closely related information (καί, →59.20), which nevertheless is somehow distinct from the preceding context (δέ, →59.16) (*and on the other hand, and furthermore, and ... as well*):

(110) ... Ξενοφῶντι, ὁρῶντι ... πελταστὰς πολλοὺς καὶ τοξότας καὶ σφενδονήτας καὶ ἱππέας δέ ... , καλὸν ... ἐδόκει εἶναι ... (Xen. *An.* 5.6.15)

... as Xenophon's eyes rested upon a great body of peltasts, bowmen, slingers, and horsemen as well ... , it seemed to him that it was a fine thing ... *The last item (καὶ ἱππέας δέ) is set off from the rest: it is the only group of soldiers which is mounted.*

καὶ δή

59.68   Typical uses:

– in dialogue in drama, καὶ δή draws attention to the fact that an action is actually taking place before the eyes of speaker and addressee; so used, it frequently signals that an order is carried out (*there you are, see*), or marks the occurrence of an event or the entrance of a character on the stage (*see here, and look*):

(111) ΗΡ. τόλμα προτεῖναι χεῖρα καὶ θιγεῖν ξένης. :: ΑΔ. καὶ δή προτείνω. (Eur. *Alc.* 1117–18)

(Heracles:) Have the courage to hold out your hand and touch the stranger. :: (Admetus:) There, I'm holding it out. *καὶ δή signals that an order is carried out.*

(112) φίλαι, πάλαι ... | καραδοκῶ τἀκεῖθεν οἵ προβήσεται. | καὶ δή δέδορκα τόνδε τῶν Ἰάσονος | στείχοντ᾽ ὀπαδῶν. (Eur. *Med.* 1116–19)

Friends, for a long time I have been waiting to see how matters in that quarter will turn out. And look, here I see one of Jason's servants coming. *καὶ δή marks the arrival of a character.*

– in a narrative, adding new information (καί, →59.20) and asking the addressee to visualize the action reported (δή, →59.44) (*and see!, lo!, and there he ...*):

(113) ἄλλην ἔδωκα κύλικα, γιγνώσκων ὅτι | τρώσει νιν οἶνος καὶ δίκην δώσει τάχα. | καὶ δή πρὸς ᾠδὰς εἷρπ᾽. (Eur. *Cyc.* 421–3)

I gave him another cup, knowing that wine would be his undoing and he would soon pay the penalty. And lo! he fell to singing.

καὶ δὴ καί

59.69   Very common in Herodotus and Plato. Adds an extra piece of information (καί ... καί *and also*, →59.20), and singles out the addition (δή, →59.44) (*and specifically, and in particular, and above all*):

(114) ἀλλ᾽ ἔστι μέν, ὦ Νικία, χαλεπὸν λέγειν περὶ ὁτουοῦν μαθήματος ὡς οὐ χρὴ μανθάνειν· πάντα γὰρ ἐπίστασθαι ἀγαθὸν δοκεῖ εἶναι. καὶ δὴ καὶ τὸ ὁπλιτικὸν τοῦτο, εἰ μέν ἐστιν μάθημα, ... (Pl. *La.* 182d–e)

But it is difficult, Nicias, to say of anything that can be learnt that it ought not to be learnt; for it seems good to know all things. And take specifically this skill at arms, if it is something that can be learnt ...

59.70   (καὶ δὴ) καὶ frequently follows on a form of ἄλλος, singling out one specific entity from a larger group (*other(s) ... and in particular; above all*):

(115) ἔς τε δὴ ὦν τὰς ἄλλας ἔπεμπε συμμαχίας καὶ δὴ καὶ ἐς Λακεδαίμονα. (Hdt. 1.82.1)

He sent messengers to his other allies, and in particular to Sparta.

καὶ μήν

59.71   The speaker adds information (καί, →59.20), and indicates that he/she vouches for the correctness or relevance of the addition, even if the addressee may not expect it (μήν, →59.49).

- in dialogue, often in favourable reactions to e.g. a request or order (*certainly, all right, well then*):

(116) OP. ἄκου᾿· ὑπὲρ σοῦ τοιάδ᾿ ἔστ᾿ ὀδύρματα, | αὐτὸς δὲ σῴζῃ τόνδε τιμήσας λόγον. | :: ΧΟ. <u>καὶ μὴν</u> ἀμεμφῆ τόνδ᾿ ἐτείνατον λόγον. (Aesch. *Cho.* 508–10)
(Orestes:) Hear us; they are for your sake, such laments as these, and by respecting our words you gain security for yourself. (Chorus:) Well, the two of you certainly cannot be blamed for addressing him at length.

- in drama, to signal the (unexpected or unannounced) entrance on the stage of a new character (*look here, see, here is*; contrast καὶ δή, which can mark the entrance of a character without the connotation of unexpectedness, →59.68):

(117) ΚΡ. κάτω νυν ἐλθοῦσ᾿, εἰ φιλητέον, φίλει | κείνους· ἐμοῦ δὲ ζῶντος οὐκ ἄρξει γυνή. | :: ΧΟ. <u>καὶ μὴν</u> πρὸ πυλῶν ἥδ᾿ Ἰσμήνη. (Soph. *Ant.* 524–6)
(Creon:) Then go below and love them, if you must! But as long as I live a woman will not rule. :: (Chorus:) See, here before the gates is Ismene.

- moving to a new step in argumentative or narrative texts (*but, and, now, well, and in fact*):

(118) οἱ μὲν δὴ Θηβαῖοι ... παρεσκευάζοντο ὡς ἀμυνούμενοι, οἱ δ᾿ Ἀθηναῖοι ὡς βοηθήσοντες. <u>καὶ μὴν</u> οἱ Λακεδαιμόνιοι οὐκέτι ἔμελλον, ἀλλὰ Παυσανίας ... ἐπορεύετο εἰς τὴν Βοιωτίαν. (Xen. *Hell.* 3.5.17)
So the Thebans made preparations for defending themselves, and the Athenians for aiding them. And in fact the Spartans did not longer delay, but Pausanias marched into Boeotia. *μήν confirms that the Boeotians and Athenians were justified in making preparations: the Spartans definitely were a threat.*

μὲν οὖν (attitudinal μήν + οὖν)

59.72   The speaker vouches for the correctness or relevance of his/her utterance (μήν, →59.49; for μὲν in this use, →59.25), and indicates that it is presented in more relevant terms (οὖν, →59.34); the combination is used specifically in dialogue, in corrective answers/reactions, improving or enlarging on what precedes (*you'll mean, you should say, I'd rather say, rather*); in Plato, sometimes simply in assenting answers (*indeed*):

(119) ΑΓ...δοκῶν γυναικῶν ἔργα νυκτερήσια | κλέπτειν ... :: ΚΗ. ἰδού γε κλέπτειν· νὴ Δία, βινεῖσθαι μὲν οὖν. (Ar. *Thesm.* 204–6)

(Agathon:) ... because I'll seem to be stealing the women's nocturnal business. :: (Inlaw:) 'Stealing' my ass: you mean 'being fucked', by Zeus!

μὲν οὖν (... δέ) and μὲν τοίνυν (... δέ)

59.73   These combinations indicate a transition to a more to-the-point, relevant text segment (οὖν/τοίνυν, →59.34, 59.39); the transition occurs in two stages (μέν ... δέ, →59.24), with the relevant new step presented in the δέ-segment; the μέν-clause typically presents a summary or rounding-off of the preceding stretch of text:

(120) περὶ μὲν οὖν τούτων τοσαῦτά μοι εἰρήσθω· ὑπὲρ ὧν δέ μοι προσήκει λέγειν, ὡς ἂν οἷόν τε διὰ βραχυτάτων ἐρῶ. (Lys. 24.4)

Concerning these things, then, let as much as I have said suffice; as for the things about which it is fitting for me to speak, I will speak as briefly as possible. *The μέν-clause rounds off the preface of this speech, δέ starts the narrative section; οὖν indicates that the speaker is transitioning to the currently most relevant point (the narrative). Note that οὖν has scope over the entire μέν-δέ structure, not merely the μέν-clause.*

59.74   Similarly, **μὲν δή** (... **δέ**): indicates a transition to an obviously relevant text segment (δή, →59.44), occurring in two stages (μέν/δέ, →59.24); the μέν-clause sometimes contains a summary or rounding-off of the preceding stretch of text:

(121) καὶ τἆλλα μὲν δὴ ῥᾳδίως ἔσω νεώς | ἐθέμεθα κουφίζοντα· ταύρειος δὲ πούς | οὐκ ἤθελ᾽ ὀρθὸς σανίδα προσβῆναι κάτα. (Eur. *Hel.* 1554–6)

Now, the other victims we easily put on the ship, as they were light; but the bull's hoofs did not want to go forward along the plank. *δή again appears to have scope over the entire μέν-δέ structure, introducing the crucial phase in the narrative about the bull.*

οὐ μὴν ἀλλά and οὐ μέντοι ἀλλά

59.75   The speaker asserts strongly, and against expectations raised by the preceding context (μήν, →59.49/μέντοι, →59.27) that nothing other is the case than that (οὐ ... ἀλλά, →59.11) (*and yet ... nothing but ... ; still, ... absolutely ...*).

(122) ἐδυσχέρανε μὲν ἐπ᾽ οὐδενὶ τῶν γεγραμμένων, ἐπήνεσε δ᾽ ὡς δυνατὸν μάλιστα, ... · οὐ μὴν ἀλλὰ φανερὸς ἦν οὐχ ἡδέως ἔχων ἐπὶ τοῖς περὶ Λακεδαιμονίων εἰρημένοις. (Isoc. 12.201)

He did not complain about any part of what I had written, but praised it in the strongest possible terms: and yet he was plainly nothing but displeased about what had been said about the Spartans. *Note that οὐ μὴν ἀλλά here 'completes' μέν.*

οὐ μὴν οὐδέ and οὐδὲ μήν

59.76   The speaker asserts strongly, and against the expectations raised by the preceding context (μήν, →59.49) that something is also not the case ((οὐ) ... οὐδέ, →59.56)(*nor, yet; nor, indeed; not ... either, indeed,* ...)

(123)   καὶ κραυγὴ μὲν οὐδεμία παρῆν, <u>οὐ μὴν οὐδὲ</u> σιγή, φωνὴ δέ τις ἦν τοιαύτη οἵαν ὀργή τε καὶ μάχη παράσχοιτ’ ἄν. (Xen. *Ages.* 2.12)

There was no shouting, nor yet was there silence, but there was the strange sort of sound which rage and battle may produce.

60

Word Order

Introduction

60.1   A consideration of some randomly chosen sentences containing the verb ἔδωκε(ν) raises many questions about the order in which the words appear:

(1) μετὰ δὲ ταῦτα ἐπεὶ συνεγένοντο ἀλλήλοις, Συέννεσις μὲν ἔδωκε Κύρῳ χρήματα πολλὰ εἰς τὴν στρατιάν, Κῦρος δὲ ἐκείνῳ δῶρα ἃ νομίζεται παρὰ βασιλεῖ τίμια. (Xen. *An.* 1.2.27)
When they met afterwards, Syennesis gave Cyrus much money for the expedition, and Cyrus gave him gifts which are considered tokens of honour at the royal court.

(2) ἐκ δὲ τούτου πολλὰ καὶ καλὰ ἔδωκε δῶρα τῷ Ὑστάσπᾳ, ὅπως τῇ παιδὶ πέμψειε. (Xen. *Cyr.* 8.4.26)
Then he gave many beautiful gifts to Hystaspes to send to the young woman.

(3) καὶ ἔδωκεν ὁ παρελθὼν χρόνος πολλὰς ἀποδείξεις ἀνδρὶ καλῷ κἀγαθῷ. (Dem. 18.310)
And the past period offered many opportunities to an upstanding man.

(4) ἑκάστῳ δὲ ἀρχὴν πολλῶν ἀνθρώπων καὶ τόπον πολλῆς χώρας ἔδωκεν. (Pl. *Criti.* 114a)
And to each he gave leadership over many men and large tracts of land.

60.2   Word order in these sentences can be considered on several levels:

– The position of **certain types of individual words** is relatively fixed. All articles appear in front of their nouns: (1) τὴν στρατιάν, (2) τῷ Ὑστάσπᾳ, (3) ὁ παρελθὼν χρόνος. Prepositions appear in front of the noun phrase they modify: (1) μετὰ ταῦτα, εἰς τὴν στρατιάν, παρὰ βασιλεῖ; (2) ἐκ τούτου. In (1), (2) and (4) the connective particle δέ is the second word of the sentence, but καί in (3) is the first word of the sentence.

– Within **noun phrases**, it is more difficult to spot regularities. In some cases, we find the order modifier–head (noun): (3) ὁ παρελθὼν χρόνος, πολλὰς ἀποδείξεις, (4) πολλῶν ἀνθρώπων, πολλῆς χώρας. In other cases, however, we find the order head–modifier: (1) χρήματα πολλά, (3) ἀνδρὶ καλῷ τε κἀγαθῷ, (4) ἀρχὴν πολλῶν ἀνθρώπων, τόπον πολλῆς χώρας. In one case, finally, the modifier and the head noun are separated by an intervening word: (2) πολλὰ καὶ καλὰ <u>ἔδωκε</u> δῶρα.

– At the level of the **sentence or clause**, with regard to the order of **constituents**, such as Subject (S), Object (O), Indirect Object (IO) and Verb (V), many different orderings are possible: (1): S-V-IO-O (Συέννεσις ἔδωκε Κύρῳ χρήματα); (2): V-O-IO (ἔδωκε δῶρα τῷ Ὑστάσπᾳ); (3): V-S-O-IO (ἔδωκεν ὁ χρόνος ἀποδείξεις ἀνδρί); (4): IO-O-V (ἑκάστῳ ἀρχὴν καὶ τόπον ἔδωκεν) – in short, syntactic function does not seem to be the main factor determining constituent order.

60.3   The principles which govern word order on all these levels, except the first one, are not fully understood. However, the assertion, often made in grammars, that Greek word order is more or less 'free' is not true; even if much remains uncertain, a number of **tendencies** can be observed.

Words with a Fixed Position: Postpositives and Prepositives

Mobile, Postpositive and Prepositive Words

60.4   Most Greek words may occur at the beginning, at the end or in the middle of a clause; such words are referred to as **mobile**. Others, however, have a more fixed position. These are known as **postpositives** and **prepositives**.

60.5   **Postpositive** words attach themselves to the preceding word. From this it follows that postpositive words may not normally occur as the first word of a clause. The most important postpositive words are:

– many connective particles: αὖ, γάρ, δέ, μέν, μέντοι, νυν (not νῦν, a mobile word), οὖν, τε, τοίνυν;
– many attitudinal particles: ἄρα, δή, μήν, που, τοι;
– the scope particles γε, περ;
– the modal particle ἄν;
– non-contrastive personal pronouns: μοι, σοι, με, σε, etc.; also οὑ, οἱ, ἑ (μιν in Herodotus), σφων, etc.;
– non-nominative forms of αὐτός (when they function as third-person personal pronouns);
– indefinites like τις (not τίς), ποτε (not πότε), που (not ποῦ), etc.

60.6   **Prepositive** words attach themselves to the following word. From this it follows that prepositive words may be the first word of a clause, but usually not the last. The most important prepositive words are:

– articles (ὁ, ἡ, τό, etc.);
– prepositions (ἀμφί, ἀνά, ἀντί, etc.);

– some connective particles, like ἀλλά, ἀτάρ, ἤ, καί (also in its adverbial use (→59.56), οὐδέ, οὔτε, τοίγαρ;
– the attitudinal particles ἄρα (= ἦ ἄρα) and ἦ; ;
– subordinators (ἐπεί, ὅτε, ὅτι, ὡς, etc.);
– relative pronouns (ὅς, ἥ, ὅ);
– negatives (οὐ, μή).

The Placement of Postpositives

60.7   **Postpositive** words tend to occur after the first word of the sentence, clause or word group they belong to, that is, **in second position**; this rule is known as **Wackernagel's Law**. Depending on several factors 'second position' may mean slightly different things in different contexts:

60.8   Depending on the size of the unit over which they have **scope**, connective and scope-particles occur in the second position of a **sentence, clause or word group**:

(5) ἐλθὼν δὲ ἐς Λακεδαίμονα τῶν μὲν ἰδίᾳ πρός τινα ἀδικημάτων ηὐθύνθη, τὰ δὲ μέγιστα ἀπολύεται μὴ ἀδικεῖν. (Thuc. 1.95.5)
When he arrived in Sparta, he was censured for the wrongs he had privately committed against certain people, but was pronounced innocent of the gravest charges. *The first δέ connects the entire sentence to the preceding context; but this sentence is itself divided up into two contrasting clauses, each featuring a text-structuring particle (μέν ... δέ) in second position.*

(6) εἰκὸς γὰρ ἐν ἀνδράσι γε ἀγαθοῖς καὶ ἄνευ τῆς αἰτήσεως τὴν ἀκρόασιν ὑπάρχειν τοῖς φεύγουσιν. (Antiph. 5.4)
For amidst good men, at least, it is likely that the defendants receive a hearing even without asking for it. *γάρ connects the entire sentence to the preceding context; the scope-particle γε appears in the second position of the noun phrase to which it lends emphasis (with ἐν ἀνδράσι being treated as a single, indissoluble unit), →60.10.*

60.9   The first word of a clause may be followed by **more than one postpostive**. The standard order of postpositives in such cases is as follows: 'forward-linking' connective particles (especially μέν, and often τε) > 'backward-linking' connective particles (δέ, γάρ, οὖν, etc.) > other particles > indefinite pronouns > personal pronouns:

(7) ἀλογία μὲν γὰρ δή τις φαίνεται διὰ τούτων. (Theophr. *Caus. pl.* 1.13.4)
For because of these reasons, then, there appears to be a certain incongruity.

(8) εἰ οὖν τί σε τούτων ἀρέσκει ... (Thuc. 1.128.7)
If one of these things pleases you ...

Note that the author's preference for the standard order in (7) causes τις to be separated from ἀλογία, the noun it modifies; for the same reason, in (8) indefinite τι *is separated from its modifier* τούτων *by* σε. *For the accent on* τι, →24.38 n.1.

60.10   Postpositives frequently do not follow the first word (as in (9)), but the **first constituent** of a clause, which often consists of a prepositive and a mobile word (as in (10)). The first constituent is then treated as a single, indissoluble unit, effectively as a single word:

(9) οἱ δ' αὖ βάρβαροι οὐκ ἐδέχοντο. (Xen. *An.* 1.10.11)
But the barbarians once more did not wait for them. *The constituent* οἱ βάρβαροι *is broken up by the two postpositives* δ'αὖ.

(10) τῶν δούλων δ' αὖ καὶ τῶν μετοίκων πλείστη ἐστὶν Ἀθήνησιν ἀκολασία. ([Xen.] *Ath. pol.* 1.10)
Then again, among slaves and immigrants the lack of restraint is greatest in Athens. *Here, the constituent* τῶν δούλων *is treated as one, indissoluble unit, and the postpositives* δ'αὖ *follow it.*

While postpositive particles (especially connective ones) often intervene between two members of the first constituent, indefinites and personal pronouns seldom do (ἄν also only very rarely):

(11) ἡ γὰρ ἀνάγκη με πιέζει. (Ar. *Nub.* 437)
For necessity presses me down. *The connective particle* γάρ *breaks up the constituent* ἡ ἀνάγκη (*also cf.* δ' αὖ *in (9) above), but the personal pronoun* με *follows it.*

60.11   The placement of other postpositives (especially personal pronouns) is complicated by several conflicting tendencies:

– First, such postpositives tend to **cluster together after the first word or constituent of a sentence**. As a result, words which syntactically go closely together may be widely separated (12).

– Secondly, however, there is a tendency **to distribute postpositives over the sentence**, dividing up the sentence into more or less syntactically recognizable clauses and word groups (13):

(12) πολλά τε γὰρ μιν καὶ μεγάλα τὰ ἐπαείροντα καὶ ἐποτρύνοντα ἦν. (Hdt. 1.204.2)
For the reasons that impelled and encouraged him were many and great.

(13) καὶ οὐ μόνον ταῦτ' ἐστὶ τὰ ποιοῦντά με ἀγωνίζεσθαι τὸν ἀγῶνα τοῦτον. (Isae. 2.43)
And these are not the only things which impel me to engage in this lawsuit.

In (12), postpositive μιν, *the object of the participles* ἐπαείροντα καὶ ἐποτρύνοντα, *appears in the first available position of the entire sentence (after other postpositives); in (13), by contrast, the participle phrase* τὰ ποιοῦντα ... τοῦτον *functions as a separate 'clause', as can be seen from the fact that postpositive* με *appears after the first constituent of that clause.*

– Thirdly, it is possible for postpositive **obligatory constituents** with verbs to be placed **after their verb**:

(14) τούτου μὲν ἀφίημί σε. (Pl. *Euthphr.* 9c)

From this point I absolve you. *σε appears straight after the verb of which it is the object (instead of after μέν, which would also have been possible).*

- Fourthly, postpositives may be placed **after the most salient word or constituent** of a sentence:

(15) δοκοῦσι δὲ Ἀθηναῖοι καὶ τοῦτό μοι οὐκ ὀρθῶς βουλεύεσθαι, ὅτι . . . ([Xen.] *Ath. pol.* 3.10)

The Athenians seem to me to be wrong in this respect, too, that . . .

60.12   The placement of **ἄν**:

- With **optatives** (potential construction) and **secondary indicatives** (counterfactual), ἄν is occasionally **repeated**, found first in second position of the sentence or clause, and then again more closely with the verb:

(16) ὥστ᾿ ἄν, εἰ σθένος | λάβοιμι, δηλώσαιμ᾿ ἄν οἷ᾿ αὐτοῖς φρονῶ. (Soph. *El.* 333–4)

The result is that, if I could find the strength, I would make clear what are my feelings toward them.

- In subordinate clauses with **ἄν and the subjunctive**, ἄν usually directly follows the subordinator: ὃς ἄν, ὅστις ἄν (also ὅ τι ἄν), ὅπως ἄν, but connective particles may intervene (ὃς γὰρ ἄν, ὅ τι δ᾿ ἄν, →60.9). However, several temporal conjunctions and the conditional conjunction εἰ occur in obligatory crasis with ἄν (ἐπεάν/ἐπάν, ἐπειδάν, ὅταν, ὁπόταν, ἐάν/ἤν/ἄν), and in these cases connective particles do not intervene (ἐπειδὰν δέ, ὅταν γάρ).

The Placement of Prepositives

60.13   **Prepositive** words usually occupy the first position in the sentence, clause or word group (for example a noun phrase) over which they have scope.

(17) καὶ οὐδεὶς ἔτι ἄνευ Ἑλλήνων εἰς πόλεμον καθίσταται, οὔτε ὅταν ἀλλήλοις πολεμῶσιν οὔτε ὅταν οἱ Ἕλληνες αὐτοῖς ἀντιστρατεύωνται· ἀλλὰ καὶ πρὸς τούτους ἐγνώκασι μεθ᾿ Ἑλλήνων τοὺς πολέμους ποιεῖσθαι. (Xen. *Cyr.* 8.8.26)

And no one goes to war anymore without the help of Greeks, neither when they are at war with each other nor when the Greeks launch an expedition against them. But even against them they realize that they can conduct their wars only with the help of Greeks. *The connective particles καί and ἀλλά occur in the first position of the sentences which they connect, οὔτε . . . οὔτε . . . precede the temporal clauses which they negate, and both examples of ὅταν (= ὅτε ἄν) occupy the first position in the subordinate temporal clauses they introduce. All articles precede their nouns, and all prepositions precede the nouns which they modify. Adverbial καί has scope over the word group πρὸς τούτους.*

60.14 Sometimes, especially in poetry, **prepositions** are placed **after the noun phrase** they modify (**anastrophe**). When this happens, their accent recedes to the first syllable if possible (→24.37):

(18) λέγοιμ᾽ ἂν οἷ᾽ ἤκουσα <u>τοῦ θεοῦ πάρα</u>. (Soph. *OT* 95)
I may as well tell you what I have heard from the god.

In Attic prose, this construction is limited to περί + genitive (e.g. τούτων πέρι *about these things*, τίνος πέρι; *about what?*)

The Ordering of Words in Noun Phrases

Head–Modifier versus Modifier–Head

60.15 Modifiers in a noun phrase may either follow or precede their head (for these terms, →26.16): ὁ ἀνὴρ οὗτος or οὗτος ὁ ἀνήρ *that man*; (ἡ) δικαία γυνή or (ἡ) γυνὴ (ἡ) δικαία *the/a just woman*; ὁ τῶν Ἀθηναίων δῆμος or ὁ δῆμος (ὁ) τῶν Ἀθηναίων *the people of the Athenians*, etc.

The **differences between the orders** modifier–head and head–modifier are by no means always clear. On the whole, however, head–modifier is the most common and 'neutral' order, while the order modifier–head is used to convey that the modifier contains particularly salient information (i.e. the modifier is emphasized). Modifiers can be salient if they are contrastive, unexpected or particularly informative.

(19) ταφαὶ δὲ τοῖσι εὐδαίμοσι αὐτῶν εἰσὶ αἵδε· <u>τρεῖς</u> μὲν <u>ἡμέρας</u> προτιθεῖσι τὸν νεκρόν. (Hdt. 5.8)
The burial rites of the more prosperous among them (*the Thracians*) are as follows: they lay out the corpse for three days. *That funeral rites should include laying out the corpse for a certain number of days is not surprising; what is peculiar to the rites of the described Thracians is that they lay out the corpse for* <u>three</u> *(τρεῖς) days. The position of the modifier in front of the head noun suggests that this is the most important information within the noun phrase.*

(20) ἐπὶ δὴ ταύτην τὴν ψάμμον στέλλονται ἐς τὴν ἔρημον οἱ Ἰνδοί, ζευξάμενος ἕκαστος <u>καμήλους τρεῖς</u> ... αἱ γάρ σφι κάμηλοι ἵππων οὐκ ἥσσονες ἐς ταχυτῆτά εἰσι, χωρὶς δὲ ἄχθεα δυνατώτεραι πολλὸν φέρειν. (Hdt. 3.102.3)
It is for this sand that the Indians set forth into the desert, each first yoking three camels. For their camels are as fast as horses, and much better able to carry loads besides. *Since Herodotus goes on to explain why the Indians use camels instead of horses, it appears that* καμήλους *provides*

the most important and surprising information (a reader might wonder 'camels?!'); the fact that they yoke three (τρεῖς) camels is not treated as the more relevant piece of information.

(21) Ἀρτάβανε, ἐγὼ τὸ παραυτίκα μὲν οὐκ ἐσωφρόνεον εἴπας ἐς σὲ μάταια ἔπεα χρηστῆς εἵνεκα συμβουλῆς. (Hdt. 7.15.1)

Artabanus, I was initially out of my mind when I said foolish words in reply to useful advice. *μάταια and χρηστῆς are contrastive, and both precede their noun.*

60.16   **Modifiers of considerable length** (also called 'heavy modifiers') have a tendency to follow their head, even if they provide salient information:

(22) ἐπιγίνεταί σφι τέρεα ἔτι μέζονα τοῦ πρὶν γενομένου τέρεος. (Hdt. 8.37.2)

Then there happened a miracle still greater than the miracle that had happened before.

Multiple Modifiers

60.17   If a head has **multiple modifiers**, they can either precede or follow the head, but it is also possible that some precede and others follow. The ordering is determined by the same pragmatic principle of saliency described above. Furthermore, multiple modifiers may be either **co-ordinated** or **juxtaposed**:

– If co-ordinated, each modifier separately qualifies the head, and co-ordinating particles like καί, τε καί, etc. may (but do not have to) intervene between the modifiers; cf. Engl. *great and old books* or *great, old books*, i.e. 'books which are great and old':

(23) ὁ Σωκράτης ὁρῶν ... θεραπαίνας πολλὰς καὶ εὐειδεῖς ... (Xen. *Mem.* 3.11.4)

Socrates, seeing many and good-looking maids, ... *Co-ordination: Socrates sees many maids, all of whom are good-looking. The possibility that there were also less good-looking maids is not implied..*

– If juxtaposed, the first modifier qualifies both the head *and* the other modifiers, and co-ordinating conjunctions are always absent; cf. Engl. *great old books*, i.e. 'old books which are great':

(24) καὶ ἅμα ἐπιτήδεια πολλὰ εἶχον, ἄλευρα, οἶνον, κριθὰς ἵπποις συμβεβλημένας πολλάς. (Xen. *An.* 3.4.31)

They also had many provisions, flour, wine, and much barley stored as fodder for horses. *Juxtaposition: the barley that had been stored as fodder for horses was a large amount (there may have been other kinds of barley, for example the kind usually sown to provide barley for the next harvest). For the attributive participle συμβεβλημένας without article, →52.47.*

Hyperbaton

60.18   In the examples given so far, the noun phrases are **continuous**, in that no words other than postpositives intervene between the modifier and the head. However, many noun phrases are **discontinuous**, in that mobile words intervene between the modifier and the head. This phenomenon is called **hyperbaton**. Two types can be distinguished:

– Hyperbaton with the **modifier preceding the head**; this type involves strong emphasis on the modifier:

(25) ἀλλ᾿ οὐδὲν ἔχων δίκαιον εἰπεῖν <u>ἑτέρων</u> παρεμβολῇ <u>πραγμάτων</u> εἰς λήθην ὑμᾶς βούλεται τῆς κατηγορίας ἐμβαλεῖν. (Aeschin. 3.205)
But since he has nothing just to say, he wishes, by the insertion of extraneous matters, to shock you into forgetting the charge.

(26) μὴ τοίνυν λέγετε . . . ὡς <u>ὑφ᾿ ἑνὸς</u> τοιαῦτα πέπονθεν ἡ Ἑλλὰς <u>ἀνθρώπου</u>. (Dem. 18.158)
Do not say, then, that Greece has suffered such things because of *one* man.

– Hyperbaton with the **head preceding the modifier**; this type does not involve emphasis: some additional information about the head is given, which is either predictable or not particularly relevant:

(27) εἰσῆλθεν ἀνὴρ Θρᾷξ <u>ἵππον</u> ἔχων <u>λευκόν</u>. (Xen. *An.* 7.3.26)
There arrived a Thracian man with a white horse.

Alternatively, the head may be topical (→60.22), while the modifier adds new information.

(28) <u>ἐσθῆτα</u> δὲ φορέουσι οἱ ἱρέες <u>λινέην μούνην</u>. (Hdt. 2.37.3)
The priests wear only linen clothes (*or: 'As for their clothes, the priests only wear linen ones'*).

60.19   The most important syntactic restriction on hyperbaton is that at least one of the constituents interrupting a discontinuous noun phrase must be the constituent on which that noun phrase depends. For instance, in (25) ἑτέρων . . . πραγμάτων is a modifier of παρεμβολῇ; in (27) ἵππον . . . λευκόν is object of ἔχων; in (28) ἐσθῆτα . . . λινέην μούνην is object of φορέουσι.

The Ordering of Constituents Within the Clause

Asserted and Presupposed Information

60.20   In English, constituent order is a syntactic phenomenon: whether a constituent is Subject (S), Object (O), Verb (V), etc. determines its position in the clause:

(29) John$_S$ likes$_V$ Julie$_O$.

(30) Julie$_S$ hates$_V$ John$_O$.

In both sentences, the constituents could only be placed in the order given (assuming that John is doing the liking and Julie the hating), because the rules of English constituent order usually require the subject of a main clause to stand in front of the verb, and the object after it.

Greek constituent order, on the other hand, is **not primarily a syntactic phenomenon**. Instead, the ordering of constituents depends on their **information status**: a constituent's position in the clause is determined largely by how new and important the information which it adds to the context is (in English, information status is mostly expressed by intonation).

60.21 Not every part of a clause uttered in spoken or written communication is equally informative. In fact, successful communication depends on a speaker's ability to estimate the amount of relevant knowledge the addressee already possesses and to increase that knowledge by adding or linking new information to already-known information. Already-known information is called **presupposed**, added information **asserted**. The difference can be made clear by considering the following question/answer pairs:

(31) A: Whom did Claire kiss?

   B: Claire kissed *JACOB*.

The presupposed information in B's answer is 'Claire kissed X'; as A asked whom Claire kissed, B can regard the information that Claire kissed someone as already known to the addressee. The asserted information is 'Jacob', as this part of the answer increases A's knowledge. Schematically:

$\boxed{\text{Claire kissed X}}_{PRESUPPOSED}\boxed{X= \text{Jacob}}_{ASSERTED}.$

In English, 'Jacob' receives a stress accent. Indeed, 'Jacob', uttered by itself, would be a sufficient answer to the question (and is in fact more common in real-life situations). Alternatively, a cleft construction may be used in English, i.e. 'It was Jacob whom Claire kissed.'

(32) A: Who kissed Jacob?

   B: *CLAIRE* kissed Jacob.

This is the mirror image of (31). Here, the presupposed information is 'X kissed Jacob', and the asserted information is 'Claire'. Schematically:

$\boxed{\text{X kissed Jacob}}_{PRESUPPOSED}\boxed{X= \text{Claire}}_{ASSERTED}.$

In English, 'Claire' receives a stress accent, and would again be a sufficient (and common) answer uttered by itself (cf. also the cleft construction 'It was Claire who kissed Jacob.').

(33) A: What did Claire do?

    B: Claire KISSED JACOB.

Here, the presupposed information is 'Claire did X', while the asserted information is that she 'kissed Jacob'. Schematically:

$$\boxed{Claire\ did\ X}_{PRESUPPOSED}\boxed{X=\ kissed\ Jacob}_{ASSERTED.}$$

In contrast to (31) and (32), in the present clause the verb is included in the asserted information.

(34) A: What happened?

    B: Claire kissed Jacob.

In this clause, all constituents belong to the asserted information, since A's question does not presuppose any knowledge about Claire and Jacob being involved in 'what happened' nor about the nature of their involvement.

Note that in running texts, it may be more difficult to separate the presupposed and asserted information, and speakers have more freedom in deciding whether to *present* information as already known or not.

Consequences for Greek Constituent Order: Focus and Topic

60.22   In Greek, certain elements with a particular information status are given special treatment in the ordering of constituents:

– the **asserted information** of a clause, called the **focus** – this focus may lie on a specific single constituent ('narrow focus'), or on a group of constituents including the verb ('broad focus');

– certain parts of the presupposed information, called **topics**.

The following formulas summarize the strongest tendencies in the ordering of constituents in Greek (declarative) clauses. These formulas are explained in detail in the following sections. They should be regarded as tools which are useful in analysing a large number of Greek clauses, but do not represent absolute 'rules'.

Narrow-focus clause				
(Contrastive/New Topic)	**Narrow Focus**	**Verb**	(Given Topic)	(Rest)

The narrow focus immediately precedes the verb. Any contrastive or new topic precedes the focus; a given topic follows immediately after the verb, in turn followed by any other predictable information (rest).

Broad-focus clause			
(Contrastive/ New Topic)	**Broad Focus**		(Rest)
	Broad Focus I (= Verb)	(Given Topic)	Broad Focus II (= Other Focal Constituents)

The broad focus begins with the verb, followed by any other focal constituents; any contrastive or new topic precedes the focus construction; any given topic interrupts the broad focus construction (between verb and other constituents), any other predictable information (rest) comes last.

Focus Constructions: Broad and Narrow Focus

60.23   The constituents of a clause which express asserted information are called the **focus** of that clause. The focus may either be:

– a single constituent (**narrow focus**; cf. (31) and (32) above), or
– include the verb and one or more other constituents (**broad focus**; cf. (33) and (34) above).

In the narrow-focus construction in Greek, the focal constituent directly precedes the verb (35). In the broad-focus construction, the verb opens the focal part of the clause, the other focal constituents follow it (36):

(35) ΚΟ. ποῖ τοῦτον ἕλκεις; :: ΓΡ. Α. εἰς ἐμαυτῆς NARROW FOCUS εἰσάγω VERB. (Ar. *Eccl.* 1037)

(Young girl:) Where are you dragging him off to? :: (First old woman:) I'm taking him to my place. *The presupposed information in the answer is 'I am taking him to X': since the girl asked* ποῖ τοῦτον ἕλκεις, *the woman can regard the information that she is dragging the man in question somewhere as already known to the girl (to the extent that 'him' can be left unexpressed in the answer). The asserted information is limited to the single constituent* εἰς ἐμαυτῆς; *compare (31) and (32). The focus is a single constituent, and precedes the verb.*

(36) ΣΩ. οὗτος, τί ποιεῖς ἐτεόν, οὑπὶ τοῦ τέγους; | :: ΣΤ. ἀεροβατῶ καὶ περιφρονῶ τὸν ἥλιον BROAD FOCUS (Ar. *Nub.* 1502–3)

(Socrates:) Hey there, what are you doing, you on the roof? :: (Strepsiades:) I walk the air and contemplate the Sun. *The presupposed information is 'I do X': Socrates' question* τί ποιεῖς *shows that Strepsiades can presuppose that Socrates knows he is doing something. The asserted information comes in two clauses, the first of which consists of a verb (*ἀεροβατῶ*) only, and questions* *of word order therefore do not arise. In the second, as in (33), the asserted information includes the verb and a noun; in this broad-focus construction, τὸν ἥλιον follows περιφρονῶ.*

(37) $\boxed{\text{ἐπορευόμην}}$ μὲν ἐξ Ἀκαδημείας εὐθὺ Λυκείου τὴν ἔξω τείχους ὑπ' αὐτὸ τὸ $\boxed{\text{τεῖχος}}$ BROAD FOCUS· ... καί με προσιόντα ὁ Ἱπποθάλης ἰδών, Ὦ Σώκρατες, ἔφη, ποῖ δὴ πορεύῃ καὶ πόθεν; $\boxed{\text{Ἐξ Ἀκαδημείας}}$ NARROW FOCUS, ἦν δ' ἐγώ, $\boxed{\text{πορεύομαι}}$ VERB, εὐθὺ Λυκείου. (Pl. *Ly.* 203a–b)

I was making my way from the Academy straight to the Lyceum, by the road outside the wall, just under the wall... And when he saw me approaching, Hippothales said, 'Socrates, where are you going to, and from where?' 'I'm making my way from the Academy', I said, 'straight to the Lyceum.' *The first sentence is the opening of the text; none of the information can be taken for granted, and a broad-focus construction is used, with the verb in initial position and all the other focal constituents following the verb. In the final sentence, the verb πορεύομαι belongs to the presupposed information (compare πορεύῃ in Hippothales' question), and therefore a narrow-focus construction is used, with ἐξ Ἀκαδημείας preceding the verb (εὐθὺ Λυκείου is best interpreted as a new clause or a tail (→60.35), with a pause in front of it).*

60.24 Some types of expression which commonly serve as narrow focus may follow rather than precede their verb. This occurs particularly with:

– cataphoric demonstrative pronouns (→29.28), which tend to appear at the end of their clause;

– expressions marked by 'adverbial' καί (→59.56; this is sometimes called 'additive' focus):

(38) ὡς δὲ ὁ Γύγης ἀπίκετο, $\boxed{\text{ἔλεγε}}$ VERB ἡ γυνὴ $\boxed{\text{τάδε}}$ NARROW FOCUS· ... (Hdt. 1.11.2)
     When Gyges came, the woman said the following: ... ἡ γυνή is a 'given topic', →60.26.

(39) ᾧ ἂν τὸ ἕτερον παραγένηται $\boxed{\text{ἐπακολουθεῖ}}$ VERB ... $\boxed{\text{καὶ τὸ ἕτερον}}$ NARROW FOCUS. (Pl. *Phd.* 60c)
     When one of them comes to someone, the other one follows as well.

Topics

60.25 Most clauses are construed around a single constituent, which is called the **topic**. It is the entity 'about which' a statement is made, that is the entity with respect to which the addressee's knowledge is most increased. The topic belongs to the presupposed information. Depending on the kind of topic involved, it either occupies the first position of the clause, preceding the focus, or immediately follows the verb. All other presupposed information tends to occupy the, pragmatically unmarked, final position of the clause, called the 'Rest' position in the examples below.

Given Topics (Postverbal)

60.26   Topics are in many cases **given** (i.e. already known) from the preceding context. They often refer to the entity that is the most important participant in a longer stretch of the discourse – the so-called **discourse topic** – when that topic has already been 'active' for much or all of such a stretch. A given topic does not have to be overtly expressed, especially if it is the subject (→26.6–7); cf. (35)–(37), where the first-person subject is topic and left unexpressed.

   If expressed, however, **given topics tend to follow the verb immediately**; in the broad-focus construction it therefore intervenes between the verb and the other focal constituents:

(40) ... ⌈ἐπεθύμησε⌉BROAD FOCUS ⌈ὁ Δαρεῖος⌉TOPIC ⌈τείσασθαι Σκύθας⌉BROAD FOCUS
      CONTINUED. (Hdt. 4.1.1)
      Darius desired to punish the Scythians. *In the passage before this sentence, Herodotus has narrated how Darius captured Babylon; he now turns to Darius' next exploit. Darius is the given topic, and follows the verb, while the verb and its complement form a broad-focus construction.*

(41) ⌈τούτων μὲν εἵνεκα⌉FOCUS ⌈οὐκ ἔπεμψε⌉VERB ⌈Ξέρξης⌉TOPIC τοὺς αἰτήσοντας⌉REST.
      (Hdt. 7.133.2)
      So that is why Xerxes did not send the men to make the request. *Herodotus has said that Xerxes sent no heralds to Athens and Sparta, and then explains why he did not do so. The present sentence rounds off the explanation: Herodotus asserts that it was because of these reasons that Xerxes did not send heralds. Ξέρξης is the given topic and appears after the verb; the rest of the sentence is construed according to a narrow-focus construction, with one focused constituent appearing in front of the verb. Note that τοὺς αἰτήσοντας (referring to the heralds) occupies the 'rest' position, as it expresses entirely predictable, presupposed information.*

Contrastive and New Topics (Clause-initial)

60.27   In many other cases, a topic is placed **in the first position of the clause**, preceding the focus. Such topics are typically not 'given', i.e. not predictable topics already active in the preceding context. Clause-initial topics may generally be classed as either 'contrastive' or 'new'.

60.28   Most often, clause-initial topics are **contrastive topics**, which single out as topic one entity in a discourse which prominently features more than one – each would be a feasible topic and the contrastive topic makes it clear who/what the clause is actually about:

(42) $\boxed{\text{στρουθὸν}}$ TOPIC δὲ $\boxed{\text{οὐδεὶς}}$ NARROW FOCUS $\boxed{\text{ἔλαβεν}}$ VERB. (Xen. *An.* 1.5.3)
An ostrich, however, nobody managed to catch. *This sentence is part of a passage in which Xenophon lists several animals encountered in a plain through which the army is marching, and then recounts how the soldiers hunted each of them. In this sentence, he discusses the ostrich, which is the contrastive topic. The fact that nobody could catch one is the asserted information, in a narrow-focus construction.*

(43) $\boxed{\text{τὸν μὲν ἡγεμόνα}}$ TOPIC $\boxed{\text{παραδίδωσι Χειρισόφῳ}}$ BROAD FOCUS, $\boxed{\text{τοὺς δὲ οἰκέτας}}$ TOPIC $\boxed{\text{καταλείπει τῷ κωμάρχῳ}}$ BROAD FOCUS, πλὴν τοῦ υἱοῦ τοῦ ἄρτι ἡβάσκοντος· $\boxed{\text{τοῦτον}}$ TOPIC δὲ $\boxed{\text{Πλεισθένει Ἀμφιπολίτῃ}}$ NARROW FOCUS $\boxed{\text{δίδωσι}}$ VERB $\boxed{\text{φυλάττειν}}$ REST. (Xen. *An.* 4.6.1)
The guide he handed over to Chirisophus, but the other members of the family he left for the village-chief, except for his son, who was just reaching puberty. Him he gave to Plisthenes of Amphipolis to guard. *Xenophon is describing how he dealt with the family of one of the army's guides. Xenophon('he') is himself the given topic and left unexpressed. The various members of the family head their clauses as contrastive topics. In the first two clauses, we have broad-focus constructions: both the fact that Xenophon gave up his prisoners and the identity of the recipients are asserted. By the time we reach the final clause, a narrow-focus construction is used: the identity of the recipient, Plisthenes, is new and asserted, but every reader can expect a verb of 'giving' by now. Also, given the context and the verb δίδωσι, the information contributed by φυλάττειν is largely predictable, and it hence appears in the rest-position.*

The slot of contrastive topics may also be occupied by **verbs**; in such cases, the (narrow) focus follows the verb:

(44) οὗτος ὁ Κροῖσος βαρβάρων πρῶτος . . . τοὺς μὲν κατεστρέψατο Ἑλλήνων . . . , τοὺς δὲ φίλους προσεποιήσατο. $\boxed{\text{κατεστρέψατο}}$ TOPIC μὲν $\boxed{\text{Ἴωνάς τε καὶ Αἰολέας καὶ Δωριέας τοὺς ἐν τῇ Ἀσίῃ}}$ FOCUS, $\boxed{\text{φίλους δὲ προσεποιήσατο}}$ TOPIC $\boxed{\text{Λακεδαιμονίους}}$ FOCUS. (Hdt. 1.6.2)
This Croesus was the first of the foreigners to have subjugated some of the Greeks, and made allies of others. He subjugated the Ionians, Aeolians and Dorians who live in Asia, and he made the Spartans his allies. *After naming Croesus as the first to subjugate Greek peoples or ally himself to them, Herodotus elaborates on both these methods: each of the clauses is 'about' one of the methods mentioned in the previous sentence, and as such the relevant verb is topic in each case. The asserted information in both cases consists of the peoples to which the approach was applied, so the objects of the verb are focus. Note that the whole*

phrase φίλους προσεποιήσατο here takes the position of the verb (= topic): the two words express a single idea and thus go closely together filling up a single 'slot'.

60.29   In other cases, a clause-initial topic placed in the first position of the clause is not explicitly contrasted with one or more other topics in the surrounding discourse, and is thus not 'contrastive' in a strict sense. However, such topics still identify one entity (to the exclusion of others) as the one which the clause is about. Since such topics have typically not been 'active' in the immediately preceding context (contrast given topics), they may be called **new topics**; they are nevertheless treated as part of the presupposed information. Often, they activate an entity as discourse topic for a longer stretch of discourse:

(45) ἀφικνοῦνται εἰς Χάλυβας BROAD FOCUS· οὗτοι TOPIC ὀλίγοι NARROW FOCUS τε ἦσαν VERB καὶ ὑπήκοοι τῶν Μοσσυνοίκων FOCUS, καὶ ὁ βίος TOPIC ἦν τοῖς πλείστοις αὐτῶν ἀπὸ σιδηρείας BROAD FOCUS· (Xen. *An.* 5.5.1)

They came to the Chalybes. These people were few in number and subject to the Mossynoecians, and most of them gained their livelihood from iron-working. *Xenophon describes a people which his army came across. When the Chalybes are named initially, they are focal material. With οὗτοι, they are then taken up as new topic (a single mention as focus is typically not enough to allow a participant given topic status) – this is a very frequent use of the anaphoric (→29.30) pronoun. When Xenophon next 'zooms in' to their way of life, ὁ βίος is suitable for use as a new topic.*

(46) καὶ τὸ θέρος ἐτελεύτα. τοῦ δ' ἐπιγιγνομένου χειμῶνος SETTING ἡ νόσος TOPIC τὸ δεύτερον FOCUS ἐπέπεσε VERB τοῖς Ἀθηναίοις REST· (Thuc. 3.86.4–87.1)

And the summer came to an end. In the following winter, the plague struck the Athenians a second time. *The clause (preceded by a setting, for which →60.32) begins with ἡ νόσος as topic. The plague has not been mentioned for some time (not since the first time it struck), but is 'reactivated' as discourse topic in this clause. The fact that it strikes for the second time is the asserted information (τὸ δεύτερον is focus), whereas the fact that it strikes the Athenians is predictable and unmarked.*

60.30   When new participants are introduced into a text for the very first time ('all-new'), they are often not suitable to be the topic of the clause in which they are introduced, as they do not easily allow themselves to be presented as 'presupposed' information. Normally, **presentational sentences** have a broad-focus construction: they start with the verb and then introduce the new participant as focal information:

(47) Ἀγησιλάῳ μὲν δὴ … οὐδὲν ἐγένετο βαρύτερον ἐν τῇ στρατείᾳ. ἦν δέ τις Ἀπολλοφάνης Κυζικηνός, ὃς καὶ Φαρναβάζῳ ἐτύγχανεν ἐκ παλαιοῦ ξένος ὢν καὶ Ἀγησιλάῳ κατ' ἐκεῖνον

τὸν χρόνον ἐξενώθη. οὗτος οὖν εἶπε πρὸς τὸν Ἀγησίλαον ὡς οἴοιτο συναγαγεῖν αὐτῷ ἂν εἰς
λόγους περὶ φιλίας Φαρνάβαζον. (Xen. *Hell.* 4.1.28–9)

And nothing happened during the campaign which was more distressing to
Agesilaus. Now there was a certain Apollophanes of Cyzicus, who, as it happened,
was an old friend of Pharnabazus and at some point during that time had become
a friend of Agesilaus as well. This man, then, said to Agesilaus that he thought he
could get Pharnabazus to meet with him concerning friendly relations. *Xenophon
uses a presentational clause with a broad-focus construction to introduce
Apollophanes, a new participant, into the narrative. Immediately after this introduction, Apollophanes is made the new topic of the next clause, with* οὗτος; *for this use of*
οὗτος, *cf.* (45) *above.*

Occasionally, however, the new participant is immediately promoted to the function of
topic – i.e. presented as presupposed information – and then appears in the first position of
the clause:

(48) τὸν δὲ οἶδα αὐτὸς πρῶτον ὑπάρξαντα ἀδίκων ἔργων ἐς τοὺς Ἕλληνας, τοῦτον σημήνας
      προβήσομαι ἐς τὸ πρόσω τοῦ λόγου ... <u>Κροῖσος ἦν Λυδὸς μὲν γένος</u>, ... (Hdt.
      1.5.3–6.1)

And the man I know to have started with unjust acts against the Greeks, that
man I will single out and continue my story. Croesus was a Lydian by birth ...
*Herodotus here introduces Croesus into the narrative, but he is nonetheless given
the function of topic on his first appearance. The choice of this construction, rather
than* ἦν Κροῖσος *may indicate that Herodotus supposes that his audience already
knows Croesus.*

The Periphery of the Clause: Settings, Themes and Tails

60.31 Often, a clause is preceded or followed by material which is, strictly speaking,
outside the clause proper. Such material may be divided between:

– in the so-called **left-periphery** of the clause (preceding the clause itself): **settings**
  (very common) and **themes**;
– in the **right-periphery** of the clause (following the clause): **tails**.

Settings

60.32 Many Greek sentences start with one or more items of background information,
which appear before the clause itself and which provide a setting for that clause or
the entire following stretch of a text. Such **settings** detail the circumstances, place
or time in which the following actions take place. Settings typically take the form of
a circumstantial participle/genitive absolute, a temporal clause, or another kind of
adverbial modifier:

(49) $\boxed{\text{ἐν δὲ τῷ ἐπιόντι χειμῶνι}}$_{SETTING} τὰ μὲν Ἀθηναίων καὶ Λακεδαιμονίων ἡσύχαζε διὰ τὴν ἐκεχειρίαν. (Thuc. 4.134.1)

The following winter, the affairs between the Athenians and the Spartans were calm, on account of the armistice. *The adverbial modifier ἐν δὲ τῷ ἐπιόντι χειμῶνι is setting, preceding the topic τὰ μὲν . . . Λακεδαιμονίων.*

(50) $\boxed{\text{ἐπεὶ δὲ καὶ οἱ ἄλλοι στρατιῶται συνῆλθον}}$_{SETTING}, ἀνέστη πρῶτος μὲν Χειρίσοφος ὁ Λακεδαιμόνιος. (Xen. *An.* 3.2.1)

When the other soldiers had come together as well, Chirisophus the Spartan stood up first. *The subordinate temporal clause is the setting for the ensuing debate scene. Note that the word order <u>within</u> the setting-clause follows the same principles as those outlined above: (καί) οἱ ἄλλοι στρατιῶται is a narrow focus preceding its verb.*

(51) $\boxed{\text{πράττοντος δὲ τοῦ Κύρου ταῦτα}}$_{SETTING} θείως πως ἀφικνοῦνται ἀπὸ Ὑρκανίων ἄγγελοι. (Xen. *Cyr.* 4.2.1)

While Cyrus was doing these things, messengers came from the Hyrcanians as if by divine intent. *A setting in the form of a genitive absolute. Note again that the setting has its own <u>internal</u> principles of constituent ordering, with τοῦ Κύρου following the verb form (as a given topic), and the predictable ταῦτα in rest position.*

Themes

60.33   Many sentences establish a topic for a stretch of discourse by placing it in the left-periphery of a sentence. This happens especially when an entity has not been mentioned for a while. While such **themes** are not always easy to distinguish from contrastive/new topics, they are nonetheless different. In particular, themes form their own 'intonation unit' (i.e. there is a pause between them and the clause proper), and they precede the setting (while topics follow it; cf. (46) and (49)):

(52) $\boxed{\text{Πρόξενος δὲ καὶ Μένων}}$_{THEME}, $\boxed{\text{ἐπείπερ εἰσὶν ὑμέτεροι μὲν εὐεργέται, ἡμέτεροι δὲ στρατηγοί}}$_{SETTING}, πέμψατε αὐτοὺς δεῦρο. (Xen. *An.* 2.5.41)

As for Proxenus and Meno: since they are your benefactors and our generals, you should send them here. *Note that Πρόξενος καὶ Μένων precede the setting. The fact that they are not part of the clause proper can also be seen from the fact that there they are referred to again, by means of the anaphoric pronoun αὐτούς.*

(53) $\boxed{\text{οὐρέουσι}}$_{THEME} $\boxed{\text{αἱ μὲν γυναῖκες}}$_{CONTRASTIVE TOPIC} $\boxed{\text{ὀρθαί}}$_{FOCUS}, $\boxed{\text{οἱ δὲ ἄνδρες}}$_{CONTRASTIVE TOPIC} $\boxed{\text{κατήμενοι}}$_{FOCUS}. (Hdt. 2.35.3)

As for the way that they (*the Egyptians*) urinate, the women do so standing, the men sitting down. *In this case the verb οὐρέουσι is theme, as is clear from the position of μέν (indicating that αἱ starts the clause proper).*

A common way to articulate a theme is with the preposition περί + **genitive**:

(54) περὶ μὲν δὴ Φλειασίων THEME, ὡς καὶ πιστοὶ τοῖς φίλοις ἐγένοντο καὶ ἄλκιμοι ἐν
τῷ πολέμῳ διετέλεσαν, καὶ ὡς πάντων σπανίζοντες διέμενον ἐν τῇ συμμαχίᾳ,
εἴρηται. (Xen. *Hell.* 7.3.1)
About the Phliasians, it has been told how they both remained faithful to
their friends and bravely carried on in the war, and how they were steadfast in
their alliance, although they were in short supply of everything.

60.34 The concept of themes is also helpful in explaining a frequent type of 'ungrammatical'
sentence in Greek, the so-called **nominative absolute**. Such nominatives establish
a theme, but are themselves outside the syntactic structure of the sentence. Often, the
theme is expressed again later in the sentence in the form of a personal pronoun in the
appropriate case:

(55) οἱ δὲ φίλοι, ἄν τις ἐπίστηται αὐτοῖς χρῆσθαι ὥστε ὠφελεῖσθαι ἀπ᾽ αὐτῶν, τί φήσομεν αὐτούς
εἶναι; (Xen. *Oec.* 1.14)
As for friends, if one knows how to make use of them in such a way that one derives profit
from them, what shall we say they are? *Cf. also* (52) *above*.

Tails

60.35 Sometimes, a clause is followed by a separate intonation-unit (after a pause)
which serves to clarify or elaborate (an element of) the clause, almost as an
afterthought. Such expressions in the right-periphery of the clause are known
as **tails**.

– Tails are often similar to given topics, in that they identify a predictable entity as
the one which the clause is about. Tails occur when a speaker realizes that non-
expression of the topic (i.e. leaving it out altogether) may be insufficient for the
addressee to identify it:

(56) χαλεπὸν | θεῶν παρατρέψαι νόον | ἀνδρεσσιν ἐπιχθονίοις. (Bacch. 5.94–6)
It is difficult to turn aside the purpose of the gods, for mortal men. *Mortals
are the entity with respect to whom the statement is valid; it is overtly expressed
only at the end of the sentence (after a metrical break), almost as an
afterthought.*

(57) αὗται αἱ πᾶσαι . . . στρατηλασίαι μιῆς τῆσδε οὐκ ἄξιαι. τί γὰρ οὐκ ἤγαγε ἐκ τῆς
Ἀσίης ἔθνος ἐπὶ τὴν Ἑλλάδα Ξέρξης; (Hdt. 7.21.1)
All these expeditions cannot compare to this single one. For what nation did
he not lead out of Asia against Greece, Xerxes? *Xerxes, whose expedition to
Greece is front and center in this part of Herodotus' work, is a predictable
subject for ἤγαγε, and not expressed in the sentence until the very end,
presumably after a pause (though this cannot be proven in prose texts).*

– In other cases, tails are added to further clarify or elaborate an element which is already overtly expressed in the clause itself (this is syntactically speaking a form of apposition, →26.24):

(58) ἐς σὲ δὴ βλέπω, | ὅπως τὸν αὐτόχειρα πατρῴου φόνου | ξὺν τῇδ᾽ ἀδελφῇ μὴ κατοκνήσεις κτανεῖν | <u>Αἴγισθον</u>. (Soph. *El.* 954–7)
I look to you not to shrink from killing our father's murderer, Aegisthus, together with me your sister. *Αἴγισθον clarifies the phrase τὸν αὐτόχειρα πατρῴου φόνου; the name is added only at the very end of the sentence, after a metrical break. The explicit mention of the name (which is predictable, and therefore not necessary in itself) may have various effects, in this case probably a tone of scorn.*

Overview of Clauses with a Periphery

60.36   We may again summarize the above discussion in a formula:

Clauses with a periphery			
(Theme)	(Setting)	Clause (with focus, topic, etc.)	(Tail)

Any setting precedes the clause; any theme precedes the clause and (if present) the setting; any tail follows the clause.

Prolepsis

60.37   Topics of subordinate clauses which follow the matrix clause are sometimes syntactically integrated into that matrix clause. This is called **prolepsis**. The construction allows the speaker to treat the 'dislocated' constituent as the (given) topic of the subordinate clause, which otherwise contains strongly focal material.

(59) ὡς δ᾽ ἤκουσα <u>τοὺς ναύτας</u> ὅτι | σοὶ πάντες εἶεν συννεναυστοληκότες . . . (Soph. *Phil.* 549–50)
But when I heard that the sailors all belonged to your crew . . . *Lit. 'I heard about the sailors, that they all . . .'. ναύτας is the topic of the subordinate ὅτι-clause. Note that πάντες is not 'displaced' along with τοὺς ναύτας and therefore emphasized.*

(60) ἦλθε δὲ καὶ τοῖς Ἀθηναίοις εὐθὺς ἡ ἀγγελία <u>τῶν πόλεων</u> ὅτι ἀφεστᾶσι. (Thuc. 1.61.1)
The Athenians too, immediately received the news about the cities, that they had revolted (= 'the news that the cities had revolted'). *Here, the subject of the subordinate clause appears as a genitive dependent on ἀγγελία.*

In many ways, prolepsis is similar to the theme construction (→60.33–4), in that topic-like material is presented to the left of the clause in which it 'belongs' (so-called 'left-dislocation').

60.38   In some cases of prolepsis, the topic of the subordinate clause precedes the subordinate clause, but is not syntactically integrated with the matrix clause. This happens especially when the topic is the subject of the subordinate clause (and thus appears in the nominative):

(61) εἰσάγγελλε <u>Τειρεσίας</u> ὅτι | ζητεῖ νιν. (Eur. *Bacch.* 173–4)

Announce that Tiresias is looking for him. *Τειρεσίας is subject of ζητεῖ, but precedes the subordinate ὅτι-clause.*

61

Four Sample Passages

Narrative: Lysias 12.5–12

Introduction and Text

61.1   Immediately after the Peloponnesian War, Athens was briefly ruled by an oppressive oligarchic regime known as the Thirty (404–403 BCE). One of the new regime's measures was to arrest and execute a number of metics (resident aliens) and to confiscate their assets, officially in order to suppress sedition, but presumably as a quick way for the cash-strapped government to gain access to funds. Among those arrested were the speechwriter Lysias and his brother Polemarchus, whose family was originally from Syracuse. Lysias escaped, but Polemarchus was executed on the orders of Eratosthenes, one of the Thirty. Later, under the restored democracy, Eratosthenes submitted to a public examination of his conduct in court (a procedure known as εὔθυναι) and Lysias took this opportunity to prosecute Eratosthenes in person but also effectively to indict the regime of the Thirty as a whole with the speech *Against Eratosthenes*. Hence, in the passage below, members of the Thirty other than Eratosthenes play a leading role. The speech is transmitted as the only speech delivered by Lysias himself in court (whether he actually did so is uncertain). The passage below is the beginning of the *narratio* of the speech; in it Lysias relates the events leading up to his own escape and Polemarchus' death.

τοιαῦτα λέγοντες οὐ τοιαῦτα ποιεῖν ἐτόλμων, ὡς ἐγὼ περὶ τῶν ἐμαυτοῦ πρῶτον   1
εἰπὼν καὶ περὶ τῶν ὑμετέρων ἀναμνῆσαι πειράσομαι. Θέογνις γὰρ καὶ Πείσων   2
ἔλεγον ἐν τοῖς τριάκοντα περὶ τῶν μετοίκων, ὡς εἶέν τινες τῇ πολιτείᾳ ἀχθόμενοι·   3
καλλίστην οὖν εἶναι πρόφασιν τιμωρεῖσθαι μὲν δοκεῖν, τῷ δ᾽ ἔργῳ   4
χρηματίζεσθαι· πάντως δὲ τὴν μὲν πόλιν πένεσθαι τὴν δ᾽ ἀρχὴν δεῖσθαι   5
χρημάτων. καὶ τοὺς ἀκούοντας οὐ χαλεπῶς ἔπειθον· ἀποκτιννύναι μὲν γὰρ   6
ἀνθρώπους περὶ οὐδενὸς ἡγοῦντο, λαμβάνειν δὲ χρήματα περὶ πολλοῦ   7
ἐποιοῦντο. ἔδοξεν οὖν αὐτοῖς δέκα συλλαβεῖν, τούτων δὲ δύο πένητας, ἵνα   8
αὐτοῖς ᾖ πρὸς τοὺς ἄλλους ἀπολογία, ὡς οὐ χρημάτων ἕνεκα ταῦτα   9
πέπρακται, ἀλλὰ συμφέροντα τῇ πολιτείᾳ γεγένηται, ὥσπερ τι τῶν ἄλλων   10
εὐλόγως πεποιηκότες. διαλαβόντες δὲ τὰς οἰκίας ἐβάδιζον· καὶ ἐμὲ μὲν ξένους   11
ἑστιῶντα κατέλαβον, οὓς ἐξελάσαντες Πείσωνί με παραδιδόασιν· οἱ δὲ ἄλλοι εἰς   12

τὸ ἐργαστήριον ἐλθόντες τὰ ἀνδράποδα ἀπεγράφοντο. ἐγὼ δὲ Πείσωνα μὲν   13
ἠρώτων εἰ βούλοιτό με σῶσαι χρήματα λαβών· ὁ δ' ἔφασκεν, εἰ πολλὰ εἴη. εἶπον   14
οὖν ὅτι τάλαντον ἀργυρίου ἕτοιμος εἴην δοῦναι· ὁ δ' ὡμολόγησε ταῦτα ποιήσειν.   15
ἠπιστάμην μὲν οὖν ὅτι οὔτε θεοὺς οὔτ' ἀνθρώπους νομίζει, ὅμως δ' ἐκ τῶν   16
παρόντων ἐδόκει μοι ἀναγκαιότατον εἶναι πίστιν παρ' αὐτοῦ λαβεῖν. ἐπειδὴ   17
δὲ ὤμοσεν, ἐξώλειαν ἑαυτῷ καὶ τοῖς παισὶν ἐπαρώμενος, λαβὼν τὸ τάλαντόν με   18
σώσειν, εἰσελθὼν εἰς τὸ δωμάτιον τὴν κιβωτὸν ἀνοίγνυμι· Πείσων δ' αἰσθόμενος   19
εἰσέρχεται, καὶ ἰδὼν τὰ ἐνόντα καλεῖ τῶν ὑπηρετῶν δύο, καὶ τὰ ἐν τῇ κιβωτῷ   20
λαβεῖν ἐκέλευσεν. ἐπεὶ δὲ οὐχ ὅσον ὡμολόγησεν εἶχεν, ὦ ἄνδρες δικασταί, ἀλλὰ   21
τρία τάλαντα ἀργυρίου καὶ τετρακοσίους κυζικηνοὺς καὶ ἑκατὸν δαρεικοὺς καὶ   22
φιάλας ἀργυρᾶς τέτταρας, ἐδεόμην αὐτοῦ ἐφόδιά μοι δοῦναι, ὁ δ' ἀγαπήσειν με   23
ἔφασκεν, εἰ τὸ σῶμα σώσω. ἐξιοῦσι δ' ἐμοὶ καὶ Πείσωνι ἐπιτυγχάνει Μηλόβιός τε   24
καὶ Μνησιθείδης ἐκ τοῦ ἐργαστηρίου ἀπιόντες.   25

They (the Thirty) had the nerve to make such claims and yet act in a very different fashion, as I will try to call to mind by speaking first about my own affairs, and then about yours. In a meeting of the Thirty, Theognis and Pison said about the metics, that there were some among them who were disgruntled with the regime; so that there was an excellent pretext to appear to exact punishment, but in reality to acquire funds; and, they added, the city was in any case without resources, and the government needed money. And they won over their audience without difficulty: for they thought nothing of killing men, but placed a premium on getting money. So they decided to arrest ten men, two of them poor, so that they would have as an excuse with regard to the others that these measures had not been taken for the sake of money, but that they were in the public interest – as if any of their other acts had been sensible! When they had divided up the houses, they were on their way. And they found me while I was entertaining guests, whom they drove out and then handed me over to Pison. The others went to the workshop and set about making a list of the slaves. I asked Pison if he was willing to let me live in exchange for money. He said that he was, if it was a lot. So I said that I was willing to give him a talent of silver; he agreed that he would do it. Now, I knew that he has no regard for either gods or men, yet it seemed to me, given the circumstances, to be absolutely necessary to extract an oath from him. After he had sworn, calling destruction on himself and his children, to let me live in exchange for the talent, I went into the bedroom and opened the money-chest. Pison noticed this and came in, and upon seeing the contents he called two of his slaves, and told them to take the contents of the chest. And, gentlemen of the jury, now that he had not the sum that we agreed, but three talents of silver and four hundred cyzicenes and a hundred darics and four silver cups, I entreated him to give me some travel money, but he said that I should be happy if I came off with my life. As Pison and I were coming out, Melobius and Mnesithides, who were on their way from the factory, met us.

Commentary

61.2   **General Notes**

The passage contains many elements which are characteristic of Greek **narratives**. In a typical narrative a speaker (the narrator) relates a series of events that occurred in the past, usually in a basic **chronological** order; once a narrative sequence begins, if no indications to the contrary are given, it may be assumed that the successive main clauses reflect the temporal sequence of events. The tenses used are **imperfects** (and pluperfects), **aorist indicatives** and **historical presents**. Stories are normally told in the **third or first person**; both occur here. Subordinate clauses and participle phrases may provide settings (→60.32) or express less important events. As a rule, shifts of scene or perspective in a story are indicated by the particle **δέ**, while closely linked events within one scene are often connected by **καί**.

Forensic speeches are **monological** texts (the speaker holds forth for a considerable time without interruptions), but they are addressed to a specific group, male Athenian citizens who served as jurors. The passage cited here shows several signs of the presence of the jurors, who (unlike the modern reader) heard the speech only once and whose attention the speaker needed to retain throughout. For example, Lysias clearly announces the beginning of the narrative (see n. on ὡς ... πειράσομαι, 1–2) so that the jurors do not lose sight of the overall flow of the text; he includes a sarcastic aside intended to raise a laugh (see n. on ὥσπερ τι τῶν ἄλλων εὐλόγως πεποιηκότες, 10–11), and addresses the jurors directly (ὦ ἄνδρες δικασταί, 21) to call their attention to a complicated calculation.

61.3   **Detailed Notes**

1 **τοιαῦτα λέγοντες οὐ τοιαῦτα ποιεῖν ἐτόλμων**: Lysias has just briefly described the rise of the Thirty, including their claims that they would rid Athens of unwelcome elements and turn the rest of the citizens to 'justice and virtue'. **τοιαῦτα** anaphorically refers to these claims (→29.28); τοιαῦτα (rather than ταῦτα) is dismissive: it suggests that Lysias does not have to bother about being precise, because the Thirty did not act in accordance with their words in the first place.

Imperfect **ἐτόλμων**, together with the present infinitive **ποιεῖν**, suggests continuous action and so conveys what Lysias sees as a defining characteristic of the rule of the Thirty. On the textual level, the imperfect also suggests that there is more to say about this point (compare the n. on ἔλεγον at 3–8 below); and the narrative indeed consists of several illustrations of the Thirty's hypocritical behaviour. This statement can thus be understood as a 'setting' against which the following narrative is to be evaluated.

1–2 **ὡς ... πειράσομαι**: An announcement of the following narrative and an explicit signal that that narrative is to be taken as exemplifying the Thirty's mendacious actions. The aspectual value of the aorist infinitive ἀναμνῆσαι dependent on πειράσομαι suggest that the following story *as a whole* (the product of Lysias' act of 'calling to mind') will permit the jurors to conclude that the Thirty 'said one thing, but did quite another'.

2 γάρ: This particle often introduces entire narratives (→59.14), especially when preceded by a speaker's announcement of his intent to relate a story for a certain purpose. γάρ then makes explicit that the narrative indeed serves that purpose (and thus serves as 'supporting' information to the announcement): in this case Lysias uses γάρ to imply that his narrative will prove that the Thirty were lying scoundrels, precisely as he said he would.

3–8 ἔλεγον . . . καὶ . . . οὐ χαλεπῶς ἔπειθον . . . ἔδοξεν οὖν αὐτοῖς: The imperfects ἔλεγον and ἔπειθον refer to actions that reach their end-point before the next action occurs; there is no reason to suppose that Theognis' and Pison's speeches were interrupted, and the persuasion referred to by ἔπειθον was obviously successful (a 'conative' interpretation (→33.25) is ruled out by οὐ χαλεπῶς). Such imperfects, which refer to actions that are in themselves 'complete' and advance narrative time, nevertheless present those actions as the background to what follows, raising the question 'what happened next?' The local function of the imperfect to refer to 'incomplete' actions is expanded into a global, textual function: the information presented in the text segment as a whole is as yet 'incomplete' (→33.51). As such, these imperfects raise suspense, suggesting that more important consequences will soon follow. And indeed, the discussion among the Thirty leads to a decision, expressed by the aorist ἔδοξεν, and marked by the particle οὖν, which indicates a transition to the main story line (→59.34). It is this decision which sets the rest of the action in motion. The sequence of two imperfects and an aorist thus conveys a sense of climax.

2–3 Θέογνις . . . καὶ Πείσων ἔλεγον ἐν τοῖς τριάκοντα περὶ τῶν μετοίκων, ὡς . . .: Theognis and Pison are here introduced into the discourse, but since they were known members of the Thirty, they immediately appear as the topic of the sentence (followed by a broad-focus construction beginning with the verb), rather than being more elaborately introduced in a presentational sentence (→60.30). The content of their speech is presented in the ὡς-clause (indirect statement), but this clause is preceded by a theme/topic constituent (περὶ τῶν μετοίκων); this is similar to 'prolepsis', even if syntactically more firmly integrated into the matrix clause (ἔλεγον) by the preposition περί (for περί in 'left-dislocated' material, →60.33).

3–5 ἔλεγον . . . ὡς εἶέν τινες . . . καλλίστην οὖν εἶναι πρόφασιν . . . πάντως δὲ τὴν μὲν πόλιν πένεσθαι τὴν δ' ἀρχὴν δεῖσθαι . . . : The indirect statement begins with a ὡς-clause with oblique optative (εἶεν); the use of ὡς (rather than ὅτι) is suggestive of Theognis' and Pison's specious argumentation (→41.6), while the continuation of the report with accusative-and-infinitive constructions (the preferred complement for verbs of opinion; →51.19 n.1) squarely ascribes the responsibility for what is said to them. The particles (οὖν ... δέ ... μέν ... δ᾽) are embedded in the indirect statements, and articulate Theognis' and Pison's line of reasoning rather than that of Lysias.

6–8 ἀποκτιννύναι μὲν γάρ ... ἡγοῦντο, λαμβάνειν δὲ ... ἐποιοῦντο: γάρ marks this sentence as explanatory of the preceding οὐ χαλεπῶς. The infinitives (together with their objects) are contrastive topics (→60.28; note μέν ... δέ); περὶ οὐδένος and περὶ πολλοῦ are narrow focus constituents (→60.23; for the idiom, →30.31 n.1). The present infinitives suggest multiple acts of 'killing' and 'seizing' (note ἀποκτιννύναι from athematic ἀποκτίννυμι, which exists alongside thematic ἀποκτείνω).

8–10 ἵνα ... ᾖ ... ἀπολογία, ὡς ... πέπρακται, ἀλλὰ ... γεγένηται: Another indirect statement depends on ἀπολογία: again (see n. on ὡς 3–5 above), ὡς may be suggestive of the falseness of the Thirty's excuse. This may also underlie the retention of the subjunctive ᾖ in the purpose clause, and the perfect indicatives πέπρακται/γεγένηται in the ὡς-clauses (rather than optatives), presenting the purpose and content of the excuse entirely from the perspective of the Thirty (and hence not that of Lysias): →41.13, 45.3 n.1.

10–11 ὥσπερ τι τῶν ἄλλων εὐλόγως πεποιηκότες: A sarcastic aside on the part of Lysias, indicated by ὥσπερ with a participle, meaning 'as if' (→52.43). Lysias scoffs at the fact that the Thirty suddenly feel the need to come up with excuses, even though they are responsible for carrying out other bad measures without further ado. For the 'responsibility' nuance of the perfect, →33.35.

11 διαλαβόντες ... ἐβάδιζον: The narrative shifts gears as we leave the meeting and start moving; Lysias will soon be involved in the action himself. From this point on the narrative generally consists of shorter clauses, and a greater use of preposed aorist participles (such as διαλαβόντες here; also ἐξελάσαντες 12, ἐλθόντες 13, εἰσελθών 19, αἰσθόμενος 19, ἰδών 20) to narrate events in a sequence (such aorist participles will have an anterior interpretation, describing an action preceding the action in matrix clauses).

After the sequence ἔλεγον ... ἔδοξεν (3–8), ἐβάδιζον starts off a new sequence of events. The imperfect again suggests that this is a preliminary (background) action which will lead up to more central events that take place at Lysias' house. As a corollary of this scene-shifting function, imperfects like ἐβάδιζον are often said to be 'immediative' (→33.52): the Thirty had divided the houses of the ten selected metics among themselves and *were on their way* without further ado.

11–15 καὶ ἐμὲ μὲν ... οἱ δὲ ἄλλοι ... ἐγὼ δὲ ... ὁ δ᾽ ... εἶπον ... ὁ δ᾽ ...: When the members of the Thirty (as well as our narrative) arrive at Lysias' house, there is an initial flurry of activity, with our attention moving back and forth between Lysias and the assailants, and between the house and the weapons factory (owned by Lysias' family) to which everyone but Pison and Lysias moves. After that, the narrative zooms in on the interaction between Lysias and Pison. This is reflected in the constant shift of topic in these sentences; when attention has been directed to Lysias and Pison in 13, there is no recurrence of the emphatic pronoun ἐγώ, and first-person verb forms suffice. Pison is variously referred to by ὁ δέ (14, 15, 23, →28.28), by name (19), or with no explicit reference at all (18, 21; →26.7).

12 παραδιδόασιν: Lysias' transfer into Pison's custody is the first event which he highlights by means of the historical present (→33.54). Lysias uses the historical present in this speech to single out moments of particular significance for the story (see also ἐπιτυγχάνει 24), but also to mark those events which are particularly damning for Pison (and, by implication, the rest of the Thirty), such as the moment when Pison enters Lysias' bedroom to steal the contents of the money-chest (εἰσέρχεται 20, καλεῖ 20). The audience is invited to feel the effects of such moments with particular empathy, to re-live them with the participants in the story, as it were, for whom they were 'present'.

13 ἀπεγράφοντο: The imperfect in the context of two scenes that take place at different locations (note the shift from the ἐργαστήριον back to Lysias' house effected by ἐγὼ δέ) suggests that the negotiation between Lysias and Pison took place *while* the list of slaves was being drawn up by the other members of the Thirty in the factory. This is because the imperfect indicates that some people were drawing up a list, but not that they finished doing so before the shift of location in the narrative; hence a translation 'set about making a list' is appropriate. The completion of the list can be inferred from the final sentence of the passage, when two of the Thirty's members emerge 'from the factory' (ἐκ τοῦ ἐργαστηρίου 25) and the two scenes merge into one again.

14–15 ἠρώτων ... ἔφασκεν ... εἶπον οὖν ... ὡμολόγησε: As with ἔλεγον above (3–8), there is no reason to assume that these speaking turns were interrupted, so the imperfects ἠρώτων and ἔφασκε must refer to *completed* actions. The imperfective aspect suggests, again, that these first steps in the negotiation lead up to more decisive events: when the eventual offer of one talent is made and accepted, we find aorists (εἶπον, ὡμολόγησε). Again, the shift to the aorist is accompanied by the particle οὖν, indicating the transition to the more relevant point (see n. on οὖν 3–8 above).

14–15 εἰ βούλοιτό ... εἰ πολλὰ εἴη ... ὅτι ... ἕτοιμος εἴην ... ὁ δ' ὡμολόγησε ταῦτα ποιήσειν: In this quickly moving narrative, Lysias presents his conversation with Pison in indirect speech, which creates less of a sense of 'pause' than directly reported speeches do. The indirect statements and questions mostly have oblique optatives, presenting the whole from Lysias' current narratorial perspective (→41.13); ὡμολόγησε is construed with a future infinitive; the verb virtually always takes the infinitive, as it properly means 'to express the same opinion (as someone else)' (cf. ὅμοιος λόγος) and so takes the regular complement of verbs of opinion (→51.19).

16–19 ἠπιστάμην μὲν οὖν ... ὅμως δ' ... ἐδόκει ... ἐπειδὴ δὲ ὤμοσεν ... εἰσελθών ... ἀνοίγνυμι: μὲν οὖν ... δ' ... is transitional (→59.73): the μὲν οὖν-clause rounds off the dialogue which led to Pison's promise by offering Lysias' comment on what a promise of Pison is worth, the δέ-clause presents the new and relevant step of extracting an oath. The imperfects ἠπιστάμην and ἐδόκει briefly 'pause' the narrative progression to provide background information, namely Lysias' reasoning for extracting an oath from Pison. With ἐπειδὴ δὲ ὤμοσεν ... ἐπαρώμενος ... σώσειν, that oath has been provided, and we are back in the quick sequence of events. Lysias then imperceptibly changes the subject (from Pison to himself) after the long subordinate clause, as becomes clear only from first-person ἀνοίγνυμι.

16 νομίζει: this present is presumably to be interpreted as anchored in Lysias' current narratorial perspective rather than as 'retained' from his original speech; if so, this can be reflected in English by translating 'I knew that he has no regard for either gods or men' rather than by 'that he had no regard'. The effect is that Pison's moral deficiency is presented as a fixed character trait, which continues to be in force until the present day (→41.14).

18 λαβών is a predicative modifier of σώσειν rather than ὤμοσεν, that is, the sentence means 'he swore to take ... and save ...', rather than 'after taking ... he swore to save ....'.

19 The historical present ἀνοίγνυμι again marks a moment of particular significance: the money is now in play.

20 εἰσέρχεται ... καλεῖ: See 12 above.

21 ἐπεὶ δὲ ... εἶχεν: The imperfect in the temporal clause implies simultaneity (contrast aorist ὤμοσεν 18).

23–24 ἐδεόμην ... ἔφασκεν: For the value of the imperfects, cf. 3–8 and 14–15 above. They leave unresolved tension as to whether Lysias actually will escape with his life; this tension is heightened by the 'retention' of the indicative σώσω in the indirect question: in contrast to the oblique optative, the indicative presents the speech from the perspective of the narrated world, when Lysias' future (would he live or die?) was still entirely open. In the remainder of the narratio (not included here), this tension will be repeatedly heightened and released.

24–25 ἐξιοῦσι δ' ... ἀπιόντες: The participle phrase ἐξιοῦσι δ' ἐμοὶ καὶ Πείσωνι (dative complement to ἐπιτυγχάνει) serves as the 'setting' to the ensuing sentence (→60.32). The word order in ἐπιτυγχάνει Μηλόβιός τε καὶ Μνησιθείδης is suggestive of 'presentational' sentences, which introduce new participants by means of a broad-focus construction (→60.30). ἐκ τοῦ ἐργαστηρίου ἀπιόντες appears in the 'rest'-position, adding circumstantial information of no particular pragmatic importance (→60.22).

ἐπιτυγχάνει: See 12 above.

Description: Xenophon, *Anabasis* 1.5.1–4

Introduction and Text

61.4   The following passage comes from the early chapters of Xenophon's *Anabasis*, which tells of the expedition of a large mercenary army led by Cyrus (who hoped to seize the Persian throne from his brother Artaxerxes), as well as the army's flight from enemy territory after Cyrus' death in battle. The passage below details one stage in Cyrus' march towards the capital, and describes in some detail the country that he passes through.

ἐντεῦθεν ἐξελαύνει διὰ τῆς Ἀραβίας τὸν Εὐφράτην ποταμὸν ἐν δεξιᾷ ἔχων   1
σταθμοὺς ἐρήμους πέντε παρασάγγας τριάκοντα καὶ πέντε. ἐν τούτῳ δὲ τῷ   2
τόπῳ ἦν μὲν ἡ γῆ πεδίον ἅπαν ὁμαλὲς ὥσπερ θάλαττα, ἀψινθίου δὲ πλῆρες· εἰ δέ   3
τι καὶ ἄλλο ἐνῆν ὕλης ἢ καλάμου, ἅπαντα ἦσαν εὐώδη ὥσπερ ἀρώματα. δένδρον   4
δ' οὐδὲν ἐνῆν, θηρία δὲ παντοῖα, πλεῖστοι ὄνοι ἄγριοι, πολλαὶ δὲ στρουθοὶ αἱ   5
μεγάλαι, ἐνῆσαν δὲ καὶ ὠτίδες καὶ δορκάδες. ταῦτα δὲ τὰ θηρία οἱ ἱππεῖς ἐνίοτε   6
ἐδίωκον, καὶ οἱ μὲν ὄνοι, ἐπεί τις διώκοι, προδραμόντες ἕστασαν. πολὺ γὰρ τῶν   7
ἵππων ἔτρεχον θᾶττον. καὶ πάλιν, ἐπεὶ πλησιάζοιεν οἱ ἵπποι, ταὐτὸν ἐποίουν,   8
καὶ οὐκ ἦν λαβεῖν, εἰ μὴ διαστάντες οἱ ἱππεῖς θηρῷεν διαδεχόμενοι. τὰ δὲ κρέα   9
τῶν ἁλισκομένων ἦν παραπλήσια τοῖς ἐλαφείοις, ἁπαλώτερα δέ. στρουθὸν δὲ   10
οὐδεὶς ἔλαβεν· οἱ δὲ διώξαντες τῶν ἱππέων ταχὺ ἐπαύοντο· πολὺ γὰρ ἀπέσπα   11
φεύγουσα, τοῖς μὲν ποσὶ δρόμῳ, ταῖς δὲ πτέρυξιν αἴρουσα ὥσπερ ἱστίῳ   12
χρωμένη. τὰς δὲ ὠτίδας, ἄν τις ταχὺ ἀνιστῇ, ἔστι λαμβάνειν· πέτονται γὰρ   13
βραχὺ ὥσπερ πέρδικες καὶ ταχὺ ἀπαγορεύουσι. τὰ δὲ κρέα αὐτῶν ἥδιστα ἦν.   14
πορευόμενοι δὲ διὰ ταύτης τῆς χώρας ἀφικνοῦνται ἐπὶ τὸν Μάσκαν ποταμόν, τὸ   15
εὖρος πλεθριαῖον.   16

From there, he marched through Arabia, keeping the river Euphrates on his right-hand side, for five day-marches through desert country, traversing thirty-five parasangs. In this region the ground was a plain, entirely flat like a sea, and full of wormwood; and if there was any other kind of shrub or reed, they were all fragrant like herbs. There was not a single tree, but there were animals of all kinds, mostly wild asses, but also many ostriches. There were also bustards and gazelles. The horsemen would occasionally hunt for these animals: as for the asses, each time that someone was chasing them, they would run ahead and then stop dead in their tracks (for they ran much faster than the horses); and again and again, whenever the horses were coming close, they would do the same, and it was not possible to catch them, except if the horsemen took up positions at intervals and hunted them in relays. The meat of the animals that were caught was much like venison, but more tender. As for the ostriches, no one succeeded at catching one of them. And the horsemen that had chased them soon gave up, because the animal would make them go a great distance when it ran from them, by running with its feet and hoisting its wings, using them like a sail. As for the bustards, if you make a quick jump on them, it is possible to catch them. For they can only fly a short distance, like partridges, and soon tire out. Their meat was delicious. Travelling through this country, they arrived at the river Mascas, which is a plethrum in width.

Commentary

61.5   **General Notes**

In **descriptions**, the speaker/narrator expands in detail on a **geographical location**, a **custom**, an **object**, a **creature**, a **character**, etc. Unlike narratives, descriptions are **not organized chronologically**: rather, **different aspects** of the thing described are treated **in turn**. Descriptions may be set in the **present or the past**, but the flow of time is mostly irrelevant. When inserted into the larger structure of a narrative, as here, such descriptions in fact interrupt that flow – in other words, they put the question 'What happened next?' on hold.

All this can be seen most clearly from the use of **tenses**: in past descriptions, such as this one, the **imperfect** is used almost exclusively; similarly, descriptions of something in the present normally have **present indicatives** (the present and the imperfect have the same aspectual value, →33.22). The imperfect and present indicative are prevalent in descriptions because the speaker tends to describe permanent characteristics of a certain thing, or repeated habits and customs: the aspect of the present stem (expressing ongoing or repeated actions) is suitable for expressing such actions. The perfect aspect, referring to states, can also be suitable: hence, in past descriptions, the pluperfect also occurs, and in descriptions referring to the present, the perfect indicative is not uncommon.

Another aspect of the passage which is typical of descriptions is the way in which particles and word order structure the text. Unlike arguments and most dialogues (→61.8, 61.13), descriptions are usually relatively uncomplicated in design, as different features are described in turn. Accordingly, they normally have a small variety of connective particles: the text moves from topic to topic by means of the frequent use of the particle δέ, with an occasional elaboration introduced by γάρ. Attitudinal particles are rare in descriptions. Word order, too, often helps to identify points where the text moves to another aspect or topic.

Like other long historiographical texts, Xenophon's *Anabasis* is strongly **monological**; it is not addressed to a specific group of addressees. Typical characteristics of dialogic texts, such as attitudinal particles (→59.3) and direct addresses by means of the vocative, are absent from the passage cited here. The most one can say is that the comparisons of the desert landscape and the ostrich's wings to the sea and sails, respectively, indicate that Xenophon had a Greek audience in mind, since most Greeks would have been more familiar with the sea and ships than with deserts and ostriches.

61.6   **Detailed Notes**

1–2 ἐντεῦθεν ... πέντε: The first sentence of the passage is still part of the main narrative: this is evident from the verb ἐξελαύνει, which can only be historical present (a use of the present indicative found predominantly in narrative).

The historical present, as often in Xenophon, 'punctuates' the narrative by highlighting the main episodes of Cyrus' march: in this way, the historical present segments the narrative into units corresponding to the various stages of the march (→33.55).

The adverb ἐντεῦθεν serves as setting, followed immediately by a lengthy broad-focus construction (→60.23) which begins with the verb (ἐξελαύνει) and covers the location (Arabia), duration (five days) and geographical extent (thirty-five parasangs) of this stage of the march: this word order is typical for many marches in the *Anabasis*; it is not unlike 'presentational sentences' (→60.30 and 61.3, n. on 24–25).

2–6 ἐν τούτῳ ... δορκάδες: Xenophon now breaks off his narrative to give an extensive description of the country he has just mentioned in the previous sentence. The description falls into two parts: first, a purely 'geographical' description of the plant-life and the animals that populated the area, as they were found by the army (2–6); second, a digression on the repeated, mostly unsuccessful attempts by the army at hunting those animals for food (6–14). In the first section, all of the verbs (ἦν, 3; ἐνῆν, 4; ἦσαν, 4; ἐνῆν, 5; ἐνῆσαν, 6) are imperfect forms of εἰμί *be*: Xenophon is simply listing all the plants and animals that could be found in the country.

2–3 ἐν τούτῳ δὲ τῷ τόπῳ: The pronoun τούτῳ is used anaphorically (→29.32) to refer to the location just mentioned, which is taken up and repeated as the setting (→60.32) for the entire following description. Using the particle δέ, Xenophon marks this off as a new, distinct section of the text.

3–6 ἦν μὲν ἡ γῆ πεδίον ... ἀψινθίου δὲ ... δένδρον δ' ... θηρία δέ: The position of the verb ἦν is a strong signal that a description begins here: ἦν is placed initially in the clause (μέν makes it clear that this clause starts with ἦν; the preceding words are a setting), which suggests that this is a 'presentational' sentence (→60.30): 'what there was' in the country is what this section will be about; but it turns out that ἦν is actually a linking verb with the words ἡ γῆ πεδίον: 'the ground was a plain'.

Xenophon goes on to mention several aspects of the country: its shape, the type of low growth that could be found, the lack of trees, and the animals that populate it. These individual aspects are enumerated by means of the particles μέν ... δέ ... δ' ... δέ, and in each case the new, contrastive topic is placed initially in the clause, except in the case of ἐνῆσαν δὲ καὶ ὠτίδες καὶ δορκάδες, where Xenophon opts for a presentational sentence.

4 ἅπαντα ἦσαν εὐώδη: The plural verb with a neuter plural subject emphasizes that each individual species of plant-life was fragrant (→27.2).

5–6 θηρία δὲ παντοῖα ... πλεῖστοι ... μεγάλαι: Because it follows a negated clause (δένδρον δ' οὐδὲν ἐνῆν), the particle δέ is here best translated by 'but', although this is a matter of translation into English rather than an actually different 'meaning' of δέ (which merely signals a shift of topic).

The whole phrase πλεῖστοι ... μεγάλαι stands in apposition to the words θηρία παντοῖα. The apposition serves to further define and specify the general 'animals of all kinds' (→26.24).

In the configuration of στρουθοὶ αἱ μεγάλαι the adjective provides additional information necessary to identify the particular type of στρουθός meant – a στρουθός is a sparrow; only with the adjective μεγάλη added does it mean 'ostrich' (→28.11 n.2).

6 ἐνῆσαν δὲ καὶ ὠτίδες: In the particle combination δὲ καί, the first particle is a connective particle (here simply to be translated 'and', or left untranslated), and καί is an adverbial particle of scope ('also'; →59.56).

6-14 ταῦτα δὲ τὰ θηρία ... ἥδιστα ἦν: The second section of Xenophon's description concerns the attempts at hunting the animals which he has just mentioned. As this section takes up the army and their actions, it is in some ways more integrated into the narrative than the preceding geographical description (this section resembles narrative more, although the organization of the text is still not chronological: the hunt is described animal by animal, which may not reflect the order they were actually hunted in). Again, imperfects proliferate (ἐδίωκον, 7; ἕστασαν, 7 (see n. below); ἔτρεχον, 8; ἐποίουν, 8; ἦν, 9; ἦν, 10; ἐπαύοντο, 11; ἀπέσπα, 11; ἦν, 14), although there is also a single aorist (ἔλαβεν, 11) and an interesting series of presents (13–14). Other than in the first section, these imperfects mostly express repeated actions, which is made clear by the temporal adverbs ἐνίοτε (6) and πάλιν (8) and the temporal clauses with iterative optatives (→47.10), ἐπεί τις διώκοι (7), ἐπεὶ πλησιάζοιεν (8).

After a brief introductory sentence (ταῦτα ... ἐδίωκον, 6–7), Xenophon talks about each of the various animals that were hunted in turn. In each case, the animal in question comes first in its sentence (καὶ οἱ μὲν ὄνοι, 7; στρουθὸν δέ, 10; τὰς δὲ ὠτίδας, 13), marking it as a contrastive topic or theme, and the sequence is segmented by μέν ... δέ ... δέ. In the case of the two species of which some animals were actually caught, Xenophon also elaborates on the taste of the meat (τὰ δὲ κρέα, 9 and 14).

6 ταῦτα δὲ τὰ θηρία: The anaphoric pronoun ταῦτα is again used to pick up an element from the preceding context and use it as basis for the following digression (compare τούτῳ above, 2). The particle δέ serves merely to mark the break between this section and the last.

7 ... ἐδίωκον, καὶ οἱ μὲν ὄνοι: Xenophon starts off the series of animals with καὶ ... μέν, where μέν anticipates the following instances of δέ, and καί is used because the whole sequence is part of the same 'item' as the verb ἐδίωκον. We may compare the force of καί here with that of 'and' in an English paraphrase: 'As for these animals, the horsemen at times chased them *and* the outcome was that ...:'

The first time the asses were mentioned (5), there was no article with ὄνοι. From that first mention onwards, the asses are identifiable, and the article οἱ is therefore used here. Compare the use of τάς (13, but see the n. there).

7 ἐπεί τις διώκοι: The optative, in a temporal clause referring to a repeated or habitual action in the past, is highly suitable for descriptive passages such as this one. The aspect of the present optative yields a relative-tense interpretation (simultaneity, →33.57): 'each time that someone *was chasing* them, …'. The subordinate clause follows the theme οἱ μὲν ὄνοι (→60.33).

7 προδραμόντες ἕστασαν: The pluperfect ἕστασαν, as the past tense of perfect ἕστηκα, suggests the immediate and complete realization of the action of coming to a standstill (→33.53): the asses stopped dead in their tracks. At the same time, given the iterative optative δίωκοι (see above), ἕστασαν does refer to a repeated action. The order of participle and verb is significant: when a participle in the aorist precedes the main verb, this suggests a temporal sequence (→52.35–6): first, the asses run away, and then they stand still at a distance from the riders; compare the order of θηρῷεν διαδεχόμενοι below (9).

7–8 πολὺ γάρ … θᾶττον: γάρ here has its normal explanatory function, serving to explain how it was possible that the asses kept getting away from the horsemen.

8 καὶ πάλιν, ἐπεὶ πλησιάζοιεν οἱ ἵπποι, ταὐτὸν ἐποίουν: The repeated failure of the horsemen in the hunt is underlined by πάλιν and ταὐτόν, as well as by the imperfect ἐποίουν and the temporal clause with the optative. The connection with καί shows that this sentence should be seen as part of the same cycle of failed attempts (καὶ πάλιν is almost 'and again and again').

9 καὶ οὐκ ἦν λαβεῖν: The imperfect ἦν cannot (by virtue of the meaning of the verb 'to be') be interpreted as expressing a repeated action: rather, the imperfect (of an ongoing action) signals that it was consistently impossible to catch any of the asses; ἦν stands for ἐξῆν (of ἔξεστι *it is possible*).

9 εἰ μὴ διαστάντες οἱ ἱππεῖς θηρῷεν διαδεχόμενοι: This negative conditional clause ('unless') actually details how, in the end, the horsemen *were able* to catch some of the asses. The optative θηρῷεν is again used to express a repeated action in the past – the negative in such conditional clauses is slightly unusual, but here necessary to balance out the negative in the previous clause (οὐκ ἦν).

The ordering of participles around the main verb is again significant. Again, the aorist participle preceding the main verb (διαστάντες) suggests a temporal sequence: first they positioned themselves, then they hunted. The present participle following the main verb (διαδεχόμενοι), however, says something about the manner in which they executed their hunt.

9–10 τὰ δὲ κρέα τῶν ἁλισκομένων ἦν παραπλήσια τοῖς ἐλαφείοις, ἁπαλώτερα δέ: With the preceding conditional clause implying that some asses were actually caught, Xenophon goes on to talk about the meat of those that were (τῶν ἁλισκομένων, present participle referring to multiple asses). The new topic is set apart by δέ; the second δέ marks a contrast (without a preceding μέν, which is not always required).

10–11 **στρουθὸν δὲ οὐδεὶς ἔλαβεν**: The next animal species that Xenophon discusses is again introduced by putting it upfront in the sentence, connected by the particle δέ.

The aorist **ἔλαβεν**, in this passage dominated by imperfects, may seem slightly surprising, but is suitable because of the negative **οὐδείς** (no one completed the action of capturing an ostrich: the complete failure is presented, almost by way of retrospective summation, in the aorist). **οὐδείς** is the narrow focus of this sentence, immediately preceding the verb, and following the contrastive topic **στρουθόν**.

11 **οἱ δὲ διώξαντες . . . πολὺ γὰρ ἀπέσπα**: Even though, at πολὺ γάρ, the subject changes here from the chasing horsemen to the ostrich (the subject of ἀπέσπα, in the singular because it refers to a typical ostrich in one of the army's attempts), the latter subject does not need to be separately expressed. This is common in Greek when the subject is still prominently 'on the mind' (a given topic), especially when there is no chance of confusion (as here).

13–14 **τὰς δὲ ὠτίδας, ἄν . . . ἀνιστῇ, ἔστι λαμβάνειν· πέτονται . . . ἀπαγορεύουσι**: In his treatment of the last species of animal (again placed first in the sentence as theme, connected by δέ, and followed by a subordinate clause) Xenophon, who is also the author of a short treatise on hunting, suddenly shifts to the present tense and a conditional clause using **ἄν** (= ἐάν) + subjunctive (habitual use in the present, →49.13). These verbs cannot be historical present: rather, they express general truths, and as a result, this section reads much like a textbook on hunting.

It is likely that the article **τάς** with ὠτίδας ought to be read as a generic article (→28.6; the rest of the section steers our interpretation this way), although readers who first come across it will naturally think that it is used to refer back to the bustards mentioned before.

14 **τὰ δὲ κρέα αὐτῶν ἥδιστα ἦν**: With the imperfect ἦν, we briefly return to the description in the past. ἦν expresses the taste of the meat as it was perceived by the hunters at the time.

15 **πορευόμενοι δὲ διὰ ταύτης τῆς χώρας ἀφικνοῦνται . . .** : The country just described is taken up anaphorically by ταύτης τῆς χώρας, and the army's travel through it is presented as backdrop for the next phase of the narrative (the whole phrase πορευόμενοι δὲ διὰ ταύτης τῆς χώρας is setting). The verb ἀφικνοῦνται, historical present (and as such a definitive sign that the narrative has been resumed) is again the beginning of a broad-focus construction (cf. 1–2 above).

Argument: Plato, *Gorgias* 484c–485a

Introduction and Text

61.7 The following passage is part of Callicles' great monologue (ῥῆσις) in Plato's *Gorgias*, which is a philosophical discussion presented like a play, with several speakers taking turns. In his monologue, Callicles proposes a radical alternative to Socrates' philosophical views: philosophical nit-picking only results in rules and laws which are intended to constrain the men with real abilities; in political life, in which every man should participate, there is no room for the philosopher's morality. In the present section he maintains that Socrates would also be of that opinion, if only he would give up philosophy. Philosophy, he argues, may be a useful part of the education of young men, but once a man becomes politically active, it will only blur his good judgement.

τὸ μὲν οὖν ἀληθὲς οὕτως ἔχει, γνώσῃ δέ, ἂν ἐπὶ τὰ μείζω ἔλθῃς ἐάσας ἤδη   1
φιλοσοφίαν. φιλοσοφία γάρ τοί ἐστιν, ὦ Σώκρατες, χαρίεν, ἄν τις αὐτοῦ   2
μετρίως ἅψηται ἐν τῇ ἡλικίᾳ· ἐὰν δὲ περαιτέρω τοῦ δέοντος ἐνδιατρίψῃ,   3
διαφθορὰ τῶν ἀνθρώπων. ἐὰν γὰρ καὶ πάνυ εὐφυὴς ᾖ καὶ πόρρω τῆς   4
ἡλικίας φιλοσοφῇ, ἀνάγκη πάντων ἄπειρον γεγονέναι ἐστὶν ὧν χρὴ   5
ἔμπειρον εἶναι τὸν μέλλοντα καλὸν κἀγαθὸν καὶ εὐδόκιμον ἔσεσθαι ἄνδρα.   6
καὶ γὰρ τῶν νόμων ἄπειροι γίγνονται τῶν κατὰ τὴν πόλιν, καὶ τῶν λόγων   7
οἷς δεῖ χρώμενον ὁμιλεῖν ἐν τοῖς συμβολαίοις τοῖς ἀνθρώποις καὶ ἰδίᾳ καὶ   8
δημοσίᾳ, καὶ τῶν ἡδονῶν τε καὶ ἐπιθυμιῶν τῶν ἀνθρωπείων, καὶ συλλήβδην   9
τῶν ἠθῶν παντάπασιν ἄπειροι γίγνονται. ἐπειδὰν οὖν ἔλθωσιν εἴς τινα ἰδίαν   10
ἢ πολιτικὴν πρᾶξιν, καταγέλαστοι γίγνονται, ὥσπερ γε οἶμαι οἱ πολιτικοί,   11
ἐπειδὰν αὖ εἰς τὰς ὑμετέρας διατριβὰς ἔλθωσιν καὶ τοὺς λόγους,   12
καταγέλαστοί εἰσιν. συμβαίνει γὰρ τὸ τοῦ Εὐριπίδου· λαμπρός τέ ἐστιν   13
ἕκαστος ἐν τούτῳ, καὶ ἐπὶ τοῦτ' ἐπείγεται,   14
     νέμων τὸ πλεῖστον ἡμέρας τούτῳ μέρος,   15
     ἵν' αὐτὸς αὑτοῦ τυγχάνει βέλτιστος ὤν·   16
ὅπου δ' ἂν φαῦλος ᾖ, ἐντεῦθεν φεύγει καὶ λοιδορεῖ τοῦτο, τὸ δ' ἕτερον ἐπαινεῖ,   17
εὐνοίᾳ τῇ ἑαυτοῦ, ἡγούμενος οὕτως αὐτὸς ἑαυτὸν ἐπαινεῖν.   18

This is the truth of the matter, and you will recognize it if you finally abandon philosophy and move on to the more important things. Mind you, Socrates, philosophy is a delightful thing, if one touches upon it in moderation at the right age; but if one wastes more time on it than one should, it destroys people. For even if one is very gifted by nature, but engages in philosophy beyond the appropriate time of life, he will inevitably turn out to be inexperienced in everything in which a man who intends to be admirable and good and well thought of should be experienced. For such people do not become experienced in the laws of the city; in the arguments one must use in dealing with people on matters of both private and public business; in human pleasures and desires; and, in short, they do not become experienced whatsoever in all forms of human behaviour. So, when they venture into some private or political activity, they become ridiculous, precisely as, I suppose, politicians are ridiculous when they venture into those pastimes of yours and your discussions. For the upshot is Euripides' saying: 'each man shines' in this, and 'strives after this',

> allotting the greatest part of the day to this,
> where he happens to be at his best;

But, whatever a man is inferior in, that he avoids and rails against, while he praises the other thing, out of goodwill towards himself, because he thinks that in this way he is praising himself.

Commentary

61.8   General Notes

In an **argumentative** passage like the present one, a speaker makes a **claim** which he brings to the attention of his addressee and which he **supports** in some way. Unlike narratives, but like descriptions, arguments are **not organized temporally**. The verbs in main clauses do not refer to successive events. Rather, the individual sentences contain a set of claims or proposals, for which other sentences offer **proofs**, **explanations**, **conclusions**, etc. The structure of many arguments is hierarchical: some proofs and explanations pertain to the main proposal, while other proofs and explanations in turn back up more central proofs and explanations. The internal organization of Callicles' argument is established clearly by the use of **particles**, as the overview of the main structure of Callicles' argument, given below, shows.

While Callicles' monologue is long, he never loses sight of the fact that he is engaged in a dialogue with Socrates. **Dialogic elements** in the passage include the interactional particle τοι and the vocative ὦ Σώκρατες (both accompany a *captatio benevolentiae*; see n. on φιλοσοφία . . . τοί ἐστιν, ὦ Σώκρατες, . . . ἐὰν δέ . . . , 2–3; also n. on ὥσπερ γε οἶμαι οἱ πολιτικοί, 11–12), and the use of the second-person verb γνώσῃ (1, also →61.11); the use of the plural possessive pronoun ὑμετέρας (12) indicates that Callicles intends to address all philosophers via Socrates, so to speak.

61.9   The Overall Structure of Callicles' Argument

Introduction: τὸ μὲν οὖν ἀληθὲς οὕτως ἔχει, γνώσῃ δέ, . . . φιλοσοφίαν.
The first sentence rounds off the previous topic of Callicles' monologue and introduces the new one (see also below, on μὲν οὖν . . . δέ . . . , 1)

Main claim: φιλοσοφία γάρ ... διαφθορὰ τῶν ἀνθρώπων.

The main claim is introduced by γάρ. This particle often occurs after an announcement of a story or argument (see γνώσῃ; see also the remarks on γάρ in 61.3, line 2); it has its normal explanatory force to the extent that the following argument in its entirety contains the information which Socrates needs in order to realize that Callicles is right. Therefore, the scope of γάρ is much wider than the sentence in which it occurs: it pertains to the entire passage which follows. It is difficult to find an adequate translation for γάρ in such cases: often, it is sufficient simply to supply a colon (:) – 'You will recognize that I am right: ...'.

Proof: ἐὰν γάρ ... ἔσεσθαι ἄνδρα.

This sentence provides proof for the main claim that over-indulging in philosophy leads to 'the destruction of men'; γάρ has its normal explanatory force.

Clarification: καὶ γάρ ... ἄπειροι γίγνονται.

This sentence clarifies an aspect of the proof: it makes explicit what the things are in which 'a man who is to be admirable and good and well thought of should be experienced'. Again, γάρ has its normal explanatory force. Observe that this clarification explains only something about the proof: the entire argument is hierarchically structured: the clarification presents the 'deepest level' of the argument.

Conclusion of the proof: ἐπειδὰν οὖν ... καταγέλαστοί εἰσιν.

As often, the conclusion is introduced by οὖν: The entire proof gives Callicles the opportunity to maintain that the 'destruction of men' who engage in philosophy consists in the fact that they 'become ridiculous'. The particle returns the argument back to a higher level of the text.

Proof: συμβαίνει γάρ ... ἑαυτὸν ἐπαινεῖν.

In his summation, Callicles is careful to indulge Socrates by granting that, just as philosophers make bad politicians, politicians would be bad philosophers. He backs this statement up by quoting a couple of lines from Euripides, whom he apparently regards as an authority in this respect. γάρ performs its normal function.

Each of the main parts of the argument can be further divided into even smaller segments. Again, particles have an important role to play here, but demonstrative pronouns are important as well.

61.10 **Detailed Notes**

1 **μὲν οὖν ... δέ ...** : This succession of particles is very common in sentences which form a transition between two topics. In the particle combination μὲν οὖν, οὖν rounds off the previous topic, suggesting a transition to a (currently) more relevant point, while μέν looks forward to δέ, balancing or contrasting the two topics (→59.73). The fact that the first part of the sentence looks back at the previous section can also be seen from **οὕτως** 'like this', which is used anaphorically (compare anaphoric οὗτος; →29.32).

2–3 φιλοσοφία ... τοί ἐστιν, ὦ Σώκρατες, ... ἐὰν δέ ... : Callicles' main claim consists of two parts, the second of which contains the contention for which he will argue in the following. The first part is a preliminary concession to Socrates' point of view intended by Callicles to mollify his interlocutor (compare the *captatio benevolentiae* with which many speeches begin). This is shown by τοι, an interactional particle, which in this case has a concessive value: '*granted*, philosophy is something delightful'; for neuter χαρίεν, →27.8. The δέ-clause builds a contrast with this preliminary point and the particle can therefore be translated by 'but'. Both conditional clauses have (contrasting) narrow focus constituents, μετρίως and περαιτέρω τοῦ δέοντος: these carry the main point. The vocative ὦ Σώκρατες fulfils a role similar to τοι, in that it clearly marks the fact that Callicles makes the point about philosophy being delightful to indulge Socrates (remember that τοι is originally a dative of the second-person personal pronoun).

4–5 ἐὰν γὰρ καὶ πάνυ εὐφυὴς ἦ καὶ πόρρω τῆς ἡλικίας φιλοσοφῇ: For γάρ, see above. Even though the two clauses under the scope of εἰ are co-ordinated by καί, they are (exceptionally) not semantically parallel. The second provides the real condition in case of which the main clause applies: 'If one engages in philosophy beyond the appropriate age, then it is necessary etc.' The first is rather concessive: 'this even holds for someone who is very gifted'. The first καί is adverbial and to be connected with πάνυ.

7–10 καὶ γὰρ τῶν νόμων ... καὶ τῶν λόγων ... καὶ τῶν ἡδονῶν τε καὶ ἐπιθυμιῶν ... καὶ συλλήβδην τῶν ἠθῶν: An enumeration consisting of four essential spheres of life in which philosophers turn out to be inexperienced. Each element is introduced by a connective καί. The first καί belongs to τῶν νόμων, but is separated from its noun phrase by γάρ, because of Wackernagel's Law (→60.7); on the force of γάρ, see above. τῶν νόμων is separated from its modifier τῶν κατὰ τὴν πόλιν in hyperbaton, as the modifier contains fairly predictable information (→60.18). The final element of the enumeration stands apart from the others, in that it summarizes the previous elements: συλλήβδην 'in short' shows this. The third part is itself subdivided in two by τε καί: this particle combination often suggests that the elements thus co-ordinated belong closely together.

11–12 ὥσπερ γε οἶμαι οἱ πολιτικοί, ἐπειδὰν αὖ: ὥσπερ γε 'precisely as' again introduces a point which is intended to appease Socrates or to forestall a possible objection on his part: Callicles grants that politicians perform badly when they in their turn (αὖ, signalling the exactly opposite scenario of the ἐπειδὰν οὖν-clause) engage in philosophy. (Of course, in his reasoning this is a rather gratuitous concession, because the real object of a man's life should be politics, and not philosophy.) Placed after the connective ὥσπερ, the scope-particle γε has scope over the entire clause. Its force is limitative: Callicles restricts the inability of politicians only to a scenario in which they engage in philosophy.

11 οἶμαι: After the confident assertions he has made so far (on which see below), Callicles clearly marks his present statement as a mere opinion by means of a paratactic οἶμαι 'I suppose': he probably does this because he does not claim to have any experience in philosophy; it is up to Socrates to judge the truth of what he is saying. This impression is reinforced by the (as usual) emphatic use of the second-person possessive pronoun in τὰς ὑμετέρας διατριβάς (→29.22), '*your* pastimes', which marks philosophy as something that does not belong to Callicles but to Socrates and people like him.

13–14 τὸ τοῦ Εὐριπίδου· λαμπρός τε ... καί ... : τὸ τοῦ Εὐριπίδου 'the saying of Euripides' introduces a quotation from *Antiope* (a lost play), which then follows immediately, without a connective particle: asyndeton is regular after such announcements. The particle τε, of course, looks forward to καί, forging into a single idea the two statements that everybody performs splendidly at and (therefore) aims to do what he believes he does best. It is possible that the quotation is not exact, as often in Plato.

14–16 ἐν τούτῳ ... ἐπὶ τοῦτ' ... τούτῳ ... ἵν': As happens often, forms of the demonstrative pronoun οὗτος (rather than of ὅδε) refer cataphorically to a following relative clause (→29.32 n.1).

17 ὅπου δ' ... ἐντεῦθεν ... τοῦτο: ἐντεῦθεν and τοῦτο here refer anaphorically to the relative clause starting with ὅπου: this is a normal function of ἐντεῦθεν and forms of οὗτος (→8.2, 29.32).

16–17 ἵνα ... ὅπου δ' ἄν ... τὸ δ' ἕτερον: Both times δέ contrasts the previous clause with the present one; the definite noun phrase τὸ ἕτερον refers back to the ἵνα-clause. Observe the difference in mood between the two relative clauses: ἵνα is followed by an indicative, indicating that there is a fixed sphere of life in which each person happens to be at his best and which is in principle identifiable in each case. By contrast, ὅπου is followed by ἄν + subjunctive (indefinite) to indicate that there may be many other, not readily identifiable, things in which each person is inferior (→50.21).

61.11 Argumentative Tone

Not only is the structure of the passage characteristic of an argument. The tone, too, is typical of at least one kind of argument. Callicles only once weakens the force of one of his claims by means of οἶμαι 'I suppose' (see above, 11). The rest of the time, he strikes a very confident tone. For example, Callicles uses the impersonal ἀνάγκη ἐστίν 'it is inevitable' (5) to express what he thinks is a *logical* necessity. The impersonal verb δεῖ 'it is necessary' (8), fulfils a similar role: it indicates that there cannot, in Callicles' view, be a discussion about what kinds of things a good man should be experienced in. The future indicative γνώσῃ 'you will realize' (1) is a further sign of confidence: by presenting Socrates' change of mind as a future *fact*, Callicles suggests that alternative views cannot really be maintained once he has finished his exposition. To 'feel' the force of these features of Callicles' language, it is helpful to envisage possible alternatives: instead of 'it is inevitable' he might have said 'I think it is the case' and instead of 'you will realize', he might have said 'perhaps you will realize' (γνοίης ἄν, a potential optative). The result would be a more modestly proposed argument.

Perhaps the most important contribution to the confident tone is made by the use of indicatives in main clauses, which express what the speaker regards as facts. Almost all of these are in the present tense, and express timeless or habitual actions, things which are always the case (or so Callicles believes). Accordingly, the conditional and temporal clauses take the form of ἐάν/ἐπειδάν + subjunctive. In accordance with this, Callicles talks about people in general (τις, 2; τῶν ἀνθρώπων, 4), or about classes of people (τὸν μέλλοντα . . . ἄνδρα, 6; οἱ πολιτικοί, 11); these noun phrases have a generic article.

Callicles not only reinforces his point through grammatical means, but also through the use of expressive vocabulary. Thus, it is apparent that he has clear ideas about what occupations are suitable for an adult man: he refers to politics as τὰ μείζω 'the bigger things' (1) – note that the definite article implies that it is recognized by everybody that politics is more important than philosophy – while philosophy is called χαρίεν 'something delightful' (2) – note the somewhat condescending use of the neuter; later on it is referred to as αἱ ὑμέτεραι διατριβαί (12). Although this word is often used for 'discussions', there is more than a hint of its other meaning 'pastimes' here. Finally, 'engaging in philosophy' is referred to by the verb ἐνδιατρίβω 'waste one's time' (3). Instead, one should only 'touch upon it in moderation' (μετρίως ἅψηται, 3).

Finally, Plato often appears to make an effort to make his writing resemble spoken language. Spoken language is often a bit more 'sloppy', redundant and less grammatical than written language, but Plato's Greek is usually clear and easy to follow. In the present passage, the influence of spoken language is apparent in the repetition of ἄπειροι γίγνονται (7 and 10), which is triggered by the long sentence of which these words form the predicate: by the time Callicles gets to τῶν ἠθῶν, he foresees that his addressees may have forgotten by now that the genitive depends on ἄπειροι γίγνονται, and for this reason he repeats it. A further sign of the influence of spoken language is the transition from the singular τις 'someone' (2; it is the subject of ἅψηται, ἐνδιατρίψῃ, ᾗ, φιλοσοφῇ and γεγονέναι), to the plurals ἄπειροι γίγνονται, ἔλθωσιν and καταγέλαστοι γίγνονται. The change is readily understandable, once we realize that τις stands for anybody who pursues philosophy beyond the right period of life, in other words, for an entire class of people. The co-ordination of two semantically non-equivalent εἰ-clauses noted in the comments above (4–5) may be a further colloquial feature.

Dialogue: Sophocles, *Ajax* 1120–41

Introduction and Text

61.12   In Sophocles' *Ajax*, the eponymous hero, having lost his mind and having tried unsuccessfully to kill the leaders of the Greek army before Troy as they lay asleep, commits suicide. Ajax's madness is the result of his losing a contest over the weapons of the slain Achilles: the contest, in the end, was decided by vote, and Odysseus was declared winner and given the splendid weaponry. The second part of the play is concerned with the burial of Ajax: in the scene below, Ajax' half-brother Teucer and his sworn enemy Menelaus engage in an angry discussion about this burial. Menelaus, whom Teucer holds personally responsible for Ajax' defeat in the deciding vote, denies Ajax a proper burial in light of the crimes he has committed. Teucer disputes this fervently, leading Menelaus to resort to outright insults.

ME.	ὁ τοξότης ἔοικεν οὐ σμικρὸν φρονεῖν.	1120
TEY.	οὐ γὰρ βάναυσον τὴν τέχνην ἐκτησάμην.	1121
ME.	μέγ' ἄν τι κομπάσειας, ἀσπίδ' εἰ λάβοις.	1122
TEY.	κἂν ψιλὸς ἀρκέσαιμι σοί γ' ὡπλισμένῳ.	1123
ME.	ἡ γλῶσσά σου τὸν θυμὸν ὡς δεινὸν τρέφει.	1124
TEY.	ξὺν τῷ δικαίῳ γὰρ μέγ' ἔξεστιν φρονεῖν.	1125
ME.	δίκαια γὰρ τόνδ' εὐτυχεῖν κτείναντά με;	1126
TEY.	κτείναντα; δεινόν γ' εἶπας, εἰ καὶ ζῇς θανών.	1127
ME.	θεὸς γὰρ ἐκσῴζει με, τῷδε δ' οἴχομαι.	1128
TEY.	μή νυν ἀτίμα θεούς, θεοῖς σεσωμένος.	1129
ME.	ἐγὼ γὰρ ἂν ψέξαιμι δαιμόνων νόμους;	1130
TEY.	εἰ τοὺς θανόντας οὐκ ἐᾷς θάπτειν παρών.	1131
ME.	τούς γ' αὐτὸς αὑτοῦ πολεμίους· οὐ γὰρ καλόν.	1132
TEY.	ἦ σοὶ γὰρ Αἴας πολέμιος προῦστη ποτέ;	1133
ME.	μισοῦντ' ἐμίσει· καὶ σὺ τοῦτ' ἠπίστασο.	1134
TEY.	κλέπτης γὰρ αὐτοῦ ψηφοποιὸς ηὑρέθης.	1135
ME.	ἐν τοῖς δικασταῖς κοὐκ ἐμοὶ τόδ' ἐσφάλη.	1136
TEY.	πόλλ' ἂν καλῶς λάθρα σὺ κλέψειας κακά.	1137
ME.	τοῦτ' εἰς ἀνίαν τοὔπος ἔρχεταί τινι.	1138
TEY.	οὐ μᾶλλον, ὡς ἔοικεν, ἢ λυπήσομεν.	1139
ME.	ἕν σοι φράσω· τόνδ' ἐστὶν οὐχὶ θαπτέον.	1140
TEY.	ἀλλ' ἀντακούσῃ τοῦθ' ἕν, ὡς τεθάψεται.	1141

M.	The archer, it seems, has little modesty.
T.	Indeed not, for I did not acquire it as a lowly art.
M.	Your boast would be great indeed if you got a shield!
T.	Even unarmed, I would be a match for you with your weapons.

M.   How brash does your mouth make your heart!

T.   Yes, for when someone has justice on his side, he may be bold.

M.   Are you saying it was just for him to get away with murdering me?

T.   Murdering? You make quite a claim, if you still live having been killed.

M.   I live because a god is my saviour: as far as this man is concerned,
        I am gone.

T.   Well then, stop dishonouring the gods, if you are saved by them.

M.   You dare say that I would disparage the precepts of the gods?

T.   If you are here to forbid the burying of the dead.

M.   The dead who are my own enemies: for that is not good.

T.   So you state that Ajax ever stood up to you as an enemy?

M.   He hated me as I hated him: you, too, knew that.

T.   Yes, because you were found out to have robbed him in the voting.

M.   That misfortune befell him on account of the judges, not on
        account of me.

T.   You could put a good face on many a despicable act, as long as you
        did them in secret.

M.   Someone is going to regret saying that!

T.   No more, it seems, than I shall cause regret.

M.   I will tell you one thing: this man is not to be buried.

T.   But you will hear only this in reply, that he shall lie in his grave.

Commentary

61.13   General Notes

The text type is on the whole that of **argument**: both Menelaus and Teucer make a number of claims and seek to support them. However, this heated *stichomythia* (a form of dramatic dialogue in which characters speak in alternating lines), quickly degenerates into the kind of shouting match to which notions of a sustained and coherent text type are perhaps less relevant.

Rather, the text is interesting for our purposes particularly for its many **dialogic** elements: there are many **first- and second-person** verb forms and pronouns; the use of tenses alternates primarily between **presents**, **futures** and **aorists**; there is **variety in the use of moods** (the imperative is rare outside dialogue); there is a greater incidence of **interactional particles** than in other text types (and other particles are sometimes employed in different fashion, see especially the notes on γάρ below); and finally, sentences generally do not have very complex syntax (that is to say, there is little stacking of subordinate clauses, circumstantial participles, etc.). With regard to syntax, this dialogue also contains examples of a feature common to *stichomythia*, namely the 'borrowing' of one speaker's syntax by the other (see the nn. on 1131–2 below).

61.14   **Detailed Notes**

In addition to comments on the structure and coherence of the text, some attention in the notes below will be devoted to an analysis of Menelaus' and Teucer's rhetorical 'tactics', since the way the speakers organize their utterances cannot be seen independently from such considerations.

1120: A line dripping with sarcasm and disdain. ὁ τοξότης is an insult both because Menelaus uses the third person (he may direct this speech to the chorus, which is present on stage, and pretend to ignore Teucer, who is nevertheless clearly *meant* to hear it), and because it emphasizes Teucer's low status (archers fought at a greater distance from the enemy than shield-bearing hoplites, and were considered of lower rank as a consequence). With ἔοικεν οὐ σμικρὸν φρονεῖν, Menelaus is deliberately, sarcastically circumspect in his description of Teucer, saying that he 'seems' to be 'not modest': Teucer's speech preceding this passage in fact conveys his attitude towards Menelaus clearly enough. The double negative inherent in οὐ σμικρόν is called 'litotes', a form of euphemism, which suggests here that Teucer's behaviour *should* normally be modest.

1121: In dialogue, γάρ often has a less obvious explanatory force than it would in monological arguments, narratives or descriptions, because it may be used by one speaker to connect his utterance to that of another. It is used to pick up an idea of the previous speaker, on which the current speaker elaborates. Its function is therefore really the same as in other contexts: it introduces a unit of text that elaborates the current line of discussion (→59.14). In many cases, such as here and in 1125, 1128, and 1135, it may be translated 'yes, for', 'indeed, because', etc. (here, Teucer uses the device to transform Menelaus' insult into a badge of honour).

Note the ordering of adjective, article and noun in βάναυσον τὴν τέχνην (predicative placement of the adjective, →28.11–12): Teucer is saying that archery, *in his case*, is not of low status at all (refuting the implication of Menelaus' τοξότης).

The aorist ἐκτησάμην, as often in non-narrative text, is used simply to observe that an action is completed (Teucer looks back at the time of his becoming an archer in retrospect, →33.28).

1122: The 'potential' conditional sentence (εἰ + opt. in the protasis, opt. + ἄν in the apodosis, →49.8) is used by Menelaus to some rhetorical effect: he both underlines the extent to which Teucer is being brazen (the gist is: 'if you're this arrogant when you're not even of high status, what would you be like if you were?'), but also subtly points out that Teucer's acquiring a shield is only a remote possibility.

ἀσπίδ', the topic of the conditional clause εἰ λάβοις is taken out of its clause and preposed, a form of prolepsis (→60.37): the implied sense is more or less 'Your boast would be great indeed with a shield, if you actually were to *get* one' (with λάβοις focus of the subordinate clause).

1123: Teucer again retorts by taking up Menelaus' point and turning it on its head: even (καί in **κἄν**) if he weren't to acquire a shield, he would still be able to take on Menelaus, regardless of status. He also adds the threat of violence: whereas shields and weapons up to this point have primarily been expressions of status, here Teucer suggests that they might actually use them.

The particle γε (**σοί γ'**) limits and focuses Teucer's boast on Menelaus specifically: '*you* I can take any day, even without weapons' (→59.53).

1124: A contemptuous exclamation (with **ὡς**, →38.47; ὡς is a prepositive, →60.13, which is here delayed until the word it goes with most closely, δεινόν). Naturally, exclamations are usually not connected to the surrounding context by a particle (asyndeton, →59.9): a connective particle would be at odds with the *impromptu* character of an exclamation.

1125: Teucer takes up Menelaus' point (using the particle **γάρ**, see note on 1121), ignoring the sarcasm of his exclamation: he has good reason to be bold. With **ξὺν τῷ δικαίῳ**, Teucer here introduces, as new topic (→60.29), a crucial term into the dialogue (τὸ δίκαιον), and pivots the discussion to the question of whether Ajax should be buried (as 'justice' demands).

1126: Menelaus takes up the issue of justice (**δίκαια** is in topic position), but is unwilling to yield the point that it is on the side of Teucer and Ajax. In a rhetorical question, he presents his own, different view of what is just.

The question is introduced by **γάρ**: in yes/no questions, this particle may be used to interrogate the premises and/or hypotheses of the other speaker: 'are you saying that because … ?', 'do you mean to say that … ?' (again, the particle elaborates on the utterance of the previous speaker, cf. 1121 above). In rhetorical questions like the present example, this leads to the interpretation that the speaker *subverts* the premises of the other speaker (in other words, Menelaus is implying that for Teucer to say that, his concept of justice must be wrong). The particle functions similarly in 1130 and 1133.

Menelaus can use the pronoun **τόνδ'** because the dead body of Ajax is actually lying on stage. We may imagine the actor pointing towards the corpse at this point (→29.29).

The conventional relative-tense interpretation of the aorist participle **κτείναντα** (→52.4) collides, of course, with the fact that the 'dead person' is speaking. This is pointed out by Teucer (see note on 1127), after which Menelaus is forced to qualify it in 1128.

1127: κτείναντα is a direct citation of Menelaus' word in the previous line, picked up to question its validity. **γ'** concentrates Teucer's point on the word δεινόν, the narrow focus of this sentence: we can do little more in translation than provide emphasis. The aorist εἶπας (an alternative form to εἶπες; →13.32) is used simply because Menelaus' relevant utterance is completed.

καί is here a scope particle (→59.56), extending the applicability of the word ζῆς beyond what might be expected ('you actually (still) live, having died').

1128: For γάρ see the note on 1121; here it 'picks up' ζῆς. The present οἴχομαι here, as often, is resultative (it means 'be gone' rather than 'go away', →33.18); the present ἐκσῴζει here (and elsewhere) works the same way ('a god has saved me' or 'is my saviour'). The particle δ' contrasts Ajax (again referred to by a form of ὅδε) with the god: no μέν precedes.

1129: Teucer latches on to Menelaus' comment about a god to again bring the topic of conversation back to the burial. His imperative μὴ ἀτίμα is connected to the preceding context by means of the particle νυν (→59.29), which expresses that the command flows naturally from what came before (the mention of a god).

The aspect of ἀτίμα (present imperative) is significant: Teucer suggests that Menelaus *has been* dishonouring the gods by not letting him bury Ajax, and that he should cease his opposition (→38.30); a translation 'stop dishonouring the gods' is better than 'don't dishonour the gods'.

1130: Menelaus seems not to grasp what Teucer is accusing him of, and objects in general to the notion that he could ever be disrespectful towards divine νόμοι. The potential optative ἂν ψέξαιμι is stronger than an indicative would be: Menelaus denies not only that he is disparaging divine precepts, but that he ever *could* (the rhetorical question implies οὐκ ἂν ψέξαιμι, a strong denial; →34.13). For the use of γάρ, see the note on 1126.

1131: Teucer here comes to the crux of his argument: burying Ajax is just. His contribution consists only of a subordinate clause, not a syntactically complete sentence. This is possible because he 'borrows' syntax from Menelaus: Teucer's conditional clause is latched onto the sentence which Menelaus has just spoken (as such it cannot be connected by a particle). The use of οὐκ instead of the expected μή (→49.3) indicates that Teucer presents this line as a statement rather than as a genuine condition.

The participle παρών is probably added to place responsibility squarely with Menelaus: as a general of the army, and being present at the site of the corpse, he is personally responsible if the burial does not go through.

1132: Menelaus, too, borrows syntax from his opponent: the accusative τοὺς πολεμίους is object with θάπτειν from 1131, which does not need to be expressed again. By the use of the limitative particle γ' (→59.53), Menelaus limits Teucer's general τοὺς θανόντας to the specific case of his own enemies: one can forbid burial when it concerns one's own πολέμιοι, since burying them is not a morally correct thing (οὐ γὰρ καλόν).

αὐτὸς αὑτοῦ is a set phrase, used in every person. Although it is impossible to be sure as to whether the second form should be αὐτοῦ rather than reflexive αὑτοῦ (for which →29.11), the phrase is well attested with a smooth breathing in the manuscripts of Greek tragic texts, and most recent editions indeed print αὑτοῦ.

1133: Teucer detects a hole in Menelaus' argument, and calls him out on it. For Menelaus' argument to hold water, Ajax must have been πολέμιος (this word suggests actual violent conflict, rather than just emotional dislike) to Menelaus (note accented σοί 'to *you*', →29.4). In a strongly suggestive question, Teucer asks whether this was truly the case. The particle **γάρ** questions the underlying premise of Menelaus' statement (see 1126 and 1130 above), and this is reinforced by ἦ ('is it *really* the case that … ?' →59.48); in this way, the two particles together mark (indignant) surprise.

The aorist **προὔστη** (= προ-έστη, →11.52) is regular with the indefinite **ποτέ**: Teucer asks whether a single occurrence of Ajax engaging in conflict with Menelaus ever took place.

1134: Menelaus has to retreat from the word πολέμιος, but tries to deflect Teucer's question by pointing out that he must have been all too aware that there was an abiding mutual hatred between the two men. The strength of that hatred is reinforced by the imperfect **ἐμίσει** (expressing an ongoing action in the past, →33.23) and by the doubling of forms of the verb μισέω (which underscores the reciprocity). **καί** should probably be read adverbially ('you too'). **ἠπίστασο** is imperfect rather than present, as Menelaus refers to the fact that Teucer was aware of Ajax's and Menelaus' mutual hatred *while Ajax was alive.*

1135: Teucer cannot now refrain from bringing up the proverbial elephant in the room, and, with **γάρ** (see 1125 and 1128), provides the reason for Ajax' hatred of Menelaus: he is held responsible for Ajax' loss in the contest over the weapons of Achilles (decided, in the end, by a vote). Teucer here uses the word **κλέπτης**: an outright accusation that Menelaus kept Ajax from what was rightfully his. **αὐτοῦ** is an objective genitive (→30.28), signifying the person robbed (note that the verb κλέπτω governs an accusative of the person robbed). The adjective **ψηφοποιός** (which occurs only here in Greek literature; the meaning is uncertain, either 'casting a vote' or 'tampering with votes') is added in apposition (→26.24) as further elaboration of how exactly Menelaus was a κλέπτης.

1136: Menelaus deflects responsibility for Ajax' loss of the weapons to the panel of judges which held the vote: a more respectable version of the story than the vote-tampering which Teucer seems to suggest took place. The pronoun **τόδ'** is used here because the affair surrounding Achilles' weapons is now prominent in Menelaus' mind (→29.29).

1137: Teucer denies that Menelaus did not cause Ajax' loss of Achilles' weapons. He ascribes to him the ability to 'put a fair face' on all kinds of criminal actions he commits without being noticed. The focus of the sentence is **λάθρᾳ**. The use of the potential optative **ἄν ... κλέψειας** (→34.13) gives the sentence a wider applicability than just the particular case under discussion: Teucer suggests that Menelaus is still ready to put this ability into action and has probably done so on several occasions in the past.

1138-9: In these lines, the conversation finally breaks down entirely: both speakers utter threats, although both do so in an indirect way. Menelaus formulates his threat in a general way, by saying **τινι** rather than **σοι**, and he distances himself from the responsibility for the threat by making Teucer's previous utterance the subject of **ἔρχεται**: not 'I will hit you', but 'what you just said will hit you'. Teucer weakens the strong force of the future indicative **λυπήσομεν** (which presents as a future fact what is actually a mere prediction; →33.43) by adding **ὡς ἔοικεν**, 'it seems'. He also leaves out any mention of the person that will be hurt. It is difficult to say why such indirect threats are more sinister (in effect, more threatening) than direct threats, but presumably it is because by not taking responsibility for a threat one suggests that the potentially violent outcome is beyond one's control and therefore all the more dangerous.

τοῦτο ... τοὔπος (= τὸ ἔπος by crasis, →1.43) refers anaphorically to Teucer's entire previous utterance. The present **ἔρχεται** is best interpreted as an action currently in progress: Menelaus is already losing control.

1140: Menelaus uses, in **ἕν σοι φράσω**, a future indicative to announce a statement which immediately follows. Such announcements indicate that the following statement is of great importance and should be given special heed. Note, in this connection, the use of the pronoun **σοι**, which appeals directly to Teucer. The statement is appended without connective particles (asyndeton), which is regular when a statement provides the content of an announcement just made.

The impersonal expression **ἐστίν ... θαπτέον** (→37.3) is reminiscent of legal language: Menelaus speaks with all the authority of a king, who does not deign to address individual subjects. As in previous instances (1126, 1128), **τόνδε** refers to the body which is present on stage.

1141: The particle **ἀλλ'** (→59.11) conveys Teucer's rejection of Menelaus' order and its replacement by a diametrically opposed intention on his part; a translation 'no, on the contrary' is suitable.

ἀντακούσῃ can be regarded as a passive of ἀντιλέγω *refute, contradict*; again, the clause announces an important statement, which here takes the form of a ὡς-clause.

The future perfect τεθάψεται (→33.46) is an instance of one-upmanship by Teucer over Menelaus: not only will Ajax be buried, he will rest in a grave once and for all. The future perfect emphasizes the state which will result from burying him. Note how Teucer echoes Menelaus' order in that he, too, uses a passive formulation, excluding himself as the agent of the burying. Again, this may suggest that the act of burying Ajax is outside any individual's control, and thus inevitable.

Bibliography

Introduction

Full-scale bibliographies of work on Greek linguistics can be found both online and in print (see I–II below). Therefore the bibliography printed in this book can be brief: we have not aimed at exhaustiveness, but merely to give an indication of the intellectual and scholarly background to *CGCG*.

Sections I–II list some large-scale reference works and online sources with full(er) bibliographies, which may be consulted by anyone interested in following up individual topics in more detail. Also listed are a few other useful online sources. Sections III–IV list works in the fields of general and historical linguistics which have helped shape our approach to Greek grammar. Sections V–VII list those books and articles on ancient Greek whose influence is visible, we believe, in major parts of *CGCG*, or which helped form our ideas in other important ways.

Note 1: The focus in the bibliography below is, then, on linguistics and Greek grammar. Naturally, we have also relied much on the wealth of learning assembled in general dictionaries, notably Liddell–Scott–Jones, and specialized lexica, as well as in commentaries written on the works from which our examples are taken. These are not individually mentioned below.
Note 2: In the case of edited collections containing more than one relevant article/chapter, we have listed the volumes as a whole rather than the individual pieces in them.

List of Books, Articles and Online Sources

I Encyclopedias, Companions (with Full Bibliographies)

Bakker, E. J. (ed.) 2010. *A Companion to the Ancient Greek Language*. Malden: Blackwell.
Giannakis, G. K. (ed.) 2013. *Encyclopedia of Ancient Greek Language and Linguistics*. Leiden: Brill.
Meier-Brügger, M. 1992. *Griechische Sprachwissenschaft*, 2 vols. Berlin: De Gruyter.

II Online Sources

(Note: no full web addresses are given below, as these may change; the resources are in any case more easily found by way of a search engine.)

Online Bibliographies:
- A Bibliography of Ancient Greek Linguistics (by M. Buijs)
- Oxford Bibliographies Online: Ancient Greek Language (by S. Colvin)
- Linguistic Bibliographies Online (Brill): Ancient Greek (by M. Janse)

Text Databases and Search Tools:
- Perseus Digital Library
- Perseus Under PhiloLogic
- Thesaurus Linguae Graecae

Encyclopedias, Companions
Of the resources listed under section I above, Bakker 2010 and Giannakis 2013 have online versions, to which many institutions provide access.

III General Works on Language and Linguistics

Brown, G., Yule, G. 1983. *Discourse Analysis.* Cambridge: Cambridge University Press.

Bybee, J., Perkins, R., Pagliuca, W. 1994. *The Evolution of Grammar: Tense, Aspect and Modality in the Languages of the World.* Chicago: University of Chicago Press.

Comrie, B. 1976. *Aspect: An Introduction to the Study of Verbal Aspect and Related Problems.* Cambridge: Cambridge University Press.

Comrie, B. 1985. *Tense.* Cambridge: Cambridge University Press.

Cristofaro, S. 2003. *Subordination.* Oxford: Oxford University Press.

Dahl, Ö. 1985. *Tense and Aspect Systems.* Oxford: Blackwell.

Dahl, Ö. (ed.) 2000. *Tense and Aspect in the Languages of Europe.* Berlin: De Gruyter.

Dik, S. C. 1997. *The Theory of Functional Grammar*, 2nd ed., 2 vols, ed. K. Hengeveld. Berlin: De Gruyter.

Givón, T. 2001. *Syntax: An Introduction.* Amsterdam: Benjamins.

Gussenhoven, C., Jacobs, H. 2013. *Understanding Phonology*, 3rd ed. London: Routledge.

Haspelmath, M., Sims, A. D. 2010. *Understanding Morphology*, 2nd ed. London: Routledge.

Horn, L. R., Ward, G. (eds) 2004. *The Handbook of Pragmatics.* Malden: Blackwell.

Kroon, C. H. M. 1995. *Discourse Particles in Latin: A Study of* nam, enim, autem, vero, *and* at. Amsterdam: Gieben.

Ladefoged, P. 2001. *Vowels and Consonants: An Introduction to the Sounds of Languages.* Malden: Blackwell.

Lambrecht, K. 1994. *Information Structure and Sentence Form: Topic, Focus, and the Mental Representations of Discourse Referents.* Cambridge: Cambridge University Press.

Levinson, S. C. 1983. *Pragmatics.* Cambridge: Cambridge University Press.

Lyons, J. 1977. *Semantics.* Cambridge: Cambridge University Press.

Lyons, J. 1995. *Linguistic Semantics: An Introduction.* Cambridge: Cambridge University Press.

Mey, J. L. 2001. *Pragmatics: An Introduction*. Oxford: Blackwell.

Palmer, F. R. 1994. *Grammatical Roles and Relations*. Cambridge: Cambridge University Press.

Palmer, F. R. 2001. *Mood and Modality*, 2nd ed. Cambridge: Cambridge University Press.

Quirk, R., Greenbaum, S., Leech, G. N., Svartvik, J. 1985. *A Comprehensive Grammar of the English Language*. London: Longman.

Roulet, E., Filliettaz, L., Grobet, A. 2001. *Un modèle et un instrument d'analyse de l'organisation du discours*. Bern: Lang.

Smith, C. S. 2003. *Modes of Discourse: The Local Structure of Texts*. Cambridge: Cambridge University Press.

Sperber, D., Wilson, D. 1995. *Relevance: Communication and Cognition*, 2nd ed. Oxford: Blackwell.

IV Historical Linguistics (Indo-European, Greek Historical Grammar, Etymology) and Greek Dialectology

Beekes, R. S. P., Beek, L. van. 2010. *Etymological Dictionary of Greek*. Leiden: Brill.

Beekes, R. S. P., Vaan, M. A. C. de. 2011. *Comparative Indo-European Linguistics: An Introduction*. Amsterdam: Benjamins.

Buck, C. D. 1955. *The Greek Dialects*, 2nd ed. Chicago: University of Chicago Press.

Chantraine, P. 1961. *Morphologie historique du grec*. Paris: Klincksieck.

Chantraine, P. 1968–80. *Dictionnaire étymologique de la langue grecque*. Paris: Klincksieck.

Colvin, S. 2007. *A Historical Greek Reader: Mycenaean to the Koiné*. Oxford: Oxford University Press.

Colvin, S. 2014. *A Brief History of Ancient Greek*. Chichester: Wiley-Blackwell.

Fortson, B. W. I. 2004. *Indo-European Language and Culture: An Introduction*. Malden: Blackwell.

Frisk, H. 1960–72. *Griechisches etymologisches Wörterbuch*. Heidelberg: Winter.

Gary Miller, D. 2014. *Ancient Greek Dialects and Early Authors: Introduction to the Dialect Mixture in Homer, with Notes on Lyric and Herodotus*, Berlin: De Gruyter.

Horrocks, G. C. 2010. *Greek: A History of the Language and its Speakers*, 2nd ed. Malden: Wiley-Blackwell.

Kölligan, D. 2007. *Suppletion und Defektivität im griechischen Verbum*. Bremen: Hempen.

Meier-Brügger, M., Fritz, M., Mayrhofer, M. 2003. *Indo-European Linguistics*. Berlin: De Gruyter.

Palmer, L. 1996. *The Greek Language*, new ed. Norman: University of Oklahoma Press.

Rix, H. 1976. *Historische Grammatik des Griechischen: Laut- und Formenlehre.* Darmstadt: Wissenschaftliche Buchgesellschaft.

Schmitt, R. 1991. *Einführung in die griechischen Dialekte*, 2nd ed. Darmstadt: Wissenschaftliche Buchgesellschaft.

Sihler, A. L. 1995. *New Comparative Grammar of Greek and Latin.* Oxford: Oxford University Press.

Threatte, L. 1980–96. *The Grammar of Attic Inscriptions.* Berlin: De Gruyter.

V Greek: Full Reference Grammars

Bornemann, E., Risch, E. 1978. *Griechische Grammatik.* Frankfurt: Diesterweg.

Kühner, R., Blass, F. 1890/1892. *Ausführliche Grammatik der griechischen Sprache* (vol. 1: *Elementar- und Formenlehre*). Hanover: Hahnsche Buchhandlung (repr. 2015 Darmstadt: Wissenschaftliche Buchgesellschaft).

Kühner, R., Gerth, B. 1898/1904. *Ausführliche Grammatik der griechischen Sprache* (vol. 2: *Satzlehre*). Hanover: Hahnsche Buchhandlung (repr. 2015 Darmstadt: Wissenschaftliche Buchgesellschaft).

Schwyzer, E. 1934–71. *Griechische Grammatik: Auf der Grundlage von Karl Brugmanns griechischer Grammatik*, 4 vols, rev. A. Debrunner. Munich: Beck.

Smyth, H. W. 1956. *Greek Grammar*, rev. G.M. Messing. Cambridge, Mass: Harvard University Press.

VI Greek: Phonology, Morphology, Accentuation, Word Formation

Aitchison, J. 1976. 'The Distinctive Features of Ancient Greek', *Glotta* 54: 173–201.

Allen, W. S. 1968. *Vox Graeca: A Guide to the Pronunciation of Classical Greek.* Cambridge: Cambridge University Press.

Chantraine, P. 1933. *La formation des noms en grec ancien.* Paris: Klincksieck.

Devine, A. M., Stephens, L. D. 1994. *The Prosody of Greek Speech.* New York: Oxford University Press.

Duhoux, Y. 2000. *Le verbe grec ancien: Éléments de morphologie et de syntaxe historique*, 2nd ed. Louvain-la-Neuve: Peeters.

Lejeune, M. 1972. *Phonétique historique du mycénien et du grec ancien.* Paris: Klincksieck.

Probert, P. 2003. *A New Short Guide to the Accentuation of Ancient Greek.* Bristol: Bristol Classical Press.

Probert, P. 2006. *Ancient Greek Accentuation: Synchronic Patterns, Frequency Effects, and Prehistory.* Oxford: Oxford University Press.

Also from section IV above: Beekes & van Beek 2010, Chantraine 1961, 1968–80, Rix 1976, Threatte 1980–96, and all works under V.

VII Greek: Syntax, Semantics, Pragmatics, Discourse

Aerts, W. 1965. *Periphrastica: An Investigation into the Use of εἶναι and ἔχειν as Auxiliaries or Pseudoauxiliaries in Greek from Homer up to the Present Day.* Amsterdam: Hakkert.

Allan, R. J. 2003. *The Middle Voice in Ancient Greek: A Study in Polysemy.* Amsterdam: Gieben.

Allan, R. J. 2010. 'The *Infinitivus Pro Imperativo* in Ancient Greek: The Imperatival Infinitive as an Expression of Proper Procedural Action', *Mnemosyne* 63.2: 203–28.

Allan, R. J. 2014. 'Changing the Topic: Topic Position in Ancient Greek Word Order', *Mnemosyne* 67.2: 181–213.

Allan, R. J., Buijs, M. (eds) 2007. *The Language of Literature: Linguistic Approaches to Classical Texts.* Leiden: Brill.

Amigues, S. 1977. *Les subordonnées finales par ὅπως en attique classique.* Paris: Klincksieck.

Bakker, E. J. (ed.) 1997. *Grammar as Interpretation: Greek Literature in its Linguistic Contexts.* Leiden: Brill.

Bakker, S. J. 2002. 'Futura Zonder Toekomst', *Lampas* 35.3: 199–214.

Bakker, S. J. 2009. *The Noun Phrase in Ancient Greek: A Functional Analysis of the Order and Articulation of NP Constituents in Herodotus.* Leiden: Brill.

Bakker, S. J., Wakker, G. C. (eds) 2009. *Discourse Cohesion in Ancient Greek.* Leiden: Brill.

Bakker, W. F. 1966. *The Greek Imperative: An Investigation into the Aspectual Differences between the Present and Aorist Imperatives in Greek Prayer from Homer up to the Present Day.* Amsterdam: Hakkert.

Bary, C. 2012. 'The Ancient Greek Tragic Aorist Revisited', *Glotta* 88: 31–53.

Basset, L. 1979. *Les emplois périphrastiques du verbe grec μέλλειν.* Lyon: Maison de l'Orient.

Bentein, K. 2012. 'Verbal Periphrasis in Ancient Greek: A State of the Art', *Revue Belge de Philologie et d'Histoire* 90: 5–56.

Bers, V. 1984. *Greek Poetic Syntax in the Classical Age.* New Haven: Yale University Press.

Biraud, M. 1991. *La détermination du nom en grec classique.* Nice: Association des publications de la Faculté des lettres de Nice.

Boel, G. de. 1988. *Goal Accusative and Object Accusative in Homer: A Contribution to the Theory of Transitivity.* Brussels: AWLSK.

Buijs, M. 2005. *Clause Combining in Ancient Greek Narrative Discourse: The Distribution of Subclauses and Participial Clauses in Xenophon's* Hellenica *and* Anabasis. Leiden: Brill.

Chanet, A.M. 1979. 'ἕως et πρίν en grec classique', *Revue des études grecques* 92: 166–207.

Chantraine, P. 1926. *Histoire du parfait grec*. Paris: Champion.

Crespo, E. et al. 2003. *Sintaxis del griego clásico*. Madrid: Gredos.

Crespo, E. et al. (eds) 2003. *Word Classes and Related Topics in Ancient Greek*. Louvain-la-Neuve: Peeters.

Cristofaro, S. 1996. *Aspetti sintattici e semantici delle frasi completive in greco antico*. Florence: Nuova Italia.

Denizot, C. 2011. *Donner des ordres en grec ancien: étude linguistique des formes de l'injonction*. Mont-Saint-Aignan: Publications des universités de Rouen et du Havre.

Denniston, J. D. 1954. *The Greek Particles*, 2nd ed., rev. K. J. Dover. London: Duckworth.

Devine, A. M., Stephens, L. D. 2000. *Discontinuous Syntax: Hyperbaton in Greek*. New York: Oxford University Press.

Dickey, E. 1996. *Greek Forms of Address: From Herodotus to Lucian*. Oxford: Oxford University Press.

Dik, H. J. M. 1995. *Word Order in Ancient Greek: A Pragmatic Account of Word Order Variation in Herodotus*. Amsterdam: Gieben.

Dik, H. J. M. 2007. *Word Order in Greek Tragic Dialogue*. Oxford: Oxford University Press.

Dover, K. J. 1997. *The Evolution of Greek Prose Style*. Oxford: Clarendon.

Fanning, B. M. 1990. *Verbal Aspect in New Testament Greek*. Oxford: Clarendon.

Fournier, H. 1946. *Les verbes 'dire' en grec ancien*. Paris: Klincksieck.

George, C. H. 2005. *Expressions of Agency in Ancient Greek*. Cambridge: Cambridge University Press.

George, C. H. 2014. *Expressions of Time in Ancient Greek*. Cambridge: Cambridge University Press.

George, C. H. 2016. 'Verbal Aspect and the Greek Future: ἕξω and σχήσω', *Mnemosyne* 69.4: 597–627.

Gildersleeve, B. 1900–11. *Syntax of Classical Greek from Homer to Demosthenes*, with the co-operation of C. W. E. Miller. New York: American Book Company.

Goodwin, W. W. 1889. *Syntax of the Moods and Tenses of the Greek Verb*. London: Macmillan & Co.

Guiraud, C. 1962. *La phrase nominale en grec d'Homère à Euripide*. Paris: Klincksieck.

Hettrich, H. 1976. *Kontext und Aspekt in der altgriechischen Prosa Herodots*. Göttingen: Vandenhoeck und Ruprecht.

Humbert, J. 1960. *Syntaxe grecque*, 3rd ed. Paris: Klincksieck.

Jacquinod, B. (ed.) 1994. *Cas et prépositions en grec ancien: contraintes syntaxiques et interprétations sémantiques*. Saint-Etienne: Publications de l'Université de Saint-Etienne.

Jacquinod, B. (ed.) 1999. *Les complétives en grec ancien*. Saint-Etienne: Publications de l'Université de Saint-Etienne.

Jacquinod, B., Lallot, J. (eds) 2000. *Études sur l'aspect chez Platon*. Saint-Etienne: Publications de l'Université de Saint-Etienne.

Jong, I. J. F. de, Rijksbaron, A. (eds) 2006. *Sophocles and the Greek Language: Aspects of Diction, Syntax and Pragmatics*. Leiden: Brill.

Kahn, C. 2003. *The Verb "Be" in Ancient Greek*, with a new introd. essay. Indianapolis: Hackett.

Kurzová, H. 1968. *Zur syntaktischen Struktur des griechischen: Infinitiv und Nebensatz*. Amsterdam: Hakkert.

Lallot, J., Rijksbaron, A., Jacquinod, B., Buijs, M. (eds) 2011. *The Historical Present in Thucydides: Semantics and Narrative Function*. Leiden: Brill.

Lamers, H., Rademaker, A. 2007. 'Talking About Myself: A Pragmatic Approach to the Use of Aspect Forms in Lysias 12.4–19', *Classical Quarterly* 57.2: 458–76.

Lloyd, M. A. 1999. 'The Tragic Aorist', *Classical Quarterly* 49.1: 24–45.

Matić, D. 2003. 'Topic, Focus, and Discourse Structure: Ancient Greek Word Order', *Studies in Language* 27.3: 573–633.

Monteil, P. 1963. *La phrase relative en grec ancien*. Paris: Klincksieck.

Moorhouse, A. C. 1959. *Studies in the Greek Negatives*. Cardiff: University of Wales Press.

Moorhouse, A. C. 1982. *The Syntax of Sophocles*. Leiden: Brill.

Muchnová, D. 2011. *Entre conjonction, connecteur et particule: le cas de ἐπεί en grec ancien. Étude syntaxique, sémantique et pragmatique*. Prague: Karolinum.

Nijk, A. A. 2013. 'The Rhetorical Function of the Perfect in Classical Greek', *Philologus* 157.2: 237–62.

Oguse, A. 1962. *Recherches sur le participe circonstanciel en grec ancien*. Paris: Klincksieck.

Ophuijsen, J. M. van, Stork, P. 1999. *Linguistics into Interpretation: Speeches of War in Herodotus VII 5 & 8–18*. Leiden: Brill.

Probert, P. 2015. *Early Greek Relative Clauses*. Oxford: Oxford University Press.

Rijksbaron, A. 1976. *Temporal and Causal Conjunctions in Ancient Greek: With Special Reference to the Use of ἐπεί and ὡς in Herodotus*. Amsterdam: Hakkert.

Rijksbaron, A. 1991. *Grammatical Observations on Euripides'* Bacchae. Amsterdam: Gieben.

Rijksbaron, A. (ed.) 1997. *New Approaches to Greek Particles*. Amsterdam: Gieben.

Rijksbaron, A. 2002. *The Syntax and Semantics of the Verb in Classical Greek: An Introduction*, 3rd ed. Amsterdam: Gieben (repr. 2006 University of Chicago Press).

Rijksbaron, A. 2019. *Form and Function in Greek Grammar*, ed. by R. J. Allan, E. van Emde Boas, L. Huitink. Leiden: Brill.

Rijksbaron, A., Mulder, H. A., Wakker, G. C. (eds) 1988. *In the Footsteps of Raphael Kühner*. Amsterdam: Gieben.

Rijksbaron, A., Slings, S. R., Stork, P., Wakker, G. C. 2000. *Beknopte Syntaxis van het Klassiek Grieks*. Lunteren: Hermaion.

Ruijgh, C. J. 1971. *Autour de 'τε épique': Études sur la Syntaxe Grecque*. Amsterdam: Hakkert.

Ruijgh, C. J. 1985. 'L'emploi 'inceptif' du thème du présent du verbe grec: Esquisse d'une théorie de valeurs temporelles des thèmes temporels', *Mnemosyne* 38.1/2: 1–61.

Ruipérez, M. S. 1982. *Structure du système des aspects et des temps du verbe en grec ancien: analyse fonctionnelle synchronique*. Paris: Belles-lettres.

Scheppers, F. 2011. *The Colon Hypothesis: Word Order, Discourse Segmentation and Discourse Coherence in Ancient Greek*. Brussels: Vubpress.

Sicking, C. M. J. 1992. 'The Distribution of Aorist and Present Stem Forms in Greek, Especially in the Imperative', *Glotta* 69: 14–43, 154–70.

Sicking, C. M. J., Ophuijsen, J. M. van. 1993. *Two Studies in Attic Particle Usage: Lysias and Plato*. Leiden: Brill.

Sicking, C. M. J., Stork, P. 1996. *Two Studies in the Semantics of the Verb in Classical Greek*. Leiden: Brill.

Slings, S. R. 1992. 'Written and Spoken Language: an Exercise in the Pragmatics of the Greek Language', *Classical Philology* 87: 95–109.

Slings, S. R. 2002. 'Oral Strategies in the Language of Herodotus', in: E. J. Bakker, H. van Wees, I. J. F. de Jong (eds), *Brill's Companion to Herodotus*. Leiden: Brill, 53–79.

Stahl, J. M. 1907. *Kritisch-historische Syntax des griechischen Verbums der klassischen Zeit*. Heidelberg: Winter.

Stork, P. 1982. *The Aspectual Usage of the Dynamic Infinitive in Herodotus*. Groningen: Bouma's Boekhuis.

Strunk, K. 1971. 'Historische und deskriptive Linguistik bei der Textinterpretation', *Glotta* 49: 191–216.

Wakker, G. C. 1994. *Conditions and Conditionals: An Investigation of Ancient Greek*. Amsterdam: Gieben.

Willi, A. (ed.) 2002. *The Language of Greek Comedy*. Oxford: Oxford University Press.

Willi, A. 2003. *The Languages of Aristophanes: Aspects of Linguistic Variation in Classical Attic Greek*. Oxford: Oxford University Press.

Also see all works under V.

Index of Examples

Index of Subjects

As throughout the book, → stands for 'see'.

Within entries, general references are given first, followed by more specific references, organized alphabetically (with Greek words following English words). However, references to Part I (Phonology/Morphology) are listed together before those to Parts II (Syntax) and/or Part III (Textual Coherence), if both occur: they are separated by three vertical bars |||. The same divider is used to set off, at the end of entries, references to further relevant entries, of the type 'also →'.

In cases where a full overview of uses of a certain form, construction, etc., is given in a chapter or section within the book, the index in some cases gives a reference to that overview instead of individual uses.

liquid 1.30 | syllabic 1.85, 1.87 ||| *also* →
   resonant; λ; ρ
locative 6.7–8

macron 1.15
main clause 39.4 | moods in 34 | syntax
   (introduction) 26
majuscule 1.11
manner/means adv. of in –ως 6.3 |||
   expressed by adverbial adjunct 26.15 |
   expressed by circumstantial ppl. 52.42 |
   expressed by relative clause → comparison
   clause | use of cases to express 30.26, 30.44
   | use of prepositions to express 31.8–9 |||
   also → ὡς
matrix clause 39.2
matrix predicate 39.2
measurement use of cases to express 30.58
medium tantum → middle-only verb
mental (change-of-)state meaning →
   middle-passive voice
middle-only verb 35.6, 35.21–7 | with
   change-of-state meaning 35.25 |
   expressing types of speech 35.27 | with
   indirect-refl. meaning 35.22–3 | with
   mental activity meaning 35.27 | with
   reciprocal meaning 35.24
middle-passive voice 11.4 ||| (change of)
   mental state meaning 35.19–20 | change-
   of-state meaning 35.17–20 | direct-refl.
   meaning 35.11–12 | expressing types of
   speech 35.27 | impersonal pass. 36.13 |
   indirect-refl. meaning 35.8–10, 35.22–3 |
   mental activity meaning 35.27 | mid. fut.
   forms expressing pass. meaning 35.30–1 |
   pass. meaning 35.13–16 | pass. meaning
   and expression of agent 35.14 | reciprocal
   meaning 35.24 | verbs with 'synonymous'
   act. and mid. 35.32
minuscule 1.11
mixed conditional → conditional sentence:
   mixed
mobile 60.4
modifier —— **in noun phrases** 26.16–18 |
   co-ordination or juxtaposition of multiple
   60.17 | 'heavy' 60.16 | placement relative to

article and head 28.11–22, 60.15–16, *also*
   → hyperbaton —— **optional (adverbial)**
   26.14 —— **predicative** 26.26
monological text 58.8
mood 11.7 ||| in main clauses 34 | overview of
   uses 54 | overview of uses in main clauses
   34.22 | in subordinate clauses 40.5–15 |||
   also → imperative; indicative; optative;
   subjunctive —— **attraction of** 40.15 | in
   'conditional' relative clauses 50.22 n.1 | in
   temporal clauses (opt.) 47.11
motive → cause/explanation/motive/reason
movable nu → ν: movable

narrative 33.13, 58.9 | main characteristics of
   61.2 | tenses used in 33.48–56
nasal 1.29 | syllabic 1.85–6 ||| *also* →
   resonant; μ; ν
nasal infix 12.30, 12.41
negative multiple 56.3–5 | overview of uses
   56 ||| *also* → μή; μὴ οὐ; οὐ; οὐ μή
nominal sentence 26.13
nominative 30.2–6 | as appositive with whole
   clause/sentence 27.14 | in lists 26.29, 30.4 |
   marking predicative complement 30.3 |
   marking subject 30.2 | in nominal
   exclamations 38.50 | with prolepsis 60.38 |
   used as voc. 30.55 n.1
nominative absolute 60.34
nominative-and-infinitive construction
   51.20
nominative-and-participle construction
   52.12
non-restrictive relative clause → relative
   clause, digressive
noun 4 | abstract vs. concrete 23.5 | action/
   agent/event 23.6 | (de)verbal 23.6 | du.
   forms 10.3–5 | effect/result/object 23.6 |
   event 23.6 | first declension 4.1–16 |
   heteroclitic 4.28, 4.90, 4.91 | overview of
   types 4.93 | root nouns vs. derived/
   compound nouns 23.3 | second declension
   4.17–30 | third-declension 4.31–92 |||
   +dyn. inf. 51.8 —— **compound** 23.37–40 |
   accentuation 24.29 | verbs derived from
   23.50

Index of Greek Words

Full Greek words are given in their dictionary form. Archaic and non-Greek letters (ϝ, ϙ, ʏ, etc.) are listed at the end. Peculiarities in the formation of tense-aspect stems of individual verbs are generally not listed (for these, →22.8–9 and the chapters on the relevant stem types). See also the headnote to the Index of Subjects.

ἀλλά 59.10–12 | apodotic 59.12 | placement 60.6 | ἀλλ’ οὖν 59.61 | ἀλλὰ γάρ, ἀλλὰ . . . γάρ 59.57–8 | ἀλλὰ δή 59.59 | ἀλλὰ μήν 59.60 | οὐ μέντοι ἀλλά 59.75 | οὐ μὴν ἀλλά 59.75

ἀλλήλων 7.6 | du. forms 10.7 ||| 29.26 | attributive gen., placement 28.16 | attributive gen., used to express possession 29.26 n.1 | combined with reflexive pronoun 29.20

ἄλλος 29.48 | combined with (καὶ δὴ) καί 59.70 | followed by another form of ἄλλος 29.51 | εἴ τις ἄλλος 29.42

ἅμα with circumstantial ppl. 52.37 | preposition (improper) 31.9

ἁμαρτάνω + gen. 30.21

ἁμιλλάομαι voice characteristics 35.24

ἀμφί overview of uses 31.8

ἀμφιέννυμι augm./reduplication 11.57

ἀμφισβητέω + μή + inf. 51.34–5

ἀμφότερος predicative position (placement in noun phrases) 28.21

ἄμφω predicative position (placement in noun phrases) 28.21

ἄν 55 | general function in main clauses 34.4 | omitted in habitual conditional clauses 49.15 | omitted in indefinite relative clauses 50.21 n.1 | omitted in πρίν-clauses 47.16 | overview of uses 55 | placement 60.5, 60.12 | repetition 60.12 | ὥσπερ ἂν εἰ → conditional clause, comparative

ἄν (=ἐάν) → εἰ

ἀνά overview of uses 31.8

ἀναβάλλομαι + μή + inf. 51.34–5

ἀναγκάζω + dyn. inf. 51.3 n.3, 51.8

ἀναγκαῖος impers. ἀναγκαῖόν ἐστι 36.8

ἀνάγκη impers. ἀνάγκη ἐστί 36.8

ἄναξ 4.42 n.1

ἄνευ preposition (improper) 31.9

ἀνέχομαι + pres. ppl. 52.9

ἀνήρ 4.64 | accentuation 24.24 | ἀνήρ (ὁ ἀνήρ in crasis) 1.45 n.1 ||| with appositive 26.25

ἄνθρωπος with appositive 26.25

ἀνίστημι/-ίσταμαι voice characteristics 35.17 n.1, also → ἵστημι: voice characteristics

ἀνοίγνυμι → οἴγνυμι

ἀντεῖπον (no pres.) + μή + inf. 51.34–5

ἀντί overview of uses 31.8

ἄνω 6.10

ἄξιος + dyn. inf. 51.9 | + gen. 30.23

ἀπαγορεύω + pres. ppl. 52.9 | + μή + inf. 51.34–5

ἀπαλλάττω/-ομαι + acc. + gen. 30.22 | voice characteristics 35.17

ἅπαξ 9.12 | origin/formation 6.6

ἀπαρνέομαι → ἀρνέομαι

ἀπειλέω + dat. 30.39

ἀπεῖπον + pres. ppl. 52.9 | + μή + inf. 51.34–5

ἀπέχω + gen. 30.21 | ἀπέχω/ἀπέχομαι + μή + inf. 51.34–5

ἀπό overview of uses 31.8 —— ἀφ’ οὗ introducing temporal clauses 47.2

ἀπογιγνώσκω + acc. + gen. 30.22

ἀποδίδωμι/-δίδομαι indirect-reflexive mid. of 35.9

ἀπόλλυμι → ὄλλυμι

Ἀπόλλων alternative acc. 4.53

ἀπορέω + indirect question 42.2

ἀποστερέω + acc. + gen. 30.22

ἀποψηφίζομαι + acc. + gen. 30.22

ἅπτομαι + gen. 30.21

ἄρα 59.42 | placement 60.5

ἆρα placement 60.6 | in yes/no-questions 38.6 | ἆρ’ οὐ in yes/no-questions 38.7 | ἆρα μή in yes/no-questions 38.8

ἀράομαι voice characteristics 35.27

ἀρέσκω + dat. 30.39

Ἄρης 4.72

ἀρνέομαι voice characteristics 35.27 | (ἀπ)αρνέομαι + μή + inf. 51.34–5

ἅρπαξ adj. ‘of one ending’ 5.32

ἄρχω/-ομαι ἄρχομαι + dyn. inf. 51.3 n.3, 51.8 | ἄρχομαι + pres. ppl. 52.9 | ἄρχομαι, differences between complement constructions 52.27 | ἄρχω/ἄρχομαι + gen. 30.21 | ἄρχων, noun, originally ppl. 52.46 n.2

-άς, -άδος collective numeral nouns 9.8 | nominal suffix 23.10

-ας, -αινα, -αν adj., with stem in ν 5.23–4

-ᾱσι locative 6.7

ἄστυ 4.83

-αται Ion. 3 pl. ending 25.39

ἀτάρ 59.18 | placement 60.6
ἄτε with circumstantial ppl. 52.39
-ατο Ion. 3 pl. ending 25.39
ἄττα 7.24
ἄττα 7.20
αυ 'long', pronunciation of 1.22 | 'short',
    pronunciation of 1.21
αὖ/αὖτε 59.13 | placement 60.5
αὐτίκα with circumstantial ppl. 52.37
αὐτός 7.10–11 | in crasis 1.44, 7.11 | in crasis,
    Ion. 25.14 | du. forms 10.7 | gen. pl.
    combined with possessive pronoun 7.9 |||
    29.7–13 | attributive gen., used to express
    possession 29.23 | emphatic use (self)
    29.9–13 | gen. pl. combined with
    possessive pronoun 29.21–2 | overview of
    uses 29.13 | placement 28.16, 28.19, 60.5 |
    strengthening personal pronoun in the
    nom. 29.10 | strengthening reflexive
    ἑαυτοῦ 29.11, 29.19, 32.10 | with the article
    expressing identicalness (the same) 29.8 |
    used as direct reflexive (oblique cases)
    29.17 n.1 | used as indirect reflexive
    (oblique cases) 29.18 | used as non-
    contrastive third-person pronoun (oblique
    cases) 29.5, 29.7 | ὁ αὐτός + dat./καί 30.40,
    32.14 —— αὐτοῦ (adv.) 6.9, 8.2
αὐτοῦ (=ἑαυτοῦ) → pronoun, reflexive
ἀφαιρέω/-έομαι ἀφαιρέομαι + 2x acc. 30.9
ἀφικνέομαι voice characteristics 35.25
ἀφίστημι/-ίσταμαι voice characteristics
    35.17 n.1, also → ἵστημι: voice
    characteristics
ἄχθομαι + indirect statement 41.3 | + ppl.
    52.10 | voice characteristics 35.26
-άω/-άομαι derivation of verbs in 23.43 | fut.
    in 15.38 | pres. in → contract present |||
    also → verb stem, ending in ᾱ/ᾰ, η/ᾰ

β 1.1 | as numeral 9.13 | pronunciation of
    1.24, 1.26 | verb stems ending in → verb
    stem, ending in labial stop ||| also → labial
    stop
βαίνω pf. βέβηκα, conjugation 18.27–32 ||| pf.
    βέβηκα with pres. meaning 33.36
βασιλεύς declension type 4.84–5 ||| used
    without article 28.8 n.2

βιάζομαι + dyn. inf. 51.3 n.3
βοηθέω + dat. 30.39
Βορρᾶς 4.14
βουλεύω/βουλεύομαι + dyn. inf. 51.8
βούλομαι 2 sg. pres. ind. (βούλει) 12.7 n.1 |
    augm. ἠ- 11.41 ||| + dyn. inf. 51.8 | voice
    characteristics 35.26 | βούλει/βούλεσθε
    introducing deliberative questions 34.8
    n.2, 38.17, 40.1 n.1 | ὁ βουλόμενος 28.25,
    52.48 n.1
βοῦς 4.86–7

γ 1.1 | as numeral 9.13 | pronunciation of
    1.24, 1.26, 1.29 | verb stems ending in →
    verb stem, ending in velar stop ||| also →
    nasal; velar stop
γάλα 4.42 n.1
γαλῆ 4.14
γάρ 59.14–15 | in anticipation or parenthesis
    59.15 | following appositive to sentence/
    clause 27.14 n.1 | after forms of address
    59.15 | introducing narratives 59.15 | vs.
    other expressions of cause, motivation, etc.
    48.1 n.1 | placement 60.5 | ἀλλὰ γάρ, ἀλλὰ
    . . . γάρ 59.57–8 | γὰρ δή 59.62 | γὰρ οὖν
    59.63 | εἴθε/εἰ γάρ in wishes 34.14, 34.18,
    38.38–9 | καὶ γάρ 59.66 | πῶς γάρ (οὐ); in
    answers, τί γάρ (οὐ); in answers 38.21
γαστήρ 4.62–3 | accentuation 24.24
γε 59.53 | in affirmative answers 38.21, 59.53 |
    placement 60.5
γελάω verb stem in σ 12.29 n.1, 13.18, 15.19,
    23.43 n.2
γέλως heteroclitic 4.91
γεραιός comparative and superlative
    5.39
γεύω/-ομαι γεύομαι + gen. 30.21 | voice
    characteristics 35.27 n.3
γηθέω intensive pf. 33.37
γίγνομαι aor. ἐγενόμην vs. ἐγενήθην 14.28
    n.1, | pf. ppl. γεγώς, -ῶσα 18.32 n.1 ||| as
    linking verb 26.8–9 | pres. with resultative
    sense 33.18 | voice characteristics 35.25,
    35.7
γιγνώσκω + decl. inf. 51.19 | differences
    between complement constructions 52.24
    n.2 | + dyn. inf. vs. + decl. inf. 51.29 | +

contraction of 1.59–60, 1.62–4 | as
numeral 9.13 | pronunciation of 1.15 |
shortened from ω (Osthoff's law) 1.70
ὁ, ἡ, τό → article
ὅ τι ὅτι vs. ὅ τι 7.20 n.1
ὅδε 7.13 ||| combined with ἐκεῖνος *(the former
. . .) the latter* 29.33 | main uses 29.29 |
typically cataphoric when referring within
texts 29.32
ὅθεν introducing relative clauses
50.34
ὁθούνεκα introducing causal clauses (in
poetry) 48.2 | introducing indirect
statements (in poetry) 41.4 n.1
οι pronunciation of 1.21
οἵ introducing relative clauses 50.34
-οι elision of 1.38 | usually short at word end
for accentuation 24.10
οἷα with circumstantial ppl. 52.39
οἴγνυμι/οἴγω augm./redupl. 11.40 | pf.
-έῳχα/-έῳγα 18.25
οἶδα overview of forms 18.4 | pf. conjugation
18.23 | differences between complement
constructions 52.23 | + indirect question
42.2 | + indirect statement 41.3 | pf. with
pres. meaning 33.36 | + ppl. 52.10
οἴκοι locative 6.8
οἴμοι in exclamations 38.50
οἴομαι/οἶμαι 2 sg. pres. ind. (οἴει) 12.7 n.1 |
forms without them. vowel 12.14 ||| + decl.
inf. 51.19 | voice characteristics 35.26
οἷος 7.23, 8.1 ||| adverbial οἷον/οἷα for
example 50.32 | in exclamations of degree
38.47–8 | impers. οἷόν τέ ἐστι 36.8 | impers.
οἷόν τέ ἐστι + acc.-and-inf. 51.11 |
introducing indirect exclamations 42.11 |
introducing relative clauses 50.28, 50.5 |
introducing result clauses with inf. 46.10 |
relative adj. 50.1 | οἷον/οἷα with
circumstantial ppl. 52.39 | οἷός τέ (εἰμι) +
dyn. inf. 51.9
οἷς 4.77
οἴχομαι with ppl. expressing manner of
departure 52.42 n.3 | pres. with resultative
sense 33.18 | voice characteristics 35.25
ὀλίγος comparatives and superlatives 5.43 |
ὀλίγον (adv.), origin/formation of 6.4 |

ὀλίγου (adv.), origin/formation of 6.4 |||
ὀλίγου δεῖν 51.49
ὄλλυμι/ὄλλυμαι more than one type of pf. act.
18.26 ||| voice characteristics 35.17 | voice
characteristics 35.7
ὅλος 29.46
ὀλοφύρομαι voice characteristics 35.27
ὄμνυμι + dyn. inf. vs. + decl. inf. 51.31
ὅμοιος + dat./καί 32.14 | + dat. 30.40 | ὁμοίως
(adv.), origin/formation 6.3 n.2 | ὁμοίως
(adv.), combined with comparative
circumstantial ppl. 52.43
ὁμολογέω in affirmative answers 38.21
ὁμοῦ 6.9 ||| preposition (improper) 31.9
ὁμῶς/ὅμως origin/formation 6.3 n.2
ὄνειρος heteroclitic 4.91
ὅπη 8.2 ||| introducing indirect questions
42.5 | relative adv. 50.1
ὄπισθεν preposition (improper) 31.9
ὀπίσω 6.10
ὁπόθεν relative adv. 50.1
ὅποι 8.2 ||| introducing indirect questions
42.5 | introducing relative clauses 50.34 |
relative adv. 50.1
ὁποῖος 7.23, 8.1 ||| introducing indirect
questions 42.5 | introducing relative
clauses 50.28 | relative adj. 50.1
ὁπόσος 7.23, 8.1 ||| anticipated by πᾶς 50.30 |
introducing indirect questions 42.5 |
introducing relative clauses 50.28 | relative
adj. 50.1
ὁπότε 8.2 ||| anticipated by τότε 50.36 |
introducing indirect questions 42.5 |
introducing temporal clauses 47.2, 47.6,
48.3–4 | ὡς ὁπότε in comparative temporal
clauses 47.17
ὁπότερος 7.23
ὅπου 8.2 ||| introducing indirect questions
42.5 | introducing relative clauses 50.34 |
relative adv. 50.1
ὅπως 8.2 ||| in comparison clauses 50.37 |
conjunction in indirect statements 41.4 n.1
| in effort clause (with fut. ind.) → effort
clause | + fut. ind. in exhortations
(independent use) 38.34 | introducing
indirect questions 42.5 | introducing
purpose clauses 45.2 | relative adv. 50.1